A HISTORY

# TEXAS

## CROSSROADS OF NORTH AMERICA

### JESÚS F. DE LA TEJA
TEXAS STATE UNIVERSITY - SAN MARCOS

### PAULA MARKS
ST. EDWARD'S UNIVERSITY

### RON TYLER
THE UNIVERSITY OF TEXAS AT AUSTIN

*with*

## MAJOR PROBLEMS IN TEXAS HISTORY
### DOCUMENTS AND ESSAYS

*edited by*

### SAM W. HAYNES
UNIVERSITY OF TEXAS AT ARLINGTON

### CARY D. WINTZ
TEXAS SOUTHERN UNIVERSITY

HOUGHTON MIFFLIN COMPANY    BOSTON    NEW YORK

TEXAS: CROSSROADS OF NORTH AMERICA, A HISTORY
By Jesús F. de la Teja, Paula Marks, and Ron Tyler
Copyright © 2004 by Houghton Mifflin Company. All rights reserved.

Editor-in-Chief: Jean L. Woy
Sponsoring Editor: Jeffrey Greene
Associate Project Editor: Shelley Dickerson
Senior Marketing Manager: Sandra McGuire
Senior Manufacturing Coordinator: Priscilla J. Bailey

*Acknowledgment*
Poem on pages 54–55: Robert S. Weddle, *Wilderness Manhunt: The Spanish Search for La Salle* (Austin: University of Texas
Press, 1974; Revised Edition, College Station, TX, 1999). Reprinted by permission of the author.

MAJOR PROBLEMS IN TEXAS HISTORY, DOCUMENTS AND ESSAYS
Edited by Sam W. Haynes and Cary D. Wintz
Copyright © 2002 by Houghton Mifflin Company. All rights reserved.

Editor-in-Chief: Jean L. Woy
Senior Associate Editor: Fran Gay
Senior Project Editor: Rosemary Winfield
Production/Design Coordinator: Christine Gervais
Senior Manufacturing Coordinator: Priscilla Bailey
Marketing Manager: Sandra McGuire

Custom Publishing Editor: Luis Rosas
Custom Publishing Production Manager: Christina Battista
Project Coordinator: Sara Abbott

Cover Designer: Brian Moore
Cover Image: iStockphoto/Francisco Romero

This book contains select works from existing Houghton Mifflin Company resources and was
produced by Houghton Mifflin Custom Publishing for collegiate use. As such, those adopting and/or
contributing to this work are responsible for editorial content, accuracy, continuity and completeness.

Compilation copyright © 2007 by Houghton Mifflin Company. All rights reserved.

Printed in the United States of America.

ISBN-13: 978-0-618-96966-1
ISBN-10: 0-618-96966-7
1022715

3 4 5 6 7 8 9 – AB – 09 08 07

 Houghton Mifflin
Custom Publishing

222 Berkeley Street • Boston, MA 02116

Address all correspondence and order information to the above address.

# Brief Contents

## TEXAS: CROSSROADS OF NORTH AMERICA, A HISTORY

## MAJOR PROBLEMS IN TEXAS HISTORY, DOCUMENTS AND ESSAYS

# Contents

## 3 | New Spain's Northeastern Frontier, 1714–1767

## 4 | The Age of Reform, 1767–1800

## 5 | New Rivals, New Challenges, 1800–1821     122

## PART II   DEFINING TEXAS     153

## 6 | The Americanization of Texas, 1821–1835     156

## 9 | Secession, War, and Their Aftermath, 1860–1876    253

## PART III TEXAS REDEFINED    287

## 10 | Toward Modernization, 1876–1898    290

## 11 | The Early Twentieth Century: One Party, Half a Dozen Fights, 1900–1929    323

## 14 | Recognizing Old and New Realities      424

# Preface

The idea for this textbook arose out of the authors' experience as consultants for the Bob Bullock Texas State History Museum in Austin. In struggling to present the entire scope of the Texas experience within the limited confines of three floors of approximately 34,000 square feet of exhibit space, we were forced to hone the messages we wanted visitors to gain during their visit. The more we thought about the contexts that could only be hinted at in the museum, the more attractive the idea of a Texas history survey became to us. We wanted to tell a balanced story that would appeal to an increasingly diverse twenty-first-century Texas audience.

## Themes

In *Texas: Crossroads of North America,* we tell the story of this region as a dynamic process, beginning with the ways in which people—natives, adventurers, government representatives, immigrants, and residents—perceived the opportunities offered on this Indian, Spanish, Mexican, and Anglo frontier, in this republic and state. That suggests one of our first major themes—that Texas was a crossroads of intersecting geographies and cultures. People pursued these opportunities both as individuals and groups, first in the land itself, then through more complex ways of achieving social, economic, and political independence and power, which reflects our second major theme of opportunity. They found often formidable challenges, in part by coming into contact with representatives of other cultural and ethnic groups with different perspectives and agendas. As certain groups gained power—including the power to define "Texas" and "Texans" in their way—their definitions were repeatedly challenged by the vastness and energetic diversity of the state and its population, which suggests our third major theme of Texas as a "cultural centrifuge." In this geographic and cultural mix, myth and reality have combined to make and keep Texas a distinctive place.

## Approach

This is a distinctly modern history of Texas. We tell the story that constitutes one of the most dramatic and colorful histories of any state in the nation, but we try to make sense of that legacy and show how it relates to present-day Texans and those to come. We haven't lost the focus on our Hispanic, African American, or German heritage, or on the brave soldiers who participated in the Texas Revolution, the war with Mexico, the Civil War, World Wars I and II, and more recent conflicts, but we also show the many contributions of Mexican Americans, African Americans, and women to the struggle for civil rights that continues as society becomes ever more mindful of inequities in opportunity. We haven't forgotten the accomplishments of Cabeza de Vaca, Stephen F. Austin, Sam Houston, James Stephen Hogg, Lyndon B. Johnson, or the presidents Bush, but we have also told the stories of Fray Isidro Espinosa, Rosa María Hinojosa de Ballí, Ignacio Pérez, Oveta Culp Hobby, Barbara Jordan, and Michael Dell. We recognize the enduring contributions of the Texas Rangers, one of the most storied law enforcement organizations in the country, but we also tell the story of the brave citizens who helped reform the Rangers and restore them as a useful state agency when others would have disbanded them.

*Texas: Crossroads of North America* tells the story of the people who lived within the state's borders before there was any idea of Texas or when Texas was defined in very different terms than it is today. Our text recognizes that the building blocks of today's Lone Star State have been in the making for not hundreds, but for thousands and even millions of years. Instead of a static presentation of the state's geography, this book offers a dynamic introduction to Texas as a place by emphasizing the interrelationship between people and nature as soon as people arrived. It makes clear for students how the American Indians who settled the land adapted to it and, when possible, altered it to better suit their needs. The extensive survey of the cultural diversity of the native peoples of Texas, relying on recent archeological findings and newer interpretations of the ethnographic evidence, constitutes one of the stronger features of our text.

Just as *Texas: Crossroads of North America* pays greater attention to the native American background, it also gives greater emphasis to the story of Spain in Texas. The recent discovery and recovery of one of La Salle's ships, the *Belle,* from the bottom of Matagorda Bay has rekindled interest in the formative period of the state's history. Yet, La Salle's misadventure and the attendant efforts by Spain to retain control of this back door to its silver colony to the south cannot be understood without consideration of why Spain had neglected the lands north of the Rio Grande for so long. By examining the expeditions of Cabeza de Vaca, Coronado, and De Soto in greater detail, and by stressing the settlement of far West Texas in the seventeenth century, this text lays a strong foundation for understanding Spanish actions in the eighteenth and early nineteenth centuries.

Past historiographical trends have dwelt on judging the Spanish Texas experience in terms of success or failure and in isolation from events elsewhere. This book takes a different approach. By emphasizing how Spanish colonials made lives for themselves on a harsh and remote frontier, it stresses that even under such adverse conditions, early Tejanos found opportunities and a sense of belonging. The diversity of the Spanish colonial experience in what is now Texas takes us from El Paso to Padre Island and from Nacogdoches to Laredo, a sweep of space and time that the authors believe can only be done justice by devoting three complete chapters to it.

The authors feel strongly that in laying this more complete foundation of early Texas history students will better understand and appreciate the advent and process of Anglo American colonization. We strive to show more fully how this colonization occurred within the context of the new Mexican nation and of local Mexican frontier governing structures, and what opportunities and challenges it posed for the existing Mexican population of Texas. This foundation helps us make more sense of the cultural context in which our Mexican American population is more fully appreciated as part of the Texas experience.

We devote a full chapter to the Texas Revolution. In part because of its strength as a "creation myth" for Texas, it remains the most dramatically engaging point of entry into the state's modern history and a cornerstone of a distinctly Texan identity for many readers. We think it important to illuminate the confusion and complexity of the struggle, to get beyond simplistic and ethnocentric understandings, to see the revolution as an event within Mexico itself, with a varied and sometimes conflicted cast of characters.

In the Republic era, we point up the political and economic fragility of the fledgling nation, and the uncertainty of opportunity, particularly for increasingly marginalized groups. In the early statehood era, we trace Texas's increasing identification as a southern state, and therefore one willing to throw away its hard-won annexation to join the Confederacy.

We try to provide a broad and varied picture of Texas and Texans during the Civil War, including those Texans who resisted identification with the Southern cause. Our emphasis in Reconstruction is on laying out clearly the various policies and requirements of the federal government, how Texans responded, and how and why the state reverted to conservative Democratic policies as soon as possible, undercutting any hoped-for gains by African Americans.

While Texas was still largely an agricultural state in 1900, we point out in Chapter 10 that in addition to being among the most productive agriculturally, these years also witnessed the beginnings of industrialization. The huge growth in population, the spread of railroads throughout the state, the fluctuations of the cotton market, and the discovery of oil at Spindletop in 1901, particularly as the state was coming increasingly under one-party rule, as described in Chapter 11, stressed its abilities to deal with economic and cultural problems. The economic structure, based on one-crop agriculture, began to falter in the aftermath of World War I and would have collapsed under the weight of the Great Depression of the 1930s, had not the federal government come to the rescue, as described in Chapter 12. And the cultural superstructure did collapse in the face of civil rights challenges by women, Mexican Americans, and African Americans, and we have not yet finished its reconstruction.

The increasingly significant role that the federal government played in the state's development is also an issue that began as soon as federal troops replaced the Texas Rangers as the region's major defenders and has only grown more important today. World War II, in particular, spurred development in Texas, with the completion of the "Big Inch" and "Little Inch" pipelines and the construction of the world's largest petrochemical complex along the Gulf coast. Federal government expenditures in

Texas, which today dwarf the state's own budget, suggest its huge role in the state, and the state's significant role in the federal government. The impact of all these factors is seen in Chapter 13, as the Democratic Party, for decades the only relevant forum for discussion of the state's problems and goals, begins to split between its liberal and conservative branches in the face of increasing problems of taxation, civil rights, education, water, and the many other problems associated with continued growth—not to mention the growing, highly successful Republican challenge.

Recent history can easily descend into a general recitation of diverse events and developments. In dealing with the end of the twentieth century, we have identified three significant themes: the ways in which Texas exhibits old identities and new in both politics and economics; the challenges of governing a state experiencing uneven growth and opportunity; and awareness of environmental issues, particularly in regard to water needs and availability.

Throughout this work, we have tried to engage where possible with individual stories, with the ways in which people have responded to the opportunities and challenges they found in Texas, and how these responses have led to the geographic, cultural, political, and economic landscape we have today. As a result, *Texas: Crossroads of North America* is as much a history of Texans as it is of Texas.

## Teaching Aids

A printed test bank prepared by James Wilson contains multiple-choice and essay questions. These questions are also available in a computerized test bank for both Windows and Macintosh computers.

## Acknowledgments

For *Texas: Crossroads of North America* to become more than rumination we needed to find a sympathetic ear. Jeff Greene at Houghton Mifflin was kind enough to hear us out. For his encouragement and patience our deep thanks. Originally, there were four of us, and we owe thanks to Doug Barnett who, although he could not collaborate on the textbook, was generous with his time, ideas, and perspective.

In writing this book the authors benefited from discussing subject matter or having chapters read by a number of knowledgeable individuals. Among those with whom we consulted are William H. Goetzmann, Creekmore Fath, and Will Wilson, Sr., and we also wish to thank Robert Utley, Randolph B. Campbell, Patrick Cox, and William H. Goetzmann for reading portions of the text. In addition, we thank the following colleagues for their invaluable suggestions: Dallas Cothrum, University of Texas at Tyler; David Cullen, Collin County Community College; Ricky Floyd Dobbs, Texas A&M University; Juanita E. Garza, The University of Texas–Pan American; L. Patrick Hughes, Austin Community College;

Jorge Iber, Texas Tech University; Charles H. Martin, University of Texas at El Paso; Kent McGaughey, Houston Community College; Nora E. McMillan, San Antonio College; Ray Stephens, University of North Texas; Brenda Taylor, Texas Wesleyan University; and Marcus S. Turner, San Jacinto College.

Jesús F. de la Teja
Paula Marks
Ron Tyler

PART **I**

# UNDEFINED TEXAS

It was not a destination for the European adventurers who traipsed across the southern half of North America in the early sixteenth century. It was not a final destination for hunter-gatherer bands who followed the buffalo, the seasons, and the spirits throughout central North America in the same era. It was not a recognizable political unit, even for the widely dispersed and varied native peoples who made it their home then. It would be hundreds of years before Texas resembled the place we recognize today as the second largest state in the Union. For three centuries conflict, competition, and cooperation among Euro-Americans and Indians continually reshaped and redefined Texas.

The history of Texas—that is, the story that can be told from documents—begins during the age of the conquistadors. What brought the first Spaniards to Texas from the 1520s to the 1540s were the same motives that led them to explore from the Oregon coast to Tierra del Fuego: the search for fabulous treasures to plunder and civilizations to conquer and put to work. A century later other Spaniards, religious missionaries, began to explore the region with a much different purpose: the search for souls to save. These early settlers faced many obstacles: great distances between settlements, a difficult climate, and Indian resistance. Only at the turn of the eighteenth century did a motive strong enough to overcome these obstacles arise: stopping the encroachment into the region of French rivals.

Geopolitical motives rarely stir the movement of large numbers of people. And so it was that throughout the eighteenth century Mexico's far northeastern frontier, from the Rio Grande to the Red River, inspired the imaginations of very few colonial settlers. Ranching proved marginally lucrative to some, but military service or subsistence farming fed the majority of people. Missionaries worked with a variety of Indian groups, sometimes with success, sometimes with disastrous consequences, to create a Hispanic population that could hold Texas for Spain. Such was the Spanish way. The Indian was not an enemy of civilization, but rather a potential subject of both majesties (God and king). In the end, the population of Spanish Texas resembled that of much of the rest of the empire—Catholic, mixed-blood, agricultural and pastoral, poor, self-reliant—but in this case, small and isolated.

Relatively few thought of themselves as "Tejanos" (Hispanic residents of Texas). For all practical purposes Texas began at the San Antonio River (where San Antonio anchored settlement to the west and La Bahía anchored settlement to the east) and stretched all the way beyond the Sabine River into what is today western Louisiana. The ranching communities that occupied the lower Rio Grande valley were part of Nuevo Santander. The people who lived in these settlements traded with Texas, but typically thought of themselves in terms of the community in which they had citizenship: Camargo, Mier, Reynosa, Revilla, or Laredo. Least Texan of all were the residents of the Paso del Norte area, what is today El Paso-Juárez. Living on both sides of the river, these people descended from the sixteenth-century settlers of New Mexico, from some of the Pueblo groups that had allied themselves with the Spanish, and from other Spanish colonials who found the area perfect for cultivating the vine and raising livestock. There is no record of Paso del Norte ever having direct contact with Texas during the colonial period.

It took events far beyond the control of the people living north of the Rio Grande at the start of the nineteenth century to alter and expand the definition of Texas. The Louisiana Purchase, the Mexican War of Independence, and the consequent political upheavals and new migration patterns brought new and very different people into the region: Euro-Americans, African Americans, and Indians. Texas became contested ground as the newcomers saw opportunities west of the Sabine—rich cotton bottomlands, vast and fecund hunting grounds, proximity to Mexico's silver mining centers. That Texas had no large and prosperous cities, no grand cathedrals or imposing public monuments, no well-developed roads or ports, helped foster the impression that it was a wilderness ready to be tamed. Neither the millennia of Indian habitation nor a century of Spanish settlement could be easily wiped away, however. And, without understanding that history—the contest over what Texas should be and to whom it should belong—we cannot understand who Texans are today.   ■ ■ ■

# 1

# Land and Life

In the opening scene of the 1963 movie "The Wheeler Deal-ers," wildcatter Henry Tyroon and his crew stand in a dusty valley by a drilling rig on the verge of blowing in. As his ac-countant reminds him of unpaid debts and vanishing lines of credit, the wildcatter crosses his fingers and gives the sig-nal for the crew to clear the borehole. The earth groans and snorts and finally, with a mighty heave, coughs up a dust ball. Played for comedic effect, the scene depicts the true-life ex-periences of countless prospectors for black gold who have traipsed across Texas for more than a century. Many struck water or dust, but some struck vast pools of oil, eons in the making. The state's first people—the Indians—were familiar with naturally occurring petroleum deposits, which they used to waterproof and decorate pottery, as in colonial times Spanish sailors used beach tar to caulk their ships. It was not until the early twentieth century that the true potential of "Texas tea" was recognized, however. Today the search for oil and natural gas is a much more scientific endeavor, reflected in the petroleum engineering programs of Texas's premier universities. Yet, it remains a cat-and-mouse game between Earth and its most ambitious parasite—humanity. Petroleum prospecting is an activity rooted in the study of the state's natural history—a history going back countless ages, to times in which dense fern forests teeming with reptilian life and vast shallow seas nursing expanses of reefs planted the biological seeds for the mineral riches that have become such an important part of the Texas identity today.

| CHAPTER 1 | Land and Life |
|---|---|
| 1 BILLION YEARS AGO | Granite domes of Hill Country form |
| 570–245 MILLION YEARS AGO | Oil, coal, and gas fields of West Texas form |
| 245–66 MILLION YEARS AGO | Salt domes, oil and gas fields of East Texas form |
| 65–2 MILLION YEARS AGO | Gulf of Mexico begins to emerge; West Texas mountain ranges form; oil and gas fields of southeast and lower gulf coast form |
| 2.4 MILLION–15,000 YEARS AGO | Palo Duro canyon cut, Padre Island and other barrier islands begin to form |
| 9,200–6,000 B.C.E. | Arrival and spread of Paleo-Indian hunter-gatherers |
| 6,000 B.C.E.–500 C.E. | Archaic period cultures—increased cultural specialization by region |
| 500–700 C.E. | Agriculture, pottery making, bow and arrow spread |
| 800–1800 C.E. | Caddos are dominant East Texas culture; Karankawa and Coahuiltecan cultures dominant in coastal and South Texas |
| 1200–1500 C.E. | Antelope Creek people flourish on plains; Jornada Mogollón culture flourishes in Trans-Pecos |
| CA. 1500 C.E. | Arrival of Proto-Apaches on southern plains |

When humans first set foot on what is now Texas soil, the natural history of the region was already hundreds of millions of years in the making. Understanding the processes that shaped the landscapes and environments of Texas seems the best place to begin the story of the Lone Star State. As large as a continent, Texas contains all of the major land forms and most climatic environments to be found in the western hemisphere, making it a natural crossroads of North America.

Humans adapted to life in these varied ecological zones, from the semitropical riverine environment of South Texas to the humid pine forests of East Texas to the short grass plains of the Panhandle. For 10,000 years the first Texans hunted, fished, farmed, and made war in what became a crossroads of native cultures. When Europeans finally arrived on the scene, what they perceived as a wilderness was in reality the home of well-adapted and widely diverse cultures. They brought with them, however, the seeds of radical change, physical and cultural, that eventually would make Texas a crossroads of empires.

## Before the First Humans in Texas

A little over a billion years ago, give or take a hundred million years, in the last quarter of the Precambrian era, what is now North America collided with another continental plate. As in an automobile accident, some parts went flying, others crumpled, and still others were completely consumed by the collision. Mother Nature cleared the wreckage over the next few hundred million years—mountains flattened out through erosion, sediment covered depressions—but today we can still see the effects of that earth-shattering event. In Llano County, at Enchanted Rock State Park, for example, a granite dome sticks up out of the countryside, a beautiful reminder of the intense heat and pressures created by that long-ago collision that also brought granite near the surface as far east as Marble Falls. Texas underwent numerous cycles of uplifting and submergence, cooling and heating, wetness and drying out, and countless species of animals and plants arose and vanished before humans arrived to claim the land for themselves a mere 12,000 years ago.

### The Early Natural History of Texas

Plate tectonics separated North America from that other continent beginning about 600 million years go, only to smash all the continents together into the supercontinent of Pangaea about 300 million years later. Not surprisingly, another mountain range, the Ouachita Range, rose along the arc of the collision. Today this range lies buried in Texas, except near Marathon, but remains exposed in Oklahoma and Arkansas. Once again erosion began wearing down the newly created peaks and the waters, streams, and seas began filling in the low places. An important difference this time, however, was that now the surface of the earth teemed with life. Among the materials that filled in the cracks and smoothed out the rough places were the remains of primitive trees, ferns, and, later on, a wide variety of simple sea creatures whose shells made up the first reefs.

These and many similar events, which geologists group into a large block of time called the Paleozoic era, transpired between 570 and 245 million years ago. Compressed and left to stew under mounting layers of sediment, the organic remains of these long-lost worlds eventually decayed into the vast oil, coal, and gas fields of West Texas. The shells of sea creatures became limestone deposits, and the evaporation of shallow seas deposited gypsum and salt beds. Along with granite and other hard stones of the Precambrian era, which adorn the state capitol and other public buildings in Texas and around the world, the mineral wealth of the Paleozoic era constitutes a significant bounty to the state.

If the earlier two eras left Texas an ample store of natural resources, the next two would be even more generous. The Mesozoic era, which began about 245 million years ago and ended about 66 million years ago, is often referred to as the Age of Dinosaurs. A wide variety of ecosystems flourished during this long period of time. As Pangaea broke up, creating the Atlantic Ocean and Gulf of Mexico, a great inland sea stretching from Canada to Mexico advanced and then retreated through Texas, splitting the region in two for millions of years. The geological changes took place during the period in which North America drifted north, moving the Texas region from the equator at the beginning of the Mesozoic era past 30° north latitude by the end of the era.

Dense conifer and fern forests covered the uplands in the Triassic period, the first part of the Mesozoic era, when evolution brought forth the first dinosaurs and the first mammals. It was a reptilian world, however. Along the banks of streams crocodile-like giants waited for prey to come within easy reach, while lizards and turtles hunted insects. Sharks and bony fish crowded the waters, both fresh and salt. Lost in this busy world were the earliest Texas dinosaurs, relatively small creatures that represented the two main branches of the dinosaur family and first appeared about 220 million years ago.

## Texas in the Age of Dinosaurs

Texas has proven to be no Jurassic Park, however. When this second part of the Mesozoic era began about 208 million years ago the dinosaurs were on the rise and the breakup of Pangaea was underway. By the end of the period, about 144 million years ago, most of Texas was submerged in a shallow sea that covered everything east of a line from Big Bend to Wichita Falls. The shallow Gulf of Mexico often evaporated, laying down huge blankets of salt that would eventually play a major role in creating pockets of oil and gas throughout coastal Texas. Unfortunately, the rock layers that chronicle the Jurassic period are so deeply buried beneath younger rocks in Texas that it has been impossible to understand the fauna and flora of the region during those exciting times.

Texas continued its northward movement during the Cretaceous period, at the end of the Mesozoic era, as the sea that covered the eastern two-thirds of the

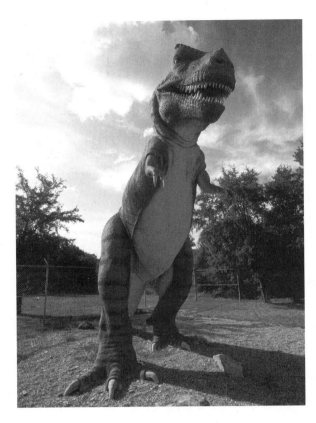

At Dinosaur Valley State Park, southwest of the Dallas-Fort Worth metroplex, visitors can follow the footprints of king lizards across streambeds and take in exhibits of fossil bones that have kept paleontologists busy for centuries. *(Photo courtesy Texas Parks & Wildlife © 2003, Glen Mills)*

state began to recede. New layers of sediment buried the reefs to create layers of limestone, sandstone, and shale formations. These heavy rock formations put pressure on the underlying salt layer, squeezing and compacting it until salt bubbles formed—what we refer to today as *salt domes*. The weight of the sediment layers also pressed the vegetable and animal matter within them to extract new concentrations of oil and gas that collected in pockets adjoining the salt domes. Millions of years later, the most famous of these, at Spindletop, hurled Texas headlong into the twentieth century.

During the late Cretaceous period, between about 80 and 66 million years ago, as Texas slowly resurfaced from yet another round of submergence, the great Age of Dinosaurs neared its end. Texas was a land of giants at that time, however, home to the Alamosaurus, the last of the giant herbivores. In the Trans-Pecos region roamed the fearsome Tyrannosaurus rex and the largest of all flying reptiles, *Quetzalcoatlus northropi,* which had a wingspan of over forty feet. Mammals, including the ancestral horse, remained tiny creatures forced to live on the margins of Cretaceous life. And by this time the air no longer belonged to tiny insects and giant pteradons alone, as birds had put in an appearance.

Yet ominous changes were underway. The fossil record shows that the ecosystems of ancient Texas were under stress. Then, one day, between the Mesozoic and Cenozoic eras, about 65 million years ago, the last of the major collisions that shaped our environment occurred. Hurtling out of deep space at 50,000 miles per hour and measuring six to seven miles in diameter, a meteorite smashed into the northern part of what is today the Yucatán peninsula in Mexico. The first shock of the impact caused an earthquake of worldwide proportions and the dispersion of a huge volume of water that tore up the sea floor, leveled hills, and killed everything in its path for thousands of miles in the direction of Texas. Then the long-term effects set in. The sky, already filled with dust and chemicals from hundreds of active volcanoes around the globe, darkened even more with the vaporized remains of the meteorite and the soils and rocks of the impact crater. Species perished as the plants they fed on died, or the animals on which they depended ceased to exist.

## The Physical Development of Modern Texas

The impact of the meteor may not have been the single cause of the extinction of the dinosaurs, but it is a convenient reference point to mark their passing. It is also a convenient reference point to mark the rise of mammals and the birth of modern geological Texas. No more would the state be swamped by ocean waters. Instead, the rivers that would come to be known as the Trinity, Brazos, and Colorado, along with a number of smaller streams, would deposit sediment to fill in more and more of the Gulf of Mexico. It would be many more millions of years before Texas would take on its modern form, but the process was underway.

The Cenozoic era, the geological era that began about 66 million years ago, is still in progress, for in geological terms the modern age is part of this most recent period of Earth's history. To the east Texas continued its expansion into the Gulf

Today's coastline continues to change in response to the same forces that have shaped it for millions of years: storm erosion, sediment buildup, and fluctuations in sea levels.

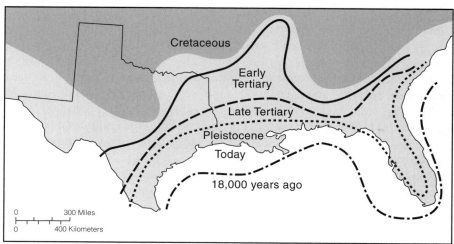

of Mexico for 64 million years, especially late in this period, which is known as the Tertiary period, when the expanding polar ice caps trapped tremendous amounts of water, causing sea levels to drop by hundreds of feet.

While the foundations of the modern gulf coast were being laid down, much was also happening in the western parts of the state. In what is now the Trans-Pecos, tensions from the last period of Rocky Mountains uplifting led to extensive volcanic activity that created the Davis and Chisos mountain ranges and other Big Bend peaks, while to the northeast the Rockies deposited sediments in the Panhandle to form the rock formations now known as the Ogallala Aquifer. Faulting between the coastal and inland formations helped produce the picturesque Balcones Escarpment.

The earth's progressive cooling during the Tertiary period contributed to change in North America's flora and fauna, with a significant impact on Texas. Evergreen tropical forests gave way to deciduous woods, which were better able to tolerate the seasonal climate that settled over North America at this time. Among the successor species were members of the walnut family, which includes the pecan tree, the state tree of Texas. Grasses also arrived on the scene during this period, contributing to the transformation of the Texas landscape. Wetter conditions in the eastern parts of the state produced lush vegetation that, in the recurring cycle of life, death, burial, and compression, produced the sandstone oil and gas fields of southeast Texas and the lower gulf coast.

Hard as it is to imagine, the exotic wildlife parks that now dot the state offer a glimpse into the variety of animal life present during the Miocene period of the Cenozoic era, between 24 and 5 million years ago. There were mastodons, rhinoceroses, camels, cheetahs, and sabre-tooth cats. Instead of zebra, there were pronghorn and as many as twelve species of horses. But most of these species died out during a great drying-out period between 5 and 2.4 million years ago. The drying of the land turned lush grasslands into the prairies known today as the Great Plains, and the western alpine forests and eastern deciduous forests were permanently separated.

The Ice Age, which lasted from about 2.4 million to 10,000 years ago, brought about the final major changes to the North American landscape, both topographical and biological, that created present-day Texas. Erosion did its job on West Texas, producing the magnificent Palo Duro Canyon and the impressive Caprock Escarpment. The state's major streams moved the eroded sediments eastward from the western formations down to the gulf coast, where they continued to add to the Texas landmass—that is, until the glaciers began to melt about 15,000 years ago. Then, sea levels began to rise rapidly, flooding the lower courses of most Texas streams to create the distinctive shallow bays and estuaries of the Texas coast. The silt and sand that continued to flow southeastward now formed barrier islands such as Galveston and Padre Island, which have proven so valuable to students seeking a respite from the arduousness of college coursework each spring.

Life in Texas was also seriously affected by the Ice Age. Mastodons and mammoths, camels, and horses all died out completely, although the latter two species, having crossed westward along the Beringian land bridge, successfully adapted to the Eurasian environment. The long-horned bison (ancestor of the American buffalo), which had crossed the land bridge eastward some 400,000 years ago, also died out by the end of the Pleistocene epoch, as this period is known to geologists. Most species of cat predators also disappeared, the mountain lion and jaguar remaining as the dominant representatives of the group in the Lone Star State. Modern bears also survived.

By the time the first Texans arrived, approximately 11,000 years ago, the land looked very much as it does today, as nature had rearranged the flora. The warming climate sent the conifer and juniper forests of West Texas back up the mountain slopes from which they had descended during the Ice Age, and grasslands returned with a vengeance to the West Texas plains. Piñon pines and junipers (Texas cedar) disappeared from the canyons of the Rio Grande and Pecos River and tributaries as this part of the state became increasingly arid. They were replaced with desert plants such as cacti and sotol. In the central Texas Hill Country, scrub oaks took the place of piñon pines next to junipers, while east of the Balcones Escarpment the older deciduous species of the Ice Age were replaced with warmer weather varieties, such as walnuts and pecans, oaks and elms. Also on the scene were loblolly pines, which although not yet dominant, made up an increasing proportion of East Texas woods. The drying of the climate also played a major hand in the retreat of South Texas scrub oaks to protected and moist areas, allowing for the spread of cacti and mesquite throughout the flat and underwatered region.

Although no Garden of Eden, the land that we call Texas today had much to offer: abundant woods and water, fertile soils and mineral wealth, and ample herds and flocks. Not surprisingly, the first Texans quickly moved to occupy just about every ecological niche the land had to offer. The human story of Texas was about to begin.

## The First Texans

Armed with spears tipped with artfully crafted stone points and traveling in extended family groups, the first people to call what is now Texas home walked into the state about 11,000 years ago, toward the end of what scientists refer to as the Pleistocene epoch. These earliest arrivals, descendants of the great game hunters who had crossed Beringia from Asia to North America at least a thousand years earlier, soon spread out through the state. They became the base population for some (but not all) of the cultures found in Texas when Europeans first arrived in the early sixteenth century. The story of the first Texans is shrouded in the mysteries of stone tools, scarred animal bones, geometrically decorated rocks, the remains of cooking pits, and several human burial grounds. Yet archeologists, with the assistance of other scientists, have begun putting more and more clues together, allowing us to understand the dawn of Texas history in ever greater detail.

## Big Game Hunters Populate the Land

There is disagreement among archeologists regarding the prehistory of Texas. Radiocarbon dating, site and artifact interpretation, and differences in methodological approaches all conspire to prevent the development of a single narrative framework for the story. Where the divisions between the Paleo-Indian, Archaic, and Late Prehistoric periods should come remains unsettled. When did the first humans arrive in Texas? Did early cultures succeed each other or did they overlap? Are the Archaic-period Indians the direct descendants of the Paleo-Indians, or were they new arrivals who occupied a land from which the earliest peoples had disappeared? Did Paleo-Indians hunt in groups or as individuals? How much and exactly what plants did they gather compared to their Archaic successors? We do know enough to tell the basic story of the original settlement of Texas, a story as full of danger, adventure, and adaptation as any from the days of Spanish explorers or Anglo American frontiersmen.

Having retreated northward during a long dry spell that broke about 12,000 years ago, the grasslands of the southern plains spread southward as far as the Rio Grande country below the Pecos River and into central Texas. Herds of mammoths, grazers stressed by the previous drought conditions, followed the expanding grasslands to find a last refuge from extinction in the well-watered meadows of southwest Texas. In their wake came the Clovis people. Not any specific tribe or clan that we can identify, for the archeological record has not clearly revealed the community size of these large-game hunters, the Clovis people made use of a lethal projectile point known by the place it was first discovered: Clovis, New Mexico.

Soon the Clovis hunters spread throughout the region, as far away as East Texas. Although they preferred to use rock shelters near springs and permanent streams, they also camped at convenient locations to carry out hunting and gathering activities that constituted a more than adequate subsistence economy. Most important, they adapted to the varieties of Texas environments that they found. Where mammoths were scarce they turned to the last remaining populations of elephant, camel, horse, and giant bison for meat. Their gathering techniques were amply rewarded by an environment rich in plant foods and smaller game.

Hunting was the principal livelihood for these first Texans, and they were efficient and resourceful killers. Given the size of their prey, Clovis hunters took special care to select the finest flints from which to make their lethal projectile points. Around cooking pits and campfires in the days and weeks preceding a communal hunt, a group's hunters sat exchanging stories and ideas and meticulously working flint cobbles collected at sites such as what is now Alibates Flint Quarries National Monument in the Texas Panhandle. Also prepared at this time were the *atlatls,* or spear throwers, hinged wooden launchers which held the stone-tipped spear and which lent both accuracy and velocity to a throw. Finally, when all was ready, the group would venture near the herd, where the Clovis hunters' strategy was to go after the matriarch or the weakened or wounded peripheral animals. When the object of the hunt was a large mammal such as a bison or camel, they scraped and dressed the hide for use as clothing, packaging, or sometimes even tent material.

The extinction of the mammoth, a gradual drying of the climate, and the spread of a new projectile form found at bison kill sites, marks the transition to the Folsom culture about 10,800 years ago. Facing a somewhat smaller, although equally dangerous prey, Folsom hunters relied on smaller, fluted projectile points, even more graceful and delicate in design than those of the Clovis, although just as deadly. At Bonfire Shelter near Langtry in Val Verde County—a butchering site since Clovis days—a particularly resourceful group of Folsom hunters drove groups of giant bison over the edge of a bluff to their deaths, dragging selected carcasses into the shelter for butchering. In other parts of the state, where no bison were to be found, or where other game animals made easier targets, campsites have been found containing stone tools and bones of some of the last remaining camels, horses, and sloths.

Just how long the good life lasted for these and other Paleo-Indian groups in Texas is not clear. A younger hunting culture, called Plainview, also relied on the longhorn bison. Their plain-sided projectile points, however, indicate a crisis in the large-game-hunting way of life. Also at this time the other remaining megafauna died out, bringing the Pleistocene epoch to an end about 10,000 years ago, and with it the Folsom and Plainview cultures that had relied on them.

The Paleo-Indian descendants of the Clovis, Folsom, and Plainview peoples of Texas had to rely on smaller game animals and, increasingly, on gathering practices that made greater use of plants. Between about 10,000 and 8,000 years ago communities of early Texans experimented with new projectile forms, none as artful and complex as the Clovis and Folsom points of the past, but all capable of bringing down the large game animals of that time: bison, deer, and antelope. A community of Golondrina culture hunter-gatherers of about 9,000 years ago hunted rabbits, rodents, and snake, and gathered walnuts, pecans, and other edible plants. Other Paleo-Indian communities also made use of fish and shellfish.

For centuries Texas provided well for Paleo-Indians. Hunting was good, water was plentiful, and bountiful crops of useful plants provided whatever they might need, even as the climate became drier and warmer. Around the campfires there was leisure time, evidenced by the production of stones with geometric designs and the presence of shells, ochre, and decorative stones, canine tooth necklaces, and bone needles. The careful burials of a young female at Leander, near Austin, and two males near Lake Whitney, along the banks of the Brazos River, suggest that Paleo-Indians also gave thought to the vastness of the universe and the possibility of a hereafter.

## Diversifying Ways of Life

Greater experimentation with tool forms, particularly projectile points, and increasing reliance on more varied foodstuffs denote the arrival of a new age in

Texas, one marked by greater cultural diversity in response to environmental changes. By 8,000 years ago the environment of Texas had assumed its modern form: hot and dry summers and cool-to-moderate winters, depending on the region. The eastern forests had retreated beyond the Trinity River, where the loblolly pine established itself as a dominant species. Elsewhere, along the state's major rivers and creeks, walnuts and pecans continued to flourish, while the western conifers, which had descended the West Texas mountain slopes during the last centuries of the Pleistocene epoch, again retreated to their alpine homes. Water became a somewhat scarce and less reliable resource, particularly in South Texas, where mesquite and other brush plants proliferated, and in the western Rio Grande country, where agave, sotol, and other desert plants began to flourish. The migratory buffalo herds of the Great Plains dominated much of western Texas, while antelope and mule deer were the only other remaining large herbivores. Bears, wolves, mountain lions, ocelots, and jaguars competed with humans as predatory mammals, while eagles and hawks did so from the air. With the disappearance of the North American ice sheet, migratory birds proliferated, making Texas the winter home of ever greater numbers of geese, ducks, and cranes.

Following these environmental changes, by 8,000 years ago the human landscape of Texas had also changed. For the next 7,000 years Texas was home to an increasing number of more regionalized hunting and gathering cultures; this period was known as the Archaic period. Population growth fostered both trade and territoriality, evidence for both of which can be found in Archaic period cemeteries such as the Ernest Witte site near the Brazos River in Austin County. At Ernest Witte, archeologists found stone artifacts from as far away as the Ouachita Mountains of Arkansas and projectile points embedded in the bones of five skeletons. Other sites contain additional evidence of the increased use of plant foods and fish and shellfish.

As the small bands of hunters who had previously roamed over large areas of Texas in pursuit of large game began to rely more on locally available resources, they made the transition from Paleo-Indian to Early Archaic ways of life. They still launched their darts, generally small points made from locally available stone, from atlatls, but now they aimed them at smaller mammals. They probably worked on developing new methods of catching animals to eat, such as traps and nets. These early Texans also probably spent a substantial amount of time experimenting with new ways of preparing the plant foods that now made up a greater share of their diet.

Successful adaptation to the Texas environment created a population boom beginning about 4,500 years ago. Over the next 1,500 years Texas hunter-gatherers became so adept at exploiting the environment that territoriality emerged as a cultural characteristic. Some groups occupied coastal bays and estuaries; other groups claimed more arid, but still fertile, environmental niches in western and southwestern Texas. From the Panhandle to central Texas some cultures maintained an ancestral connection to the bison, whereas farther south, along the middle stretches of the Rio Grande, resourceful desert dwellers relied on smaller game and a wide variety of plants. Fish and shellfish furnished a plentiful food supply to coastal groups for a large part of the year. For the remainder of the year, these groups also lived off the small game and various plants available on the coastal prairies.

These hunter-gatherer groups adapted so successfully to their local environments that the temporary rock shelters and stream-side camps they had established in the past became more permanent camps. A sense of home is evident among Archaic peoples in their treatment of the dead, their evolving aesthetic, and the diversity of their material goods. Well-defined cemeteries were established in which men, women, and children found a final resting place close to their band's favorite site. These sites cannot be considered villages in the modern sense, for the hunter-gatherer bands needed to move, at least seasonally, to ensure adequate food sources. Within their well-established ranges, which would also have included mineral and flint deposits, campsites were used over numerous generations and provided the groups with a sense of identity.

Seasonally occupied village sites at rock shelters became canvases for the group's imagination. Archaic artists decorated their dwellings with imaginative representations of the natural and supernatural world around them. Much as modern graffiti artists express their relationship to a place by elaborate decoration

Rock shelters such as Fate Bell at Seminole Canyon State Historical Park, near the confluence of the Rio Grande and Pecos River, served as housing for early Texans. Paintings on the shelters' walls have survived thousands of years of weathering to remind us of our kinship with the Paleo-Indians, who dreamed of great hunts and spiritual journeys. *(Photo courtesy Texas Parks & Wildlife © 2003, TPWD)*

Late Prehistoric Indian cultures in the context of modern environmental conditions.

with spray paint, or urban gangs "tag" the boundaries of their turfs, Archaic rock artists transformed anonymous caves and megaliths into a band's possessions. Each succeeding generation reinforced the group's association with a place by adding to the earlier artwork, creating a historical record the meaning of which is lost to us today.

Elaborate burials attest to the increasing value placed on status and material possessions. The presence of stones from as far away as the Ouachita Mountains of Arkansas is evidence that territoriality had fostered the development of long-distance trade, another sign of increased materialism. Shell ornaments, chert knives, and even deer skulls in some graves may have been intended to introduce the departed as an important individual in the afterlife. Dart points embedded in the bones of some corpses bespeak the darker side of increased contact between groups—violent competition for land and resources.

The last centuries of the Archaic period also mark the end of a purely hunter-gatherer Texas. Far to the south, in today's central and southern Mexico, human cultural evolution had followed a similar track until about 6,000 years ago, when people started planting the seeds of various plants whose wild relatives they had been gathering for generations. By about 5,500 years ago, early gardeners had transformed the wild *teosinte* into domesticated corn, and soon this most versatile grain had begun to spread in all directions. Farming eventually produced sedentary populations of considerable size, with increasingly sophisticated cultures. In time their technologies spread northward into the American Southwest, where they had an impact on the cultural development of Texas. Between 1,500 and 1,300 years ago, three important technologies—agriculture, pottery making, and the bow and arrow—all arrived in the Lone Star State, contributing to the cultural landscape that Europeans discovered when they arrived in the early sixteenth century.

# The Agricultural Revolution Arrives

The colonization of Texas by frontier agriculturalists was neither an Anglo-American accomplishment of the early nineteenth century, nor a Spanish colonial achievement of the early eighteenth century. By the time the Spanish arrived in Texas, farmers had been raising corn, squash, beans, and sunflowers for about 1,000 years. Representing two very different cultural traditions, the Desert and Mississippian agriculturalists of far West and East Texas tie the state to cultural developments in adjoining parts of North America. They are important elements in the ever diversifying cultural landscape of Late Prehistoric Texas.

## Desert Farmers of West Texas

Along the course of the Rio Grande, from El Paso to Presidio, and northeastward as far as Midland, the native people of West Texas began combining some gardening with their hunting and gathering ways at the latest by 500 C.E. For hundreds of years various hunter-gatherer groups experimented with gardens of corn, squash, beans, and local plants, while still relying on foraging and hunting for their basic subsistence needs. Influenced by the Mogollón culture of southern Arizona and New Mexico, these part-time farmers built pit houses next to their fields of corn and beans. As soon as the harvest was in, however, it was off to hunt and gather in order to meet the rest of the year's subsistence needs. Seasonally occupied villages thus became a common settlement pattern for hundreds of years.

Even in the best of times, farming was a challenge in this perennially arid region. There is no evidence that the Jornada Mogollón people ever attempted irrigation agriculture on a sizable scale, as the Hohokam did in Arizona, but they did divert runoff. By placing their fields at the foot of a mountain, the Jornada Mogollón could tap spring rain runoff to give their crops a chance. Nevertheless, this was a hit-and-miss proposition, and many farming and village sites had to be abandoned after a year or two, when they were unable to support group needs.

At a select few sites, conditions were right for long-term settlement. As the pit-house dwellers succeeded in raising surpluses of corn and beans, they began to construct simple adobe pueblos, usually consisting of a number of apartments arranged in a row and containing a large room thought to be a ceremonial or communal space. Builders often plastered the floors of their pueblos and built a variety of outbuildings and cooking pits. Even in pueblo times the Jornada Mogollón did not entirely abandon their traveling ways. In some villages, including Firecracker Pueblo (so named for an abandoned fireworks stand across the road from the site north of El Paso), they scooped out storage pits in which to keep corn and other food supplies during their absences.

Increasing dependence on corn made the Jornada Mogollón people focus increasingly on agriculture and support activities. They had to make *manos* and *metates* (hand stones and grinding slabs) and transport them to the village from wherever the stone deposits were, sometimes a considerable distance away. They had to make pottery on a regular basis, given its fragility, for storage, cooking, and eating purposes. Utilitarian as the pots, bowls, pitchers, and ladles they made were, the human need for artistic expression found its way into animal motifs and geometric designs that have acquired the designation "El Paso polychrome style."

The Jornada Mogollón people were more gatherers than hunters, even in their pre-pueblo days, but animal protein, leather, bone, and sinew were essential products that could only be obtained through the hunt. Whereas rabbits, rodents, birds, and snakes provided everyday meals, deer, antelope, and bison supplied not only the village table, but its workshops as well. Killed, skinned, and butchered in the field, the animals' hide, meat, and useful bones were brought back to the village for processing. Because the Jornada Mogollón people used stone tools, they were forced to spend a considerable amount of time preparing arrow tips, dart points, scrapers, knives, and hammers from stones that sometimes came from hundreds of miles away.

And travel, whether to hunt, gather, or procure stone for tools, brought the Jornada Mogollón into contact with neighboring groups and cultures. Sometimes they brought back a pot or bowl from one of the western Mogollón or Hohokam villages, or from an Anasazi pueblo. From exchanges with other hunting parties, they obtained obsidian, turquoise, and even seashell beads. Although more important symbolically than economically, these interactions provided the

Jornada Mogollón with vital links to the technological and cultural trends of the region.

By the early fourteenth century, the peoples of the Trans-Pecos were entering a period of crisis. So successful during earlier (and wetter) times in establishing a corn-farming subsistence base for themselves, they had outstripped their capacity to survive prolonged drought and underproduction. This was not unique to the Jornada Mogollón, for the Hohokam, Anasazi, and western Mogollón were suffering from the same combination of environmental and demographic factors. Drought conditions emptied reservoirs and meant that not enough runoff came down mountain slopes to allow the large pueblos to survive. Dispersing in their efforts to survive, some of the Jornada Mogollón moved north into the Rio Grande valley of central New Mexico to join Anasazi migrants from the northwest. Other Jornada Mogollón groups entirely abandoned agriculture and returned to a hunter-gatherer way of life, especially the easternmost groups, which had easy access to migratory buffalo herds on the southern Plains.

By the time they arrived in the region, sixteenth-century Spaniards identified various Indian groups inhabiting the lower parts of the southern Plains and parts of the Trans-Pecos as Jumanos. Although they described some of these groups as purely bison-hunting societies, they described others as floodplain agriculturalists. At least some of these groups were undoubtedly the descendants of the Jornada Mogollón culture, some of whom had clung to their semisedentary agricultural ways and others of whom had become important traders across Texas. Slowly over the next two centuries, the Jumanos disappeared from the scene, some incorporated into other regional culture groups and others absorbed into northern Mexican colonial society.

## Mound-Building Farmers of Southeast Texas

As late as the last decades of the seventeenth century Jumano traders were crossing the great expanse of Texas to trade with agricultural peoples, the Caddoans, who inhabited the eastern fringes of the Great Plains and the river valleys of the Mississippi basin. Some of these Caddoans lived as far west as the Trinity River and represented an even more successful Texas agricultural tradition than the Jornada Mogollón. By the time the Spanish arrived, their colonization of East Texas extended back about a thousand years, and they would continue to be an important factor in Spanish colonial Texas history up to the eve of Mexican independence.

About 500 C.E., when Caddoan groups began their southwestward migration into what is today East Texas, that part of the state was home to descendants of Paleo-Indian and Archaic-period cultures. Some of these groups, having traded with both Plains hunters to the west and agriculturalists to the east, had established substantial societies in which gardening had become a minor element of their subsistence strategy. Their settlements consisted of seasonally occupied villages of modest numbers of people. These Late Archaic people were certainly in no position to stop the Caddoan migration that swept westward over the next few centuries.

The Caddoans who moved into Texas were themselves descendants of a series of increasingly sophisticated cultures that had flourished in the Mississippi basin for hundreds of years before the Caddo emerged as a distinct society about 800 C.E. The Adena and Hopewell cultures, which flourished in the Midwest between 2,800 and 1,600 years ago were ancestors of all of the later "mound builder" societies of North America. These societies were characterized by sophisticated agricultural practices, the development of copper working, and the burial of prominent people in increasingly larger mounds. During Hopewell times, long-distance trade and a population boom led to the establishment of a hierarchical society and tribute system that extended for hundreds of miles along the basins of the Mississippi and its eastern tributaries.

Competition for resources and other undetermined factors contributed to the decline of Hopewell culture by about 400 C.E., yet its accomplishments were not forgotten. Even as Hopewell was in decline, however, a similar culture was emerging in the same area of the central Mississippi Valley. Some 1,700 years ago the Mississippian culture, with strong roots in Adena and Hopewell, but better adapted to changed conditions, had established itself in several locations. This new culture carried on the mound-building tradition of Hopewell but built its subsistence strategy on corn agriculture.

Among the regional variants of Mississippian culture was one that developed in what is today western Louisiana. This distinctive culture, which has come to be known as Caddoan, emerged by about 500 C.E., and in the course of the next three centuries spread through the area along the Red, Sabine, Angelina, Neches, and Trinity rivers of Texas. The people who brought it to Texas spoke one of a number of related languages called Caddoan today, of which Wichita, Pawnee, and Osage are other examples. In time the Caddos became the dominant society of the region, spreading elements of their culture to neighboring non-Caddo speakers.

That process took place over hundreds of years during which Caddoan culture developed into a sophisticated system of interrelated kinship-based political entities that late seventeenth-century Europeans described as confederacies. In fact, the three confederacies of historic times—the Kadohadacho, Hasinais, and Natchitoches—were the product of successful adaptation to environmental conditions in East Texas, western Louisiana, southwestern Arkansas, and southeastern Oklahoma. In this well-watered and heavily forested region, early Caddoan pioneers found abundant natural resources that enabled them to establish scattered communities which by 1,000 years ago had become completely dependent on corn as the principal staple. Squash, beans, sunflowers, and a variety of other annuals rounded out the agricultural base of Caddo society. Caddoans also hunted deer and rabbit to meet the balance of their dietary requirements and, along with the occasional bear and buffalo, to provide leather and furs for other needs.

Like Mississippian cultures to the east, the Caddoans were prolific mound builders. As their culture became more sophisticated, they developed a settlement

At Caddoan Mounds State Historical Park, the agricultural way of life of early Texas farmers has been unearthed through years of archeological excavation. Mural paintings at the visitors center colorfully illustrate their long-vanished way of life. Although Caddos no longer reside in Texas as a tribe, a group from Oklahoma returns to the park each year for commemorative ceremonies. *(Photo courtesy Texas Parks & Wildlife © 2003, Nola Davis)*

pattern based on scattered agricultural villages of conical-shaped thatch dwellings, a few important towns, and specialized ceremonial centers. Mounds near villages continued to serve the basic purpose of containing the remains of high-status individuals, and mounds at ceremonial centers served to elevate small temples in which Caddo priests and leaders could commune with the spirit world.

The prosperity indicated by widespread mound building is also evidenced by extensive interregional trade and sophisticated crafts activities. Through Plains intermediaries, the Caddo exchanged their hardwood bows, ceramics, tanned goods, and perhaps even corn, for turquoise from New Mexico, copper from the Great Lakes region, seashells from the Gulf of Mexico, and buffalo hides from Plains. They produced sophisticated agricultural and woodworking tool kits of stone and shell that included digging tools, hoes, and axes for clearing timber. In the stone-scarce environment in which they lived, the Caddo even relied on wood to make the large mortars and long wooden pestles they used to grind corn into meal. Caddo pottery and basketry from the centuries immediately preceding the arrival of Europeans was among the finest in North America. French and Spanish descriptions of their tanned and decorated animal-skin apparel indicate a long tradition of craftsmanship.

Due to extensive observation by Europeans in the late seventeenth and early eighteenth centuries, a great deal can be inferred about Caddo society on the eve of the arrival of Europeans. Overall, the Caddos were largely peaceful tribes before the eighteenth century, although defensive warfare was part of life. At the most basic level of society—the family—organization was matrilineal, meaning that descent was traced on the mother's side. Marriage took place between members of different clans, and families were grouped in clans, usually named for animals, which were hierarchically ranked. Commoner families typically lived in individual homesteads surrounded by the agricultural field assigned to them.

Political organization outside the home combined egalitarian and hierarchical practices and was partly theocratic in nature. Chiefdoms composed of groups of these scattered homesteads, one or more central villages, and a ceremonial center, were under the leadership of a hereditary *caddi,* or community chief. He governed with the support of elders called *canahas,* but in times of war, villages would select war chiefs from among proven warriors. Religious leadership in each Caddo tribal group was in the hands of the *Xinesi,* also a hereditary position in the male line, who conducted ceremonies to communicate with the spirit world. His mediation with the supreme being, and his leadership during important annual feasts to celebrate planting, harvesting, and the hunt, were indispensable to the continuation of Caddo society.

By the early fifteenth century Caddo society faced the same period of crisis that confronted the other agricultural societies of North America. Overpopulation may have combined with changing environmental conditions to create violent competition. Corn, a soil-depleting crop, may not have been planted in the proper balance with beans and other soil-enriching plants to maintain adequate production levels. Whatever the case, a reduction in the number of long-distance trade items found in Caddo archeological sites, the discontinuation of mound building, and the abandonment of many sites throughout East Texas, indicate that by the time Europeans arrived Caddoan culture was well past its prime.

The decline of Caddo fortunes, which continued throughout the colonial period, was intensified by a number of factors. Warfare with neighboring Indian groups such as the Choctaws, Osages, Wichitas, and Tonkawas became more violent as the region's animal resources became a source of contention in trade relations with the French. Epidemic diseases, which probably struck even before the first European set foot in East Texas, decimated whole villages, forcing survivors to consolidate into fewer and fewer groups. Attempting to adapt to the changing conditions of the eighteenth century, the Texas Caddos began to hunt bison on horseback, an adaptation that brought them into the realm of people for whom the buffalo had always been at the core of life and culture.

## Buffalo Peoples and Fishermen

While people in eastern Texas experimented with becoming agricultural societies, from central Texas to the Panhandle the American bison and other large mammals remained basic to human subsistence. Along the Texas coast in the southernmost prairies, Indian cultures relied on seasonal migration to exploit locally available resources. All of these native groups were active in the east-west and north-south trade system that made Texas a crossroads of cultural and technological exchange long before the Spanish, the French or Anglo Americans ever set foot in the state.

### Buffalo Hunters of Western Texas

In the case of central and Panhandle Texas, the lack of archeological evidence makes it difficult to tie Archaic and Late Prehistoric populations to those groups encountered by Spaniards in the sixteenth, seventeenth, and eighteenth centuries. The case of the Panhandle-Llano Estacado region appears to be the easier of the two to piece together. Late Archaic hunter-gatherers either were absorbed by eastward-moving Pueblos and Mogollón peoples, or were pushed farther east to the Hill Country of central Texas. The result was that between 800 and 500 years ago, during a period called the Antelope Creek phase, the broad expanse of northwestern Texas was home to a culture that combined bison hunting with horticulture and the construction of permanent dwellings.

Antelope Creek people may well have been Pueblo colonizers expanding eastward in pursuit of permanent water sources at the beginning of the great drought age that eventually transformed the Anasazi and Mogollón into the modern Pueblo tribes. Settling near permanent springs fed by the Ogallala Aquifer, these groups adapted to local conditions by taking up buffalo hunting as an important subsistence strategy, coming back to their villages at spring planting and fall harvest times. Besides hunting, Antelope Creek people became important traders with surrounding cultures. With buffalo hides and, perhaps, dried meat as trade items, they acquired ceramics from both the Pueblos to the west and the Caddos to the east. They also traded turquoise, obsidian, and seashells, making it clear that their exchange system functioned beyond the utilitarian level.

Successful as they were in adapting to conditions on the southern Plains, the Antelope Creek people were incapable of meeting the challenge of a new intruder group that arrived in the Panhandle region about 500 years ago. For hundreds, if not over a thousand years, Athabaskan-speaking bands of hunter-gatherers had been moving down the eastern slopes of the Rocky Mountains, adapting to conditions on the fringes of the Great Plains on the way to becoming the most formidable pre-horse buffalo people of Texas. In historic times these people came to be known as Apaches. Some groups of Apaches settled east and others west of the Rockies. Highly adaptive, the eastern Apaches not only became the most proficient bison hunters of West Texas, but they also took up gardening, mimicking the subsistence strategy of the Antelope Creek people they replaced. Arriving on the eve of the arrival of the Spaniards to the interior of North America, the ancestral Plains Apaches were among the earliest people to be described by Spanish explorers.

Unfortunately, the same cannot be said for the people inhabiting central Texas. Because European penetration of this region came rather late—in the last decades of the seventeenth century—the prehistory of the area is not definitive. For a long time informed opinion was that the Tonkawas, the people thought to have inhabited the area west of the Caddoan home territory in the early eighteenth century, were the descendants of the region's Archaic Indians. It may well be, however, that the Tonkawas represent the coming together of late-arriving southern Plains hunters and the remaining central Texas hunter-gatherer bands that were no longer independently viable.

Regardless, for a thousand years before the arrival of Europeans, central Texas was home to a succession of Archaic-period hunter-gatherer cultures that relied extensively on the buffalo for subsistence. Highly mobile, and continuing to make use of rock shelters, by 1,300 years ago these Indians had adopted the bow and arrow and made use of pottery. Within the next few centuries, the central Texas Indians joined in the interregional trade system that had developed across the expanse of Texas. Ceramics imported from Caddoan lands to the east, seashells, and stone from hundreds of miles away survive to point out the extent of this trade. But the life of these Toyah-phase people (the name given to the central Texas culture dated to 1300–1600 C.E.) was not an entirely idyllic life of following the buffalo and gathering berries and nuts. They were, it seems, basically territorial, as the presence of cemeteries associated with them attests. Numerous burials, with arrowheads found among the skeletal remains, indicate that the deceased suffered violent deaths.

### Hunter-Gatherers and Fishermen of South Texas and the Gulf Coast

The violence experienced by the Toyah-phase people may have been the result of conflict with their southeastern neighbors. To the Spaniards the various hunter-gatherer groups that inhabited most of southern Texas and neighboring northern Coahuila came to be known as Coahuiltecos, a name that has remained popular with scholars of early Texas. Yet the Coahuiltecans consisted of a number of distinct cultures and language groups that had evolved in the South Texas environment over hundreds of years since Archaic times.

Generally, Coahuiltecan cultures shared a number of characteristics that distinguish them from other Texas hunter-gatherers. Very mobile, they normally occupied open campsites, relying on temporary brush or hide shelters to protect them from the elements. About 1,000 years ago the bow and arrow and a simple form of pottery made an appearance among them, although the absence of *manos* and *metates* at their sites suggests that they did not experiment with corn.

As hunter-gatherers, the ancestral Coahuiltecans had relied mostly on small mammals such as rabbits and rodents, snakes, and freshwater fish and shellfish for the meat portion of their diet. As the bison moved south in the centuries immediately preceding the arrival of Europeans, the Coahuiltecans increasingly hunted buffalo, an adaptation that may well have brought them into conflict with buffalo hunters to the north as their hunting ranges overlapped.

The territoriality of Coahuiltecans varied greatly, with some groups being more attached to specific locations than others. In the interior of South Texas, between San Antonio and the Rio Grande, the preference for isolated burials indicates that even at the end of the prehistoric period these band peoples remained not only extremely mobile, but also unattached to specific sites. Coahuiltecans in the lower Rio Grande valley, on the other hand, were attached to specific sites, and cemeteries are much more numerous in that area.

The Brownsville Complex people, as the Late Prehistoric Coahuiltecan culture of the lower Rio Grande region is known, are distinct from other Coahuiltecans in other respects. Most important, they developed a material culture that made extensive use of marine resources. They employed seashells for a wide variety of purposes: whelks became hammers, sunray clams became scrapers, and conch and clam shells were turned into projectile points. They used shells to create jewelry and other ornamentation for exchange purposes. In time the Brownsville Complex people sought to trade their shell creations with other hunter-gatherer cultures of the interior and with the Mesoamerican cultures of central Mexico, from whom they received ceramics, obsidian, and jadeite.

Up the coast from the Rio Grande delta Coahuiltecans lived another coastal culture with distinct characteristics and a long history of interaction with Euro-Americans in historic times. Collectively known as the Karankawas, these people of the bays and barrier islands from Corpus Christi to the lower Brazos River can be traced through the archeological evidence to about 1,200 years ago. With access to substantial marine as well as upland animal and plant resources, the Karankawa Indians developed an annual cycle of migration based on the seasonal availability of specific species. In the fall and winter of each year extended family groups and small bands gathered together at traditional coastal sites, where through early spring they could exploit the ample supply of drum- and redfish that spawned in the shallow bays and estuaries. Shellfish, particularly clams and mussels, made up a significant portion of their diet, but mammals, mostly white-tailed deer, only a fractional amount.

Arriving at their winter campsite in the fall, the Karankawa families erected simple brush and hide huts intended to keep out only the worst of the elements. They repaired or constructed canoes, which were of dugout design and shaped with shell adzes and scrapers. Some members of the group prepared fishing nets and traps. Others chipped away at flint cobbles to make the arrowheads and other stone tools necessary to process the catch of fish and shellfish on which the group would feed until early spring.

Each member of the camp had duties to perform, but also considerable leisure time. Although drum- and redfish were the principal meat resource for the group until early spring, an occasional white-tailed deer or rabbit not only added variety, but provided hide and bones for the group's clothing, tools, and ornaments. Some group members did not go fishing or hunting, but went out to gather roots, nuts, and leaves for food, basketry, and dyes. Some returned to camp at the end of the day with supplies of clay for pottery and asphaltum (naturally occurring marine tar) with which to coat or decorate pottery and to waterproof baskets.

The Karankawas were as concerned with the hereafter as any of their neighbors and, indeed, as just about all human cultures. A simple people with little social stratification and few measures of status and wealth, the group's members shared in both times of bounty and scarcity. If the practices described by Spanish observers in the eighteenth century stretch back to prehistoric times, then Karankawa celebrations were truly joyful affairs of group dancing ceremonies that lasted for days and wrestling and other skills competitions among the adolescent and adult males.

In late spring the camp broke up into extended family hunting and gathering groups. Moving inland to occupy sites along the coastal prairie's many streams, these smaller groups set up hunting camps to take advantage of the substantial population of bison and white-tailed deer present during Late Prehistoric times. Consistent archeological evidence indicates that this upland movement went no farther than about twenty-five miles, a boundary at which Coahuiltecan sites begin. Also evident in the remains of the camps of both Rockport-Karankawas and Coahuiltecans is shared use of this boundary area, for the sites of the former indicate spring-summer use while the camps of the latter indicate fall-winter use.

Access to a rich and varied diet made the Karankawas a strong and healthy people. Spanish observers remarked on their tall stature and robust builds, evidence of which extends into prehistoric times in the archeological record. One interesting example of their adaptation to coastal conditions that proved repellent to Spanish and Anglo American observers because of the odor was their habit of rubbing themselves in alligator grease to protect themselves from mosquitoes, a practice shared with their coastal neighbors. There is no evidence in the archeological record, however, to support the common Euro-American misconception that the Karankawas were cannibals. In fact, there is little evidence that they were significantly more bellicose than other Texas Indians in prehistoric times. It seems clear that on the eve of European contact the Karankawas were enjoying the simple prosperity of a bountiful natural environment.

So too were their neighbors to the north. Along the coast from Galveston Bay eastward and inland into the coastal prairie lived hunter-gatherers with many of the same characteristics as the Karankawa people. Known as the Galveston Bay Focus, they appear to have practiced the same kind of seasonal migration and balanced reliance on marine and upland resources as their southern neighbors. They may have been ancestors of some of the Atakapans (Akokisas, Deadoses, and Atakapans proper) that Europeans would encounter in the eighteenth century.

## Conclusion

It took millions of years for Texas, as we now know it, to form. Texas is a land of geological marvels: the product of continental collisions, meteor impacts, glacial expansions and contractions, and erosion due to wind, temperature, and precipitation. It is a land of extinct volcanoes and submerged mountain ranges, of granite hills and mud flats. It contains hundreds of miles of coast, as well as hundreds of thousands of square miles of underground rivers and lakes. Also below its surface are the relics of those eons of change: dead forests and animal matter compressed into coal, gas, and oil fields that have fed the engines of industry for the last century; limestone and shale that were once an unfathomable number of sea creatures forming reefs in the shallow seas that once covered much of the state.

The diversity of Texas's geology is more than matched by the variety of its environments. The sub-humid forests of East Texas for centuries sheltered the most successful agricultural society to emerge within the state. The Plains and prairies stretching from northwestern Texas to the southern coast provided such a rich animal subsistence base in the form of bison, deer, and antelope, that full-time agriculture, or any agriculture at all in some cases, proved an unnecessary adaptation. Even in the harshest environment Texas had to offer—the desert far west—there were enough water, animal, and plant resources to meet the needs of a particularly hardy group of early Texans.

Consequently, at the beginning of the sixteenth century the land we now call Texas had already been a cultural crossroads for thousands of years. It was the meeting place of Woodlands, Plains, and Southwestern cultures. It was home to both simple hunter-gatherers and sophisticated agriculturalists. Its people spoke a number of unrelated languages and maintained widely varying traditions, although their cultures all made pottery and used stone tools and bows and arrows. Almost all Texas Indians had something else in common: To one degree or another they all made use of the buffalo, a grazing animal that due to changing environmental conditions in the Late Prehistoric period was extending its range southward and eastward across almost the entire breadth of Texas.

Not a single Indian living within the state's present boundaries would have understood the concept of Texas, however. With the exception of the complex, hierarchical, socially-stratified Caddos, no prehistoric Texas Indian group appears to have had much use for any kind of political organization beyond the local chief or head man and his group of trusted advisors. And, although most cultures had become territorial by Late Prehistoric times, that territoriality was at most a simple defense of hunting grounds or a finely tuned subsistence strategy based, as in the case of the Karankawas, on seasonal exploitation of locally available resources.

In other words, the land that the Spaniards encountered in the first half of the sixteenth century was not a wilderness or a land of savages. Crisscrossed by trade networks that tied the Rockies to the Mississippi and the Great Lakes to the Gulf of Mexico, its people were exposed to and influenced by, to one degree or another, the major technological changes of pre-Columbian North America. Occupying every possible ecological niche the state had to offer, its people had adapted to conditions with amazing dexterity.

Most of these adaptations, which relied on extensive rather than intensive exploitation of the land, seemed odd and primitive to the technologically advanced and socially complex Europeans who encountered them. Certainly, the early cultures of Texas paled in comparison to the technological and social complexity of some Mesoamerican and Old World civilizations. And so they were unprepared to meet the challenge of the new world. In the course of the next 500 years, this new world would leave no room for the descendants of the first Texans to call the state home.

## SUGGESTED READINGS

The study of early Texas requires a little ingenuity, given the existing nature of the literature. Entries in the *New Handbook of Texas* (*NHOT*) covering most of the subjects treated in this chapter (except dinosaurs) will prove extremely useful as a basic introduction. The essay "Geology" in the *NHOT* gives a clear overview that complements the information in *Roadside Geology of Texas* by Darwin Spearing (1991). Dividing the state into sections, focusing on the geological features encountered on or near the state's byways, and profusely illustrated, *Roadside Geology of Texas* is a great companion for weekend excursions. Terry G. Jordan et al., *Texas: A Geography* (1984), remains the best survey on the subject.

### Prelude to Human Texas

Massive amounts of technical information are available on the evolution of life in Texas and North America, most of it of such scientific rigor as to be inaccessible to the general reader. Fortunately, there are some writers who are able to make the work of scientists intelligible to the rest of us. One fascinating view of how the interaction between land and life has shaped North America, including Texas, is Tim Flannery's *The Eternal Frontier: An Ecological History of North America and Its People* (2001). Both readable and informative, it surveys the natural history of the northern part of the western hemisphere during the last 65 million years, since the meteor crashed into the northern Yucatán, helped kill off the dinosaurs, and set mammals on the road to world domination. Taking the story backwards for Texas, specifically, is Louis Jacobs's *Lone Star Dinosaurs* (1995), a nicely illustrated and easy-to-read overview of the state's paleontologic record by a practitioner.

### The First Texans

The archeological literature on Texas largely consists of highly technical reports of fieldwork and efforts to reconcile findings in different parts of the state from approximately the same time frame. Although no single-author, single-volume synthesis of Texas during prehistoric times exists, the story can be pieced together from a few select sources written for students and the general public. The reader is forewarned that archeologists do not all agree on the boundaries between prehistoric periods, or on the precise taxonomy to apply to their findings, although they do tend to agree broadly on Paleo-Indian, Archaic, and Late Prehistoric as the major periods. These issues, along with many others, are presented by Linda Cordell in *Archaeology of the Southwest* (2nd ed., 1997). Although concerned only with western Texas as part of her definition of "Southwest," the text is very useful in understanding the general currents of development during Paleo-Indian times in Texas. A brief but extremely useful summary of Texas prehistory is Thomas Hester's article on the subject in the *NHOT,* as well as the appropriate parts of his *Digging into South Texas Prehistory: A Guide for Amateur Archaeologists* (1980). Now out of date with regard to the vast amount of archeological work done in Texas over the last forty years, but still useful for explaining basic lines of development in early Texas, is W. W. Newcomb, Jr.'s *The Indians of Texas: From Prehistoric to Modern Times* (1961). Newcomb also provided the text to a marvelously illustrated volume on *The Rock Art of Texas Indians* (1967), the paintings for which were done by Forrest Kirkland from original sketches and photographs.

## The Agricultural Revolution Arrives

Texas Indians during Late Prehistoric to historic times have received unequal attention from scholars. Articles in the *NHOT* on individual tribes are uneven in how up-to-date they are, but generally serve as a good introduction to the background of each group. The evidence for the mysterious Jumanos, their possible origins, and what might have happened to them is presented by Nancy Parrott Hickerson in *The Jumanos: Hunters and Traders of the South Plains* (1994). As for the advanced agricultural Caddos, most of the writing about them for prehistoric times, as with all Indian groups, is highly technical. The opening parts of three works provide a useful introduction: *Caddo Indians: Where We Come From,* by Cecile Elkins Carter (1995); an overview of Caddo history down to the present, *"The Caddo Nation": Archaeological and Ethnohistoric Perspectives,* by Timothy K. Perttula (1992); and *The Caddo Chiefdoms: Caddo Economics and Politics, 700–1835* (1998) by David LaVere.

## Buffalo Peoples and Fishermen

Aside from the material on them in Cordell's *Archaeology of the Southwest,* there is little available to the general reader on the pre-Apache peoples of the Texas Plains. The story of the Tonkawas and their status as "ancient" Texas Indians remains an archeological tug-of-war largely inaccessible to the general public. The story is better with regard to the Coahuiltecans, as Hester's *Digging into South Texas Prehistory* gives a clear picture of the variety of Coahuiltecan cultures. The work of Robert A. Ricklis—in particular *The Karankawa Indians of Texas: An Ecological Study of Cultural Traditions and Change* (1996)—has revolutionized our understanding of these long-maligned people. The Atakapans and other East Texas Indians are the subjects of Lawrence E. Aten, *Indians of the Upper Texas Coast* (1983).

Finally, for those readers who wish to dig into Texas Indian prehistory themselves, there are a number of out-of-print works that can serve as invaluable guides: Parker Nunley, *A Field Guide to Archeological Sites in Texas* (1989); Ellen Sue Turner and Thomas R. Hester, *A Field Guide to Stone Artifacts of Texas Indians* (1985); and, of course, Hester's *Digging into South Texas Prehistory.*

# 2

# First Meetings, First Conflicts, 1492–1693

Looking out from behind the dune vegetation of what is now Follets Island on a crisp November morning in 1528, the island's inhabitants beheld a strange sight. In the wreckage of a large makeshift boat, a group of strangely dressed men sat close together, shivering and muttering in an incomprehensible language. In the days that followed, the scene was repeated three more times on other Texas barrier islands. In all, over two hundred members of Pánfilo de Narváez's Florida expedition had by happenstance become the first Europeans to arrive in Texas. This first recorded meeting between Texas Indians and Europeans took place on peaceful terms. The Indians offered fish, roots, and nuts, while the Spaniards reciprocated with hawkbells and beads. The chronicler of this meeting, Alvar Núñez Cabeza de Vaca records that when he and his men were unable to relaunch their boat and lost all their possessions in the heavy surf, "the Indians, at sight of what had befallen us, and our state of suffering and melancholy destitution, sat down among us, and from the sorrow and pity they felt, they all began to lament so earnestly that they might have been heard at a distance, and continued so doing more than half an hour." In the months to come the shrinking number of survivors, undernourished, suffering from exposure, and increasingly at odds with the local inhabitants, would transfer some of their negative feelings to the island, naming it *Mal Hado,* or "Misfortune." Eventually, only four men, Cabeza de Vaca and two other Spaniards along with the North African slave of one of them, returned to Christendom. Their adventures inspired others to venture into the interior of North America and take part in the initial chapter of Texas history.

| 1492 | Columbus's voyage opens Western Hemisphere to European exploitation |
| 1519 | Álvarez de Pineda becomes first European to explore Texas coast |
| 1521 | Cortés completes Spain's conquest of the Aztec Empire |
| 1528 | Narváez's expedition to Florida marooned on Texas coast; survivors Alvar Núñez Cabeza de Vaca and companions provide earliest information on Texas Indians |
| 1541 | Coronado visits the Texas Panhandle during his 1540–42 expedition to Arizona, New Mexico, and the Plains |
| 1542 | Moscoso leads the remains of the Soto expedition (1539–43) into East Texas before returning to the Mississippi River |
| 1554 | Hurricane wrecks Spanish treasure fleet off Padre Island, confirming accounts of hostile Indians |
| 1573 | Philip II issues new colonization laws aimed at making expansion of Spanish rule more orderly |
| 1598 | Oñate's expedition crosses the Rio Grande at Paso del Norte |
| 1659 | Fray García de San Francisco establishes Mission Nuestra Señora de Guadalupe, first Spanish settlement at Paso del Norte |
| 1680 | Pueblo Revolt leads to founding of Ysleta for friendly Tigua Indians, and other settlements at Paso del Norte |
| 1685 | La Salle expedition lands at Matagorda Bay, builds Fort St. Louis |
| 1690 | San Francisco de los Tejas becomes first Spanish settlement in the province of Texas |
| 1693 | Spaniards abandon Texas |

When Europeans first set foot on what is now Texas soil, they claimed by right of discovery land that for thousands of years had been the home of native peoples. The first encounters between Europeans and Texas Indians, which took place during the Age of the Conquistadors in the first half of the sixteenth century, had very different outcomes for both sides. The diseases that the Spaniards brought with them quickly began to take their toll on the native population, setting off a chain reaction of events that would last for centuries. For the Spaniards, disappointment marked their contacts with Texas. The vast expanses of the land, the dearth of precious metals, and, to their view, backward Indian cultures argued against devoting many resources to the settlement of the region. Having claimed the land and foreseeing no European challengers to the claim, Spaniards quickly forgot about Texas as they turned their attention to the more immediate task of establishing a successful colony among the civilizations of Mesoamerica.

It was not until the mighty struggles for empire that enveloped Spain, France, and England from the end of the sixteenth century onward that Spaniards began to pay attention to their long-neglected far northern frontier. Only reluctantly did Spaniards return to Texas, and when they did they were indecisive and ill equipped to meet the challenges posed by the country. And only in the El Paso area was a secure Spanish presence established before the end of the seventeenth century.

## Dawn of Texas History

The first Spaniards to explore Texas lived during that restless period of frenzied searching for precious metals and great civilizations known as the Age of the Conquistadors. From their experiences in the Caribbean and Mesoamerica (Mexico and Central America), Spaniards looked upon the conquest of Indian peoples and the plunder of their wealth as legitimate goals of exploration. In fact, it was Hernán Cortés's triumph over the Aztec empire that created high expectations for what might be found in the rest of North America. From the 1520s through the 1540s numerous expeditions made their way north from Cuba and the land of the Aztecs seeking other Mexicos. Eventually, members of three of these expeditions came into contact with most of Texas's geographic regions and many of its culture groups.

### Spain and America

When Pánfilo de Narváez presented his petition to King Charles I of Spain (better known as Charles V, Holy Roman Emperor) to conquer Florida in 1526, he was hoping to surpass the accomplishments of his rival and personal enemy, Cortés. From various slaving expeditions and explorations in the 1510s, including one by

Álvarez de Pineda in 1519 that mapped the entire gulf coast from Florida to Tampico, Spaniards became curious about the vast land north of Mexico that came to be known as Florida. Narváez, who had sided with the governor of Cuba against Cortés during the conquest of Mexico, had lost an eye in battle attempting to arrest Cortés. Captured, humiliated, and abandoned, he had returned to Spain intent on getting his due; this, he believed, could be accomplished in Florida.

The broad sweep of the royal *capitulación,* or charter, Narváez received in 1526 granted him all the lands between the Soto la Marina River in Mexico and the Atlantic seaboard, a vague expanse known as Florida from the time of Juan Ponce de León. This territory, he firmly believed, held within it rich and populous kingdoms capable of compensating him and his followers for their considerable expenses. For, like the other conquistadors, the members of Narváez's *entrada* (conquest, colonization, or settlement expedition) had signed up for service without any compensation except a share in the spoils and rights to land. If truly fortunate, the conquistadors might also receive an *encomienda,* a grant of a certain number of Indian tributaries as reward for their services in the expedition, but only under obligation to Christianize and protect the Indians—an obligation more often honored in the breach than in the performance. If the members of this *entrada* were like the men who followed Cortés, they had gone into debt to equip themselves. A successful venture would not only make them rich, but lords of the land. For, although some conquistadors were members of the Spanish nobility, most were not, and the prospects of becoming *hidalgos* (literally sons of something, the lowest rung of Spanish nobility), served as a powerful motive.

To be sure, daring and resourceful as the conquistadors were, they were not without their critics. One of these was the prominent Dominican clergyman Bartolomé de Las Casas. For fifty years, from the conquest of Cuba until his death in 1566, Las Casas worked tirelessly for the welfare of the native populations of the New World. He opposed everything conquistadors like Narváez represented. Indian slavery was not only unjustified, but reprehensible. The sole purpose of the Spanish enterprise in the New World should be to convert its peoples to the one true faith; to do anything else was to exploit naturally free and rational beings.

The defender of the Indians struggled mightily against a society steeped in the martial spirit, ruled by a monarch wrapped in the mantel of divine right, and equipped with the technological tools to construct a modern empire. Having expelled the last of the Muslim feudal lords in 1492, after seven centuries of religious warfare known as the *Reconquista,* King Fernando and Queen Isabel united much of the Iberian peninsula through a series of centralizing measures that gave the crown more control at the expense of free cities and the nobility. Fernando, in particular, carried the war to northern Africa, where he sought to expand the power of the Kingdom of Aragón, which had previously played second fiddle to Isabel's Kingdom of Castile. For most Spaniards, the distinction that Las Casas attempted to draw between Muslims and pagans was mere hair-splitting. War against non-Christians was justified, and there was no better proof of God's approval than the riches with which he had rewarded Spanish arms.

To further unify the country, the Catholic Kings (a title granted to Fernando and Isabel by the papacy in recognition of their religious zeal) issued ultimatums to the Jews and Muslims of Spain: convert to Christianity or leave the country. This effort at religious unification had negative consequences for Spain, however, as a large proportion of the learned and skilled population abandoned the Iberian peninsula for other parts of the Mediterranean, and those who chose conversion lived under the taint of their past religious convictions. The large population of "new Christians" also strengthened the power of the Holy Office of the Inquisition, a branch of the Catholic Church dedicated to rooting out heresy and Judaizing (continuing to practice Jewish customs after conversion). The Spanish monarchy also used the Inquisition to eliminate political enemies. Not surprisingly, the Protestant Reformation stood no chance of gaining a foothold in Spain. With the election of Fernando and Isabel's grandson Charles I as Holy Roman Emperor, a Spanish king became the successor to the Holy Roman Empire. Charles's son, Philip II, would carry his religious zealotry to the extreme, bankrupting Spain in his efforts to destroy Protestant England and defeat his rebellious and heretical Dutch subjects.

That the Spain of Las Casas was able to juggle so many balls at the same time was in large part due to its having embraced and combined a number of technologies, most of which were of foreign origin. By the late fifteenth century, Portuguese ship-building techniques had produced vessels large enough to successfully negotiate deep-ocean crossings. Improvements in instrumentation made dead-reckoning navigation a more standard practice. With these sailing technologies, the Spaniards followed their Iberian neighbors into the Atlantic Ocean in an effort to discover new sources of riches. The printing press abetted these efforts, making possible the speedy and widespread distribution of star charts and travel guides that gave sailors more confidence in challenging the unknown waters to the west. By the early sixteenth century, the crown had established the *Casa de Contratación* (House of Trade), a clearing-house for navigational information that gave Spaniards an early lead in establishing a New World presence.

Columbus's failure to reach Asia had, nevertheless, opened up a whole new hemisphere to this confident and zealous nation. The oft-quoted motto of the conquistadors, "God, gold, and glory," really did capture the ethos of the times. Steel blades, gunpowder, and horses certainly were advantages in the Spaniards' conquest of the New World, but so was their attitude and worldview. Convinced of the superiority of their God and their civilization, the conquistadors paid little heed to the pleadings of a clergyman who did not have the stomach for the job of empire building.

## The Narváez Expedition: First Contact

For Charles I, granting Narváez a charter to such a vast territory represented great potential and no risk, even as it demonstrated Spanish ignorance of the true geographic dimensions of North America. As king of Castile and León, the largest and most powerful of the Iberian kingdoms that made up late medieval Spain, Charles exercised jurisdiction over the New World under the terms of Pope Alexander VI's *Inter Caetera*, a 1493 bull (papal decree) that granted the Catholic kings dominion over the western hemisphere in return for a commitment to Christianize all lands conquered in their name. Narváez's charter legitimized the undertaking without exposing the crown to financial risks. In case of success, the crown stood to gain the *quinto real* (royal fifth), a percentage of all acquired wealth to which it was entitled by virtue of its jurisdiction over the land.

Although the papacy had legitimized Spanish claims in the New World, some of the clergy, particularly Las Casas and his fellow Dominicans, vehemently protested the methods employed by the conquistadors. Largely due to their efforts, the crown had decreed use of the *Requerimiento* in every Spanish New World expedition. This document, drawn up in Spain in 1511 as a result of a debate over whether or not Indians, as pagans, were subject to enslavement, attempted to deal with the problem in a typically medieval and scholastic manner. The document consisted of a brief history of the world from the Judeo-Christian perspective, including an explanation of how the pope as successor to St. Peter had given the Spanish monarchs sovereignty over the New World, followed by the admonition that refusal to accept Spanish rule would bring forced conversion and the possibility of slavery. In other words, slavery was the Indians' fault for not willingly accepting their conquest by Christians. This document, although unacceptable to Las Casas and his colleagues, was just the pretext the crown needed to soothe its conscience while continuing to follow an expansionist colonial policy.

There would be no *quinto real* from this venture, however, and no spoils for Narváez and his men, either. Misfortune arrived shortly after the expedition's five small ships reached the Caribbean. One hundred forty men deserted at Santo Domingo, then a hurricane off the Cuban coast sank two ships and killed the sixty men on board. After wintering in Cuba, the expedition again set sail in February, encountering other storms that threatened disaster. Finally, in April 1528, the Spaniards reached the gulf coast of Florida, where they entered a large bay, probably Tampa Bay. Their luck did not improve, however. Despite the warnings of his treasurer, Alvar Núñez Cabeza de Vaca, that the land forces should not separate from the fleet, Narváez marched his men inland in a futile attempt to reach the supposedly gold-rich Kingdom of Apalachen. After four months of hostilities with Indians, and forced marches through swamps and jungles, the men had found no gold or other tangible wealth, and there was no sight of the expedition's fleet. The *entrada's* morale was broken. In September the men constructed crude boats at St. Mark's Bay, Florida, and toward the end of the month the five small craft, overcrowded with almost 250 survivors, set sail for Mexico.

Sailing westward across the northern gulf, the unfortunate expeditionaries drifted toward what they thought was the safe haven of Mexico. Soon after passing the mouth of the Mississippi, however, a storm battered the boats toward the Texas coast. Exhausted, with no water, and forced to survive on handfuls of raw corn, the survivors were in desperate straits. When Cabeza de Vaca requested orders from Narváez, the disheartened *adelantado* (governor with broad powers) replied that "it was no longer a time in which one should command another; but that each should do what he thought best to save his own life." Narváez was never heard from again.

In the first days of November, one after another of the three remaining craft beached just south of Galveston Island. Suffering from exposure, starvation, and dehydration, the would-be conquistadors were at the mercy of the Indians who inhabited the area. The initially friendly meeting between Indians and Spaniards soon took a turn for the worse as misunderstandings between the two cultures developed. Some Spaniards died of exposure and others disappeared in attempts to reach civilization; a fortunate few found "employment" among the Indian groups that took them in. Of the dwindling number of expeditionaries, only four would live to tell the tale. One of these four was Cabeza de Vaca.

For six years the survivors dwelt among the Atakapan, Karankawan, and Coahuiltecan Indians of coastal and south Texas, sometimes as "slaves," sometimes as merchants, but also as healers. In 1532 Cabeza de Vaca finally abandoned his single remaining companion, Lope de Oviedo, and made his way inland. Captured by another group of Indians, he soon discovered the presence in the region of three other expeditionaries, Captains Alonzo del Castillo and Andrés Dorantes and the latter's North African slave, Estebanico. Two years of planning resulted in a successful escape from their captors, and the beginning of an odyssey that took the four Christians across parts of present-day Texas, New Mexico, and northern Mexico, from the Gulf of Mexico to the Gulf of California between 1534 and 1536.

### The First Texas Literature

Cabeza de Vaca and his companions told stories that combined personal experience with rumor. Living hand to mouth, they soon came to understand the Indians' hunting and gathering practices and how they could adapt to them. The humbled conquistador recalled: "I bartered with these Indians in combs that I made for them and in bows, arrows, and nets. We made mats, which are their houses, that they have great necessity for; and although they know how to make them, they wished to give their full time to getting food, since when otherwise employed they are pinched with hunger."

The conquistadors' healing powers made them honored guests wherever they went. In at least one case Cabeza de Vaca practiced surgery to remove an arrowhead from an Indian's chest. Most often their practice of medicine consisted of praying over their patients, but, according to Cabeza de Vaca, in every single instance the Indians who received their ministrations claimed complete recovery.

Cabeza de Vaca's detailed descriptions of the various Indian groups the four Christians encountered are a cornerstone of Texas ethnography. Among the hunter-gatherers of Texas, he reported, "all the Indians whom we saw have the custom from the time in which their wives find themselves pregnant, of not

Unlike his conquistador contemporaries, Alvar Núñez Cabeza de Vaca, along with the three other survivors of the Narváez expedition, was forced to "go native" in order to survive. He was also among the few to write extensively of his experience, becoming the first author in Texas history. His report to Emperor Charles V was first printed in 1542 and was published in slightly different form in 1555 along with accounts of his adventures in South America. *(South Western Writers Collection, Alkek Library, Southwest Texas State University)*

sleeping with them until two years after they have given birth. The children are suckled until the age of twelve years, when they are old enough to get support for themselves. We asked them why they reared them in this manner; and they said because of the great poverty of the land."

Cabeza de Vaca also recorded some of the local lore. He gave one account of "Badthing," a monster in the form of a man who stalked the Indians of coastal Texas and made his home in a hole in the ground. Cabeza de Vaca was convinced that the creature was an evil spirit, who would disappear if the Indians accepted Christianity.

Cabeza de Vaca and his companions were astute observers of nature as well as of the people they encountered. Descriptions of fauna, flora, terrain, and climate abound in Cabeza de Vaca's account. His is the first report of that quintessential North American mammal, the buffalo. His first-hand description of this "cattle" in Texas is as colorful as his account of the "Badthing":

> Three times I have seen them and eaten of their meat. I think they are about the size of those in Spain. They have small horns like the cows of Morocco; the hair is very long and flocky like the merino's. Some are tawny, others black. To my judgment the flesh is finer and fatter than that of this country. Of the skins of those

not fully grown the Indians make blankets, and of the larger they make shoes and bucklers. They come as far as the sea-coast of Florida, from a northerly direction, ranging through a tract of more than four hundred leagues [approximately 1,000 miles]; and throughout the whole region over which they run, the people who inhabit near, descend and live upon them, distributing a vast many hides into the interior country.

By the time Cabeza de Vaca and his companions took up the last leg of their journey in the present-day Mexican state of Sonora, they were accompanied from village to village by hundreds of men, women, and children. They were careful to preserve the illusion that they were "sons of heaven," which allowed them to maintain their positions of power: "We possessed great influence and authority: to preserve both, we seldom talked with them. The negro was in constant conversation; he informed himself about the ways we wished to take, of the towns there were, and the matters we desired to know."

The Spaniards' reports of wealthy kingdoms to the north of where they had traveled fueled a competition for the conquest of North America among Viceroy Antonio de Mendoza and the conquistadors Hernán Cortés and Hernando de Soto. This competition would again bring Spaniards to Texas in a futile search for quick riches.

## Elusive Riches—Harsh Realities

Cabeza de Vaca and his companions arrived in Mexico City, capital of the newly created viceroyalty of New Spain (a jurisdiction that encompassed what is today Mexico, Central America, and Caribbean), to a heroes' reception. Every Spaniard, from Viceroy Antonio de Mendoza to Hernán Cortés to the most threadbare recent arrival from Spain put the best possible spin on the wanderers' accounts and was excited about the possibility of untold riches to be found.

In the fifteen years since the conquest of the Aztecs, Spanish expeditions had fanned out north, south, and west from the Valley of Mexico in an unrestrained and often brutal quest to replicate Cortés's success. Kingdoms had been conquered, idols smashed, and whole villages baptized into the Christian faith at once, but in the end New Spain did not contain enough material wealth to repay European investors and creditors. Nevertheless, tales of adventure and the promise of a boundless country yet to be explored brought a growing number of would-be conquerors to the viceregal capital in the hopes that the next discovery would prove the big one.

Some Spaniards had quickly lost interest in the dreams of Amazon kingdoms and lost civilizations and instead turned to a more tangible source of wealth—slaving. A number of conquistadors led raids into Indian territory solely for the purpose of capturing slaves, under the pretext that the Indians refused to submit peacefully under the terms of the *requerimiento*. The most brutal of these slavers was Nuño de Guzmán, rival of Cortés and founder of Guadalajara and other

Spanish towns in western Mexico. It was one of his parties that had stumbled upon Cabeza de Vaca and his companions during a slave raid in Sonora.

## Coronado and the Exploration of the Panhandle

Antonio de Mendoza, first viceroy of New Spain, had only recently arrived in the New World when Cabeza de Vaca came out of the northern wilderness. For Mendoza, underwriting an expedition to discover and conquer the "Seven Cities of Cíbola" that the wanderers reported hearing about would be financially rewarding, would reduce the slaving that contributed to social and economic instability in the country, and would be a way to rid central Mexico of the large number of idle Spanish "gentlemen" who were a constant source of trouble. A prudent and sensible administrator, however, Mendoza was not about to invest his limited financial resources and reputation on unsubstantiated rumor. To establish the veracity of Cabeza de Vaca's reports he sent out a scout: a Franciscan friar with considerable New World experience, Marcos de Niza. He was to be guided by none other than Estebanico, the slave whom the viceroy purchased from Dorantes because none of the three Spaniards were willing to retrace their steps into the wilderness.

The Niza-Estebanico expedition turned out to be an utter disaster, the unforeseen consequences of which again brought Spaniards into what is now Texas. In the spring of 1539 Fray Niza set out with a large contingent of Indians and the irrepressible African, who soon moved far out in front of the rest of the party. By the time Niza crossed into southern Arizona, Estebanico had already reached the Zuni country, where he alienated the local population and was put to death. Hearing this news as he approached the same pueblo, the friar settled for a view of the town from a distant bluff. He then hurried back to report on this first city of Cíbola, which he judged "bigger than Mexico City," an utterly fanciful claim.

Mendoza had the answer he wanted, however, and the man to carry out the conquest. Francisco Vázquez de Coronado, who had come to New Spain with Mendoza, was a dashing and able young man with a bright future. By 1538 he was both an alderman of Mexico City and governor of Nueva Galicia. Now his benefactor bestowed on him, at age 30, the honor of leading an expedition that would bring new glory and subjects to the crown, new souls to Christ, and great wealth to himself, the viceroy, and those sturdy enough to see the enterprise to its conclusion. A thousand Spanish men-at-arms, thousands more Indian servants and camp followers, and immense herds of horses, mules, and cattle, and flocks of sheep and goats, marching out of Culiacán, Sinaloa in April 1540 must have presented an imposing spectacle.

What the villagers of Hawikuh, a Zuni Pueblo in eastern Arizona, thought of the Spaniards in their armor, riding huge beasts, and making unintelligible demands for shiny yellow and white metals they had never seen, can only be imagined. Coronado, not to be denied, took the town by storm on July 7, 1540, and set an unfortunate pattern of employing force for the rest of the expedition.

Long considered one of Coronado's campsites, Palo Duro Canyon, now a state park, has lost favor among recent historians, who consider Tule or Blanco canyons as the more likely location for the *barranca grande* mentioned in expedition journals. From their camp Coronado marched northeastward in search of Quivira, only to return to the Texas canyon country that summer. Even had they beheld Palo Duro's magnificent vistas the Spaniards, by now dejected by their failure to find rich kingdoms, would have been unimpressed. *(Photo courtesy Texas Parks & Wildlife © 2003, Earl Nottingham)*

Disappointed with the first city of Cíbola, the Spaniards moved on to the others, then eastward to the Rio Grande and Pecos River *pueblos* (settlements), where bloodshed and disappointment mixed. Niza's enthusiasm had been proved a lie, but at the Pecos River pueblo of Cicuye the Indians gave reason for hope. Far to the east, beyond the great flat lands, they promised, was the Kingdom of Quivira, where gold and silver awaited the Spaniards in plenty.

To get to Quivira, Coronado and his men had to cross a portion of northwestern and Panhandle Texas. In the spring of 1541 they visited the Blanco and Tule canyons region, where their encounter with the now-famous Texas weather provides us with the first description of a North American hailstorm: "While the army was resting in this ravine . . . a tempest came up one afternoon with a very high wind and hail, and in a very short space of time a great quantity of hailstones, as big as bowls, or bigger, fell as thick as raindrops, so that in places they covered the ground two or three spans or more deep."

Members of the Coronado expedition also recorded their impressions of the unprecedented flatness of the land, the immense bison herds of the region, and the tipi-dwelling, buffalo-hunting Querechos and Teyas who made the southern Plains their home. Pedro de Castañeda, the best of the expedition's chroniclers, described them in very favorable terms, as more numerous than the pueblo dwellers: "They have better figures, are better warriors, and are more feared. They travel like the Arabs, with their tents and troops of dogs loaded with poles and having Moorish pack-saddles with girths. . . . These people eat raw flesh and drink blood. They do not eat human flesh. They are a kind people and not cruel. They are faithful friends. They are able to make themselves very well understood by means of signs."

Quivira turned out to be another disappointment for Coronado and his men. The Wichita villages of central Kansas were not rich in gold and silver, or anything else for that matter. Although some of his men desired to stay in the pueblo country, Coronado, broken both psychologically and physically (a fall from his horse had caused permanent injuries), brought his humbled expeditionaries back to Culiacán in the spring of 1542 with nothing to show for their efforts. Their reports on the Rio Grande country, although optimistic about future prospects for the region, did not encourage Spanish settlement. The High Plains of Texas, remote and almost totally devoid of human residents, offered even fewer attractions. One lasting legacy of Coronado's bold venture seems to have been a lingering resentment on the part of the town-dwelling Indians, who henceforth would be called Pueblos by the Spaniards, and who within fifty years would confront more determined Spanish conquerors.

The viceroy was a different man when Coronado returned with his disappointing news. So many Spaniards had participated in the expedition that Nueva Galicia had been left vulnerable to Indian rebellion. The ensuing Mixtón War (1540–42), the first great Indian insurrection after the conquest, overwhelmed Spanish frontier defenses and forced the viceroy to take the field against the rebellious Indians. The costly war intensified Mendoza's disappointment with Coronado, especially as his investment in the expedition was a total loss. Although Coronado was eventually cleared of most charges brought against him for failures in leadership, he died in 1554 under a cloud of dishonor (despite the fact that fellow Spaniards who attempted the conquest of Florida were as unsuccessful as he had been).

## Conquistadors in East Texas

Cabeza de Vaca had his own ideas about how Spanish settlement of Florida might best be carried out, and he hoped to gain permission from Emperor Charles V to attempt a new colonization effort. He returned to Spain in the summer of 1537 to find that he had been preempted by one of the heroes of the conquest of the Inca Empire, Hernando de Soto. This ruthless conquistador had come away from the Peruvian adventure a rich and powerful man. For him, as for most of his contemporaries, adventure and conquest had become an addiction. God, gold, and glory, although usually not in that order, were the driving motives for these men.

In the spring of 1536 Soto arrived in Spain laden down with his share of the booty taken from the Incas. Although he made a significant loan to the crown, purchased a magnificent palace, feasted with his companions in a spendthrift manner, and married into a prominent family by the end of the year, Soto found time to work on gaining his very own *capitulación* from Charles V. Impressing the most powerful monarch of the western world was no easy matter, but Soto's stories of how he and the other 130 adventurers led by Francisco Pizarro had vanquished an empire of millions did the trick. By the end of April 1537 Soto had obtained the governorship of Cuba, a knighthood in the Order of Santiago, and a charter to colonize Florida. Wisely, Cabeza de Vaca turned down Soto's offer of a place in his expedition when the conquistadors later met.

By the spring of 1539, after almost a year of final preparations in Cuba, Soto landed his 600-man expedition somewhere in the Tampa Bay area of Florida's gulf coast. He was much better equipped than Cortés had been twenty years earlier in Mexico, or than Narváez had been a decade earlier on his Florida misadventure. His quest for the wealth that had eluded Narváez and that Cabeza de Vaca and his companions had told him about led him through much of what is now the southeastern United States between May 1539 and May 1542. Wherever he and his men traveled, the least resistance from the Indians was met with steel, lead, and war dogs. Finally, racked with fever and discouraged by his failure to find the precious metals that lured him to North America, Soto died on the banks of the Mississippi River, leaving behind only a legacy of slaughter and destruction that imperiled the expedition's survival.

Succeeding Soto in command was Luis Moscoso de Alvarado. His first act as leader of the expedition, which now became known as the Moscoso expedition, was to hold a council at which the Spaniards decided to abandon the enterprise. With the most direct course for withdrawal being an overland march to New Spain, Moscoso led his men across the Red River in the summer of 1542 and got them at least to the Trinity River before determining the effort impracticable. Only slightly less brutal now that Soto was no longer in command, expedition members fought and tortured their way through the Caddo country of northeast Texas. Despite claims to the contrary by the Gentleman of Elvas, the most eloquent of the expedition's chroniclers, the Caddos encountered by the Spaniards in Texas, known as the Hasinais, must have had word of the Spaniards ahead of time. For, according to the Portuguese chronicler, as soon as Moscoso and his men approached,

> the people were called out, who, as fast they could get together, came by fifties and hundreds on the road, to give battle. While some encountered us, others fell upon our rear; and when we followed up those, these pursued us. The attack continued during the greater part of the day, until we arrived at their town. Some men were injured, and some horses, but nothing so as to hinder travel, there being not one dangerous wound among all. The Indians suffered great slaughter.

The Indians, anxious to rid themselves of the pillaging strangers, resorted to the same tactic the Pueblos had employed with Coronado: They convinced the

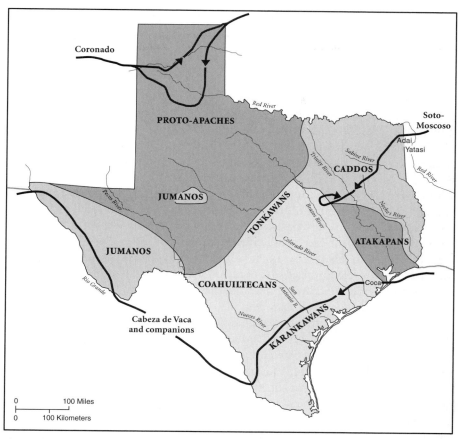

Sixteenth-century Texas conquistadors and native peoples.

Spaniards that if only they would travel on for some distance, they would arrive in a country where they could find their compatriots. The farther into Texas the conquistadors ventured, the greater their frustration with the country: "The country was very poor, and the want of maize was greatly felt. . . . For twenty days the march was through a very thinly peopled country, where great privation and toil were endured."

Despite the rumors of Christians far to the south or the west, and certain knowledge that New Spain lay to the southwest, Moscoso and the other expedition leaders based their decision to abandon the overland march on Cabeza de Vaca's experience. They recognized the country they were entering to be the one in which, according to Cabeza de Vaca, "the Indians wandered like Arabs, having no settled place of residence, living on prickly pears, and the roots of plants, and game; and that if this should be so, and they, entering upon that tract, found no provision for sustenance during winter, they must inevitably perish."

At that point, the conquistadors retraced their steps to the Mississippi, where they wintered and built boats to carry them to New Spain. In September 1543 the surviving 311 members of Soto's great expedition arrived at Pánuco. They left behind a trail of destruction from the Atlantic coast to central Texas. Most disruptive were epidemic diseases that soon wreaked havoc on the native populations of the southeastern United States, including the Hasinais of Texas.

The disheartening results of the Coronado and Soto-Moscoso expeditions convinced the Spanish to direct their attention to other parts of the New World. The absence of precious metals, the unsuitability of the native peoples for assimilation, and the difficulty of access to the region argued against a permanent Spanish presence. The absence of any foreign threat in the Gulf of Mexico further disinclined the crown from expending more resources there. Consequently, for the next four decades the little contact Spaniards did have with what is now Texas was restricted to the gulf coast, where hurricanes and other storms sometimes drove Spanish ships sailing between Veracruz and Havana.

The most famous of these incidents, the 1554 wreck off Padre Island of the *Santa María de Yciar, San Esteban,* and *Espíritu Santo,* three of four ships in a treasure fleet containing over two million pesos in gold and silver, did nothing to improve the reputation of Texas. The 250 castaways who attempted to march back to Spanish-held territory overland were attacked by Indians the whole way. The lone survivor, Fray Marcos de Mena, told stories of cannibal Indians and a waterless desert by the sea. The salvage expedition sent to recover the 1.5 million pesos on board the three ships found the shallow waters off Padre Island treacherous and lacking in adequate anchorages. If the interior of Texas offered few attractions for the fortune-seeking conquistadors, the coast of the Gulf of Mexico represented only danger for the sailing men bearing treasures from the New World to the old.

## The Paso del Norte Corridor

In the years after Coronado returned from the land of the Pueblos, tensions between Spanish colonials and the Indians of northern New Spain again erupted into armed conflict. The native peoples involved, referred to collectively as *Chichimecas,* a derogatory term employed by the Aztecs for the hunter-gatherers of the region, actively resisted encroachment of their hunting grounds by Spanish ranchers intent on expanding the developing livestock industry of the colony. A series of silver strikes, beginning in 1546 at Zacatecas, brought about a new type of colonial expansion, however—the silver rush.

### Development of the North Mexican Frontier

The native peoples in the mining frontier area were very different from the sedentary Aztecs and Maya. Fierce and mobile, the Chichimecas resisted Spanish encroachment in what became known as the Chichimeca War, a conflict that lasted most of the latter half of the sixteenth century. Instead of being able to exploit well-developed and sophisticated native societies, Spaniards found themselves having to build towns, start farms and ranches, open roads, establish fortifications, and settle the country. A lucky few made fortunes as miners, merchants, and *hacendados* (owners of large landed estates producing both livestock and crops for market). The vast majority, however, simply sowed the seeds of modern North Mexican society.

The northern frontier society that populated these new agricultural and mining centers was a mixed lot. At the top a relatively few European-born Spaniards, known as *peninsulares,* filled the highest administrative and commercial posts. Accompanying them from the Old World were numerous people—mostly men—of African heritage, whose status as slaves placed them at the beck and call of the dominant Spaniards. The demand for labor in the sparsely settled north also required the recruitment, both voluntary and forced, of large numbers of Indians.

In time an important new element was added to this mixed lot of Spaniards, Africans, and Indians—the *mestizo.* Because migration from the Old World in the decades following the conquest was overwhelmingly male, it was Indian women who provided the sexual companionship, both willing and unwilling, for Spaniards and Africans alike. *Mestizaje,* as the process of blending has come to be known, created an ever increasing population of mixed-blood people that collectively came to be called *castas.* The ordering of society according to a racial-ethnic hierarchy was called the *sistema de castas.* Often the product of extra-legal unions or of rape, the mestizo population found the expanding northern frontier more welcoming to them. Military service, ranching, farming, and other economic activities were more accessible on the frontier, as was the possibility to "pass" into the ranks of the *criollos,* that is, the American-born Spaniards who occupied the top level of colonial society with the *peninsulares.*

At the same time that Spaniards, Africans, mestizos, and acculturated Indians flocked to each new *bonanza* (rich mineral deposit), Spanish missionaries established new centers for the conversion of the small local Indian populations. The Catholic religious order primarily responsible for undertaking the conversion of the Chichimecas was the Franciscans. Having arrived in New Spain in the mid-1520s at the behest of Cortés, their job had at first seemed a strictly religious one—to turn the Aztec and other "civilized" Indian societies of central Mexico away from the devil and toward Christ. The farther north they expanded their efforts, however, the more complicated the problem became. Preparing hunter-gatherers and semisedentary people for life in the Spanish empire was not merely a matter of religious reeducation but of completely transforming their ways of life. Indians gathered together in communities known as missions were subjected to the regimentation of European civilization: strict and complex divisions of labor, regular work schedules, and monogamy. Although the friars were the ultimate authorities in the missions, the Indians were trained in the ways of Spanish local government and responsibilities to the greater colonial society. The search for Indians who might prove amenable to the Christian life became part of the colonization process, the goal of which was the re-creation of Spanish social, political, and economic institutions. The mass of Indians would serve as the lower strata of society, whereas European and American-born Spaniards became the lords of the land.

## New Mexico and Far West Texas Explored Again

As the silver frontier expanded northward, it was only a matter of time before the Pueblos again drew the attention of the Spaniards. Following the 1567 silver strike at Santa Barbara (in present-day southern Chihuahua), Spanish prospectors, slavers, and missionaries fanned out through the far north in search of other mines, new labor supplies, and souls to save. Byproducts of this frontier activity included the founding of Saltillo in the 1570s and contact with Indians who told tales of city-dwelling peoples north of a great river. The long-forgotten reports of the Coronado expedition might have quelled new rumors of rich kingdoms, but the northward extension of the silver corridor along the Sierra Madre Occidental argued for the most optimistic view of what might lie far to the north.

By 1581 Franciscan missionaries working in the Santa Barbara area were ready to investigate the rumors of sedentary peoples to the north. On June 5, Friars Agustín Rodríguez, Francisco López, and Juan de Santa María, accompanied by Captain Francisco Sánchez Chamuscado, eight soldiers, and nineteen Indian servants, headed northward, following the Conchos River to its juncture with the Rio Grande, a site that came to be known as Junta de los Ríos. Following the great river upstream on the counsel of the various Indian groups they encountered, in August they finally arrived in the El Paso area, which came to be called Paso del Norte because of the broad valley the Rio Grande cut between mountain ranges. Continuing northward, the Rodríguez-Chamuscado expedition entered the Pueblo country. At some point in the next few months Fray Santa María left for Mexico City to report to the viceroy, but was killed by Indians along the way. During this time his companions explored the region and made plans to establish missions. When their military escort decided to return to Santa Barbara in early 1582 the Franciscans chose to remain and begin work among the Pueblos.

Fueled by the Chamuscado party's wild tales of precious metals and a rich country, Antonio de Espejo seized the opportunity to "rescue" Friars Rodríguez and López. A Spaniard who had been implicated in the murder of one his servants, he had fled to the frontier, where he saw his chance to redeem his fortunes by opening up the Pueblo country. His party left Santa Barbara in November 1582, following the same route as the Rodríguez-Chamuscado expedition. Like the earlier group, Espejo's men heard stories of wealthy cities to the north, the earlier presence of three Spaniards and a black man (the Cabeza de Vaca group), and the abundance of silver to the west. Upon arrival in the Pueblo country, they got word of the death of Friars Rodríguez and López at the hands of the Tiguex Pueblos, but Espejo was undeterred and conducted a wide-ranging exploration west and east of the Rio Grande. About thirty miles south of present-day Santa Fe, he struck eastward to the Pecos River, which he followed south to its juncture with the Rio Grande. He returned to Santa Barbara very enthusiastic about the prospects of New Mexico and was on his way to Spain in 1585 to personally lobby the king for a *capitulación* when he died in Havana.

## Juan de Oñate and the Founding of New Mexico

King Philip II was quite interested in this "new" Mexico, as the Pueblo country had come to be called, not only for the reports of silver and other riches, but for its large population of sedentary peoples. Spain's European rivals had been probing the peripheries of Spanish dominions for over a decade, and there continued to be talk of a northern water passage between the Atlantic and Pacific oceans. With little sense of the true geography of North America, Spaniards were becoming increasingly alarmed that the English might find a way to approach their rich colony of New Spain from the north. Spanish occupation of New Mexico, especially if the stories of rich mines and populous cities proved true, would keep them at bay.

Having deliberated the matter carefully, the royal council on colonial affairs, the Consejo de Indias, advised the king to seek out an *adelantado* who would occupy New Mexico under the terms of the colonization laws of 1573. Concerned by continued complaints from clergy with regard to the treatment of Indians in newly conquered areas, the conflicts among rival claimants to territory, and other abuses, Philip II and his councilors devised a new set of rules for subjugation of native lands. The new code of law emphasized the religious and philosophical ideals of the monarchy and required nonviolent pacification of new territories and fair treatment of the inhabitants whenever possible. To assure that men of good character led these enterprises and to minimize conflict among potential rivals, the code also called for all exploration to be carried out only under royal license. The search for a suitable candidate, that is, one who could underwrite the cost of colonization himself, with the appropriate experience on the frontier, and willing to abide by the new rules, took more than a decade.

In 1595, twelve years after Philip II's order, the viceroy settled on an acceptable candidate for *adelantado* of New Mexico. Juan de Oñate was the son of one of the discoverers of the Zacatecas silver mines and the husband of Isabel Tolosa Cortés Moctezuma—granddaughter of the conqueror of the Aztecs and great-granddaughter of the conquered emperor. Oñate was rich, well connected, and had substantial administrative experience. Finally, late in 1597 Oñate received the king's permission to proceed.

The permanent colonization of New Mexico had begun. Oñate's expedition included about 130 Spanish soldier-settlers and their families, over two hundred other soldiers, and hundreds of Indian servants. The religious goals of the *entrada* were represented by ten Franciscans who hoped to be worthy successors of Fray Rodríguez and the other missionaries who had first attempted to convert the

Pueblos in the 1570s. Herds and flocks accompanied the colonists, who hoped to establish a successful mining colony among the sedentary Pueblo Indians. After a three-month crossing of the Chihuahuan desert, Oñate's caravan arrived at the banks of the Rio Grande at the site of present-day Juárez-El Paso. El Pasoans today claim that by virtue of the April 30, 1598, celebration of their safe arrival, Texas can claim to be the site of the first Thanksgiving. According to one of the colonists, "there was a sermon, a great ecclesiastical and secular celebration, a great salute and rejoicing, and in the afternoon, a comedy." Although a number of Indian groups lived along the banks of the river below El Paso, Oñate and the Franciscans who accompanied him had their eyes set on the Pueblos of the upper Rio Grande valley.

As Oñate took control of the upper Rio Grande valley he sent out expeditions to explore the region. In 1601 he repeated Coronado's trek across the Texas Panhandle in search of the mythical Kingdom of Quivira. As disappointed as Coronado had been before them, Oñate's group settled for establishing a modest colony among the Pueblos. A few hundred Spanish colonists lived among thousands of agricultural Indians who were under the tutelage of Franciscan missionaries. New Mexico became a land of sheep ranches and subsistence farms, hardly the prosperous and populous colony that Oñate and the crown had envisioned.

Despite the lack of development, Spanish New Mexico needed to be able to communicate with rest of New Spain; the only route by which this could occur lay along the Rio Grande and the Paso del Norte. Spanish convoys headed to and from Santa Fe regularly stopped there to rest and take on water, but for many years no one thought to establish a mission, presidio (garrison), or town at the crossing. Not until 1659 did Fray García de San Francisco gather a group of local Manso Indians in Mission Nuestra Señora de Guadalupe de los Mansos. (This was more than a century after Cabeza de Vaca had first visited them and sixty years after Oñate had claimed their land for the Spanish crown.) Within a short time a number of Spanish settlers established farms in the area and in 1665 the Franciscans started a second mission, San Francisco de los Sumas, for another of the local native groups. During this time Paso del Norte was officially incorporated into the province of New Mexico with the appointment of an *alcalde mayor,* or lieutenant governor, under the authority of the governor in Santa Fe.

## The Pueblo Revolt and the Growth of Paso del Norte

Life at Paso del Norte was uneventful until the Pueblo Revolt of 1680. The rebellion resulted from continued Spanish abuse of the Pueblos: The missionaries had suppressed local beliefs and humiliated traditional leaders; Spanish settlers had exploited Indian labor; and missionaries and secular officials had fought over control of the province and Indian labor. Although their numbers had declined significantly due to epidemic diseases and dropping fertility rates, the Pueblos still numbered in the tens of thousands in 1680, whereas the Spanish population included only about 3,000 men, women, and children. In a coordinated assault on

Spanish farms, missions, and the town of Santa Fe, the Pueblos killed 21 missionaries and almost 400 settlers. The survivors fled to Paso del Norte, arriving with little more than the clothes on their backs.

When Governor Antonio de Otermín took stock of the refugees in October 1680, he found that fewer than 2,000 had made it out safely; among them were over 300 Piro and Tiwa Pueblos whose close association with the Spaniards put them at odds with other Pueblos. With no prospects of reoccupying the upper Rio Grande valley in the immediate future, Otermín set about establishing settlements for the Spanish and Indian populations. By 1684 a string of five communities lined the south bank of the river: Guadalupe, San Lorenzo, Senecú, Ysleta, and Socorro. Although the last three of these settlements were intended to serve the friendly Pueblo refugees, Spanish settlers soon moved in among the Indians. For the next 150 years these settlements, along with a small number of haciendas and smaller ranchos, flourished in New Mexico's southernmost district. The area became an important wine-producing and Indian trade center and the key way station on the Santa Fe–Chihuahua Camino Real (royal road).

With the Spaniards' expulsion from New Mexico a group of Franciscan missionaries turned their attention to Indians who had been visited in the 1580s and who periodically came to trade at Spanish outposts. East of the Mansos and Sumas, in what is today western Texas, southeastern New Mexico, and northern

The expansion of Spanish colonization in the direction of the Rio Grande in far West Texas altered Indian ways of life even in areas where the Spaniards never gained a foothold. At Meyers Springs, just east of the Big Bend, a rock shelter contains Indian artists' rendering of these contacts in the form of church towers with crosses. *(From the collections of the Texas Memorial Museum, The University of Texas at Austin)*

Chihuahua, lived various indigenous groups known collectively as Jumanos by the Spaniards. Among these groups there were both sedentary agriculturalists, some of whom had been visited by Cabeza de Vaca, and nonsedentary buffalo hunters and traders. Over the course of the seventeenth century various groups of Apaches had moved southward into the area and had begun engaging in cycles of warfare and trade with the Pueblos and other Indian groups in the interior. Also finding their way into this area were groups of Indians from Spanish frontier settlements fleeing harsh working conditions and loss of their traditional ranges. Thus, by the late seventeenth century there were thousands of Indians in the area with enough knowledge of the Spanish and enough interest in European trade goods to foster trade and missionary contacts.

In 1681 the Jumano chief Juan de Sabeata arrived in Paso del Norte asking for missionaries to visit his country. Sabeata spoke Spanish, claimed to have been baptized at the mining town of Parral, and had conducted many trade expeditions to the Hasinai country of eastern Texas, where he exchanged Spanish wares and horses for dressed hides and other Indian trade goods. In response, Governor Domingo de Cruzate, responding to the opportunity to gain additional Indian allies, sent his lieutenant, Juan Domínguez de Mendoza, and Fray Nicolás López to investigate the possibility of establishing a Spanish presence among the Jumanos in the vicinity of the Conchos-Rio Grande junction, an area that came to be called La Junta de los Ríos. Between December 1683 and June 1684, the Mendoza-López expedition visited Jumano and other groups at La Junta and ventured as far northeast as the Edwards Plateau, somewhere along the Colorado River. There the escort hunted for buffalo hides while Fray López and his companions baptized a number of Plains Indians and made plans for establishing a permanent mission field.

When Mendoza and López returned to Paso del Norte they left behind two missions, La Navidad and Apóstol Santiago, near what is today Presidio, Texas. Fathers Juan de Zavaleta and Antonio de Acevedo, who were left in charge, were soon forced to withdraw to Parral, however, when the Julime and other tribes in the area joined a general insurrection against the Spaniards. Word of the successful rebellion of the Pueblos soon spread among other tribes under Spanish control, and the whole northern frontier was aflame in an insurrection that has come to be called the Great Northern Revolt. Missions and *haciendas* burned, missionaries became martyrs, herds were scattered, stolen, and slaughtered. Communications between outlying posts and more established settlements became erratic. It took over a decade for the Spaniards to restore a measure of control and resume the process of expansion.

Despite various efforts to reestablish the La Junta missions in the years that followed, neither La Navidad nor Apóstol Santiago proved sustainable in the long run. The Spaniards turned their attention to recovering New Mexico, where their honor and their strategic interests had been wounded by the first major successful Indian revolt against Spanish rule in New Spain. As the Franciscans returned to their burned-out churches, their torn-down friaries and abandoned fields, they poured what resources they could muster into New Mexico. Little could be spared for the marginal stations at La Junta. Nevertheless, it was at these missions that Spanish authorities in Mexico first received word of the first successful intrusion by other Europeans into the colony's territory.

## La Salle and the Spanish Rediscovery of Texas

Fathers Joaquín Hinojosa and Agustín de Colina were working at La Junta late in 1687, reestablishing the missions abandoned three years earlier during the Great Northern Revolt, when Chief Juan Sabeata of the Jumanos arrived with disturbing news. He had returned from the annual Indian trade fair in Hasinai country with word that other Spaniards were actively trading with the Indians of the region. Asked to bring back proof, Sabeata returned from the next fair at the beginning of 1689 with pages torn from French books, a picture of a ship with French verse inscribed on it, and the reassuring news that other Indians had attacked and destroyed the French settlement and all its occupants. In this way the Spaniards first learned of the whereabouts and fate of the La Salle colony.

Evidence of a long-distance Indian communication network across Texas comes from this unlikely source, a drawing of a European sailing vessel on which two of the La Salle expedition members wrote a message. The parchment was carried by Jumano Indians as far as the Spanish mining center at Parral, the first conclusive proof of a French landing in Spanish territory. *(Jean L'Archeveque Items, CN 02178 a, b, The Center for American History, The University of Texas at Austin)*

## The French Threat

Spanish authorities had not been unaware of the Frenchman's plan. Since the fall of 1685, when a Spanish naval squadron had captured a French pirate ship in the Caribbean, colonial officials were aware that René Robert Cavelier, Sieur de La Salle, was leading a large expedition headed for the Mississippi, with the purpose of establishing a colony on the Gulf of Mexico coast. The Spaniards, having neglected the Gulf of Mexico for over a century, found themselves ill prepared to meet the French challenge. Fortunately for them, La Salle himself was poorly equipped for his enterprise, and his expedition's misfortune proved a godsend to the Spaniards.

From the time of his arrival in the vicinity of Montreal in 1666, La Salle, a French-born Canadian, took an interest in the fur trade and in creating a commercial empire in the interior of North America. He discovered the Ohio River, opened up the Great Lakes to navigation, built a string of trading posts in the upper Midwest, and in 1682 reached the mouth of the Mississippi River, claiming the entire basin, which he named Louisiana, for France. La Salle intended the name to flatter Louis XIV, before whom in late 1683 he had laid out a plan to establish a fortified colony at the mouth of the river. From a warm water port there, the French could both control the fur trade of much of the continent and pursue the conquest of the silver mining districts of nearby New Spain.

Misfortune dogged the expedition from the beginning. Soon after the four-ship fleet sailed in July 1684, its naval escort vessel had to turn back for repairs. Later, a hurricane scattered the fleet and a Spanish pirate ship captured the fleet's smallest ship. Desertions at Saint-Domingue, where La Salle had made port to reprovision, left the expedition with considerably fewer than the 400 men, women, and children with which it had started. In January 1685 the fleet sailed past the mouth of the Mississippi, finally making landfall at Matagorda Bay, where the expedition's supply ship soon foundered. When the French naval commander decided to take his ship home, a significant number of expedition members chose to abandon the venture, including the sole engineer in the company. Finally, during the following winter La Salle lost his last ship, *Belle*, which sank in Matagorda Bay during a storm.

Nothing seemed to work in La Salle's favor. The first settlement site on the bay turned out to be unhealthy (brackish water and mosquito and snake infested) and exposed to attack. La Salle soon discovered a better location on Garcitas Creek, where a small compound, which came to be known as Fort St. Louis, began to take shape in the summer of 1685. A number of the weaker members of the party died during the first months, and the "artisans" recruited for the expedition turned out to be a rather useless lot overall. The company proved ill equipped to farm under the prevailing conditions, and the first crops were lost. In addition, the local Karankawas, whom La Salle had initially decided to treat as hostile, kept the settlement under siege.

By the time the first winter arrived, work was far enough along for La Salle to feel comfortable in undertaking his first substantial exploration of the country.

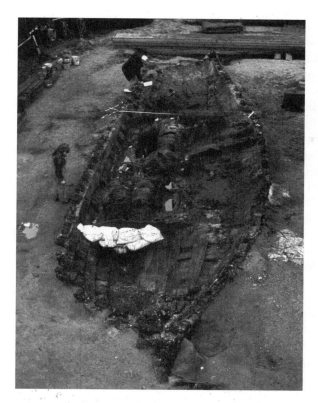

The *Belle,* one of La Salle's ships, foundered in Matagorda Bay within a year of its arrival on the Texas coast in 1685. Discovered by archeologists from the Texas Historical Commission, the ship was excavated in 1996–97. Its restoration was entrusted to Texas A&M's Marine Archeology Laboratory. (*Texas Historical Commission*)

Contradictory reports and self-serving claims make it difficult to know where he went and how he dealt with the native peoples he encountered. In April 1686 La Salle and twenty men began an unsuccessful march to the northeast in an effort to find the Mississippi and seek help for the colony in the Illinois country. They made it only as far as the Hasinai country between the Trinity and Neches rivers. Only eight men made it back to the French settlement. The others had died of illness, gotten lost, or, in one case, fallen victim to an alligator.

Desertion also took its toll on the colony. Not only did men abandon the post, but some deserted La Salle during his exploration of the country. Henri Joutel remarked that two sailors had gone native:

> They had . . . so perfectly enur'd themselves to the Customs of the Natives, that they were become meer Savages. They were naked, their Faces and Bodies with Figures wrought on them, like the rest. They had taken several Wives, been at the Wars and kill'd their Enemies with the Firelocks . . . but having no more Powder nor Ball, their Arms were grown useless, and they had been forc'd to learn to shoot with Bows and Arrows.

Another member of the expedition had done so well among the Coahuiltecans who had taken him in that by the time the Spanish found him he was the chief of a sizable village. With each desertion or death by snakebite, alligator mauling, or disease, the colony became weaker. La Salle had to act.

The last chapter of the La Salle colony began in January 1687. The settlement was down to about forty people, including some women and children, and under constant attack by the Karankawas. On January 12 La Salle and the strongest seventeen men among the colonists again set out for the Mississippi to seek help. Arrogant and abusive toward his men, he forced them to carry their own supplies so that the few horses acquired from the Indians could transport his and his brother's trade goods and personal possessions. By March 19 a number of men in the party had had enough and mutinied, killing La Salle, his brother, and two servants. Eventually, six men made it to Canada, including Henri Joutel, who wrote the best existing account of the La Salle expedition and its tragic end.

At the post, conditions worsened as food ran out and disease felled the survivors. Although a temporary truce was reached with the Karankawas, the end came during Christmas 1688, when a large war party attacked the compound. Among the dead was the first child of European parents known to have been born in Texas.

## The Spanish Search for La Salle and the First Occupation of Texas

The Spaniards had no way of knowing that the Texas coast and its native peoples had taken care of their problem for them. With only a rough idea of which direction La Salle's ships had sailed, colonial authorities organized a number of maritime and land expeditions to search for the French. Although five voyages to the northern Gulf of Mexico failed to turn up evidence of a French presence, they did produce the first detailed maps of the region and became the basis for Spanish occupation of the Florida panhandle in the 1690s.

Ultimately successful in locating the site of the French colony was Alonso de León, governor of Coahuila and seasoned frontiersman. Born in Nuevo León in 1639, he had studied in Spain and served in the Spanish navy before returning to the frontier and becoming an accomplished Indian fighter. Between 1686 and 1688 he made three reconnaissance expeditions in search of the French colony, pausing in between to put down an Indian revolt. In 1689 he and the Franciscan Friar Damián de Massanet undertook a fourth land expedition during which they came upon the ruins of the French post. The sight of human remains, of loose pages torn from books, of everyday household belongings scattered within the compound moved one of León's men to compose a poem commemorating the event. The first verse, as translated by La Salle historian Robert Weddle, reads:

> Sad and fateful site
> where prevails the dark of night
> because misfortune's whim
> brought thy people death so grim,
> here alone I contemplate

thou epitome of fate,
of the inconstancy of life;
since in the fierceness of the strife
the cruel enemy pressed
his heartless hand upon thy breast,
upon thy innocence so mild,
sparing not the smallest child.

Although the smallest child had not been spared, five children had survived the final Indian attack. Karankawa women protected four of the Talón family children and one other boy, all of whom were adopted into the tribe. During their 1690 expedition León and Massanet managed to ransom three of the five. The other two children were acquired from the Karankawa by Domingo Terán de los Ríos the following year.

In the spring of 1690, when León and Massanet returned to Texas together for the last time, La Salle's colony was no longer a threat but there was no clear evidence that the French were entirely gone from the region. At the same time Massanet's contacts with the Hasinai (who the Spaniards believed called themselves Tejas) led him to believe that it would be easy to convert these sedentary peoples to Christianity and incorporate them into the colonial system without the need for a military presence. León believed the Indians, although friendly, should not be trusted and that the Spaniards would need a string of four presidios to properly hold the province.

After carrying out the viceroy's orders to burn the French post, León proceeded to the Kingdom of the Tejas, where, assured of the Hasinais' continued interest in conversion, he placed Fray Massanet in charge of Mission San Francisco de los Tejas on May 25, 1690. He also invested the village head man with the symbols of Spanish authority:

> I delivered to the governor a staff with a cross, giving him the title of governor of all his people, in order that he might rule and govern them, giving him to understand by means of an interpreter that which he should observe and do, and the respect and obedience which he and all his people ought to have for the priests, and that he should make all his families attend Christian teaching, in order that they might be instructed in the affairs of our holy Catholic faith so that later they might be baptized and become Christians. He accepted the staff with much pleasure, promising to do all that was desired of him, and the company fired three salutes.

Afterwards he gathered the remaining Talón children from the colony and returned to Coahuila, reporting to the viceroy the disturbing news that a French trader had been among the Hasinais trying to undermine their loyalty to Spain.

Henri Tonti, a trader from French Illinois, had made the journey down the Mississippi late in 1689, in a second effort to locate survivors of the La Salle colony. He had visited among the various Caddo tribes, exploring trade opportunities and the possibilities of an anti-Spanish alliance, but had no success. His exploration and the arrival of the La Salle expedition survivors in New France reinvigorated French interest in the Gulf of Mexico region, however. It would not be long before better equipped and better informed Frenchmen arrived to reassert La Salle's claim to the area on behalf of Louis XIV.

## Spain Abandons the Kingdom of the Tejas

León's report of continuing French activities among the Tejas reached Mexico City about the same time as news of France's renewed hostilities against Spain. In the face of the mounting challenge it became obvious that a single Franciscan mission so far from the settlement frontier in Coahuila was inadequate to protect Spanish interests. The question for the viceroy's council was whether to accept Fray Massanet's plan for a string of missions but no presidios or León's plan for a strong military presence. Given the limited resources at their disposal and the requirement of royal approval for the establishment of presidios, the question answered itself.

The Kingdom of the Tejas, that portion of modern Texas that extends from the Trinity River eastward, first became a Spanish province with the appointment of Domingo Terán de los Ríos as its governor in January 1691. An experienced colonial official, Terán de los Ríos accepted the assignment to found seven new missions, explore the country east of the Tejas, and determine the proximity of foreign colonies; however, he protested being subordinated in all important decisions to Fray Massanet.

The Terán de los Ríos-Massanet expedition, which lasted from May 1691 to April 1692, proved that Spain was not ready to occupy Texas. Throughout the *entrada* the governor and missionaries quarreled. Even before arriving in Hasinai country they learned of an epidemic which had swept their villages and taken Fray Miguel de Fontcuberta's life along with those of many Indians. The epidemic, drought, and exhaustion of supplies began to turn the Hasinais against the Spaniards. The winter of 1691–92, which caught Terán de los Ríos in what is now the Red River country of Texas, Louisiana, and Arkansas, proved harsh and sapped what was left of the expedition's morale. In the end Terán de los Ríos had nothing to show for his year-long wanderings through East Texas: He had not founded any missions; he had not explored the country to the degree required by his instructions; and he had not established adequate lines of communication between the Kingdom of the Tejas and the interior of New Spain.

Spain's first occupation of Texas was coming to an end in the months following Terán de los Ríos's departure. Given the change in attitude on the part of the Hasinais, six of the missionaries had chosen to return to Coahuila, leaving only Fray Massanet and two companions behind. Mission Santísimo Nombre de María, which had been founded before the arrival of Terán de los Ríos, had been washed away by a flood, its Spanish residents forced to move into San Francisco de los Tejas. Efforts to resupply the missions overland from Monclova had largely failed as a result of the weather, evidence of the logistical obstacles to occupying a far-flung outpost without intermediate way stations.

Fray Massanet had tragically miscalculated his chances of success in bringing Christianity and Spanish civilization to the Hasinais. He had persuaded the viceroy and his council that missionaries working among peaceful and sedentary Indians, without the disruptions and corruption of Spanish colonial soldiers, could secure Texas for the crown. The Indians, however, lost all respect for the Franciscans, refusing to participate in religious instruction, and came to associate the waters of baptism with death. The Franciscans had misunderstood the intentions of the Hasinais in inviting the missionaries to live among them. Their real interest in courting the Spanish had not been in religious conversion, but in obtaining gifts and trade goods previously available only in limited amounts from the Jumanos and other Indian traders. When the gifts dried up and it became obvious that these Spaniards had little interest in establishing reciprocal trade relations on their terms, the Tejas saw little incentive in supporting, or even accepting, a Spanish presence among them. Finally, in October 1693 Chief Bernardino, now sporting a French suit of clothes, warned the Spaniards to leave. By the end of the month Friars Massanet and Francisco Hidalgo and a handful of soldiers were on their way to Coahuila. Ironically, waiting for them in Monclova, the capital of Coahuila, when they arrived in February 1694 was an order from the viceroy to abandon the province of Texas.

## Conclusion

Happenstance brought the first Europeans to the northwest corner of the Gulf of Mexico, to a land that had no name, no boundaries, and in no way approximated modern Texas. The accidental exploration of present-day coastal Texas and much of what is today northern Mexico by Cabeza de Vaca and his fellow survivors of the Narváez *entrada* was followed by the more purposeful exploits of the Moscoso and Coronado expeditions: Dreams and tales of treasure had brought these conquistadors into the forests of East Texas and the plains and canyons of West Texas. The great disappointment at finding no new Aztec empires to conquer dampened their enthusiasm. This vast and sparsely settled land turned out to be nothing more than the least inviting corner of Spain's North American backyard.

And that part of Texas that was eventually settled by Spaniards and their Indian allies in the course of the seventeenth century was, in fact, not part of Texas at all. The Spanish colonials, missionaries, soldiers, and Indians who made up the Paso del Norte communities, along the Rio Grande, considered themselves New Mexicans. It would not be until the middle of the nineteenth century that the descendants of some of these people began to call themselves Texas Mexicans.

Finally, with the arrival of La Salle the Spaniards were forced to explore the long-forgotten corner of their backyard. What they found was the Kingdom of the Tejas, Caddoan-speaking, agricultural villagers more correctly referred to as <u>Hasinais,</u> whose word for "friend" or "ally"—spelled Texas in the Spanish of the times—served as the name for their country. La Salle's own wishful thinking and exaggerated expectations met disaster in the tough and unforgiving Karankawa country.

At the end of the seventeenth century Texas remained a vague abstraction that included only a fraction of its current territory. Except for the vicinity of Paso del

Norte, which was developing as an important part of the province of New Mexico, the rest of what is now Texas was well beyond the frontier line of settlement and remained unknown territory. Although the expeditions that had found La Salle's post and established contacts with the Hasinais had stressed the apparent fertility and plentiful waters of the region, few saw any immediate opportunities in a land so far removed from established lines of communication. There were plenty of Indian souls in need of salvation who were closer to central New Spain to bother much with the fickle Caddos. The long-neglected corner of the backyard was still securely a Spanish possession—clearing it, farming it, and building on it could wait a little longer. The next chapter in the Texas story would be written when the French again appeared in Louisiana to challenge Spain's claim to the Kingdom of the Tejas.

## SUGGESTED READINGS

Several works provide overviews of Spanish North America, including the area that is now Texas, from the Age of the Conquistadors through the end of the first Spanish occupation of Texas. Anyone with a deeper interest in the conquest of Mexico and the establishment of Spanish institutions in North America can begin to explore the subject in Michael C. Meyer, William L. Sherman, and Susan M. Deeds, *The Course of Mexican History* (6th ed., 1999). The first six chapters of David J. Weber's *The Spanish Frontier in North America* (1992) provide a comprehensive survey of what is now the southern half of the United States through the end of the seventeenth century. The same chronological period is covered, in a very different, but highly entertaining way, in the first eight chapters of John L. Kessell, *Spain in the Southwest: A Narrative History of Colonial New Mexico, Arizona, Texas, and California* (2002). For those interested specifically in Texas, the most complete survey of this era can be found in chapters 2–5 of Donald E. Chipman, *Spanish Texas, 1519–1821* (1992). Emphasizing the Indian side of the story are two very different works: Elizabeth A. H. John, *Storms Brewed in Other Men's Worlds: The Confrontation of Indians, Spanish, and French in the Southwest, 1540–1795* (reprint; 1996), and Gary Clayton Anderson, *The Indian Southwest, 1580–1830: Ethnogenesis and Reinvention* (1999). For an understanding of Spain in the age of exploration and the age of the conquistadors, see J. H. Elliot, *Imperial Spain, 1469–1716* (1964).

### Dawn of Texas History

Of the conquistadors who traveled across Texas, none has received more scholarly attention than Alvar Núñez Cabeza de Vaca, who set down the story of his adventures in North America in a work titled *Relación*. It has been translated numerous times, including the very readable and well illustrated *Castaways: The Narrative of Alvar Núñez Cabeza de Vaca*, ed. Enrique Pupo-Walker, trans. Frances M. López-Morillas (1993). Cabeza de Vaca's experiences have also produced a cottage industry of anthropological and ethnohistorical work and literary criticism on

Indian-Spanish contact. One example of this more recent work is Nancy Hickerson, "How Cabeza De Vaca Lived With, Worked Among, and Finally Left the Indians of Texas," *Journal of Anthropological Research* (1998). A more established tradition is the effort of historians and naturalists to pin down Cabeza de Vaca's route across Texas and northern Mexico. Two recent examples of this type of work are Donald E. Chipman, "In Search of Cabeza de Vaca's Route Across Texas: An Historiographical Survey," *Southwestern Historical Quarterly* (1987), and Donald W. Olson et al., "Piñon Pines and the Route of Cabeza de Vaca," *Southwestern Historical Quarterly* (1997).

### Elusive Riches—Harsh Realities

Interpretation of the Coronado and Soto-Moscoso expeditions has changed significantly over the last century. The first historian to put together the story of Soto-Moscoso was the mestizo historian Garcilaso de la Vega, whose *The Florida of the Inca,* which first appeared in 1605, has been translated and edited by John Grier Varner and Jeannette Johnson Varner (1980). Bringing up to date the state of research on Moscoso's route in Texas is James E. Bruseth and Nancy A. Kenmotsu, "From Naguatex to the River Daycao: The Route of the Hernando De Soto Expedition Through Texas," *North American Archaeologist* (1993). A very good brief summary of the expedition can be found in Robert S. Weddle, *Spanish Sea: The Gulf of Mexico in North American Discovery, 1500–1685* (1985), chapter 12. The current trend in research on the Coronado expedition can be found in Richard Flint and Shirley Cushing Flint, eds., *The Coronado Expedition to Tierra Nueva: The 1540–1542 Route Across the Southwest* (1997). The best short summary of Spanish exploration in West Texas during this period is John Miller Morris, *El Llano Estacado: Exploration and Imagination on the High Plains of Texas and New Mexico, 1536–1860* (1997), part 1.

### The Paso del Norte Corridor

The various early expeditions and Juan de Oñate's conquest of New Mexico in 1598 are covered in *El Paso: A Borderlands History* by W. H. Timmons (1990), which also traces the seventeenth-century history of the area. Marc Simmons's *The Last Conquistador: Juan de Oñate and the Settling of the Far Southwest* (1991), also discusses Spanish activity in the El Paso area up to 1598. The poetically inclined might wish to look up the Oñate story in epic poem form, *Historia de la Nueva México, 1610,* by Gaspar Pérez de Villagrá (1992), originally published in 1610. A very readable account of the Pueblo Revolt and the Spanish flight to the El Paso area in 1680 is Andrew L. Knaut, *The Pueblo Revolt of 1680: Conquest and Resistance in Seventeenth-Century New Mexico* (1995).

### La Salle and the Spanish Rediscovery of Texas

No one has produced more work on La Salle's expedition and its consequences than Robert S. Weddle. His most recent work, *The Wreck of the* Belle, *the Ruin of La Salle* (2001), is an exhaustive study of the explorer from his early Canadian ventures to his death in East Texas. A quarter-century older, but still the best narrative of the Spaniards' efforts to find the French colony is Weddle's *Wilderness Manhunt: The Spanish Search for La Salle* (1973). Another writer who has made significant contributions to our understanding of this period is William Foster. His edition and annotation of Juan Bautista Chapa's *Texas and Northeastern Mexico, 1630–1690* (1997), ties the history of Texas to that of Nuevo León and Coahuila. Also of value are chapters 2 through 5 of his *Spanish Expeditions into Texas, 1689–1768* (1995), in which he tries to pin down the routes of the various *entradas* of the late seventeenth century.

# 3

# New Spain's Northeastern Frontier, 1714–1767

Tired, sick, but full of hope and enthusiasm for their work, the nine Franciscan priests who participated in the reoccupation of Texas finally sat down together on July 22, 1716, to pen a joint petition to the viceroy seeking further aid for their work. "We have conceived great expectations that this province will become a New Philippine, having, firstly, Your Excellency's protection and, on the Indians' part, the great friendliness with which they have received us. We believe that their docility and good demeanor merit that our generous and Catholic King and Lord (whom God protect) attend to them as his beloved children, and extend his powerful hand to put in ours the wherewithal for them to cover their nakedness, cultivate their lands, and raise livestock for their subsistence." With a bit of hyperbole, they hoped to flatter King Phillip V by comparing their work among the Hasinais with the efforts of earlier missionaries in the Philippine Islands under Phillip II 150 years earlier. These friars and their successors represented one of the principal tools of Spanish colonial expansion, although royal support was never as generous as they hoped it would be. Along with presidios and ranches, missions were an indispensable institution of the Spanish North American frontier until the last third of the century. Missionaries firmly believed that their work served both majesties—glorifying God and expanding the dominions of the king. In Texas both these assumptions would be tested and the reality of Spanish imperial might put to the test.

| | |
|---|---|
| 1699 | French occupy central Gulf of Mexico coast |
| 1700 | Mission-presidio complex of San Juan Bautista del Río Grande established |
| 1714 | St. Denis founds Natchitoches and makes contact with Spaniards at Rio Grande |
| 1716 | Ramón expedition reoccupies East Texas for Spain |
| 1718 | Governor Alarcón founds mission-presidio complex of San Antonio de Béxar |
| 1720 | Mission San José y San Miguel de Aguayo, "Queen of the Missions," founded by Fray Antonio Margil de Jesús |
| 1721 | Marqués de Aguayo establishes Presidio de los Adaes as capital of Texas; founds mission-presidio complex of La Bahía |
| 1727 | Rivera inspection |
| 1731 | Querétaro missions from East Texas transferred to San Antonio; Canary Island immigrants establish first civil settlement at Béxar |
| 1746 | Mission-presidio complex of San Xavier begins to form |
| 1749 | Escandón orders transfer of La Bahía to present location; settlement of lower Rio Grande valley begins |
| 1755 | Laredo founded |
| 1758 | Mission San Sabá, established for Apaches, destroyed by Indians hostile to Apaches |
| 1759 | Norteño defeat of Spanish-Apache expedition at Red River marks end of Spanish ambitions to expand northward |
| 1767 | Distribution of land grants in lower Rio Grande valley begins |

In the years following Spanish withdrawal from Hasinai country, Spanish officials remained concerned about the French threat to their dominion of the Gulf of Mexico region, and Franciscan missionaries remained interested in the prospect of converting the native peoples of the northeastern frontier. They all failed to see the thriving and dynamic world that the diverse Indian peoples of the region had created for themselves. The various culture groups in what is now Texas had developed a vast and sophisticated trade network based on regular exchange gatherings in the Colorado-Brazos area of central Texas. Indian trade fairs included a wide variety of products, including buffalo robes and dried meat, tools, pottery, mass-produced stone projectile points, corn, some jewelry, and, most prized of all, horses. This Indian world was only vaguely understood by the Spanish, who could not accept that an Indian political economy might complement rather than threaten the Spanish imperial system. It would take much of the eighteenth century to bring Spanish policy-makers around to accepting that Indians could be allies or trade partners rather than merely enemies or heathens awaiting salvation.

Consequently, for a half century after it was reoccupied in 1716, Texas and the rest of New Spain's northern frontier were pawns in a great geopolitical contest for empire. While policy-makers in Madrid, Paris, and London maneuvered to expand and consolidate their colonies, settlement of the frontier was driven by a combination of fear and opportunity. The native peoples were seen as the prize of this imperial contest, and the frontiersmen were expected to sacrifice and forebear.

By mid-century Spanish Bourbon policy-makers were exploring new ways of colonizing and had begun distancing themselves from the missionary approach. Texas, occupied during this period of transition, proved a largely insurmountable challenge to Spanish religious, political, and economic principles.

## The French Challenge

Overextended and underpopulated, by the end of the seventeenth century the Spanish empire was a feeble power—just like its king, the sickly and often irrational Charles II, who was the last of the increasingly incompetent Spanish Hapsburgs. Convinced that Pensacola Bay in west Florida was strategically the best place from which to maintain control of the Gulf of Mexico, Spanish colonial officials moved to occupy the area in 1698. If the tactic worked, there would be no need to occupy the more hazardous and inaccessible Texas coast; Pensacola would protect the entire northern gulf at minimal cost to the crown. Such optimism quickly evaporated when in January 1699 a French squadron sailed past Pensacola on its way to the Mississippi. Totally unprepared to challenge the intruders, the Spanish could do little but watch as French Louisiana came into being, first at Biloxi, then at Mobile and along the lower Mississippi River. Further complicating the situation was the death of the childless Charles II, whose vacillation over naming a successor had created competing claims by French Bourbons and Austrian Hapsburgs.

When Philip of Anjou, grandson of Louis XIV, ascended the Spanish throne in 1700 the War of the Spanish Succession (known as Queen Anne's War in English North America) followed. France and Spain were allied against the English, Austrians, Dutch, and various German states. France took advantage of the situation to claim that its expansion in Louisiana was as much an effort to protect its Spanish ally's interests in the Gulf of Mexico as it was to defend its North American colony. By the end of the war in 1714, the French were well entrenched in a series of Indian trading posts and a handful of strategic ports. It was clear to the Spanish that their erstwhile allies were now their most serious rivals in North America.

### A French Trader Helps Spain Settle Texas

The new French threat did not take long to materialize. Governor Antoine de la Mothe, Sieur de Cadillac, charged with making Louisiana profitable, soon began to probe New Spain for weaknesses. He attempted, unsuccessfully, to establish trade at Veracruz, colonial Mexico's principal port. Cadillac also ordered traders westward to establish trade relations with the western Caddo chieftanships, and entrusted a most sensitive assignment to one of the oldest and most experienced residents of Louisiana, Louis Juchereau de St. Denis. St. Denis's mission was to establish contact with the Spanish on the northern frontier as a prelude to opening direct trade with the legendary silver mining region of Nueva Vizcaya.

St. Denis was in command at Biloxi at the time Governor Cadillac chose him as emissary to the Texas Caddos and the Spanish frontier. A vigorous, Canadian-born Indian trader and royal official, the thirty-seven-year-old Frenchman already had a dozen years of experience among the lower Mississippi tribes. In September 1713 he ventured up the Mississippi to the mouth of the Red River, then westward to the site of a Caddo village, where he established his post of Natchitoches and began trading with the Indians. In the course of the next few months St. Denis slowly made his way southwestward in search of a Spanish outpost. With him were Pierre and Robert Talón, who as children had survived the La Salle expedition. Finally, in July 1714 he crossed the Rio Grande near present-day Guerrero, Coahuila (about thirty-five miles southeast of Piedras Negras-Eagle Pass), and approached Presidio San Juan Bautista del Río Grande.

The story St. Denis told the commander of the small post, Diego Ramón, reveals how religious, commercial, and political forces combined to make the frontier such a fascinating place. According to the Frenchman, Governor Cadillac had sent him on a mission to find the Franciscan missionary Fray Francisco Hidalgo, who had written the French governor of Louisiana two years previously requesting assistance in the conversion of the Hasinais. So, now he was here, ready to help Fray Hidalgo in his religious work while at the same time offering to open trade between Louisiana and New Spain.

Fray Hidalgo's request for assistance may have been an excuse for Cadillac and St. Denis's efforts to establish commercial links with northern New Spain, but it was much more. It represented yet another effort on the part of the Colegio de Propaganda Fide de la Santa Cruz de Querétaro to restore its Texas mission field so precipitously abandoned two decades earlier. By the 1680s, in an effort to re-capture the missionary zeal of a century earlier the Franciscans had settled on a new system for carrying out their frontier work. Missionary colleges such as Querétaro (1683), Nuestra Señora de Guadalupe at Zacatecas (1707), and San Fernando at Mexico City (1734) sent priests and lay brothers to the northern frontier. The colleges operated as independent institutions. Each served as a base of operations as well as a training center, especially in the languages and customs of the Indians. Recruiting was done both in New Spain and in Spain, and candi-dates for missionary work had to display a special vocation for the rigors of fron-tier life. The naive zeal of the Querétaro College Franciscans in the years immediately after its establishment had contributed to the initial failure in east Texas by 1693, but that setback had not dampened the missionaries' enthusiasm for work among the Tejas.

Fray Hidalgo, in particular, had opposed abandoning the mission to the Hasi-nais and had returned to Querétaro determined to make another attempt with them. By the late 1690s he had been assigned to the new mission field in northern Coahuila, and in 1700 he was involved in founding missions San Juan Bautista and San Francisco Solano on the Rio Grande. There, in a model of missionary frontier expansion, the missions were clustered in the vicinity of a presidio, also called San Juan Bautista del Río Grande, whose troops had responsibility for defending the missions. Together, soldiers and friars would educate the missions' Indian occu-pants in Spanish colonial agricultural, architectural, and artesanal practices, and teach them to dress, eat, and speak as humble subjects of the crown.

With the arrival of St. Denis at the Rio Grande outpost, Fray Hidalgo must have believed his prayers answered. The friar knew that the appearance of a Frenchman on the Coahuila frontier would create a panic in the viceroy's palace. He also knew that circumstances on the frontier had not changed appreciably since the Spanish had abandoned Texas twenty years before: The country was still misunderstood; the Indian peoples of the region remained totally independent of Spanish sovereignty; and the colonial population of northern New Spain was not large enough to populate yet another province. The missions, with their role of converting the natives into Christian subjects of His Catholic Majesty, were the only way Spain might hold such a vast and remote region against the French.

The news that came back from Mexico City in the summer of 1715 was just what Fray Hidalgo had been waiting to hear. St. Denis's testimony before the viceregal court provided conclusive evidence of French designs, not only on Texas, but on the interior mining provinces. The viceroy issued orders for the reoccupation of Texas on terms favorable to the Franciscans as well as to the French: four missions to be protected by a garrison of twenty-five men, to be es-tablished as close as possible to the westernmost French post. Fray Hidalgo would now return to the country of the Tejas and Governor Cadillac had his point of contact with New Spain.

The vanguard of Spanish colonization in Texas consisted largely of Franciscan missionaries such as Antonio Margil de Jesús. A native of Spain with over thirty years of experience in Central America and Mexico, the Texas mission field proved to be his last great effort. Judged by modern, cultural relativistic standards, his work seems misguided and destructive to Indian society, but in his day he was seen to epitomize Christian virtues. *(The San Jacinto Museum of History, Houston)*

## Spain's Return to Texas

In command of this important expedition was Captain Domingo Ramón, son of the commander of Presidio San Juan Bautista and an experienced frontiersman. Setting out from Saltillo in February 1716, he continued to collect materiel and people along the way. By the time the caravan arrived in the country of the Tejas in June, it consisted of twenty-six men, seven of them married and with their families, twelve missionaries, and a number of civilians, including St. Denis, who served as guide. The missionaries included representatives of both the Querétaro and Zacatecas colleges, one of whom was the now aged Fray Hidalgo. In his thirty years of service in New Spain, Fray Hidalgo had helped establish the college he represented as well as numerous missions, and was now given the honor of becoming the first resident priest at Nuestro Padre San Francisco de los Tejas, the first mission established by the Ramón expedition. Continuing to the northeast, Querétaro friars established a second mission, Nuestra Señora de la Purísima Concepción, on the Angelina River. Still farther east, friars from the Zacatecas College established Mission Nuestra Señora de Guadalupe at the head Nacogdoche village and future site of the town of Nacogdoches. Finally, Ramón established a third Querétaro mission, San José de los Nazonis, a few miles to the north at the village of that group. Clustered between the Neches and Angelina rivers, the four missions came under the protection of Presidio Nuestra Señora de los Dolores.

Officially the leader of the Zacatecas missionaries was Fray Antonio Margil de Jesús, the most renowned Franciscan in early eighteenth-century New Spain and cofounder of the Zacatecas College, who had been too ill to make the initial *entrada* with Ramón. Early in 1717 he directed the founding of two new missions to the east, closer to the French post of Natchitoches. At the site of present-day San Augustine he founded Nuestra Señora de los Dolores at an Ais Indian village. Still farther east, in what is today the vicinity of Robeline, Louisiana, he established San Miguel de los Adaes. The considerable distance between these two missions and the presidio-mission complex on the Neches could only mean that Fray Margil had accepted St. Denis's assurance of protection and assistance. It was a decision he and his fellow friars would soon regret.

Although they had made a good start, Ramón and the missionaries were uncomfortable with the precariousness of their outpost. The Indians, happy to receive the gifts brought by the Spaniards to establish friendly relations, proved indifferent to the friars' preaching once all the goods had been distributed. The two-dozen-man garrison was certainly not big enough to provide protection to the new settlement, carry out construction and escort duties, and keep watch for the French. Also, the immense distance between the Neches presidio-mission complex and the Rio Grande settlement, more than 400 miles, made for exceptional hardship in communicating with the interior and obtaining supplies.

The missionaries' letters, a memorial by Fray Olivares, and reports by the Ramóns (father and son) reached Mexico City about the same time as new warnings that St. Denis and the French in Louisiana were intent on the commercial penetration of northern New Spain. The viceroy was determined not to let this occupation of Texas duplicate the 1690–93 experience, and not to let the French gain the upper hand. When his war council recommended occupying strategic locations on the coast and on the San Antonio River, he moved quickly. He made Martín de Alarcón governor of Coahuila and Texas and ordered him to establish a settlement-mission complex on the upper San Antonio River and resupply the East Texas establishments.

Alarcón proved to be the wrong man for the job, however. His recruitment efforts were half-hearted; he had barely enough men to carry out the first part of his mission—establishing a settlement on the San Antonio River. Fray Olivares was so upset with the governor, especially over the quality of the recruits, that he refused to travel in his company. Trailing along with all the property and a few Indian servants from the now-closed Mission San Francisco Solano, the friar met Alarcón at the San Antonio River on May 1, 1718. There he immediately took possession of land and water in the name of the local Indians for the founding of Mission San Antonio de Valero. Four days later Alarcón founded a town that he called the Villa de Béxar, in honor of the viceroy's brother, the Duke of Béjar. Failing to attract civilian settlers, however, the town quickly faded into memory, leaving Presidio San Antonio de Béxar to serve as the core Spanish settlement in the area for the next dozen years.

Governor Alarcón, having accomplished his primary objective, moved on to inspect the rest of his far-flung province. Traveling east to Matagorda Bay with fewer than thirty men, he failed to establish an outpost on the coast. Although he did visit all of the East Texas missions later in the fall, he also failed to reinforce Presidio de los Tejas. He antagonized the missionaries and other Spanish residents, further alienated the local Indians, and provoked the nearby French by confiscating their trade goods. By the time of his Texas service, Alarcón, a Spaniard with previous service in the Spanish navy, had well over twenty years of military experience in New Spain. Well past his prime, he was ill prepared to deal with the challenges of a province that existed more on paper than in reality and was unable to prevent the province's Indians from trading with the French. When hostilities that erupted between Spain and France in 1719 reached the Texas-Louisiana frontier, the viceroy sought a more vigorous man to take charge of the situation.

In the aftermath of the War of the Spanish Succession, Spain had been an unwilling party to the Treaty of Utrecht, which parceled out various Hapsburg possessions, including the islands of Sardinia and Sicily. When Spain attempted to retake these former possessions, France joined in a general European war against Spain. Word of this conflict reached Spanish Texas in a curious way. One morning in June 1719 a small troop of French soldiers from Natchitoches surprised the missionary and guard at Mission San Miguel, and took prisoner all the occupants of the mission henhouse. While Lieutenant Philippe Blondel and his men returned to their post with their feathered booty, Captain Ramón ordered the abandonment of East Texas. The episode, known in Texas history as the "Chicken War," set off a chain of events that expanded and solidified Spain's hold on Texas.

### Spanish Texas Reinforced

By the time word of the French action reached Mexico City, officials were already preparing to secure their border with Louisiana. A royal decree had arrived in May ordering construction of fortifications at Matagorda Bay, the strengthening of missionary activity at San Antonio, and military protection for all missions. Fortunately for the viceroy, the selection of a leader for this expedition proved a simple matter. The Marqués de San Miguel de Aguayo, a Spanish nobleman who had married into one of the richest families in New Spain, had had his eye on Texas for some time; the prospect of serving the king by going to the Texas missionaries' rescue might further his ambitions to expand his wealth and property. Aguayo volunteered not only to lead an expedition to expel the French, but to foot the bill as well. The offer, however, turned out to be too good to be true, and the royal treasury eventually bore the brunt of the expedition's cost.

As governor of Coahuila and Texas, Aguayo found it difficult to muster the necessary resources to march on the Louisiana frontier. Insurrections among Indian groups close to home forced him to deploy men in Texas. Drought followed by floods killed livestock by the thousands, decimating the herds he needed to support the full-scale campaign he had in mind. In the meantime, he did authorize Fray Margil to establish a mission for the Zacatecas College at San Antonio. Dedicated on February 23, 1720, Mission San José y San Miguel de Aguayo was destined to become the "Queen of the Missions." Even before setting foot in Texas, the Marqués de Aguayo had already carried out one part of his instructions—to strengthen the missionary effort at San Antonio. It was more than a year before he arrived in Texas and began carrying out the rest of his orders.

Whereas previous expeditions to Texas had been makeshift, under-prepared, and largely unsuccessful, the Aguayo expedition proved an unqualified success. By the time it set out from Monclova in mid-November it consisted of almost 600 men, about 4,000 horses, thousands of head of cattle, sheep, and goats, and hundreds of pack-mules. It was the largest and best equipped Spanish force ever to enter Texas. Delayed in crossing the Rio Grande, which was swollen beyond its banks, Aguayo ordered his second-in-command, Fernando Pérez de Almazán, forward to San Antonio with over 100 men to forestall its occupation by the French. He also dispatched Domingo Ramón with forty men to occupy Matagorda Bay at the site of La Salle's post. By the time Aguayo and St. Denis (who had returned to French service and was again in command of Natchitoches) met on August 1, 1721, Aguayo's mission was all but complete. Various Caddo chiefs had already pledged their loyalty to the Spanish king, and St. Denis was pleased at the opportunity to do business with the restored missions and the new presidio that Aguayo had been ordered to build.

For the next few months Aguayo executed his plan for strengthening and reinforcing Texas. Plans for new presidios at Los Adaes and La Bahía del Espíritu Santo and for the reconstruction of Presidio de los Tejas and Presidio de Béxar reflected the expansion of military personnel in the province from approximately 50 to over 250. Aguayo reopened all of the East Texas missions that had been abandoned in 1719 and authorized the construction of new ones, including one at La Bahía called Nuestra Señora del Espíritu Santo de Zúñiga. More important, Aguayo seems to have done a good job at Indian relations and left the Spanish at peace with all of the Indians except the Apaches, who inhabited the Edwards Plateau and remained beyond the Spanish sphere of influence.

## Spanish Texas Takes Shape

Fray Hidalgo did not return to the East Texas mission field following Aguayo's restoration of Spanish settlements there in 1721. He remained in San Antonio, where he labored at Mission Valero. It was an exciting and dangerous time at the presidio-mission complex on the edge of the Edwards Plateau. The south-central Texas native peoples who entered the missions spoke a variety of Coahuiltecan dialects and were sometimes antagonistic toward each other. Their hunting and gathering ways were so at odds with Spanish notions of civilized life that misunderstanding, resistance, and, sometimes, violence colored their relations with Spanish colonials. A mission, Fray Hidalgo well understood, was a risky undertaking, and failure could come from the most unexpected source.

### Early Spanish-Indian Relations

Mission San Francisco Xavier de Nájera was a good case in point. Chief Juan Rodríguez of the Sanas, one of several central Texas Indian groups collectively known as the Ranchería Grande, had quickly befriended the Spanish and offered his services and those of his people in return for a mission of their own. Early in 1722 he and fifty families of Sanas arrived in San Antonio eager to start a new life. Their eagerness was in part due to depredations from Apache Indians, whose increasing raids against them made the Sanas all the more interested in alliances with the Spanish. Months turned into years as missionaries and Indians waited for official permission to proceed. A new viceroy with orders from the king to reduce the cost of defending the frontier refused to authorize the project and the Querétaro College pleaded lack of resources.

Eventually, Chief Rodríguez and the remaining dozen warriors, fearing annihilation at the hands of the Apaches if they stayed at the unprotected Nájera site, befriended the Xarames at Mission Valero and took up residence there. As for the Sanas who had returned to the Ranchería Grande, they made their sentiments clear: "The Spaniards want us to work for them; we want to be their friends and to fight no more; but to live near them, or be placed in a mission, we do not want even to speak of it." The collapse of Mission Nájera would not be the last Spanish failure with the Ranchería Grande.

The Sanas's concerns with Apache attacks was well founded. Lipan Apache raids made life dangerous in San Antonio, both at the presidio and at the missions. Retaliatory campaigns by the Spanish only increased the level of enmity. Soon the friars of the Querétaro College came to see the Apaches not as aggressors, but as the victims of corrupt military commanders and their debauched troops. So convinced were the friars at Mission Valero of the possibility of peace with the Apaches, that in 1725 Fray Hidalgo, now in his late sixties, offered to go out and preach among them. His request denied by his superiors, Fray Hidalgo retired to San Juan Bautista del Río Grande, where he spent the last year of his life.

A chronic state of warfare between Apaches and Spaniards existed for the next twenty years. The presidio-mission complex made an inviting target for these plains hunters who were slowly migrating to the south in the early eighteenth century. As the eastern Apache tribes came under pressure from the Comanches, who cut off their access to the Pueblos and Spanish New Mexico, they raided Spanish Texas horse herds to replace mounts lost to their enemies and supply convoys for manufactured items they did not have access to. Human beings also became the objects of raiding, as both the Apaches and the Spanish took women and children as hostages and slaves. The Apaches perceived that the Spanish had allied themselves with their enemies: the Hasinais, Ranchería Grande, and other eastern Indians. Apache enmity for the Spanish was reinforced as they took into their bands other Indians who had fled Spanish control in Coahuila, Nuevo León, and Nueva Vizcaya. From these forced migrations, and the addition of captured and escaped non-Apaches and Spanish colonials emerged the Lipan Apaches, whose presence in the Edwards Plateau west of San Antonio would be at the heart of Texas's Indian problems throughout the eighteenth century.

Conflict was not confined to the Apaches, however, as the Karankawan tribes along the Texas coast also proved to be antagonistic to a Spanish presence at Matagorda Bay. Shortly after its founding, Mission Espíritu Santo attracted members of various Karankawa bands, but relations between the military and the Indians in the missions soon deteriorated. The souring of relations with most of the coastal Karankawa groups frustrated efforts to remain at the Matagorda Bay site; by 1726 the new commander at La Bahía had arranged for the presidio-mission complex to relocate at what is today called Mission Valley in Victoria County. The new location was more healthful (higher ground, better water supply) and secure, and the missionaries of Espíritu Santo were able to attract bands of Aranamas and Tamiques, Coahuiltecan-speaking residents of the coastal prairies, who helped build the mission into Texas's first important ranching center. Unfortunately, even at its new location La Bahía was an extremely isolated community and was unable to attract civilian settlement. For the next twenty years Presidio La Bahía, understaffed and undersupplied, struggled to survive, until one final move in 1749 brought it to a location where increasing contacts with the outside world allowed development to take place.

Perhaps the greatest disappointment to friars and officials alike was the lack of progress they had made with the Caddoan villagers in eastern Texas. As in the 1690s and just before the Chicken War, the Hasinais and other Caddo groups quickly lost interest in the Christian conversion program. The Indians also blamed the Spanish for the epidemics and crop failures they experienced. Within a few years of their reestablishment, the missions were almost completely devoid of Indians, who preferred to live in their own villages and tolerate the occasional visits of the friars. Consequently, neither the missionaries nor the presidios could feed their residents, and they were forced to rely increasingly on either the Indians, French Natchitoches, or far-off San Antonio. Conditions in Texas, then, did not bode well for the province's long-term survival. An infusion of new blood was needed.

### A New Plan to Colonize Texas

From the perspective of Mexico City, the northern frontier, Texas in particular, seemed to be little more than a money pit, where missionaries, governors, and presidio commanders exchanged charges of corruption, incompetence, and cruelty toward the natives. The viceroy, determined to get the situation under control, appointed Colonel Pedro de Rivera to carry out a thorough inspection of the frontier defense system with the goal of saving money and instilling discipline.

Armed with broad powers not only to inspect everything he deemed proper, but to issue orders on the spot, the newly promoted brigadier left the viceregal capital in November 1724; he was not to return for three and a half years.

When Rivera arrived in Texas in August 1727, he was tired and in no mood to hear excuses. What he found was shocking and troubling. In East Texas there were no Indians at the missions, and the presidios were overstaffed, given the peaceful relations with both the Hasinais and the French. At San Antonio and La Bahía the missionaries were more gainfully employed, but the presidio companies were similarly overstaffed as they had successfully handled the Apaches. Rivera's draconian reforms called for abandonment of Presidio de los Tejas, the closing of East Texas missions, reductions in the complements of the remaining three presidios, and recruitment of colonists.

The viceroy was extremely pleased with Rivera's efforts, and as a reward made him special counsel for frontier matters. Spanish Texans were not so pleased with the penny-pinching measures that resulted from the brigadier's recommendations. Instead of four presidios and 269 men, the Texans were left with only three garrisons with a total of 144 billets, with all except the officers at reduced pay. The Franciscans were also displeased, not only because the Querétaro missionaries were forced to abandon East Texas, but because they would get less assistance from the remaining smaller garrisons.

Rivera, in his rush to please his superiors, overlooked the importance of military settlements. The symbiotic relationships between presidios and missions were crucial to what little success Texas had enjoyed. Presidios served as seed settlements in regions where it was difficult to attract civilian settlers, and Texas, indisputably, was such a region. Governor Pérez de Almazán commented in 1724 that recruiting soldiers for service in Texas was a difficult task, not only because they had to be sought outside the province, but also because "some time is needed to court them, and they must be given some assistance for their costs besides their salaries, because of the resignation with which they all come to this country." Missions, if they were to evolve into permanent communities of hispanicized Indians, needed nearby presidios to protect them as well as to serve as markets for the food crops and animals that the neophytes produced.

Because the development of Texas could not rest solely on a few soldiers and christianized Indians, Rivera agreed with Spanish officials who had recognized the need for civilian settlement since the time of the Aguayo expedition. In 1719 the Council of the Indies, the royal policy-making body on colonial affairs, had recommended bringing 2,000 families from the Canary Islands and northern Spain and 100 Tlaxcalan Indian families to help instruct neophytes at the missions. Three years later the Marqués de Aguayo and the viceroy added their support for crown-sponsored immigration, and in 1723 the king relented and issued an order for the recruitment of 200 families in the Canary Islands. Years passed, and in 1727 another order was issued without effect. In 1728, Rivera explained to the viceroy how civilian settlement at San Antonio would help reduce costs: "the location being so fertile and pleasant, . . . it is particularly suited for the settlement of twenty-five families, who would fully protect the land and induce others to imitate them in settling other sites as may seem convenient." The viceroy and officials in Madrid hoped that such settlement might eliminate the annual 17,500-peso expense that Presidio de Béxar represented.

Finally, in 1729 the first ten families of a proposed 400 set out from the Canary Islands for Texas by way of Havana and Veracruz, then overland to Mexico City and onward to the frontier. The experiment proved so costly, time-consuming, and inefficient that the viceroy did not want it repeated. The fifty-six Isleños (Canary Islanders) who arrived in San Antonio on March 9, 1731 were the only product of a decade of schemes and royal decrees, but they were a fortunate lot. Dating back to the early years of colonization in the sixteenth century, the crown had granted certain privileges to the first settlers of new communities. (Unfortunately for the soldier-settlers of San Antonio, La Bahía, and Los Adaes—between 200 and 250 at each settlement in 1730—the military status of their communities precluded similar consideration.)

Treated as *primeros pobladores* (first or original settlers) the Isleños were granted a variety of privileges by the king, which must have created considerable envy among the province's already-established residents. He granted the Canary Islanders the title of *hidalgo;* he granted them land and water rights; and he authorized them to form a town government, with those selected for office getting life appointments. Most practical of all, the king granted the Isleños a year's stipend and the necessary supplies to establish themselves as farmers.

## The First Civil Government of Texas

Captain Juan Antonio Pérez de Almazán, commander of Presidio de Béxar and *justicia mayor* (district magistrate), was a busy man in 1731. It must have seemed as if all the world were descending on him as missionaries, Isleños, and military settlers lined up for a piece of the San Antonio River valley. His biggest worry was keeping the Canary Islanders alive in the face of Apache hostilities and the raw wilderness conditions in which they lived. Despite the viceroy's orders that the Isleños establish a separate community, Almazán reasoned that their survival rested on the defense the presidio could provide and the instruction the experienced frontiersmen of San Antonio could supply these Old World farmers. Consequently, the captain decided to grant the Isleños farmland and a site for a town between the presidio and Mission Valero. They named the town San Fernando in honor of the heir to the Spanish throne. (For the sake of clarity, we will use the terms Béxar or San Antonio for the settlement). The decision, although expedient, brought about considerable conflict with the already-established military settlers and nearby Mission Valero.

Just four days before the Isleños arrived, Captain Almazán had begun dealing with the other group of land claimants that had descended on the fertile and well-watered valley. He had carried out the act of possession for Mission Nuestra Señora de la Purísima Concepción de Acuña at the site of the defunct Mission Nájera. The Querétaro College friars had successfully lobbied the viceroy to allow them to move the three missions near Presidio de los Tejas after it closed in 1729;

following a brief effort at what is now Barton Springs in Austin, the missionaries decided that the San Antonio River was both a safer and more convenient location. Along with Mission Concepción, Captain Almazán assigned land and water to missions San Juan Capistrano (formerly San José de los Nazonis) and San Francisco de la Espada (formerly San Francisco de los Neches). Located downstream from Mission San José, these last two stations completed the presidio-mission complex that over the centuries would blossom into the city of San Antonio.

By the end of 1731 San Antonio de Béxar, or simply Béxar, as the district was collectively known, had evolved from a simple stopover on the trail to the Texas capital at Los Adaes to the province's most diverse settlement. The friars of its five missions, which occupied rich farmland on alternating banks of the river, were busy building sophisticated irrigation systems, laying out village compounds, and attempting to transform the region's wandering bands of hunters and gatherers into villagers. They relied on *mayordomos* (overseers), usually soldiers and former soldiers, to help train, discipline, and supervise the Indians. Missions Valero and San José, which had been in operation for over a decade by then, both produced

San Antonio's Plaza de las Islas (Main Plaza) commemorates the city's early Canary Islands settlers. What is now the French gothic San Fernando Cathedral started out as the humble San Fernando church, the construction of which began under the direction of Canary Islanders in 1738. *(The Institute of Texan Cultures at UTSA)*

surpluses that the friars could sell to the presidios, the proceeds going toward the needs of the missions and the neophytes.

Similarly, the Isleños, who at first had been housed among the military settlers, were busy putting up their first homes, expanding the *acequia* (irrigation ditch) system and agricultural land they had inherited from the military settlers, and accustoming themselves to running a town government. The king's orders provided for the Canary Islanders to be a self-governing community, with a *regimiento* (town council) of six *regidores* (aldermen), two *alcaldes ordinarios* (municipal magistrates), an *alguacil mayor* (constable or sheriff), a *procurador* (municipal attorney), and *escribano* (public scribe). As a further concession to the original colonists, all the positions except those of *alcalde* were extended to the original holders for life, thus giving the Isleños sole control of local authority for well over a decade after the town's founding.

Thus the military settlers, a number of whom had retired or were about to retire and hoped for land, water, and house lots in the community, were at first excluded from this town-building activity. The presidio, although adjacent to the new town, represented a separate jurisdiction, and its commander continued to exercise exclusive authority over soldiers, their dependents, and any settlers not considered *vecinos* (citizens) of the town. Most Isleños, concerned about competition from retired soldiers in selling their crops to the presidio, made every possible effort to exclude military settlers, whom they referred to as *agregados* (additional or secondary settlers), from access to water and agricultural land. And the Old World immigrants, now bearing noble status, considered themselves racially superior to the mixed-blood military population, many of whom were descended from the unions of Spanish men and Indian and Afro-Hispanic women.

Time and numbers were not on the Isleños' side, however. On the one hand, construction projects, supply convoys, and retirements and recruitments at the presidio all brought people to San Antonio, reinforcing the non-Isleño population. On the other hand, it soon became apparent that no more Canary Islanders would come to reinforce the initial contingent. Isleño offspring soon began looking for spouses among the military families. Lacking business ties and appropriate economic skills, some Isleños formed partnerships with military settlers. A few Isleños even abandoned civilian life for the financial security of military service. To cement these partnerships and to foster family alliances, *agregados* and Isleños established ritual kinship relations through *compadrazgo* (godparenthood) and support for selected non-Isleños to participate in town government.

Squabbling between Isleños and *agregados* was not San Antonio's most pressing problem; that honor went to the continued hostilities with the Lipan Apaches. It was a situation at least in part of the settlers' making, however, or so thought the missionaries. Fray Benito Fernández de Santa Anna complained after a major campaign in 1739 that "the expedition was profitable only to those who had horses and other goods, which they sold at excessively high prices . . . and had greater hopes of a considerable prize of horses, hides, and Indian men and women to serve them." Whether it was the Lipans who retaliated for unprovoked campaigns by the settlers, or the settlers who exacted a measure of retribution from the Apaches for their continual depredations, the result was that everyone was at constant risk: mission Indians tending herds and flocks, settlers among their crops, and muleteers carrying supplies into and out of the province. Finally, following a major campaign in which the Spaniards pursued the Apaches deep into the Edwards Plateau, the Lipans were ready to call a truce in 1745. The cease-fire lasted until August 1749, when, at a formal treaty ceremony held at San Antonio, Lipan chiefs, military officers, the missionaries, and town officials literally buried the hatchet. Into a great hole dug in the presidio plaza the participants threw a live horse, arrows, a lance, and a ceremonial hatchet. As the hole was covered, they held hands and embraced.

# The Rio Grande Frontiers

The Apache peace at Béxar came just as colonial New Spain underwent its last and most successful colonization effort on the northeastern frontier. For a number of years officials in Mexico City had been increasingly concerned about Spain's weak presence along the Gulf of Mexico coast between Tampico and La Bahía. The rugged mountain chains of the Sierra Madre Oriental, the mosquito-infested lowlands of the immediate coast, and the semiarid expanses north of the Rio Grande had all contributed to discouraging Spanish interest in the area. As a result, the Seno Mexicano, as the area was commonly called, remained home to numerous hunter-gatherer groups and became a haven for Indians fleeing Spanish domination, who then turned around and launched highly destructive raids into Spanish areas. Increased foreign activity in the gulf added to government concerns, especially in view of growing tensions between England and Spain over colonial boundaries and trading privileges. English occupation of any portion of the Seno would be a strategic disaster for Spanish interests. The Seno Mexicano had to be settled.

## New Times, New Methods for Settling the Frontier

Colonial officials charged with defending New Spain, crown jewel of the empire, faced a daunting problem: how to effectively gain control of the vast and isolated coastal territory between Tampico and Texas while spending as little as possible from the royal coffers. Not wanting to rely on missionaries, policy-makers searched for an individual willing to organize and underwrite a systematic colonization of the Seno. After considering a number of proposals in the 1730s and early 1740s, José Escandón y Elguera's plan emerged as the favorite.

Escandón was a Spanish-born military officer who had made a name for himself as an honest and successful Indian fighter. He received his appointment in September 1746, along with the title of lieutenant general to the viceroy, which was a high honor. Given his military background and the contradictory and incomplete information available about the vast area in question, Escandón determined that before colonization could begin he would need to mount a comprehensive exploration. Only by determining the best trails, most fertile and well-watered locations, and the territories of existing Indian groups, could the project achieve quick success. In early 1747 he organized seven expeditions that penetrated the Seno from the south, west, and north.

From the reconnaissance of the region, Escandón came up with a bold plan to gain Spain complete control of the coastal region. Colonists would enter the Seno from neighboring provinces and occupy strategic locations as far north as the Nueces River. To facilitate contacts with Texas, Escandón ordered the relocation of La Bahía from its Mission Valley site to its present location on the San Antonio River. For his part, Escandón would recruit families to settle a new town on the Nueces River, near present-day Corpus Christi, to serve as the northern limit of Nuevo Santander. Although the Nueces River settlement never materialized, La Bahía flourished at its new location. Captain Joaquín Orrobio y Basterra, who directed the transfer, liked the new location, commenting on the availability of timber and stone for construction, open prairies for farming and grazing, plentiful water in the San Antonio River, and a prominent hill on which to build the presidio. His successor, Captain Manuel Ramírez de la Piscina, who took over in early 1750, was similarly impressed and predicted a quick increase in civilian settlement.

The missionaries shared the optimism of the military community. At Mission Espíritu Santo the Indian population quickly recovered from the move, and by 1758 they had replaced the initial wooden church and friary with stone-and-mortar structures. This success prompted renewed efforts among various Karankawa groups, as Fray Juan de Dios María Camberos gathered hundreds for a new mission. Not waiting for an official reply to his request for permission, Fray Camberos established Mission Nuestra Señora del Rosario about five miles west of Espíritu Santo in 1754.

Throughout the 1750s and 1760s La Bahía made steady progress despite the advent of Apache and Comanche raiding. Until the early 1760s La Bahía had only had to contend with the minor depredations of the coastal band peoples. The Karankawas had a fierce reputation, but for the most part they did little damage to the presidio and mission. After the establishment of Mission Rosario, most Karankawa bands remained at peace with the Spanish, even though they refused to become full-time mission dwellers. As the Comanches and other northern tribes put pressure on the Lipan Apaches, the Lipans moved farther east, launching their first raids on La Bahía in 1762. Their enemies soon followed them, with devastating results on local cattle herds and considerable loss of human life.

Nevertheless, the herds grew, the mission populations remained constant, and the number of civilian settlers increased. From just a handful of civilians in 1749, the settlement's population increased to forty-six civilian households in 1767. Marriage among the presidio company added to the nonmilitary population, and by the 1760s the sons of former soldiers were themselves enlisting in the company. At the missions, although the numbers fluctuated, populations numbered in the hundreds, more than enough to perform all the essential functions at the mission compounds and at the outlying ranches.

Increased economic activity centered on livestock. Thousands of head of cattle grazed the open ranges of the coast. Mission Espíritu Santo, although it could only count a few thousand branded head, claimed over 40,000 animals between the San Antonio and Guadalupe. Captain Piscina's Rancho San José, which occupied thousands of acres on the west bank of the San Antonio, was so productive that he employed both civilians and enlisted men in its operation. Over time the community's growing prosperity encouraged the appearance of the first merchants and craftsmen.

Of importance to the history of Texas was not only the relocation of La Bahía, but Escandón's founding of a series of settlements along the Rio Grande. By the end of March 1749 he had authorized two settlements along the south bank of the lower Rio Grande: Camargo, under the leadership of Blas María de la Garza Falcón, a member of a leading stock-raising family from Coahuila; and Reynosa, under another wealthy *hacendado*, Captain Carlos Cantú of Nuevo León. As families continued to respond to Escandón's initial success, new settlements were founded over the course of the next few years. In 1750 Vicente Guerra, another Nuevo León landowner, established Revilla upstream from Camargo on the south bank of the Rio Grande, and José Vázquez Borrego, a stockman from Coahuila who had been grazing his animals in the area for some time, received permission to establish Rancho de Dolores on the north bank. Two years later José Florencio Chapa of Nuevo León received permission from Escandón to found a village on the south bank, downstream from Revilla, known as Mier. Finally, in 1755 yet another wealthy stockman, Tomás Sánchez, received permission to found the town of Laredo on the north bank of the Rio Grande.

Late in 1755 Escandón stepped back to make an account of his efforts. In the previous six years he had authorized the founding of twenty-three civilian settlements, including five along the Rio Grande, fifteen missions, and two mining camps. By his reckoning he was responsible for the settlement of 1,337 civilian and 144 military families, for a total of 6,385 persons. In the fifteen missions under the direction of the Colleges of Zacatecas and San Fernando there were 2,837 neophytes. These accomplishments had been possible even in the face of adverse conditions: three years of drought that required purchase of corn in neighboring provinces, followed by severe flooding that had brought on epidemics and malaria, and the continued hostility of some of the region's native people. The contrast with Texas, where settlement had not successfully expanded beyond the three mission-presidio complexes left behind by the Marqués de Aguayo in 1722, and which contained a Spanish population of only 1,800, could not be more stark.

## The Roots of Hispanic South Texas

Escandón's reports were one thing, independent verification another. In 1757 the viceroy instructed José Tienda de Cuervo, an experienced administrator, to carry out a thorough inspection of the province. The viceroy was impressed with what he found. The population had increased to almost 9,000 settlers and 3,500 neophytes, and the number of missions had increased to eighteen. The number of mines had increased to eleven, and five salt deposits were being exploited. It was obvious that this was livestock country, especially the area north of the Rio Grande, where the largest ranches were located. In all, the province had 58,000 horses, 25,000 cattle, and 288,000 sheep and goats. The inspection went so far as to describe the residents of Revilla, Camargo, and Reynosa as rich from the livestock and salt trade.

The people of Nuevo Santander, like those of Texas and the rest of New Spain's northern region, were ethnically and socioeconomically mixed. *Criollos* made up about one-third of the population, *castas* about half, Christianized Indians approximately 15 percent, and peninsular Spaniards only 1 or 2 percent. These proportions were a source of disappointment for Escandón, who preferred *peninsulares* for important positions, but had few from whom to choose. Many of the people of Nuevo Santander, as one local official reported in 1757, were poor families that had no home of their own, but lived off the seasonal employment they could obtain from *hacendados*. Escandón was more blunt, declaring that his recruiting success, which continued long after the initial expeditions, were a result of the colonists fleeing the abuses of local officials and "the slavery in which they lived, having been made debtors to the hacienda owners, and aspiring to free themselves." Presaging the Anglo-American immigration trend of the 1820s and 1830s in Texas, many of the new arrivals were fugitives from the law fleeing prosecution for debt, theft, and even murder. Without a doubt, however, the Nuevo Santander-South Texas frontier offered opportunities for those intrepid enough to face the risks.

Although Escandón had made exceptional progress in transforming Nuevo Santander into a secure and productive province of New Spain, there were problems. The missionaries complained that rather than carrying out their primary mission of converting the Indians, they were forced to serve the civilian population. Most missionaries, therefore, had become little more than parish priests. Worse, the *reducción* (gathering of nonsedentary Indians in formal missions) of the native peoples had become the means by which prominent landowners and military men throughout the province exploited their labor. The friars accused the governor of "having not the slightest interest in the most important and proper matter of the pacification and settlement of the Indians." As a result, the most peaceful Indian groups had fallen into virtual slavery and the most aggressive ones had abandoned the missions and started preying on outlying ranches and settlements. Under these conditions, the missions quickly declined; by the 1760s many contained no neophytes at all. By the 1790s the mission system in Nuevo Santander had completely collapsed. An Indian population in the territory estimated at approximately 25,000 in 1750 stood at less than 2,000 at the end of the century.

The missionaries were not Escandón's only critics. Many settlers, especially those of substantial means, complained that although they had repeatedly been assured of land titles (one of the recommendations of the Tienda de Cuervo inspection), none had as yet been distributed. Although he could deflect or ignore the missionaries' complaints, the governor did have to account for the unsettled state of land ownership in the province. Escandón's explanation to the viceroy was that his extensive duties kept him from attending to the matter and that he had no qualified subordinate to see that the job was done properly. Moreover, because settlers continued to arrive, some of whom he considered of better quality than the original settlers, he wanted to wait longer and make sure the land went to those most capable of making the best use of it.

Determined not to allow such a promising start to descend into chaos, the viceroy appointed a royal commission to carry out a general inspection and distribution of lands to the settlers of Nuevo Santander in 1767. By the time the commission reached the Rio Grande settlements, it had worked out a very efficient system of land distribution. The commissioner named local leaders as subordinates and individuals with experience appraising land as surveyors. Thus, the locals had primary responsibility for establishing which lands were to be granted for ranching, farming, common use, and town use. Conditions along the river created unique problems: abundant water in the Rio Grande, but a scarcity of fresh water away from it, especially on the north bank; an adequate amount of good bottomland available for agriculture, but high flood banks that limited irrigation on the south side and made it impossible on the north bank. Naturally most people wanted to stay close to the river and to the settlements, especially in light of continued Indian depredations. As stockmen, they needed large parcels of land, but also access to drinking water for their herds.

What the local experts came up with was a unique solution to the complicated set of issues. After setting aside the required amount of land for each town and mission tract, all of which, except for Laredo, were located on the south bank of the river, they prioritized the limited amount of agricultural land in favor of the oldest settlers. When it came time to distribute grazing land the experts gave each family access to the Rio Grande. They laid out each tract of approximately 8,000–10,000 acres with a very narrow frontage on the river. Some families, given their status, received more than one tract and, because of the delay in distribution, others had sons who could claim tracts of their own. These long, narrow lots, which received the name *porciones,* allowed stockmen to move their herds and flocks close to the river during the dry season and graze them away from the stream during rainy periods. So efficient were the surveyors that in some settlements, such as Laredo, a considerable number of *porciones* went undistributed for a number of years.

On their departure for Mexico City in fall 1767, the commission left behind a well settled and quickly expanding ranching kingdom. The commission had issued land grants to over a thousand settlers, most for tracts intended for ranching purposes. Even the territory north of the Rio Grande, the most exposed to hostile Indians and the most arid, saw a steady advance in cattle operations that produced many *ranchos* (the root of the English term ranch) measuring in the

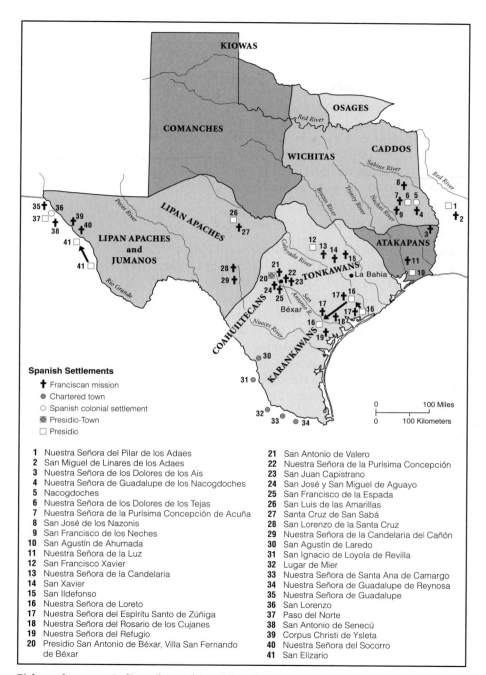

Eighteenth-century Indian tribes and Spanish settlements.

**Spanish Settlements**

✝ Franciscan mission
● Chartered town
○ Spanish colonial settlement
◉ Presidio-Town
□ Presidio

1  Nuestra Señora del Pilar de los Adaes
2  San Miguel de Linares de los Adaes
3  Nuestra Señora de los Dolores de los Ais
4  Nuestra Señora de Guadalupe de los Nacogdoches
5  Nacogdoches
6  Nuestra Señora de los Dolores de los Tejas
7  Nuestra Señora de la Purísima Concepción de Acuña
8  San José de los Nazonis
9  San Francisco de los Neches
10  San Agustín de Ahumada
11  Nuestra Señora de la Luz
12  San Francisco Xavier
13  Nuestra Señora de la Candelaria
14  San Xavier
15  San Ildefonso
16  Nuestra Señora de Loreto
17  Nuestra Señora del Espíritu Santo de Zúñiga
18  Nuestra Señora del Rosario de los Cujanes
19  Nuestra Señora del Refugio
20  Presidio San Antonio de Béxar, Villa San Fernando de Béxar

21  San Antonio de Valero
22  Nuestra Señora de la Purísima Concepción
23  San Juan Capistrano
24  San José y San Miguel de Aguayo
25  San Francisco de la Espada
26  San Luis de las Amarillas
27  Santa Cruz de San Sabá
28  San Lorenzo de la Santa Cruz
29  Nuestra Señora de la Candelaria del Cañón
30  San Agustín de Laredo
31  San Ignacio de Loyola de Revilla
32  Lugar de Mier
33  Nuestra Señora de Santa Ana de Camargo
34  Nuestra Señora de Guadalupe de Reynosa
35  Nuestra Señora de Guadalupe
36  San Lorenzo
37  Paso del Norte
38  San Antonio de Senecú
39  Corpus Christi de Ysleta
40  Nuestra Señora del Socorro
41  San Elizario

tens of thousands of acres and some measuring hundreds of thousands of acres. These *ranchos* became the progenitors of the famous Texas ranches of later generations.

Escandón had not been perfect: He had taken advantage of the Franciscans to gain easy access to religious services for his colonists; he had allowed extensive exploitation of the local native population, despite his stated intentions to bring them the benefits of civilization; he had taken care of his personal and family interests, and those of colleagues, before the interests of the general population of colonists. Nevertheless, the settlement of Nuevo Santander had been a spectacular success, especially in contrast to the continued struggle for survival experienced by its neighboring province of Texas throughout this time.

## The Desert Blooms at Paso del Norte

Hundreds of miles upstream from the developing ranching communities of the lower Rio Grande valley a very different type of settlement activity had produced a thriving set of communities at Paso del Norte. Located at a crucial juncture of the road between New Mexico and Chihuahua, the residents of Paso del Norte prospered from providing services to travelers, but the area also had products to offer. A combination of climate, soil, and the waters of the Rio Grande made the area a desert oasis and ideal viticulture country. By mid-century Paso del Norte's wines, brandies, and raisins were in great demand throughout northern New Spain. Farming extended to the cultivation of wheat in well-irrigated fields that produced substantial surpluses for export to the mining camps to the south. In fact, the use of farmland for grapes and wheat meant that in some years residents did not harvest enough corn to meet local needs.

Economic success brought population growth to the communities that made up the district. Despite increased raiding by Apaches, the population of the district grew from about 1,000 people at the turn of the century to almost 5,000 in 1765. The civil-military settlement located on the south bank of the river, El Paso del Río del Norte, was home to over 2,800 residents. The presidio company of 49 men and their families, 230 persons in all, made up less than 10 percent of the total. Indians and *genízaros* (New Mexico term for detribalized Indians incorporated into Spanish society) made up about 20 percent of the population. The remaining 70 percent consisted of *criollos* and *castas,* usually referred to as mestizos, but also including mulattoes. Some of the genízaro families had even managed to gain *vecino* status, that is, they were considered full citizens of the settlement, an indication that economic and social opportunities on the frontier conspired to downplay the social and racial labels that restricted social mobility elsewhere.

Also prospering were the three mission communities established for area Indians—Guadalupe, Senecú, and Socorro—and Ysleta, the settlement established for the Tigua Indians who fled New Mexico with the Spaniards at the time of the Pueblo revolt of 1680. Although all three communities had substantial numbers of non-Indians living in them by the middle of the eighteenth century, each retained its distinctive Indian character. Franciscan missionaries supervised these communities, in addition to providing spiritual services to the non-Indian population of the area.

As successful as the Paso del Norte district was, it shared a major problem with Texas, Coahuila, and the other northern frontier provinces: Apache Indian raids. As in Texas, the most important factor contributing to the increase in hostilities was the pressure from the north being put on the eastern Apache tribes (those located east of the Rio Grande) by advancing Comanches. The problem had been at its worst in the first decades of the eighteenth century, until reorganization of the presidio led the raiders, mostly Gileños, Mescaleros, and Natagés, to choose targets farther south. Nevertheless, sporadic depredations took their toll, mostly in lost horses and mules, which the Apaches used both for transportation and for food, but also in the occasional killing of a field hand. Given the strategic and developing economic importance of the Paso del Norte district, however, the problem was manageable.

# The Failure of Missionary Expansion in Texas

Unlike Nuevo Santander, where José de Escandón directed an essentially civilian colonization effort, or Paso del Norte, which occupied a significant economic niche, much of what is today Texas remained fundamentally a religious-military frontier. Efforts at expansion in Texas during the 1740s and 1750s were tied to the twin objectives of bringing more Indians into the fold of the Catholic church and preventing French penetration of Spanish territory.

## Missionary Expansion into Central Texas

For Fray Mariano Francisco de los Dolores y Viana, missionary at San Antonio de Valero since the mid-1730s, the appearance at Béxar of a delegation from the Ranchería Grande tribes on June 2, 1745, was an answer to his prayers and years of patience and hard work. For over a decade while out in search of runaway neophytes, he had taken the opportunity to preach the benefits of mission life to independent Indian groups he encountered. Now representatives of Tonkawan, Atakapan, and Ervipiame that made up the Ranchería Grande requested that a mission be established in their territory—a large area of central Texas between the Colorado and Trinity rivers. They insisted, however, that the friars come to them, as San Antonio was too far from allies and hunting grounds.

Not waiting for authorization from his superiors, Fray Mariano obtained the services of five presidio soldiers and with a group of trusted neophytes headed for the Ranchería Grande. He caught up with the Indians in January 1746 near the junction of the San Gabriel River and Brushy Creek (present-day Milam County). He soon had a makeshift mission in operation, describing the land as "much better than that found in San Antonio, and there is an abundance of *cíbolos* (buffalo), deer, turkeys, fish, persimmons, prickly pears, and other fruits used by the Indians." Although other reports were less optimistic, the viceroy ultimately consented to the project, creating a garrison out of detachments of soldiers from Los Adaes and La Bahía.

Despite the enthusiasm of Fray Mariano and the other friars, the San Xavier settlement was short-lived and marked by tragedy. The missionaries accused the soldiers of debauchery and corrupting the Indians. Supplies at the missions were inadequate; a smallpox epidemic killed more than forty Indians, and there were mass desertions. Matters only got worse when Captain Felipe de Rábago y Terán, the new garrison commander, arrived with his fifty-man company in December 1751. He found only 100 neophytes at Mission San Xavier, none at San Ildefonso and just twenty-five at Candelaria. Disappointed in the missionaries and the remote location, he recommended abandonment of San Xavier in favor of a site on the San Marcos River, which he considered much more favorable. Having been sharply rebuked by the friars for his affair with the wife of one of his men, Rábago refused to discipline his men, whom the friars accused of adultery and rape. The situation deteriorated until May 1752, when one of the missionaries and the man whose wife Rábago y Terán had been living with were murdered. In the aftermath of the crime (which the captain blamed on Indians, but which the missionaries blamed on him), most of the neophytes fled the missions.

### A Mission for the Apaches

Would it be possible to salvage something from the failure of the San Xavier project? The Spanish had lost the trust of the Indians; a severe drought had shown the area to be unsuitable for a presidio-mission complex, and disease had decimated both the remaining Indian population and the garrison. Even Fray Mariano surrendered to the inevitable and in September 1753 added his voice to those of the presidio officers and other missionaries calling for the removal of the missions and presidio to a more promising location.

A number of friars had dreamed for many years of converting the Lipan Apaches. Periodically, individual Apache chiefs approached the missionaries claiming to want the benefits of Spanish civilization; accordingly, the Franciscans blamed the Spanish colonists for the hostilities. Fray Mariano's insistence on the potential for peace with the Lipans if a mission were established for them in their own territory led to expeditions into the hill country northwest of San Antonio. Expeditionaries returned with a favorable impression of the area, particularly at the indications of silver deposits and the friendliness of the Indians.

In 1756 the Franciscans got their wish. When Fray Alonso Giraldo de Terreros's rich cousin stepped forward to help underwrite the project, the viceroy issued orders for a new mission-presidio complex for the Lipan Apaches. He placed Colonel Diego Ortiz Parrilla, a former frontier governor and veteran soldier, in charge of the military component of the expedition, but gave Fray Terreros independent authority to negotiate with the Indians. The colonel, cynical about the Indians' intentions, soon quarreled with the missionaries. He complained to the viceroy that "the state in which we have found the Apaches is so different from

No greater gift could a man give God than to sacrifice himself in the cause of the faith. So thought the Franciscans who achieved the "crown of martyrdom" at Mission San Sabá, when they became victims of an Apache-Norteño struggle for control of western Texas. *(Destruction of Mission San Sabá in the Province of Texas and the Martyrdom of the Fathers Alonso Giraldo de Terreros, Joseph Santiesteban, by José de Páez [attrib.], ca. 1763. Oil on canvas. 83" × 115". Courtesy Instituto National de Anthropología e Historia, Mexico City)*

what I expected that I assure you the method of their pacification is a major concern to me."

Indeed, when the *entrada* arrived at the site of present-day Menard and pitched camp, the Lipans were nowhere in sight. Construction soon began on a mission and presidio, but each passing day gave another indication that the San Sabá complex was not to flourish. Three thousand Apaches appeared near the mission in June, but soon departed to hunt buffalo and raid their enemies, the Norteños. With the Apaches unwilling to settle down and no prospects for attracting other groups, some of the missionaries gave up on the project, leaving Mission San Sabá in the hands of Fray Alonso and two colleagues from the San Fernando College. During the fall and winter of 1757–58 various Apache bands made rest stops at the mission, but all refused to stay. They did bring rumors, however, that the Norteños, including the Comanches, were massing to attack the Apaches and their allies at San Sabá.

The end came in March 1758. At the beginning of the month a war party attacked the presidio's horse herd and made off with sixty-two mounts. On March 16 a large group of warriors, including Caddos, Tonkawas, Atakapans, Wichitas, and Comanches encircled the mission compound, many of them bearing French muskets and swords. After ransacking the buildings, the warriors turned on the mission's residents, killing friars Alonso and José Santiesteban along with a few of the assistants and soldiers. Fray Miguel Molina and a few others took refuge in an office and survived the burning of the compound. Unwilling to challenge the military directly, the Indians approached but did not attack the presidio.

Unable to pursue the attackers, Colonel Parrilla sought revenge in a more deliberate way. Parrilla offered to lead a campaign not only to avenge the deaths of two friars and eight other Spanish subjects, but also to demonstrate to the Norteños that they could not act with impunity. In a January 1759 meeting between Parrilla, the governors of Texas and Coahuila, and the region's presidio commanders, it was decided that they would mount a 500-man expedition against the Wichitas and Tonkawas that summer.

Although it achieved a minor victory against a Tonkawa camp near the Clear Fork of the Brazos, the expedition's encounter with the Wichitas was a disaster. The Wichita village, at present-day Spanish Fort on the Red River, was not only fortified but was also flying a French flag. The Wichitas, armed with French muskets, were every bit a match for the ragtag force under Col. Parrilla. The engagement turned into a rout: The Wichitas repulsed the Spanish assault and the Lipan

Today the ruins of the Spanish Empire's last effort to expand into western Texas rest next to a golf course in Menard. Photographs and captions chronicle a failed reconstruction effort in the 1930s, documenting how for many years the locals continued to believe the stone presidio was the remains of the wooden mission destroyed by the Norteños in 1758. *(Photo by Frank de la Teja)*

Apache allies fled. Although the Spanish suffered only fifty-two casualties, the humiliating defeat spelled the end of Spain's hopes of expanding into the southern plains from Texas.

The San Sabá episode illustrated two major problems with Spain's frontier system in Texas①the inadequacy of the presidio-mission system for expanding Spain's territory and the②inability to prevent foreign access to Indians. At San Sabá, as at San Xavier earlier, the Spanish came into contact with Indians bearing French muskets, wearing French clothing, and boasting of their ties to Louisiana. Spanish security along the Louisiana frontier proved so lax that by the early 1750s a small party of Frenchmen under the direction of Joseph Blancpain was able to establish a trading post on the lower Trinity River.

Discovery and arrest of the Frenchmen probably reflected the governor's effort to protect his own pocketbook (he was involved in contraband himself) rather than to defend imperial interests, but it did set off another abortive attempt to expand Spanish control over Texas. In 1756 Viceroy Marqués de las Amarillas authorized a presidio-mission complex for the lower Trinity River. By the end of the year a thirty-man post had been established, named Presidio San Agustín de Ahumada in honor of the viceroy. (Agustín de Ahumada y Villalón, Marqués de las Amarillas holds the distinction of being the only viceroy to have two presidios named for him.) A mission named Nuestra Señora de la Luz had also taken shape near present-day Anahuac in Chambers County.

El Orcoquizac, as the complex was commonly referred to, proved a complete disaster from the beginning. The Akokisa and Bidai Indians, for whom Mission Nuestra Señora de la Luz was built, showed as little interest in settling down permanently at this location as they had at the San Xavier missions a few years earlier. The thirty-man garrison at the presidio suffered great privation as flooding and the stifling heat and humidity made it difficult to keep the presidio store stocked and the crops growing well. About the only thing that made life bearable for the garrison was trading in contraband—the very thing they were there to prevent.

## Conclusion

By the early 1760s there was a marked contrast between Texas and the neighboring provinces of Nuevo Santander and Coahuila. José de Escandón had fired the imaginations of thousands of Spanish frontiersmen with his offers of generous land grants and effective measures against the Indians of the region. Towns, ranches, and mining camps soon dotted the Nuevo Santander countryside from the area just north of Tampico to the Rio Grande valley. Even the least settled part of the new province, the semiarid prairies of what is now south Texas began to see the expansion of a ranching culture that played a significant role in New Spain's economy. Similarly, in Coahuila, although the progress was slower, the subjugation of the province's Indians led to the founding of new towns and great haciendas. The Apaches remained a constant menace, but the province showed signs of flourishing, especially in the realm of livestock production.

In Texas, however, Spanish civilization was stalemated by Indian cultures capable of successfully fending off both its military might and its religious blandishments. Of the early settlements, only San Antonio de Béxar seemed to have the necessary natural resources and diversity of population to sustain itself. Béxar did not offer many attractions for migrants from the interior of New Spain; La Bahía and Los Adaes offered even fewer. With royal resources insufficient to meet frontier needs, officials played a shell game with the few soldiers and missionaries at their disposal. The successive failures at San Xavier, San Sabá, and El Orcoquisac largely discredited the presidio-mission system of frontier expansion. (California, however, founded in 1769, seems to have been the great exception that proved the rule.)

Fortunately for the Spanish, events that took place far away from the prairies and forests of Texas brought about a radical change of circumstances in 1763. Spain had allied itself with France in a European conflict known as the Seven Years' War (called the French and Indian War in America) and lost. Forced to give up Florida to England in return for recovering Havana, France made it up to Spain and prevented England from gaining most of North America by ceding Louisiana to the Spanish Crown. With Louisiana no longer a foreign colony, Texas ceased to be a border province. French traders would no longer undermine Spanish authority among the province's Indians, and the Spanish could move the line of defense against foreign aggression eastward to the Mississippi River. The last third of the eighteenth century offered Spain a new opportunity to make something of Texas, if it could simply overcome the other great barrier to development: the objections of the Norteños, the Comanches, and the Apaches to becoming part of the Spanish Empire.

## SUGGESTED READINGS

The first half of the eighteenth century coincides with the arrival of the Bourbon dynasty on the Spanish throne. David Weber's overview of the imperial rivalries and realignments that brought Spanish Texas into being in chapters 6 and 7 of *The Spanish Frontier in North America* makes very interesting reading, as do chapters 8 and 9 of John Kessell's *Spain in the Southwest.* Those interested in the social history of northern Mexico and the American Southwest at that time can turn to the very readable *Los Paisanos: Spanish Settlers on the Northern Frontier of New Spain* by Oakah L. Jones, Jr. (1979, 1996). Understanding the Spanish frontier military system is vital to an appreciation of colonial Texas history, and the work that does the best job of explaining that system is Max L. Moorhead's *The Presidio: Bastion of the Spanish Borderlands* (1975). The most controversial of Spanish frontier institutions is the mission. Missions were traditionally viewed as the great civilizing force through which the Spanish brought both salvation and enlightenment to the native peoples; see, for example, the introductory chapter in Marion A. Habig, *The Alamo Chain of Missions: A History of San Antonio's Five*

*Old Missions* (1968). A newer generation of scholars has come to focus on the negative effects of the missionary project on the target populations; see, for example, David Sweet, "The Ibero-American Frontier Mission in Native American History," in Erick Langer and Robert H. Jackson, eds., *The New Latin American Mission History* (1995).

## The French Challenge

When Louis Juchereau de St. Denis arrived at San Juan Bautista del Río Grande in 1714 the first Spanish missions of Texas had already been abandoned for twenty years. Texas remained a mostly unknown land, despite a few *entradas* north of the Rio Grande by missionaries and military men. In chapters 6–9 of *Spanish Expeditions into Texas,* William Foster discusses the expeditions that brought the Spanish back to Texas permanently. Louis Juchereau de St. Denis not only instigated the permanent occupation of Texas by Spaniards, but founded Natchitoches and a French colonial dynasty there, a story well told in "Tios and Tantes: Familial and Political Relationships of Natchitoches and the Spanish Colonial Frontier," by Patricia R. Lemée, *Southwestern Historical Quarterly* (1998). Ross Phares, *Cavalier in the Wilderness: The Story of the Explorer and Trader Louis Juchereau de St. Denis* (1952) is a full-scale biography of St. Denis. Essays on "Francisco Hidalgo/Louis Juchereau de St. Denis," "Antonio Margil de Jesús," and "Marques de San Miguel de Aguayo/Pedro de Rivera y Villalón" in *Notable Men and Women of Spanish Texas* by Donald Chipman and Harriett Denise Joseph (1999) provide a good understanding of the backgrounds of the military and religious leaders of early Texas.

## Spanish Texas Takes Shape

Rivera's record of his inspection of Texas in 1727 provides a good description of the province ten years after its founding. His diary and report, along with an assessment, are included in *Imaginary Kingdom: Texas as Seen by the Rivera and Rubí Military Expeditions, 1727 and 1767,* ed. Jack Jackson, annot. William C. Foster (1995). Updating our understanding of Spanish-French rivalry in Texas is David LaVere, "Between Kinship and Capitalism: French and Spanish Rivalry in the Colonial Louisiana-Texas Indian Trade," *Journal of Southern History* (1998). Historical work on colonial Texas has overwhelmingly centered on San Antonio, the province's largest and most diverse community. The story of its founding and early development appears in *Tejano Origins in Eighteenth-Century San Antonio,* ed. Gerald E. Poyo and Gilberto M. Hinojosa (1991) and Jesús F. de la Teja, *San Antonio de Béxar: A Community on New Spain's Northern Frontier* (1995).

## The Great Colonizer

What is now South Texas, from Corpus Christi to Laredo to Brownsville and South Padre, was the northern half of Nuevo Santander during the colonial period. Most of the historical work on this region has been done by Mexican scholars, and remains untranslated although there is a handful of very useful recent works on the subject in English. The colonization and early development of this vast region that became the home to huge ranching estates is told by Armando Alonzo in the early chapters of *Tejano Legacy: Rancheros and Settlers in South Texas, 1734–1900* (1998) and in "José de Escandón y Elguera," chapter 7 in *Notable Men and Women of Spanish Texas*. A useful synthesis of what is known of the aboriginal peoples of that area is found in *Indians of the Rio Grande Delta: Their Role in the History of Southern Texas and Northeastern Mexico,* by Martín Salinas (1990). The story of La Bahía has yet to receive comprehensive scholarly treatment, but two works, along with the article "La Bahía" in *The New Handbook of Texas,* provide basic information: Kathryn Stoner O'Connor, *Presidio La Bahia, 1721–1846* (1966), and Craig H. Roell, *Remember Goliad! A History of La Bahía* (1994). For developments at Paso del Norte, W. H. Timmons offers a good overview in chapter 2 of *El Paso: A Borderlands History* (1990).

### The Failure of Missionary Expansion in Texas

The collapse of Spanish expansion efforts in Texas centers on two pivotal events: the disintegration of the San Xavier mission-presidio complex and the successful Norteño and Comanche resistance to a Spanish punitive expedition following their destruction of Mission San Sabá. Herbert E. Bolton's *Texas in the Middle Eighteenth Century: Studies in Spanish Colonial History and Administration* (1915, 1970) remains the best survey of Spanish activities in the region, except the San Sabá story. That tale, and the followup Spanish effort to punish the Indians responsible, is told by Robert S. Weddle in *The San Sabá Mission: Spanish Pivot in Texas* (1964, 1988). The Norteño-Comanche destruction of the San Sabá mission, which the Spanish built for the Lipan Apaches, is also notable for having produced the first artwork with a Texas theme, a large allegorical painting executed in Mexico City in the early 1760s. The painting itself has an interesting story, nicely summarized by Sam D. Ratcliffe in "'Escenas de Martirio': Notes on *The Destruction of Mission San Sabá,*" *Southwestern Historical Quarterly* (1991).

# 4

# The Age of Reform, 1767–1800

In October 1770 Athanase de Mézières, the French-born lieutenant governor for the Natchitoches district of Louisiana, traveled to the Kadohadacho village of San Luis on the Red River to meet with various groups of Caddo and Wichita-related Indians. He brought word to the skeptical chiefs and elders of the new colonial order in Louisiana and the wishes of His Catholic Majesty to forget the unpleasantries of San Sabá and to establish a lasting peace:

> Do not forget that there are now no Frenchmen in these lands, and that we are all Spaniards. I have and will keep in mind your promises in order to report them to my chief, to whom they will undoubtedly be pleasing, and he will receive you into the number of his children and of the happy subjects of our monarch. But meanwhile it is fitting, since you have committed so many insults, robberies, and homicides in San Antonio de Vexar and vicinity, that without loss of time you should journey to that city. . . . There you will humble yourselves in the presence of a chief of greatest power who resides there, and whose part it is to ratify the treaty which you seek, since you have established yourselves within his jurisdiction, and to name the light and easy conditions to which you must conform in order not to incur the misfortune of being deprived of so desirable a boon.

Mézières's words reflected both the challenges and opportunities that the acquisition of Louisiana represented for Spain. On the one hand, Spanish officials had to gain the respect and loyalty of a large number of tribes that until recently had been incited by the French to hostility against Spaniards. On the other hand, without a European rival on the doorstep of New Spain, colonial officials could look for ways to reorganize the frontier in more efficient and thriftier ways.

| CHAPTER 4 | The Age of Reform, 1767–1800 |
|---|---|
| 1766 | Marqués de Rubí begins inspection tour of Texas region at Paso del Norte |
| 1772 | *Reglamento de 1772*, intended to reorganize frontier defense system, issued |
| 1773 | Presidio Los Adaes and East Texas missions suppressed; San Antonio de Béxar becomes capital of Texas |
| 1774 | Refugees from Los Adaes found settlement of Nuestra Señora del Pilar de Bucareli at Trinity River crossing of Camino Real |
| 1777 | Comandancia General de las Provincias Internas organized |
| 1778 | Commandant General Croix holds war council in Béxar, establishes Mesteña tax on unbranded livestock |
| 1779 | Nacogdoches established when Bucareli abandoned following Comanche raids and flooding |
| 1785 | Governor Cabello makes peace with Comanches and Norteños |
| 1790 | Commandant General Ugalde defeats the Apaches at Sabinal Canyon |
| 1793 | Secularization of Texas missions begins with San Antonio de Valero (the Alamo) |
| 1797 | La Bahía missions exempted from secularization |
| 1800 | First permanent bridge across the Rio Grande in operation at Paso del Norte; Rosa María Hinojosa de Ballí controls ranching empire of 1 million acres |

For Charles III, his ministers, and their subordinates throughout the Spanish Empire there was much work to do in the aftermath of the Seven Years' War. The defeat of the Spanish military in the Old World and the New revealed superficiality and inadequacy of the military reforms and rebuilding programs of Philip V and Ferdinand VI, Charles's father and brother. Charles III, determined to recover Spain's fortunes as a world power, committed himself to bold action. Only a radical shakeup in colonial policies and institutions could overcome the inertia of colonial officials and the inadequacy of military preparedness. Charles thought that only peninsular Spaniards had the necessary detachment and training to carry out the reforms. In the long run, this policy shift away from American-born Spaniards alienated many *criollos* who came to resent their lack of opportunities, but in the short term, it seemed to bear good results.

Charles was a son of the Enlightenment, a movement born in the France of Louis XIV, his great-grandfather, and brought to Spain by his father, Philip V. True to Enlightenment ideals, Charles believed in the progressive and absolute power of the monarchy and the value of scientific knowledge and rational thought. Like his fellow Enlightenment monarchs throughout Europe, he was determined to curb the power of the Catholic church, which remained a useful instrument of government, but represented the old, less rational, less modern way of doing things. Although his immediate predecessors had focused on reforming the political, economic, and social institutions of peninsular Spain, Charles turned his attention to the empire by sending out like-minded officials with broad powers to shake up a colonial system over 250 years in the making.

The most prominent of this new breed of enlightened administrators was José de Gálvez. An accomplished judge with a no-nonsense attitude, in 1765 Gálvez became *visitador* (inspector general) for New Spain, with power to implement immediate reforms to increase revenue, foster government efficiency, and strengthen the colony's defenses. When he did not get along with the viceroy, the king replaced the viceroy with the more collegial Marqués de Croix. Between them, Gálvez and Croix initiated a series of measures intended to strengthen Spanish control in North America. During his six years in New Spain, Gálvez established a tobacco monopoly and other royal monopolies, overhauled the tax structure, and began designing a new administrative system which, although not implemented until 1786, divided New Spain into eleven large districts called *intendencias*. He also ordered the occupation of Alta California (what is today the state of California) in order to forestall Russian moves in that direction. With regard to the Catholic church, he removed the Jesuit order from New Spain in response to the king's decree expelling the Jesuits from the empire on charges of disloyalty. The Spanish Enlightenment legacy of Charles and his ministers would extend even to far off and neglected Texas.

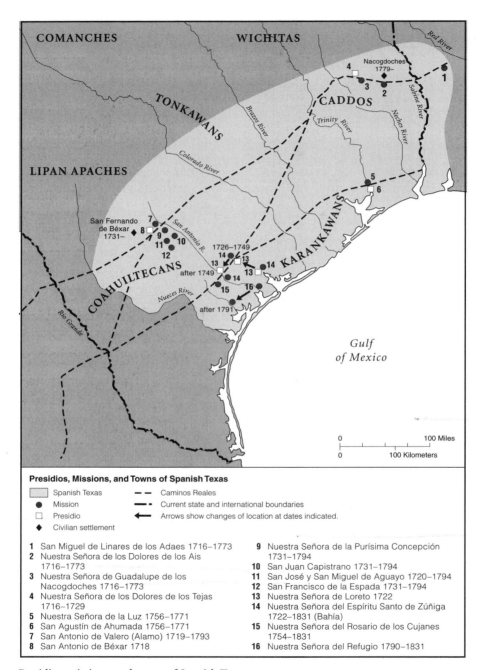

**Presidios, Missions, and Towns of Spanish Texas**

- ▢ Spanish Texas
- ● Mission
- ▢ Presidio
- ◆ Civilian settlement

- – – Caminos Reales
- –▪– Current state and international boundaries
- ← Arrows show changes of location at dates indicated.

**1** San Miguel de Linares de los Adaes 1716–1773
**2** Nuestra Señora de los Dolores de los Ais 1716–1773
**3** Nuestra Señora de Guadalupe de los Nacogdoches 1716–1773
**4** Nuestra Señora de los Dolores de los Tejas 1716–1729
**5** Nuestra Señora de la Luz 1756–1771
**6** San Agustín de Ahumada 1756–1771
**7** San Antonio de Valero (Alamo) 1719–1793
**8** San Antonio de Béxar 1718

**9** Nuestra Señora de la Purísima Concepción 1731–1794
**10** San Juan Capistrano 1731–1794
**11** San José y San Miguel de Aguayo 1720–1794
**12** San Francisco de la Espada 1731–1794
**13** Nuestra Señora de Loreto 1722
**14** Nuestra Señora del Espíritu Santo de Zúñiga 1722–1831 (Bahía)
**15** Nuestra Señora del Rosario de los Cujanes 1754–1831
**16** Nuestra Señora del Refugio 1790–1831

Presidios, missions, and towns of Spanish Texas.

# Reorganization of the Frontier

Maximizing royal revenues and streamlining colonial government were not Charles III's only concerns in New Spain: There was the critical matter of the military. The weaknesses of the colonial army and navy had come to light during the Seven Years' War, when the English captured Havana and other Caribbean ports, forcing Spain to give up Florida to the English in order to recover Cuba. New Spain's military establishment was small, consisting of only a couple of garrisons protecting the major ports; its militias were disorganized and poorly trained, and the navy was outdated and in disrepair. On the northern frontier, the presidio system, despite the reforms implemented following Brigadier Pedro de Rivera's inspection tour of the 1720s, was in disarray. There was little standardization in anything: uniforms, equipment, or training. Chains of command were mixed, with some commanders reporting to the local governor and others to the viceroy, and there was little cooperation among units. Furthermore, the acquisition of Louisiana required a rethinking of frontier military strategy, particularly with regard to Texas.

## Texas Comes Under Inspection

The job of reforming frontier defenses in response to the new international situation fell on Cayetano María Pignatelli Rubí Corbera y Saint Climent, Barón de Llinas, Marqués de Rubí, a career military officer holding the rank of field marshal and a knight in the Order of Alcántara. Rubí had come to New Spain in 1764 and had already undertaken a number of reform projects when he received his orders in August 1765. The king wanted him to inspect "all the presidios of this Kingdom, examine their condition, their location, inspect their troops, review the old price regulations under which they subsist, and, having assessed things time has changed since their establishment . . . propose changes appropriate to the present situation and spell out everything else that for their better government and defense you consider necessary." To assist him, the viceroy appointed two engineers, Nicolás de Lafora and Joseph de Urrutia, who eventually produced a series of detailed maps and plats of the region including Texas.

Rubí's inspection tour left Mexico City in March 1766 and visited the western frontier for over a year. In August 1766 he visited the Paso del Norte area, which at the time consisted of a presidio, a civilian settlement, and various haciendas and missions. Rubí found the Paso del Norte district to be flourishing, which prompted him to recommend moving the presidio to Carrizal, about seventy miles to the southwest. A detachment from the presidio had already been assigned to that location. A militia company could easily protect the area's settlers and peaceful Indians.

It was not until spring 1767 that Rubí's entourage headed for the eastern frontier provinces of Coahuila, Texas, and Nuevo León, reaching the Rio Grande at what is today Eagle Pass on July 14, 1767. His first inspection stop in what is now Texas occurred at Mission San Lorenzo, where a detachment of thirty-one men from Presidio San Sabá was stationed. Mission San Lorenzo (near present-day Camp Wood, Real County) and another mission, Candelaria (near present-day Montell, Uvalde County), had opened in 1762 and in a followup attempt to convert the Lipan Apaches after the disaster at Mission San Sabá. Located along the upper Nueces River, the missions were collectively known as El Cañon. Conditions at the sites were dismal: Mission Candelaria was completely abandoned, there were no Indians at San Lorenzo, and the detachment was totally destitute.

Moving on to San Sabá, which remained under the direct authority of the viceroy, Rubí's immediate assessment was that the presidio there was about as useful "as a ship anchored in mid-Atlantic would [be] in preventing foreign trade with America." He found the presidio's walls badly constructed, its horse herd under constant assault from the Comanches and Norteños, and the men poorly equipped and prone to desertion. Captain Felipe Rábago y Terán, who had been exonerated of all charges in the San Xavier murders of a decade earlier, had taken command in 1760 and tried to make San Sabá an efficient and vital post. He had sent detachments to explore a possible route to New Mexico, accommodated the Franciscans in establishing their missions at El Cañon, and spent lavishly on presents for Indians and supplies for his command (although much of what was requested never made it to the missions or the presidio). As the years wore on and Mexico City continued to ignore the plight of San Sabá and El Cañon, conditions deteriorated and Captain Rábago turned to profiteering. Isolated and unable to attract civilian settlers because of constant assaults by the Indians, the soldiers and their families, numbering approximately 300 individuals, lived in constant terror. Rubí rode out of Presidio San Sabá on August 4, 1767, already formulating his final recommendation—abandonment of the site and transfer of the handful of civilian families to Béxar.

Nothing could have prepared Rubí for conditions at San Antonio when he arrived on August 8. In the forty years since Rivera's inspection San Antonio de Béxar had undergone considerable change. To the two missions Rivera had found in 1727 another three had been added, and the presidio now shared the space between the San Antonio River and San Pedro Creek with the municipality of San Fernando de Béxar. The combined civilian and military population of Béxar had grown to over 700 individuals, representing a diverse ethnic mix of *criollos, castas,* and acculturated Indians. At each of the missions the friars led 200–350 neophytes, for a total population of over 1,200 men, women, and children from a dozen or more Coahuiltecan, Karankawa, and Apache tribes. General farming and a limited amount of ranching supported the majority of the population, and textile manufacturing was beginning at some of the missions. Unlike Paso del Norte, Béxar was still in no position to defend itself, especially as the mission Indians remained prone to flight, but the location showed promise in its fertile and irrigated fields, its vast grazing lands, and its healthy climate.

For all the development over the course of its first fifty years of existence, Béxar remained a decidedly backward place. This was due to decisions years earlier to deprive the presidio of its fighting strength: Rivera's recommendation to reduce the garrison from fifty-four to forty-four in 1729 and the viceroy's decision to take twenty-two men from Presidio de Béxar for service at San Sabá in 1757. A decade later Rubí found a garrison that was ill equipped, undisciplined, and overextended. The presidio was in disrepair in part because only seven men were available to the captain at any one time; the other fifteen were assigned to mission guard duty. Captain Luis Antonio Menchaca was more businessman than officer: he had his men uniformed in a colorful mix of lace, silk, and silver, which kept his pockets full and the men in want of basic necessities. The shortcomings of the garrison went beyond the men's uniforms, however, as the horse herd was depleted and many of the animals unfit for service. Although the soldiers were armed, their weapons were of many different calibers and a number of them were unserviceable.

Never a successful settlement despite being the capital of Texas from 1720 to 1773, Los Adaes remained an isolated military outpost that was often dependent on nearby French Natchitoches. José de Urrutia's map and elevation of the presidio accentuates both its isolation and its architectural distinctiveness from other Spanish colonial settlements. *(By permission of the British Library)*

Compare Urrutia's map of Los Adaes (p. 97) and this one of Paso del Norte. Note the number of structures along roads, the agricultural fields, and extensive irrigation system. By the time the Marqués de Rubí and Urrutia visited what is now the El Paso-Juárez area, the missions, presidio, and civilian settlement had a flourishing economy combining ranching, viticulture, and subsistence crop production. *(By permission of the British Library)*

On receiving Rubí at his headquarters at Los Adaes on September 11, interim Governor Hugo Oconor must have been terribly embarrassed by conditions at the "capital" of Texas. He had assumed command of the province just a month earlier from Ángel Martos y Navarrete, whose tenure had been marked by disaster (the destruction of Mission San Sabá), scandal (his arrest order for the presidio commander at Orcoquisac had resulted in the death of a soldier and the burning of the presidio), and dishonesty (he had made huge profits on the sale of goods to his men). The goods he had sold to his men were goods he had purchased illegally at French Natchitoches. Presidio Los Adaes exhibited the scars of Martos's neglect: Serviceable weaponry among the company of sixty-one soldiers consisted of two muskets, seven swords, and six shields; instead of the regulation 500–600 horses, the company herd contained just 117, only twenty-five of which were fit for service; a number of soldiers lacked basic items of dress, including shirts, shoes, and hats. The former governor had illegally employed the men in his command as cowboys and farmers on his private ranch and had sold back to them part of the crop that they had grown in the company's communal farm. Oconor's memories of the poor conditions at Los Adaes would lead him to strongly support Rubí's recommendations.

Spanish East Texas, the marqués found, did not meet expectations for a Spanish provincial capital. The settlement lacked a substantial civilian population beyond the soldiers' families, although there may have been as many as 100 families living on ranches in the forest clearings and at former Hasinai Indian village sites in the countryside. In general, the approximately 500 people who lived in East Texas lived off subsistence farming, trapping, Indian trade, and contraband commerce with Louisiana. The steadily declining Caddo population, having experienced a series of epidemics as well as the adverse climatic conditions of much of the eighteenth century, had never been converted; the area's three missions contained not a single neophyte.

If Los Adaes had proven to be a viable settlement, Rubí's judgment might not have been so harsh. As matters stood, however, the Texas capital was a drain on the viceroyalty's overextended resources. As was the case throughout Texas, in Paso del Norte, and the rest of the northern frontier, each missionary received a yearly stipend of 450 pesos from the government. This sum might have been justifiable in the case of San Antonio, where the missions had healthy neophyte populations, but was unjustified where the friars had no Indians to instruct and only a few civilian settlers for whom to provide spiritual care. Keeping soldiers at government expense when they did little more than work on their commander's private estate was equally unacceptable. With Natchitoches in Spanish hands, and with its French residents on good terms with the area Indians, what need was there to maintain Los Adaes? As the inspector's entourage departed for Orcoquisac, Rubí must already have arrived at the solution to reinforcing San Antonio: close down the presidio and transfer the local population to Béxar, where plentiful lands awaited the civilians and genuine military service awaited at least some of the soldiers.

Following a circuitous and tortuous route through woods and swamps, it took the Marqués de Rubí from September 28 to October 15 to reach Presidio San Agustín de Ahumada and Mission Nuestra Señora de la Luz del Orcoquisac. Since its founding in 1756 near present-day Wallisville, Chambers County, to counter French penetration of southeast Texas by way of Galveston Bay, El Orcoquisac had failed by every measure. The garrison itself had turned to contraband and Indian trade in the absence of any opportunity to raise its own food or meet its other needs. The presidio suffered from constant desertions; the mission had failed to attract the local Atakapa-speaking Indians; and no civilian population had established itself in the vicinity. Best for all concerned—the royal treasury, missionaries, and beleaguered soldiers and their families—was the complete abandonment of the site.

In November 1767, when Rubí reached La Bahía (his last stop in Texas) he was in sore need of some good news. Although conditions were not perfect at Presidio La Bahía, they were better than conditions anywhere else in the province. This was due in large part to Captain Manuel Ramírez de la Piscina, whose seventeen-year tenure had begun when the complex had been moved to the lower San Antonio River. Although the old captain, who had died the previous July, had some of the same faults as his contemporaries at the other Texas posts—he overcharged for the goods he sold to his soldiers and had soldiers work at his ranch—he had kept his command disciplined and relatively well supplied. Most of the horses and firearms were in good condition, and all fifty soldiers were properly uniformed, if somewhat dirty, threadbare, and lacking in shields and lances.

Unlike the situations at San Sabá, Los Adaes, and El Orcoquisac, settlement at La Bahía seemed to be moving in the right direction. The number of families was increasing, from under ten in 1762 to about twenty-five at the time the marqués made his inspection. Although there was no formal town as yet, the more than 300 inhabitants of the presidio settlement seemed to be flourishing. Captain Ramírez had successfully dealt with the Karankawas and Coahuiltecans of the area, and the missionaries had learned to be patient with these hunter-gatherers who could not fully adjust to the sedentary life of Spanish colonial society. As a result, La Bahía was an oasis of peace and relative efficiency. As far as Rubí was concerned, it was worthy of serving as the eastern anchor in the presidio line he was about to recommend to the viceroy.

### Rubí's Blueprint for the Reorganization of Spanish Texas

Bypassing Laredo, which did not have a presidio, Rubí and his retinue visited Presidio del Río Grande in November 1767, before arriving in Mexico City the following February. There he prepared a *dictamen* (official opinion) regarding matters on the frontier. It was not favorable in the least. The twenty-four presidios then in operation were in random, and sometimes ill-advised locations, and their commanders for the most part lacked the necessary training and abilities and seemed more interested in turning a profit than carrying out their duties. The men were poorly trained, ill equipped, alternately underutilized and overburdened, and in general taken advantage of by their commanders. To remedy this situation, Rubí proposed that the entire frontier, from the Gulf of California to the Gulf of Mexico be considered a single unit, so that officials could base their decisions on overall strategic considerations rather than immediate tactical or local interests. Further, he proposed a complete reform of the organization, command structure, and financial management of the presidios, which would produce cost savings to the crown and better conditions for the soldiery.

Rubí's recommendations were incorporated into a series of reforms carried out in the 1770s that streamlined not only military policy but political and religious administration as well. The first, known as the *Reglamento of 1772*, called for a complete overhaul of the presidio system. With the exception of Santa Fe and San Antonio (which was to become the capital of Texas) all the presidios would now line up roughly along 30° north latitude, from Altar in Sonora to La Bahía in Texas. Presidios above or below that line would be relocated or closed, according to regional needs, so that in the end a string of fifteen presidios, approximately 100 miles apart from each other, could effectively coordinate their activities. In Texas that meant closing El Orcoquisac and Los Adaes and transferring San Sabá to a site on the Rio Grande under the jurisdiction of Coahuila. In order to curb the abuses of the presidio commanders, who also controlled the purse strings of their individual garrisons, each company was to elect a commissary officer who would be held strictly accountable for his financial dealings. Soldiers' salaries would be reduced in light of reforms certain to lower their expenses, and they would receive part of it in cash. Training and duties were to be standardized, as were soldiers' uniforms, and presidio commanders were to keep regular muster rolls and enlistment papers.

The big winners in Texas were Presidios de Béxar and La Bahía. At San Antonio the *Reglamento* called for a company commanded by the governor and manned by eighty officers and men, and a chaplain. Presidio La Bahía was to be manned by its captain, fifty officers and men, and a chaplain. Not all Tejanos (Texans of Spanish-Mexican descent) were happy with the reforms, however, and the new governor assigned to the province had his hands full attempting to placate the disgruntled and dispossessed denizens of East Texas while pleasing his superiors in Mexico City and Madrid.

## The Death and Rebirth of Spanish East Texas

Colonel Juan María Vicencio, Barón de Ripperdá, a Spanish-born career military man, accompanied by his Mexican-born wife, Mariana Gómez de Parada Gallo y Villavicencio, arrived in San Antonio early in 1770, marking the beginning of a new chapter in Texas history. Technically, his command was Presidio Los Adaes, but the pressing needs of reorganizing and strengthening defenses at Béxar, not to mention the perils and inconveniences of taking his new wife to East Texas, led him to take up residence in the *casas reales* (town hall). He and the baroness must have been greatly relieved when late in 1771 Viceroy Antonio María de Bucareli denied Ripperdá's half-hearted request to transfer to Los Adaes with the admonition that because Natchitoches was now in Spanish hands, he should remain where he was. Although San Antonio de Béxar was not officially to become the provincial capital until 1773, Ripperdá's presence there from 1770 signaled the complete acceptance of Rubí's recommendations for the reorganization of Texas.

### Colonial Frontier Society

Although they were members of the elite, the baron and his wife's arrival in Texas was an example of a common occurrence at the time: the migration of families to the frontier. The myth of a European, male-only frontier does not stand up to close scrutiny in the Texas case. La Salle had attempted to establish a well-rounded colony by bringing a number of French women along on his tragic expedition of 1685. The Spanish Crown, always interested in establishing stable colonial communities, had encouraged married soldiers to move to Texas from the time of the Ramón and Alarcón expeditions of 1716–18. One of the viceroy's counselors commented that married soldiers were a double benefit, as "they will be able to fill their presidios with the children that their wives bear them," and they would be less likely to make advances to the neophyte females and take advantage of them. The effort to bring Canary Islanders to Texas had also been predicated on the migration of families, rather than single individuals; of the fifty-five who eventually made it to Béxar in 1731, only four were single adult males.

Of course, frontier conditions made Texas essentially a male-dominated society, and Spanish females were always in short supply. Women like the Baroness de Ripperdá, a high-born *criollo*, were rare. Most Spanish women in Texas had been born on the frontier, and their "Spanish" status was often based on social convention rather than biological grounds. Beginning with the conquests of the sixteenth century, exclusively male undertakings, many men had found companionship in Indian women, and some took women of African descent as wives. Over the course of generations, if family circumstances improved, the children of such mixed couples might "pass" into the ranks of the "Spanish"; by the late eighteenth century the term "Spaniard" was more a recognition of social status than an ethnic label, especially on the frontier. In the case of Texas, although the evidence points to considerable ethnic mixing, "Spaniards" were reported to make up a majority of the population. The continued infusion of significant numbers of acculturated Indians (and a smaller number of individuals of African descent) into the Hispanic population, kept the reported Indian population consistently at about 25 percent and the mixed-blood population at about 20 percent.

For all women, Texas was a harsh environment. Aside from her relative wealth, the Baroness de Ripperdá was fortunate in a number of respects. Her husband, despite his military career, lived out his stay in Texas, whereas many other Tejanas could expect to be widowed once or twice if they did not die in childbirth, in one of the periodic epidemics that swept through the province, or during an Indian attack. The baroness delivered six children during her husband's tenure in Texas, at least two of whom died in infancy. Her experience was not uncommon: Most women in Texas, indeed throughout New Spain, could expect to lose half of their children in infancy (from birth to two years).

Although the baroness did not have to worry about food or shelter (despite her husband's repeated complaints about their quarters' poor state of repair), the overwhelming majority of her contemporaries faced lives of unremitting toil. With the exception of a few families who had one or more servants—sometimes a hired hand, sometimes a captured Apache or Comanche child who was brought up in the household as a *criado* (someone having servant status)—women worked long hours to maintain their households. The large number of widows meant that many women had to take on the role of sole provider for their families. As heads of households, they engaged in a variety of occupations outside the home such as seamstress, midwife, and shopkeeper. A few women acquired property through inheritance and marriage and became leading ranchers and farmers in their communities. For some, economic reversals and lack of other opportunities prescribed a life of prostitution, an activity which seems to have been grudgingly accepted in colonial Texas.

Active public participation in the economic life of Texas required women to have legal rights that afforded them considerable protection in what was a man's world. Thus the Baroness de Ripperdá and all women, from the best-positioned Spanish matriarch to the lowliest Indian maid, benefited from a legal system that recognized them as individuals. Women had the right to their own separate property, including those goods and real estate they had acquired before marriage or that had been bequeathed to them. Moreover, after marriage they were entitled to half the property that husband and wife acquired as a couple. The right to defend one's property and honor required that women play a role in legal proceedings, so they could initiate legal actions and give testimony. These rights extended even to slaves, who on a number of occasions successfully petitioned to be removed from the homes of abusive masters. And, as theirs was a Roman Catholic society, women could file for divorce from abusive or runaway husbands, although neither party could remarry before the death of his or her former spouse.

## The First Capital of Texas Abandoned

Los Adaes, despite the Marqués de Rubí's dismissive assessment of East Texas, was the second largest settlement in the province of Texas, and the most ethnically diverse. Over 500 Spanish subjects lived among the remaining aboriginal inhabitants, members of various Hasinai and Atakapan groups, and a growing number of Louisianians, white and black. The death warrant for the fifty-year-old capital of the Province of the Tejas and Nuevas Philipinas had long since been signed, however, and it fell to the Baron de Ripperdá to execute it. In the process he and the policy-makers in Mexico City came to discover just how deep-rooted the local Tejanos' attachment was to their homes in the woods and swamps of East Texas.

In January 1773 Viceroy Bucareli informed Ripperdá that it would be his responsibility to carry out Spain's withdrawal from the Texas side of the Louisiana border. His instructions were draconian: Not only were the existing missions to close, but the governor was to see that the two presidios were destroyed and the entire Hispanic population of the area relocated to San Antonio. Ripperdá arrived in Los Adaes in early June 1773 and made the bad news official. Resentment and resistance emerged on all sides. Some families fled to Natchitoches and others into the isolated woods where they had cleared fields and built their cabins. The various Hasinai groups in the vicinity took the withdrawal as evidence that the Spanish had allied with the Apaches, and were preparing to make war on them. After the governor failed to adequately reassure them, the refugees had to leave two families behind at Nacogdoches in a sign of goodwill.

The overwhelming majority of refugees from Los Adaes arrived in Béxar on September 26 to a less than enthusiastic welcome. They were instructed to look for house lots and farmlands in the vicinity, but without disturbing the property of Bexareños or missions. This was impossible without moving so far away from the settlement that they would be exposed to Indian attack and have no access to irrigation water. Some families did find places for themselves, either as share-croppers at the missions, hired hands for some of the better-off residents, or in military service at the presidio. At least half of the refugees, however, were deter-mined to return to East Texas, and soon after their arrival they petitioned for per-mission to establish a new settlement at the site of the former Mission Nuestra Señora de los Ais (at present-day San Augustine).

The Adaesanos' petition had Governor Ripperdá's support. He was not only sympathetic to the plight of the dispossessed Tejanos, but their return to East Texas would buttress the Indian policy he favored: forming alliances with area Indians through trade. Of particular importance was establishing friendly rela-tions with the Wichita groups that had moved into north central Texas. The Wi-chitas seemed well disposed toward the Spanish, but were actively trading with Louisiana. Ripperdá believed that removing the Hispanic East Texas population would not solve the illegal Indian trade problem, but would only serve to under-mine the authority and respect officials in San Antonio commanded among the Indians of the region. His opinions were not shared by Oconor or the viceroy, both of whom wished to tow the line in regard to closing Texas off from Louisiana, prohibiting trade in firearms with the Indians, and sticking to Rubí's presidio line of defense. Eventually, the baron's refusal to carry out instructions he regarded as counterproductive cost him his office.

As for the Adaesanos, although he could not grant their request, Ripperdá gave them permission to carry their petition to the viceroy. When the viceroy re-sponded that he would not allow them to settle so close to Louisiana, but that they could select an intermediate location, the governor had the necessary ap-proval to authorize settlement at the Camino Real crossing on the Trinity River. More than 120 families made the decision to move while about sixty or seventy families remained behind.

As for the new settlement, Nuestra Señora del Pilar de Bucareli required gov-ernment and protection. No presidio or army detachment had been authorized for Bucareli so the governor organized a militia, pending the viceroy's approval. Ripperdá named <u>Antonio Gil Ybarbo</u> captain of the militia and *justicia mayor,* ef-fectively making him lieutenant governor for the district. It is difficult to imagine anyone better suited to the job of running what was essentially a renegade settle-ment of smugglers and Indian traders. A native of Los Adaes, Ybarbo was schooled in various Indian languages and French, adept at contraband trade, and skilled in the arts of political survival. His rather loose interpretation of property

On the campus of Stephen F. Austin University in Nacogdoches sits a reconstruction of the "Old Stone Fort." Antonio Gil Ybarbo built his *casa de piedra* shortly after founding Nacogdoches in 1779. For more than a century the building served as home, store, government headquarters, and saloon, until it was demolished in 1902. In 1936, the stones from the original structure were used to construct the replica, which today serves as a museum of early East Texas history. *(East Texas Research Center at Stephen F. Austin State University)*

rights had landed him in jail in New Orleans by order of Governor Oconor in the late 1760s, when he was caught with horses alleged to have been stolen by Indians from various Texas settlements. Any enemy of Oconor's was a friend of Ripperdá, and the Texas governor soon obtained Ybarbo's release from jail. The two men saw eye-to-eye on a variety of issues: the need for a continued Spanish presence in East Texas; the need for broad and sympathetic trade relations with the northern tribes; and the need to maintain commercial ties with Natchitoches.

### Indian Relations Transformed

Under Ybarbo's guidance Spanish East Texas was reborn, even as the settlers were forced to abandon Bucareli for the site of Mission Nacogdoches in early 1779 because of hostilities with the Comanches and flooding on the Trinity River. The abandonment of Bucareli and the settlement of Nacogdoches coincided with administrative changes both at the local and the viceregal level. In late October 1778 Colonel Domingo Cabello y Robles, Governor Ripperdá's replacement, arrived in Béxar. A career army officer like his predecessor, the fifty-three year old had considerable experience in colonial matters, but none in frontier Indian affairs. He had served in Cuba twice, displaying conspicuous valor during the English capture of Havana in the Seven Years' War. His gallantry earned him the governorship of Nicaragua, a position he held for almost twelve years before receiving the Texas post.

Cabello must have wondered what he had done to deserve such a posting. Texas had such a bad reputation in the viceregal capital that his cook, "a very good one that I employed at Cádiz in 1763, when I went to serve in the government of Nicaragua, was told so many things about this place as soon as we arrived in Mexico City last year, that he came to believe that the Indians would eat him, for which reason he resigned from my service. And the same thing happened with my manservant and a secretary. . . . Although I recognize that they did right, because this [place] is worse than Siberia and Lapland." There were, of course, no cannibals in Texas, but Cabello's comments reflect the general perception of the Texas frontier as a savage land.

By the time Cabello assumed office the most revolutionary of the frontier reforms was underway: the creation of an independent administrative and military jurisdiction for the frontier provinces. The Comandancia General de las Provincias Internas, as the new entity was called, represented José de Gálvez's attempt to make government in northern New Spain more responsive and efficient. The region, including the provinces of Sonora, Sinaloa, Nueva Vizcaya, New Mexico, Coahuila, and Texas, would be administered by a commandant general, a military official holding both military and political authority, and independent from the viceroy.

On January 1, 1777, Caballero Teodoro de Croix became the first commandant general of the Interior Provinces. Croix was an experienced army officer who had served in various political capacities under his uncle, a former viceroy. He was acquainted with the situation on the northern frontier and in Texas, and did not agree with the policies of either the current viceroy or Inspector General Oconor. He soon replaced Oconor, and began to carry out an inspection tour of his jurisdiction that included holding a war council at San Antonio de Béxar.

As far as Texas was concerned, Croix was in accord with Ripperdá and Athanase de Mézières: make peace with the Nations of the North and the Comanches, and make war on the Apaches. Athanase de Mézières, a native of Paris and former French army officer and Indian trader, had served at Natchitoches beginning in the 1740s. Louisiana governor Alejandro O'Reilly appointed De Mézières, who had readily accepted Spanish rule, lieutenant governor for the Natchitoches district, a post in which the Frenchman could help the Spanish maintain good relations with the frontier tribes. De Mézières quickly won over Governor Ripperdá to his ideas on Indian relations, particularly regarding whom should be considered friend versus foe. Beginning in 1770 he had undertaken a series of missions to various East Texas tribes on behalf of the Spanish Crown.

Not surprisingly, the war council held by Croix at San Antonio in January 1778 placed blame of Texas's Indian problems squarely on the shoulders of the Apaches, especially the Lipans, and called for all-out war against them. The Nations of the North and the Comanches had not been hostile to Spanish interests until the Spanish had made peace overtures to the Apaches and built missions and a presidio for them. Even worse, because the Apaches refused to keep their word, Spanish Texas had ended up at war against all these groups. The council also approved Ripperdá's agreements with the Nations of the North negotiated through De Mézières. "Although some have groundlessly regarded these treaties as deceitful, all the nations except the Comanches have scrupulously kept them." Only all-out war against the Apaches, combined with concerted diplomacy toward the Nations of the North and the Comanches, could bring peace and prosperity to the province. And only Athanase de Mézières had the necessary diplomatic skills to bring the province's Indians into an alliance against the Apaches. De Mézières's declining health did not permit him to accept Commandant General Croix's offer of the Texas governorship, however. He died in San Antonio in November 1779, having made peace between the Nations of the North and the Spanish and still advocating diplomacy toward the Comanches and war against the Apaches.

The situation was not so clear to Governor Cabello, however. On his arrival he was confronted by Comanche raids on Bucareli and friendly visits from Lipan and other Apache chiefs. From Cabello's brief survey of the situation, De Mézières's insistence that the Comanches were not the problem made little sense. Consequently, Cabello decided not to take sides. Unfortunately, De Mézières's death left Cabello with no one to help him keep the peace with the Nations of the North, and during the early 1780s Spanish Texas was exposed to increased raiding. Only in 1785, after implementing a new policy of gift-giving and diplomacy and after experienced translators became available to him, was Cabello able to work out new agreements with various Texas tribes, including the Comanches. The program, also known as "peace by purchase," required Spanish officials to make regular gifts to the Indians and allow trade with settlers, including, ultimately, muskets and ammunition. Until well after the turn of the century only the various Apache tribes and occasional groups of young independent warriors troubled Spanish Texas. It was the longest period of relative peace that the province would enjoy for decades to come.

## Sunset for the Missions

Reform and change marked the religious realm as well as the military and political spheres of life in late eighteenth-century Texas. The mission system, backbone of Spanish policy on the frontier, had given way to a more secular and economic perspective of Spanish-Indian affairs. In Texas the East Texas missions had failed to produce tangible results among the Hasinais in over fifty years of existence, and the mid-century experiments at San Sabá and El Cañon with the Lipans, San Xavier with the Ranchería Grande, and El Orcoquisac with the Akokisas had been disastrous. Even the active missions at Béxar and La Bahía faced new challenges that would prove insurmountable in the long run.

## ◀ The Missions in Decline

For all intents and purposes the only active missions in Texas were located at Béxar and La Bahía. These missions had made such remarkable progress in physical terms through the early 1770s, that there was considerable animosity between Hispanic settlers and the friars over livestock, land, and water rights. The missions controlled some of the best grazing land in the San Antonio River basin, having established their ranching operations long before the civilian population had begun to venture into the countryside. The Béxar missions, having claimed their land before the arrival of the Canary Islanders, had gained control of the best agricultural land in the region, on which they had built extensive and sophisticated acequia systems. The mission compounds included large stone churches, workshops, granaries, and living quarters. In effect, the missions were independent communities that competed with civilian settlements for both resources and markets.

Despite all these physical advantages the missions had always faced one important hurdle in becoming the ideal Christian Spanish communities the friars wanted them to be: maintaining adequate Indian populations. The Ranchería Grande, Coahuiltecans, and Karankawas on whom the Franciscans of Béxar and La Bahía had depended to populate their missions had never been numerous peoples to begin with. Life at the missions often proved detrimental to the health of these hunter-gatherers. Dietary changes combined with different hygiene regimens weakened immune systems already under assault from a variety of pathogens alien to the region. Periodic epidemics of smallpox, measles, and other Old World diseases took a great toll on all residents of Texas, but particularly on the Indians. In addition, the missionaries' efforts to impose European values, particularly in the areas of division of labor, work routines, and sexual relations, contributed to the Indians' frequent flight.

In time the mission system faced a population crisis that the Spaniards were unable to overcome. Although the Béxar missions had averaged more than 200 neophytes each during the 1750s and 1760s, by the mid-1770s there were fewer than 200. At La Bahía, there had been a large number of Indians at Espíritu Santo and a new station, Nuestra Señora del Rosario, had been constructed for local groups in the 1750s. Neither establishment contained more than fifty families by the 1770s. The collapse or flight of neophyte populations forced friars to undertake frequent forays into the countryside to round up runaway neophytes or recruit new ones, but these were increasingly unproductive. The Coahuiltecans were becoming scarce. Coastal Indian groups, which proved particularly well insulated from Spanish encroachment, found that they could incorporate the missions into their annual cycle of seasonal migration without having to accept unwanted aspects of Spanish civilization. The Lipan and other Apaches might flirt with the missions, but as groups they proved unwilling to abandon their independent way of life, even in the face of increasing pressures from their Norteño and Comanche enemies. Missions were never able to attract the most populous tribes of Texas Indians, the Comanche and Wichita of northern and western Texas. As a result missions came to depend on a small core of acculturated Indians and increasingly larger numbers of non-Indian residents to maintain operations.

Presidio-mission complexes had operated fairly amicably with the community in East Texas and at La Bahía, because for the most part, in East Texas the missions never developed substantial resources and at La Bahía the civilian community remained small. Such was not the case at Béxar, however. From the time of the Canary Islanders' arrival, there had been considerable tension between the civilian and mission communities. There was competition over land, water, cattle, and the sale of agricultural products to the presidio market; the settlers attempted to gain access to the labor of neophytes; and the friars felt that the settlers were corrupting their Indians. These were the complaints that royal officials regularly received from both sides.

These circumstances combined to increase pressure on the Texas mission system to scale down its operations. The first missions to close were the remaining East Texas stations, those among the Hasinais as far east as Los Adaes and the one for the Akokisas on the lower Trinity River. This was a result of Rubí's claim that East Texas was not worth the investment in money and resources. These closures released Zacatecas College friars for duty at the four Béxar missions operated by

For Spanish colonial administrators, including Teodoro de Croix, first commandant general of the Provincias Internas, Texas posed a series of frustrating and seemingly insurmountable problems. Arriving in San Antonio in January 1778 for a council of war, Croix experienced first-hand the penury of the Tejanos, the struggles of the missions, and the neglect of the presidio system in the province. Later he would comment that Texas "did not deserve the name of the Province of Texas . . . nor the concern entailed in its preservation." (*Teodoro de Croix and the Northern Frontier of New Spain, 1776–1783, Alfred B. Thomas, University of Oklahoma Press*)

the Querétaro College, which abandoned Texas to concentrate on its more successful operations in Sonora and Arizona.

The pressure mounted with the arrival of Commandant General Croix for his 1778 war council in San Antonio. Croix listened to the complaints of settlers and missionaries about each other. He certainly understood the problems, and as a member of the new breed of more secular and regalist officials that the Spanish Bourbons were employing to modernize the empire, his actions favored settler and government interests. As far as the province's livestock was concerned, he strictly enforced the property rights of all parties, including the crown. As for the dispute over resources between Mission Valero and the townspeople of San Antonio, he ordered the suppression of the mission. Each Indian family would gain agricultural land and a house lot from the distribution of mission property, after which the Adaes settlers and other civilians would have access to the remaining farmland and lots. It was not until the early 1790s that both of these decisions were implemented, however, as lawsuits and reprieves wound their way through the imperial bureaucracy.

## Secularization Begins

When the president of the Texas Franciscans, Fray José Francisco López, sat down to make his report on the state of the missions in 1789 there was little positive to say. Nine friars attended to the needs of the province, one at each of the six operating mission communities, another two at the Nacogdoches settlement, and one as a substitute wherever he was needed. Only San José and Espíritu Santo counted more than 100 Indian residents, most of whom spoke imperfect Spanish even after such a long time in residence. In fact, the missions had become multiethnic communities, "the Indians," as Fray López wrote about Valero, "having married mulattoes and mestizoes." The physical plants of the missions varied widely in quality and state of repair, with Valero and the abandoned Rosario in the worst shape, and Espíritu Santo and San José in good condition. Various construction projects had had to be abandoned for lack of Indian labor, including larger churches at Valero (the main part of today's "Alamo chapel") and at Capistrano.

Although the Texas missionary enterprise seemed to have some life left to it in the coastal environs of La Bahía, conditions at Béxar were such that the Zacatecas College could no longer justify operating five stations there. Fray Manuel Julio de Silva had proposed a plan for converting all the coastal Indians from Nuevo Santander to the Mississippi, which required a redistribution of the college's resources. Although the plan ultimately foundered and only the Copano Bay mission, Nuestra Señora del Refugio, was built, the project did set in motion the suppression process for the Texas missions.

Governor Manuel Muñoz received the viceroy's order for the suppression of San Antonio de Valero in February 1793. Suppression, or secularization, was the final stage in the life cycle of a mission, and marked the successful transition of a new Christian community to parish status. Secularization was not a mark of failure, therefore, but of success for the religious, as it marked the formation of a permanent Catholic community. The goods and property of the mission were divided among the Indians, who had farmed communally and, except for a limited amount of self-governance, followed the directives of the friars. They were now considered adult Christians and full citizens in Spanish colonial society. Leftover land and water could be used by the community to attract additional settlers, in this case, the Adaesanos and other worthy San Antonio families, or held in reserve for the children of current families. In the spring of 1793, therefore, San Antonio de Valero became a separate civilian community (although, as far as religion was concerned, it became part of San Fernando parish).

On April 10, 1794, a year to the day from when secularization of Mission Valero began, Commandant General Pedro Nava issued a decree for the secularization of all missions more than ten years old in the Provincias Internas. The order had two principal objectives. First, it was meant to address the complaints of ranchers, farmers, and mine owners throughout the region that the missions only served the interests of the friars, who had sole access to Indian labor. Suppression of missions would free up valuable and scarce water and land for the expanding civilian population. Second, a reduction in the number of missions would mean a real savings to the crown, which had to provide each friar with an annual stipend. In addition, with the reduction in the cost of guards, escorts, and incidental expenses, the savings to the royal treasury would be substantial.

In Texas the decree meant closure, not only of the remaining four Béxar stations, but also of Espíritu Santo and Rosario. Typical of the confused and contradictory "enlightened" reform effort of the Spanish Bourbons, the decree gave the mission Indians their freedom, granting them all the rights and privileges enjoyed by *gente de razón* (people of reason, that is, full members of Spanish society), while at the same time ordering governors to appoint local officials as *justicias* (magistrates) to oversee the activities and property of Indians, so that they would not be victimized and they would not become lazy and debauched. The Indians were no longer under the supervision of the missionaries, who were now limited to looking after their spiritual welfare, yet they were not completely independent either.

Governor Muñoz was skeptical about whether secularization would be successful, particularly in the case of the La Bahía missions, where populations consisted of Indians only recently brought under instruction. Consequently, he decided to start with the four Béxar missions, where he carried out the distribution of property during July 1794. Beginning at Espada, and moving northward to Capistrano, San José, and Concepción, he took inventory of all property, made surveys of agricultural land, and distributed it to the resident Indians, with most of the land set aside for future use. Concerned that there were still a few Indians under instruction, he divided responsibility for the mission residents between the *justicias,* who had authority over those Indians deemed civilized enough to participate in the new order, and the friars, who remained in charge of neophytes.

Nevertheless, it seems clear that the four missions continued much as they had in the past. The friars continued to exert considerable influence over the activities of the Indian residents. The residents continued to elect a governor and *alcalde* annually. The farming and animal husbandry that went on was mostly on a subsistence basis. Every once in a while a small group of Indians would appear at the gates of the mission compounds and come in for instruction. The one significant change was the steady growth in the number of settlers who occupied farm and ranch land in the vicinity of each mission. By the turn of the century, Concepción, Capistrano, and Espada all had a majority of non-Indian residents.

Having completed his work in Béxar, Governor Muñoz traveled to La Bahía early in the fall of 1794 to inspect the missions there. He found too few of the Indians at Espíritu Santo and Rosario ready for "civilized" life and so petitioned the commandant general for an exemption. It took until May 1797 for the commandant general to decide to grant the two La Bahía missions a five-year exemption from the secularization decree. In that time Mission Nuestra Señora del Refugio, which had first been founded in 1793 as part of Fray Silva's project for the conversion of coastal Indians, had found a permanent home at the site of present-day Refugio. At the end of the eighteenth century the three La Bahía missions represented the only fully authorized Franciscan missions in the province.

## The Birth of the Texas Cattle Kingdom

By the time secularization of the San Antonio missions began in 1793, all of the Franciscan establishments in the San Antonio River basin had long ceased to play an important role in the province's economy. In fact, because they controlled valuable irrigable farmland near Béxar and vast expanses of grazing land as far away as the coast, the missions stood in the way of progress. Although they had been instrumental in establishing the first successful livestock concerns in Texas, by the 1780s the missions could no longer train or employ enough Indian herders to maintain themselves or challenge the increasingly aggressive civilian ranchers who were encroaching on mission ranch land.

### The First Texas Ranches

Stock raising had been an important economic activity from the very beginning in Texas. The early expeditions introduced herds of horses and cattle, and sometimes sheep and goats. The Marqués de Aguayo brought thousands of head of stock, not only to supply his army, but also to help seed the presidios and missions he left in the wake of his expedition. One of the wealthiest ranchers in northern New Spain, he might have been using his visit to Texas to scout out the country for potential expansion of his haciendas. In the end, neither he nor any of the other great stockmen—sheep- and cattlemen known as *hacendados*—established operations as far north as Texas.

A few of the early military settlers managed to build up small herds. Mateo

Pérez, an early soldier who died in 1748, left over 200 head of cattle and 50 horses in his will. Early soldiers Bernabé Carbajal and Francisco Hernández had herds large enough by the 1730s that they obtained grants of grazing land, but their operations were limited by the threat of Indian attacks and their own meager economic means. In fact, it was the very limitations of livestock raising in Texas that influenced use of the term *rancho* (small ranch) rather than *hacienda* (large estate) for Texas livestock properties.

It was the missions, particularly those at La Bahía and Béxar, that first developed herds and flocks large enough to require construction of ranch compounds. At first the mission herders, specially trained neophytes with civilians or soldiers acting as overseers, maintained their animals in the vicinity of the missions. As the herds grew, however, it became necessary to move them farther away. Except for Mission San José, which headquartered its operations south of Béxar on the Atascosa River, the other San Antonio missions established their ranches southeast of the settlement. East of these ranches, between the San Antonio and Guadalupe rivers, Mission Espíritu Santo claimed land in what are today Victoria, Goliad, DeWitt, Gonzales, and Karnes counties.

Of all the mission ranches established in Texas, the one with the best story to tell is Rancho de las Cabras (Goat Ranch), the livestock enterprise of Mission San Francisco de la Espada, and today a state historical park. By the 1740s the southernmost of the Béxar missions had established its pastures along the south bank of the San Antonio River opposite present-day Floresville. The ranch was more than a goat ranch, however, as flocks of sheep and herds of cattle and horses also required the attention of a growing number of neophyte ranch hands (making these Indians among the first Texas cowboys). In time the operation grew to comprise an impressive complex of structures that were the envy of the area's civilian ranchers. From the extensive archeological remains, we know that red sandstone walls enclosed a large compound that contained a sturdy stone chapel, dwellings for the ranch families, and utility buildings and corrals. For defensive purposes two *torreones* (towers) served as bastions at the northwest and southeast corners of the compound.

Although its stonewalls could protect the residents of Rancho de las Cabras, nothing could protect the open range claimed by the mission from the assaults of both settlers and Indians. Following the 1749 treaty with the Apaches, a number of families with livestock interests moved into the countryside in force, claiming what pastures and watering places the missions had not reserved for themselves, and conflict soon arose. The missionaries charged that the so-called ranchers were moving next to the mission ranches in order to efficiently despoil the neophytes of their livestock. They argued that all the cattle in the countryside, branded and unbranded, belonged to their Indians because the missions had brought the first cattle to the area.

The ranchers responded that their parents and grandparents too had brought cattle and horses into the province. As one San Antonio *alcalde* reported to a Mexico City judge hearing a complaint from the missionaries: "this so distant

Province could be no less populous than that of Saltillo, because its land is pleasingly fertile, with abundant places to take water, and fields and plains sufficient to receive and maintain large populations; but as these waters and lands are only diverted in order for the missions to make ranches, the nonholding *vecinos* do not benefit nor does His Majesty in that his dominions are not settled."

While the ownership issue slowly made its way through the courts and various layers of bureaucracy, Indian warfare had created a crisis situation. By 1772 only Ignacio de la Peña's ranch and Rancho de las Cabras had withstood the Indian assaults that had resulted in the destruction or abandonment of all the other ranches in the area. Construction of a military post, Fuerte de Santa Cruz del Cíbolo, halfway between Béxar and La Bahía on Cíbolo Creek, was ineffective. The fort was conceived by the Marqués de Rubí as a way to repopulate the area by offering immediate protection against Indian assaults. Governor Cabello, never happy with the location of the understaffed and overextended fort, eventually prevailed upon the commandant general to destroy and abandon it in 1782.

Governor Ripperdá had attempted to mediate the complaints of both camps, only to find himself the subject of complaints. When Commandant General Croix arrived in Béxar in January 1778 to hold his war council, he was forced to listen to days of grievances from governor, missionaries, and ranchers alike. Although the positions of friars and stockmen were similar—the unbranded stock belonged to them—the governor had a larger agenda. Ripperdá pointed out to Croix that the uncontrolled and indiscriminate slaughter and export of cattle from the province was bound to lead to its extinction. Also, here was a public source of wealth being exploited by people who paid no direct taxes to the crown.

The commandant general responded by issuing what can be considered Texas's first environmental regulation. His ordinance of January 11, 1778, declared all unbranded stock property of the crown, required licensing of all cattle exports from Texas, established a tax on all unbranded stock captured either for export or slaughter, and imposed heavy fines for the unlicensed slaughter of unbranded cattle. Through this measure Croix hoped to raise revenue from a province that had always been a drain on the royal coffers while protecting the cattle population and ending the ownership dispute. The *mesteña* (unbranded stock) fund, as the livestock tax was commonly known, proved extremely controversial, and was challenged by all stock raisers in the province. Efforts by succeeding governors to control the consumption of breeding cows, a particularly detrimental practice, only served to increase animosities. Only in 1795 did one of Croix's successors, Pedro de Nava, reaffirm the measure, forgiving back taxes owed, but granting all legitimate stockmen just one year to gather *mesteño* cattle and horses before taxes were assessed again.

The governmental regulations putting the missions on a par with the ranchers in regard to unbranded stock contributed greatly to the demise of the Texas mission system. Continued Indian depredations and an inability to recruit neophytes took their toll on Rancho de las Cabras, which, although it still had twenty-six residents when Croix and Fray Morfi passed through on their way to

La Bahía early in 1778, was already in decline. The murder of six to eight Espada herdsmen by raiding Indians in 1780–81 was an almost insurmountable loss, especially when hiring civilian cowboys cost one peso a day, the highest wage for any skilled work in colonial Texas. When Governor Cabello ordered a branding roundup at the end of 1780, Rancho de las Cabras was unable to participate. In fact, Valero was the only Béxar mission able to field a roundup and branding crew; the rest of the participants were private ranchers.

## Triumph of the Ranchers

By the time Governor Cabello managed to negotiate a general peace with the Comanches and Norteños in 1785, the end of the mission ranches was in sight. Cabello's successor, Rafael Martínez Pacheco, who was sympathetic to the plight of all Texas stockmen, crafted a series of roundup agreements in 1787 that allowed the missions and ranchers to round up as many animals as they could within assigned territories. Fray Pedro Noreña, representing Espada, was optimistic that somehow he could field a crew and revive the fortunes of Rancho de las Cabras. Such was not the case, however. When Martínez Pacheco issued his final report on the roundups, neither Espada nor any of the other Béxar missions had managed to capture a single animal. Only Mission Espíritu Santo had branded cattle: 1,418 head, compared to 6,231 cattle and 183 horses branded by the ranchers.

Without neophyte *vaqueros* (cowboys) to maintain the mission's ranching interests, Espada's missionaries, along with the friars at the other missions, had long since begun to make compromises with encroaching stockmen, which led to the eventual transfer of Rancho de las Cabras to civilian ownership. Ignacio Calvillo had occupied land in the vicinity of Rancho de las Cabras as early as 1774, and had gained the mission's approval by 1778. Within three years he was the recognized owner of Rancho Paso de las Mugeres. Similarly, Juan Barrera, a native of Coahuila and tithe collector for Texas, moved into the area during the 1780s. He operated a ranch he called Santa Gertrudis, possibly only renting the land so he could pasture the stock he collected as *diezmero* (tithe collector). Soon after secularization the two men moved to complete their takeover of Rancho de las Cabras, Calvillo taking the upper portion of the mission ranch, including the site of the headquarters compound, and Barrera taking the lower portion, which came to be called Las Cabras Viejas. This process was repeated at the other San Antonio missions.

The return of mission grazing lands to the royal domain that accompanied suppression was the ultimate victory for the civilian stockmen of Béxar who had vied with the missions for control of this valuable asset for more than half a century. Ranchers won in two ways. First, they acquired large numbers of unbranded cattle that roamed the prairies of south-central Texas. Second, in the three decades following secularization, civilian stockmen moved onto the former mission ranches and claimed them for themselves.

By the turn of the century, ranching had become the principal economic activity of Texas, despite adverse climatic conditions, severe financial constraints, persistent though greatly diminished Indian raids on herds, and continued reliance on natural reproduction of the semi-wild stock on the open range. At Béxar, where there were fourteen recognized ranch owners in 1791, there were thirty-five in 1810. Nacogdoches too saw a boom in ranching, particularly in horse breeding, during the 1790s, as the final collapse of the area's Caddo population left a number of clearings open for the taking. By 1810 there were more than twenty registered ranch owners in East Texas, including a number of Anglo and French Americans who had made their way into the area as authorized Indian traders, government agents, and squatters.

### Ranching Empires of the Lower Rio Grande Valley

By the time secularization of the Texas missions began in the 1790s Nuevo Santander had become an even more successful ranching region than its neighbor to the north, Texas. No one knew this better than Rosa María Hinojosa de Ballí, matriarch of its most powerful ranching clan. From the various explorations of the region, José de Escandón had come to believe that this part of Nuevo Santander, which is sometimes referred to as the trans-Nueces, was best suited to a stock farming way of life, and he had encouraged *hacendados* from Coahuila and Nuevo León to establish sheep and cattle operations in the region. With no missions to stand in the way of occupation, one of these hacendados, Captain Juan José Hinojosa, with his relatives, friends, and a select group of other families, fanned out from the Rio Grande settlements in the last three decades of the eighteenth century to establish ranches as far north as today's Nueces County.

Among these stockmen was militia captain José María Ballí, whose father had brought his family to Reynosa in the earliest days. Like other prominent heads of family, Ballí served as a militia officer as well as *alcalde*. By the late 1750s, the Hinojosas and Ballís were two of six families, all interrelated, that controlled the economic and social life of Reynosa. The alliance between the two clans was further cemented through the marriage of Hinojosa's daughter Rosa María to Ballí, and during the 1770s and 1780s father-in-law and son-in-law worked as business partners to build up a ranching empire. The partnership included making joint application for a 37-*sitio* (166,500-acre) grant along the Rio Grande east of Hinojosa's *porciones* in the Reynosa jurisdiction.

Hinojosa must have seen something special in his daughter from early on. Unlike the vast majority of women in the Spanish world, including many elite women, Rosa María received an education under the direction of a local priest. Later, she received business training from her father and husband. As a result, upon their deaths in the late 1780s she was more than ready to handle the family's affairs. By age 38 she had become matriarch of the Ballí family and was known to many area residents as *la patrona* (the mistress).

Not only did she inherit property from her husband and her father, but she inherited their debts and obligations. Between 1790 and 1803, the year of her

Wealth entailed social responsibility, even on the frontiers of Texas and Nuevo Santander. Doña Rosa María Hinojosa de Ballí, matriarch of the wealthiest ranching family of the lower Rio Grande valley, was an important contributor to worthy causes, including the construction of Nuestra Señora de la Purísima Concepción Church in Mier. The church, construction of which began in 1780, is part of a binational heritage corridor that includes numerous sites on both sides of the river from Laredo to Brownsville-Matamoros. *(Photo by Frank de la Teja)*

death, she not only reversed the family's financial fortunes but more than doubled its land holdings. In the process she became a pillar of the community, serving as witness to legal proceedings, becoming godmother for dozens of children born to friends and employees, and serving as lender to fellow ranchers and benefactor to the churches in Reynosa, Camargo, and Matamoros.

The Hinojosa-Ballí land empire was Doña Rosa's greatest accomplishment. A shrewd businessperson, she spent much of her time during the 1790s expanding upon the 12 sitios (54,000 acres) she inherited from her husband, and her 3-sitio inheritance from her father. On behalf of one son she applied for 72 sitios (324,000 acres) to the northeast of other family holdings, a grant known as San Salvador del Tule. As financier for her brother Vicente she obtained 12 sitios out of the 35-sitio Las Mesteñas grant she helped him obtain. In partnership with another son, Nicolás, a diocesan priest by calling, she acquired an interest in the lower portion of Isla de Santiago (now Padre Island). Purchases and other transactions brought tens of thousands of additional acres under her control, so that at the beginning of the nineteenth century the Ballís controlled about 1,000,000 acres of grazing lands in what are now Cameron, Hidalgo, Willacy, Kenedy, Kleberg, and Nueces counties.

These vast holdings were managed principally from Doña Rosa's headquarters on the La Feria estate. Like the other few major ranch owners in the region, she maintained one residence in town (in her case, Reynosa) and another at the ranch headquarters. Although some subsistence farming took place, the primary sources of income came from grazing horses, cattle, and sheep and leasing out pastures to landless or land-poor ranchers.

Despite her impressive accomplishments Doña Rosa was representative of a society and an economic system that was land-rich, but money-poor. Many ranchers of the trans-Nueces owned little, if any, land at all, and grazed their small herds and flocks on the more marginal and isolated, as yet unclaimed, land in the area. Others leased land from the better-off stockmen who were able to establish legal title to large tracts that often contained what little permanent water was available in an area. The marginal quality of most unimproved land meant that even the major stockmen, such as the Ballís, ran only a few thousand head of all types of stock combined. With the relatively low prices the ranchers received for the animals and byproducts they produced, few ranchers had the means to improve their production capabilities. For example, the obstacles to effectively fencing the trans-Nueces range meant that selective improvement of stock was impossible. Animals mated in the field, to be rounded up only for branding, slaughter, or sale.

Nevertheless, Doña Rosa and the other leading ranchers were the *patrones* (masters) in a social system in which hierarchical relationships were all-important. *Patrones* met the needs of their employees (sometimes referred to as *peones*), and employees were expected to have unconditional loyalty to their *patrones*. Especially at Reynosa, the large ranchers held the local political and military posts, so their interests and concerns had a better chance of being addressed than those of the majority of the settlers, the rancheros, and the mestizos, mulattoes, and Indians that made up the majority of the population.

## Conclusion

In the last third of the eighteenth century Texas and neighboring Mexican provinces made considerable strides toward development. Rubí's reforms and the creation of the Comandancia General de las Provincias Internas had reinforced Béxar and La Bahía and even presented an opportunity for Tejano frontiersmen to establish a civilian community in East Texas. All three communities experienced significant population and economic growth—none more so than Béxar, where the increasing number of merchants and artisans attested to expanding market opportunities.

The new policy of making war on the Apaches and pacifying the other independent tribes eventually bore fruit. From the Spanish perspective, the most spectacular demonstration of the efficacy of the new policy was the defeat that Commandant General Juan de Ugalde and his troops and Indian auxiliaries inflicted on over 300 Lipans, Lipiyans, and Mescaleros at Sabinal River canyon in 1790.

The increasing security of the countryside allowed Tejanos to expand the boundaries of settlement beyond their rather small and marginal communities, especially with the decline of the missions. The markets for colonial beef, hide, tallow, and other beef byproducts provided an incentive for civilian ranchers to challenge missionaries for control of the countryside in Texas and to meet the challenge of the semiarid prairies of the trans-Nueces. In the last third of the eighteenth century Texas became a cattle empire, establishing a legacy for centuries to come.

At Paso del Norte, too, the reduction in Indian hostilities was noticeable in a number of ways. Rapid population growth brought the number of residents in the district to almost 6,000 by the end of the century. Paso del Norte had become the only part of New Mexico connected to the rest of the Provincias Internas by a regular mail system. Economic activity along the road between the rest of the province and the interior of New Spain had increased to such a degree that the first permanent bridge across the Rio Grande—500 feet long and 17 feet wide—was in operation by 1800.

The birth of new ways to foster the development of the frontier brought the death of old ways. The missions, which had played such an important role in the permanent occupation of Texas, no longer had anything to offer. The remaining Indians of Texas were either friendly to the Spaniards, had been co-opted through better trade relations and ritualized gift-giving, or were sorely weakened enemies. Although young Apache, Comanche, and Norteño warriors sometimes tested their mettle by launching minor raids on cattle and horse herds, mechanisms were in place for resolving conflict without the terror of generations past.

Texas and surrounding areas were headed in the right direction, an observer at the end of the eighteenth century might have concluded. Population and economic growth were evident, peace with all of the native peoples was in sight, and Louisiana now served as a buffer to foreign threats. Then it happened: The nineteenth century blew in like a blue norther.

## SUGGESTED READINGS

In the last third of the eighteenth century, Texas and all of northeastern New Spain again came under the scrutiny of royal officials eager to make the empire more efficient and defendable. The broad outline of this story, and Texas's place in it, is presented in chapters 8 and 9 of David Weber's *The Spanish Frontier in North America,* and in chapters 10 and 11 of John Kessell's *Spain in the Southwest.* Works from the first half of the twentieth century remain our best English-language sources for the two most important figures in frontier reform efforts: *José de Gálvez, Visitor General of New Spain, 1765–1771* by Herbert I. Priestly (1916, 1980) and *Teodoro de Croix and the Northern Frontier of New Spain, 1776–1783* by Alfred B. Thomas (1941). The economic expansion of New Spain, from which Texas benefited only marginally, is well covered by David A. Brading in *Miners and Merchants in Bourbon Mexico, 1763–1810* (1971). Donald Chipman continues the story of Texas during this time frame in chapters 9 and 10 of *Spanish Texas, 1519–1821.*

### Reorganization of the Frontier

Reform had to be based on firsthand knowledge, and so the Marqués de Rubí, on instructions from José de Gálvez, set out in 1766 on an inspection tour of the Indian frontier from the Gulf of California to the Gulf of Mexico. The Texas portion of his travels is covered in Jackson and Foster, *Imaginary Kingdom.* A second opinion on Texas appears in *The Frontiers of New Spain: Nicolas de Lafora's Description, 1766–1768,* ed. Lawrence Kinnaird (1958). V. A. Vincent discusses the consequences of the Rubí inspired regulations of 1772 in "The Frontier Soldier: Life in the *Provincias Internas* and the Royal Regulations of 1772, 1766–1787," *Military History of the Southwest* (1992).

### The Death and Rebirth of Spanish East Texas

The reorganization of Texas and the restructuring of Spanish-Indian relations fell to a high-born Spanish governor and two frontiersmen, one a native of East Texas and the other a long-time resident of French Louisiana. Although the Spaniard, Governor Barón de Ripperdá, has yet to receive the separate attention he deserves, his role in the abandonment of Los Adaes and establishment of Bucareli is covered well in the chapters on "Athanase de Mézières" and "Marqués de Rubí/ Antonio Gil Ibarbo" in Chipman and Joseph, *Notable Men and Women of Spanish Texas.* Ripperdá's successor, Governor Domingo Cabello, does get his own chapter in *Notable Men and Women of Spanish Texas.* On the development of Nacogdoches as the heterogenous center of Spanish East Texas, see Patrick J. Walsh, "Living on the Edge of the Neutral Zone: Varieties of Identity in Nacogdoches, Texas 1773–1810," *East Texas Historical Journal* (1999).

### Sunset for the Missions

The secularization of the Texas missions was a drawn-out process that only began in the 1790s. As with other subjects in Spanish Texas history, most work has focused on the San Antonio area. The process of secularization in the context of rivalry between mission communities and the civilian population of Texas is treated in Félix D. Almaráz, Jr., "San Antonio's Old Franciscan Missions: Material Decline and Secular Avarice in the Transition from Hispanic to Mexican Control," *Americas* (1987). A missionary's view of the need for secularization at San Antonio is presented in "Report on the San Antonio Missions in 1792," ed. Benedict Leutenegger and Marion A. Habig, *Southwestern Historical Quarterly* (1974). Although secularized, the San Antonio missions survived as living communities with their own folklore, essential portions of which were gathered by Adina de

Zavala early in the twentieth century and published under the title *History and Legends of the Alamo and Other Missions in and around San Antonio* (reprint, 1996).

## The Birth of the Cattle Kingdom

Given the state's heritage of cattle raising, it is not surprising that a number of authors have addressed the Hispanic elements of the Texas livestock industry. An exhaustive narrative history, focusing on political struggles among civilians, missionaries, and royal officials is Jack Jackson, *Los Mesteños: Spanish Ranching in Texas, 1721–1821* (1986). Much shorter, and focusing on the practices and institutions is *The Ranch in Spanish Texas, 1691–1800* by Sandra L. Myres (1969). A useful short essay on the subject, somewhat dated in light of more recent research, is Odie B. Faulk's "Ranching in Spanish Texas," *Hispanic American Historical Review* (1965). The difficulties of creating a safe environment for cattle operations in Spanish Texas is one of the principal subjects of *El Fuerte del Cíbolo: Sentinel of the Béxar-La Bahía Ranches*, by Robert H. Thonhoff (1992). For South Texas, in addition to the appropriate parts of Armando Alonzo's *Tejano Legacy*, Jesús F. de la Teja looks at the interrelationship between environment, economics, and legal practices in "'Only Fit for Raising Stock': Spanish and Mexican Land and Water Rights in the Tamaulipan Cession," in *Fluid Arguments: Five Centuries of Western Water Conflict*, edited by Char Miller (2001).

# 5

# New Rivals, New Challenges, 1800–1821

Benito de Armiñán, interim governor of Texas in the spring of 1814, had an impossible task to perform. In the aftermath of the royalist victory over the latest rebellion in the province families had been broken up by the death or flight of husbands, fathers, and sons; crops had been destroyed or consumed by the contending forces; and the little commerce the province enjoyed had been subject to disruption by Indian attack. Ill and depressed Armiñán sat down to write his superior, Commandant General Joaquín Arredondo, to explain why he might have to resort to force to keep his men fed if higher authorities did not see fit to send relief immediately. "They are hopelessly lost in their misery. They have been weakened by their past misfortunes. They are complaining most pitiously over the lack of sustenance for themselves and their families. They are lamenting over the crisis and weeping bitterly over their fate—especially when they remember the terrible misery which lies before them." Relief did not come for Armiñán and it did not come for his successors. What did come were adventurers, pirates, and Indian raiders who made life as precarious as it had been at the height of the Indian wars of the 1770s and 1780s. The news that Spain and the United States had agreed on a border that respected Spanish claims to Texas was of little consolation to frontier officials or the surviving Tejano population. A decade of destruction and terror had left them so "hopelessly lost in their misery" that they greeted Mexican independence with no great jubilation. Rather, they began to heal the wounds that had divided families; they began to think about hoping again.

| 1800 | Napoleon forces Spain to return Louisiana to French control |
| 1801 | Philip Nolan killed during his fourth trip to Texas since 1791 when he resists Spanish efforts to arrest him for spying |
| 1803 | Louisiana Purchase |
| 1805 | Baron of Bastrop proposes to colonize Texas with Louisiana families |
| 1806 | Neutral Ground Agreement between Col. Herrera and Gen. Wilkinson averts war between Spain and the United States over Texas; town of Santísima Trinidad de Salcedo founded |
| 1808 | Town of San Marcos de Neve founded |
| 1810 | Father Hidalgo launches revolt against Spanish rule |
| 1811 | Casas revolt in Texas fails; Father Hidalgo executed |
| 1812 | Gutiérrez-Magee expedition begins invasion of Texas |
| 1813 | Republic of Texas proclaimed; Gen. Arredondo defeats Republican Army of the North at battle of Medina |
| 1815 | Rebels under Father Morelos declare Mexican independence; filibusters and pirates occupy Galveston Island |
| 1818 | French settlement Champ d'Asile fails |
| 1819 | Adams-Onís Treaty recognizes Spanish title to Texas; James Long launches first expedition to liberate Texas for the United States |
| 1820 | Moses Austin proposes to colonize Texas with Catholic families from the United States |
| 1821 | Mexico gains independence; second Long expedition fails |

The last two decades of Spanish rule in Texas found the province battered by political storms that its few Spanish residents were ill equipped to weather. First, Louisiana changed hands from Spain to France to the United States. Napoleon Bonaparte had had dreams of reconstructing a great French empire in America and in 1800 had forced the weak Charles IV of Spain to return Louisiana to the French. In 1803, when the cost of his empire became too great, Napoleon sold the territory to a very willing Thomas Jefferson. But what, exactly, was Louisiana? The Americans thought it should include all the territory to the Rio Grande. Thus Texas became a bone of contention between the oldest empire of the New World and its first republic. Its population boomed as Spanish troops, Louisiana exiles, and displaced Indian groups from east of the Mississippi sought the protection of Spanish territory.

Second, a whirlwind of revolution brought insurgents, filibusters, and royalist armies into Texas in destructive waves of violence. The destruction caused by warfare was compounded by the depredations of Comanche, Norteño, and Apache bands determined to take from Tejanos what they could no longer obtain in trade and gift exchanges. At the end of this tumultuous era Texas lay in ruins, its ranches largely abandoned, its fields largely untilled, its remaining people largely destitute. The future would belong to those who were the first to take hold of the shattered remains and build a new Texas.

## Louisiana

In 1800 no one in Texas or Mexico City, or even in Madrid, could have foreseen the chain of events that left the Spanish empire in ruins and Texas as part of an independent Mexico. For more than a decade New Spain had fought against United States expansionism along the Mississippi River and its eastern tributaries. Although the situation was precarious, it was not out of control.

Spanish officials recognized U.S. expansionism as a dangerous successor to British imperialism and moved to counter the threat with the meager resources at their disposal. Forced to be flexible, beginning in the 1780s local officials took matters into their own hands and allowed Protestant families to settle in Louisiana. These settlers, often English or Anglo American royalists who no longer had a home on the U.S. side of the Mississippi River, in time were joined by other Anglo Americans more interested in the economic opportunities available in Spanish Missouri, Natchez, and Louisiana. Spanish officials in Florida and Louisiana also took advantage of Indian dissatisfaction with Anglo American pioneers to keep the United States at bay. A number of southeastern tribes took refuge on the Spanish side of the border or conducted raids against intruding Anglo American settlers with the support of local Spanish authorities. Slavery was legal in the Spanish world, but slaves from U.S. territory were granted their freedom in Spanish Florida and Louisiana: another method of fending off Anglo American encroachment of Spanish territory.

After Spain was drawn into the French Revolution and the Napoleonic wars, it proved impossible to maintain adequate commercial contacts with its American empire or to properly defend it against outside threats. As tensions over trade, Indian relations, and slave flight mounted, Madrid forestalled a direct confrontation with Washington by entering into the Treaty of San Lorenzo in 1795. By the terms of the treaty, U.S. citizens enjoyed navigation rights on the Mississippi River and the right to use New Orleans as a trans-shipment port for their products. In addition, both countries would restrain the Indians on their side of the border from conducting depredations on the other side.

### Philip Nolan: Horse Trader or Spy?

It was in these circumstances that adventurers like Philip Nolan and the self-styled Baron of Bastrop, made their way to the Louisiana-Texas frontier. The two men could not have been more different. As a young man Philip Nolan had immigrated from Ireland to the western frontier of the new United States, where he became a protégé of General James Wilkinson. The American military man, who maintained very friendly relations with the Spaniards (at one point in his career he was actually employed by the Spanish Crown), soon had Nolan acting as his business agent in New Orleans.

While in the Louisiana capital the twenty-year-old Irish American learned about the Indian trade opportunities in Texas, which led in 1791 to the first of a number of trips there for him. Officially, commercial contacts between Texas and Louisiana were forbidden under Spain's tightly regulated mercantile system. Despite a series of reforms intended to expand trading opportunities among its various American colonies, Spain's mercantilist policies remained the most restrictive of the European empires—that is, on paper. In reality, an inefficient and corrupt customs and administrative system meant that contraband, graft, and incompetence were rife. At the time of the American Revolution the Spanish Crown had consented to a limited livestock trade between Texas and Louisiana, and it was this authorization that adventurers like Nolan took advantage of in order to trade with Texas Indians. The governor of Spanish Louisiana did not think twice about giving Nolan a passport to gather livestock in Texas.

To Texas authorities Nolan's trading license was not valid. They suspected the Irish American tradesman of being a spy, a contrabandist, or both, and officials in Nacogdoches confiscated his merchandise. Financially ruined and in no hurry to return to Louisiana, Nolan chose to spend some time living with various Texas Indian tribes, among them the Comanches. Although Nolan claimed that "the freedom, the independence of the savage life was always congenial to my nature," he also admitted that he could not completely "indianify."

Between 1794 and 1799 Nolan made two more successful trading expeditions to Texas. It was not just the province's Indians who welcomed the opportunity to trade for higher-quality manufactured goods that Nolan's company brought with him: Tejanos also did business—illegally—with the American. Nolan eventually sold the horses, hides, and furs he collected in Texas as far east as Frankfort, Kentucky, attracting even more interest among American frontiersmen in the Texas trade.

Nolan had caught Texas fever, but he had also caught the attention of Spanish authorities. Their suspicions were confirmed by his decision to return to Texas in the fall of 1800 leading a large body of men in the face of Spanish disapproval. In fact, a deserter from the expedition, Mordecai Richards, later declared that Nolan "had maps of all the rivers, marked all the distances, and explored everything more attentively than a man would do who had not other ends in view than that of catching horses—that he had told him many times that there were mines in this country, and moreover that he had assured his men that if the Spaniards killed a single one of them he would take a commission as an English general . . . and would take possession of all this country."

It was not one of his men, but Nolan himself who died at the hands of the Spaniards. He had built corrals and begun catching horses and trading with Wichita and Comanche bands in what is now Hill County, but a Spanish patrol caught up with him in March 1801. After Nolan was killed by a cannonball his men quickly surrendered, claiming that their only goal had been to capture mustangs. Authories remained unconvinced, however.

### The Baron of Bastrop: Would-be Colonizer

Another adventurer who eventually turned to Texas for new opportunities was the Baron of Bastrop. A native of Dutch Guiana, Philip Hendrik Nering Bögel had moved to Holland as a child and had grown up to become a tax collector. Accused of embezzlement in 1793, he fled the country, adopting the title by which he would henceforth be known. After arriving in Louisiana in 1795 he undertook a variety of business ventures, including real estate development, all with only minor success.

As a would-be colonizer Bastrop joined a number of Anglo American and European entrepreneurs who saw great opportunities in Spain's desperate effort to reinforce Louisiana and Texas in the face of the United States challenge. Some had big schemes, like Pennsylvania Dutch innkeeper Pedro Paulus, who offered to settle 3,000 families as long as they had freedom of worship, local self-government, and generous land allotments. (His plan never amounted to anything.) Some had more modest ambitions, like William Barr, another Irish immigrant who became a Spanish subject in Louisiana before moving to Nacogdoches in 1793. Barr established himself as an Indian trader and entered into partnership with Natchitoches merchant Peter Samuel Davenport. Having gained a monopoly on Indian trade in northern Texas, the House of Barr and Davenport had made Barr a wealthy man by the time he died in 1810.

Bastrop fell somewhere in between. Shortly after his arrival in Louisiana he received permission to settle families along the Ouachita River. During a recruiting trip to the United States in 1797, a new governor arrived in Louisiana who opposed settlement by Protestant Anglo Americans and suspended Bastrop's project. With this turn of events Bastrop saw his land schemes evaporate and he turned to the Indian trade as a means of recovering his fortunes. Although he obtained a contract to supply the Indians along the Ouachita River with merchandise, the sale of Louisiana to the United States in 1803 brought an end to his monopoly and to his profits.

Bastrop, like a number of other Louisiana land promoters, now turned his attention to Texas. Bearing a letter of recommendation from his friend, the former governor of Louisiana, in the fall of 1805 he arrived in San Antonio, where he proposed to establish a colony between Béxar and the Trinity River. The settlers would be some of the families he had previously brought to Louisiana along with friendly and agricultural Choctaws. Having learned his lesson from the Ouachita project, he pledged to introduce only Catholic families.

Both Texas Governor Antonio Cordero and Commandant General Nemecio Salcedo thought the project worth pursuing, as it fit with their plans to expand settlement in Texas in the face of U.S. occupation of Louisiana. Immediately after the territory's transfer to the United States, President Thomas Jefferson, basing his position on French documents, had claimed that all the lands as far as the Rio Grande were included in the purchase. Spanish colonial authorities, facing what the baron called the "daring land-hunger of the infamous class of Americans" along with Jefferson's claims, naturally grasped at the colonization proposals of Bastrop and other Louisianians in order to create a first line of defense in Texas. Although none of the plans ever took shape, the baron soon settled in San Antonio, where he became a leading member of the community. A decade later he would become involved in a colonization project beyond his wildest dreams.

## Neutral Ground

Whatever disappointment Governor Cordero felt about the results of Bastrop's mission could not have measurably added to the distress he already suffered. In 1805 United States troops had arrived in the vicinity of Natchitoches and asserted U.S. claims to the area. By early 1806 both sides were convinced that the other was preparing for war. In March President Jefferson reported to the United States Congress: "Some time since, however, we learnt that the Spanish authorities were advancing into the disputed country to occupy new posts and make new settlements."

Jefferson responded by ordering U.S. troops to chase out the Spanish detachment that Governor Cordero had ordered to occupy the Los Adaes district, in response to which the Texas governor ordered the militia to reinforce Nacogdoches. To defuse the situation Commandant General Nemecio Salcedo proposed establishing a neutral ground between Natchitoches and the Sabine River while the boundary between United States and Spanish territory was negotiated.

To these developments were added the complications of the Aaron Burr conspiracy and U.S. reconnaissance of the Red River country. Dissatisfied with his

Los Adaes State Historic Site, outside Robeline, Louisiana, preserves a piece of Spanish Texas. Although Spanish forces briefly reoccupied the long-abandoned first capital of Texas following the Louisiana Purchase, it, along with the rest of the territory west to the Sabine River soon became part of the Neutral Ground, and then part of the United States under the Adams-Onís Treaty of 1819. *(© Alex Demyan/Fineart Photography)*

prospects in the United States, Burr, the volatile former vice president, developed a scheme with a number of associates to separate the trans-Appalachian states from the Union and combine them with the Louisiana Purchase and the silver mining region of northern New Spain into a great empire. As soon as rumors of Burr's scheme reached Salcedo, he advised Cordero "it is a very grave matter . . . that some 10,000 men, subjects of the United States, are being prepared in Kentucky with the object of overpowering the uninhabited provinces of this kingdom and our Indian allies, with no respect for the boundaries of Louisiana. You will, therefore, take extraordinary precautions toward putting the country in a good state of defense by bringing up all the auxiliaries."

The commandant general's response to another incident was even more confrontational. In the spring of 1806 an exploratory expedition under Major Thomas Freeman began to ascend the Red River. When he received news of this obvious violation of Spanish territory, Commandant General Salcedo issued orders to stop the expedition from continuing westward. Freeman had managed to travel 600 miles up the Red River before he was confronted by a large Spanish detachment and decided to turn back.

Throughout these months the Spanish had been reinforcing the small Texas garrisons with auxiliary units from other provinces. First to arrive was a light cavalry unit from Coahuila known as the Second Flying Company of San Carlos del Alamo de Parras. The unit arrived in Béxar in 1803 and occupied the abandoned buildings of Mission San Antonio de Valero, lending its name to the site, which would ever after be known as the Alamo. Militia units from Nuevo Santander and Nuevo León brought total troop strength in the province to over 1,000 by early summer.

Despite growing war hysteria along the U.S. frontier and the troop buildup on the Texas side, cooler heads prevailed. Wilkinson arrived unopposed at the Sabine River on October 29 and immediately sent a message to the Texas governor proposing an agreement by which the Spaniards would not recross the Sabine and the Americans would retreat to Natchitoches and not recross the Arroyo Hondo until the boundary had finally been negotiated. While Cordero hesitated, Lieutenant Colonel Simón Herrera seized the moment and on his own authority accepted Wilkinson's terms. On November 5, 1806, at the U.S. Army camp on the Sabine, General Wilkinson and Inspector Francisco Viana signed what came to be called the Neutral Ground Agreement. Cordero could now turn his attention to preparing the rest of Texas for what he was sure would be an inevitable onslaught of Anglo Americans.

## Fortress Texas

Governor Cordero and his superiors knew that troops alone could not hold the province. Defending the Texas frontier of New Spain from the land-hungry Anglo Americans would depend on increasing the population. The times seemed propitious for a concerted population drive as Spanish subjects in Louisiana deserted what was now U.S. territory and relative peace reigned between Texas's remaining native peoples and their Spanish colonial neighbors. It would not be easy to overcome the obstacles of distance and climate, but there was reason for hope among the long-suffering Tejanos that this might be their day in the sun.

### Still a Country of Indians

Antonio Cordero y Bustamante had been thrown into a difficult situation, but this was not the first time in his long and successful career as a frontier officer. Born in Cadiz, Spain, in 1753, he had come to New Spain as a cadet and soon found himself fighting Indians on the northern frontier. He distinguished himself in campaigns against various western Apache tribes before being assigned to the Coahuila theater of action in 1795. Throughout this time he strengthened presidio defenses and organized new settlements, activities that he continued after becoming governor of Coahuila in 1798. Commandant General Nemecio Salcedo turned to the popular Cordero in the summer 1805 to assume the reins of command in Texas when the health of the incumbent took a turn for the worse. About a month after Cordero's arrival, Juan Bautista Elguézabal, the incumbent who himself had been serving in an interim capacity since 1799, died. It would be up to Cordero to make sense of the increasingly chaotic situation.

The interim governor could see that there was much work to do in Texas. Formal settlement remained confined to San Antonio de Béxar, the capital of the province, the presidio-mission complex of La Bahía del Espíritu Santo, and the village of Nacogdoches. Of these population centers Béxar was by far the largest, containing over 2,000 men, women, and children, the other two having roughly 900 Tejanos each. Also during the 1790s an informal settlement of 100 to 200 persons called Bayou Pierre had begun to form in the old Los Adaes district. In addition, in 1803 the Alamo company added considerably to the military population of the province and put Cordero's available fighting strength at about 350 soldiers when he arrived in Texas.

Cordero also inherited the difficult problem of Louisiana émigrés. The Baron of Bastrop was not the only Louisiana subject of His Catholic Majesty who sought to start a new life in Spanish Texas. A number of individuals and families petitioned for Texas land. Commandant General Salcedo, suspicious of the situation, especially as the United States was claiming Texas as part of the Louisiana Territory, allowed the settlement of people who could prove their loyalty to the crown, while absolutely forbidding the admission of Anglo Americans. The latter were particularly suspect, because they seemed intent on undermining Spanish-Indian relations on the frontier.

As for the Indian peoples of Texas, some groups were in decline and facing extinction, others were expanding, and there were opportunities for new arrivals. By the early nineteenth century many Coahuiltecan bands had died out completely as separate culture groups. A similar trend was evident among the elusive Tonkawas of central Texas, who at several hundred tribe members, were at least holding out better than the Bidai and Akokisa, who numbered no more than 100 or 200. The Caddoan speakers of East Texas had also experienced drastic drops in number, most tribes consisting of no more than a few hundred individuals. Many villages had been abandoned and their surviving members had moved in with Caddo relatives on the Louisiana side of the frontier.

For Cordero the Indians requiring serious attention were the various Apache, Wichita, and Comanche tribes that still ranged freely on the western peripheries of Spanish Texas. The combined pressure of Comanches and Norteños on the Apaches, especially the Lipans, had forced the Lipans southward until, by the end of the eighteenth century, they inhabited a territory southwest of San Antonio and stretching into northern Coahuila. There Mescaleros and Lipans had made peace with each other and, in relative terms, with Spanish colonials, whose main complaints continued to be loss of livestock to young warriors.

*Cutchatés.*

Among the Indian tribes from east of the Mississippi River that sought the protection of Spanish authorities in Texas at the beginning of the nineteenth century were the Alabamas and Coushattas. In time the two small bands joined together on a single reservation in Polk County, where they remain today. This watercolor of Coushatta warriors by Lino Sanchéz y Tapia captures the degree to which southeastern Indians had adopted Western dress and technologies. (*Lino Sánchez y Tapia,* Cutchatés, *plate xviiii, from the collection of Gilcrease Museum, Tulsa, Oklahoma*)

More formidable were the Comanches and Wichitas. Their commercial contacts with Louisiana and New Mexico and their large numbers gave them an independence that required Spanish officials to deal with them as equals. Governor Cordero continued the successful policy of peace by purchase, but faced a new challenge in Anglo American tradesmen who moved onto the southern plains in an effort to gain the friendship—economic and political—of these peoples. Numbering in the thousands, mobile and aggressive, they posed the most serious threat to Spanish Texas in the first decade of the nineteenth century.

Another type of Indian challenge developed at this time in the form of immigrant tribes from U.S. territory. Spain's rivalry with the United States made Texas an attractive destination for groups seeking to escape Anglo American control. Small bands of Indians from a number of tribes began making their way into Spanish territory during the 1790s, particularly into the eastern part of the province, where the decline of the Caddos had left a considerable amount of land suitable for settlement. Among the immigrant tribes that Cordero had to deal with during his service in Texas were Alabamas, Apalaches, Cherokees, Chickasaws, Chocktaws, Coushattas, Pascagoulas, and Shawnees.

## Defensive Colonization

Cordero concluded that settlement should concentrate on the Camino Real between Nacogdoches and San Antonio. Occupation of strategic sites along the road would expedite communications within the province and make it easier for the new settlers to transport their goods. By the end of September 1805 Governor Cordero was requesting permission to found towns on the Trinity and Brazos rivers with a mix of native Tejanos and Louisiana émigrés. In December 1805 five families from Béxar that had been recruited for the project were on their way to the Trinity, where they discovered a group of Louisiana émigrés waiting for them. Early in 1806 they founded the town of Santísima Trinidad de Salcedo, most often referred to as Salcedo, under the supervision of a military officer from Béxar. By late January, titles to house lots and agricultural land were being issued, and construction began on a number of buildings. So successful was this first settlement effort under Cordero that families from Nacogdoches petitioned for permission to relocate to the new town.

Despite Salcedo's approval of Cordero's initial settlement plan, the two men did not see eye to eye on how best to utilize the growing pool of immigrants. In particular, Cordero saw the Louisianians, many of whom wished to remain in the Nacogdoches area, as the only means to populate East Texas in the absence of any significant migration from the interior of New Spain. This was especially important as the Tejano population of that part of the province was unable to supply provisions to the growing number of troops. Salcedo, concerned about the ever-present contraband problem and suspicious of the loyalties of many of the new arrivals, refused to allow them to locate permanently east of the Trinity.

His superior having made clear his hard line on settlement in the Nacogdoches region, Governor Cordero turned his attention to promoting new settlements farther west. He now requested permission to found towns on the Colorado, Guadalupe, and San Marcos crossings of the Camino Real, a request that was granted by the commandant general. The first and only one of the three towns that was actually established was San Marcos de Neve. Cordero worked out a deal with Felipe Roque de la Portilla, a fellow army officer from Spain who had seen service in Nuevo Santander. In return for a sizable land grant and a sizable subvention to the families he recruited, Portilla gathered a group of followers and a substantial number of animals and brought them to San Marcos in April 1808.

Of the five authorized settlements in Texas only Salcedo and San Marcos were established. Unlike Salcedo, which was made up of Bexareños and Louisianians, San Marcos was settled mostly by families from below the Rio Grande. Whereas Salcedo enjoyed military protection from the beginning, San Marcos had no garrison and was therefore exposed to Indian depredations. Salcedo enjoyed modest growth until its abandonment, but San Marcos attracted no new settlers after the first few months. Both ultimately suffered the same fate, however, falling victim to the warfare that engulfed Texas during the Mexican War of Independence.

## Last Efforts at Reform

In the summer of 1808, much to Cordero's relief, his replacement arrived. The new governor turned out to be none other than Nemecio Salcedo's thirty-two-year-old nephew, Manuel María de la Concepción Josef Agustín Eloy de Salcedo y Quiroga. Despite his young age, Manuel came with considerable experience: he had assisted his father, who had served as the last Spanish governor of Louisiana. To assume his post Manuel Salcedo and his family had traveled by way of the United States, landing at New Bedford, Massachusetts, going on to New York City, then to Philadelphia and Pittsburgh, Pennsylvania. Riverboat travel down the Ohio and Mississippi rivers brought them to Natchez. From there they traveled by coach to Natchitoches. In Natchitoches Salcedo met with U.S. government officials before proceeding to Nacogdoches, where he arrived in early October 1808. By the time he reached the Texas capital at Béxar at the end of the month, Salcedo must have been fully aware of the challenges that confronted him.

Manuel Salcedo took over the most exposed province of a colony under assault. Not only had Texas territory been compromised through establishment of the Neutral Ground Agreement in 1806, but the United States continued to claim the Rio Grande as the true boundary of the Louisiana Purchase. Also, various foreign agents had penetrated the province before his arrival. One of these, Zebulon Montgomery Pike, had succeeded in crossing the southern plains to arrive in New Mexico early in 1807. Treated well by the Spaniards, he collected considerable information on the state of Spanish defenses on the northern frontier, including conditions in Texas, through which he passed on his return to Louisiana. A year later another foreign adventurer, the Napoleonic agent Octaviano D'Alvimar, crossed from Louisiana into Texas with instructions to sow insurrection in New Spain. Captured by Texas troops, he was brought before Governor Cordero, who shipped him off to the interior before he could cause much harm to Spanish interests. The presence of runaway slaves and U.S. Army deserters also added to tensions.

The aggressive moves of the United States along the border were only one concern for Salcedo, who also had to consider recent events in Spain and Mexico City. Napoleon had forced the abdication of the Spanish Bourbon King Charles IV and his son Ferdinand VII in favor of his brother Joseph Bonaparte. That move had met with resistance both in Spain and throughout the colonies. From Mexico City had come news of an abortive move by the colonial capital's criollo elite to take over the government, an effort that had been frustrated by the powerful resident peninsulares. The peninsulares replaced a pro-criollo viceroy with one of their own. Eventually word arrived that a revolutionary Cortes (parliament) in Spain had declared the empire a constitutional monarchy. Traditional lines of authority were being disrupted, the legitimacy of the crown was being questioned, and misinformation and disinformation were rife.

Conditions, therefore, were ripe for an Anglo American move against Texas, and Salcedo pleaded for reinforcements and extensive economic investment in the province. His request was grounded in what he perceived to be essentially a problem of political economy. Like his predecessor, Salcedo considered the government responsible for existing conditions because it had failed to provide the necessary resources with which Tejanos could develop the province.

> The industry of these inhabitants is nonexistent, because neither have they had nor do they have elements for it. And one even marvels at how most of them cultivate their lands without the necessary farming tools by substituting for them as best they can, how some have built houses without artisans and how others suffer the rigorous cold and hot weather in those homes that they have made with sticks and shed-roofs of straw, and lastly at how in this poverty they have been able to dress themselves and their families, since this province has no other port of entry than that of Veracruz distant more than five hundred leagues.

Certainly there was some exaggeration in the governor's description of the situation, but not much. A few families at San Antonio and a few at La Bahía and Nacogdoches were living above a subsistence level, enjoying the meager profits of the livestock trade, an occasional sale of provisions to the local military, or participation in contraband activities. The province's few artisans could not practice their crafts on a regular basis, but relied on subsistence agriculture to make ends meet. If not for the military payrolls, there would have been practically no business for the few legitimate merchants, who themselves combined a variety of economic pursuits and credit schemes to keep their doors open and feed their families.

Governor Salcedo's plans required money and more communication between Texas and the outside world, of course, and Commandant General Salcedo was not in a position to grant the former or allow the latter. A port at Matagorda Bay would only create increased opportunities for smuggling and illegal immigration from Louisiana. The expense of raising, equipping, and maintaining the kind of force Governor Salcedo proposed was impossible. No, Texas would have to get by on what it already had.

Short of resources (his uncle would not even permit him to hire a secretary), Governor Salcedo took up the task of reforming the frontier province in every imaginable way. He issued orders on the proper preparation and filing of legal documents and he attempted to increase the efficiency of the mail system. He reorganized troop deployments, hoping to put soldiers lacking weapons to work on military construction projects for which no labor funds were available. Officials at La Bahía and Nacogdoches were snowed under by Governor Salcedo's constant requests for information and detailed instructions on just about every issue. In particular, they had to adjust to the commandant general's change of heart regarding immigrants, as the governor ordered that former Spanish subjects from Louisiana were to be received openly and warmly in Texas.

At San Antonio de Béxar, capital of Texas since 1773, Governor Salcedo took a personal hand in bringing order to a people that previous governors had considered unruly and untrustworthy. He issued ordinances on everything from the licensing of midwives to the licensing of ox carts (in effect, the first vehicle registration law in Texas history). He restructured local government and organized the countryside into police jurisdictions. He established a curfew, instituted a noise ordinance, and required owners to keep their properties clean and well maintained. Unfortunately for Manuel Salcedo and the other representatives of the Spanish monarchy, these last efforts at enlightened government could not hold back the tide of rebellion that began to sweep New Spain toward independence.

## Insurrection on the Frontier

The urgency of Governor Salcedo's appeals to the loyalty and patriotism of Tejanos intensified as rebellion broke out in the central parts of the viceroyalty. At the beginning of the nineteenth century New Spain was rife with the social and economic contradictions that have often made for revolution. A tiny percentage of the population lived in opulence in Mexico City, Guadalajara, and a handful of other major urban centers, whereas the overwhelming majority of colonial Mexicans lived in abject poverty. Although the silver mines of the colony remained the driving engine of the economy, most people relied on subsistence agriculture for a living. In the very small manufacturing sector, consisting mostly of second-class textiles and ceramics, as well as on the large agricultural estates, abusive labor practices predominated.

### The Causes of the Mexican War of Independence

Spanish colonial institutions were antiquated and corrupt. The church represented the largest and richest property owner in the colony, recipient of a tithe that the government collected for it and beneficiary of innumerable bequests. The church, consequently, served as the colony's principal landlord and lender. Yet, in the countryside many parish priests lived a poor, hand-to-mouth existence that led many to become disaffected. Exploitation of the rural Indian and *castas* population also came at the hands of an underpaid and, therefore, extremely corrupt local officialdom. Bourbon reform efforts ultimately failed to solve any of these problems, as they only replaced one group of corrupt petty officials with another. Although the *intendentes,* the regional administrative heads who exercised considerable economic and political power, were themselves well educated and well paid, their local subordinates, known as *subdelegados*, were not, and they came to rely on graft and extortion just as the *alcades mayores* and *corregidores* they replaced had.

Compounding these problems, which to one degree or another were endemic to most polities of the time, was the complex and oppressive ethnic ordering of society inherent in the *sistema de castas*. Spanish colonial society, which consisted of about 6 million people at the turn of the century, was divided into two large groups, the *república de indios* and the *república de españoles,* with separate codes of law governing each. Mexico's 3.5 million Indians remained perpetual wards of the crown, with a protective legal structure governing their economic and political dealings. The overwhelming majority lived in ancestral villages, spoke their native languages, and practiced syncretic forms of Catholicism. Local representatives of the crown took advantage of their authority over the Indians to exploit their labor and monopolize business dealings with them.

The rest of the population, about 15,000 *peninsulares,* 1 million *criollos,* and 1.5 million *castas*—the *república de españoles*—was governed by a legal code that operated on the assumption that all men were not created equal. Punishment for criminal offenses was based on ethnicity: Spaniards often received fines whereas the *castas* were subject to corporal punishment of varying degrees. The legal code, which was intended to preserve the position of Spaniards, dictated who could ride a horse, carry different types of weapons, and wear certain types of clothing. "Purity of blood" did matter, even to the point of restricting the access of *castas* to membership in some of the religious orders.

The legal distinctions among the various social groups extended to opportunities for advancement in both the public and private sectors. The late Bourbon push to entrust positions of higher authority such as *intendente,* bishop, and high court judge to *gachupines* (a derogatory term for European Spaniards) troubled the considerable number of well-educated *criollos* who saw their prospects limited. In the many guilds and associations that governed New Spain's economy *castas* could not hope to rise to the top ranks of the organization or fully participate in the government. Although *criollos* made up the overwhelming number of hacienda and mine owners and occupied the vast majority of local government posts, they did not run the viceroyalty. Although blacks, mulattos, and mestizos made up the bulk of the non-Indian population, they were denied full opportunities for personal advancement.

At the same time that the crown and its advisers were consolidating power and "modernizing" the empire in Madrid, they were ignoring the needs and wishes of their colonial subjects. In America, meanwhile, *criollos* were developing a sense of nationalism. American-born Spaniards began to resent the superior attitude and privileged status of *gachupines* and advocated a new relationship to mother Spain. *Criollo* intellectuals began to feel pride in their early civilizations and to regard their accomplishments as no less worthy than those of ancient European societies. They challenged the idea that the New World environment was intrinsically inferior to that of the Old World. The American provinces were no different from, and certainly not inferior to, the European possessions of the crown, and the American colonies should be governed by Americans.

Added to this long-simmering disaffection, economic and political upheavals in the first decade of the nineteenth century precipitated insurrection. First, cut off from its American possessions by whichever enemy—England or France—it happened to be fighting at the time, Spain's normal commerce was disrupted; European imports flooded colonial markets, disrupting domestic manufacturing.

Second, in 1804, desperate for revenues with which to fund its war effort, the crown confiscated church assets, eliminating the single largest source of available capital in the viceroyalty. Third, drought late in the decade produced famine and widespread rural unemployment, especially in the Bajío, the colony's most productive economic region. Fourth, although New Spain's elites unanimously rejected Joseph Bonaparte as their sovereign in 1808, a power struggle between the *criollo* and *peninsular* elites of the capital left the latter in control of the viceregal government.

## The Struggle Begins

In this atmosphere of political and economic turmoil, groups of discontented *criollos* and mestizos began to conspire to overthrow the government. One such group, centered at Querétaro, a major agricultural center in the Bajío, included the man who would come to be known as the father of Mexican independence, Miguel Hidalgo y Costilla, parish priest of the small agricultural town of Dolores. Hidalgo, along with the lower-rank military and political officials who made up the conspiracy, was a *criollo* of rather liberal bent and broad interests. The conspirators had read the writings of French Enlightenment thinkers and were informed about the political thought behind American constitutionalism. They did not entirely reject their ties to Spain, indeed Hidalgo never declared the outright independence of Mexico from the mother country, but they did believe that Mexico should be governed by Mexicans rather than *peninsulares*. Unlike the majority of their fellow *criollos*, whose fear of the masses kept them allied to the *gachupines*, they were willing to gamble on their ability to control the Indians and mixed-bloods who would bear the burden of fighting.

Unfortunately for the conspirators, their plans were discovered and Hidalgo had no choice but to launch his revolt before preparations were complete. In the early morning hours of September 16, 1810, the bells of his church signaled to townspeople and nearby peasants that something was wrong. He stepped out on the front steps of his church and made an impassioned speech to the gathering crowd. He said, in part, "my friends and compatriots, for us there no longer exist either king or tributes; this shameful burden fit only for slaves, we have borne for three centuries as a sign of tyranny and servitude, a terrible stain that we shall wash away with our own efforts." In contradiction to this first line of the speech, he is said to have ended it by uttering his famous *grito* (cry): "Long live Religion! Long live our Blessed Mother Guadalupe! Long live Ferdinand VII and death to bad government!"

News of the revolt made its way northward within days, where at first there seemed to be little support for expanding the insurrection. The north did not have large numbers of disgruntled and hungry Indians and had only a few *peninsulares*, so discontent in the region appeared to be under control. In fact, however, the same class of disaffected *criollos* and *castas* that existed in the more central portions of the colony also existed in the northeastern provinces. In addition, the large number of frontier troops, overwhelmingly locals serving either in the frontier presidio companies or in militia units, had conflicted loyalties. Unlike regular army troops these men had been recruited from the frontier population to serve as a sort of home guard. They were accustomed to fighting Indians to protect their homes. How would they respond to their Spanish officers' efforts to employ them against insurgents?

The answer to that question was alarming to royal authorities, as they discovered in December 1810. The military units in Nuevo Santander revolted against the royalist government when told to prepare to march on the rebels farther south. Early in January, the entire command of the well-liked but royalist Antonio Cordero defected when confronted by a rebel force of 7,000–8,000. When insurgent envoys arrived in Nuevo León soon thereafter, that province too allied itself with the insurrection. Of the northeastern Interior Provinces only Texas remained under royal control.

## Texas Joins the Revolt

In Texas Governor Salcedo desperately attempted to retain the loyalty of the inhabitants of the province. Arrests of suspected instigators (both Tejanos and outsiders), speeches on the need for loyalty to king and God, and assurances of the safety of the population from Indian attack did little to quell a growing unrest. From Natchitoches, American agents reported to the U.S. government that substantial numbers of Tejanos, including members of leading San Antonio families, were preparing to overthrow the royalist authorities. The troops stationed in Béxar were uneasy about the possibility of being marched south to confront the insurgents, in the process leaving their families exposed to Indian attack. This unease only increased with news of the revolt's spread through neighboring provinces.

Texas, however, was awash in disaffection. Some Tejanos were upset with the crown's lack of responsiveness to the needs of the province. For all of Governor Salcedo's efforts, there were few signs that the necessary investment in money and people were coming any time soon. At San Antonio, where the reforms of Governors Cordero and Salcedo had most affected traditional patterns of leadership, there was resentment. There was also resentment among those whose economic interests had been hurt by the military's efforts to curtail contraband. Even more critical was the anxiety that Salcedo had created among the troops when he announced that the entire garrison at San Antonio might have to march south against the insurgents.

The man who led Texas's first revolt against Spanish rule, Juan Bautista de las Casas, was himself a retired *criollo* militia officer. He later claimed he was a loyal subject of Ferdinand VII and that his sole purpose in deposing Governor Salcedo had been to prevent the province from falling into anarchy, but his actions indicated otherwise. Although his motives may never be known, much weighed against him: the participation of a number of known Hidalgo sympathizers and disgruntled citizens of San Antonio in his coup, his constant communications with the insurgency's leadership in the interior of Mexico, and his orders for the

Texas presidial troops at the beginning of the nineteenth century were poorly equipped to handle a well-armed adversary. Smooth-bore carbines and pistols, often in disrepair, were considered less reliable than the lance, short sword, and shield. Leather jackets with cotton padding provided added protection from arrows. (© *Ministerio de Educación, Cultura y Deporte. Archivo General de Indias, MP-UNIFORMES. Diseño de uniforme de las fuerzas de Caballería que guarnecen la línea de frontera de las nueve Provincias Internas de Nueva España, Soldado de Cuera, 1804*)

arrest of all *gachupines* in the province as well as anyone who did not recognize him as governor.

The Casas revolt, which took place on January 21, 1811, was on shaky ground almost from the very beginning, however. Many among the province's leading families had stayed on the sidelines, unwilling to risk alienating a government that, although it might not be as responsive as they wanted, still paid for the defense of Texas against hostile Indians. News of Hidalgo's defeat at Guadalajara on January 17 and the flight of the insurgent leadership toward the frontier contributed to the sense of unease among prominent Tejanos. Casas's own arbitrary rule antagonized members of San Antonio's elite families who rallied instead around Father Juan Manuel Zambrano, a native of Béxar with aspirations of his own.

On March 17, not three months after his assumption of power, Casas was overthrown by Zambrano and his supporters. Most of his followers quickly switched allegiance and royalist officials throughout the province soon took up their posts again. Restored to the governorship, Manuel Salcedo now governed a province that was very different from the one he had lost the previous January. The Comanches and Norteños resumed large-scale raiding, dissatisfied that Spanish officials no longer had the gifts and merchandise that had been the basis of the peace that had existed for a quarter century. Salcedo considered the 1,136 men who formed the province's military defense largely untrustworthy. They had already mutinied once, and they continued to be exposed to the revolutionary rhetoric of disloyal kinsmen and ever-present foreigners. Every day shortages mounted: Paper, clothing, candles, even horses, were all in short supply. But, most troubling of all were reports filtering in from Louisiana of preparations for an invasion of Texas by a force of insurgents and Anglo American mercenaries.

### The Struggle Takes a New Twist

The reports were not rumors. Mexican revolutionaries had fled to the United States at the time of Hidalgo's debacle and were attempting to enlist U.S. support for their cause. In the aftermath of the royalist capture and execution of Hidalgo on March 21, 1811, leadership of the war against Spanish rule devolved upon another cleric, Father José María Morelos, a mestizo whose more realistic grasp of the situation and better organizational skills brought him considerable initial success. Under his leadership a revolutionary congress finally declared independence from Spain, abolished slavery, and drafted a constitution for Mexico. Still, Morelos proved unable to convince enough *criollos* to back the cause. In November 1815 Father Morelos was captured and executed in southern Mexico. By that time Texas had experienced a second failed insurrection and was teetering on the brink of utter devastation.

José Bernardo Gutiérrez de Lara was a *criollo* and a native frontiersman. He had been born in the Rio Grande valley town of Revilla (now Guerrero Viejo, Tamaulipas) in 1774, the son of pioneer settlers in Escandón's colony. By 1810 he was a family man, a petty merchant, blacksmith, and, like many settlers of the area, a landowner. He was also disaffected. When the Hidalgo revolt erupted he immediately embraced the cause. As a result he played a prominent role in helping the insurgents achieve early success in Nuevo Santander.

The defeat of the rebellion in the early months of 1811 did not discourage Gutiérrez de Lara. Claiming to have been assigned to seek assistance in the United States, he traveled to Washington, D.C., in July. Although he failed to obtain overt assistance from the U.S. administration, it is obvious that Gutiérrez de Lara received tacit approval for his plans. Back in Louisiana by the spring of 1812, he met with local authorities and began recruiting for what eventually became the Republican Army of the North. His most important collaborator in organizing the invasion was a U.S. Army officer, Augustus Magee. The West Point graduate resigned his commission to take up military leadership of the Anglo American volunteers in the army, which came to consist of about equal numbers of Anglo Americans and Mexicans.

When the Gutiérrez-Magee expedition crossed the Sabine River in August 1812 it encountered little resistance and had quick success. It arrived in Nacogdoches to find the local troops unwilling to fight. In September, now grown to 300 effectives, the Republican Army of the North took Santísima Trinidad de Salcedo. Discovering that Governor Salcedo had marched to the Guadalupe River to obstruct their advance on Béxar, Gutiérrez and Magee turned southeast to La Bahía, where they occupied the presidio in early November. Between November 1812 and February 1813 the royalists besieged La Bahía, but were unable to dislodge the insurgents, who finally went after Salcedo's army as it retreated to Béxar. The royalists made one last stand about nine miles southeast of San Antonio on March 29. At the battle of Rosillo about 1,200 men under Colonel Simón Herrera met the approximately 800-man Republican Army of the North. Having lost hundreds of men, more than a thousand horses, all of his field artillery and most other equipment, Salcedo had no choice but to surrender. On April 1, 1813, the Republican Army of the North, under the command of Gutiérrez de Lara and Samuel Kemper, Magee's successor, took San Antonio. The first Texas republic was born.

## The First Republic of Texas

The process of nation building began with bloodshed. On the evening of April 3, Salcedo and his subordinates, a total of fourteen *gachupines,* were assassinated a few miles outside of Béxar as they were being "escorted" out of the province. Kemper and a number of other Anglo Americans were outraged by the brutal action. A declaration of independence adopted on April 6 and a constitution that the Mexican insurgents drew up in the following days completed the alienation of many Anglo officers, who took their leave and returned to Louisiana. According to the Constitution, the state of Texas was to be governed by a "president-protector," whose power would be shared only with a *junta* of five men that enjoyed a merely advisory role. Catholicism remained the established religion. If anything served to partially appease some of the filibusters, it was the constitutional provision for land grants of approximately 4,500 acres to each volunteer.

In short order factionalism overwhelmed the republicans. Gutiérrez de Lara and his supporters, mostly Mexican insurgents and sympathizers, faced off with the Anglo American volunteers and U.S. government agents, who perceived Gutiérrez de Lara as an arbitrary and divisive leader. Pressing for the removal of Gutiérrez de Lara was William Shaler, a U.S. State Department official who championed José Alvarez de Toledo as the solution for the problems of the republic of Texas. In the days following his arrival in Béxar on August 1, 1813, Toledo and Gutiérrez de Lara fought over control of the government. In the end, Toledo won and Gutiérrez de Lara withdrew to Louisiana.

By this time it was clear that Viceroy Calleja was determined not to allow the murders of Salcedo and the other Spaniards to go unavenged or to have Texas remain in the hands of filibusters. The man he charged with recovering control of the errant province was General Joaquín Arredondo, who had recently been promoted to commandant general for the eastern Interior Provinces. Arredondo had considerable experience fighting insurgents in the north, having served as military governor of Nuevo Santander and having put down the rebellion in that province in 1812. With an army of over 1,800 men, Arredondo moved north toward San Antonio in early August for a final showdown with the Texas insurgency.

On August 18, 1813, Arredondo's royalist army fought Toledo's 1,400-man Republican Army of the North a few miles south of the Medina River, near the Laredo-San Antonio road. The daylong battle was a complete disaster for Toledo's army of Mexicans, Anglo Americans, and Indians. Colonel Ignacio Elizondo, the man who had captured Hidalgo, was now turned loose on the fleeing insurgents. With a 200-man force he pursued what remained of the Republican Army of the North northward and by September had reached Nacogdoches. He reported having executed 71 rebels and taken over 100 people captive, mostly women and children. Arredondo, meanwhile, had executed hundreds more and imposed martial law in San Antonio. He began his final, and rather inflated, report on the campaign: "The ever victorious and invincible arms of our Sovereign, aided by the powerful hand of the god of war, have gained the most complete and decisive victory over the base and perfidious rabble commanded by certain vile assassins ridiculously styled a general and commanders." Texas was again in the royalist fold.

## A Howling Wilderness

Spanish Texas in the fall of 1813 was a land devoid of hope. From across the border in western Louisiana, Juan Martín Veramendi, Francisco Arocha, Vicente Travieso, and Francisco Ruiz, all Tejanos who had participated as local leaders in Gutiérrez de Lara's republican experiment, heard the news that they were not included in the general amnesty granted to contrite rebels. Yet others, such as Erasmo Seguín, were caught between loyalties. The one-time Béxar postmaster and leading member of Zambrano's revolt against Casas had been accused of providing letters of introduction for insurgents, for which crime all of his property had been confiscated. It took years for him to clear his name. Some unrepentant Tejano insurgents continued to work actively against Spanish rule. One such insurgent was Vicente Tarín, a former officer in the Alamo Company who had joined the Gutiérrez-Magee expedition. He organized a small company of like-minded men and roamed throughout northern Texas, bartering with the Indians and inciting them against the Spaniards. For the general population of Texas, even those who had remained steadfastly in the royalist camp, the abandonment of crops, the sequestration of property, impressment into military or other public service, and the constant menace of Indian attack meant a precarious existence.

### Indians, Filibusters, and Pirates

One Tejano who saw his fortunes rise was Ignacio Pérez. Descended from original military settlers and Canary Islanders, he had become a prominent rancher and militia officer at Béxar. He was also a staunch loyalist (his daughter was married to former governor Cordero). Among his services to the crown would be an eight-month stint as interim governor of Texas between 1816 and 1817. Pro-

Presidio La Bahía, which by the early nineteenth century consisted of a stone enclosure with battlements, was the scene of repeated attacks by insurgents and filibusters. The fortification has been rebuilt by the diocese of Victoria and today serves not only as a museum, but as a favorite living-history location for reenactors of the Texas War of Independence. (© *Cathi M. Bunn*)

moted to lieutenant colonel for his service against the Gutiérrez-Magee expedition, he became a trusted field commander in the Indian war that followed the insurgency.

Hostilities with Comanches, Wichitas, and other Norteños had already been going on for years by then, brought on by a combination of factors over which Spanish authorities had little control. With the onset of Hidalgo's revolt, crown resources for placating Indian demands completely dried up. Wichitas and Comanches, formerly enemies of the Lipan Apaches, now joined together with them to raid Spanish settlements from San Antonio to the lower Rio Grande valley, causing settlers to abandon San Marcos de Neve, Santísima Trinidad de Salcedo, and many of the ranches south of the Nueces River.

By the time Antonio Martínez arrived in Texas to take over as governor in May 1817, things had reached the breaking point. Agriculture in the province had completely broken down and grain shipments from Coahuila were unreliable and inadequate to meet Texas's needs. With Ignacio Pérez and most of the other able-bodied men in the province impressed into active militia service, cultivation of even subsistence crops proved extremely difficult.

The situation was not new, but it had become critical as Texas faced a new wave of invasions from the United States and beyond. In late 1815 a former U.S. military officer and member of the Gutiérrez-Magee expedition, Henry Perry, organized a successful though minor invasion of Galveston Bay and occupied the mouth of the Trinity River. He was joined in the area in September 1816 by Louis Michele Aury, a pirate who had sold his services to a group of New Orleans conspirators intent on turning the Mexican War of Independence to their own advantage. Setting up headquarters on Galveston Island under the authority of Mexican rebel agent Manuel de Herrera, Aury was soon joined by other pirates, the brothers Jean and Pierre Lafitte. Spanish authorities, aware of these activities, could do little but stay informed and bide their time.

An abortive invasion of Mexico agreed upon by Perry, Aury, and the newly arrived insurgent Francisco Xavier Mina in April 1818 became the basis of the first filibustering expedition since Gutiérrez-Magee. After a fallout among the three leaders, Perry decided to lead his men to La Bahía. When Governor Martínez received word of Perry's arrival at Matagorda Bay, he transmitted the information to Commandant General Arredondo, along with a general assessment of how things stood:

> The pitiful condition of [La Bahía commander] Castañeda's few forces—in addition to his lack of supplies for subsistence, they are unmounted and barefooted—does not permit him even to select parties to go out on observation duty and those whom he does send in this condition go at full risk, and I am almost in the same situation. Now I cannot furnish him any kind of assistance. In regard to the forces, I have fifty men at Río Grande to transport corn, as I have already told you, and 100 men commanded by Lieutenant Colonel *Don* Ygnacio Pérez have had to go out to punish large bands of Indians who raid us quite frequently. I am alone in this capital with thirty or forty men, most of whom are ill, and I cannot count on those who are not because they are on foot and the arms they have are useless. My sole protection depends on the few citizens who without exception are in exactly the same condition I have said the troops are in.

Fortunately for the royalists, on June 18 one of Martínez's subordinates caught up with Perry and his forty-three men north of La Bahía and defeated the filibusters.

Despite the problems, and his limited ability to carry out any consistent reconnaissance beyond the vicinity of Béxar and La Bahía, Martínez was resourceful enough to confront the major challenges that presented themselves in the last three years of Spanish rule. Certainly the presence of the Lafitte brothers, who had usurped Aury's position in Galveston, was not a critical issue for the Texas governor. The pirates were interested in maritime conquests and Texas was receiving no seaborne traffic that might be affected. The Indians too were an intractable problem, but they had been so for a century. No, the challenge that concerned Martínez was the one posed by foreign invaders who might seize Texas.

One such challenge arose in 1818, when a large group of Napoleonic exiles attempted to establish a French outpost on the Trinity River. Charles Lallemand, a general in Napoleon's armies, led more than 150 men and a few women and children to a spot near the present town of Liberty, where they built a fort called Champ d'Asile. Although Lallemand claimed that his followers were peaceful agricultural colonists, the military nature of the encampment—with 600 muskets and 12,000 cartridges—and the failure of the colonists to clear land and plant crops points to other purposes. From the Spanish ambassador to the United States came word that Lallemand's intention was to occupy part of New Spain in order to proclaim Joseph Bonaparte king of Mexico.

Martínez could do little but send out scouting parties during the months following initial word of the arrival of the French. It was only in mid-September that Captain Juan de Castañeda, former commander at La Bahía and now in charge of the Alamo company, set out for the Trinity with 240 men. His orders, beyond expelling the French intruders, included driving out squatters and Indian traders, punishing the local Indians who had sided with the filibusters, and destroying the abandoned settlement of Nacogdoches. Fortunately for Castañeda, when he arrived at Champ d'Asile he found that the French had already abandoned the fort and taken refuge on Galveston Island. Although he sent an ultimatum ordering them to immediately depart or surrender, he had no boats to cross the bay and was in no position to attack. Neither was he in a position to carry out a punitive campaign against East Texas Indians or even to drive out squatters and illegal Indian traders. Castañeda had to be content to tear down the French fortifications and cabins and head back to Béxar.

## From the Adams-Onís Treaty to Mexican Independence

The good news that Captain Castañeda brought back from Galveston Bay marked a temporary improvement in Spanish fortunes in Texas. U.S. interests in the last remaining vestige of the Spanish empire in eastern North America brought more good fortune to Spanish authorities in New Spain the following spring. Although the United States had continued to claim Texas as part of the Louisiana Purchase, General Wilkinson's acceptance of the neutral ground in 1806 had weakened the U.S. position. During and after the War of 1812, Spanish Florida had become a haven for Creek and other Indians hostile to the United States, leading to two invasions of the province by Andrew Jackson's army. Expediency demanded that U.S. Secretary of State John Quincy Adams and Spanish ambassador Luis de Onís reach an agreement. In February 1819 they reached a compromise: Spain would keep Texas but give up Florida.

Perhaps Adams and President James Monroe concluded that Spain would not long be in control of Mexico and that Texas would naturally fall to the United States soon thereafter. Whatever the case, the Adams-Onís Treaty (also known as the Transcontinental Treaty) did not win the approval of western political interests, who had long been advocating Anglo American expansion in that direction. Certainly the speculators who had backed Perry, Aury, and Mina would not sit still for the Yankee secretary of state giving away American rights to Texas. Meeting in New Orleans in May, the group began organizing a filibustering expedition

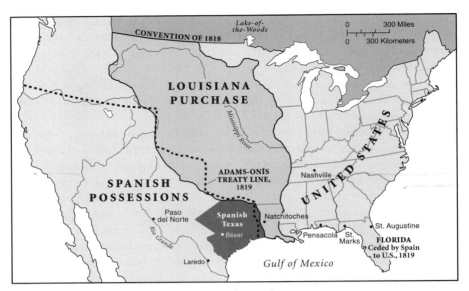

Texas at the end of the Spanish Empire in North America.

to "liberate" Texas from Spain. At Natchez too, irate citizens of the West organized to bring about a proper resolution to the situation. The conspirators found the man to lead the liberation of Texas in James Long, a Natchez merchant and veteran of the War of 1812.

What has come to be known as the first Long expedition began in June 1819, when an advance party of 120 men crossed the Sabine and occupied Nacogdoches. Long arrived later in the month and immediately organized a government that declared the independence of Texas on June 23, 1819. The document, drafted by Long and a group of Anglo American supporters, presumed to declare, "The citizens of Texas have long indulged the hope, that in the adjustment of the boundaries of the Spanish possessions in America, and of the territories of the United States, that they should be included within the limits of the latter." One of the new government's first acts was to grant each soldier in the army 6,400 acres as compensation for service. Within a month Long had more than 300 men at his service, including Mexican insurgent Bernardo Gutiérrez de Lara, Tejano rebel Vicente Tarín, the Anglo American Indian agent John Sibley, and former Spanish Indian agent Samuel Davenport.

To counter this new threat to Spanish sovereignty in Texas, Governor Martínez turned to Ignacio Pérez. The governor was unsure of the size of the threat—reports filtering in ranged from several hundred to several thousand invaders—but no better man could be entrusted with the mission than Lieutenant Colonel Pérez. Mustering 550 men, two cannons, 425 pack mules, and enough horses to provide each man with two or three remounts, the small army left Béxar on September 27,

1819. Pérez's instructions were not only to drive out all foreigners from East Texas, but to punish any Indians in the area who had supported the filibusters.

By the time Pérez and his now reinforced command of 650 men reached Nacogdoches, Long and most of his men had withdrawn to Louisiana. A few stragglers were captured, but the danger seemed to have passed. Pérez pardoned some of the remaining residents of Nacogdoches on the grounds that they had joined the rebels only because they could not resist.

The expedition returned to San Antonio by February 1820, a resounding though not total success. Pérez had captured forty-four Anglo American filibusters and Mexican rebels, not including a large group of squatters he had allowed to cross over into the Neutral Ground and the residents of Nacogdoches he had pardoned. Just as important, he had managed to free ten residents of Béxar, Laredo, and Camargo being held by the Comanches. He had also managed to take a large amount of booty, including valuable tools and dry goods. Pérez had not destroyed another squatter settlement at Pecan Point as he had wished to do, however, and he had not been able to establish a military post at Nacogdoches from which the Spanish could watch the border.

After fleeing to Natchitoches, the president of the Supreme Council of the republic of Texas proceeded to New Orleans. There he met with another Mexican insurgent, José Félix Trespalacios, a native of Chihuahua who had recently escaped a royalist dungeon in Mexico and was now preparing his own invasion of Texas. The two men decided to join forces and by early 1820 Long had established new headquarters at Point Bolivar. There he remained until September 1821, when, not having heard or not being interested in the news of Mexican independence, Long marched for La Bahía. He captured the presidio on October 4, but was forced to surrender to Ignacio Pérez, who was now in the service of the new Mexican nation.

The writing on the wall that Long had failed to see or chosen to ignore had been clearly visible for some time. A revolt by a Spanish army waiting to sail for Spanish America to put down independence movements had forced Ferdinand VII to restore the liberal Constitution of 1812. For *criollos,* many of whom had lost faith in the legitimacy of the Spanish government, the changes merely symbolized the continued instability of royal authority. One of these *criollos* was a royalist officer named Agustín de Iturbide. Sent into the field to crush the leading rebel, Vicente Guerrero, Iturbide instead reached an agreement with him for the separation of Mexico from Spain. The Plan of Iguala, signed by the two men on February 24, 1821, consisted of three important clauses: 1) the continued special status of the Catholic church in Mexican society, 2) the independence of Mexico as a constitutional monarchy, and 3) equality between *peninsulares* and *criollos.*

Curiously, many staunch royalists in northern New Spain, who until the beginning of the year had still been fighting the insurgents, accepted the inevitable with great aplomb. At his headquarters in Monterrey, Commandant General Arredondo took the oath pledging support of the Plan of Iguala in June and sent word to all his subordinates to do likewise. He soon resigned his position and withdrew to Cuba. In Coahuila Governor Cordero took the oath and continued in service to Mexico as commandant general of the western Interior Provinces until his death in 1823.

Hesitant to appear rebellious after carefully cultivating their royalist connections since August 1813, Béxar's leaders waited until the very last moment to endorse independence. On July 19, two months before Iturbide's triumphant Army of the Three Guarantees entered Mexico City, with a large part of the community drawn together in the main plaza, civilian and military officials, including Lt. Col. Ignacio Pérez, took the oath to the new nation. A few days later word arrived from La Bahía that its officials had also taken the oath. Spanish Texas was no more.

## Conclusion

In the second decade of the nineteenth century the progress of the previous century had been almost totally undone. The extent of the damage done by filibusters, insurgents, royal armies, and hostile Indians made Texas appear to be a "wild, howling, interminable solitude," to Stephen F. Austin as he traveled from the Sabine toward San Antonio in the summer of 1821. Austin's father, Moses, one of the Anglo Americans who had settled in Spanish Louisiana, had lost everything during the panic of 1819 and had looked to the green pastures and rich bottom lands of Texas to restore his fortunes. He had come to Béxar in December 1820 with a proposal to settle 300 Anglo American Catholic families on the Brazos or Colorado River. And Governor Martínez and Commandant General Arredondo had been so desperate to do something for the forlorn province that they had agreed to the plan.

A survey of what was left of Texas gives an idea of why Austin might have had big dreams for Texas and why Spanish officials would accept his offer. Salcedo and San Marcos, two towns established by Antonio Cordero in the first decade of the century, had been totally wiped out by the end of August 1813. Nacogdoches was a virtual ghost town, although a few buildings remained standing and a handful of families remained in the vicinity.

Texas, then, consisted of little more than the San Antonio River valley settlements of San Antonio de Béxar and La Bahía del Espíritu Santo, with a population of about 3,000. Ranches throughout the area were largely abandoned and most crop land lay fallow. The settlers of La Bahía were able to reap only a meager harvest that could not possibly meet even subsistence needs. The presidio company had no horses and remained barefoot. Conditions at San Antonio were equally bad. A major flood in July 1819 had added to the local misery, as had field fires intentionally set by hostile Indians. As a result, harvests were poor or nonexistent and the towns found themselves at the mercy of whatever convoys of corn and flour could make it up the road from Río Grande and Laredo.

Men who had not seen their homes for the better part of a decade, some with families, returned to Béxar, Nacogdoches, and La Bahía under such conditions.

Former royalists and former republicans were now all Mexicans. Surprisingly, it appeared to work. Ignacio Pérez continued to serve in the military as if there had been no change in sovereignty. Erasmo Seguín, who had been suspected of collaborating with insurgents but who had vehemently protested his loyalty to the crown, eventually represented Texas at the congress in Mexico City that framed the country's first republican constitution. Juan Martín Veramendi, who had been pardoned and had returned to San Antonio, soon reentered public life, first as a customs agent and later as chief executive of the state. Vicente Tarín and Francisco Ruiz, who had stayed on the run, were commissioned by the new government to negotiate with the Indians who had helped bring Spanish Texas to its knees.

Could this partnership between former enemies be successful and could it extend to the Anglo Americans so eager to make Texas their home? With the odds stacked against them, old-stock Tejanos and newly-minted Texians got to work on answering that question.

## SUGGESTED READINGS

Texas was no longer an isolated and backward Indian frontier province after 1800. Events over which colonial officials and Tejanos had no control thrust the poor and underpopulated colony into the thick of international politics and revolution. The literature on the major international events of this period—the Louisiana Purchase, the Aaron Burr conspiracy, the War of 1812, and the Napoleonic Wars—is too voluminous to discuss adequately here. Some understanding of the processes by which the Spanish empire collapsed, particularly in Mexico, can be gained from *The Independence of Latin America,* ed. Leslie Bethell (1987). In chapter 10 of *The Spanish Frontier in North America,* however, Weber provides a useful summary of events along the Spanish borderlands, as does John Kessell in chapter 13 of *Spain in the Southwest.* Don Chipman surveys the era from the Texas perspective in the aptly titled chapter 11 of *Spanish Texas,* "The Twilight of Spanish Texas, 1803–1821."

### Louisiana

Just as Spanish Texas had its beginnings in the French occupation of what eventually came to be known as Louisiana, so too is the end of Spanish Texas tied to its eastern neighbor. For the story of the most representative of the early intruders, see Maurine T. Wilson and Jack Jackson's *Philip Nolan and Texas: Expeditions to the Unknown Land, 1791–1801* (1987). Although Charles A. Bacarisse's doctoral dissertation on the Baron of Bastrop was never published, he did prepare an article summarizing his research: "Baron de Bastrop," *Southwestern Historical Quarterly* (1955). Extensive accounts of Spanish efforts to stop Anglo American penetration of Texas appear in *Jefferson & Southwestern Exploration: The Freeman & Custis Accounts of the Red River Expedition of 1806,* by Dan L. Flores (1984), and Jack D. L. Holmes, "Showdown on the Sabine: General James Wilkinson vs. Lieutenant Colonel Simon de Herrera," *Louisiana Studies* (1964).

## Fortress Texas

*The Opening of Texas to Foreign Settlement, 1801–1821*, by Mattie Austin Hatcher (1927; reprint 1976) remains unsurpassed in telling the story of Spain's desperate efforts to hold back the tide of Anglo American westward expansion. Spanish policy in Louisiana, which helped shape attitudes in Texas, is the subject of Gilbert C. Din's "Spain's Immigration Policy in Louisiana and the American Penetration, 1792–1803," *Southwestern Historical Quarterly* (1973). The colorful and competent Governor Antonio Cordero still awaits a biographer, but his successor has received much closer scrutiny in *Tragic Cavalier: Governor Manuel Salcedo of Texas, 1808–1813* by Félix D. Almaráz (1971). The problems these officials had in keeping undesirable people and ideologies from taking hold in Texas is the subject of Odie Faulk's "The Penetration of Foreigners and Foreign Ideas into Spanish East Texas, 1793–1810," *East Texas Historical Journal* (1964). Chapter 6 of F. Todd Smith's *The Wichita Indians: Traders of Texas and the Southern Plains, 1540–1845* (2000) gives considerable attention to the Indian side of Spanish troubles during this period.

## Insurrection on the Frontier

No period of Texas colonial history has received more attention than that of 1811–13, when the province was caught up in the whirlwind of the Mexican War of Independence. Julia Kathryn Garrett's *Green Flag Over Texas: A Story of the Last Years of Spain in Texas* (1939) remains a very readable narrative of the entire period. A number of more specialized studies add to or provide a different perspective on events. An essay appearing in *Tejano Journey, 1770–1850*, edited by Gerald E. Poyo (1996), "Rebellion on the Frontier," by Jesús F. de la Teja, discusses local political conditions, especially in San Antonio, and how these contributed to partisanship during the war of independence. A very interesting collection of documents related to the first revolutionary episode was translated by Frederick C. Chabot in *Texas in 1811; the Las Casas and Sambrano Revolutions* (1941). The story of how San Antonio's elites restored royal government is told by J. Villasana Haggard in "The Counter-Revolution of Béxar, 1811," *Southwestern Historical Quarterly* (1939). A good summary of the Gutiérrez-Magee expedition that is also a detective story about the author's efforts to pin down the site of the battle of Medina is Ted Schwartz, *Forgotten Battlefield of the First Texas Revolution: The Battle of Medina, August 18, 1813*, edited and annotated by Robert H. Thonhoff (1985).

## A Howling Wilderness

The history of the last years of Spanish Texas has been given over to stories of pirates and filibusters. The classic study in the field is Harris G. Warren, *The Sword Was Their Passport: A History of American Filibustering in the Mexican Revolution* (1943). Other useful readings include Fane Downs, "Governor Antonio Martínez and the Defense of Texas from Foreign Invasion, 1817–1822," *Texas Military History* (1968), and Ed Bradley, "Fighting for Texas: Filibuster James Long, the

Adams-Onís Treaty, and the Monroe Administration," *Southwestern Historical Quarterly* (1999). The story of French exiles who made a brief, unsuccessful attempt to establish themselves on the lower Trinity River is told by Kent Gardien in "Take Pity on Our Glory: Men of Champ d'Asile," *Southwestern Historical Quarterly* (1984). On the ever-popular Jean Laffite story, Jack C. Ramsay, Jr.'s *Jean Laffite, Prince of Pirates* (1996) makes entertaining reading. The anticlimactic change of sovereignty is the topic of Félix D. Almaráz's *Governor Antonio Martínez and Mexican Independence in Texas: An Orderly Transition* (1979).

PART **II**

# DEFINING TEXAS

In 1821 the Mexican government, newly independent from Spain and seeking ways to populate its northern frontier, permitted a colony of families from the United States to settle on the coastal and blackland prairie lands of southeastern Texas. This officially sanctioned effort led to other colonization attempts by and for immigrants from the United States and Europe, and to independent immigration. As a result, Texas developed along new political, social, and economic trajectories. The present-day state took shape, and a distinctive Texas identity was forged, but not without tremendous struggles or significant costs.

Initially, the newcomers agreed, at least nominally, to abide by the rules and regulations of the Mexican government and the Catholic faith. Most had been propelled westward by the prospect of cheap and fertile farmlands, but increasingly they were joined by adventurers looking for diverse political and economic opportunities. Arriving primarily from the southern states, the immigrants adopted some Mexican practices and policies but held allegiances to the U.S. form of government and to the southern agricultural system in which cotton was central and slave labor was promoted.

The settlers' view of the government's role in their lives clashed with the realities of their status as remote residents of a vast Mexican state, Coahuila y Texas, and with the government's turn away from republican reforms included in the 1824 Mexican Constitution. In the quest for increased political recognition and autonomy that ensued, new Texans—together with disaffected Tejanos—acted from a mix of idealistic, practical, and self-serving motives. At first calling for recognition of Texas as a separate Mexican state, they soon called for—and won—independence from Mexico.

Most voting Texans were in favor of annexation to the United States as the next step, but in this desire they were rebuffed by a U.S. government wary of Mexico's reaction and of bringing another slave state into the Union.

So, rather haphazardly, Texas not only became a nation but remained one for almost a decade. Rejected by the United States, still threatened by a Mexico that refused to recognize Texas independence, harassed by Comanche raids, and struggling economically, Texans developed a strong sense of their separate identity and even entertained dreams of empire. They sought to claim most of present-day New Mexico as part of the Republic, and some contemplated extending Texas's rule into Mexico or to the Pacific.

Such grand imperialistic vision and pride in "going it alone" did not disappear when Texas was eventually annexed as a state in a changed U.S. political climate. Although Texans voted decisively for statehood, knowing the stability and development possibilities it would confer, they continued to nurture a sense of their own exceptionalism. The U.S. government reinforced this feeling by allowing the state to control its own land sales, for example, and paying the Texas government to relinquish its New Mexican land claims.

At the same time, however, Texans were firmly developing their state's southern identity. Statehood increased the flow of immigrants from the American South. Gins overflowed with "King Cotton." A planter class wielded political, social, and economic power. African Americans were held as slave labor, and Tejanos were pushed to the periphery of public life and cut off from economic opportunity. By the eve of the Civil War, the majority of Texas citizens were Anglo Americans who identified with the systems and philosophies of the antebellum South.

Thus, in 1861 Texas voters overwhelmingly favored secession from the Union that they had entered in 1846. Although a few flirted with the idea of independent nationhood once more, most were ready to join the Confederate States of America in its assertion of states' rights and its defense of the southern slave system.

There were dissenters, and the war years brought not only privation and loss of Texas soldiers but severe tensions among Texans themselves. Many Unionists were killed for their beliefs. The war years also exposed other serious problems within the state, such as lack of adequate frontier defense along the western border of settlement and lack of industrial development to sustain a war effort.

The defeat of the Confederacy was felt as bitterly in Texas as in other southern states. An Anglo majority had defined the state based on an agricultural system that was no longer politically or morally acceptable. Cotton remained Texas's premier cash crop, but it could no longer be the fulcrum of political, social, and economic power. The plantation system had been broken, and new forms of economic enterprise were developing, born along on the burgeoning tracks of the railroads that not only connected the settled regions but helped open up West Texas for settlement and development.

Reconstructionists sought to dismantle the old political structure in favor of one in which Unionists and African Americans participated freely. Although the plantation system had been broken, however, old political structures and beliefs were harder to erase, and in the gubernatorial election of 1874, antebellum southern forces regained much of the power they had lost. Theirs was still essentially an agrarian vision, and one strongly favoring Anglo hegemony. But new social and economic forces coalescing would force new definitions for Texas, including new political ones. ■ ■ ■

# 6

# The Americanization of Texas, 1821–1835

He had been unsure of the venture at first, so much so that his father had written, "I hope and pray you will Discharge your Doubts, as to the Enterprise." But trusted friends had been enthusiastic, and all the arrangements had been made. In Natchitoches, Louisiana, a delegation headed by Erasmo Seguín met twenty-seven-year-old Stephen Fuller Austin and in July 1821 escorted him across the Sabine into Spanish Texas, where he was to meet his father Moses and commence their colonizing work. Barely had the traveling party started, though, when word came of Moses's death in Missouri. Now it would be up to Stephen F. Austin himself to start the Anglo colony that had been his father's dream. As the party moved deep into the interior of Texas, to the Brazos River and beyond, he encountered few settlers; aside from the reduced settlement of Nacogdoches through which he had passed, most of the Mexican population was concentrated at San Antonio de Béxar and far off along the Rio Grande. He saw no Indians. Austin noted with enthusiasm the abundant wildlife, the fertile soil, the clear-running rivers, the pleasing way in which woodland alternated with prairie. He was bound for San Antonio, hoping and trusting that the Mexican officials there would allow him to carry out his father's deathbed wish that his son replace him in the Texas enterprise. Outside the town, an advance party returned with the news that Mexico had declared its independence and Texas was no longer under Spanish rule. This news posed another complication for Austin, but by now he was fully committed to the vision of a U.S. colony flourishing in Texas. His work toward that end would prove crucial to the reshaping and redefining of nineteenth-century Texas.

| | |
|---|---|
| 1821 | Stephen F. Austin arrives in Texas and proceeds with his father's colonization plans |
| 1824 | Federalists create a republican constitution for independent Mexico; Mexican Congress passes National Colonization Law; Texas becomes part of Mexican state of Coahuila y Texas |
| 1826 | Empresario Haden Edwards and his supporters stage the Fredonian rebellion |
| 1828–29 | Gen. Manual Mier y Terán travels in Texas and reports back to Mexican government |
| 1830 | Law of April 6 seeks to greatly restrict U.S. immigration into Texas |
| 1832 | First Anahuac disturbance erupts in conflict between garrison commander and colonists; Texas colonists, including a Tejano delegation from Goliad, hold convention to take concerns to Mexican government |
| 1833 | Santa Anna is elected president of Mexico as federalist but moves quickly toward centralist rule; second colonist convention convenes and prepares a provisional state constitution |
| 1834 | Stephen F. Austin is arrested in Saltillo, returning from Mexico City to Texas |
| 1835 | Second Anahuac disturbance reflects, helps stimulate political unrest in Mexican Texas |

## Colonization Efforts, 1821–1829

In San Antonio, Spanish governor Antonio María Martínez continued to oversee the political affairs of Texas in the wake of Mexican independence. Mexico's independence both followed upon and fed the country's severe economic distress and political divisiveness, ensuring that the new nation would be unable to mount colonization efforts from within to protect its northern frontier. Having originally accepted Moses Austin's settlement project as a necessary means of building and reinforcing Mexico's Texas frontier, Martínez now approved of Stephen Austin's moving forward with it. Other Tejano leaders, too, welcomed Austin's efforts, as evidenced by the guidance and counsel of Erasmo Seguín, Juan Martín de Veramendi, and other political and cultural leaders who wished to build on mutual interests: the economic development and political stability of Texas.

### Austin's Colony

Governor Martínez asked the younger Austin to devise a plan for land grants to the colonists. Austin complied, specifying that families would receive 320 acres of farming land and 640 acres of grazing land, with extra allotments provided to the head of the household for each family member and each slave. From the beginning, then, the extension of antebellum slavery from the American South characterized the Americanization of Texas, despite Mexican objections to the practice.

Austin found that the region his father and Mexican officials had been considering for colonization would indeed sustain agricultural settlers. It stretched southward from the Nacogdoches–San Antonio trail he had just traveled, encompassing a sweep of present-day Southeast Texas. In surveying the region after his initial visit to San Antonio, Austin observed not only pleasing pastoral vistas but plenty of timber, water, and good river-bottom soil. His first colony would be bordered on the east by the San Jacinto River, on the west by the Lavaca, with long, fine stretches of the Brazos and the Colorado between them. This constituted the best farming land in Texas. Initially, Austin would obtain an empresario grant for the land all the way to the coast, where these rivers emptied into the gulf and where ports could be established.

Austin's contract specified that he could settle 300 families, and he had begun recruiting efforts before leaving New Orleans. In December 1821, his colonists began arriving and locating along both the Colorado and the Brazos. Overwhelmingly, the newcomers were American farm families of English origin migrating from nearby U.S. states, especially Louisiana and Alabama.

Barely had the settlement begun when Austin made his way to Mexico City to get his grant confirmed by the government there. He spent almost a year in the Mexican capital, witnessing a dizzying array of political reversals: Augustín de Iturbide was crowned emperor; one congress dissolved to be replaced by a junta

Stephen F. Austin led the colonization of Texas from the United States. This watercolor, done by British artist William Howard in 1833, highlights Austin as a pioneer leader even as empresario Austin faced some of his most intense challenges in the role. *(Prints & Photographs Collection, CN 01436, The Center for American History, The University of Texas at Austin)*

charged with congressional duties; a rebellion spread; the federal cabinet was pressured into resigning; another congress convened; and Iturbide abdicated.

Out of all of this turmoil, however, came a generous colonization law for Mexico's Texas frontier and specific approval for Austin's effort. The Imperial Colonization Law of 1823 set up an empresario system that surpassed Austin's initial allotments, offering a square league, or *sitio,* of about 4,428 acres to each family involved in stock raising and a *labor* (Spanish colonial unit of cropland), or 177 acres, for a family's farming operation. It provided further inducements as well, such as a six-year moratorium on taxes. Austin would not receive payment for his colonization efforts from the government until he had settled at least two hundred families, at which point he would receive choice lands of his own. Until then, he had to rely on the moderate fee he charged settlers to offset his surveying and administrative costs, although he offered to accept whatever items of value the colonists might have to offer, from beeswax and deerskins to livestock.

During the period from 1821 to 1824, Austin would exceed the 200-family requirement for his own land, and by 1827 he would approach the projected number of settlers, with 297 families, later referred to as the "Old Three Hundred," receiving land titles. By the terms of settlement laid out in 1823, they were to be "of unblemished character, good Morals, Sobriety, and industrious habits," each man "also hav[ing] sufficient property to begin with either as a farmer or mechanic besides paying for his land." They were also supposed to be Catholics; for the overwhelmingly Protestant settlers, this was a conversion in name only. Austin would have to remind them repeatedly that "the Roman Catholic is the religion of this nation."

As a group, Austin's colonists had high literacy rates for the era and were people of some means. Of those who had settled by the fall of 1825, sixty-nine families possessed slaves. Jared Groce of Alabama, the wealthiest colonist, brought with him ninety slaves whose labor quickly helped him consolidate his wealth and position in their new location beside the Brazos.

The Mexican government and Mexican public in general did not favor slavery, but the government allowed concessions to enhance the colonization efforts. Austin won the first such concession on that initial trip to Mexico City. He felt that the colony's success would depend in large part on its ability to attract slaveholders such as Groce—and would-be slaveholders—from the American South. The colonization law allowed slaves to enter Texas but did not allow slave trading, and it specified that the children of slaves should be freed at age fourteen. Austin won his colony's exemption from such measures. By 1825, slaves made up almost 25 percent of the population of 1,800 in Austin's colony. From the earliest years, then, the institution of slavery was a significant part of the economic development of Anglo Texas.

## Other Colonizing Efforts

As word of Austin's enterprise spread, other empresarios responded to the opportunities that Texas offered for colonization. And in its 1824 immigration law, the Mexican government declared itself "desirous of augmenting by all possible means the population of its territory; of encouraging the cultivation of its fertile lands, the raising of stock, and the progress of arts and commerce." The government sought to refine colonization laws, so that subsequent empresario contracts were somewhat different from that of Austin's first colony. But with a grant from the government and six years to settle a requisite number of families, these empresarios—primarily Anglo, but also Mexican, German, Scottish, and Irish—could promise families more land at a lower rate than what they could obtain in the United States and the opportunity to make their own fortunes in the bargain.

Martín De León, member of an aristocratic Mexican family, had petitioned the Spanish government as early as 1807 to establish a colony south of the land Austin claimed. De León had come to Texas in 1805 and developed a ranching empire. In 1824, he won a contract to locate forty-one Mexican families on the lower Guadalupe River. Although Mexican authorities had questioned De León's loyalties, he would be the only colonizer to bring predominantly Mexican families in to Texas.

Just to the north of De León, in 1825 Green DeWitt, a former Missouri sheriff, with the help of Austin and the Baron de Bastrop, was awarded a grant bordering Austin's on the west and was authorized to locate 400 families further inland on the Guadalupe. As with the other colonizers, his contract with the government

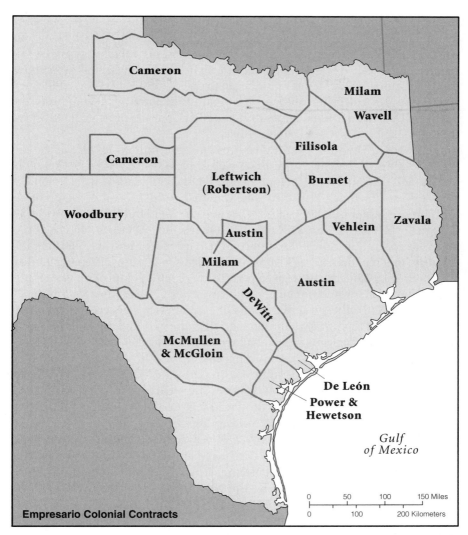

Map of Texas and adjoining states. Compiled by Stephen F. Austin. Published by H. S. Tanner, Philadelphia, 1836. Shows the boundaries of the empresario "grants."

specified that they were to be Catholic families of "good moral character"; DeWitt was not to admit "criminals, vagrants, or persons of bad morals," and should they enter the colony, he was to "cause them to leave the republic, by force of arms if necessary."

In each colony, a core settlement came into being. For Austin's, it was San Felipe de Austin, set on a bluff on the west bank of the Brazos River. San Felipe was never very prepossessing; adventurer and blacksmith Noah Smithwick would remember it in 1827 as "[t]wenty-five or perhaps thirty log cabins strung along the [river] bank," with "every fellow buil[ding] to suit himself." Yet San Felipe was vital to the colony's identity and to Americanization in general; it proved a fulcrum for political, economic, and social activity for colonists and newcomers from the United States. As San Felipe began to thrive, in 1824 De León established Nuestra Señora Guadalupe de Jesús Victoria on the lower Guadalupe, and the next year DeWitt's surveyor, James Kerr, founded Gonzales near the point where the Guadalupe and San Marcos rivers met.

Between 1825 and 1829, various empresarios and empresario companies won grants to most of present-day Texas, as well as parts of New Mexico, Colorado, Kansas, and Oklahoma, which Texas later tried to claim as its own. As a result of the Mexican Congress's National Colonization Law of 1824, they were not allowed to colonize within ten leagues of the gulf coast without federal approval, although Austin and De León successfully made cases for their own original grants to the coast. Mexican officials had hoped in vain for more Mexican colonizers and colonists to strengthen Texas's Mexican identity. On a map, entrepreneurs like Scotsman John Cameron were given permission to settle colonists on vast swaths of West Texas that would not be home to anyone but Native Americans until after the Civil War. Others received grants of land in Texas's eastern and southern regions, in closer proximity to the United States, the gulf, and the rest of Mexico. Arthur Wavell, an Englishman who had served as a brigadier general in the Mexican army and had assisted Austin in his colonization, in 1826 won a grant in northeast Texas, primarily consisting of what is now Red River, Lamar, and Bowie counties. Other Europeans with Mexican ties also secured grants. Irishmen James Power and James Hewetson had both located in Coahuila, engaging in mining and other enterprises, and in 1828 received a grant to settle both Mexican and Irish families in the coastal area between the Lavaca and Guadalupe rivers. John McMullen and James McGloin, also Irish merchants in Mexico, took over an empresario contract from two Anglo entrepreneurs in 1828 and brought Irish men, women, and children recently arrived in New York City to their colony in the brush country of South Texas.

By 1834, about 150 Irish families would be settled in the colonies of Refugio and San Patricio. Most of the colonizers, however, had little success in attracting a significant number of settlers: Only one-third would manage even to bring colonists to Texas. Even in East and Central Texas, empresarios experienced major difficulties.

## The Fredonian Rebellion

One difficulty the would-be colonizers had was encountering people who already occupied the land. These people included both Native Americans and earlier immigrants of European and Mexican extraction. On his initial surveying expedition, Austin had encountered a band of Cocos Indians, a branch of the Karankawas. Their meeting was peaceful, and Austin hoped to avoid conflict, but he anticipated that "there will be no way of subduing them but extermination." The dwindling Karankawas did not have a strong enough presence to challenge the part of Austin's colony that infringed on their traditional grounds. Instead, they moved in and out of the colony boundaries, quickly coming to be considered a nuisance and a threat because of occasional attacks they made on solitary colonists or small parties. The Tonkawas and other small tribes further inland had been weakened by the Spanish presence, wars with other Indian groups, and disease and cultural change. The Wacos and Tawakonis retained strength in their solid agricultural communities and intermittent alliances with the Comanches to the west and north, but these two groups, like the Tonkawas, became known primarily as horse stealers to Austin's colonists.

There were also immigrant Indian groups pressed westward by Anglo migration: Alabamas, Coushattas, Shawnees, Choctaws, Chickasaws, and Cherokees. The Cherokees figured in a major land dispute in the Nacogdoches area in 1825 and 1826. Empresario Haden Edwards, a wealthy former U.S. senator from Kentucky and Mississippi plantation owner, had lobbied with Austin for the colonization laws in Mexico City; for his efforts he had gained authorization to locate 800 families in Nacogdoches and to the west and south of the decimated far East Texas community. There were other groups, however, already established not only in the town but in the outlying areas. "Old settlers"—both Mexican and Anglo—had held on to their homesteads through the political intrigues and official neglect of the region and possessed their own land grants from the government. Shortly before Stephen F. Austin entered Texas, approximately sixty Cherokee families forced westward by Anglo settlement in Arkansas had crossed the Sabine and begun attempts to gain title to land in the Nacogdoches area. And various "squatters" had settled in the area, gambling on gaining title to land at some point.

Edwards antagonized the "old settlers" and even the squatters, some of whom had lived in the area for a number of years, by posting notices stating that they would have to document their land claims or their lands would be given to his colonists. When residents complied, Edwards questioned the validity of some of their titles. With those he judged legitimate, he attempted to extract payments, claiming that he was now empresario over the lands and charged more per grant than the government did, so the settlers would have to make up the difference.

The antagonism Edwards engendered only intensified after an election for *alcalde* in January 1826. Edwards's Irish son-in-law Chichester Chaplin, a lawyer recently arrived from Louisiana, garnered more votes than "old settler" Samuel Norris, a Maryland native. Norris's supporters claimed vote fraud, and in March 1826 political chief José Antonio Saucedo in San Antonio ordered that Norris be installed as *alcalde*.

In another blow for Edwards, the Mexican government soon judged that he was not abiding by the terms of his colonization contract and voided it. Edwards had already poured considerable money into the enterprise and had gathered around him colonists who shared his dissatisfaction with the turn of events. In

November, a group led by Edwards supporter Martin Parmer simply took captive a number of the key players in the political struggle, including Norris and Edwards himself. Edwards was quickly released, but members of his faction tried and convicted Norris and others of "oppression and corruption in office" and installed their own *alcalde.*

This was just the kind of extralegal maneuvering that Mexican officials had hoped to avoid by controlling the issuance of colonization contracts in the first place. Now Lieutenant Colonel Mateo Ahumada was dispatched from San Antonio with a force of dragoons and infantrymen. Edwards, his brother Benjamin, and Parmer responded by declaring the institution of a separate republic in the Nacogdoches region, the republic of Fredonia.

In doing so, they enlisted the support of the Texas Cherokees. Just north of Nacogdoches, occupying lands that were partially in the northern boundaries of Edwards' colonization grant and partially in the grant of empresario Frost Thorn, these immigrant Indians had cleared land, planted crops, constructed homes, and integrated themselves into the life of the region. Mexican officials saw them as a buffer against uncontrolled Anglo settlement. But they were regarded with suspicion by native tribes, by some officials, and by other settlers. The repeated and vigorous efforts of Cherokee representative Richard Fields and John Dunn Hunter to negotiate a land title from the government in Mexico had proven futile. The Cherokees could only surmise that they would again be forced out as more United States immigrants arrived.

The Fredonians had not recruited as many men for the cause as they hoped, and Benjamin Edwards turned to the Cherokees, offering them the land they currently occupied and much more land to the west if they would fight along with the Edwards faction. The Fredonian Declaration of Independence, then, claimed to speak for "the White and Red emigrants from the United States of North America" in its resistance to "an imbecile, faithless, and despotic government, miscalled a Republic." But as soon as they heard of the Cherokees' involvement, representatives of the Mexican government in Texas began trying to dissuade the Indian leaders by holding out the promise of a land grant from the government. Stephen F. Austin joined these government representatives; as the leading empresario in Texas, he took seriously his responsibility for the orderly implementation of colonization efforts as the Mexican government required. The Cherokee peace chiefs under Chief Bowl, also known as Duwali or Chief Bowles, heeded the government's counsel and withdrew their support of Edwards, going so far as to order the execution of Fields and Hunter in an attempt to reassure Texas authorities that they had no wish to foment trouble.

With Mexican troops and a militia from Austin's colony on the way, the Fredonian rebellion fell apart, and Haden Edwards escaped temporarily to Louisiana. The conflict had demonstrated to Mexican officials some of the dangers of allowing colonization from the United States, but the Edwards faction's failure to recruit many colonists, the Austin colony's response, and the reversal of

Cherraquis.

Cherokus: *Indigenes les C.U. du S. Amerique emigris aux environs de Nacogdoches.*

Cherokees who had been pushed westward preceded colonists from the United States and hoped to gain title to the East Texas lands they occupied. This watercolor of "Cheraquis" in Texas by Lino Sánchez y Tapia was based on descriptions from the 1828 Mier y Terán expedition. *(Lino Sánchez y Tapia,* Cheraquis, *plate xv, from the collection of Gilcrease Museum, Tulsa, Oklahoma)*

the Cherokees' position seemed to indicate that they could maintain peace, order, and governmental authority in the face of such threats.

### Continued Colonization Difficulties

Land disputes, however, continued to contribute to uncertainty and strife in Mexican Texas. Wavell's grant overlapped a section of southwest Arkansas. De León's boundaries were unspecified, and the Mexican government wound up including his colony within DeWitt's grant, leading to boundary clashes between De León and DeWitt, followed by boundary clashes between De León and Power and Hewetson.

Boundaries were not the worst of their problems. Empresarios had difficulties attracting colonists to regions remote from Mexican and U.S. supply centers. They also had trouble transporting those who responded and then following through on promises to provide basic services. Even East Texas was still remote from U.S. cities and supply routes. Austin and his colonists fared better than the others, and Austin extended his colonization grants northward, westward, and southward in a series of five grants, gaining land from the gulf coast to the heart of Texas. Austin's success was due to several factors: He captured some of the best river bottomlands for farming; his settlements were located close to major rivers and the gulf coast; there was only a limited threat from Indians in southeastern Texas; he had selected colonists of some means, education, and experience in reestablishing themselves successfully; and, finally, he paid constant attention to myriad aspects of the colonization, including the all-important relations with the Mexican government.

This does not mean that Austin or his colonists had an easy time of it. Austin learned Spanish and worked ceaselessly to cultivate government officials in Mexico City, in Coahuila, and in Texas, adjusting to frequent changes in government and government policy regarding empresario contracts. His work—and that of other empresarios and of Mexican officials in Texas—was complicated by the fact that the fledgling Mexican government was struggling against serious odds to administer the North American empire it had won from Spain.

After the 1823 abdication of Iturbide, who had sought to establish a constitutional monarchy in independent Mexico, there was political competition between two groups throughout the rest of the decade. Centralists were regarded as conservatives: They continued to favor old imperial models of government, including an authoritarian national government. Federalists looked in part to the United States for a more liberal alternative: They espoused republican principles and the transfer of many governmental powers to the Mexican states. The federalists, including Texas representative Erasmo Seguín, managed to pass a constitution in 1824 that resembled the U.S. Constitution in its emphasis on a free republic. A president with limited powers was to be elected every four years by the legislatures in the Mexican states, and a national Congress was to convene annually. The Constitution garnered enthusiastic support from Tejano and Anglo American leaders in Texas.

A more dubious development for Texas, especially with the two groups vying for control of the Mexican government, was the designation of Texas as part of a larger state of Coahuila y Texas. In fact, all of Texas from the Sabine to the Nueces was initially designated simply the "Department of Béxar." (Distant El Paso and other western Rio Grande settlements were part of the state of Chihuahua, whereas the far southern Rio Grande, now the tip of Texas, was included in the state of Tamaulipas.) This meant that the interests of Mexican citizens in Texas, whatever their origins, were subsumed into those of their larger neighbor Coahuila. Coahuila's state government was based in Saltillo, across the Rio Grande, deep in Coahuila, and high in the Sierra Madre Occidental mountain range. This relationship took on new importance in 1825, when the new federalist legislature passed a national colonization law giving the states authority over colonization contracts. Coahuila officials would decide who received these contracts in Texas. The leaders and people of both Coahuila and Texas, however, were ill served by a shifting government in Mexico City with limited ability to address the needs of far-flung areas.

Struggling with some of these external issues, Austin also worked tirelessly on internal issues in his colonies: dealing with Indian threats, administering land grants, setting up internal colonial civil codes, addressing disputes and potential disputes among colonists, and responding to colonist complaints against his administration, particularly in the matter of land grants, which many considered inequitable. He wielded extensive judicial power within his colonies without deviating significantly from Mexican codes of law or overstepping government control. His capital, San Felipe, remained a rude collection of cabins, its often-muddy, often-dusty thoroughfares still forested with raw tree stumps. Reports of crop failures and other woes in the colony made their way to U.S. newspapers and no doubt deterred some would-be colonists.

Those who settled in Austin's colony in these early years faced frontier isolation, danger, and crude living conditions. Mary Crownover Rabb, who arrived in Austin's colony from Arkansas as a young woman with her husband John in 1823, would remember, "We come to [the Colorado River] where LaGrange now is, but there was no house there then nor nothing but a wilderness, nor even a tree cut down to mark that place." They settled with relatives in the small community of Indian Hill, further upriver, but John grew impatient with the constant Indian depredations. The couple moved from one isolated farming location to another, camping out or creating rudimentary log shelters. In the U.S. colonial tradition,

Mary Crownover Rabb and her husband John were among Austin's "Old Three Hundred" settler families; Mary left a vivid and engaging account of frontier life. (*Prints & Photographs Collection, CN 00878, The Center for American History, The University of Texas at Austin*)

they produced what they needed at home: John constructed a loom and Mary sat under a tree weaving mosquito netting—"a thing quite indispensable," another early immigrant wrote—before their cabin was constructed. Later, often left alone with her children at the cabin for long periods, Mary dealt with her loneliness and Indians ranging nearby by working late into the night and sprinkling shelled corn on the floor for the family pigs, noting "by the time I got in the bed, all them little pigs would be in the house cracking corn until I would be asleep and the Indians gone and the pigs gone."

In other colonies, conditions were even more precarious. Noah Smithwick visited DeWitt's colony two or three years after its founding and found that the inhabitants, "consisting of a dozen families, were living—if such existence could be called living—huddled together for security against the Karankawas, who, though not openly hostile, were not friendly." Smithwick provided a particularly vivid picture of the lives of the women, who lamented "old homes and friends left behind" and did not share the men's excitement about hunting and exploring:

> They had not even the solace of constant employment. . . . There was no house to keep in order; the meager fare was so simple as to require little time for its preparation. There was no poultry, no dairy, no garden, no books, or papers. . . . no schools, no churches—nothing to break the dull monotony of their lives. . . ."

Despite the struggling character of the colonies, other colonizers continued to advance their own settlement plans, fired by the opportunity to gain access to vast tracts of land, develop a vision of settlement and trade, and add to their own status and wealth. In 1822 Sterling Robertson, a Tennessee plantation owner, joined other stockholders in a "Texas Association" planning a settlement in Mexican Texas. In 1825 his colleague Robert Leftwich secured a grant to settle 800 families in what is now central Texas but was unable to follow through. Robertson continued his attempts to recruit settlers in Tennessee and Kentucky but would not be able to advance the colonization under his own name until the 1830s. David G. Burnet, a New Jersey native, Ohio lawyer, and Louisiana trader with the Comanches on the Brazos, obtained a grant in central East Texas in 1826 and spent the following years trying to raise money and colonists for the enterprise. Joseph Vehlein, a German trader in Mexico, received two 1826 grants south of Burnet's, but also lacked the resources to follow through. Lorenzo de Zavala, an accomplished political leader in Mexico, obtained an empresario grant in East Texas between Vehlein's and the Sabine in 1829. One stimulus to colonizers and colonists was an 1829 homestead exemption rule provided by the Mexican government, which secured from creditors colonists' land and the tools to work it.

In 1830, however, the picture in Mexican Texas would change considerably, the challenges for colonizers growing more difficult. Spurred by a report from Mexican Brigadier General Manuel de Mier y Terán, officials within the Mexican government were questioning the wisdom of allowing colonization efforts from the United States.

# Growth of Political and Cultural Tensions, 1829–1833

In many ways, the government of Mexico had been accommodating to the colonizers and settlers from the United States. Not only had the federal government and the government of Coahuila encouraged immigration with generous land grants, but despite general Mexican opposition to slavery, exceptions were made for U.S. immigrants, and an 1828 decree declared that slaves would be considered contract labor or indentured servants. Even when President Vincente Guerrero officially abolished slavery in 1829, he issued an exemption for Texas. Yet political problems were mounting between the government and its citizens in Texas, particularly the newcomers from the United States.

## Tensions and the Law of April 6, 1830

There were four contributing factors to the tensions that existed in Texas at this time: First was the general restiveness of the recent immigrants under Mexican and empresario authority. A number of colonists and other immigrants settled on land without authorization, ignored the government's other conditions of residence, and sought at the local level to replicate American political and legal customs. In other words, many continued to think of themselves as Americans. Further, many continued to think of themselves as American Southerners—and to consider slaveholding an inalienable right, even as the Mexican government continued its efforts to restrict or end the practice in Texas.

The second factor was the dissatisfaction of Tejanos and immigrants alike with Texas's status as part of Coahuila y Texas. The 1827 Constitution of Coahuila y Texas provided for a twelve-person legislature: eleven representatives from Coahuila and one from Texas. A third factor was the federalist/centralist power shifts in Mexico. Tejano and Anglo leaders continued to favor the federalists, with their republican ideals and rejection of a strong, authoritarian central government. Yet a Coahuila y Texas state government that really worked for Texans could not develop in the fluid political climate of the 1820s, a fact that affected Tejanos as well as immigrants. Béxar's population and status as a political center declined in the 1820s, and the soldiers of its garrison, deprived of pay and necessities, became a drain upon the citizens rather than a ready market for their goods. Tejanos, like the immigrants, had little influence in Mexico City, and could only observe as centralists in 1829 firmly took control of the Mexican government.

The final factor was the Mexican government's own concerns over immigration from the United States. Whether federalist or centralist, officials watched this migration with growing alarm: It was neither as orderly nor as controlled as previous officials had envisioned. Adding to their concerns was the fact that U.S. President Andrew Jackson was trying to purchase much of present-day Texas for the United States. Although Mexican officials rebuffed these overtures, they found them disquieting evidence of American designs on Mexican soil. Also disturbing was the report they received from General Terán, who traveled on government business in Texas in 1828 and 1829. On an expedition called the Comisión de Límites (Boundary Commission), Terán moved northward through the American settlements to establish the Mexican-United States boundary on the east and north but also to assess the American presence in Texas.

Terán, who had served in the first independent Mexican Congress, working specifically on how the new nation could colonize its frontier regions, was disturbed by the "smoldering fires" he found. He spoke bluntly in an 1828 letter to President Guadalupe Victoria: "I am warning you to take timely measures. Texas could throw the whole nation into revolution." In Nacogdoches in particular, he found a lack of necessary authority and order. New immigrants from the United States were streaming in and simply appropriating plots of land, many of them "fugitives from our neighbor republic and bear[ing] the unmistakable earmarks of thieves and criminals," although he noted that some of these "have reformed and settled down to an industrious life." The Mexican population in Nacogdoches he judged "comprising what in all countries is called the lowest class—the very poor and the very ignorant." Terán found the population mix to be volatile, with Anglo immigrants, Indian immigrants, and slaves naturally growing restive in a Mexican Texas less restrictive than the American South.

On one issue, however, he found most Texas residents in agreement, from Austin's colony northward: the need to separate Texas from Coahuila. Terán cited reasons such as the impracticality of having to seek recourse from a state capital in Coahuila "so distant and separated from this section by deserts infected by hostile savages" and the friction resulting from "the mixing of [Texans'] affairs with those of Coahuila."

The general's subsequent report indicated that Mexico stood in real danger of losing Texas to the United States. He recommended that the government expend more effort in recruiting Mexican and European settlers, in developing trade with the Mexican interior, and in encouraging foreign trade along the gulf coast.

Terán's report formed much of the basis of the Law of April 6, 1830, a centralist decree that attempted to restrict and control American immigration into Texas. Among other provisions, this law halted most of the empresario efforts at colonization, and thus most U.S. immigration. It was clearly aimed at U.S. empresarios and immigrants, not Mexican or European colonization. With Terán's blessing, Austin won an exception for his colony and DeWitt's; the next grant, however, in 1831, went to Vincente Filisola, a Mexican official who was allowed to settle 600 families in East Texas with the understanding that they were not to be Anglo Americans. The Mexican government installed its soldiers, forts, and officials along Texas's border with Arkansas and Louisiana and along the gulf coast to discourage independent immigration. It also closed the legal loopholes on bringing slaves into Mexican territory. It made Mier y Terán commandant general for the Eastern Interior Provinces of Mexico, including Coahuila y Texas, and charged him with enforcing the new law—which was appropriate, but also ironic, as he had not recommended or anticipated some of its stricter provisions.

From the conservative Mexican perspective, however, officials were acting prudently to stem a threat to Mexican control of Texas. And from this perspective, the threat could still be considered manageable. The empresario attempts were faltering anyway; even DeWitt, despite a reprieve, would fail to fulfill his contract in 1831 and would not ask for a renewal. True, there were thousands of colonists and independent adventurers from the United States now inhabiting Texas after a decade of immigration, many of them with continuing allegiance to their own homeland, but they were not organized or united on any broad level. The most cohesive group might be said to have been Austin's colonists, but they numbered only a few thousand and often disagreed among themselves on political allegiance and governance questions. Other potential immigrants from the United States had stayed away, uncertain about American fortunes in Mexican Texas and uneasy as early as 1822 over its reputation as a haven for American criminals.

Yet the Law of April 6 drew the first stirrings of unified protest. Among the protesters were members of Austin's colonies and federalist Tejanos who still rejected the centralists and welcomed the economic and republican promise of the American influx. The federalist Tejanos were joined by political and economic leaders in Coahuila, other federalists who continued to welcome Anglo settlement and enterprise in their state. Austin himself still professed strong loyalty to the Mexican government, rejecting the criticisms he suffered from "bawling democrats who know nothing of liberty but licentiousness," but his loyalty had limits, as he indicated to T. F. Leaming in July 1830.

> As to my colony I can say that we have been true and religiously faithful in our acts and in our views, to Mexico—and so we will remain—but I also say that Mexico cannot oppress us alive—we may be overwhelmed & anihilated—but we cannot be treated like children nor like slaves. . . .

With more Mexican soldiers at Nacogdoches, Goliad, and San Antonio and new presidios on the coast, immigration from the United States slowed but did not stall. One complication was created by empresarios De Zavala, Vehlein, and Burnet, who in 1830, having been unsuccessful, had passed their grant rights to the Galveston Bay and Texas Land Company. In violation of law, this company began selling land scrip to immigrants as if it had full authority to establish titles to the 13 million acres encompassed by the three grants.

### Trouble at Anahuac

The next major event in the struggle over Texas identity occurred in 1832, in what became known as the first of two Anahuac disturbances. Anahuac, perched above the mouth of the Trinity River on Galveston Bay, had been established as a coastal fort after passage of the Law of April 6. The commander of the garrison, John (or

General Manuel de Mier y Terán worked diligently to address problems for the Mexican government as American colonization in Texas—legal and illegal— continued, but he despaired of maintaining effective control of the frontier.

Juan) Davis Bradburn, was a Virginian by birth who had become a Mexican military officer. General Terán had sent Bradburn to establish the fort at Anahuac and enforce Mexican laws. In 1831, Bradburn was joined by customs collector George Fisher. The exemption from tariffs had expired for Austin's colonists, and the government wanted to collect the monies to use to fund its Texas forts. Fisher angered Texans not only by insisting on imposing the customs duties, which was, after all, his job, but by decreeing that all ships in Texas ports had to obtain permission to sail at Anahuac. This meant that ships at Brazoria had to make a trip of more than a hundred miles to gain official government approval to operate from the Texas coast. Even Austin protested the situation at Anahuac, asking Bradburn if it was the government's goal to have Texas "totally broken up and all commerce totally annihilated?" An exasperated General Terán, who had learned of ships defiantly sailing by Anahuac, their commanders refusing to pay customs duties, replied pointedly, "You want the government to adopt a more liberal policy. You should say what liberality you long for beyond that which you already receive." Terán did, however, establish a customs house at Brazoria to address the problem.

Anahuac remained a trouble spot, for tensions had also quickly developed between Bradburn as a representative of the centralist government and the feder-alists as well as prickly Anglo immigrants impatient with Mexican government restraints in general.

The first problem surfaced in Bradburn's feud with Jose Francisco Madero, another Mexican official, but a member of the federalist state's-rights camp. Madero had been sent by the state of Coahuila y Texas to Anahuac to issue land titles to residents of the area who had arrived before 1828. Bradburn, citing the National Colonization Law of 1824, argued that Madero had no authority to do so within the ten-league coastal reserve.

Madero, briefly jailed by Bradburn, nonetheless issued the land titles and also formed an *ayuntamiento,* or local government, at a nearby Trinity River commu-nity which quickly became known simply as "Liberty." It was within Madero's au-thority to create a municipality with its own governmental structure, but this further rankled Bradburn as a representative of the centralist government.

The Anglo settlers of Liberty and the surrounding area embraced the *ayun-tamiento.* They resented the garrison, whose members included former convicts and a handful of runaway slaves. Further, the settlers were increasingly annoyed by Bradburn's attempts to regulate them; under orders from Terán, Bradburn was checking land titles and the licenses of Anglo American lawyers. Meanwhile, Fisher continued to impose customs duties on ships already anchored in Galve-ston Bay and on the Brazos River.

Tensions escalated when Bradburn imprisoned Anglo law partners William Barret Travis and Patrick Jack. The two men had entered Texas from the Ameri-can South, Jack in 1830 and Travis in 1831, clearly after the Law of April 6, 1830; however, both had obtained land grants in Austin's colony. An Alabama lawyer, Travis in a few years would become an icon of Texas history; like so many other new immigrants, he was both fleeing the past—in his case, an apparently un-happy marriage—and seeking an opportunity to distinguish himself economi-cally, socially, and politically in the new environment. As he practiced law and learned Spanish in Anahuac, he and Jack had already organized a citizens' "mili-tia." Ostensibly it was for defense against Indians, but their antagonism against the Mexican garrison was already obvious. The pair then tried by roundabout means to convince Bradburn that a large American force from Louisiana was coming to claim the runaway slaves in the garrison.

When an exasperated Bradburn placed Travis and Jack in jail, a group of An-glo colonists marched to within six miles of the fort, capturing the nineteen cav-alrymen attached to the Anahuac garrison and stopping at Turtle Bayou. The colonists sent a delegation to Brazoria to obtain a cannon to use against the fort. When the military commander at Velasco, Domingo de Ugartechea, attempted to stop the ship carrying the cannon, the battle of Velasco ensued. An estimated 100–150 Texans fought 90–200 Mexicans under Ugartechea, and there were cas-ualties on both sides. Ugartechea had to surrender when his troops ran out of ammunition.

Meanwhile, on Turtle Bayou, the insurgents produced the Turtle Bayou resolutions. Significantly, they represented themselves not as wishing to sever Texas from Mexico but as supporting the federalists in Mexico. Federalist forces were still battling the centralists and had just achieved a major military victory under the leadership of Antonio Lopez de Santa Anna, who nine years earlier had been instrumental in toppling Emperor Iturbide. With a somewhat hazy understanding of what was happening in Mexico, the resolution framers pledged their "lives and fortunes" in support of "the highly talented and distinguished Chieftain—General Santa Anna."

One outcome of the federalist-centralist battles and the growing troubles with Anglo settlers was the suicide of General Terán. Terán had served Mexico under both federalist and centralist regimes only to see civil war divide Mexico and daunting problems multiply in Texas. Terán had support throughout Mexico as a strong enough leader to end Santa Anna's revolt and bring federalists and centralists together. But he recognized the precariousness of his position as a representative of the centralist government, and he despaired over Texas. On July 2, he wrote presciently to another Mexican official, "How could we expect to hold Texas when we do not even agree among ourselves. . . . As it is, we are lost. . . . Texas is lost. . . . What will become of Texas? Whatever God wills." The next day, he killed himself with his sword.

The controversy at Anahuac ended—temporarily—when Bradburn's military superior, Colonel José de las Piedras, replaced the unpopular garrison commander and released the prisoners. (Bradburn's cavalry had already been released.) But Travis and Jack continued to cause trouble. The centralist government still controlled the fort at Anahuac, and the two Anglo attorneys encouraged garrison members to reject its authority. Finally, a federalist officer relocated the whole garrison to the Rio Grande.

## Growth of Political Opposition

In reviewing the first Anahuac disturbance, it is important to note that not all colonists supported Travis and Jack, considering them rash troublemakers. In fact, newcomers and observers in Mexican Texas often found that many colonists cared little for political turmoil, being determinedly individualistic and concerned with building their own fortunes in the demanding but bounteous regions of eastern and southeastern Texas. And overall, despite the Law of April 6 and the furor surrounding Bradburn, the Mexican government had imposed only intermittent and limited controls on their presence.

Many Texans, however, were frustrated and impatient with the government's continued political shifts and its attempts to exercise authority even as it failed to provide for the safety and well-being of its citizens. In 1832 Béxar Tejano leaders sent a petition to the Mexican Congress in which they complained of the "inaction and apathy" of the government as Comanches scourged their area, in the absence of any sizable and effective frontier military. Texas trade was languishing, and the Law of April 6 had only ensured that "capitalists and industrious and honorable" immigrants from the States were kept out, whereas "wicked adventurers and others who constitute the dregs of society" kept arriving.

The primarily Anglo colonists—along with others who had slipped into Texas without the sanction of empresario contracts—also spoke out. In October 1832, fifty-eight representatives of the colonists met at San Felipe and petitioned the Mexican government for, among other things, a repeal of the Law of April 6 and separate statehood for Texas. Stephen F. Austin presided, walking a fine line between his responsibilities to the government and to the colonists. To the delegates, the convention was their way of democratically advancing political agendas, but to Mexican officials, it was illegal, as only the Coahuila y Texas legislature could file petitions. Further, the meeting was evidence of insurgency. The idea of a Texas separated from Coahuila also sparked Mexican fears of a Texas separated from Mexico itself.

Among the Tejano settlements, only Goliad had sent a delegation to the convention, and Austin particularly wanted to get the *ayuntamiento* of San Antonio involved as well, as Béxar leaders favored reform and would be important allies in convincing the Mexican government that the petitioners were still loyal Mexican subjects. He was working toward this end when Anglo colonists called for a second convention in April 1833 at San Felipe. In the meantime, the federalist Santa Anna won election as Mexico's president, leading to hopes in Texas that the new government would look more favorably on the idea of statehood and accept a great degree of local autonomy.

At the convention of 1833, Austin recapped why the delegates had been called together: "The political system under which Texas has heretofore been governed, tends to check the growth of the country, and to produce confusion and insecurity, rather than to extend protection to lives liberty and property."

The convention called for the repeal of the Law of April 6, for frontier defense, for tariff exemptions, and for more effective and efficient handling of criminal acts and legal disputes. It again petitioned that the union of Coahuila and Texas be "dissolved, abrogated, and perpetually cease," with Texas residents "authorized to institute and establish a separate state government, which will be in accordance with the federal constitution." This time delegates went so far as to prepare a provisional state constitution.

The convention appointed Austin, Erasmo Seguín, and physician James B. Miller to take the petition to Mexico City. Some of his own colonists did not trust Austin, given his previous attempts to placate the Mexican government. One of these, John P. Coles, wrote ominously, "[I]f for the want of proper Exertion on his part the application should fail Col. Austin will be a Ruined man in Texas." But Austin had come to the conclusion that he must press for statehood, and that if the petition failed, he and Texas would have to prepare for war.

Miller, tending victims of a cholera epidemic, was unable to make the trip. Seguín had tried to anticipate such a petition in 1824 when he served in the Mexican constitutional congress that had combined Coahuila and Texas. At that time, he had labored to insert a provision allowing Texas to petition for separate statehood. Now, however, although he continued to favor separation, he declined to make the trip.

Thus, Austin made the journey by himself in the late spring of 1833, nearing Mexico City in a countryside still ravaged by civil war, with a revolt against Santa Anna's new federalist government already in progress. Austin was ready to align himself with this government and aware that "[t]he consequence of a failure [to win statehood] will no doubt be war." He pledged, "So soon as I am convinced that there is no hope of success I shall return as quick as possible by water." Austin was right in his assessment of the seriousness of the situation, but he would be unable to follow through on his pledge. He would not see Texas again until the late summer of 1835.

## The Burgeoning American Presence and the Impetus to Revolution, 1833–1835

In 1835, the number of Texas residents who had migrated from the United States reached approximately 30,000. Many were diligent settlers, others were young male adventurers who might or might not settle down. Most were drawn by the potential of Mexican Texas for farming, stock-raising, trade, town-building, and/ or land ownership and speculation. Many were "pushed" from the States, not necessarily fugitives from the law but people who were trying to leave financial and other failures behind. One visitor from Louisiana noted, "[W]hen a new-commer averred that he had *ran away from his creditors* ONLY, he was regarded as a gentleman of the *first water*." Whatever their circumstances, their participation in the definition of an American identity would have significant consequences for everyone involved with the province.

### Continued Immigration and Colonization

When Austin left for Mexico City in 1833, families and adventurers from the United States continued to cross the Sabine illegally, disregarding the Law of April 6 and hoping to seize the opportunity to build homes and/or find prosperity in Mexican territory. Some were drawn by an 1833 book on Texas by Austin's widowed cousin from Connecticut, Mary Austin Holley. The cultured Holley had made an initial tour of the Texas settlements in 1831. Her travel account provided a detailed picture of life in the Anglo colonies. Among other observations, she noted the work necessary to establish one's family in the colonies, and the lack of ready and regular supplies: Mattress cases brought from the States, she advised, could be stuffed with tree moss, perhaps with "some layers of wool, well carded" on top of the moss for warmth.

Despite the constant need to create whatever one wanted or needed, Holley noted that "even privations become pleasures" as "people grow ingenious in overcoming difficulties." She characterized the Texans she met as "kind and hospitable,"

In frontier Texas, the natural environment often provided challenges to travelers. With this illustration from an 1834 book titled *A Visit to Texas,* J. T. Hammond conveys the size of the thick cane breaks through which travelers found and forged routes. *(CN 11582, The Center for American History, The University of Texas at Austin)*

like many travelers in the settlements finding them generous with what they did have. And she spoke glowingly of the natural abundance of the country.

Others were less sanguine about the privations of life in Texas. Ann Coleman, arriving in Brazoria in 1832, noted with humorous consternation the common practice of sharing a room—and even a bed—with one's hosts when visiting at isolated cabin homes. Carolyn Ernst von Roeder von Hinueber, daughter of German settlers who arrived in 1831, would write, "No one can imagine what a degree of want there was of the merest necessities of life, and it is difficult for me now to understand how we managed to live and get along under the circumstances, yet we did so in some way."

In spite of the challenges, land speculators as well as farm families continued to be undeterred by the Law of April 6, eager to claim tracts of land unsettled by Mexicans or U.S. or European immigrants, and able to devise strategies to do so. Jane McManus Storm Cazneau is an example. Daughter of a New York congressman, Cazneau arrived in Texas in December 1832 with scrip from the Galveston Bay and Texas Land Company and a recommendation from former U.S. vice president and speculator Aaron Burr stating that she could "send out one or two hundred substantial settlers in less time . . . than any man or half a Dozen men whom I this day Know." At San Felipe, she was designated a Mexican citizen and received the transfer of an eleven-league grant through the approval of the San Felipe *alcalde*. Stymied in her own efforts to settle a colony of Germans, she sought to act as an agent providing immigrants to Austin's colonies and was a speculator in Texas lands for many years.

In the meantime, Power and Hewetson moved forward with a series of empresario contracts, because they, too, were seeking to settle Europeans. In 1833, Power journeyed to Ireland and returned with more than 300 settlers, most from his home parish on Ireland's southeast coast. Most of these immigrants would die of cholera, either en route in New Orleans or shortly after reaching Texas, but the remainder would join a group of Mexican settlers enticed from Coahuila.

Another colonization effort had gotten underway in late 1832 with the blessings of the Mexican government. James Grant, a Scotsman who had established himself in the political hierarchy of Coahuila and Texas, and Englishman John Charles Beales, a Mexico City–based surgeon, obtained a land grant far to the west of the settled colonies, between the Nueces and the Rio Grande in South Texas. They were allowed to bring 800 European families. Beales traveled in late 1833 and early 1834 to the area with fifty-nine colonists—some German, some English, and some American. They settled on a creek near the head of the Nueces and surveyed their surroundings with some despair. Although their new settlement—named Dolores, after Beales's Mexican wife—was well chosen, much of the country was desert. They found little game to provide meat; crops could not thrive without irrigation in an area of so little rainfall and such intense heat; wood for building was some distance away; and the Comanches regularly passed through the area and harassed its occupants.

No one except the Comanches would contest Grant and Beales for their chunk of South Texas desert, but in the more desirable areas, by 1834 the land ownership situation was hopelessly tangled among the various empresario and other claims. Over the years since the grants had begun, settlers had located outside the perimeters originally determined or had established settlements under competing authorities. DeWitt's and De León's colonists continued to argue over boundaries. To the south and west, long-term Mexican residents and newer immigrant residents occupied a checkerboard, claiming title based on Goliad *ayuntamiento* authority or on the empresario grants of De León, McMullen and McGloin, or Power and Hewetson. Hundreds of immigrants from the United States were squatting on the lands east of Austin's colony, which Vehlein had turned over to the Galveston Bay and Texas Land Company. Sterling Clack Robertson was angrily disputing the claims of the absent Austin to the grant Robertson had failed to colonize, which had become the "upper colony" of Austin and his friend and partner Samuel May Williams. Eleven-league grants to Mexican citizens from the Mexican government had passed into the hands of speculators in Texas and the United States.

One group consistently left out was the Texas Cherokees. They had made repeated attempts to gain title to the lands north of Nacogdoches. They lived, farmed, maintained towns, raised livestock, and traded with their Mexican, Anglo, and Indian neighbors on these lands. But the government included these lands in various unfulfilled empresario grants. As commandant general, Terán had tried in 1831 to secure land title for them, and in 1833 Chief Bowles and other tribal leaders had journeyed to Monclova, then the capital of Coahuila and Texas, in an attempt to have their claims recognized. Not only did these efforts fail, but new U.S. immigrants swelled settlements to the east, west, and south of the Cherokees, pressing in upon them.

Texans of African extraction also found themselves constantly hard-pressed. Free Africans lived increasingly uncertain lives and had little hope of gaining a plot of land, while slaves continued to work land for their owners.

Many of the immigrants arriving in the early 1830s, and particularly in 1833 and after, had little patience with Indian or even Mexican land claims. Neither did they feel the necessity of allegiance to the Mexican government; whether they settled in Austin's colonies or other areas, they were more likely to align themselves with the Travises and Jacks of Texas. They were inclined to be contemptuous of slow diplomatic efforts when their freedom to locate where they pleased and do what they pleased was at issue.

## Tejano Perspectives

What of the Mexican population, many of whose roots coiled deep in Spanish and Mexican Texas? Some still lived their lives far from the U.S. immigrants' influences. Along the Rio Grande far to the west, in 1833 El Paso boasted a population of 5,801 and continued, as part of the Mexican state of Chihuahua, to develop as a Mexican trading center with no "Texas" identity. Its leading citizens were more concerned with frequent Apache depredations than with the political disruptions to their south in Mexico or to their east in Texas, although they kept a wary eye on American expansion in general.

Many of the 4,000 Mexicans within the Texas portion of the state of Coahuila y Texas had become disillusioned with the Anglo presence. This was particularly true in Victoria and Goliad, where Tejanos and Anglos had been at odds since DeWitt's colony had been established. Tejanos complained that Anglos violated the law, rustling cattle and smuggling and generally being rude and disruptive. Religious differences had become painfully apparent, with few Anglo colonists even keeping up the pretense of adherence to Catholicism, and many expressing a prejudice against Catholics as "papists." The Anglo immigrants combined republican spirit with a Protestant belief in free will and an individual relationship with God, impatient or suspicious of the ritualized and hierarchical Catholic faith.

Some Tejanos continued to see a partnership with Anglo immigrants as the economic lifeblood of Texas, the only clear hope for a region that had suffered too long from the crudest frontier conditions. For this reason, liberal Tejanos

Vista del Presidio de Goliad antes Bahia del Espiritu Santo (Texas)

In 1834 Lino Sánchez y Tapia drew this view of the Goliad presidio from a late-1820s sketch, providing an early depiction of the site that would soon figure in the Texas Revolution. *(The Yale Collection of Western Americana, Beinecke Rare Book and Manuscript Library)*

continued to support the Anglos' attempts to win exceptions to Mexican laws against slavery. With slaves and the right techniques, they could grow enough cotton to be exported, building an economy beyond subsistence and barter. Added to this economic interest was the shared desire among many Tejanos and Anglos for an end to the vacillating political regimes in Mexico City and the triumph of a consistent liberal federalist agenda.

Tejano leaders had reason to be proud of the regional political system they had nurtured before and during the influx of U.S. immigrants. The Tejanos had developed a workable and often farsighted range of solid frontier adaptations, from water systems to livestock roundups, from educational initiatives to military response units. The more thoughtful of their Anglo colleagues were beginning to learn from and build upon these adaptations.

However, there is no denying that by late in the Mexican period, Tejano communities were beginning to feel cut off from and out of step with their Anglo neighbors. One Anglo observer noted that "[t]he Mexican population is Entirely sepperated from the N. American people in Texas." Tejanos continued to share much of the Anglos' impatience with the Mexican government; in fact, Tejanos at Goliad had held their own meeting in January 1833 and concluded in their memoria, "[L]et's be republicans, let's be men, let's defend our rights, or let's not exist at all." But too often they found the Anglo declarations and actions to be precipitate and intemperate. As newcomers, they became political agitators without any sense of the intricacies of Texas's frontier relationship with the Saltillo and Mexico City governments.

## Austin and the Developing Crisis

Stephen F. Austin continued to pursue the careful diplomatic course, working dutifully in Mexico City for Texas statehood. He spent months in the Mexican capitol, enduring a devastating cholera epidemic, fluctuating responses from Santa Anna's government, and concerns about the outcome of a cholera outbreak in his own colonies. Finally, in October 1833, deeply frustrated, he informed Vice President Valentín Gómez Farias "that Texas must be made a state by the Govt. or she would make herself one." He also wrote a fateful letter to the *ayuntamiento* of San Antonio recommending that the Texas *ayuntamientos* "unite in a measure to organize a local government independent of Coahuila, even though the general government withholds its consent."

Austin continued to meet with Mexican officials, winning such concessions as a repeal of the suspension of unfulfilled empresario contracts in the Law of April 6. The Mexican Congress agreed to officially allow U.S. immigration into Texas again, beginning in May 1834. But the officials remained cool to the idea of statehood for Texas. In December, Austin started home, feeling that he had made some progress even on the statehood question. In January of 1834, however, when he reached Saltillo, the capital of Coahuila y Texas, he was arrested by the commandant there, on orders from Mexico City. Austin's remark to Farias had caused suspicion, and officials had learned of Austin's letter to San Antonio and considered it treasonous.

Austin was held in a series of prisons in Mexico for almost a year, then waited in Mexico City through early 1835 for resolution of his case. Shortly after Austin's arrest, Farias dispatched Colonel Juan N. Almonte to inspect the various political regions of Texas. In his 1834 report, Almonte noted many of the same conditions that Terán had noted in 1828, but did not sound any significant alarms about the loyalties of the population, whom he found generally peaceful. He did note the constant influx of immigrants from the United States in the Nacogdoches area and the need for adequate troops to maintain Mexican law.

The Coahuila y Texas Congress of 1833—still largely federalist and, in general, friendly to Anglo immigration and economic activity—had actually passed a number of liberal reforms advantageous to developing Texas, including approval of English as a legal language. The next year, while Austin was held in prison, the state government passed further political reforms to benefit Texans, including some needed judicial reforms and the addition of another Texas representative in the state legislature. Such measures helped to quiet the Texas frontier while Austin was imprisoned. In the colonies, this gave a "peace party," including empresario David Burnet and various Austin supporters, the upper hand against a "war party," including Travis and Austin colonist Jared Groce's son-in-law William Wharton. The latter group consisted in general of younger, brasher, less-established immigrants (those who had entered Texas in the early 1830s), as well as more-established settlers disillusioned with controversies over land titles and the general state of the region under Mexican rule. Land speculator A. C. Allen of Nacogdoches noted, however, "The people generally appear to be satisfied with what has been done for the present [and] are willing to defer the state question. They consider their pro[s]pects truly cheering."

Ultimately, though, any hope of bringing Texans smoothly under a liberal Mexican system of state government was undermined by the government's instability and the escalating demands of Texas residents, whether newly arrived or long-term. Texans were accustomed to freedom from much government control. Hope was also undermined by Santa Anna's surprising 1834 shift to centralist policies, and his declaration that he was the sole Mexican government authority.

## Centralists and Colonists

In 1835, as Santa Anna installed centralist officials and his new Congress dismissed the federal Constitution of 1824 for a set of centralist laws, the Coahuila and Texas governor, Agustin Viesca, tried unsuccessfully to rally Texas as well as Coahuila residents against the repressive measures.

Texas residents, confused and divided over the appropriate response to this latest and spectacular shift of power, were unable to see the possible dire consequences for their region. Many had considered Santa Anna a good federalist, and they had reservations about supporting the state government of Coahuila y Texas, which appeared to favor a few Texans in land speculation, in a fight with the federal government. Only Béxar sent a group of militiamen under Erasmo Seguín's son Juan to help defend the state at its new capital of Monclova; by the time they arrived, however, Viesca backed down.

Through the early summer of 1835, Texas residents had discussed what to do; some, including leaders in the Austin colony capital of San Felipe, argued that the new centralist regime posed a real and immediate threat. But even Anglo settlers considered members of the "war party" counseled "union, concert, and moderation."

Meanwhile, tensions at Anahuac had erupted again over the collection of tariffs, and William Barret Travis again emerged at the center of the resistance, in late June leading fifty men in an attack on the fort that forced the commander's surrender. This action sparked no rebellious unity among Texas colonists; in fact, many rushed to disassociate themselves from Travis's action. Mexican and Anglo settlers alike seemed to wish to adjust to the new government and go about their business. Mexican and Anglo officials either accepted the centralist agenda or vacillated between rebellious and conciliatory rhetoric.

There were disturbing—and true—rumors, however, of a Mexican military force on its way to Texas to subjugate a rebellious populace swollen and agitated by people from the United States who were not Mexican citizens. Santa Anna's brother-in-law, Brigadier General Martín Perfecto de Cos, had been troubled by reports of an increased influx of immigrants from the United States. Observers called the 1835 migration "astonishing," with reports of 250 families locating in the Nacogdoches area in one month and a thousand colonists reaching the Brazos River in January, with another thousand in February.

Cos was also angered by reports of the immigrants' continued resistance to government policies, as evidenced by the troubles at Anahuac. Reassured by the minister of war that troops would be available after they suppressed a revolt in the Mexican state of Zacatecas, Cos wrote that such an expedition would let "[t]hose ungrateful strangers know that the Govno. has sufficient power to repress them" and that they should leave Mexico "if they do not want to submit themselves to its laws."

Hints of this impending punitive action from Mexican troops sparked new talk of concerted opposition in Texas. Public meetings were held across the frontier communities, and people began to talk of a convention, or consultation, to address the governmental threat. Both those who wanted to move cautiously but purposefully and those who breathed open defiance saw a convention as a vehicle for action.

So did Stephen F. Austin, who had been released from his extended imprisonment and detention, in part through the influence of Almonte, and returned to Texas via New Orleans. In that city, he called—defiantly now—for new immigrants, asserting "I wish a great immigration this fall and winter from Kentucky, Tennessee, every where . . . any how." Austin was ready to declare with other members of the former "peace party" that "Texas shall be effectually, and fully, Americanized."

Both firebrand orators and respected leaders were warning that the centralist forces would disrupt and destroy the settlements—particularly the Anglo settlements—and deny the rights of their citizens, all in violation of the overturned federal Constitution of 1824. Instigators of rebellion argued that the centralist government, not the residents of Texas, had abrogated Mexican liberal principles, and in this way they sidestepped the question of whether it was right and moral for Anglo Americans to seize control of Texas from Mexico. But this was the implicit agenda for many as Anglo Texas communities in particular galvanized into military preparedness against the oncoming army. At the end of September 1835, Texas was teetering on the edge of revolution.

## Conclusion

In 1820 and 1821, Spanish and Mexican officials saw U.S. colonization efforts as an opportunity to strengthen Mexico's devastated northern frontier and to offset the threat of U.S. expansion by controlling and limiting immigration through an empresario system. When Stephen F. Austin first entered Béxar, this had seemed a feasible course to follow in Texas: What did a new republic of 6 million have to fear from a few attempts at colonization in its remote regions? Few Mexican citizens could be drawn to these colonies. And what did Mexico have to lose? Either the colonizers would do their work well and reinforce Mexican claims by occupying and cultivating the land and building towns and trade networks or they would forfeit the grants, and the officials would devise another remedy for the problems of maintaining the northern frontier.

In Austin, Mexican authorities had found an Anglo entrepreneur initially devoted to his charge to uphold a Mexican Texas. They had also selected other empresarios, such as Martin De León, Joseph Vehlein, and Vincente Filisola, who could be expected to remain loyal to the republic of Mexico. The government had offered the colonizers generous terms in establishing settlers.

When it became clear that colonization was not working as authorities had hoped it would, the centralist government attempted to stop most immigration from the United States with the Law of April 6. Even after this, however, the Mexican Congress and the state government in Coahuila continued to establish policies favorable to settlers wishing to participate in the development of Mexican Texas.

Yet it became clear that the immigration from the United States had spiraled beyond Mexico's control. Texas residents had different perceptions of their loyalties and relationship with the government than did the officials in Mexico City and Coahuila. From Texans' vantage point, their needs had been neglected, particularly with the constant political upheaval in the Mexican capital. They had had to struggle at the local level with disputes over land titles, troubles with hostile Indians, and lack of an economy beyond a system of barter. In a way, the isolated life had suited them, for most residents demanded considerable autonomy, but this demand was constantly undercut by Texas's position as part of a larger Mexican state.

Tejanos and U.S. immigrants alike chafed under the sometimes indifferent, sometimes apparently arbitrary rule of a federal government always in flux. They also chafed under the government's retreat from the republican principles in the Mexican Constitution of 1824.

At the same time, some Anglo immigrants cared little for Mexican claims to the region, and they behaved in more exclusionary ways as their numbers grew. Such changes demonstrated that Anglo hegemony was growing. The term "manifest destiny" had not yet been coined, but the feeling it represented—that Anglo Americans had both the God-given right and the duty to claim and develop the continent to their own ends—was increasingly evident. Anglo Americans had little regard for the rights of Tejanos, Indians, and African Americans and were dissatisfied with any attempts of the Mexican government to exert its authority.

Who, then, would have the power to define Texas in the future? In the following months, that question was to be fought out from Béxar to the South Texas plains to the coastal marshes and bayous bordering the San Jacinto.

## SUGGESTED READINGS

The arrival and settlement in Texas of the first significant numbers of Anglo-Americans has been heavily researched over the years. Eugene Barker led in his work on the chief Anglo colonizer, Stephen F. Austin, and his colony, *The Austin Papers* (1924–1928) and *The Life of Stephen F. Austin: Founder of Texas, 1793–1836* (1969), but Gregg Cantrell's *Stephen F. Austin: Empresario of Texas* (1999) supersedes the Barker biography. Among other works focusing on Anglo pioneers in this period, the most prominent and popular has been Noah Smithwick's *The Evolution of a State, or Recollections of Old Texas Days,* first published in 1900; despite concerns about its veracity, it is an entertaining and illuminating first-person look at early Texas life.

In addition to the focus on Anglo pioneers, there has been scholarship on the dynamics of Mexican rule in this period. In particular, Paul Lack's *The Texas Revolutionary Experience, A Political and Social History, 1835–1836* (1992) provides insight into the ways in which Mexico governed this portion of Coahuila y Texas and the challenges the government faced in the years leading up to the Revolution.

Recent scholarship has also explored Mexican self-government and experience in Texas in this period. The most prominent work is Andrés Tijerina's *Tejanos and Texas under the Mexican Flag, 1821–1836* (1994), which in part argues that Mexican Texans had already established many frontier government forms adopted by emerging Anglo leaders. Useful regional sources are Jesus F. de la Teja and John Wheat's "Béxar: Profile of a Tejano Community, 1820–1832," *Southwestern Historical Quarterly* (1983), and W. H. Timmons's "The El Paso Area in the Mexican Period, 1821–1848," *Southwestern Historical Quarterly* (1980).

For the origins of American-imported slavery in Texas, a key source is Randolph B. Campbell's *An Empire for Slavery: The Peculiar Institution in Texas, 1821–1865* (1989). For an examination of a forming Texas identity, see Mark E. Nackman, *A Nation Within a Nation: The Rise of Texas Nationalism* (1975).

### Colonization Efforts, 1821–1829

Lester G. Bugbee pioneered in documenting "The Old Three Hundred," Austin's early settlers, with his article of that title in *The Quarterly of the Texas State Historical Association* (1897). For early Anglo women's experiences, part 1 of Jo Ella Powell Exley's *Texas Tears and Texas Sunshine: Voices of Frontier Women* (1985) provides three early first-person accounts, and Dianna Everett's *The Texas Cherokees: A People Between Two Fires, 1819–1840* (1990) chronicles the Cherokees' attempts to establish a home in East Texas. For information on prominent people and events of the period, the *New Handbook of Texas* (1996), edited by Ron Tyler, Douglas Barnett, and Roy Barkley, is invaluable; the reader will find clear and specific entries for such subjects as the individual empresarios and the Fredonian rebellion.

### Growth of Political and Cultural Tensions, 1829–1833

With Stephen F. Austin remaining a key political figure, Cantrell's *Stephen F. Austin: Empresario of Texas* helps explain the overall political tensions and developments, as does "The Austin-Leaming Correspondence, 1828–1836," edited by Andreas Reichstein, in the *Southwestern Historical Quarterly* (1985). Much primary material for the events in this period and those immediately surrounding it can be found in Ernest Wallace, David M. Vigness, and George B. Ward, eds., *Documents of Texas History* (1994).

### The Burgeoning American Presence and the Impetus to Revolution, 1833–1835

Continuing empresario attempts are chronicled in such works as Linda S. Hudson's *Mistress of Manifest Destiny: A Biography of Jane McManus Storm Cazneau 1807–1878* (2001) and Carl Coke Rister's *Comanche Bondage,* first published in 1955 and republished in the 1980s. The former deals in part with Cazneau's attempts to colonize in Texas, the latter with John Charles Beale's attempt to establish a colony between the Nueces and the Rio Grande. For a detailed look at a colonization effort, see Malcolm D. Maclean, ed., *Papers Concerning Robertson's Colony in Texas,* seventeen volumes published between 1974 and 1991.

For Tejano experience and relations with Anglos, see not only the works cited above but also Timothy M. Matovina's *Tejano Religion and Ethnicity, San Antonio, 1821–1860* (1995) and Arnoldo de León's "Early Anglo Settlers View Mexicans with Hostility" in Sam W. Haynes and Cary D. Wintz, eds., *Major Problems in Texas History* (2002).

The variety of people seeking refuge in Texas is represented by the Cherokees, with Everett's *The Texas Cherokees* the standard, and by the beginning of German migration, as chronicled in Crystal Sasse Ragsdale's *The Golden Free Land: The Reminiscences and Letters of Women on an American Frontier* (1976).

# 7

# Revolution, 1835–1836

By September 1835, Juan Seguín had become convinced that the time for revolution was "close at hand." The twenty-eight-year-old political chief in San Antonio had been baptized as an infant in the community, as had his father, Erasmo, and his grandfather, Santiago. The Seguíns had successfully navigated a number of Spanish and Mexican political shifts that affected their community. Juan had his father's example of befriending and partnering with the new Anglo immigrants to Texas. The Seguíns had even taken in Stephen F. Austin's younger brother, James, and introduced him to the Spanish language and Mexican culture.

Now the younger Seguín wanted to take a stand against Santa Anna. In the spring his militia had been the only one from Texas to respond to Coahuila y Texas governor Agustín Viesca's call for resistance to Santa Anna's imposition of centralist control in Mexico. When that attempt failed in Monclova, Seguín and his company returned in June, as he wrote in his memoir, "pledg[ing] to use all our influence to rouse Texas against the tyrannical government of Santa Anna." Yet both within his own native community and among the settlements made up primarily of U.S. immigrants, people either tried to avoid actions that would affect their private fortunes and daily lives, or they remained confused and divided on what actions to take in response to the centralist control and the looming threat from Mexican troops.

On September 27, Seguín traveled to Salvador Flores's ranch to convince the Mexican ranch owners along the San Antonio River that they should arm themselves against the current Mexican government. He was to play an active role in

| CHAPTER 7 | Revolution, 1835–1836 |
|---|---|
| SEPT. 1835 | Gen. Martín Perfecto de Cos reaches the Texas coast |
| OCT. 1835 | Texians refuse to give up Mexican cannon in incident near Gonzales; Cos arrives in San Antonio de Béxar; Texian volunteers march on San Antonio and camp at nearby creek; colonists' "Permanent Council" attempts to devise a revolutionary government |
| NOV. 1835 | "Consultation" continues work of Permanent Council; Texians remain camped outside San Antonio |
| DEC. 1835 | The Texian volunteer siege force takes San Antonio; small volunteer force remaining in San Antonio fortifies the Alamo for siege |
| FEB. 1836 | Provisional Texian government has fallen apart; Santa Anna begins siege of Alamo |
| MARCH 1836 | Texian convention meets at Washington-on-the-Brazos, declares independence, and sets up new interim government; Alamo falls; Texas residents flee Santa Anna's troops in the Runaway Scrape; James Fannin and his troops are captured by Gen. José de Urrea and most are executed (Fannin Massacre) |
| APRIL 1836 | Sam Houston's troops defeat Santa Anna's at San Jacinto and Santa Anna is captured |

the upcoming struggle. The participation of Seguín and other Mexican residents with deep Texas roots reminds us that the Revolution was not a simple battle between Anglo colonists and Mexican troops. It was a complex redefining of Texas carried out—often with much tension and confusion—by people with different experiences of and expectations for the region.

## The Revolution—Early Months (October–December)

In the fall of 1835, the *Telegraph and Texas Register* newspaper began publication in San Felipe de Austin. It promptly dealt with an issue of some debate, an appropriate name for the people of Texas, concluding, "We believe that, both by the Mexican and American residents of the country, the name commonly used is Texians." Among those responding to Santa Anna's political and military threat, many would soon claim the name "Texian" as an independent—and revolutionary—identity.

### Come and Take It

As Juan Seguín rode to the Mexican ranches to encourage revolt, others rode out of San Antonio on a different mission: A company of 100 dragoons under Francisco de Castañeda was being sent by Domingo de Ugartechea, military commander of Texas, to retrieve a cannon provided to the citizens of Gonzales in 1831 for defense against Indians. In the charged political climate, Ugartechea felt it was dangerous for the colonists to possess the cannon, especially because they had already refused to turn it over to one squad sent to retrieve it.

The town of Gonzales, the center of Green DeWitt's colony on the Guadalupe River, had been vulnerable to raids by bands of Indians, and its citizens had gratefully accepted from the Mexican government the protection of a six-pound cannon. Further, they had refused to succumb to the revolutionary fervor circulating through the colonies since 1832. Yet a Mexican soldier had attacked a colonist in September, and there was a sense that the government might be as harsh and uncompromising as some of the revolution-minded were claiming. The cannon quickly became a symbol of potential resistance not to the Indians but to the Mexican government.

This was the situation Ugartechea sought to address by sending the dragoons, with orders to try to retrieve the cannon peaceably. Upon reaching the outskirts of Gonzales, however, the soldiers found their passage blocked: The Guadalupe was rain-swollen and the colonists had removed the ferry. On the other side of the river stood eighteen colonists led by Albert Martin, a local storekeeper. When a Mexican courier swam across the river, Martin informed him that the force must remain on the other side of the river until the local *alcalde,* Andrew Ponton, returned to Gonzales. The colonists then used the time to bury the cannon in a peach orchard and to send out a call for resistance to volunteers from neighboring settlements.

Camped on a high mound across the river, Casteñada repeatedly tried to convey that he had not come to fight and was eager to talk with the colonists' representatives. But volunteer forces were arriving from Fayette and Columbus. The militiamen elected Henry Moore of the Fayette contingent as their commander and applauded the rhetoric that linked their resistance with that of the patriots of the American Revolution. They unearthed the cannon and loaded it with metal scraps, as cannonballs were not available.

Casteñada moved to a less exposed site on the riverbank. But the Texians, now 180 strong, moved across the river during the evening of October 1 and approached the Mexican military camp in the early hours of October 2. They were discovered quickly and there was a short burst of gunfire followed by defensive scrambling on both sides. As the daylight arrived, the two sides skirmished again, the settlers falling back from a 40-man Mexican cavalry charge. Casteñada and Moore then parleyed, without result, Casteñada protesting that he, too, was a supporter of the Constitution and that he had no order, and no desire, to force the cannon issue.

With a makeshift flag flying—white with an outline of the disputed cannon and the emblem "Come and Take It"—the Texians began firing the cannon and their Kentucky rifles as well. Castañeda withdrew rather than "compromis[e] the honor of Mexican arms," for his carbines were no match for the Texians' rifles. The Mexicans had suffered only one or two casualties, the Texians none. Thus ended the first "battle" of the Revolution, significant not for its scope but for its effect: Texians were in open defiance and had shown they would fight.

### An Army and Government Form

Meanwhile, the rumored military force sent to require Texas's allegiance to the current Mexican government had arrived, all too real, on Texas soil. General Cos had sailed into Copano Bay with 500 soldiers on September 20, and he scoffed at the revolutionaries' motives, writing, "[I]t is quite useless and vain to cover them with a hypocritical adherence to the federal constitution." Meanwhile, the formerly conciliatory Stephen F. Austin was writing that Cos's own motive was "to destroy and break up the foreign settlements in Texas," concluding that, in response, "WAR is our only resource."

Cos quickly moved his troops to the presidio of La Bahía at Goliad. A volunteer Texian force, made up primarily of Anglo men from Matagorda but including Mexican *vaqueros* (cowboys) and African American freedman Samuel McCulloch, hurriedly gathered to storm La Bahía, but Cos continued moving. Just eight days after the confrontation at Gonzales, these Texians took the inadequately-manned presidio and also took control of Goliad, whose Mexican officials had initially protested, despite some sentiment among the Mexican population in favor of the insurgents. Cos had already arrived with his battalions in San Antonio de Béxar, with every intention of imposing military control over Texas, including disarming colonists and arresting and banishing insurgents. To help him in this endeavor, he had a well-fortified position, a well-trained cavalry, and twenty cannons.

In Gonzales, in the wake of the successful resistance there, volunteer forces began to coalesce into an army: an army bent on winning San Antonio de Béxar away from Cos. Yet this was no well-defined, well-disciplined fighting force. With no clear governing structure to this volunteer enterprise, companies voted on their commanders. As new combinations of militias formed, however, the elected leadership often changed, and there was no commander-in-chief. Enlistment periods were unclear or unenforceable. In many cases, the volunteers—especially young, single men with little to lose—were just looking for a good fight, and almost all militiamen remained fiercely individualistic. Lorenzo de Zavala, the Mexican empresario and statesman casting his lot with the revolutionaries in Texas, warned Stephen F. Austin that although there was "individual patriotism," a "unified patriotism" did not exist: "They will defend their private rights until death; but still they do not realize the necessity for cooperation."

Nonetheless, Austin accepted the role of commander-in-chief when those present in the Gonzales volunteer camp voted on October 11. He was not a military man, and not in very good health, but Austin seemed to be the one candidate on whom the volunteers could agree. No sooner had a commander been chosen than the Texas volunteer army at Gonzales began its march on San Antonio de Béxar. Their course led them directly westward, over the oak-studded savanna and the prairies interspersed with stands of post oak, blackjack oak, and hickory. Along the way, other volunteers joined. Austin had summoned Juan Seguín and, when he arrived, promptly made him a captain. The new captain and Plácido Benavides, *alcalde* in Victoria, both brought Texas Mexican contingents to the revolutionary force. By October 19, this force drew near to San Antonio de Béxar, making camp on Salado Creek.

As the volunteers set up camp on the creek, Texians were struggling toward a rude revolutionary governing system. Almost 100 delegates had been elected to a "Consultation" scheduled for October 15, but with all the military activity and confusion, most delegates were slow in arriving. In the meantime, a "Permanent Council" made up of representatives from San Felipe and a few other communities met and dispatched supplies to Austin's army; they also directed that the land offices be shut down to reduce the tension and turmoil over land claims and took steps to raise funds in the United States for the Revolution.

The Permanent Council was anything but permanent, however, for on November 1, the Consultation took over. With only fifty-eight of the delegates ever in attendance, over the next two weeks this group wrestled to establish the ideological stand to take, whether insistence on a return to the Constitution of 1824 with Texas as a Mexican state or complete independence from Mexico. The divided delegates argued for both courses, with the result that both the principles of the Constitution and Texians' sovereignty were affirmed.

The Consultation also hammered out the structure an independent provisional government should take, devising a general council made up of representatives

Juan Seguín, like his father, Erasmus, a San Antonio native and political leader, sided with the Anglo new-comers in the fight for Texas's freedom from Santa Anna's centralist government. *(Texas State Library and Archives Commission)*

from each municipality. In theory, these representatives were to aid a new executive authority, the Texas governor, sharing in his duties and even extending his powers if and when they deemed it necessary. In reality, the plan would prove troublesome, as would the Consultation's authorization of a regular army, governed by U.S. Army regulations, in addition to the volunteer forces already in the field.

This new Council could authorize a regular army, but it couldn't produce one. It did, however, produce a commander—the popular Sam Houston, already commanding the volunteer troops from Nacogdoches—and give him the rank of major general.

Houston was about to become one of the major figures in Texas history, but he was already a figure of some renown in the United States. A native of Virginia, he had a dramatic past, which included a three-year sojourn with a Cherokee band as a teenager and notable service in the 1814 battle of Horseshoe Bend during the War of 1812. The latter brought him to the attention of General Andrew Jackson. As Jackson's political star rose in the 1820s, Houston had become a leading "Jacksonian Democrat," loyal to a war hero of the frontier who championed a vision of America as an egalitarian republic for Anglos and who seemed to represent the common man against privileged interests. Living in Tennessee after the war, Houston rose to become state governor, acting as "unofficial campaign manager" in Jackson's successful bid for the U.S. presidency in 1828.

Soon thereafter, Governor Houston married nineteen-year-old Eliza Allen, but the marriage ended quickly, mysteriously, and disastrously, with Eliza returning to her parents. Houston then left Tennessee. He had helped the Cherokee band of which he had been a part when the U.S. government "removed" them to Oklahoma Territory, and he now joined them for another three years.

Eventually, Houston again traveled back to the East Coast. In Washington, D.C. in April of 1832 he felt insulted by an Ohio congressman and beat him with a cane. Tried and reprimanded by the House of Representatives, Houston, like many Americans seeking a new start, looked to Texas. He hoped to become an agent for the Galveston Bay and Texas Land Company. When that did not work out, he determined to go anyway.

Houston did, however, have a mission, one provided by his old friend President Jackson: to parley with the Comanches as members of southeastern tribes were pushed toward their territory and to assess the Indian situation in Texas in general. Jackson was particularly interested in the tribes that might act as "buffers" between the Comanches and those tribes being pushed westward.

In Mexican Texas, Houston had set up a law practice and immediately become involved in the political unrest. He served as a delegate to both the Consultation of 1833 in San Felipe and the current Consultation that named him major general of a nonexistent regular army.

In late October Houston had visited the volunteer army camped outside Béxar, finding the men divided as to when to attack the town. Houston suggested that they wait until they had obtained more cannons and were more fully trained. Austin was still the commander, and the army's numbers ebbed and flowed as some men chose to go home and re-provision or see to business there while others arrived.

## The Siege of Béxar

The siege began with the volunteer army's arrival outside Béxar, but the first engagement of any note occurred on October 28, when Austin dispatched a ninety-two-man contingent under famed frontiersman James Bowie to locate a site closer to Cos's defenses. Bowie, too, had traveled to Texas with a messy past and an eye to opportunity. Known as a scraper in his native Louisiana, he was already renowned for his use of the "Bowie knife" in a Natchez duel that ended in a violent melee. Bowie had engaged in apparently fraudulent land speculation and "slave running" (taking captured slaves from the Caribbean and selling them in Louisiana). Turning to entrepreneurial opportunities in Texas, he had applied for Mexican citizenship in 1830, won huge land grants, and married Ursula de Veramendi, member of a leading San Antonio family. Veramendi and her influential father, Juan Martín de Veramendi, died in an 1833 cholera epidemic; Bowie continued to try to build his Texas holdings while advocating for war.

Now Bowie's contingent had spent the day of October 27 searching out various sites and had found a good one, at a bend in the San Antonio River near the Mission Concepción, but by then nightfall was approaching. Bowie and his men camped at the mission for the night rather than return to the main army.

This gave Cos an opportunity to attack the small group, and he dispatched 100 infantry and 300 Mexican dragoons. The Texians dug in against the riverbank. In the battle that ensued, the Mexicans' advance with muskets and belching cannons proved ineffective against the Texians' long rifles, accurate at a greater distance than the muskets, and their "snipe-and-hide combat." Only one Texian was fatally wounded. Approximately seventy-six men in the Mexican force were killed or wounded.

Austin, anticipating a clash, had been busily moving the rest of the volunteer army forward and came upon the scene shortly after the Mexican soldiers had retreated. Heartened by the apparent ease with which the contingent had forced the Mexican troops back, Austin wanted to press forward into San Antonio itself. Cooler heads prevailed, however, reminding him of the defensive fortifications into which the soldiers had retreated. Again, the volunteer army made camp, this time at the bend in the San Antonio River.

Now the opposing forces sat and waited—Cos for reinforcements, Austin for reinforcements and for a siege gun or guns that would breach Cos's defenses. Neither could wait with any complacency. On November 2, Austin wrote Dimitt at Goliad, "Whether the army can be kept together long enough to await the arrival of reinforcements, and the necessary supply of heavy battering-cannon and ammunition, I am sorry to say is somewhat uncertain."

Indeed, some men left again, impatient with the lack of action or eager to get home and get more clothing as the weather turned cold. Those who stayed did not take well to attempts at regimentation. Many fell ill, without medication or treatment available. Enough men drank heavily to create new problems in the camp. Tied to these problems were a lack of strong, decisive leadership and a shared understanding of what they were trying to accomplish. Seguín's men and other mounted volunteers patrolled the roads into San Antonio to keep supplies from reaching the town and to alert their encampment if Cos's reinforcements showed up. Minor skirmishes ensued, but November dragged on.

A bright spot for the Texians was the acquisition of a number of pieces of artillery, which they put into use against the Mexican fortifications, although with little effect. Many were also cheered by the arrival of the Greys, a company formed in New Orleans. The Greys brought visible volunteer support from the United States, a development that galled Mexican officials and heightened their suspicions of U.S. designs on Mexican territory. (Volunteer companies to fight in Texas were formed in Kentucky, Mississippi, Georgia, and Alabama as well.) One of the Greys, Herman Ehrenberg, would remember that the camp stretched "at least half a mile wide," surrounded by dormant corn fields and prairies, the latter "overgrown in places by mesquite brush and by enormous groups of gigantic cactus."

Many volunteers were growing deeply disenchanted. Austin, who wrote dejectedly on November 8 that he had "[n]ever pretended to be a military man," still tried to rally the troops, even after receiving word on November 18 that the provisional government had made him a commissioner to the United States and had therefore given him ample reason to resign his command. In fact, on November 21 Austin ordered his troops to prepare for an attack, relying on reports that the Mexican force was demoralized and desertions were common.

Austin's officers had to tell him that no more than 100 men would obey this order; the others had become disillusioned with his command. There are hints in the record that Houston may have been behind some of the dissatisfaction, as he had made no secret of his concerns about the wisdom of the siege and of his desire to do things differently with a regular army under his own command. Reluctantly, Austin rescinded his order and, acknowledging that he could better play a diplomatic role, assembled the troops on November 24. He determined that more than 400 were ready to stay and fight under an elected leader, and they voted for Colonel Edward Burleson to fill this role. On November 25, Austin left the camp for San Felipe.

A resident of Texas since 1830, Burleson had been active in protecting the frontier against Indian raids. Under Austin, he had served as lieutenant colonel of the infantry. The provisional government would recognize his new status as commander of the volunteer army on December 1. Despite the men's vote of confidence, he inherited a fractured and debilitated fighting force, one ready to strain at any rumor. Thus, when a scout entered camp on November 26 with a report of a hundred men in a large pack train headed toward San Antonio, word quickly spread that it was a company of dragoons that had been dispatched from Béxar about two weeks earlier, and that they were returning carrying silver as payment for the garrisoned Mexican soldiers.

Burleson sent James Bowie with a hundred mounted men to survey the pack train, warning him to refrain from engagement, if possible. But on finding the train beside a creek south of town, the pugnacious Bowie immediately attacked them. Meanwhile, most of the volunteer soldiers left behind, driven to distraction by the idea that their fellows would get to the silver first, simply rushed to the scene of the fight, disregarding orders. With little bloodshed on either side, the Mexican column, at a disadvantage with their muskets, abandoned the pack train for the safety of the Béxar fortifications.

The Texian volunteers found only grass in the packs; the train had been a foraging party trying to supply the hungry horses in the garrison, evidence that the Mexican garrison was indeed in difficult straits. Burleson, who had been considering withdrawal, began to think seriously about ordering an attack.

Further confirmation of the Mexican garrison's plight came when Cos released two Anglos living in San Antonio, John Smith and Samuel Maverick, on the condition that they return to the United States. Instead, they made their way to the ranch of José Antonio Navarro, a revolution-minded Mexican citizen, and thence to the Texian camp. They brought encouraging reports of the garrison's vulnerability. Burleson gave the order to attack, but he had not reckoned with strong internal dissent. Officers responded with further arguments, and Burleson, like Austin before him, rescinded the order. Those who had finally been preparing to fight responded with anger. An estimated 250–300 men left camp, and the others sank into gloom.

Burleson decided that his only recourse was to give up the siege and retreat to Goliad to establish winter quarters. Many of the troops responded to his announcement of this decision on December 4 with palpable anger and frustration. Why had they marched to the outskirts of Béxar and lived for as long as seven weeks on short rations and rumors?

## Divided Opinion

It is tempting to speculate what would have happened if the volunteer army had indeed retreated at this point. Revolutionary allegiances had built in the Texas settlements and been reinforced by the arrival of young, restless, and aggressive adventurers such as the New Orleans Greys. But opinion was still divided, both outside Texas and within it. Abolitionist Benjamin Lundy would charge that U.S. land speculators and slave interests threatened by Mexican policies against slavery stood behind the uprising. He warned, "Influential slave-holders are contributing money, equipping troops, and marching to the scene of the conflict."

There was some truth to Lundy's charges, as leading slaveholders in the American South were seeking ways to protect and expand the institution of slavery against threats from the American North and vacillation on the issue from the Upper South (states bordering the northern states). In Texas, colonists, most of whom were from the American South, continued to argue publicly against any Mexican threat to their human "property." Their fears had been heightened by a slave revolt on the Brazos River in October, an uprising that ended with one observer noting "many whipd nearly to death some hung etc."

But beleaguered revolutionary leaders could only hope for such aid as Lundy suggested, for southern slavery leaders were too involved in their own political battles in the United States. And even within Texas the revolutionaries found significant lack of interest among the citizens. Revolutionary leaders despaired when Anglo settlers—including some prominent ones—avoided aiding the war effort in any way; They did not share their food or other resources, and the men did not even serve in local militias.

The response was uneven from other groups as well. Although some Tejanos joined the war effort, those in the Nacogdoches area were already being unmercifully pressed by Anglo immigrants, who were suspicious of all Mexicans and had reason to be wary of a revolutionary effort that could leave them even more at the mercy of this group. A local Tejano militia would be formed at the instigation of revolutionary leaders, its commander a prominent area landowner, Vincente Córdova. But Córdova and his fellows carefully distanced themselves from the war against the Mexican government, instead concentrating on trying to defend Tejano rights and Tejano participation in the local power structure. In the meantime,

Irish settlers had fought alongside the Mexican military when, in a side action in late October, Goliad commander Dimitt had sent a small force to take the Mexican post of Lipantitlán on the Nueces River. The Irish of San Patricio shared allegiances with their Mexican neighbors in South Texas, who had assisted them in getting settled in and shared a Catholic church with them.

The Irish of Refugio, on the other hand, sided with the Texians. But Houston was having little luck recruiting for his regular army. Despite the work of the Permanent Council and the Consultation, efforts to resist allegiance to Santa Anna's government or to declare outright independence remained confused, piecemeal, diffuse. This sullen, ragtag volunteer army camped outside San Antonio was, for better or worse, the most united, potent force the Texas revolutionaries had. And this army was about to move the conflict to a new level, to make it indisputably a revolution.

## The Revolution—Victory and Defeat (December–March)

Benjamin Rush Milam had both a deeper and more checkered past in Texas than most of his fellow volunteers at the Siege of Béxar could imagine. A veteran of the War of 1812, by 1818 he had made his way to Spanish Texas, where he traded with the Comanches. In New Orleans the following year, he had joined James Long's first filibustering expedition, traveling to Vera Cruz and Mexico City. Although he spent time in jail in the capital, after the Constitution of 1824 introduced republican government, he became a Mexican army colonel. As an unsuccessful empresario in Texas, he took his case for land titles to Agustín Viesca in 1835, just as Viesca's resistance to Santa Anna formed, and wound up captured and jailed with Viesca. Escaping, he had made his way northward to the Goliad area. Here the Texian detachment sent to take Goliad had found him, weary and alone, hidden under a tree. Then and there Milam had become a member of the volunteer army. It was Milam who refused to accept Burleson's order to retreat, thereby providing the spark for the next series of revolutionary events.

### The Taking of Béxar

Returning to camp from a scouting mission to find his compatriots packing up on December 4, Milam went first to Colonel Frank W. Johnson; then both men went to Burleson. Milam prevailed on Burleson to agree that, if he could convince enough of the remaining men to storm the city, Burleson would stay with the others as a reserve force to cover a possible retreat. Milam emerged from the meeting asking the legendary question, "Who will follow old Ben Milam into San Antonio?" Three hundred of those remaining in camp—about six out of ten—said they would.

Milam and other officers devised a plan: to attack in two columns. Milam's column advanced up Acequia Street toward the Garza house, while Johnson's scurried up Soledad toward the Veramendi house. When a sentry discovered the invaders, however, the Mexican artillery released a rain of canister shot, and the Texians sought cover within the homes that lined the streets. Fighting erupted wherever the Texians and the soldiers encountered each other, on the streets and in the dwellings. The Texians climbed onto roofs, hoping to use them as vantage points, but Mexican soldiers were already positioned on other roofs and in the San Fernando Church bell tower, from which they could pick off the enemy.

What followed were four confused days of fighting within Béxar. Although many San Antonio families no doubt simply wished for the fighting to move elsewhere, Erasmo Seguín supplied the rebels with livestock and grain from his ranch. At least a few dozen Tejanos joined with other Texians in the slow infantry advance, although most of them, skilled horsemen, were more comfortable on a horse.

The Texians fought hard and well, as did many of the soldiers under Cos. When Ugartechea finally arrived with a relief column on the afternoon of December 8, most of the men he brought with him to be soldiers were recalcitrant and shackled convicts. Unshackled, the convicts proved not only resistant to taking orders but disruptive and violent.

By this time, the heavy artillery fire from both sides had created a landscape of "blackened tree-stumps, battered walls, smoldering ash heaps." Cos was running out of supplies and workable defense plans. Over the objections of some of the soldiers who had been defending their fortifications for the past four days, on the morning of December 9, Cos had one of his men unfurl the white flag of truce. Colonel José Juan Sánchez-Navarro negotiated surrender terms with volunteer army commander Burleson and Colonel Johnson. Colonel Milam did not live to witness the capitulation, having been struck down by a sniper's bullet during the fighting. He was one of only four Texians who died, with an estimated fourteen wounded. Mexican losses were estimated at 150 dead and wounded.

Burleson and Johnson granted liberal terms to Cos, among other things allowing him time to remove his wounded and supplying him with "such provisions as can be obtained" for the troops' retreat to the Rio Grande. In turn, Cos promised not to take up arms against the rebel forces again. As he directed the removal of his troops, residents of San Antonio who had been forced to flee the fighting returned. Juan Antonio Chávez remembered, "When we returned we found the house badly shattered with shot and shell. The doors were riddled with bullets and grape shot from the cannon and escopetas [muskets] and the rifle balls." Although some Béxar residents supported the Texians and some the Mexican government, a bond that transcended these differences was that of citizens subjected to war in their own community.

The men who had taken San Antonio felt that they had sent a decisive message in favor of a return to the Constitution of 1824 that would serve as a rallying signal for a general Mexican revolt against Santa Anna. At the same time, many Anglos clearly favored complete independence, either long-term or as a means of

Antonio López de Santa Anna had appeared to be a strong federalist leader for Mexico, but his switch to centralist policies and his authoritarian presidency greatly fed unrest in Mexican Texas. (*The San Jacinto Museum of History, Houston*)

transferring the region to the United States. A couple of weeks after the Texians' victory at Béxar, the Goliad garrison proclaimed its independence from Mexico. A Texas official in New Orleans collecting supplies for the Texians expressed his sense that "a very large majority of the people wish to come into the Union with Uncle Sam." Yet in general, Anglo leaders remained cautious about advocating a full break from Mexico.

### Readying for War

Santa Anna sought to contain and crush the rebellion in Texas. He had already tried to send word to Cos that the rebels were to be given no quarter. He even "stepped down" as president in order to lead an army across the Rio Grande. Even as the Goliad garrison was making its declaration of independence, Santa Anna was amassing his troops at San Luis Potosi. By the end of the month, they were on the march toward San Antonio.

Santa Anna's threat to the fledgling rebellion was very real but the Mexican force had its own problems: Many of the recruits had only minimal training, and many were draftees who would welcome a chance to bolt; the officers relied on outdated tactics of warfare; there was a serious lack of basic supplies and medical treatment for the widespread illness; there were periodic Indian threats; and the cold was bone-chilling, which proved especially hard on the recruits from tropical Yucatán.

The Texian army had serious problems as well, problems of almost farcical proportions. In November the Consultation had voted an independence advocate, Henry Smith, into the provisional governorship of revolutionary Texas. He and the Council established by the same body had quickly split. The split was in part over a scheme to take Matamoros by federalist José Antonio Mexía and volunteer army leaders, including Frank Johnson and empresario James Grant. The Council supported the enterprise, one of the goals of which was to rally federalists in the other regions of Mexico. Smith stood adamantly against such a brazen gamble with limited forces even as Santa Anna responded to the rebel victory at Béxar.

The Council appointed Johnson and James Fannin as commanders of a Matamoros expedition. Fannin was another veteran of the siege of Béxar and an ardent revolutionary. He had attended West Point, which gave him an added cachet in revolutionary war circles. Immediately after the siege, Houston commissioned him a colonel in the regular army.

Governor Smith insisted that Houston take control of the Matamoros expedition, if there was to be one, and dispatched him to Goliad, the rallying point. Here Houston found James Grant claiming to be acting commander-in-chief. With Grant directing the volunteers, Houston simply joined the enterprise and bided his time.

Soon word came that the Council had rescinded Houston's appointment as commander-in-chief and directed that James Fannin command the expedition. The Council had also deposed Governor Smith after he tried to dissolve it. Houston continued taking orders from Smith, leaving the expedition (which soon fell apart) and going to East Texas to persuade the Cherokees not to align themselves with the Mexican army. A regular army was still a chimera, and the volunteer army was fragmented and confused.

Back in San Antonio, however, J. C. Neill was directing a concerted effort to resist Santa Anna's thrust into Texas. Neill was an artilleryman who had provided cannon-firing distraction as the siege of Béxar began. In the wake of the Texian victory over Cos, the Council had given him a regular army commission as lieutenant colonel of artillery and had left him in command of the volunteers remaining in San Antonio. Neill wrote to Smith and the Council on January 14, "There can exist but little doubt that the enemy is advancing on this post, from the number of families leaving town today." But the Matamoros expedition leaders stripped Neill of men and much-needed supplies; he complained that soldiers who "had not been in the army more than four days" commandeered the clothing sent by the Council for those who had "endured all the hardships of winter

This 1836 view of the Alamo, sketched by Alamo siege participant Lieutenant Colonel José Juan Sánchez-Navarro, indicates that Texians flew the flag of Coahuila y Texas over the old mission, thereby couching the resistance as a struggle of Mexican subjects against the centralist government. *(Benson Latin American Collection, University of Texas at Austin)*

and who were not even sufficiently clad for summer." With only a hundred men, he chose to fortify the old Alamo mission.

In this effort, at least, he had plenty of weaponry—all the artillery left by Cos. Neill and his men mounted the guns on the walls and made other preparations for a siege. Even as they did so, Houston was ordering James Bowie to the Alamo and reportedly instructing him to destroy the mission and remove the troops.

When Bowie arrived on January 19, however, he found Neill's improvements compelling justification to maintain the Alamo as a Texian post, and he entered enthusiastically into preparations for a siege. He also notified Smith that he and Neill were resolved to stay and defend the position. In response, a convinced Smith ordered William Barret Travis, now a regular-army lieutenant colonel, to raise volunteer reinforcements for the post.

Travis balked. He could raise a company of only thirty men, few well-armed. "I am willing, nay anxious, to go to the defense of Béxar, but sir, I am unwilling to risk my reputation (which is ever dear to a soldier) by going off into the enemy's country with such little means, so few men, and with them so badly equipped." Nevertheless, Travis led his meager contingent into the Alamo on February 3.

They were joined on February 8 by a small volunteer force from Tennessee, including one of Tennessee's most famous sons, David, or Davy, Crockett. As a frontier character, Crockett was already the subject of popular literature. A former frontier militiaman and U.S. congressman from Tennessee, he had lost a congressional re-election campaign, and Texas had beckoned as a new avenue for his political and economic aspirations. Like other enthusiastic volunteers, he judged the region "the garden spot of the world. . . . a world of country here to settle."

Furthermore, he anticipated "being elected a member to form a constitution for the province" while "making a fortune yet for myself and family."

At the Alamo, Crockett did not press for a leadership position, which was just as well, as there was already dissension over who would be in command. J. C. Neill was called home by illness in the family on February 14. Travis, with his regular army commission, technically succeeded him, but the volunteers lobbied for Bowie, an elected colonel, to be commander. A vote split along predictable lines: the regulars for Travis, the volunteers for Bowie. Bowie promptly got drunk, then sobered up and suggested that they share the command along the lines already established. Travis agreed, and none too soon, for Santa Anna crossed the Rio Grande on February 16. The next day, General José Urrea crossed as well, his objective to "sweep . . . the coastal prairies" and reclaim Goliad. At about the same time, Jesse Badgett left the Alamo garrison as its delegate to a new convention called by the Council at Washington-on-the-Brazos for March 1; the other garrison-elected delegate, Samuel Maverick, remained.

The convention was a desperate necessity. The provisional government had dissolved in squabbling, leading one citizen to write Sam Houston, "I sincerely hope the Convention will remedy the existing evils and calm the Public since if not Texas must be lost." And squabbling had occurred over who was allowed to elect delegates. Many of the Anglo revolutionaries looked upon the Tejanos with suspicion, although it was finally decided that Tejanos who were against the Mexican government could vote. Two natives of Texas, José Antonio Navarro and José Francisco Ruiz, were elected, along with relative newcomer Lorenzo de Zavala, who had resigned his appointment as a Mexican diplomat in Paris to protest Santa Anna's shift to centralism. Brash recent arrivals including a group of Kentucky volunteers vociferously protested their exclusion from voting, forcing a place for themselves at the ballot box and influencing the election in favor of proindependence candidates unconcerned with a return to the Mexican Constitution of 1824.

When Badgett left to join the other elected delegates, the Alamo defenders still felt that Santa Anna would not be able to reach San Antonio before mid-March. They were wrong. On February 20, some of the local citizens began to depart, accompanied by some of the Tejano members of the garrison. On February 22, a messenger reported that an advance Mexican force was camped only eight miles south of town. The next morning, even more Béxar residents left hastily. By afternoon, garrison members could view from their parapets an ominous sight: Mexican troops flowing into and around the town.

### Siege and Fall of the Alamo

Santa Anna began by demanding that the rebels surrender and "place themselves immediately at the disposal of the Supreme Government from whom alone they may expect clemency after some considerations are taken up." Travis responded with a defiant cannon shot. The Mexican army then began shelling the Alamo walls.

Everyone knew that the walls had to give at some point. The only advantage the Texians enjoyed in this regard was that the Mexicans' heavy siege guns had not yet arrived, and their attempts to position their small cannon close to the structure were met with withering fire from the rebels' accurate long rifles.

Nevertheless, the walls would eventually crumble. Further, supplies and ammunitions within the Alamo would dwindle quickly. The Texians' only real hope lay in the arrival of reinforcements. Bowie and Travis wrote to Fannin at Goliad urging him to bring his force.

The Texians placed their artillery at strategic points, but with only about 150 men, they couldn't hope to keep the Alamo's perimeters covered. Nor did the old mission have defensive firing ports. Even when it had served as a barracks for Mexican troops, the thick adobe walls had not been strong enough to withstand Indian attacks. Now men had to stand, "upper bodies . . . exposed," to pick off approaching soldiers. Even the cannon were exposed to enemy fire.

That fire rained unceasingly upon the compound. On February 24, Travis sent Gonzales resident Captain Albert Martin out to raise volunteer reinforcements. Martin rode to his hometown with Travis's famous "Victory or Death" letter": "*I shall never surrender or retreat.* Then, I call on you in the name of Liberty, of patriotism & everything dear to the American character, to come to our aid with all dispatch." At Gonzales, Martin recruited the Gonzales Ranging Company of Mounted Volunteers, two dozen or so men ranging in age from sixteen to forty-one. A few others joined them on the seventy-mile ride to the Alamo's defense. Nevertheless, the thirty-two reinforcements must have looked paltry indeed when the defenders opened the gates to them on February 29.

Yet these were the only reinforcements the besieged garrison would receive. Fannin had started toward Béxar, then turned around, citing as his reasons an ox-cart breakdown on the road and the warnings of his officers, and arguing that he needed to defend Goliad, as Santa Anna had targeted it, too, and "Both places [Goliad and San Antonio] are importent [*sic*]."

Travis had suspected that Fannin was not coming, and a courier, James Butler Bonham, on March 4 confirmed his apprehension. In the meantime, the Mexican forces, working repeatedly under cover of darkness, extended their batteries so close to the north wall that every volley caused it to disintegrate further.

As the end drew near on March 5, Santa Anna called a meeting of his officers. Many of them listened in consternation as their commander outlined plans for an attack. In their view, the siege was wearing down the Texians garrison, which was running out of provisions. The heavy artillery should arrive in a couple of days and the walls would come down. Why attack at all?

Santa Anna was adamant, arguing that the action would improve the soldiers' morale. But it is clear that what he wanted was a violent retributive victory. Travis, too, had called a meeting of his men. (Their number was long thought to be 189, but modern-day researchers believe there may have been as many as dozens more than this.) The story of Travis's drawing a line in the sand and asking those who would fight to the death to step over the line is apparently only that—a story. But he did apparently offer all of his men the opportunity to slip away if they chose; according to legend, only one—a Frenchman named Louis Rose—did so. Couriers had managed to come and go; Samuel Maverick had finally departed for the Washington-on-the-Brazos convention on March 2; and Juan Seguín had taken Travis's appeals for aid to the settlements, remaining in Gonzales under Houston's orders. By some accounts, Travis also promised the remaining men that they would surrender or attempt to escape if help did not arrive. He even sent an intermediary to Santa Anna in an attempt to discuss surrender terms, only to be rebuffed.

Santa Anna was busy readying the final assault: four columns coming from each direction, with the commander himself overseeing the reserve troops. At the head of one column was General Cos, who had been persuaded by his brother-in-law, Santa Anna, that a promise given to rebels was not binding.

The Mexican forces began their attack at 5:30 A.M. on March 6, the soldiers who had waited through the cold night marching silently into position. The Texians were asleep, their dozing sentinels easily dispatched by an advance guard of light infantry. A few in the Mexican ranks, however, could not resist rallying cries, which woke the Alamo defenders to the sight of the columns already drawing near to the walls.

There followed a bloodbath for both sides. The Texian cannons quickly began spitting grapeshot and followed it with nine-pound iron balls. The metal shards ripped through the tight columns, the iron balls adding to the general destruc-

H. A. McArdle's painting "Dawn at the Alamo" dramatically portrays the battle that began in the early morning hours of March 6, 1836, with carnage on both sides. The Texians' defeat galvanized support for their cause. (*Texas State Library and Archives Commission*)

tion. At the same time, Texians were being picked off the wall at close range by the soldiers' Baker rifles, British arms with great short-distance accuracy. But even the Mexican army's muskets were hitting their marks.

Soldiers scaled the walls. Although they had only a few ladders, they found enough footholds on the north wall that some men were able to slip over and open the north gate. Ironically, the long rifles that had served the Texians so well proved a poor defense at this point, for they took too long to reload, and the troops were pouring into the breach. The invaders even turned the captured cannon on the doors through which the defenders were firing by means of loopholes.

Travis fell early in the fighting, with a bullet in the forehead. Some Texians tried to surrender by waving white cloths, but others fired on the advancing troops. Bowie was killed in his sickbed. The chapel was overrun last, James Butler Bonham and Almeron Dickenson dying beside the cannon they had manned.

Various accounts stated that a few of the defenders fought to the last and were taken prisoner, then executed upon Santa Anna's orders. Certainly the Mexican commander had made it clear that he would grant no quarter. Among those captured and executed, it was rumored, was David Crockett.

The diary of Mexican officer José de la Peña confirmed these accounts. Although the validity of the diary has been challenged, many historians agree that it is legitimate and that Peña's description of events provides an important eyewitness record. In Peña's account, fighting officers, including General Manuel Fernández Castrillón, wanted to spare the six or seven captives, but Santa Anna reacted in disgust, insisting that they be executed. Some of his staff officers, seeking to curry his favor, set upon the captives with bayonets.

San Antonio resident Eulalia Yorba and her children had gone to the home of a Spanish priest to get some food and watched from there as the shooting began. "It seemed as if there were myriads of soldiers and guns about [the Alamo,]" she recalled. "There was volley after volley fired into the barred and bolted windows," with answering volleys and "puffs of smoke from within the Alamo." She observed that "The din was indescribable."

Yorba related that a Mexican colonel came and asked those in the house to minister to the dying Mexican soldiers. When she emerged to do so, "The roadway was thronged with Mexican soldiers with smoke and dirt begrimed faces, haggard eyes and wild, insane expression," she related. In the Alamo itself, she observed doors "splintered and battered in," floors "crimson with blood," the air "dark with powder smoke" and "hot and heavy." Tending to the wounds of some of the Mexican soldiers, she saw dead Texians lying "singly and in heaps of three or four, or in irregular rows here and there all about the floor of the Alamo, just as they had fallen."

Santa Anna summoned Béxar mayor Francisco Antonio Ruiz to identify Travis, Bowie, and Crockett. He also ordered Ruiz to see to the interment of the dead Mexican soldiers, estimated at 600, or one-third of the attack force. But Ruiz did not have the resources to bury so many dead, and his workers threw many in the San Antonio River, where they jammed up in the curves. Pablo Díaz remembered that the sight of the bodies in the river and their stench made him ill, "for they lined the river's course and banks all the way from Crockett Street to more than a mile below."

The Alamo defenders met a different fate, for Santa Anna ordered two funeral pyres built for them. Díaz recalled these ten-foot-high pyres with alternating layers of corpses and firewood. "Grease of different kinds, principally tallow, was melted and poured over the two pyres," he noted. "I saw ashes, as well as the blackened chars of the different anatomical fragments. They emitted an odor even more sickening than did the corpses of those who had been thrown into the river. . . ."

The only Alamo defender to receive burial was Gregorio Esparza, who had served under Juan Seguín in the siege of Béxar and had stayed in his command afterward. Esparza's brother Francisco had served under General Cos. Francisco went to Cos and got permission to take his brother's body. "I proceeded to the Alamo," Francisco would relate, "and found the dead body of my brother in one of the rooms," with "a ball in his breast and a stab from a sword in his side."

Not everyone in the Alamo died. The old mission had also sheltered a number of noncombatants, most of whom survived the carnage. Most famous in Anglo annals are Susannah Dickenson, wife of Almeron, and the Dickensons' child Angelina. But there were also African Americans, chief among them Travis's slave Joe, and a number of members of Tejano families, including Gregorio Esparza's wife and children. One of the children, Enrique, would later relate his mother's courage and pain. The family was marched to the home of Ramón Músquiz, a merchant and political leader who had argued for Anglo American colonization but remained loyal to the Mexican government. Enrique's mother began searching for food in the house for the children and the other refugees. When Músquiz warned her that she was under guard and should not be moving about, "[s]he told him she did not care whether she was under guard or not, she was going to have something to eat for herself, her children, and her companions whom she intended to feed if Santa Anna did not feed his prisoners." Enrique noted, "[a]fter our release we went back to our home and my mother wept for many days and nights."

## The Revolution—The Winning of Independence (March–April)

At the Alamo, a small contingent of men had come together—natives and immigrants, Mexicans, Anglos, and Europeans, old settlers, more recent immigrants, and newly arrived adventurers. They had all sensed opportunity—for glory, for a return to republican principles, for land, for a separate Mexican state of Texas or a Texas tied to the United States. Now their deaths would provide a rallying point for the Texian cause.

## At the Independence Convention

Now delegates to the independence convention were at work at Washington-on-the-Brazos anxiously awaiting news of the Alamo defenders. On March 2, they still thought that Fannin was headed to the Alamo's aid, and they adopted a Texas declaration of independence, decisively breaking with the idea of Texas continuing as part of a federalist Mexico. "The necessity of self-preservation," they concluded, ". . . now decrees our eternal political separation. . . . the people of Texas do now constitute a FREE, SOVEREIGN, and INDEPENDENT REPUBLIC."

Fifty-nine delegates would arrive by March 11, and these members—primarily from the American South, with only one in six residing in Texas before January 1830—set about creating a constitution modeled on the U.S. Constitution and fulfilling as much as possible the functions of a government.

There was no word from or of the Alamo. Lawyer William Fairfax Gray, a land agent traveling in Texas, attended the convention and wrote on the 13th, "The anxiety begins to be intense." Houston, again named military commander-in-chief by the convention, had not tried to hurry to the Alamo's relief, even though Travis's final appeal to the Council, where Houston was a delegate, had arrived on March 5. By one account, Houston doubted the reports from Travis and from Fannin, considering them political grandstanding. Departing on March 6 for Gonzales, however, he had just begun to put together a new force composed of both volunteers and militia, and even if he had hurried, he would have been too late.

News of the Alamo's fall reached Gonzales on March 11, the same day as Houston's arrival, and was quickly followed by the arrival of noncombatant survivors. With so many of the townsmen in the Alamo and now dead, the community took on a horrified mourning. Houston resolved not to be trapped in any one place and retreated to Burnham's Crossing on the Colorado. With both Santa Anna's and Urrea's forces threatening the western settlements, he ordered that Gonzales be burned and abandoned—no doubt adding to the grief and disorientation of its residents. He had already sent word to Fannin at Goliad to join him, with plans to combine Fannin's volunteer army of about 400 with his own force of about the same size.

At Washington-on-the-Brazos, delegates worked hurriedly to define laws and the governmental structure of a new republic. They followed some Spanish and Mexican precedents, for example, in laws on homestead exemptions and debtor relief. The delegates tried to address the thorny issue of land claims through such measures as voiding some eleven-league claims and questionable titles, noting that "one of the great duties of this convention" was "the protection of the public domain from unjust and fraudulent claims, and quieting the people in the enjoyment of their lands."

Convention members used a definition of citizenship that included Tejanos but excluded "Africans, the descendants of Africans, and Indians" and affirmed the continued practice of slaveholding. The republic Congress would not "have power to emancipate slaves," although an owner who did so would either need the Congress's approval or have to "send his or her slave or slaves without the limits of the Republic," because congressional approval would be required for a freedman or -woman to reside in the state.

The governmental structure devised by the convention reflected the American system: executive, legislative, and judicial branches; a Senate and a House of Representatives; and supreme, district, county, and justice courts.

On March 17, members approved the document in an atmosphere of continued anxiety and uncertainty. They settled on an interim government that included empresarios David G. Burnet as president and Lorenzo de Zavala as vice president, with Samuel P. Carson as secretary of state, Robert Potter as secretary of the tiny Texas navy, David Thomas as attorney general, Bailey Hardeman as treasurer, and Thomas Jefferson Rusk as secretary of war.

## Further Setbacks: The Runaway Scrape and the Fannin Massacre

As the independence convention ended, a general panic swept the settlements with the news of the Alamo's fall and Houston's retreat. Families began a pell-mell rush eastward and southeastward in what became known as the Runaway Scrape. "Deserters were constantly passing us on foot and on horseback," remembered Rosa von Roeder Kleberg, who had settled outside San Felipe. "The old men who were with the families laughed at them and called to them, 'Run! Run! Santa Anna is after you!'" Frances Meneffee Sutherland, mourning the loss of her son, William DePriest Sutherland, in the Alamo, reported, "We went to the Colorado, forty miles, but after some time, [Houston] thought proper to retreat farther and of course we had to go, too." At the Brazos River, they stopped for a few days, her husband leaving to join the republic army. But news came that the Mexican army was drawing near, and the settlers continued their confused flight. "I wish you could know how the people did as they kept going about trying to get somewhere," Sutherland wrote, "but no person knew where they were going to get to."

Families suffered greatly. Dilue Rose Harris, "near eleven years old" when the Alamo was under attack, would later remember her family's desperate flight: "We left home at sunset, hauling clothes, bedding and provisions on the sleigh with one yoke of oxen." At the Lynchburg ferry on the San Jacinto River, they found "fully five thousand people trying to get across," including a number of slaves. After waiting three days to cross, they proceeded onto a prairie where her uncle's wagon bogged down. At the next stage of the journey, the crossing of the Trinity River, again people were jostling to cross. One of Harris's sisters had fallen ill, and the family was allowed to cross first, but their boat flooded and Harris's little sister "was in convulsions." (The girl would later die on the five-week journey.) For some, however, the advancing Mexican troops evoked a quite different response. Some slaves, rather than aiding in the retreat, simply rushed to meet the troops, gaining protection and freedom, for Santa Anna and General Urrea no longer countenanced the practice of slavery.

As many Texians scrambled, wondering if they would ever be able to return to their frontier homes, Houston continued to fall back—and Fannin failed to appear to join forces with him. Fannin had his own escalating troubles. He had ordered a company to Refugio to evacuate settlers there, only to have them run into a detachment of Urrea's troops. Urrea had been making a successful incursion into the coastal prairies, crushing what was left of the Matamoros expedition at San Patricio. His troops now bested the Goliad company and the battalion sent to reinforce it, the Georgia battalion. Most of the latter managed to get away, but Urrea was helped by loyal Tejano residents of the Refugio-San Patricio area, some of whom had received highhanded treatment from the Texian volunteers.

The Goliad garrison consisted almost entirely of very recent newcomers to Texas, Fannin being one of the exceptions with about a year and a half residence. Fannin was also unusual because he had some formal military training, although it did not serve him well. His situation was unfortunate, but he compounded it, with fatal consequences.

Fannin had not wanted to leave his troops at Refugio, but when he received word of their defeat on the afternoon of March 17, he still failed to follow Houston's orders to retreat. This gave Urrea's scouts time to start reconnoitering the garrison. By the evening of the 18th, Fannin was trying to get the march started, but the night was deemed "too murky for a proper march." The next morning, the garrison members delayed further, failing to make use of an obscuring fog. Fannin, ignoring Houston's order to dump the nine cannons in the river, instead burdened underfed oxen with baggage and artillery. When the troops finally departed, the oxen proved agonizingly slow. Garrison member Herman Ehrenberg noted "disgust at the creeping pace of our column induced us finally to abandon all our equipment."

In perhaps his most inexplicable move, Fannin called the column to a halt for a rest break in the middle of a prairie after only six miles of travel. Some of his men protested, eyeing the relative safety of a distant tree line, but he apparently felt that the Mexican troops would not attack a 400-man contingent. Fannin's troops rested for an hour without incident, but soon after resuming the march, they looked back to see numerous Mexican cavalrymen spilling from the timberline two miles away.

Again, Fannin rejected the idea of trying to reach the tree line ahead, despite the arguments of his officers that it would be better to push toward a defensive position even if casualties were high along the way. Fannin had the men "form a hollow square, with the artillery posted at the corners." In the early afternoon, the Mexican dragoons began the attack. Fannin's men were able to direct withering rifle, musket, and artillery fire on the advancing troops, but Mexican sharpshooters picked off the Texian gunners. The Mexicans mounted charge after charge, and Fannin, to his credit, bravely led the defense. But the Texian force had run out of water, and the Mexican troops had shot the oxen, making it impossible to move the baggage and the wounded. With nightfall came a cessation in the fighting, aside from sporadic sniper fire, but also the knowledge that Urrea's troops had them surrounded.

The only possible escape seemed to be a stealthy nighttime retreat, but Fannin's men agreed that they could not do this for it would mean abandoning the wounded. They tried through the night to erect breastworks, but when the morning dawned, they were greeted with reinforcements and more artillery on the Mexican side. An injured Fannin called a truce and approached General Urrea to discuss terms. Urrea offered him only the opportunity to "surrender at discretion." Fannin interpreted this to mean their lives would be spared.

Fannin's command surrendered. On the Texian side, nine had been killed, fifty-one wounded; among the Mexican troops, fifty had been killed, 140 wounded. The prisoners would be held in Goliad, and joined by members of the Georgia battalion captured by Mexican cavalry. Urrea was one of a number of Mexican officers who disagreed with Santa Anna's edict that captured rebels should be killed; he wanted to spare the men. He even allowed Fannin to go to the coast with a German in Mexican service, Colonel Juan Holsinger, to see about gaining passage for the prisoners on a ship bound for New Orleans. But no ship was available, and Santa Anna reiterated his edict.

On Palm Sunday, March 27, the order was carried out. The Texians were divided into four groups and told they were being marched to Matamoros. Instead, after a short march, with the groups now isolated from each other, Mexican infantry opened fire on them, with lancers backing them up. Three hundred and forty-two of the prisoners died outside Goliad that day; twenty-eight would

"The March to the Massacre," by Andrew Houston, depicts James Fannin's troops leaving Goliad as prisoners. Told they were being marched to Matamoros, instead most were executed a short distance from Goliad. (*The San Jacinto Museum of History, Houston*)

manage to escape the carnage, including two doctors spared because they were desperately needed to tend the Mexican troops. A firing squad executed Fannin separately, his mortal wound a bullet through the face. Again, the Mexicans burned the Texian dead. The killings would become known to Texans as the "Fannin Massacre."

### Sam Houston and San Jacinto

During this time Secretary of War Thomas Jefferson Rusk, a South Carolinian who had joined Burnet's colony in 1835, was active in moving the interim government to the relative safety of Harrisburg and in organizing militias to defend against the eastward-moving Mexican forces. He also found himself in the unenviable position of trying to coordinate with and direct General Houston. Despite grumblings from his army, Houston had retreated again on March 19, judging the Burnham's Crossing location indefensible and a poor strategic location to keep Santa Anna from striking the settlements. At his new location, Beason's Crossing, he welcomed a sizable number of new volunteers, residents of the settlements who had tried to stay out of the conflict but now had been galvanized by news of the Alamo's fall. Here, however, on March 23 he received news of Fannin's defeat and surrender. It was a terrible blow. Along with the news that Santa Anna had dispatched General Joaquín Ramírez y Sesma to Beason's Crossing with a large force, it caused Houston to retreat again, this time to San Felipe.

Houston's decision brought him further censure and even desertion among the troops, who resented the apparent weakness of such a move. Historians, however, have generally concluded that an engagement at Beason's Crossing would not have helped the Texian cause, at least not in the long run.

In the meantime, Urrea's troops had been effective, especially in the victory over Fannin and in shutting off to the Texians all coastal ports except Galveston. Yet torrential spring rains had slowed the movement of the entire Mexican army, and Santa Anna was just rousing himself to leave San Antonio. He joined Sesma and General Eugenio Tolsa, their goal an attack on San Felipe, Houston's new headquarters and the heart of the Anglo colonies.

At San Felipe, to the dismay of many of his troops, Houston ordered another retreat, to Jared Groce's plantation twenty miles away. He left two companies guarding the San Felipe and Fort Bend crossings and departed with the rest of the army, now numbering about 500.

Santa Anna's combined forces pressed toward San Felipe, arriving nine days after Houston's departure. By this time, the remaining Texians had burned the town and disappeared. But Santa Anna had discovered that the Texian government was in nearby Harrisburg, to the east of the army, whereas Houston's force was to its west. Santa Anna saw an opportunity to seize the rebel government and at the same time cut off Galveston Bay, the one remaining "rebel lifeline to the United States."

The rebel government, like many of the soldiers, chafed at Houston's inaction.

President David Burnet sent a missive to Houston: "Sir: The enemy are laughing you to scorn. You must fight them. You must retreat no further. The country expects you to fight. The salvation of the country depends on your doing so."

Houston's army had swollen again—to 900—and the two weeks at Groce's plantation had allowed them to rest and recuperate from a host of ills brought on by hard camp living and relentless rain. They had also drilled in some of the rudiments of warfare. Rusk had been told to seize command from Houston if he still refused to attack, and some of the troops clearly wanted Rusk to do so. But the secretary of war listened to Houston's justifications for his actions up to this point and responded by joining the army. On April 12, Houston started them eastward.

Santa Anna's advance troops made it to Harrisburg late on April 15, but the governor and his cabinet escaped to New Washington, a short distance to the south on the San Jacinto River. As Santa Anna's troops pursued, they moved away again, to Galveston Island. Santa Anna was still between Houston and the Texas government. Learning that Houston was moving eastward toward the Trinity River, the Mexican general prepared to block the Texian march at the Lynchburg Crossing on Buffalo Bayou near Harrisburg.

Houston's plans and motives at this point remained unclear; some of his officers later maintained that he was seriously considering taking his force across the Sabine to Louisiana to recruit more volunteers. The Texian army was coming to a crucial crossroad: If Houston ordered them to go north, they would be headed toward Nacogdoches and away from Santa Anna. If he ordered them to follow the road to Harrisburg, they would be almost sure to fight.

As it turned out, the army did not await a command, but simply surged toward Harrisburg when they reached the crossroad. Houston was simply carried along by the tide, his intentions still unknown. The army would fight.

Santa Anna was in New Washington, with about 660 of his men. Houston learned this from letters seized from a captured Mexican messenger and realized that he had a good opportunity to strike. He had had to leave almost 250 men ill at Harrisburg, but his numbers were swelling again, and he finally exhorted the troops, urging them to remember the Alamo. The troops added a cry of "Remember Goliad!" and commenced the tricky crossing of Buffalo Bayou, then marched till about midnight. The next morning, they learned that the Mexican troops were headed toward Lynch's Ferry. Whoever reached it first would gain the advantage of the best tactical position from which to fight.

The Texians arrived first and established themselves in a high oak grove, a position particularly well suited for their riflemen. Santa Anna had to take a relatively risky position, but he immediately sent men to test the Texians' defenses. They were greeted by fire from two cannons, dubbed the Twin Sisters, and responded with their own twelve-pounder, but the Texians won this initial skirmish, forcing the Mexican artillery back into a wood.

Some Texians wanted to press on immediately. Although Houston said no, he did allow the hotspur Sidney Sherman to reconnoiter with a group of mounted riflemen. Sherman immediately ignored orders and charged the Mexican cavalry.

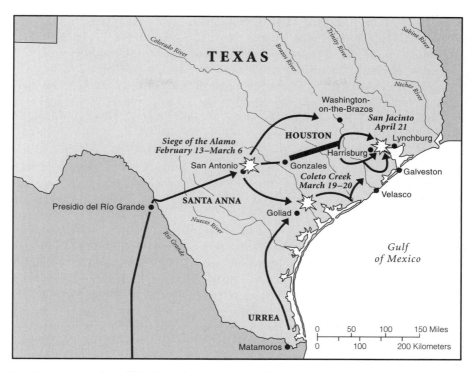

Revolutionary battles—"The Texas Revolution, 1836."

When he asked for infantry assistance, Houston refused. But again, the Texian army took the decision out of their commander's hands, a whole infantry regiment responding to Sherman's plea and deliberately ignoring Houston's order to turn around. This time the Mexicans successfully repulsed them.

Both armies settled down for the night, although the Mexicans were busy building breastworks in their relatively vulnerable position. They were also eagerly awaiting the arrival of General Cos, on his way with reinforcements. At 9 A.M. the next morning, Cos appeared with about 540 men.

This, of course, shifted the numerical advantage: Houston had 910 men, Santa Anna about 1,200. Historians have asked why Houston did not attack during the night, as he knew Cos was on his way. Houston's troops asked the same thing. Many of them were also furious when the whole morning went by with no action on Houston's part. What if further reinforcements arrived? Houston and his officers met from noon to 2 P.M., with differing accounts of the meeting. But finally, as the afternoon wore on, Houston himself ordered the men into battle positions, to advance in two lines over a rise that had separated them from the Mexicans' view. Houston had at first denied Juan Seguín's detachment a place in the battle force because many of the other soldiers had demonstrated considerable animosity toward Mexicans in general; Houston was afraid that some of the

Mexicans might be shot by their own compatriots as the battle raged. But Seguín and his men had argued for the opportunity to fight, reminding Houston of their unflagging commitment to the cause. They went into battle wearing cardboard insignias on their hats to distinguish them from Santa Anna's forces.

Santa Anna had kept a close watch through most of the day but had grown complacent, despite the worries of some of his officers. Houston had not mounted a full attack yet; why should he now, just after the Mexican force had built breastworks and received reinforcements?

Thus, the Texians' artillery unit advanced "within two hundred yards of the enemy's breastworks" and opened fire. This was immediately followed by a Texian cavalry charge. Houston had the infantry hold their fire, but once they had fired the first volley he lost command of them and they fell to skirmishing, some using their rifles as clubs.

The Mexican officers also struggled to organize their startled, confused, and frightened troops and get them to listen to orders, but without success. With Texians scaling the barricades, the eighteen-minute battle became a rout—and a bloodbath. The Texians were bent on revenge, and they killed indiscriminately and often brutally. Even the Tejano volunteers proved ruthless. Many Mexican soldiers jumped into a nearby lake, calling desperately "Me no Alamo—me no Goliad!" but they were easy targets for the Texian guns, and the lake soon ran red with their blood.

This William Huddle painting of Houston accepting Santa Anna's surrender after the battle of San Jacinto shows Houston reclining as a result of an ankle wound sustained in the battle. *(Texas State Library and Archives Commission)*

Six hundred and fifty Mexican soldiers were killed, most of them after the brief battle, and most of the rest were captured quickly. The victory for the Texians was decisive but not complete. They had subdued only a part of the Mexican army. At first, they even feared that Santa Anna had escaped them, but he was apprehended after spending the night of April 21 hiding in a marsh. Under terms of his surrender, Santa Anna ordered his second-in-command, Vincente Filisola, to retreat to Béxar. Filisola judged the campaign lost, with Santa Anna captured and Mexican supply lines stretched thin. He refused to listen to some of the other Mexican officers who counseled continued warfare, especially the able Urrea, and instead retreated not just to Béxar but all the way across the Rio Grande.

## Conclusion

The volunteer army had made the independence declared at Washington-on-the-Brazos a reality. Texas was now a nation born in conflict—not only the conflict between the Mexican government and its recalcitrant Texas subjects, but conflict among those subjects as well. There had been the war and peace parties, and within the war party those fighting for recognition of a separate Mexican statehood and those fighting for separation from Mexico. There had been those who simply wanted to be left alone and were drawn unwillingly into the conflict. There had been tensions between newcomers and established Texians, with the roles constantly shifting. Newcomers did not have the perspective of residents of a year or two; residents of a year or two did not have the perspective of Austin's Old Three Hundred; and Austin's Old Three Hundred did not have the perspective of Tejano residents. There had been tensions between Anglos and Tejanos, even as some of them had worked and fought well together. There had been tensions among the Anglos dominating the new military and the new government, with pro- and anti-Houston factions, pro- and anti-Smith factions.

Somehow, in part due to Santa Anna's harsh and arrogant conduct of the war in Texas, all of this had added up to a victory for the revolutionaries. But there were still many tensions to be resolved. The Mexican government would refuse to recognize Texas independence; Mexicans were bitter about losing part of their territory so early in their own history as an independent nation, with many struggling to maintain republican principles shared with the United States. The United States would see the developments in Texas as both a blessing and a curse: With possible annexation, Texas provided an opportunity for U.S. westward expansion, but it would also be a catalyst for further problems between the slaveholding antebellum South and the North. Texas slaves themselves saw any hope of an improvement in their status and for freedom disappear. With Anglos from the American South overwhelmingly in positions of power, racial and ethnic differences would become more significant. Juan Seguín would find post-revolution Texas more difficult to endure than the sieges of Béxar and the Alamo and the battle of San Jacinto, until he became, as he said, "a foreigner in my native land."

But he was indisputably one of the most prominent revolutionary veterans, and he would continue in the service of the republic. To him was given the task of burying the remains of the Alamo defenders. Shortly before the first anniversary of the Alamo's fall, he located the heaps of ashes from the cremation and interred them after a sober procession, with "three volleys of musquetry . . . fired over the grave by the whole Battalion." Seguín did not have enough powder to fire the larger guns, "but every honor was done within the reach of my scanty means." The Alamo would ever loom large in Texians' memory, but old and new challenges awaited.

## SUGGESTED READINGS

The Texas Revolution—particularly the defense of the Alamo—has generated copious scholarship and dramatic conjecture. A classic scholarly work is Amelia Williams's "A Critical Study of the Siege of the Alamo and of the Personnel of Its Defenders" in *Southwestern Historical Quarterly* (1932–33). Paul Lack's *The Texas Revolutionary Experience, A Political and Social History, 1835–1836* (1992) is a key scholarly source for understanding the events of the Revolution. Another key source is Stephen L. Hardin's clear and informative *Texian Iliad: A Military History of the Texas Revolution (1994).* A good brief overview is provided in "Colonization and Revolution," the first chapter of Richard Bruce Winders's *Crisis in the Southwest: The United States, Mexico, and the Struggle over Texas* (2002). The *New Handbook of Texas* (1996) has a detailed "Texas Revolution" entry and helpful entries on the key events and participants.

Despite the debates as to its veracity, José Enrique de la Peña's *With Santa Anna in Texas: A Personal Narrative of the Revolution* is an important source for the period. For other primary sources, consult *Documents of Texas History* (1994), eds. Ernest Wallace, David M. Vigness, and George B. Ward; *The Papers of the Texas Revolution* (1973), compiled by John H. Jenkins; and "Revolutionary Texas, 1835–1836," in Sam Haynes and Cary D. Wintz's *Major Problems in Texas History* (2002).

### The Revolution—Early Months (October–December 1835)

In addition to the works above, Gregg Cantrell's *Stephen F. Austin, Empresario of Texas* provides good secondary material on the early months of the war. Alwyn Barr focuses on the siege of Béxar in his *Texans in Revolt: the Battle for San Antonio, 1835* (1990). Interesting primary accounts are included in Noah Smithwick's *Evolution of a State* and Herman Ehrenberg's "The Fight for Freedom in Texas," included in Natalie Ornish's *Ehrenberg: Goliad Survivor, Old West Explorer* (1997). Graham Davis's "Models of Migration: The Historiography of the Irish Pioneers in South Texas" in *Southwestern Historical Quarterly* (1996) includes an analysis of how one ethnic group split in its loyalties between the Mexican government and the revolutionaries.

### The Revolution—Victory and Defeat (December 1835–March 1836)

William C. Davis's *Three Roads to the Alamo: The Lives and Fortunes of David Crockett, James Bowie, and William Barret Travis* (1998) examines in detail the three men's paths to the Alamo and provides a brief account of the Alamo's fall. *A Line in the Sand: The Alamo in Blood and Memory* (2001), by Randy Roberts and James N. Olson, examines both the events at the Alamo and the myths surrounding them. Primary accounts of the period leading up to the Alamo battle and the Alamo's fall appear in Bill Groneman's *Eyewitnesses to the Alamo* (1996), Ron Jackson's *Alamo Legacy: Alamo Descendants Remember the Alamo* (1997), and Timothy M. Matovina's *The Alamo Remembered: Tejano Accounts and Perspectives* (1995).

### The Revolution—The Winning of Independence (March–April 1836)

Good primary accounts are included in Jackson's *Alamo Legacy,* in editor Paul Lack's *The Diary of William Fairfax Gray from Virginia to Texas, 1835–1837* (1997), in Crystal Sasse Ragsdale's *The Golden Free Land* (1976), and in the reminiscences of Dilue Rose Harris, included in Jo Ella Powell Exley's *Texas Tears and Texas Sunshine.* Juan Seguín's story from this period is told in *A Revolution Remembered* (1991), edited by Jesús F. de la Teja.

Sam Houston comes to prominence in this portion of the Revolutionary story; there have been numerous biographies of this leading Texas figure. A good one for reference is Randolph B. Campbell's *Sam Houston and the American Southwest* (1993).

# 8

# Texas Independent, Texas Annexed, 1836–1859

**P**leasant and Margaret Fowler were bringing their young family home to their farm in Austin's colony near the gulf coast, the Runaway Scrape over, independence a fragile reality. The family arrived after dark and camped, having heard that Mexican troops had vandalized their house. When morning dawned, they found hogs exiting its front door, floorboards pulled up, and their possessions scattered. Pleasant immediately began plowing, while Margaret shocked daughter Dilue Rose by veering from religious observance and doing the family wash on a Sunday. Neighbors were filtering back, tired and threadbare. Bread was hard to come by. Across the settlements, homes had to be restored, cattle reclaimed or replaced, food provisions renewed. "Mother was very despondent," Dilue would write, "but father was hopeful. He said Texas would . . . become a great nation."

The challenges in this assessment were immense. Mexico was refusing to recognize its newly won independence, and other nations—including the United States—would be slow with official recognition. The populace lived under a continued threat of renewed attack from Mexico, as well as from the Comanches and other hostile tribes to the north and west. All of the old problems of living on a frontier had been exacerbated by the losses and disruptions of the war. Many residents now openly advocated annexation to the United States, both because most of the population had strong American roots and because of the need for stability and security. Yet annexation would be long in coming, and when it finally occurred, new struggles over identity would stress and eventually fracture the state.

## CHAPTER 8 — Texas Independent, Texas Annexed

| | |
|---|---|
| 1836 | Sam Houston becomes first elected president of Republic of Texas |
| 1837 | U.S. recognizes Republic of Texas but rebuffs Texas attempts to win annexation |
| 1838 | Mirabeau B. Lamar succeeds Houston as republic president; Vicente Córdova leads Córdova rebellion |
| 1839 | Cherokees are forced from Texas |
| 1842 | Houston again becomes republic president; Mexican troops twice invade Texas, which Mexico refuses to recognize as independent; Somervell and Mier expeditions are mounted in retaliation |
| 1844–46 | German stock company Adelsverein transports thousands of German immigrants to Texas |
| 1845 | Mexico offers to recognize Texas if the republic will not annex itself to another country, but Texas wins annexation to the U.S. |
| 1846 | War between Mexico and the U.S. begins; Baylor University opens in Independence |
| 1848 | Treaty of Guadalupe Hidalgo cedes Mexican holdings in American Southwest and West to U.S. |
| 1850 | Compromise of 1850 limits Texas boundaries but gives the state a financial boost |
| 1859 | Indians on West Texas reservations are expelled to Indian Territory; Juan Cortina leads insurrection in South Texas |
| 1860 | Texas slave owners make up just over a quarter of the population but hold three-fourths of the wealth; Texas is strongly identified as a southern state |

Dilue Rose Harris was only eleven years old when she participated in the Runaway Scrape of 1836; she would remain a Texan, watching the Houston area grow, marrying, and bearing nine children. *(The San Jacinto Museum of History, Houston)*

## The Quests for Annexation and Empire, 1836–1841

The captive Santa Anna had been sent to Washington, D.C., but not before signing two treaties at Velasco: a public one in which he promised not to engage in warfare against Texas, and a private one, in which he agreed to work to get the Mexican government to recognize Texas's independence. But for many an independent Texas was simply a prelude to annexation to the United States. As interim president David G. Burnet struggled to get the government on a solid footing, setting national elections for September 1836, the ballot would include the proposition that Texas seek annexation.

### Sam Houston's Administration

In the new republic, old antagonisms and factions had resurfaced, men jockeying for positions of influence and power in the new order. The situation was intensified by the volatile mix of newcomers who had arrived during the Revolution and by the lack of a strong, well-established governmental structure.

Many were concerned about the new state of affairs. Revolution veteran

Mirabeau B. Lamar lamented that Texas was "upon the verge of anarchy, with too little credit abroad, and too much of the fiery elements of discord at home." Thomas Jefferson Rusk, the popular commander-in-chief of the postwar army of Texas, wrote in August: "If we do not soon adopt some system and some rules of Law to govern the angry passions of men we shall forfeit all our claims to the benefits of that kind providence to whom we owe our success so far."

Rusk refused to run for president of the republic. Stephen F. Austin was being promoted in some quarters and agreed to serve if elected, but many—especially newcomers and those who had served or were serving in the army—saw him as too vested in the empresario system, still tied to old ways of relating to Mexico. Another candidate, strongly opposed to Austin, was the volatile former provisional governor Henry Smith. However, the enmities that had developed between him and other officials during his provisional governership were deeply troubling; Texas could ill afford another situation with such divisive leadership.

On August 20, a third candidate entered the race: Sam Houston. Houston had had strong critics throughout the Revolution, and the victory at San Jacinto had not completely silenced them. But Houston brought to the table the glory of the victory, a strong public identity and presence, and a background in both political and military affairs. He announced that he was stepping forward because "the crisis requires it."

In the election that followed, both Houston and the annexation proposal won resounding victories. Measures to approve the Constitution hammered out at Washington-on-the-Brazos and to authorize the new Texas Congress to make changes to that constitution also passed.

Thus, even as they approved the document that spelled out their independence, Texas voters favored annexation. In doing so, they were saying from shortly after the birth of the republic that they preferred to identify with the United States, that they preferred the security and definition of being part of that nation to "going it alone." Yet annexation was beyond the control of Texans and would not occur for longer than many expected or hoped. The quest for annexation would color the decade Texas spent as a republic, especially the politics of the era, even as new Texans—the term "Texian" no longer widely used—and new developments altered the social and economic landscape.

When Sam Houston took office in October 1836, Texas had already begun to press the U.S. government for annexation. Interim president Burnet had sent two representatives to Washington that summer. They had made little headway. Houston also declared a commitment to Texas's annexation to the United States, proclaiming in his inaugural address, "The appeal is made by a willing people. Will our friends disregard it? . . . We are cheered by the hope that they will receive us to a participancy of their civil, political, and religious rights, and hail us welcome into the great family of freemen."

Despite Houston's optimistic plea, the U.S. government was wary of even providing diplomatic recognition of the new republic. In December, President Andrew Jackson told the U.S. Congress that they should delay recognition, as

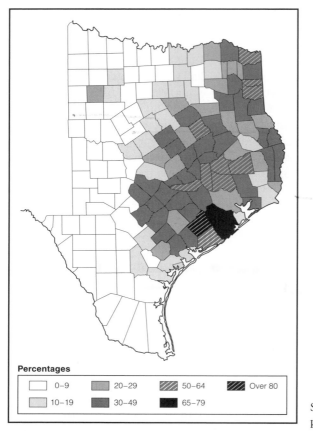

**Percentages**

| | | | |
|---|---|---|---|
| 0–9 | 20–29 | 50–64 | Over 80 |
| 10–19 | 30–49 | 65–79 | |

Slaves as a percentage of total population, 1860.

acknowledging Texas's shaky independence would only deepen the Mexican government's anger and convince it that the United States was in league with the Texans in plotting annexation. Also, Jackson was wary of the powerful antislavery forces opposing annexation in Washington.

The North and South had been increasingly at odds on this issue since the inception of the American republic. When President Thomas Jefferson completed the Louisiana Purchase in 1803, there were no stipulations against slavery in this vast tract west of the Mississippi, stretching from Louisiana in the South all the way to present-day Montana.

Missouri was one of the first areas in the region to be settled by U.S. emigrants. When Missouri applied to be admitted to the Union as a slave state in 1819, much bitter wrangling ensued among proponents of slavery and aggressive expansion of the slave system (mostly in the Lower South), those adamantly opposed to it (mostly in the North), and those with more tentative or limited proposals in the middle (mostly in the Upper South). These different views reflected different economic and political realities and visions, pitting the North with its growing emphasis on industrialization, free labor, and republicanism against the

Lower South, burgeoning economically through the cultivation of cotton with a large, captive work force and defining itself by old paternalistic models of privilege and responsibility. The Missouri Compromise that ultimately emerged involved maintaining the balance between slave and free states in the Union, establishing a latitudinal boundary, and admitting Missouri as a slave state and Maine as a free state at about the same time.

Aside from these serious divisions over slavery, which would continue to affect Texas's fortunes, it was unclear whether Texas was even going to survive as a republic. A U.S. agent had noted in August that Texas "may still be considered a mere experiment upon independence which the loss of friends or of a single battle may disperse to the winds."

With Texas agents in Washington working feverishly, Congress recognized the Republic of Texas in the spring of 1837. Yet Texans were disappointed, having hoped for annexation. As one observer wrote, the prospect was grim for a "Texas independent, and compelled to fight her own battles and pay her own debts."

Yet this was the reality, and republic officials had begun trying to address the challenges. In the fall the first Congress had established the new town of Houston as the temporary capital and had identified twenty-three counties, based primarily on the Mexican municipalities already in existence. They had set up a Supreme Court with a chief justice and four associate justices, as well as a county court system. They had approved development of an army, a navy, a small force of mounted rangers, a militia, and frontier forts and trading posts. In December, they had also attempted to establish the southern and western boundaries of Texas: the length of the Rio Grande as it arced from its source in what is now southern Colorado and vertically bisected present-day New Mexico, then veered southeastward, forming the extended southern boundary of Texas and emptying into the Gulf of Mexico.

The Adams-Onis Treaty of 1819, which affirmed U.S. claims to Florida and Spanish claims to Texas, had established the eastern boundary of what was then Spanish Texas along the Sabine River, and the northern and northwestern boundaries along the Red River westward and northward to the Arkansas River. Texas and Louisiana would continue to quibble over the exact location of the eastern boundary. But far more problematic was the action of the First Congress regarding the southern and western borders. First, Mexican officials were not prepared to accept any borders between Mexico and an independent Texas, having rejected any treaties Santa Anna signed at Velasco. Second, the Nueces River, in some places more than 150 miles north of the Rio Grande on its west-to-east course, seemed a likelier southern border to some; there was very little Texas settlement beyond it. The same argument could be applied to Texas's grandiose claims to the Rio Grande on its vertical course through New Mexico, as republic settlement barely extended westward to what is now central Texas. These border issues would take on more and more significance.

Even as Texas leaders sought to claim an extended domain, however, most Texans continued to look toward annexation to the United States as the answer to many of their problems—in particular, defense against a Mexican invasion, protection against hostile Indians, and debt relief. The new republic had started with a debt of $1,250,000 and had little hope of doing anything but adding to it.

In the summer of 1837, Houston started diplomatic negotiations with Great Britain and France in hopes of strengthening Texas's position through further recognition and political and economic alliances. At the same time, Texas formally asked the U.S. government for annexation. The administration of Martin Van Buren argued that such a move would violate U.S. treaty agreements with Mexico. But again, there was another factor behind the government's reluctance: strong resistance in the North to the specter of another slaveholding state entering the Union. The request languished until the following summer, when Houston appointed Anson Jones minister to the United States and instructed him to withdraw it.

In the last days of the first Houston administration, officials pursued two courses simultaneously: developing Texas's ability to stand alone by establishing alliances with European nations and enticing United States officials to reconsider annexation.

## Mirabeau Lamar's Administration

Major changes occurred, however, with the election of Houston's vice president, Mirabeau B. Lamar, to the presidency in November 1838. The Constitution had prohibited the first president of the republic from seeking a second consecutive term. Lamar had emerged as one of the heroes of San Jacinto. A native of Georgia, he had been a Georgia state senator before two failed attempts at a congressional seat. After arriving in Texas and participating in the Revolution, he had briefly and unsuccessfully acted as major general and commander-in-chief of the chaotic Texas army.

Lamar differed from Houston in many ways. He had an intense interest in education and the arts and was known as the "poet-president" of Texas. Early on he succeeded in passing a land act for public education that set the stage for the development of public education in Texas.

Lamar's differences from Houston were more evident, however, in his attitude regarding Texas independence. Lamar was an unabashed proponent of an empire for the Republic of Texas. In other words, he had little use for talk of annexation. Instead, he looked to strengthen and expand the republic—even as far as the Pacific Ocean. As one step in this process, Lamar moved the capital of Texas from Houston, near the gulf coast, to the ragged little settlement of Waterloo on the eastern edge of the Edwards Plateau in what was then far West Texas. Rechristened Austin in honor of Stephen F. Austin, who had died in a bout with pneumonia in December 1836, the remote settlement on the banks of the Colorado River would serve as the seat of Lamar's administration—and his projected empire.

Under Lamar, the Texas Congress ratified Jones's withdrawal of the annexation request. The diplomatic work abroad begun by Houston continued, as Texas struggled to take its place among other nations. Some European nations gradually began to realize that it would be in their best interests to acknowledge the new

This lithograph of Austin, the new capital of Texas in 1840, appeared in an 1844 emigrants' guide. It shows a rudimentary settlement, with Congress Avenue stopping at the site of the future state capitol. *(CN 01547, The Center for American History, The University of Texas at Austin)*

republic. In September 1839, France, embroiled in a war with Mexico, recognized the independence of Texas. The government of England had also become more receptive to the republic's request for recognition. England faced a possible war with the United States and wanted to maintain a flow of cotton, which Texas could help provide. It also did not want France to gain the upper hand in trade and negotiations with Texas. In 1840, English and Texan representatives signed three treaties acknowledging Texas's independence and setting trade and navigation guidelines.

Lamar also sought to stanch the threat from Mexico, where Santa Anna had regained power. Released in Washington, D.C. less than a month after the battle of San Jacinto, Santa Anna had temporarily retired, then reemerged as a military leader in an 1838 conflict between Mexico and the French, becoming acting president of Mexico in 1839 and dictator in 1841. Not only had the Mexican Congress rejected his Velasco treaties, but the Texas government had not fulfilled all of the treaties' stipulations, and Santa Anna himself had little use for these promises made under duress.

A member of the Lamar administration, former South Carolina lawyer Bernard Bee, served as a diplomatic agent to the government of Mexico. He sailed to Veracruz in May 1839, carrying an offer of a $5 million payment if Mexico would recognize Texas's independence and accept the Rio Grande as the southern and western boundary between the two nations. Santa Anna, however, rejected a meeting, and the Mexican Council of State quickly rejected the proposal.

Lamar sent envoys to Mexico in late 1839 and in early 1841, but again without results. Meanwhile, he looked to other means of establishing Texas's claims to the plateaus, prairies, and plains to the west. He also recognized the need to bring trade dollars into Texas, as the republic treasury had never been adequate for the demands made upon it, much less for expansionist plans, and Lamar was significantly adding to Texas's debts. Thus the Santa Fe Expedition of 1841 was born.

### The Santa Fe Expedition

In 1840, Lamar had enlisted three citizens of Santa Fe as commissioners for Texas. The three were to offer Santa Fe citizens the opportunity to declare their allegiance to the Texas republic. This extension of empire reflected Lamar's political plans, but it also fit well with plans for economic expansion, as there was a considerable amount of potentially lucrative trade in Santa Fe. Via a letter carried by one of the commissioners, Lamar promised Santa Fe residents that other representatives of the Texas government would arrive in Santa Fe to discuss the plan and effect a union with them.

The Texas Congress, fearing to provoke the Mexican government, refused to endorse this plan. It had appropriated money for a commercial expedition, however, so Lamar made it a volunteer venture. The subtext was still to bring the New Mexico settlements within Texas's political sphere, but the aim stated in the call for volunteers in Texas newspapers also rang true: "for the purpose of opening a commercial intercourse with the people of Santa Fe; for which purpose troops are necessary to escort the merchandise through the Comanche wilderness."

In June 1841, more than 300 men started out from a fort north of Austin. The expedition included merchants, teamsters, four civil commissioners, and a large volunteer military contingent of six companies under twenty-six-year-old Hugh McLeod, a Georgian who in 1836 had resigned his U.S. army lieutenant's commission to cast his fortunes with Texas. Here he had quickly become a leader in Indian warfare and risen to the rank of brigadier general.

The expedition headed north into unsettled territory, planning to reach the Red River and follow it westward toward Santa Fe. With "not a single map of the route among them," however, they cut their way through the dense timberlands called the Cross Timbers rather than detouring around them. Upon reaching the Wichita River, they mistook it for the Red River and began traveling along its valley. With Comanches and Kiowas threatening them and water and provisions running low, they tried to correct their course, again striking northward for the Red River. But the Caprock Escarpment that divides the rolling plains of West Texas from the High Plains proved daunting for the wagons.

With progress agonizingly slow, McLeod authorized about one-third of the expedition members to ride ahead. This group arrived in the Mexican settlements of New Mexico to find Governor Manuel Armijo had marshaled his troops to meet them, and first the advance group, then the main expedition were forced to surrender their arms and become prisoners of the Mexican government. They began a harrowing forced march to Mexico City, with summary executions along the way.

As members of the expedition staggered southward, Texans were again contemplating whom to elect as president of the republic. The failure of the expedition pointed up the unrealistic nature of Lamar's expansionist plans for the republic. Sam Houston, now in the Texas Congress, had been a steady critic of Lamar's vision, and of the fact that he was spending Texas money to achieve it even as the republic sank deeper into debt—debt that now totaled more than $8 million. In the election of fall 1841, Houston won the presidency again. And once again Houston would seek a solution for many of independent Texas's woes through the pursuit of annexation to the United States.

## Challenges and Opportunities in the Republic of Texas

Because of the unsettled state of affairs and the remoteness of much of the available land, not as many people immigrated to the republic as promoters and other Texans hoped. Simply getting to Texas and traveling within it remained a challenge, transportation problems during this period judged by some "the chief obstacles to prosperity." Continuing frontier conditions and political uncertainty proved vexing, but not insurmountable to certain groups.

### Challenges

Immigrants continued to haul wagons over the primary travel route, from Natchitoches in Louisiana through Nacogdoches, fighting choking dust at times, oceans of sticky mud at others. By the late 1830s those who came by sea to the coastal settlements could travel in impressive steamboats, although most couldn't afford the cabins and crammed into steerage or took deck passage. Within Texas, despite the advent of a few stagecoaches, the standard modes of transportation continued to be horseback, wagon, and ox cart.

The Texas rivers had already proven a disappointment in terms of moving people and goods. Even steamers designed for shallow rivers could not navigate the Trinity, the San Jacinto, the Colorado, the Guadalupe, the San Antonio, or the Nueces. The Brazos was barely navigable on its lower reaches, between Washington-on-the-Brazos and the gulf. And the republic was far too poor to mount railroad and canal projects. Only Buffalo Bayou between Houston and Galveston would develop into an important commercial waterway during the republic period; it, too, was difficult to navigate but had some natural canal-like qualities.

All of this meant that the settlements of the Republic of Texas were a series of remote sites, difficult to reach and particularly difficult to supply with goods, except along the gulf coast. In addition, there were uncertainties over hostilities with Mexico, the Mexican government still insisting on sovereignty over the region, and with warring Indian tribes, particularly the Comanches. Mexican troops invaded Texas twice in 1842. The first time, General Rafael Vásquez's troops sparked a second Runaway Scrape, leading President Houston to try—unsuccessfully—to move government records from Austin to Houston in what became known as the Archive War. The second time, General Adrián Woll in September took a few dozen prisoners and began marching back to the Rio Grande, in the process killing thirty-six members of a volunteer force gathered to stop him at Salado Creek. Such incidents heightened the uncertainty that Texas immigrants felt about their long-term prospects in their new home. Even two years later, many Texans were reportedly still in "a State of excitement and apprehension truly painful" regarding further Mexican invasions.

After Texas became a state and immigration increased, the first state census in 1847 counted about 142,000 Texas residents, more than a quarter of them African Americans, fewer than 1 percent of whom were free. This population total is probably low, but it reflects the fact that immigration to Texas was still limited, with the Missouri frontier and even distant Oregon beckoning many from the United States and Europe.

Stephen Pearl Andrews, a Houston lawyer, reasoned that slaveholders stayed away from the republic because of the political and economic uncertainties and others stayed away because of the slavery. Convinced that slavery was holding back economic development, he tried in the early 1840s to persuade others, but many Texans identified strongly with the American South and would not countenance talk of eliminating slavery. Andrews soon tired of the effort and left the republic.

Those who arrived in Texas and stayed had various reasons for abandoning old homes for this frontier. Many had been propelled westward in part by a spirit of adventure and wanderlust and/or by the specter of previous business, political, and personal losses. But common to virtually all was the hope for economic opportunity. In the American South, from whence most of the emigrants came, economic opportunity was tied up with the ownership of land for farming, ranching, and/or speculating and colonizing.

And Texas had plenty of it—more than 250 million acres of public domain as the Republic era began. More than 26 million acres had already been granted through a hodgepodge of Spanish, Mexican, and empresario claims. But the new government was more than ready to use much of the rest as an inducement to settlers.

The Constitution allowed for a league and a labor for every head of household in Texas at the time of independence and for one-third of a labor for every single man, although African Americans and Indians were excluded from this liberal policy. The Texas Congress followed up with a series of grants for new arrivals in the period from March 1836 through December 1841. These newcomers had to live in Texas for three years before gaining clear title to the land, but grants were still generous.

As a further inducement, on January 26, 1839, the Texas Congress passed a homestead exemption act to protect debtors from seizure of their homes. Although this act had its origins in the Mexican period, when the legislature of Coahuila y Texas had enacted a similar statute, it was a first in American jurisprudence, stipulating that a citizen was protected in retaining "fifty acres of land or one town lot, including his or her homestead, and improvements not exceeding five hundred dollars in value."

When even the homestead measure did not stimulate enough migration, in 1841 the Texas Congress authorized the president to implement another empresario contract system. The following year, a colonization law stipulated that the new empresarios would receive "ten premium sections, each to be settled by one hundred families," with the government holding on to alternate sections to sell after the original sections were settled.

As with the previous empresario efforts, the results were uneven at best. They depended in large part on European immigration. William Peters established a colony in the vicinity of present-day Dallas, with the assistance of both English and American investors, thrusting settlement far northward, close to the Red River. Henri Castro brought Catholic Alsatians from Europe and settled them deep in an expanse west of San Antonio and the Medina River, pushing the Texas frontier westward. Henry F. Fisher and Burchard Miller contracted to introduce a large number of German immigrants to Texas; although they faltered, others picked up the challenge, and the resulting colonies, like Castro's, extended the western frontier.

Nineteenth-century painter Carl G. von Iwonski titled this painting "Log Cabin, New Braunfels." It provides one picture of antebellum Texas farm and frontier life. *(Courtesy Daughters of the Republic of Texas Library)*

Visitors and immigrants continued to be excited by the agricultural potential of the lands they saw in traveling through the settlements. Cotton cultivation in particular was developing, and with it a planter class that depended heavily on slave labor. In the republic era, however, most immigrants were looking for that initial golden opportunity. In 1845, a Texan wrote, "All are land-hunting, seeking sugar, cotton and stock farm lands, but are as much at a loss in their selection as children in a toy-shop."

Merchandising offered another economic opportunity; the field was wide open for the buying and selling of goods. Merchants or traders would buy items on credit and then sell them to farmers, planters, townspeople, even to other merchants, often taking crops in place of cash. Many merchants, however, suffered in the financial instability of the republic, with its paper money worth only twelve cents in exchange with the U.S. dollar, and in the extended aftermath of the global economic Panic of 1837. Adolphus Sterne, a merchant who had been in business in Nacogdoches since 1826, would complain in May 1842, "[T]imes have never been so hard in Texas, like they are now, I have never known the want of two bits until now,—!!!!!"

Sterne was also a land agent, and many like him tried to seize the opportunities to make money in land speculation. The empresarios hoped to make a profit from their colonization efforts. Land agents and land lawyers bought and sold and took commissions, "organiz[ing] the land market in the new territories" and serving as "critical intermediaries" between the Tejano elite who still owned title to desirable lands and those who wanted them. In a well-established American tradition, speculators bought up whatever lands they could in hopes of realizing vast profits, but many bought on credit, then saw the acreage drop in value.

Some used the fledgling towns both as objects of speculation and as bases for it. A visitor to Houston in 1837 found "the spirit of speculation . . . afloat," with lots "selling at enormous prices, in some instances as high as four and five thousand dollars apiece." Few of the towns could be said to be flourishing, however, and some would even decline during the republic years: By 1844, Brazoria was looking distinctly rundown. Texas entrepreneurs, like their government, lacked a vital trade system, a stable currency, and hope of attracting outside investors.

Most Texans, whatever their location and pursuits, still could expect to have very rudimentary homes. In general, Tejanos had one-story stone or adobe homes or even simple structures with picket walls and thatched roofs; Anglo settlers lived in log cabins, known as "dog-trot" cabins because they were designed with a room on either side of a central "dog-trot" breezeway. The floors consisted of clay or dirt.

Food was usually equally simple—beef, cornbread, coffee. Wheat flour proved so scarce throughout the period that many families relied on cornmeal instead. "Raising corn," wrote one German settler, "was a matter of life and death, since upon it depended the existence of the colony." Others grew their own wheat. Many were happy to get a cow; as one young woman who arrived shortly after the republic period explained to her father: "[F]or over three months we had neither a scrap of butter or a drop of milk, but we got by nicely and oh how wonderful did the first cup of coffee with milk and the first piece of cornbread with butter taste to us!"

## Anglos and Europeans

In these challenging times, those who were best able to seize opportunity were Anglo men of some means from the American South, men who had previous experience with American forms of economic and/or political power. They resembled—and in many cases were—the architects of the late revolution, men who knew their way around a cotton farm and a courtroom, a plantation and a political office. They had migrated primarily from the Lower South—Alabama, Louisiana, Mississippi—bringing with them strong proslavery views. Many had experienced failure—business reverses, lost political elections, fractured personal lives—yet they maintained a sense of unbridled optimism and entitlement. In the United States, only white males could exercise that most basic right of citizenship, the vote. These men had absorbed the concept of manifest destiny, although it still did not yet have a name: They saw themselves as representatives of a culture and a race destined for greatness and control of the American continent.

European men, too, found opportunities, although most of them were new to the continent and had to adjust to American ways as well as the presence of Mexicans and Indians. To a great extent, the immigrant European groups stayed together, setting up their own small German, Alsatian, Czech, and Norwegian enclaves; however, the men moved about freely and engaged in farming and business along with their American counterparts. The largest European immigrant group by far was the Germans, whose numbers would be estimated at more than 11,600 by 1850. Germans had migrated to Texas as early as the 1820s. By the late 1830s, numerous Germans were looking to do so. Merchants and craftsmen had been losing economic ground in Germany with the advent of industrial production and population growth. They were finding it prohibitively expensive to maintain even a small business. And land was a powerful allure. Especially after the failed German revolution of 1848, many political dissenters came looking for freedom in Texas; these new arrivals became known as the "Forty-Eighters."

The 1842 Fisher and Miller contract to bring German colonists to Texas was expanded in 1844, but the two men soon sold it to a German organization called the Adelsverein, or Society for the Protection of German Immigrants in Texas. In exchange for a flat fee, the Adelsverein, now a joint-stock company, promised to transport German colonists to America and then to Adelsverein lands in Texas. Because the Fisher-Miller grant was so remote, located between the Colorado and Llano rivers, the Adelsverein selected and purchased a site on the Guadalupe River closer to the edge of Anglo settlement.

The Adelsverein brought an estimated 5,200 German immigrants to Texas between 1844 and 1846. Many journeyed with difficulty from Indianola on the coast to the Guadalupe site, New Braunfels, established in 1845. The travelers

John O. Meusebach (center), Commissioner General of the German immigrant company the Adelsverein, led the German colonists in parleying with Comanche chiefs near the lower San Saba River in March 1847. Two months later, the chiefs signed the Meusebach-Comanche Treaty. (*Courtesy Gillespie County Historical Society*)

were already weary from the long sea voyage, and the Adelsverein had not been able to make the small coastal settlement of Indianola an adequate staging area for the long journey inland. Travelers struggled with illness, incessant rains, and oxcarts mired in mud.

The first commissioner-general, or leader, of the Adelsverein colonization was Prince Carl of Solms-Braunfels, who cut quite a swath through Texas frontier society. A tireless worker in the colonization effort, he was nonetheless best remembered for his aristocratic and eccentric ways, including the cock feathers he and members of his entourage wore in their hats. Following him in the role was Otsfried Hans von Meusebach, who in Texas became John O. Meusebach and guided the Adelsverein colonists well, establishing a second center of settlement, Fredericksburg, some sixty miles northwest of New Braunfels.

In the ideology of the era in America, women were to stay at home, to maintain the "private sphere," while Anglo and northern European men engaged in the business and politics of capitalistic empire building. This division of labor was reinforced by women's frequent pregnancies and, in Texas as on frontiers elsewhere, by the very real work of maintaining a frontier home whose residents had to rely to a large extent on their own self-sufficiency and inventiveness rather than on nonexistent or erratic supply networks.

Yet the same frontier conditions also gave Anglo and European women some autonomy. They ran farms and businesses as well as homes in the absence of their menfolk; many of these absences were frequent and prolonged. They operated boarding houses, participated in a frontier bartering economy, hunted and harvested as need dictated, and worked to establish schools and churches. These Texas women also had more rights under the Hispanic-influenced community property laws than did women in the United States, for economic gains in a marriage were considered both the woman's and the man's.

They could also expect some court protection against abusive or wayward husbands; recognizing the isolation and vulnerability of many frontier wives, republic lawmakers established standards penalizing abandonment and cruelty in their 1841 divorce act. State lawmakers would follow with anticruelty standards "among the most liberal found in the antebellum South." Nonetheless, political opportunities remained off-limits, economic opportunities meager; legally, women could not accumulate property or sell it without the permission of their husbands.

## Marginalized Groups in the Republic

If women of the increasingly dominant Anglo and European American culture faced restrictions, women and men of different ethnic groups found their opportunities even more restricted. Increasingly, African Americans, Tejanos, and Native Americans found far more challenges to survival than opportunities to thrive in the Republic of Texas.

### African American Experience

Of course, African American slaves lived the most circumscribed lives. Most arrived in Texas with their masters, rather than being brought to Texas to be sold. Some historians have noted that the shared pioneer enterprise with its intimate working conditions on the Texas frontier created stronger bonds for both owners and slaves. Whereas most slaves in the southern states lived on large plantations, in Texas most lived on small isolated farms, both in the republic era and in the early statehood era. Even in 1860, more than half of the slaveowners in Texas held four slaves or fewer, only 1.5 percent claiming to own more than fifty.

In a land of rough conditions, however, slaves experienced the worst. William Fairfax Gray would judge some of the slave homes he saw in the midst of a chilling norther in 1837 "more open than the log stables in Virginia." But rough living conditions were not all they faced. The Republic of Texas government meted out harsh punishments for any crimes or even perceived crimes committed by slaves. "Insulting or abusive language" directed at a white person earned twenty-five to a hundred lashes. White owners could hire out slaves at will and controlled all their transactions, as it was forbidden for anyone to buy something from a slave without written permission from his or her master. There were harsh penalties, too, for anyone harboring an escaped slave or in any way encouraging or abetting his or her escape. Marriages of African Americans and Anglos were simply outlawed.

The few liberties a slave might enjoy depended upon the kind of owner the slave had: Would the owner, for example, allow the slave to marry someone on a neighboring plantation, or even to visit him or her? Even under a relatively lenient master, slaves could not choose their own marriage partners, learn to read, or escape arbitrary punishment. And there was no guarantee that their families would remain intact if the owner needed funds and chose to sell one or more of them.

Free African Americans were restricted as well. The punitive legal codes applied to slaves also applied to them, and the Constitution of 1836 required them to receive special permission to live in the republic. In 1837 Congress qualified this requirement, allowing those in Texas at the time of independence (approximately 150 people) to reside in the republic "as long as they choose." One of those affected by these laws was Samuel McCulloch, Jr., who had fought in the Revolution as a member of the Matagorda volunteer company. After passage of the 1836 law, McCulloch had petitioned for citizenship and land grants; the 1837 law had automatically granted him citizenship but left his land grant request in limbo.

In 1840, Congress again reversed itself, passing a law barring the immigration of free blacks to Texas and stipulating that all free men and women must leave within two years or be sold into slavery. Although this draconian plan was not fully implemented—for example, McCulloch and four relatives won exemption—free African Americans faced an uncertain existence at best.

The lives of African Americans in Texas reflected the long-lasting effects of the slave system in the South. Blacks coming to Texas, usually through no choice of their own, knew all too well the ways in which their lives could and would be restricted and constricted. In the republic era, however, many Tejanos were just beginning to comprehend the full implications of the growing Anglo presence for their own future.

### Tejano Experience

Immediately after the Revolution, Tejanos were pushed, prodded, and deprived of opportunity in a variety of ways. Members of the Tejano elite who had worked with Anglo leaders were increasingly excluded from or moved to the margins of the developing power structure of the republic. Tejano settlers near the Anglo colonies found themselves, their homes, and their livestock targeted by former soldiers bitter toward Mexicans. It didn't matter whether the Tejanos had actively aided the revolutionary effort, remained loyal to the Mexican government, or tried to be neutral. Many were driven from their homes, particularly those who lived near the Austin and DeWitt colonies, as immigrants spilled onto accessible lands with little or no regard for Mexican land titles. (These titles were clouded by confusion over previous land claims under earlier governments but also by Anglos having taken control of political and legal systems.)

The Rio Grande region contained relatively intact Mexican enclaves; Laredo was still considered a part of the Mexican state of Tamualipas and El Paso still a town of the state of Chihuahua. But former Texian soldiers raided south of the Nueces, in one of the territories disputed by the Texas and Mexican governments. Emboldened by a republic decree that Mexican livestock was public property, the former soldiers took cattle belonging to Mexican residents, many of whom had sought refuge in the Rio Grande towns during the war.

Far to the east in Nacogdoches, tensions between Tejanos and Anglos continued to ignite. In the wake of the Revolution, emigrants from the United States decisively outnumbered Tejano residents and showed little interest in or respect for Mexican social and political structures and history. Some Tejano residents rallied around Vicente Córdova, the Nacogdoches-area landowner and former *alcalde* and militia commander. Tired of the conspiracy rumors surrounding him and the continued intimidation of Tejanos, Córdova had been in touch with Mexican authorities intent on disrupting Republic of Texas affairs. Now he gathered supporters from among the local Tejano and Indian populations in what would come to be known as the Córdova rebellion.

In early August 1838, Thomas Jefferson Rusk, now major general of the militia, received word that Córdova and a hundred or more Mexicans had set up camp on the Angelina River. As Rusk readied the local militia, President Houston issued a proclamation aimed at Córdova banning unlawful assembly and the carrying of arms.

Córdova and eighteen companions signed a proclamation in response, asserting that they had been stripped of their rights but would die defending them. A detachment sent by Rusk and led by Major Henry W. Augustine, a veteran of the Revolution and former republic senator, tracked and set upon Córdova's band, which now had a few hundred Indians added to its numbers.

Córdova escaped and traveled to Mexico, but as a result of the incident, thirty-three men of Mexican heritage faced treason charges in the Nacogdoches and San Augustine district courts. Only one, a former Nacogdoches official, would be found guilty. Sentenced to hang, he eventually received a pardon. But the ultimate result of the troubles in the Nacogdoches area was that more than a hundred Mexican families were forced out the following year.

In San Antonio, as in Nacogdoches, the old cooperative structures were crumbling, with land and power rapidly shifting into Anglo hands. Some newcomers voiced suspicion of the Mexican population, but others acknowledged the plight of the Tejanos. Many of the elite Tejanos, in particular, were caught between economic and political ties with Anglos—even personal ties, as daughters of leading Tejano families married prominent or soon-to-be-prominent Anglo men—and their Catholic, Spanish, and Mexican identity and heritage. Despite conditions on the frontier, the Tejanos of San Antonio had preserved their heritage through attention to religious practice, nationalistic and religious celebrations, and schooling for their children. Increasingly, Anglos ignored or paid little attention to this heritage.

Juan Seguín, however, remained an influential figure—an indisputable war hero who had an ability to bridge the Mexican and Anglo communities. He was repeatedly elected to the republic Senate, where he was the only Tejano. Returning to San Antonio, he generated enough support in the Anglo community as well as the Tejano community to be elected mayor in late 1840. As mayor, he found that "[a]t every hour of the day and night my countrymen ran to me for protection against the assaults or exactions of those adventurers."

Seguín, who had connections with Mexico through his continued support of the federalists against the centralists, soon found himself suspected of collaborating with the Mexican government against the Texas republic by giving away information about the ill-fated Santa Fe expedition. Yet, denying the charge, he won reelection as mayor. More trouble awaited, however. Seguín requested from Mexican frontier commander General Rafael Vásquez a pass to travel to Mexico "for a drove of sheep," and the manner of Vásquez's reply led Seguín to surmise "that an expedition against Texas was in preparation for the following month of March." Without further credible information of an impending Mexican army invasion of San Antonio, Seguín could not get the secretary of war to send aid, and he did not think he could defend the town without help. Thus, he, his family, and other Tejano residents left town for outlying ranches as Anglos in San Antonio tried to set up a defense.

The Mexican troops arrived and occupied the town for two days in March 1842. Seguín served in a company that pursued the troops, but when he returned to San Antonio he found "reports about my implausible treason were spreading widely." Seguín heard daily threats: "All the parties of volunteers en route to San Antonio declared 'they wanted to kill Seguín.'" He resigned as mayor in April, reluctantly preparing to move to Mexico to escape the "constant wretchedness" his family was experiencing.

### Cherokee and Comanche Experience

If Seguín had been caught in a cultural and political crossfire in San Antonio, the same could be said of Chief Bowles, or "Duwali," and the Cherokee Indians in East Texas. They were beset by conflicting claims on their loyalties, by factionalism within the tribe, and by possibilities of alliances with other Indians. During the war, Chief Bowles had signed the treaty pledging loyalty to the independence movement in return for clear land title, and Houston had reassured him, saying, "You will get your land as promised in our Treaty." Now, after the war, the Cherokees faced increased suspicion and hostility from Anglo neighbors, and they had no treaty for the land they had cultivated as long as Austin's early colonists had cultivated theirs. When Mexican agents continued to move around Texas, attempting to weaken the republic and reassert Texas claims by enlisting the tribes, some Cherokees were ready to listen in order to survive.

In August 1836, the republic government received a report that the Cherokees, Comanches, and a number of smaller groups were preparing to attack settlers. When Sam Houston took office in October, he attempted to defuse the tension created by the reports by enlisting some of the Cherokees as rangers against the Comanches and other hostile Indians. This did not deter some Cherokees from meeting with Mexican officials planning a spring 1837 attack on the settlements; when spring arrived, however, Chief Bowles went as an emissary from the Texas government to the Comanches and other western tribes.

Later that year, a Texas Senate committee rejected the Houston-Bowles treaty of 1836, calling the Cherokees, who had proven the most adept of the five "civilized" tribes in adopting Anglo ways, "the most savage and ruthless of our frontier enemies." This harshly worded rejection only fueled the pro-Mexican faction among the Cherokees. At the same time, new immigrants were pushing onto the lands occupied by the tribe, rendering even Chief Bowles desperate. He sent an emissary to the Cherokees already in Indian Territory asking for warriors and promising Cherokee land titles for them, but without success.

Then came the Córdova rebellion, in which a few hundred Indians, including many Cherokees, clearly aligned themselves with the Mexican plotters. Houston tried to prepare against the threat militarily while still reaching out to the Cherokees, ordering a survey of the boundaries of the land claimed by the Cherokees, even though the treaty had been rejected.

Events continued in this contradictory vein. Survivors of autumn 1838 Indian raids in the settlements implicated Cherokees, and Thomas Jefferson Rusk led the Texas militia in a show of force through the Cherokees' region. With feelings running high, tribal members, whether aligned with the Mexicans or not, had to take measures for self-defense, even as the surveyors finished marking the boundaries of their disputed land.

Mirabeau Lamar's election to the presidency effectively sealed the Cherokees' fate. If there was a second major difference between Houston and Lamar, beyond their opposing attitudes toward annexation and expansion, it was in their attitude toward Indians. Houston, with his experience among the Cherokees, had been remarkable for his era in his attempts to treat the Indians fairly. To Lamar, as to many frontiersmen, Indians were simply hostile or potentially hostile nuisances to be removed without compunction by whatever means necessary.

One of Lamar's first stated intentions in office was to remove the Cherokees. In the meantime, Vicente Córdova was still building alliances from Mexico. The group that would later be known as the Texas Rangers had been formed in 1837, largely in response to Indian threats, and in May 1839, rangers took from a Mexican agent letters addressed simply to "the various immigrant chiefs." Lamar used them as evidence of collusion by the Cherokees and ordered their removal. In July Lamar sent Rusk to begin the forced removal. The Cherokees were told they would be paid for their improvements and their crops. Many balked at the news that they would have to remove the gunlocks from their weapons and accept a militia escort. When the militia attempted to force the terms, the Indians simply left on their own, pursued by the militia.

On July 16, the militia caught up with the Cherokees, as well as with allied Delawares, Shawnees, and Kickapoos. Chief Bowles was shot and killed, and the Indians were scattered, some to Mexico, some to other tribal groups.

The Cherokees' story vividly demonstrates the limits of opportunity in Texas for those who were perceived as a threat or a nuisance by members of the dominant immigrant culture. The Comanches, who perceived the surveyor's compass as "the thing that steals the land," posed a much larger threat. They remained violently resistant to attempts to encroach upon the land they ranged and to restrict their mobility, freedom, and autonomy.

Texas had barely become independent when a sizable force of Comanches, with some Kiowa and Kichai allies, rode up to a settler enclave known as Parker's Fort near the headwaters of the Navasota River. Inhabitants fled in fear as the Indians speared and killed several and took five captives, including Rachel Plummer, who left a dramatic account of her captivity, and her cousin Cynthia Ann Parker, who would grow up among the Comanches and become the mother of the last Comanche chief, Quanah Parker.

The Comanches and their allies continued to kill settlers and to pluck captives from the settlements as companies of rangers tried to pursue and punish them in a lurching yet escalating warfare. This conflict flared on the streets of San Antonio in the Council House Fight of March 1840. A delegation of Penateka Comanche leaders had come to the town to negotiate a peace treaty with representatives of the Texas government eager to redeem Comanche prisoners. Yet the Indians had brought only a handful. The Texans demanded other prisoners; the Indians responded that they had no direct control over the others. When the Texas officials tried to take the assembled chiefs hostage in a ploy to redeem the other prisoners, a general bloody melee broke out, spreading through the Main Plaza and into the side streets. Many of the Indians were killed, others held hostage, but the incident only heightened Comanche resistance. In retaliation the Comanches raided even deeper into the settlements, in August penetrating all the way to Victoria and Linville. They were led by Buffalo Hump, a war chief of the Penateka Comanches. A volunteer army met the Indians on their return, on the banks of Plum Creek near Lockhart, and defeated them. But Buffalo Hump and other warriors escaped to fight again insisting that the republic keep settlement to the east of the Edwards Plateau.

In his second term as president, Houston negotiated a treaty with the Comanches and their allies near what is today Waco. This 1844 Treaty of Tehuacana Creek declared that "the tomahawk shall be buried, and no more blood appear in the path" between the parties, but the grievances on both sides endured. The continued incursions of adventurers and settlers onto the lands occupied by the Comanches led to further raids, both by the warriors against settlers and travelers and by Texas Rangers against Indian camps.

In response to the Indian threats, as well as the Mexican threats, the republic could mount only a limited and scattershot defense. For this and other reasons, Sam Houston and most of his fellow Texans remained convinced that they needed the protection and resources annexation would bring. But how could they obtain it?

# The Annexation Quest Continues, 1841–1845

Houston's election to the presidency in 1841 again brought the issue of annexation to the fore. Lamar had declared in his inauguration speech that the "imposing considerations which at one time rendered [annexation] seemingly desirable" no longer existed, but in fact, the republic was now in even deeper economic distress. During Lamar's administration, not only had the government's debts spiraled, but the vast amounts of paper money the Texas treasury printed beginning in 1839 had become virtually worthless. Republic leaders could not develop trade and settlement with vigor or effectively protect the citizenry. Thus, Houston again quietly began trying to build support for the republic to become part of the United States.

Yet the officials of the U.S. government remained indifferent, hesitant, or even hostile to the idea. Not only did they wish to avoid further difficulties with Mexico, but many national leaders actively resisted the idea of another slave state entering the Union. Meanwhile, Houston grappled with an impoverished treasury and the unrelenting threat from Mexico.

## The Mier Expedition

The Mexican incursions of 1842 stimulated the fighting spirit of many Texas volunteers, who signed up in San Antonio after Woll's departure. Houston preferred diplomatic maneuvering but sent Brigadier General Alexander Somervell to control and direct the angry, combative forces. In late November 700 men marched south under Somervell and seized Laredo, but many of the men remained undisciplined and greedy for both revenge and plunder. One hundred and eighty-five headed home after the capture of Laredo. Somervell led the rest in the capture of Guerrero, but it became apparent to him that they could not hope to further the campaign. He ordered the volunteer army disbanded.

Many of the volunteers resisted. Revolution veteran William S. Fisher, a captain in the expedition, assumed command of the more than 300 men who refused to disband, wanting at least to raid the Mexican settlements for horses and cattle. On December 23, this group crossed the Rio Grande into Mier and demanded supplies, then retreated across the river to wait for the goods that the town residents had nervously pledged. Meanwhile, however, the Mexican military arrived in Mier and stopped delivery. With no supplies forthcoming and news of the Mexican force's presence, the volunteers crossed the river again on Christmas Day and fought a battle with the soldiers. Although the Mexicans suffered heavy losses, they prevailed and took most of the Texan force prisoner. The Texans were scheduled for execution, then spared and marched toward Mexico City. They attempted an escape, but almost all were recaptured.

In "The Mier Expedition: Drawing the Black Bean," well-known late-nineteenth-century artist Frederic Remington depicted the fateful ceremony in which men of this expedition drew beans to determine who among them would be executed by Mexican troops. In this way, seventeen of the 176 prisoners received their death warrants. (*The Museum of Fine Arts, Houston; The Hogg Brothers Collection; gift of Miss Ima Hogg*)

This account provides the background for the famous "black bean" episode, in which the 176 prisoners were each required to draw a bean from an earthen jar. Those who drew the seventeen black beans were slated for execution. The Mier expedition thus came to a tragic end: The seventeen black bean holders were shot and Ewen Cameron was executed, on an order by Santa Anna, because of his leadership in the escape attempt. Other members of the expedition gradually won their freedom from a Mexican prison.

### Changing Climate for Annexation

In the meantime, opportunities to further the cause of annexation to the United States presented themselves in Texas. England was eager to continue to deal with Texas as an independent nation in hopes of building a viable commercial trade, arresting U.S. westward expansion in the Southwest, and indirectly exerting some control over American slavery and tariff issues. The British were actively working against annexation. A worried President John Tyler, who shared southern attitudes on slavery, reopened communication on the subject with Houston.

Sam Houston moved cautiously—too cautiously for many in Texas. One member of the republic legislature worried that Washington didn't understand how devoutly most Texans hoped for annexation and concluded "We are obliged to leave much to [Houston], and I am sorry to leave in such suspicious keeping a thing so valuable to us all." Nonetheless, Houston had deftly played American authorities against the British, with Texas minister in Washington, James Pinckney Henderson, reporting in February 1844, "All things prove now the *very great* desire of the U.S. to annex us."

Houston, however, was worried about reactions from Mexico and wanted U.S. troops in place in Texas before any news of annexation negotiations leaked out. Negotiation attempts limped along until Tyler's negotiator, the energetically proslavery John C. Calhoun, signed a proposed treaty of annexation with Henderson and second Texas minister Isaac Van Zandt. But antislavery forces again opposed the idea of admitting another slave state; they and others also argued against the move on the grounds that it would bring on war with Mexico. The U.S. Senate in June 1844 rejected the document by more than a two-to-one margin.

Five months later, expansionist James K. Polk of Tennessee won election as U.S. president, in part through advocating annexation of Texas, and added weight to Tyler's efforts to bring Texas into the American republic. At about the same time, Houston was succeeded by Texas secretary of state and Houston supporter Anson Jones. Jones sensed that Texas now had a fair amount of bargaining power given Polk's election, American fears of a Texas-British alliance, and the potential British brokering of a Texas-Mexico peace. Jones refused to request annexation again without assurance that the U.S. Senate would now approve it.

Tyler continued to work toward this end, and on March 1, 1845 won congressional passage of an annexation agreement. The agreement was designed to please Texas leaders, allowing Texas to enter the Union as a slave state and hold onto "all the vacant and unappropriated lands lying within its limits." This was a major victory for the South, as northerners still vigorously protested admitting another slave state to the Union.

Now, however, the Texas government was also being courted seriously by England and France in an attempt to stave off annexation to the United States. The British and French representatives convinced Jones to delay an answer and pressured Mexican officials to belatedly recognize the still-shaky republic rather than confront the specter of a strong United States on their border. In late April 1845, Mexican officials tentatively recognized the independence of the Republic of Texas if Texas would not annex itself to another country.

Thus, Jones was able to offer the republic Congress, meeting in special session in June, both the annexation agreement and an alternate choice: continuation of the republic under a treaty of peace with Mexico, with the stipulation that Texas would not annex itself to the United States. The congressmen unanimously chose annexation, but their choice had to be approved by "the representatives of the people of Texas in convention assembled." On July 4, by a vote of 55 to 1, representatives led by Thomas Jefferson Rusk resolved that the territory of the republic "may be erected into a new State, to be called the State of Texas . . . in order that the same may be admitted as one of the States of [the American] Union."

In "The Republic of Texas Is No More," illustrator Norman Price envisioned the annexation ceremony of February 19, 1846, with President Anson Jones leading in the lowering of the republic flag. *(Prints & Photographs Collection—Annexation File, CN 03085a, The Center for American History, The University of Texas at Austin)*

The Convention then proceeded to create a state constitution, the Texas Constitution of 1845, providing for election of a governor, a lieutenant governor, and a legislature, as well as the appointment of other state officials. On October 13, Texas voters overwhelmingly approved both the document and annexation to the United States. In a special election they proceeded to vote for J. Pinckney Henderson as the first governor. Meanwhile, the U.S. Congress also approved the state constitution, and on December 29 President Polk signed the act making Texas a state.

On February 19, 1846, with the first meeting of the state legislature in Austin, Jones turned over the reins of government to Henderson in a ceremony at noon in front of the capitol. With the republic flag lowered and the American flag raised to fly over it, Jones proclaimed to the gathered crowd, "The lone star of Texas . . . has . . . become fixed forever in that glorious constellation . . . the American Union." According to a newspaper report, many in the crowd cried, but few of them would have wished for a different course for Texas, given the American origins of most of the citizenry and the experiences of the previous ten years. "Thank God, we are now annexed to the United States," wrote Mary Maverick, "and can hope for home and quiet."

# The New State Takes Shape

With annexation, the struggles over Texas's identity seemed to recede into the past. New state officials busily worked to bring Texas into the federal system. Two prominent leaders since the Revolution, Thomas Jefferson Rusk and Sam Houston, headed to Washington, D.C., as U.S. senators. Texans looked to a more stable future, and to increased growth and development.

## The Mexican War and Texas Territory

Texans could now even regard the outbreak of a U.S. war with Mexico with little trepidation. And war broke out almost immediately, in part because of the annexation treaty and continuing boundary disputes, including the one over the Rio Grande. Polk had sent General Zachary Taylor and troops to a post at the mouth of the Nueces River in the summer of 1845. Polk's representative, sent to Mexico to negotiate in November, was rebuffed by officials angry about the annexation proceedings. Shortly after the American flag was raised over the Texas state capitol, Taylor's troops were dispatched to the Rio Grande, where Mexican troops were also massing. On April 23, 1846, Mexico declared a defensive war against the United States. President Polk won a declaration of war as well, citing a late-April incident in which Mexican troops had crossed the Rio Grande near Matamoros and fought an American patrol. The first substantial conflict, the battle of Palo Alto near Brownsville on May 8, grew out of American troops' attempts to supply the Fort Texas Rio Grande border post (later Fort Brown) from Port Isabel to the east and Mexican troops' attempt to stop them.

There was serious opposition to the war in the United States, especially among prominent members of the Whig political party, which had been established in the 1830s to challenge President Jackson and the Jacksonian Democrats. Many felt that Polk, an expansionist Democrat, had provoked the conflict in a bid to seize Mexican holdings stretching to California. In Texas, public sentiment among the Anglo American majority was decidedly prowar, with resentment and even bitter hatred against the Mexican government still lingering.

Governor Henderson asked the legislature to release him to command the Second Texas Regiment, and he led this unit in the U.S. forces' taking of Monterrey in September. The Texas Mounted Rifles under Colonel John Coffee "Jack" Hays also participated in this victory. Major Benjamin McCulloch's spy company contributed to the American victory at the battle of Buena Vista in February 1847, and Hays, now leading a company of Texas rangers, aided General Winfield Scott on his march to Mexico City. With the fall of Mexico City in September 1847, the United States claimed ultimate victory. The 1848 Treaty of Guadalupe Hidalgo that followed shifted to the United States Mexican claims on a great swath of the West, including California, New Mexico, and Arizona, and portions of Utah, Nevada, and Colorado.

For Texans, the treaty secured their southern Rio Grande border for the state and the nation, and meant that they would need to negotiate with the federal government regarding their continuing claims to a large portion of New Mexico.

Within six weeks of the treaty being signed, Texans tried to further these claims by creating Santa Fe County, with boundaries extending through most of eastern New Mexico. The next year, the state redrew these boundaries and added three more counties in the disputed territory. Governor Peter Hansborough Bell sent Robert Simpson Neighbors, a former volunteer ranger and the first Indian agent for Texas, to organize the four counties. Neighbors was successful with El Paso County but met resistance from antagonistic New Mexicans intent on bidding for separate statehood.

Texans continued to cling fiercely to their claims to New Mexican territory, winning an advantageous compromise in September of 1850. Texas would relinquish most of its New Mexico claims except for the El Paso region. In exchange, the federal government offered the state $10 million. Voters approved the offer, two to one, and in November 1850 Bell signed the compromise, fixing the present boundaries of Texas and giving Texas a tremendous economic boost. The federal government retained half of the $10-million award to settle "revenue debt" owed

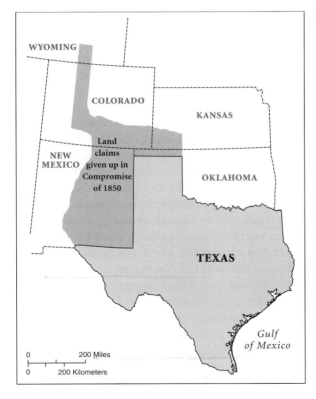

Compromise of 1850.

to those holding Republic of Texas securities. But with the other half, state officials were able to pay off all claims by participants in the Texas Revolution and suppliers of the Texas army and still have $3.75 million left. With these funds, they would set up an endowment for public schools, provide loans to railroads in hopes of developing rail lines in Texas, and remit most county taxes for a number of years, enabling the counties to use the money for development.

Although the money was a tremendous boon to a government just a few years removed from the financial ruin of the republic, Texas was not yet able to attract viable railroad projects. The lack of fast, efficient transportation remained an obstacle, within the settlements and especially beyond the lines of settlement, to the west and northwest. With annexation, immigrant numbers were swelling, with the population reaching 212,592 in 1850, including 58,161 slaves. One of the primary tasks for the state and federal government in the late 1840s and through the 1850s became the establishment of a line of forts through central, north, and west Texas, in preparation for trade routes through and immigration onto the plateaus and plains of the region.

Soldiers were dispatched to establish posts along a south-to-north frontier line running through Austin, from Fort Brown (1846) at the southern tip of Texas to Fort Worth (1849) at the junction of the Clear Fork and West Fork of the Trinity River in the north, a short distance west of the small settlement of Dallas. Fort Belknap (1851), beyond Fort Worth, was the northernmost of these posts, with Fort Bliss (1848) and Fort Quitman (1858) the westernmost, along the Rio Grande near El Paso. In between, a host of forts dotted the Texas frontier, from the Rio Grande northward to the southern reaches of the Llano Estacado, or "Staked Plains." Although settlement would not reach to most of these forts in the 1850s, it did push westward into the Texas Hill Country and northward through the Eastern Cross Timbers.

Soldiers partnered with merchants and others intent on finding the best routes through the vast and often forbidding stretches to the west. In 1848, a civilian expedition under the command of Jack C. Hays and financed in part by San Antonio merchants teamed with a small military force under Captain Samuel Highsmith to try to map out a trade route between San Antonio and El Paso. The Hays-Highsmith expedition helped spur two more the following year, a topographical engineers' expedition which established a "lower route" across West Texas and an expedition led by Neighbors. First moving northward to where the new town site of Waco was being plotted, Neighbors used his contacts with the Indians to trace a northern route to El Paso. In the meantime, Captain Randolph B. Marcy of the U.S. Army explored a wagon route across the Texas Panhandle to Santa Fe.

## Pressures on Indians and Tejanos

All of this activity, of course, periodically incited Comanches and their allies on the southern plains in the late 1840s and the 1850s. Neighbors, appointed Texas Indian agent again under a new federal administration, worked to set up two western Indian reservations in 1855. (A third, established the previous year in East Texas, was for the Alabama and Coushatta Indians who had migrated from Alabama to Spanish Texas beginning in the 1780s.)

About half of the Penateka Comanches agreed to occupy the reservation on the Clear Fork River in Throckmorton County; the other western reservation, at the junction of the Brazos and Clear Fork rivers, was home to what remained of a hodgepodge of tribes, including Waco, Caddo, and Tonkawa. Neighbors labored tirelessly to get the Indians onto these reservations and to protect them once they were there. Settlers pressed unmercifully, however, contending that Indians from the reservations were responsible for depredations against them, rather than blaming nonreservation Indian bands or even Anglo outlaws. Neighbors had to employ federal troops to protect the western reservation Indians, many of whom had helped frontier volunteers and the military in campaigns against the hostile bands of Indians. The situation grew so bad that Neighbors requested and received permission from the Commissioner of Indian Affairs in Washington to remove the reservation Indians across the Red River to Indian Territory. Even removal of the western Indians, however, did not occur fast enough for armed bands of Indian hunters among the Anglo population. In late summer 1859, Neighbors accompanied his charges across the river to Indian Territory, only to be shot and killed at Fort Belknap en route home, the victim of an attack by an Anglo immigrant. At about the same time, hostile Comanches and Kiowas began mounting extremely severe raids along the Texas frontier, forcing Sam Houston, now elected governor of the state, to dispatch a large force of Texas Rangers who in turn raised militia companies.

More and more immigrants were pouring into Texas, filling up the eastern regions, swelling the population of such now-major towns as Houston, Galveston, and Marshall, venturing westward in search of opportunity along the frontiers. They were still overwhelmingly from the states of the Lower South, Arkansas, and Missouri. And the hostility many of them felt toward Indians in general was matched by hostility toward residents of Mexican heritage. There was increasingly less tolerance for the presence of Mexican Texans. Some simply left the areas of the Anglo settlements, thereby contributing to their marginalization. But some were strongly pressured into leaving. In September 1854, Seguin residents tried to ban Mexicans "of the peon class" from visiting or living in Guadalupe County, and in Austin a similar movement forced out all except "those vouched for by 'respectable citizens.'" In 1857, journalist Frederick Law Olmstead observed that most Tejanos had voting rights but few used them. If they did vote in a place such as San Antonio, where they might be able to prevail in an election, Olmstead surmised that it could result in a "revolution" among the Anglos, who "constantly distinguish[ed] themselves as 'white folks,'" superior to Tejanos as well as to African Americans and Indians.

The principle activity of the Tejano men was hauling goods between the coast and inland towns, but even this was not to be allowed. More successful than rival Anglo freighters, beginning in 1855 the Tejano haulers faced the threat of theft, destruction of their carts, and physical attacks. In the summer of 1857, "cart war" attacks became common, and by November, Governor Elisha M. Pease was announcing, "It is now very evident that there is no security for the lives of citizens of Mexican origin engaged in the business of transportation, along the road from San Antonio to the Gulf."

The state legislature approved a militia to protect the freighters, but the pattern was clear. Economic opportunity and any kind of power—economic, political, and social—were to be the provenance of the Anglos. Not only did the Mexican freight business not recover, but even the remaining Mexican elite in San Antonio were now relegated to lower-level positions.

South and west of the Nueces, in traditionally Mexican cultural territory (especially in Laredo), some families managed to hold onto their land and some of their power, but many of the greediest and most prejudiced newcomers tried to uproot the populace and lay claim to land. In El Paso, Anglos assumed control of the town while Tejanos held sway in the country. Resentments festered among the Mexican Texans; it took an incident on the streets of Brownsville for these resentments to crystallize into a challenge to Anglo hegemony.

Juan Cortina had grown up the eldest heir of the second family of José Narcisco Cavazos, who owned a large grant in the area of Brownsville. Although Cortina and his family held legal title to the grant, his father's first family sold it to Charles Stillman, who with two partners established the town of Brownsville in 1848.

Cortina fought not only the appropriation of his land but that of the land holdings of other Mexican Texans in the area as well. Then, on July 13, 1859, he observed the Brownsville city marshall abusing and arresting a former Cortina employee. Cortina shot the marshall and departed with the former employee. A few months later, he returned with a force of men and took over the town. Persuaded to abandon the occupation by a Mexican official from Matamoros, he retreated, but also produced a manifesto on the wrongs done to Mexican Texans and his intention to punish the wrongdoers. He also petitioned Governor Houston to protect the rights of Mexican Texans.

Cortina's force reportedly grew to 400 men, and he engaged in repeated skirmishes with Texas rangers before retreating into Mexico. "Our object," he had insisted, ". . . has been to chastise the villainy of our enemies," who had robbed and harassed with impunity "without any cause, and for no other crime on our part than that of being of Mexican origin." He would mount a second challenge to Anglo Texas during the Civil War, a reminder of a Texas vastly different from the image upheld by many of its citizens: that of a southern state deeply and irrevocably committed to the institution of slavery.

## Texas as a Slave State

In the years 1845 to 1860, the Texas economy revolved more and more around the production of cotton, with more than 58,000 bales produced in 1849–50, but more than seven times that much only ten years later. Cotton cultivation continued to expand in the older settled areas but also in central Texas. The number of slaves jumped from 30,505 in 1846 to almost 183,000 in 1860; this was one-third of the Texas population. In thirteen counties, slaves accounted for over half the population. Yet throughout this period, most Texas citizens did not own slaves; of those who did, most owned only one to four.

Nonetheless, by 1860, the 27 percent of the population that owned slaves held almost three-fourths of the wealth in Texas. The bulk of that wealth was concentrated among the elite—the approximately sixty owners of more than 100 slaves. Texas's identity—economic, political, and social—had become intricately tied to the "peculiar institution."

It is not hard to see how Texas developed an identity as a slave state, from the concessions Stephen F. Austin had won from the antislavery Mexican government to the fact that the largest group of immigrants had come from the American South with proslavery attitudes. National events had also helped shape Texas responses. Even before Texas became a republic, South Carolina had attempted to override, or "nullify," federal law, in late 1832 holding a Nullification Convention to reject high tariffs the federal government was imposing on imports. The nullification controversy, which was tied to a defense of slavery as well, had ended due to lack of support in the South for such an extreme step and President Jackson's upholding of federal power. But the stage had been set for further divisiveness, especially as the nation continued to expand. In 1854, the Kansas-Nebraska Act repealed the Missouri Compromise outlawing slavery north of a certain latitude. Now the people of Kansas and Nebraska were to determine whether they would become part of slave or free territory. The act caused great consternation in the United States and led to near-anarchy in Kansas after vote fraud gave the win to the proslavery forces. The Kansas situation remained volatile through the late 1850s, feeding national tensions and southern intransigence.

Southerners justified slavery on a number of grounds, primarily the sheer necessity of having a large labor force and their feeling that the slaves, as an inferior, childlike people destined for servitude, benefited from the benevolence of their masters and the material conditions they provided. As fanciful and morally reprehensible as this argument was, it was an accepted tenet of southern thought. Those who questioned it usually knew to keep their mouths shut; those who did not often aspired to become slaveowners themselves.

As in the Lower South, then, Texas institutions reflected the acceptance and promotion of slavery. By the late 1850s, the "Calhoun Democrats," staunchly in favor of states' rights, were in ascendance. For much of Texas's brief history as a republic and a state, politics had been a distinction between those who supported Democrat Sam Houston and those who didn't. The Whigs had made inroads in Texas in the early 1850s, as had the nativist Know-Nothing party in the mid-1850s, the latter an unabashedly anti-Catholic and antiforeign organization. Both of these parties had quickly faded from the Texas scene, leaving two primary groups: the Jacksonian, or Unionist, Democrats, and the Calhoun, or states' rights, Democrats.

Now preachers extolled the institution of slavery from their pulpits and editors from their newspaper columns, and the Texas legislature actually considered voting in favor of resuming an African slave trade. Part of the feeling directed against Mexican Texans in this era stemmed from the perception that they encouraged slaves to escape to Mexico (by 1851, an estimated 3,000 had done so).

The conditions of slavery as it developed in Texas varied. Some slaves were brutalized, forced to work incessantly, kept hungry and ragged, even whipped to death. Former Texas slave Lulu Wilson would recall that the master and mistress "nearly beat us to death," working their slaves incessantly from early childhood on and feeding them poorly: "For years all I could get was one little slice of sowbelly, a puny little piece of bread and a tater. I never had enough to stave the hongriness out'n my belly." Although Lulu was able to stay with her mother, the owner spirited other children away for sale when Lulu's mother was working in the fields.

For others, life was not as harsh. A fair number of slaves were allowed to hire themselves out, despite an 1846 law prohibiting this passed by the first state legislature. Some gained limited protection from juries against cruel treatment. But none of them were free.

To Anglo and European Texans, who overwhelmingly shared a sense of racial superiority, the slavery of African Americans was an accepted means of pursuing the best economic opportunity in the state: the growing of cotton. And most would defend that course with vehemence. The 1850s were rife with incidents that demonstrated the allegiance to the South of a sizable and vocal segment of the dominant culture. For example, in 1854, when German "Forty-Eighters" called a political convention at San Antonio and denounced slavery as an "evil," the outcry was instant and vitriolic, even though the Germans had also argued for the right of the state to decide without federal intervention whether to perpetuate slavery or not. In 1855, Galveston lawyer Lorenzo Sherwood received encouragement for his plan for economic development for the state, which involved making banking and railroad building "semipublic enterprises." Sherwood viewed slavery as a "temporary institution" incompatible with democracy, a view long held by many in the Upper South as well as the North. Sherwood was forced from office, faced censure by the House, and was denied the opportunity to speak publicly in Galveston.

This public reaction did not represent the feelings of the full voting populace, as evidenced by the fact that in 1859 Sam Houston, still an ardent Jacksonian Democrat, defeated incumbent Democrat Hardin Runnels, who had signed a bill encouraging free blacks to enslave themselves by selecting a master. In fact, antisecessionist feeling was strong in some areas; in the same year, an audience at a public debate near Paris, Texas, left after the Union speaker's talk, despite his urgings that they stay to hear the secessionist. He was told, "no damned Secessionist could speak there, or if he did, he would speak to an empty house."

But Texas in the 1850s was rapidly defining itself in opposite terms. "Vigilance committees" sought to stanch any signs of slave uprisings or attempts by others to encourage slaves toward freedom. In 1857 the *Galveston Weekly News* announced, "Those who denounce slavery as an evil, in any sense, are the enemies of the South. . . ." The architects of antebellum Texas—southerners invested culturally and emotionally, if not financially, in the slave system—were ready to take a stand.

# Conclusion

Through the republic and early statehood periods, some of Texas's identity questions seemed to have been answered. The difficulties of maintaining an independent republic, much less trying to build an extended empire, had proven formidable; in the near-decade of independence, the fledgling nation had fallen more deeply into debt and remained an uncertain frontier plagued by external threats and internal divisions. Most Texans had been glad to see Texas enter into American statehood. Texas then began to develop as a state in the Union—but, significantly, as a southern state aligned with the other states that championed slavery, a state in which cotton was "king" and slavery was increasingly to be defended at all costs. In commenting on Lorenzo Sherwood's mild criticism of the "peculiar institution," the Dallas *Herald* had vehemently editorialized, "A man, a Texan, a southerner who could get up in the legislature of a southern State, of the most southern State, and deliberately outrage the feelings of the whole people . . . possesses a heart too callous to be reached by votes of censure."

"The most southern State"—it was a curious identification for a former Spanish and Mexican province, a former republic, a state with a strong Mexican heritage, a state with thousands of European immigrants, a state that was made up of people from all over the American South and all over the Union as well. That the newspaper could write so blithely of Sherwood's "outrag[ing] the feelings of the whole people" indicated not only a moral obtuseness but a dangerous blindness to Texas's heritage and diversity. The state was headed into another crisis of identity, one that would prove to be both extended and costly.

## SUGGESTED READINGS

The Republic era stands as a very distinct period of almost a decade in Texas history, a period in which Texas leaders struggled to create a stable government and economy and to withstand challenges from Mexico while residents struggled to survive and thrive under continued frontier conditions. Readings that focus on this period include William Ransom Hogan's classic *The Texas Republic: A Social and Economic History,* first published in 1946, Stanley Siegel's *The Political History of the Texas Republic, 1836–1845* (1956), and John Edward Weems's *Dream of Empire: A Human History of the Republic of Texas 1836–1846* (1971). The *New Handbook of Texas* (1996) has a good "Texas Republic" entry and entries for various events of the era.

On the subject of Texas annexation, Frederick Merk's *Slavery and the Annexation of Texas* (1972) is considered a classic. Subsequent works have built on and challenged Merk, significantly William W. Freehling's *The Road to Disunion: Secessionists at Bay, 1776–1854* (1990) and Sam W. Haynes's "Anglophobia and the Annexation of Texas: The Quest for National Security" in *Manifest Destiny and Empire: American Antebellum Expansion* (1997).

Much of the scholarly research on the early statehood period, from annexation to the Civil War, as well as in the Republic period, focuses on ethnic groups or individual families; some of these are noted below under "Challenges and Opportunities in the Republic of Texas" and "Marginalized Groups in the Republic." A useful source for understanding gender and ethnicity issues is Mark M. Carroll's *Homesteads Ungovernable: Families, Sex, Race, and the Law in Frontier Texas, 1823–1860* (2001). The *New Handbook of Texas* contains many useful entries for the early statehood period—for example, on the Mexican War and the "Cart Wars."

For primary documents of the republic and the early state, see *Documents of Texas History* (1963, 1994), edited by Ernest Wallace, David M. Vigness, and George Ward. For primary accounts, see *Rip Ford's Texas* (1963, 1987), edited by Stephen B. Oates; *Texas Tears and Texas Sunshine: Voices of Frontier Women* (1985), edited by Jo Ella Powell Exley; and Crystal Sasse Ragsdale's *The Golden Free Land* (1976). An oft-quoted account of Texas in early statehood is Frederick Law Olmsted's *A Journey Through Texas, or a Saddle-Trip on the Southwestern Frontier* (1857, 1978).

To place Texas's movement toward secession at the end of this period into a national context, an excellent resource is Freehling's *Road to Disunion*.

### The Quests for Annexation and Empire, 1836–1841

Randolph B. Campbell's *Sam Houston and the American Southwest* (1993) provides an accessible overview of the first Houston presidential administration. Because Sam Houston was such an important Texas figure throughout the periods covered in this chapter, the Campbell work is also more broadly useful, as is Sam W. Haynes's "Sam Houston and His Antagonists" in *Major Problems in Texas History* (2002). For a detailed account of the Santa Fe expedition, see Paul N. Spellman's *Forgotten Texas Leader: Hugh McLeod and the Texan Santa Fe Expedition* (1999).

### Challenges and Opportunities in the Republic of Texas

In addition to the general works on the republic, individual family fortunes are traced in Margaret Swett Henson's and Delolece Parmalee's *The Cartwrights of San Augustine: Three Generations of Agricultural Entrepreneurs in Nineteenth-Century Texas* (1993) and Paula Mitchell Marks's *Turn Your Eyes Toward Texas: Pioneers Sam and Mary Maverick* (1989). Two good sources for German immigration and settlement are Terry Jordan's *German Seed in Texas Soil: Immigrant Farmers in Nineteenth-Century Texas* (1966) and Walter Struve's *Germans & Texans:*

*Commerce, Migration, and Culture in the Days of the Lone Star Republic* (1996). A good source on women is Fane Downs's "Tryles and Trubbles: Women in Early Nineteenth Century Texas," *Southwestern Historical Quarterly* (1987).

### Marginalized Groups in the Republic

Sources on African Americans include Randolph B. Campbell's *An Empire for Slavery: The Peculiar Institution in Texas, 1821–1865* (1989), Elizabeth Silverthorne's *Plantation Life in Texas* (1986), and Alwyn Barr's *Black Texans: A History of African-Americans in Texas, 1528–1995* (1996). Sources on Tejanos include Timothy M. Matovina's *Tejano Religion and Ethnicity, San Antonio, 1821–1860* (1995), Jesus F. de la Teja's *A Revolution Remembered* (1991), David Montejano's *Anglos and Mexicans in the Making of Texas, 1836–1986* (1987), and Andrés Tijerina's *Tejano Empire: Life on the South Texas Ranchos* (1998). Dianna Everett's *The Texas Cherokees: A People Between Two Fires, 1819–1840* remains the best source of information on the Cherokees' tragic end in East Texas.

### The Annexation Quest Continues

The annexation sources cited above prove useful for understanding the final movements toward annexation within and outside Texas as well. For the Mier expedition, the best source is Sam W. Haynes's *Soldiers of Misfortune: The Somervell and Mier Expeditions* (1990).

### The New State Takes Shape

Most of the sources above also deal substantially with the early statehood period, as reflected in some of their subtitles. A good source on Texas and the Mexican War is Richard Bruce Winders's *Crisis in the Southwest: The United States, Mexico, and the Struggle Over Texas* (2002). For the Compromise of 1850, see Mark J. Stegner's *Texas, New Mexico and the Compromise of 1850: Boundary Dispute and Sectional Crisis* (1996). For Texas's development as a southern state, see Freehling's *Road to Disunion* and Walter Buenger's "The Roots of Texas Secession" in *Major Problems in Texas History* (2002), eds. Sam W. Haynes and Cary D. Wintz. For resistance to this southern definition for the state, see David Pickering and Judy Falls's *Brush Men & Vigilantes: Civil War Dissent in Texas* (2000).

# 9

# Secession, War, and Their Aftermath, 1860–1876

Texas Congressman Sam Maverick was in a quandary. Decades earlier, he had left his home in South Carolina in part because he disagreed with the widely-held states' rights and secessionist views in that state. Now, after a quarter-century as a Texan, once again he found himself surrounded by calls for states' rights and secession. With another national presidential election approaching, in April 1860 secession advocates dominated the state Democratic convention in Galveston, some arguing for Texas to become an independent nation again. Meanwhile, at the national Democratic convention, the Democratic party split in two. Northerners nominated Stephen A. Douglas, the U.S. senator from Illinois who had argued that territories could not be compelled to pass laws protecting slavery. White southerners, on the other hand, were looking for someone who held their strong proslavery views. They held a separate convention, naming Kentuckian John C. Breckenridge as their Democratic presidential candidate.

The Republican Party had coalesced in the mid-1850s in the North, largely to battle the extension of slavery. Delegates to its convention in Chicago now nominated lawyer Abraham Lincoln, a leading Illinois Republican, for president.

Maverick had strong feelings about maintaining the Union—to the extent that, despite his own frequent criticism of Sam Houston, he had supported Houston's 1859 gubernatorial bid, concluding "Old Sam is the right man for this delicate occasion." Maverick had also judged that a curse

| 1860 | Republican Abraham Lincoln is elected U.S. president |
| 1861 | Texas joins other southern states in seceding from the Union |
| 1862 | Federal troops make inroads on Texas gulf coast; suspected Unionists are executed in the "Great Hanging at Gainesville" |
| 1863 | Confederates retake or defend key points on Texas gulf coast |
| 1865 | War ends with South's defeat; on June 19 in Galveston Gen. Gordon Granger declares slaves in Texas to be free, providing basis for the Juneteenth holiday; President Andrew Johnson begins mild presidential Reconstruction |
| 1866 | New state constitutional convention meets as a condition of Texas's reentry into the Union |
| 1867 | First Reconstruction Act of U.S. Congress ushers in congressional Reconstruction |
| 1868–69 | Another constitutional convention meets under requirements of congressional Reconstruction |
| 1870 | Under Republican governor E. J. Davis, Texas gains readmittance to the Union and home rule |
| 1872 | State elections favor resurgent "Old South" Democrats |
| 1873 | Democrat Richard Coke is elected governor over Davis |
| 1875 | Another constitutional convention meets and produces the Texas Constitution of 1876, still in use (with multiple amendments) into the twenty-first century |

seemed to hang over a slave country but had determined "to use without abusing the institution." He held a few slaves and as a lawyer and land speculator was included among the wealthy southern elite of Texas. He became "a good Breckenridge man," still hoping that secession could be averted. But this time he could not avoid a fateful decision.

## Texas and the Confederacy

In the summer of 1860, much of Texas simmered with unrest and suspicion. There was a series of mysterious fires in North and East Texas during the scorching season, with temperatures hitting 114 degrees. Parts of downtown Denton and Dallas went up in flames. Proslavery agitators began attributing these fires to slaves and their northern sympathizers, and slaves were coerced into "confessions" as a panicked vigilantism mounted. Vigilantes killed at least thirty people, perhaps many more. Even in September, when the panic was subsiding, a posse chased down and hung Anthony Bewley, an antislavery Methodist minister suspected on questionable evidence of provoking the arsons.

The "Texas Troubles," as they came to be called, were both a sign and a cause of the Texas secession that was to follow. Although the fires were subsequently determined to have been the result of high temperatures and the spontaneous combustion of new phosphorus matches, the proslavery propagandizers' manipulation of racist fears showed how strongly many Texans identified with the South and made them even more combative.

### Secession

In the elections of 1860, southern Democratic candidate John C. Breckenridge garnered 858,356 votes, with major support across the South and in Texas. Yet to the horror of many southerners, from South Carolina to Texas, Abraham Lincoln was elected president, garnering 1,865,593 votes, and Hannibal Hamlin vice president. Southerners felt that the northern states had prevailed in electing, in the words of Texas's subsequent declaration of secession, "two men whose chief claims to such high positions are their approval of . . . long-continued wrongs, and their pledges to continue them to the final consummation of these schemes for the ruin of the slave-holding States." In Texas, as in the rest of the South, Lincoln was viewed as an archfiend, his party as "behind the Texas Troubles."

Texas secessionists began to clamor for a state convention that would declare a complete break with the U.S. government. As governor, Houston remained adamantly opposed to furthering this cause. On December 17, in response to secessionists' call for a January convention, he reluctantly called the legislature into session for January 21, hoping that moderates in that body would prevail, forestalling such a gathering. In the meantime, South Carolina seceded from the Union. When the Texas legislature met in the new year, delegates had already been elected to a Texas secession convention a week later. The legislature simply voted to authorize the scheduled convention. As a member of the House, Maverick reluctantly cast his vote for this convention. In doing so, he had unwittingly placed himself in the middle of the latest struggle for the identity of Texas.

On January 28, the convention met, with O. M. Roberts, Texas Supreme Court judge and avid secessionist, presiding. Members moved speedily to vote in favor of breaking away from the United States. They insisted that "the governments of the various States . . . were established exclusively for the white race, for themselves and their posterity," with "the African race . . . rightfully held and regarded as an inferior and dependent race."

Houston and others favoring federal union and compromise had insisted that the people of Texas vote as well. With this vote set for February 23, both supporters and opponents of secession took their arguments into the voting districts and to the newspapers of the state, printing and distributing copies of the ordinance of secession in English, Spanish, and German. In the meantime, the convention appointed a Committee of Public Safety to authorize volunteer troops and force the U.S. military to turn over the 2,700 federal soldiers, twenty-one forts, and weapons stores in Texas. On February 16, Texas volunteer troops arrived in San Antonio and effected the surrender of military personnel, sites, and stores.

A week later, Texas voters approved secession by a vote of 46,129 to 14,697. To understand why Texas voters approved secession, it is important to remember the developing sectionalism between the North and South of the United States throughout the early nineteenth century, most of it in regard to slavery. Factors included the delay in Texas annexation, the Compromise of 1850, the Kansas-Nebraska Act, the emergence of the Republican Party, and Lincoln's election. Those Texans who could vote—overwhelmingly, white southern males—favored a southern economic system based on cotton cultivation, and, by extension, on slave labor. They also favored a caste system that valued white over black. And they valued states' rights over continuing in a Union controlled by people who opposed the continued growth of a slave system.

In eighteen counties in Northeast and Central Texas and one in East Texas, however, the vote actually went against secession. Counties with significant numbers of Germans or immigrants from the Upper South—in Texas, primarily former residents of Missouri, Arkansas, and Tennessee—and from the North were far less likely to approve secession than were those with immigrants from the Lower South, especially those with large slave populations. But despite the opposition—which would continue during the war—the convention had its mandate and made the break with the Union official on March 2. Texas quickly joined the Confederacy, requiring everyone in office to take a loyalty oath to the new confederation. When Sam Houston and his secretary of state, E. W. Cave, refused to do so, they were removed, with Lieutenant Governor Edward Clark put in Houston's place. Less than a month later, the Civil War commenced with the Confederate firing on the federals' Fort Sumter, South Carolina.

Although Samuel Maverick had long opposed secession, he finally voted in favor of a Texas secession convention and became a leading Confederate supporter in San Antonio. *(Courtesy of the Witte Museum, San Antonio, Texas)*

Where was Sam Maverick as all of this transpired? As one of the three members of the Committee of Public Safety charged with appropriating federal troops and stores, he became a leading Confederate official, taking the loyalty oath and voting that those who did not should be deposed. His wife Mary, who would join in the war effort herself by leading the Ladies Aid Society and the women's wing of the Southern Defense Aid Society in San Antonio, offered an explanation: "At last he came to believe the quarrel was forced upon us, and that there was before us an 'irressible [*sic*] conflict' which we could not escape, no matter where we turned." The decision would cost them dearly.

### Texans as Part of the Confederacy

Even before the citizen vote for secession, Texas had dispatched seven delegates to a Confederate government organizing convention in Montgomery, Alabama. Once Texas entered the Confederacy, it was obliged to acquiesce to central Confederate authority in such matters as conscription laws, use of slave labor, and cotton trade with Mexico, and to recruit increasing numbers of its men of fighting age to serve the Confederacy. At the same time, it had its own representatives and influential men in the Confederate government: Texans Louis T. Wigfall and W. S. Oldman became members of the Confederate Senate, and John H. Reagan, Texas lawyer, judge, and legislator, became postmaster general of the Confederacy.

There were occasional tensions between the state and Confederate government over policy and procedure, such as when to give men exemptions to Confederate service so as to retain a defense force in Texas. And throughout the war, both governments would contend with deserters and evaders of the conscription laws. But in the recruiting of fighting men, Texas built an impressive record. Within ten months of the firing on Fort Sumter, Texas had 25,000 men in the Confederate army. Two-thirds of them were in cavalry units; eventually, almost 59,000 Texans would serve in the cavalry. Although Governor Francis Lubbock's November 1863 estimate of a total of 90,000 Texans in Confederate service has been dismissed as too high for any one time, historians say that the figure probably has validity for the whole war effort—this in a fighting-age population estimated at 100,000 to 110,000.

Texans were well represented, too, in the Confederate officer ranks, with numerous brigadier generals and colonels. The highest-ranked officer was General

Nineteenth-century Texas painter Carl G. von Iwonski created this dramatic portrait of four members of Company B, Eighth Texas Cavalry, better known as Terry's Texas Rangers. This unit participated in some of the major battles of the Civil War. *(Courtesy of the Witte Museum, San Antonio, Texas)*

Albert Sidney Johnston, a veteran of the Texas Revolution and the Mexican War, who assumed command of the Western Department of the Confederacy but died leading troops at the battle of Shiloh in 1862. John Bell Hood rose from captain to colonel to brigadier general in charge of Hood's Texas Brigade in Robert E. Lee's Army of Northern Virginia. A promotion to major general followed, then one to lieutenant general. Hood commanded the Army of Tennessee in the later months of the war.

Major generals from Texas were Tom Green, Samuel Bell Maxey, and John A. Wharton. Wharton, a wealthy planter, first served as captain of Company B, Eighth Texas Cavalry, better known—and celebrated—as Terry's Texas Rangers. After the deaths of Colonel B. F. Terry and his lieutenant colonel, Wharton led the Rangers at the battle of Shiloh, then received rapid promotions. He was killed before the end of the war in a dispute with another Confederate officer.

The highest-ranking Tejano Confederate commander was Santos Benavides, a descendant of the founder of Laredo, county judge of Webb County in 1859, and colonel of the Thirty-Third Texas Cavalry. Benavides, aided by his brothers Refugio and Cristóbal, led efforts to protect the Mexican border, pushing back both Union guerillas and Juan Cortina, who in 1861 again tried to rally supporters on the Texas side of the border. The Thirty-Third built an impressive record, but Tejanos also served throughout the Texas Confederate forces. More than 300 enlisted in the Eighth Texas Infantry, and there are estimates that at least 2,500 Tejanos were Confederate soldiers, in encounters from Virginia to New Mexico.

Not all Texans who fought or commanded did so for the Confederacy. Many who opposed Texas's stance joined Union troops. E. J. Davis, another Texas judge, had resigned rather than take the Confederate loyalty oath and traveled to New Orleans, where he organized the First Texas U.S. Cavalry to fight against the Confederacy. The Second Texas Cavalry comprised Tejanos and Mexicans from the Rio Grande, drawn by the bounty money they received for enlisting but also propelled by grievances about their treatment by Texas officials and by opposition to slavery.

Most Texas Confederate troops—about two-thirds—stayed in the western theater, or west of the Mississippi, many serving in the Louisiana and New Mexico campaigns. In fact, Texas became the base for two attempts to extend the Confederacy westward in an echo of previous Texan attempts to claim New Mexico.

In the first attempt, John Baylor, lieutenant colonel of the Second Texas Mounted Rifles, had simply been told to protect the overland route to El Paso. Upon reaching nearby Fort Bliss, however, he was determined to invade the Mesilla Valley and claim New Mexico for the Confederacy. This effort would quickly founder as Baylor antagonized even his Confederates.

Meanwhile, Brigadier General Henry Hopkins Sibley was proceeding with a similar conquest plan, having convinced Confederate President Jefferson Davis that he could take a group of Texas volunteers, arm them from the federal forts and arsenals now under Confederate control, and seize New Mexico in "the westernmost campaign of the Civil War." The Confederacy would then be in a position to move its troops onward to claim Colorado and the Southwest all the way to southern California. This would bolster the rebel economy and its chances of being taken seriously as a viable republic by nations other than the United States.

Sibley, a West Point graduate who had five years of military service on the Texas frontier, began recruiting in San Antonio in August 1861. By late October, he had more than 3,000 men in three regiments and in supply and artillery units. They marched out along the San Antonio-El Paso Road in detachments, their numbers staggered to make use of the limited water holes.

Following Baylor's steps—and incorporating some of Baylor's volunteers—in January 1862 Sibley made Mesilla his base of operations. Meanwhile, to meet the Confederate threat, Colonel Edward R. S. Canby, commander of the federal Military Department of New Mexico, was busy amassing federal troops and volunteers from Colorado and New Mexico at the Union post of Fort Craig.

In February, Sibley began moving most of his force toward Fort Craig, where twenty-one captured volunteers were being held. Canby, however, had fortified Craig to the point that the Confederates dared not try an assault. Instead, they detoured eastward around the fort and drew Canby's troops out for a battle at Valverde Ford on the Rio Grande.

This engagement was followed by a Confederate push to Albuquerque and to Santa Fe and by a series of clashes, the most significant of which is known as the battle of Glorieta, which occurred near Glorieta Pass on March 28, 1862. With Sibley still in Albuquerque, Lieutenant Colonel William R. Scurry led the main Texas force against 850 Union fighters. When these fighters destroyed the Confederate supply train, the Texas troops began a slow retreat.

The suffering on the return trip to San Antonio was intense. A San Antonio resident who had seen the brigade march out the previous October, "finely dressed, splendidly mounted and elegantly equipped" now observed fewer than half their number "come straggling back on foot, broken, disorganized in an altogether deplorable condition." Not all of the missing were accounted for, but approximately 500 had died, either from wounds or disease, and another 500 had been taken prisoner and marched to Illinois. Like previous Texas attempts to expand westward, this Confederate one had ended badly.

Particularly in the eastern theater, as battle piled upon battle, casualties soared in ways few could have anticipated. Texan W. R. Bell of Blossom wrote of the aftermath of the battle of Franklin, Tennessee, "I helped bury the dead . . . and I think I could have walked all over the battlefield on dead men." Battlefield deaths, injuries, illness, and desertion all took their toll; B. F. Carpenter of Gainesville would recall, "Our regiment went out of Texas with 1180 men and when we surrendered at Canton, Mississippi, there were 240 at roll call."

# The War in Texas and Its Impact

There were few and limited Civil War battles in Texas, and Texans did not experience the invasion and destruction visited upon the Old South; one need only think of Union General William Tecumseh Sherman's burning of the city of Atlanta and punishing "March to the Sea." The war did reach Texas, however, and it affected the state and its citizens in very important ways.

## Military Conflict in Texas

In the wake of the Confederates' firing on Fort Sumter, Union naval vessels began blockading southern ports, extending the blockade to Texas very quickly. Confederates tried to strengthen the Texas coastal positions, but in the fall of 1862 Union ships were shelling the sites. On the Texas coast, the bark USS *Arthur,* the yacht *Corypheus,* and the steamer *Sachem* harassed trade and Confederate positions, seizing Confederate sloops and schooners. In August the *Arthur*'s commander tried to follow up by taking the town of Corpus Christi but was repulsed in two engagements by a Confederate force of 700, a combination of local volunteers and four companies of the Eighth Texas Infantry battalion.

Despite this victory, the Texas coast remained vulnerable as the war seesawed in the East. The battle of Antietam in September put an end to Robert E. Lee's attempt to press into Union territory in Maryland. That same month, a federal blockade patrol shelled the Texas coast at Fort Sabine, constructed by local residents to protect the community of Sabine Pass, near the juncture of the Sabine River and the Gulf of Mexico. Damage to the fort and an outbreak of yellow fever caused local militia and Texas infantrymen to abandon the post. In October, a squadron of Union ships sailed into Galveston harbor, with their commander demanding surrender of Galveston Island as well. Confederate Brigadier General Paul O. Hébert, in charge of the Confederate District of Texas, judged the island to be indefensible, and Confederate troops removed to the mainland.

This military abandonment of the island dealt a blow to the spirits and fortunes of many Texans. The town of Galveston on the island had been developing as a significant commercial and transportation center, with steamers taking people and goods to Houston and back through Galveston Bay and Buffalo Bayou. A railroad company had even built a bridge to the island in 1860 and constructed a short railroad line. Now this vital coastal artery was severed.

Major General John Bankhead Magruder, a Virginian and Mexican War veteran, followed Hébert as commander of the district. He assumed command on November 29 and immediately began planning to retake Galveston using two river steamers for a naval attack as well as infantry and cavalry forces.

On New Year's morning 1863, the Confederates struck, the troops crossing

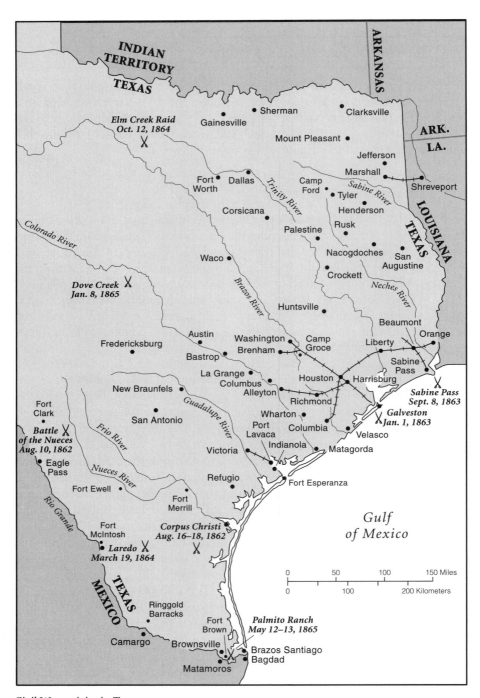

Civil War activity in Texas.

over the railroad bridge and the two steamers opening fire from behind the Union ships. Twenty-six Confederates were killed and 117 wounded, whereas the Union had about 150 casualties. The federal ships departed, leaving Union infantrymen in Confederate hands. Magruder had retaken Galveston.

This victory was followed by news of Lee's December victory over the Army of the Potomac near Fredericksburg, Virginia, and by the January 21 retaking of Sabine Pass. On January 30, Mary Maverick, busy with relief efforts for soldiers and their families, wrote to her son in Confederate service, "With all our grand victories & all their losses, won't we have peace soon think you?"

But the war was far from over, the southern secession far from secured. In summer 1863, the biggest single battle of the war occurred at Gettysburg, Pennsylvania, where Lee's southern troops were pushed back and combined casualties—dead, wounded, or missing—topped 43,000. Further Union victories in the South positioned the federal forces to control the Mississippi River and freed Major General Nathan Banks to look toward a conquest of Texas.

His first attempt came at the previously contested Sabine Pass, from which Banks hoped to capture Houston, recapture Galveston, and gain entrance to the state's interior. Banks sent 4,000 troops by ship, and the U.S. Navy dispatched four gunboats to cover their landing.

At Sabine Pass, the Davis Guards, Company F of the First Texas Heavy Artillery Regiment, had been busy fortifying the site and preparing for an attack by sea. When one of the four gunboats, the *Clifton,* appeared and began shelling them from a distance on the morning of September 8, the Confederates bided their time. The other three ships joined the Clifton in the afternoon, advancing on the pass. Under Lieutenant Dick Dowling, a genial Houston saloon owner from Ireland, the forty-seven-man Confederate force made good use of its six cannons, firing more than 100 times in a thirty-five minute battle.

The small Confederate force turned back the invasion, the federal troops returning to New Orleans. The Confederates also captured two of the gunboats and more than 300 Union soldiers. General Banks, however, maintained pressure on Texas. In particular, he was eager to capture Brownsville, which had become a key import/export center for the western Confederacy, with southern cotton going to Europe through Matamoros and war supplies and other essentials coming in to Texas. In November Banks took Brazos Island, off the mouth of the Rio Grande near Brownsville, forcing Confederate troops to abandon defense of the town. Banks's occupation of Brownsville and disruption of trade there would be temporary, but federal soldiers worked their way along the Texas coastline, occupying the port of Indianola as well. Eudora Moore, a fifteen-year-old resident of the port town, would later recall the federal soldiers "digging rifle pits and building forts on the prairie back of town" and appropriating the family's cattle. Soon Galveston and Sabine Pass were the only ports remaining in Confederate hands, and as far inland as San Antonio, residents prepared to flee.

In yet a third thrust, Banks and General Frederick Steele planned a two-pronged attack into East Texas, Banks from Lousiana and Steele from Little Rock,

THE CONFEDERATES EVACUATING BROWNSVILLE, TEXAS.—[Sketched by an English Artist.]

**EVACUATION OF BROWNSVILLE BY THE CONFEDERATES.**

Brownsville lies on the Texas side of the Rio Grande opposite Matamoras, which is two miles distant. We present above the hasty departure from this place of the Confederate garrison on November 2, 1863. The occasion of this sudden flight was the anticipated arrival of our fleet of transports off Brazos, Santiago. For two days every means of transit across the river was overcrowded with goods, furniture, cotton, and luggage, while upon both banks were piled, in confused heaps, bedding, cotton bales, luggage, vehicles, and merchandise of every description. The garrison buildings in the mean time were burned, and all cotton and stores that could not be removed. On the 6th the Federal troops occupied Brownsville, where is now the head-quarters of General Herron. It was General Banks who originally occupied the position.

In January 1864 the *London Illustrated News* ran this wood engraving titled "The War in America: The Confederates Quitting Brownsville, Texas, on Hearing of the Approach of Federal Transports." Confederate troops under John S. (Rip) Ford reoccupied the town in summer 1864 and held it until the end of the war. *(CN 01535, The Center for American History, The University of Texas at Austin)*

Arkansas. But in spring 1864, Steele was halted by Confederate troops—including Texas brigades—at Camden, Arkansas. Banks's troops met the Confederates at the battles of Mansfield and Pleasant Hill in Louisiana but then fell back east of the Mississippi. One Texan, John Howard King of Gilmer, remembered of Pleasant Hill, "Here was the wildest shooting that I saw during the war. They shot the tops of the trees all to pieces. . . ."

As the war dragged on for another year, Texas troops retook Brownsville and other points along the coast. But the Army of the South was faring badly. In September 1864, Sherman took Atlanta in a terrible blow to the Confederacy. By the end of the year, John Bell Hood's Army of Tennessee had been devastated. In truth, southern manpower and resources had been strained to the breaking point. The greatest blow to Confederate hopes would come in the East on April 9, 1865, when Lee surrendered the army of Northern Virginia to Grant at Appomattox Courthouse, Virginia. Nine days later, Joseph E. Johnston surrendered "the last major Confederate army."

The war was essentially over, but in early May Lieutenant General Edmund Kirby Smith, commander of the Confederate Trans-Mississippi Department, announced that his western Confederate forces would continue to fight. In the meantime, the Union commander on Brazos Island was negotiating unsuccessfully for a Confederate surrender at Brownsville. This continued resistance brought to Texas soil the last engagement of the Civil War—the battle of Palmito Ranch.

Learning of the surrenders in the East, many soldiers in the Brownsville area left for home, but others continued to occupy and hold the town. They skirmished twice with Union forces before Colonel Benavides and Colonel John Salmon "Rip" Ford appeared with Confederate reinforcements. Ford was one of the more ubiquitous and colorful characters in this era of Texas history. He had arrived in Texas immediately after the Revolution and had worked as a medical doctor, Texas military officer, state senator, Texas ranger, and newspaper editor. His nickname stemmed from his dispatches reporting deaths of American troops during the Mexican War; he would use "RIP" as shorthand for "Rest in Peace." He, too, had engaged in extensive border service during the war.

At Palmito Ranch, the numbers were now nearly even. With their field artillery firing, Ford and Benavides's forces attacked the Union troops from the left, the right, and the center, forcing them into a rout. The federal troops hurried back toward Brazos Island with the Confederates in pursuit, the four-hour battle ending when the federal troops reached reinforcements near Brazos Island.

Even as the battle raged, Kirby Smith and other western Confederate officials acknowledged the futility of a continued Confederate resistance. Federal officers entered Brownsville to arrange a Confederate surrender. On June 2, Smith formally turned over the Confederate Trans-Mississippi Department to General Canby, who had stopped the early Confederate advance into New Mexico.

After four years of conflict, the loss would rankle those Texans who had embraced the identity of Texas as an extension of the American South. But whatever one's political stance, the war in Texas had had a significant impact, in spite of the fact that invasion had been confined to the coast. The war effort had both drained Texas resources and development and created division and new uncertainties about Texas's identity.

### Wartime Conditions

During the war years, more and more men were conscripted into Confederate service. At first, the call was for men aged 18 to 35, but by war's end, with Confederate losses mounting, conscription acts included men from 17 to 50. Unpopular laws, the Conscription Acts of 1862 allowed those overseeing twenty slaves an exemption from Confederate service, but the great majority of Texas men either volunteered or were conscripted. Some of the youngest and oldest recruits served in the "Home Guards" in each county. Farming, ranching, and businesses naturally suffered with the absence of men of fighting age. But many women, following the American colonial tradition of women as "deputy husbands," took over the management of farms, plantations, ranches, and businesses during this period.

Union blockades and the disruptions of war meant that Texans learned to make do or do without. Texans learned to concoct coffee substitutes out of peanuts, corn, barley, and even okra. Eudora Moore would recall her mother constructing a pair of pants from a "parlor table cover." When items previously in good supply did appear, they commanded exorbitant prices. In early February 1864, Mary Maverick squeezed into the crowded Mutual Aid store in San Antonio, getting for her efforts and $180 a bolt of domestic cloth, a pair of shoes, and a dozen candles.

Homespun and handwoven clothing became a symbol of patriotic pride; Governor Francis R. Lubbock was inaugurated in a homespun suit in 1861, and the chorus of the Confederate song "Bonny Blue Flag" noted "My homespun dress is plain I know/My fan is homemade too/But then it shows what Southern girls/For Southern rights will do." Despite the severe shortages at home, girls and women also worked hard to clothe the soldiers and provide them with medicine and food, as the Confederate and state governments struggled to provide them with the most basic necessities.

Texas did enjoy an important trade advantage over other southern states in its proximity to Mexico. At Matamoros, on the Rio Grande across from Brownsville, and at Bagdad, Tamaulipas, bordering the mouth of the Rio Grande, Texas cotton was shipped out, helping shore up the Texas and western Confederate economies, and items such as medicine and tobacco intermittently made their way to inland Texas. Mexican, Tejano, and Anglo merchants operating on the Rio Grande made "small fortunes" in trade during the war years as blockade-running vessels carrying supplies and cotton evaded the Union ships in the gulf.

Nonetheless, the war greatly hurt economic and cultural development in Texas. The state was just beginning to establish the transportation arteries necessary for increased trade and growth when the conflict broke out. For example, railroad projects of the 1850s, although limited and short-lived, had already made a difference in Texas travel. A thirty-six-mile trip northwest from Houston to the Hockley area took a day and a half by stagecoach (through mud) in 1854; the same trip over the same ground took an hour and forty minutes by rail in 1857.

The war played havoc with fledgling railroad efforts. Although a few short railroad lines in Texas were actually completed and put in service during the war years, others had to shut down. In some cases, their rails were dug up and used as military fortifications or laid elsewhere as part of the military supply effort. Meanwhile, many railroad construction efforts simply stopped midway through.

By the same token, work ground to a halt on other community development efforts. For example, since her first arrival in San Antonio in 1838 Mary Maverick had longed to worship in an Episcopal church, practicing the faith in which she was raised. By 1850, a small core congregation had been formed, but despite the efforts of the Mavericks and others, attempts to build a church repeatedly faltered. Construction on St. Mark's Episcopal church finally commenced in the midst of the statewide agitation over secession, but was suspended with the advent of the war.

At its most extreme, the war pushed Texans back into uncertain frontier conditions, not only in terms of supplies and community development but in terms of safety. During the early statehood period, American and European immigrants had moved westward through the Texas Hill Country, pushing settlement onto the Edwards Plateau. To the north, they had moved onto the grand prairies and into the western cross timbers of north central Texas, pressing westward to the prairies beyond. In both cases, they were drawing near to the rolling plains still occupied by embattled Indians. Although the early months of the war were relatively quiet on Texas's western frontier, with the northern and southern states at war and men and resources being drained for the fighting, the remaining free-roaming Comanches, in particular, began to use the situation to their advantage. They mounted punishing raids on the outlying western settlements, hitting hard in Cooke, Denton, Montague, Parker, and Wise counties. Texans "forted up," as they had in earlier days, families coming together and stockading for protection.

From the outset of the war the state government had tried to address the need for frontier protection, from Indians as well as other threats. In December 1861 the Texas legislature authorized a Frontier Regiment to replace a Texas Confederate regiment briefly assigned to home-front protection. Led by Colonel James M. Norris, the new force of more than 1,000 men established a frontier defense line a short distance west of the settlements, from the Red River on the north bordering Indian Territory southward to the Rio Grande, with a string of sixteen forts bisecting the state, north to south. (In the south along the Rio Grande, a Confederate regiment patrolled the border area.)

In spring 1862, Confederate President Jefferson Davis responded to complaints about lack of protection by Texas governor Francis R. Lubbock and Missouri's governor by establishing a Trans-Mississippi Military Department with Edmund Kirby Smith commanding. But the Confederacy's military attention and resources remained directed eastward.

At first, Norris's troops patrolled regularly from fort to fort, but the Comanches and their allies from other tribes, discerning the pattern, stepped up their attacks on temporarily exposed areas. In 1863, Governor Lubbock reorganized and expanded the Frontier Regiment, which was rechristened Mounted Regiment, Texas State Troops. It abandoned the patrol system in favor of an aggressive series of scouting parties beyond the line of defense.

As the frontier force sought to quell the Indian threat, state officials and President Davis sparred over its status. State officials wanted the regiment to be a Confederate force, but to remain under state control to respond quickly and knowledgeably to Indian threats. Davis wanted the regiment to be subject to all Confederate rules and regulations, which meant that its members could be pulled from the Texas frontier and used elsewhere.

In an agreement that became official in March 1864, the regiment was switched to Confederate service and divided, some of the companies moving elsewhere in Texas. On the western frontier, those remaining were joined by more than 4,000 local militia men, like other "Home Guard" units mostly older men and teenage boys too young for service.

Indian depradations continued, the most prominent of which was the Elm Creek raid of October 1864. Comanches and Kiowas rode into the Elm Creek Valley in Young County and raided the settlements, killing eleven residents and five Confederate troopers and capturing seven women and children.

### Dissent Within Texas

In the waning months of the war, the Comanches and their allies shifted their attentions away from the Texas frontier, a move that should have ensured a much-needed peace. But the frontier—and much of North Texas—remained chaotic and strife-filled, the remaining companies riding out not only after outlaws but after deserters and those who refused to serve in the Confederacy or Home Guard. In October 1864, General Edmund Kirby Smith noted, "The frontier counties . . . are . . . a grand city of refuge where thousands of able-bodied men have flocked to escape service in the Confederate Army." The conscription evaders and the deserters were called "brush men" because they hid in the brush. All attempts to corral and control them ended in failure. Henry McCulloch, commander of the Northern Sub-District, offered the deserters an amnesty in the fall

In the year this photo was taken, 1859, Sam Houston was about to mount a victorious campaign for the governorship of Texas. But when he refused to take a loyalty oath to the Confederacy in 1861, he was removed from the office. *(Sam Houston Memorial Museum, Huntsville, Texas)*

of 1863 and included those who responded in the "Brush Battalion," charged with chasing down other deserters and protecting against Indians. But the members of the battalion were so troublesome, and prone to desert, that McCulloch disbanded it in March 1864.

McCulloch's experience points up one impact of the war in Texas: increased divisiveness. Not only had some Texans chosen to fight for the Union, but some of those who stayed refused to commit to the war effort, or actively opposed it. At first, many Texans excused immigrants from Europe, in particular, from embracing the cause with fervor. But as the casualties began to mount, and as the Confederacy fought for survival, dissent or even neutrality was viewed as suspect at best, traitorous at worst. In San Antonio, as one resident noted, "It was like living in an asylum where every one was crazy on one especial subject; you never knew what dangerous paroxysms were about to begin."

Secessionists perceived opposition to the southern cause among the Germans of central Texas and the immigrants from the Upper South living in frontier north Texas. Although members of both groups enlisted and fought for the Confederacy, their numbers did include staunch antislavery contingents, people who felt that slaveholding provided an unfair advantage in an agricultural society and was at odds with the principles of democracy. Further, there were avowed Unionists in both groups; many of the North Texans were rumored to be members of a Union League formed during the war as a means of pledging continuing fidelity to the United States. The opposition of the two groups was explained in part by the fact that many Germans had left their home country disappointed by its failure to reach unification, and by the fact that the Upper Southerners, whether or not they favored slavery, felt that the issue should be resolved without secession.

Some Upper Southerners moved on to Kansas or California, and some Germans left for Mexico. One such group of German Unionists, en route to Mexico and camped beside the Nueces River in Kinney County, were set upon by Confederate troops in August 1862. Of the sixty-plus members of the traveling party, nineteen were killed in the "battle of the Nueces," along with two Confederates. Confederates executed the nine wounded Germans as well.

Many Upper Southerners in North Texas felt secure and well established in their independent views. After all, they lived in an area of the state where slavery had only a tentative foothold, and many had arrived in the 1830s and 1840s. Yet immigrants from the Lower South, especially those holding slaves and with more wealth, in general, had arrived in the 1850s. Some of these representatives of antebellum southern culture, spurred in part by stories of the Union League, in part by tales of North Texans' collaboration with Kansas abolitionists and Indians across the Red River, began to form vigilante groups to ferret out Union sympathizers.

This atmosphere led to a series of vigilante killings of suspected or known Union sympathizers in Cooke, Grayson, Wise, and Denton counties. The most notorious killings occurred in Cooke County and became known collectively as the "Great Hanging at Gainesville."

Suspicions had been provoked when a number of Cooke County citizens

This oil painting, done by C. B. Clauss in 1888, depicts the "battle of the Nueces" in August 1862, when Confederate troops set upon more than sixty German Unionists camped beside the Nueces River en route to Mexico. Two troopers and nineteen Germans were killed and nine wounded Germans were executed. (*Comfort Historical Museum, Comfort, Texas*)

signed a petition protesting the Conscription Acts of April 1862 because the acts exempted men in charge of at least twenty slaves. The acts had caused grumbling statewide, but resistance was stronger and more vocal in the northern counties, where dissenters were unhappy about being drafted or seeing their sons drafted. When rumors began to circulate of a Unionist plot to seize the militia arsenals at Sherman and Gainesville, the commander of the Gainesville-area militia district authorized the arrest of any able-bodied men who failed to respond to a call to arms. Colonel James G. Bourland, a former state senator and plantation owner, led state troops in arresting more than 150 men on October 1. They were to be tried by a "citizens' jury" organized by Bourland and Confederate colonel and fellow slaveholder William C. Young, who happened to be home on leave.

None of the accused owned slaves, but seven of the twelve jurors did. The jurors proceeded to convict seven leading Unionists of "conspiracy and insurrection" or "disloyalty and treason." These seven men were summarily hung, but the jury was exonerating others when a mob demanded more convictions. Fourteen more men were turned over to the vigilantes, escorted by Bourland's troops, and hung from a large elm tree on the banks of Pecan Creek just east of Gainesville.

In Gainesville, it appeared that the rest of the prisoners would be released, but then William Young and another man were ambushed and killed by unknown assailants. Many of the prisoners were immediately retried, and nineteen more were executed. In all, forty men were hung and two killed while trying to escape before the troubles in Gainesville came to an end. A family member of one of the executed men charged that most of the dead "were old settlers in this country, and had fought the Indians from their doorsteps. And they did not want to be crowded back on the back seat by a few newcomers that was trying to take the lead and run the country."

The war left a palpable bitterness between those who had wholeheartedly embraced the cause and those who could not and would not do so. In San Antonio, as people like the Mavericks struggled to comprehend and accept the defeat of a cause to which they had given time, energy, money, and sons, Confederate veterans raided and looted, defending their actions on the grounds that San Antonians had not fully supported the war effort.

## Aftermath

Even without the internal enmities, the military and political loss festered. "Our humiliation in defeat . . . is harder to bear, than all the exposure, hunger and wounds during the war," former Confederate soldier J. L. Greer of McKinney would write. "It rankles me in my heart still. . . ."

The war, then, left many Texans exhausted, disheartened, and divided, with not only the plantation system but their towns and farms in disorder and decay. Galveston's population had declined, and a local newspaper reported that even Confederate troops had "torn [fine residences] to pieces merely for fuel during the whole war, and that too while there has been an abundance of wood at the head of the bay." Beaumont had been growing in promise and prominence before the war as a sawmill and ranching town and a railroad transportation hub, but after the war the sawmills sat deteriorating, the railroad bridges and roadbeds untended and unused. In the countryside, much farming land lay uncultivated, its cash value diminished, and farms had deteriorated.

If any group had reason to rejoice at the South's capitulation, it was African Americans, most of them slaves. Texas had more slaves than ever at war's end—an estimated 250,000—because of the southern practice of sending them beyond the reach of the Union army. The feeling of freedom was sweet to people who had lived so long without it; Annie Hawkins would remember, "We was the happiest folks in the world when we knowed we was free."

Nevertheless, former slaves had reason to be uneasy. General Gordon Granger had arrived in Galveston on June 19 and proclaimed enforcement of the Emancipation Proclamation in Texas, an event that would later spark the creation and observance of "Juneteenth" celebrations among African Americans. But even the wording of the proclamation seemed to send mixed messages. It demanded "an absolute equality of rights and rights of property between former masters and slaves," yet also suggested that the slaves "remain at their present homes and work for wages" and warned that "they will not be allowed to collect at military posts" or be "supported in idleness, either there or elsewhere." Some even had to overcome the deception of their owners; Lulu Wilson's owner told her stepfather that adults had been freed, but children had to remain with masters until they reached adulthood.

Many of Texas's leaders and voting citizens had defined Texas as part of a southern Confederacy built on cotton culture; its most powerful citizens were those who managed large-scale cotton cultivation with slaves. They had separated Texas from the very Union it had sought to enter in the 1830s and 1840s. Now Texans were going to have to redefine themselves and their relation to that Union, including expanding definitions of citizenship—or accept definitions imposed from outside.

## Reconstruction in Texas

With the defeat of Texas and other seceded states, the federal government faced the problem of bringing them back into the Union and ensuring their adherence to federal law, including the emancipation of former slaves. President Lincoln considered this an executive branch responsibility and in December 1863 had issued the Proclamation of Amnesty and Reconstruction by which southern voters were to pledge their loyalty to the U.S. Constitution and the Union.

By the time Edmund Kirby Smith surrendered the western Confederate forces, President Lincoln had been assassinated, and his vice president and successor, Andrew Johnson, had already offered amnesty to most Confederates if they would take a loyalty oath to the United States. Like Lincoln, Johnson saw the southern states' attempt to withdraw from the Union as an illegal action that the executive branch should handle through a program of "reconstruction." But powerful Republicans in national government had a different interpretation: The southern states had given up their statehood in the Union. Because it was the responsibility of the U.S. Congress to admit new states, Congress should direct the "reconstruction," and do so in such a way as to ensure the rights of the former slaves and advance Republican principles. At first Johnson prevailed, allowing the old southern power order to begin reasserting itself. Then Congress took over, trying to force the old southern electorate to accept enhanced federal control and rights for African Americans. In Texas, as elsewhere in the South, some sought to construct a new order as others sought to reclaim the old one.

### Presidential Reconstruction

A former Democratic senator from Tennessee who had become vice president in 1864, Johnson proceeded with his mild restructuring plan. He ordered a constitutional convention "to restore [Texas] to its constitutional relations to the federal government." Delegates would have to take the loyalty oath, but again, all but the most prominent Texas Confederate leaders would be allowed to participate in the new political order.

John H. Reagan, the Texan who had served as postmaster general in Jefferson Davis's cabinet, wrote from prison in Boston to "the People of Texas" in August 1865 urging that they "accept the present condition of things, as the result of war, and of inevitable necessity," accepting "the supreme authority of the Government of the United States" and the abolition of slavery as conditions for regaining "the blessings of local self-government" and banishing military rule.

Johnson had appointed Andrew J. Hamilton provisional governor of Texas. The controversial Hamilton embodied many of the political dilemmas of the era. An Austin lawyer and former Democratic state representative, Hamilton had been among those moderate Democrats who tried to fight the secessionist tide in the 1850s. His popularity was such that he won a U.S. congressional seat in 1859 and a special election to the Texas Senate early in the war. But by mid-1862, he felt harassed for his views and left Texas. In the U.S. cities of the Northeast, he lectured on the evils of slavery and slave owners' power. With the North anticipating the occupation of Texas, Hamilton was actually appointed military governor of the state and participated in the Union troops' foray into South Texas in the fall of 1863. But he waited out the later stages of the war in New Orleans.

Despite Reagan's admonishments to Texans to accept federal measures, Hamilton and other Unionists encountered intense enmity. Many Texans remained bitter in defeat and unwilling to tolerate newly freed slaves as anything but a controlled labor force whose conditions were not that different from their previous conditions. Nor did the disaffected Texans have much to fear from military enforcement, as few federal troops were stationed in Texas or remained in the South. The Unionists had their own record of wrongs to settle from the war years. Hamilton tried to place only staunch Unionists in high-level state positions as well as in positions at every other level—district, county, and precinct; even the most nominal Confederates, people who had served in minor governmental roles during the war years, were denied positions. Even under Johnson's mild version of Reconstruction, former Confederates often felt the wrath of those the secessionists had silenced and marginalized. Minyard H. Harris of Kirvin, whose Confederate duties had included chasing down deserters and forcing them back to their units, reported himself after the war "in constant danger of being caught and shot or hanged."

Overall, however, in most parts of the state, the old southern order managed to reassert itself fairly quickly, in part thanks to Johnson's lenient pardoning policy. Many Confederate leaders were elected to serve, along with Unionists, in the federally required constitutional convention of early 1866. For readmission to the Union, members were expected to repudiate the right of secession, to ratify the Thirteenth Amendment to the U.S. Constitution outlawing slavery, to determine fairly and objectively the "social and political status of freedmen," and to repudiate the state's war debt.

Members agreed to nullify Texas's act of secession, but not to do so *ab initio* (from the beginning) as this would mean that they had had no right to secede in the first place and would also nullify all laws and transactions made in Texas since 1861. They skated around ratification of the Thirteenth Amendment; because it had already become national law the previous year, they argued, in agreeing to support the Constitution, they were also supporting the amendment. They repudiated the war debt and acknowledged certain freedman rights, including protection of person and property, but they rejected any idea of freedmen voting or holding public office. None of this was likely to satisfy Reconstructionists in Congress, and it did not.

In June, Texas voters approved the resulting constitution and chose their first elected postwar governor in a contest between two moderates: the constitutional convention's chair, J. W. Throckmorton, and former Texas governor E. M. Pease. Throckmorton, a member of the Texas legislature before the war, had held out against secession until it was accomplished. He had endeared himself to supporters of the war, however, by enlisting quickly in frontier defense, then in the Sixth Texas Cavalry. A former surgeon and soldier in the Mexican War, Throckmorton had fought in various Civil War engagements, eventually serving as Edmund Kirby Smith's Confederate commissioner to the Indians.

Elisha Pease possessed exceptionally strong Texas credentials as well, having participated in the writing of the Republic constitution in 1836 and having served in a variety of government roles since that time, including two terms as an able governor of the state in the 1850s. Like Throckmorton, he had resisted secession; unlike Throckmorton, he had chosen not to participate in the Confederacy but had quietly continued to adhere to Union principles.

In the election, Throckmorton emerged the victor, in part because Pease's support of even limited African American voting was perceived as "radical" by "unreconstructed" Texans. With the power structure of the Old South reasserting itself, even many southern moderates refused to support some of the most basic citizenship rights for African Americans. When the Eleventh Legislature convened in August 1866, it not only appointed leading secessionist O. M. Roberts to the U.S. Senate but set "black codes" limiting African Americans' movements in Texas—for example, specifying labor contracts that required them to get permission to leave the home workplace.

In truth, African Americans found precious little freedom or independence after the war and much hostility to their assuming any role but a variation of the slave role. Because they remained landless, they had few choices but to labor for whites as tenants. The best hope for many became an agency established in March 1865 to be administered by the U.S. Army; the Freedman's Bureau came to Texas in September of that year.

Agents of the bureau—including military men, northerners, and some Texans—were charged with helping former slaves make the transition into citizenship. This included ensuring that blacks had the same protections under the law as whites, helping them set up schools and providing teachers, monitoring the freedmen's labor contracts for fair terms, and helping former slaves unite with scattered family members. One of the most active agents, George T. Ruby, soon established himself in Texas politics. A freeborn native of New York who had traveled extensively, Ruby moved to Galveston from Louisiana after the war. Here he served as a *New Orleans Tribune* correspondent, started his own Galveston newspaper, and taught school. Soon he was administering the Bureau's schools in a number of counties.

At its peak, the bureau had fifty-nine agents in fifty-nine districts in Texas. The difficulties of travel and communication, as well as resistance to the bureau's efforts by many white Texans, made the agents' job a hard and dangerous one. Even though Andrew Johnson in late August 1866 declared "the insurrection which heretofore existed in the State of Texas is at an end," violence—especially violence directed against African Americans and representatives of the national government—was all too prevalent.

Nationally, the picture was equally dismal. Only Tennessee among the Confederate states had been induced to ratify the Fourteenth Amendment, granting citizenship rights to former slaves. In the eyes of Republican leaders, presidential Reconstruction had failed miserably, allowing the old southern hierarchy to begin to reassert itself, and members of the U.S. Congress refused to seat Roberts and other members of the Texas delegation when they arrived in Washington.

## Congressional Reconstruction

Republican leaders wrested control of Reconstruction from the executive branch. They began passing Reconstruction legislation over Johnson's veto and in 1868 the House of Representatives impeached him over his attempt to remove a secretary of war. Although Johnson would barely survive the impeachment in a close Senate vote, by 1867, he had lost almost all support. Congress now assumed military control of the southern states and forced them to do what most had failed to do under presidential Reconstruction: involve African American men in the reconstruction of state government and grant freedmen voting rights.

The First Reconstruction Act, signed on March 2, 1867, essentially reestablished and reasserted military rule in the South. Two more acts followed, specifying who was disqualified from voting and authorizing military commanders to "suspend or remove" and replace any officeholders in their districts. Congress also stipulated that the southern states must have new constitutional conventions that would support the Fourteenth Amendment, which penalized states for denying adult male citizens the right to vote ("except for participation in rebellion, or other crime") and made it more difficult for former Confederates to gain a pardon. General Charles Griffin, who had risen to major general as a Union commander during the war, now had federal authority over the Department of Texas and pursued an ambitious agenda of new voter registrations, black and white. He repeatedly clashed with Governor Throckmorton, the governor charging that the military was taking on too much civil authority and Griffin charging that the governor was being obstructionist and allowing violence against blacks and Unionists. Griffin complained to his superior, General Philip H. Sheridan, and got Throckmorton removed. Although Sheridan appointed the seasoned and respected E. M. Pease in Throckmorton's stead, this blatant use of military power only hardened many Texans against the occupation.

Like former provisional governor Hamilton, Griffin also replaced other former

Confederates holding office with Union men. He enforced the congressional voting restriction by which officials, candidates, potential jury members, and even voters had to swear that they had never taken an oath to uphold the U.S. Constitution, then participated in rebellion. Radical Reconstructionists reasoned that these exclusions were necessary, at least temporarily, in order to carry out congressional Reconstruction. After Griffin died suddenly in the summer of 1867 in a yellow fever epidemic, his successor, Joseph J. Reynolds, stepped up the removals of state, county, and local officials who had any ties to the Confederacy.

Given the major restructuring going on, it was no surprise when the elections for a new constitutional convention in Texas yielded a distinctly different set of delegates from previous conventions. In addition to supporting the Fourteenth Amendment, Congress expected the delegates to revisit the *ab initio* question and nullify the original secession decision and any laws in the state that followed from it. Congress also expected them to support the Thirteenth and Fifteenth Amendments, the latter a flat statement that voting rights would not be denied "on account of race, color, or previous condition of servitude."

Many Democrats were adamantly opposed to the new convention and a new constitution, and many of them simply stayed away from the polls or were barred from them by the loyalty voting restriction. For the first time, African American men voted, and voted in large numbers, spurred on by the voter registration campaign administered by the military. Ten of the ninety delegates elected were African Americans, the most prominent of whom was probably George T. Ruby. Ruby had not only administered schools for the Freedman's Bureau in their most successful Texas program but had served as president of the Union League, a Unionist organization effective in involving African Americans in politics. Although there were a few Democrats, most of the delegates were Republicans who had opposed the old southern leadership in one way or another. A. J. Hamilton, in something of a shift, now led the moderate Republicans loyal to Pease. One contingent consisted of the "radical" Republicans intent on forcing Texans into line with federal mandates and keeping all former Confederates out of power. This group was led by A. J. Hamilton's brother, Morgan C. Hamilton, and Edmund J. Davis. Davis had first been appointed a district judge by Pease in the 1850s but had won the undying hatred of many Civil War Texans by joining the federal forces as a cavalry colonel and participating in the Union's attempted invasions of Texas.

The delegates, with Davis presiding, argued interminably, with the *ab initio* issue again receiving much attention: Should nullification extend to the initial act of secession? Another primary issue at this convention was whether to divide Texas into two states, east and west. Delegates from both East Texas and West Texas favored this move as a means of addressing the fact that East Texas remained in many ways an extension of the American South, whereas West Texas—represented most vocally by the radical Republicans—had a more independent population less tied to the cotton culture of the South.

After three months, the money set aside for convention expenses ran out, and the delegates adjourned without even getting to the wording of a constitution, although they did call for ratification of the Thirteenth and Fourteenth Amendments by the first legislature to assemble under the new constitution. Everyone waited to see what shifts the national presidential election would bring. When Union General Ulysses S. Grant won the presidency, the radical Republicans felt affirmed in their vision of a reconstructed Texas, which not only included a state of West Texas but delayed statehood for East Texas because of the continuing hostility against Reconstruction manifested there.

The convention met again in December 1868 and again delayed producing a constitution, breaking up in early February. Its members had done some visionary work, particularly in the area of education, setting aside monies from the sale of public lands for a permanent school fund to be used to educate Texas children "irrespective of race and color." But they had drawn up only a partial constitution for the state, one signed by only half the delegates. Subsequently, a committee appointed by General Reynolds completed the work, using records from the convention.

The document that went before voters in November 1869 both softened the restrictions against former Confederates' political participation and finally affirmed voting rights irrespective of "race, color, or former condition." It contained the far-reaching public education plan under a state superintendent of public instruction. Perhaps the most important aspect of the constitution in the short run was its centralized vision of government. This vision was at odds with the Jacksonian democracy that had underpinned Texas politics in the decades before the Civil War, when many Texans had taken as a tenet of faith the idea that the "common man" in the Anglo population played a part in governmental decision making and compromise agreements. The constitution gave great powers to the governor, who would have a longer term—four years—and would appoint district judges and some key state officials who had previously been chosen in elections. As part of the consolidation of control, elections were to be held at the county seats, not at precincts, and county commissioners were eliminated, with justices of the peace taking over county court functions.

At the same time voters were asked to weigh in on the new constitution, they were also asked to vote for new state and county officials. For the first time, black candidates appeared on a number of ballots. The race for the governorship was key to the next stage of Reconstruction. As a candidate, former provisional governor Hamilton continued to adopt a more conservative course than he had in the early days of Reconstruction, opposing the radicals' attempt to form a state of West Texas and even backing off from support for black suffrage. His opponent, E. J. Davis, continued to represent radical Republicanism—and was supported and assisted by military commander Joseph Reynolds, whose cavalry Davis had commanded in the later stages of the war. Reynolds, continuing to exercise his power over even local appointments, saw to it that supporters of Davis filled the voter registration boards and so angered Governor Pease that Pease resigned in protest in September.

With leading Democrats disenfranchised or disaffected and divided on how to combat the new Republican-driven constitution, the constitution was approved in the November election. Two African Americans were also elected to the Texas Senate—Ruby and Matthew Gaines, a Baptist preacher who had been born a slave in Louisiana—and twelve African Americans were elected to the Texas House. In the gubernatorial race, charges and countercharges of vote fraud flew during and after the elections, and there may well have been fraud on both sides. Davis emerged the victor by a narrow margin, helped along by the heavy turnout of African Americans. They recognized in him a champion of new definitions for Texas in which blacks could play roles previously denied them.

### Conditions in Texas

Davis took office in 1870 in a state still scarred, battered, and divided. Land values had dropped, cotton prices had been cut almost in half just since 1866, and sharecropping—the farming of someone else's land in exchange for a place to live and a third to a half of the money earned—was becoming a way of life for many whites and blacks alike. A young Englishman who had immigrated to Texas the previous year wrote, "Times are awful hard now in Texas. Money is scarce, land is worth almost nothing . . .things generally are in a state of stagnation."

There were signs of economic health, however: The rate of population growth was higher in Texas than in the nation as a whole; industry was developing; key towns were growing again, with Galveston and San Antonio leading the way; and the 1870 census showed that 60 percent of employed Texans were "property-holding farmers, businessmen, members of professions, or skilled tradesmen." The ranks of the wealthiest Texans were shifting, with merchants and bankers replacing plantation owners and farmers. Yet most of the wealthy Texans had deep roots in the state, and none more so than Sam Maverick, the only member of the Independence Convention of 1836 to be listed among the wealthiest Texans in the 1870 census.

Despite his continued holdings, Maverick's experience demonstrates the difficulties encountered by many former Confederates in this period. After passage of the First Reconstruction Act, he and fellow secession commissioner Thomas Devine were "summoned to appear before the Federal Court to answer for the three million dollars worth of U.S. property they receipted for as Rebel commissioners." The case was suspended indefinitely, but it left the accused in limbo. In 1869 he wrote to his sons in college that they would have to come home or teach school, as the U.S. government was refusing to pay rent on some of his lands, the Reconstruction San Antonio mayor was threatening to sue him, and "several conspiracies [have been] got up here against me financially." A beleaguered Maverick would die of a "wasting illness" early in the Davis administration.

Whatever one's social, political, and economic standing and fortunes, Texans through the Reconstruction period found violence continuing and intensifying. Local and regional feuds erupted, the most extended and violent the Sutton-Taylor Feud in DeWitt County. Indians had continued to scourge and push back the Texas frontier, Kiowa leader Satanta arguing vehemently that the Kiowas and Comanches owned West Texas. The U.S. government had provided a limited, ineffective force for frontier Texas forts, and Congress had tried unsuccessfully to stop the raiding and get all of the Indians onto reservations in Indian Territory with an 1867 parley between a commission and southern Plains Indian leaders at Medicine Lodge Creek, Kansas. But by 1870, the attacks were worsening.

There were also outlaw gangs to contend with, such as that of Cullen Baker, a resident of northeast Texas whose murderous tendencies were already documented before the war. After the conflict, in which he served intermittently as a Confederate soldier, he turned his ire against African Americans and Reconstruction representatives, he and his band killing a number of people, including Freedman's Bureau agents.

Meanwhile, the Ku Klux Klan, first formed by Confederate veterans in Tennessee in 1866, had spread to Texas by spring 1868. This secret organization, loosely organized in Texas, had among its goals resistance to Reconstruction and restoration of white supremacy. Members throughout eastern Texas—particularly the northeastern region—targeted African Americans, "carpetbaggers" (northerners representing federal control and privilege), and even Republicans in general. They destroyed crops, stole horses, burned houses, beat and murdered victims, and intimidated local authorities. Some forced former slaves into registering to vote as Democrats. Similar secret organizations arose, promoting a rhetoric of white superiority, the Knights of the Golden Circle pledging to "maintain and defend the social and political superiority of the White race on this Continent; always and in all places to observe a marked distinction between the White and African races. . . ."

A committee for the 1868–69 constitutional convention had determined that of the 939 murders reported by county officials between 1865 and 1868, almost half were committed by whites against other whites and 40 percent were committed by whites against blacks. Many other murders and other crimes remained unreported. Military commander Reynolds had been at least partially effective in prosecuting some of the more flagrant lawless acts, but many problems remained.

### Home Rule

When Davis and radical Republican legislators took office, they acted quickly to pull Texas out of Congressional Reconstruction, in part by adopting the Fourteenth and Fifteenth Amendments. With a constitution acceptable to Congressional Reconstructionists in place and adoption of these amendments, on March 30, 1870, Texas gained official readmittance to the Union. It now had home rule, although "unreconstructed" Confederates considered it as far from their own rule as possible.

Davis and the Republican-dominated Twelfth Legislature moved to create some far-sighted policies. Most significantly, they passed laws in 1870 and 1871 that made public schooling free and compulsory, to be supported with an adequate tax base. They also tried to address the continuing violence and chaos by creating a state police force. The Police Act of July 1870 was only one of what came to be known by resistant white Texans as the "obnoxious acts," but it was probably the most hated. The force would answer to Davis as governor and be able to move at will about the state, having local law officers who failed to cooperate removed from their positions. This force, which reached a size of about 200, contained African American and Tejano men as well as Anglos and both former Union soldiers and former Confederate ones. The majority, not surprisingly, were Republicans. Some abused their authority, yet much of the ill-feeling against the state police grew from its oversight by Davis and the fact that 40 percent of the troopers were African American.

Other controversial measures which Davis and the legislature enacted included a militia bill which authorized him to declare martial law and enroll and command any able-bodied males in Texas, ages 18 to 45, if he deemed local or state policing too weak. The legislature gave him even more power to select state, district, and county officials previously elected by citizens. It also delayed the regular election until November 1872, advocates citing the need to bring state and congressional elections in line. To Democrats and dissatisfied Republicans, however, this simply looked like another power play, for Davis and the Republican legislators now had another year on their terms.

To add further fuel to the fires of resentment, Davis did not hesitate to use martial law in various counties. His calling out the militia was often to protect African Americans against some very real threats, but at other times it smacked of intimidation against Democrats. And the Democrats, with many of their number no longer excluded from voting and holding office, were gaining in power. They continued to resist citizenship rights for African Americans, and they saw Davis's presence in the governor's mansion as yet another feature of federal Reconstruction. In the elections of 1872, they would be ready.

### The "Redeemers" in Control

Democrats and conservative Republicans demonstrated their active resistance to Governor Davis's administration in September 1871, with a Taxpayers' Convention in Austin. Former governor Pease presided as they protested not only Davis's expenditures but his "despotic power." The demands of congressional Reconstruction had brought a concentration of power which most Texas citizens would not have accepted in other circumstances. Now delegates charged Davis with a "violation of nearly every private right of the citizen" in the Police Bill. In sum, the delegates concluded, "The . . . people of the State no longer govern themselves, but are governed by E. J. Davis, as completely as if there were no Constitutions, State or Federal." The next month, Democratic candidates won all four Congressional seats. The editor of the *Neches Valley News* crowed, "[T]he people of Southeast Texas have done handling political issues with gloves and intend to do their share in tearing down and uprooting the government policy implemented by Eastern fanatics."

Democrats continued to seek to "redeem" Texas from the hands of the radical Republicans. In the fall elections of 1872, they won a majority in the House and decisive election victories throughout the state. In part, this shift reflected the intimidation of freedmen in exercising their voting rights. In part, it reflected the disenchantment of former Davis supporters, some of whom had participated in the Taxpayers' Convention. In large part, it reflected the continuing southern sentiment among Anglos, especially with the steady influx of southerners into Texas; in 1873, an estimated 80 percent of the 125,000 immigrants would be from southern states.

When the Thirteenth Legislature convened in January 1873, even many of the Republican members jumped into a dismantling of the previous legislature's acts. The state police force was eliminated, some of the governor's appointments were changed to elective office, and the governor's power to declare martial law was erased. Voting could be moved back to precincts, and the school system was broken up, with much authority shifting to local school boards. By the elections of November 1873, the radical Republicans in office were the remnants of radical home rule serving out their terms.

It was no surprise, then, when Davis was decisively voted out of office in favor of Democratic candidate Richard Coke, a Waco lawyer, Confederate veteran, and district and state judge under Presidential Reconstruction. But what followed only added to the abundant partisan ill-feeling and left Davis in an impossible position.

The governor still had supporters, and they identified two issues that made the transfer of executive power problematic. First, the state constitution gave two dates for the transition: "the first Thursday after the organization of the legislature"—in this case the second Thursday in January 1874—and the end of the four-year term, which would be April 28, 1874. Second, the constitution said one thing about the length of time the polls should be open, while the statute passed by the Thirteenth Legislature to govern the 1873 elections specified another. Davis supporters challenged the constitutionality of the statute, and thus of the election results.

In December, the state attorney general ruled that the governor's term should run a full four years. Further, on January 5, 1874, the state Supreme Court agreed with the Davis supporters in judging the election unconstitutional, thereby voiding results not only in the governor's race but in all other categories—and opening the door to legal challenges to anything the new slate of state and county officers would do governmentally.

Davis had stayed removed from the court challenges. Now, however, he felt obliged to uphold the rulings of the attorney general and the Supreme Court even as the Democrats proceeded with plans to convene the legislature and inaugurate Coke in January. Davis sent President Grant a request for federal troops to delay the seating of the Fourteenth Legislature. He also wanted Grant to address

Douglas Jerrold's sketch of the inauguration of Richard Coke as governor in January 1874 illustrates a turning point in Texas political history, as Democratic "redeemers" replaced the Reconstruction government of E. J. Davis. *(PICA 26678 Austin History Center, Austin Public Library)*

the issue of the body's legitimacy: Would Grant recognize the election results as valid, essentially overruling the state Supreme Court?

Grant refused to send troops and failed to respond to Davis's repeated requests for an authoritative response on whether the election could or would be considered valid by the president. Meanwhile, the Democrats convened the legislature on January 13. Davis finally disbanded his supporters and stepped down after the president again rebuffed his request for troops and a ruling.

As a political player and as governor, Davis had been punitive and controlling, but he had also been genuinely concerned with the law, with the problems post-Civil War Texas faced, and with the rights of freed African Americans. In the other camp, even his moderate detractors had acquiesced to a condemnation of "the unseemly advances of the Negro" under Davis. Their racist rhetoric and their desire to overturn progressive Reconstruction policies were apparent, yet they had also championed a theoretically more balanced and less centralized government.

Coke and his supporters lost no time in consolidating their power, placing Democrats in district judge positions and seeing to it that Democrats filled all five positions on a new state Supreme Court. Another matter would take more time: the revision or replacement of the Constitution of 1869.

In particular, Democrats wanted to dismantle the centralized powers born of Reconstruction and spelled out in this constitution; they wanted to limit the governor's and legislature's authority and to do away with the voter registration provisions that had kept many of them from the ballot box.

At first, a legislative commission tried simply to revise the 1869 constitution, but this method still smacked of centralized government. So in August 1875 the new legislature asked voters to approve yet another constitutional convention. Among the representatives elected, there were five Democrats for every Republican, but the fifteen Republican delegates included six African Americans. A number of the delegates had served as officers in the Confederate army; there were also a few U.S. Army veterans. Significantly, more than 40 percent of the delegates belonged to a newly formed farmers' organization, the Patrons of Husbandry, or the "Grange," a cooperative to protect and improve the lives of farm families who were feeling threatened in their livelihoods and increasingly marginalized after the economic Panic of 1873.

The document that resulted called for economy and limited power in state government, especially in the governor's office. Government salaries and expenditures were to be kept low, and terms of office were shortened even as the framers shifted many of the offices from appointed to elected. The governor would not be able to call out the militia or fill vacancies by appointment without approval of the Senate, nor did he have any constitutional control over the other state executive officers. The legislature was to meet regularly only every other year, its members receiving a modest sum. To support such fiscally conservative measures, delegates built in lower tax rates. They also included a homestead exemption protecting family homes and limited acreage from forced sale, reflecting both Mexican precedent and the "pro-debtor, anti-bank" attitudes long held by Texans. This distrust of corporate power was also reflected in a ban on state-chartered banks and in attempts to regulate the railroads by declaring them "common carriers" and having the legislature set limits on freight and passenger rates. In education, the convention followed the Thirteenth Legislature by gutting the Davis administration's centralized public school system, rejecting compulsory attendance and essentially creating segregated schools administered locally. They provided for some taxation and continued the idea of a permanent school fund, establishing one that would grow substantially, first through land sales and leases and later through off-shore oil leases and fuel taxes. But by cutting the local tax base for schools at the same time it mandated local control, the new constitution left Texas schools in an untenable position.

The delegates made no provisions for another constitutional convention, and their involved, detailed document, approved by voters on February 15, 1876, would remain the law of the land in Texas, with increasingly frequent amendments. It was a document that reflected the interests and priorities of most of the delegates, and of most of the voters in 1876, their definitions of what Texas should be and how its government should function. But ultimately, it also reflected an old agrarian outlook, with vestiges of the old plantation South but depending for its definitions on a rather homogenous population engaged primarily in independent farming. In this sense, it was a poor document for a Texas which contained thousands of tenant farmers and people engaged in nonfarming pursuits as well as an ethnically diverse population which included free African Americans, approximately 24,000 Tejanos, and another increasing immigration of Europeans. And the constitution was a poor document for a Texas that was beginning to develop industrially and geographically far beyond the old antebellum definitions.

## Conclusion

As a state—as a southern state—Texas had chosen to define itself apart from the American Union it had sought during the republic years. The resulting war had temporarily drained the state of most of its manpower and, despite the trade at Brownsville, had retarded growth and development, extending or renewing frontier conditions. It had also fed serious divisions, both between the American North and South and among Texans. The extent of these divisions became abundantly clear in the troubled Reconstruction period. As the federal government sought to "reconstruct" the southern states, first with fairly mild measures, then with more stringent ones, Texans struggled to determine who they were going to be outside the familiar dimensions of antebellum southern life. For the first time, African Americans as a group were able to seek opportunity, but found little, as proponents of a racial caste system reasserted it with a vengeance. Many Texans became concerned about their agricultural prospects, what they had considered their livelihood. Although farming—especially the farming of cotton—remained the chief economic activity, it was growing difficult to make a living in this way, especially as cotton prices slid downward. Some Texans were beginning to move into the drier areas of the state, areas that initially seemed less suited to agriculture. The movement called for a different identity, a western one.

Meanwhile, modernizing influences were beginning to alter old understandings, offer new ways of living and connecting. As Texas came out of Congressional Reconstruction, railroad construction took off, linking Texas markets and culture with other parts of the nation, especially the powerful Northeast. Manufacturing began to develop in the state, most of it initially connected to farming, but sawmills, textile mills, and iron smelters and foundries signaling steps toward industrialization. Towns were becoming cities, the largest, Galveston, boasting not only colleges, banks, theaters, and concert halls, but such modern amenities as street cars and gas lights. More and more, Texas would become firmly linked culturally and economically to the rest of the nation. But it would carry its southern legacy as well, in attitudes toward government, political parties, and race.

## SUGGESTED READINGS

Good primary sources for the Civil War and Reconstruction periods can be found in Ernest Wallace, David M. Vigness, and George B. Ward, *Documents of Texas History* (1994) and in chapters 8 and 9 in Sam W. Haynes and Cary D. Wintz, *Major Problems in Texas History* (2002). Because these are two very distinct crisis-ridden periods, the sources for each are specified below.

### Texas and the Confederacy

The *New Handbook of Texas* has a number of useful Civil War–related entries, including one on the "Texas Troubles" and entries on various military units, battles, and campaigns. A good source for understanding Texas's decision to secede from the Union is Walter L. Buenger's "The Roots of Texas Secession" in Haynes and Wintz, *Major Problems in Texas History,* pp. 230–237. For general Civil War information, readers are encouraged to look at the work of Ralph A. Wooster: *Texas and Texans in the Civil War* (1996) and *Lone Star Generals in Gray* (2000). For the story of the Confederacy's thrust into the Southwest, see Donald S. Frazier, *Blood and Treasure: Confederate Empire in the Southwest* (1995) and Jerry Thompson's *Civil War in the Southwest: Recollections of the Sibley Brigade* (2001). Thompson has also written about Mexican Texans in the war: *Mexican Texans in the Union Army* (1986) and *Vaqueros in Blue and Gray* (1976). Evault Boswell's *Texas Boys in Gray* (2000) offers reminiscences by Confederate soldiers.

### The War in Texas and Its Impact

For African Americans' experience in the war, see the accounts in Haynes and Wintz and Randolph B. Campbell's *An Empire for Slavery* (1989). Jo Ella Powell Exley's *Texas Tears and Texas Sunshine* (1985) contains some women's accounts of the period; Paula Mitchell Marks in *Turn Your Eyes Toward Texas* (1989) charts the Maverick family fortunes during the war. David Montejano's *Anglos and Mexicans in the Making of Texas, 1836–1986* (1987) deals briefly with the war years. For dissent in Texas, see L. D. Clark, ed., *Civil War Recollections of James Lemuel Clark and the Great Hanging at Gainesville, Texas in October 1862* (1997) and David Pickering and Judy Falls, *Brush Men & Vigilantes: Civil War Dissent in Texas* (2000).

### Reconstruction

General works on Reconstruction in Texas include the Charles W. Ramsdell classic, *Reconstruction in Texas* (1910), but there are various late-twentieth-century reassessments, including Edgar Sneed's "A Historiography of Reconstruction in Texas: Some Myths and Problems" in Ralph A. Wooster and Robert Calvert, *Texas Vistas: Selections from the Southwestern Historical Quarterly* (1980), Carl Moneyhon's *Republicanism in Reconstruction Texas* (1980), and Barry Crouch's "'Unmanacling' Texas Reconstruction: A Twenty Year Perspective" in the *Southwestern Historical Quarterly* (1995). More recent general Reconstruction studies include Randolph B. Campbell's *Grass-Roots Reconstruction in Texas, 1865–1880* (1997).

The *New Handbook of Texas* has an excellent entry on Reconstruction and useful entries on the constitutional conventions and constitutions produced in this period.

For information on African American leaders in Reconstruction, see Alwyn Barr and Robert A. Calvert, *Black Leaders: Texans for Their Times* (1981), James M. Smallwood, *Time of Hope, Time of Despair: Black Texans During Reconstruction* (1981), and Carl Moneyhon, "George T. Ruby and African American Politics During Reconstruction" in Haynes and Wintz, pp. 260–269.

An interesting view of Texas life in this period is provided by Robert J. Robertson, *Her Majesty's Texans: Two English Immigrants in Reconstruction Texas* (1998). The endemic violence is discussed in Barry A. Crouch's "White Violence in Reconstruction Texas" in Haynes and Wintz, pp. 252–260. Also see Crouch's work on the Freedmen's Bureau: *The Freedmen's Bureau and Black Texans* (1992). Ralph A. Wooster's "Wealthy Texans, 1870" examines economic, political, and social power in Wooster and Calvert's *Texas Vistas,* pp. 75–186.

A good study of the end of Radical Reconstruction is Carl H. Moneyhon's "Edmund J. Davis in the Coke-Davis Election Dispute of 1874: A Reassessment of Character" in *Southwestern Historical Quarterly* (1996).

PART **III**

# TEXAS REDEFINED

In 1936, in the middle of the Great Depression, Texans threw themselves a big six-month-long party in Dallas, ostensibly to celebrate the centennial of Texas's independence from Mexico. The live show "Cavalcade of Texas" described four centuries of Texas history in documents and maps and artifacts, recalling the halcyon days of the Texas Revolution and republic, Stephen F. Austin's "Old Three Hundred," and Sam Houston. University of Texas historian Walter Prescott Webb published his still-popular *The Texas Rangers,* and historical museums were established throughout the state—in Austin, Huntsville, Gonzales, Lubbock, and El Paso.

The real theme of the Centennial, however, was the modernization of the state. A lot had happened to Texas since its reentry into the Union following the Civil War, and the Centennial organizers wanted the people of Texas as well as the larger public to know the story. The cotton planter, represented by Dallas *Morning News* cartoonist John Knott's "Old Man Texas," might still have been the state's most widely recognized symbol, but oil production had eclipsed cotton as the most important product in the state's economy in 1929. Railroads crisscrossed the state, giving Texas more miles of railroad track than any other state by 1911. By 1940 there were 19,000 miles of road. In addition, the Texas population had increased significantly in every decade following 1870, and the growth did not slacken until the depression year of 1930. From a state that was 93.3 percent rural in 1870, Texas had become a state with the majority of its population in cities by 1950; that same year, Houston, with a population of 596,163, ranked fourteenth in the nation. By 1990 Texas contained three of the largest ten cities in the nation—Houston, Dallas, and San Antonio—and was the third most populous state.

With futuristic glimpses of automobiles, television, and air conditioning, the Centennial organizers suggested that opportunity awaited in Texas. They hoped to attract tourists by marketing the state in a different way—as part of the new West rather than the Old South—and adopted the cowboy and a more western look as the theme for the celebration. In addition to the palm trees of the Lower Rio Grande valley and the Spanish missions of old San Antonio, the Centennial publicists used the stunning mountain scenery of the Big Bend, in the Trans-Pecos region, soon to become Texas's first national park. Helping to deliver the message of the new, modern Texas, but one nourished by its historical roots, was the celluloid cowboy from Tioga, Texas, Gene Autry.

In 1939, Texas was on the threshold of a new, modern, industrial age. How did the state transform itself from a rural, slaveholding member of the

Confederacy with a one-crop economy to the diverse, multiracial economic juggernaut that we know today, third only to California and New York in population and with a gross national product (GNP) greater than that of most European nations? Here is that story.   ■ ■ ■

# 10
# Toward Modernization, 1876–1898

As Texas began to recover from the economic impact of the Civil War and Reconstruction, the cattle drives up the Chisholm Trail brought thousands of Longhorns through Fort Worth, a former army post on the Clear Fork of the Trinity River, and the "cow town" began to grow. The North Texas *Epitomist* published what became known as the "tarantula map," which showed Fort Worth as a regional center with rail lines (spider legs) extending in every direction; cattle buyers, professional people, and merchants moved to the city with the understanding that it would soon become a railhead. In the spring of 1873, 116 new buildings were erected, and forty new stores opened within one week.

Then came the Panic of 1873, one of the worst economic depressions that the country had seen. It began when one of the most respected firms on Wall Street, Jay Cooke and Company, failed. The New York stock market closed for ten days in September; a month later trail drivers arriving in Kansas either found no market for their herds or had to sell at a considerable loss. As the shock waves spread, the Texas & Pacific (T&P) Railroad, which had expected to reach Fort Worth that year, stopped construction at Eagle Ford, six miles west of Dallas, and Fort Worth's overnight boom turned just as quickly into a bust. Dozens of businesses closed and hundreds of economic refugees flooded the wagon road east to Dallas as the city's population dropped from an estimated 4,000 to approximately 1,000. One of the defectors, newly

| CHAPTER 10 | Toward Modernization, 1876–1898 |
|---|---|
| 1870s | Windmills in widespread use in West Texas |
| 1874 | Invention of barbed wire |
| 1874–75 | Indian wars end |
| 1875 | Scott Joplin moves to Texarkana with his family |
| 1876 | State adopts present constitution; the Agricultural and Mechanical College (now Texas A&M University) opens |
| 1877 | The Compromise of 1877 ends Reconstruction; Texas Farmers Alliance established |
| 1883 | Cowboy Strike in the Panhandle; University of Texas opens in Austin |
| 1885 | Open range trail drives decline |
| 1888 | New Texas state capitol inaugurated |
| 1891 | Texas Railroad Commission established |
| 1898 | Spanish-American War; Texas public domain exhausted |

arrived in Dallas, published a letter in the newspaper saying that Fort Worth was so desolate that he had seen a panther "sleeping undisturbed in the business district which was as quiet as a cemetery."

Refusing to accept defeat, Fort Worth citizens took matters into their own hands. In 1875 they formed the Tarrant County Construction Company to grade the railroad bed so that the T&P could lay the track, and the city gradually began to recover its confidence. The T&P had to reach Fort Worth by the time the legislature adjourned the following spring in order to receive the 15-million-acre land grant that the state had promised. As the deadline drew near, Tarrant County employed 100 laborers to prepare the roadbed and called for volunteers to assist in the effort; the T&P sent 300 mule teams and 1,000 men to lay the track. And, according to legend, as the road approached Fort Worth, Tarrant County's representative, Nicholas H. Darnell, who was seriously ill, had to be carried on a cot into the House chamber each day for fifteen days to cast his vote against adjournment. Finally, the track was completed on July 18, and the first train arrived the next day.

As businesses returned—many boasting the word *Panther* in their names as a proud response to the newspaper article—Fort Worth became a shipping center for cattle, buffalo hides and bones, lumber, cotton, and groceries and a supply depot for the cattle trade as well as expansion into West Texas. As the railroad grew during the last quarter of the nineteenth century, it brought similar economic benefits to every region of the state.

Although the last quarter of the nineteenth century was dominated by agrarians, who constituted the large majority of the state's population and controlled the writing of the 1876 Constitution, it also saw the beginnings of industrialization and the birth of the modern state. During these years, most people in Texas still earned their living from the land, and many joined organizations such as the Patrons of Husbandry, or the Grange, and the Farmers' Alliance. But these years also witnessed a tripling of the state's population, a huge increase in industrial output, the birth of labor unions, and unprecedented growth in railroads, pushing the state from twenty-eighth in miles of track in 1870 to first in 1904. This was what economic historian Walt Rostow called the "take-off" phase of industrialization that occurred between 1843 and 1900 in the United States but occurred several decades later in Texas.

In 1870 there were more Texans than ever—818,579, according to the census—with more than 93 percent of the population living in rural areas. The state's continuing need for population spurred the establishment in 1871 of the Texas Bureau of Immigration, abolished in 1876, but only after its generous land grant policies had had significant impact. The state continued that official effort with the publication of the "forgotten census of 1887," an attempt to "call attention of the overcrowded population of the East . . . to our millions of acres of rich virgin soil, which can be had almost for the asking." Preemption and homestead grants and cheap land policies made acquisition of land relatively easy until 1898, when the Texas Supreme Court declared the public domain to be exhausted.

Aside from the natural population increase, immigrants—blacks as well as whites—came mostly from the Southern states, such as Arkansas, Alabama, Mississippi, and Tennessee, that had been devastated by the Civil War. Despite the immigration, the state's established cultural patterns remained largely intact. By 1900 the population had grown to 3,048,710, with almost 83 percent still living in rural areas.

At the same time, however, the value of the state's manufactured items increased from one-fourth of the gross farm income in 1870 to one-half in 1900. But more people probably were involved in non-farm sectors of the economy than the raw census data would suggest. In 1860, for example, although 89 percent of the people lived in rural areas, only 59 percent of all Texans considered themselves to be involved in agricultural pursuits. Ten percent claimed to be involved in manufacturing, and 11 percent pursued one of the professions, owned or worked for a business, or worked in transportation. By 1870 all but thirty of the state's 324 sawmills, the largest industry, had converted from waterpower, which was sometimes undependable, to steam. The average mill was larger, and a number of them had begun to specialize, for example, in planing lumber.

## Economic Recovery

Three major changes occurred in the 1870s that greatly influenced the economic development of the state. The first was the adoption of an agrarian-dominated constitution in 1876, which enabled Texans to nurture the political will and organization to permit industrialization to occur. But the fact that most of the capital for this development came from eastern investors and banks, and that the changes wrought by the industrial revolution initially took capital out of the state at a time of depression, created significant opposition. Reeling from what they considered an abusive and dictatorial Republican government under Reconstruction, the agrarian Democrats and ex-Confederates did all they could to ensure that taxes would be low and the government would remain weak. The delegates took advantage of the only asset that the state possessed—land—and continued the cheap land policy that the state had been following. The two other major changes that occurred in the 1870s were expansion into West Texas and the accumulation of enough capital to accommodate huge projects such as the construction of railroad tracks, the improvement of port facilities, and the growth of large businesses, including the state's first multimillion-dollar corporation. These three changes helped fuel the state's rapid growth.

### Texas Industries Develop

The leading industries in the state in 1870 were what economic historian John S. Spratt called "migratory," meaning that the owners had little capital invested and they could easily move from one community, source of raw materials, or market

Joseph Landa built a complex of water-powered mills at Comal Springs in New Braunfels and established Landa Mills during the 1890s. Photograph by Henry Stark. *(Courtesy Dallas Historical Society)*

to another. Flour and grist mills were the leading industry, and virtually every community was home to a mill of some kind. But only about 1 percent of the population—fewer than 8,000 wage earners—was employed in all of the 2,400 manufacturing shops in the state. The total value of the capital invested in the more than 500 mills was little more than $1 million, and the value of all manufactured goods produced in the state was less than $12 million, less than 25 percent of the value of agricultural products. By 1900 the value of manufactured items had jumped to more than $92 million, which was one-half the value of the state's agricultural products.

The first big change came in the timber industry. East Texas was a veritable woodland of yellow pine, extending westward from the Louisiana border across perhaps 20 million acres of heavily timbered terrain but concentrated in what is known as the Big Thicket, now a national preserve. By 1870 only about 100 million board feet of lumber were being cut annually in Texas, and that primarily by commercial mills in Orange, Beaumont, and Houston. More of the early settlers undoubtedly would have cut timber, had their routes to mills and markets not been limited to the Neches and Sabine rivers and to rough wagon roads.

Another initially limiting factor was the wood itself, for most lumbermen considered the Upper Midwestern white pine superior to the Texas yellow pine. But as supplies of white pine began to run short, entrepreneurs looked again at East Texas, encouraging the construction of railroad lines into timbered areas. The *Galveston News* noted in 1880 that there were twenty sawmill towns located on the Texas & Pacific Railroad east of Dallas with a combined capacity of 595,000 board feet of lumber daily. Indeed, as railroad expansion increased in the 1880s, the subsequent demand for wooden rail ties further stimulated the industry, with the T&P ordering 500,000 crossties in 1880 alone. The railroads provided the inexpensive transportation needed to propel lumbering into the forefront of Texas industry by the end of the century, and Texas into one of the top ten lumbering states in the nation.

Lack of capital was also a problem, but the arrival of entrepreneurs like Henry J. Lutcher and G. Bedell Moore from Pennsylvania in 1877 marked a change in the East Texas industry. Lutcher and Moore built sawmills near Orange, and established both a domestic and an international trade. John Henry Kirby and Nathan D. Silsbee, who acquired more than a quarter of a million acres of pine forests, built large corporations that brought order to the industry. They constructed company towns that often included churches, schools, stores, and homes and virtually controlled the life of their employees, one-third of whom were African Americans. By the turn of the century, although individuals still owned half of the lumbering plants, corporations so dominated the industry that they employed three-quarters of the workforce, produced three-quarters of the industry's total value, and were growing at an accelerated rate. The total value of lumber and other timber products produced in the state was $16,296,473, with a capital investment of $19,161,265 (another characteristic of the take-off phase is reinvestment of capital), and the Kirby Lumber Company, chartered the following year, became the state's first multimillion-dollar company.

The same kind of concentration occurred in the flouring and gristmill industry. Although the industry had slipped to third in the state in overall value by 1900, and the number of mills had decreased by almost 50 percent, total capital investment had increased significantly, and total output had increased almost 600 percent, to $12,333,730. In 1877 mills in Dallas County alone produced $2.75 million worth of flour for a market that ranged from Shreveport and Jefferson on the east to Austin and San Antonio in the southwest. This total exceeded the entire 1870 output of the state by more than $300,000. No longer was every town required to have its own mill; larger mills ground grain more cheaply than the small mills and shipped it inexpensively by rail.

The largest and most productive industrial city in the state in 1870 was Galveston, with a population of 13,818 and more than $1.2 million in total value of manufactured products. Second was Jefferson, the state's leading river port, at the head of Big Cypress Bayou in Marion County. But the city that benefited most from the developing East Texas lumber industry was Houston, by virtue of its location at the southwestern edge of the thick forests to the east and north. Timber fueled the industrial revolution nationwide, providing power for railroads, steamboats, and city-based factories, and Texas was no exception. As the nearby supplies were depleted, Houston's business leaders organized and built a narrow-gauge railroad into the Big Thicket to ensure a continuing supply of wood. The city's population grew from 9,382 in 1870 to 27,557 in 1890, despite the fact that it lacked a reliable source of coal—even poor-grade coal, which had to be shipped in at almost prohibitive expense. (By the 1880s, coal had become the fuel of choice in the industrial East and Midwest.) Still, the growth continued, with Houston's population reaching 44,633 in 1900 and the total value of manufactured products $13 million, making Houston the top producer in the state.

Dallas was the state's second largest manufacturing city in 1900, followed by El Paso, San Antonio, and Fort Worth. Galveston, focusing its efforts on obtaining a deepwater port and solidifying its position as the major Texas trade center, had fallen to sixth in manufacturing value. The completion of the railroad lines to Marshall, Longview, Texarkana, and other cities in Jefferson's economic sphere ended the city's dominance of Northeast Texas because rail transportation was more reliable than the untimely steamboats. East Texas cotton began to flow toward St. Louis, an important rail center, rather than the gulf port of New Orleans. While Galveston struggled to recover from the devastating hurricane of 1900, the discovery of oil at nearby Spindletop in 1901 would stimulate Houston's growth even further in the twentieth century.

As Texas cities grew, citizens expressed their civic pride in public architectural monuments. The new state capitol in Austin, designed by Michigan architect Elijah E. Myers and completed in 1888, was the most important new public building. Inspired by the nation's capitol, the new Texas state capitol is some 562 feet long by 287 feet deep. The star that the Goddess of Liberty holds in her hand is 311 feet above the ground. Restored and greatly enlarged with an underground expansion during the 1990s, the structure still serves as the seat of the state's government. The capitol, in turn, inspired several county courthouses, for example, those in Fort Worth and Marshall. County seats in Anglo American communities sited the courthouse in a public square, whereas communities of European origin, such as San Antonio, Castroville, and New Braunfels, reserved open spaces for public activities and located the courthouse prominently nearby. Both plans provided residents the opportunity to make a symbolic statement, and dozens of counties built impressive courthouses during these years, including Austin, Galveston, Houston, Dallas, Fort Worth, El Paso, and San Antonio. Many of these turn-of-the-century palaces of justice still serve today as centers of government (in Fort Worth, Albany, San Antonio, Lockhart, and New Braunfels, to name only a few), whereas others have been converted for use as public libraries (in Brazoria and Fredericksburg), museums (in Marshall and Tascosa), and community centers (in Blanco and Clairemont) or some kind of private use (in Brownsville).

One of the most prominent architects working in the state at this time was J. Reilly Gordon of San Antonio, who designed a number of the most distinctive courthouses. His buildings in Decatur, Giddings, Gonzales, La Grange, Lockhart,

New Braunfels, San Antonio, Sulphur Springs, Stephenville, Waxahachie, and Victoria still serve as government centers. Frederick E. Ruffini of Austin designed the old main building at the University of Texas as well as courthouses in Blanco, Paint Rock, and Franklin, and Nicholas J. Clayton of Galveston, who is perhaps better known for his many commercial buildings on The Strand and residential structures in Galveston, also designed the main building for the University of Texas Medical Department in Galveston, the Galveston County Courthouse, and St. Edwards University in Austin. County governments, working in many cases with the Texas Historical Commission, have restored many of these distinctive courthouses in communities such as Albany, Belton, Cameron, Brazoria, Canton, Cuero, Del Rio, and Gatesville, which are still in use as governmental seats.

At the same time, a lesser-known manifestation of civic pride and promotion was the publication of dozens of lithographic bird's-eye views of Texas cities sold by itinerant salesmen and produced by out-of-state printing firms. Although part of a national fad that included the publication of almost 5,000 views of American cities during the century, the Texas images ranged from the largest cities in the state—Houston, Galveston, San Antonio, Dallas, Fort Worth, and El Paso—to some of the smallest, such as Wolfe City, Sunset, and Clarendon. Chauvinistic residents apparently constituted a ready market for the handsome pictures, which depicted the cities from an imaginary point high in the air—sort of a combination of a panoramic view and a map—and merchants and city fathers used them to advertise the communities as well as individual businesses. In truth, one can tell a great deal about a community from these images, just as modern satellite photography provides information about landforms, patterns of settlement, and the growth of a community—all the way down to individual blocks and residences. And the fact that almost sixty-five different views of Texas cities were produced between 1871 and 1900, along with dozens of guides to the state, suggests the enthusiasm with which Texans promoted their communities.

## The Impact of Railroads

The most important element of industrialization—and the catalyst for so much of the economy—was the expansion of railroads into almost every part of the state by 1900. As the nation slowly recovered from the Panic of 1873, Texas entered its greatest era of railroad building, and one of the greatest in the nation. The state had only 1,650 miles of track in 1875, all in East Texas, but more than half of the total railroad construction in Texas occurred during the next decade. In part, this was because the Constitution of 1876 authorized land grants to railroads to encourage their construction. The state awarded sixteen sections of land for every mile of track laid, and Texas rail companies collected 32,153,878 acres of land in return for 2,928 miles of track. The era of land bonuses came to an end in 1882, when state officials were embarrassed to discover that the supply of public land had been exhausted and that they had commitments for 8 million acres more than they could supply. In 1877 Texas led the nation in miles of track built

Grand Central Depot on Washington Street in Houston, 1894, with rail cars loaded with bales of cotton. *(Houston, 1880–1910, CN 02747, The Center for American History, The University of Texas at Austin)*

and in the following year more track was laid in Texas than in all the other states and territories combined.

Although such a vast state had a genuine need for economical transportation, and construction of the railroad lines clearly spurred the industrial revolution along, the spurt in railroad building also resulted from outside factors, including competition between two of the most powerful and storied railroad moguls of the Gilded Age: Jay Gould, who acquired the Texas & Pacific Railroad in 1879, and Collis P. Huntington, who owned the Southern Pacific. Together, they owned or controlled more than half the track mileage in Texas. The T&P began construction westward from Fort Worth in April 1881, and the Southern Pacific reached El Paso in May of that year.

This competition is reflected in the track mileage built in Texas during those years: 1,527 miles of track were laid in 1881 and 1,349 miles in 1882. By 1900 Texas had almost 10,000 miles of track, approximately 5 percent of the total railroad mileage in the United States, and every city of significant size had service, with cities such as Denison, Greenville, Dallas, Fort Worth, San Antonio, and Houston being served by multiple lines.

## The Growth of Labor Unions

One response to the growing industrialization of the state was the establishment of labor unions. Before the Civil War, for the most part Texas unions were limited to typographers and carpenters, because most of the workers lived in widely separated rural areas, which was not conducive to the organization of unions. Public sentiment initially seemed to be neutral or sympathetic toward unions, but that changed as the unions began to engage in what many regarded as bothersome if not "revolutionary" activities. The flashpoint was an 1886 strike, called by the Knights of Labor against the T&P and Jay Gould. Thousands of men, many of whom had hoped to improve their lot by moving west with the railroad, became disappointed when they got caught in the squeeze of economic depression and declining wages and walked off the job, seriously affecting service in North and West Texas. Gould himself was caught in a similar squeeze, as he attempted to negotiate the fine line between tough competitors and expansion, made more problematic by the same depression that bedeviled the workers. When he refused to compromise with the workers, an armed clash occurred in Fort Worth, and Governor Ireland sent the Texas Rangers and the state militia to restore peace. The affair was settled when the T&P passed into the hands of a federal receiver, and the court held the strikers in contempt. The Knights' power declined rapidly thereafter; however, they played a role in the successful boycott of the contractors building the new capitol in Austin because they had imported Scottish granite cutters, a violation of the Alien Contract Labor Law.

African Americans were usually barred from white unions, although some were members of the Knights of Labor, including David Black, who served on the union's state executive board. Concentrated in East Texas and in the coastal cities, they were able to establish their own unions, such as Negro Longshoremen's Association in Galveston. Most Mexican Americans, by virtue of their residence in South Texas, were not involved in unionization activities, although two dozen Hispanic laborers worked for the Texas and Pacific Coal Company in Thurber by 1900. Because the state was largely rural and the electorate increasingly suspicious, Texas labor unions remained weak as the nineteenth century drew to a close.

## Expansion into West Texas

Because the state had no navigable rivers, Texans any distance from the coast were for all practical purposes landlocked. The extension of railroads into the western portions of the state offered a solution to this problem, but, first, the hostile Indians on the northwestern and western frontiers had to be subdued. The U.S. Army reoccupied the frontier forts of Texas and resumed the frontier defense following the Civil War, and the slaughter of the great southern buffalo herd, undertaken to supply Eastern factories, became an integral part of that process.

The transcontinental railroad, completed in 1869, had divided American bison into two huge herds, one in the north and the other in the south. The southern herd ranged deep into Texas, coming into contact with the advancing cattle and farming frontier and with the deadliest killers that the bison had yet encountered—white hunters. J. Wright Mooar, a Kansas buffalo hunter, glimpsed the potential of the buffalo trade in 1871 when he sent fifty-seven hides to relatives in New York with instructions to try to sell them. A Philadelphia tanner purchased the lot for $200. When the hides proved to make fine leather, he gave the Mooar brothers an order for 2,000 more, and by the mid-1870s there were, perhaps, 3,000 buffalo hunters roaming the Texas Panhandle in search of what was left of the once great Southern herd. The slaughter that would bring the American bison almost to extinction had begun.

## The Slaughter of the Buffalo

Whereas the Plains Indians depended upon the bison for every aspect of their lives, white men had previously killed them for sport and food, primarily for the crews building the transcontinental railroads. Now they slaughtered them for their hides, which could be quickly converted into cash, and left the carcasses on the ground to rot. "No mercy was shown the buffalo," plainsman and Indian fighter Billy Dixon recalled of his 1874 hunt. "I killed as many as my three men [skinners] could handle, working them as hard as they were willing to work. This was deadly business, without sentiment; it was dollars against tenderheartedness, and dollars won."

The buffalo hunters were engaged in an unprecedented slaughter of what General Philip H. Sheridan had called the "Indians' commissary," and he concluded that they had "done more in the last two years and will do more in the next year to settle the vexed Indian question than the entire regular army has done in the last 30 years." Within five years, the last hostile tribe had been defeated and settled on a reservation, ending the conflict that had raged along the Texas frontier for more than half a century and opening West Texas to ranchers and farmers, which set the state on a course different from that of the other Southern states.

After the hunters came the "bone pickers." Northern industries had been using buffalo bones for buttons, combs, and knife handles for some time, but they soon realized that bones could be ground into meal or charred and used to remove the color from sugar. Fresh bones also provided calcium phosphate ash for bone china furnaces. By the mid-1870s, bone pickers got from $7 to $9 per ton for bones and $12 to $15 for hooves and horns. And the prairie was littered with the bleached bones of the millions of animals that the hunters had killed and left to rot. Pickers hauled wagonloads of bones to the railroad right of way and stacked them by the tracks, some of the mounds reaching a height of sixteen feet and stretching for half a mile. Texas led the world in bone production for a brief period during the early 1880s, and prices got as high as $22 to $23 per ton. Within a few years, however, the bone pickers had gathered virtually all of the bison skeletons and by the turn of the century industries were using cow bones instead.

## Displacement of the Indians

At the same time, even though they were issued government rations and provisions on the Fort Sill Reservation in the Indian Territory, the Kiowas and Comanches continued to raid the Texas frontier and into Mexico. The much-acclaimed "peace policy" of President Ulysses S. Grant afforded Texans little relief, for it barred the army from pursuing raiding Indians onto the reservation. When the Salt Creek massacre of 1871 resulted in the deaths of seven teamsters and almost snared General William T. Sherman himself, however, the army obtained permission to operate against marauders, even in their Fort Sill "city of refuge." The conflict approached its climax when Comanches, Kiowas, and Cheyennes attacked a camp of buffalo hunters at Adobe Walls, northeast of what is today Borger, in June 1874. Indians of all three tribes fled their reservations and took refuge on the Staked Plains of the Texas Panhandle. Army columns advanced from five directions but fought few battles. The most notable was Colonel Ranald S. Mackenzie's surprise attack on a camp in Palo Duro Canyon. Because the Indians were elusive and would fight only under favorable conditions, the army resorted to brutal tactics such as slaughtering their horses, ravaging villages, and confiscating food, weapons, and anything the Indians needed to survive. So relentlessly did the army harass the Indians through the winter of 1874–75 that most returned to their reservations and surrendered. The Red River War ended Indian hostilities on the southern Plains and brought to a close more than fifty years of bloodshed and plunder on the Texas frontier.

The final defeat of Indians in Texas occurred in the summer of 1880, when units of "buffalo soldiers" of the Tenth Cavalry stationed at Fort Davis confronted the wily Apache Chief Victorio and his band. The Indians called the black troops, who served in both the Ninth and Tenth Cavalry and the Twenty-fourth and Twenty-fifth Infantry, buffalo soldiers, probably because the texture of their hair reminded the Indians of the buffalo. The black troops realized that the Indians regarded the buffalo as sacred and accepted the term as a compliment. One of the ablest Apache leaders, Victorio had rejected the intolerable life on Arizona's barren San Carlos Reservation and for several years had tried to get along on the Fort Stanton Reservation in New Mexico. When that proved impossible, he and his band raided ranches on both sides of the border as well as stagecoaches and travelers on the San Antonio-El Paso Road. They led military columns on a wild chase across New Mexico, Mexico, and Texas. Rather than pursue them further, in August 1880, Colonel Benjamin H. Grierson and his buffalo soldiers established impregnable positions commanding seasonal water holes at Tinaja de las Palmas, fifteen miles southeast of Sierra Blanca, and Ratttlesnake Springs, forty miles north of present-day Van Horn. Grierson knew that the Apaches could not make it through the dry desert country without water. Unable to displace the soldiers,

Victorio and his band fell back into Mexico. There, in October, Mexican troops assaulted him on the rocky slopes of Tres Castillos, wiped out nearly all of his followers, and killed the dynamic chief himself.

The human suffering and drama on both sides of the Indian wars was deplorable and poignant. "The Indian loves to live as well as the white men," Buffalo Good, a Wichita, had said in 1871, "and [we] can't help being there." But, as anthropologist W. W. Newcomb observed, "the obliteration of Texas Indians was but a small part, a footnote really, to the nineteenth-century development and emergence of a new, and in technological terms, a tremendously powerful nation-state."

## The Impact of Barbed Wire

About the time of the defeat of the Plains Indians, the introduction of a new type of fencing encouraged the settlement of West Texas. Fences had always been a problem. In East Texas, where timber was plentiful, most fences were made of board, split rail, or, in some cases, rock. On the plains, lacking timber or rock, ranchers used hedges, with bois d'arc being the favorite because, planted along a line, the scrubby trees could be bent and shaped into an almost impenetrable barrier.

That changed when J. F. Glidden of Illinois invented barbed wire in 1874. Meeting with only limited success in Illinois, Glidden's agents, Henry B. Sanborn and Judson P. Warner, moved to Texas. Barbed wire was controversial when it was first introduced: People thought that it would not restrain wild cattle or horses, and, if it did, that the animals would be severely injured when they threw themselves against it. Sanborn and Warner made their first sale in Gainesville in the fall of 1875, and barbed wire soon proved to be a huge success. It was cheap and effective in fencing livestock, and in only a few years it changed the nature of western agriculture. Now ranchers could keep livestock out of farmlands and selectively breed their animals by controlling access. With all these conditions in place, the stage was set for accelerated growth in the Texas economy.

## The Cotton Culture Expands

Farmers, as unlikely as it may seem, were also among the first to feel the effects of modernization. Just as in industry, the trend in agriculture was toward concentration and efficiency, and in Texas that meant cotton. Cotton had been the major cash crop in Texas prior to the Civil War, and the move into West Texas did nothing to lessen its dominance. In West Texas, farmers had to dig deeper to find water, there were few springs, and gypsum rendered most of the stream water undrinkable. But, by 1875, windmills offered a solution to the problem of deep wells by harnessing the power of the ever-present West Texas wind to pump ground water, and in the late 1880s and early 1890s farmers developed several techniques

The eclipse windmill was the most popular one on the plains and made settlement of the plains possible. This one was located on the XIT Ranch. *(Courtesy Panhandle-Plains Historical Museum)*

that enabled them to make the dry but fertile land productive, and the number of acres devoted to cotton climbed steadily throughout the last quarter of the century.

Another factor contributing to the increase in cotton production was the proliferation of tenant farmers. Tenant farming—whether the farmers are renters or sharecroppers—although often perceived in a negative way, can enable people with no savings to get a start; however, in Texas at this time the conditions under which credit was extended, the owners' pressure on tenants to produce the most profitable crops, and the economic depression of the 1890s combined to leave most tenants little hope of improvement. As long as inexpensive or free public

Plowing the field on a farm near Bonham. Photograph by Henry Stark, 1895–96. *(Courtesy Dallas Historical Society)*

lands were available in West Texas, renters had the option of settling a homestead there, but sharecroppers, mostly African Americans, were usually so indebted that they could not move. And, at about the same time that the public land was exhausted, in 1898, population had increased significantly, depression drove some families from the cities back to the farms, and cotton prices declined precipitously—to 5.7 cents per pound.

As farmers adapted to this new environment, the line of settlement moved rapidly westward. It reached the northern Panhandle, the South Plains, and the Trans-Pecos region in the 1880s. The number of acres under cultivation skyrocketed—from 36,292,000 in 1880 to 51,407,000 in 1890, and 125,807,000 in 1900. It would be thirty-five years before that total was exceeded. Additional counties were organized until, by 1900, all but twenty-four of Texas's 254 counties had been established. The "almost unprecedented tide of immigration," according to an Agricultural Commission report, had brought the Texas frontier to a close. And, at the same time, immigrants to East Texas—in many cases, African Americans from other Southern states—had more than replaced the population that had moved west.

The expansion of cotton farmers onto ranch lands was not always harmonious. The newcomers always sought land near streams and rivers and often

## Acreage in Texas Farms, 1850–1960

Taken from *Historical Statistics of the United States, Colonial Times to 1970*

fenced the water off from the cattlemen, who had in some instances been grazing their livestock on public land for years. J. L. Driskell of Austin, for example, began with a herd of only 800 cattle in 1873 and by 1884, courtesy of the state's free grass, was worth an estimated $800,000. The ranchers' practice was to buy the land with the water and use the rest. Most ranchers felt they were entitled to free use of the state's land because they had suffered the risks and hardships of settling the frontier. But the increased use of barbed wire—by 1883 almost $1 million worth was sold in Texas annually—resulted in extensive fencing, even in West Texas. This precipitated such widespread fence cutting that the Texas Rangers had to be called in. The farmers were not always the catalyst in these cases, nor the rancher always the perpetrator, for competition between ranches sometimes produced a similar result.

Following a heated debate, the legislature passed a law in 1884 declaring that fence cutting and setting grass fires were felonies punishable by one to five years in prison. Knowingly fencing public lands, or lands belonging to others, without permission became a misdemeanor. And, if a fence blocked access to a public road, the builder was required to place a gate every three miles and to keep the gates in repair.

Production of all the major crops—wheat, corn, oats, and cotton—increased during these decades, but, abetted by tenant farming, cotton far outpaced the others with a more than fourfold increase, from 805,284 bales produced on 2,178,435 acres in 1879 to approximately 3,500,000 bales produced on 7,178,915 acres in 1900. The expansion of railroads into the cotton-producing areas helped to make this possible. Farmers, who had lived in a barter economy and maintained subsistence farms that supplied virtually all of their family's needs, now turned almost wholly to cotton. They could ship their crop to market and obtain consumer goods via the new railroads.

Despite these innovations, there were those who warned against dependence upon a single crop. "Plant cotton," the editor of the *Albany News* counseled, "not all cotton, but some cotton." The logic of the warning became apparent when the price of cotton declined in the 1890s, and all farmers were hurt, especially the tenant farmers and sharecroppers, who found themselves deeply in debt. As farmers continued the move toward commercialized agriculture, organizations like the Patrons of Husbandry and the Farmers' Alliance proposed solutions for their problems, and many farmers were ready to join.

### The Growth of Ranching

The open range of South Texas seemed made for cattle, and they bred and multiplied in the wild as well as under the care of the mission priests and *rancheros.* It was here that the Spanish *vaqueros* developed the techniques and costume that later spread throughout the American West. Anglo Americans and African Americans contributed their own sets of skills to the handling of cattle when they began to arrive in large numbers in the 1820s. The cattle industry of South Texas, the home of the Ballí, King, Kenedy, O'Connor, and other large ranches, grew rapidly during the postwar period. Led by Gail Borden's invention of the meat biscuit (made of dehydrated meat and flour) in 1849, Texas boasted fifteen factory-size meatpacking plants in 1870. After the Civil War, as the U.S. Army moved the line of defensive forts farther westward, the cattlemen resumed their westward march. By 1876 ranchers like Charles Goodnight had passed the 100th meridian all the way from Kimble County in the Edwards Plateau to Childress County in the eastern Panhandle. By the mid-1880s, enterprising salesmen and drillers had solved one of the most difficult problems for plains ranchers: how to get adequate water in a land of little rain. Goodnight installed his first windmill in 1886 to pump water from the Ogallala Aquifer, a huge, natural underground reservoir that stretched from the High Plains of Texas to South Dakota.

Ranchers had already begun to address another serious concern—how to get their cattle to market. Because it was cheaper to walk the beef to market, feeding it on free grass and water, than to slaughter and pack it in Texas, by 1880 the number of packing plants declined to three; throughout the heyday of the trail drives (1867–85) the second most lucrative part of the business, after raising and selling the cattle, was the service that the drovers provided in getting them from ranch to market. Men like Goodnight, Thomas S. Bugbee, and C. C. Slaughter pushed into West Texas, New Mexico, and Colorado to occupy the newly cleared land. By the mid-1880s, Texas-style ranchers had extended their operations as far north as Alberta and Saskatchewan to take advantage of the free grasslands.

### The American Cowboy

Out of these trail drives came the most popular folk character in American history: the cowboy. The real Texas cowboy was usually a young, small, wiry character with a knack for herding animals, hardly a hero in the normal sense.

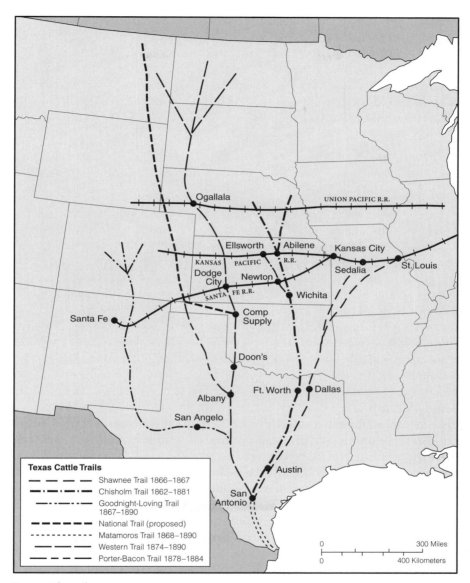

Texas cattle trails.

**Texas Cattle Trails**

— — — — Shawnee Trail 1866–1867
— ·— ·— · Chisholm Trail 1862–1881
— ··— ··— · Goodnight-Loving Trail 1867–1890
▬ ▬ ▬ ▬ National Trail (proposed)
· · · · · · · · Matamoros Trail 1868–1890
——————— Western Trail 1874–1890
— — — Porter-Bacon Trail 1878–1884

The highlight of his year was the spring and summer cattle roundup and drive to one of the Kansas railheads. Except in the way the Texas cowboy practiced it—cowboys usually were hired specifically for the trail drive, as opposed to ranch hands who remained at home and worked year-round—the trail drive itself was not unique. His cow-handling predecessors in Europe and colonial America had driven cattle to market, but the cowboy lived with the cattle, camped out for the

A Texas cowboy. Photograph by William Henry Jackson. *(Courtesy Colorado Historical Society, CHS-J1005)*

three months of the drive, and slept on the ground nightly. He got up before the sun rose to begin his work and did not turn in until it had set. In between he stood his turn at watch, losing two or three hours of sleep. Throughout the drive the cowboy ate only the chuck that the cook had on his wagon. The day was filled with hard, difficult work, for a herd of 3,000 cattle did not maintain itself.

The cowboy is personified by Charles A. Siringo, who was born to an Italian father and an Irish mother in Matagorda County in 1855, became a cowboy at the tender age of fifteen, and thirty years later wrote the first cowboy autobiography, *A Texas Cowboy; or, Fifteen Years on the Hurricane Deck of a Spanish Pony—Taken from Real Life,* which proved to be immensely popular, particularly among cowboys themselves. But there are many other representative types; one historian has estimated that perhaps as many as one-third of the drovers were Hispanic or black.

Sometimes the experience was more than hard work, because the trail drive was often dangerous. In *Lonesome Dove,* a fictional treatment of Goodnight and Loving's stories, among others, Texas novelist Larry McMurtry has enshrined the water moccasin attack in the river as one of the dreaded events of the trail. But becoming unhorsed in midstream was equally perilous, for few of these dry land laborers could swim. One of the main advantages of the Chisholm Trail was the absence of large rivers. Of course, one stood a good chance of getting caught in a lightning- or hailstorm or stampede, and had to endure blistering sun that dried up the streams and turned the cattle into thirst-crazed creatures that might stampede at the slightest incentive. Rain and bone-chilling cold wind were equally certain to make the trip north as miserable as possible.

Despite the demanding hours and even more demanding work, countless youngsters who read about cowboys in Siringo's book or in dime novels tried to imitate them. They hit the trail inspired to challenge "Texas Jack" Omohundro's or "Buffalo Bill" Cody's greatest feats. The trail drive was not just a character-building experience for ambitious wanderers, but also an original piece of Americana. In many ways it resembled a military expedition, as the boss gathered his crew, rounded up the cattle, and set out for Dodge City, Abilene, Sheridan, or one of the other small cattle towns that dotted the Kansas Pacific and Union Pacific railroad lines.

The storied camaraderie of the campfire helped to combat the loneliness of a three-month trip, but, as E. C. "Teddy Blue" Abbott (a young Englishman turned cowboy) said, they had "told each other everything we knew in a week." But even the trail drives, supposedly the epitome of freedom and independence, fell victim to the changes wrought by the industrial revolution. By the time he quit the range in 1884 and located in Caldwell, Kansas, where he became a merchant, Siringo was aware of the changes going on around him. The first trail drives were for the purpose of getting mature cattle to market for slaughter. But when the Missouri, Kansas and Texas Railroad reached Denison, near the Red River, and the Texas & Pacific reached Dallas, it became easier and less expensive for ranchers to ship their mature cattle by rail. Yearling steers made up most of the drives by 1880, driven north for the purpose of stocking the northern ranges, and the Kansas railheads became clearinghouses where northern ranchers purchased stock rather than shipping points.

One of the reasons that the Texas cowboy is such a folk hero today may be that he stands as a symbol of all the workers whose lives changed under the pressure of industrialization. But specialization, one of the byproducts of barbed wire and the industrial revolution, affected the freedom-loving cowboy every bit as much as it did the sodbuster.

Perhaps the most famous illustration of the changing management-worker relationship is the Cowboy Strike of 1883. With the end of open-range cattle ranching came stock farming and the improvement of herds, which encouraged many eastern and European investment companies to get into the business and brought about innovations that many cowboys considered a threat to their livelihood. In earlier years ranch hands could take part of their pay in calves, brand mavericks for themselves, and graze their small herds on their employers' land. But the new managers often represented absentee owners who wanted hands to work for wages only and who provided none of the opportunities of the past. To the cowboys it seemed that the more conventional roles of owner/manager and worker were replacing the traditional, more fraternal relationships that they had enjoyed.

In 1883 Tom Harris of the LS Ranch led a small group of cowboys in drafting an ultimatum demanding higher pay and threatening a strike against several ranches, which they believed to be controlled by corporations or individuals who were involved in ranching only for quick profit. Twenty-four men signed the document, which set March 31, 1883, as the strike date and promised limited assistance to strikers who needed money. Harris and others attempted to recruit all the cowboys in the area, but no one knows for sure how many actually participated; it might have been anywhere from thirty to 325. With a combination of temporarily higher wages for those who defied the strike, immediate firing of those who participated, and rumors of violence on the part of the strikers, the stockmen defeated the fledgling union within two and a half months, and the spring roundup occurred without incident. But the failed strike was a clear indication that modernization and industrialization had changed ranching. Many of the old-timers like Siringo had gone into ranching themselves or into some other line of work, and the new breed of ranch hand represented the working class more than the undisciplined, freedom-loving character of popular culture.

Historians disagree as to whether this strike was part of the larger labor movement in Texas, but the fact that it seemed to share some of the same causes as other labor unrest—growing anonymity on the job, changing worker-employer relationships—has invited such speculation, especially because it occurred at the same time as the Knights of Labor's greatest successes.

## The Political Will, 1876–1898

Politics reflected the economic realities that Texans faced during the last quarter of the century. Supporters of the new governor, Richard Coke, elected in 1874, represented what they called the New South and proposed to industrialize Texas by enticing railroads, lowering taxes, holding down government expenses, and creating an inexpensive labor supply. Largely ex-Confederates, these men felt that Republican misrule during the years after the Civil War had destroyed Southern prosperity by upsetting the traditional relationship between the races. Although they represented the party of slavery, secession, and defeat, they now cast themselves as the redeemers of the Democratic Party of their forebears and the true South, and the 1876 Constitution, still in effect today, was an effort to erase all traces of the Republican regime.

### Texas Uses Its Land

Just as before the Civil War, the state was dependent upon one crop—cotton—and was in debt, and its only asset of any consequence was the land itself. Because per capita income in Texas was only 63.2 percent of the national average at the end of the decade, more than 5.5 percent lower than the average personal income in the adjacent states of Louisiana and Arkansas, and because of a nationwide depression in 1873, Democrats felt that their only option was retrenchment. Coke resigned the struggle in 1876 to accept appointment to a seat in the U.S. Senate, and Richard B. Hubbard replaced him. Hubbard was denied the 1878 nomination, however, because critics claimed that he had not done enough to reduce the state's debt. Instead, the Democratic convention nominated ex-Confederate Oran M. Roberts, of Tyler, who had served as chairman of the secession convention of 1861 and was now chief justice of the state supreme court. With Roberts leading the way, the Democrats began to decrease taxes and instituted what many considered draconian measures to restore the state's financial stability.

Roberts also wanted the state to "get out of the land business" and led efforts to dispose of public land as quickly as possible. Such policies hurt the big landowners, the railroads, and the Capitol Syndicate, a group that had accepted land in return for building additional railroad tracks and the new state capitol. Under the law, the railroads had to dispose of their land within eight years of receipt, but when they tried to sell it, they found that the state, with its cheap land, was their main competitor. The Syndicate, which had ultimately received more than 3 million acres of Panhandle lands that had been set aside for the construction of the new capitol building, had initially hoped to subdivide its land and sell it to settlers at a profit. But the state's land policies kept prices so low that the Syndicate established a ranch instead: the famous XIT Ranch, which was at one time the largest piece of fenced property in the world, with 6,000 miles of single-strand wire fence ringing its ninety-four pastures and outer perimeter. The imposing, new red granite capitol building opened in the spring of 1888 with a gala party, marred only by the huge leak in the roof that drenched the celebrants during a typical Texas thunderstorm.

Roberts's land policies engendered widespread opposition. The ferocity of the conflict may well have been the reason that he did not seek a third term. But he had compiled a formidable fiscal record. By the time he left office, he had balanced the state's budget, reduced the debt by $500,000, and gathered a treasury surplus of $300,000.

### New Political Issues

Issues that would dominate the state's politics for decades gradually emerged over the next few years. Roberts's successor, Governor "Oxcart John" Ireland (1883–87), had earned his nickname by opposing land grants to the railroads when he was a member of the legislature, but he continued the probusiness policies that had prevailed, and the railroads continued to build.

Consumption of alcoholic beverages became a growing concern during the administration of Lawrence Sullivan Ross (1887–91), one of the state's most popular Texas Rangers and military heroes. He was the person who had brought Cynthia Ann Parker back (albeit unwillingly) from Comanche captivity in 1860. The Women's Christian Temperance Union, United Friends of Temperance (the first statewide prohibition organization), and other groups had been preaching prohibition for decades; now the message began to resonate, especially among the fundamentalist Protestants, and found supporters among such capable politicians as Senator John H. Reagan. The state constitution authorized local option elections, but prohibitionists now called for a statewide ban on the sale of alcoholic beverages and convinced the legislature to put a constitutional amendment on prohibition before the electorate in 1887. Even though it carried only thirty-two counties and failed by a vote of 220,627 to 129,270, the prohibitionists vowed to continue the fight.

A third reality of the political scene was the decreasing importance of the Republican Party. Known as the party of African Americans ever since its organization in 1867, the Texas Republican Party suffered a devastating blow when the Democrats returned to office in 1873 and 1874. With the percentage of African Americans in the state's population decreasing from 31 percent in 1870 to 20 percent in 1900, the Republicans realized further losses when whites began to split from the party (the "lily-whites") and to disenfranchise African Americans through the organization of white men's political clubs, the legal process, and intimidation (it is likely that as many as 300 to 500 African Americans were lynched during the last quarter of the century). Norris Wright Cuney, an able African American politician from Galveston, became head of the party when former governor Davis died in 1883. As sergeant-at-arms during the Twelfth Legislature (1870–71), Cuny was skilled in the use of political patronage, especially after President Benjamin Harrison appointed him collector of customs in Galveston in 1889. He even survived various modifications in the election code, such as the elimination of the use of colored paper ballots to aid illiterate voters, and was resourceful enough to continue to get Republicans elected to office in a few counties in East Texas and along the gulf coast. But he could not prevent the passage of such Jim Crow segregation laws as the one offered in 1889 by the state senator from Marshall, William H. Pope, requiring railroads to provide separate coaches for African Americans and whites. As the Republican Party became increasingly marginalized, Cuney tried to maintain his power by allying with a Democratic Party faction or with a third-party movement.

### Populism Challenges the Status Quo

The status of farmers in the newly evolving economy led them to search for new solutions too. The state's reliance on one crop became all too apparent when farmers received 22 percent less income between 1887 and 1890 despite harvesting 25 percent more cotton. Feeling the brunt of extensive societal changes as well, they expressed their concern through the Grange, or the Patrons of Husbandry, Greenback clubs, and the Farmers' Alliance.

The Grange began in 1867 as a secret social and educational society, but soon began to advocate political and cooperative solutions to agrarian problems. The primary allure of the Greenback Party to farmers was its campaign for an inflated currency through issuance of paper money (greenbacks) not backed by coin (gold). By the 1880s, the Texas Farmers' Alliance had become the dominant agrarian

Reformer James Stephen Hogg served as attorney general from 1886 to 1891, then as the first native son to be elected governor, 1891–95. *(James Stephen Hogg Photographs, 1836–1969, CN 05612, The Center for American History, The University of Texas at Austin)*

group in the state. From its beginning in Lampasas in 1877, it had been more political than the Grange and demanded wholesale economic changes rather than modest reforms. The Alliance shared many goals with the Greenback Party, advocating the establishment of a subtreasury system, the abolition of the national banking system, abandonment of the deflationary gold standard in favor of free coinage of silver, adoption of an income tax, an eight-hour workday, direct election of senators, the Australian (secret) ballot, and referendum and recall, but it made fewer and less radical demands than its counterparts in other states with regard to issues such as government ownership of the railroads and the establishment of a new political party. The group took no stand on the sale of alcoholic beverages, perhaps because the farmers saw it as too divisive an issue. Seeing no place for themselves in the evolving economy, many of the have-nots of society would later rally first under the People's Party and then the Populist Party banners.

Although these agrarian movements attracted many voters, the person who most effectively voiced these concerns in Texas was Democrat James Stephen Hogg, a crusading East Texan, who had served as attorney general under Governor Ross and in 1891 became the first native-born Texan to be elected governor. As attorney general, Hogg had zealously defended the public lands, regaining over 1.5 million acres for the state. He demanded that out-of-state insurance companies comply with Texas law and drove from the state those who did not. He sought to regulate railroads under the Constitution of 1876, breaking up the Texas Traffic Association, and helped to write the second state antitrust law in the nation. But he soon realized that neither the legislature nor his small office could deal effectively with the railroads and campaigned for governor in 1890 on a platform that included passage of a constitutional amendment that would enable the establishment of a railroad commission.

A tall man who weighed more than 250 pounds, Hogg was an energetic campaigner with a common touch, a love of the vernacular, and a native understanding of people. He easily ingratiated himself with rural audiences, who seemed immediately to identify with a man named Hogg. It is difficult to imagine the task that campaigners faced in addressing the huge outdoor crowds in those days. When Hogg opened his campaign for the governorship at Rusk in April 1890, for example, perhaps 3,000 people gathered in a shady grove outside of town for the event. Without the benefit of the public address systems we have today, Hogg's strong and intelligible voice gave him a big advantage over his opponents in such situations; even the men and boys in the trees near the edge of the crowd could hear him. Once he tore into the railroads and others who took advantage of farmers, he could hold an audience for hours. As the temperature rose on a hot summer afternoon, he would fling off his coat, loosen his suspenders, and gulp water to refresh his throat and maintain his strength. At times his plain speech may have offended the ladies, but still they came even though they could not vote. His zeal and personality earned him a long list of enemies by the time he decided to run for governor, but, fortunately for Hogg, he also had a much longer list of friends.

### Hogg's Reforms

Hogg called for a number of policies in the 1890 campaign, such as reform of the state's land policy, longer school terms, an endowment for the University of Texas and the Agricultural and Mechanical College, a home for disabled Confederate veterans, and, regrettably, separate railroad coaches for African American and white passengers, but he focused on the need for a constitutional amendment to enable the state to regulate railroads. In doing so, he appropriated one of the main tenets of the Farmers' Alliance, or the Populist Party, as they became known, and appealed to them to join his campaign. Five Democrats announced against him at one time or another, and the railroads favored each of them in turn, but only Lieutenant Governor Thomas Benton Wheeler stayed in the fight until the convention. The railroads helped finance Hogg's opponents and resorted to such practices as laying off engineers and canceling planned new construction in certain areas "until the commission question was settled." But the agrarians remained with Hogg, whom they saw as their defender even though he did not endorse a subtreasury, and he had only token opposition. He swept into office, and the constitutional amendment permitting a railroad commission also passed handily.

Hogg quickly established the Railroad Commission as an appointive body and convinced John H. Reagan, who as a member of the U.S. House of Representatives had shepherded the Interstate Commerce Act through Congress in 1887, to resign his new seat in the U.S. Senate to become chairperson. Reagan's appointment drew widespread praise, but the Alliance had wanted an elective commission, and Hogg added fuel to the flickering fire by declining to appoint any of their supporters to it. The People's Party, or the Populists, formally organized into a third national political party in St. Louis in April 1892, leading conservative Democrats, who had opposed the establishment of the commission, to believe that their more liberal colleagues might desert the party, enabling them to unseat Hogg in the next election.

Hogg's election represented a rebuke to the Bourbon, or conservative, wing of the Democratic Party, leading them to bolt in the 1892 election. Hogg might not have survived had his campaign not been masterminded by one of his close friends, who later became one of the most unusual, mysterious, and influential figures in American politics. Edward Mandell House of Austin had enjoyed a privileged youth as the son of a wealthy Houston merchant, banker, and landowner and had moved to Austin in 1885 to escape the heat of Houston and to be closer to his cotton plantations. There he befriended a number of political leaders, including Governor Hogg. He admired Hogg, especially his reform efforts, and learned politics from him. "When I found out that the railroads and the entire corporate interests of Texas were combined to defeat Hogg," House later wrote, "I enlisted actively on his behalf." It would be largely through House's guidance and organizing skills, both at the state and national levels, that Hogg would gain reelection and that Texas would later become a major influence in the federal government before the other states of the old Confederacy.

As the Democrats gathered in Houston in August 1892 for what would become known as the "street car barn" convention, the Hogg forces were in control. More or less according to plan, the conservatives bolted, held their own convention, and nominated Waco attorney George W. Clark, a staunch supporter of the railroads, to oppose Hogg. The race for the governorship soon became a three-way contest with the entry of Thomas L. Nugent, the Populist candidate. Able African American leaders such as John B. Rayner of Calvert hoped that they could bring Republican Party chair Cuney and other African Americans into the Populist fold, but Cuney had other plans. Thinking that the liberal votes would be split between the Democrats and the Populists, he formed a coalition with Clark in an effort to gain some of the spoils that he believed the Republicans and the conservative Democrats would be able to win. In fact, the coalition abetted a split that was already under way in the Republican Party itself. Objecting to continued African American domination of the party, the small white faction known as the lily-whites held their own convention and nominated A. J. Houston, Sam Houston's youngest son.

Hogg also made a serious appeal to African American voters. He campaigned vigorously on the issues, including his opposition to lynching, which he eloquently expressed in a Brenham speech in June. He pardoned several African American prisoners in an obvious attempt to influence the electorate, and African American speakers volunteered to campaign for him and organized

"Hogg clubs" throughout the state. This was the first election in which large numbers of African American voters deserted Cuney and the Republicans to vote for the Democratic candidate.

The Populist campaign, meanwhile, took on the aura of a religious crusade. Men like former Methodist minister H. S. P. "Stump" Ashby, labor leader W. R. Lamb, and Ben Terrell, a well-known Southern Alliance orator, fanned out across the state, holding camp-meeting style rallies on Nugent's behalf. They used Biblical rhetoric to tell familiar stories and substituted political slogans for the words of well-known hymns. Hoping to challenge the Democrats with a biracial coalition, they promised equal protection under the law as well as guaranteed suffrage, regardless of race.

Ultimately, Hogg won the bitter race, but only by a plurality—190,486 votes to Clark's 133,395 and Nugent's 108,483. Populist candidates drew even more support at the congressional level, finishing second in ten of thirteen races. The election served notice to the Democrats that a Populist alliance with the Republicans could be a real threat, especially if they were unable to heal the breach in their own party.

Now wary of the Populists, Hogg continued his reform program. He had already begun to incorporate many of their issues into his own platform—making the railroad commission elective rather than appointive, for example—but he refused to go so far as to endorse a subtreasury system. He signed the Perpetuities and Corporations Land Law with the intention of keeping companies "whose main purpose of business is the acquisition or ownership . . . of lands" from owning lands, but it missed its main targets, the great land and cattle companies, because they defined their primary activity as cattle raising. He signed the Stock and Bond Law of 1893 in an effort to keep railroads from issuing "watered," or overvalued, stock and another law restricting the amount of indebtedness that counties or municipalities could incur. He established the Board of Pardon Advisors to review the hundreds of clemency pleas and make recommendations to the governor, extended the public school term from four to six months, and increased the appropriation for the new University of Texas.

House became Hogg's closest advisor. He visited with the governor virtually every day and was the man to see if one wanted a political appointment or to petition the governor on any subject. He also continued his correspondence with his far-flung network of friends and confidants that he began to refer to as "our crowd." Although Hogg offered him several political positions, House refused them all, finally accepting the honorary title of Lieutenant Colonel, which the press quickly shortened to Colonel. House had begun to perfect the behind-the-scenes political machinations that would ultimately take him to Washington as a personal advisor to President Woodrow Wilson in 1912.

## Women and Minority Rights

Hogg was also more active than any other governor in trying to bring an end to lynchings in Texas, which one authority has estimated might have resulted in the deaths of 300 to 500 African Americans between 1870 and 1900. Hogg called those who would lynch a fellow citizen "bands of murderers" who had "no respect for constitutional guarantees or the stability of government or the lives of human beings." When a mob seemed about to threaten the life of an African American man arrested for murder in Bastrop County, Hogg notified the sheriff that he had posted a $1,000 reward for the arrest and conviction of each member of the mob if a lynching occurred; the mob dissipated. Then, responding to the horrible torture and burning death of Henry Smith at Paris in 1893, Hogg called the affair a disgrace to Texas and unsuccessfully petitioned the legislature to pass an anti-lynching bill.

One issue that neither Hogg nor the Populists would touch was women's suffrage. It had been an issue for a number of years, but both constitutional conventions, in 1868–69 and 1875, had refused to take any action. Rebecca Henry Hayes of Galveston led in the establishment of the Texas Equal Rights Association at a Dallas meeting in May 1893, but the effort to get the three major political parties to include a suffrage plank in their platforms failed the following year. She and others were successful in arousing interest in the cause as auxiliaries spread to a number of cities, and newspapers began to take notice of their efforts. But the organization split after it failed to get the state House of Representatives to recommend a constitutional amendment in 1895.

Another trend became apparent while Hogg was in office. The state census of 1887 counted only about 83,000 Hispanics, about 4 percent of the population, and they lived mostly along the border. But Mexican immigration had begun to increase before the American Civil War and continued to grow into the 1890s. Mexicans were not so much attracted to Texas as they were driven from Mexico by the developing social chaos, the increased population, the collapsing economy, and the spread of entrepreneurs, who drove the village farmers from their *ejidos* (common lands) in the name of government-approved development. The newcomers were generally limited to hard labor such as grubbing and picking cotton, sheepherding, and ranch work, but because they constituted a large majority of the population in the counties along the Rio Grande, they were generally able to keep their culture intact, including language, religion, holidays, foods, folk medicine, and family structures. The 1900 census showed that there were perhaps as many as 165,000 Mexican Americans in Texas, some 71,000 of them born in Mexico. There was similar growth in the Anglo population, it is true, but with far fewer foreign-born.

Although he could easily have won a U.S. Senate seat, Jim Hogg, who had no means of support except his job, announced at a "harmony meeting" in Dallas in January 1894 that he would not be a candidate for political office. In debt and feeling that he should tend to his family's needs, he entered into what became a lucrative legal practice in Austin, serving the same corporations and railroads that he had attacked while in public office. After the discovery of oil at Spindletop in 1901, he moved his practice to Houston and became involved in the oil business, helping to organize the Texas Company, which ultimately became Texaco, with Joseph S. Cullinan and others. Some ten years after his death, oil was discovered on property that he had purchased near West Columbia, making his three children "oil rich."

## Business-Oriented Democrats

Hogg's 1892 reelection was only the beginning for Colonel House, who controlled the state Democratic Party machinery for the next decade, orchestrating the elections of a series of business-oriented Democrats to the governorship. Each of the Democratic factions fielded candidates again in 1894, the most reputable of whom was former U.S. Senator and railroad commissioner John H. Reagan, the "old Roman," whom Hogg favored. But Charles Allen Culberson, a reformer who had supported Hogg's platform and as attorney general had enforced the laws that he passed, entered the race with House's assistance. Culberson stood with Hogg on most state issues, but not on many national issues, such as the free coinage of silver. The House organization went into action, blanketing the state with hundreds of letters to "our crowd" as well as to influential Democrats in every section, arranging for speakers at local meetings, and making sure that Culberson's views made it into the press and into thousands of brochures. While Culberson was on the stump, House remained in Austin, handling the arrangements for his appearances—from publicizing events and making sure that the right people would be there to meet him to deciding upon the refreshments. Culberson's headquarters sent out bales of campaign literature and copies of his speeches. The turning point proved to be Reagan's withdrawal, when the convention produced a platform document that he could not support, and his votes went to Culberson.

In the general election, Culberson had to contend with an invigorated People's Party that had increased its influence by taking over most of the Farmers' Alliance structure in the state and made its best showing to date in Texas with 35 percent of the vote. Realizing that he had lost a number of voters both to the Populists and to Hogg in 1892, Cuney and the Republicans fielded their own candidate in this election, as did the "reform" Republicans (lily-whites) and the Prohibitionists. Culberson won by a plurality, 216,373 votes to 159,676 for Nugent, again the Populist candidate, and 57,147 for the "regular" Republican, W. K. Makemson. The growing Populist totals did not bode well for the Democrats.

Unfortunately, no one will ever know what the actual vote might have been, for both the Democrats and the Populists had honed a number of techniques to sway the African American vote. White sheriffs intimidated African Americans with guns or courted them with whiskey. In some counties, the parties paid influential African American men to pressure their friends and neighbors. In others, they sponsored all-night parties with lots of food and drink; the next morning mounted and armed white men escorted the African Americans to the poll, supplied them with ballots, and paid them twenty-five or fifty cents. Such practices gave credence to the Greenback and Farmers' Alliance charges of vote fraud and their campaigns for the Australian (secret) ballot and an honest count.

House's organizing genius was needed even more in Culberson's reelection bid two years later, because the feared union between the Populists and the Republicans became a reality. In the midst of a national depression, Culberson was an easy target. "Almost every working man is idle," former Confederate colonel and Democratic state senator John S. "Rip" Ford wrote from San Antonio that summer. "If these things increase how can common people procure the means of livelihood?" Many shared his view and joined the Populist crusade. Populist candidate Jerome C. Kearby campaigned hard on issues such as the free coinage of silver, direct election of U. S. senators, and an income tax and made a genuine effort to attract African American voters, at one point serving with two African Americans on the state executive committee and using talented spokesmen such as Rayner. But Kearby was greatly disenchanted when the great Populist orator and champion of free silver, William Jennings Bryan of Nebraska, accepted the nomination of the Democratic Party as well as that of the Populists.

House's political instincts were still good. He relied upon the proven formula of thousands of personal letters to local and regional leaders, tons of brochures and leaflets, and large rallies with talented speakers, including the African American Republican William M. "Gooseneck Bill" McDonald, who refused to go along with his party because he opposed many of the planks in the Populist platform. House even had one of Culberson's speeches translated into Swedish. Kearby polled 44 percent of the vote, the largest total that the Populists would ever receive in Texas, but he still lost to Culberson by an official count of 298,528 to 238,692. The Populists elected twenty-two state representatives and two senators. The Democrats claimed that 47 percent of the African Americans voted for them, but the election is generally considered one of the most corrupt in the state's history, with the widespread use of "influence" men on both sides, and historians generally doubt the claim. The coercion that occurred in Franklin, the county seat of Robertson County, is representative of what occurred, as armed white Democrats patrolled the streets all day, turning away African American would-be Populist voters. In Hearne, white men stood in front of the polls and fired pistol shots into the air to break up a crowd of African Americans who were attempting to vote. Some historians think that an honest election might have resulted in a Populist victory.

Following the 1896 election, the Populist coalition in Texas broke up. Part of the reason was that the national Democratic Party had adopted some of the Populist positions after Bryan became its candidate for president. Race was an issue in some precincts, particularly in East Texas, and a genuine conflict with Republican ideology left others no choice but to return to the Democratic Party, the Socialist Party, the Farmers' Alliance, and other organizations. The impact of the People's Party on the state was the same as its impact on the nation, because the Democrats adopted a number of its proposals, but it ultimately had little direct influence on Texas because the party elected only a few members of the legislature and never gained control of the executive office. At the same time, it attracted so many agrarians that the Democratic Party became more urban and conservative, reducing the number of farmers and farmer sympathizers serving in the legislature. It is possible that their absence from the Democratic Party made possible Culberson's 1894 nomination.

Colonel House, meanwhile, continued his influence over the state's politics by allying himself with a long-haired, smooth-talking Southern orator named Joseph Weldon Bailey. Originally from Mississippi, Bailey had come to Texas in 1885 and settled in Gainesville, where he practiced law. His outgoing personality and flair for spinning yarns in the Jim Hogg style soon won him many friends, who urged him to run for Congress. Elected in 1890, he became a spokesperson for the silver Democrats and by 1897 had become the House minority leader. With Texas Senator Roger Q. Mill's seat becoming vacant in 1899, Bailey lent his support to Culberson, who cinched the nomination when House convinced his main opponent to quit the race. With his reputation as a political kingmaker enhanced, House turned his attention once again to the statehouse.

Several able candidates, including Attorney General Martin M. Crane, had announced for the 1898 race. Crane was a well-known politician who, as attorney general, had won some of the most impressive legal victories in support of Hogg's reforms. He did not ask for House's support because he was not particularly close to the colonel and probably thought he would face only token opposition. So, when Congressman Joseph D. Sayers of Bastrop, whom House had assisted in his 1896 race, asked for help, House agreed and quietly began lining up newspaper support throughout the state. House's accomplishment in this race was that he convinced "our crowd," the Hogg-Culberson network that he had helped create, to support Sayers, rather than Crane, who appeared to be the natural heir to the mantle.

House's strategy of tight organizational control paid off in an unexpected way. He had learned the value of organizing early conventions in counties favorable to his candidate to create a bandwagon effect. As county after county declared for Sayers in the weeks before the convention, the ploy worked, and, in a fit of depression, Crane withdrew from the race. The night of his withdrawal a reporter for the *Dallas Morning News* called House at midnight to inform him of it and to ask for a statement. House recalled that he "lay awake for nearly an hour, enjoying" the fact that he had taken a mediocre candidate and beaten the obvious choice. This incident suggests that, rather than pushing a political agenda, House enjoyed the feeling of power that he gained by manipulating other men, and he extended his influence over the Texas Democratic Party.

## Conclusion

Some of the men who served in office during these years are among the most popular and capable Texans in the state's history. Oran M. Roberts, although generally faulted for viewing government in narrow, legalistic terms, returned the state to financial solvency. After leaving office, the "Old Alcalde" served for ten years as professor of law at the University of Texas and became the founding president of the Texas State Historical Association in 1897. Lawrence Sullivan Ross's two terms were so peaceful and prosperous that historians have often referred to his tenure as an "era of good feeling." The people so revered the "Old Roman," John H. Reagan, that Jim Hogg felt that only he could bring to the new railroad commission the credibility it needed to succeed. Colonel House will forever be regarded as the cagey Texas kingmaker who would go on to succeed in the same low-key and personal manner at the national level. And most historians still consider Jim Hogg, who personified the reform movement in Texas, one of the best chief executives the state has ever had.

Nevertheless, these men left unresolved some of the most troubling and complex issues of the day, including prohibition, segregation, civil rights, and women's suffrage. An issue ever since the days of the republic, support for prohibition was particularly strong in most rural areas of the state and gradually increased as the decades passed. Prohibition would recover from its resounding defeat at the polls in 1887 to become a virulent political issue as the twentieth century dawned. Although legally prevented from voting during this time, women used voluntary organizations to address legal and social problems; when supporters of these two issues—prohibition and women's suffrage—merged, beginning with the state branch of the Woman's Christian Temperance Union in 1883, the issues become even more compelling to Texas voters. The abolition of segregation and the expansion of civil rights would require more time.

The last quarter of the nineteenth century brought tremendous change to Texas. Although the population was still largely rural in 1900, it had increased by more than 370 percent, and many citizens felt that Texas had fulfilled its vision as a land of promise. Railroads had spread throughout the state, encouraging immigration, urban growth, and labor unions, exhausting the public domain through land grants, helping to close the hostile frontier of more than half a century, and engaging in excesses that required governmental regulation. Although industry now accounted for half as much production as agriculture, farmers had greatly increased their output through commercialization, used the expanded railroad network to ship their produce greater distances, and responded to national and even international markets. Although one may credit the state's successes to the indomitable spirit and resilience of the early settlers, it is also important to remember that these two and a half decades also witnessed the virtual extinction of the buffalo, the overgrazing of West Texas rangelands, and the first large-scale exploitation of the East Texas timberlands. Indeed, many of the coming twentieth-century political battles would revolve around the state's use of and/or protection of the environment as Texas became even more populous and urban.

## SUGGESTED READINGS

The best overviews for the latter part of the nineteenth-century are Billy Mac Jones, *The Search for Maturity* (1965), and Alwyn Barr, *Reconstruction to Reform: Texas Politics, 1876–1906* (1971).

## Economic Recovery

For the beginnings of industrialization, see John S. Spratt, *The Road to Spindletop: Economic Change in Texas, 1875–1901* (1955), and Robert S. Maxwell, *Sawdust Empire: The Texas Lumber Industry, 1830–1940* (1983); Thomas L. Miller, *The Public Lands of Texas, 1519–1970* (1972); and S. G. Reed, *A History of the Texas Railroads* (1941).

## Expansion into West Texas

There are literally hundreds of studies on the ranching industry and the cowboy, but the most helpful are Ernest S. Osgood, *The Day of the Cattleman* (reprint, 1957); William C. Holden, *Alkali Trails, or, Social and Economic Movements of the Texas Frontier, 1846–1900* (1930); Jimmy M. Skaggs, *The Cattle-Trailing Industry: Between Supply and Demand, 1866–1890* (1973); and Joe B. Frantz and Julian Ernest Choate, *The American Cowboy: The Myth and the Reality* (1955).

Information on the Indian wars may be found in Rupert Norval Richardson, *The Comanche Barrier to South Plains Settlement: A Century and a Half of Savage Resistance to the Advancing White Frontier* (1933); William H. Leckie, *Military Conquest of the Southern Plains* (1963); and Robert Wooster, *Soldiers, Sutlers, and Settlers: Garrison Life on the Texas Frontier* (1987). For the settlement of West Texas, see Frederick W. Rathjen, *The Texas Panhandle Frontier* (1975). For information on the agrarian movement, see Roscoe C. Martin, *The People's Party in Texas* (reprint, 1970).

## The Political Will

Useful biographies for the period include Robert Cotner, *James Stephen Hogg* (1951); Ben H. Procter, *Not Without Honor: The Life of John H. Reagan* (1962); Gregg Cantrell, *Kenneth and John B. Rayner and the Limits of Southern Dissent* (1993); John Anthony Moretta, *William Pitt Ballinger: Texas Lawyer, Southern Statesman, 1825–1888* (2000); and Rupert Norval Richardson, *Colonel House: The Texas Years* (1964).

For information on minorities and women, see Alwyn Barr's *Black Texans: A History of African Americans in Texas, 1528–1995* (reprint, 1996); Arnoldo De León, *Mexican Americans in Texas: A Brief History,* 2nd ed. (1999); and Ann Patton Malone, *Women on the Texas Frontier: A Cross-cultural Perspective* (1983).

The *Southwestern Historical Quarterly* and the *New Handbook of Texas,* both published by the Texas State Historical Association, contain dozens of useful articles relating to the period. The *New Handbook* is available free of charge on the Internet at www.tsha.utexas.edu.

# CHAPTER

# 11

# The Early Twentieth Century: One Party, Half a Dozen Fights, 1900–1929

Jim Ferguson was a virtual unknown when he stepped up to the makeshift outdoor podium on the main street of the small Central Texas town of Blum, northwest of Hillsboro. Almost 600 men and perhaps a dozen women stood for two hours in the "penetrating cold and raw, damp chill" on March 21, 1914, to hear the first speech of his campaign for governor. Backed by fluttering American flags and red, white, and blue bunting draped from a storefront awning, Ferguson told the rural audience that "I am the thirteenth candidate for governor of Texas, announcing in the year 1913, on the thirteenth day of the month in the thirteenth year of my married life, and my platform was completed on Friday. . . . I have caught the black cat tail of superstition and I intend to twist and pinch it until I am inaugurated Governor of this great State on or about the thirteenth day of next January."

Ferguson was a handsome forty-three-year-old banker from Temple, looking like "the substantial business man of farm origin that every town in Texas knows well." He was a political neophyte but not an innocent. He had some formal education, including a working knowledge of the classics, which he revealed from time to time, quoting Adam Smith in his Blum talk, but he also reverted to "country talk" to emphasize his points. Prohibition was the overriding social and political concern of the day, but Ferguson rejected it, telling the farmers, "If I am elected Governor, and the Legislature puts any liquor legislation up to me, pro or anti, I will strike it where the chicken got the ax."

| | |
|---|---|
| **1900** | Galveston hurricane |
| **1901** | Oil discovered at Spindletop |
| **1902** | Poll tax enacted |
| **1903** | Terrell election law disfranchises blacks |
| **1904** | Texas ranks first in railroad track mileage |
| **1913** | Sixteenth (income tax) and Seventeenth (direct election of U.S. senators) Amendments to the U.S. Constitution ratified |
| **1914** | Houston Ship Channel opens |
| **1915** | *Plan de San Diego* discovered |
| **1917** | U.S. enters World War I |
| **1918** | Legislature ratifies Eighteenth Amendment (prohibition) to the U.S. Constitution |
| **1919** | Legislature grants women the right to vote in Texas primaries |
| **1929** | Value of crude oil production in Texas exceeds the value of the cotton crop, and Texas is the world's leading supplier of crude oil |

Instead, he addressed a greater evil, one that kept the majority of farmers economically prostrate and threatened our political system. The amount of rent that many landlords were now charging tenants, Ferguson shouted, amounted to usury, which was against God's law and man's. It had led to statewide poverty and the rise of the Socialist Party. "As long as the tenant was treated fairly and equitably," he reasoned, "the claims of the Socialist were a matter of fine spun theory. Take away the abuses of the present rent system, and the Socialist would not have a leg to stand on." No other politician in the Democratic Party proposed such a radical measure. To the *Dallas Morning News* reporter at the scene, he was "frank and outspoken," but a neighbor recalled that Ferguson could "electrify and sway audiences to the near frenzy of a wild mob." The Socialists would claim that he had stolen their thunder, and the farmers had found their champion.

The first two decades of the twentieth century, give or take a few years, are generally known as the Progressive Era in American history. Although this is an unsatisfactory, and in many ways misleading, term, it has been used historically to embrace the social and political reforms that a rising middle class and agrarian and social reformers proposed during the early years of the twentieth century.

Texans, nevertheless, shared many of the reformers' concerns, some of which are evident in the four primary factors that facilitated the state's drive toward modernism during these opening decades of the twentieth century. The first was a good economy, rooted in ranching and cotton production and greatly bolstered in January 1901 by the discovery of what was, at that time, the world's largest oil deposit at Spindletop. Second was the political and cultural climate—one-party control—that permitted and at times even encouraged the reforms; indeed, one historian of the era even refers to the state as a "bastion of reform" during these years. Third were the reforms themselves, which originated from societal needs and pressure to modernize as well as to maintain Democratic Party control. And the fourth factor, but by no means the least important, was the role of the federal government, the role that Texans played in it, and the fact that Texans were willing to look to it for assistance when other Southern states had not yet overcome the divisive effect of the Civil War.

It is difficult to categorize these reformers as a movement because of the increasing political, economic, cultural, and racial diversity of Texas society during these years. Almost 200,000 Mexicans probably immigrated to Texas between 1890 and 1910, for example, producing a more than 300 percent increase in the number of Mexicans in Texas, whereas the state's overall population grew by only 75 percent. This represented the largest increase in the Mexican population in Texas since the Texas Revolution in 1836 and meant that in Texas those who called themselves Progressives, whose social and political goals were largely based on a homogeneous society, sometimes could not agree on social and political agendas. And it meant that, from the perspective of a Hispanic, African American, or poor white, there were many events during these years that would not have been considered "progressive" at all.

## The Texas Economy in 1900

Agriculture—farming and ranching—still fueled the state's economy in 1900. Since the mid-1870s, Texas farmers had led the South in the production of cotton. By the turn of the century, the state produced more than 3.5 million bales on 7,178,915 acres of land, and there was still arable land yet to bring under the plow.

Cotton production dipped when the boll weevil, a native Mexican insect, began to make its way northward from South Texas, where it was discovered in 1894. The weevil flourished in the semitropical warmth of much of South and East Texas and proved resistant or immune to most known insecticides and poisons. In 1904, the small weevil destroyed more than 700,000 bales of cotton, in 1910 6 percent of the entire cotton crop, and in 1921 34 percent, costing farmers millions of dollars.

The pest's susceptibility to freezing temperatures spurred the migration of farmers to West Texas and the High Plains, which had begun with the aid of barbed wire and the construction of railroads. Despite the boll weevil infestation, even as late as 1927 the value of the state's cotton crop was still more than three times the value of its oil production.

The fact that agriculture was flourishing did not mean that Texas farmers earned as much as their counterparts in other regions of the country. Texas led the South in farm income per family during these years by a wide margin, but it trailed the Midwest and much of the rest of the nation.

### Tenant Farmers

Despite the fact that state law declared that every Texan was entitled to a homestead of 160 acres, little tillable land remained to be distributed by 1880, and tenants operated about 37 percent of Texas farms. After the state Supreme Court declared in 1898 that unappropriated public lands were exhausted, that figure jumped to more than 49 percent in 1900, a direct result of the continuing population increase and the devastating depression of the 1890s, and to nearly 52 percent by 1911.

Some were "share tenants," who furnished their own tools, plows, work animals, seed, and food, and bargained over the percentage of the crops that they paid the landowner. In a common arrangement, a tenant farmer would provide the landlord with one-third of the cotton crop and one-fourth of the corn crop ("third and fourth" renters). But others—"halfers" or "croppers"—simply worked for the landlord, providing nothing but their labor in return for the proceeds from one-half of the crop, less any debts they might have accumulated during the year. As one would have expected in a segregated state, most of the share tenants were white, whereas most of the "halfers" were African Americans and Mexicans.

## Number and Value of Cotton Bales, 1900–1932

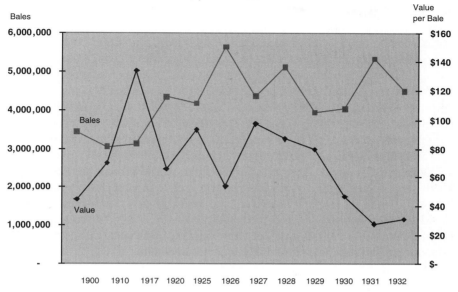

As agricultural prices dropped, farmers and their supporters attempted to organize to improve their conditions. The Renters' Union of North America established more than 200 chapters throughout the state and tried to set rules for tenancy and improve the marketing of agricultural products. Originating in Emory, Texas, in 1902, the Farmers' Union became the 140,000-member Farmers' Educational and Cooperative Union of America (ECUA) by 1914, with a Colored Farmers' Union providing services for African Americans. The ECUA constructed some 1,300 cotton warehouses and marketing cooperatives throughout the state and operated more than 100 cotton gins, but it is best known for the "plowup campaign of 1908," in which it tried to create a shortage of cotton by destroying one-third of the crop. Another result of the increasing number of tenant farmers was the rise of the Socialist Party in Texas. The most successful of all the organizations was the Farm Bureau, more conservative than its forebears and focused on landowners rather than tenants or sharecroppers, but also dedicated to getting more credit for the farmer and helping to sell the crops at the highest prices possible. Ultimately, in terms of the average farmer of the 1920s, they all failed.

### The Lumbering Bonanza

With the huge East Texas forest at its disposal, the state's lumbering industry reached its zenith in 1907, cutting 2.25 billion board feet (a board foot is a square foot of lumber one-inch thick), the third highest production rate in the United

States. Entrepreneurs such as Henry J. Lutcher, G. Bedell Moore, Thomas L. L. Temple, and John Henry Kirby had changed the industry by establishing complete plants and company towns in remote parts of East Texas—Camden, Fostoria, Kirbyville, Diboll—that received the logs from the forest and delivered finished lumber to the railhead. The work was long, difficult, dangerous, and low-paying. The workers averaged about ten hours a day on the job between 1900 and World War I, then nine hours a day until World War II, and only the most skilled employees earned more than a common laborer's pay. In many cases these poor conditions persisted until companies, following a "cut out and get out" policy and expecting the cleared land to become farms, began to exhaust their timber holdings and the industry declined in the 1920s.

Despite the status of agricultural and lumber workers, most people view the 1920s as good economic years. The average Texan's income was almost three-quarters that of the average American, and World War I had increased the demand for lumber (for wooden ships) and boosted the price of cotton to 20.9 cents per pound in 1919. But the relative economic position of the farmer slowly sank during that decade and many forests were decimated.

### The Discovery of Oil

Like other places in the United States, Texas had been home to a modest oil industry for decades before the legendary discovery at Spindletop in 1901. The state's first producing field came in at Corsicana until 1894, and the real estate developers who owned it recruited several Pennsylvania oilmen—James M. Guffey, John H. Galey, and J. S. Cullinan—to help them develop the field, which, by 1900, was producing 836,000 barrels a year. Cullinan built the first refinery in the state there in 1898 to produce primarily kerosene. It was still generally true in 1900 that if a Texan drilled a well, he or she was looking for water, a far more precious substance than oil, especially in the western part of the state.

That began to change on January 10, 1901. The Gladys City Oil, Gas, and Manufacturing Company had been drilling for oil on Spindletop Hill near Beaumont ever since 1893, but they had been foiled by their out-of-date cable-tool drilling rig and the tricky sands of the salt dome formation and had run out of money. Anthony F. Lucas, the leading American expert on salt dome formations, leased the rights from the company and joined in the search in 1899. Initially, he suffered the same fate as the Gladys City company, but, convinced by his experience in Louisiana, he did not give up.

A new rotary drilling technique, combined with Lucas's experience in drilling in salt domes and money from the Mellon banking interests in Pittsburgh, brought success. On January 10, shortly after mud began bubbling from the well, the newly released pressure blew six tons of four-inch drilling pipe from the hole. Everyone watched, stunned, as the well seemed to settle down for a few minutes, then a geyser of mud, gas, and, finally, oil burst out of the hole. The oil spewed more than 100 feet into the air at an estimated rate of 100,000 barrels a day for

Burkburnett, near Wichita Falls, was one of the wildest of the early Texas oil boomtowns in 1918. Here, horse-drawn wagons loaded with tools and equipment jam the roads with a forest of oil derricks in the background. *(Archives Center, National Museum of American History, Smithsonian Institute)*

nine days—until the workers finally managed to cap it. By the time it was brought under control, a huge pool of oil surrounded the well, along with hundreds of oilmen, speculators, and onlookers. Inspired by the Spindletop discovery, wildcatters rushed into every part of the state looking for oil.

The first genuine oil boom in the state greatly expanded the regional economies.

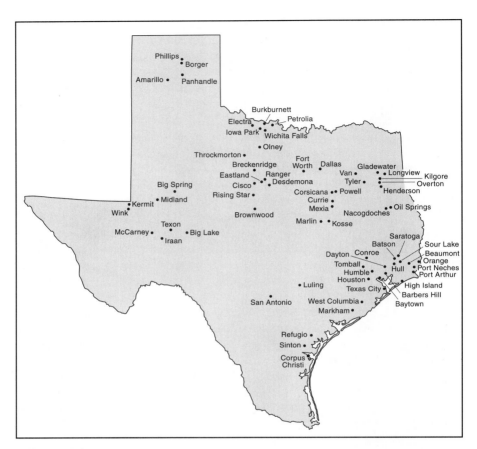

Early Texas oil centers.

Texas had produced approximately 1,000 barrels of oil in 1896; that figure jumped to 21 million in 1902. Thousands of people moved into the area from Houston to Beaumont to Port Arthur, and real estate became more expensive—prohibitively so in some cases. Related manufacturing companies such as machine shops and distribution facilities relocated to the gulf coast. Augmenting the facilities at Galveston, the Houston Ship Channel opened in 1914, the same year that the Panama Canal opened, and Texas began to attract shipping from around the world.

The industry produced new terms and personalities to take their place alongside the cowboy in the pantheon of Texas characters: the "go-for-broke" wildcatter, the hard-working, hard-playing roughneck, and the "get-rich-quick" oilman. These characters were firmly established by the 1920s, but Edna Ferber gave them stereotypical expression in the fictional persona of Jett Rink, a merging of the cowboy and the get-rich-quick oilman, in her popular novel (which became a motion picture) *Giant* (1952).

Wildcatters drilled cheek by jowl with other rigs in boomtowns because there were no laws preventing it; more than 200 derricks rose within the city limits of Breckenridge, with several thousand more in the immediate area. Oil overflowed storage tanks and spilled into streams and polluted the air. There were shortages of food and fuel. Heavy rains and constant oilfield traffic turned dirt roads into mud bogs. When torrential rains fell in Desdemona in 1919, influenza and typhoid quickly reached epidemic proportions. Violent crime accompanied the gambling houses and brothels, and law enforcement officials chained prisoners to trees when jails became overcrowded. When the onslaught overwhelmed city and county services, the state intervened. The governor dispatched the Texas Rangers to Desdemona in 1920, Borger in 1927, and Wink in 1927 and again in 1928 and 1929, and the state militia to Mexia in 1922 and Borger in 1929.

Creation of the vast petrochemical complex on the gulf coast, today one of the world's largest, began soon after the discovery at Spindletop as dozens of small refineries located in the vicinity. In 1902, Guffey established a large refinery there (renamed Gulf Oil Corporation in 1907) to produce kerosene. That same year he and the Texas Company (later Texaco and now Shell) connected the pipelines between Spindletop and their Oklahoma field, and by 1916 Gulf's production capacity reached 50,000 barrels of crude oil per day. Sun Oil Company, Houston Oil Company, and Security Oil Company (a subsidiary of Standard Oil Company, later Magnolia Petroleum Company, one of the forebears of ExxonMobil Corporation) also established sizable installations on the gulf coast.

The state began taxing oil production at the rate of 1 percent of the value of the product in 1905, collecting $101,403 during the first full year of taxation. But by 1919 tax revenues from oil exceeded $1 million, and in 1929 they had reached almost $6 million. The state would become increasingly dependent upon this source of revenue.

## The Climate for Reform

The second factor in building a modern Texas was the political and cultural climate that encouraged development and permitted various reforms to occur. Governor Hogg had introduced significant improvements during his two terms in office; the growing economy, one-party rule, with its inherent factions, and an emerging cultural transformation created an environment in which additional changes could be made; and the election of several progressively minded governors during these years encouraged reform. The major exceptions were two of the state's most famous governors, James E. Ferguson and his wife, Miriam Ferguson, the first woman to be elected governor of the state, and even they seem only mildly retrograde when compared with some of the governors of other southern states.

The cultural change that became apparent in Texas as the twentieth century dawned was important because it permitted Texans to throw off the emotional shackles of the "lost cause," provided them with a positive outlook, and encouraged them to accept modernity in the form of new ideas, including increased participation in and assistance from the federal government.

Historian Walter Buenger says that Texans shifted from an allegiance to the South to an allegiance to Texas itself, which he defines as resembling the American dream in that it contained neither the burden of slavery nor the defeat of the Civil War; the fact that Texans successfully resisted Union invasion during the Civil War enabled many to persist in the belief that they had not been conquered. The commemoration of Texas uniqueness had begun as early as 1886 when orators throughout the state celebrated the fiftieth anniversary of the state's independence, comparing Stephen F. Austin and Sam Houston to George Washington and Thomas Jefferson rather than Robert E. Lee and Jefferson Davis. By 1900 the state had acquired more than 330 acres of the San Jacinto battlefield as a memorial; by 1905 it had purchased additional parts of the Alamo and turned it over to the Daughters of the Republic of Texas to administer as a shrine. And in 1901 artist Henry McArdle loaned his two large paintings of significant moments in Texas history, *Dawn at the Alamo* (1905) and *Battle of San Jacinto* (1895), to the state for exhibition in the new capitol. Today they hang in the Senate chamber and have been reproduced in Texas history books for decades.

At the same time, the Texas State Historical Association, founded in 1897, had begun to publish heroic stories of early Texas in its journal. Later directors of the association, Eugene C. Barker and Walter Prescott Webb, would write great books—Barker's biography of Stephen F. Austin (1926) and Webb's *The Great Plains* (1931) and *The Texas Rangers* (1936)—that focused on the state's westernness rather than its southernness. In 1906, *Dallas Morning News* editorial cartoonist John Knott personified the state in a character that became famous as "Old Man Texas," known for his belief in fiscal responsibility, low taxes, and honesty in government, just as the character of Uncle Sam represents those values for the country as a whole. In addition, generations of schoolchildren learned the history of the state from an enormously popular comic strip, *Texas History Movies*, first published in the *Dallas Morning News* beginning in 1926, then distributed to the schools by Magnolia Petroleum Company for years.

The result, according to Buenger, is that Texans like novelist Walter Humphrey grew up reenacting the battle of the Alamo in their childhood games instead of the battles of Bull Run and Gettysburg. This developing "Texanness" led the state's residents to associate themselves with victory at San Jacinto rather than defeat at Appomattox. It culminated in the state's centennial celebration in Dallas in 1936, by which time cowboys, cowgirls, and the Big Bend mountains had officially replaced planters, southern belles, and East Texas cotton fields as the state's symbols, despite the fact that the state's two largest cities, Houston and Dallas, are in East Texas. By then one could hardly tell if Knott's "Old Man Texas" was an East Texas planter or a West Texas rancher. This does not mean that the cult of Texas exceptionalism had only positive effects, but it did provide the intellectual underpinning for a newer and more positive culture in Texas than in the other Southern states.

Nor did it mean that vestiges of the "bloody shirt," the Southern penchant for recalling Yankee horrors committed during the Civil War, no longer existed, for these years also saw the installation of dozens of Confederate monuments overlooking courthouse squares, parks, and cemeteries throughout the state. Sculptors such as Pompeo Coppini, an Italian who first moved to Texas in 1901, earned their living from commissions such as the Confederate monument on the capitol grounds (1901–03), the statues on the south mall of the University of Texas at Austin, the Confederate soldier in Victoria (1911), and the John H. Reagan Memorial in Palestine (1911), featuring a personification of the "lost cause," a Roman soldier sitting pensively at Reagan's feet, contemplating defeat. In most cases, it meant that Texans saw no conflict in thinking of themselves as both Texan and Southern.

## The Conservatives Take Charge

With the breakup of the Populism movement, the last significant opposition to the Bourbon Democrats faded and the back-to-back elections of Joseph D. Sayers (1899–1903) and Samuel W. T. Lanham (1903–07) as governor and Culberson as senator (1899–1923) confirmed their hold on power. Supported by House and "our crowd," Sayers and Lanham were both former members of the U.S. Congress and were the last two Confederate veterans to serve as governor. Neither Sayers nor Lanham (1903–07) was as reform-minded as Hogg. They were sophisticated men but lacked his transforming zeal and realized that the modernization of Texas depended on the vast oil reserves at Spindletop and the continued exploitation of the East Texas timberlands. In a political party divided by factions, House had virtually negotiated their nominations, almost arguing that their administrations would be "caretaker" administrations rather than proactive ones. As House bluntly put it, "the people wanted no disturbance" in 1902 and Lanham "managed to say nothing in a most convincing and masterly way." The resulting friendly business climate was reflected in a decline in the proportion of farmers in the legislature; both Sayers and Lanham, however, continued to prosecute antitrust violations and, together, brought more cases in Texas than the federal government prosecuted in the entire nation during the same period. Lanham was the last governor that House actively supported before turning his attention to national politics, and, House left behind no real machine or organization because his power was based on personal contacts and influence.

It was also during their administrations that the Bourbon Democrats, with traditional motives as well as a desire for genuine reform, overhauled the state's election laws, which admittedly were a confusing mélange of local laws. Block voting and ballot stuffing were endemic, and the state needed a good system of voter registration. But, disturbed by the fact that the combination of African American Republicans and Populists almost brought victory in 1896, the Democratic legislature moved in 1902 to institutionalize the one-party rule as well as solve the registration problem. The legislature first recommended a constitutional amendment that would permit a poll tax (which passed with a 65 percent majority), then in 1903 enacted a series of "reforms" that encouraged the counties to continue the all-white primaries (which, in this case, was interpreted to include Mexicans as well, to accommodate the South Texas political bosses), made third-party competition more difficult, and established a poll tax that had to be paid six months before the primaries and nine months before the general election.

A majority of middle- and upper-class whites favored the poll tax, as did reformers who reasoned that it would be an efficient way of registering voters and discouraging block voting and manipulation of voters. Former legislator Alexander Watkins Terrell was one of those who had advocated a poll tax for years, and he made clear his intention to prevent "the thriftless, idle and semi-vagrant element of *both races*" from voting. The poll tax did make the job of ward politicians and brewing interests more expensive, but they continued to buy the votes of large blocks of workers, tenant farmers, railroad employees, and opponents of prohibition. And, it was effective in reducing the number of people who voted. Political scientists estimate that at the high tide of Populism, 1896, more than 80 percent of those eligible to vote actually participated in the election. That figure dropped to approximately 35 percent in 1904, the first year the poll tax was enforced, and to less than 25 percent in 1906.

Terrell returned to the legislature in 1903 to offer further reforms that would, at the same time, make it even more difficult for minorities to vote. The stated intent of the laws that bear his name was to standardize voting across the state and eliminate fraud. They required, for example, that all counties hold their conventions on the same day, preventing manipulators such as Colonel House from scheduling early conventions in favorable counties. An even more pervasive law enacted in 1905 required primary elections for those parties that had received at least 100,000 votes in the previous general election (later raised to 200,000, then to 20 percent of the vote) and defined the process by which candidates would be nominated for office as well as who would be permitted to vote. Known collectively as the Terrell election laws, these statutes culminated the Bourbon Democrat effort to institutionalize one-party rule. A disgruntled Republican realized as early as 1912 that "the primary election law . . . [is] so effectual . . . that today, a nomination in the Democratic primaries is tantamount to election."

This revamping of the election law, however, did not include women. The Texas Woman Suffrage Association organized in Houston with the intent of establishing chapters throughout the state, but the group's activities stopped when one of its main leaders, Annette Finnegan, left the state in 1905. A small group in Austin carried on the fight until the movement gained greater public support a few years later. In the meantime, women took pride in the fact that the concerted action of many groups, including the Texas chapter of the Woman's Christian Temperance Union, the Grange, the Texas Federation of Women's Clubs, and the Texas Woman's Press Association, led to the establishment of Texas Woman's University in Denton in 1903.

## Half a Dozen Fights

With its newfound dominance, the Democratic Party became the only serious venue for discussion of the state's social and economic problems. It also became home to a number of factions, that, although based on such strong characteristics as class, race, and ideology, moved in and out of the party from time to time and followed one or another of the charismatic leaders who vied for center stage. Powerful orators such as Senator Joseph W. Bailey and Governor Oscar B. Colquitt attempted to persuade the faithful with regard to issues such as voting, workers' and women's rights, tenancy and land ownership, political corruption, railroad law, regulation of insurance companies, penal and tax reform, antitrust legislation, education, conservation, and creation of a highway system, with no one faction gaining dominance. The astute Jim Hogg had helped the party find a middle ground between the conservative, prorailroad wing and the more radical Populist demands, and Colonel House had negotiated between various factions of the party for another decade. But no such passionate and domineering a figure as Hogg appeared again until an unknown forty-three-year-old independent-minded Temple banker-turned-politician, James E. Ferguson, announced for governor in 1913, and he did so by casting aside the overriding political and cultural issue of the day—prohibition.

Others were not as bold. To Thomas B. Love of Dallas, speaker of the Texas House of Representatives in 1907, and Thomas H. Ball of Houston, who ran against Ferguson for the Democratic gubernatorial nomination, prohibition was a sincere motive, but they also recognized it as an issue that motivated voters. The railroads had submitted to the regulating authority of the Railroad Commission, and other "foreign" corporations had either fled the state or reconciled themselves to Texas's parochial commercial interests. Lacking a genuine corporate bully, urban abuses, or corrupt political bosses (outside of South Texas) to rally against, Texas reformers soon united around the prohibition question. Most, like Love and Ball, were fervent in their conviction, but it was also good politics. The typical Texas resident was white, ethnocentric, conservative, and had roots in the South. He or she also lived in a rural area, farmed, and espoused traditional values, as opposed to the sinful vices associated with the growing cities. That also made them naturally suspicious of racial and ethnic minorities who, it seemed, consistently opposed prohibition.

With no threat to their power, the Democrats could afford these intraparty struggles, but the overriding issue that seemed to cut across all the others was prohibition, which inspired endless debate, with Bible-quoting evangelists such as J. B. Cranfill of Dallas and J. Frank Norris of Fort Worth on one side and on the other the majority of Roman Catholics, members of less evangelical Protestant sects, African Americans, Mexicans, urban dwellers, and Democratic conservatives. "We have only one political party in Texas," Governor Colquitt told a Dallas audience in 1911, "but there are enough political fights in that one for half a dozen."

## Texas and the Federal Government

Even as the Democratic party in Texas reorganized and strengthened itself it was on the verge of bringing Texas to national political prominence. The presidential election of 1912 ushered the Democrats back into the White House and a number of Texans into significant positions in the federal government. Part of this resurgence was due to Colonel House's personal friendship with the new president, Woodrow Wilson of New Jersey, but an equal part of it was the team of talented officeholders that the state sent to Washington. Even before Wilson began his run for the presidency, Texans had elected Morris Sheppard of Pittsburg, in northeast Texas, to the Congress in 1902; he would become a member of the U.S. Senate in 1913. John Nance Garner of Uvalde joined Sheppard in the House in 1903, and he would later become Speaker of the House and vice president under President Franklin D. Roosevelt. Sam Rayburn of Bonham, who would also serve as speaker, joined this distinguished company as a member of Congress in 1912.

Although House played no role in Wilson's nomination—indeed, he had concluded that the governor could not be nominated and suggested to his friend Senator Culberson that he support someone else—the Texas delegation to the Democratic convention in Baltimore did. In a close ballot—and through forty-six roll calls—the Texas delegation, or the "immortal forty," as they became known, remained loyal to Wilson and lobbied others to join them, and Wilson did not forget the Texans. With Colonel House as one of the president's closest advisors, the state found itself in an ideal position to play a major role in the new government.

While he took a much-needed vacation, Wilson left Colonel House to come up with nominations for his cabinet and other appointments. After House recommended a number of Texans, the Lone Star State also found itself in an excellent position to influence federal legislation and programs at the same time as the growing political changes within the state had led Texans to expect more of their government. Texans were pleased to see a Treasury Department that took more interest in the South, and they welcomed the Federal Reserve Act (1913), the Federal Farm Loan Act (1916), aid to agricultural education, lower tariffs, and increased military appropriations in the state as World War I loomed. These federal programs and the largess made the social reforms that often accompanied them a bit more palatable to the conservative state; the coming war in Europe provided the ideal opportunity for Texas to exercise its influence, as army bases were established throughout the state, and Texas oil began to play an important role in the national economy. The state Democratic Party platform of 1920 endorsed the actions of the Wilson administration in direct contradiction to Senator Bailey's lament of the "growing tendency to regulate everything by law."

# Pressure for Reform

Aware of the national campaign to reform government and industry, widely publicized by muckraking journalists such as Lincoln Steffens, Ida M. Tarbell, and

Ray Stannard Baker, Texas reformers, lacking a political base during the years between governors Hogg and Campbell, began at the grass-roots level. A new labor group, the State Federation of Labor, organized in 1898, joined with the even newer Farmers' Union to develop a legislative program and to lobby for its implementation. The Texas Federation of Women's Clubs, founded in 1897 and with more than 230 clubs and more than 5,000 members by 1903, took on other aspects of the Progressive agenda, such as better schools and libraries. The Texas Local Option Association organized in 1903 to defend the state's local option laws, but its members also concerned themselves with moral issues of the day as well as labor and agriculture reforms.

Although different groups focused on different issues, the causes seemed to fall in three areas: monopolistic business practices, individualistic excesses, and social engineering and increasing efficiency. Among the goals on the various reformers' agendas were improving government; ending political corruption; curtailing the influence of large, particularly out-of-state, corporations; and improving all aspects of life, from the farm to the city and from schools to prisons and charitable institutions. The reformers believed that such social goals could be achieved through efficient bureaucracies, the application of scientific research and training, and public education.

But prohibition was, in fact, the dominant issue in Texas politics for much of this period. It cut across political factions and classes and gained additional support when women won the right to vote. Progressives believed that "demon rum" would corrupt a democratic society and the fact that most Germans, Mexicans, and other ethnic groups opposed prohibition only seemed to reinforce the point that it would benefit the Anglo-Saxon society. Having failed in previous attempts at statewide prohibition in 1887 and 1911, antiliquor forces concentrated on local-option laws, vowing to dry up the state one precinct at a time.

The "wets," as those who were against prohibition were called, responded with similar propaganda and organization. Although the wets had prevailed, 237,393 to 231,096, in a statewide election in 1911, they now faced an aroused nation and state. On February 28, 1918, the legislature ratified the Eighteenth Amendment, a prohibition amendment to the U.S. Constitution that outlawed the sale of alcoholic beverages, and immediately enacted a statewide prohibition law.

## Government Reform

One of the first reforms to sweep the state in the twentieth century was a new form of municipal government. Although it was not a result of the devastating hurricane that struck Galveston Island on September 8, 1900, that tragic event, the greatest natural disaster to strike North America, hastened its implementation.

Galveston had been engaged in an all-out civic struggle with Houston for dominance in gulf shipping, but the hurricane tipped the balance decisively in Houston's favor. Nevertheless, the people of Galveston struggled back heroically. Under the leadership of a group of wealthy businessmen, who feared that the city

Walking along the Galveston beach after the storm, with some of the devastation apparent in the background. *(Courtesy of the Rosenberg Library, Galveston, Texas)*

would never recover its prosperity with the current city council, the city changed its governmental structure. The oligarchy devised a plan to elect commissioners at large, rather than from specific wards or precincts. The commissioners would then elect the mayor from among their number, and the commission would be both a policy-making and administrative body: Individual commissioners would also serve as heads of specific departments. The intent of the plan was to bring increased expertise and efficiency to the rebuilding of the city. Progressives did not object to the elite running the city as long as they made the correct decisions.

The effective and businesslike manner in which Galveston recovered from the storm—including building a seventeen-foot seawall on the gulf side of the island, raising the grade level of the city, and building an all-weather bridge to the mainland—caught Governor Campbell's attention, and he encouraged other cities to implement the commission form of government. Houston adopted it in 1905. Dallas, Fort Worth, Denison, Greenville, and El Paso followed in 1907, and by 1920 seventy other Texas cities had implemented the plan along with more than 400 cities nationwide. The Galveston Plan, or the "Texas Idea" as it was known outside the state, continued to spread across the country, but it further eroded minority representation. The at-large elections meant that a majority population could determine the makeup of the entire commission.

## Educational Reforms

One of the most important Progressive goals, second in importance only because of the tragedy at Galveston, was educational reform. In general, there were two types of schools at the turn of the century: common schools, which were usually rural and independently governed by trustees who organized for the purpose of hiring a teacher and operating and maintaining the school, and independent districts that usually resembled the present-day school system. Critics of the common schools usually argued that the one-teacher, one-room rural schools offered an inferior education and proposed consolidating these schools and transporting students to the regional schools at no charge. Progressives, further, insisted upon compulsory attendance, an increase in the tax base, increased teacher qualifications, and free textbooks. They wanted all school districts to use the same books, offer similar courses, and have the same requirements for graduation and teacher certification. They created the new State Board of Education to oversee the curriculum and textbooks.

Because of the state's relative poverty, only a few of the changes could be implemented. A newly created Normal School Board of Regents began oversight of the teacher-training schools. Perhaps the Progressives' major impact on education in the state, however, was a change in philosophy. Progressives advocated practical training, but they also thought education should be more relevant to students' lives and supported curriculum changes that introduced the new social sciences of psychology and sociology. Schools took on additional duties, including supervised recess periods, supervised athletic and academic competitions (under the University Interscholastic League at the University of Texas, 1910), and improved health care. The goal of public schools significantly changed from imparting technical skills to improving the social order. By 1930, white Texans had a wide range of choices for higher education at a relatively low cost, and student enrollment increased more than tenfold from 2,148 in 1900 to 23,134 in 1929.

## Social Reforms

The initial success of the Galveston Plan seemed to indicate that Progressives were right in their contention that science and training could lead to efficiency. They sought further governmental reforms in the areas of prisons, where they hoped to end inhumane treatment, improve health and sanitation, and regularize paroles. They favored segregated facilities so that women would not be housed with men, juvenile offenders with adults, those who had committed minor violations with murderers. The legislature addressed the problem in 1911, ending contract leasing of prisoners in 1912. It established the Gainesville School for Girls in 1917, and transferred the Gatesville School for Boys to the State Board of Control in 1919, with instructions that the school emphasize reform and education. It replaced hanging as the preferred method of execution with the electric chair, thought to be more humane, in 1923, and established the Texas Prison Board in

Minnie Fisher Cunningham (right) became the first woman from Texas to campaign for the U.S. Senate when she ran for the office in 1928. *(PICA 16817 Austin History Center, Austin Public Library)*

1927 to reorganize the system. But Progressives and most Texas citizens wanted the prison system to be self-supporting, so further solutions had to be found.

Because the federal Social Security program had not yet been enacted, other Progressive efforts focused on establishing county poorhouses and hospitals for the indigent and improving conditions in state asylums, and all such organizations were placed under the State Board of Control. Not all the reforms were carried out, because most citizens felt that the state was too poor to support such programs, while other reforms, such as women's suffrage, continued to be defeated at the ballot box. Minnie Fisher Cunningham, Jane Y. McCallum, Annie Webb Blanton, Jessie Daniel Ames, and others worked hard for the cause, unsuccessfully seeking legislative approval of suffrage amendments in 1915 and 1917.

### Good Roads

Although many national issues, such as urban political machines, did not really apply to Texas, others did. In addition to prohibition and women's suffrage, Progressives in Texas also campaigned for good roads and conservation of timber. The demand for good roads emerged around 1910 as the number of automobiles increased. Because the Texas constitution relegated road upkeep and maintenance to the counties, the state had no network of roads and those that did exist were in appalling condition, often being little more than rocky trails that followed along old Indian routes, circled around hills, large trees, and boulders, forded creeks, and zigzagged in right-angle turns along fence-lines. Some stretches of flat road developed a ripple pattern known as the "washboard" and there were no barriers to keep motorists from skidding into ditches along the road or signs to warn of upcoming hazards such as a dip. During the seasonal torrential rains, dirt roads became quagmires and often held water or flowed like a creek on the rise. A publicity-shrouded trans-continental drive sponsored by five Southern newspapers, including the *Dallas Times Herald* and the *Houston Post,* almost came to a halt in 1913 when the automobile became mired in the impassable black gumbo soil of Hill County, en route from Waco to Dallas. The first modern road from Austin to San Antonio was built only when Travis, Hays, Comal, and Béxar counties each agreed in 1914 to pay their share of the $140,000 required to convert the old wagon road to a sixteen-foot wide roadway covered with a foot of gravel. Governor Colquitt "plowed the first furrow for the great highway" behind a "big road plow drawn by six restless mules," according to a reporter for the *New Braunfels Herald,* and the Austin–San Antonio Post Road was completed a year and one-half later.

Advocates of good roads began working in various parts of the state as early as 1903. They organized auto tours, encouraged volunteer road work and posted directional signs for travelers. In 1910 they met at the state fair to promote the idea of a central authority to oversee and maintain a statewide network of roads. Hoping to overcome the traditional objection to centralization of power and to educate both the legislature and citizens of the growing need, they organized the Texas Good Roads Association in 1911. In 1916, the first year of automobile registration, 194,720 Texans registered cars and trucks. But the good road enthusiasts faced formidable opposition, because the county commissioners courts did not have the money to finance the roads and did not want to give up their authority.

The national Progressive agenda came to their rescue, however, as Congress enacted the Federal Aid Road Act in 1916, offering matching funds to all states that created a central planning authority and joined the national highway network. The following year the legislature created the Texas Highway Department (THD), now the Texas Department of Transportation, overseen by a three-member commission appointed by the governor.

### Conservation

The Progressives were not as successful with conservation. Their primary focus was East Texas, where the timber industry had enjoyed outstanding years during the first decade of the century with an average cut of more than 2 billion board feet a year. As World War I came on, lumbering grew to the point that it threatened the very existence of the vast pine forests. W. Goodrich Jones, a Temple banker, led the effort to regulate the timber industry and implement a program of reforestation.

After attending President Theodore Roosevelt's White House Conference of Governors on Conservation in 1908, Jones returned to Texas and organized the Texas Forestry Association, which espoused a statewide program of forest conservation that called for prevention of fire, selective cutting, sustained yield, and reforestation. Because of the Association's encouragement—and Jones's lobbying of fellow Temple resident Governor Jim Ferguson—the legislature established the Texas Department of Forestry as a part of the Agricultural and Mechanical College. Despite much good work on the part of the agency, however, the legislature failed to follow through in other ways. By the 1920s, the intensive lumbering had virtually destroyed the great virgin forests of East Texas, and the boom came to an end. The Progressives got their agency, but it had little power, and by 1932 Texas timber production had decreased to its lowest point since 1880.

## Reformers in Charge

Despite the factionalism, all of the candidates in the 1906 gubernatorial campaign identified themselves as reformers who called for antilobby, antitrust, and protax legislation and support for the state's educational and charitable institutions. With no Colonel House to orchestrate the results, Palestine lawyer Thomas M. Campbell returned to the fray and swept his three primary opponents aside. Although the electorate remained divided on key issues, Campbell's administration, along with the Thirtieth Legislature, became the most reform-oriented government in the state's history. Together, they enacted a number of laws characteristic of reforms throughout the South such as several antirailroad laws that former Governor Hogg supported, an antinepotism law, prolabor laws, antitrust laws, and insurance regulations. During his four years in office, Campbell created a department of agriculture and a library and historical commission and encouraged prison and public school reforms. The Robertson Insurance Law (1907) required insurance companies to invest their policy reserves in the state. Campbell's administration also stopped the contract lease system for prisoners and implemented more humane treatment. Under his administration the legislature even passed a law taxing the intangible assets of corporations, thereby doubling the value of assets on the tax roll. Although he failed in his effort to enact an income tax, Governor Campbell's efforts led to the only major increase in state revenue before oil began to play a major role in the state's economy.

The more conservative Oscar Branch Colquitt (1911–15) continued some of the progressive reforms, such as regulation of child labor, factory safety standards, women's work hours, and the state's first workers' compensation law, when he was elected in 1910. But, unlike Campbell, he was against prohibition and that, along with his pro-German sentiments as World War I approached, alienated many Democrats. Ultimately, Governor Colquitt had to spend most of his time dealing with two problems. One, the tax system, was chronic. As the progressive governors increased spending on the state's institutions, it became apparent that the Texas did not have a broad enough tax base. Colquitt had inherited a $1 million debt from Campbell and, although he had campaigned on the basis of lowering taxes, he soon had to increase them to pay for growth in public education, prisons, and bureaucracies.

The second problem related to the disturbances along the Rio Grande border resulting from economic chaos and revolution in Mexico. Increased numbers of Mexican refugees had been arriving for some time, and events such as the so-called Garza War of 1891, in which journalist Catarino E. Garza became a folk hero by using a base in Texas to launch a rebellion against Mexican President Porfirio Díaz, did nothing to calm the furor. Governor Hogg had called for assistance from the U.S. Army and had sent a small Texas Ranger force to deal with the matter. Garza finally slipped away into exile in Central America, leaving his followers to return to their South Texas and northern Mexican *ranchos*.

Colquitt never felt that the federal government did enough to protect Texas citizens or to keep Mexican insurgents from using Texas as a safe haven to arm themselves and plan their assaults. He sent the Texas National Guard to join the small Ranger force in an effort to maintain control, but the problem flared into open warfare when U.S. troops invaded northern Mexico on at least two different occasions. These incidents resulted in long-standing disputes and hard feelings between the Anglos and Mexicans in South Texas.

## Fergusonism and Texas on the World Stage

The "farmer's friend," James "Pa" Ferguson was a self-made man who aimed his message at the long-suffering rural population of the state. Having been born to a central Texas farm family and found his early employment in the fields and work gangs of backcountry Texas, he understood the problems of country folk. Having moved up in life by combining a law practice with real estate and banking, he understood the needs of an evolving economy. Ferguson and his wife Miriam ("Ma"), who became the first woman governor of the state, despite their shortcomings tended to represent the modern ideals of fair government and greater economic opportunity for most Texans.

### Ferguson's Rise to Power

In shunning prohibition as a rallying cry, James E. Ferguson did not give up the ability to excite voters, for he focused on what he considered to be a greater societal ill and, at the same time, a greater source of support in a state where the political system was still dominated by rural voters. Farm tenancy had occupied the attention of academics and agricultural journals for a number of years, but it had been ignored by state and national governments, despite the organization of the Land Renters' Union of North America in Waco in 1911. Rising land prices and high interest rates made it difficult for tenants to become landowners and move up the economic ladder, and their children toiled in the fields rather than attend school, dooming them to the same fate. "There is something rotten in Texas when over 50 per cent of our farm families are homeless renters," the *Houston Chronicle* editorialized in 1912. The number was 10 percent higher in the state's richest cotton growing area, the Blackland Prairie, where Ferguson grew up. "One of these days" the editor continued, "this issue is going to fly up and hit our lawmakers slap in the face; they'll know they have met it."

The Temple banker would ensure that they would meet it. Ferguson knew the plight of the tenant farmers, although his bank was apparently no more forgiving of their debts than his competition; as one who had worked in the fields himself as a young boy, he understood the hardships and despair of such a life. Although he had studied for a time at Salado College and later passed the bar, his campaign persona belied that heritage, especially when he lapsed into the dialect that his wife, Miriam, the daughter of a well-to-do Bell County farmer, called "country talk."

And he was good at it, an orator who purposely maligned his opponents with a unique mix of bad grammar, acerbity, libel, and wit: "He spoke the language of the corn rows and the vernacular of the country stores," a veteran Austin newspaper editor recalled. He called himself "Farmer Jim" and said he spoke for the "boys at the forks of the creek." His record of opposing local option prohibition in Bell County quickly brought him to the attention of the brewing interests. Like Jim Hogg before him, he co-opted some radical proposals, such as limiting the amount of rent that a landowner could charge a tenant.

Ferguson's second major campaign issue targeted what he considered to be the next most difficult problem that the state faced: a poor educational system that ranked thirty-eighth nationally and lagged in such categories as teacher salaries, spending per student, length of school year, and percentage of school-age children in school. His desire to improve the schools stemmed, again, from his own rural heritage as well as an understanding of his constituency and a conviction that education was one of the skills that could most quickly improve people's lives. In his campaign announcement, he declared that Texans should "buy all the education that we can pay for," beginning with "the little schoolhouse on the country road." Although he also talked about running a "business administration" in Austin, he spent most of his time campaigning in poorer agricultural districts, where he made more than 90 percent of his speeches.

Ferguson used homey props like a gourd and a wooden water bucket in his appearances, and relentlessly attacked the prohibitionist candidate, Thomas H. Ball. Ball was an experienced candidate. He had served in Congress, practiced law in Houston, and seemed the early favorite to win the race. Even veteran observers such as Colonel House felt that he would be the next governor. He fought back as best he could, but his schedule was leisurely compared to Ferguson's, and he could not excite a crowd as "Farmer Jim" could. He accused Ferguson of being under the influence of the Catholic church because he had received the endorsement of a priest in Temple. He quoted the banker as saying that "My pocket book is my principles" and suggested that his dealings with farm clients then belied his campaign on behalf of tenants now. But after hearing Ferguson at a campaign stop in Denton, one observer warned, "his cunning and knowledge of the class to which he is appealing will render him a formidable opponent for Col. Ball."

Even the endorsement of President Wilson and Secretary of State William Jennings Bryan could not save Ball. He did not speak the language of the majority of rural voters who cared more about their economic situation than about prohibition. Also, the brewing interests backed Ferguson with a well-financed campaign to reach voters in urban areas, South Texas, and the German district of Central Texas, claiming that prohibition diverted attention from the state's real problems. Ferguson handily defeated Ball with more than 55 percent of the vote, and his charismatic personality and his "vest-pocket vote" of thousands of tenants, small farmers, and laborers would flavor Texas politics for the next two and a half decades.

Ferguson's first term was relatively harmonious. He fulfilled his campaign pledge by getting a farm tenant bill through the legislature, but it was soon declared unconstitutional. He also followed up on his other main platform pledge with continued educational reform, increased appropriations for higher education, and the creation of a State Department of Forestry.

## Trouble on the Border

There were early rumors of malfeasance on Ferguson's part, but they took a back seat to the continuing disturbances on the border. Reports from South Texas noted an increase in raiding as early as January 1915, but local authorities continued to see the raids as nothing more than "bandit activity" until officials arrested one of the insurrection organizers and discovered the *Plan de San Diego,* a revolutionary charter that called for Hispanics on both sides of the border to rally in a combined revolution and race war. Their goal was to seize the territory that Mexico had lost to the United States in 1848 and to establish an independent republic. The South Texas area was fertile ground for such a movement because it had absorbed literally thousands of Mexican immigrants in the preceding decade as well as an influx of Midwesterners who engaged in citrus farming, bringing about a wrenching transition from a pastoral, ranching economy to commercial agriculture. A way of life had changed, and many Tejanos were displaced in the process, sometimes now working for wages on property that they or their family had once owned. This tragedy was complicated by the revolution in Mexico and World War I, which had begun in Europe in August 1914, and included the threat of German activity in a disrupted Mexico.

The sporadic raids increased in July, and a number of Americans were killed in both Texas and Mexico. Ferguson sent the entire Texas Ranger force to the valley and called for additional U.S. troops. There were probably no more than fifteen or twenty Regular Rangers on the border, but they served as leaders, role models, and participants in the events that followed, supplemented by Ferguson's patronage appointment of many "Special" Rangers, probably including most of the local law enforcement officers. The raids peaked on August 8 when sixty Mexicans carrying a red flag emblazoned with the slogan *Igualdad e Independencia* ("Equality and Independence") attacked Las Norias Division of the King Ranch. The Rangers and local law enforcement officials immediately retaliated with a "systematic manhunt," brutally killing more than 100 Mexicans and perhaps as many as 300 in the process. Ferguson called out the Texas National Guard the following year to supplement federal forces under General John J. Pershing, who ultimately invaded Mexico in an effort to capture Pancho Villa, the Mexican rebel leader who had raided Columbus, New Mexico, on March 9, 1916. Virtually the entire combat-ready American army, almost 50,000 troops, was assigned to the border. As the Mexican Revolution drew to a close, and the United States recognized the Carranza government, the raids came to an end. This suggests, of course, that the raiding was directly related to the situation in Mexico, but the raiders would not have been as successful if conditions in South Texas had not been ripe.

These were tragic years on the border, with much of the Angelo community traumatized by the raiders and the Mexican American community brutalized by the lawless Rangers, Special Rangers, local officials, and vigilante groups who were ill prepared for the overwhelming situation they faced. This reign of terror on the Rio Grande came to an end in 1919, when both a U.S. Senate investigating committee and a legislative committee led by Brownsville representative J. T. Canales documented so many atrocities committed by the Rangers—some sources claim that as many as 5,000 Mexicans had been murdered—that the force was reorganized, or "purified," to use Canales's word, and reduced to four regular companies of seventeen men each.

### Ferguson's Downfall

By contrast, Ferguson's escalating conflict with the University of Texas during his second term might seem trivial, but surprisingly, it, rather than the bloodbath in the valley, led to his impeachment and conviction. As early as 1915 Ferguson had disagreed with acting university president William J. Battle over the university's budget and had accused the startled scholar of duplicity. Battle, of course, was appalled by the governor's charges and resented his micromanagement. When the university's board of regents selected Robert E. Vinson, president of the Austin Presbyterian Theological Seminary, as the new president of the university without consulting the governor, who was courting his own candidate, Ferguson was further angered and determined to oust the university "clique." That summer he inserted a clause in the Democratic Party platform calling for each item in the university budget to be listed separately.

The evolving conflict probably could have been prevented had Ferguson and Battle managed to overcome the initial problem, but it would have been difficult to find two more opposite personalities. Battle was a slender, balding professor of Greek, Ferguson a rough-and-tumble politician who had far more in common with the masses who had elected him than he did with a Harvard-educated classicist. Perhaps Ferguson even harbored an inferiority complex similar to the one President Lyndon Johnson felt regarding the Ivy League graduates in the Kennedy administration. "I knew Battle for perhaps fifteen of his latter years," historian Joe B. Frantz later recalled, "and he was the essence of politeness. But I could never feel quite comfortable in his presence, as if he were measuring me. Jim Ferguson must have felt the same way."

Despite the increasing suspicions of his own financial malfeasance, Ferguson won reelection in 1916 over a lackluster but surprisingly strong candidate, Charles H. Morris of Winnsboro, and then stepped up his charges against the university, demanding the immediate dismissal of six professors whom he accused of forming an "oligarchy." To the board of regents he described the faculty as "tenants at will," and, in answer to a question about why the president of the university and the designated faculty members should be fired, he replied, "I don't have to give any reasons, I am Governor of the State of Texas."

The university was ably defended by a group of ex-students led by forty-three-year-old Will C. Hogg of Houston, son of the former governor and a member of the board of regents. Calling Ferguson a "pothouse politician," he and other ex-students began to gather information about the governor's finances and conduct in office. Others, whom Ferguson had spurned, ignored, or defeated, joined in the fight. The prohibitionists had not forgotten about the way he had embarrassed Colonel Ball, and the Texas Equal Suffrage Association, led by Minnie Fisher Cunningham, and women's clubs all over the state joined in because Ferguson was a staunch opponent of women's suffrage.

But the governor was a formidable opponent. He knew that a legislative committee was looking into his financial affairs, so he began to put them in order. Needing more than $150,000 to repay overdrafts to his old Temple bank, he approached friends in the brewing industry and asked for a loan. Then he launched his attack, calling the university's board of regents to his office on May 28, 1917, to inform them that he was going to veto the university's entire appropriation.

Then, on July 27, the Travis County grand jury indicted Ferguson and some of his aides on charges of embezzlement and misuse of public funds. The Speaker of the House issued what was surely an illegal call for a special session of the legislature to consider charges against the governor, but Ferguson legitimized it by issuing a call himself the day before the legislators got to Austin. Using information gathered by a special committee during the regular session and the grand jury, former attorney general Crane, as special counsel, led the legislature in listing twenty-one charges against Ferguson. Ferguson defended himself for more than two hours before the Senate and wrote an open letter to the public, but the Senate convicted him on ten of the charges, seven of which dealt with his finances. Ferguson resigned rather than submit to impeachment, but the Senate rendered its decision anyway, removing him from office and banning him from holding any future state offices. Ferguson's arrogance in office thoroughly provoked the growing urban, industrial, educated, and more progressive segment of the population. The trends that would shift the residual political power of agrarians to the urban dwellers were already in evidence by 1917. Thus did thirty-nine-year-old William P. Hobby, former journalist and editor from Houston, become governor of Texas on August 25.

"Before the time of Ferguson," wrote the political scientist V. O. Key, Jr., in *Southern Politics,* "elections were contested on issues that held deep meaning for the people of Texas. How the state was to protect its citizens from organizations of wealth, what the state was to undertake by way of public services for its citizens, for what citizens these services were intended, and who should pay the tax bill—these are ultimately the great concerns of democratic government, second only to maintenance of the democratic processes themselves in their importance to the citizenry." After Ferguson, and continuing into the late 1930s, the issue changed to "Fergusonism."

## World War I Brings Change and Reform

Although Europe had gone to war in the summer of 1914, Texans initially saw no reason for the United States to get involved. The state was divided over President Wilson's initial efforts to prepare the nation for possible entry into the war, and many Texans agreed with the *Dallas Morning News* that the state's large German population bore at least a portion of the blame. That conviction intensified in March 1917 with the revelations in the infamous Zimmerman telegram. Alfred Zimmerman, the German foreign secretary, had instructed the German minister in Mexico City that, in the event of war with the United States, the minister should propose an alliance between Germany and Mexico that, if successful, would regain for Mexico all its lost territory in Texas and the Southwest. The British had intercepted the message and given it to Wilson. Coming, as it did, on the heels of the *San Diego* insurrection in South Texas, many Texans interpreted the telegram as confirmation that Mexico had inspired the raids, and it solidified the president's support across the country. Less than a month later, President Wilson called on the United States to enter the war to make the world "safe for democracy."

Almost a million Texans registered for the draft, including 449 women who served as nurses; 197,789 men actually served, and approximately 25 percent of these were African American. More than 5,000 Texans died in the conflict, many as the result of the Spanish influenza epidemic in 1918, and many more were injured. Most of the Texas troops trained at four large camps that the federal government established at Fort Worth, Houston, Waco, and San Antonio. But there were many other training sites in the state as well, such as a basic flight instruction school at the University of Texas. The mild climate and vast amounts of open space also led the government to establish other training facilities for fledgling aviators, the primary one at Kelly Field in San Antonio. Randolph Field, constructed in San Antonio in 1928, became "The West Point of the Air."

On the home front, the legislature acted to help those in the service by compensating them for economic losses while on active duty and forbidding the sale of a serviceman's property until one year after he had been discharged. Another act eliminated the poll tax for servicemen, and the Texas Council of Defense was organized to oversee the efforts of the more than 15,000 county and community defense councils. Unfortunately, some of them also became vigilante groups, harassing people with German names, especially if they refused to purchase war bonds or displayed pictures of the Kaiser in their home. The Socialist newspaper, *The Rebel,* which had attained a circulation of 23,000, was also shut down by government order. Using authority granted by the Hobby Loyalty Law of May 1917, Governor Hobby appointed almost 1,000 Special Rangers, whose primary duty, it seemed, was to insure Hobby's election in 1918.

Although welcome for many reasons, the vast infusion of federal resources also had an adverse effect in that it set off an inflationary spiral that greatly outpaced incomes and more than doubled the cost of some of the new state programs, such as the improved school system. The legislature also acted to limit the negative effects of the large military installations on communities—bars and prostitution—but did nothing to stem the racial tensions that existed. In Huntsville a white mob killed an African American man and six members of his family when he was accused of evading the draft, but an even worse incident occurred in Houston in 1917. The federal government had brought in the Third Battalion of the African American Twenty-fourth U.S. Infantry to guard two military installations that had been established near the newly opened Houston Ship Channel. On August 23, following a summer of growing tensions, a riot broke out with more than 100 armed and mutinous African American soldiers marching on the Fourth Ward police station. Fifteen whites, including five policemen, died, and eleven others were seriously wounded. Four African American soldiers also died, two accidentally shot by their own men. The army quickly removed the troopers to New Mexico, where, under wartime conditions, the military courts handed down harsh punishments: Nineteen soldiers were hanged and sixty-three sentenced to life in prison.

The war revived prohibition efforts in Texas. Prohibitionists called for a ban on alcohol within ten miles of military bases or schools and attacked its manufacture as wasteful in a time of war, its brewers as agents of the German Kaiser, and its effect on military personnel as unhealthy. When Secretary of War Newton D. Baker let it be known that the government would continue to send large numbers of soldiers to Texas bases if they insured "conditions of cleanliness and wholesomeness" nearby, Hobby submitted these new rules to a special session of the legislature in February 1918. With a majority in both houses of the legislature, the drys first approved a bill relating to military bases, then ratified the prohibition amendment (the Eighteenth Amendment) to the U.S. Constitution, which went into effect in 1919. From the depths of disappointment over the Ferguson victory in 1914, the drys had now put the finishing touches on nationwide prohibition.

Finally, the legislature amended the election law to require a runoff in primaries if no candidate received a majority and to extend the right to vote in primaries to women. The drafting of large numbers of men for World War I helped the women's suffrage movement nationwide. With so many men in the military, numerous home-front jobs opened up for women, and their new wartime responsibilities gave the movement impetus, even eliciting President Wilson's less than ardent support. After the legislature extended women the right to vote in primaries, Annie Webb Blanton was elected state superintendent of education, but women would have to wait until the Nineteenth Amendment to the Constitution was ratified, in 1920, before they could vote in the general election.

The enthusiasm from that special session carried Hobby through the 1918 gubernatorial election. Despite his impeachment and conviction, "Farmer Jim" Ferguson was on the ballot. His allies on the party's executive committee allowed him to run and he was still able to inspire an audience of farmers. After a slow start, however, Hobby proved to be an able campaigner, and his run took on the aspects of a patriotic rally. With prohibitionists and suffragists strongly behind him, he received a total of 461,479 votes to Ferguson's 217,012. No runoff was necessary.

The war came to a close a couple of months later, on November 11, when the Allies and the Germans signed the armistice. It had brought a measure of prosperity to Texas, as cotton production soared, but it had also brought a growing cultural conformity as the drive to unite a heterogeneous population for war continued long after the peace. The legislature made it a crime to criticize the U.S. government, the flag, the war effort, or soldiers' uniforms, and required that schools teach patriotism, fly the American flag, and teach all classes except foreign language classes in English. In 1919 Hobby vetoed the appropriation for the German department at the University of Texas, and most high schools dropped the language from their curriculum. The 1917 Russian Revolution had called the public's attention to what many perceived as a growing Bolshevik threat, and many Texans believed that union and civil rights activists were evidence of the menace at home. Oil producers rumored that a 1917–18 oilfield workers strike in Louisiana and Texas was inspired by the Industrial Workers of the World, and a violent and prolonged dock strike in Galveston led Governor Hobby to place the city under martial law. Lynchings and intimidation of African Americans continued as well; there was a race riot in Longview and an official of the National Association for the Advancement of Colored People (NAACP) was beaten by a white mob in Austin during what became known nationwide as the "red summer" of 1919.

By 1920, the population shift from rural to urban areas was becoming apparent. Meanwhile, the economic difficulties of farmers were temporarily obscured by two years of abundant crops that helped make up for the falling postwar prices. Governor Hobby would have encouraged the urban growth and economy but declined to do so in the face of a reluctant legislature and a "leave well enough alone" public attitude.

But that was not because the state did not have problems. Lynching was on the decline but still occurring from time to time, and economic refugees were arriving from Mexico in ever-increasing numbers, with perhaps as many as 126,811 settling in Texas between 1910 and 1920. The burgeoning oil and gas industry had spawned some swindlers and the usual lawlessness that, on occasion, required the intervention of the Texas Rangers and, on at least one occasion, the Texas National Guard; the cause of most of the crime, however, was undoubtedly the Volstead Act of 1919, which implemented the new prohibition amendment.

The decade of the 1920s soon became known throughout the nation as the Jazz Age, which was defined by the rise of cities, the decline of religion (coupled with the teaching of evolution), bootleggers and speakeasies, the growth of the Socialist Party and the "red scare," increased European immigration, and the advent of the "New Woman." And perhaps the prototypical Jazz Age flapper was Gordon Conway, born in Cleburne and reared in Dallas. An extremely productive commercial graphic artist and costume designer for stage and film in New York, London, and Paris, Conway produced paintings and drawings of the New Woman for *Vogue, Vanity Fair, Harper's Bazaar,* and many other publications, including her hometown newspapers, from World War I into the Depression. Conway's New Woman was, in many ways, a parody of New York society women involved in charity work, but the new type caught on. The New Woman and the flapper became icons of the 1920s.

## The Elements of Jazz

From the hard-scrabble cultures of the cotton farms and lumber mills of East and Central Texas came one of the truly American forms of music, jazz, which, because of its varied folk roots, has been called a true expression of democracy. One strand of jazz can be traced to Texarkana in the 1880s, when Scott Joplin, a young son of a former slave, learned music from a German teacher and began to perform in medicine shows and vaudeville. Joplin, composer and pianist, known as the "father of ragtime," developed his musical talent in the saloons and brothels of Saint Louis, Missouri, and named his best-known composition, the "Maple Leaf Rag," after an employer, the Maple Leaf Club in Sedalia, Missouri. "Maple Leaf Rag" included some of the syncopated rhythms and structure that would later be incorporated into jazz. Joplin's music was featured in the soundtrack of the 1973 Hollywood movie *The Sting,* and he was posthumously awarded a Pulitzer Prize in 1976 for *Treemonisha,* the first grand opera by an African American. Another ragtime composer from Texas, Euday L. Bowman of Fort Worth, composed "Twelfth Street Rag" sometime around 1915, which trumpeter Louis Armstrong made famous with his 1927 recording. And Eddie Durham of San Marcos, who played in a number of regional bands during the 1920s before moving on to Kansas City and New York City, perhaps contributed as much to jazz history as any other Texas musician.

A second strand of jazz is the blues, which can be traced to East Texas as early as 1890 and is represented by two of its most famous practitioners, Blind Lemon

Jefferson (1897–1929) and Huddie "Leadbelly" Ledbetter (1888–1949), who were active in the 1920s and actually played together for a while in the Deep Ellum district of Dallas. A third strand was "barrelhouse-style piano," perhaps better known as boogie-woogie, which probably came out of the lumber camps of East Texas. Itinerant musicians and traveling bands spread these various musical styles along the railroad tracks, in the prisons, and in the communities. Because of the rural nature of the state, many of these performers and composers moved to Kansas City, where they were among the first generation to compose, perform, and record jazz.

Another icon of the Jazz Age was the lawlessness accompanying the oil boom that gained nationwide publicity as the veterans returned from World War I. The oil boom only hastened the migration from rural to urban areas, and Texans were quick to display the decline of moral values that was supposedly going on throughout the nation. Less than a year after passage of prohibition, bootlegging was so widespread in Texas that a still with a 130-gallon capacity was found on the Austin-area farm of U.S. Senator Morris Sheppard, the author of the Eighteenth Amendment.

### Reaction to Reform: The Ku Klux Klan

The Achilles' heel of the Progressive movement—indeed, of virtually all political movements of the day—was racism. During the early part of the twentieth century the rights that African Americans had gained after the Civil War were systematically taken away. Shocked by the near-success of the Populist Party coalition of poor African American and white farmers, the Bourbon Democrats had embarked upon a campaign to divide the poor by claiming that African Americans were inherently inferior and a threat to society. Their goal was to segregate African Americans into a separate society, divided by law and custom and governed by leaders for whom they could not vote. They largely succeeded.

There were 670,722 African Americans in Texas by 1900, 854,964 by 1930, most of them living in rural areas and working as tenants and farm laborers. But others had attempted to escape the racial and economic conditions of rural life by moving out of the state—to northern cities and to Louisiana and Oklahoma—or to Texas cities such as Houston and Dallas. The urban African American population increased from 19 percent in 1900 to 32 percent in 1930; the number of African American males employed in nonagricultural jobs increased from 57,000 to almost 115,000 during that same period, most still in manual labor or servant jobs. Ministers and teachers made up most of a small African American bourgeoisie that also consisted of doctors, dentists, lawyers, and undertakers. There were more than 1,700 African American–owned retail stores in the state in 1929, most of them mom-and-pop operations such as grocery stores, drugstores, and restaurants. Hobart Taylor, Sr., of Houston, who invested in insurance and taxicabs, may have been the first African American millionaire in the state. Prairie View A&M offered courses for African Americans at both the high school and college level, with emphasis on technical, agricultural, and educational training.

The Ku Klux Klan reached a membership of approximately 90,000 in Texas during the 1920s. Here, the Klan is shown parading in Beaumont on November 10, 1922. *(Tyrrell Historical Library, Beaumont, Texas)*

The first step toward racial segregation had occurred when the Redeemers won control of the state government in 1876. The second step was African American disenfranchisement, accomplished by the Terrell election laws. When the Supreme Court, in *Nixon v. Herndon* (1927), agreed that all-white primaries violated the Fourteenth Amendment, Texas responded by defining political parties as private organizations that could select their own qualified voters. The court agreed, and African Americans remained effectively shut out of the electoral process.

Next came the segregation of public facilities. Passenger trains had been segregated by race as early as 1891. In 1910 and 1911 the legislature required the establishment of separate waiting rooms in railroad stations and separate drinking fountains and restrooms in public facilities. Several cities adopted residential segregation laws after 1910, but the U.S. Supreme Court invalidated them. Cities got around the Court by resorting to zoning regulations. That led to a degradation of health and recreational services and city services such as utilities, paving, and police protection in the African American areas. By the 1930s, African Americans could no longer attend sports or cultural events, eat at restaurants, or stay in hotels unless those facilities provided separate accommodations. Although these laws were not passed with the Mexican population in mind, community cultural mores often denied Mexicans many services and opportunities.

Where laws did not sufficiently enforce segregation, vigilante action often did. The Ku Klux Klan of the 1920s was a relic of Reconstruction. William Joseph Simmons, an ex-Methodist minister near Atlanta, Georgia, reorganized the Klan in 1915 as an antidote to what he perceived as moral deterioration and a lack of patriotism. He sent field representatives (kleagles) to organize new chapters (klaverns) throughout the nation and by 1922 the Klan had more than 700,000 members, by 1925 perhaps as many as 5 million. Its militant fundamentalism and anti-Catholicism appealed to many in the South and the Midwest, including progressive reformers in the urban areas, where the new middle class, usually with rural values still intact, identified with the Klan's goals. With issues such as prohibition foremost in society, the Klan attracted progressive reformers who did not object to enforcing a moral code so long as it was theirs. Thomas B. Love of Dallas, who had supported Wilson for the presidency, characterized the Klan as "made up almost wholly of misled and misguided good people who are on the moral side of moral questions and on the progressive side of economic questions" who would quickly grow tired of the effort. The Klan moved into Texas in 1920.

The Klan gained many adherents in North, East, and Central Texas. Membership was not nearly so high in heavily Catholic South Texas. Despite the fact that the Klan resorted to such extralegal practices as flogging, tar-and-feathering, and branding to enforce its will (there were more than fifty cases of Klan violence during 1921 alone), many prominent citizens, including Governor Neff, refused to speak out against it. With oil boomtowns bursting out of control on occasion and the Mexican Revolution troubles on the border, the Klan claimed that unparalleled lawlessness forced it to act, and Governor Neff seemed to agree. By playing on fears aroused by race riots, labor disruptions, and rumors of Bolshevik influence, the "invisible empire" gained many members; by 1922 these members included a sympathetic U.S. Senator, Earle B. Mayfield, who triumphed over "Farmer Jim" Ferguson in a bitter contest.

With prohibition now law, the Klan itself became the main issue in Texas politics during the early 1920s, as major newspapers in Dallas, Houston, and El Paso attacked it. As Imperial Wizard of the Klan, Hiram W. Evans of Dallas instituted a policy of political action rather than violence and intimidation. The Klan denied responsibility for any of the lynchings that took place during these years, but it is likely that the emotionalism and moral passion of its rallies incited them, at the very least. Miriam Ferguson's victory in the 1924 governor's race over the Klan-backed candidate for governor, Felix D. Robertson of Dallas—the choice between "a bonnet or a hood"—marked the end of significant Klan influence in Texas politics.

## The Fergusons Return

The "business progressivism" of Governors Hobby and Neff had provided Texans with a respite from "Fergusonism," but Miriam Ferguson signaled a return to the populism of her husband. Miriam Ferguson won the election because the cult of personality continued to dominate the Democratic Party in 1924, and the dominant personality of the last decade had been her husband, "Farmer Jim" Ferguson. Ferguson had continued to publish his newspaper, *Ferguson's Forum*, ever

Miriam Ferguson, the first woman to be elected governor of Texas, delivering her inaugural address in the House chamber on January 20, 1925. *(The Institute of Texan Cultures at University of Texas, San Antonio)*

since his impeachment, claiming that the major newspapers had "submarined the truth." Still able to energize a rural audience, he had run for president on the American Party ticket in 1920 and for senator in 1922. Although he clearly disagreed with the Klan on the issue of prohibition, the 1922 election may have been the first time that he ran afoul of the organization. Unable to get his name on the Democratic primary ballot in 1924, he came up with the ruse of running his wife, Miriam, and the main issues of the campaign became prohibition and the Klan itself in another insulting, mud-slinging contest. He stumped the state on behalf of his wife, proclaiming "two governors for the price of one" and referring to Imperial Wizard Evans as the "Grand Gizzard." Again, the prohibition candidate was no match for the crafty veteran, and Miriam Ferguson won the primary runoff by almost 100,000 votes.

Once in office, and with her husband at her side, Mrs. Ferguson struck back at the Klan, securing passage of a law that prohibited the wearing of masks in public. She vetoed a number of line items in the University of Texas appropriation and granted more than 2,000 paroles, pardons, and extensions, many of which went to prohibition violators. She lamented the fact that most of those convicted of such violations were poor whereas the wealthy continued to have access to drink in their private clubs and she offered a $500 reward for the arrest and conviction of any liquor-law violator who had property worth more than $5,000. But her term was also tainted by charges of graft and scandal. "Pa," it seems, acted as attorney for many of the successful pardons that she granted and saw to it that state contracts for school textbooks and highway construction were awarded to those who bought ads in the *Ferguson Forum*. A final irony may have been the fact that most people who supported the vote for women expected them to clean up corruption in politics, but Miriam Ferguson's election put her cunning and scandal-plagued husband back in power. Attorney General Dan Moody successfully brought suit to cancel a number of highway contracts that had been awarded to Ferguson friends and allies.

Those charges proved to be the basis of Moody's successful campaign against Miriam Ferguson in 1926. The main issue was "Fergusonism" and corruption, and the self-styled liberals in the Democratic Party rallied to Moody's reform banner. Moody was a personable, thirty-two-year-old who had successively been elected to office as the Williamson County attorney, district attorney of the Twenty-sixth Judicial District, and attorney general. With his business-progressive point of view, he set about reorganizing several government departments. He led an ostensibly prosperous and increasingly urban state for four years as it sank, along with the nation, into the worst depression that the country has ever known. Few noticed that 1929, the same year that the New York stock market crashed, was also the first year in which the value of crude oil production in Texas ($322,520,000) exceeded the value of the cotton crop ($315,200,000).

## Conclusion

In 1929, Texans seemed about to enjoy the rewards of more than two decades of reform and progress. Farming and ranching had certainly suffered during the 1920s, but that was largely disguised by the booming economy nationwide and the growing influence of oil on the state's economy. Prohibition was now a national law, thanks, in part, to platoons of righteous women voters. The "business progressives" had apparently beaten back the Fergusons, and the state seemed to be coming of age in other ways. Progressive historians at the University of Texas led the way in investigating the state's past with the founding of the *Southwestern Historical Quarterly* in 1897. George Pierce Garrison began teaching the first course in Texas history that year, and two and a half decades later his protégé, Eugene C. Barker, published his classic biography of Stephen F. Austin. At the same time, Paris-trained Dallas artist Frank Reaugh was leading his students on summer expeditions into West Texas and extolling the virtues of interpreting the Texas landscape. Most Texans were outraged at the publication of Dorothy Scarborough's novel, *The Wind* (1925), because of its haunting and inhospitable portrait of West Texas. They took pride, however, in the work of one of the state's most distinguished writers of fiction, Katherine Anne Porter, who grew up in Kyle and San Antonio, but whose Texas-based short stories gained her international fame.

## SUGGESTED READINGS

Useful general studies of the first three decades of the century include Lewis L. Gould, *Progressives and Prohibitionists: Texas Democrats in the Wilson Era* (1992); Walter L. Buenger's *The Path to a Modern South: Northeast Texas Between Reconstruction and the Great Depression* (2001); and Seth S. McKay and Odie B. Faulk, *Texas After Spindletop* (1965).

### The Texas Economy

Works on economic history include Donald E. Green, *Land of the Underground Rain: Irrigation on the Texas High Plains, 1910–1970* (1973), and Diana Davids Olien and Roger M. Olien, *Oil in Texas: The Gusher Age, 1895–1945* (2002).

### The Climate for Reform

A useful work on politics and reform is Evan Anders, *Boss Rule in South Texas: The Progressive Era* (1982). The best work on the Galveston storm of 1900 is Erik Larson, *Isaac's Storm: A Man, a Time, and the Deadliest Hurricane in History* (2000). Excellent works on urban history include David G. McComb, *Galveston, A History* (1986); McComb, *Houston: A History* (1986); David C. Humphrey, *Austin, an Illustrated History* (1985); and Patricia Everidge Hill, *Dallas: The Making of a Modern City* (1996).

### Ferguson and Texas on the World Stage

Norman D. Brown, *Hood, Bonnet, and Little Brown Jug: Texas Politics, 1921–1928* (1984) contains an excellent discussion of much of the Ferguson era. For information on the border troubles, see Don M. Coerver and Linda B. Hall, *Texas and the Mexican Revolution: A Study in State and National Border Policy, 1910–1920* (1984), and David Montejano, *Anglos and Mexicans in the Making of Texas, 1836–1986* (1987). Works on women and minorities include Judith N. McArthur, *Creating the New Woman: The Rise of Southern Women's Progressive Culture in Texas, 1893–1918* (1998); Alwyn Barr, *Black Texans: A History of African Americans in Texas, 1528–1995* (1996); and Arnoldo De León, *Mexican Americans in Texas: A Brief History,* 2nd ed. (1999). For information on the Texas Rangers, see Robert M. Utley, *Lone Star Justice: The First Century of the Texas Rangers* (2002). Biographical essays on Edward M. House, Morris Sheppard, John Nance Garner, Tom Connally, and Sam Rayburn are included in Kenneth E. Hendrickson, Jr. and Micael L. Collins, Eds., *Profiles in Power: Twentieth-Century Texans in Washington* (1993).

# 12

# Depression and War, 1929–1945

"In 1929, my father was employed as a locomotive engineer," recalled Robert Ozment of the years just before the Great Depression struck. Ozment and his family lived in Temple, a Central Texas farming and railroad center. "We had a new Overland Whippet auto, were buying a home, had money in the bank, and plenty of food and clothing. By 1933 all this was gone except the Whippet. We were living in a rent-free house which bordered the Negro section of Temple. We often had little to eat but oatmeal, we were without electricity, and had few clothes. I remember this house well because it had no coverings on the splintery old floors. My one pair of shoes had to be saved for winter use, and during the summer my feet were constantly bandaged from the . . . splinters.

"I also remember the Whippet. We had no money for either gas or tires so it just sat in the shed. It became a kind of physical symbol of the times to me because, like some of the humans, it was waiting [for] a chance to go to work and did not understand why it could not. All it could do was to waste away its productive years waiting and hoping until the inexorable end should arrive. We sold it for five dollars in 1939 . . .

"I once asked my mother what had caused the depression they talked about so much. Considering the fact that neither we nor any of our family were farmers, her answer may seem a bit peculiar. She said: 'The bottom fell out of the cotton market.' To a person living in Bell County, it was just that simple: the bottom fell out of the cotton market. I was just old enough to remember the physical deprivations which my family suffered," he concluded, "but none of the psychological trauma."

| 1929 | New York stock market crashes; LULAC founded |
| 1930 | East Texas oil field discovered; price of oil falls to 8 cents per barrel |
| 1931 | Price of cotton falls to 5 cents per pound |
| 1933 | Eighteenth Amendment is repealed |
| 1935 | Texas repeals its prohibition law |
| 1936 | Texas Centennial |
| 1937 | Soil Conservation Service recorded 72 dust storms on the plains |
| 1938 | U.S. Congressman Martin Dies becomes the first chair of the House Un-American Activities Committee |
| 1941 | Japanese attack Pearl Harbor, U.S. enters World War II |
| 1942 | Bracero program adopted |
| 1943 | "Big Inch" pipeline completed |
| 1944 | "Little Inch" pipeline completed; Texas's all-white primary held to be unconstitutional by the U.S. Supreme Court |

In 1945, Texas emerged from World War II fully industrialized and one of the most rapidly growing urban areas in the nation. The two economic dynamos—oil and agriculture—continued to propel the state forward, and the federal government became even more important during the turbulent years from 1930 to 1945. During these years, Texas and the nation faced two of their greatest challenges—the Great Depression and World War II—and the state's inability to act forcefully to combat the ravages of the depression required the federal government to play an even more significant role than it had. But another force, almost as powerful as the economy, according to some, was the sense of Texas chauvinism and modernism that emerged in the midst of the Great Depression of the 1930s and was celebrated at the centennial of Texas independence in 1936. It was a chauvinism based on the state's colorful history and honed in the hard work on a thousand cotton fields, ranches, and oil fields.

As the presidential election of 1928 approached, many Texans reflected on the good economic times of the Roaring Twenties, when the state's population had increased by almost 25 percent, to more than 5.8 million and cotton, lumber, truck and citrus farming, livestock, and oil and gas fueled the economy, apparently more efficiently than ever. By 1929 the state was the world's leading supplier of crude oil, having produced more than 2 billion barrels, and the development of the Houston Ship Channel had made that city the state's busiest port. Electrical appliances, lights, radios, telephones, and plumbing facilities had greatly improved urban life, and several Texas cities—Dallas, Houston, and San Antonio—were among the most rapidly growing in the country. The number of automobiles, which facilitated the move to urban areas, increased to the point that Texans owned one car for every 4.3 residents. Such affluence led to talk of "Coolidge prosperity," after President Calvin Coolidge (1925–29), and the general feeling that the nation had created a permanent cornucopia.

## The Great Depression

But the economy had a soft underbelly. Texas farmers, like those of other states, had suffered hard times throughout the seemingly prosperous decade. Farmers had not adjusted their production at the end of World War I and quickly accumulated surpluses that brought a sharp decline in prices in 1920–21. Instead of reducing production, they increased it. The number of Texas farms increased from 436,038 to 495,489, and the amount of cultivated land grew by 3.5 million acres, while at the same time, printed notices of sheriff's sales, business failures, and bankruptcies became characteristic of the farm country, and newspaper editors resorted to homilies—"many a family that has lost its car has found its soul. . . ."

Few people were aware of the nation's deeper economic problems. Inequitable distribution of wealth, with a mere 2 percent of the population controlling 28 percent of the wealth whereas the bottom 60 percent controlled only about 24 percent, was only one of the harbingers of the coming difficulties. But economic crisis was hardly on the minds of Texans as they went to the polls in 1928 to vote against a wet Catholic and for a continuation of the good times. The Democrats had nominated Governor Alfred E. Smith of New York, a Catholic and an antiprohibitionist, at their Houston convention, but Texans voted *en masse* for Herbert Hoover, the first Republican presidential candidate to carry the state.

## The Stock Market Crash

Before Hoover had completed his first year in office, however, the failing economy grabbed the nation's attention in a spectacular way: The New York Stock Exchange crashed. The steady advance of the market, which had begun in the mid-1920s and encouraged many investors to speculate by purchasing stocks on margin (with borrowed money), came to an end in September, 1929, and only got worse throughout October. "Black Thursday," October 24, was bad, but the worst occurred on October 29, when 16 million shares of stock, more than ever before, changed hands and the *New York Times* industrial average dropped nearly forty

San Antonio bank depositors wait for access to their safety-deposit boxes at City-Central Bank and Trust on October 1, 1931, the first day they were allowed access to their boxes after the bank failed to open on September 28. The City-Central Bank and Trust was one of 298 U.S. banks that failed that month. *(The Institute of Texan Cultures at University of Texas, San Antonio)*

points. A coalition of New York bankers tried but could not stem the tide, and by November exchange listings had declined an average of 37.5 percent. Because relatively few of them owned stock, Texans felt insulated from the troubles of the market. They seemed to agree with the editor of the *Taylor Daily Press,* who said that his concern was "Jim Rural" and "Joe Normal," whom he expected would continue to do business as usual, and with the editor of the *Houston Post-Dispatch,* who suggested that "the changes in stock prices are purely an affair of and for stock speculators." Governor Moody finished his term in office without feeling the full force of the coming depression or taking any action to prepare for it.

Nor was the economy the chief concern of voters in the gubernatorial election of 1930. Citing his need to enter the private practice of law to pay his debts, Governor Moody declined to run for a third term, and Ross S. Sterling, a founder and former president of Humble Oil and Refining Company, carried the business-progressive mantle in the campaign. His primary opponent was former governor Miriam Ferguson, who filed after the state Supreme Court had refused to let her husband put his name on the ballot.

Sterling called for prison reform, better roads and labor conditions, and more support for education. His service as Moody's able chair of the State Highway Commission led him to champion a $300–$350 million bond issue for state highways. James Ferguson, who did most of the campaigning for his wife, initially did not take seriously the heavy-set Sterling, who had once been introduced to an audience as "your fat boy from Houston," and Miriam Ferguson led Sterling in the primary by more than 70,000 votes. But personalities came to the fore as she and Sterling met in the runoff. The added influence of former Governor Moody and other officials, who announced for Sterling and began making speeches on his behalf, pushed him to victory, and he won by almost 90,000 votes.

## The Depression Deepens

The election was, however, a sideshow to the main event, as cotton prices continued to fall and unemployment soared. The Hoover administration offered little more than the appearance of action—an endless series of meetings, each of which seemed to culminate with hollow statements of confidence that "prosperity is just around the corner." The optimism continued into 1931, with the *Fort Worth Star-Telegram,* for example, claiming that Texans did not "know what hard times are," and pointing to increased construction, railroad traffic, and oil production, and stable cattle and poultry sales. Even as late as 1933, Jesse H. Jones, the Houston banker whom President Hoover had appointed to the board of the Reconstruction Finance Corporation, told a Dallas audience that, "The most important thing before the nation today is to balance the budget."

In Temple, meanwhile, the impact of the Wall Street crash came in 1930—sooner than anyone had expected—when the local banks began to lay off experienced employees. As early as January, 1930, labor union officers asked San Antonio officials to vote bonds to provide work for the growing number of unemployed construction workers, and in Houston a local news vendor reported that his business was up because people who "don't look like they have much more than the price of a newspaper in their pockets . . . are buying them now to read the want ads." New oil softened the blow in a few places such as Taylor and Kilgore, but in Midland oil prices crashed because of overproduction in the East Texas field, which led to declining leases and drilling and more unemployment. The population of Midland dropped by perhaps 1,000 between 1930 and 1932. Between Black Thursday and 1932, more than 5,000 banks failed and 100,000 businesses closed nationwide, and the national income was halved—from $80 billion to $40 billion.

By 1933 more than 7 percent of Texas families were on relief, compared to 10 percent nationally. The number in Texas increased to about 13 percent the following year. Some historians have suggested that rural Texans did not suffer as much as city dwellers because they had gardens and continued to raise much of their food. But, as the economy faltered, the average wage paid for the backbreaking labor of picking cotton dropped from $1.21 per 100 pounds in 1928 to 44 cents in 1931. By then farmers had other concerns as well. "I did not go to . . . [church tonight]," William G. DeLoach of Crosby County in the Texas Panhandle recorded in his diary in 1931. "I am afraid to go. That is[,] all of us go away at night. Some people are losing their canned goods. We have quite a lot of foods of different kinds canned up, can't afford to take a chance on some road tramp coming here and getting it, so I stayed home."

Family and friends initially rallied to help those who fell victim to unemployment, and when their resources were expended, private charities helped out. When charitable funds were depleted, only the local and state governments remained to help. Some cities established public works programs to offer temporary aid to the unemployed, but usually tried to limit it to local residents. Midland and other cities sent police officers to train stations to make sure that transients got back on the train. Houston, meanwhile, reserved relief for whites, denying it to African Americans and Mexican Americans. A typical "buy at home" campaign urged Austinites to "talk Austin, write about Austin, work for Austin, and live for Austin." School districts and retail merchant associations issued scrip when they ran out of money. Some school districts refused to employ single women and, on the assumption of only one breadwinner per family, fired married women if their spouse had a job. Finally, the depression became so severe that only the federal government stood between the country and complete collapse.

## The Dust Bowl

Even if the depression did take longer to arrive in Texas than in other parts of the country, it was no less devastating. Conditions on the farm got even worse as a combination of poor land maintenance and a devastating drought created what became known as the Dust Bowl on the Great Plains. Growing numbers of enthusiastic young farmers had moved onto the plains since the turn of the century,

Dust storm rolls into Spearman, Hansford County, in April 1935. *(The Texas Collection, Baylor University, Waco, Texas)*

and in just a few years, through cattle raising and row-crop agriculture, they had destroyed most of the native grasses that held the dirt in place. Between 1925 and 1930, with the new gasoline tractors, entrepreneurs like the movie mogul Hickman Price, who in 1929 established a fifty-four-square-mile factory farm in Swisher County, plowed up the vegetation on millions of acres of the Southern Plains in what one writer has called "the great plow-up."

The rain stopped abruptly in late 1931, and one of the periodic droughts that plague the semiarid region set in and lasted through 1934. But this was not an ordinary drought. With almost 33 million acres of plains land bare and open to the characteristically high winds, the phenomenon known as the Dust Bowl began. The onset of a polar air mass that might, in an ordinary year, have produced common "sand blows" now incited "black blizzards" that were sometimes accompanied by fantastic displays of lightning. Atmospheric electricity lifted the windblown dirt as high as 7,000–8,000 feet—until it looked like a winter blizzard or a huge thunderstorm. In 1932 the Soil Conservation Service counted fourteen dust storms on the plains. That number increased to thirty-eight in 1933, twenty-two in 1934, forty in 1935, sixty-eight in 1936, and seventy-two in 1937, the worst year on record.

The storm of April 1935 was the worst. As it blew in on April 9, William De-Loach recorded that visibility fell to 200–300 yards. His family remained in the house for several days. On Sunday, while the rest of the family was at church and he sat reading, the worst of the storm hit: "One could hardly get breath," he wrote.

The well-known photographer Dorothea Lange made this photograph of a young cotton picker in South Texas in August 1936. *(Library of Congress, Prints & Photographs Division, FSA/OWI Collection, LC-USF34-009828-E)*

"I thought I would choke when I went to bed." Even in Austin, legislators and staff wore gauze face masks in the capital.

Thousands of tenants and sharecroppers, and even some landowners, gave up and left. Many joined the exodus to California, a trek that John Steinbeck made famous in his novel *The Grapes of Wrath* (1939). But a large number of the Dust Bowl migrants were not victims of drought, windstorm, and grasshoppers. A number of them were tenants who had been forced off the land by tractors and wage laborers; others had been replaced by Mexican laborers who had been im- migrating northward in increasing numbers since the turn of the century and were willing to work for less. The net result was a reduction of almost 200,000 in the number of people living on farms in Texas between 1930 and 1940.

Even in the face of such tragedies, Governor Sterling apparently agreed with the Hoover administration that his first responsibility as governor was to re- duce the state's expenses. He vetoed a number of bills passed by the forty-second legislature, usually because they did not provide taxes to cover their costs. Despite the fact that the legislature met for 131 days, little was done to assist in the state's crisis during what was characterized as a "do-nothing session." This pay-as-you-go approach was traditional in Texas, and the state constitution required it.

## Chaos in the East Texas Oil Field

Sterling's greatest concerns were the state's two largest economic engines—oil and agriculture—and, ironically, overproduction was the problem in both cases. Overproduction of oil was a problem even before Sterling took office. By 1930, oil had been discovered all over Texas, and the new wells in the Yates field in West Texas were so productive that many industry experts began to warn of overproduction. Then, in October 1930, Columbus Marion (Dad) Joiner brought in the Daisy Bradford No. 3 near Kilgore and the boom was on. The East Texas field was even bigger than Spindletop. Within two years it boasted more than 10,000 producing wells, and the price of oil fell from a little over a dollar a barrel in 1930 to eight cents a barrel in 1931. In the peak year of 1933 the East Texas production reached 204,954,000 barrels of oil, more than the rest of the state combined.

The East Texas field was an anomaly for at least two reasons. The first was its sheer size. Within a few months of Joiner's discovery, successful wells had been drilled into this huge reservoir in five counties spread over 140,000 acres. Experts estimated that it contained about 5.5 billion barrels of oil, approximately one-third of the nation's then-known oil reserves.

The second anomaly—the absence of major oil companies—brought a new element into the industry. This field became known as "the promised land of independent producers and small royalty owners," and they, along with entrepreneurs, swindlers, prostitutes, hustlers of all kinds, gathered around the oil field workers in Kilgore, the center of most of the activity. When the wildcatters realized that they were not drilling in separate fields, as they had thought, but into one giant pool, the frenzy began in earnest. The rule of capture—the law governing the development of oil fields ever since a Pennsylvania Supreme Court decision in 1889—meant that the person who pumped the oil owned it, even if it had migrated from an adjoining lease. Landowners began to sell leases that were measured in feet rather than acres, and, ultimately, one city block in Kilgore contained forty-four wells. The massive overproduction soon forced the price of oil down, and kept it down, as the unusual circumstances of this particular field ensured that everyone would continue to drill and pump as fast as they could. No one would agree to limit production unless they all did.

Governor Sterling first suggested that the Railroad Commission act, under the authority granted by the legislature in 1917. But the problem was not easily resolved. Conservationists and the major oil companies were concerned that unrestrained production not only wasted natural resources but also threatened the very existence of the East Texas field by reducing the internal pressure that made the oil flow. The independent producers refused to stop pumping, because their survival was at stake. Most of them were operating on a shoestring or on borrowed money, and slowing down or stopping would have meant bankruptcy. Second, they suspected the motives of the major producers, whose reserves would diminish significantly in value if the price of oil remained low. The independents argued that such restrictions were not for the sake of conservation, but were, in fact, illegal price fixing.

The Railroad Commission initially ordered production limited to about 1,000 barrels per day at each well, but a federal court struck down the order on the grounds that it was price fixing. Through three special sessions in the summer of 1931 the legislature was unable to reach a solution. In the meantime, the major producers, who owned the refineries, stopped buying East Texas oil, claiming that they did not need it. The independents established "teakettle" refineries and their own gasoline stations. Finally, with more than a million barrels of oil a day pouring from the East Texas field, and agreement among the operators apparently not possible, Governor Sterling declared martial law in four counties and sent in the National Guard. The fact that he was a former president of Humble Oil and that the National Guard commander in the field, General Jacob F. Walters, was an attorney for the Texas Company gave the independents grounds to doubt the state's objectivity in the matter.

The "hot" oil, that is, oil produced in violation of the Railroad Commission's orders, continued to flow, and the secrecy required to circumvent the National Guard also made it extremely difficult to determine the amount of oil produced, who owned it, and whether correct royalties were being paid. In another special session, in the fall of 1932, the legislature authorized the Railroad Commission to prorate production according to market demands and in 1932, at the request of Ernest O. Thompson, chair of the Railroad Commission, the governor sent a force of Texas Rangers to stop the flow of hot oil.

The chaos in the East Texas field was the immediate impetus for Roosevelt's secretary of the interior, Harold Ickes, to propose federal control of the oil industry. As he saw it, the price of oil needed to be higher in the interest of the country's financial recovery, so the unchecked flow of hot oil constituted a problem for the country as well as the industry. His efforts at federal control met fierce resistance, particularly among the independent oil producers whose point of view was well represented by the Texas congressional delegation. By 1933 the Rangers had restored some measure of order to the East Texas field, and in January 1934 a federal court upheld the Railroad Commission's right to prorate oil production. But it was not until later that year, with the establishment of the Federal Tender Board and the threat of prison, that the flow of hot oil declined sharply. When the Supreme Court declared unconstitutional the National Recovery Administration, under whose auspices the federal government had acted, Texas Senator Tom Connally sponsored the Connally Hot Oil Act of 1935 specifically to make interstate transportation of hot oil illegal.

Within a few years, most of the small independents had sold out to the stronger, better-capitalized major producers, who owned 80 percent of the East

Texas field by the time World War II broke out. Later in the century, when the Organization of Petroleum Exporting Countries (OPEC) nations were struggling to control their own overproduction, they found their model for stabilizing the international price of oil in the Texas Railroad Commission. Sterling had dealt successfully with the East Texas oil crisis, but in doing so he had alienated large numbers of East Texas voters.

### Agricultural Overproduction

Sterling's other problem grew out of the continuing agricultural depression. The price of cotton, already low at 9–10 cents per pound in 1930, fell drastically in 1931, bottoming out at around 5 cents per pound that fall. The prices of other commodities fell as well, but not as much. The net result was that farmers' purchasing power was about one-third of what it had been before World War I.

The problem would not have been as severe if Texas farmers had been more diversified or had voluntarily limited production. They had tried several different marketing cooperatives, including the Federal Farm Board and the Texas Marketing Association, both of which failed in the face of the 1931 crop of more than 17 million bales of cotton nationally (5.32 million in Texas), the second largest in history.

Any action to limit Texas cotton producers would have failed without the cooperation of the other cotton-producing states, so, in response to a joint resolution of the legislature, Sterling called a governor's conference for the summer of 1931 to try to come up with a plan for unified action. Five states sent representatives, who agreed to limit cotton production if Texas would. During one of the special sessions of 1931, the legislature passed a law limiting the 1932 cotton acreage to 30 percent of the 1931 crop. Most farmers simply ignored the law, and a few days later the courts held it to be unconstitutional. The 1932 yield in Texas alone was 4.5 million bales.

### Fergusonism Revived

James Ferguson, an astute and veteran observer of the political scene, concluded that 1932 could be a good "Ferguson year," and Miriam Ferguson filed to run against Sterling, along with seven other candidates. As always with the Fergusons, personalities rather than issues seemed to inspire the voters. The Fergusons accused the wealthy Sterling of trying to buy the election, of misusing the highway fund, and employing political allies in the highway department. Sterling accused them of voter fraud, and probably with reason. The Ferguson strongholds of East Texas issued only 359,667 poll tax receipts, but reported that 397,386 votes were cast in the July primary. Sterling lost the runoff by fewer than 4,000 votes out of almost 1 million cast, but was unable to get the fourth special session of the legislature to investigate the election or to get the Supreme Court to keep Miriam Ferguson's name off the general election ballot.

Miriam Ferguson accomplished little during her second term because the legislature was wary of all proposals that she presented, and because the early efforts of newly elected President Franklin D. Roosevelt to deal with the depression overshadowed and preempted state actions. She resumed her policy of liberally pardoning prisoners and turned the Texas Rangers into a form of political patronage by appointing 2,344 "Special Rangers." Plans to consolidate state agencies and reorganize the state's higher education system failed. The Twenty-first Amendment to the U.S. Constitution, which repealed the Eighteenth Amendment and once again left the management of alcoholic beverages up to state and local officials, was ratified in December 1933, but Texas did not repeal its prohibition amendment until August 1935. Essentially, the depression had overwhelmed local, state, and private efforts, and, with the election of Franklin D. Roosevelt in 1932, Texas, along with the rest of the nation pinned its hopes for recovery on the federal government.

## The New Deal

We know in hindsight that no president could have prevented the depression or quickly returned the nation to prosperity, but President Hoover's lackluster personality and political ineptness made him a ready scapegoat, and Texans were ready to return to the Democratic fold in 1932. "Truly, I have been hit hard," one penitent voter wrote, "but I deserve no sympathy, I voted for Hoover." When Speaker of the U.S. House of Representatives John Nance Garner of Uvalde accepted second place on the ticket with Roosevelt, that sealed the deal as far as Texans were concerned: More than 88 percent of the state's voters supported Roosevelt and Garner in their call for a "New Deal for the American people."

With Garner as vice president and de facto head of the Texas delegation, the state was well positioned within the federal government. Some historians consider Garner to have been the most powerful vice president in history, because, as a former Speaker of the House who knew virtually every legislator personally, he wielded enormous influence. Sam Rayburn, the congressman from Bonham and Garner's long-time associate and protégé, headed the Interstate and Foreign Commerce Committee. Six other Texans chaired House committees, and in the Senate Tom Connally chaired Public Buildings and Grounds and Morris Sheppard headed Military Affairs. In addition, Roosevelt elevated Hoover-appointee Jesse Jones to the chair of the Reconstruction Finance Corporation (RFC), which soon became one of the most powerful agencies in Washington.

Congress structured the RFC as an independent agency, but in reality it was a government bank that made loans, received repayment of loans, and earned interest, and, from time to time, added to its capital. The RFC funded some of the most significant New Deal agencies, but perhaps the most important thing it did was save the banking system itself by purchasing preferred stock in threatened banks. Of course, Jones gained support in Congress by funding a pet project on occasion, but his real source of power was Garner and the Texas delegation, who usually stood united on the important issues. By January 1936 the RFC had disbursed more than $8 billion, received $3.2 billion, and earned $294 million in interest.

All of these federal programs had an impact on Texas. The Federal Emergency Relief Administration provided funds for direct relief as well as work relief. RFC money went to banks and to state and local bodies for relief efforts; because of the requirement that the state governments share the burden, Texans had to amend the 1876 Constitution so that the state could provide $20 million in matching "bread bonds" to feed the hungry. Other programs provided jobs: The Civilian Conservation Corps; the National Youth Administration, directed for awhile by the young Lyndon B. Johnson; the Federal Emergency Administration for Public Works; and the Works Progress Administration employed thousands of Texans. The federal dollars went for relief, for civic construction projects, and for culture. Interviewers paid by the federal government documented the lives of literally thousands of Texans—former slaves, old cowboys, Indians, and pioneer residents in all parts of the state—and federally funded artists painted and sculpted historically based public art works for courthouses and post offices throughout the state. All told, the federal government, through public works and relief programs, invested some $351,023,546 in Texas between 1933 and 1936. State and local funds provided another $80,268,595 in assistance.

Unfortunately, many of the poor received little help. Programs that encouraged lower production in an effort to forestall sinking prices for the farmer drove up the price of food for the consumer, making it difficult for those below the poverty line to maintain an adequate diet; Mexican American and African American families were among those who suffered the most. Programs that rewarded owners for taking land out of production and mechanizing their farms drove tenants off the land. Meanwhile, although there was a higher percentage of African American workers on relief than white workers, African American workers in Houston received 25 percent less per month than whites. Some relief agencies placed African American workers only in unskilled jobs, and others would not hire them at all. These agencies also denied Mexicans work on the grounds that they were not citizens. At the same time, because of large-scale unemployment, the federal government undertook a deportation campaign. All told, perhaps as many as half a million Mexicans were deported from the United States during the 1930s, with almost half of that number coming from Texas. Despite widespread discrimination, some agencies had a better record than others—the National Youth Administration under Lyndon Johnson, for example—and the New Deal caught the attention of Texas African Americans, who realized that the Democratic Party of Franklin Roosevelt, despite the wage differentials and hiring discrimination, would offer them more opportunity for economic relief than the Republicans.

In 1934, Texas Attorney General James V. Allred campaigned for governor by identifying with Roosevelt and the New Deal. Although conservative criticism of the president and his programs had begun to surface, Roosevelt still had the support of a huge majority of Texans. And Allred, who had come to public attention as an opponent of out-of-state monopolies and political lobbies, probably had better name recognition than any of his opponents after Miriam Ferguson declined to run, as she said, because of the two-term tradition. The evangelical Allred attracted attention, one Houston reporter likening him to an actor with expert political and oratorical skills. Nevertheless, his call for a Public Utilities Commission, restrictions on lobbies, and a modest tax on chain stores to limit out-of-state competition did not arouse large numbers of voters. A reporter for the *Austin Statesman* claimed that most voters had responded with a "wide yawn." A *New York Times* correspondent called the response "apathetic." Allred led the first primary over five other candidates, but he knew that he had a fight on his hands against Tom Hunter, an independent oil man who was the runner-up.

Allred had been emphasizing his opposition to federal control of the oil industry with the slogan that "Texans should rule Texas." In an effort to increase voter interest in the runoff, he decided to make Jim Ferguson an issue. Although "Ma" Ferguson did not run, "Pa" had actively supported Charles C. McDonald, a former Texas secretary of state, and switched his support to Hunter for the runoff. Allred began to interest the voters when he charged that Hunter had made a corrupt bargain to gain the former governor's support. In the two weeks before the runoff, Allred managed to associate Hunter with a sales tax proposal and edged him out by only about 40,000 votes out of more than 950,000 cast.

## A New Image for Texas

One of Allred's more enjoyable duties as governor was to preside over the Texas Centennial in 1936. The main celebration took place in Dallas, but the Centennial was acclaimed all over the state as a watershed event for a society on the cusp of a modernized economy as well as a mature concept of itself. The voters approved a constitutional amendment to establish the Texas Centennial Commission in 1932, and Governor Ferguson appointed the first commission in June 1934. Because it presented the best-funded and best-organized proposal, Dallas was chosen as the site of the official celebration over what many people considered the more historically interesting cities of Houston, near the site of the battle of San Jacinto, and San Antonio, home of the Alamo.

The primary goals of the Centennial, to introduce Texas to the world and to bring out-of-state tourists to Texas, suggested to the committee that the state needed a public relations makeover. Believing that most people thought of Texas as a primitive, frontier area, or as an extension of the culturally and economically backward South, the committee decided to take advantage of the state's romantic history and myth. It was then that, in the words of Centennial historian Kenneth B. Ragsdale, "ten-gallon hats, six-shooters, high-heeled boots, Texas Rangers, bluebonnets, and sex" became the icons of the celebration. The committee's success was assured when Texan Janice Jarratt, the model regularly seen throughout the nation in newspaper and magazine ads as the Chesterfield cigarettes girl, agreed

Governor James Allred tries on a new pair of cowboy boots in preparation for the Texas Centennial in 1936. *(Austin History Center, Austin Public Library)*

to be the "Sweetheart of the Texas Centennial." A picture of her dressed in western style and waving the official Centennial hat on the patio of the spanish Governor's palace in San Antonio was displayed all over the state.

The Centennial itself opened on June 6 and carried out this theme in its most popular attraction, *The Cavalcade of Texas,* a historical pageant depicting four centuries of Texas history. The *Cavalcade* was an instant hit, selling out two performances a day and playing before 60,000–70,000 people a week. Children who had grown up playing the battles of the Alamo and San Jacinto and cowboys and Indians now had a fully articulated historical myth of their own to celebrate. That image was further popularized in what was probably the best-attended attraction outside the main Centennial celebration, the Billy Rose–produced extravaganza in Fort Worth, featuring the "Frontier Follies," the "Winning of the West," and the stripper Sally Rand. "Let Dallas . . . educate the people," the always-quotable Rose told reporters. "We'll entertain them in Fort Worth."

Nor did the focus on Texas history and legend fade away with the passing of the Centennial: The Texas Centennial Commission placed a marker in every county indicating the date of its establishment and the source of its name. Historical buildings and museums received assistance, and new ones were established,

Janice Jarrett was the poster girl for the Texas Centennial celebrations of 1936. Cover of "Pictorial Parade of Texas," published by the Texas Centennial Committee. *(From the Gov. James V. Allred Papers Courtesy of Special Collections & Archives, University of Houston Libraries)*

including the Texas Memorial Museum at Austin, the Sam Houston Memorial Museum at Huntsville, the Corpus Christi Centennial Museum, the El Paso Centennial Museum, the West Texas Museum at Lubbock, the Big Bend Historical Museum at Alpine, and the San Jacinto Monument near Houston. In many ways, the Centennial personified the new Texas identity as a part of the West, and scholarly publications such as Walter Prescott Webb's *The Great Plains* and *The Texas Rangers,* lent academic credibility to it, and the Texan producer/director King Vidor made a popular movie of *The Texas Rangers* in 1936.

### Recovery from the Depression

On the political front, Allred had to face the grim realities of the depression. He fulfilled one of his campaign promises when the legislature approved the chain store tax in 1935 during the first of three special sessions, but the primary problem with his initiatives was that the state lacked sufficient money to fund them. Another problem was that many of the New Deal programs that offered assistance—such as the Social Security Act of 1935—required matching state funds, which meant that the federal government dictated much of the governor's tax agenda. The act established the Social Security program that we know today, funded by both the employee and the employer, as well as federal-state programs to cover unemployment insurance, care of dependent mothers, children, disabled and blind persons, public health services, and a pension to assist destitute persons over age sixty-five.

Another problem was the violence that sprang from a society in turmoil. It seems to have begun with the agricultural slump of the 1920s, prohibition, the revival of the Klan, labor and industrial conflict, and the wild and lawless oil boom towns like Kilgore, Desdemona, Mexia, Wink, and Borger, followed by a nationwide depression. There were bootleggers in every county, gambling in most Texas cities, and a series of bank robberies and other crimes throughout the state. At the same time, Miriam Ferguson's election in 1924 and again in 1932 brought a return of her husband's practice of appointing Special Rangers—"a contemptible lot by any standard," according to one historian—who soon became more a part of the problem than the solution.

With the exploits of John Dillinger, Pretty Boy Floyd, and others making headlines throughout the Midwest, Texas too seemed plagued by an epidemic of such infamous criminals as George "Machine-Gun" Kelly, Raymond Hamilton (who made two successful prison breaks), and Clyde Barrow and Bonnie Parker in the Dallas–Fort Worth area, and the Whitey Walker gang in Central Texas, who robbed and murdered apparently at will. State and local authorities seemed outwitted and outgunned, and most Texans were aware of the problem: "A Ranger commission and a nickel can get you a cup of coffee anywhere in Texas," one newspaper editor sardonically remarked. The situation was so bad that in May 1934 Governor Ferguson was forced to go outside the Texas Rangers, to Senior Captain Frank Hamer, who had resigned in protest when she was elected, to find a man to track down Bonnie and Clyde.

The Texas Centennial did not aid law enforcement officials either. As Dallas geared up for the celebration, newspaper publisher and civic leader Amon Carter, Sr. of Fort Worth allegedly reached an accommodation with the liquor control board that would permit the open sale of liquor at the well-publicized "Frontier Follies," which he and others in Fort Worth had organized to compete with the official centennial in Dallas. Not wanting to be upstaged, Dallas officials decided to "open up" their city so they could compete with "Cow Town."

When Allred took office in early 1935, he understood that reorganization of the state's law enforcement agency was one of his most urgent tasks. He immediately proposed a bill creating the Texas Department of Public Safety, which would consist of a new three-person Public Safety Commission to oversee the Texas Rangers, the Highway Patrol, and the Headquarters Division in Austin, which was to be a new, modern scientific crime laboratory. The Fergusons had left the Rangers in complete disarray, and one of the first acts of the new commission was to rehire the Rangers who had been fired and give them tenure. The commissioners also established standards for the operation of the agency.

Recovery from the depression continued to dominate Allred's agenda after he was reelected in 1936. An Allred-backed state constitutional amendment permitting establishment of an old-age pension passed handily that fall, so one of his first goals was to get the pensions funded. The state had estimated that there might be about 63,000 people eligible for pensions, but by the fall of 1936, 81,000 applications had already been filed, and the commission administering the program estimated that number might go as high as 125,000. The state tightened the eligibility requirements, but still lacked funding for such a large program, so Allred opted for a middle course, advocating pensions only for the needy elderly. Most of the money for his plan came from increased taxes on liquor. When Allred proposed new taxes on oil, gas, carbon black, and sulfur to cover other needed programs, the legislature balked. He had to call two special sessions of the legislature in 1936 to work out the details of the program. Even so, when Allred declined to run for another term in 1938 and accepted appointment as a federal judge, the state was $19 million in debt.

## The Impact of Radio and Old-Age Pensions

As the 1938 gubernatorial race got underway, thirteen candidates announced for the office. Attorney General William McCraw was the early favorite in what appeared to be a routine race, but the political establishment had no idea that the state's politics were about to be turned upside down. In May of that year, a Fort Worth flour salesman, Wilbert Lee O'Daniel, who had been advertising and performing for several years on a radio program that featured country-and-western music, told his audience that several listeners had written him suggesting that he run for governor. He feigned lack of interest in the idea, but asked members of the audience to write him if they thought he should run. After receiving more than 54,000 letters in one week, O'Daniel announced that he was a candidate for governor. In keeping with the homilies that he delivered on his program, he claimed that his motto would be the Golden Rule and his platform the Ten Commandments.

O'Daniel was not the hillbilly that he portrayed on his radio program. An Ohio native, he had moved to Fort Worth in 1925 to become general manager of a milling company. He discovered the potential of the relatively new medium of radio when he fired the "hillbilly" band, the Light Crust Doughboys—including the creator of "western swing," Bob Wills—that performed on a program his company sponsored. Thousands of fans wrote requesting that the show be put back on the air. O'Daniel did not like the band's music, but he recognized the opportunity. He rehired the Light Crust Doughboys, took over as master of ceremonies for the program, moved it to the strongest radio station in the area, WBAP in Fort Worth, and put it on the Texas Quality Network during the prime-time noon hour each day. After being fired from his general manager job, O'Daniel organized his own band, the Hillbilly Boys, and was soon selling "Hillbilly Flour" under his own label. His program began with a woman's voice asking, "Please, pass the biscuits, Pappy," and O'Daniel was soon known throughout the state as "Pappy."

Texas politicians underestimated W. Lee O'Daniel's bid for governorship because they did not realize how popular he was because of the radio. The placement of this huge, cabinet-model radio in the middle of this Hidalgo County couple's living room in 1939 suggests its importance. Photograph by Russell Lee. *(Library of Congress, Prints & Photographs Division, FSA/ OWI Collection, LC-USF34-TO1-032010-D)*

O'Daniel would not have been such a political surprise if politicians had taken note of the impact of the new medium of radio. President Roosevelt had proved its power while he was still governor of New York, and his fireside chats as president had become legendary throughout the 1930s. But commercial radio had only come to Texas in the early 1920s and had spread slowly because of the rural nature of the state; even by 1940 some sections of Texas still had no broadcasting stations, and fewer than 1 percent of the residents of the Hill Country, for example, had radios in their homes. Politicians had begun to use radio in their campaigns—Allred had made liberal use of it in his 1934 campaign—but apparently it had no demonstrable impact on elections.

O'Daniel's program, on the other hand, consisted of hillbilly music, homely stories, advice on family life, and maudlin poems such as "The Boy Who Never Got Too Old to Comb His Mother's Hair," and became one of the most popular programs on the air. Although he was a bit aloof, even austere, in person, O'Daniel affected a folksy voice that worked on the radio; he even composed and sang his own songs, such as "Beautiful Texas" and "Put Me in Your Pocket." O'Daniel had

O'Daniel campaigning for governor in 1938. *(Jimmie A. Dodd Photograph Collection, 1937–1966, CN 08129, The Center for American History, The University of Texas at Austin)*

never thought seriously about politics and probably considered himself a performer rather than anything else but by the time he ran for governor he may have been, according to some political observers, the best-known personality in Texas because of the popularity of radio. Roy Bedichek, who traveled frequently in his job as head of the University Interscholastic League at the University of Texas, recalled seeing men all over the state "slapping their thighs with delight around filling station radios" as they listened to O'Daniel.

Once in the race, O'Daniel employed the same showmanship in his political campaign that he had in his flour business. He fitted out an old bus with a loudspeaker and, with his hillbilly band, traveled from town to town, drawing thousands of people at every stop. After entertaining the crowd with music, he would launch into his stump speech, proclaiming that he was for "less Johnson grass and politicians; more smokestacks and businessmen." Then he would ask for contributions to his campaign, and his daughter would walk through the crowd with collection plates that had been made in the form of barrels labeled "Flour—Not Pork." Some doubted that he was serious about the race—at one point he told a reporter, "I don't know whether or not I'll get elected, but boy! It sure is good for the flour business"—and few realized that it was all an act, that some of his most unpretentious comments and much of the campaign itself was the product of the fertile and expert mind of Dallas public relations executive Phil Fox.

The other candidates initially underestimated the attraction the voters had for "Pappy." When it became clear that he was a serious candidate, the opposition began to ridicule him as "the big town hillbilly candidate" and "the banjo man from Fort Worth." But he handled the attacks with aplomb. When a reporter asked how he would govern under his platform of the Ten Commandments, O'Daniel smiled and said, "Well, take the fourth commandment, Honor Thy Father and Thy Mother: Doesn't that mean old-age pensions just as plain as day?" The increasingly large crowds loved it. Former chair of the Railroad Commission, Ernest O. Thompson, who had been one of the favorites in the race, confessed that he "didn't even see O'Daniel. The first thing I knew he passed all of us and left me with a cloud of flour dust in my eyes."

Even an old pro like "Farmer Jim" Ferguson, who sat out this race, had to be impressed. O'Daniel conducted his campaign like an old-time religious revival, holding the rallies outside, "basking in God's sunlight." And he presented the issues in the same way as the camp meeting preacher: They were black or white, you were for him or against him, good for Texas or bad for Texas. Having never paid a poll tax or voted, O'Daniel called for abolition of the poll tax and capital punishment. Novelist George Sessions Perry of Rockdale aptly remarked that had O'Daniel "been even slightly less astute, had he made a slightly less careful analysis of his own talents and the emotional requirements of his constituents, he might very well have gone on the road with a medicine show." O'Daniel won without a runoff in one of the biggest upsets in state history, with his largest majorities coming from the WBAP listening area around Fort Worth.

## The Conservative Backlash

Although O'Daniel appeared to some to be little more than a popular personality, his homilies cloaked his conservative agenda. He invoked President Roosevelt's name on the campaign trail, but in reality was more representative of the remnants of the Jeffersonian Democrats, a conservative group that had organized in an almost fatalistic attempt to defeat Roosevelt in 1936. The Jeffersonian Democrats adamantly opposed the "court packing" plan and saw the attempted purge of anti-Roosevelt Democratic members of Congress in 1938 as un-American. As some measure of prosperity returned to the middle class, their message of limited government, lower taxes, and individual freedom gained adherents. Knowing that they had no chance as a third party, however, they worked against New Deal programs and candidates from within the Democratic Party; they undoubtedly played a role in the 1938 defeat of liberal congressman Maury Maverick of San Antonio and in the return to Congress of Martin Dies of Orange, initially a Roosevelt supporter but now chair of the House Un-American Activities Committee (HUAC), an ardent anti–New Dealer. Men of such stripe were O'Daniel's friends, advisors, and supporters.

Congressman Martin Dies, speaking perhaps in San Antonio in 1940, established and chaired the House Un-American Activities Committee (HUAC) until 1945. *(Courtesy of Sam Houston Regional Library and Research Center)*

Because of the deficit that O'Daniel had inherited from the Allred administration, everyone realized that taxation would be the dominant issue of his term. The state was still trying to catch up with its side of the funding under the Social Security Act, which had grown to $48–$60 million, but was so poor that members of the House had sat through the last legislative session with umbrellas when it rained because there was no money to repair the capitol roof. It was clear that the governor and the legislature would have to work together to come up with that much new money.

O'Daniel had denounced a sales tax during the campaign but had not revealed where he would find the money to cover the deficit or the pensions that he had promised, and speculation began to spread that he would endorse an income tax. He waited until his inaugural, which attracted a crowd of approximately 60,000 to the University of Texas Memorial Stadium in January 1939, to unveil his plans for a "transactions tax" of 1.6 percent. It was a thinly disguised and regressive sales tax, of course, something that he had condemned during the campaign. He also scaled back on his primary campaign platform of universal old-age pensions to assistance for those over age sixty-five who did not have an income of at least $30 per month. Unable to get even these modest measures through the legislature, he identified those who opposed him in his folksy Sunday morning radio addresses from the porch of the governor's mansion, and the legislature soon was inundated with warnings from voters that the lawmakers should quit playing politics and support the governor. His tax plan had no chance of passing, but many of those who opposed him either did not run in the next election or were defeated.

Meanwhile, claiming lack of funds, he vetoed money for new buildings at state hospitals and cut more than 50 percent from the state Highway Department's budget. He slashed the Texas Rangers' budget to the point that they had to borrow bullets from Highway Patrol officers. O'Daniel began appointing ultra-conservative businesspeople to the University of Texas Board of Regents with the intent of gaining control of the university without enduring the public drubbing that Ferguson had suffered. The plan would come to fruition under his successor, Coke Stevenson, when the conservatives took over the board and fired several professors before dismissing President Homer P. Rainey himself. The legislative session ended with no tax bill and an increase of some $10 million in the state's deficit.

# World War II

War came to Europe in the fall of 1939 with a suddenness that few in Texas anticipated. There had been adequate warnings: Japan had invaded Manchuria in 1931 and China in 1937 and had gradually expanded its influence over the western Pacific. In the meantime, Germany, bristling under the onus of its World War I defeat and subsequent treaties, began its regeneration under Chancellor Adolf Hitler, while Benito Mussolini took power in Italy. Italy attacked Ethiopia in 1936, and the following year Germany successively occupied Austria, the Sudentenland (German-speaking Czechoslovakia), and Czechoslovakia itself. But it was the German invasion of Poland in 1939 that began the European phase of the war, and in April 1940, the German blitzkrieg overcame Denmark, Holland, and Belgium. France fell only a few weeks later. Then Hitler turned his bombers toward Britain.

## Texans and National Politics

As President Roosevelt struggled with the delicate task of helping Britain while at the same time preparing a reluctant nation for war, he also had to decide whether he would seek a third term. O'Daniel faced a similar decision about his own political future in Texas. But, unlike Roosevelt, whose sense of duty called, O'Daniel's failure to accomplish even the more modest of his platform goals seemed to diminish his interest in reelection. Indeed, his poor performance inspired several challengers. The old veteran, "Pa" Ferguson, believed that the governor had made such a mess of things that "Ma," now almost sixty-five years old, would be a shoo-in to retake the mansion. Highway Commissioner Harry Hines announced. Jerry Sadler, a member of the Railroad Commission, joined the fray. Political observers anticipated the moment when "Pa" and "Pappy" would square off, but it did not happen. Ferguson tried. Still wearing his trademark black hat and string tie, he baited O'Daniel, calling him a "slickhaired banjo player who crooned his way into the governor's office" and "has been giving the people of Texas a song and dance ever since."

O'Daniel stuck to what he did best. He began his campaign on the radio, wondering aloud whether he should run for reelection. A few weeks later he announced that "thousands of my friends" had beseeched him to run and that he would honor their request. Despite the fact that Europe was engulfed in war, he offered the same clichés as his platform, decried that state agencies were nothing more than "juicy play-pretties for professional politicians," and denounced the "powerful oligarchies" in Austin. In his few campaign appearances he took little notice of the fact that the Nazis had occupied Paris and the Luftwaffe was bombing London, except to claim that he had sent President Roosevelt a telegram detailing the activities of fifth columnists in Texas, which, needless to say, he did not follow up on after the election. He won again without a runoff, and Miriam Ferguson's poor fourth-place finish finally retired the duo that had dominated Texas politics for more than two decades.

Vice President Garner momentarily diverted attention from the statehouse when he allowed his name to be put forward for the presidency in 1940 in an effort to keep Roosevelt from winning a third term. Garner had been a conservative influence on Roosevelt from the beginning, warning him to slow down in the spring of 1934 and calling some of the New Deal program just "plain damn foolishness" in 1935. But the greatest rift occurred when, in his second inaugural address in 1937, Roosevelt shocked the political establishment by calling for expansion of the U.S. Supreme Court. The conservatives on the Court had declared both the National Recovery Act and the Agricultural Adjustment Act, as well as several other pieces of legislation, unconstitutional in a series of five-to-four decisions in the spring of 1936. Roosevelt felt that adding a few friendly justices to the Court might solve the problem. Garner was only one of many who fiercely opposed this proposal, and he became the silent leader of the Democratic opposition. Another Texan, Hatton Sumners, chair of the House Judicial Committee, blocked the "court packing" plan in the House, and the conservatives ultimately defeated it in the Senate. The difficulty passed when vacancies enabled Roosevelt to make several new appointments to the Court, but the split with Garner was irreparable. After the 1940 election, the seventy-one-year-old vice president joined the Fergusons in retirement.

O'Daniel began 1941 with a renewed mandate, but he still had to face the need for a tax bill, and he again submitted his plan for a 1.6 percent transactions tax and a tax on natural resources and public utilities. The legislature virtually ignored him, and his bills died one by one in various committees. Eventually, the legislature put together its own plan, which became known as the Morris omnibus tax bill, and it passed both houses overwhelmingly. O'Daniel salvaged an anti-labor bill but the session was an open rebuke of the governor, and the state seemed on the verge of another political crisis.

A solution of sorts appeared when U.S. Senator Morris Sheppard, who had served the state in the Senate since 1913, died on April 9, 1941. O'Daniel saw an opportunity to take his antilabor campaign national, and many of his detractors saw an opportunity to get him out of the governor's mansion. The legislature even passed a resolution requesting that he appoint himself to the Senate. Instead, O'Daniel selected the ailing, eighty-seven-year-old son of Sam Houston, Andrew Jackson Houston, to replace Sheppard and announced it in his typically heavy-handed and ostentatious manner: He elbowed aside University of Texas folklorist and author J. Frank Dobie, the guest speaker at the San Jacinto Day ceremonies at the monument, to present Houston as the new senator, then led the crowd in singing "Beautiful Texas." It was only a ploy to reserve the position for himself in the upcoming election, of course, and Houston managed to attend only one committee meeting before he died.

O'Daniel then filed as a candidate in the 1941 special election to fill the seat, facing the young New Deal congressman from Johnson City, Lyndon Baines Johnson, who had the support of President Roosevelt; East Texas Congressman Martin Dies; and Attorney General Gerald Mann. Johnson ran a modern, well-financed campaign focusing on the president's support. To counter O'Daniel, he, too, hired a hillbilly band, staged "patriotic rallies," and allowed the entertainment to take precedence over his carefully written and rather pompous speeches. He also bought time on the radio, but his stilted performance was no match for Pappy. O'Daniel stepped up his radio messages, broadcasting from the governor's mansion every day at noon and at 6:00 A.M. on Sundays. He declared that his platform remained "one hundred percent approval of the Lord God Jehovah, widows, orphans, low taxes, the Ten Commandments, and the Golden Rule." If the United States had to get involved in the war, he mused, then perhaps Texas should have its own army and navy, and he emphasized his one legislative accomplishment, the passage of the antistrike law, which he said had driven labor organizers out of the state.

"Pa" Ferguson was able to play his last political trick in this election. Ferguson protégé Lieutenant Governor Coke Stevenson would advance to the governor's office should O'Daniel be elected to the Senate. Ferguson also had reasons to dislike O'Daniel, aside from "Ma's" 1940 defeat. O'Daniel was a staunch prohibitionist who had tried unsuccessfully to appoint three prohibitionists to the Texas Liquor Control Board and complained when the Senate turned down these "good clean honest Christian dry citizens." With a few well-placed telephone calls to old friends in East Texas, "Pa" set in motion the process by which O'Daniel was elevated to the U.S. Senate and Coke Stevenson into the governor's office.

According to Jake Pickle, one of Johnson's young staff members who later represented Austin in the U.S. Congress, the election process was imperfect in Texas in 1941, and a shrewd candidate would have his supporters withhold a final count of their votes until the situation became clear. If the vote were close, the candidate would know how many votes were needed to win, and the candidate's friends around the state who had not yet certified their results would then discover "uncounted" ballots in their precincts. This was how Miriam Ferguson had defeated Sterling in 1932. But Johnson and his twenty-four-year-old campaign manager, John B. Connally, were novices, and, because Johnson wanted to appear to be winning early on, Connally instructed George Parr, the self-styled political boss of Duval County and one of Johnson's good friends, to report his votes as soon as the polls closed. With 96 percent of the vote counted the morning after, Johnson led by approximately 5,000 votes. But as the Ferguson strongholds in East Texas began to report their official tallies, the gap between Johnson and O'Daniel began to close.

Connally pleaded with Parr to report more votes, but the "Duke of Duval County" had already served one jail term, and he refused, saying he would not risk prison again. The young congressman had made a rookie's mistake: He had let the opposition know how many votes they needed, and now with outright fraud, and in some cases the actual switching of votes from Martin Dies to O'Daniel, they were harvesting them from the same fertile East Texas fields that had been so good to the Fergusons over the years. Johnson might have filed a protest but for the glaring irregularities and clear violations of election law in his own campaign. Lyndon Johnson had learned a hard lesson that he would never forget.

## Texas in the War

Many Texans had continued to feel that a European war did not concern them, but on Sunday, December 7, 1941, a ham radio operator in South America picked up the news from Hawaii of the Japanese attack on the American naval base at Pearl Harbor and relayed it to amateur radio operators in Texas. The worst was soon confirmed: Nineteen ships had been sunk—most of the U.S. Pacific fleet—hundreds of men killed, and the harbor badly damaged. Before U.S. Senator Tom Connally could get to the capitol the next morning to introduce the resolution declaring war against Japan, young Texans had already lined up in front of recruiting offices. Germany and Italy declared war on the United States three days later.

O'Daniel's departure for Washington did nothing to calm state politics, because he had to run again in the regular election in 1942 to hold onto his seat. He prepared for the campaign by introducing several antilabor, antistrike bills in the Senate, never gathering more than a handful of supportive votes, yet he later had the audacity to claim that he had enabled the United States to win World War II because his antilabor efforts had prevented strikes.

Two former governors—James Allred and Dan Moody—opposed him this time, and he ridiculed them as the "gold dust twins," charging that "Communistic labor leader racketeers" and professional politicians were financing their campaigns. He wondered aloud why Allred would leave his "$10,000-a-year job" as a federal judge to run for the Senate unless he were being paid off by the Communists. Allred and Moody attacked O'Daniel for opposing the draft, but O'Daniel countered by talking about his son, who was now serving in the armed forces. They hired private investigators who uncovered damaging information about the senator—he was single during World War I yet failed to serve in the military; his flour-milling business in Kansas had gone bankrupt and some alleged fraud; and he had not paid all of his property taxes in Tarrant County—but the magic had not entirely faded. With Moody falling by the wayside in the primary, O'Daniel defeated Allred in the runoff by almost 20,000 votes. Despite his poor record in office, O'Daniel had done a remarkable thing: He had won four contested, statewide elections in five years. His proposed transactions tax foreshadowed the sales tax that is today by far the state's largest revenue generator, and his suggestion that the state find a way to import water from the spring floods in the Rocky Mountains would be much more welcome today that it was in 1941 when he introduced it.

O'Daniel's return to Washington did bring a period of relative political calm to the state, as Texans pitched into the war effort. For one thing, Coke R. Stevenson from Junction, the new governor, was a much quieter person, a man of few words. He smoked a pipe and had a habit of drawing on it several times before responding to a question, which led the capitol press corps to nickname him "Calculating Coke." Even then, his response was usually brief and uninformative. He was a seasoned official, having served as speaker of the House of Representatives before being elected lieutenant governor, and he managed to establish a cordial relationship with the capitol press corps by visiting with them frequently on an informal basis and inviting them to his ranch in the summers. Probably seeing himself as the guardian of the state's financial stability rather than as a politician, Stevenson espoused the simple life and conservative politics, meaning that he opposed expansion of federal powers. Expansion of the state's economy during the war enabled him to balance the budget without excessively cutting services, and he oversaw several improvements in the highway and educational systems. He faced no serious opposition and was easily reelected to the office in 1942 and 1944.

Ever since World War I, Texas had been a military training center, with the Third Army headquartered at Fort Sam Houston, and aviators stationed at Randolph, Brooks, and Kelly airfields, all in San Antonio. That infrastructure expanded during World War II. Fifteen major army camps in Texas trained more than 1.2 million troops between 1940 and 1945, and several prisoner-of-war camps were built in the state, ultimately housing almost 80,000 German, Italian, and Japanese prisoners of war by June 1944.

Approximately 750,000 Texans served in the armed forces, including 12,000 women, more than any other state. Two of the war's greatest military commanders were born in Texas—General Dwight D. Eisenhower at Denison and Fleet Admiral Chester W. Nimitz at Fredericksburg—and Audie Murphy of Farmersville became the war's most decorated hero before coming home to pursue a career in the movies. Texas A&M University alone, which at the time was a male-only, military-

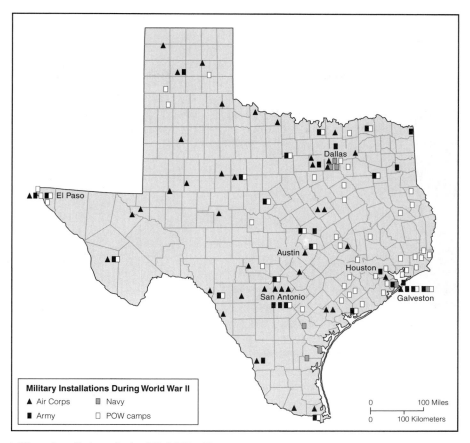

**Military Installations During World War II**

- ▲ Air Corps
- ■ Army
- ■ Navy
- □ POW camps

0    100 Miles
0    100 Kilometers

Military installations during World War II.

oriented institution, provided some 14,000 officers during the war, more than both the U.S. Military Academy and the U.S. Naval Academy combined.

The war finally brought an end to the depression. As the federal payroll stimulated local businesses, Texans sacrificed for "our boys overseas" and bought war bonds and planted "victory gardens," as they had during World War I. Rationing of sugar, coffee, meat, shoes, rubber, automobile parts, and gas became a way of life. Governor Stevenson accepted the rationing of everything except gasoline because, he said, Texas had plenty of it and with such vast distances to cover, it was as necessary as "the saddle, the rifle, the ax, and the Bible." Farmers now put all their land back in cultivation, got high prices for their crops, and helped feed the Allies.

With the assistance of the federal government, the largest petrochemical complex in the world developed along the gulf coast. Crucial to its growth was the construction of two pipelines from Texas to the Midwest and the East Coast. As

J. R. Parten, director of the Transportation Division of the Petroleum Administration, inspects construction of the "Big Inch" pipeline that would carry Texas oil to the East Coast. June 1943. *(Jubal R. Parten Papers, CN 09603, The Center for American History, The University of Texas at Austin)*

early as 1940, Interior Secretary Ickes realized that German submarines might interfere with tanker ships along the coastline and urged the construction of the pipelines. It was not until the attack on Pearl Harbor, however, that he persuaded independent oilman J. R. Parten to head the Petroleum Administration for War and to undertake the construction of the pipelines. With financing from the RFC, construction was completed on the "Big Inch" (24 inches in diameter), to deliver Texas crude from East Texas to Illinois and then on to the East Coast, in August 1943; the "Little Inch" (20 inches in diameter), from the Houston-Beaumont area to New Jersey, was completed in 1944. After the war the pipelines were acquired by Texas Eastern Transmission Corporation, formed by George and Herman Brown and their partners.

Other wartime industries were established all over the state: steel mills in Houston and Daingerfield; the largest tin smelter in the world at Texas City; aircraft factories at Garland, Grand Prairie, and Fort Worth; huge shipyards at Beaumont, Port Arthur, Houston, Galveston, and Corpus Christi. The war reinvigorated the paper and wood-pulp industries in East Texas and supported synthetic rubber and munitions plants in other parts of the state. The number of

The Standard Oil (New Jersey) Refinery in Baytown, 1946. *(Standard Oil Collection, Photographic Archives, University of Louisville)*

wage earners tripled, with opportunities now available in the work force for minorities and women, including positions that had formerly been reserved for men. The popular song "Rosie the Riveter" heralded the accomplishments of women in new roles such as pipe fitter, lathe operator, and assembly-line worker. All told, manufacturing increased fourfold between 1939 and 1944, from $453 million to $1.9 billion. This newfound prosperity enabled Governor Stevenson to sweep away the $42 million debt that the state had accumulated and, at the same time, improve state highways, raise teaching salaries, and undertake a building program at the University of Texas. Still, one of his most important contributions was the adoption, early in his term, of the constitutional amendment (Article III, Section 49a) that put the state on a "pay-as-you-go" basis; it prohibits the legislature from spending more than the State Comptroller (tax collector) certifies will be on hand when the bills come due.

## Minorities and the War

African Americans from all over the country trained in and staffed Texas camps, and they were expected to conform to the local customs regarding segregation. They lived separately from white troops, trained separately, and were not welcome in the white service clubs or movie theaters or had separate seating. Almost

258,000 African American Texans registered for the selective service, and about one-third of them were assigned to segregated units, usually commanded by white officers. As would be expected, there were racial incidents under such circumstances, and African American leaders protested the discrimination. The Fair Employment Practices Commission conducted investigations in some fifty cities, which in some cases heightened the existing tensions.

The urban areas were even more volatile because of the wartime growth. African Americans already made up one-third of the population in the Beaumont-Port Arthur area, but that number increased by 20 percent in the three years after 1940. On a hot summer night in 1943, the city erupted into racial violence as 2,000 white shipyard workers rioted in the African American section of Beaumont because it had been rumored (falsely) that an African American man had raped a white woman. Two people were killed and more than seventy injured before the local authorities, the Texas Rangers, and the National Guard restored order.

President Roosevelt acted preemptively to maintain good relations with Mexico and the other Latin American countries by establishing the Office of Inter-American Affairs (OIAA). When Mexico banned laborers from coming into Texas under the 1942 Bracero program, which had been negotiated to ensure a supply of wartime field hands and other laborers, the OIAA brought the matter to Governor Stevenson's attention, and the following year he appointed a Good Neighbor Commission, funded by the OIAA. The commission worked to improve the treatment and living conditions of Mexicans in Texas, and became a state agency in 1945.

Although many minorities, both African Americans and Mexican Americans, fell between the cracks during the New Deal, the government programs and the war created an increased political awareness among them that enabled them to improve their situations. African American businesspeople and civil rights leaders such as Maceo Smith and Juanita Craft in Dallas and Hobart T. Taylor, Sr., Carter W. Wesley, and Lulu B. White in Houston took leadership roles in the local chapters of the NAACP. The NAACP's challenge to the state's white primary law led to the 1944 Supreme Court decision, *Smith v. Allwright,* in which the Court held that the white primary was unconstitutional. Mexican Americans, meanwhile, had formed the League of United Latin American Citizens (LULAC) in an effort to eliminate racial prejudice and win equal rights. LULAC was largely a middle-class organization that opposed strikes, demonstrations, boycotts, and other acts that might be interpreted as disloyal. It encouraged Mexican Americans to vote and sent delegations to protest inequity and police brutality. In El Paso, Mexican American women protested their low wages, and in San Antonio 12,000 pecan shellers, mostly Hispanic women, walked off the job in protest of low wages. In 1942 the United States and Mexico signed the Mexican Farm Labor Program Agreement, known as the Bracero program, to permit much-needed Mexican laborers to come into the United States to help alleviate the labor shortage. The agreement guaranteed the workers a minimum wage of 30 cents an hour and humane treatment. Because of the record of discrimination and mistreatment of Mexicans in Texas, however, the Mexican government—despite the legislature's passage of the Caucasian Race Resolution in 1943, which guaranteed Mexicans equal rights in public places—refused to let Mexican laborers come into Texas under the program until 1947.

## Conclusion

The labor shortage was only one indication of the major changes that had taken place in agriculture during the war. The diversification of crops continued, with increases across the board in the production of grain sorghums, cattle, sheep, goats, horses, turkeys, tomatoes, onions, spinach, pecans, and roses, in addition to cotton. The number of farms decreased during the war, but the average size of farms grew and total production increased by as much as 30 percent because of the increased use of machinery.

By 1945, Texas industry, fueled by the needs generated by the war, had greatly outstripped agriculture in production. The state once again had a financial surplus, for which Governor Stevenson claimed credit, but which, in fact, was due more to the federal expenditures that poured into the state during and after the war. In addition to the federal payroll—perhaps one out of every ten members of the armed services trained in Texas—private industry expanded at an unprecedented rate. Fort Worth, Garland, and Grand Prairie boasted aircraft factories; Houston, Port Arthur, Orange, and Beaumont had new shipyards; and the huge petrochemical industry was firmly established on the coast. In addition, munitions plants, steel mills, and the world's largest tin smelter (at Texas City) added to the state's industrial muscle. Needless to say, the older, established industries, such as the oil and lumber industries, did equally well, and by 1945 Texas had replaced California as the leading petroleum producer in the nation.

Although Governor Stevenson was reelected in 1942 and 1944 virtually without opposition, the war years saw the beginning of a liberal-conservative rift in the Democratic Party that became even more pronounced after the war. The party remained united behind Vice President Garner as the U.S. presidential election approached in 1940, but when Roosevelt decided to run for a third term, Texas conservatives, who called themselves the Texas Regulars, split from the New Deal faction of the party. Two episodes, in particular, ignited their fury. The first was the supposed infiltration of the University of Texas by Communists and other subversives, which led to the ultraconservative board of regents firing the president, Homer P. Rainey, an ordained Baptist minister, in November 1944. The second was the U.S. Supreme Court's *Smith v. Allwright* decision in April 1944, which brought an end to the all-white primaries. Within a few decades, this liberal-conservative split would evolve into the two-party system that characterized the state's politics at the close of the twentieth century.

## SUGGESTED READINGS

Overviews of this period include Donald W. Wisenhunt, *The Depression in Texas: The Hoover Years* (1983); Lionel V. Patenaude, *Texas Politics and the New Deal* (1983); and James Smallwood, *The Great Recovery: The New Deal in Texas* (1983).

### The Great Depression

For information on the Great Depression in Texas, see Robert C. Cotner et al., *Texas Cities and the Great Depression* (1973) and Kenneth B. Ragsdale, *Centennial '36: The Year America Discovered Texas* (1987). Robert S. Maxwell, *Texas Economic Growth, 1890 to World War II: From Frontier to Industrial Giant* (1981), is also helpful. For information on agriculture, see Donald E. Green, *Land of the Underground Rain: Irrigation on the Texas High Plains, 1910–1970* (1973).

### The New Deal

George Norris Green, *The Establishment in Texas Politics: The Primitive Years, 1938–1957* (reprint, 1984) is the best treatment of politics during this period. Robert Dalleck, *Lone Star Rising: Lyndon Johnson and His Times, 1908–1960* (1991), and Robert A. Caro's *The Years of Lyndon Johnson: Means of Ascent* (1990) and *The Path to Power* (1982) are the best treatments of Lyndon B. Johnson. See also Seth S. McKay, *W. Lee O'Daniel and Texas Politics* (1944), and biographical essays of Morris Sheppard, John Nance Garner, Jesse Jones, Tom Connally, Sam Rayburn, and Johnson in Kenneth E. Henderickson, Jr., and Michael L. Collins, eds., *Profiles in Power: Twentieth-Century Texans in Washington* (1993).

Information on minorities and women may be found in Alwyn Barr, *Black Texans: A History of African Americans in Texas, 1528–1995* (1996); Julia Kirk Blackwelder, *Women of the Depression: Caste and Culture in San Antonio, 1929–1939* (1984); and Rebecca Sharpless, *Fertile Ground, Narrow Choices: Women on Texas Cotton Farms, 1900–1940* (1999).

### Texas in World War II

The best information on Texas in World War II is found in *The Handbook of Texas* and the *Southwestern Historical Quarterly.*

# 13

# A "Confluence of Anxieties": Texas from 1946 to 1972

In 1949 a forty-one-year-old Texan named V. O. Key, Jr., who was then a professor at Johns Hopkins University in Baltimore, published the results of his seminal study of the electoral process in the South, *Southern Politics in State and Nation*. The South had long been recognized as the most depressed part of the nation, especially after President Roosevelt identified it as such in 1938. The question was how it would prevail over its problems to participate in the prosperity that the rest of the nation enjoyed. Many people assumed that the most difficult problem the South had to overcome was racism and segregation; Key agreed that years of race baiting on the part of the ruling oligarchy to maintain the loyalty of poor whites had worsened the situation. Although Key was not a Marxist, he concluded that the lack of class conflict in the South prevented economic and electoral progress. In Texas, however, Key saw a glimmer of hope, suggesting that the beginnings of a class conflict had erupted there in the liberal-conservative split in the Democratic Party. He predicted that the one-party system, by which the ruling elite held power, would gradually succumb to the forces of urbanism, industrialism, and organized labor and would transform into a two-party system, with one liberal party and the other conservative. Because "politics generally comes down, over the long run, to a conflict between those who have and those who have less," he argued, the issues in most disputes are taxation and expenditure: who pays the taxes, and how the money is used. It was almost as if he had written a script for the postwar decades in Texas.

| 1949 | Gilmer-Aiken laws passed; fifty-first legislature adopts the state's first billion-dollar budget |
| 1950 | U.S. Supreme Court decides *Sweatt v. Painter* and Heman Sweatt admitted to University of Texas Law School; 59.8 % of the state's population live in cities and towns; Korean War begins |
| 1953 | U.S. Congress enacts legislation confirming Texas ownership of its tidelands out to three leagues |
| 1954 | Texas Instruments produces first silicon transistor and first portable radio |
| 1956 | U.S. Congress approves national system of interstate highways |
| 1957 | Senator Lyndon B. Johnson is instrumental in the U.S. Congress's passage of the first civil rights act in more than eighty years; Soviet satellite Sputnik launches space race |
| 1958 | Texas pianist Van Cliburn wins the prestigious Tchaikovsky Piano Competition in Moscow |
| 1960 | John Tower becomes the first Republican U.S. senator from Texas since Reconstruction |
| 1961 | Legislature passes 2 % general sales tax, and Governor Daniel permits it to become law without his signature |
| 1963 | President Kennedy assassinated in Dallas |
| 1964 | President Johnson's Great Society program, including the Civil Rights Act of 1964 and the Voting Rights Act of 1965; the Twenty-fourth Amendment to the U.S. Constitution declares poll taxes illegal in federal elections; Southwest Airlines founded; Dr. Michael DeBakey of Methodist Hospital in Houston performs the first successful coronary artery bypass graft procedure |
| 1965 | The Astrodome, the world's first enclosed, domed, multipurpose sports stadium, opens in Houston |
| 1965 | First U.S. combat troops sent to Vietnam |
| 1966 | Rio Grande valley farm workers march on the state capitol |
| 1967 | Governor Connally leads in reorganizing higher education, including establishment of the University of Texas system |
| 1968 | Dr. Denton Cooley performs the first heart transplant in the U.S. at St. Luke's Hospital in Houston |
| 1969 | Neil Armstrong speaks first words from the lunar surface, "Houston, the Eagle has landed." |
| 1971 | Sharpstown scandal |
| 1972 | Equal Rights Amendment to the Texas constitution adopted |

As World War II ended, Texan veterans came home to a changed state. Industrialization and a large population increase brought on by the war effort had transformed the economic, social, and political fabric of the state, and it would take some time before most people understood the ramifications. Opportunities in Texas, including the huge growth of the oil industry, even attracted out-of-state veterans, such as the future president George Herbert Walker Bush, who came to Midland with his growing family after graduating from Yale in 1948. The "modified class politics" that Key had documented in Texas was not the product of a plantation oligarchy, as in other Southern states, or of an "upthrust of the masses" that had forced the upper class to defend itself, but the result "of the personal insecurity of men suddenly made rich who are fearful lest they lost their wealth." And it quickly became apparent during the biennial gubernatorial races and subsequent sessions of the legislature as various constituencies fought over the commonly accepted solution: tax revenue—where to get it and how to use it. Rapid urbanization and increased population forced the state to expand its educational institutions, social services, and bureaucracy, which, of course, required additional taxes. But increased taxation challenged the traditional agrarian-inspired approach to Texas government—that low taxation would attract new industry, and the only relatively new source of money in the state, the oil industry, had accumulated enough political and economic clout to ensure that it would not have to bear the brunt of these new initiatives.

## Stressing the One-Party System

The party harmony that had prevailed during World War II, which saw Coke Stevenson virtually unopposed as governor, dissolved after the war, as liberal and conservative factions renewed their battles. As the first postwar gubernatorial campaign began in 1946, the favorite seemed to be Homer P. Rainey, the former president of the University of Texas who was searching for vindication for his firing by the board of regents. Hosting a radio show in which he defended his official behavior, Rainey drew increasing support from liberals and newly-enfranchised African Americans. He espoused, to one degree or another, academic freedom, civil rights, labor union rights, and taxes on natural resources; his opponents suspected him of, and accused him of, supporting integration—the kind of race-baiting that Key described—although he was on record against it. Rainey's opponents included three conservative officeholders who attacked him either on personal issues or for permitting Communist infiltration of labor unions and the University of Texas and for supporting integration of public facilities. Rainey's proposed tax on natural resources was anathema to the oil industry, and, with the exception of a few liberal stalwarts such as independent oilman J. R. Parten of Madisonville, the industry unified behind the more moderate Beauford H. Jester, a member of the Railroad Commission, who positioned himself between the conservative trio and the liberal Rainey.

Rapid wartime industrialization had led to increased union membership in Texas. By 1946 approximately 350,000 Texans had joined unions, some 225,000 of them in unions affiliated with the American Federation of Labor (AFL), the largest labor group in the country. Another 60,000 belonged to unions associated with the Congress of Industrial Organizations (CIO), the second largest labor group, which had its state headquarters in Dallas and was making significant gains in East Texas. The largest numbers of union members were located in the heavily industrialized areas of Houston-Beaumont and Dallas–Fort Worth, although many unions were located in areas of specific industry, such as Daingerfield (steelworkers), Greenville (auto workers), and Tyler (oil field workers). At the same time, the state CIO became active in politics in 1944 and in 1946 supported Rainey for governor, which further tainted the former university president in the eyes of the conservative businesspeople. As election day neared, and the nation endured hundreds of strikes by union laborers trying to keep up with postwar inflation, including work stoppages at the General Tire and Rubber Plant in Waco and Consolidated Vultee Aircraft in Fort Worth, the electorate began to see Rainey in a new and, to them, more dangerous, light.

## Modified Class Politics

The more conservative Jester ran a well-financed campaign, positioning himself as a moderate, whereas Rainey had to spend most of his time refuting charges of being a political and personal extremist. Jester portrayed Rainey as a super-liberal, when, in fact, the scholar was a New Deal Democrat. Jester campaigned on the basis of no new taxes, states' rights, and opposition to labor unions. The Rainey campaign was the first in the state to profit from the emerging urban coalition of labor, minorities, and independent progressives that would ultimately challenge the state's Democratic establishment for control of the party itself, and it was here that Key had seen a flash of what he perceived as a budding "modified class politics." Although Rainey led in the polls right up to election day, Jester took a small lead in the first primary and concluded with a resounding victory in the runoff.

Candidate Jester had urged enactment of several labor laws in his 1946 campaign, such as voluntary mediation and arbitration in contract disputes and binding arbitration in public and quasi-public utility disputes; with conservative business support, however, the legislature went even further in 1947, passing laws requiring an "open shop," forbidding strikes by public employees, severely limiting picketing, and prohibiting picketing of utilities. Meanwhile, Jester's own proposals died for lack of support. Jester did not really agree with the antiunion laws, but he did not fight them, and an expanding, postwar economy enabled him to keep his promise of no new taxes. He swept into office a second time in 1948 without really having to campaign.

Other Texans had the reform spirit as well. Several of the state's cities were still plagued by organized crime. Gambling, bootlegging, and various kinds of rackets were prosperous endeavors for a number of notorious characters, including Lester "Benny" Binion of Dallas, who had become the local kingpin as the war

Governor Beauford Jester delivering his inaugural address, January 22, 1947. (*The Institute of Texan Cultures at University of Texas, San Antonio*)

ended. The Maceo brothers still ruled Galveston, where the local police commissioner bragged to an attorney that he was on the payroll of almost fifty brothels. A number of veterans, just home from making the world safe for democracy, felt that the gangsters threatened democracy at home and embarked on reform. In 1946 a crusading district attorney, Will Wilson, chased Binion out of Dallas to Las Vegas, where he became a fixture of the gambling establishment in that city. In 1949 Attorney General Marion Price Daniel, Jr. sent investigators into cities across the state to look into rumors of bookies and gambling and, on August 15, sent Texas Rangers on successful raids in Fort Worth, Odessa, and Beaumont. Advance warning permitted operators in Galveston, perhaps the most wide-open town in the state, to hide their equipment and escape prosecution, but in 1957 they fell victim to newly-elected Attorney General Will Wilson, who closed them down.

### The 1948 Elections

The 1948 elections sharply delineated the kind of liberal-conservative conflict that Key described, both on the national and state levels. The presidential race pitted President Harry S. Truman against New York's Republican Governor

Thomas E. Dewey, and the U.S. Senate race featured former governor Coke Stevenson and Congressman Lyndon B. Johnson. By comparison, the gubernatorial contest between Jester and seven other candidates was a mere sideshow, with Jester winning without a runoff.

Truman inherited all the anti–New Deal sentiment that had built up in Texas when he succeeded Roosevelt in 1945. Many of the conservatives who had called themselves the Texas Regulars and organized around Senator O'Daniel and Congressman Martin Dies and campaigned against Roosevelt now joined with the Dixiecrats and nominated Strom Thurmond of South Carolina to challenge Truman. They opposed Truman on the basis of his continuation of New Deal policies, his foreign policy, and, specifically, his civil rights initiatives of 1947 and 1948. Truman won the nomination, however, carrying Texas by more than a million votes, his largest majority of any state, and upset Dewey. Governor Jester maintained control of the Democratic Party and helped Truman to his huge majority.

The senatorial primary was equally dramatic. Coke Stevenson represented the Texas establishment and was heavily favored over Lyndon Johnson, but the contest turned out to be one of the closest elections in the state's history. Stevenson had served as wartime governor for almost three terms (finishing O'Daniel's second term, then being elected twice on his own). Lyndon Johnson, his more liberal opponent, had gone into the campaign believing that he had been cheated out of victory in the 1941 special election against O'Daniel and determined not to let it happen again.

Johnson had continued to serve as a member of Congress from the Hill Country and had earned a reputation as a New Dealer. He was only forty years old in 1948 and tried to depict himself as a modern politician, relying heavily on radio commercials and crisscrossing the state in a helicopter named the "Johnson City Windmill." Johnson also worked twenty hours a day and ran a well-organized campaign, whereas Stevenson's campaign was poorly organized and haphazard. Johnson contrasted what he depicted as Stevenson's old-fashioned conservative, antigovernment views with his own stance as a responsible official who was attentive to his constituents. Campaign manager John Connally, a future Texas governor, had his advance team in each town ahead of Johnson to prepare for the brief visit. The helicopter brought out the crowds, enabling the candidate to talk to more voters, and during June and July Johnson visited 118 cities in seventeen days. He portrayed the sixty-year-old Stevenson as old, old-fashioned, and out of touch. He expected to win in the first primary, but finished more than 71,000 votes behind the better-known Stevenson. Only the fact that the third candidate in the race, Houston attorney George Peddy, got enough votes to force a runoff saved Johnson from defeat.

Stevenson's runoff campaign was even more disorganized than the primary, and he soon made his biggest blunder of the election. A special session of Congress provided the occasion. The governor had announced that he would visit Washington to talk with federal officials and foreign policy experts, undoubtedly an attempt to discount any advantage that Johnson might have in the runoff

Senatorial candidate Lyndon Baines Johnson campaigning in 1948 with a thunderstorm behind him. The first candidate to use a helicopter in his campaign, Johnson made 370 stops in five weeks, including several "flyovers" of his opponent Coke Stevenson's rallies. *(LBJ Library Photo)*

because of his experience and wide acquaintance in the capital. When Stevenson looked at possible office space in the Senate Office Building and met with real estate agents about purchasing a home, it appeared to many that he was taking the election for granted. But Stevenson's real difficulty occurred at a press conference. In what many considered an effort to appear more conservative than Stevenson, Johnson had supported the Taft-Hartley Act, which reaffirmed workers' rights to join unions, bargain collectively, and strike, but prohibited closed shops, permitted states to pass "right-to-work" laws, and enabled the president to get a court-ordered injunction for an eighty-day "cooling off" period before unions could close down an entire industry. As a result, the Texas AFL had endorsed Stevenson, despite his antiunion record, and Stevenson had refused to take a position on Taft-Hartley during the primary. If he had opposed it he would have lost his conservative backers, and if he had favored it he would have lost the support of the AFL. So Johnson suggested that one of the reporters ask Stevenson to explain his position on the Taft-Hartley Act. At first Stevenson refused to answer, saying that his comments had already been published. When the reporter persisted, Stevenson lamely replied, "All my notes and papers are back in Texas. I am facing these questions without any material." The syndicated columnist Drew Pearson, a friend of Johnson's, was unmerciful the next day, writing that Stevenson "evaded more issues and dodged more questions than any recent performer in a city noted for question dodging." The Johnson team spread thousands of copies of the column across the state as the runoff approached, and "Silent Coke's" refusal to take a stand became the theme of the Johnson runoff campaign.

Johnson returned to Texas and continued to work until the last votes were in. His final strategy was to use the same tactic in 1948 that he was convinced had defeated him in 1941: He had his supporters hold their vote totals in the precincts where he was strongest, in South Texas, until he knew how many votes he needed. Everyone knew that the election would be close. The day after the runoff, with Stevenson leading by only a few hundred votes, the *Dallas Morning News* declared, "Anything can happen." During a period of thirty-four hours, the Texas Election Bureau, a consortium of news organizations, unofficially reported that the lead changed almost every five hours as election officials all over the state filed and refiled their returns. Both Stevenson and Johnson knew what was going on. It was only a question of whose supporters would file last, and whether they could get away with it. Bob Murphey of Nacogdoches, Stevenson's nephew and driver throughout the campaign, later acknowledged that Stevenson was at a huge disadvantage at this stage because of Johnson's better organization. A week after election day, officials in Jim Wells County finally reported an additional 200 votes for Johnson, enough votes to give him the victory—by eighty-seven votes. (No one is certain how many extra votes were reported. Some sources say that it was 200, and others say that it was 201, with one vote for Stevenson. Still others report that it was 202 with two votes for Stevenson.)

Johnson had not contested O'Daniel's controversial victory in 1941 because he knew that his campaign could not withstand investigation itself, but Stevenson had no such qualms (despite knowledge that some of his supporters in East Texas had been equally devious) and immediately charged that Johnson had stolen the election. Rather than call for a statewide recount, which might have confirmed Johnson's victory, Stevenson felt that he could find evidence in the boss-ruled counties of South Texas that Johnson supporters had stuffed the ballot box and that he could have those votes disqualified. He went to Alice with long-time friend and ex-Texas Ranger Frank Hamer, who had tracked down Bonnie and Clyde, to investigate the matter of Box 13 in Jim Wells County, which had reported the additional 200 votes for Johnson a week after the election. They found their evidence: The last 200 names on the voting list were written in the same hand, but a different hand from the rest of the list, in a different color ink than the rest of the list, and in alphabetical order. Stevenson's attorneys even took depositions from several people whose names were on the list but who said that they had not voted.

Stevenson took his evidence directly to the state Democratic Election Committee, which upheld Johnson's victory by a vote of 29 to 28. Then, with fistfights punctuating the meeting and a delegate who suffered a heart attack in the hotel lobby assigning his proxy to a Johnson supporter before being taken to the hospital, the state convention confirmed the committee's decision. Stevenson challenged the election in U.S. District Court and got a temporary restraining order keeping Johnson's name off the general election ballot, but with Abe Fortas, whom Johnson later appointed to the Supreme Court, planning the strategy, the Johnson forces convinced Supreme Court Justice Hugo Black to set the order aside. The full Court later affirmed Black's ruling, and Johnson went on to win the general election. Stevenson, still unwilling to give up, contacted several Republican senators in an effort to have the Senate refuse to seat Johnson. But the Democrats won control of the Senate that fall, and Johnson had enough friends among them that no challenge would have been successful. Johnson realized that he entered the Senate with the reputation of a wheeler-dealer and a cloud of illegality hanging over his head, and he gave himself a nickname based on the event: In a radio speech, he jokingly referred to himself as "Landslide Lyndon" because of his eighty-seven-vote runoff victory, and it stuck.

Because the fight occurred in the Democratic Party primary, and because both sides were thought to have participated in the shenanigans, little in the way of election reform resulted. After confronting Johnson with rumors of illegalities in his 1941 campaign, reporter Jack Anderson summed up the matter in a memo to his boss, syndicated columnist Drew Pearson: "The circumstantial evidence, at least, is overwhelming against Lyndon. At the same time, he gave me such a sales talk that I can't help believing he is so much better than the crowd fighting him that I hate to play into their hands. . . . On the whole, Lyndon's record has been far better and more progressive than the average Texan."

Johnson's election would help the Texas delegation regain some of the power it had lost with the departure of Garner and others. Sam Rayburn had become Speaker of the U.S. House of Representatives in 1940 and served until the Republicans took over the House in 1947. He would return to the Speaker's chair in 1950, and two years later Johnson began his rapid ascent in the Senate, first with his election to minority whip (1952) and then to majority leader in 1955. Johnson's first committee assignments were Armed Services and Interstate and Foreign Commerce, which permitted him to push for more military bases in Texas, and to shape legislation that affected his friends in the oil and natural gas business. He soon had a hand in legislation that helped to build more houses around military bases, subsidized the tin smelting business in Texas City, loaned money to the Lone Star steel plant in northeast Texas, and sold surplus war equipment to the University of Texas for use in government-contracted research. Such results turned more than a few "recalcitrant and hardened Ag'inners" into "I told you so supporters," according to one business leader.

## Jester's Reforms

With Jester's easy reelection, he unveiled an ambitious plan to deal with some of the state's increasingly serious problems. Unlike those who preceded and followed him, Jester was a moderate. Working with the legislature, he initiated an antilynching law and prison reforms and appropriated more money for the elderly and for the state's health services. They reformed the state's educational institutions, providing more money for higher education and establishing Lamar University in Beaumont. But the most important reforms they made were in the area of public education, where the Gilmer-Aikin laws brought about many changes: The laws consolidated 4,500 school districts into 2,900; instituted state equalization funding, based on attendance, which supplemented local taxes; required a minimum of 175 teaching days per year; and raised teacher salaries as well as educational requirements. Finally, the appointed nine-member State Board of Education and the elected state superintendent of public instruction became an elected twenty-one-member board with the power to appoint a commissioner of education, subject to confirmation by the Texas Senate, and a new agency, the State Department of Education (now the Texas Education Agency) was created to support the board and the commissioner.

Jester also supported the Colson-Briscoe Act of 1949, which appropriated $15 million a year from the Omnibus Tax Clearance Fund to be used in the construction of what became known as farm-to-market roads. The highway commission had authorized construction of 7,500 miles of rural roads funded equally by the state and federal government in 1945, immediately after the war. This proved to be a popular program, and the legislature increased the appropriation in 1962 so that a minimum of $23 million would be spent each year. By March 1989 the Texas farm-to-market system included almost 42,000 miles of paved roads, the most extensive network of secondary roads in the world.

Along with other Southern governors, Jester opposed President Truman's civil rights program, but he advised University of Texas officials in the spring of 1949 that they would have to admit qualified African American students to medical school at Galveston unless the legislature created a separate medical school at Texas State University for Negroes (now Texas Southern University) in Houston. An African American applicant to the law school, Heman Sweatt, had already filed suit against the university in 1946, claiming that he had been turned down for admission because of his race and challenging the segregation system itself. As that suit wound its way through the courts, two African Americans filed for application to the medical school in Galveston in 1949, and one of them was admitted that fall.

Although the fifty-first legislature passed the state's first billion-dollar budget in 1949, many of Jester's reforms needed additional funding, and he vetoed much of the second year of the biennial appropriation because the comptroller ruled that there was insufficient income. The state still needed other sources of revenue because, in addition to increased expenses, the growing competition from Middle Eastern crude had cut into the state's oil revenues. The Gilmer-Aikin law, for example, was financed by a selective consumer tax. Jester had also convinced the legislature to propose a series of constitutional amendments to repeal the poll tax, prohibit discrimination on juries, establish civil-service protections, and require the legislature to meet annually. But before he could pursue these proposals, he died of a heart attack on July 11, shortly after the session ended. Lieutenant

Governor Allan Shivers succeeded him, and that fall the voters rejected all of the proposed amendments.

## The Conservatives Take Charge

Allan Shivers had begun his political career as a prolabor member of the legislature from Jefferson County. Like Jester, he graduated from the University of Texas, where he had been president of the student body. He earned the respect of his colleagues while in the legislature and emerged as a leader. In 1937 he married Marialice Shary, daughter of a wealthy Rio Grande valley land developer, John H. Shary, who was called the father of the Texas citrus industry. After service in the army during World War II, he returned to Texas in 1946 and was elected lieutenant governor (and reelected in 1948); he instituted changes that brought considerable power to the office, enabling him to become the first lieutenant governor to influence and shape the state's legislative agenda by controlling Senate committee appointments. Although he was considered a moderate, Shivers pursued a more conservative course on social and economic issues after election to statewide office.

Governor Allan Shivers campaigning for reelection in 1954. (*Russell Lee Photograph Collection, 1935–1977, CN 09623, The Center for American History, The University of Texas at Austin*)

Whether one agrees with Shivers or not, it is clear that he was one of the ablest chief executives in the state's history. In preparation for a special session of the legislature in 1950, Shivers called a number of lobbyists and business leaders to the governor's mansion to convince them of the need for new taxes, then called a special session of the legislature for January 1950 to address the matter. In his speech before that session he still exhibited some of his early liberal ideals. He also instituted administrative changes that, ironically, because he is generally known as one of the stronger chief executives, weakened the power of the governor but improved efficiency: He created the Legislative Council to research and draft bills and the Legislative Budget Board, with the lieutenant governor and Speaker of the House as chair and vice chair, to prepare the annual budget. Previously, each agency had submitted a memorandum to the governor, who determined what to recommend to the legislature.

The reforms continued during the 1951 legislative session. Shivers asked the legislature for more money for roads, prisons, schools, and the mentally ill. He supported safety inspections for automobiles and liability insurance for motorists, with the intent that motorists must prove that they had sufficient resources to cover any accident that they might cause. The legislature also passed the first redistricting bill in thirty years, which began a long process of transferring power from the rural areas with diminishing population to the growing urban areas.

As Shivers expanded his political power, he began to express his conservative views more clearly. Early in 1951 he supported a measure that permitted candidates for public office to cross-file—that is, they could file in both the Democratic and Republican primaries. Liberals objected to some of the more conservative, antilabor legislation that Shivers had supported during the last session, and they finally broke with him when, because of the tidelands issue, he decided to support the Republican candidate, Dwight D. Eisenhower, in the 1952 presidential election. In what V. O. Key would have considered a prime example of the rising class conflict, Shivers won control of the executive committee of the state Democratic Party that year and purged the more liberal members.

### The Tidelands

Ownership of the tidelands, the submerged land from the point of low tide to three leagues (about ten and a half miles) out in the Gulf of Mexico, further split the Democratic Party and made Shivers a stronger states' rights advocate. After oil was discovered in the tidelands, federal officials claimed that the offshore lands belonged to the nation. California was the first state to press its claim to tidelands in 1945, but the Supreme Court decided against it. Congress even passed legislation guaranteeing California's ownership of the tidelands, but President Truman vetoed it, asserting national ownership. Texas pleaded that it was in a different situation than California, and President Truman seemed to agree, saying during a presidential campaign stop in Austin in 1948 that "Texas is in a class by itself; it entered the Union by Treaty." In the meantime, Texans had miffed Truman by awarding leases in the tidelands without consulting him, and after the election (in which he handily carried Texas) he instructed his attorney general to file suit against the state, claiming that these lands too belonged to the nation. The Supreme Court ruled against Texas by a vote of 4 to 3 (with two abstentions). In 1952 Rayburn pushed another bill through Congress that would have given Texas possession of its tidelands, but Truman vetoed that one too. With Texas Attorney General Price Daniel leading the fight, the tidelands became the foremost issue during the upcoming presidential election and one of the most serious conflicts between states and the federal government during the twentieth century.

The tidelands dispute split the state Democratic Party. Adlai Stevenson of Illinois, the Democratic presidential candidate, supported the Truman administration's position but native Texan Dwight D. Eisenhower, the Republican presidential candidate and revered commander of Allied forces in Europe during the war, supported the Texas claim. Maintaining control of the party machinery, Governor Shivers led a Democrats for Eisenhower campaign. Liberal Democrats, including the state's two most important national leaders, Sam Rayburn and Lyndon Johnson, remained loyal to Stevenson, but Texas voted Republican for only the second time in the twentieth century. In the governor's race Shivers defeated Ralph Yarborough, a liberal attorney and former judge, by more than 400,000 votes. In 1953 the Congress passed and Eisenhower signed a quitclaim bill that recognized that the tidelands extended three leagues into the Gulf of Mexico along the coast of Texas and the west coast of Florida. The General Land Office reported that by 1987 the Texas public school fund had received nearly $2 billion from leases, rentals, and royalties on this property.

In retrospect, the 1952 election marked the beginning of an increasingly harsh rhetoric between liberal and conservative forces that signified deeper change in the state's politics—change that V. O. Key had predicted and that would continue until most of the conservatives had joined the Republican Party. The demographics of Texas had changed as a result of the war. Increasing numbers of immigrants from the North and the Midwest fueled the state's move toward urbanization, then suburbanization. As racial and ethnic minorities—African Americans and Mexican Americans—began to exercise political power, old political allegiances faltered. The Democratic Party was splitting into liberal and conservative factions, but the conservative faction maintained control of the party apparatus.

## The Cold War and Class Politics

Shivers drifted toward conservatism on the tidelands issue as well as the wave of anti-Communism in America. The "red scare" or McCarthyism of the 1950s was partly a result of the undocumented charges by Wisconsin Senator Joseph McCarthy that Communist party members had infiltrated the government, especially the State Department. But Texas had its own brand of anti-Communism in

Martin Dies, who became the first chair of the U.S. House of Representatives Un-American Activities Committee in 1938, and in the Texas Senate committee, established in 1941 for the purpose of ferreting out Communists. Many political figures also mixed red-baiting with race-baiting. Key would have recognized it as a Cold War variation on a theme.

Many date the Cold War from the famous 1945 Yalta Conference between President Roosevelt, British Prime Minister Winston Churchill, and Soviet Premier Joseph Stalin—from the moment that Stalin asserted Russia's authority in Eastern Europe, dividing Europe along what Churchill dramatically called the "iron curtain" in a speech at Fulton, Missouri, the following year. By the end of 1949, the Soviet Union had detonated its first atomic bomb, ending the U.S. monopoly on atomic power, and the Communists had driven the nationalists out of China; in June 1950 North Korean troops crossed the 38th parallel that separated the Communist north from the western-oriented south, pushing the poorly-prepared defenders before them. President Truman responded quickly, committing U.S. troops under the United Nations banner. But as the war dragged on, and the Chinese entered the conflict on the side of the North Koreans, Americans became increasingly frustrated. Shivers was among those who called Truman soft on Communism and claimed that he was committed to a "no win" policy in Korea.

Such difficulties provided a following for Senator McCarthy, which included Houston oilman Hugh Roy Cullen and Jesse H. Jones, publisher of the *Houston Chronicle,* which supported the Wisconsin Senator through much of his career and publicized his 1950 speech in Houston. By the spring of 1951 chapters of the Minute Women of the U.S.A., whose goals were to fight Communism in government and education and ensure that schools and colleges taught American heritage, had formed in Houston, Dallas, San Antonio, and Wichita Falls. Among other things, the Minute Women forced the Houston school superintendent out of office. The legislature required loyalty oaths of all public employees, but the crusade to get Communists out of the public schools resulted in only one dismissal out of more than 65,000 employees. In Dallas, Jerry Bywaters, director of the city-supported Dallas Museum of Fine Art, came under attack from conservative citizens who claimed that the museum exhibited paintings by Communist artists. Although some citizens may have been concerned about Spanish artist Pablo Picasso's Communist sympathies, later research proved, ironically, that the accusations originated with a group of realist artists who probably felt threatened by the modernist and abstract works that the museum was exhibiting rather than by the artists' political sympathies. The real problem was that the "red scare" and the Cold War combined with social changes such as urbanization and the expansion of civil rights to threaten the status quo, causing many citizens to identify these needed changes as also un-American.

## Civil Rights

Another issue that split the state Democratic Party was integration. Although the state had established Alta Vista Agricultural College (now Prairie View A&M University) in 1878, before Sweatt's lawsuit African Americans had to go outside the state to pursue a professional education as a lawyer, doctor, engineer, or architect. But civil rights litigants had been increasingly successful in the federal courts after World War II, and the Houston chapter of the NAACP, with the support of Thurgood Marshall, the well-known attorney and future Supreme Court justice, challenged segregation in Texas. Heman Sweatt, a graduate of Wiley College in Marshall and a former medical student at the University of Michigan and now a postal employee and civil rights advocate in Houston, had become interested in law and applied to the University of Texas law school in 1946. Marshall successfully sued the university in the U.S. Supreme Court (*Sweatt v. Painter*), winning a major decision in 1950. Shivers led the segregationist forces, and the state attempted to resolve the dilemma by creating a law school for African Americans as part of the newly created Texas State College for Negroes (now Texas Southern University), but the Court held that the new school did not meet the "separate but equal" provision required by the 1896 *Plessey v. Ferguson* case and ruled that the university had to admit him. This decision, however, did not apply to undergraduate education.

The decision that made racial separation illegal was *Brown v. Board of Education* in 1954, which was far more sweeping in its effect. In that decision the court brushed aside the "separate but equal" argument and held that segregation of the public schools was unlawful because to separate children "from others of similar age and qualifications solely because of their race generates a feeling of inferiority . . . that may affect their hearts and minds in a way unlikely ever to be undone."

The majority of Texas voters opposed racial integration, and it became one of the central issues of the 1954 gubernatorial race, pitting Governor Shivers, seeking an unprecedented third term, against the garrulous and liberal Ralph W. Yarborough, an Austin attorney and former judge whom Shivers had defeated in 1952. The election confirmed several of Key's conclusions: that the poll tax and other repressive measures kept poor citizens from voting, that the coalition of organized labor and poor rural folk was developing, and that the liberal-conservative class conflict, represented by Yarborough and Shivers, was at hand. As the race grew closer, and after the Supreme Court had handed down the *Brown v. Board of Education* decision, Shivers charged not only that "Communist labor racketeers" supported Yarborough but that Yarborough also advocated full integration. Yarborough forced Shivers into a runoff, but Shivers won by fewer than 100,000 votes.

Integration continued to be an issue after the election. Conservative Attorney General and fierce state's rights advocate John Ben Shepperd contended that the Supreme Court decisions did not apply to Texas. But the University of Texas and Texas Western College did admit their first African American undergraduate students in 1955. The San Antonio and El Paso school districts began integrating their schools in 1956. But when three African American students attempted that same year to enroll in the Mansfield school, near Fort Worth, members of the local community resisted federal court orders, and Shivers, by then a lame-duck governor, sent Texas Rangers to preserve the status quo.

### Scandal Hurts Shivers

Shivers's historical reputation probably would have been better served if he had not run for a third term. The school crisis was an ugly affair, and he was beset with charges of corruption as insurance scandals eroded public confidence in his administration. Reporters exposed illegal operations in the Veterans' Land Board that resulted in the sentencing of General Land Office Commissioner James Bascom Giles to six years in the penitentiary. Even worse were the insurance scandals. The state's regulation of the insurance industry was so lax that more insurance companies called Texas home than any other state. So many had failed that Yarborough made it an issue during the 1954 campaign. One of the largest failures was U.S. Trust and Guaranty, which had grown quickly into a large company that controlled seventy-four other insurance companies in twenty-two states, but more troubling politically was the failure of the Insurance Company of Texas. Its founder, Ben Jack Cage, was indicted for bribery and embezzlement and fled to Brazil, where he lived for the rest of his life.

Shivers again led Eisenhower's campaign in Texas in 1956, but the state Republican Party nominated only a few candidates for office, preferring to vote for the conservative Democrats who had cross-filed as Republicans as well. The liberal Yarborough made his third run for the governor's office, but lost to the moderate Price Daniel, who had the support of Johnson and Rayburn and who resigned his U.S. Senate seat to become governor. Johnson, Rayburn, and Daniel formed a coalition with liberals to wrest control of the party machinery away from Shivers and the conservative establishment, and, in the major liberal victory of the decade, Yarborough won the open senatorial seat with only 38 percent of the vote in a winner-take-all special election over twenty-one other candidates.

President Eisenhower had taken no action in the school integration crisis because he was in the midst of a reelection campaign and Texas was a crucial state. But the following year, when Governor Orville Faubus of Arkansas attempted to keep nine African American students from enrolling in Little Rock's Central High School, Eisenhower sent federal marshals to enforce the Court's ruling. Shivers, meanwhile, appointed an Advisory Committee on Segregation in the Public Schools with the specific instructions that they prevent "forced integration." The committee presented a number of racist proposals to the legislature. In the debate, state senator Henry B. González of San Antonio, the lone Mexican American in the legislature, became a hero to liberals when he filibustered against the proposals. He had many supporters, but two of the bills eventually became law: 1) Local voters had to approve integration before state funds could be used for an

When African Americans, led by NAACP attorney Thurgood Marshall (second from left), prepared to sue to integrate the Dallas independent school district in 1956, the school board voted to integrate. With Marshall are (left to right): U. S. Tate, C. B. Bunkley, and W. J. Durham. *(R. C. Hickman Photographic Archive, 1949–1961, 1969, CN 08028, The Center for American History, The University of Texas at Austin)*

integrated school, and 2) Any reason on a list of approved reasons could be legally used to prevent integration. Price Daniel, who succeeded Shivers as governor, signed the bills into law but made no effort to enforce them. Daniel had pledged to support local boards of trustees in their decisions, implying his support of segregation, but the new attorney general, Will Wilson, recognized that federal laws and Supreme Court decisions did apply to Texas, and segregation gradually came to an end in Texas over the next two decades.

Mexican Americans also defended their rights in several notable federal court cases. *Delgado v. Bastrop ISD* (1948), prosecuted by the League of United Latin American Citizens and the American G.I. Forum of Texas, forced local school districts to cease de facto segregation; in 1954 they won the *Hernández v. State of Texas* case, which prohibited discrimination based on class. World War II veteran Dr. Hector García had organized the forum in 1948 to help Mexican American veterans get the benefits due them under the G.I. Bill of Rights of 1944, but quickly began to address other concerns. One such concern was the refusal of a Three Rivers funeral home director to permit the use of his chapel for the funeral of Félix Longoria, an American soldier who was killed in the Philippines during the last days of World War II but whose body had just been recovered. García wrote to a number of Texas senators and members of Congress, and Senator Lyndon Johnson was the only one to respond. He arranged for Longoria to be buried in Arlington National Cemetery in 1949.

## Better Roads

The press of urbanization threatened to leave agricultural and rural areas of the state behind because Texas was, until the admission of Alaska in 1959, the largest state in the nation. Throughout the 1930s, rural Texans felt isolated from their neighbors and often had to drive for hours over unpaved roads to reach the nearest market community. The state tackled the problem in 1949 with the passage of the Colson-Briscoe Act (Dolph Briscoe would later be elected governor) for construction of farm-to-market roads. The real push came during the decade of the 1950s, however, when the federal government took the lead in the construction of superhighways as a part of national interstate highway construction.

A new road system was high on President Eisenhower's agenda when he took office. Ever since he had made a cross-country trip with an Army convoy in 1919, he had realized how badly the nation needed good roads. The trip from Washington, D.C. to San Francisco had taken sixty-two days, and the soldiers had encountered all kinds of difficulties caused by poor roads and extreme temperatures. Like most Americans, Eisenhower was impressed with the German *autobahns* and noted how much more rapidly American forces moved once they reached the good German roads. President Roosevelt and Congress had made several false starts on improving the roads during the 1930s, then postponed everything as the war effort consumed the country's attention and economic resources. Eisenhower began to work on the National System of Interstate and Defense Highway Act as early as 1954, and Congress approved it in 1956. The goal was to link every major population center with a modern, high-speed expressway. The states had to finance the expensive roads, but the federal government reimbursed them for 90 percent of the cost. Texas was a major beneficiary of the system because of its size and geographical location. By 1989, the state had 3,234 miles of superhighway, more than any other state.

Better highways combined with war-related industrialization and the large number of military bases across the state greatly accelerated urbanization. In 1940, 45.4 percent of the population lived in cities; that figure increased to 59.8 percent by 1950, slightly higher than the percentage for the country as a whole (58.6 percent). There were more than 34,000 miles of highway in the state that year; increased construction of farm-to-market roads, the interstate highway system, and freeways such as North Central Expressway in Dallas (1954) accelerated the process during the next decades until, by 1995, Texas had 183,150 miles of improved roads. This led to the development of the suburbs, as mobility permitted workers to live outside the city centers. And that, in turn, led to the development of what one author has termed "edge cities"—suburban business districts, minicities, or service cities—smaller city cores outside the central business district of the larger cities, the Galleria areas in Houston and Dallas, for example, and Las Colinas in Irving. Today these edge cities are marked by the presence of office towers and hotels and are usually located near interstate highway junctions.

Growing cities, and the long distances between them, also fostered the development of commuting by air. Texas cities had long been served by Braniff Airways (founded in 1928) and Texas International Airways (founded in 1947 as Trans-Texas Airways), but their flights served primarily as one leg of a longer, out-of-state flight. Meanwhile, Rollin King's small air-taxi service gave him the idea of establishing a commuter service between the state's three major cities: Houston, Dallas, and San Antonio. King joined with his attorney, Herb Kelleher, to create Southwest Airlines, which, by the turn of the century, had become one of the leading airlines in the nation.

### Governor Price Daniel

The most important issues facing Texas as Price Daniel took the governor's office were taxation and expansion of state services such as water (the worst drought in the history of the state occurred from 1949 to 1956), schools, highways, care of the elderly, law enforcement, and prison reform. But the state's antiquated tax system creaked and groaned under the pressure, and little could be done without increased revenue. Daniel favored "sin" taxes (for example, on tobacco and liquor) and business taxes, but, after two special sessions in 1961, and despite his public objections, the legislature presented him with a 2 percent general sales tax, which he permitted to become law without his signature. The regressive nature of the tax was somewhat tempered by the exemption of food, drugs, clothing, farm supplies, and some other items, but the subsequent need for additional funds has since caused some of those items to be added to the tax list. Daniel ran for an unprecedented fourth term in 1962 but was defeated because much of the electorate blamed him for the new sales tax.

Although Daniel would not be called a champion of civil rights, he clearly stood to the left of Shivers, and neither he nor Attorney General Wilson agreed with the positions taken by Shivers and Shepperd. On the national scene, meanwhile, Johnson took a leading role in passing the 1957 Civil Rights Act, while Rayburn supported it behind the scenes so as not to offend voters in his home district. The act provided for a civil rights commission, a civil rights division within the Justice Department, and a compromised voter rights section.

## The Lyndon Johnson Era

Johnson's support of the 1957 Civil Rights Act was based on his personal convictions as well as his belief that he needed a dramatic achievement to advance his national political aspirations. Johnson had grown up in the Hill Country and

Speaker of the U.S. House of Representatives Sam Rayburn, John B. Connally, and Vice President Lyndon Johnson on the occasion of Connally's appointment as secretary of the navy. *(LBJ Library Photo by DOD Signal Corps)*

graduated from Southwest Texas State Teachers College (now Texas State University) in San Marcos, where he earned his elementary teacher's certificate in 1928. He spent a year as principal and teacher at Cotulla, in South Texas, where the poverty of his students and their families deeply impressed him. His first important political job in 1935 was as director of the National Youth Administration in Texas, a job that he left in 1937 to run for Congress, and then for the Senate in 1948. Johnson apparently had his eyes on the presidency all along and viewed the Civil Rights Act as necessary both for racial harmony in the South and for his political career. But racial harmony was immediately disrupted by Arkansas Governor Faubus's stand against integration of Central High School in Little Rock; polls showed that Johnson's popularity suffered as a result, because people in Texas linked him with Eisenhower's program. Johnson was able to regain significant ground when the Soviets launched *Sputnik I,* the first artificial earth satellite, later that year, and he seized the moment to convene hearings on its impact and the American response. He received a large part of the credit when the Democrats gained twenty-eight seats in the Senate in the 1958 midterm elections.

Rather than immediately announce for the presidency in 1960, Johnson remained in Washington, presenting the image of a hard-working senator doing his job. Rayburn and others portrayed him as a seasoned leader whose accomplishments and wisdom made him a far better choice than the young and inexperienced

Gubernatorial candidate Paul Eggers, senatorial candidate George H. W. Bush, Senator John Tower, and President Richard Nixon, campaigning in Texas. When Tower won election to the U.S. Senate and Bush to the U.S. House of Representatives, it was apparent that Texas was becoming a two-party state. *(From* Two Party Texas, *by John Knaggs, Eakin Press)*

John F. Kennedy of Massachusetts, who was already campaigning hard around the country. Johnson felt that Kennedy's weaknesses would become apparent during the campaign and that a deadlocked convention would then turn to him as the only truly qualified candidate to lead the party. He had protected his Senate seat, however, by getting the Texas legislature to move the state's primary to May so that he could be a candidate for both the Senate and the presidency.

Nominated on the first ballot at the Los Angeles convention, Kennedy was shrewd enough to realize that he needed Johnson's help to carry Texas and other crucial Southern states. He offered Johnson the vice presidential slot, and, against the advice of Rayburn and his closest advisors, Johnson accepted. The Republicans nominated Vice President Richard Nixon for president and Henry Cabot Lodge III for vice president. The 1960 campaign featured the first televised debates between presidential candidates.

Everyone had predicted a close vote in Texas, and an incident in Dallas may have swung it toward the Kennedy-Johnson ticket. Campaigning with his wife, Lady Bird, in downtown Dallas, Johnson encountered some aggressive supporters of Dallas

Republican congressman Bruce Alger, who cursed them, one of them hitting Lady Bird with a campaign sign, probably by accident. But the news media covered the event, and when the Alger camp showed little or no remorse, a number of voters probably expressed their disapproval at the ballot box. Another event that surely helped the Kennedy-Johnson ticket was Henry B. González's gubernatorial campaign of 1958. Although González had finished a poor second to Daniel, his political organization was still intact in 1960 and delivered a large percentage of the Hispanic vote to the Democrats; reversing the trend of the last two presidential elections, the Democrats carried Texas (by fewer than 50,000 votes out of the almost 2.3 million cast). Nationwide the margin was only 118,574 votes out of the more than 68 million cast. Kennedy was actually a minority president, garnering only 49.7 percent of the vote. Johnson had literally made it possible for him to become president.

Although their party had lost the presidency, Texas Republicans saw the 1960 election as something of a turning point. Despite their loss, Nixon and Lodge had captured more votes in Texas than any Republican candidate ever had. John Tower, an unknown assistant professor from Midwestern University (now Midwestern State University) in Wichita Falls, had polled more than 900,000 votes against Johnson for the Senate seat; he then won the special election over conservative Democrat William Blakely and dozens of other candidates in a runoff to fill Johnson's vacant seat and became the first Texas Republican senator since Reconstruction.

### John Connally

As the Republicans grew to become a mature political party, the Democrats engaged in a divisive ideological battle that at times became quite personal. In 1962 John B. Connally, Jr. challenged five other candidates, including the incumbent, Price Daniel, for the governorship. Connally had long been a friend of Johnson's and had served as manager for all of Johnson's major campaigns so he had the makings of a statewide network in place.

Many noticed a big difference between Connally's campaign and previous Democratic establishment efforts. Johnson's election to the vice presidency as well as the newly found potency of the liberal wing of the party, evidenced by Yarborough's election to the Senate, influenced Connally to openly court the votes of labor, African Americans, and Hispanics. After a close election, Connally took office saying that he wanted to be the "education governor" because he believed that education was the key to addressing the pressing social problems of race relations and poverty.

In hindsight, many have suggested that the incident in which Johnson and his wife were jostled—particularly when coupled with a later incident in which UN Ambassador Adlai Stevenson was heckled and hit with a placard—was illustrative of the sentiment in Dallas in the early 1960s. Dallas was home to retired general Edwin A. Walker, who had resigned from the army when he was reprimanded for distributing right-wing propaganda to his troops and had recently taken to flying the American flag upside down at his residence as a distress sign because of the federal government's integration policy. It was also home to others of similar sentiment, such as H. L. Hunt, the wealthy oilman who financed extremely conservative causes.

It was in that setting, on November 22, 1963, that President Kennedy was assassinated as he rode in a motorcade through downtown Dallas. He had come to Texas primarily in an attempt to heal the liberal-conservative rift in the state Democratic Party and to raise funds for his coming reelection campaign in 1964. Riding in the same car with the president, Governor Connally was seriously wounded, apparently by the same sniper, Lee Harvey Oswald, shooting from the Texas Schoolbook Depository. Many blamed the city's conservatism for Kennedy's death, but the Warren Commission, established immediately after the assassination, concluded in 1964 that Oswald acted alone. In 1979, after reviewing the Warren Commission findings and gathering new information, the House Select Committee on Assassinations concluded that Kennedy "was probably killed as the result of a conspiracy," but was unable to identify any participants other than Oswald or the person or persons who planned the assassination. Despite passage of the President John F. Kennedy Assassination Records Collection Act in 1992, which unsealed all of the federal records pertaining to Kennedy's assassination, conspiracy theories continue to abound.

Kennedy's assassination changed the course of both national and state politics. Lyndon Johnson became president, and John Connally, who had narrowly defeated a political unknown in 1962, now became virtually unbeatable as governor. He won reelection in 1964 by a 3–1 margin and in 1966 with 72 percent of the vote. At the same time, Johnson's ascendance was a setback to state Republicans, and he momentarily stymied their surge in Texas and quieted the battle within the state Democratic Party. Johnson led the Democratic ticket in 1964 against Republican Barry Goldwater of Arizona, defeating him by more than 700,000 votes. The future Republican president, George H. W. Bush, who had represented a Houston district in Congress for two terms, failed in his bid to unseat Yarborough in the Senate race, and the Republicans lost both of their congressional seats and all but one of their legislative offices.

Safely elected on his own, President Johnson embarked upon an ambitious program. He had already signed the Civil Rights Act of 1964, the most far-reaching civil rights act in the nation's history, which addressed voting rights, public accommodations, and discrimination both in education and on the job, and had begun to talk about the Great Society program, which would include a "war on poverty" as well as other social programs like health care for the elderly (Medicare) and the Neighborhood Youth Corps. Along with more than 200 other bills passed during Johnson's first two years, Congress passed the Voting Rights Act of 1965. The other bills included the National Museum Act, the Public Broadcasting Act, and the national endowments for the arts and humanities. At the same time, Lady Bird Johnson called attention to the environment with her well-received beautification program. Unfortunately, Johnson also prosecuted the growing war in

Vietnam, which ultimately divided the country and eroded his political base to the point that he declined to run for reelection in 1968.

The Great Society had an immediate impact on Texas. Governor Connally had opposed the public accommodations section of the 1964 Civil Rights Act but endorsed the Head Start program, thinking that Johnson might have taken the idea from a language program for Mexican American children that he had begun in Texas. In other areas of the domestic legislative package, however, Connally feuded with Johnson, because, in Connally's view, they reduced the power of the state too much and actually vetoed an eleven-county Neighborhood Youth Corps project.

## Higher Education

With his new popularity and the political assistance of a new Speaker of the House, his protégé Ben Barnes, Connally began to push his programs in higher education, increased tourism, and recruitment of out-of-state industry, and he proved himself to be one of the ablest and most powerful of the state's twentieth-century governors. Connally looked like most people thought a Texas governor should, tall in his elegant boots, with distinguished wavy gray hair frequently hidden under his white Stetson. He was articulate and, on occasion, rose to the level of oratory. *Dallas Morning News* political reporter Richard Morehead claimed that Connally was the only governor in the nation who could hold his own with California Republican governor Ronald Reagan at the annual governors conferences, where he frequently found himself defending Johnson's policies against Reagan's charges. Now he applied that power of persuasion and salesmanship to implementing his campaign promises. Early in his term, Connally had described his goal to State Department counselor and later Johnson aide Walt W. Rostow: He wanted to unify Texas, and in his opinion the best way to do that was to focus on higher education. There was plenty of room for improvement. Eighty-six percent of the graduates of the University of Texas at Austin who pursued graduate studies did so elsewhere; faculty salaries were forty-sixth in the nation; and New York produced five times more Ph.D.s annually than did Texas. Connally believed that education would be the engine that drove his other two goals.

Connally's record of achievement is impressive. He established a coordinating board for higher education and raised taxes so that he could increase faculty salaries, enlarge campuses, and create the University of Texas system in 1967. Under the leadership of his close friend, Frank C. Erwin, whom he appointed to the board of regents, appropriations for the flagship campus in Austin increased in little more than a decade from $40.4 million to $349.7 million. The system's enrollment also increased rapidly, from 29,940 to 77,437 during the same period.

Connally's programs, plus a large infusion of federal grants from the Great Society program, also led to a major increase in medical research and the number of medical schools in the state. As World War II ended, the state had only three medical schools—the University of Texas Medical Branch at Galveston, Baylor College of Medicine in Houston, and Southwestern Medical College in Dallas— that graduated about 200 doctors per year, not enough to care for the state's growing population. With the availability of federal funding, however, Texas established four new schools during the 1960s and 1970s. Although it was a private institution, Baylor would begin to receive some state funds during the 1980s.

With increased federal financing for medical research as well as the Lyndon B. Johnson Space Center (originally known as the Manned Spacecraft Center), which the National Aeronautics and Space Administration (NASA) had located near Houston, doctors at several of the Texas medical schools produced distinguished treatments and research. Perhaps the best known are Michael E. DeBakey of Methodist Hospital and Denton Cooley of St. Luke's Hospital in Houston, who have been in the forefront of heart surgery and transplants since the 1960s. DeBakey performed the first successful coronary artery bypass graft procedure in 1964, and Cooley performed the first heart transplant in the United States in 1968. Both have continued their research by working on mechanical hearts. In Dallas, meanwhile, Joseph L. Goldstein and Michael S. Brown of the University of Texas Health Science Center performed research in physiology and medicine that would be recognized with the Nobel Prize in 1985.

## The Arts

Connally's establishment of the Texas Fine Arts Commission (now the Texas Commission on the Arts) in 1965, which also receives funds through the National Endowment for the Arts, called attention to the state's growing cultural facilities. Long famous for its philanthropists, Texas is fortunate that a number of them chose to establish museums. One of the first to do so was Jessie Marion Koogler McNay of San Antonio, who left her Mexican-Mediterranean style mansion and art collection as a private museum, which opened in 1954. The Amon Carter Museum, designed by New York architect Philip Johnson, followed in 1961. Five years later the Museum of Fine Arts in Houston opened Bayou Bend, the mansion that architect John F. Staub had designed for Ima Hogg and her brothers, as a decorative arts center. Perhaps the best known of the Texas museums is the Kimbell Art Museum in Fort Worth, which opened in 1972 but one of the most eclectic, which opened to the public in 1978, is the Stark Museum of Art in Orange, containing H. J. Lutcher Stark's vast collections of Americana.

Museums also seemed to lead the way for modern architecture in the state. In 1950 John and Dominique de Menil hired architect Philip Johnson to design an International Style house for them in Houston. He went on to design the campus plan and several of the buildings for the University of St. Thomas in Houston in 1958, the same year that Ludwig Mies van der Rohe, one of the pioneers of the International Style, designed Cullinan Hall as an addition to the Museum of Fine Arts. At the same time, San Antonio architect O'Neil Ford was designing the campus of Trinity University with the revolutionary lift-slab construction technique that cut building costs considerably. Other distinguished architecture can be seen in the San Antonio Art Museum, which moved into the spectacularly renovated Lone Star Brewery in 1981; the new (1984) Dallas Museum of Art designed by Edward Larrabee Barnes; the Louis Kahn–designed Kimbell Art Museum in Fort Worth; and the new Museum of Fine Arts and the Menil Collection in Houston.

Perhaps the most recognizable building in the state after the Alamo is the Astrodome, the world's first fully air-conditioned, enclosed, domed, multipurpose sports stadium, which opened as the home of the Houston Astros baseball team in 1965. When it was determined that baseball players could not see fly balls against the bright glare of the plastic roof and crisscrossed girders during daylight, Judge Roy M. Hofheinz, head of the Houston Sports Association, ordered the roof painted. The lack of sunlight meant that natural grass could not grow in the stadium, so in a well-publicized event, Hofheinz obtained an artificial grass called Astroturf®. The Houston Oilers football team played there until moving to Nashville in 1997, and the domed stadium has hosted dozens of other sporting events as well as concerts, conventions, and religious meetings. Today the Astrodome is a relic, with both the Astros and the Houston Texans football team playing in other stadiums, but it continues to be popular with tourists, averaging approximately 4 million visitors a year since it opened.

Music in Texas still reflects the state's heterogeneous character. For years German music could be heard in the beer halls and gardens of San Antonio, while just a few streets over, in La Plaza del Zacate or Haymarket Square, Tejanos played Mexican folk and popular music. Adopting the accordion from German musicians, Tejanos created the *conjunto* style, now popular through Texas and Mexico. Meanwhile, the folk music of the South combined with the cowboy style of Texas to create what became known as "hillbilly" music, which later evolved into the upscale country-and-western tunes that most of the state's radio stations now play. The first national country-and-western star may have been the singer Jimmy Rogers, who moved to Kerrville in 1929. A few years later, Bob Wills borrowed from such great jazzmen as Benny Goodman to create "western swing" and became popular as part of the band on W. Lee O'Daniel's radio program. Maurice Woodward "Tex" Ritter carved a niche for himself and other singing cowboys in what became known as "western music" and smoothed the way for the stars of the B-grade western movies of the 1950s. One such star was Gene Autry (from Tioga), who parlayed his matinee stardom into a chain of radio stations and, ultimately, ownership of the California Angels major league baseball team and the establishment of the Autry Museum of Western Heritage in Los Angeles. Ernest Tubb took country music in another direction and pioneered what was widely known as "honky-tonk" music, whereas performers like George Jones retained his "country" style but moved more toward the popular genre. Meanwhile, Willie Nelson and a few others who had become disaffected with the growing mainstream of country music moved to Central Texas, where they developed the "Austin sound." Tejanos have contributed to country-and-western music, too, with singers like Trini López, Freddy Fender, Johnny Rodríguez, and Selena.

African Americans have also added much to the Texas arts mix. Ornette Coleman of Fort Worth has revolutionized the way the saxophone is used in what has been called "free jazz." Weldon Leo "Jack" Teagarden of Vernon became a famous jazz trombonist and orchestra leader and played with Benny Goodman, Louis Armstrong, and Paul Whiteman, among others. Perhaps the most famous African American Texan artist, however, is Alvin Ailey of Rogers, who debuted on Broadway in 1954 and stayed on in New York to study ballet and modern dance, founding the Alvin Ailey American Dance Theater in 1958. Drawing upon his "blood memories" of Central Texas, the blues, spirituals, and gospel music, he choreographed his masterpiece, *Revelations,* in 1960, and the company remains popular today with its unique blend of modern and African American expression.

Classical music in Texas also boomed in postwar Texas. Although the state had three major symphony orchestras during the 1950s (in Dallas, Houston, and San Antonio), it was pianist Van Cliburn's triumph at the prestigious Tchaikovsky Piano Competition in Moscow in 1958 that really attracted the public's attention. Van Cliburn was born in Shreveport, Louisiana, but grew up in Kilgore. After winning international fame, in 1962 he helped establish the Van Cliburn International Piano Competition in Fort Worth. Meanwhile, smaller orchestras gained prominence and proficiency in Amarillo, Fort Worth, Austin, Wichita Falls, Corpus Christi, Beaumont, and Lubbock, and other cities. Opera companies perform throughout the state, but there are professional companies in San Antonio, Fort Worth, Houston, Dallas, and Austin. In addition, pianist James Dick performs and administers the International Festival-Institute at Round Top, established in 1971 to provide advanced musical instruction to gifted young musicians.

### After Johnson and Connally

Both Johnson and Connally announced that they would not run again in 1968. Johnson was driven from office by the social unrest and urban riots accompanying the war in Vietnam. He returned to the Hill Country, where he wrote his memoirs and supervised construction of the Lyndon Baines Johnson Library and Museum on the campus of the University of Texas at Austin.

When Connally stepped down after three terms, Preston Smith of Lubbock, who had served the same length of time as lieutenant governor, was elected governor in 1968. Having grown up on a West Texas farm and worked his way through high school and college, Smith was a plainspoken, uncharismatic but sensitive person who suffered by comparison with Connally and was offended by suggestions that he lacked a vivid or humorous personality. His trademark polka-dot tie (Governor Price Daniel had advised him to wear something distinctive) seemed only to call attention to his bland personality. "He doesn't look very good," an editorial writer once said in comparing him to the former University of Texas All-American quarterback, Bobby Layne, also from Lubbock, "all he can do is beat you. . . ."

Smith was an informal governor, who often answered his own telephone and placed calls himself, but Smith seemed to have an inherent mistrust of city dwellers, and the feeling was mutual. He immediately set the tone for his administration when he was called to Washington in the spring of 1969 to learn the details of a federal plan designed to ease slum housing problems. He opposed the plan, he told reporters, because "some people just like to live in slums." Elected at the same time as Smith was Lieutenant Governor Ben Barnes, almost Smith's polar opposite and the apparent heir of the Johnson/Connally mantle. He had been the youngest person to serve as Speaker of the Texas House when he was elected in 1965 at age twenty-six and polled more votes than any other Texas politician—more than 2 million—to win the lieutenant governor's office.

The third member of the leadership was House Speaker Gus Mutscher, who assumed the office with the opening of the legislative session in 1969. A conservative from rural Washington County, Mutscher soon exercised surprising control over the House (even more than Barnes had exercised) by sticking to his motto, "never quit politicking and never underestimate your opponent." With Mutscher as Speaker and Barnes as lieutenant governor, Smith proposed a program that met with only limited success. He got a pay raise for schoolteachers, but his water plan, which proposed transferring water from East Texas or from outside the state to needy areas like West Texas, went down to defeat at the hands of East Texas legislators. He supported the establishment of two new medical schools, one in Houston and the other in Lubbock, and got funding for a minimum wage and for vocational education. In the face of a "housewives' revolt," he was embarrassed to have to back away from a Barnes/Mutscher proposal to add food to the list of items subject to a sales tax.

### The State and the Federal Government

Federal interventions during the 1960s and early 1970s continued to alter the social and political fabric of Texas, much as Key had anticipated. First, U.S. Supreme Court decisions continued to have an impact: *Baker v. Carr* (1962) and *Reynolds v. Sims* (1964) brought about what became known as "one-man, one-vote," which meant that both houses of a state legislature had to be reapportioned regularly so that each representative and each senator would represent approximately the same number of citizens. Subsequent decisions affecting Texas held that a county could have more than one member of the Senate and more than seven members of the House. These were important legal victories for urban areas, for the first time permitting neighborhoods such as Houston's largely African American fifth ward to have its own representation.

Federal actions also continued to broaden the electorate. The Twenty-fourth Amendment to the U.S. Constitution in 1964 made it illegal to require a poll tax to vote in federal elections. The big change, however, came with the Voting Rights Act of 1965, which outlawed state and local restrictions on voters as being prejudiced against minorities and provided federal officials to monitor elections. Even after adoption of the Twenty-fourth Amendment, Texas had kept the poll tax for state elections, but it succumbed to the Voting Rights Act in 1966 when Judge Homer Thornberry, a Johnson protégé on the U.S. Court of Appeals of the Fifth Judicial Circuit, ruled it to be a violation of the Fourteenth Amendment. Subsequent to these reforms, Barbara Jordan from Houston's fifth ward became the first African American to be elected to the Texas Senate since Reconstruction, and Curtis Graves and J. E. Lockridge were elected to the House. In 1971, the Twenty-sixth Amendment to the U.S. Constitution gave eighteen-year-olds the right to vote.

These changes also opened up local elections and changed the face of governing bodies in Texas. The political complexion of the Senate changed overnight, for example, as moderates or liberals gained office. The impact of these changes also reached the local level, and organizations such as the Citizen's Charter Association in Dallas and the Good Government League in San Antonio, which had dominated local politics for years, lost their control.

Coupled with these federal acts, African Americans and Hispanics continued to campaign for their rights. Nonviolent protests that began in Greensboro, North Carolina in 1960 spread to Texas. Students at two historically African American colleges, Wiley and Bishop, staged nonviolent demonstrations that year, and the following year students at Texas Southern, the University of Texas, North Texas State, and other colleges protested against segregated theaters and restaurants. James Farmer, a native Texan, headed the Congress of Racial Equality (CORE). Fear of bad publicity and federal laws gradually brought segregation to an end. In Houston, for example, local businesspeople quietly reached an agreement with a group of college students and community leaders that if they would not demonstrate, public facilities would be integrated. While cities throughout the nation dissolved into confrontations and riots, for the most part Texas cities remained calm.

Meanwhile, the Hispanic takeover of the city council of Crystal City, the G.I. Forum, Henry González's losing gubernatorial campaign, and the 1960 presidential race had all encouraged Mexican Americans to participate in the political process. The result was the Political Association of Spanish-speaking Organizations (PASO), which, assisted by Teamsters officials, helped organize the Hispanic voters in Crystal City in 1963. Their new majorities on both the city council and school board sent a message to the white minority population throughout South Texas that their rule would no longer go unchallenged, and there were subsequent victories in Carrizo Springs and Cotulla.

This new-found Hispanic activism resulted in one of Governor Connally's most embarrassing moments in the summer of 1966. In an effort to get the legislature to adopt a minimum wage of $1.25 per hour, organizers in South Texas decided to march the almost 500 miles from Rio Grande City to the capital to focus publicity on the effort.

Although he had planned to be out of the capitol building on Labor Day, when the marchers were scheduled to arrive, Connally told Speaker of the House Ben Barnes, "I don't think it's right for them to just march up here and nobody be here." With Barnes and Attorney General Waggoner Carr in tow, he headed to New Braunfels, where he found the bedraggled little band. Shaking hands all around, Connally urged them to call off their march because "things can get out of hand in marches," a veiled reference to the riots, violence, and bloodshed that had occurred throughout the nation, and said that he would not receive them in Austin because he did not want to "lend the dignity" of his office to any such demonstration. When state labor leaders arrived at the scene, the mood turned more confrontational and developed into a standoff, and Connally, Barnes, and Carr departed in their executive limousine.

The marchers rallied and continued gathering supporters as they neared Austin and as word of Connally's rather highhanded attempt to stop them spread. Senator Yarborough met the marchers at the capitol on Labor Day along with a number of supporters, including labor leader Cesar Chavez of the United Farm Workers and Connally's brother, Golfrey, an economics professor at San Antonio College. The minimum wage law did not pass that year, but historian Arnoldo de León considers this incident one of the formative events of the Chicano movement.

Some of the most dramatic changes during this time gave women many rights that they had been long denied. One woman who epitomized women's rights was Oveta Culp Hobby, wife of the former governor, who had been the head of the Women's Interest Section in the army during the war and then became the first commander of the Women's Army Corps. She supported Eisenhower for president in 1952 and was named to his cabinet as the first secretary of health, education, and welfare in 1953. When she returned to Houston in 1955, she resumed her position as president and editor of the *Houston Post* and, in 1956, became chair of the board of directors of the newly organized Bank of Texas. Another prominent woman in Texas at this time was Dallas attorney Hermine D. Tobolowsky, president of the Texas Federation of Business and Professional Women. Tobolowsky had been active in women's rights issues since the 1940s and had identified a number of laws that she considered discriminatory, such as the denial of women's right to control property they owned at marriage or had inherited. Tobolowsky testified before a state Senate committee hearing in support of a bill that would have changed a number of these laws. The bill failed, and her treatment before the committee caused her to resolve instead to support an equal rights amendment to the Texas Constitution. She traveled around the state speaking to women and civic groups, rallying support for the amendment. It was introduced at each session of the legislature from 1959 until it was finally passed in 1972, after the introduction of the federal Equal Rights Amendment in Congress provided greater credibility for the effort. Tobolowsky became known as the mother of the Texas Equal Rights Amendment.

As the feminist movement gained strength nationally, many Texas women began to pay attention. The National Organization for Women (NOW) established chapters in Texas, and the Texas Women's Political Caucus encouraged women to get involved in the political process. New methods of birth control (such as the birth control pill) influenced many women to delay marriage and family while pursuing an education or a career. Again, actions of the federal government had an impact. Title VII of the 1964 Civil Rights Act (upheld by later court decisions) gave women control of their property and prohibited discrimination in the workplace. Title IX of the 1972 Education Amendments required universities receiving federal funds to allow women to participate in many activities that had been closed to them. In sports, for example, universities organized a number of teams for women athletes that had not existed before Title IX. That same year Texan attorney Sarah Weddington argued and won the case of *Roe* v. *Wade* in the U.S. Supreme Court, which struck down many state laws forbidding abortion.

### The Sharpstown Scandal

Another federal intervention in Texas helped bring down the curtain on an era. In 1971 the Securities and Exchange Commission (SEC) charged several state officials and others with illegally profiting from a quick-turnover stock deal. According to the SEC, Houston businessman Frank Sharp wanted a banking bill passed that would provide state-backed depositor's insurance to exempt his bank, Sharpstown State Bank, from regulation by the Federal Deposit Insurance Corporation; he bribed several current and former state officials by loaning them money from his bank to purchase stock in one of his companies, the National Bankers Life Insurance Company, with the understanding that once the bill had passed, they could sell their stock at a handsome profit. Governor Smith included the bank bill in the agenda for the second special legislative session in 1971, and Speaker of the House Gus Mutscher, Jr. and his allies pushed it through. Smith later vetoed the bill on the advice of the state's banking law experts, but not until he and several others had sold their stock at a profit. A Travis County grand jury indicted Mutscher, Representative Tommy Shannon, and Rush McGinty (an aide to Mutscher) for bribery and conspiracy, and in March 1972 they were convicted by an Abilene jury and given a sentence of five years' probation. The SEC alleged that Governor Smith, state Democratic chair and state banking board member Elmer Baum and others had been bribed, but did not charge them.

The result was a political house-cleaning and modest shift to the left in the state's politics. Conservative rancher Dolph Briscoe of Uvalde, who had run in 1968, swept the gubernatorial primary with a "Mr. Clean" image. This election ended the political career of Lieutenant Governor Barnes, who had also borrowed money from Sharp's bank, even though he was not named in the scandal, and was, therefore, connected to it in the minds of most voters. The same fate awaited Governor Smith, who ran a poor fourth.

The vengeful voters elected moderate Houston newspaper executive William P. Hobby, Jr., son of Governor Hobby, as lieutenant governor over seven other Democratic candidates, and reform-minded moderate Democrat John L. Hill of Houston, a former secretary of state, defeated the popular three-term attorney general, Crawford C. Martin, who had been criticized for his handling of the stock fraud scandal and for his own relationship with Frank Sharp. The makeup of the legislature also changed significantly, with many newcomers winning election to both the House and the Senate. Virtually all of these newly elected officials were committed to reform of some kind, and Briscoe did not try to control the party machinery in the same way that his predecessors had.

The Sharpstown scandal proved a boon to Republicans. Coupled with it was former Governor John Connally's service as secretary of the treasury in Republican President Richard Nixon's administration and his support of Nixon against Democrat George McGovern in the 1972 presidential election.

# Conclusion

Although by 1972 the state was not engaged in the kind of class conflict that Key had foreseen, there was no denying that Texas had changed. The post-war growth of the oil and gas industry (including the state's acquisition of the Tidelands) had major impact on the economy, but not sufficient to offset the dramatic growth in population. The percentage of population growth in Texas outpaced that of the nation throughout the twentieth century. In 1962 the state passed the 10-million mark in population, reaching 11,197,730 in 1970, and most Texans lived in the cities. Rather than being restructured, however, the state's antiquated tax system was merely amended, primarily by the 1961 sales tax, which by 2000 supplied 55 percent of the state's revenue. By the election of 1972, economic and political power had shifted to the cities, raising the issues of urban poverty, crime, and pollution for Texas that had long plagued eastern urban centers. The state's cultural institutions flourished after the war, with new museums, orchestras, and educational facilities being established, but, again, these improvements hardly kept pace with the needs that an increased population demanded.

Major changes in governing procedures opened up the Democratic Party, tilting it toward the liberals, despite Governor Shivers' conservative influence. Lyndon Johnson's long career had a great impact on the state, but with his departure from office, the move back to the right, and to the Republican Party, resumed and included even his long-time friend and campaign manager, John Connally. These issues, along with the perennial problem of water, would dominate political dialogue during the last quarter of the twentieth century.

## SUGGESTED READINGS

### Stressing the One-Party System
The best overview for these years is George Norris Green, *The Establishment in Texas Politics: The Primitive Years, 1938–1957* (1984).

### Conservatives Take Charge
One of the key books of the era is V. O. Key, Jr., *Southern Politics in State and Nation* (1949). Chandler Davidson, *Race and Class in Texas Politics* (1990) provides a

thoughtful update and analysis of Key's theories. See also Paul Casdorf, *A History of the Republican Party in Texas, 1865–1965* (1965); Roger M. Olien, *From Token to Triumph: The Texas Republicans Since 1920* (1982); and Don E. Carleton, *Red Scare: Right-Wing Hysteria, Fifties Fanaticism, and Their Legacy in Texas* (1985).

For agriculture, see Donald E. Green, *Land of the Underground Rain: Irrigation on the Texas High Plains, 1910–1970* (1973).

## Lyndon Baines Johnson Era

Among the more useful and readable biographies of Lyndon Johnson are Robert A. Caro, *The Years of Lyndon Johnson: Means of Ascent* (1990) and *Master of the Senate* (2002); Robert Dalleck, *Lone Star Rising: Lyndon Johnson and His Times, 1908–1960* (1991); also see Dorsey B. Hardeman and Donald C. Bacon, *Rayburn: A Biography* (1987); Sam Kinch, Jr. and Stuart Long's *Allan Shivers: The Pied Piper of Texas Politics* (1974); James Reston, Jr.'s *The Lone Star: The Life of John Connally* (1989); Don E. Carleton's *A Breed So Rare: The Life of J. R. Parten, Liberal Texas Oilman, 1896–1992* (1999); and Patrick Cox's *Ralph Yarborough: The People's Senator* (2001).

For information on African Americans, see Alwyn Barr, *Black Texans: A History of African Americans in Texas, 1528–1995* (1996); Robert D. Bullard, *Invisible Houston: The Black Experience in Boom and Bust* (1987); Merline Pitre, *In Struggle Against Jim Crow: Lulu B. White and the NAACP, 1900–1957* (1999). For material on women, see Ruthe Winegarten, *Black Texas Women: A Sourcebook* (1996). Good studies relating to the history of Mexican Americans include Carl Allsup, *The American G.I. Forum: Origins and Evolution* (1982), and Guadalupe San Miguel, Jr., *Let All of Them Take Heed: Mexican Americans and the Campaign for Educational Equality in Texas, 1910–1981* (1987).

# 14
## Recognizing Old and New Realities

**D**on't go for it unless it's already in your pocket," Lyndon Johnson had advised Texas state senator Barbara Jordan when she contemplated running for a seat in the U.S. Congress. Having the seat in her pocket must have been hard to imagine in her first two attempts to gain election to a Texas legislative seat in the early 1960s. Then, the African American attorney from Houston's fifth district had campaigned hard as part of a liberal Democratic coalition, only to see many of the white males in the coalition get elected while she did not. At the time, her family—loving and supportive but reflecting the traditional values of the era—had encouraged her to curtail her political activity and think about getting married.

The political picture for Jordan and other minority candidates had begun to change with the federal actions of the mid-1960s: The Voting Rights Act had struck down some of the barriers to voting African Americans had experienced, the "poll tax" that had kept many poor people and minorities from exercising their franchise had been abolished, and the Supreme Court had mandated redistricting efforts, giving urban areas with larger populations more representatives than rural areas and moving from at-large legislative seats to officeholders representing specific areas.

All of this meant that Jordan could run again in a new Houston eleventh district with a significant percentage of African American voters. In 1966, she won a state senate seat and by 1972 had proven herself a skilled team player, enjoyed the support of former president Johnson, and served as vice chair of the newest senate redistricting panel, allowing her to help control the shape her district would take. Running for the U.S. Congress seat from herdistrict, she was opposed by another African American legislator, Curtis

| Year | Event |
|------|-------|
| 1972 | Women and minorities gain greater visibility in Texas political elections |
| 1974 | State legislators reject new state constitution |
| 1975 | State legislators approve revised new constitution, but voters reject it |
| 1978 | William Clements, Jr. becomes the first Republican governor of Texas since Reconstruction |
| 1979 | Juneteenth is made an official state holiday |
| Mid-80s | The oil business in Texas goes from boom to bust; Michael Dell begins his successful personal computer business |
| 1985 | Joseph L. Goldstein and Michael S. Brown of the University of Texas Health Science Center in Dallas win Nobel Prize in medicine for their research on cholesterol |
| 1989 | Southwest Airline revenues top $1 billion |
| 1992 | U.S., Canada, and Mexico enter into North American Free Trade Agreement (NAFTA) |
| 1997 | Senate Bill 1 creates a new state water-planning system |
| 1998 | After two decades of alternating Democratic and Republican administrations, Republicans consolidate control of state offices |
| 2000 | George W. Bush wins U.S. presidency; Hispanics are largest ethnic group in four major Texas cities |
| 2001 | Enron Corporation declares bankruptcy in Houston |
| 2002 | Rio Grande runs dry |

Graves. She had such solid support, how-ever, both within the Texas political power structure and within her home district, that she became the "first black woman from a southern state to serve in Congress," the first African American elected to Congress from Texas, and one of only two African American representatives elected from the South, which had not sent an African American to Congress since 1900. Chosen to speak before the Democratic National Convention in 1976, she would tell delegates, "[M]y presence here is one additional bit of evidence that the American Dream need not forever be deferred." Jordan's political success symbolized some of the changes that were taking place in Texas and the nation.

As Texans moved through the final decades of the twentieth century and into the twenty-first, their actions and attitudes as individuals and groups, along with broader economic and political trends, were redefining Texas identity. The state continued to have a significantly diverse population, but now that diversity was increasingly acknowledged and reflected in the political structures and culture of Texas. The state continued to be a land of economic opportunity, but this opportunity increasingly took new forms—or new variations on old forms. Texans continued to value independence and limited government, but now these values had to be balanced even more than before with the challenges of dynamic urban growth, rural decline, and federal-state relations. Finally, the state continued to be defined in large part by the scope and character of its land, but Texans continued to be drawn to the cities; the remaining farmers and ranchers found the challenges of working and managing the land more and more daunting; and Texans, in general, faced the challenges of preserving natural features and natural resources that they had previously taken for granted.

## Diversity in Texas Politics and Culture

The entrance of women and minorities into the political arena reflected a new diversity in Texas politics, due in part, to the rise of the liberal coalition in the Democratic party anticipated by Keys. This new political diversity also came from Republican inroads into, and eventual dominance of, state political power structures as Texans reacted to the shift in the Democratic Party by choosing more conservative candidates.

### Women Entering Texas Politics

Women—Mexican American, African American, and Anglo—began setting political agendas and winning local elections. In the late 1960s, Anita Martinez of Dallas had already become the first Mexican American woman to win a city council seat in Texas, and Wilhemina Delco had become the first African American, male or female, to be elected to the Austin school board. But the year 1972 proved to be a watershed for Texas women in politics. Other women saw Barbara

Jordan campaigning for the U.S. Congress and Sissy Farenthold for the governorship and began to see opportunities for themselves. Farenthold had directly challenged the power structure in her three years in the House. She would recall, "I went there knowing blacks weren't represented, knowing Mexican Americans weren't represented. I found that Texans weren't even represented." She and Jordan cosponsored the Equal Legal Rights amendment to the Texas constitution.

Sefronia Thompson, a former junior- and senior-high-school teacher, would recall being galvanized by Jordan's and Farenthold's campaigns: "I just wanted to be part of this big harvest, so I ran. And I won." Thompson was one of a record half-dozen women elected to the Texas legislature, along with a young lawyer named Sarah Weddington, who was about to win a landmark Supreme Court case, *Roe v. Wade,* that legalized abortion in the United States. Among the other five were two African American women, Thompson and Eddie Bernice Johnson, and two Republican women, Betty Andujar and Kay Bailey.

Farenthold, perceived to be too liberal by many, lost to Dolph Briscoe in the 1972 runoff, but at the Democratic National Convention that year, she finished second in the voting for the vice presidential slot on the Democratic presidential ticket. Forty percent of the delegates were women—compared to a mere 13 percent only four years before. At the Republican convention as well, a previously unheard-of 30 percent of the delegates were women.

Throughout the 1970s women would continue to emerge in positions of local and regional political power. In 1973 Lucy Patterson became the first African American woman elected to the Dallas city council. In 1975 Lila Cockrell became the first female mayor of a major Texas city, in this case, San Antonio. The next year, Irma Rangel, a former teacher and lawyer from Kingsville, became the first Mexican American woman to take a seat in the Texas House of Representatives, and Ann Richards, on her way to the governor's mansion, became a Travis County commissioner.

After election, these women found themselves facing an entrenched power structure. "There was a great deal of questioning and suspicion and challenge we could see on the faces of those who had been there longer, because this was a new crop of people for a new era," Eddie Bernice Johnson would recall, "and we ushered in that era, and we made a lot of changes."

Johnson worked on bills to eliminate credit discrimination against women and housing and home loan discrimination against minorities. She also labored to see that poor children got school breakfasts and pregnant teachers got benefits and job security. She and most of the other women in these new roles supported the federal Equal Rights Amendment (ERA), first introduced in 1923 to promote gender equality and resurrected in the fertile activist climate of the late 1960s. The U.S. House and Senate had passed the measure. Now enough states needed to ratify the ERA to make it law, and the Texas legislature was among the first in the southern states to do so, having recently also ratified the Equal Legal Rights amendment to the state constitution sponsored by Jordan and Farenthold.

By the late 1970s, the national mood had become more conservative and national ERA ratification failed. Nonetheless, many of the 2,000 delegates to the 1977 International Women's Year National Conference in Houston remained energized by the possibilities of addressing social, legal, and economic ills and inequities in government. Charged by the federal government with preparing a national plan, they produced a host of resolutions dealing with women's rights and general societal improvements.

### Minorities Entering Texas Politics

Even as women focused on bringing gender issues into the public forum, members of ethnic minorities—male and female—continued to fight for their own distinctive identities as Texans and for inclusion in the political power structure. African Americans were building on the civil rights movement of the 1950s and the activism of the 1960s. So were Texas Hispanics, primarily Mexican Americans and Mexicans but also those with roots in other Central and South American countries.

In 1970, the census showed 2 million Mexican Americans in the state—about one in every five Texans. They were concentrated in the major cities, but also spread through the agricultural and cattle-raising towns of South and West Texas. Although many were laborers, an increasing number—some 40 percent—constituted a Mexican American middle class. Activism was growing among young urban Hispanics, particularly with the rise of the Mexican American Youth Organization (MAYO) after a 1967 activist meeting in El Paso and 1968 meetings in San Antonio and Laredo. MAYO leaders felt that institutional racism in the United States was so entrenched that only an alternate educational system delivered by Mexican Americans for Mexican Americans and through a separate political party could address their concerns. Their activism led to another political coup in Crystal City—and to a serious run by candidates of a Mexican American party for the offices of Texas governor and lieutenant governor.

The earlier Crystal City "electoral revolt" had come to naught by 1965, leaving many of the town's Mexican Americans wary when José Angel Gutiérrez returned to the town as a MAYO organizer in 1969. Gutiérrez, who had participated in the 1963 revolt as a college student, found that despite the wariness, many in the community were upset over the stipulation that candidates for the Crystal City High School homecoming queen and court must have a parent who had graduated from the school. In this era of limited schooling for most Mexican Americans, this requirement eliminated most Hispanic students. Now Gutiérrez, his wife Luz, activist Virginia Músquiz, and others organized a response that put pressure on the school board and mounted a student boycott that emptied the high school of almost 65 percent of its students.

By spring, a new political party was coalescing across South Texas—*La Raza Unida* (United Race or United People), which would come to be known as RUP (*Raza Unida* Party). In Crystal City, Gutiérrez and other RUP candidates captured school board and city council seats. Gutiérrez would explain, "We were chicanos [a

1970s term for activist Mexican Americans] who were starved for any kind of meaningful participation in decision making, policy making and leadership positions."

Similar victories occurred in other South Texas towns, with RUP leaders pushing an agenda of Chicano power and pride, although the results were not as dramatic as in Crystal City, where Gutiérrez became school board chair. Here Anglo teachers uneasy with the new regime were replaced with RUP supporters; much of the curriculum centered on Mexican American experience; and militant stances became the norm—for example, the boycott of lettuce picked by exploited migrant workers.

On the heels of the RUP victories came a barrage of legal challenges to the party's place on the ballot and, in the next local South Texas elections, significant vote fraud against the activists. Gutiérrez, anticipating opposition from Mexican American Democrats, among others, felt that the party was not ready for statewide races in 1972; other activists overruled him, however, and Gutiérrez assisted in selecting an RUP candidate for governor, a twenty-nine-year-old attorney from Waco and MAYO member named Ramsey Muñiz.

Muñiz, a former lineman on the Baylor University football team, traveled the state in a red 1962 Plymouth announcing that "the days of being led to the polls to vote straight ticket for these two other parties are over." He was personable and energetic, militant without being overbearing, and his campaign gained momentum when Dolph Briscoe beat Farenthold for the Democratic nomination, for Briscoe, to many, was an old-style Democrat unfriendly to minorities.

Muñiz's running mate for the lieutenant governor slot, Alma Canales, was only twenty-four years old, more radical, and less able or less inclined to court the middle class, whether Mexican American or Anglo. Her presence on the ticket signaled the depth of Tejana activism. In fact, in 1971 in Houston, Mexican American women had put together "the first national conference ever organized to deal specifically with Mexican-American women's concerns." Even the relatively conservative LULAC Women's Affairs Committee in this election year had a Texas convention at which they urged LULAC to work for women in important governmental positions.

With Muñiz officially a candidate, Gutiérrez became his campaign manager, and they drew an array of not only militant but moderate Mexican Americans and liberal Anglos to consider voting for the third party. At the same time, they drew the ire of liberal Democrats unhappy with Briscoe but unwilling to desert the party. Lawyer Mark Smith warned ominously, "A vote for La Raza Unida . . . is nothing more than a vote for destruction of the liberal wing of the Democratic Party in Texas. It can only result in destroying any hope for a two-party state in which the Democratic Party is representative of the voice of the people and their aspirations for justice."

On election day, Muñiz's 6.28 percent of the vote may have looked negligible to some, but it was sufficient to worry the leaders of the Texas Democratic Party, for Muñiz almost became the spoiler in a race in which Briscoe could have expected the RUP votes.

La Raza Unida continued to challenge the traditional political power structure. Gutiérrez, who would go on to become judge for Zavala County, called for education and urban renewal that would take into account Mexican American claims, plans, and dreams for their city communities. Many of the activists advocated a brand of cultural nationalism that seemed as exclusive in its way as that of the Anglo-dominated institutional structures; these activists split off both from other Mexican American groups and from the RUP, with different ideologies and political plans. But they stimulated older organizations, such as the G.I. Forum and LULAC, to address issues of equality more boldly, and they demonstrated that Tejanos and Tejanas could and would participate in defining local and state government issues. Another organization, the Mexican American Legal Defense and Education Fund (MALDEF) led the way in creating court challenges to the imbalances in power.

## The Rise of the Republican Party

For more than a century, the traditional power structure in Texas had been strongly, consistently based in the Democratic Party. But with the changes of the 1960s and 1970s, liberals had gained power within the party and had drawn activist reformers and minority voters in to it. Most of the women and minorities entering politics in the 1970s did so as Democrats. More conservative Texans—including many concerned with the rapid rate of societal and political change they saw the activists advocating—switched to the Republican Party. This was already evident in 1972, when white middle-class voters uneasy with Lyndon Johnson's Great Society and affirmative action elected seventeen Republicans to the House and three to the Senate. Among these new legislators were the two Republican women mentioned earlier, Betty Andujar and Kay Bailey. In the state elections of 1978, for the first time since Reconstruction, a Republican—Dallas oilman William Clements, Jr.—was elected governor of the state. His victory, albeit by a narrow margin, surprised his opponent, Attorney General John Hill, and was attributed in part to Democratic president Jimmy Carter's declining popularity.

In the 1980s, Texas was clearly a two-party state. Democrat Mark White defeated Clements in the election of 1982, but four years later, their positions were reversed, with Clements defeating the incumbent White.

Minorities and women continued to make inroads. In 1981, Democrat Henry Cisneros was elected mayor of San Antonio; not since the administration of Juan Seguín 140 years earlier had a Hispanic headed the city government. That same year, El Paso native Sandra Day O'Connor was appointed to the U.S. Supreme Court by the Republican administration of Ronald Reagan, and became the first woman on the Court. In 1982, Democrat Ann Richards won election as Texas state treasurer; not since the second election of Ma Ferguson in 1932 had a woman achieved election to statewide office.

In 1986, Democrat Judith Zaffirini of Laredo joined the Texas state senate as its first Mexican American woman. A former volunteer lobbyist for the mentally ill and mentally retarded, Zaffirini set out to effect what she termed a "momma agenda," advocating legislation that reflected her concerns as a mother, such as requiring immunizations for Texas children. She playfully reminded a fellow legislator, "[Y]ou study legislation from the perspective of Bubba. I study legislation from the perspective of Momma."

Zaffirini entered the senate as conservatism continued to grow nationally. The American South as a whole shifted heavily from Democratic to Republican, the majority voting in national elections for Ronald Reagan for president, then for his former vice president and former Texas congressman George H. W. Bush, who was elected president in 1988. In Texas, Clements could enjoy a "veto-proof" second term, as the 1986 elections had given Republicans more than one-third of the House votes. Then in 1990 former Travis County commissioner and state treasurer Ann Richards outpolled Republican oilman and rancher Clayton Williams in the governor's race. At the same time, Republican Kay Bailey, now Kay Bailey Hutchinson, won election as state treasurer, earning recognition as the first Republican woman to secure a statewide elective position, and Democrat Dan Morales became the first Hispanic attorney general. Two years later, Morris Overstreet became the first African American to gain statewide office with his election as a judge on the Texas Court of Criminal Appeals.

Despite these gains—and Richards's appointments of women, Hispanics, and African Americans to various boards and commissions—the percentages of women and minority officeholders remained low. For example, in the early 1990s, city councils in Texas, on average, had one Hispanic for every twenty members, even though the Hispanic population statewide was one in five. In 1997, the Texas House and Senate had thirty-three women members, but this constituted less than 20 percent of the total membership.

The biggest political story of the 1990s was the consolidation of Republican power in the state. George W. Bush, son of the former president, won the governorship in 1994 and again in 1998, making Republican inroads even in heavily Hispanic counties identified with the liberal Democrats. In 1998 Republicans also won the offices of lieutenant governor, attorney general, comptroller, land commissioner, and agriculture commissioner. Republicans were a majority in the Texas state senate and close to a majority in the House. Among these numbers were women and minorities; for example, Susan Combs served as the first female agriculture commissioner, and Michael Williams, an African American, became a railroad commissioner.

The growing power of the Texas Republican Party in the 1990s reflected national events, including a "Republican revolution" in 1994 during the administration of Democratic president Bill Clinton. The Republican Party vowed to regain the control it had lost when incumbent George H. W. Bush lost the presidency to Clinton in 1992, and it did so in large part by propelling Texas governor George W. Bush into the White House in the election of 2000. Governor Bush ran against Democrat Al Gore, Clinton's vice president, for the presidency. Vote-count problems, particularly in Florida, delayed election results, but a Supreme Court ruling on the returns confirmed totals that led to Bush's victory in the electoral college.

## Cultural Diversity

The political ferment of the 1960s and 1970s had made clear that Texans were not homogenous. It gave rise to a new or more widely shared appreciation for different cultural roots and ways of life. The Institute of Texas Cultures, first opened in 1968 as part of the San Antonio World's Fair at Hemisfair Plaza, began producing exhibits and information on Texans of various ethnic origins, its mission statement to "enhanc[e] the understanding of the history and diverse cultures of Texas." In 1973 San Antonio students and community members of Mexican heritage staged an original play, *El Alamo: Our Version of What Happened.* Visitors flocked to celebrations of traditional German holidays such as Oktoberfest and those adapted from their experiences in Texas, such as the Easter Fires pageant in Fredericksburg, which combines ancient custom with Texas frontier legend. Texans of African American descent reinvigorated the celebration of "Juneteenth," a holiday originally established to mark the public recognition of Texas slaves' freedom—the reading of the Emancipation Proclamation in Galveston with the arrival of federal troops after the Civil War. In 1979, the legislature voted to make the date, June 19, a state holiday.

The Hispanic population of Texas, primarily Mexican and Mexican American, continued to grow, with census figures doubling between 1970 and 1990. Holidays such as Cinco de Mayo and Mexican Independence Day were more widely celebrated. In many parts of the state, Hispanic families staged elaborate *quinceaneras* (fifteenth-birthday parties) for their daughters, complete with formal dresses and tuxedos for the honoree and attendants, with dances and dinners. In this era, Tejano music became more widespread and prevalent. The biggest Tejana sensation in this period was a young woman from South Texas, Selena Quintanilla Perez, who became the "queen of Tejano music." Known only as Selena, she achieved national prominence in the early 1990s, before her untimely death in 1995.

By the time of Selena's death, Texas's cultural diversity was apparent to the most casual observer, much of it of a strong ethnic character and much of it simply reflecting a range of cultural expression. New immigrants to Texas, most of them urban, added to the mix of perspectives and experiences. They joined long-term residents in both challenging and celebrating the stereotypes of Texans as oil-rich ranchers, as "urban cowboys" and rural ones, as "outlaws" in keeping with the country music scene of the 1970s, when Willie Nelson, Waylon Jennings, and others brought a fresh Texas-based perspective to the genre. Texans could navigate the steps of the cotton-eye Joe in country dance halls and attend local opera productions in Houston, Dallas, Fort Worth, San Antonio, Austin, and Beaumont. They could visit exhibits of art produced in the state and also study the paintings of the old masters at the Kimbell Art Museum in Fort Worth; they could camp out at the Kerrville Folk Festival and attend the symphony orchestra productions in Texas's major cities.

The new acknowledgment of cultural and ethnic diversity did not come without some friction. Prominent Hispanic author Sandra Cisneros sparked controversy by painting her house a vivid shade of purple in the King William district of San Antonio, a historic area in which homeowners agreed to restrictive codes to maintain nineteenth-century appearances. When some neighbors and other city residents complained, Cisneros argued before the San Antonio Historic Review Board that the color was historically accurate for the population of Mexican heritage. The new exterior paint stayed.

There were larger issues based on ethnic identity, such as historic claims to land ownership, with Hispanics descended from pre-Revolution Spanish and Mexican families fighting in court for title to lands taken over years before by Anglos. Prominent in this regard was the Balli family, which included hundreds of descendants of a Spanish priest who had received an eighteenth-century grant to what is now Padre Island. The Ballis had arrived in Spanish Texas in 1749 and had amassed "more than a million acres of ranchland by 1800." By 1938, however, the family was struggling economically, and eleven family members sold their portions of the island to a New York lawyer named Gilbert Kerlin.

Family members contended in subsequent lawsuits that Kerlin had cheated them out of agreed-upon mineral rights and had failed to return a portion of the island to them in a 1942 settlement of competing claims. Generations of the Balli family vowed to carry on the fight as Kerlin's wealth, in part from oil and gas royalties from Padre Island, soared. In late 2000, a Brownsville jury sided with them, granting almost 300 family members a judgment of $2.7 million.

Another issue was the rights of the three remaining Native American tribes in Texas. The Alabama-Coushattas of East Texas, a small group with long ties of loyalty and friendship to the state, had been recognized by the state as a tribe in the nineteenth century. The Kickapoos, who in the nineteenth century had sought refuge from land and cultural pressures by moving through Texas to Mexico, had established enough of a presence on the Rio Grande border that in 1983 they were granted recognition from the U.S. government and land in Texas near El Indio. The Tiguas of Ysleta had been considered virtually extinct and had received no state or federal recognition, and therefore had no official tribal identity or claim to government benefits. The Tiguas' quest for federal recognition and the introduction of gambling operations by the three tribes reminded other Texans of the continued presence of Native American groups and of the challenges posed by the new awareness of diversity.

In the 1960s, El Paso city officials contacted the Bureau of Indian Affairs to report that the Tiguas, descendants of Pueblo Indians who had settled near El Paso after the 1680 Pueblo revolt against the Spanish, were living in the expanding city on land tribal members had occupied "for centuries" and were unable to pay their property taxes.

The Tiguas had never been under the jurisdiction of the Bureau of Indian Affairs, but the federal government rather grudgingly acknowledged the Tiguas as a tribe, leading the way to tax exemption. It insisted, however, that the state rather than the federal government act as their trustee. State funds proved inadequate and uneven, and the Tiguas continued a marginal existence, relying in large part on the development and management of a restaurant and tourist center.

Then, in 1984, state attorney general Jim Mattox ruled that it was against the state constitution for Native American tribes to have "special rights." This meant that the Tiguas would lose both the limited state funds and their tax exemption. Tribal members responded by petitioning for federal trust status, along with the Alabama-Coushatta tribe, which was seeking a restoration of this status.

In August 1987, the Tiguas—1,124 individuals—won federal trust status, thereby protecting their land claims and securing federal funds and services. Some tribes nationally were turning to gaming operations to improve employment rates and living conditions the federal government had not effectively addressed. As part of the trust agreement, however, the Tiguas acknowledged that gambling would not occur "where gambling is not permitted in Texas." The state government did not want to open the door to Native American gaming, and the Tiguas were expected not to maneuver around this stipulation by claiming federal reservation rights.

But when the state entered the lottery business in 1992, the Tiguas argued that gambling was now permitted across Texas, and they opened a bingo hall, then a high-stakes gambling casino. By 1999 the casino was pulling in almost $60 million a year in profits and had become a major economic force in the El Paso area, employing 800 people, less than half of whom were tribal members.

In 1999 Texas attorney general John Cornyn filed suit against the Tiguas, arguing that they had violated the 1987 trust status provision against gambling where gambling was not permitted in the state. In September 2001 he won against the Tiguas in district court, and in early 2002, having lost an appeal, they closed the casino. The ruling also affected the Alabama-Coushattas, who only briefly opened a casino in 2002, but despite the judgment, the state was unable to stop a Kickapoo gaming operaion at Eagle Pass on the Mexican border.

In the 2000 census, Native Americans added up to .5 percent of all Texans; the African American population continued to hover at about 12 percent of the state total; and the Hispanic population was growing rapidly, at 32 percent constituting almost one-third of the census total. Although a little over half of the population was categorized as "white," by 2000, in El Paso and San Antonio as well as Houston and Dallas, Hispanics were the largest ethnic group, outnumbering African Americans and Anglos. The effect of such shifts was dramatically demonstrated in the Democratic primary runoff for the governorship in 2001, when for the first time the two contenders, Dan Morales and Tony Sanchez, publicly debated in both English and Spanish.

The changes in public perceptions could be profound. After winning her seat in the U.S. Congress, Barbara Jordan had gone on to become a national figure: a

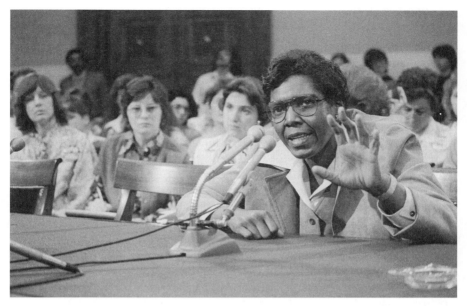

Barbara Jordan built upon her experience as a Texas legislator to mount a winning run for the U.S. Congress in 1972; as "the first black woman from a southern state" in Congress, she became a powerful national political figure. *(© Bettmann/CORBIS)*

formidable member of the House Judiciary Committee during the 1974 Watergate hearings, keynote speaker at the 1976 and 1992 Democratic National Conventions, professor at the Lyndon Baines Johnson School of Public Affairs in Austin, and ethics advisor to Governor Ann Richards. Jordan had traveled a long way from her modest beginnings in Houston's Fifth Ward and from the double challenge of growing up black and female in an era when African Americans did not share in the power structure and women were expected to focus on being wives and homemakers. After Jordan's death in 1996, Texas playwright Larry King's play *The Dead President's Club* included an appearance by God in the form of a strong, articulate black woman. No one could miss the resemblance to Jordan.

## Developing Economic Opportunity

As new faces and agendas appeared on the Texas political scene, the economic landscape of the state was changing as well. One then-unheralded sign of these changes was Michael Dell's arrival at the University of Texas in fall 1983 to begin his freshman year. He was starting college as a premed student, but had brought three computers with him and a lot of ideas about making and selling them. Dell's future, like the Texas economy, was about to take some interesting turns.

## The Oil Industry

During the 1970s and early 1980s, economic opportunity in Texas remained largely defined by the state's status as the chief oil-producing state in the nation. The 1974 Arab embargo on oil to the United States led to higher prices for Texas oil, and the oil and gas industry continued to fuel the Texas economy to the extent that the state gained a great degree of economic independence. Nationally, worries over the availability of foreign oil proliferated as high oil prices prevailed, taking another spike upward as a result of the Iranian revolution and reductions in Saudi Arabian oil production. By 1981, the industry generated more than one-fourth of the state's economic revenues and provided a bonanza of funds both for the state and for private enterprise. These funds gave the state legislature a surplus and stimulated prolific business growth and real estate speculation.

Then, when the Middle Eastern Organization of Petroleum Exporting Countries dropped its prices, Texas oil revenues stopped climbing and soon began to drop. In the mid-1980s, the economy built on oil teetered and crashed. Rigs closed down; large numbers of oil workers lost jobs. Even more ominous for the state as a whole, the state government lost revenues from oil and property taxes from oil producers and was forced to cut back services. At the same time, the spiraling real estate market that had been tied to oil prosperity took a nosedive; people were suddenly stuck with mortgages that far exceeded the new value of their property, and new office space now sat empty.

Then, to make things worse,, the savings and loan industry in Texas blew apart. With recent federal deregulation by the Reagan administration, savings and loan institutions had been operating with little restraint and foresight, offering generous interest rates to depositors, generous loans to the real estate speculators and energy developers, and—in many cases—generous payouts to their top personnel. As an economic recession took hold, the savings and loans failed at a rate not seen since the Great Depression of the 1930s, and out-of-state investors claimed them, again undercutting an independent Texas economic base. The whole banking industry in Texas was affected, the ten largest banking operations passing out of the control of state corporations by 1990.

By 1993, money generated by the oil and gas industry had dropped to 7 percent of total state revenues, and one-third of the jobs in the petroleum industry from the early 1980s had vanished. This trend continued as oil prices remained low— at $10 a barrel in 1999, less than a third of what the prices had been in the early 1980s. The same year, 6,658 wells were drilled, less than a quarter of the number drilled in the peak year of 1984.

Although oil prices started rising in 2000, even the most optimistic observers no longer saw the petroleum industry as a viable foundation for the Texas economy. The lesson of the mid-1980s was to diversify, and Texans had done so, reviving the economy with a variety of enterprises by the mid-1990s.

## Private and Public Enterprise

Perhaps the most prominent success stories were in the field of electronics and computer technology. Texas businessman H. Ross Perot had already become a billionaire in the 1960s with his Electronic Data Systems (EDS) in Dallas, which supplied software and services for the fledgling computer industry. Dallas-based Texas Instruments, which had introduced "the first portable hand-held calculator" in 1971, struggled in the 1970s and early 1980s. But it rebounded, continuing to provide electronics and electronic research for the military and for commercial use, extending its research and development into computer graphics and related areas. Microelectronics and Computer Technology Corporation (MCC), begun by people in computer and semiconductor manufacturing in Austin in 1982, became one of the biggest research and development consortia for the U.S. electronics industry; it drew together government and university researchers, high-tech companies, and users of their technologies.

Another significant research and development venture got underway in Texas in the early 1990s. The U.S. Department of Energy had selected the state as the location for a superconducting super collider, a huge particle accelerator that would serve as a research tool for particle physicists studying the dynamics of matter by accelerating the subatomic particles in an extended tunnel. With congressional funding, more than 2,000 employees were brought together at a site outside Waxahachie, where a laboratory and tunnel were under construction. As the cost of the project climbed, however, a nervous Congress withdrew funding, halting progress on the project in 1993.

In the midst of all of these scientific and technological ups and downs, Michael Dell became a phenomenal success story. In his one year at the University of Texas, he had registered his own company, PC's Limited, with the state of Texas, and by the end of that school year had incorporated the company under the name Dell Computer Corporation. On the proceeds of his direct sales of "upgraded PCs, upgrade kits, and add-on components to people in the Austin area," he rented office space in North Austin and hired an engineer to use the newly available chip sets (streamlined versions of the chips necessary to put together a PC) to create Dell's first computer. Dell developed a business model that allowed the company to avoid the costs of high levels of inventory by building the computers according to customer specifications.

By 2002 Dell Computer Corp. claimed 14 percent of the global market in computers and appeared poised to continue increasing its share. "If you want to be in the PC business, you have to compete against Dell," noted the chief executive officer (CEO) of another company, "and that is very, very difficult." Dell Computer Corp. became the largest employer in Austin and Michael Dell became the richest individual under the age of 40 in the world.

Other innovative, entrepreneurial growth appeared as solid but proved chimerical. In 1986, Enron Corporation, an energy-trading firm that had grown out of a small gas-pipeline operation, moved its headquarters to Houston and in an

When energy-trading giant Enron Corporation crashed in late 2001, workers at its headquarters facility and individual stockholders were not the only Texans affected; Houston lost a major source of philanthropic funding, and state teacher and employee retirement systems suffered heavy stock and bond losses. *(© Reuters NewMedia Inc./CORBIS)*

age of energy deregulation proceeded to become "the world's largest energy-trading company"; by 2000 Enron reported over $100 billion in annual revenues and mounted what was touted as "the most successful Internet effort of any firm in any business." The company built a handsome forty-story headquarters, with a million-dollar hand-etched glass relief map of the world suspended in the atrium. It subsidized the arts in Houston and the Astros baseball stadium, putting its distinctive "E" logo on the facility, and even sponsored a venture capital initiative to aid and nurture minority businesses in Houston's Fifth Ward.

In late fall 2001, however, it became clear that Enron's reported revenues had little basis in fact. Not only did thousands of Enron employees and individual investors lose their substantial investments in the company, but Texas's teacher retirement system and employee retirement system together lost almost $60 million in stocks and bonds. In the litigious aftermath of Enron's fall, Houston itself felt the pinch as not only jobs but a variety of vital community funding disappeared.

More stable economic activity in this period centered on other enterprises. The timbering industry employed almost 100,000 people in 1999. Tourism drew more than 1 million international visitors in 1999; the overall tourist rate was second only to California's, and the Sea World Amusement Park in San Antonio rivaled—but did not surpass—the Alamo as the top tourist attraction. The construction industry was robust, and exports in 2001 made up more than 13 percent of all U.S. exports. Most of these exports fell into four categories: "electronics, industrial machinery (including computers), chemicals and petrochemicals, and transportation equipment." Also significant were retail trade, health services, and some manufacturing.

The aerospace industry continued to develop. In the 1990s NASA partnered with other agencies, private firms, and Texas universities to develop new methods of exploring outer space. The airline industry in Texas continued to grow as well. American Airlines, which had relocated its headquarters from the New York area to the Dallas–Fort Worth area, set up the first of a series of hubs at Dallas–Fort Worth airport in 1981. Meanwhile, entrepreneur Herb Kelleher persevered in his vision of a "no-frills" airline based in Texas to create Southwest Airlines with the aid of Rollin King, owner of a small Texas flying service, and former Universal Airline president Marion Lamar Muse. The first in-state flight took off from Love Field in 1971, and by 1973, the airline had become profitable, despite fares as low as $10. In 1989, Southwest's annual revenues topped $1 billion, and it would go on to become the United States's "most consistently profitable airline" in the 1990s.

Other Texans with a vision made their fortunes in a wide variety of ways. Houston native Mary Kay Ash started a modest beauty business in the 1960s with a formula for face cream and parlayed it into an industry bringing in $2 billion annually.

As some Texans parlayed their visions into corporate enterprises, others found employment in the major cities. By 2000, eighty-four out of every 100 Texans lived in urban areas, and eight out of every ten new jobs were located in only five "magnet" cities: Dallas, Fort Worth, Austin, San Antonio, and Houston. In these cities, the average wage was about $40,000 a year, whereas in the rest of Texas it remained about $29,000 a year. The latter figure seemed large in many rural counties; in the four counties at the bottom of the personal-income scale, all located along the Rio Grande, average annual income ranged from $8,588 to $10,826.

Organized labor had been in a decline since the 1970s, as workers increasingly entered fields without strong unionizing traditions—fields such as retail trade and government—and as employment shrank in jobs associated with unions, such as oil and manufacturing. From the early 1970s to the early 1990s, the percentage of the labor force employed in "highly unionized industries" dropped by more than half, from 47 percent to 21 percent. Other factors were involved as well, including a political climate less receptive to unionizing, corporate practices such as contracting with outside firms and individuals, and development of the computer and other industries in which management proved resistant and workers unresponsive to labor organizing.

One controversial economic measure in this era was a national free trade agreement that promised to impact Texas more than it would other states. In 1992, President George H. W. Bush joined Canadian and Mexican leaders in signing the North American Free Trade Agreement (NAFTA). This agreement promised a gradual reduction of trade barriers throughout North America, making it easier and more economical for the three nations to move their goods across the borders. It greatly altered U.S.-Mexican trade, and most of that trade centered in or moved through Texas. Critics feared that the increased Mexican truck traffic would strain the state's highways and that there would be environmental costs, especially along the border where Mexico's *maquiladoras* (industrial plants) multiplied under the new agreement. But the pact did significantly increase commerce between Texas and Mexico, infusing money and thousands of jobs into the state economy. One study by the Texas Public Policy Foundation showed that trade with both Mexico and Canada had increased Texas exports to these countries by $16 billion between 1993 and 1999. Further, 70 percent of all American exports to Mexico moved through Texas.

### Ranching and Farming in Texas

The three components of an earlier state economy—farming, ranching, and oil—seemed far removed from the lives of most Texans. Large operations and small remained, however. The fabled King Ranch, invigorated by oil and gas royalties totaling more than $1 billion between 1945 and 1994, had become a corporation with its own exploratory oil and gas division and international cattle operation. Most Texas ranches were far more modest in scope, even economically marginal, but the flush oil years of the 1970s and early 1980s had stimulated the ranching business in some areas of the state. A study of Washington County, a portion of Stephen F. Austin's old colonies, showed oilmen and other wealthy investors buying up ranches after World War II and making improvements to the land and to the breeding of the cattle. This "rural gentrification" became more pronounced in the 1970s, as wealthy Houston residents continued to buy Washington County farms and ranches and raise cattle, often consulting with local agricultural extension agents. There was a certain extravagance and simple hobbyist mentality to much of the activity in the late 1970s and early 1980s, as the "mink and manure set" gave lavish parties to show off their pricey purebred cattle. The phenomenon was fueled primarily by their ability to sink large amounts of money into ranching. But many of them did preserve and improve the ranch lands and participate in the modernization of ranching practices.

By the 1990s, only about 1 percent of Texas workers were "directly engaged in agriculture," and the number of people in the ranching industry had dwindled as well. Nevertheless, Texas continues to claim an important role nationally in farming and ranching. In 1999, even though the number of Texas farms had dropped by more than 40 percent since 1940, the 227,000 remaining constituted the largest number of farms in any American state, as did the land they covered—131 million acres. They also were valued at more than 18 times their 1950 prices. Texas continued to lead all states in cotton production in most annual tallies, producing one-fourth of all cotton grown in the United States and exporting large amounts to Mexico, Japan, and South Korea. In the meantime, ranchers were contributing almost 65 percent of the agricultural revenues in Texas, with almost

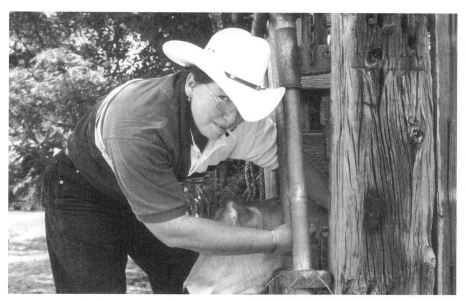

Despite the economic challenges, many Texans continue to be drawn to ranching. Sandy Faison is representative of those who made a shift to part- or full-time ranching after years of employment in urban areas. (© *Robert Burns, Texas Cooperative Extension*)

all of the 254 counties ranking cattle first among their agricultural revenues. The state was also unmatched in the United States not only in beef cattle but also in cattle "on feed," wool, mohair, goats, sheep, and lambs.

These achievements required great diligence and modern approaches. Many people were surprised to learn that more cattle were being raised in East Texas and more cotton grown in West Texas, the latter thanks to extensive irrigation. But heat and drought, frigid and changeable winters, rains at the wrong time, the heavy expenses of maintaining a farm or a ranch—all conspired to keep farmers and ranchers sweating out their profit margins. Those ranchers who could do so depended on oil production on their ranch land to help finance their livestock and other agricultural losses.

Most farmers and ranchers continued in these occupations because of a deep attachment to the work, to the land and the cattle. In a 1998 interview on his ranching operation, famed baseball pitcher Nolan Ryan explained, "It's an emotional attachment you have. . . . Those cows, they live with you day in and day out, and you have raised them from the first day they hit the ground to the day they become a producing cow in your herd."

With all the challenges of raising crops and cattle, however, farmers and ranchers knew to use the technology at their disposal. They employed computers to maintain business records, information, and projections on crop treatments and yields and cattle development. "There's a record that follows the calf all the way to the end product," ranch manager Tom Woodward of the Broseco Ranch would explain, with computer files showing "everything that was done to that calf from the day he was born, even before he was born," including his diet and vaccines. Ranchers even used technological imaging to determine the state of a live animal's hide.

Farmers and ranchers employed a range of scientific management techniques, including pest- and disease-control, efficient irrigation, improved breeding and crossbreeding of plants and animals, improved medical treatment for the cattle, and wildlife management. Ranchers used improved grazing systems, such as "time controlled grazing."

With a continued increase in mechanization and improved equipment, many of the old jobs of farm and ranch were completed more efficiently. With state-of-the-art working pens, Woodward noted, "our guys can put a herd of 300 cows and 300 calves in the pens and have them worked before lunch."

Innovations were fueled in part by the work in research facilities, such as the Institute of Biosciences and Technology at the Houston Medical Center and the Crop Biotechnology Center at Texas A&M, both established in the 1990s. Research goals included the strengthening and diversifying of crops and cattle breeds to avoid such situations as a disease wiping out one's whole crop or herd.

In many ways, farmers and ranchers simply learned to work smarter—for example, videotaping cattle for sale rather than taking them to market (cattle often lose valuable weight in the process), and purchasing already trained horses rather than using ranch resources to raise them.

These people still intimately tied to the land, however, also faced the vagaries of the weather in ways the majority of Texans could no longer fully appreciate. In the extended drought of 1994–96, farmers lost their crops and ranchers sold off their cattle, but the cattle market then became saturated and prices fell. In the meantime, the feed on which ranchers depended in dry times for their remaining herds grew more expensive. A frigid winter in 1996–97 compounded problems for many, and when it was followed by more drought conditions in 1998, 1999, and 2000, farmers and ranchers faced billions of dollars of agricultural losses, including an estimated $515 million in 2000 alone. Some gave up on staple crops; even though cotton remained big business in Texas in 2002, farmers could not sell it for even half of what it cost many of them to grow it.

In the Rio Grande valley, continuing drought combined with the Mexican government's failure to deliver on a shared water treaty to turn the Rio Grande into a trickle and leave farmers' fields high and dry. Third-generation farmers converted citrus groves to goat pastures and cotton, vegetable, and sugar cane fields into grain sorghum fields, the latter a good dry-weather crop but one that produces little profit. Almost half of the valley's irrigated cropland had become dry farmland in only six years. Bud Wentz, a long-term farmer outside Brownsville, told a reporter, "I used to want to keep the farm for the next generation. Now, I could care less." He expressed an eagerness to walk away "if I could sell every acre for a decent price."

Most held on, however, and the overall productivity remained impressive, with agriculture generating almost $28 billion of business in the state in 2000. The Texas economy itself performed well that year, given a boost by improved export markets and by a new upturn in oil and gas activity. Unemployment rates were lower than they had been in more than twenty years. Texans continued to look for ways to innovate and diversify in a new world in which "knowledge work" and service work predominated, the former based on the use, manipulation, interpretation, and transmission of information. The economic growth of the cities, however, generated new problems, including how the cities could absorb the new immigrants and continue to provide jobs. Further, the social and economic disparities between the vital cities and the rest of the state became more pronounced, leading Pampa representative Warren Chisum to note that "rural Texas is in real trouble." In the meantime, Texas government officials sought to address the shifting contours of Texans' lives and work.

## Governing a Changing State

Through this period, Texas government had to adapt to the needs and pressures of a burgeoning citizenry, to continued movement of Texans and out-of-state immigrants to key cities, to the changes in the state economy, and to increasingly complex relations with the federal government. And it had to do so with a constitution that was already dated when it was first adopted in 1876, with its emphasis on agrarian interests and a limited state government. Further, while redistricting in the 1970s had "broken the conservative male domination of the legislature," the legislature continued to operate with traditional and limited responses to many pressing modern problems.

### Government in the 1970s and 1980s

In the early 1970s, reformers began pushing to rewrite the state constitution rather than continue the unwieldy system of multiple amendments. It took a constitutional convention amendment to start the process, which voters approved in 1972. Legislators were to meet for this purpose in January 1974. In the meantime, a commission appointed by state officials prepared a new constitution for their consideration. Among its changes: convening the legislature every year rather than every other year and granting the governor more power.

When the legislature met as a convention, it rejected the document; the measure failed by three votes to gain the necessary two-thirds majority approval. Some had argued that the changes did not go far enough, others that they went too far. The governor at the time, Dolph Briscoe, had appeared indifferent to the initiative, and ultimately came out against it. The next legislature, in 1975, tried a different tack: Members put together eight amendments to the old constitution that resembled the one rejected the previous year. They won passage of the amendments in the legislature, but not among the voters. Texas would continue into the twenty-first century with the 1876 Constitution and its elaborate set of amendments—ninety-one were approved in the decade of the 1980s alone, a total of more than 350 passed into law by the mid-1990s. It would also continue under this constitution with a chief executive with very limited powers and a legislature that shut down for long periods.

Governors of the 1970s and 1980s provided uneven and generally uninspired leadership as they continued to grapple with where to get and how to use tax money, most of them focusing on educational initiatives and budget matters. Briscoe's predecessor, former legislator and lieutenant governor Preston Smith, demonstrated an impressive insider's knowledge of state government. His emphasis on school funding did yield a number of new colleges, professional schools, and branches of technological institutes, including some in his native West Texas, which had had few higher education options. But overall, as his comment on people "lik[ing] to live in slums" indicates, his administration largely maintained the status quo.

Briscoe focused primarily on his pledge of "no new taxes," in part by transferring much school funding from the state to local school districts. Republican governor Clements also focused on cost-cutting measures, in part by requiring state agencies to justify their existence and their work forces.

After the gubernatorial election of 1982, when attorney general and Democrat Mark White defeated Clements, White put much emphasis on education. Students continued to swell the state's college population, particularly at its two flagship public universities, the University of Texas and Texas A&M University, as well as at other state schools funded and regulated by a legislatively-approved coordinating board. White led in the legislature's passing of House Bill 72, or the Educational Reform Act, a weighty and far-reaching education law that reconfigured the state board of education. The bill instituted a "no pass, no play" requirement for students in public schools—barring students who had failed a class from participating in extracurricular activities in the next grading period—and tried to balance the state funding allocated to poor and wealthy districts. Many saw the "no pass, no play" law as aimed at student athletes and feared it would undermine high school sports programs in a state where high school football has often been a focal point for whole communities. After a legal challenge in which a Texas court upheld the rule, the U.S. Supreme Court refused to consider the issue. The law stood, although it was modified in the mid-1990s, shortening the suspension period and allowing the suspended student to practice or rehearse with the extracurricular group.

## School Funding

Although the "no pass, no play" rule was controversial, most problematic was the attempt to balance the funding allocated to Texas K-12 school districts. Because most of the money for schools came from property taxes in the areas served by the schools, wealthier communities received more money per student than poorer communities. Thus, in the late 1980s the Alamo Heights independent school district had more than fourteen times the property value per student of the Edgewood independent school district, also in Béxar County.

Unsatisfied with White's attempts at reform, the Edgewood independent school district pursued a lawsuit asserting that the state's reliance on local property taxes made its educational system imbalanced and unconstitutional.

Clements returned and defeated White in 1986, as White struggled with the education issues and as the state experienced the economic downturn brought on by falling oil prices. Facing loss of one-fourth of the state's revenue as a result, Clements, too, struggled to keep the state government functioning, reluctantly abandoning his own "no new taxes" stance and dealing with a new state court ruling that indicated the need for more taxes to maintain the public schools. Under his administration, the legislature continued to work to equalize school expenditures per student across the state, as poorer districts still had less than half of what the richer districts had to spend per student. In the meantime, as a result of the Edgewood lawsuit the Texas Supreme Court in 1989 instructed the legislature to put into place an equitable system before school started in the fall of 1990.

A series of legislative initiatives resulted, each deemed unacceptable by the courts. Finally, in 1993, the legislature offered a plan whereby each school in the wealthy districts would aid redistribution in one of five ways: by combining its tax base with that of a poorer district, by giving the state money "to help pay for students in poorer districts," by "contracting to educate students in other districts," by simply consolidating with another district or other districts, or by "transferring some of its commercial taxable property to another district's tax roles."

By the end of the twentieth century, this new refinement of a so-called Robin Hood law had led to much dissatisfaction. The limited but important state funding for schools declined and districts judged "wealthy" fought to hang onto their resources, many of them in the midst of major spurts in enrollment. In 2001, a number of these school districts sued to get "Robin Hood" overturned, but a district judge affirmed its legality.

### Other Governing Challenges

The governors of this era also contended with federal government involvement in Texas affairs. Federal courts enforced integration plans for public schools in the early 1970s. Federal agencies such as the U.S. Justice Department, the Occupational Safety and Health Administration, and the Environmental Protection Agency required compliance with federal regulations. The federal government at varying rates supplemented state coffers for public schools, for cities, for highways and transportation, and for welfare costs, but Texas continued to rank low in federal grants awarded to states.

In the 1980s prison reform became an issue illustrating the tensions and complexities of federal-state relations. Texas had been convicting and incarcerating

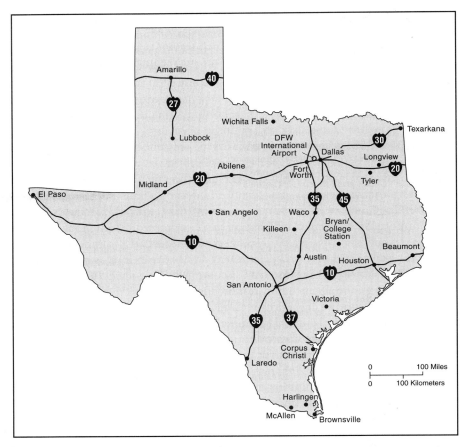

Texas interstates and cities with commerical airports.

convicts at a rate far exceeding the national average, and although the state population had grown 19 percent between 1968 and 1978, the prison population had doubled. David Ruiz, an inmate who had been convicted of armed robbery, led other Texas inmates in filing suit against prison system director W. James Estelle in 1972, citing overcrowding and other substandard prison conditions. In 1980 federal judge William Wayne Justice agreed that the conditions constituted "cruel and unusual punishment," outlawed by the U.S. Constitution. He ordered the state to make major penal changes. Officials scrambled to comply, in part by establishing new prison facilities. But the prison population continued to swell disproportionately to the general population.

Texas also became a lightning rod for national and international debate in its use of the death penalty. The death penalty had been reinstated by the state legislature during the Briscoe administration, reflecting a national trend in which most Americans polled favored it. But Texas became far more rigorous than other states in employing capital punishment. By 2002, Texas's thirty-three executions for the year made up almost half of the U.S. total for the year.

The governors of the 1990s continued to struggle with such issues, but in an improving economy. Texas was changing rapidly in this decade. Not only was the minority population becoming the majority in many cities, but key cities and outlying areas were experiencing staggering population growth. In the oil boom of the 1970s and early 1980s, Texas had attracted 2.5 million immigrants, making it the third most populated state. Now, in the 1990s, as more people were drawn to business opportunities or high-tech jobs and the warm climate, it shot to second place, behind California. By 2002, despite some slowdown in growth and employment, three of the fastest-growing counties in the nation were located in Texas.

In El Paso and other urban areas outside the five magnet cities, rapid growth was the rule, but not prosperity. City governments faced infrastructure problems, including clogged highways, urban sprawl, crowded new schools, and a general drain on city services. Even in the magnet cities—primarily Dallas, Houston, and Austin—unemployment sometimes jumped dramatically, as more hopefuls poured in and the economy shifted.

In the midst of such urban challenges, there remained among much of the populace a resistance to local, state, and federal government regulation. At its most pronounced, this resistance was manifested in the separation of the Branch

Traffic jams, urban sprawl, and other growth issues kept local, county, regional, and state officials busy as Texas in the 1990s became the second most populous state in the nation, with some of the fastest-growing counties in the United States. (© *Ralph Krabner/Index Stock Imagery, Inc.*)

Davidians under David Koresh until their final fatal encounter with federal agents at the Branch Davidian compound outside Waco in 1993, and in the 1990s activities of a group in West Texas calling itself the "Republic of Texas" and asserting that Texas remains independent of the United States. On a milder level, Texans have repeatedly rejected the idea of a state income tax, including a brief attempt by officials to introduce one in the late 1980s. Residents of Houston in the 1980s also resisted attempts to institute standard zoning measures that would regulate the city's growth; in doing so, they maintained Houston's record as "the largest unzoned city in the United States." Smaller communities wrangled over the rules and regulations that would come with incorporation, particularly those involving land use.

At the state level, although the economy was strong during the administrations of Ann Richards and her successor, George W. Bush, many problems remained. For example, in 1998, Texas ranked first among the states in people without health insurance, second in the number of people in state prisons, and third in the number of people living below the poverty level. There also remained a violent strain of racism, as evidenced that year by the dragging death of African American James Byrd, Jr., by three white men in East Texas. The men were captured and tried, and hate-crime legislation was developed to address such crimes of racism and prejudice. With Bush vacating the governorship for the presidency, the post passed to Lieutenant Governor Rick Perry, who signed this legislation and identified transportation and higher education as his priorities.

As Texas moved into the twenty-first century, government officials grappled with urban and suburban growth and rural decline, lack of a state income tax, and Texas's low ranking in a number of health-and-welfare areas, including welfare payments, mental health care, and immunizations. They also faced the knowledge that Texas ranked first among the states in releases of toxic chemicals into the air and was developing serious problems in meeting the water needs of communities, farms, ranches, and industries. Although conservation efforts were underway, much of the Texas landscape had been polluted, depleted, and scarred.

## Tending the Land

In the last few decades of the twentieth century, the federal and state governments passed legislation reflecting a new awareness of the need to preserve and protect the land and its resources. In this they were aided or spurred by national environmental organizations such as the Sierra Club and Audubon Society and also by local Texas grass-roots organizations concerned about vanishing species, an altered landscape, and air, ground, and water pollution. In particular, water pollution, shortages, and anticipated shortages began to come to the fore as a major issue for twenty-first-century Texas.

## The Environment

Most of the Big Thicket, a biological treasure trove in East Texas, gained federal protection as the first national biological preserve in 1974. Here were found "relict" plants, located nowhere else and nurtured by the unique combination of soil and humidity. In the late 1990s the preserve provided sustenance for hundreds of bird and plant species, as well as fifty kinds of reptiles and sixty mammal species.

Yet the Texas environment was much altered and diminished from the days when the Spanish explored its grasslands and flowing rivers. Texas in the 1700s had over 12 million acres of Blackland Prairie, over 16 million acres of bottomland hardwood forests, and over 12 million acres of coastal wetlands. By the late 1990s all of these had been reduced by more than half, endangering a range of plants and animals—from ocelots to brown pelicans, from red-cockaded woodpeckers to Kemp's ridley sea turtles.

Texas had boasted the largest expanses of prairies in the United States, with as many as 300 native plant species and with great stands of Indian grass, switchgrass, big bluestem, and little bluestem predominating. Yet even on the remaining prairie acreage, plowing had destroyed the native grasses.

The picture was far from uniformly grim. Environmental organizations were seeking to preserve and expand the pockets of native grasses, rich in nutrients and part of a healthy ecosystem. The East Texas forests had benefited from efforts by the U.S. Forest Service and the Civilian Conservation Corps of the 1930s, as well as improved timbering practices by companies in the late twentieth century, so significant reforestation occurred in some of the areas already stripped or "farmed out."

In addition, farmers, ranchers, and even suburbanites had worked with biologists, game wardens, and other state and federal officials on stewardship of their land and its resources. The federal Endangered Species Act of 1973 with its rules for habitat protection had not always been popular in the state, as landowners struggled with requirements that sometimes seemed harsh and unreasonable. Many landowners were deeply committed to caring for their property but felt constrained by government regulations made at a distance. Yet good land-use and wildlife management practices, whether imposed by law or sought out and adopted, had yielded thriving wild turkey and deer populations and made Texas the premier bird-watching area in the world.

The government and citizens' groups tried to stop or reduce industry pollution in Texas as aging smokestacks continued to belch out sulfur dioxide and nitrogen oxide compounds. For example, in late 2001, the Central Texas environmental group Neighbors for Neighbors spurred the state to investigate Alcoa, Inc.'s Rockdale plant by charging that it was releasing unsafe amounts of these chemicals into the air, then in 2002 joined a lawsuit to force the plant to spend hundreds of millions of dollars to clean up emissions.

Even relatively benign development, such as light, "clean" industry or housing, put a strain on those cities and counties that were burgeoning; officials and neighbors of the new development struggled with everything from traffic problems and school overcrowding to loss of natural habitat for animals and plants. But increasingly, the greatest strain became how to ensure enough clean water.

## Water Challenges

Water quality and availability in the late twentieth century became a chief concern for Texans, from the wetlands of the coast to the *playas* (shallow rainwater pools of the High Plains far to the northwest), from the state's many southward flowing rivers to its aquifers, the ancient, shallow underground seas fed by rainwater. The legislature, prodded by Lieutenant Governor Bob Bullock, slowly awoke to the issue, in 1997 passing Senate Bill 1, which split the state into sixteen water-planning areas. In each area, a regional water-planning group would project water needs and strategies for the next fifty years; all of these plans would be consolidated in 2002 and updated every five years.

The coastal wetlands, in particular, had suffered from the industrial development of the twentieth century. The Texas gulf coast shared with the Louisiana coast a distinction as "the petrochemical center of the nation," the Texas portion claiming almost 60 percent of American petrochemical capacity. Galveston Bay, the seventh largest estuary in the United States, remained a busy port and the site of extensive petroleum refining and chemical production. Although the Texas Solid Waste Disposal Act of 1969 helped protect Galveston and other gulf bays from direct discharge of industrial waste, this estuary, also the location of a vital fisheries industry, continued to absorb pollution from the Houston Ship Channel, which connects it to the city of Houston. The channel, still narrow and shallow despite mid-twentieth-century attempts to improve it, continued to be the site of oil spills and other freighter, barge, and tanker accidents and collisions, many of the damaged ships carrying poisonous cargo.

Far away on Texas's High Plains the *playas* hosted more than a hundred species of migrant waterfowl, such as lesser Canada geese and mallards, and were home to sandhill cranes and other bird species. Almost half of the *playa* region was in Texas; beginning in the 1980s, the United States, Mexico, and Canada shared an agreement to protect these sites.

Major concern centered on Texas rivers. By 2002 some had appeared on lists of the most endangered U.S. rivers, among them the Clear Creek, the Trinity, the San Jacinto, the Concho, and the Guadalupe and its tributaries. In the last case, the environmental group American Rivers charged, the state was allowing too much of the Guadalupe's water to be used by urban areas, industries, and farmers, thereby adding to the ravages of drought and not only affecting water quality and flow but also doing damage to the coastal estuaries that normally received that flow. In 1993 the Rio Grande, a vital water source for Mexico, New Mexico, and Texas and the second longest river in the nation, was named one of the top ten endangered rivers in the United States and came to be known as the "Sewer Grande." In its more than 40,000 square miles of drainage in Texas, it provided irrigation for the cotton, pecan, and vegetable crops of West Texas and the citrus fruits, cotton, and vegetables of the lower Rio Grande valley in South Texas. But dams, drought, and too many people relying on what water existed took their toll. In addition, the proliferation of *maquiladoras* along the river border meant more human crowding, with inadequate sanitary conditions, and more industrial water and air pollution, with associated hazardous waste disposal issues.

These water woes were exacerbated by the treaty struggle between the United States and Mexico that had Rio Grande valley farmers worried and incensed. A 1944 agreement specified that Mexico would "provide the U.S. with one-third of all water that flows from six Rio Grande tributaries, or a minimum of . . . about 114 billion gallons." In exchange, the United States would provide Mexico "at least 1.5 million acre-feet of water per year from the Colorado River," with an acre-foot being the amount of water it takes to inundate an acre to the depth of a foot. By 1950, the United States was fulfilling its part of the agreement. But over the years between 1944 and 2002, Mexico built up a huge water debt while increasing irrigated acreage and claiming deferments based on drought conditions. In September 2001, the debt stood at 350,000 acre-feet.

With recurring droughts, water-sharing troubles with Mexico, and aquifers being pumped at a rapid rate, water issues in Texas have become critical. Various state and private organizations now seek to preserve and conserve Texas's water resources. (© *Bob Boerner, Texas Water Quality Association*)

In the meantime, the Rio Grande shrank dramatically in just twenty years (1982–2002), its flow at El Paso reduced from 33.39 cubic meters per second to 11.79 cubic meters. In spring 2002, the river simply ran dry before reaching its gulf outlet near Brownsville.

Aquifers presented an equally troubling picture. Texas was blessed with an abundance of these underground water sources—nine major ones (including the Edwards Aquifer) and twenty smaller ones spreading under four-fifths of the state. The problems with their depletion were illustrated when businessman Ron Pucek tapped the Edwards Aquifer, which spread through a maze of channels, fractures and limestone formations underlying nine central Texas counties. In 1991, Pucek spent $1 million drilling "the world's largest water well" into the aquifer to create the 85-acre Living Waters Artesian Springs Catfish Farm, confident that he could do this under the "right of capture" on which Texas water law is based: the idea that a landowner can draw as much water as he can pump from underneath his land.

In the same year, a scientific study showed that the Edwards Aquifer was being rapidly depleted and warned what would happen if a drought of the severity of the 1950s struck central Texas again. San Antonio alone made heavy demands upon the aquifer for its municipal water supply, being "one of the largest cities in the world that relies solely on a single ground-water source" for this purpose. Yet by some estimates Pucek, whose well could pump 40,000 gallons a minute, was using as much water as the city of San Antonio needed for a quarter million people, or one-fourth the population of the city.

In part, this meant that Pucek had a viable operation; the heavy flow of water helped ensure that the fish would be healthy, and the Medina River, into which his operation discharged, would remain unpolluted by the enterprise. In fact, the water discharge from the farm, although not usable as drinking water, promised to help "the downstream environment and the bays and estuaries of the Gulf Coast." Of course, the question arose as to whether Pucek should have the right to such vast amounts of a resource that could renew only slowly. Although the right of capture had made some sense in an earlier era when untapped ground water could not be accurately mapped or measured, most states had adopted more cautious approaches to groundwater supplies. Pucek's defenders argued that the water was available for reuse and that farming operations should take precedence over watering lawns in urban and suburban areas.

After just one season of operation, a series of challenges stopped the catfish farm operation. Finally, in 2000, after almost a decade of legal wrangling, Pucek sold the catfish farm and most of his water rights for $9 million to the trustees of the San Antonio water system. Legally, he had retained the right of capture, and he walked away a financial winner by selling the water rights. In the meantime, the city struggled with whether to allow new ventures that would impact its water supply. In 2002 some city officials endorsed a proposed Professional Golf Association resort with three planned golf courses to be perched over the Edwards Aquifer. Critics pointed out that one golf course normally used hundreds of thousands of gallons of water a day, as well as draining fertilizers and pesticides into the ground.

As Texas entered the new century, the tapping of groundwater, primarily for farmer's irrigation and use by cities but also for ranching, mining, and manufacturing, was still depleting the aquifers faster than they could refill through the natural slow percolation of rainwater. The largest aquifer, the Ogallala Aquifer underpinning the Texas High Plains, had been pierced by more than 50,000 irrigation wells. It is estimated that the natural refilling of the Ogallala would take 6,000 years. Yet the Department of Commerce warned in the 1990s that by 2020, if groundwater use continued at the same rate, two-thirds of this aquifer would be empty.

Water projections were grim in many areas of the state. In Williamson County, one of the three Texas counties among the ten fastest-growing in the United States, it was estimated that by 2050, the county "would face a shortfall of as much water as it takes to fill Lake Georgetown." Planners were considering a variety of costly options, including piping water from the Carrizo-Wilcox Aquifer. But this would require landowners in nearby counties to grant pumping rights, a risky proposition for the grantees.

More troubling for many was the state water plan compiled from the regional water-planning groups established by Senate Bill 1 in 1997. Houston *Chronicle* editorial writer Ken Kramer noted in May 2001 that in an era of water conservation, too many of the plans depended on "major new dams and pipelines" costing almost $17 billion. Dallas had actually projected an increase in per-capita water use to be supported by a costly dam when, Kramer contended, the dam "would be unnecessary if the per capita water use in Dallas is kept in line with more conservation-minded cities." Kramer and others made it clear that water issues would only grow more pressing.

# Conclusion

In the last three decades of the twentieth century, recognition of old realities and new shaped a Texas for the twenty-first century. The historical experience of all who called Texas home took on greater meaning, diversity was acknowledged, and members of groups formerly excluded from political power began to share in that power. New ways of making a living and a fortune developed to reshape the Texas economy, but the old economic staples of oil, ranching, and farming remained integral to the economy through ups and downs and to Texans' sense of identity. An old independent spirit wary of government had to be balanced with challenges born of rapid, shifting population growth and the intricacies of state-federal relations. The land and its resources no longer seemed endless and therefore needed renewed care and communal effort.

All of these changes brought to the fore issues of Texas identity, and Texas myth: the stories about Texas identity that Texans—and non-Texans—have created or absorbed as part of their understanding of the world. Of course, these stories had been shaped through the region's history in a number of ways, from "Texians" embracing images of their land as a cradle of liberty in the Revolutionary era to the conscious adoption of western images by framers of the Texas Centennial. Key stereotypes ranged from stalwart pioneers, Texas Rangers, ranchers, and cowboys to larger-than-life businessmen engaged in boom-and-bust enterprise. Key elements included an emphasis on rugged individuality and a rather testy and exploitative frontier mentality. As Professor Betty Sue Flowers of the University of Texas has noted, "Texas stayed in a kind of perpetual state of primal, rural independence of mind."

But myths evolve. By the twenty-first century, some of the old myths have been exposed as skewed in favor of the group getting to tell the story; for example, many Anglos over the course of the nineteenth and twentieth centuries accepted and transmitted negative characterizations of Mexicans and Tejanos. Some myths can be seen to lack the basis in truth they may have had in an earlier era—for example, the images of Texas as having limitless land and resources. Some can be affirmed and adapted: If Texas is distinctive as a place, then its environment is worth protecting and preserving.

Many of the changes described in this chapter, then, are attempts to rewrite the myth, to address old ways of thinking that turned out to be wrong, no longer viable, or true in a different, more complex sense. In the process, Texas has retained a distinctive dynamic. In December 2002, *The Economist* published an article arguing that Texas had emerged as the most influential state in the American union, one leading the way into an American future, in part through its "sheer size and dynamism," in part through its citizens' "entrepreneurship" and cultural and ethnic diversity.

The Texas entering the twenty-first century, then, was poised to further sharpen and enhance its identity as a distinctive land of opportunity and diversity. It remained immense with possibilities for new economic, social, and political visions, new forms of innovation, new community configurations. Possessed of a rich, checkered, and complex history, it remained a place to, in the words of republic president Anson Jones, "commence the world anew."

## SUGGESTED READINGS

Information on this era comes largely from the *Texas Almanac* (2001) and from newspaper articles listed in the bibliography; much of the history of Texas in the late twentieth century remains to be written. For discussions of Texas myth, see "Texas Values/Texas Future," in the Philosophical Society of Texas *Proceedings of the Annual Meeting at Austin, Dec. 3–5, 1999,* and Robert F. O'Connor, ed., *Texas Myths* (1986).

### Diversity in Texas Politics and Culture

For information on the life of Barbara Jordan, consult Barbara Jordan and Shelby Hearon, *Barbara Jordan: A Self-Portrait* (1979) and Mary Beth Rogers, *Barbara*

*Jordan, American Hero* (1998). Other useful works that deal with Texas women in politics during this era include *Capitol Women,* by Nancy Baker Jones and Ruthe Winegarten (2000); *Texas Women Frontier to Future* (1998), by Ann Fears Crawford and Crystal Sasse Ragsdale; and *Claytie and the Lady: Ann Richards, Gender, and Politics in Texas* (1994), by Sue Tollison-Rinehart and Jeanie R. Stanley. For information on Mexican American activism in the 1970s, see Ignacio M. Garcia's *United We Win: The Rise and Fall of La Raza Unida Party* (1989) and Arnoldo DeLeon's *Mexican Americans in Texas: A Brief History* (1993). For one account of Mexican family land claims, see Abel Rubio's *Stolen Heritage: A Mexican-American's Rediscovery of His Family's Lost Land Grant* (1998). Information on the Tiguas appears in Jeffrey M. Schulze's "The Rediscovery of the Tiguas: Federal Recognition and Indianness in the Twentieth Century" in *Southwestern Historical Quarterly* (2001).

### Developing Economic Opportunity

In addition to the *Texas Almanac* and newspapers, the *New Handbook of Texas* contains numerous helpful entries on public and private enterprises in Texas—see, for example, "AMR Corporation" and "Southwest Airlines." Michael Dell's story can be found in his *Direct from Dell: Strategies that Revolutionized an Industry* (1999).

Newspaper articles chronicle the challenges of farming, but ranching continues to draw loving book-length appraisals; see, for example, Lawrence Clayton's *Contemporary Ranches of Texas* (2001) and Kathleen Jo Ryan's *Deep in the Heart of Texas: Texas Ranchers in Their Own Words* (1999), from which some of the quotes in this section were drawn. Also useful is Mark Friedberger's "'Mink and Manure': Rural Gentrification and Cattle Raising in Southeast Texas, 1945–1992" in *Southwestern Historical Quarterly* (1999).

### Governing a Changing State

Although it provides only a brief overview of the governors since 1969, a good reference work is Kenneth E. Hendrickson, Jr.'s *The Chief Executives of Texas from Stephen F. Austin to John B. Connally, Jr.* (1995). Donald Walker provides a positive assessment of Governor Smith in "Governor Preston E. Smith," *West Texas Historical Yearbook* (1999). The *New Handbook of Texas* includes useful information on this period on such topics as education and the prison system.

### Tending the Land

A good general source is Richard C. Bartlett's *Saving the Best of Texas* (1995). Information on Ron Pucek's catfish farm and other environmental matters can be found on the Internet at the Edwards Aquifer home page, *www.edwardsaquifer. net.* Consult the *New Handbook of Texas* for a variety of related articles—see, for example, "Environmental Health."

# A

# Texas Governors

## Governors of Spanish Texas

| | |
|---|---|
| Domingo Terán de los Ríos | 1691–92 |
| Gregorio de Salinas Varona | 1692–97 |
| Francisco Cuerbo y Valdez | 1698–1702 |
| Mathías de Aguirre | 1703–5 |
| Martín de Alarcón | 1705–8 |
| Simón Padilla y Córdova | 1708–12 |
| Pedro Fermín de Echevérs y Subisa | 1712–14 |
| Juan Valdez | 1714–16 |
| Martín de Alarcón | 1716–19 |
| Joseph de Azlor, Marqués de Aguayo | 1719–22 |
| Fernando Pérez de Almazán | 1722–27 |
| Melchor de Media Villa y Azcona | 1727–30 |
| Juan Antonio Bustillos y Ceballos | 1730–34 |
| Manuel de Sandoval | 1734–36 |
| Carlos Benites Franquis de Lugo | 1736–37 |
| Prudencio de Orobio y Basterra | 1737–41 |
| Tomás Felipe Wintuisen | 1741–43 |
| Justo Boneo y Morales | 1743–44 |
| Francisco García Larios | 1744–48 |
| Pedro del Barrio Junco y Espriella | 1748–51 |
| Jacinto de Barrios y Jáuregui | 1751–59 |
| Angel Martos y Navarrete | 1759–66 |
| Hugo Oconor | 1767–70 |
| Barón de Ripperdá | 1770–78 |
| Domingo Cabello | 1778–86 |
| Bernardo Bonavía | 1786 (appointed, but did not serve) |
| Rafael Martínez Pacheco | 1786–90 |

| | |
|---|---|
| Manuel Muñoz | 1790–99 |
| José Irigoyen | 1798–1800 (appointed, but never served) |
| Juan Bautista de Elguézabal | 1799–1805 |
| Antonio Cordero y Bustamante | 1805–8 |
| Manuel María de Salcedo | 1808–13 |
| Juan Bautista Casas | Jan.–Mar., 1811 (insurgent governor) |
| Cristóbal Domínguez | 1813–14 |
| Ignacio Pérez | 1816–17 |
| Manuel Pardo | May–Oct., 1817 |
| Antonio Martínez | 1817–22 (continued to serve after Mexican independence) |

### Governors of Provincial Texas

| | |
|---|---|
| José Félix Trespalacios | 1822–23 |
| Luciano García | 1823 |

### Governors of Coahuila y Texas

| | |
|---|---|
| Rafael Gonzales | 1824–26 |
| José Ignacio de Arizpe | 1826 |
| Victor Blanco | 1826–27 |
| José Ignacio de Arizpe | 1827 |
| José María Viesca y Montes | 1827–31 |
| José María Letona | 1831–32 (died in office) |
| Rafael Eca y Músquiz | 1832–33 |
| Juan Martín de Veramendi | 1833 (died in office) |
| Francisco Vidaurri y Villaseñor | 1833–34 |
| Juan José Elguézabal | 1834–35 |
| José María Cantú | 1835 |
| Marciel Borrego | 1835 |
| Agustín Viesca | 1835 |
| Miguel Falcón | 1835 |
| Bartolomé de Cárdenas | 1835 |
| Rafael Eca y Músquiz | 1835 |

### Provisional Governor of Texas During Texas Revolution

| | |
|---|---|
| Henry Smith | Nov. 1835–Mar. 1836 |

## Presidents of the Republic of Texas, 1836–1846

| | |
|---|---|
| David G. Burnet | Mar.–Oct., 1836 (interim) |
| Sam Houston | Oct. 1836–Dec. 1838 |
| Mirabeau B. Lamar | Dec. 1838–Dec. 1841 |
| Sam Houston | Dec. 1841–Dec. 1844 |
| Anson Jones | Dec. 1844–Feb. 1846 |

## Governors of the State of Texas

| | |
|---|---|
| J. Pinckney Henderson | Feb. 1846–Dec. 1847 |
| George T. Wood | Dec. 1847–Dec. 1849 |
| Peter Hansborough Bell | Dec. 1849–Nov. 1853 |
| J. W. Henderson | Nov. 1853–Dec. 1853 |
| Elisha M. Pease | Dec. 1853–Dec. 1857 |
| Hardin R. Runnels | Dec. 1857–Dec. 1859 |
| Sam Houston | Dec. 21, 1859–Mar. 1861 (removed from office by Secession Convention) |
| Edward Clark | Mar. 1861–Nov. 1861 (appointed to office by Secession Convention) |
| Francis R. Lubbock | Nov. 1861–Nov. 1863 |
| Pendleton Murrah | Nov. 1863–June 1865 |
| Andrew J. Hamilton | June 1865–Aug. 1866 (appointed by President Andrew Johnson) |
| James W. Throckmorton | Aug. 1866–Aug. 1867 (removed from office by Gen. Philip H. Sheridan during Reconstruction) |
| Elisha M. Pease | Aug. 1867–Sept. 1869 (appointed by Gen. Philip H. Sheridan but resigned in protest of radical Reconstruction policies) |
| Edmund J. Davis | Jan. 1870–Jan. 1874 |
| Richard Coke | Jan. 1874–Dec. 1876 |
| Richard B. Hubbard | Dec. 1876–Jan. 1879 |
| Oran M. Roberts | Jan. 1879–Jan. 1883 |
| John Ireland | Jan. 1883–Jan. 1887 |
| Lawrence Sullivan Ross | Jan. 1887–Jan. 1891 |
| James Stephen Hogg | Jan. 1891–Jan. 1895 |
| Charles A. Culberson | Jan. 1895–Jan. 1899 |
| Joseph D. Sayers | Jan. 1899–Jan. 1903 |
| S. W. T. Lanham | Jan. 1903–Jan. 1907 |
| Thomas Mitchell Campbell | Jan. 1907–Jan. 1911 |
| Oscar Branch Colquitt | Jan. 1911–Jan. 1915 |

| | |
|---|---|
| James E. Ferguson | Jan. 1915–Aug. 1917 |
| William Pettus Hobby | Aug. 1917–Jan. 1921 |
| Pat Morris Neff | Jan. 1921–Jan. 1925 |
| Miriam A. Ferguson | Jan. 1925–Jan. 1927 |
| Dan Moody | Jan. 1927–Jan. 1931 |
| Ross S. Sterling | Jan. 1931–Jan. 1933 |
| Miriam A. Ferguson | Jan. 1933–Jan. 1935 |
| James V. Allred | Jan. 1935–Jan. 1939 |
| W. Lee O'Daniel | Jan. 1939–Aug. 1941 |
| Coke R. Stevenson | Aug. 1941–Jan. 1947 |
| Beauford H. Jester | Jan. 1947–July 1949 |
| Allan Shivers | July 1949–Jan. 1957 |
| Price Daniel | Jan. 1957–Jan. 1963 |
| John Connally | Jan. 1963–Jan. 1969 |
| Preston Smith | Jan. 1969–Jan. 1973 |
| Dolph Briscoe | Jan. 1973–Jan. 1979 |
| William P. Clements | Jan. 1979–Jan. 1983 |
| Mark White | Jan. 1983–Jan. 1987 |
| William P. Clements | Jan. 1987–Jan. 1991 |
| Ann W. Richards | Jan. 1991–Jan. 1995 |
| George W. Bush | Jan. 1995–Dec. 2000 |
| James Richard Perry | Dec. 2000 to present |

*Sources:* Vito Alessio Robles, *Coahuila y Texas desde la consumación de la Independencia hasta el Tratado de Paz de Guadalupe Hidalgo,* 2 vols. (1945, reprint, Mexico: Editorial Porrua, 1979); Arturo Berrueto González, comp., *Diccionario biográfico de Coahuila* (Saltillo: Gobierno del Estado, 1999); H. P. N. Gammel, comp., *The Laws of Texas, 1822–1897,* vol. 1 (Austin: Gammel Book Co., 1898); "About Texas," Texas State Library Website <http://www.tsl.state.tx.us/ref/abouttx/prerepub.html>; *Handbook of Texas Online* <http://www.tsha.utexas.edu/handbook/online/index.html>.

# B

# Comparative Population Statistics

| Year | Province of Texas[1] | New Spain[1] |
|---|---|---|
| 1731–39 | 1,499 | |
| 1740–49 | 3,203 | |
| 1750–59 | 3,683 | |
| 1760–69 | 3,436 | |
| 1770–74 | 3,076 | |
| 1780–89 | 2,919 | |
| 1790 | | 4,636,074 |
| 1790–99 | 3,316 | |
| 1803 | | 5,764,731 |
| 1805–9 | 4,329 | |
| 1810 | | 6,122,354 |
| 1815–19 | 3,778 | |
| 1820 | | 6,204,000 |

| | Department of Texas[1] | Mexico[2] |
|---|---|---|
| 1834–35 | 23,621 | 6,854,193 |

| | Republic of Texas[3] | |
|---|---|---|
| 1845 | 125,000 | 7,263,246 |

| | State of Texas[4] | United States[4] |
|---|---|---|
| 1850 | 212,592 | 23,191,876 |
| 1860 | 604,215 | 31,443,321 |
| 1870 | 818,579 | 38,558,371 |
| 1880 | 1,591,749 | 50,189,209 |
| 1890 | 2,235,527 | 62,979,766 |
| 1900 | 3,048,710 | 76,212,168 |
| 1910 | 3,896,542 | 92,228,496 |
| 1920 | 4,663,228 | 106,021,537 |
| 1930 | 5,824,715 | 123,202,624 |
| 1940 | 6,414,824 | 132,164,569 |
| 1950 | 7,711,194 | 151,325,798 |
| 1960 | 9,579,677 | 179,323,175 |
| 1970 | 11,196,730 | 203,211,926 |
| 1980 | 14,229,191 | 226,545,805 |
| 1990 | 16,986,335 | 248,765,170 |
| 2000 | 20,851,820 | 281,421,906 |

*Sources:* [1]Colonial-period estimates exclude independent Indian groups, which Meacham estimates to have declined in population from 35,600 in the seventeenth century to 20,100 early in the nineteenth century. Movement of Indians in and out of missions, the opening and closing of new mission fields, and the transfer of troops all kept the colonial-period population in flux. Estimates based on the work of Tina Laurel Meacham, "The Population of Spanish and Mexican Texas, 1716–1836" (Ph.D. diss., The University of Texas at Austin, 2000).

[2]"Population: 1821–1910," *Encyclopedia of Mexico: History, Society & Culture* (Chicago: Fitzroy Dearborn, 1997).

[3]"Census and Census Records," *Handbook of Texas OnLine,* www.tsha.utexas.edu/handbook/online/articles/view/CC/ulc1.html

[4]http://www.tsl.state.tx.us/ref/abouttx/census.html

# Glossary of Spanish Terms

*acequia:* irrigation ditch

*adelantado:* governor with broad powers; usually reserved for the leader of a royally chartered expedition

*agregado:* additional or secondary settler

*alcalde mayor:* district magistrate

*alcalde ordinario:* municipal magistrate

*alguacil mayor:* constable, sheriff, jailer

*ayuntamiento:* town government

*bracero:* from *brazo,* arm; one who works with his hands; term applied to field laborers, particularly those who came to the United States during and after World War II

*capitulación:* royal charter

*casas reales:* town hall

*castas:* general term for mixed-bloods

*compadrazgo:* ritual kinship, godparenthood

*corregidor:* district magistrate

*criado:* reared or raised; a servant who is part of the household

*criollo:* American-born Spaniard

*dictamen:* official opinion

*diezmero:* a tithe collector

*empresario:* colonization agent; one who contracts with the government to introduce families into Texas

*encomienda:* grant of Indian tributaries to a Spaniard as a reward for services in an *entrada*

*entrada:* conquest, colonization, or settlement expedition

*escribano:* public scribe, notary

*gachupín:* derogatory term for European Spaniards, particularly popular at the end of the colonial period

*genízaro:* New Mexican term for a detribalized Indian incorporated into Spanish society

*gente de razón:* people of reason; term applied to all members of colonial society excepting Indians

*grito:* yell, scream, cry; a political declaration

*hacendado:* the owner of a *hacienda*

*hacienda:* large landed estate producing both livestock and crops for market

*hidalgo:* literally, "son of something"; lowest rung of Spanish nobility

*intendencia:* late colonial administrative unit based on French model intended to replace the old Hapsburg colonial structure

*intendente:* administrative head of an *intendencia*

*junta:* committee, governing directorate

*justicia mayor:* district magistrate

*labor:* tilling or plowing; an agricultural field; a Mexican era unit of land measure of approximately 177.1 acres.

*mayordomo:* overseer

*mesteña* or *mesteño:* unbranded stock

*mestizaje:* term applied to the process of race mixing among the European, African, and Indian populations of Spanish America

*mestizo:* offspring of a Spaniard and an Indian

*patrón:* master

*peninsular:* European-born Spaniard

*peón:* lowest category of permanent *hacienda* employee

*porción:* portion or allotment; long lot along the Rio Grande originally surveyed in 1767

*primeros pobladores:* first or original settlers

*procurador:* municipal attorney

*pueblo:* village, settlement, people; in New Mexico and Arizona, term applied to the various town-dwelling Indian tribes

*quinto real:* royal fifth; Spanish Crown's portion of treasure taken in an expedition or precious metals mined

*rancho:* term for a mixed-use, small-to-medium rural property that in Texas referred to a large livestock estate

*reducción:* gathering of nonsedentary Indians into a mission community

*regidor:* alderman, town councilman

*regimiento:* town council

*república de españoles:* one of two major divisions of Spanish colonial society composed of all non-Indians covered by a separate code of law

*república de indios:* one of two major divisions of Spanish colonial society composed of all Indians under Spanish rule covered by a separate code of law

*requerimiento:* summons, demand; formal statement of Spanish right to dominion in the New World, required to be read to Indians before war could be made on them

*sistema de castas:* ordering of Spanish American society according to racial-ethnic characteristics

*sitio:* place; a unit of land equivalent to approximately 4,500 acres of grazing land

*subdelegado:* district magistrate under the *intendencia* system

*Tejano:* a Texan of Mexican heritage

*vaquero:* cowboy

*vecino:* citizen

*visitador:* inspector general

# Bibliography

Abbott, E. C., and Helena Huntington Smith. *We Pointed Them North: Recollections of a Cow-puncher.* Norman: University of Oklahoma Press, 1955.

Alessio Robles, Vito. *Coahuila y Texas desde la consumación de la Independencia hasta el Tratado de Paz de Guadalupe Hidalgo.* 1945. Reprint, Mexico City: Editorial Porrúa, 1979.

———. *Coahuila y Tejas en la época colonial.* Mexico City: Editorial Cultura, 1938.

Allen, Henry E. "The Parrilla Expedition to the Red River in 1759." *Southwestern Historical Quarterly* 43 (July 1939): 53–71.

Allen, Ruth A. *East Texas Lumber Workers.* Austin: University of Texas Press, 1961.

———. *The Great Southwest Strike.* Austin: The University of Texas Bulletin No. 4214, 1942.

Allsup, Carl. *The American G.I. Forum: Origins and Evolution.* Austin: University of Texas Press, 1982.

Almaráz, Félix D., Jr. *Governor Antonio Martínez and Mexican Independence in Texas: An Orderly Transition.* 1975. Reprint, San Antonio: Bexar County Historical Commission, 1979.

———. "The Legacy of Columbus: Spanish Mission Policy in Texas." *Journal of Texas Catholic History and Culture* 3 (1992): 17–36.

———. "San Antonio's Old Franciscan Missions: Material Decline and Secular Avarice in the Transition from Hispanic to Mexican Control." *Americas* 44 (July 1987): 1–22.

———. *Tragic Cavalier: Governor Manuel Salcedo of Texas, 1808–1813.* Austin: University of Texas Press, 1971.

Alonzo, Armando. *Tejano Legacy: Rancheros and Settlers in South Texas, 1734–1900.* Albuquerque: University of New Mexico Press, 1998.

Ambrose, Stephen E. *Eisenhower: Soldier and President.* Rev. ed. New York: Simon & Schuster, 1990.

Anders, Evan. *Boss Rule in South Texas: The Progressive Era.* Austin: University of Texas Press, 1982.

Anderson, Gary Clayton. *The Indian Southwest, 1580–1830: Ethnogenesis and Reinvention.* Norman: University of Oklahoma Press, 1999.

Anderson, H. Allen. "The Delaware and Shawnee Indians and the Republic of Texas, 1820–1845." *Southwestern Historical Quarterly* 94 (October 1990): 231–260.

Aten, Lawrence E. *Indians of the Upper Texas Coast.* New York: Academic Press, 1983.

Bacarisse, Charles A. "Baron de Bastrop." *Southwestern Historical Quarterly* 58 (January 1955): 319–330.

Bagur, Jacques D. *A History of Navigation on Cypress Bayou and the Lakes.* Denton: University of North Texas Press, 2001.

Bainbridge, John. *Super-Americans.* Garden City, NY: Doubleday, 1961.

Banks, Jimmy. *Money, Marbles, and Chalk.* Austin: Texas Publishing Co., 1971.

Barksdale, E. C. *The Meat Packers Come to Texas.* Austin: Bureau of Business Research, 1959.

Barnes, Donna A. *Farmers in Rebellion: The Rise and Fall of the Southern Farmers Alliance and People's Party in Texas.* Austin: University of Texas Press, 1984.

Barr, Alwyn. *Black Texans: A History of African-Americans in Texas, 1528–1995.* Norman: University of Oklahoma Press, 1996.

———. *Reconstruction to Reform: Texas Politics, 1876–1906.* Austin: University of Texas Press, 1971.

————. *Texans in Revolt: The Battle for San Antonio, 1835.* Austin: University of Texas Press, 1990.

Barr, Alwyn, and Robert A. Calvert, eds. *Black Leaders: Texans for Their Times.* Austin: Texas State Historical Association, 1981.

Barta, Carolyn. *Bill Clements: Texian to His Toenails.* Austin: Eakin Press, 1996.

Bartlett, Richard C. *Saving the Best of Texas.* Austin: University of Texas Press, 1995.

Bartley, Earnest R. *The Texas Tidelands Controversy: A Legal and Historical Analysis.* Austin: University of Texas Press, 1953.

Benavides, Adán, Jr., comp. and ed. *The Béxar Archives (1717–1836): A Name Guide.* Austin: University of Texas Press, 1989.

Benson, Nettie L. "A Governor's Report on Texas in 1809." *Southwestern Historical Quarterly* 71 (April 1968): 603–615.

————. "Bishop Marín de Porras and Texas." *Southwestern Historical Quarterly* 51 (July 1947): 16–40.

————. "Texas Failure to Send a Deputy to the Spanish Cortes, 1810–1812." *Southwestern Historical Quarterly* 64 (July 1960): 14–35.

Berrueto González, Arturo. *Diccionario biográfico de Coahuila.* Saltillo: Gobierno del Estado de Coahuila, 1999.

Bethell, Leslie, ed. *The Independence of Latin America.* Cambridge, UK: Cambridge University Press, 1987.

Biles, Roger. *The South and the New Deal.* Lexington: University of Kentucky Press, 1991.

Bishop, Bill. "Major Urban Areas See Most of Texas' Growth: As Cities' Amenities Attract Talented Workers—Companies, Jobs Follow." *Austin American Statesman* 3 March 2002—A1. <http://archives.statesman.com>.

Bixel, Patricia Bellis, and Elizabeth Hayes Turner. *Galveston and the 1900 Storm.* Austin: University of Texas Press, 2000.

Blackwelder, Julia Kirk. *Women of the Depression: Caste and Culture in San Antonio, 1929–1939.* College Station: Texas A&M University Press, 1984.

Blodgett, Jan. *Land of Bright Promise: Advertising and the Texas Panhandle and South Plains, 1870–1917.* Austin: University of Texas Press, 1988.

Bolton, Herbert E. *Coronado: Knight of Pueblos and Plains.* 1949. Reprint, Albuquerque: University of New Mexico Press, 1964.

————. *The Hasinais: Southern Caddoans as Seen by the Earliest Europeans.* 1987. Reprint, Norman: University of Oklahoma Press, 2002.

————. *Texas in the Middle Eighteenth Century: Studies in Spanish Colonial Administration.* 1915. Reprint, Austin: University of Texas Press, 1970.

Bolton, Herbert E., ed. and trans. *Athanase de Mézières and the Louisiana-Texas Frontier, 1768–1780.* 2 vols. Cleveland: Arthur H. Clark, 1914.

Boswell, Evault. *Texas Boys in Gray.* Plano: Republic of Texas Press, 2000.

Brading, David A. *Miners and Merchants in Bourbon Mexico, 1763–1810.* Cambridge, UK: Cambridge University Press, 1971.

Bradley, Ed. "Fighting for Texas: Filibuster James Long, the Adams-Onís Treaty, and the Monroe Administration." *Southwestern Historical Quarterly* 102 (January 1999): 323–342.

Bricker, Richard W. *Wooden Ships from Texas: A World War I Saga.* College Station: Texas A&M University Press, 1998.

Brown, Norman D. "Garnering Votes for 'Cactus Jack': John Nance Garner, Franklin D. Roosevelt, and the 1932 Democratic Nomination for President." *Southwestern Historical Quarterly* 104 (October 2000): 148–188.

————. *Hood, Bonnet, and Little Brown Jug: Texas Politics, 1921–1928.* College Station: Texas A&M University Press, 1984.

Bruseth, James E., and Nancy A. Kenmotsu. "From Naguatex to the River Daycao: The Route of the Hernando de Soto Expedition Through Texas." *North American Archaeologist* 14 (1993): 199–225.

Bryant, Keith L., Jr. *Arthur Stillwell: Promoter with a Hunch.* Nashville: Vanderbilt University Press, 1971.

———. *History of the Atchison, Topeka and Santa Fe Railway.* New York: Macmillan, 1974.

Buckley, Eleanor C. "The Aguayo Expedition into Texas and Louisiana, 1719–1722." *Quarterly of the Texas State Historical Association* 15 (July 1911): 1–65.

Buenger, Walter L. *The Path to a Modern South: Northeast Texas Between Reconstruction and the Great Depression.* Austin: University of Texas Press, 2001.

Buenger, Walter L., and Robert A. Calvert, *Texas Through Time: Evolving Interpretations.* College Station: Texas A&M University Press, 1991.

Bullard, Robert D. *Invisible Houston: The Black Experience in Boom and Bust.* College Station: Texas A&M University Press, 1987.

Calvert, Robert A., and Arnoldo De León. *The History of Texas.* 3d ed. Wheeling, Ill.: Harlan Davidson, Inc., 2002.

Campbell, Randolph B. *An Empire for Slavery: The Peculiar Institution in Texas, 1821–1865.* Baton Rouge: Louisiana State University Press, 1989.

———. *Sam Houston and the American Southwest.* New York: HarperCollins, 1993.

Cantrell, Gregg. *Kenneth and John B. Rayner and the Limits of Southern Dissent.* Urbana: University of Illinois Press, 1993.

———. "Racial Violence and Reconstruction Politics in Texas, 1867–1868." *Southwestern Historical Quarterly* 93 (January 1990): 333–356.

———. *Stephen F. Austin: Empresario of Texas.* New Haven: Yale University Press, 1999.

Carleton, Don E. *A Breed So Rare: The Life of J. R. Parten, Liberal Texas Oilman, 1896–1992.* Austin: Texas State Historical Association, 1999.

———. *Red Scare: Right-Wing Hysteria, Fifties Fanaticism, and Their Legacy in Texas.* Austin: Texas Monthly Press, 1985.

Carlson, Paul H. *The Plains Indians.* College Station: Texas A&M University Press, 1998.

———. *Texas Woollybacks: The Texas Sheep and Goat Industry.* College Station: Texas A&M University Press, 1982.

Carmody, Kevin. "Guadalupe Is in Jeopardy, Group Warns: Water Rights Issue Puts River System on Conservationists' List." *Austin American Statesman* 2 April 2002—B1. <http://archives.statesman.com>.

Caro, Robert A. *The Years of Lyndon Johnson: Master of the Senate.* New York: Alfred A. Knopf, 2002.

———. *The Years of Lyndon Johnson: Means of Ascent.* New York: Alfred A. Knopf, 1990.

———. *The Years of Lyndon Johnson: The Path to Power.* New York: Alfred A. Knopf, 1982.

Carraro, Francine. *Jerry Bywaters, A Life in Art.* Austin: University of Texas Press, 1994.

Carroll, John M., ed. *The Black Military Experience in the American West.* New York: Liverwright, 1971.

Carroll, Mark M. *Homesteads Ungovernable: Families, Sex, Race, and the Law in Frontier Texas, 1826–1860.* Austin: University of Texas Press, 2001.

Carter, Cecile Elkins. *Caddo Indians: Where We Come From.* Norman: University of Oklahoma Press, 1995.

Casdorf, Paul. *A History of the Republican Party in Texas, 1865–1965.* Austin: Pemberton Press, 1965.

Cashion, Ty, and Jesús F. de la Teja, eds. *The Human Tradition in Texas.* Wilmington, Del.: SR Books, 2001.

Castañeda, Carlos E. *Our Catholic Heritage in Texas.* 7 vols. Austin: Von Boeckmann-Jones, 1936–1958.

Chabot, Frederick C., ed. *Texas in 1811: The Las Casas and Sambrano Revolutions.* San Antonio: Yanaguana Society, 1941.

Champagne, Anthony. *Congressman Sam Rayburn.* New Brunswick, N.J.: Rutgers University Press, 1984.

Chapa, Juan Bautista. *Texas & Northeastern Mexico, 1630–1690.* Austin: University of Texas Press, 1997.

Chávez, Thomas E. *Spain and the Independence of the United States: An Intrinsic Gift.* Albuquerque: University of New Mexico Press, 2002.

Chipman, Donald E. "In Search of Cabeza de Vaca's Route Across Texas: An Historiographical Survey." *Southwestern Historical Quarterly* 91 (October 1987): 127–148.

———. *Spanish Texas, 1519–1821.* Austin: University of Texas Press, 1992.

Chipman, Donald, and Harriett Denise Joseph. *Notable Men and Women of Spanish Texas.* Austin: University of Texas Press, 1999.

Christian, Garna L. *Black Soldiers in Jim Crow Texas, 1899–1917.* College Station: Texas A&M University Press, 1995.

Clark, L. D., ed. *Civil War Recollections of James Lemuel Clark and the Great Hanging at Gainesville, Texas in October 1862.* Plano: Republic of Texas Press, 1997.

Clayton, Lawrence. *Contemporary Ranches of Texas.* Austin: University of Texas Press, 2001.

Coerver, Don M., and Linda B. Hall. *Texas and the Mexican Revolution: A Study in State and National Border Policy, 1910–1920.* San Antonio: Trinity University Press, 1984.

Conkin, Paul. *Big Daddy from the Pedernales: Lyndon Baines Johnson.* Boston: Twain, 1986.

Connor, Seymour V. *Texas: A History.* New York: Thomas Y. Crowell Co., 1971.

Cook, John R. *The Border and the Buffalo: An Untold Story of the Southwest Plains.* 1907. Reprint, Austin: State House Press, 1989.

Copelin, Laylan. "As Enron Sank, State Pension Funds Invested, Lost." *Austin American Statesman* 26 December 2001—A1. <http://archives.statesman.com>.

Cordell, Linda. *Archaeology of the Southwest.* 2d ed. San Diego: Academic Press, 1997.

Cotner, Robert C. *James Stephen Hogg.* Austin: University of Texas Press, 1951.

Cotner, Robert C., et. al. *Texas Cities and the Great Depression.* Austin: Texas Memorial Museum, 1973.

Cox, Patrick. *Ralph Yarborough: The People's Senator.* Austin: University of Texas Press, 2001.

Crawford, Ann Fears, and Crystal Sasse Ragsdale. *Texas Women Frontier to Future.* Austin: State House Press, 1998.

Crawford, Ann Fears, and Jack Keever. *John B. Connally: Portrait in Power.* Austin: Jenkins Co., 1973.

Crouch, Barry. *The Freedman's Bureau and Black Texans.* Austin: University of Texas Press, 1992.

Cruz, Gilbert R. *Let There Be Towns: Spanish Municipal Origins in the American Southwest, 1610–1810.* College Station: Texas A&M University Press, 1988.

Cummins, Light T. "Church Courts, Marriage Breakdown, and Separation in Spanish Louisiana, West Florida, and Texas." *Journal of Texas Catholic History and Culture* 4 (1993): 97–114.

Cutrer, Emily F. *The Art of the Woman: The Life and Work of Elisabet Ney.* Lincoln: University of Nebraska Press, 1988.

Dabbs, J. Autrey. "The Texas Missions in 1789." In *Preparing the Way: Preliminary Studies of the Texas Catholic Historical Society III.* Austin: Texas Catholic Historical Society, 2000.

Dallas Morning News. *Texas Almanac 2002–2003.* Dallas Morning News, 2001.

Dalleck, Robert. *Lone Star Rising: Lyndon Johnson and His Times, 1908–1960.* New York: Oxford University Press, 1991.

Dary, David. *Cowboy Culture: A Saga of Five Centuries.* Lawrence: University Press of Kansas, 1989.

Davidson, Chandler. *Race and Class in Texas Politics.* Princeton: Princeton University Press, 1990.

Davis, Graham. "Models of Migration: The Historiography of the Irish Pioneers in South Texas." *Southwestern Historical Quarterly* 99 (January 1996): 326–348.

Davis, William C. *Three Roads to the Alamo: The Lives and Fortunes of David Crockett, James Bowie, and William Barret Travis.* New York: HarperCollins, 1998.

Dawson, Sr., John C. *High Plains Yesterdays: From XIT Days Through Drouth* [sic] *and Depression.* Austin: Eakin Press, 1985.

De León, Arnoldo. *Mexican Americans in Texas: A Brief History.* 2d ed. Wheeling, Ill.: Harlan Davidson, Inc., 1999.

———. *They Called Them Greasers: Anglo Attitudes Toward Mexicans in Texas, 1821–1900.* Austin: University of Texas Press, 1983.

De Zavala, Adina. *History and Legends of the Alamo and Other Missions in and Around San Antonio.* 1917. Reprint, Houston: Arte Publico Press, 1996.

Deaton, Charles. *The Year They Threw the Rascals Out.* Austin: Shoal Creek Publishers, 1973.

Dell, Michael. *Direct from Dell: Strategies That Revolutionized an Industry.* New York: HarperBusiness, 1999.

Din, Gilbert C. "Spain's Immigration Policy in Louisiana and the American Penetration, 1792–1803." *Southwestern Historical Quarterly* 76 (January 1973): 255–276.

Dixon, Olive K. *Life of "Billy" Dixon.* Austin: State House Press reprint, 1987.

Doughty, Robin W. *At Home in Texas: Early Views of the Land.* College Station: Texas A&M University Press, 1987.

Downs, Fane. "Governor Antonio Martínez and the Defense of Texas from Foreign Invasion, 1817–1822," *Texas Military History* 7 (spring 1968): 27–43.

———. "'Tryels and Trubbles': Women in Early Nineteenth Century Texas." *Southwestern Historical Quarterly* 90 (April 1987): 35–56.

Dugas, Vera Lee. "Texas Industry, 1860–1880." *Southwestern Historical Quarterly* 59 (October 1955): 151–183.

Dugger, Ronnie. *Our Invaded Universities: Form, Reform and New Starts: A Nonfiction Play for Five Stages.* New York: W. W. Norton, 1974.

———. *The Politician: The Life and Times of Lyndon B. Johnson.* New York: W. W. Norton, 1982.

———. *Three Men in Texas: Bedicheck, Webb, and Dobie.* Austin: University of Texas Press, 1967.

Dunn, William E. "Apache Relations in Texas, 1718–1750." *Quarterly of the Texas State Historical Association* 14 (January 1911): 198–274.

Eckhardt, Gregg A. "Ron Pucek's Living Waters Catfish Farm." *The Edwards Aquifer Home Page.* 28 June 2002. <http://www.edwardsaquifer.net/pucek.html>.

Elliot, J. H. *Imperial Spain, 1469–1716.* New York: St. Martin's Press, 1964.

Everett, Dianna. *The Texas Cherokees: A People Between Two Fires, 1819–1840.* Norman: University of Oklahoma Press, 1990.

Exley, Jo Ella Powell. *Texas Tears and Texas Sunshine: Voices of Frontier Women.* College Station: Texas A&M University Press, 1985.

Faulk, Odie B. *The Last Years of Spanish Texas, 1778–1821.* The Hague: Mouton, 1964.

———. "The Penetration of Foreigners and Foreign Ideas into Spanish East Texas, 1793–1810." *East Texas Historical Journal* 2 (October 1964): 87–98.

———. "Ranching in Spanish Texas." *Hispanic American Historical Review* 45 (May 1965): 257–266.

Faulk, Odie B., and Laura E. Faulk. *Defenders of the Interior Provinces: Presidial Soldiers on the Northern Frontier of New Spain.* Albuquerque: Albuquerque Museum, 1988.

Flannery, Tim. *The Eternal Frontier: An Ecological History of North America and Its People.* New York: Atlantic Monthly Press, 2001.

Flint, Richard. *Great Cruelties Have Been Reported: The 1544 Investigation of the Coronado Expedition.* Dallas: Southern Methodist University Press, 2002.

Flint, Richard, and Shirley Cushing Flint, eds. *The Coronado Expedition to Tierra Nueva: The 1540–1542 Route Across the Southwest.* Niwot: University Press of Colorado, 1997.

Flores, Dan L. *Jefferson and Southwestern Exploration: The Freeman and Custis Accounts of the Red River Expedition of 1806.* Norman: University of Oklahoma Press, 1984.

Foik, Paul J. "Captain Don Domingo Ramón's Diary of His Expedition into Texas in 1716." In *Wilderness Mission: Preliminary Studies of the Texas Catholic Historical Society II.* Austin: Texas Catholic Historical Society, 1999.

Foley, Neil. *The White Scourge: Mexicans, Blacks, and Poor Whites in Texas Cotton Culture.* Berkeley: University of California Press, 1997.

Forman, Maury, and Robert A. Calvert, *Cartooning Texas: One Hundred Years of Cartoon Art in the Lone Star State.* College Station: Texas A&M University Press, 1993.

Forrestal, Peter J., trans. "The Solís Diary of 1767." In *Preparing the Way: Preliminary Studies of the Texas Catholic Historical Society I.* Austin: Texas Catholic Historical Society, 1997.

Foster, William C. *Spanish Expeditions into Texas, 1689–1768.* Austin: University of Texas Press, 1995.

Frantz, Joe B. *Texas: A Bicentennial History.* New York: W. W. Norton, 1976.

Frantz, Joe B., and Julian Ernest Choate. *The American Cowboy: The Myth and the Reality.* Norman: University of Oklahoma Press, 1955.

Frazier, Donald S. *Blood & Treasure: Confederate Empire in the Southwest.* College Station: Texas A&M University Press, 1995.

Freehling, William W. *The Road to Disunion: Secessionists at Bay, 1776–1854.* New York: Oxford University Press, 1990.

Friedberger, Mark. "'Mink and Manure': Rural Gentrification and Cattle Raising in Southeast Texas, 1945–1992." *Southwestern Historical Quarterly* 102 (January 1999): 269–293.

"The Future Is Texas." Reprinted from *The Economist. Austin American Statesman* (5 January 2003): H1+.

Galbraith, John Kenneth. *The Great Crash, 1929.* Boston: Houghton Mifflin, 1955.

García, Ignacio M. *United We Win: The Rise and Fall of La Raza Unida Party.* Tucson: University of Arizona Press, 1989.

García, Mario T. *Desert Immigrants: The Mexicans of El Paso, 1880–1920.* New Haven: Yale University Press, 1981.

Gard, Wayne. *Frontier Justice.* Norman: University of Oklahoma Press, 1949.

Gardien, Kent. "Take Pity on Our Glory: Men of Champ d'Asile." *Southwestern Historical Quarterly* 87 (January 1984): 241–268.

Garrett, Julia K. *Green Flag Over Texas: A Story of the Last Years of Spain in Texas.* New York: Cordova Press, 1939.

Gee, Robert W. "Dry Fields Threaten Way of Life for Valley Farmers." *Austin American Statesman* 17 March 2002—A1. <http://archives.statesman.com>.

Gerhard, Peter. *The Northern Frontier of New Spain.* Princeton: Princeton University Press, 1982.

Goodwyn, Lawrence. *Democratic Promise: The Populist Movement in America.* New York: Oxford University Press, 1976.

Gould, Lewis L. *Progressives and Prohibitionists: Texas Democrats in the Wilson Era.* Austin: Texas State Historical Association, 1992.

Graham, Joe S. *El Rancho in South Texas: Continuity and Change from 1750*. Denton: University of North Texas Press, 1994.

Green, Donald E. *Land of the Underground Rain: Irrigation on the Texas High Plains, 1910–1970*. Austin: University of Texas Press, 1973.

Green, George Norris. *The Establishment in Texas Politics: The Primitive Years, 1938–1957*. 1979. Reprint, Norman: University of Oklahoma Press, 1984.

Green, James R. *Grass-Roots Socialism: Radical Movements in the Southwest, 1895–1943*. Baton Rouge: Louisiana State University Press, 1978.

———. "Tenant Farmer Discontent and Socialist Protest in Texas, 1901–1917." *Southwestern Historical Quarterly* 81 (October 1977): 133–154.

Groneman, Bill. *Eyewitness to the Alamo*. Plano: Republic of Texas Press, 1996.

Habig, Marion A. *The Alamo Chain of Missions: A History of San Antonio's Five Old Missions*. Chicago: Franciscan Herald Press, 1969.

Hackett, Charles W. "The Neutral Ground Between Louisiana and Texas, 1806–1821." *Louisiana Historical Quarterly* 28 (October 1945): 1001–1128.

Hackett, Charles W., ed. and trans. *Pichardo's Treatise on the Limits of Louisiana and Texas*. 4 vols. Austin: University of Texas Press, 1931–1946.

Haggard, J. Villasana. "The Counter-Revolution of Béxar, 1811." *Southwestern Historical Quarterly* 43 (October 1939): 222–235.

Haley, J. Evetts. *Charles Goodnight, Cowman and Plainsman*. Norman: University of Oklahoma Press, 1949.

———. *George W. Littlefield, Texan*. Norman: University of Oklahoma Press, 1943.

Hardeman, Dorsey B., and Donald C. Bacon. *Rayburn: A Biography*. Austin: Texas Monthly Press, 1987.

Hardin, Stephen L. *Texian Iliad: A Military History of the Texas Revolution*. Austin: University of Texas Press, 1994.

Harmon, Dave. "The Fight for a Historic Birthright: Padre Island Ruling Gives Hope to Latino Families." *Austin American Statesman* 10 January 2000—A1. <http://archives.statesman.com>.

Hatcher, Mattie Austin. "The Expedition of Don Domingo Terán de los Ríos into Texas." In *Wilderness Mission: Preliminary Studies of the Texas Catholic Historical Society II*. Austin: Texas Catholic Historical Society, 1999.

———. *The Opening of Texas to Foreign Settlement, 1801–1821*. 1927. Reprint, Philadelphia: Porcupine Press, 1976.

Haynes, Sam W. "Anglophobia and the Annexation of Texas: The Quest for National Security." In Sam W. Haynes and Christopher Morris, eds. *Manifest Destiny and Empire: American Antebellum Expansionism*. College Station: Texas A&M University Press, 1997.

———. *Soldiers of Misfortune: The Somervell and Mier Expeditions*. Austin: University of Texas Press, 1990.

Haynes, Sam W., and Cary D. Wintz, eds. *Major Problems in Texas History: Documents and Essays*. Boston: Houghton Mifflin, 2002.

Henderson, Richard B. *Maury Maverick, A Political Biography*. Austin: University of Texas Press, 1970.

Hendrickson, Jr., Kenneth B. *The Chief Executives of Texas: From Stephen F. Austin to John B. Connally, Jr.* College Station: Texas A&M University Press, 1995.

Hendrickson, Jr., Kenneth E., and Michael L. Collins, eds. *Profiles in Power: Twentieth-Century Texans in Washington*. Arlington Heights, Ill.: Harlan Davidson, Inc., 1993.

Henson, Margaret Swett, and Deolece Parmalee. *The Cartwrights of San Augustine: Three Generations of Agricultural Entrepreneurs in Nineteenth-Century Texas*. Austin: Texas State Historical Association, 1993.

Hester, Thomas R. *Digging into South Texas Prehistory: A Guide for Amateur Archaeologists.* San Antonio: Corona Publishing, 1980.

Hickerson, Nancy P. "How Cabeza de Vaca Lived with, Worked Among, and Finally Left the Indians of Texas." *Journal of Anthropological Research* 54 (summer 1998): 199–218.

———. *The Jumanos: Hunters and Traders of the South Plains.* Austin: University of Texas Press, 1994.

Hight, Bruce. "Tiguas Roll Snake Eyes in Court Fight; El Paso Tribe Must Close Casino after Nine Years but Can Continue Appeal." *Austin American Statesman* 12 February 2002—A1. <http://archives.statesman.com>.

Hill, Patricia Everidge. *Dallas: The Making of a Modern City.* Austin: University of Texas Press, 1996.

Hinojosa, Gilberto M. *A Borderlands Town in Transition: Laredo, 1755–1870.* College Station: Texas A&M University Press, 1983.

Hodge, Frederick W., and Theodore H. Lewis, eds. *Spanish Explorers in the Southern United States, 1528–1543.* 1907. Reprint, Austin: Texas State Historical Association, 1990.

Hogan, William Ransom. *The Texas Republic: A Social and Economic History.* 1946. Reprint, Austin: University of Texas Press, 1969.

Holden, William C. *Alkali Trails, or, Social and Economic Movements of the Texas Frontier, 1846–1900.* Dallas: Southwest Press, 1930.

Holmes, Jack D. L. "Showdown on the Sabine: General James Wilkinson vs. Lieutenant-Colonel Simon de Herrera." *Louisiana Studies* 3 (1964 ): 46–76.

Hudson, Linda S. *Mistress of Manifest Destiny: A Biography of Jane McManus Storm Cazneau, 1807–1878.* Austin: Texas State Historical Association, 2001.

Humphrey, David C. *Austin, an Illustrated History.* Northridge, Calif.: Windsor Publications,1985.

Hyman, Harold. *Oleander Odyssey: The Kempners of Galveston, Ca. 1850–1987.* College Station: Texas A&M University Press, 1990.

Iber, Jorge. "Bridal Aguero and *El Editor* Newspaper: The Varied Roles of a Spanish Surnamed Entrepreneur in a Lubbock, Texas Barrio, 1977–1999." *West Texas Historical Association Yearbook* 75 (1999): 54–61.

Jackson, Jack. *Los Mesteños: Spanish Ranching in Texas, 1721–1821.* College Station: Texas A&M University Press, 1986.

Jackson, Jack, ed., William C. Foster, annot. *Imaginary Kingdom: Texas as Seen by the Rivera and Rubí Military Expeditions, 1727 and 1767.* Austin: Texas State Historical Association, 1995.

Jackson, Ron. *Alamo Legacy: Alamo Descendants Remember the Alamo.* Austin: Eakin Press, 1997.

Jacobs, Louis. *Lone Star Dinosaurs.* College Station: Texas A&M University Press, 1995.

Jasinski, Laurie. *Hill Country Backroads: Showing the Way in Comal County.* Fort Worth: Texas Christian University Press, 2001.

John, Elizabeth A. H. *Storms Brewed in Other Men's Worlds: The Confrontation of Indians, Spanish, and French in the Southwest, 1540–1795.* College Station: Texas A&M University Press, 1975.

John, Elizabeth A. H., ed., John Wheat, trans. "Inside the Comanchería, 1785: The Diary of Pedro Vial and Francisco Xavier Chaves." *Southwestern Historical Quarterly* 98 (July 1994): 27–56.

Jones, Billy Mac. *Health Seekers in the Southwest, 1817–1900.* Norman: University of Oklahoma Press, 1967.

Jones, Billy Mac. *The Search for Maturity.* Austin: Steck-Vaughn Co., 1965.

Jones, Nancy Baker and Ruthe Winegarten. *Capitol Women.* Austin: University of Texas Press, 2000.

Jones, Oakah L., Jr. *Los Paisanos: Spanish Settlers on the Northern Frontier of New Spain.* Norman: University of Oklahoma Press, 1979.

Jordan, Barbara, and Shelby Hearon. *Barbara Jordan: A Self Portrait.* Garden City, NY: Doubleday, 1979.

Jordan, Terry G. "A Century and a Half of Ethnic Change in Texas, 1836–1986." *Southwestern Historical Quarterly* 89 (April 1986): 385–422.

———. *German Seed in Texas Soil: Immigrant Farmers in Nineteenth-Century Texas.* Austin: University of Texas Press, 1966.

———. *North American Cattle-Ranching Frontiers: Origins, Diffusion, and Differentiation.* Albuquerque: University of New Mexico Press, 1993.

———. *Texas: A Geography.* Boulder, Colo.: Westview Press, 1984.

———. *Trails to Texas: Southern Roots of Western Cattle Ranching.* Lincoln: University of Nebraska Press, 1981.

Kearns, Doris. *Lyndon Baines Johnson and the American Dream.* New York: Harper & Row, 1976.

Kessell, John L. *Spain in the Southwest: A Narrative History of Colonial New Mexico, Arizona, Texas, and California.* Norman: University of Oklahoma Press, 2002.

Key, Jr., V. O. *Southern Politics in State and Nation.* New York: Alfred A. Knopf, 1949.

Kinch, Jr., Sam, and Ben Procter. *Texas Under a Cloud.* Austin: Jenkins Publishing Co., 1972.

Kinch, Jr., Sam, and Stuart Long. *Allan Shivers: The Pied Piper of Texas Politics.* Austin: Shoal Creek Publishers, 1974.

King, Larry L. *Confessions of a White Racist.* New York: Viking Press, 1971.

Kinnaird, Lawrence, ed. *The Frontiers of New Spain: Nicolás de Lafora's Description, 1766–1768.* Berkeley, Calif.: Quivira Society, 1958.

Knaggs, John R. *Two Party Texas: The John Tower Era, 1961–1984.* Austin: Eakin Press, 1986.

Knaut, Andrew L. *The Pueblo Revolt of 1680: Conquest and Resistance in Seventeenth-Century New Mexico.* Norman: University of Oklahoma Press, 1995.

La Vere, David. "Between Kinship and Capitalism: French and Spanish Rivalry in the Colonial Louisiana-Texas Indian Trade." *Journal of Southern History* 64 (May 1998): 197–218.

———. *The Caddo Chiefdoms: Caddo Economics and Politics, 700–1835.* Lincoln: University of Nebraska Press, 1998.

La Vere, David, and Katia Campbell, eds. and trans. "An Expedition to the Kichai: The Journal of François Grappe, September 24, 1783." *Southwestern Historical Quarterly* 98 (July 1994): 59–78.

Lack, Paul D. *The Texas Revolutionary Experience, A Political and Social History 1835–1836.* College Station: Texas A&M University Press, 1992.

Lack, Paul D., ed. *The Diary of William Fairfax Gray from Virginia to Texas, 1835–1837.* Dallas: De Golyer Library and William P. Clements Center for Southwest Studies, Southern Methodist University, 1997.

Larson, Erik. *Isaac's Storm: A Man, a Time, and the Deadliest Hurricane in History.* New York: Vintage Books, 2000.

Lemée, Patricia R. "Tios and Tantes: Familial and Political Relationships of Natchitoches and the Spanish Colonial Frontier." *Southwestern Historical Quarterly* 101 (January 1998): 341–358.

Leutenegger, Benedict, ed., and Marion A. Habig. "Report on the San Antonio Missions in 1792." *Southwestern Historical Quarterly* 77 (April 1974): 487–498.

Lindell, Chuck. "Texans Take Mexico Water Fight to D.C.; Growers Want U.S. to Push Mexico on Releasing Water to Rio Grande." *Austin American Statesman* 25 April 2002—B1. <http://archives.statesman.com>.

Linsley, Judith Walker, Ellen Walker Rienstra, and Jo Ann Stiles. *Giant Under the Hill: A History of the Spindletop Oil Discovery at Beaumont, Texas, in 1901.* Austin: Texas State Historical Association, 2002.

Little, Carol Morris. *A Comprehensive Guide to Outdoor Sculpture in Texas.* Austin: University of Texas Press, 1996.

Malone, Ann Patton. *Women on the Texas Frontier.* El Paso: Texas Western Press, 1985.

Marks, Paula Mitchell. *Hands to the Spindle: Texas Women and Home Textile Production, 1822–1880.* College Station: Texas A&M University Press, 1998.

———. *Turn Your Eyes Toward Texas: Pioneers Sam and Mary Maverick.* College Station: Texas A&M University Press, 1989.

Martin, Robert L. *The City Moves West: Economic and Industrial Growth in Central West Texas.* Austin: University of Texas Press, 1969.

Martin, Roscoe. *The People's Party in Texas: A Study in Third-Party Politics.* 1933. Reprint, Austin: University of Texas Press, 1970.

Matovina, Timothy. *Tejano Religion and Ethnicity in San Antonio, 1821–1860.* Austin: University of Texas Press, 1995.

———. *The Alamo Remembered: Tejano Accounts and Perspectives.* Austin: University of Texas Press, 1995.

Maxwell, Robert S. *Sawdust Empire: The Texas Lumber Industry, 1830–1940.* College Station: Texas A&M University Press, 1983.

McArthur, Judith N. *Creating the New Woman: The Rise of Southern Women's Progressive Culture in Texas, 1893–1918.* Urbana, Ill.: University of Illinois Press, 1998.

McCarty, Kieran. "Before They Crossed the Great River: Cultural Background of the Spanish Franciscans in Texas." *Journal of Texas Catholic History and Culture* 3 (1992): 37–44.

McCaslin, Richard B. "Wheat Growers in the Cotton Confederacy: The Suppression of Dissent in Collin County, Texas, During the Civil War." *Southwestern Historical Quarterly* 96 (April 1993): 527–539.

McComb, David G. *Galveston, A History.* Austin: University of Texas Press, 1986.

———. *Houston: A History.* Austin: University of Texas Press, 1986.

———. *Texas: A Modern History.* Austin: University of Texas Press, 1989.

McConal, Patrick M. *Over the Wall: The Men Behind the 1934 Death House Escape.* Austin: Eakin Press, 2000.

McKay, Seth S. *Texas and the Fair Deal.* San Antonio: Naylor Press, 1954.

———. *Texas Politics, 1906–1944.* Lubbock: Texas Tech University Press, 1952.

———. *W. Lee O'Daniel and Texas Politics.* Lubbock: Texas Tech University Press, 1944.

McKay, Seth S., and Odie B. Faulk. *Texas After Spindletop.* Austin: Steck-Vaughn Co., 1965.

McMath, Robert C., Jr. *American Populism: A Social History, 1877–1898.* New York: Hill and Wang, 1993.

———. *Populist Vanguard: A History of the Southern Farmer's Alliance.* Chapel Hill: University of North Carolina Press, 1975.

Meinig, D. W. *Imperial Texas: An Interpretive Essay in Cultural Geography.* Austin: University of Texas Press, 1969.

Meyer, Michael C. *Water in the Hispanic Southwest: A Social and Legal History, 1550–1850.* Tucson: University of Arizona Press, 1984.

Meyer, Michael C., William L. Sherman, and Susan M. Deeds. *The Course of Mexican History.* 6th ed. New York: Oxford University Press, 1999.

Miller, Thomas L. *The Public Lands of Texas, 1519–1970.* Norman: University of Oklahoma Press, 1972.

Moneyhon, Carl. "Edmund J. Davis in the Coke-Davis Election Dispute of 1874: A Reassessment of Character." *Southwestern Historical Quarterly* 100 (October 1996): 131–151.

Montejano, David. *Anglos and Mexicans in the Making of Texas, 1836–1986.* Austin: University of Texas Press, 1987.

Moorhead, Max L. *The Presidio: Bastion of the Spanish Borderlands.* Norman: University of Oklahoma Press, 1975.

Morehead, Richard. *Fifty Years in Texas Politics.* Burnett: Eakin Press, 1982.

Morfi, Juan Agustín. *History of Texas, 1673–1779.* Trans. and ed. Carlos E. Castañeda. 2 vols. Albuquerque: Quivira Society, 1935.

Morris, John Miller. *El Llano Estacado: Exploration and Imagination on the High Plains of Texas and New Mexico, 1536–1860.* Austin: Texas State Historical Association, 1997.

Murph, Dan. *Texas Giant: The Life of Price Daniel.* Austin: Eakin Press, 2002.

Myers, Sandra L. *The Ranch in Spanish Texas.* El Paso: Texas Western Press, 1969.

Nackman, Mark E. *A Nation Within a Nation: The Rise of Texas Nationalism.* Port Washington, N.Y.: Kennikat Press, 1975.

Navarro García, Luis. *Don José de Gálvez y la Comandancia General de las Provincias Internas del Norte de Nueva España.* Seville: Escuela de Estudios Hispano-Americanos de Sevilla, 1964.

Neu, Charles E. "In Search of Colonel Edward M. House: The Texas Years, 1858–1912." *Southwestern Historical Quarterly* 93 (July 1989): 25–44.

Neugebauer, Janet M., ed. *Plains Farmer: The Diary of William G. DeLoach, 1914–1964.* College Station: Texas A&M University Press, 1991.

Newcomb, W. W., Jr. *The Indians of Texas: From Prehistoric to Modern Times.* Austin: University of Texas Press, 1961.

———. *The Rock Art of Texas Indians.* Paintings by Forrest Kirkland. Austin: University of Texas Press, 1967.

Nunley, Parker. *A Field Guide to Archeological Sites in Texas.* Austin: Texas Monthly Press, 1989.

O'Connor, Kathryn Stoner. *Presidio La Bahia del Espiritu Santo de Zuniga, 1721–1846.* Austin: Von Boeckmann-Jones, 1966.

Oates, Stephen B., ed. *Rip Ford's Texas.* Austin: University of Texas Press, 1963.

Olien, Diana Davids, and Roger M. Olien. *Oil in Texas: The Gusher Age, 1895–1945.* Austin: University of Texas Press, 2002.

Olien, Roger M. *From Token to Triumph: The Texas Republicans Since 1920.* Dallas: Southern Methodist University Press, 1982.

Oliphant, Dave. *Texas Jazz.* Austin: University of Texas Press, 1996.

Olmsted, Frederick Law. *A Journey Through Texas, Or, A Saddle-Trip on the Southwestern Frontier.* 1857. Reprint, Austin: University of Texas Press, 1978.

Olson, Donald W., et al. "Piñon Pines and the Route of Cabeza de Vaca." *Southwestern Historical Quarterly* 101 (October 1997): 174–186.

Ornish, Natalie. *Ehrenberg: Goliad Survivor, Old West Explorer.* Dallas: Texas Heritage Press, 1997.

Osante, Patricia. *Orígenes del Nuevo Santander (1748–1772).* Mexico: Universidad Nacional Autónoma de México, Instituto de Investigaciones Históricas, 1997.

Owens, William A. *A Season of Weathering.* New York: Scribner, 1973.

Pate, J'Nell L. *Livestock Legacy: The Fort Worth Stockyards, 1887–1987.* College Station: Texas A&M University Press, 1988.

Patenaude, Lionel V. *Texas Politics and the New Deal.* New York: Garland Publishing, 1983.

Paulissen, May Nelson, and Carl McQueary. *Miriam: The Southern Belle Who Became the First Woman Governor of Texas.* Austin: Eakin Press, 1995.

Pérez de Villagrá, Gaspar. *Historia de la Nueva México, 1610.* Albuquerque: University of New Mexico Press, 1992.

Perttula, Timothy K. *"The Caddo Nation": Archaeological and Ethnohistoric Perspectives.* Austin: University of Texas Press, 1992.

Pickering, David, and Judy Falls. *Brush Men and Vigilantes: Civil War Dissent in Texas.* College Station: Texas A&M University Press, 2000.

Pitre, Merline. *In Struggle Against Jim Crow: Lulu B. White and the NAACP, 1900–1957.* College Station: Texas A&M University Press, 1999.

———. *Through Many Dangers, Toils and Snares: The Black Leadership of Texas, 1868–1900.* Austin: Eakin Press, 1985.

Platt, Harold L. *City Building in the New South: The Growth of Public Services in Houston, Texas, 1830–1915.* Philadelphia: Temple University Press, 1983.

Powers, John, and Deborah Powers. *Texas Painters, Sculptors and Graphic Artists: A Biographical Dictionary of Artists in Texas before 1942.* Austin: Woodmont Books, 2000.

Poyo, Gerald E., ed. *Tejano Journey, 1770–1850.* Austin: University of Texas Press, 1996.

Poyo, Gerald E., and Gilberto M. Hinojosa, eds. *Tejano Origins in Eighteenth-Century San Antonio.* Austin: University of Texas Press, 1991.

Priestley, Herbert I. *José de Gálvez, Visitor General of New Spain, 1765–1771.* 1916. Reprint, Philadelphia: Porcupine Press, 1980.

Prindle, David F. *Petroleum Politics and the Texas Railroad Commission.* Austin: University of Texas Press, 1981.

Procter, Ben H. *Just One Riot: Episodes of Texas Rangers in the Twentieth Century.* Austin: Eakin Press, 1991.

———. *Not Without Honor: The Life of John H. Reagan.* Austin: University of Texas Press, 1962.

Pupo-Walker, Enrique, ed., and Frances M. López-Morillas, trans. *Castaways: The Narrative of Alvar Núñez Cabeza de Vaca.* Berkeley: University of California Press, 1993.

Ragsdale, Crystal Sasse. *The Golden Free Land: The Reminiscences and Letters of Women on an American Frontier.* Austin: Landmark Press, 1976.

Ragsdale, Kenneth B. *Centennial '36: The Year America Discovered Texas.* College Station: Texas A&M University Press, 1987.

Ramsay, Jack C., Jr. *Jean Laffite, Prince of Pirates.* Austin: Eakin Press, 1996.

Ratcliffe, Sam D. "'Escenas de Martirio': Notes on *The Destruction of Mission San Sabá.*" *Southwestern Historical Quarterly* 94 (April 1991): 507–534.

Reed, S. G. *A History of the Texas Railroads.* Houston: St. Clair Pub. Co., 1941.

Reichstein, Andreas, ed. "The Austin-Leaming Correspondence, 1828–1836." *Southwestern Historical Quarterly* 88 (January 1985): 247–282.

Reindorp, Reginald C. "The Founding of Missions at La Junta de los Ríos." In *Preparing the Way: Preliminary Studies of the Texas Catholic Historical Society III.* Austin: Texas Catholic Historical Society, 2000.

"Republican Party of Texas." <www.txgop.org/library/history.asp>.

Reston, James, Jr. *The Lone Star: The Life of John Connally.* New York: Harper & Row, 1989.

Reston, Maeve. "Growth Drains Williamson Water Supplies." *Austin American Statesman* 18 August 2000—B10. <http://archives.statesman.com>.

Rhinehart, Marilyn D. *A Way of Work and a Way of Life: Coal Mining in Thurber, Texas, 1888–1926.* College Station: Texas A&M University Press, 1992.

Rice, Lawrence D. *The Negro in Texas, 1874–1900.* Baton Rouge: Louisiana State University Press, 1971.

Richards, David. *Once Upon a Time in Texas: A Liberal in the Lone Star State.* Austin: University of Texas Press, 2002.

Richardson, Rupert N. *Colonel Edward M. House: The Texas Years, 1858–1912.* Abilene: Hardin-Simmons University Publications in History, 1964.

Richardson, Rupert N., Adrian Anderson, and Ernest Wallace. *Texas: The Lone Star State.* 8th ed. Englewood Cliffs, N.J.: Prentice-Hall, 2001.

Ricklis, Robert A. *The Karankawa Indians of Texas: An Ecological Study of Cultural Traditions and Change.* Austin: University of Texas Press, 1996.

Rister, Carl Coke. *Comanche Bondage.* 1955. Reprint, Lincoln: University of Nebraska Press, 1989.

Roberts, Randy, and James S. Olson. *A Line in the Sand: The Alamo in Blood and Memory.* New York: The Free Press, 2001.

Robertson, Robert J. *Her Majesty's Texans: Two English Immigrants in Reconstruction Texas.* College Station: Texas A&M University Press, 1998.

Rodnitzky, Jerry L., and Shirley R. Rodnitzky. *Jazz Age Boomtown.* College Station: Texas A&M University Press, 1997.

Roell, Craig H. *Remember Goliad! A History of La Bahía.* Austin: Texas State Historical Association, 1994.

Rogers, Mary Beth. *Barbara Jordan, American Hero.* New York: Bantam Books, 1998.

Rosenbaum, Robert J. *Mexicano Resistance in the Southwest: The Sacred Right of Self Preservation.* Austin: University of Texas Press, 1981.

Rubio, Abel. *Stolen Heritage: A Mexican-American's Rediscovery of His Family's Lost Land Grant.* 1986. Austin: Eakin Press, 1998.

Rundell, Walter, Jr. *Early Texas Oil: Photographic History, 1866–1936.* College Station: Texas A&M University Press, 1977.

Ryan, Kathleen Jo. *Deep in the Heart of Texas: Texas Ranchers in Their Own Words.* Berkeley, Calif.: Ten Speed Press, 1999.

Salinas, Martín. *Indians of the Rio Grande Delta: Their Role in the History of Southern Texas and Northeastern Mexico.* Austin: University of Texas Press, 1990.

Sanders, Leonard. *How Fort Worth Became the Texasmost City.* Fort Worth: Amon Carter Museum, 1973.

San Miguel, Guadalupe, Jr. *Let All of Them Take Heed: Mexican Americans and the Campaign for Educational Equality in Texas, 1910–1981.* Austin: University of Texas Press, 1987.

Santos, Richard G. *Aguayo Expedition into Texas, 1721: An Annotated Translation of the Five Versions of the Diary Kept by Br. Juan Antonio de la Peña.* Austin: Jenkins Publishing, 1981.

Schmelzer, Janet L. *Where the West Begins: Fort Worth and Tarrant County.* Northridge, Calif.: Windsor Publications, 1985.

Schulman, Bruce J. *From Cotton Belt to Sunbelt: Federal Policy, Economic Development, and the Transformation of the South, 1938–1980.* New York: Oxford University Press, 1991.

Schulze, Jeffrey M. "The Rediscovery of the Tiguas: Federal Recognition and Indianness in the Twentieth Century." *Southwestern Historical Quarterly* 105 (July 2001): 15–39.

Schwartz, Jeremy. "Wimberley Seeks to Restore Harmony After Bitter Campaign." *Austin American Statesman* 12 May 2002—B1. <http://archives.statesman.com>.

Schwartz, Ted. *Forgotten Battlefield of the First Texas Revolution: The Battle of the Medina, August 18, 1813.* Ed. Robert H. Thonhoff. Austin: Eakin Press, 1985.

Serwer, Andy, and Julia Boorstin. "Dell Does Domination." *Fortune* (Asia) 145, 2 (21 January 2002): 43.

Sharpless, Rebecca. *Fertile Ground, Narrow Choices: Women on Texas Cotton Farms, 1900–1940.* Chapel Hill: University of North Carolina Press, 1999.

Shockley, John S. *Chicano Revolt in a Texas Town.* Notre Dame: University of Notre Dame Press, 1974.

Sibley, Marilyn. *The Port of Houston.* Austin: University of Texas Press, 1968.

Silverthorne, Elizabeth. *Plantation Life in Texas.* College Station: Texas A&M Press, 1986.

Simmons, Marc. *The Last Conquistador: Juan de Oñate and the Settling of the Far Southwest.* Norman: University of Oklahoma Press, 1991.

Skaggs, Jimmy M. *The Cattle-Trailing Industry: Between Supply and Demand, 1866–1890.* Lawrence: University Press of Kansas, 1973.

Smallwood, James. *The Great Recovery: The New Deal in Texas.* Boston: American Press, 1983.

Smith, F. Todd. *The Wichita Indians: Traders of Texas and the Southern Plains, 1540–1845.* College Station: Texas A&M University Press, 2000.

Smithwick, Noah. *The Evolution of a State, or Recollections of Old Texas Days.* 1900. Reprint, Austin: University of Texas Press, 1983.

Soukup, James R., et al. *Party and Factional Division in Texas.* Austin: University of Texas Press, 1964.

Spearing, Darwin. *Roadside Geology of Texas.* Rev. ed. Missoula, Mont.: Mountain Press, 1991.

Spellman, Paul N. *Forgotten Texas Leader: Hugh McLeod and the Texan Santa Fe Expedition.* College Station: Texas A&M University Press, 1999.

———. *Spindletop Boom Days.* College Station: Texas A&M University Press, 2001.

Spratt, John S. *The Road to Spindletop: Economic Change in Texas, 1875–1901.* Dallas: Southern Methodist University Press, 1955.

Spratt, John S. *Thurber, Texas: The Life and Death of a Company Coal Town.* Austin: University of Texas Press, 1986.

Stewart, Kenneth L., and Arnoldo De León. *Not Room Enough: Mexicans, Anglos, and Socioeconomic Change in Texas, 1850–1900.* Albuquerque: University of New Mexico Press, 1993.

———. *Tejanos and the Numbers Game: A Socio-Historical Interpretation from the Federal Censuses, 1850–1900.* Albuquerque: University of New Mexico Press, 1993.

Struve, Walter. *Germans and Texans: Commerce, Migration, and Culture in the Days of the Lone Star Republic.* Austin: University of Texas Press, 1996.

Sweet, David. "The Ibero-American Frontier Mission in Native American History." In Erick Langer and Robert H. Jackson, eds., *The New Latin American Mission History.* Lincoln: University of Nebraska Press, 1995.

Taylor, Alex. "Little Divides Manor Hopefuls: Schools Candidates Unified in Opposition to Wealth-Sharing Laws." *Austin American Statesman* 26 April 2002—B7.

Taylor, Virginia H., trans. and ed. *The Letters of Antonio Martínez, Last Governor of Texas, 1817–1822.* Austin: Texas State Library, 1957.

Teja, Jesús F. de la. "'A Fine Country with Broad Plains—the Most Beautiful in New Spain': Colonial Views of Land and Nature." In *On the Border: An Environmental History of San Antonio,* ed. Char Miller. Pittsburgh: University of Pittsburgh Press, 2001.

———. "'Only Fit for Raising Stock': Spanish and Mexican Land and Water Rights in the Tamaulipan Cession." In *Fluid Arguments: Five Centuries of Western Water Conflict,* ed. Char Miller. Tucson: University of Arizona Press, 2001.

———. *San Antonio de Béxar: A Community on New Spain's Northern Frontier.* Albuquerque: University of New Mexico Press, 1995.

———. "Spanish Colonial Texas." In *New Views of Borderlands History,* ed. Robert H. Jackson. Albuquerque: University of New Mexico Press, 1998.

Teja, Jesús F. de la, ed. *A Revolution Remembered: The Memoirs and Selected Correspondence of Juan N. Seguín.* 2d ed. Austin: Texas State Historical Association, 2002.

Teja, Jesús F. de la, and John Wheat. "Béxar: Profile of a Tejano Community, 1820–1832." *Southwestern Historical Quarterly* 89 (July 1983): 7–34.

"Texas Values/Texas Future." *Proceedings of the Annual Meeting at Austin, December 3–5, 1999.* Austin: The Philosophical Society of Texas, 2002.

Thomas, Alfred B. *Teodoro de Croix and the Northern Frontier of New Spain, 1776–1783.* Norman: University of Oklahoma Press, 1941.

Thompson, Jerry. *Mexican Texans in the Union Army.* El Paso: Texas Western Press, 1986.

———. *Vaqueros in Blue and Gray.* Austin: Presidial, 1976.

Thompson, Jerry, ed. *Civil War in the Southwest: Recollections of the Sibley Brigade.* College Station: Texas A&M University Press, 2001.

Thonhoff, Robert H. *El Fuerte del Cíbolo: Sentinel of the Béxar-La Bahía Ranches.* Austin: Eakin Press, 1992.

Tijerina, Andrés. *Tejano Empire: Life on the South Texas Ranchos.* College Station: Texas A&M Press, 1998.

———. *Tejanos and Texas Under the Mexican Flag, 1821–1836.* College Station: Texas A&M University Press, 1994.

Timmons, W. H. *El Paso: A Borderlands History.* El Paso: Texas Western Press, 1990.

———. "The El Paso Area in the Mexican Period, 1821–1848." *Southwestern Historical Quarterly* 84 (July 1980): 1–28.

Tjarks, Alicia V. "Comparative Demographic Analysis of Texas, 1777–1793." *Southwestern Historical Quarterly* 77 (January 1974): 291–338.

Tolleson-Rinehart, Sue, and Jeanie R. Stanley. *Claytie and the Lady: Ann Richards, Gender, and Politics in Texas.* Austin: University of Texas Press, 1994.

Tous, Gabriel, trans. "The Espinosa-Olivares-Aguirre Expedition of 1709." In *Preparing the Way: Preliminary Studies of the Texas Catholic Historical Society I.* Austin: Texas Catholic Historical Society, 1997.

———. "Ramón Expedition: Espinosa's Diary of 1716." In *Preparing the Way: Preliminary Studies of the Texas Catholic Historical Society I.* Austin: Texas Catholic Historical Society, 1997.

Turner, Elizabeth Hayes. *Women, Culture and Community: Religion and Reform in Galveston, 1880–1920.* New York: Oxford University Press, 1997.

Turner, Ellen Sue, and Thomas R. Hester. *A Field Guide to Stone Artifacts of Texas Indians.* Austin: Texas Monthly Press, 1985.

Utley, Robert M. *Lone Star Justice: The First Century of the Texas Rangers.* New York: Oxford University Press, 2002.

Vega, Garcilaso de la. *The Florida of the Inca.* Trans. and eds. John Grier Varner and Jeannette Johnson Varner. Austin: University of Texas Press, 1980.

Vigness, David M. *Spanish Texas, 1519–1810.* Boston: American Press, 1983.

Vincent, V. A. "The Frontier Soldier: Life in the *Provincias Internas* and the Royal Regulations of 1772, 1766–1787," *Military History of the Southwest* 22 (spring 1992): 1–14.

Walker, Donald. "Governor Preston E. Smith." *West Texas Historical Association Yearbook* 75 (1999): 6–17.

Wallace, Ernest, and E. Adamson Hoebel. *The Comanches: Lords of the South Plains.* Norman: University of Oklahoma Press, 1952.

Wallace, Ernest, David M. Vigness, and George B. Ward. *Documents of Texas History.* 1963. Reprint, Austin: State House Press, 1994.

Walsh, Patrick J. "Living on the Edge of the Neutral Zone: Varieties of Identity in Nacogdoches, Texas, 1773–1810." *East Texas Historical Journal* 37 (1999): 3–24.

Warren, Harris G. *The Sword Was Their Passport: A History of American Filibustering in the Mexican Revolution.* Baton Rouge: Louisiana State University Press, 1943.

Weaver, John D. *Brownsville Raid.* 1973. Reprint, College Station: Texas A&M University Press, 1992.

Weber, David J. *The Spanish Frontier in North America.* New Haven: Yale University Press, 1992.

Weddle, Robert S. *The French Thorn: Rival Explorers in the Spanish Sea, 1682–1762.* College Station: Texas A&M University Press, 1991.

———. *San Juan Bautista: Gateway to Spanish Texas.* Austin: University of Texas Press, 1968.

———. *The San Saba Mission: Spanish Pivot in Texas.* Austin: University of Texas Press, 1964.

———. *Spanish Sea: The Gulf of Mexico in North American Discovery, 1500–1685.* College Station: Texas A&M University Press, 1985.

———. *Wilderness Manhunt: The Spanish Search for La Salle.* Austin: University of Texas Press, 1973.

———. *The Wreck of the* Belle, *the Ruin of La Salle.* College Station: Texas A&M University Press, 2001.

Weems, John Edward. *Dream of Empire: A Human History of the Republic of Texas, 1836–1846.* New York: Simon & Schuster, 1976.

Whisenhunt, Donald W. *The Depression in Texas: The Hoover Years.* New York: Garland Publishing Co., 1983.

Whisenhunt, Donald W., ed. *Texas: A Sesquicentennial Celebration.* Austin: Eakin Press, 1984.

Willoughby, Larry. *Texas, Our Texas.* Austin: Holt, Rinehart and Winston, 1993.

Wilson, Maurine T., and Jack Jackson. *Philip Nolan and Texas: Expeditions to the Unknown Land.* Waco: Texian Press, 1987.

Winders, Richard Bruce. *Crisis in the Southwest: The United States, Mexico, and the Struggle Over Texas.* Wilmington, Del.: SR Books, 2002.

Winegarten, Ruthe. *Black Texas Women: A Sourcebook.* Austin: University of Texas Press, 1996.

———. *Texas Women: A Pictorial History, from Indians to Astronauts.* Austin: University of Texas Press, 1986.

Winegarten, Ruthe, and Sharon Kahn. *Brave Black Women: From Slavery to the Space Shuttle.* Austin: University of Texas Press, 1997.

Wooster, Ralph A. *Lone Star Generals in Gray.* Austin: Eakin Press, 2000.

———. *Texas and Texans in the Civil War.* Austin: Eakin Press, 1996.

Wooster, Ralph A., and Robert A. Calvert. *Texas Vistas: Selections from the Southwestern Historical Quarterly.* Austin: Texas State Historical Association, 1980.

Wooster, Robert. *Soldiers, Suttlers, and Settlers: Garrison Life on the Texas Frontier.* College Station: Texas A&M University Press, 1987.

Zamora, Emilio. *World of the Mexican Worker in Texas.* College Station: Texas A&M University Press, 1993.

# Index

Abbott, E. C. "Teddy Blue," 309
abortion, 421, 427
accordion, 416
*acequia* (irrigation), 75
Acevedo, Antonio de, 50
Adams, John Quincy, 145
Adams-Onís Treaty, 128*f*, 145, 223
*adelantado* (governor), 36, 47
Adelsverein (Society for the Protection of German Immigrants), 231–32
Adena culture, 20
adobe pueblos, 18
aerospace industry, 439
African Americans. *See also race entries;* slavery
  "buffalo soldiers," 301
  citizenship rights, 274, 280, 282
  civil rights activities, 419
  Civil War impacts on, 271–72, 285, 286
  colonization and, 179
  cowboys, 308
  disenfranchisement of, 312, 318–19, 353
  Emancipation Proclamation and, 271–72
  integrated education for, 405
  Ku Klux Klan and, 352–54
  labor unions and, 299
  legal system and, 233–34
  lynchings, 312, 316–17, 350, 448
  medical school admissions, 400
  music, 417
  New Deal and, 370
  outlaw gang hostilities against, 279
  percentage of population, 434
  political appeals to, 315–16
  as political candidates, 277–78
  political parties and, 312, 315–16
  political power of, 403
  post–Civil War conditions, 284
  Progressive Era and, 325–26
  relief programs denied to, 363
  school integration and, 406–7
  sharecropping by, 304
  in state police, 280
  tenant farming, 326
  in Texas republic, 228, 233–34, 252
  transition of slaves to freemen, 274–75
  voting rights, 276, 318–19, 424
  World War I and, 348
  World War II and, 387–88
agrarianism, 322
  constitution and, 283–84
  modernization and, 292
  populism and, 312–14
  urbanization and, 393
*agregados* (additional or secondary settlers), 75
Agricultural Adjustment Act, 381
agriculture, 455. *See also* cotton production; farming; ranching
  desert farmers (Jornada Mogollón people), 17–19
  Dust Bowl, 363–66
  economy and, 360
  farms, number of, 360, 365, 440
  Great Depression and, 368
  irrigation systems (*acequias*), 75
  Isleños and, 75
  Mexican War of Independence and, 143
  missions and, 108
  mound-builders (Caddoan people), 19–22
  overproduction, 368
  post–Civil War, 284
  post–World War II, 389
  prehistory, 17–22, 29
  sharecropping, 278
  technology and, 441–42
  tenant farming, 303–4, 325, 326–27, 343–44, 365
  trends, 440–43
Aguayo, Marqués de San Miguel de, 68–69, 72, 78, 112
Ahumada, Mateo, 164

# MAJOR PROBLEMS IN TEXAS HISTORY

## DOCUMENTS AND ESSAYS

EDITED BY

## SAM W. HAYNES

UNIVERSITY OF TEXAS AT ARLINGTON

## CARY D. WINTZ

TEXAS SOUTHERN UNIVERSITY

*To Adrian Haynes, Jason Wintz, and Alexander Wintz,*
*a new generation of Texans*

# Contents

C H A P T E R   4

*Populating Texas During the Late Spanish and Mexican Periods, 1810–1835*

Page 79

C H A P T E R   5

*Revolutionary Texas, 1835–1836*

Page 111

C H A P T E R   6
## The Fragile Republic: Building New Communities, 1836–1845
### Page 146

C H A P T E R   7
## Texas Joins the Union: Changing Roles for Tejanos and Women in the New State, 1845–1860
### Page 175

CHAPTER 8
*Secession and Civil War, 1861–1865*
Page 208

CHAPTER 9
*Race, Politics, and Reconstruction, 1865–1875*
Page 238

# C H A P T E R  1 0
## *Conquering and Populating the Frontiers, 1860–1890*
### Page 271

CHAPTER 11

*Suffrage and Beyond: Texas Women and Reform, 1885–1925*

Page 307

CHAPTER 12

*Oil, Industrialization, and Urbanization, 1900–1940*

Page 337

## C H A P T E R   1 3
## Defining Mexican American Identity in Texas, 1910–1950
### Page 371

## C H A P T E R   1 4
## The African American Struggle for Civil Rights in Texas, 1940–1960
### Page 405

CHAPTER 15

*The Rise of the Republican Party and the Transformation of Texas Politics, 1960–2000*

Page 437

# *Preface*

More scholarly and popular history has been written about Texas than perhaps any other state. Indeed, so much attention has been devoted to some of the more colorful aspects of Texas history—the Revolution, the cattle drives, and the oil boom spring instantly to mind—that they have become etched indelibly on the American popular consciousness. In recent years, however, scholars have begun to challenge some of the most basic and time-honored assumptions about the state's past. To a large degree, they have been inclined to reject the Anglocentric perspective that has shaped much of the scholarship on the American West—a view steeped in lore and insulated by myth. In its place, they have constructed a new narrative, one that is informed by a greater appreciation of the state's multiethnic character.

Today, historians are much more inclined than their predecessors to view the state's past through the broadest possible lens. In addition to adopting a more inclusive approach with regard to issues of ethnicity and race, they have employed the categories of gender, technology, urbanization, class formation, and community development to expand our knowledge of the state's past and, in so doing, link it to the history of the nation. At the same time, Texas historians have come to appreciate the power of myth in shaping historical memory, recognizing that the way we create myths about the past can often tell us as much about ourselves today as the past itself.

At the start of the twenty-first century, scholars at colleges and universities in Texas and throughout the country are actively engaged in the process of creating a new synthesis for Texas history. But historians alone do not deserve all the credit for these major contributions to the field. Their work has been sponsored and assisted by professional organizations and publishers who have helped redefine Texas history and dramatically raised the standards of scholarship. For example, the Texas State Historical Association and its journal, *Southwestern Historical Quarterly* (both of which recently celebrated their one-hundredth anniversaries) have embraced the new perspectives on Texas history, and they have provided important forums for the new scholarship. For information about the association and journal, see their website at www.tsha.utexas.edu. In addition, Texas A&M University Press (which recently celebrated its twenty-fifth birthday) has published a disproportionate number of the new books on Texas history in recent years, contributing greatly to our knowledge of the state's past.

To fully understand Texas, one must first come to terms with the myths that have played such a central role in defining it. In Chapter 1, Mark E. Nackman argues that Anglo-Texans developed a unique identity during the early decades of the nineteenth century. Walter Buenger and Robert A. Calvert view the process of identity formation as one grounded more in misconception than reality and suggest that Texas historians deserve a fair share of the responsibility for promoting and perpetuating the myth of Texas exceptionalism. Yet these stereotypes about the state continue to thrive today, Benjamin Soskis reminds us, because they serve the agendas and interests of those who employ them. The process by which Texans have developed and promoted certain myths about the state is also the focus of several essays in subsequent chapters. In Chapter 5, David J. Weber explains how Texans have romanticized their struggle for independence with Mexico. In a similar vein, Chapter 12 challenges the stereotype of the freewheeling Texas entrepreneur, noting that urban growth in early twentieth-century Texas took advantage of national and international economic and political developments and was accompanied by a rather "un-Texas" concern with urban planning. Chapter 15 chronicles and attempts to explain the unraveling of another Texas myth—the Texas Democratic Party's absolute control over Texas politics.

In view of the ethnic diversity that has long been one of the region's constant features, it should come as no surprise that racial conflict and accommodation are dominant themes in several of the chapters that follow. Chapter 2, for example, examines the dislocating effects that the arrival of Europeans in Texas had on Native Americans and studies the ways in which indigenous peoples sought to adapt to those upheavals. Chapter 4 deals with the tensions that arose soon after large numbers of Anglo-Americans moved into Mexican Texas. In Chapter 5, which focuses on the Texas Revolutionary period, Eugene Barker portrays the conflict as a clash of disparate political cultures. At the same time, however, the interaction of ethnic groups must not always be viewed strictly in terms of a collision between immutable, monolithic forces. As Gregg Cantrell (in Chapter 4), David J. Weber (in Chapter 5), and David Montejano and Jane Dysart (in Chapter 7) remind us, Anglo-Mexican relations were nothing if not complex and frequently characterized by cooperation and collaboration. The challenges faced by African Americans in Texas in the nineteenth and twentieth centuries are also given attention in several chapters. In Chapter 8, slavery historian Randolph B. Campbell examines the "peculiar institution" as it existed in Texas. In Chapter 9, Barry Crouch, who has written extensively on the state's Freedman's Bureau, details the violence that freedmen confronted during this period, while Carl Moneyhon demonstrates how some blacks assumed positions of political power, albeit briefly.

While the issue of ethnic conflict is woven throughout the fabric of the book, another theme that figures prominently in several chapters is the process of community building and formation. Chapter 3, for example, focuses on the obstacles Spain encountered in its attempts to establish a permanent presence north of the Rio Grande, while Chapter 6 examines the challenges Anglo-Texans faced as they set about the task of nation-building after the Revolution. In Chapter 8, Walter L. Buenger seeks to place antebellum Texas firmly in a southern regional context and thereby helps to explain the path Texans chose in their decision to join the Confederacy in 1861. Similarly, Chapter 10 examines the settlement of the frontier in post-Civil War Texas, emphasizing the diversity of the cultural forces and human participants in this process.

Several chapters also reflect historians' interest in gender issues. Chapter 7 focuses in part on the special challenges that Mexican American and Anglo American women faced in the new state. Chapter 11 focuses on the role of women in the political and social movements of the late nineteenth and early twentieth centuries. Subsequent chapters also focus particular attention on the role that women have played in the struggle for racial and civil rights. In Chapter 13, Irene Ledesma examines Mexican American women who challenged the norms of their own community as well as the Anglo male-dominated labor movement as they struggled for their rights in the workplace, while Merline Pitre and Yvonne Davis Freer describe, in Chapter 14, the leadership role of African American women in the state's early civil rights movement.

This volume adheres to the format of other volumes in the Major Problems series, introducing students to some of the most important issues in the field of Texas history through a mix of primary sources and scholarly interpretations. Chapter introductions and headnotes for the documents and essays seek to provide historical context, as well as to help students view the material in a conceptual manner by posing questions for further consideration. Organized chronologically, the documents and essays in each chapter highlight a particular problem or theme in Texas history and are designed to encourage students' critical thinking skills and stimulate classroom discussion. The documents are drawn from a wide variety of sources, including letters, diaries, oral histories, poems, songs, broadsides, government reports, political and institutional papers, court rulings, legislative acts, and newspaper editorials and columns. The interpretive essays represent classic writers of the state's history and the most innovative scholars working in the field of Texas history today. Some essays were selected because they draw wholly divergent conclusions from the same materials; others were chosen for the way in which they complement one another, by approaching a particular topic from different perspectives. In both cases, the selections are intended to demonstrate that the past should be viewed not as a single narrative but from multiple viewpoints, each valid in its own way. At the end of each chapter is a Further Reading section that alerts students to some of the most significant new scholarship as well as classic studies.

The authors would like to thank Thomas G. Paterson, general editor of the Major Problems in American History series, and Jean Woy, sponsoring editor at Houghton Mifflin, for asking us to prepare a volume of documents and essays on Texas history. Our editor at Houghton Mifflin, Frances Gay, patiently shepherded this manuscript through every stage of the publication process, while Rosemary Winfield kept us on task during the production phase of the project.

The authors are indebted to many historians who gave freely of their time and expertise for this project. Walter Buenger of Texas A&M University helped us rethink the direction and focus of significant portions of this book. Juliana Barr of Rutgers University, and David E. Narrett of the University of Texas at Arlington offered numerous helpful suggestions regarding the documents and essays that appear in some of the early chapters. Jimmy L. Bryan, a graduate student at Southern Methodist University, helped track down some particularly elusive documents that appear in Chapter 6. Tom Kreneck, of Texas A&M, Corpus Christi, and Barry Crouch of Gallaudet University provided suggestions, advice, and guidance in identifying and locating documents for the later chapters. Equally helpful was the staff of the Special Collections of the University of Texas at Arlington and at the Barker Center for American History at the University of Texas at Austin. Francine Cronshaw translated Spanish-language documents into English, and Adrian Anderson contributed suggestions and inspiration. Although most of the selected essays are reprinted from previously published sources, four historians—Gregg Cantrell of the University of North Texas, Robert Fairbanks of the University of Texas at Arlington, Merline Pitre of Texas Southern University, and Yvonne Davis Freer of Texas A&M University—kindly agreed to write essays specifically for this volume. We also thank the following reviewers of this volume: Walter Buenger, Texas A&M University; Caroline Castillo Crimm, Sam Houston State University; Arnoldo De Leon, Angelo State University; Charles H. Martin, University of Texas at El Paso; and James A. Wilson, Southwest Texas State University, who offered numerous helpful comments and specific citations for documents and essays when this project was in its earliest stages of development.

Most of all, we want to acknowledge the role that our friend and colleague Robert A. Calvert played in the inception and development of this project. Initially he planned to be a coeditor but was obliged to withdraw as his health failed. We know he would recognize his influence on the organization of the book, and we hope that he would be pleased with the way it turned out. We regret that he will not be with us to celebrate the publication, but we will toast his memory.

Finally, this book is dedicated to Adrian Haynes, Jason Wintz, and Alexander Wintz, a new generation of Texans.

S. W. H.
C. D. W.

*Major Problems in*
*Texas History*

# CHAPTER
# 1

# *Enduring Myths and the Land*

*Texas has always been defined as much by its myths as by its past. Perhaps more than any other state, Texas can claim a vibrant popular history, one that is familiar not only to natives of the state, but to many people far beyond its borders. At the core of this popular history are such events as the revolution against Mexico, Indian wars, the cattle drives and the open range, the oil boom—episodes that are often cited as evidence of the state's unique frontier heritage and the spirit of individualism that it purportedly engendered. Yet these images are so deeply ingrained in the popular consciousness that they often tend to obscure other facets of the historical record. To regard Texas history as the narrative of Anglo males engaged in a process of triumphant conquest over alien enemies and a hostile environment is to provide an unbalanced and distorted view of the state's past.*

*This popular version of the state's history has proven remarkably resilient to revisionist challenge. Certainly Hollywood and television—the twin engines of American cultural myth production—have done their part to promote Texas stereotypes, inoculating Texans from the disquieting realities of change and modernization. For much of the twentieth century, Texas historians were also willing recruits on behalf of this traditional interpretation. To a large degree, scholars took their cue from the American historian Frederick Jackson Turner, who attached special importance to the Anglo-American westward push across the continent in his famous address, "The Significance of the Frontier in American History," in 1893. According to Turner, the process of "taming the wilderness" endowed earlier generations with a frontiering spirit that became embedded in the American character. Texas, with its history of violent conflict with Mexico and various Indian tribes, appeared to be a template for Turner's frontier thesis. Some scholars even set about to prove what the general public had long suspected—that the state's frontier heritage had stamped Texans with a unique identity, an exaggerated form of "Americanness."*

*In recent years, Texas historians have tended to reject this interpretation, and the chauvinism that has so often accompanied it. Reflecting the concerns of historians in other fields, they have pursued new areas of interest that include gender relations, ethnicity, class formation, and urban and technological change. In short, they are no longer fixated on the martial heroics of Anglo alpha males. The state's*

*demographic and economic landscape has also led historians to move in new his-*
*toriographical directions. It is estimated that Hispanic Americans will become*
*the state's largest ethnic group by 2025. Oil and gas, the mainstays of the Texas*
*economy in the twentieth century, are being eclipsed by a burgeoning information*
*technologies industry. Texas, still often characterized in popular literature as a*
*rugged wilderness, has become an urban state: 85 percent of its population lives*
*in cities. As Texas enters a new century, it offers few vestiges of its frontier heritage,*
*prompting present-day historians to question whether that period of the state's past*
*has been given undue emphasis.*

   *These debates serve to highlight the fundamental but frequently overlooked*
*fact that history and historical memory are rarely if ever the same. The traditional*
*interpretation of Texas history may continue to appeal to many Anglo-Texas males,*
*but it cannot have the same resonance for women, nor for non-white ethnic groups,*
*such as Mexican Americans and African Americans. The past can be seen from*
*multiple perspectives, each valid in its own way, but necessarily incomplete. Only*
*by adopting a more inclusionary approach can historians hope to present a reason-*
*ably complete version of the past.*

# E S S A Y S

The study of history is rarely static; more often it is subject to constant revision,
shaped and reshaped according to the shifting perspectives of those who write it. The
three essays offered in this chapter are indicative of the manifold changes that have
occurred in the study of Texas during the last twenty-five years.

   In the first essay, Mark E. Nackman, author of a 1975 study on Texas nationalism,
offers a vigorous defense of the orthodox view that Anglo-Texans possessed a unique
identity, one that set them apart from other Americans. According to Nackman, notions
of Texas exceptionalism have their roots in the 1830s and 1840s, when Anglo settlers
won their independence from Mexico and set about to establish a sovereign nation. This
brief, turbulent chapter in its history, Nackman argues, enabled Texas to claim a mythic
past that was the foundation of the state's identity for the next century and a half.

   While Nackman concedes that Texas nationality had no meaning for ethnic minorities, his exclusively Anglo focus puts him at odds with newly developing trends
in Texas scholarship. In the second essay, written in 1991, Walter L. Buenger, an historian at Texas A&M University, and the late Robert A. Calvert offer a critique of the
traditional interpretation, which has enjoyed an unduly long "shelf life," and more
generally fault Texas historians for their slowness in incorporating new historiographical developments into their scholarship.

   In the third and most recent essay, written on the eve of the 2000 presidential
election, journalist Benjamin Soskis examines some of the modern day myths—
favorable and unfavorable—that continue to be an integral part of popular perceptions
of the state's identity. According to Soskis, the modern state of Texas bears little relation to the heroic stereotypes of legend, but resembles other parts of the country in its
attitude toward responsible urban growth, environmental controls, and ethnic accommodation. Yet despite the state's high-tech economy, diverse population, and a political culture that is progressive in a number of respects, Texas is still often defined by its
frontier myths. The "New Texas" Soskis describes is a curious amalgam of nineteenth
century stereotypes and caricatures, grafted anachronistically onto a modern, complex society. Perhaps, one might argue, in its readiness to cling to the past even as it
embraces the future, Texas is exceptional, after all.

# The Roots of Texas Exceptionalism

### MARK E. NACKMAN

Texan nationalism, like American nationalism, did not give birth to the nation-state. Both nationalisms surfaced with the creation of the state itself. The Texas nation was from the start a homogeneous one and national unity through social integration was achieved almost immediately. The "nation" spoken of in this study is the "Anglo" nation, embracing white Americans and Europeans. Other racial and ethnic groups on the land—Mexicans, blacks, and Indians—were not assimilated and remained powerless. With rare exceptions, they did not contribute to the political state. Language, religion, and custom isolated the Mexican, race and slavery excluded the black, and a wide cultural chasm separated the Indian. Thus, Texan nationality had little or no meaning for these groups. The Anglo-Americans dominated and enjoyed certain advantages in the quest for nationhood: a common language, religion, ethnicity, and political heritage. Even class differences were slight among the generations up to the Civil War. They made a coherent group and a credible petitioner for nationality. Like all nationalists, they wanted to convince others (particularly other governments) that they were entitled to a nation-state. No one could deny their territorial conquests, least of all the Mexicans. From a cultural standpoint, however, did they truly constitute a nation? To be recognized as a separate and distinct people, they should have certain distinguishing characteristics. Wherein did the Texans differ from the American friends and relatives they had left behind in the States?

I must say at the outset that a separate culture is not a *sine qua non* of nationality. Nor must there be, where there is a separate nationalism, a culture of equivalent separateness. Whether the Zionists of the twentieth century who settled in Palestine and founded the state of Israel became culturally distinguishable from the Jews remaining in their native countries is a moot question. Whatever the verdict, it is undeniable that they considered themselves deserving of their own nation and nationalism was a natural outgrowth of that determination. One might also observe that Americans of the revolutionary era were highly Anglicized. It may then seem paradoxical that they revolted from England at the very time they most resembled their English rulers. Where cultural antagonisms exist (as between the Anglo-Americans in Texas and their Mexican masters), the potential for revolt is greater, but the drive for self-determination does not depend on cultural differentiae. Whether the Texans differed significantly from their American brethren or from other frontiersmen is not germane to the rise of nationalism. But it should be borne in mind that personal circumstances cast them into a similar mold and that their subsequent historical experience departed from the American norm.

Up to 1846, they had this in common: they were all expatriates. The very fact that they had abandoned home and country to settle in an unknown and untamed wilderness marked them as a breed apart. We may ask why any sober individual would choose Texas, a country infested with "wild" Indians and banditti, and

Mark E. Nackman, *A Nation Within a Nation: The Rise of Texas Nationalism* (Port Washington, NY: Kennikat Press, 1975), 3–12. Copyright © 1975 by Mark Nackman. Reprinted with permission of the author.

threatened continually after 1836 by a hostile Mexico. Why should they volunteer for such a land in preference to their own American frontier, which at least enjoyed the protection of federal laws and a national army? A good many, it seems, were debtors or criminals seeking refuge from economic hardship or the hot breath of the law. Some fancied themselves empire-builders who never blinked at national boundaries, many more wished only for anonymity and a place in the vast landscape to hide from a hounding wife, or creditor, or sheriff. Others, doubtless, were ordinary farmers and businessmen no more ambitious or desperate than their counterparts in Iowa or Arkansas. Or were they? The vexing question remains: why should they take their chances in Texas?

An army wife stationed in Texas in the 1850s encountered an individual whom she considered the epitome of the Texan. This was one Henry Clay Davis of Rio Grande City, who had in a few years established himself as a prosperous ranchero while earning a reputation for fighting prowess as the leader of a local ranger company. "Clay Davis was a true specimen of the Texan, tall and athletic," she wrote. Indeed, Davis's past seemed to fit perfectly into the mold of the typical Texan. Seeking adventure, he had left his Kentucky home at the age of fifteen and while still a youth got into a bloody fight on a Mississippi steamboat, apparently killing a man. He took off for Arkansas, a fugitive from justice, without friends or money. As he grew to manhood, he learned the necessity of self-reliance. His many escapes from danger imparted to him a recklessness which he would put to good use in the Texas Revolution. When he reached Texas, the woman concluded, "He found himself among men of tastes and dispositions similar to his own. . . . Fighting simply for the love of it, he cared less for the result than for the pleasurable excitement it produced."

Many American visitors came away convinced that Davis was the stuff of which the average Texan was made. Whether from the security of the United States or in the nerve-fraying atmosphere of Texas itself, persons acquainted with Texans before the Civil War concluded that a daredevil spirit and volatile temperament were part of their being. Those who got to know them at first hand sometimes felt themselves rubbing elbows in situations too cozy for comfort. "I saw at the breakfast table one morning," related one, "four murderers who had sought safety in this country; and a gentleman assured me, that on one occasion, he had set down with eleven." Another reported that he had once spent the night at an inn where he found himself in the company of fourteen men, "all of whom freely acknowledged that they had absconded from their native country, and were drawn into Texas as a last resort." Samuel E. Chamberlain, whose knowledge of Texans came from what he saw of them in the Mexican War, did not hesitate to generalize: "Take them all together with their uncouth costume, bearded faces, lean and brawny forms, fierce wild eyes and swaggering manners, they were fit representatives of the outlaws who made up the population of the Lone Star State."

Contemporaries also testified to certain ennobling qualities. "What a race!" marveled the French minister to the Republic in 1839. "What can the Mexicans do against men of this kidney!" An English settler found the country "full of enterprising and persevering people" ("the timid and the lazy generly [sic] return to the States"), and the British chargé in Austin doubted there was anywhere in the world a race of men "more enterprising and energetic." To a traveler from Germany, the Texans fully deserved "all the praises which impartial observers have heaped upon them in the past. Even the really bad Texan is no common, low, vulgar, debased criminal, but in his character and conduct there is still discernible a certain degree of greatness." The Scotch militarist, General Arthur Wavell, had known the men of Texas since the days of the early filibusters. In 1844, he offered this assessment to the British Foreign Office:

> To as much if not more natural Talent, and energy to call it into play, and knowledge of all which is practically useful under every Emergency of the most Civilized Nations, they add a reckless hardihood, a restless spirit of adventure, resources and confidence in themselves, keen perception, coolness, contempt of other men, usages, and Laws, and of Death, equal to the Wild Indian.

The many travelers who visited Texas during the antebellum years tried to fathom what they felt certain was a distinct Texan character. In doing so, they made the Texans acutely conscious of their specialness. The Texan found himself to be a curiosity, almost a legendary figure in his own lifetime. Half-alligator, half-horse; villain, desperado, Indian fighter, wild man—he personified the exoticism of the far western frontier. Some, like William "Bigfoot" Wallace, enjoyed telling tall tales and yarns to the folks back home in Virginny, and the very dimensions of his physique persuaded his eager listeners that the mythical Texan was real. Texans could not depart the boundaries of their country without being surrounded by curiosity seekers. "What has contributed very much to my daily annoyance is the circumstance of my being a Texian," wrote Sam Maverick to his wife from Charleston in 1846. "I leave it to you to imagine for I cannot describe the fatigue I constantly suffer by continual calls from my very friendly but exceedingly uninformed acquaintance & kindred." From London, the self-effacing Texan ambassador to the Court of St. James related a diplomat's experience:

> I dined a few evenings since, by special invitation, with Sir John Herschell the great astronomer, and Mr. Tytler the eminent Scotch historian. Several other literary gentlemen of distinction were present. . . . I of course was modest and reserved in such company—and yet they would bring me out on the subject of Texas and the U states—we discussed the affairs of the two nations—their prominent men—institutions etc. They listened with much deference to all I said about those countries—but evidently with delight to the accounts of our Indian fights—prarie [sic] life—buffalo hunting etc.

As every historian of Texas will insist, the majority, perhaps the vast majority of settlers were decent, law-abiding folk. Visitors to the country gratefully commented upon their friendliness and hospitality, while admitting to their intelligence, their fortitude, and even their morality. It may have been a goodly flock; nevertheless one is struck by the evident profusion of black sheep in it. Their ubiquity was remarked upon by nearly every traveler who journeyed to the country in the formative years.

> Texas generally may with safety be regarded as a place of refuge for rascality and criminality of all kinds—the sanctuary to which pirates, murderers, thieves, and swindlers fly for protection from the laws they have violated in other countries, and under other governments. . . . Many innocent and deluded people are certainly mixed up with this vile population, and some mercantile men of respectability, education, and probity; but, in the main, scoundrelism, under one shape or another, constitutes the larger portion of the present population of Texas.

As early as 1822, the *Niles' Register* called Texas "a rendezvous for criminals," and soon the initials "G.T.T." ("Gone to Texas") would become infamous. As an American explained to an Englishman, "When we want to say shortly that it's all up with a fellow, we just say 'G.T.T.', just as you'd say gone to the devil, or the dogs." The place was known as the "Elysium of rogues," and its people as "renegades and ruffians." Anson Jones, who later became a president of the Texas Republic, was living in New Orleans and failing in business in 1833 when he was urged to try his luck in Texas. "My impressions of Texas were extremely unfavorable," he recalled. "I had known it only as a harbor for pirates and banditti." When the fires of the Texas Revolution were about to blaze in 1835, the Opelousas, Louisiana *Gazette* opined that if Texas and Mexico went to war, "The world would lose many bad citizens and the devil would gain some faithful servants—that everybody knew that the immigrants to Texas were vagabonds and refugees from justice." The heroics of the Revolution made Texans world renowned for their fighting prowess but did nothing to diminish their notoriety for plunder and thievery. The widely circulated exposés of Benjamin Lundy, William Ellery Channing, and others stigmatized the revolutionary effort as a land-stealing escapade and a conspiracy to advance the domain of slavery. Purportedly executed by a cadre of audacious adventurers, the Revolution made the names Sam Houston, Jim Bowie, William Travis, and Davy Crockett household words in America and kept Texas in the public mind for years to come.

As a fledgling nation, Texas fared little better with the American press that it had as a Mexican province, particularly as the question of annexation rose and fell. The New York *Sun* remarked in 1839 that few Texans had "the conscience to abstain from plundering whatever they can lay their hands on," and gave the country faint praise by declaring its president, Mirabeau B. Lamar, "the only man in Texas, whether of high or low degree, who possessed a character unstained by villainy of some sort or other." As annexation came to be more and more an issue in the mid-forties, an avalanche of epithets descended upon the Texans. Horace Greeley in the *Clay Tribune* cast Texas as a "den of thieves" and a "rendezvous for rascals of all the continent." At an anti-annexation meeting in New York, Philip Hone was shocked by the behavior of a gang of "prizefighters and pardoned felons" who riotously broke up the gathering by hissing, groaning, and shouting, "Hurrah for Texas!" The Hartford *Courant* labeled Texas "the land of Bowie knives and Toothpicks." In a scathing editorial against annexation, the paper urged the nation's legislators not to sully America's good name by adding a population "composed mainly of a wild and desperate set of men." The debate over Texas in the 1844 presidential campaign featured a widely disseminated cartoon showing candidates Polk and Dallas wooing "Lady Texas," while a sanctimonious Henry Clay stood to the side with folded arms, saying: "Stand back, Madam Texas! for we are more holy than thou! Do you think we will have anything to do with gamblers, horse-racers, and licentious profligates?"

The leading spokesmen for Texas had for some time deplored the sayings of the "foreign press." "We have been most dreadfully slandered in the U.S. papers," complained Stephen F. Austin to a Philadelphian. "Such publications have injured us dreadfully . . . it is really a cruel & unjust thing to have the best interests of a whole community, and a new & rising one, injured and men jeopardised by a set of silly scribblers." Texans suspected that a conspiracy of sorts existed to discourage desirable citizens and families from emigrating. The Houston *Telegraph and Texas Register* in 1841 accused American publicists of "unwarranted and reckless jibes and taunts," which had darkly colored the image of the Republic. "It is to be regretted, that so many blackguards and grossly ignorant men are still conducting public journals in the United States; while this state of things continues, we must expect to experience the effect of calumny and detraction."

Texans were, of course, aware of the political considerations operating against them. Their stuttering bid for annexation to the United States marshaled an array of forces, particularly in New England, opposed to the extension of slavery. In answer to William Ellery Channing's open letter to Henry Clay in 1837, a modest Texan, George L. Hammeken, allowed that if the Bostonian's denunciation of the Revolution contained merely his objections to slavery and to annexation, he would have left it to "abler pens" to respond. "But no man of honor and feeling, however incompetent to cope in fine language," he asserted, "should remain quiet when the character and motives of his friends and countrymen are so unjustly vilified." Hammeken conceded that Texas was filled with men who had been "unfortunate in commerce, or been ruined by their kindness to swindlers," but he insisted that there were no more than three or four hundred fugitives from justice, and they had no influence on the inhabitants in general.

Still, the Texan reputation was not confined to Northern opinion subserving the purposes of political anti-slavery. Southerners, too, entertained the notion that Texans were, according to William H. Wharton, "a set of adventurers, of young men of desperate fortunes" bent on conquest and glory. "To the contrary," argued Wharton, the first Texas minister to the United States, "the people of Texas [are] generally unpretending farmers and planters from the middle walks of life, [and] all they desired on earth was the privilege of cultivating in peace those fertile lands which they had so dearly earned by the perils and privations consequent upon the colonizing of a wilderness." Other Texans stoutly maintained that theirs was a decorous society, that young men did not come to town loaded down with pistols and knives, and that Texas had no call for an "anti-Duelling and Peace-Making Society" such as had been organized in Mississippi in 1844. Moreover, as Guy M. Bryan grandly announced to his Kenyon College mate, Rutherford B. Hayes, Texas could boast its "circles of beauty & accomplishment & intellect that will vie or bear comparison with the proudest & best of your land." Upon Texas's debut as a state in 1846, local editors implored the voters to exercise discretion in their selection of U.S. congressmen. We should impart to the world, the LaGrange *Intelligencer* admonished, "a just and proper impression of our moral and intellectual character."

> It is a matter of infinite moment on our first entrance into the fold of the confederacy, that a gross delusion under which a great many honest and intellectual minds have long labored, in regard to our moral, social, and intellectual condition should be at once and forever removed. We should take a peculiar degree of pride and satisfaction in convincing our sister states, that we . . . possess a large fund of moral and intellectual wealth . . . by sending to the councils of the nation gentlemen who will compare to advantage with any of their fellow members. . . . We should delight to show such puny snarlers [revilers of Texas], not only that something good can come out of Texas, but some of the most precious and elevating goods which this world may boast.

A Matagorda newspaper in 1844 observed that since the Revolution eight years earlier, "It has been the fate of Texas to attract the attention of the world to a greater extent than was ever done by the same number of the human family in any age." It was a fair estimation. If nothing else, the unwelcomed publicity advertised Texas to an audience far and wide. Foreigners were perhaps more amused than disheartened by the halo of evil surrounding the Lone Star. "When every other land rejects us," the Englishman William Bollaert punned, "here is the land which freely takes us (Texas)." . . .

For all these refugees, Texas became a homeland. Its broad boundaries gave them room to roam and enveloped them in a protective shell. They, in turn, embraced Texas. As a society of pariahs, the Texans could achieve self-respect and self-realization through identification with a virile state. The citizen's supreme loyalty went eagerly to his fellow nationals, and the vehicle of their joint aspirations was the state. The achievement of nationhood, reinforced by such palpable effects as a constitution, a flag, an army, a navy, fired their nationalism. Nationhood gave them security; nationality told them who they were. With the Republic of Texas they became "Texians" and nothing else. No longer need they be men without a country.

## The Shelf Life of Truth in Texas

### WALTER L. BUENGER AND ROBERT A. CALVERT

Professional historians often see their mission as stripping away myth and exposing unvarnished truth. Yet cultural biases bind historians just as they do society at large. As purveyors of written culture historians may arrive at only the near-truth, a truth relevant to current problems. This should cause no dismay, for understanding what historical truth has been releases society from the blinders of tradition. Realizing the limited shelf life of history allows for the pursuit of a new understanding of our past and present culture.

Escaping the enfolding snares of past writings on a society requires understanding their origin. Scholars must investigate not only the past, but how past generations looked at the past. Practitioners of history call this process historiography: the history of historical writings and changing intellectual points of view. For Texas the key historiographic question is: Why have historians not subjected the myths of the state to rigorous cyclical examination? Certainly, different cultures interpret their myths of origin differently. A "diversity of Texas myths" exists based on which ethnic group describes its origins. Nevertheless, the dominant culture has created and added to the myth in such a way that few openly challenge its premises. Thus the macho myth of Anglo Texas still reigns.

The Texas myth has been both a part of and separate from the older frontier myth of the Anglo United States, which was born in the Puritan heritage of the City

Walter L. Buenger and Robert A. Calvert, *Texas Through Time: Evolving Interpretations* (College Station: Texas A&M University Press, 1991), xi–xv, xviii–xxi, xxxi–xxxv. Reprinted by permission of the Texas A&M University Press.

on the Hill and honed by the Manifest Destiny advocates of the mid-nineteenth century. The North American myth celebrated the past. It assumed, at least until the Vietnam War, that the United States was invincible in wartime, magnanimous in peacetime, and destined to bring peace, prosperity, Christianity, and democracy to first the continent and then to the globe.

The Texas myth accepted the North American version, adopted it, and typically exaggerated it. The outlines of the Texas myth are well known. For all practical purposes it begins with the Alamo and ends with San Jacinto. Mythic Anglo Texan male heroes—Crockett, Bowie, and Travis—die for the nation. Women are either subservient and supportive—Susanna Dickinson carries the message of heroism to Sam Houston—or sultry and seductive—Emily Morgan gives her all to detain the dictator. A foreigner, Moses Rose, refuses to cross Travis's line and flees the battle. A loyal black slave, Joe, a noncombatant, accompanies Susanna and describes the fall of the Alamo. A Tejano, Juan Seguín, leaves the Alamo as a messenger and then serves as a scout. Later disillusioned, Seguín goes to Mexico, but still represents the "good" Mexican as compared to the barbarous Santa Anna, who is saved from the cruel death he dealt to Texas heroes by Houston, the generous Anglo victor at San Jacinto, who went on to help found a republic based on freedom. The creation of the nation—the Texas Republic—separates the Texas myth from the Anglo North American myth and gives to the culture a Texas nationalism and romantic vision that transcends geography and creates, as Willie Nelson sings, a Texas state of mind.

Only recently has cyclical revisionism appeared in Texas history and the myth come under considerable criticism. Like other myths it is only partially true. The actual character of the historic individuals no doubt has little correlation to their mythic presence, but debunking them makes scant difference in the perception of the myth. Selective historical memory persists and Texas elites in particular still profess at least a limited subscription to that romantic concept of Texas. The myth then creates a sense of what a Texan is that precludes many of the state's citizens from identifying themselves as Texans. Moreover, the myth also defines the presumed role of all of Texas' multicultural citizens and describes the alleged characteristics of non-Anglo males. The result is that in much the way that oral myths sustained a cultural identity and gave a society shared values and common goals, written myths and folklore have shaped the goals and perceptions of those who have governed and controlled Texas for most of the twentieth century. . . .

Demands for an inclusionary history, for intellectual toughness and honesty, however, have usually run aground on the rock of Texas provincialism. One root of this provincialism grows from the mixed perception that Texans have of their own identity. Partial responsibility for this unfocused identity rests with historians who have failed to nurture cyclical revisionism. Affected by a frontier heritage that is depicted as larger than life in both fiction and folklore, university professors translated into the official history of Texas what many citizens viewed as the unique experience of Anglo-Saxon males wresting the wilderness from savage Indians and venal Mexicans. The universities were largely Anglo male preserves and research and teaching represented that bias. Further, as late as the 1950s, historians still worked within the intellectual constructs of Frederick Jackson Turner's frontier thesis. They saw the frontier as the agent that shaped and made the United States unique. In this Texas historians simply followed the lead of their teachers.

At the University of Texas, which dominated the training of professional historians interested in Texas as a field of study, the first generation of historians who came on the scene in the early twentieth century took Turner's concept and applied it to the history of the state. Although judicious, some still saw a war of civilized Anglos versus barbaric cultures. George P. Garrison, for whom the building that houses the University of Texas history department is named, entitled one of his books *Texas: A Contest of Civilizations* and argued that competition on the frontier produced the superior Texas character that civilized the state and vanquished aboriginal and Spanish cultures. Garrison believed strongly in scientific history. He also believed that history demonstrated progress, and that social Darwinism caused progress. The Texas frontier represented for Garrison the movement across the North American West of the Teutonic values that gave western European culture world domination. Where Garrison left off Eugene C. Barker picked up. Although his work was highly professional and more dispassionate than most, as the subtitle of his most famous work reveals, Barker also saw a "manifest destiny" in the expansion of Anglo Texas. For him the Texas Revolution was a clash of Anglo and Hispanic cultures that was almost inevitable once Spain and Mexico invited energetic and freedom-loving Anglos into Texas.

The tendency to romanticize the frontier continued into the second generation of historians working in the 1930s. Both Walter Prescott Webb, who was influenced by Garrison, and J. Frank Dobie, who was not an historian but certainly shaped intellectual life in Texas through the 1950s, saw the frontier as a source of positive values relevant to modern life. They feared that the loss of the frontier heritage of Texas would weaken the state and make it like all others. This need to glorify the past led novelist Larry McMurtry to ask if there existed an unsentimental Texas historian. . . .

The tendency to look toward historic Texas frontiers and Anglo culture as explanations for the causes for most events also skewed the direction of historical studies. It gave Texas history a strong nineteenth-century bias that is still in effect. . . . Until recently most historians simply did not write on twentieth-century topics. By ignoring them they were not forced to ask critical questions about cultural and economic injustices. The historians were not forced to look at the limited shelf life of history.

This avoidance of culturally relevant topics and the concentration on writings in the heroic mode was also at least partially subconsciously defensive, and this defensiveness sprang from anticolonialism, another root of Texas provincialism. In a state whose economy was clearly a colonial one and whose cultural developments were limited by its rural heritage and its commitment to a yeomanlike concept of agrarian goodness, memories of the frontier past saved the society from looking deeply into the bleakness and poverty of much of the historical period through the 1930s. . . .

This resentment did not recede when the prosperity of World War II turned into the recently ended sustained economic growth. Expansion forced Texans to consider the issues of urban growth, outside population migrations, and a transition into an industrial economy. Texans both welcomed the changes and feared

them as intellectual and cultural colonialism. Some believed that the frontier produced an expansive imagination and a concept of risk taking that would be lost if
the frontier heritage were lost; others insisted that modernization would make
Texas like all other states and that its folk culture and heritage should be preserved
to protect Texans' sense of place.

Clearly both groups wanted a usable myth for the twentieth century. The Texas
macho myth hung on—less pronounced but more damaging. Once it had given
many Texans purpose and identity. Now for many it had become a "Hollywood"
caricature that encouraged greed and a lack of individual responsibility for society
as a whole. Others saw attacks on the Anglo Texas tradition as an elitist endeavor
that would destroy the past and therefore the state's *Zeitgeist.* Historical writings
became a battleground between proponents representing both parts of the state's
identity crisis: modernists who welcomed change and wanted to verify it historically, and traditionalists who wanted writings that preserved the perceived cultural heritage. The more numerous traditionalists glorified the historic past to
deter the onslaught of technocratic and cultural vandals and proclaimed that frontier individualism explained the present economic accomplishments and social
stability of the state. . . .

Perhaps this identity crisis also springs from the inability of Texans to place
themselves within the broader region of West or South. Not knowing if Texas be-
longs with the slaveholding South or the cattle-ranching West has allowed Texans
to ignore the more innovative scholarship in those areas and to argue that Texas
has always been unique. The insistence on uniqueness, added to the persistent impact of past scholars, precluded until recently a full-scale study of Texas slavery.
Just as Texans cannot place themselves in the Sunbelt, then, they cannot place
their history or their identity in the analytical framework of either the South or the
West. The insistence by some Texas historians on the state's uniqueness and an
inability to accept an analytical framework had encouraged the provincialism of
outsiders who observe the doings of Texas historians. Often deservedly, historians
from outside the state minimize the work done on Texas, because it fails both to
draw comparisons between Texas and other similar places and to set Texas in a
larger national focus.

Nowhere has this identity crisis come into sharper focus than in the economic
history of the state. Historians . . . have exhibited a curious "flight from modernity." On the one hand they celebrate growth and profits. On the other they flee
the implications of a modern life created by growth and profits. The ranch remains
the most studied and probably least significant major aspect of the Texas economy.
Besides being a traditional topic acceptable to the old masters, ranches are romantic, close to a preindustrial past, and uniquely Texan—at least in the popular view.
Texas historians choose ranch histories as ideal topics, for they fit within the
framework of past giants, and they fire another round at the modernists. Popular
culture also supports such ventures, for, tellingly, ranch histories usually outsell all
other Texas books.

Moreover, most economic and business histories record a fascination with a
golden age, a bygone age, where things were better and the heroes and villains
were clearly discernible. In this golden era the old myth of the Anglo-Saxon male
triumphing over all odds without the aid of government runs rampant. Issues of

class, community, gender, and ethnicity are ignored because they conflict with the pristine past. Current legends are perfect examples of the avoidance of modern realities by editing out all complexities and subtleties. Unlike history, in legends events are resolved without contradictions. The writers often ignore the evolution of twentieth-century Texas, because its development challenges earlier legends. Ironically, then, descriptions of the business would have inherited and adapted the Anglo Texan myth, encapsulated in the Alamo. Even possibly more ironic, the part of the historical discipline most closely linked to the "dismal science" of economics and to factual data seems currently to also be the one that is most enamored with myth and chained by an identity crisis. . . .

A new history would be particularly useful if it adjusted our myths and values to our current situation, if it helped to resolve the identity crisis associated with being Texan, if it demonstrated the importance of opening up new ways of looking at ourselves. . . . The image of Texas as a homogeneous state has only recently come under attack and the critique of that image has not been widespread. The strength of earlier writings on Texas history was that they perpetuated a pride in the state, a myth of what it meant to be a Texan that could lead us to value the past and refuse to accept a second-rate status. Yet until all of the population feel a part of the myth, excluded groups will be alienated from the state's history and potentially from the state itself.

## The New Texas

### BENJAMIN SOSKIS

Election 2000 may come down to Texas—not its electoral votes, which are safely in the pocket of George W. Bush, but its political identity. Both presidential campaigns realize that Texas is to this race what Massachusetts was to 1988: if you can define the state, you can define its governor. For Bush, that means aligning himself with his state's reputation for boundless opportunity, vast self-confidence, and relaxed good humor. In their answer to the Clinton campaign's legendary *The Man From Hope,* the biographical film that introduced the Arkansas governor to the country in 1992, the Bush campaign at the Philadelphia GOP convention showed W. on a prairie in Crawford, Texas, site of his yet-to-be completed ranch. He spoke about his hometown. "There used to be a slogan in Midland that said 'The sky is the limit,' which really is such an optimistic slogan," Bush mused. "It's how I feel about America, really." Clad in blue jeans and a cowboy hat, he extolled the virtues of the Texas frontier. He waxed lyrical about "dreamers—the doers who take risks and sometimes failed, but then rose above failure to achieve greater good things." Then he climbed into his blue pickup truck and, passing a well-placed calf, drove off toward the horizon.

Al Gore, of course, is trying to evoke a different image: Texas as economic and cultural backwater. If Bush has the "Proud of Texas Committee," which touts the

Benjamin Soskis, "Lone Star Joining: Why Texas Is Like America," *The New Republic,* September 18, 2000. Copyright © 2000. Reprinted with permission.

state's old-fashioned virtues, Gore has the "Texas Truth Squad," which notes endlessly that Texas ranks near the bottom of the nation in categories that connote enlightenment (child health care, clean air) and near the top in those that connote primitivism (incarceration, gun violence, cow-manure production). By Election Day, one Democratic strategist boasts, Gore will have turned Texas "into a Third World country."

Gore and Bush aren't trying to create stereotypes of Texas. They're doing something far easier—tapping into stereotypes that already exist. They're playing on the flip side of Texas's reputation as exceptional, a state whose cultural distinctiveness has uniquely withstood homogenizing national influences. Even before this campaign, many liberals viewed Texas as a world apart, a state where, in the words of lefty *New York Times* columnist Bob Herbert, "compassion is virtually illegal." Just as conservatives didn't need much convincing to believe that Massachusetts was a place of oppressive taxation and rampant political correctness, liberals already believed that Texas abused its poor—Al Gore just filled in the details. Likewise, conservatives didn't need much convincing to believe that Bush supports self-reliance and personal freedom, because, after all, his state is one of the few places where they still reign.

There is, of course, some truth to both images. It probably is easier to start a business in Texas than in New York. And swaths of the Lone Star State really do suffer from deep social underdevelopment and government neglect—neglect Gore and the press would be derelict to ignore. But the odd thing about the Bush-Gore fight over the meaning of Texas is that its very premise, Texas exceptionalism, is increasingly anachronistic. By buying into one side or another of the Texas frontier myth—by accepting that the state is somehow set apart, either by its rugged individualism or by its prideful backwardness—the candidates and the press have ignored the striking new reality on the ground: Texas is becoming more like the rest of the nation than anyone, Texan or non-Texan, wants to admit.

It started with the oil bust. For much of the postwar era, Texas's reputation as distinct from the rest of the country stood on firm economic ground: its economy was countercyclical. When the price of oil was high, as in the Carter years, the nation foundered but Texas boomed. When the price of oil dropped and the country rebounded under Ronald Reagan, Texas crashed. "When I first came here," says Rice University sociologist Stephen Klineberg, "the rule of thumb was, if things are good in Boston, they're going to be bad for us in Houston, and vice versa."

But the 1980s oil bust, which hit harder and lasted longer than almost anyone had predicted, changed that. Third-lowest in the country in 1980, the state's unemployment rate was ninth-highest by 1990. Over the same period, the number of Texans living in poverty grew 47 percent. Slowly and painfully, the economy began to diversify, as companies that once fixed oil rigs retooled to service computers and televisions. In 1982, around 30 percent of state revenue came from severance taxes on oil and gas; by 1988, that figure had dropped to 8 percent.

Since then, the state has nursed itself back to economic health by embracing the same industry that has remade the economy nationally: technology. Two decades ago, high tech accounted for just over 5 percent of the state's economic output; today, it accounts for nearly 9 percent. Indeed, more Texans now work in high tech as work in oil, gas drilling, refining, and agriculture combined. According to a recent study by the American Electronics Association, Texas ranks second in semiconductor and office-computer manufacturing and is the nation's second-largest electronics exporter. In fact, according to a study by Bernard Weinstein of the University of North Texas, the state's economy has so dramatically aligned itself with the rest of the country's that, for the first time in modern history, rising gas prices do Texas more harm than good: every $1 increase in the price of natural gas cuts economic activity by some $3.4 billion a year and adds another 35,000 people to the ranks of the unemployed. "For a long time Texas was different," Weinstein explains. "Well, it ain't another country anymore."

That could be the unofficial motto of Tyler, Texas. A few months ago, I visited this friendly town of 84,000 in the green, eastern part of the state. Tyler is best known for its fall Rose Festival—an archaic, lavish blend of debutante ball and Mardi Gras. Recently, though, the town has gained another distinction: it is one of the state's hottest technology hubs, ranked the fourteenth-fastest-growing tech town in the nation by the California-based Milken Institute.

For most of the twentieth century, Tyler's economic fortunes depended on oil. In 1930, a 70-year-old wildcatter struck black gold at the Daisy Bradford Farm, 20 miles away. The discovery ushered in the East Texas oil boom, and Tyler, whose paved streets distinguished it from many nearby towns, became the regional service center for the fledgling industry. Tyler shrugged off the Depression and thrived for the next few decades, attracting a number of major manufacturing firms. Then the bust hit. Between 1981 and 1989, the number of residents employed in the oil and gas industries dropped by more than half. "It knocked everyone out of the saddle," says Kevin Eltife, the town's 41-year-old mayor. "We had to create a whole new city."

Now Tyler is a boomtown again. But it's a different sort of boom. The town boasts two nationally ranked not-for-profit hospitals, and medicine has become one of its largest employers. Three years ago, the University of Texas granted its Tyler satellite full four-year status, and soon afterward, a College of Engineering opened, followed by a $20 million cultural center. The College of Engineering, which will churn out 30 graduates a year, helps provide Tyler with the kind of tech-savvy labor pool that attracts employers. Indeed, the number of tech employees in town has doubled in the last decade to nearly 3,000, twice as many people as are employed in the town's famed oil and gas sector.

To be sure, Tyler retains touches of East Texas folksiness: just as Eltife, the son of Lebanese immigrants, brandishes a convincing drawl, so the downtown eateries have names like "The Feed Lott" written in lasso-like fonts. But mostly Tyler is co-opting old images to serve a new reality, appropriating styles and symbols of the nineteenth century to adorn the twenty-first. At the Jordan Plaza technology park, for example, the architectural style is distinctively ranchlike: twelve wide, low-roofed buildings face a 20-acre wooded park, which will be allowed to remain "wild." But it is as thoroughly "new economy" as anything you'd find in Boston or San Jose: the 60-acre complex is full of firms like SPEA International, a company based in Turin, Italy, that builds microchip testers and plans to recruit 50 engineers to the town in the next five years; GeoInfo Ltd., whose 50 employees specialize in geographic information systems and mapping technology; and Fair Point Communication, a 25-person telecommunications firm.

Tyler still has a ways to go before it becomes another Silicon Valley. Its nightlife, according to some of the town's younger residents, could use some work. David Buhrkuhl, a semiretired businessman who serves as head of SPEA's American division, actually worries that until the nightlife improves, SPEA might have a hard time attracting twentysomething engineers. " You can't compare Tyler to South Hampton," admits Eltife. But when I ask the Birkenstock-clad mayor whether Tyler might look more like Austin after a decade of development, he pauses for a moment—perhaps contemplating images of Austin's frolicking hippies and militant environmentalists—smiles, and replies, "Sure."

And the transformation I saw in Tyler is playing out on a much grander scale in Texas's large metropolitan centers. In 1940, the state was 80 percent rural; now it is 85 percent urban. Of the 570,000 domestic migrants to Texas in the '90s, more than 80 percent settled in the high-tech suburbs outside Houston, Dallas, Fort Worth, and Austin. Last year, for instance, Yahoo! set up shop in an abandoned warehouse in Dallas's Deep Ellum district, once one of the nation's most infamous skid rows, prompting at least a dozen Internet-related firms to follow; Dell Computer has called Austin home for years. Dallas now ranks fourth nationally in number of high-tech workers; Houston ranks fourteenth; Austin, fifteenth. Even Waco, a city that doesn't exactly enjoy a reputation for forward thinking, has witnessed a 60 percent growth in high-tech output over the last five years.

Texas's economic changes are sparking social ones. The state has experienced surges of professional migration before. The greatest expansion of Anglos in the state, for instance, occurred during its 1970s oil boom, when nearly one million people settled in Houston alone. But to attract today's high-tech migrants, the state is not simply relying on its traditional enticements—low cost of living, low taxes, minimal regulation, and an oil-rich substratum. The new migrants, according to conventional wisdom, demand a healthy environment and functioning social services. And this has led a growing number of Texans to challenge a prominent tenet of their state's secular religion: the unfaltering belief that development is always good, you can always use another highway, and there is always more land. Last year, in a highly publicized statewide poll, more than half the respondents named urban sprawl as a major concern. "This reflects a real change in Texas attitudes," state historian T. R. Fehrenbach told a local newspaper at the time. Previously," it was practically considered Communistic to oppose growth."

Ground zero for this insurgency is Austin, where environmentalists routinely play kingmaker in city elections—this year, every candidate elected to the city council ran on an environmentally friendly platform. And today, after years of feuding, business groups (spurred by local high-tech leaders) have joined Greens to promote "smart growth" and improve the city's quality of life. According to Robin Rather, a former chairwoman of Save Our Springs (Austin's largest environmental organization) and currently head of a reform-minded alliance of high-tech CEOs, a local consensus is emerging that the imperatives of the market require some attention to environmental standards. "I think what we've proven is that if you cut through the rhetoric and look at what's in everybody's best interest, it's quality of life." she says. In fact, Save Our Springs has joined forces with the city's Chamber of Commerce and the Real Estate Council to buy 50,000 acres of open space in the nearby Hill Country, to protect the city's aquifer. "It's sort of an anti-sprawl measure," Rather suggests, a bit taken aback by the phrase.

Texans, of course, have long viewed Austin as an exotic isle of liberalism, toler-ated as if it were the older sister who cut her hair short and went off to Berkeley. But notions of smart growth are also catching on in Houston, a city whose name is prac-tically synonymous with sprawl. Last April, Houston's environmentalists won a stunning victory over development titans when the city council voted down a pro-posal to build an airport on the Katy Prairie, a wildlife-rich wetland 30 miles outside the city. In the wake of the victory, environmentalists established a political action committee, Houston Conservation Voters, to push for clean air and open-space poli-cies. The refineries and developers "are still in control," says Jim Blackburn, the PAC's director. "But there is certainly more willingness to discuss issues, and to be open to ideas, than I have previously seen in this part of the world."

The stats bear out Blackburn's wary optimism. According to Rice University's Klineberg, who has been polling Houstonians for nearly two decades, as many voters support spending city funds on inner-city mass transit as support funding highways to the suburbs, and they prefer investments in education and public serv-ices to tax cuts—both stark changes from the past. In 1999, 70 percent of those Klineberg polled supported emissions testing for all vehicles in Houston, up from 38 percent just four years earlier. And Houston's business community is finally catching on. This June, the city's largest business organization, the Greater Houston Partnership, officially came out in support of "sensible growth." Even Tom DeLay has taken notice. After the House majority whip, who represents the southwest Houston suburbs, shot down federal funding for an inner-city rail system, he re-ceived a significant number of complaints from his conservative constituents. "I think he was surprised by how much sentiment there was out there in the suburbs to quit just pouring concrete and think about new solutions," says Richard Murray, a political scientist at the University of Houston. This July, in a rare slap in the face to the third-highest-ranking congressional Republican, city officials chose to ignore DeLay's opposition and, if necessary, give up on federal funding and finance the rail project locally.

If Texas's high-tech migration is upsetting a long-held consensus on develop-ment and the environment, a broader migration is challenging long-standing stereotypes about the state's racial identity. For decades an unofficial demarca-tion, running from San Antonio to Corpus Christi, separated Texas's Hispanic south from its more Anglicized north, which was itself starkly divided between white and black. But in recent years a tide of Mexicanization has breached that divide, reshaping the political and cultural identities of the state's largest cities. Houston, for example is now one of the most racially diverse cities in America— 34 percent Hispanic, 31 percent white, 29 percent black, 6 percent Asian. Austin, too, is now more than one-quarter Hispanic, with a rapidly growing Asian com-munity that includes a large population of Indian techies who left Silicon Valley, lured by Austin's cheaper rents and multicultural vibrancy. In fact, at current growth rates, in 20 years Asians will surpass blacks as Austin's second-largest minority. Even Dallas, epicenter of good-old-boyism, is now nearly one-quarter

Hispanic. And, according to census projections, that number will reach 40 percent in 30 years.

More impressive than the ethnic diversification itself is that Texas has experienced it without much of the violence and antagonism that has plagued its supposedly more liberal counterpart, California. The Lone Star State has produced no successful Proposition 187-style campaigns to restrict the rights and benefits of immigrants, and politicians hostile to the largely Hispanic immigrant community frequently suffer at the polls. For instance, after Jim Mattox, a former state attorney general and front-runner for the Democratic senatorial spot in 1994, suggested using the military to patrol the border, his campaign plummeted. When Bush ran for governor, by contrast, he made a point of signaling to voters that he supported immigration and considered Texas's relationship with Mexico one of the state's most valuable assets. Bush won in 1994 "because he wasn't Pete Wilson," says Andrew Hernandez, author of the *Almanac of Latino Politics,* referring to the California governor who championed Prop 187. "He got credit for saying, 'We are not that kind of state.'"

This isn't to say Texas is always racially enlightened. The state's shamefully decrepit criminal justice system leaves many poor black and Hispanic defendants without competent counsel. Texas still witnesses spasms of racial violence—the brutal dragging death of Jasper resident James Byrd two years ago being among the most terrifying. In parts of East Texas, the tolerance enjoyed by Texas Latinos is often denied to African Americans; and in the border regions the poverty and dropout rates among Tejanos remain much higher than the statewide averages. For the most part, however, race relations in Texas confound the traditional liberal paradigm of a white majority oppressing a brown or black underclass. The state's supposedly reactionary business elite, for instance, has largely accepted multiculturalism as a way of life. Houston and Dallas, neither of which has a black majority, both recently elected black mayors, and they did so without much of the racial hostility that accompanied similar breakthroughs in Los Angeles, Chicago, and New York. "There is an understanding that the future is increasingly a non-Anglo future," notes Klineberg, "an understanding that if you're going to make money in the twenty-first century, you're going to have to make coalitions."

One reason for the absence of ethnic vendettas is that in Texas, Hispanic and Anglo culture are more deeply intertwined than in California or even New York. "Texas Latinos are more likely to be multigenerational Americans and have greater distance from the immigrant experience than do their counterparts in California," writes Gregory Rodriguez, a fellow at the New America Foundation, a Washington, D.C., think tank. Three years ago, when a town across the border from El Paso hoisted a gigantic Mexican flag and the local paper polled residents about whether it should plant an American flag in response, a greater percentage of Hispanics than non-Hispanics said yes.

And if Hispanic Texans don't see a contradiction between being culturally Mexican and fully American, neither, it seems, do the state's Anglos. Unlike in California, Texas's white politicians have never crusaded against bilingual education; George W. explicitly supports it. In fact, in more than 30 districts—from El Paso to Dallas to Houston—schools encourage "two-way" bilingualism so that Anglo students can also gain proficiency in Spanish. According to Josefina V. Tinajero, president of the National Association for Bilingual Education, attitudes toward bilingual education in California are hampered by a sort of liberal paternalism, which she describes as a "let's help these poor little kids who don't speak English" attitude. In Texas, on the other hand, where more than 70 percent of all English-as-a-second-language elementary school students are educated in both Spanish and English, compared to just 30 percent in California, bilingualism is considered "an asset . . . an intellectual accomplishment," and a wise business investment. She points to a partnership between the San Antonio Chamber of Commerce and the city's school districts to ensure that all high school graduates are fluent in both languages. "From an economic point of view," Tinajero says, "the leadership in Texas has seen that bilingual education is good for our kids."

But prognosticators who expect that Texas's "sleeping giant" Hispanic population will usher in an era of Lone Star liberalism when Hispanics become a plurality of the state's population (expected by 2025) are probably deluding themselves. Texas, unlike California, boasts a Hispanic Republican congressman and a Hispanic Republican state official. And even many Hispanic Democrats, like El Paso's law-and-order, pro-life Representative Silvestre Reyes, hold political views far to the right of national Latino advocacy groups like the National Council of La Raza.

But if one explanation for Texas's lack of a white backlash is the political moderation of its Hispanic population, another is the underappreciated moderation of its white population as well. In fact, despite the high-profile antics of the state's Republican Party, whose recent platform demanded the abolition of the IRS and the Federal Reserve, there is substantial evidence that, on a host of social issues, Texans are not much more conservative than the nation as a whole. According to a March Scripps Howard Texas Poll, 44 percent of Texans consider themselves pro-choice, while 46 percent lean pro-life (the national figures, according to a March Gallup Poll, are 48 percent pro-choice, 43 percent pro-life). And, according to statewide polling by Rice's Klineberg, nearly half of all Texans believe that "government should do more to solve our country's problems" and that homosexuals should be granted equal civil rights. For years, writes Rice sociologist Chandler Davidson, Texas has suffered from a "myth of overwhelming conservatism," encouraged by hard-right politicians who "self-servingly portray themselves as spokesman for a homogenous conservative population." But now, despite the Gore camp's best intentions, that myth, like the 25,000 abandoned oil wells that litter the state, might finally run dry.

Or maybe not. Because it's not just the presidential candidates who seem determined to wrap Texas in outdated caricatures; so do many Texans themselves. Dallas residents might complain about the unfair portrayal of their city as a gaudy boomtown and tout their cosmopolitan art scene. But in the next breath they'll proudly advertise their city's second-largest tourist attraction: Southfork, the ranch from the TV show "Dallas," which celebrates exactly the image they claim to loathe. And linguists have recently discovered that the much-maligned Lone Star drawl correlates not so much with geographic location or time spent in the state as with positive feelings about Texas. A 1993 statewide poll found that more than 60 percent of Texans believed themselves to be "particularly unique" compared with other Americans.

Ironically, Texans have historically promoted their state's cultural uniqueness so strenuously precisely because of its lack of true unity and cohesion. In the nineteenth century, the legends of the cowboy (appropriated from eighteenth-century northern Mexican folk culture) and the Alamo held together a fragile coalition of five ministates, each with its peculiar culture, topography and climate. (The annexation treaty of 1845, which incorporated Texas into the Union, included a provision allowing the state to splinter into those five regions if it chose to do so.) Politicians, in particular, have burnished the old myths to stoke Texas chauvinism and unite the populace. Lyndon Johnson, for instance, used the image of the spirited rancher to transcend his Germanic, peach-farming, central Texas origins and broaden his appeal to the entire state. And, once Johnson became president, the national press eagerly bought into the stereotype he and his Texas constituents had worked so hard to create. If, along with self-sufficiency, entrepreneurial savvy, and bravado, that stereotype included buffoonery, anti-intellectualism, and violence, LBJ and the rest of the state seemed happy with the bargain. They would take the bad rap if they could keep the swagger.

And today's Texans, no matter how much they change their state's reality, seem just as happy with the deal. Back in May, Bush admitted to *U.S. News & World Report* that, compared to "bigger-than-life characters" like LBJ and John Connally, he represented "the newer Texas," someone who didn't "fill the screen quite as big." But then there he was, in that convention film, leading a camera crew in his pickup truck around the site of his future ranch, singing Midland's praises. How ironic, since few Texas cities have done a worse job of adapting to the state's new realities. Midland, which once boasted one of the highest per capita rates of millionaires in the nation, has proved unable to tap into Texas's high-tech boom and is now an economic disaster; last year the city's unemployment rate reached 9 percent. In April, town elders invited Tyler Mayor Eltife to come explain how he turned his East Texas town around.

It is Tyler, not Midland, that represents the real story of "entrepreneurial pioneers" and Texas optimism—a story about how the state revived itself by becoming more like the rest of America. Yet each presidential candidate, for his own, very different reason, seems determined to bury it. And the people of Texas appear happy to play along.

## FURTHER READING

Daniel D. Arreola, "The Texas-Mexican Homeland," *Journal of Cultural Geography* 13 (Spring/Summer 1993)

Walter L. Buenger, "Texas and the South," *Southwestern Historical Quarterly* 103 (January 2000)

Walter L. Buenger and Robert A. Calvert, *Texas Through Time: Evolving Interpretations* (1991)

Robert A. Calvert and Arnoldo de León, *The History of Texas* (1990)

Richard Francaviglia, *The Shape of Texas, Maps as Metaphors* (1995)

Don Graham, *Giant Country: Essays on Texas* (1998)

John H. Jenkins, *Basic Texas Books* (1988)

Terry G. Jordan, "The Anglo-Texan Homeland," *Journal of Cultural Geography* 13
    (Spring/Summer 1993)
D. W. Meinig, *Imperial Texas: An Interpretive Essay in Cultural Geography* (1969)
Robert F. O'Connor, ed., *Texas Myths*, (1986)
Rupert N. Richardson, Earnest Wallace, Adrian N. Anderson and Cary Wintz, *Texas the
    Lone Star State* (rev. ed. 2000)
Texas State Historical Association, *Handbook of Texas* (rev. ed., 1996)
Emilio Zamora, Cynthia Orozco, and Rodolfo Rocha, *Mexican Americans in Texas History:
    Selected Essays* (2000)

CHAPTER
2

# Contested Empires:
# The Native Americans of Texas
# and European Contact

*The first Europeans to arrive in Texas encountered a complex set of distinct tribal cultures of nomadic hunters and sedentary agriculturalists, perhaps numbering as many as 50,000 people in the late seventeenth century.*

*Although conflict and accommodation were not new to Texas—or to North America—prior to European contact, the arrival of the Spanish and French profoundly upset the geopolitical and cultural equilibrium of the Texas tribes. As the documents and essays in this chapter indicate, a vast cultural divide separated Native Americans and Europeans. Throughout the western hemisphere, devastating pandemics wreaked havoc on Native Americans when they first encountered Europeans, and Texas was no exception.*

*Yet the Indians of Texas were not simply passive victims of European disease. Despite the debilitating effects of depopulation, many Texas tribal groups emerged as active agents in the contest for empire between France and Spain. Indeed, European forays into Texas during the first two centuries of Indian-European contact proved so sporadic and tentative that Native Americans were usually in a position to dictate the terms of their encounters with European visitors. Not until the eighteenth century, with the arrival of the Spanish in sufficient numbers, coupled with the rapid decline of the indigenous population, was Spain able to establish a limited degree of political and cultural sovereignty over east and south central Texas. How did Europeans and Native Americans attempt to bridge the cultural chasm that separated them during the early years of contact? What forces and conditions often stood in the way of mutual understanding?*

 DOCUMENTS

Document 1 is an excerpt from the memoir of Alvar Nunez Cabeza de Vaca. The treasurer of the ill-fated Narvaez expedition, Cabeza de Vaca was one of 600 soldiers and colonists who sailed from Cuba in June 1527, in search of riches in Florida. After several setbacks, Narvaez' men attempted the following year to sail to Mexico in make-shift boats. De Vaca was one of about one hundred and sixty members of the expedition who were washed up along the Texas coast. After a lengthy captivity by coastal Indian tribes, De Vaca and three survivors trekked across Texas, Mexico, and the American Southwest, reaching the Spanish settlements of Sinaloa, in western Mexico, in 1536.

Cabeza de Vaca's peregrinations encouraged Spanish authorities to undertake further expeditions into the borderlands, two of which converged on Texas in the early 1540s. Francisco Vásquez de Coronado followed rumors of golden cities into the southwest, crossing the Texas panhandle and traveling as far east as Kansas before returning to Mexico. Hernando De Soto led an expedition from Florida across the Gulf Coast region. When De Soto died near the Mississippi River, Luis de Moscoso assumed command and led his men into East Texas. Document 2 is an account of Moscoso's trek to the Trinity River. Discouraged by the failure to uncover new sources of mineral wealth, Spanish authorities declined to authorize any new expeditions into the borderlands until the end of the century.

Almost one hundred and fifty years would pass before European adventurers would return to Texas. In 1682, René La Robert Cavalier, Sieur de la Salle, sailed down the Mississippi River and claimed the region for the French. Two years later he embarked on a second expedition from France, accompanied by 280 colonists, but was unable to find the mouth of the river and landed on the Texas coast. LaSalle was murdered by disgruntled members of the expedition in 1687. Henri Joutel, one of La Salle's loyal subordinates, lived among the Caddoes before leading a group of survivors to Canada. In Document 3, Joutel describes a Caddo war party.

Alarmed by reports of the French presence in Texas, the Spanish government promptly renewed its efforts to control the area, authorizing several expeditions under Alonso de León. In Document 4, Father Damian Massanet describes the remnants of Fort St. Louis, built by La Salle and his men on Matagorda Bay in 1685. Father Francisco Casanas de Jesús Maria spent a year and a half among the Caddo Indians; his report to the viceroy of Mexico on the favorable conditions for undertaking missionary work in East Texas is excerpted in Document 5. As Jesus Maria had anticipated, however, the absence of Spanish women posed a serious obstacle to amicable Hispanic-Indian relations. Sexual depredations committed by the male soldiery, coupled with the dramatic increase in Indian mortality rates as a result of exposure to European disease, soon antagonized the Caddoes, and Spain was obliged to close its mission in 1694.

# 1. Cabeza de Vaca Encounters the Indians of Texas, 1535

Castillo and Estevanico went inland to the Yguazes. This people are universally good archers and of a fine symmetry, although not so large as those we left. They have a nipple and a lip bored. Their support is principally roots, of two or three kinds, and they look for them over the face of all the country. The food is poor and gripes the persons who eat it. The roots require roasting two days: many are very bitter, and withal difficult to be dug. They are sought the distance of two or three

Frederick W. Hodge and Theodore H. Lewis, eds., *Spanish Explorers in the Southern United States 1528–1543* (Austin: Texas State Historical Association, 1990): 64–66; 95–97. Copyright Texas State Historical Association. Reprinted with permission.

leagues, and so great is the want these people experience, that they cannot get through the year without them. Occasionally they kill deer, and at times take fish; but the quantity is so small and the famine so great, that they eat spiders and the eggs of ants, worms, lizards, salamanders, snakes, and vipers that kill whom they strike; and they eat earth and wood, and all that there is, the dung of deer, and other things that I omit to mention; and I honestly believe that were there stones in that land they would eat them. They save the bones of the fishes they consume, of snakes and other animals, that they may afterwards beat them together and eat the powder. The men bear no burthens, nor carry anything of weight; such are borne by women and old men who are of the least esteem. They have not so great love for their children as those we have before spoken of. Some among them are accustomed to sin against nature. The women work very hard, and do a great deal; of the twenty-four hours they have only six of repose; the rest of the night they pass in heating the ovens to bake those roots they eat. At daybreak they begin to dig them, to bring wood and water to their houses and get in readiness other things that may be necessary. The majority of the people are great thieves; for though they are free to divide with each other, on turning the head, even a son or a father will take what he can. They are great liars, and also great drunkards, which they became from the use of a certain liquor.

These Indians are so accustomed to running, that without rest or fatigue they follow a deer from morning to night. In this way they kill many. They pursue them until tired down, and sometimes overtake them in the race. Their houses are of matting, placed upon four hoops. They carry them on the back, and remove every two or three days in search of food. Nothing is planted for support. They are a merry people, considering the hunger they suffer; for they never cease, notwithstanding, to observe their festivities and *areytos*. To them the happiest part of the year is the season of eating prickly pears; they have hunger then no longer, pass all the time in dancing, and eat day and night. While these last, they squeeze out the juice, open and set them to dry, and when dry they are put in hampers like figs. These they keep to eat on their way back. The peel is beaten to powder.

It occurred to us many times while we were among this people, and there was no food, to be three or four days without eating, when they, to revive our spirits, would tell us not to be sad, that soon there would be prickly pears when we should eat a plenty and drink of the juice, when our bellies would be very big and we should be content and joyful, having no hunger. From the time they first told us this, to that at which the earliest were ripe enough to be eaten, was an interval of five or six months; so having tarried until the lapse of this period, and the season had come, we went to eat the fruit.

We found mosquitos of three sorts, and all of them abundant in every part of the country. They poison and inflame, and during the greater part of the summer gave us great annoyance. As a protection we made fires, encircling the people with them, burning rotten and wet wood to produce smoke without flame. The remedy brought another trouble, and the night long we did little else than shed tears from the smoke that came into our eyes, besides feeling intense heat from the many fires, and if at any time we went out for repose to the seaside and fell asleep, we were reminded with blows to make up the fires. The Indians of the interior have a different method, as intolerable, and worse even than the one I have spoken of, which is to go with brands in the hand firing the plains and forests within their reach, that the mosquitos may fly away, and at the same time to drive out lizards and other like things from the earth for them to eat.

They are accustomed also to kill deer by encircling them with fires. The pasturage is taken from the cattle by burning, that necessity may drive them to seek it in places where it is desired they should go. They encamp only where there are wood and water; and sometimes all carry loads of these when they go to hunt deer, which are usually found where neither is to be got. On the day of their arrival, they kill the deer and other animals which they can, and consume all the water and all the wood in cooking and on the fires they make to relieve them of mosquitos. They remain the next day to get something to sustain them on their return; and when they go, such is their state from those insects that they appear to have the affliction of holy Lazarus. In this way do they appease their hunger, two or three times in the year, at the cost I have mentioned. From my own experience, I can state there is no torment known in this world that can equal it. . . .

. . . Among the articles given us, Andrés Dorantes received a hawk-bell of copper, thick and large, figured with a face, which the natives had shown, greatly prizing it. They told him that they had received it from others, their neighbors; we asked them whence the others had obtained it, and they said it had been brought from the northern direction, where there was much copper, which was highly esteemed. We concluded that whencesoever it came there was a foundry, and that work was done in hollow form.

We departed the next day, and traversed a ridge seven leagues in extent. The stones on it are scoria of iron. At night we arrived at many houses seated on the banks of a very beautiful river. The owners of them came half way out on the road to meet us, bringing their children on their backs. They gave us many little bags of margarite and pulverized galena, with which they rub the face. They presented us many beads, and blankets of cowhide, loading all who accompanied us with some of every thing they had. They eat prickly pears and the seed of pine. In that country are small pine trees, the cones like little eggs; but the seed is better than that of Castile, as its husk is very thin, and while green is beaten and made into balls, to be thus eaten. If the seed be dry, it is pounded in the husk, and consumed in the form of flour.

Those who there received us, after they had touched us went running to their houses and directly returned, and did not stop running, going and coming, to bring us in this manner many things for support on the way. They fetched a man to me and stated that a long time since he had been wounded by an arrow in the right shoulder, and that the point of the shaft was lodged above his heart, which, he said, gave him much pain, and in consequence, he was always sick. Probing the wound I felt the arrow-head, and found it had passed through the cartilage. With a knife I carried, I opened the breast to the place, and saw the point was aslant and troublesome to take out. I continued to cut, and, putting in the point of the knife, at last with great difficulty I drew the head forth. It was very large. With the bone of a deer, and by virtue of my calling, I made two stitches that threw the blood over me, and with hair from a skin I stanched the flow. They asked me for the arrow-head after I had taken it out, which I gave, when the whole town came to look at it. They sent it into the back country that the people there might view it. In consequence of this operation they had many of their customary dances and festivities. The next day I cut the two stitches and the Indian was well. The wound I made appeared only like a seam in the palm of the hand. He said he felt no pain or sensitiveness in it whatsoever. This cure gave us control throughout the country in all that the inhabitants had power, or deemed of any value, or cherished. We showed them the hawk-bell we brought, and they told us that in the place whence that had come, were buried many plates of the same material; it was a thing they greatly esteemed, and where it came from were fixed habitations. The country we considered to be on the South Sea, which we had ever understood to be richer than the one of the North.

## 2. Luis de Moscoso Explores East Texas, 1542

The Governor set out from Nondacao for Soacatino, and on the fifth day came to a province called Aays. The inhabitants had never heard of the Christians. So soon as they observed them entering the territory the people were called out, who, as fast as they could get together, came by fifties and hundreds on the road, to give battle. While some encountered us, others fell upon our rear; and when we followed up those, these pursued us. The attack continued during the greater part of the day, until we arrived at their town. Some men were injured, and some horses, but nothing so as to hinder travel, there being not one dangerous wound among all. The Indians suffered great slaughter.

The day on which the Governor departed, the guide told him he had heard it said in Nondacao, that the Indians of Soacatino had seen other Christians; at which we were all delighted, thinking it might be true, and that they could have come by the way of New Spain; for if it were so, finding nothing in Florida of value, we should be able to go out of it, there being fear we might perish in some wilderness. The Governor, having been led for two days out of the way, ordered that the Indian be put to the torture, when he confessed that his master, the cacique of Nondacao, had ordered him to take them in that manner, we being his enemies, and he, as his vassal, was bound to obey him. He was commanded to be cast to the dogs, and another Indian guided us to Soacatino, where we came the following day.

The country was very poor, and the want of maize was greatly felt. The natives being asked if they had any knowledge of other Christians, said they had heard that near there, towards the south, such men were moving about. For twenty days the march was through a very thinly peopled country, where great privation and toil were endured; the little maize there was, the Indians having buried in the scrub, where the Christians, at the close of the day's march, when they were well weary, went trailing, to seek for what they needed of it to eat.

Arrived at a province called Guasco, they found maize, with which they loaded the horses and the Indians; thence they went to another settlement, called Naquiscoça, the inhabitants of which said that they had no knowledge of any other

Frederick W. Hodge and Theodore H. Lewis, eds., *Spanish Explorers in the Southern United States 1528–1543* (Austin: Texas State Historical Association, 1990): 243–246. Copyright Texas State Historical Association. Reprinted with permission.

Christians. The Governor ordered them put to torture, when they stated that farther on, in the territories of another chief, called Naçacahoz, the Christians had arrived, and gone back toward the west, whence they came. He reached there in two days, and took some women, among whom was one who said that she had seen Christians, and, having been in their hands, had made her escape from them. The Governor sent a captain with fifteen cavalry to where she said they were seen, to discover if there were any marks of horses, or signs of any Christians having been there; and after travelling three or four leagues, she who was the guide declared that all she had said was false; and so it was deemed of everything else the Indians had told of having seen Christians in Florida.

As the region thereabout was scarce of maize, and no information could be got of any inhabited country to the west, the Governor went back to Guasco. The residents stated, that ten days' journey from there, toward the sunset, was a river called Daycao, whither they sometimes went to drive and kill deer, and whence they had seen persons on the other bank, but without knowing what people they were. The Christians took as much maize as they could find, to carry with them; and journeying ten days through a wilderness, they arrived at the river of which the Indians had spoken. Ten horsemen sent in advance by the Governor had crossed; and, following a road leading up from the bank, they came upon an encampment of Indians living in very small huts, who, directly as they saw the Christians, took to flight, leaving what they had, indications only of poverty and misery. So wretched was the country, that what was found everywhere, put together, was not half an alqueire of maize. Taking two natives, they went back to the river, where the Governor waited; and on coming to question the captives, to ascertain what towns there might be to the west, no Indian was found in the camp who knew their language.

The Governor commanded the captains and principal personages to be called together that he might determine now by their opinions what was best to do. The majority declared it their judgment to return to the River Grande of Guachoya, because in Anilco and thereabout was much maize; that during the winter they would build brigantines, and the following spring go down the river in them in quest of the sea, where having arrived, they would follow the coast thence along to New Spain,—an enterprise which, although it appeared to be one difficult to accomplish, yet from their experience it offered the only course to be pursued. They could not travel by land, for want of an interpreter; and they considered the country farther on, beyond the River Daycao, on which they were, to be that which Cabeça de Vaca had said in his narrative should have to be traversed, where the Indians wandered like Arabs, having no settled place of residence, living on prickly pears, the roots of plants, and game; and that if this should be so, and they, entering upon that tract, found no provision for sustenance during winter, they must inevitably perish, it being already the beginning of October; and if they remained any longer where they were, what with rains and snow, they should neither be able to fall back, nor, in a land so poor as that, to subsist.

The Governor, who longed to be again where he could get his full measure of sleep, rather than govern and go conquering a country so beset for him with hardships, directly returned, getting back from whence he came.

## 3. A Caddo War Party Returns Home, 1687

One morning at daybreak a troop of women enter our hut who were painted and smeared. When they had all entered, they began to sing various songs in their language at the top of their voices; after which, they began a kind of circle dance holding each other's hands. For what purpose were they performing this ceremony that lasted a good two or three hours? We learned that it was because their people had come back victorious over their enemies. As soon as the village had heard it, they all gathered in the way that I have told. Their dance ended with a few presents of tobacco that those in the hut made to the women who had come. I noticed during their dance that, from time to time, some of them took one of the scalps that was in the hut and made a show of it, presenting it first from one side, then the other, as if to jeer at the tribe from which the scalp had come. At noon, one of the warriors also arrived at our hut, apparently the one who had brought the news of the enemies' defeat.

This Indian told us that the people of his village had indeed killed 40 of the enemy and that the others had taken flight; at this news, everyone displayed great joy. But what disturbed me then was to see that, as joyful as these women were, they broke out crying. I was fearful, as always, of some malicious plan against us according to what I had heard in the past. After all these ceremonies, the women went to work; pounding corn, some parching it and others making bread. They were preparing to bring the food to the warriors. . . .

We learned then of the way they had proceeded: they had met, surprised and struck terror into their enemies with a few gunshots fired by our men who, having killed a few of them, drove the others to flee. Indeed, before any of them had been killed, the enemy was waiting staunchly, not demonstrating any fear. But hearing the shots from the guns, of which they had no understanding, they ran as fast as possible. In this way, our Indians killed or captured 48 individuals, men as well as women and children. They killed several women who had climbed trees to hide as they could not escape by running, not having enough time to follow along with the others.

Few men found themselves thus defeated, but the women were left for victims because it was not the Indians' custom to give any mercy except to children. They cut off the scalp of a woman still alive, after which they asked our people for a charge of powder and a bullet which they gave the woman and sent her back to her tribe telling her to give that to her people as a warning that they should expect the same treatment in the future.

I believe I have spoken elsewhere of this practice of taking scalps. In involves cutting the skin all around the head down to the ears and the forehead. They then lift the entire skin which they take care to clean and taw to preserve and display in their huts. They thus leave the sufferer with an exposed skull, as they did with this woman whom they sent back with word to her tribe.

William Foster, ed., *The LaSalle Expedition to Texas: The Journal of Henri Joutel, 1684–1687,* (Austin: Texas State Historical Association, 1998): 204–207. Copyright William C. Foster. Reprinted with permission.

The warriors brought another woman to the women and girls who came to meet them with food. Then they gave to the women and girls this unfortunate captured woman to be sacrificed to their rage and passion according to the account of our men who were witnesses. When these women arrived and learned that there was a captive, they armed themselves, some with short heavy sticks, others with wooden skewers they had sharpened, and each one struck her as caprice seized her, vying with each other. The unfortunate woman could do nothing but await the finishing stroke, suffering as it were the martyr's role, for one tore away a handful of hair, another cut off a finger, another dug out an eye. Each one made a point of torturing her in some way; and in the end there was one who struck a hard blow to her head and another who drove a skewer into her body. After that she died. They then cut her up into several pieces which the victors carried with them, and they forced several other slaves taken earlier to eat the pieces. Thus the Indians returned triumphant from their war. Of the 48 persons whom they took, they gave mercy only to the young children. All their scalps were brought back, and several women who had gone to war with the others even carried some heads they brought back. . . .

On the next day, the 20th, the Indians assembled and went to the chief's hut where all the scalps were carried as trophies along with the heads. Then they began to rejoice which continued all day in that hut, and the ceremony continued for three more days. After that, they proceeded to the huts belonging to the most eminent among them whom they called *cadis* which means chiefs or captains. They invited the six Frenchmen who had accompanied them to participate in their festivities just as they had participated in their victory. As we were staying in one of the most important chief's huts, they came there after concluding their celebration at the hut of the head chief.

I was astonished at the way they conducted themselves. After all had arrived, the elders and the *cadis* took their places on the mats upon which they sat down. Then one of these elders, who had not been with them but who seemed to be an orator, began to speak as master of ceremonies. He delivered a kind of eulogy or oration of which I understood nothing. A short time later, each warrior who had killed in battle and had scalps marched forward preceded by a woman carrying a tall cane and a deer skin. Then came the wife of the warrior carrying the scalp; the warrior followed with his bow and two arrows. When they arrived before the orator or master of ceremonies, the warrior took the scalp and placed it in the hands of the orator who, on receiving it, presented it to the four quarters of the compass, saying many things that I did not understand. After this he placed the scalp on the ground on a mat spread for this purpose. Another warrior approached in the same manner until each one had brought his scalp as a trophy. When all this was done, the orator gave a kind of address, and they were served food. The women of the hut had cooked *sagamité* in several large pots knowing the assembly would come. After they had eaten and smoked, they began to dance in an unclosed circle formation. They set a sort of rhythm that they stamped with their feet and waved with fans made from turkey feathers; in this way they adapted all this to their songs which seemed too long to me because I could not understand anything.

Their ceremony ended with a few presents of tobacco which those from the hut gave to the elders and the warriors. I must mention too that the master of ceremonies brought food and tobacco to the scalps as if they were in condition to eat or smoke. They also had two young boys whom they had captured and given mercy. One was wounded and could not walk; therefore they had put him on a horse. They brought pieces of flesh of the woman they had tortured, and they made these two young boys eat some of it. They made a few other slaves, whom they had captured another time, eat pieces of her flesh as well. As for them, I did not notice whether they ate any themselves. After they had finished, they went off to a few other huts, and this ceremony lasted there for three days.

## 4. Spain Reacts to the French Presence in Texas, 1689

We left Coahuila on the twenty-sixth of March in the year 1689, and went as far as the Rio del Norte, which, in the said province of Coahuila, is called the Rio Grande, our guide still being the Indian Juanillo, and when we reached the said river, I sent for the Indian who knew the country and had been among the Frenchmen, whom I call Quems, because he belonged to the Indian nation of that name. We travelled on towards the northeast and at times east-northeast, until we reached the river of Our Lady of Guadalupe. And here I asked this Indian whether the dwellings of the French were still a long way off, thinking that when we should be distant from them a day and night's journey, some of us might push forward in order, unnoticed, to take a survey of the village. The Indian replied that the village was about fifteen leagues distant from that river.

On the morning of the next day Captain Alonso de León asked me what we should do in order to ascertain the number of Frenchmen and the condition of things in their village. With regard to this there were various opinions, mine being that, since we had with us the Quems Indian, who was well acquainted with the country, we should all have a mass sung in honor of the Blessed Virgin of Guadalupe that very morning, at the very place in which we were; also that when we should succeed in the reaching the dwellings of the Frenchmen we should have another mass celebrated, in honor of Saint Anthony of Padua. All consented very readily to this, and, soon, at about nine o'clock in the morning, the mass to the Virgin was sung.

After that it was arranged that, the two Indians, Juanillo the Papul and the Quems Indian, serving as guides, twenty-five men should travel on with us until we should come upon the French village in the early morning, while the remaining soldiers with the beasts of burden should come behind us and camp when they reached a suitable spot. This spot they should then not leave until we returned, unless by the express command of Captain Alonso de Leon. When we started out, the rear-guard received orders to proceed slowly, watching cautiously lest any Indian should appear; in case any did, they were to seize him without doing him the least harm, and notify us of the capture.

After travelling some four leagues, the rear-guard saw an Indian come out of a dense wood, and called to him, and he went towards them without any show of resistance. They sent us word, and we halted. On the arrival of the Indian the two we

"Letter of Father Massanet to Don Carlos de Siguenza, 1690," Herbert E. Bolton, *Spain's Exploration in the Southwest, 1542–1706* (New York: Scribner's, 1916): 355–364.

had along asked him whether there were thereabouts any of the white people who dwelt further on. He said that, as to those living further, they used to inhabit houses which now no longer existed, for, two moons previous, the Indians of the coast had killed all but a few boys, whom they had carried off; that he himself lived in the ranchería of the Emet and Lavas Indians, which was about two leagues out of the route which we were following towards the bay of Espiritu Santo. We went with this Indian to the ranchería of which he spoke, and reached it at about three in the afternoon. As soon as the Indians became aware of our presence, they made for the wood, leaving to us the ranchería, together with the laden dogs, which they had not been able to drive fast enough when they fled. The Indian who served as our guide himself entered the wood, and called to the others, declaring that we were friends, and that they should have no fear. Some of them—and among these was their captain—came out and embraced us, saying: *"Thechas! techas!"* which means "Friends! friends!" One of those who came out first was a big young fellow about twenty years old, who wore a Recollect friar's cloak, and when we saw that it was the cloak of a friar, we gave him a blanket, and I took the robe from him.

The said Indians told how, two days previous, two Frenchmen had passed by with the Tejas Indians. That very afternoon we started in pursuit of the said French-men, and at sunset, we reached the ranchería of the Toxo and Toaa Indians, who told us that the said Frenchmen had passed by with the said Tejas, and had been un-willing to remain there with them. That night we slept near the ranchería, and at eight in the evening some Indians came to the place where we were, one of them dressed after the fashion of the French. And they brought some French books and a Holy Bible. The next morning we set out in quest of the said Frenchmen, passing through some very dense woods; and at about two o'clock in the afternoon we came to some ranchitos of Emet Indians. On our inquiring concerning the French-men, these Indians pointed out to us an Indian who had just arrived and who had conducted them (the Frenchmen) as far as the San Marcos River, and when we wished to cross they told us that we would not be able to cross the said river. We told the Indian who had led the Frenchmen that if he would take them a paper and bring an answer we would give him a horse, and that he should take the answer to the houses where the Frenchmen lived. Captain Francisco Martinez wrote the letter in the French language because he was master of it.

We returned where the camp was, five leagues beyond the Guadalupe River, and we learned that three days previous the horses had stampeded, and a number having been recovered, fifty were still missing, and in pursuit a soldier had lost his way. This man remained missing four days, and in the meantime he met with some Indians who were skinning a buffalo, who took him home with them at nightfall to their ranchería, giving him to eat of the buffalo meat, and whatever else they them-selves had. On the day after this, an Indian belonging to the same ranchería came there with a small bundle of tobacco. This Indian was the one who had been with us, and he made a long harangue to all the Indians who were in the ranchería. As to the soldier who was lost, when he met with the Indians who had the buffalo, they spoke to him by signs, and he understood them to tell him to make a fire. This he must have inferred from seeing the meat they had, or he was frightened at seeing himself lost among barbarian Indians; he spilled on his cloak the powder he was carrying in a flask, and on his striking the light a spark fell on the powder, and it burned his whole side from head to foot. When the Indians learned that we were in their territory they must have come to the conclusion that, since that man was lost, his comrades would be sure to look for him. The next day they brought him his horse, and, since he was so badly burned that he could not help himself, the Indians themselves saddled it for him, and assisted him to mount, telling him by signs to go with them. They brought him very near to the place where we were, just a couple of shots away. The Indians who brought him, not wishing to approach us, signified to him that he should go on, using signs to indicate to him where we were, at the foot of a hill which he saw there. At the foot of that hill, on the other side, they left him, and he reached us at nine in the morning, which was for all a source of great satisfaction. We felt very sorry when we saw how badly burnt he was.

On the following day we left for the settlement of the Frenchmen, and when we were about three leagues from it there came out some twenty-five Indians. Now the old Frenchman who accompanied us took occasion to say that the settlement of the Frenchmen was not in the place to which the two Indian guides were taking us. On the way this Frenchman tried several times, by means of an Indian of the Cavas nation whom he had with him, to make our two Indians desert us, or say that it was very far, and that we should not be able to cross the rivers which were on the way. I resented so much that the Frenchman should be given occasion to speak that I grew angry, and Captain Alonso de Leon said to me: "Father, we are going wherever you wish." We continued following the two guides quite three leagues; we arrived at a stream of very good drinking water, and the two Indians said to me: "Lower down on the bank of this stream are the houses of the French, which must be about three leagues off." Then the old Frenchman saw that there was no help, and that we were certain to come upon the village. He then said: "Sir, now I know very well, yea, very well, that the houses are on this little river."

We started the next morning, and three leagues off we found the village of the Frenchmen on the bank of the stream, as I had been told by the two Indians, the Quems and Juanillo the Papul. We arrived at about eleven in the forenoon, and found six houses, not very large, built with poles plastered with mud, and roofed over with buffalo hides, another larger house where pigs were fattened, and a wooden fort made from the hulk of a wrecked vessel. The fort had one lower room which was used as a chapel for saying mass, and three other rooms below; above the three rooms was an upper story serving for a store-house, wherein we found some six loads of iron, not counting scattered pieces, and some steel, also eight small guns and three swivels made of iron, the largest pieces being for a charge of about six pounds of shot. The pieces and one swivel were buried, and Captain Alonso de Leon carried off two of the swivels. There was a great lot of shattered weapons, broken by the Indians—firelocks, carbines, cutlasses—but they had not left the cannon, only one being found. We found two unburied bodies, which I interred, setting up a cross over the grave. There were many torn-up books, and many dead pigs.

These Frenchmen had a piece of land fenced in with stakes, where they sowed just a little corn, and had an asparagus bed; we found also very good endive. This place affords no advantages as to situation, for good drinking-water is very far off, and timber still further. The water of the stream is very brackish, so much so that in five days during which the camp was pitched there all the horses sickened from the brackish water.

The next day we went down to explore the bay of Espiritu Santo, and coasted it until we succeeded in finding the mouth; in the middle of this there is a flat rock, and all along the shore of the bay there are many lagoons which it is very difficult to cross. Blackberries are abundant, large and fine, and there are a number of stocks which seem to be those of grape vines, but no trees, and no fresh water. The Indians dig wells for drinking water.

After exploring the bay we returned to the main body of our party, whom we had left in the village; we arrived there at noon, and remained there that afternoon, and the next day they bent the large iron bars, making them up into bundles, in order to carry them with ease. We found the Indian with the reply to the letter which we had written to the Frenchmen; they said that we should wait for them, that they would soon come, that another Frenchman was further on, and that they were waiting for him in order that they might come all together. The Indian received the horse, as we had ordered. As to the fort, Captain Alonso de Leon would not have it burnt down, and it remained as it was.

The next day we set out on our return trip to the Guadalupe River, and when we got halfway, since we saw that the Frenchmen did not come, Captain Alonso de Leon, with twenty-five men, went to the ranchería where they were, and the main party went on as far as the Guadalupe River, where it remained waiting three days. The Frenchmen were in the ranchería of the Toaa Indians, with the Tejas; they came to the Guadalupe with Captain Alonso de Leon and arrived there on the 2d of May, '89. Two Frenchmen came, naked except for an antelope's skin, and with their faces, breasts, and arms painted like the Indians, and with them came the governor of the Tejas and eight of his Indians. Through that day and night I tried my utmost to show all possible consideration to the said governor, giving him two horses, and the blanket in which I slept, for I had nothing else which I could give him. Speaking Spanish, and using as an interpreter one of the Frenchmen whom we had with us, I said to the governor that his people should become Christians, and bring into their lands priest who should baptize them, since otherwise they could not save their souls, adding that if he wished, I would go to his lands. Soon the afore-mentioned governor said he would very willingly take me there, and I promised him to go, and to take with me other priests like myself, repeating to him that I would be there in the following year, at the time of sowing corn. The governor seemed well pleased, and I was still more so, seeing the harvest to be reaped among the many souls in those lands who know not God.

The next day was the day of the Holy Cross—the 3d of May; after mass the governor of the Tejas left for his home and we for this place. We arrived at Coahuila, and Captain Alonso de Leon sent two Frenchmen—the one named Juan Archebepe, of Bayonne, the other Santiago Grollette—from Coahuila to Mexico, with Captain Francisco Martinez, and His Excellency the Conde de Galbe had the Frenchmen provided with suitable clothes and dispatched to Spain on shipboard in the same year, '89.

All this news did not fail to create excitement and to give satisfaction not only to His Excellency but also to other men of note in Mexico, and there were several meetings held in order to consider measures not only for keeping the French from gaining control of those regions and settling in them, but also for the introduction of religious ministers.

## 5. A Franciscan Reports on Prospects for Converting the Caddo Indians, 1691

I trust that by the grace of the Most High, through the protection of our Most Holy Mother and the good wishes of our Catholic Majesty and of your Excellency, all these tribes will be subdued. This will be true if those who come from Spain to this country to live will furnish a good example. This done, and the spirit of the evangelical ministers being joined therewith, it is inevitable that much glory and fruit for the two Majesties can be expected. . . .

The dissatisfaction of all the Indians is great when the Spaniards live among them without their wives. I say also from what I have experienced that, if it be possible, it would be to our interest if no man came without his wife. . . . Before I left the mission of Santiago, a letter was written me giving me information of the people that were on their way to Texas, and of the flocks they were bringing. I read this letter to the captains and nobles who were altogether in a council. The first thing they noticed in the letter was that the men were coming without their wives, and they knew that there would [necessarily] be additional men to guard the stock. If objections be made to these few, how much greater objection will be raised, your Excellency, if a great number come into this country to stay. Every day these Indians ask me whether the Spaniards are going to bring their wives with them when they come back. I tell them yes. But in spite of everything they do not give me any credence. They tell me that I must write to Your Excellency, their great captain, and tell you in this missive that they want to be friends, but if the Spaniards want to live among them it must be under such conditions that no harm will be done the Indians by the Spaniards if they do come without their wives; but, if the Spaniards bring their wives, the Indians will be satisfied.

I must say that the demand of these Indians is just and reasonable. And it has already been agreed to. I know from experience gained upon two occasions when duty to the church called me to the work of conversion that this will be wise; and it will be well to leave for my protection three or four unmarried men. I have been much distressed and feared to lose all the fruit that might be produced; and, therefore, prostrate at your feet, I beg of Your Excellency to look with favor upon this work which is so pleasing to the Lord, that it should not be lost. And do not send criminals taken from the prisons, or bachelors, or vagabonds, who, when they are here, away from home where there are no Christians, would commit great atrocities, and, by their depraved lives and bad example, counteract the efforts of the minister, depriving them of the fruit of these souls of the Indians. It would be better for that class of men to be sent somewhere else where they can be kept down with lash in hand. In this way, and in no other, may their souls be saved. For, God knows, souls cannot be saved by one who does not regard his own soul; by one who does not believe in human justice nor acknowledge the justice of God. What a pity. But the evangelical ministers can be confident, since they know that they have the

"Descriptions of the Tejas or Asinai Indians, 1691–1722," trans. Mattie Austin Hatcher, *Southwestern Historical Quarterly*, vol. 29 (July, 1925–April, 1926): 287–290; 300–303. Copyright Texas State Historical Association. Reprinted with permission.

protection of Your Excellency whom we all know watches over the work with more ardent love and desire than we do ourselves. . . .

I trust by the Grace of God that, as soon as the ministers are able to speak the language perfectly and when we have the protection and watchful care of the Spaniards, we will uproot all the discord which the mortal enemy of our souls has sown in this country and that the faith will be planted with greater perfection than in other sections; especially as we enjoy the protection of our Catholic king and of Your Excellency who tries to encourage this work with so much zeal and order by sending ministers and by doing everything else which you may think necessary, since it is for the service of God, our Lord, without which all that has already been done will be lost, if God does not intervene. I say all this because the devil will lay many snares and hindrances in our way in order that the cause of the Most High may not triumph.

Most Excellent Sir, from the information I possess my pen might run on concerning the things I have so far recorded, particularly in regard to their ceremonies, rites, and superstitions, which are so great that those I have myself seen and carefully examined would fill a quire of paper. However, time offers me only the alternative of closing this work. However, what I have related so far contains the most essential features. If Your Excellency will permit me to amplify these notes in greater detail, I shall be very prompt in executing the order. The Lord knows that in this whole matter I am inspired only by the desire I have that not a single soul shall be lost and that these poor miserable people may die only after receiving the holy baptism. It would certainly be a great misfortune if they should perish for want of encouragement because it has not yet been ascertained, nor is it not known, whether there are other unconverted tribes who are more civilized and settled than these Indians and their more immediate neighbors; for all of them cultivate their fields. They do not lack for food. They never abandon their houses nor their country, although they do go to war with their enemies.

They are an industrious people and apply themselves to all kind of work. Indeed, if during the year and three months I have been among them if I had had some bells, some small clasp knives, some glass beads, and some blue cloth—which they greatly prize,—some blankets, and other little things to exchange with these Indians, I could have started a convent with the articles it would have been possible to make from the best materials that are abundant here. I, therefore, declare that it will be well for the ministers to have some of these things—not that one person only should have them—because the Indians are of such a nature that they have no love save for the person who gives them something. So strong is this characteristic that only the person who gives them something is good while all others are bad. They do not even want to receive the holy sacrament of baptism except from some person who has given them a great many things. Even the ministers are not able to persuade them, nor will it ever be possible to develop the mission without these presents. During my stay of one year and three months in this country and during the ten months since I started this, Your Excellency's mission, under the name of Santíssima Nombre de María, I have not had a scrap or anything else. I have torn even my tattered garments up to give to some Indian for helping me. The governor of this mission of yours can vouch for this. . . .

All the ministers may take courage and comfort themselves, first because the language of all these tribes is easy to learn; and then because all the infidels of this section of the country are very tractable. The ministers should not be discouraged even when some of the Indians are very obstinate and are not willing to receive the holy baptism. In two cases I realized that it was impossible to succeed in inducing them to receive it and so they died without it. But cases have come up that demand great prudence so that the fruit may not be lost through some unimportant thing. I do not prophesy what may happen, but it will be well for the ministers who come to this country to know that, in time and upon a closer acquaintance, they will discover cruelties which the Indians practice. Mothers have killed their newborn children because the fathers did not want them. On one occasion they set fire to a house and left two little children to burn, declaring that they were good for nothing.

Most Excellent Sir, according to the information I have received about three thousand persons among all the friendly tribes of the *Tejias* must have died during the epidemic which the Lord sent during the month of March, 1691. The disease was worse in some provinces than in others. As to our own province, I have already stated that the deaths probably reached the number of three hundred—in other provinces the number was sometimes greater, sometimes less.

I have information that the *Cadaudacho* have hopes that the French will return, because they promised when leaving the country that they would return when the cold season again set in, and that a great many of them would have to come in order to occupy the country completely. This is nothing but Indian gossip, though for several reasons it is to be feared that they speak as they are instructed to speak. The French may also be compelled to return on account of their companions whom they left here. I know nothing more of this matter than that in the month of February there were nine or ten Frenchmen at a feast which the Indians had in a neighboring province, about thirty leagues from us called the province of *Nacaos.*

Most Excellent Sir, I know well that much of what I have related does not concern me, but I have had no motive in so doing save the desire I have of bringing souls to the Lord. Although there are many of the tribes who have died, there is no lack of material for conversion for all the ministers who may come. In the name of our Saviour and that of the blessed Mary, prostrate at their feet, I pray for aid and protection and that His Divine Majesty may grant you good health in order that Your Excellency may be the patron of a work which is so pleasing to God.

## ❧ E S S A Y S

The area today known as Texas experienced rapid depopulation as a result of European diseases. The first essay, by the late Smithsonian anthropologist John C. Ewers, presents a grim picture of the devastating toll which these epidemics took on the indigenous peoples of Texas, a process that was well underway even before Europeans arrived in large numbers. Nonetheless, as the second essay by Daniel A. Hickerson reminds us, the disastrous impact of disease was only one component, albeit the most important one, of the sociocultural changes which the Indians of East Texas experienced as a result of European contact. When the Spanish, spurred by reports of French encroachment, arrived in the pine forests of East Texas in the late seventeenth century to establish their claim to the region, they encountered an agricultural people, the Caddo Indians, living under a highly developed political system as members of the Hasinai Confederation. But the lives of the Caddoes had already been profoundly altered by the Spanish presence in North America. Hickerson offers several reasons for the creation of the confederacy, all of which suggest the extent to which the prior arrival of the Spanish in distant regions of the borderlands had transformed native cultures in Texas even before direct contact occurred there.

# The Impact of European Diseases on Texas Indians

### JOHN C. EWERS

That Europeans introduced epidemic diseases into the Americas which drastically reduced the numbers of Indians during the historic period is a fact well know to both historians and anthropologists. But the long range effects of successive epidemics on the populations of particular tribes have not been sufficiently studied, and the effects of these epidemics on the beliefs and customs of the Indians who survived them have been little considered by scholars.

Texas provides a fertile field for studying the influences of epidemics on neighboring tribes of different cultures over an extended period. Nowhere else in the American West did tribes of so many cultures live in such close proximity in the historic period. In Texas alone, buffalo-hunting nomads of the plains met not only horticultural tribes of the plains and woodlands, but also hunter-gatherers of the southwestern deserts and fishermen of the Gulf Coast. . . .

In view of the difficulties in evaluating early estimates of Indian populations, it is not surprising that most anthropologists have relied upon the figures cited in James Mooney's posthumously published study, *The Aboriginal Population of America North of Mexico*. Because Mooney's industry was enormous, his knowledge of Indians and of the literature was great, and his integrity was beyond question, this study of Indian population became the classic work in its field. Nevertheless, A. L. Kroeber, who carefully reviewed Mooney's estimates for the entire North American continent, concluded that "the best of Mooney's estimates can hardly pretend to be nearer than 10 per cent of the probable truth, and some may be 50 per cent or more from it" [see Table 1]. . . .

On the whole, Mooney's estimates for the Indian tribes of Texas appear to be conservative. He may have erred more grievously in underestimating some of the more populous tribes than in overestimating some of the smaller ones. A total population for the tribes considered of at least 50,000 might not be excessive.

By 1890 census figures for these same tribes indicate that their total populations had declined to 12,243, or less than 25% of Mooney's "aboriginal" total for these tribes (Table 1, columns 5–6). Before 1890 the Karankawan, Atakapan, and Coahuiltecan tribes had become extinct. The Caddoan and Tonkawan tribes, as well as the Lipan Apache and Comanche, appear to have suffered reductions of more than 75%. Only the Kiowa, Kiowa-Apache, Mescalero Apache, Arapaho, and Cheyenne appear to have been reduced by less than 50%. It is noteworthy that, with the exception of the Mescalero Apache, all of the last group of tribes

John C. Ewers, "The Influence of Epidemics on the Indian Populations and Cultures of Texas," *Plains Anthropologist: Journal of the Plains Conference,* vol. 19, no. 60 (May 1973): 104–113. Reprinted by permission from Plains Anthropologist. Copyright © 1973 by Plains Anthropological Society.

**Table 1.    The Depopulation of the Indian Tribes of Texas**

| Tribe or Group of Related Tribes | Linguistic Stock | Mooney Est. for 1690 | Mooney Est. for 1780 | Census for 1890 | Per Cent Reduction |
|---|---|---|---|---|---|
| Karankawan tribes | Karankawan | 2,800 | | Extinct | 100% |
| Akokisa | Atakapan | 500 | | Extinct | 100% |
| Bidai | Atakapan | 500 | | Extinct | 100% |
| Coahuiltecan tribes | Coahuiltecan | 7,500* | | Extinct | 100% |
| Tonkawan tribes | Tonkawan | 1,600 | | 56 | 97% |
| Caddoan tribes of East Texas | Caddoan | 8,500 | | 536 | 94% |
| Wichita group of tribes | Caddoan | 3,200 | | 358 | 89% |
| Kichai | Caddoan | 500 | | 66 | 87% |
| Lipan Apache | Athapascan | 500 | | 60** | 88% |
| Mescalero Apache | Athapascan | 700 | | 473 | 32% |
| Kiowa-Apache | Athapascan | | 300+ | 326 | +9% |
| Comanche | Shoshonean | 7,000 | | 1,598 | 77% |
| Kiowa | Kiowa-Tanoan | | 2,000 | 1,140 | 43% |
| ‡Arapaho | Algonquian | | 3,000 ⎤ | 5,630 | 13% |
| ‡Cheyenne | Algonquian | | 3,500 ⎦ | | |

\*   Coahuiltecan tribes in Texas estimated at one-half Mooney's total for these tribes in Mexico and Texas.
\*\*  Includes 20 Lipan among Tonkawa and 40 among Mescalero Apache in 1890.
+   Yet Mooney (1898:253) states: "They have probably never numbered much over three hundred and fifty."
‡   All figures for Cheyenne and Arapaho include both Northern and Southern divisions, although only the Southern ones lived on the frontiers of Texas.

had limited contacts with whites prior to 1790, and none of them were missionized during the Spanish Period.

Epidemics certainly were not the sole cause of this radical reduction of more than 75% in the population of these tribes during the period prior to 1890. Intertribal warfare and wars with Spaniards, Mexicans, Texans, and citizens of the United States also took their toll. Overindulgence in liquor on the part of Indians living near white settlements also contributed to this decrease, as did venereal disease, malnutrition, and starvation. Nevertheless, Mooney's contention that epidemics were *the major cause* of marked population decrease among the tribes of North America prior to 1900 appears to have been true of the Indians of Texas.

Mooney listed but five "great epidemics" in Plains Indian history which decimated some or all of the tribes of Texas: an unidentified disease reported to have killed 3000 Caddoans in East Texas in 1691; widespread smallpox epidemics in 1778, 1801, and during the late 1830's; and a widespread cholera epidemic in 1849. Yet I found references to no less than *thirty* epidemics which appeared among one or more of the tribes of Texas (as I define them) between 1528 and 1890. There was still another one in 1892. Even this may not be a complete record. The absence of references to any epidemic among these Indians during the 146-year-period 1528–1674 may reflect our paucity of information more accurately than it does their state of health, or freedom from epidemics.

Contemporary writers did not identify the diseases involved in a number of the epidemics of the pre-1800 period. However, Dr. Pat Nixon, a San Antonio physician who reviewed the literature on these early epidemics, suggested the diseases on the basis of the symptoms described. Throughout the entire period, smallpox was the most common cause of epidemics.

There were smallpox epidemics in 1674–5, 1688–9, 1739, about 1746, 1750, 1759, 1763, 1766, 1778, 1801–02, 1816, 1839–40, 1861–2, and 1864. Although the Indians of present Oklahoma were vaccinated against smallpox in 1865, an epidemic of this disease occurred among the Mescalero Apache in New Mexico in 1877. Yet another smallpox epidemic was averted among the Mescalero during the winter of 1882–1883, when timely vaccination enabled these Indians to escape "without a single case of smallpox."

Next to smallpox, measles and cholera appear to have been the most deadly, although epidemics of malaria, whooping cough, and influenza also took their tolls of Indian lives.

The frequency of epidemics within a tribe must be regarded as a very important factor in the progressive decline of Indian population, for it inhibited the recovery and growth of tribal populations. The French biologist, Jean Louis Berlandier, who explored Texas in 1828 and subsequent years, reported that smallpox occurred among the Indian tribes "every sixteen years, making great ravages for a year at a time." He was not precisely accurate in defining the interval between epidemics, but the record is clear that there was a smallpox epidemic among one or more of the tribes of Texas at least once each generation from 1739 to 1877. Losses in these epidemics must have been high among children and teenagers who never lived to reproduce. Older people (including women beyond child-bearing age), who gained immunity by exposure to previous epidemics, presumably survived. . . .

Indian beliefs regarding the causes of epidemics varied. Interestingly enough, the fragmentary records of two of the earliest epidemics indicate that the afflicted Indians initially, and probably correctly, blamed the whites for these plagues. Cabeza de Vaca wrote that the Karankawa at *first* blamed his Spanish party for communicating the epidemic of 1528 to them, "believing we had killed them and holding it to be certain, they agreed among themselves to kill those of us who survived." But one Indian saved the Spaniards' lives by pointing out that if the white men had "so much power" they would not have suffered so many of their own men to perish.

Caddoan survivors of the disastrous epidemic of 1691 among the Indians of the East Texas missions at first blamed the high mortality upon the priests' practice of baptizing the stricken Indians during their death throes. But Father Casañas believed that he convinced even the most hostile Indian medicine men that the priests attentions had not caused the Indian deaths. . . .

The common practice among the nomadic tribes of scattering once an epidemic struck one of their camps, as well as their avoidance of the locality of the initial outbreak for a considerable time thereafter, must have helped to minimize losses among them. The desertion of the missions by some of the missionized Indians during the epidemic of the 18th century must have had a similar effect. The loyal neophytes who remained with their priests perished, while many of the dispersed apostates survived.

Significantly, the greatest population losses during the 18th century and the early years of the 19th century were suffered by the least mobile tribes. These were the mission Indians and the Caddoan farming tribes. The latter, as well as the Wichita and the tribes of East Texas, lived in compact, semi-permanent villages of multi-family lodges, where conditions were as favorable for the rapid communication of diseases as they were in the mission compounds. . . .

Early accounts of the Karankawan and Caddoan tribes of East Texas refer to the common practice of infanticide. It was also the custom of the Caddo to bury a live, nursing infant with its dead mother, and of the Comanche to kill a warrior's wife at his grave. These customs do not appear to have survived among these tribes beyond the middle of the 19th century. Why? Did not the continued decline in tribal population encourage the abandonment of customs so wasteful of human life?

The population decline also may have brought about significant changes in Indian war practices during the 19th century. Eighteenth century accounts indicate that the eating of prisoners, the hideous torture of captives, and the trade of captives as slaves were common among the Indian tribes of Texas. As the 19th century progressed only the Tonkawa continued to practice cannibalism to any extent, and both the torture and sale of captives became less common. Captives became more valuable as adopted members of a family—to replace children, wives, and husbands who had been lost in epidemics—than as human sacrifices or human trade goods. . . .

Epidemics strongly affected Indian tribal organization—or more properly disorganization and reorganization. Certainly the Karankawan, Atakapan and Coahuiltecan tribes, all of whom were repeated victims of epidemics, suffered the ultimate in social disorganization—extinction. The Lipan Apache lost their political and social autonomy and survived only as minority groups of a few individuals living among friendly Apache tribes in Oklahoma and New Mexico. Remnants of the Tonkawa were preserved from extinction under the protection of the United States Army at Fort Griffin during the waning years of the intertribal wars. The horticultural Caddoans, who numbered nearly thirty tribes before the epidemic of 1691, were reduced to three small tribes, identified as Caddo, Kichai, and Wichita, by the end of the frontier period.

There is need for a thorough study of the process by which the Caddoans managed to survive, through repeated combinations and reorganizations into fewer and fewer units as their numbers declined. In this process the names of many of the earlier tribes became almost forgotten. But they survived (to a degree) biologically long after they lost their political identity. There are indicators of tribal combinations following the deaths of important chiefs and many of their followers during the 18th century epidemics. Why the names of some of these tribes, such as Anadarko, survived, while those of other once equally numerous and prominent tribes disappeared, needs explanation. . . .

The cumulative effect of 30 or more epidemics among the Indians of Texas played a major role in the marked decline in population among these tribes during the historic period prior to 1890. Even though our best available set of early population estimates for these tribes, those of James Mooney, cannot be considered exact, comparison of them with 1890 census figures for the surviving tribes clearly indicates both a general population decline and a differential rate of decline among the different tribes. The sedentary, missionized and horticultural tribes suffered the most severe losses. Some of them became extinct; others sacrificed their tribal independence as their numbers decreased but insured their biological survival by combining with other linguistically and culturally related tribes. This practice was most common among the Caddoan tribes of East Texas. The nomadic tribes of the northern periphery appear to have suffered least, due to a combination of factors such as their relative remoteness from Whites until the early years of the 19th century, their common practice of scattering once they learned of the presence of disease among their people, and their very positive efforts to recruit additional tribal members through raiding for captives—both Indian and non-Indian.

# The Caddo Confederacy

### DANIEL A. HICKERSON

The Hasinai Confederacy was a loosely centralized group of Caddoan agricultural communities located along the Neches and Angelina Rivers in eastern Texas during the seventeenth and eighteenth centuries. Recent research has focused on introduced disease, and resulting population coalescences, during the protohistoric period (ca. A.D. 1520–1680) as an important factor in the formation of this confederacy and other similar groupings. Though the importance of disease cannot be denied, other factors contributed to the political and social situation of the Hasinai in the early historic era. Among these factors were trade in European goods, Apache aggression, and the natural defensive advantages of the Hasinai region. . . .

. . . Once the disease factor has been recognized, there exists a strong temptation to overstate its impact on bringing about those cultural changes, protohistoric or historic population movements, and shifts in settlement or subsistence patterns, and political and economic life for which evidence is found. This temptation can be dangerous for at least two reasons. First, despite recent attempts to use demographic research to interpret the archaeological record, the true extent of demographic decline in the Caddoan region has yet to be adequately established. And second, the protohistoric period in this region (ca. 1520–1680) was characterized by a number of large-scale historical changes, each of which culturally affected local populations over a wide area, and only one of which was the introduction of Old World epidemic diseases to the New World.

In other words, we should view disease within a larger context, as one of several large-scale processes of change that resulted directly or indirectly from European activity in North America and Mesoamerica. Each of these historical processes contributed to sociocultural changes among the Caddo and other Native American peoples. Even where disease plays a significant and documented role in a sociocultural change, it cannot entirely determine how the change is played out. For example, the spread of disease may have brought about the abandonment of some areas in North America, but other social, political, and environmental factors may have played a role in determining or influencing where the survivors moved.

Daniel A. Hickerson, "Historical Processes, Epidemic Disease, and the Formation of the Hasinai Confederacy," *Ethnohistory,* 44:1 (Winter 1997): 31–48. Copyright © 1997, American Society for Ethnohistory. All rights reserved. Reprinted by permission of Duke University Press.

I begin with the premise that the Hasinai area of eastern Texas was the site of a protohistoric population coalescence, that the core of the historic Hasinai Confederacy was a combination of groups or communities long resident in the area, and that they were joined by other Caddoan communities during the late protohistoric period, possibly during the mid- to late seventeenth century. Several such amalgamations took place in the protohistoric southeast. The Creeks and the Choctaws were both societies that developed as a result of protohistoric population coalescences. The spread of epidemic disease may have been one event that brought about pressure for such coalescences. The abandonment of some areas, and subsequent amalgamations of survivors in a diminished number of continuing or new settlements, has been identified as a response to depopulation from epidemic disease.

But population movements took place for other reasons in addition to depopulation. During the protohistoric and early historic periods there were many political and economic changes, some originating many miles away, with far-reaching impacts; and there were social and environmental factors other than disease that influenced the movements of groups of people—that influenced whether or not they moved their settlements, and to what destinations. In this article I briefly discuss the role of disease in protohistoric population movements. I then focus attention on three additional factors—warfare, the physical environment, and trade—and discuss how changes in these factors combined to influence the creation of the historic alliance known as the Hasinai Confederacy.

## The Hasinai Confederacy in the Seventeenth Century

The Hasinai Caddo occupied the Neches and Angelina river valleys and neighboring areas in eastern Texas. In the late seventeenth and early eighteenth centuries, the Hasinai lived in nine to twelve communities. Collectively, these communities were grouped politically into what anthropologists have called a "confederacy," and which we might think of as a loosely centralized chiefdom. The Hasinai Confederacy was one of three such groupings in the late seventeenth and early eighteenth centuries in the Caddoan area of present-day northeastern Texas, northwestern Louisiana, southwestern Arkansas, and southeastern Oklahoma. The other two, the Kadohadacho and Natchitoches confederacies, were located on the Red River, to the north and east of the Hasinai.

In 1691, the Spanish missionary Fray Francisco Casanas de Jesus Maria listed the following communities as comprising the Hasinai: Nabadachos, Nechas, Nechavis, Naconos, Nacachaus, Nazadachotzis, Cachaes, Nabitis, and Nasayayas. Later lists, made after 1715, differed slightly, with additions and omissions of certain names. To what extent these inconsistencies reflect changes in the composition of the Hasinai, and to what extent they resulted from errors in observation or in the recording of names, is unclear. There is little doubt, however, that changes in the makeup of the Hasinai Confederacy occurred, both before and after European entry into the region.

Each Hasinai community consisted of several widely separated hamlets, which were probably the residences of local lineage groups. Each hamlet consisted of seven to fifteen houses, which were usually located in or near river or creek bottoms and were surrounded by fields of corn, beans, squash, melons, tobacco, and other crops. Father Anastius Douay noted of a Hasinai community in 1686, "This village is one of the largest and most populous that I have seen in America. It is at least twenty leagues long, not that it is constantly inhabited, but in hamlets of ten or twelve cabins."

Hasinai society was hierarchical, with several status positions, the two highest of which were hereditary and probably reserved for members of a central lineage. The xinesi was the recognized leader of the Hasinai Confederacy. He performed no labor, and his household was supported with tribute collected from the members of the communities. The duties of the xinesi were primarily ceremonial, including the performance of numerous rituals, many connected to the agricultural cycle, regular sacrifices of food to supernatural beings, and the maintenance of the sacred, perpetual fire in a ceremonial structure near his house.

Each community was governed by a caddi (pl. caddices), or chief. Like the xinesi, the caddices performed ritual functions, but they also had a number of political duties. The caddi of each community coordinated communal work efforts, acted as judge in disputes between individuals or kin groups, and had some authority in the conduct of war. On most matters of importance, the caddi consulted a council of elders, who were probably heads of the lineages that made up each community. Each caddi also acted as an intermediary between his own and other communities. This last function included receiving visiting representatives of other communities and groups, both Caddoan and non-Caddoan, who regularly came to trade with the Hasinai.

The first Europeans to enter the territory of the Hasinai were the surviving members of the de Soto expedition, who briefly entered eastern Texas in 1542 before they were forced to turn back to the Mississippi River. The next European contact was not made until 1686, when the ill-fated French party led by LaSalle, stranded on Matagorda Bay on the Texas Gulf Coast, twice passed through the Hasinai territory while in search of a route to the Mississippi. Shortly thereafter, in 1690, Spanish officials, alarmed by reports of the French settlement, sent missionaries to the Hasinai, with the primary purpose of reinforcing Spanish claims to the territory. French fur traders began to make regular visits to the Hasinai by the first decade of the eighteenth century, visits that became more frequent after the establishment of a French post at Natchitoches, on the Red River in western Louisiana, in 1716. For nearly a century thereafter, the Hasinai would occupy the frontier between Spanish and French colonial territory.

## Hasinai Population and Epidemic Disease

. . . When drawing comparisons with the demographic trends elsewhere in the protohistoric Southeast, it must be kept in mind that settlements in the Caddoan area were, in general, more dispersed and less densely populated than the Mississippian period settlement systems of the Southeast, and thus were likely to be less susceptible to the spread of epidemics. Within the Caddoan culture area, the populations of eastern Texas, particularly those of the relatively lightly settled Hasinai area, appear to have been less severely affected by introduced diseases than the populations of the more densely populated Arkansas and Ouachita river valleys, both of which were abandoned before direct contact with Europeans could take place. The de Soto party, which passed through the Caddoan area early in the protohistoric period, found it to be less densely populated, with smaller and more scattered settlements, than those areas of the Southeast through which they had passed earlier. This trend was first noted during their passage through Naguatex, located on the Red River and their point of entrance into eastern Texas.

Epidemics of introduced diseases might be sufficient to explain the abandonment of, or significant demographic reduction in, some areas, and the concentration of settlements in others, in the Arkansas, Ouachita, and Red river regions during the protohistoric period. However, given available information, comparisons of settlement patterns and epidemic disease trends are not adequate to explain the abandonment of the less densely populated upper Cypress Creek basin toward the end of the protohistoric or the very early historic period. Nor do these factors adequately explain the coalescence of population around this time along the Neches and Angelina Rivers, the site of the historic Hasinai Confederacy. . . .

## Warfare

One political factor that clearly influenced population movements during the protohistoric period is warfare—specifically, the increased aggression by the Apaches in the southern Plains. The inroads of Apache Indians were a major concern for the Hasinai and their neighbors, and violent encounters that frequently took place with the Apaches were noted by nearly all of the European observers who lived for an extended time among the Hasinai. It is important to understand that, although the Spanish priests may have believed the wars between the Hasinai and the Apaches to be the result of the "ancient hostility between them," the rise of the Apaches as a major threat to the settled tribes at the margins of the Plains was actually, as of the late seventeenth century, of quite recent origin. Before the seventeenth century, the Apaches wandered the western Plains on foot, hunting bison and other game, and trading with the Pueblo peoples who lived along the Rio Grande to the west of the Plains. Indeed, it appears that the Apaches only became a significant threat to their eastern neighbors around the middle of the seventeenth century. The development that created this threat took place several hundred miles to the west, with the introduction of the horse into New Mexico by the Spanish colonists who occupied the Rio Grande valley.

The first horses, and the knowledge required to ride and maintain them, were probably acquired by the Apaches through trade with Puebloan Indians. The possession and mastery of those first horses gave the Apaches the means to build up their supplies through raiding, and by 1660 they were taking horses in frequent attacks on the Spanish and Puebloan Indian settlements in New Mexico. It was around this time that the Apaches acquired their reputation among the Spanish as the fearsome and hostile warriors who dominated the southern Plains, a reputation that stayed with them well into the eighteenth century.

Horses, along with Spanish weapons acquired in New Mexico, made the Apaches a serious threat to the settled agricultural villages occupied by Caddoan Indians on the eastern fringe of the Plains. They became, in the words of one Spanish observer, "enemies of one and all" on and near the Plains. In 1690 Alonso de Leon, who led the initial Spanish expeditions to the territory of the Hasinai, noted that "the war that the Tejas (Hasinai) fight continuously is with the Apache Indians, who are from the land to the west of their settlements." Father Massanet, a Franciscan missionary who worked among the Hasinai, reported in 1691 that the Apaches "are at war with all the other nations. . . . they dominate all the other Indians." Father Isidro Felix de Espinosa, a Franciscan missionary priest who chronicled the Franciscan effort in this area, noted that when the Hasinai went to the Plains to hunt bison, they "go well-armed, because at this time, if they encounter the Apaches, they cruelly murder each other."

Other tribes that had lived on the southern Plains, and had served as a buffer between the Apaches and the Caddoan groups, had been driven south and west by the 1680s, as the Apaches expanded across the entire width of the Plains. In 1686 Alonso de Posada described the Apache nation, "which possesses and is owner of all the plains of Cibola [the southern Great Plains]. . . . The Indians of this nation are so arrogant, haughty and such boastful warriors that they are the common enemy of all nations who live below the northern region. . . . They have destroyed, ruined, or driven most of them from their lands." Posada noted that the Apaches were at war with the Hasinai, and listed several nations, including the Jumanos, that they had driven from the region of the Nueces River southward to the Rio Grande.

The Hasinai themselves began to acquire horses and Spanish weapons of their own through trade some time before the 1680s. In 1686 the French party under René Robert Cavelier Sieur de LaSalle found among the Hasinai many horses, which they freely traded to the French explorers. Father Espinosa stated that the Hasinai had possessed many horses "since the first entry of the Spaniards," which had taken place in 1690. The acquisition of horses allowed the Hasinai and their allies to meet the Apache on more equal terms, and occasionally to take the offensive in battle.

However, at the same time, they were also actively seeking allies to stand with them in these battles. These allies included a large number of native groups, both Caddoan and non-Caddoan, which the Hasinai hosted regularly at feasts and trading fairs. Father Espinosa described the loyalty of these allies, who, he says, "are so faithful in observing their treaties that they do not delay even one day from the appointed time, to gather all together for the march in search of their enemies, the most adamant of which are the Apaches." In the eyes of Hasinai leaders, their potential allies also included European newcomers. In 1687, according to Father Douay of the LaSalle party, a party of Hasinais persuaded some of the French colonists to join them in battle with the Canoatinno, which may have been an Apache group living on or near the Colorado River. Indeed, military alliance may have been expected, even assumed, of the friends and neighbors of the Hasinai. A few years later, in a letter of 1693, Father Massanet noted that among the reasons for the dissatisfaction that the Hasinai had with the Spanish, "they have said many times that if we do not go with them to their wars and to kill their enemies, that we should return to our land."

The rise of hostility between the Hasinai and the Apache on the southern Plains, and the resulting increased danger from raiding and warfare, clearly exerted pressure on the Hasinai and their neighbors, both Caddoan and non-Caddoan, to seek close alliances and in some instances to concentrate their settlements for the benefit of mutual protection. This factor alone, however, does not explain the selection of the specific region of the Neches and Angelina Rivers, the homeland of the Hasinai, as the site of a population coalescence.

## Environment

The location of the Hasinai in the woodlands along the Neches and Angelina Rivers in itself provided a measure of protection from mounted raiders of the Plains. Many Titus phase settlements, particularly those on the upper reaches of the Big Cypress Creek and on the nearby Lake Fork Creek, were located in oak-hickory forest that was less dense, and closer to the Plains, than the oak-pine forest occupied by the historic Hasinai. The threat from the Apaches, and other real or potential enemies, may have been a significant factor that determined or influenced the movement of populations into this area during the seventeenth century.

The dense forest that covered most of this area was a hindrance to travel by any means, but especially to horseback warriors wishing to strike suddenly and then retreat quickly. The advantages of this natural protective barrier were noted by European observers. In 1690 Father Massanet described the two roads from the south by which the Hasinai could be reached. The first road "goes straight north to the Texas. But the Apaches are in the habit of coming to it, and these Apaches are enemies both of the Texas [i.e., the Hasinai] and of the Spanish." The second road ran to the northeast, and was "more secure, because there are no enemies, nor do the Apaches come to it because of the dense forest and the distance." . . .

Historical accounts also indicate that during part of the year river flooding presented as significant a barrier to travel as did the dense forest. The most difficult period of travel was in the fall, which coincides with one of the two peak rainfall periods for eastern Texas, late September or October; the other peak period occurs in May. In 1689 a Jumano Indian being questioned by Spanish authorities investigating French activity on the Gulf coast was asked about the approach to the country of the Hasinai. He replied, "When the rains begin it is not easy to enter or come out of that land because of the flooded rivers and marshes which do not permit passage. . . . After it begins to rain in those parts it is not possible to come out until winter sets in." Father Massanet wrote, in 1693, to the Viceroy Conde de Galve, explaining why a promised report from the province of the Hasinai, which he had sent in the care of two soldiers in October, was several months late. "It pleased the majesty of God," he explained, "that the Colorado River would not allow them to pass, nor lessen its flow until the past month of April." . . .

The combination of the dense forest and the sometimes impassable rivers made travel in the country of the Hasinai always difficult, and sometimes impossible, for anyone unfamiliar with the territory, whether they be horseback raiders from the Plains or Franciscan priests from New Spain. As the Apaches, supplied with horses taken from the Spanish settlements of New Mexico, expanded their hunting territory on the Plains, threatening all challengers, such a country must have provided a particularly attractive homeland for displaced or remnant Caddoan groups from the country farther north and northwest. Caddoan peoples had occupied the Neches and Angelina basin long before horses were introduced to the Plains peoples. However, in the early to mid-seventeenth century, when those Plains peoples began their rapid expansion, this quality of the country around the

Neches and Angelina could hardly have been overlooked by Caddoans who had previously occupied the less densely forested, more exposed territory to the north and northwest, closer to the edge of the Plains.

## Trade

Another aspect of the geographic position of the Hasinai may have exerted an equally strong attraction for the Caddoan peoples who occupied eastern Texas during the protohistoric period. Although archaeological data are not conclusive on this point, there is strong historical evidence that during the mid- to late seventeenth century, the Hasinai communities were a gateway for trade in European goods and horses brought from Spanish settlements in northern Mexico and New Mexico.

Evidence exists for trade contacts between the East Texas Caddo and the regions to the west, particularly the Puebloan area of New Mexico, in both the archaeological and the historical records. Father Douay, with the LaSalle party, noted in 1686 that the Hasinai "have intercourse with the Spaniards through the Choumans [Jumano], their allies." These allies brought to the Hasinai "many things which undoubtedly came from the Spaniards, such as dollars and other pieces of money, silver spoons, lace . . . clothes and horses." Douay also noted the presence of several Jumano "ambassadors" among the Hasinai. A few months later, on their second passage through the territory of the Hasinai, the LaSalle party was greeted by a Hasinai man dressed in Spanish clothing, and saw several others who carried Spanish sword blades. . . .

The Jumanos are most frequently mentioned as middlemen who brought Spanish goods to the Hasinai. However, there is no reason to suppose that other groups, including the Coahuiltecans, were not involved in this trade network as well. Jumanos, displaced from the southern Plains, are known to have been present in northern Coahuila around the time of the report cited above, and Coahuiltecan groups resident in that area may have accompanied the Jumanos on their trading visits to eastern Texas. Indeed, the "Coahuiles" mentioned by the Bishop of Guadalajara may have even included Jumanos. European observers, including the members of the Teran de los Rios expedition of 1691–92, noted the presence of members of a number of other tribes, probably "Coahuiltecan," who accompanied the Jumanos on their journeys to the Hasinai around 1690.

If the reports concerning the Hasinai made to the Bishop of Guadalajara by the Indians were accurate, which we have no reason to doubt, then it would appear that the xinesi (the "Great Lord" mentioned in the quote above) maintained strict control of the border regions of the Hasinai territory. The local chiefs, the caddices, of the outlying provinces or communities of the Hasinai Confederacy, appear to have been instrumental in maintaining this border control. These caddices, or "casique(s) . . . named by the Great Lord," were probably members of the same lineage as the xinesi, if the Hasinai conformed to the pattern of southeastern chiefdoms, in which status positions were held by members of a central lineage within a system of ranked clans and lineages.

There is no direct evidence from the historical descriptions of the Hasinai, other than this one indirect account, that the xinesi appointed the caddices. It is more likely that the xinesi rose from the ranks of the caddices, either through seniority or through personal influence—he may have been, as Kathleen Gilmore termed it, the "biggest big man" among big men. An observation by Father Casanas suggests that this may have been the case, when he requests that the viceroy of New Spain direct that a gift be sent for him to present to the xinesi, the "principle chief of all this province." He then reveals that this chief, whom Casanas had already presented with a baton symbolizing his command, "is no more than a Caddi, subject with those of the other eight of these nine nations to the Grand Xinesi," but that because of the gifts and recognition by the Spanish, "it will be impossible that he should not be recognized as the Xinesi."

However, it is also quite likely that the xinesi could direct the placement of caddices, who were probably younger relatives, among the Hasinai villages. The purpose of their control of the frontier and the points of entry into the Hasinai territory would have been, at least in part, to control the inflow and distribution of incoming trade goods, both among their supporters among the Hasinai and to representatives of other groups allied with them.

Identification of the historical processes taking place in the material and social environment are important to any understanding of the influences on sociocultural changes, such as those that created the late-seventeenth-century Hasinai Confederacy. It is also important to remember that such historical processes can have their origins in far-flung locations, hundreds or even thousands of miles distant from the point of observation.

This article has addressed four separate historical factors that, at the end of the protohistoric period and the beginning of the historic period, were present and which exerted significant pressure on the Caddoan peoples that comprised the Hasinai Confederacy. These factors were epidemic disease, the rise of Apache aggression and hostility on the southern Plains, the development of a regular trade in European goods and horses from Spanish colonial settlements in northern Mexico and New Mexico, and the location of defensible territory. This combination of factors led to the migration of Caddoan populations south to the protohistoric and early historic Hasinai territory. This migration provided the foundation for the subsequent development, during the late protohistoric period, of a formal political alliance and nascent chiefdom . . . first called the Hasinai Confederacy. . . .

. . . Ewers emphasizes that the movement of groups and their combination with other communities was a frequent response to demographic decline among the historic period Caddo, and notes that the population of a Caddo community rarely dropped below 150 before it would leave its territory and join another group. Of course, the population of a village would not have to drop to this critical level if other factors dictated a decision to shift to a new location. And other pressures besides disease could have made it advantageous for communities to move nearer to more well-positioned allies and trading partners, and thus might have been responsible for population movements.

The Spanish occupation of northern New Spain, accompanied by the introduction of Spanish goods and horses, encouraged the creation of a native trade economy centered on the movement of European goods and horses across the southern Plains, from New Mexico and far western Texas to the Caddoan region of eastern Texas. The groups involved in this trade network probably included many of the same peoples who were involved in earlier exchange in native objects, which had brought goods from the Puebloan region to the Caddoan villages along the Red River.

However, during the late seventeenth century, middleman groups, notably the Jumano, began to follow a more southerly route across the Plains than did the earlier traders, a development that was almost certainly a response to Apache expansion and aggression. As a result of this southerly shift in the native trade route across the Plains, the Hasinai communities of northeastern Texas became the eastern terminus of this route, and thus became the regional gateway for the entrance of Spanish trade goods and horses into the Caddoan region.

Apache hostility also made it advantageous for other Caddoan peoples to concentrate their settlements near the Hasinai, for its relatively protected positions, for the safety to be found in numbers, and for the Spanish horses and weapons to be found there, which allowed them to meet the Apaches on relatively equal ground. The Hasinai leaders were able to use their position as a gateway for the distribution of trade goods to help them gain a close circle of Caddoan allies, forming the Hasinai Confederacy, as it is now known to historians and anthropologists. They were also able to attract a looser, less formal, alliance network of groups, both Caddoan and non-Caddoan, that they could count on as allies and as trade partners. Finally, the desire of the Hasinai and Jumano Indians, and their allies, to maintain open trade routes across the southern Plains in the face of increasing Apache raiding may, by the late 1600s, have led the Hasinai to encourage the establishment of Spanish missions in their territory.

✪ *F U R T H E R     R E A D I N G*

Herbert E. Bolton, *The Hasinais: Southern Caddoans as Seen by the Earliest Europeans,* Russell M. Magnaghi, ed. (1987)

———, *Coronado on the Tourquoise Trail: Knight of Pueblo and Plains* (1940)

Donald E. Chipman, *Spanish Texas, 1519–1821* (1992)

Donald E. Chipman and Harriet Denise Joseph, *Notable Men and Women of Spanish Texas* (1999)

William C. Foster, *Spanish Expeditions into Texas, 1689–1768* (1995)

Jack Jackson, *Flags Along the Coast: Charting the Gulf of Mexico, 1519–1759* (1995)

———, *Shooting the Sun: Cartographic Results of Military Activities in Texas, 1689–1829* (1999)

Elizabeth John, *Storms Brewed in Other Men's Worlds: The Confrontation of Indians, Spanish, and French in the Southwest, 1540–1795* (1975)

David La Vere, *Caddo Economics and Politics, 700–1835* (1998)

William W. Newcomb, Jr., *The Indians of Texas: From Prehistoric to Modern Times* (1961)

Martin Salinas, *Indians of the Rio Grande Delta: Their Role in the History of Southern Texas and Northern Mexico* (1990)

F. Todd Smith, *The Caddo Indians: Tribes at the Convergence of Empires, 1542–1854* (1995)

David J. Weber, *The Spanish Frontier in North America* (1992)

Robert S. Weddle, *Spanish Sea: The Gulf of Mexico in North American Discovery, 1500–1685* (1985)

CHAPTER
3

# *The Challenges of*
# *Spanish Colonization:*
# *Struggles and Accommodation*
# *in the Eighteenth Century*

Spain's program to Hispanicize the borderlands met with decidedly mixed results.
Vast distances, poor communications, and warring Indian tribes were only a few of
the obstacles Spain faced. By the mid-eighteenth century, the religious communities
and civil settlements established by Spain remained little more than isolated islands
in a vast region very much dominated by its indigenous peoples. As the century drew
to a close, Spain, like other European colonial powers, sought to implement a more
streamlined, efficient administrative system designed to reduce government expenditures. Known as the Bourbon reforms, they included a complete review of Spain's
borderlands empire. Accompanied by the diminishing political influence of the
Catholic Church, these reforms also led Spain to cut costs by secularizing many of
the missions it had built in Texas and the American Southwest.
    Students of early Texas and the American Southwest owe a great debt to
Herbert E. Bolton, an historian writing in the early twentieth century whose work
inspired a generation of borderlands scholarship. Rejecting an Anglocentric view of
early American history that focused primarily on the English colonies of the eastern
seaboard, Bolton called attention to Spain's colonization efforts and urged historians
to integrate the Hispanic Southwest into the narrative of European settlement in
North America. Bolton and the many historians he influenced viewed the borderlands as part of a larger process of Spanish imperial expansion in the western
hemisphere. This perspective gave particular attention to the institutional structures
of Spain's empire, a grand design imposed on the borderlands by Spanish officialdom in which colonists, clerics, and Indians were all dutiful participants.
    More recently, however, historians (including the two whose works are
excerpted in this chapter) have devoted less attention to royal policies and edicts

*and more attention to the inhabitants themselves. By emphasizing community
formation and development, a new generation of historians has gained a better
understanding of the obstacles and challenges which the peoples of the borderlands faced in their efforts to settle Texas in the seventeenth and eighteenth
centuries. Challenging, at least implicitly, traditional assumptions of European
"conquest," some historians have stressed the ways in which Native Americans
resisted and ultimately shaped Spanish rule. Similarly, Spanish settlers are
viewed less as obedient subjects of the crown than as active participants in the
creation of a unique borderlands community, who managed to adapt to the harsh
realities of their wilderness environment. An understanding of the problems
which these communities faced will enable students to see why Mexico turned to
external sources to populate Texas in the early nineteenth century (see Chapter 4).
What problems did Hispanics encounter in their struggles to establish permanent
settlements in the Texas borderlands? To what extent were Native Americans
successfully assimilated into these communities?*

 D O C U M E N T S

The first two documents in this chapter reflect the squabbling and discord that initially characterized relations between the Franciscan missionaries and civil settlers of
Spain's borderlands communities. In 1731, fifteen families from the Canary Islands
arrived in Villa San Fernando de Bexar (later known as San Antonio), and promptly
found themselves in competition with the local missionaries and presidial soldiers
for the area's limited resources. In Document 1, the Canary Islanders complain to the
viceroy in Mexico City of the hardships and difficulties which they have encountered
in San Antonio. In Document 2, the Franciscans present their version of the reasons
for the friction between the isleños and the area missions in an appeal written by
Father Benito Fernández. On the basis of Father Fernández' statements, the viceroy
rejected the isleños' petition.

The five missions of the San Antonio area became the centerpiece of the
Spanish mission system in Texas in the eighteenth century. In Document 3, Father
Gaspar José de Solís gives an enthusiastic report on productivity at the San José
mission. Franciscan efforts to establish a Catholic presence in northern Texas, on the
other hand, encountered far stiffer resistance from indigenous tribes. In Document 4,
Father Miguel de Molina gives an account of the attack on the San Sabá mission by
Comanches and Wichitas in 1758.

During the second half of the eighteenth century, Spanish authorities gradually
reached the conclusion that their northernmost American holdings were more of a
burden to the empire than an asset. Document 5 is an excerpt from the Rubí Dictamen,
issued by Marqués de Rubí following his extensive inspection of presidios and civil
settlements in the Southwest. Rubí recommended the consolidation of Spain's frontier
population in Texas, urging the abandonment of all missions and settlements with
the exception of San Antonio and La Bahía. By the end of the century, ecclesiastical
authorities, bowing to royal pressures to administer the mission system with a greater
degree of economic efficiency, were also ready to give up their efforts in Texas. In
Document 6, Father José Francisco López, president of the Texas Missions, advocates
the secularization of the five missions in San Antonio, in order to release missionaries
for evangelical work elsewhere.

# 1. The Canary Islanders State Their Grievances to the Viceroy, 1741

The first hardship which these miserable people suffer is the lack of a church in which Mass can be said and divine services held. They must, therefore, attend services in a room of the presidio, and during the rainy season this cannot be done because of the heavy rains. Mass is then said in the room of the guard, which is an open porch. Both places are unbecoming for the celebration of the august Mystery. Some citizens, who want a decent church, have agreed to contribute towards building a church, in so far as their meagre means allow. This is clear from the testimony given by the governor of this province, which I duly present. But they have been unable to contribute what they promised because of their great needs. Would Your Excellency be so kind as to give orders to proceed with the building of a church and assign from the royal treasury the amount Your Excellency would be pleased to grant, and appoint a person to look after the accounts. The citizens are ready to help with their personal labor.

Likewise, may I mention to Your Excellency that these miserable settlers have no way whatsoever to maintain themselves, because this province has no trade or anything which can give them work, unless it be farming their land, which they cultivate with their own hands. Even by this one occupation that they have, they cannot obtain a life's sustenance, because there is no place to sell the corn they harvest. If they want to go outside the province, besides the danger from savages, their expenses soar so high, that they have nothing left. On the other hand, if they want to sell in the presidios, the captains do not want to buy, even though the Marqués de Casafuerte has given regulations for the captains to buy at the price of three pesos to supply the presidios. The reason why the captains do not buy from the Islanders is the fact that the missionaries sell corn at two pesos, since they have no expense in harvesting it. The Indians of the missions are obliged to work for the missionaries and cultivate the fields, but the settlers are unable to get the Indians for work in their fields even though they pay them. In view of this, would Your Excellency order those captains, especially Captain Don Gabriel Costales to buy the corn they need from these citizens who are ready to sell at two pesos, which is a very moderate price.

Also, my parties feel the disadvantage of not being able to obtain from the missionaries permission for the Indians to work in their fields, though they would be paid in cash for their work. The missionaries have put a stop to all communication between the Spaniards and the Indians; they also prevent the Indians from cultivating the fields of the Spaniards. . . .

Since my parties also suffer continuous damage in their fields from the cattle of the missions, though the fields are fenced in, would Your Excellency give orders so that these cattle do not enter the fields of the Islanders; also, because their animals and horses are harmed, would Your Excellency command Captain Don Joseph de Urrutia to see to it with all care that the citizens suffer no harm in themselves, in

"Memorial of Father Benito Fernández, 1741," *Southwestern Historical Quarterly*, vol. 79 (January, 1979): 274–276. Copyright Texas State Historical Association. Reprinted with permission.

their fields, nor among their cattle and animals? For all that has been here requested, may a penalty be imposed to insure observance, and the needed dispatch
be issued and sent to Captain Urrutia with a penalty attached to enforce it; and may
the writings I have presented be returned to me, as they are needed by my parties?
Therefore, I ask Your Excellency that after the presentation of these writings or
provisions, would you give orders as I have requested, and give your decision to
the general auditor?

## 2. Father Benito Fernández Refutes the Canary Islanders' Complaints, 1741

The hardships and labor, which the families have endured since the first days of
their arrival, are ordinary ones which human nature must put up with in all parts of
the world; compensation is had by obtaining help from others who are in the same
difficulties in this Kingdom of New Spain. The lands given by the King our Lord
were opened and cleared, and they vie in richness with lands in the rest of the world.
The land was fertilized already and a great supply of running water was ready to
be drawn. This work had been done previously by the soldiers and settlers. During
the time the Islanders were building their homes, they lived with the citizens and
soldiers. With help from the royal treasury they were decently clothed and were
supplied with implements, seed, and other needed items. To no one did they pay tax,
nor do they now pay tribute to the King our Lord; a few extortions took place, but
they were common in the entire province. There is war with the Apache Indians; and
problems that cause war in Europe are met with. These problems loom large but are
far less than the problems caused by hostile Indians in these regions. And so the
notable discomforts and hardships which (as the Islanders say) they suffer, are, or
seem to be, those of delicate women rather than those of manly men, who are called
the first founders and settlers of a villa in the vast province of Texas. . . .

If the citizens of the Villa San Fernando would work together to build a new
church (whose walls are already almost finished, for they had more than two years
to do this and the wood was cut [for them]), without doubt the building now would
be complete and they would not have to ask the royal treasury to pay all the expenses. It is not true to say that they were ready to work together and give personal
labor to build their church, for, as I have said, there is not much more to do to finish
it, and the soldiers and citizens are not refusing cooperation in doing what they can
in that construction, if only the families would divide the work and would not engage in quibbling and walkouts that end up in untruths.

The attorneys say that the only work the families have to maintain their livelihood is farming. If this is true, then the Islanders are lazy, for their fields are full of
undergrowth. When the King our Lord gave them the land, it was clean and cleared.
Since it is not just to accuse them of the crime of laziness, for then the purpose of
His Majesty in bringing them to this province from the Islands would be frustrated

"Memorial of Father Benito Fernández, 1741," *Southwestern Historical Quarterly,* vol. 79 (January,
1979): 277–278. Copyright Texas State Historical Association. Reprinted with permission.

with rising cost for the royal treasury, it must be stated that the families do not have only one kind of work, that of farming, for many of them roam about. In truth, the families of the Canary Islands could not exceed sixteen, and those who are only farmers are least in number. It is a fact that one of the attorneys is not a farmer; he is the high constable; neither are Señor Francisco Arrocha, Señor Antonio Rodríguez, Dionis [Manuel de Niz?], and others [farmers]. Señor [Antonio] Santos works more at bricklaying than at farming. The three Leales are more merchants than farmers. One of the Islanders is a carpenter and four are soldiers. The breeding of cattle, raising vegetables and fruit, and making cheese do not bring exceptional profit in these regions. And so the attorneys do not speak well in saying that the only work of the families is farming their lands.

They also say that in this province one cannot engage in trade and so it is necessary to be employed only in the work of farming. They ought to cite the family of the deceased Don Miguel Núñez and of Joseph Antonio Rodríguez, citizens, as also the high constable, an Islander, who maintain themselves quite comfortably by trading; there are others who maintain a livelihood by trade alone. And so it is not true to say that in the province there is no trade nor that one cannot be sustained by this work but that all are forced to the hard work of farming. . . .

The missionaries do not allow the Indians to work for outsiders not because of personal interest but to safeguard the spiritual and temporal welfare of the Indians and to reach the goal set by His Majesty and the Most Excellent Lord the Viceroy. And that goal is to have the Indians, after their conversion to the holy faith, form a new settlement for the Crown, where the new children and subjects live as comfortably as they can (this is what our royal monarch desires). . . .

. . . These Indians of the missions (as said before) are born in the forest and do not do the work which civilized life brings with it; now they work in their own pueblos with great moderation and even this means great hardship for them and some Indians leave the mission for that reason. If these Indians would be obliged to do a day's work to keep alive and clothe themselves, it seems certain that they would draw back and revert to the full freedom of the forest and live only to hunt and in complete liberty. . . .

Every day the missionaries see to it that the Indians of all ages and conditions of life recite the Christian Doctrine and by this gentle influence gain good knowledge; at the same time the missionaries go on explaining the sacred mysteries. This could not be done if the Indians were day laborers; they could not then be maintained as they are now cared for at the mission; nor could they attend catechism instruction regularly. The missionary thinks it best for the Indians to form their pueblo leisurely and attend daily catechism and not be forced to work every day. Besides—the planting done in the missions and all the work is performed by the community. Only the Indian who is a Christian and is strong enough to take care of the old, the infirm, and the non-Christian unfamiliar with work, is capable of becoming a day laborer. When these Indians become day laborers, they and their wives and children maintain themselves with difficulty. If those who can work daily are working for the Islanders, then the others in the mission would necessarily die, for no planting would be done in the mission. Not only would the Indians suffer hardship, as was said, but the rest of the province would be forced to go to the granaries of the Islanders and buy food at rising prices, which is the purpose of the petition presented to the higher tribunal of His Excellency by the attorneys for the families. That this would be so is very evident. In each mission there is only one corn field and only one granary for all the Indians and beyond this there is no planting done, neither by the missionaries nor by anyone else. This would be ascribed then to them, to the missionaries, and to their own interests; in the end no mission would plant and products could be sold at the price desired by the Islanders. I spoke to Señor Juan Leal, one of the lawyers, and made the same remark to him. He replied that it was not his intention to hinder the planting done by the Indians but only that they should not sell corn that is left over at the regular price. But this is what they intend in their dubious claim, which I hold to be unjust in both Spains, for it is completely opposed to natural reason. These Indians are settlers and natives; the Islanders are settlers and foreigners. . . . The King our Lord wants and commands that the natives live a civilized life and go clothed and walk in our holy Faith. Means are not wanting for the Islanders to clothe themselves. It seems to be something beyond reason to expect these pueblos of Indians to give out goods they need themselves for clothing, and other items needed to live a civilized life and establish their pueblos. It is something beyond an irremediable crime to begin to think that the King our Lord brought from the Canary Islands men who thought to justify such injustice to the natives. And so the claim of the lawyers made that they found things unreasonable is contrary to what our royal monarch wants and commands.

### 3. Father Gaspar José de Solís Praises the Productivity of Indians at the San José Mission, 1768

The condition of this mission of Señor San Joseph de San Miguel de Aguayo, as I saw it in the inspection which I made personally in this year of 1768, is as follows: it is so pretty and well arranged both in a material and in a spiritual way that I have no voice, words or figures with which to describe its beauty. The structure consists of a perfect square of stone and lime, each side is two hundred and twenty varas long and has a door; there are towers in opposite corners, each one guarding its two sides. The dwellings of the Indians are built against the wall from five to six varas in length and four in width. Within each there is a little kitchen of four varas in length, a chimney and loopholes which fall on the outside for defence against the enemy; there is an arched granary of stone and lime, [and] three cannon; there is a work-shop where woolen blankets and very good cotton and woolen cloth is woven. They make a great deal of the latter. They have a carpenter shop, an iron shop, a tailor shop, a furnace in which to burn lime and brick, and an irrigating ditch so large and carrying so much water that it seems like a small river, and it has a great number of fish in it. This canal waters many fertile fields, all of which are fenced in for more than a league. In these fields they have sown corn, brown beans, lentils, melons, water-melons, peaches, sweet potatoes, Irish potatoes, sugar-cane. From all of these things they take large and abundant harvests, so that this mission

"Diary of Fray Gaspar José de Solís, 1767–68," *Southwestern Historical Quarterly,* vol. 35 (July, 1931): 50–52. Copyright Texas State Historical Association. Reprinted with permission.

gives food to others, and to the presidio of San Antonio, Bahía del Espíritu Santo, San Saba, the Orcoquisac and Los Adais. It has a garden in which they grow all kinds of vegetables and many fruit trees, especially peaches, one now and then of a pound in weight, little more or less.

Although this mission does not actually have a church it is building a very adequate one of stone and lime in the shape of an arch which serves as a church. Some of the closed arches of the *portales* of the dwellings of the ministers are of fair size. They are sufficient for all of the offices that are necessary. The jewels of silver, the sacred vessels, the large cup of the *custodia,* the ornaments and all things pertaining to the Divine Worship, are good and neatly arranged. Its baptismal font, its shell, and small vials for the Holy Oil are made of silver, also small vessels for the Holy Water and hyssop are of silver. This mission has from ten to twelve leagues of ranch that is called El Atascosa, where there are about ten droves of mares, four droves of burros, about thirty pair, and about fifteen hundred yoke of oxen for plowing. It has all of the tools, such as rakes, plows, hoes, sticks, axes, varas and all that are necessary; and about five thousand head of sheep and goats.

The Indians take care of all of this without the necessity of having white people to look after it and administer it. The same Indians serve in the work-shop, in the carpenter shop, the iron shop, the tailor shop and the quarry; in short for all that is to be done in the mission. They are industrious workers and very skilful in every thing; they serve as mule drivers, stone-masons, cow-herders, shepherds and in short do everything, since they do not employ any one for anything who does not belong to the mission.

The nations among whom this mission of Señor San Joseph and San Miguel de Aguayo was founded, in the year 1716 or '17, by the Minister Reverend Father Friar Antonio Margil de Jesús, are the Pampoas, Mesquites, Pastias, Camamas, Cacames (Tacames), Canos, Aguastallas and Xaunaes. Between young and old of both sexes, there are about three hundred and fifty men advanced in years, learning and experience; and of these skilled in managing arms there are about one hundred and ten, forty-five of whom are armed with guns, sixty-five with bows and arrows, lances and other arms. All the Indian men and women are very well trained in civilized customs and christianity. All of them know how to pray the christian doctrine and the mysteries of our Holy Faith; all speak the Spanish language, except those who came from the forest when grown and who have remained untamed and wild, but all know how to pray and have been baptized. Most of them are skilled in playing on the guitar, some on the violin and others on the harp. All have sonorous voices, and on Saturdays, each 19th day and the feast days of the Christ and the Most Holy Mary they take out their rosary, singing with four voices, soprano, alto, tenor and bass, being accompanied with the corresponding instruments, and it is glorious to hear them. . . .

All of the Indians, both men and women, know how to sing and dance after the manner of the white people from the land outside, and perhaps with more skill and beauty; they are all decently dressed, each having two suits, one for work days and another better one for feast days. The Indians are not ugly, and the Indian women are comely and very graceful, except one now and then who is surly and lazy. The Indian men occupy themselves with the work that is to be done. The old men make arrows for the soldiers; the young Indian women spin and untangle the wool and sew; the old women spend their time fishing in order that the Fathers may eat; the boys and girls go to school and pray in their turn.

Although the mission is so cultured, following the inclination that the Indians have for their *mitotes* at times when the Fathers are careless, the men and the women go off to the woods and dance the *mitotes* with the pagan Indians. This is carefully watched for, and those who are caught are punished severely. They all have their beds in high places with their large warm blankets of cotton and wool, woven in the work-shop of the mission, their sheets and blankets, and their buffalo hides which serve them as a mattress. In short the Indians of this mission are so well trained in civilized life and so cultured that the Indians from the outside, who are among white people, and for a long time have been reduced and settled, will need time to become like them.

## 4. Father Miguel de Molina Describes the Attack on the San Sabá Mission, 1758

I certify fully and swear upon my word as a priest that shortly after sunrise . . . a furious outburst of yells and war cries was heard outside the gate of the enclosure. It seemed to come from the distance of a musket shot in the direction of the fords of the river, which at that point flows northward. Soon afterward, some of the men and women of the Mission cried out that the Indians were upon us. I immediately went to the church to warn the Father who was starting to say his Mass, of what was going on, and to advise him, in view of the state of affairs, not to continue. He followed my advice, removing his sacred vestments, but remained in the church.

I returned very quickly to the quarters of the Father President, where several persons had taken refuge, while others had sought safety in various buildings and offices, for a great horde of Indians, firing their muskets, had surrounded the stockade and houses. The barbarians took note of our precautions and our preparations for defense, and they found out too that the gates were not open and that it would not be easy to carry out their evil designs without effort or risk, as they had supposed. Therefore they resorted to offers of peace and friendship, which they made from outside the enclosure, some in the Castilian language, and some by means of signs and gestures.

They succeeded in convincing Corporal Ascencio and another soldier, the son of Juan Antonio Gutiérrez and the two soldiers entered the quarters of the Reverend Father President to inform us of the good will and peaceful intentions of the Indians. The Corporal assured us that the promises of the Indians were genuine, and that he recognized them as members of the Texas, Tancague, Vidae, and other nations from farther inland, with whom he had had experience on many previous occasions.

Thereupon the Father President went out into the courtyard. I accompanied him, filled with amazement and fear when I saw nothing but Indians on every hand, armed with guns and arrayed in the most horrible attire. Besides the paint on their

Paul D. Nathan, trans., Lesley Byrd Simpson, ed., *The San Saba Papers: A Documentary Account of the Founding and Destruction of the San Saba Mission* (San Francisco: John Howell-Books, 1959), 84–91. Copyright Southern Methodist University Press. Reprinted with permission.

faces, red and black, they were adorned with the pelts and tails of wild beasts, wrapped around them or hanging down from their heads, as well as deer horns. Some were disguised as various kinds of animals, and some wore feather head-dresses. All were armed with muskets, swords, and lances (or pikes, as they are generally called), and I noticed also that they had brought with them some youths armed with bows and arrows, doubtless to train and encourage them in their cruel and bloody way of life.

As soon as the wily enemy became aware of the confidence we placed in them, many dismounted and, without waiting for us to unlock the gates, opened them by wrenching off the crossbars with their hands. This done, they crowded into the inner stockade, as many of them as it would hold, about 300, a few more or less. They resorted to the stratagem of extending their arms toward our people and making gestures of civility and friendliness. When I noticed that many chieftains had approached with similar gestures, I advised and persuaded the Father President to order that they be given bundles of tobacco and other things they prize highly. This he did most generously. I myself presented four bundles to an Indian who never did dismount and whom the others acknowledged as their Great Chief. He was a Comanche, according to the barbarians themselves, and worthy of respect. His war dress and his red jacket were well-decorated, after the manner of French uniforms, and he was fully armed. His face was hideous and extremely grave.

When I gave him the four bundles of tobacco, he accepted them cautiously, but with a contemptuous laugh, and gave no other sign of acknowledgment. I was dis-concerted at this, all the more so because I had already seen that the Indians, heed-less of their promises of peace, were stealing the kettles and utensils from the kitchen, and the capes of the soldiers. They also took the horses from the corral, and then demanded more. When they were told there were no more, they asked whether there were many horses at the Presidio. The Fathers and soldiers told them that there were indeed many horses at the Presidio, as well as equipment and supplies of all kinds—a reply we thought expedient to make them fully aware that nothing was lacking for the defense of the Presidio. When we asked the cunning enemy whether they intended to visit the Commandant at the Presidio, they replied that they did, and asked us to give them a note to him. We did not consider this request inoppor-tune, but rather thought it might be an effective way of clearing the Mission of the enemy, for they still had it completely surrounded and were causing great damage by their thievery, as they boldly ransacked all the buildings and offices.

The Father President decided to give them the paper, which was taken by a chieftain of the Texas Nation, who went to the corral and took one of the remaining horses, the personal mount of the Father President, saying he needed it to take the note to the Presidio. When the Father President objected, he took up his musket and aimed it at the horse, whereupon the Father let him keep the horse and resumed his conversation with several Indians, who were telling him about the state of affairs in the Texas country, concerning which the Father, having visited there, had some knowledge. All this while the barbarians persisted in their hostile actions, surround-ing, searching, and looting the various buildings.

Meanwhile, other Indians were talking with me and my companions, trying to convince us that they had no intention other than to fight the Apaches, who had killed some of their people. They asked whether there were any at the Mission; but, since the enemy had already declared their desire to kill Apaches, we had managed to shelter and conceal [the latter] in the quarters of the Father President, the entrance to which was protected by a constant guard of soldiers.

I further certify that, a short time after the departure of the Texas Indian from the Mission post, he returned with a large number of his followers, saying that he had not been allowed to enter the Presidio and that three of his companions had been killed and another wounded with knife cuts. To which the Father President and I answered that he must have approached the Presidio with too large a party and they must have behaved badly; that, if he wished to go again, the Father President would go with him. He replied that he would do so. With this decision the Father ordered the horse saddled that had been left for him, and another for a soldier.

The Father President and the soldier Joseph García mounted in order to accompany the Indian. I observed the Father President looking for the Indian chief who was to go with him, but without finding him; nor was he to be seen among the rabble that thronged the courtyard. Therefore the Father President started toward the gate to look for him outside the enclosure; but, as he approached the gate, a shot was heard and the said Father President cried out. At once other shots were fired at the mounted soldier, and then began a cruel attack against all, and thus I became fully convinced of the treachery and falsehood of the enemy and my suspicion of evil intentions on their part was confirmed. I was now certain that the story of the crafty Texas chieftain about the killing of his Indians was a lie and a snare. I managed to escape to the quarters of the Father President; others did likewise, and still others sought refuge elsewhere. I also assert that, at the very moment the Father President and the soldier Joseph García were shot, [the Indians] set raging fires on all sides of the stockade, where they had provided themselves with ample supplies of firewood. All this I and the other refugees saw through the loopholes in our room. Therefore I believe—indeed, I am sure—that they had been planning and preparing their violence from the start, and that they began it as soon as they had the wood ready, the buildings reconnoitered, and the roads occupied. It is my opinion that their number exceeded 2,000—an estimate I made by observing for more than half an hour the space they occupied while carrying on their trickery and mischief.

From our closed room we fired through loopholes prepared in advance and thus defended ourselves until after midday. The Indians busied themselves meanwhile with pillage and plunder of the provisions stored for the Apaches who were to be settled at the Mission. They were confident that the fires they had set in and around the Mission post would consume us all without any further effort on their part. Therefore they became careless and afforded us the opportunity to make our way to a house next the church, because our former quarters were already burning. But our move was discovered by the enemy, who again attacked us with shots and fed the fires they had previously set, so that we had to flee once more. We went into the church itself, which was less badly ruined, although it too was on fire. There we remained until past midnight, when all of us escaped except Juan Antonio Gutiérrez, who could not on account of a serious wound in the thigh. . . .

The number and resourcefulness of these enemies of religion, divine and human, is very great, and the inhabitants of this region cannot be converted, even by the strongest efforts and the best planning, unless the territory between this river and our own settlements is occupied by our troops. For it is likely, if in this case the attackers numbered about 2,000 equipped with at least 1,000 firearms, that in another attack their numbers will be still greater because of the many nations now involved in the war. Intent as they are on robbery and plunder, they will not desist from such activities, nor cease to carry out their diabolic schemes. Therefore I consider it impossible to reduce and settle these Apache Indians along the San Sabá, or for many leagues roundabout, even with the aid of the King's forces; nor will they be pacified by the utmost favor and aid. For having become aware, as they have done, of the evident threat and danger from their enemies, they are certain to try to escape from them, as they are now doing. It is well-known that the home of the Apaches is far away, closer to our settlements along the rivers. I am of the opinion that it would be an inhuman action to try to reduce them to this region, for experience shows that it is not proper or right to subject them to the dread of ill treatment and cruelty by their more numerous and warlike barbarian enemies. Nor is it possible, as is being attempted, to reduce all the Apaches [into Christian settlements].

Although it is only a little more than two months since I arrived at this post, obeying the orders of my College, I have become well-versed in the affairs, events, and actions affecting the Apache Indians and their objections to being reduced and settled in this region. I believe that the strongest reason for their reluctance is dread and fear of their enemies. They have not openly said so, even when given the opportunity, so as not to admit their terror or show their anxiety and fear, for they are well-known to be very proud, haughty, and petulant. I am well-aware that some of them have often admitted their uneasiness to our soldiers. These fears, together with the ice, snow, cold weather, and the continual high winds of winter in this region, make it difficult for them to take care of their horses and other animals, and since we have experienced the cruel and hateful conduct of the enemies of the Apaches, we must give the latter some credence and continue trying to find refuge for them in other parts, where they will be able to support themselves and be less reluctant to accept conversion. This is my unalterable opinion.

## 5.  Retrenchment in the Borderlands: The Rubí Dictamen of April 10, 1768

Let the presidio and town of San Antonio de Béxar remain, . . . because they have been so much expense to the royal treasury, in the conveying of families from the Canary Islands; in the building of a church, which could be sumptuous; in the inducements distributed to the settlers for the provision of tools for their tilled fields, which they neglect, and arms for the service, which they do not perform except at the cost of new inducements from the accounts of the King. Also let the five missions—not composed of Indians native to that spot, but of those brought or extracted from the coast of the Colony of Nuevo Santander and from other, more interior locations to which the missionaries go to do their spiritual recruiting—remain in their pleasant valleys. However, since this settlement is more than a degree

Pedro de Rivera, in Jack Jackson and William C. Foster, eds., *Imaginary Kingdom: Texas as Seen by the Rivera and Rubí Military Expeditions, 1727 and 1767* (Austin: Texas State Historical Association, 1995), 183–185, 196, 197. Copyright Jack Jackson. Reprinted with permission.

farther north than the other presidios placed on a line along the banks of the Rio Grande, it is necessary to take precautions, in the best way possible, against the risks which are presented by its location and distance of more than fifty leagues from the Presidio of San Juan Bautista del Río Grande.

With San Sabá evacuated as has been advised, and with the presidio and the little settlement of Los Adaes (presently being finished off by its own misfortune) extinguished or incorporated into the Department of New Orleans—the extremely unsuitable Presidio of Orcoquizá being withdrawn at the same time to this town [San Antonio] or another location in its vicinity—the town of San Antonio will remain finally the most advanced of our frontier in the province of Texas. . . .

For a greater increase of forces, trade, circulation, and consumption of merchandise and money, it will be convenient that the governor, relieved of the cumbersome care of Los Adaes, should reside in this settlement [San Antonio] adding to it the command of the Presidio of San Juan Bautista del Río Grande, which would then be taken away from that of the governor of Coahuila. Perhaps the governor of Texas will propose to bring the other presidios located on the banks of the Rio Grande, beginning with the presidio at the confluence of this river with the Conchos, in Vizcaya, closer to this settlement of San Antonio, according to the respective distance at which they may then be located. If so, it may be at the cost of moving this Presidio of San Juan Bautista somewhat forward from its present location on the banks of the river in order to shorten and even up the distance from the latter to the aforementioned settlement of San Antonio. . . .

From the Presidio of Los Adaes, distant only seven leagues from the Fort of Natchitoches [of the colony] of New Orleans, it is 240 [leagues] to the town of San Antonio de Béxar, which I have set as the most advanced limit of our frontier; and 200 leagues, approximately, to the Presidio of La Bahía, the last one of our line. For these two lines of communication, which are the only ones frequently used for entering Los Adaes, we have two narrow paths. These we share with the various subdivisions of the coastal Indians, the reduction of whom leaves this transit somewhat open, but not completely free of their petty larcenies. In this whole extension there is not one single settlement of ours to be found, nor should we promise ourselves one for many years, as far as the Mission of Nacodoches, distant forty-six leagues from Los Adaes, where, without there being a single converted or catechized Indian, there has been a friar established since the last entry made by the Marqués of San Miguel de Aguayo in the year 1721.

Next after this mission, on the same route, at a distance of less than twenty leagues, is the Mission of Los Aes, with the appellation of Los Dolores, where two other friars reside in the same inaction, having only one Indian for whom to carry out their ministry. From this mission one comes to Los Adaes, in which—besides the company, the stationing of which costs 27,765 pesos per year—the King maintains another mission with two friars. Frustrated in their principal purpose of converting the heathen, they administer spiritual nourishment to the troops of the presidio and to the small neighboring population of its surrounding farms. These are becoming depopulated by misfortunes and by the scarcity of water, and did not number even thirty families at the time of my review. To the south-southwest of this presidio, at a distance of 120 leagues, is located, among a thousand inconveniences and infelicities, the Presidio of Orcoquizá with its company of thirty-one enlistees.

Here is also an imaginary mission—without Indians, with two missionary ministers, and no citizenry—for it was found to be impracticable, despite the offer to construct it, which the founder and creator of this presidio pledged himself to do.

This region's two presidios, and the stipends for the religious at the four cited missions, are a cost to the King of 44,151 pesos per year. Multiplied by the number of years since their creation, beginning with the twenty-first year of this century [1721], it is a very considerable sum, without our being compensated for this exorbitant expense in any manner at all, either spiritual or political. As to the conversion of the heathen, we will not lose a single Christian, nor even a single neophyte, if the aforementioned four missions are suppressed. And as to the defense of our true dominions, more than two hundred leagues from this imaginary frontier, we shall substitute for this weak barrier one that is being established in a more respectable fashion along the Colorado [Red] and Missouri Rivers by the present governor of that colony [Louisiana], Don Antonio de Ulloa, and thus the communication and transit therefrom to the dominions of this kingdom will be made much more difficult, as the King intends.

So it may be legitimate for me to ask now if, in the abandonment of the presidios of Los Adaes and Orcoquizá, and their imaginary missions, the King will lose the vaunted extension of his dominions, or if he will obtain the saving of more than 44,000 pesos that their [annual] maintenance costs him? Therewith I satisfy this objection, which has seemed to me an essential one.

## 6. Father José Francisco Lopez Advocates Secularizing the Missions in San Antonio, 1792

The first point I make is obvious from the fact that in the sixty and more leagues surrounding these missions of Béjar there is no nation of pagan Indians which can be converted. Those who are at a greater distance to the east, north, and south, cannot be taken out of their land without violence to their nature, without offending the laws of humanity, the pontifical regulations, and repeated decrees of his Majesty, nor has it been possible for the missionaries to win them over by favors and kindness, so that they freely leave their lands and congregate in one of the missions. At different times from 1703 till the present year of 1792 various and costly experiments have been made in vain toward this end.

Secondly, it is evidently true, shown not only by the long time of eighty-nine years since the mission of San Antonio was founded, bur felt also in the trade and communication with those Indians, that although they have not given up entirely the traits that are proper to and inseparable from their natural low way of living and their fickleness, they nevertheless are seen to be more civilized and cultured than many other Indians and pueblos in lands beyond.

Finally, the experience of so many years has taught us that the best fruit we can promise ourselves for the future of these Indians will be only to preserve in them the

"Report on the San Antonio Missions in 1792," trans., Benedict Leutenegger, *Southwestern Historical Quarterly*, vol. 77, no. 4 (April, 1974): 490–497. Copyright Texas State Historical Association. Reprinted with permission.

faith and Christianity they have received, just as it is preserved in the other christian pueblos by the help and preaching of their pastors. But no apostolic increase in spreading the faith can be made among them, and yet this is the proper and special office of the missionaries, to which alone our efforts ought to be directed. . . .

. . . I consider it highly important that without making any changes in the Missions of Espíritu Santo and Nuestra Señora del Rosario de la Bahía, the other four missions on the River of San Antonio be reduced to two by joining Mission Espada to Mission San José, and Mission San Juan Capistrano to Mission Purísima Concepción, both because of the advantage of having the first two on one side of the river and the last two on the other side, and also because the lands and goods are joined in their respective boundaries, and those of Mission Concepción are also adjacent to those of San Juan Capistrano. Thus only two missionaries will be in charge, and they should reside in Mission San José and Concepción, since their churches and the houses for the missionary are larger and better. The other two missions will be pueblos or settlements of visitation [mission-stations]. In this way and by giving over the Mission of San Antonio and the administration of Nacogdoches to the bishop, the holy College can make greater progress in converting the infidels, which is the main objective of its apostolic zeal and the only purpose I have in writing this report. In this way the King Our Lord will be spared new expenses, and our College, without increasing the number of missionaries, will be able to use these five superfluous missionaries for new conversions which, it seems, can be made on the coast of San Bernardo, in Refugio, Brazos de Dios, and Orcoquiza. Thus the faith will be spread in that direction and the aforesaid missions will not be abandoned. At the beginning of their foundations it was judged necessary to have more missionaries, but at the present time they can be adequately maintained by only two missionaries, if the union which I have suggested is accepted.

But one must remember that this is possible only by leaving the administration of temporal affairs to the Indians, by keeping them in their respective pueblos without merging their lands and goods, and by freeing the missionaries from the administration and care of temporalities, so that they will look after only the spiritual welfare of the Indians, who will work for themselves and seek their own well-being. . . .

It is certain that as soon as the Indians receive the goods, they will misuse them, sell them and give them to the Spaniards, and by using up their small patrimony in games, drunkenness, and other vices, they will want more when they return to the house of their Father missionary, asking for help to alleviate their hunger and to clothe them; and when the poor missionary will have to dismiss them from his door in sorrow, not being able to help them sufficiently, even by sharing with them the bread of his own sustenance, he will have to practice patience, charity, and compassion, and will see many of his poor Indians go hungry, naked, and dejected, and exposed to serve the Spaniards to get food. But since these are consequences that will follow from transferring the goods to their awkward management and misconduct, they are also unavoidable conditions which keep the Indians in the natural sphere with all the rest of them. This is neither surprising to the Indians, nor is it proper for the apostolic institute to strive to suspend the course of divine Providence, which in its hidden design maintains all the natives of this America in the condition of the most lowly, humble, poor and abject men.

The most zealous, prudent, and holy missionaries, who have been in these Indies from the beginning of the conquest up to this day, as we know from history and as can be seen in the abundant fruit obtained by their evangelical preaching in all the converted pueblos, thought undoubtedly that they fulfilled their task of preaching and exercised their apostolic zeal by instructing the Indians in the catholic religion, by teaching them to live as Christians, as obedient sons of the holy Church and true subjects of our Sovereign. The true charity, which impelled them to win so many souls, did not influence them to draw the Indians from their natural place of abode, to help them in their bodily miseries, to lift them up from their humble dejection, and to throw on their shoulders the duty of protecting and defending these helpless men, except in so far as these duties were conducive to the teaching and instruction by which they tried to educate them. And when, through the goodness of God our Lord we can say that in these four missions of which we speak our missionaries have now done all the duties imposed by the apostolic institute, having all the Indians in their care (except a few who have come recently) well instructed and nourished in Christianity, and in all that is required by necessity and precept to reach salvation if they want to be saved. We sympathize surely on seeing the miserable state in which they would be left by the surrender of their goods, and we shall be content in having, after all, imitated our venerable predecessors. We shall make known to all who till now have been deceived, and who have entrusted to us the management of temporalities, that we have used them only in so far as they have been conducive to keeping the Indians together and as a help in instructing and teaching them. This, for the most part, has been achieved. . . .

Finally, some could object to this report, claiming that the Indians, should they lack the shelter and protection from the missionary, would abandon themselves and become lazy by not cultivating their land, by leaving the missions, and some perhaps would join pagan nations to make war against us, tired of the heavy yoke of Christianity and apostatizing in great numbers from the faith and thus lose their souls. But just as the pastor, the preacher, the confessor are not responsible for these and greater willful evils committed by bad Christians because of temporal discomfort and not because of lack of instruction and teaching, neither can the apostolic missionary be held responsible for the fatal results that come to the bad Indians of his mission because of the lack of material things. In truth, if the Indians have not apostatized up to this day and have remained in the mission, submitting to the yoke of Jesus Christ after so many years of instruction, if this has been due to the temporal comfort which they have had under the protection of the missionary, little or nothing has our apostolic institute achieved. This is not easy to believe when we see that the more unskilled Indians of these missions, with the exception of one or the other, have received more instructions than many other pueblos in lands beyond. Thus if perchance they are lost, we can tell them what God told Israel: *perditio tua ex te*. These Indians will perish . . . because of the evil inclination which prompts all evil Christians to permit themselves to be carried to perdition. Although the missionaries must deplore their perdition, it is not their task to try to remedy the situation by means of material help. Otherwise, charity would compel them to care for the widows, orphans, helpless men and women, who perhaps would not be given to so many vices, if the help of clothing and food would be given to them as it is given to the Indians.

## 🌟 E S S A Y S

The following two essays examine the problems and challenges of community build-ing on Spain's northern frontier, each from a different perspective. In the first essay, Gilberto M. Hinojosa, an historian at the University of Texas at San Antonio, focuses on the mission system in Texas, which was modeled after the Franciscans' long tradi-tion of Indian conversion in Mexico and South America. Contrary to the widely held view that the Franciscans were primarily dedicated to the goal of assimilating native groups into Hispanic society, Hinojosa argues that the monastic orders of Texas sought instead to build separate utopian communities, and for the most part abandoned inte-gration as a long-range goal. For almost a century, the Franciscans endeavored to build permanent, self-sustaining communities; ultimately, however, economic and demo-graphic pressures led to the absorption of the missions into the larger community of San Antonio.

In the villa of San Antonio, the same need for self-sufficiency resulted in a very different set of solutions. As Jesús F. de la Teja, an historian at Southwest Texas State University, argues in the second essay, the region's limited resources tended to erode social divisions based on race and caste. Rejecting the long-held view that the Isleños represented a traditional ruling elite over the San Antonio community, de la Teja argues convincingly that the town's small size and remote position on the edge of Spain's north-ern frontier required a significant level of cooperation among San Antonio residents.

## Self-Sufficiency and the San Antonio Missions

### GILBERTO M. HINOJOSA

### Forces of Exclusivity in Mission Life

Although certain facets of mission life seemed to encourage the eventual integration of the Indians into Hispanic colonial society, overall the padres strove to build and maintain communities that were completely separate from the neighboring settle-ment of San Fernando. In the missions natives were to become acquainted with farming and grazing and certain crafts, gain some fluency in the Spanish language, and adopt selected cultural traditions. The overriding goal of the friars was, after all, to settle the Indians and inculcate in them the Christian faith and the moral virtues it required, all very important elements of Spanish society and culture. However, accul-turation of the natives was not absolutely essential to the functioning of mission pueblos and the fulfillment of the friars' goals. As for assimilation of the Indians into the Hispanic society of San Fernando, it does not appear to have been seriously considered. Quite the contrary, the work and life in the missions and the building programs directed by the padres were designed to create permanent communities completely separate from the other institutions on the frontier. The survival and de-velopment of the missions for almost a century attests to the strength of those ideals of segregation and independence.

Gilberto M. Hinojosa, "The Religious-Indian Communities," in Gerald E. Poyo and Gilberto M. Hinojosa, eds., *Tejano Origins in Eighteenth Century San Antonio* (Austin: University of Texas Press, 1991), 68–82. Copyright © 1991. By permission of the University of Texas Press.

A dispute in 1736 between the missionaries and the governor in San Antonio concerning a bridge over the river that separated Mission San Antonio de Valero and the town-presidio settlement exemplifies this commitment of the friars to build and maintain separate communities. The bridge had been built by the Indians under the direction of the padres to facilitate mission business with the presidio, but no sooner had the crude span been set up than settlers and soldiers began using it to visit the Indian pueblo for personal reasons. This unrestricted access to the mission interfered with the scheduled work, the teaching of crafts, and catechism and prayer. Some of the intruders allegedly cheated the neophytes out of food and household goods or stole these outright. Supposedly the soldiers also slaughtered mission cattle, indulged in public drunkenness, and molested native women. To prevent these disruptions and abuses the missionaries removed the beams that served as a bridge. Thereupon the settlers and soldiers affected by this action took their objections to the top provincial authority, Carlos Franquis de Lugo, who eagerly jumped into the fray on their side. Without hesitation the governor brazenly ordered the missionaries to send some Indians to help reconstruct the bridge. The friars refused, but the soldiers forced a handful of natives to carry out the governor's wishes nonetheless. The padres retaliated by posting a guard in front of the mission, an action that enraged Franquis de Lugo. Set on resolving the conflict personally, he dashed across the river, forced his way into the mission, and confronted the religious superior in his cell, threatening him with his cane. The missionary stood his ground, however, and, although the bridge remained, the friars discontinued the tradition of allowing settlers and soldiers to worship in the mission chapel.

The bridge story is illustrative of the friars' attempts to control all interaction between the natives and all others and to protect mission property. Fray Benito Fernández de Santa Ana observed that, while presidiales and townspeople could trade with the mission residents, these outsiders should not be allowed to enter the Indian pueblo or even talk to the natives unless supervised by a missionary. By the same token, intruders and squatters on mission lands were to be assessed the stiff penalty of 200 pesos and evicted. The maintenance of two distinct societies was critical to the functioning of the friars' institutions. Indeed, as padre Mariano Francisco de los Dolores y Viana reminded the governor, strict separation of Indians and Spaniards was decreed by the laws of the realm.

As prescribed by the friars, life and work within the mission walls was directed to the exclusivity and permanence of those institutions. The friars set out to teach the Indians to farm and graze livestock and to build suitable dwellings, but they did so at the most elementary levels. The evidence suggests that the missionaries utilized the neophytes mostly in work gangs that provided unskilled manual labor. Bolstered by supply trains which brought a variety of finished or nearly finished goods to the missions, the padres could direct the energies of the residents to clearing the fields, constructing the irrigation canals, and erecting the buildings needed in the pueblo. Occasionally some Indians took up butchering, tanning, tailoring and sewing, smithing, carving, and sculpturing. Most frequently, however, Spaniards or mestizos from the villa or from central Mexico were in charge of these skilled tasks, while the natives were engaged in the labor-intensive functions that ensured the subsistence, profit, and long-range endurance of the missions.

These overriding objectives interfered with goals directed to the acculturation of the natives, such as teaching the Spanish language. The padres did prefer their own mother tongue over Indian dialects which lacked the terms for the new tools and crops and, most importantly for the abstract concepts of Christianity. But teaching Spanish to the natives proved to be more difficult than learning the Indian languages. The use of a Coahuiltecan dictionary-catechism in the missions bears this out and in fact suggests that the padres even attempted to establish a Coahuiltecan lingua franca among the natives. To have carried out an efficient acculturation program as their ideals called for, the friars would have needed to have started each mission with only a few Indians, as one friar advised, and increased their numbers only gradually. But that process would have impeded the construction projects, which involved many workers, and learning Spanish did not appear to be as important for missionization and Christianization as did the work habits and moral behavior fostered by a settled village life.

The friars had, in fact, directed substantial efforts in the early years to Hispanicizing the Indians, but these endeavors were thwarted by their own manpower limitations. Ideally one of the two friars stationed at a mission was to devote himself entirely to teaching the new language, Spanish customs, and Christian doctrine and morals, but, given the relatively large number of Indians, this was hardly sufficient for effective cultural change. Consequently the friars demanded that some mission families send their young boys to reside in the monastery wing in order to imbue them with the European world view, values, and traditions. By midcentury, when widespread commitments drained available personnel and only one priest was assigned to each mission, the friars deemphasized cultural endeavors and at times even spiritual ideals and placed more attention on the "temporalities" in order to guarantee the primary goal of institutional survival.

The building program reflected the self-sustaining impulse pervasive in the missions. Generally the first structures erected after a mission's founding were makeshift, temporary jacales (mud and stick, thatched-roof huts) because the padres wanted to ascertain the location's suitability and because priority was given to clearing the fields and digging the acequias, undertakings that required a couple of decades to complete. However, small stone churches were built shortly after a permanent site was selected. Typically these structures were converted into other uses once the major projects were well on the way in the 1740s and construction began on bigger churches and on conventos (monasteries for the friars). In the following decade storage buildings and workshops were erected. Later, stone houses were built for the residents, and the pueblos were enclosed. Within these fortresslike villages the friars then expanded the churches and conventos, impressing residents and visitors alike with the success of the mission enterprises. From their pulpits and offices the padres directed mission life and operations, fully confident that their institutions would always form important, separate communities in the area.

Even serious demographic changes did not alter for a long time the direction of these institutions towards exclusivity. When a decline in the mission population became evident in the 1780s, the friars shifted construction priorities from the addition of decorative features in the churches to the expansion of utilitarian structures such as mills, granaries, and workshops. Most of the buildings had, in fact, been erected previously, in the early period which coincided with population peaks (from the 1740s to the 1770s).

During those years, and indeed since their foundation in the 1720s, the San Antonio missions had averaged more than 150 residents, having at times as many as 260 (in one exceptional year Mission San Jose reported 350 Indians). But in the mid-1770s the population of each institution declined by 50 to 100 natives. Then, in the late 1780s, it dropped precipitously, reaching the lowest marks after 1792, approximately when partial secularization began. In those twilight years the still physically imposing structures housed very few Indians (from twenty-seven to forty-five residents each). However, given the more than sixty years of sustained relatively high populations and strong support from the interior of the colony, the mission communities stood apart and independent from the other institutions in San Fernando.

This trend towards creating insular communities, so evident in the drive for mission self-sufficiency and in the physical barriers, minimized the need for inter-action between Indians and the soldier-settlers and town dwellers. Consequently the movement of acculturated natives to San Fernando—if, in fact, it was ever intended—appears minimal until the end of the century. The number of mission Indians marrying outside their racial group was inconsequential. The mission system was simply not designed towards making integration a reality. Indeed, contrary to prevailing historical interpretation, the padres did not, until the very end, contemplate the demise of their institutions and full assimilation of the natives into the Hispanic society. Throughout most of the century the letters and reports of the missionaries never expressed a desire for a fully integrated society. Quite the opposite, the padres' words and actions attest to the hope of permanent, separate towns. Up until the 1790s the friars launched new building programs, continued to consolidate their institutions, and even made efforts to expand their landholdings. These mission complexes, with prominent churches and conventos, reflected a large-scale, somewhat utopian, plan to create distinct Indian communities directed by the friars—a re-creation of the centuries-old República de Indios common to central Mexico.

The independence of the missions could not be sustained indefinitely, however. Along with the pull towards exclusion, the system contained internal pressures directing it towards integration. Furthermore, external forces, such as governmental policies and economic and social developments beyond the control of the padres, interfered with mission objectives. The friars themselves also had a change of heart, or at least of interest, in their work in Texas, and this also weakened the intrinsic in-stitutional drive for autonomy. Consequently by the end of the century the missions were shorn of their corporate status and secularized. Lands were deeded to residents and opened to settlers, while the religious duties of missionaries were turned over to the diocesan clergy. The dissolution of these once-separate religious entities broke down the barriers to their becoming a part of the larger Béxar community.

To a certain extent, the seeds of the dissolution of the missions were evident in the very foundation of the province. The padres had never been able to imple-ment their goals in East Texas, where large groups, such as the Hasinai, who lived on isolated farms, proved "insolent" and "obstinate," resisting the padres pressures to congregate them. For a time the missionaries were heartened by the number of deathbed baptisms (it appears that the Indians who were seriously ill hedged their bets on the hereafter by availing themselves of both Indian and Spanish rituals). Eventually, however, since the padres were unable to procure the military support to create the necessary social structure for conversion, they became disillusioned with their work among these Indians and retreated to the San Antonio River valley.

The Béxar "way stations" quickly became the core religious settlements from which missions for the large northern Indian groups were planned and launched. However, these ambitious new efforts failed. The Comanches, the Wichitas, and other northern tribes were prospering in their commerce with the French and remained beyond direct Spanish control throughout the colonial period. When Spain did try to bring the Norteños (Nations of the North) into its sphere in the mid-1700s, the Crown adopted a policy of trading with these natives rather than attempting to settle them. For geopolitical reasons, the government also refused to assist the missionaries in reducing and Christianizing the Apaches. Still, in the face of these failures and constraints, the padres never questioned their strategy for evangelization; rather, they continued to be committed to their vision of creating permanent Indian villages.

Unable to evangelize the larger native groups, the missionaries contented themselves with recruiting from small Central-Texas and coastal bands, a limitation which was an asset in many respects but which ultimately proved to be the undoing of the missions as separate communities. Small bands of Coahuiltecans and Karankawas, which were easily recruited and controlled, were the most likely candidates for missionization. Having a dozen or so of these groups in a mission provided an element of stability to the work force because, if one band left with all its members (as happened on one occasion at San José), the entire pueblo's population would not suffer significantly, and the construction projects could continue without interruption. This strategy of depending on small bands worked well until the last quarter of the eighteenth century. At that time, these groups no longer subjected themselves to the padres' demands for social and cultural conformity to Spanish ways and turned instead to the Norteños to improve their lot. The lack of neophytes to replenish mission populations would in time spell the end of those institutions.

Recruitment was critical for the survival of the missions since the Indian towns were unable to increase, or even maintain themselves, numerically. At Valero, for example, during the sixty years for which data is available (which includes mostly years with high populations), births outnumbered deaths only in five years. On the average, for every seven babies born annually, ten persons died. The disproportionate death rate was directly linked to a high infant and childhood mortality. Over two-thirds of 319 Indians baptized and buried at Valero died during the first three years of life. Only fifty reached what may have been considered adulthood, twelve years of age. Of these, only fourteen lived into their twenties, and a mere eight into maturity (thirty to forty-five years).

Various factors contributed to the overall low rate of natural increase among mission Indians. For example, there were considerably fewer women than men, a phenomenon that resulted from the numerous deaths of mothers while giving birth and possibly from female infanticide. This latter practice appears to have been a common form of population control among Indians facing limited resources, and the natives may have continued this custom even after missionization. Fatal accidents, murders, and deaths at the hands of attacking Indians contributed minimally. Plagues also took their toll on the mission residents because of the Indians' lack of immunity to European diseases, but the data suggests that deaths occurring during epidemic years were not considerably higher than usual. It appears, however, that the most important contributor to the high death rate was the generally poor health of the mission Indians.

According to the missionaries, the Indians themselves were to blame for this condition. Fray Mariano observed that common illnesses were fatal to the natives because they ate unwholesome foods gathered in el monte (the wilderness) nearby. Supposedly these had debilitating effects on all, especially on nursing infants. Moreover, the padre noted, the Indians were usually dirty and did not use purges, sweating, or other accepted remedies, relying instead on wild herbs for their cures. They also engaged in " sexual excesses" which resulted in the spread of venereal diseases. Fray Mariano also complained that the natives did not adequately protect themselves from the elements. They appeared more concerned with eating and roaming than with building comfortable houses and weaving in order to clothe themselves. While Fray Mariano's observations may reflect a strong European prejudice, they may also suggest that the missions were not attracting physically strong bands and that life in the mission did not substantially alter the lifestyles of those Indians or make up for the poor health in which they arrived.

Indeed, mission life itself may have had limited effects on the Indians and may have, in fact, exacerbated the Indians' health problems. Undoubtedly the nutrition of mission residents improved—sufficient corn and beef appears to have been distributed year-round, and vegetables and fruits were available seasonally—but the very change of diet may have affected the Indians' health. Whereas, during the roaming days the natives had eaten a large variety of roots, fruits, nuts, wild game, and fish, their mission fare was largely starches (corn) and red meats (beef). Then, too, while their caloric intake may have been suitable for moderate activity, Indians were made to work in different and more demanding work patterns than their previous tasks required. The highly supervised life of labor, prayer, and learning was probably very stressful for these once-free natives, and constant psychological pressures, we now know, are as injurious to health as any virus or malnutrition.

Besides being more constrained and crowded in the Indian pueblos than they had been in el monte, the natives actually did not enjoy adequate housing in the missions. The construction program had concentrated on clearing the fields, digging the acequias, and building the churches and storage rooms. Indeed, as late as 1776, Fray Benito Fernández de Santa Ana admitted that some "Indian houses . . . [were still] impermanent and rickety, their household goods . . . [were] few, not much more than a metate [corn-grinding stone], a skillet, and a thin mat on which to sleep." Despite benefits natives received by accepting the padres' invitation, life in their new surroundings apparently did not improve their health significantly and may have worsened it. Whatever the cause, the troubling reality was that mission populations had serious difficulties maintaining themselves.

Indian resistance to demands of mission life also contributed to the demise of those institutions. The task of changing the natives' cultural outlook and lifestyles was a major challenge for the missionaries, who continually had to exhort and pressure backsliding neophytes to comply with their new religious responsibilities. The padres' charges did not easily give up their sexual mores or their mitotes (nature-dance rituals). Under the observant eye of friars and soldiers, the mission Indians were marched to church like schoolchildren to attend mass, sing the alabanzas (hymns), and fulfill the Easter duty of receiving the Sacrament of Penance. In the confessional the neophytes rarely volunteered any information of their offenses, acknowledging them only when prodded and excusing their reticence by claiming "You did not ask me" or "I thought it would upset you." When pressed to admit sexual sins, they usually denied these were willful acts. But the missionaries were not discouraged by their limited success in changing the natives. They merely doubled their efforts of persuasion and force, including greater supervision and the use of whips and stocks to discipline those remiss in their obligations.

Chafing under the monastic work-and-prayer routine, the Indians resorted to passive protests such as carelessness and work slowdowns or desertion. "It takes four of them to accomplish what I can do alone," grumbled one missionary, adding that the simple task of cleaning the sanctuary lamp would not get done unless the priest supervised the assignment. The neophytes often claimed ignorance or lack of dexterity as reasons for not performing their duties, or they feigned illnesses, a strong sign, according to one friar, that they were preparing to desert. Indeed, when pressed too severely to comply with the work rules or to change their ways, many residents simply ran away. "These Indians are not difficult to convert," observed one padre, meaning that they could be easily persuaded to enter the mission, "but they are bothersome [to keep]," thus explaining the large population turnover in the missions.

Desertions aggravated the demographic crisis. Unbeknownst to the natives, in joining the missions they had entered into a binding legal commitment, equivalent to receiving baptism, matrimony, or Holy Orders, or to taking religious vows. Thus, when the Indians abandoned their new homes to go back to their old habitats, they became "apostates," individuals rejecting the faith or abandoning the monastery. Usually soldiers accompanied the padres to ensure the return of escapees, but the padres did not receive this assistance after midcentury. By then the government had adopted a policy of befriending and trading with the larger Indian nations and refused to alienate them by demanding they surrender mission runaways who had joined them. This inability to retrieve escapees, coupled with a decline in new recruits, dealt a heavy blow to the missions.

The demographic crisis led to the greater contact between the religious institutions and the town. Despite restrictions, mission residents had, in fact, always traded with the soldier-settlers and interacted with them in various other settings. On occasion Indians accompanied the presidial companies on military campaigns against warring Indians, and some soldiers were almost always stationed in the missions because their assistance, as Fray Mariano observed, was indispensable "in order to direct and instruct them [the natives] in their work, and to subdue, teach, control, and punish" them. Without the soldiers' help, another missionary advised, the Indians would revert to their inherent laziness, neglect to plant and harvest the corn crop, and commit all kinds of excesses and crimes right under the very roof of the mission. Furthermore, unless closely watched, the natives might just run away. Two or three soldiers sufficed to maintain order and work because their presence reminded the Indians that the entire presidial company was nearby. Towards the end of the century the influence of these few presidiales increased as fewer natives remained in the missions.

The same happened with other outsiders. The padres had always hired some five to ten vecinos (townspeople) in each mission for skilled crafts. As the Indian population declined, additional outsiders worked at the missions in order to keep them economically viable. The vecinos residing in the Indian pueblos increased not only in absolute numbers but also in proportion to the declining native population. For every one Spaniard, mestizo, or mulatto living in the missions, there was an average of twenty-eight Indian residents in 1772, thirteen in 1792, and only six in 1806. As the proportion of vecinos from San Fernando working and living in the missions grew, their cultural impact on the remaining natives increased, a situation that hastened secularization. Thus, while the friars had at first insisted on segregation, in time they increasingly brought into the missions more soldiers and townspeople who unavoidably acted as agents of acculturation for the mission residents, and by the end of the century, the once-Indian pueblos came to resemble Hispanic villas in practically everything save legal status.

A downturn in the economic fortunes of the missions further weakened those once self-sufficient institutions and threatened their very survival as separate communities. In the 1750s San José had been a thriving enterprise with approximately 2,000 sheep and 3,000 head of cattle, bustling carpentry and smithing workshops, active looms where the Indians made most of their clothing, a full granary, and a sugarcane storage building. But "now [three decades later] everything, everything is turned around," lamented one of the friars. "There are few Indians and many hired hands. There are few cattle, and even so, no one to sell them to because there are too many grazers. Even if the missions had an abundance of corn, there are too many farmers, so many that some have abandoned agriculture. The resources that [once] sustained the missions have [now] been reduced." As this observer suggested, part of the padres' problem stemmed from developments outside the mission walls. By the second half of the century some of the town dwellers from San Fernando had not only secured their agricultural resources but also had expanded their cattle-grazing enterprises. These ranchers had found a market for their herds in Louisiana and prospered from this trade, openly disregarding the royal decrees prohibiting it. The padres, who relied on subsidies from the Crown, could not act so boldly. Furthermore, as the roundup of wandering, unbranded cattle spread throughout the river valley down to the coast, the rancheros competed vigorously with the missions, with the result that the institutional herds dwindled considerably and the padres found themselves in a serious economic impasse. . . .

Yet these economically depressed and demographically small communities continued to control immense properties, resources that the town dwellers and the soldiers quite naturally wished to exploit. To achieve that goal, the latter urged the government to end the corporate privileges of the missions and allow them (the settlers) to exploit the lands and herds used by so few residents, who were only technically "Indian."

The Crown agreed in part with the petitioners and applied to the mission herds the same tax it collected on all mesteños (unclaimed livestock on the range). The vecinos avoided the assessment on their herds by various appeals and by ignoring the decree altogether, but the padres apparently lacked the stamina for the long, drawn-out legal battle and, more importantly, did not have the manpower to compete with the settlers in the race to round up the remaining livestock. By the end of the century the herds were largely depleted, and the issue of the tax became moot, even though the padres repeatedly blamed the decline of the missions on the levy on mesteños. Faced with all these difficulties, the friars found the governing of the missions an all-consuming task. Overseeing the farming and grazing operations took so much time, one padre complained, that he had little time for the doctrina (religious education for the natives) and even for his own prayer and meditation. Maintaining the missions was draining the resources available locally and straining the order's assets and its ability to raise funds for the San Antonio institutions. Furthermore, the expulsion of the Jesuits from the Spanish Empire in 1767 had left an enormous vacuum in the northwestern frontier, a vacuum the Franciscans were called upon to fill. Facing this new challenge and disappointed by their ventures in Texas, the friars willingly agreed to partial secularization in the 1790s and all but abandoned the province in the early 1800s.

When the missions were secularized, title to many of their lands was turned over to individual residents. Some Franciscans remained to minister spiritually to their former charges, but the mission era was over. The institutions that had dominated the San Antonio valley from the early 1700s to the 1780s experienced a rapid decline in the last decade of the century. Originally established with the idealistic goal of "civilizing" and Christianizing the natives, the missions developed into separate Indian pueblos but ended as Hispanic communities barley distinguishable from the neighboring town of San Fernando. At the close of the century that villa, its military establishment, and the missions merged into the settlement later known as San Antonio.

In a sense, the closing of the missions and the distribution of lands was in keeping with the friars' long-range goal of integrating the Indians into the Hispanic society, and to that extent the missions accomplished the purpose for which they were founded originally. In reality, however, the friars had not operated their institutions with this end in mind. They had set out to establish segregated Indian towns with certain corporate legal rights and a very distinct character. Many aspects of mission life were geared towards self-sufficiency, permanence, and the exclusion of external influences. Nevertheless, critical demographic patterns beyond the control of the padres worked against the survival of those autonomous Indian pueblos. In this regard, the problem of desertions was aggravated by minimal or nonexistent population growth, leaving the missions dependent on continued immigration, which ceased once the economically dependent bands found a better alternative in joining the Norteños. When the prospects of recruiting neophytes at the earlier levels faded, it then became impossible to justify the cost and personnel involved in maintaining those large enterprises for so few residents. Challenges by the townspeople and the government resulted in the termination of the autonomous corporate status the missions had enjoyed. By the time this happened, those institutions were already changing. Vecinos and soldiers had moved into the missions, and Indians had been drifting into the civilian town. Thus the once-separate Franciscan-Indian pueblos merged with the larger community of the villa of San Fernando de Béxar.

# The Making of a Tejano Community

## JESÚS F. DE LA TEJA

To understand community development in San Antonio during its first eighty years of existence, it is first necessary to agree on the meaning of the term "community." At its simplest, community is synonymous with place, and historians often use the two terms interchangeably. Community, however, can be defined as the product of shared attitudes, experiences, and cultural traits without reference to place. . . . In a broader perspective, community may also embody shared space and shared experience. . . .

To analyze the development of the San Antonio community, one must examine its origins. In 1718 Governor Martín de Alarcón led an expedition that resulted in the founding of San Antonio. Crown officials perceived the new settlement as a multifaceted project, not a purely military one, even though San Antonio's primary function remained strategically defensive in nature. The presidio was to serve as a way station between the Río Grande missions and the Louisiana-border outpost of Los Adaes and to protect area missions as they began the work of bringing the natives into the Spanish fold. The original settlement also was to be the nucleus for a Spanish town. With these purposes in mind, Alarcón was instructed to recruit civilians with families, not just soldiers. Accordingly, many of Béxar's first residents came to settle as much as to protect imperial interests. They were not professional soldiers but frontiersmen recruited in Coahuila and Nuevo León to tame the wild new province.

Isolation and shared purpose made the forging of community ties natural. The presidio formed the settlement's core, and all inhabitants, military and civilian, looked to its commander for political and judicial as well as military leadership. Families, many of whom were interrelated, lived in a compact settlement, civilians and military residing side-by-side. The soldiers shared many responsibilities with the handful of civilians—farmers, muleteers, construction workers, and assistants to the missionaries. As their enlistments expired, soldiers became civilian settlers, but their roles remained much the same. In essence, the settlement consisted of families facing the dangers, duties, and adventures of the frontier.

Mission records at San Antonio de Valero bear witness to the emergence of this early community. Beginning in 1720, marriages between soldiers and the daughters of soldiers occurred frequently, and those unions produced the first generation of native Bexareños. From its founding in 1718 to 1731, forty-seven couples married and 107 children were baptized at Mission Valero. Some weddings were performed for people from other Texas outposts, but most of these marriages helped forge communal bonds within the new settlement.

The small, isolated population's need for unity required a loosening of caste boundaries. Although evidence indicates that San Antonio's original population was ethnically mixed, it was not a matter to which the settlers paid undue attention.

Jesús F. de la Teja, "Indians, Soldiers and Canary Islanders: The Making of a Texas Frontier Community," *Locus: An Historical Journal of Regional Perspectives on National Topics,* vol. 2, no. 1 (Fall 1990), 84–96. Reprinted by permission of the author.

In registering the civilian population, the missionaries at Valero did not indicate an individual's ethnic status unless he or she was considered Spanish. For instance, there is evidence of only one interracial marriage at San Antonio, that between a Spanish settler and an Indian servant of the commander. Even when a groom was identified as the son of a Spaniard and an Indian, he was listed as Spanish, not mestizo, in the marriage register. Such obfuscation permitted descendants of racially mixed individuals to "pass" as Spaniards, the preferred social category in the larger colonial society. Clearly, the society that developed at San Antonio between 1718 and 1731 reflected the unifying influence of a number of factors. The necessities of survival in a frontier outpost, including protection from hostile Indians and production of food, drew the settlers together both physically and in terms of shared experiences.

In order to understand fully the impact of the Isleños upon this nascent community, and vice versa, it is important to realize that prior to 1731 the settlement at San Antonio bore little resemblance to an organized town. In the absence of a civil government, the presidial commander was the sole source of political authority. The arrival of the Canary Islanders in 1731 and the creation of a formal municipality altered this situation and completely disrupted the existing community.

Concerns for defending northern New Spain's mining districts led the crown and the Council of the Indies to consider various plans for fostering the growth of Texas, including the settlement of Old World families. Although a proposal to recruit Canary Islanders was first presented in 1719, not until February 14, 1729, did a group of ten Isleño families arrive at Veracruz en route to the San Antonio area. Preceding the new settlers were directives from the viceroy of New Spain to Juan Antonio Pérez de Almazán, captain of the presidio, which explained the economic, social, and political position that the Islanders were to occupy. Among other things, the instructions required that the immigrants be settled apart from the existing presidial community in order to avoid conflict. It was this part of the instructions that Captain Almazán felt compelled by circumstances—Apache hostilities, availability of irrigation water—to set aside.

Following procedures established by the Laws of the Indies, which codified Spanish colonial law, each of the Isleño founders of the new town, called San Fernando de Béxar, received a promotion to the rank of nobility, carrying with it the title of hidalgo. Only the hidalgos had the right to hold places on the town council and to serve in other town offices, including sheriff (*alguacil*) and official secretary (*escribano de cabildo*). In addition, only these town officers could elect local alcaldes to administer justice.

Along with the foreordained political power, the Isleños received daily allowances during their first year in Texas, and they were provided with the seeds necessary for raising their first crop. Each family also received a quantity of sheep, goats, cattle, and horses. In addition to the already cleared agricultural land given to them, Captain Almazán distributed among the Isleños other arable land as well as town lots on or near the main plaza of the new town. All of this was done to the exclusion of San Antonio's creole settlers.

The privileged position of the Canary Islanders produced considerable rancor as well as numerous petitions and appeals to Spanish officials by the original settlers and, in response, by the Isleños. It worked, however, to define more clearly the status of the various groups within the new, complex social structure that evolved in the town's first years. At the bottom of the emerging hierarchy stood the soldiers and a growing number of *agregados,* who took advantage of the availability of town land to build homes and start gardens and orchards. Most of them lived in *jacales* that stood in marked contrast to the stone homes of the wealthy few. In spite of vice-regal efforts to regulate prices for goods going to the presidos, venality in the system kept most soldiers on the edge of poverty. The same was true of the agregados. With nowhere else to go, some became servants or day laborer, others lived off the products of their gardens and small herds. By 1745 the agregados numbered forty-nine families, all of whom chafed under the predominance of the Canary Islanders.

Above the mass of agregados were a smaller group of civilian settlers, some of whom had been present at San Antonio's founding in 1718 and had amassed enough property to be of some consequence. Along with the handful of craftsmen, blacksmiths, carpenters, and tailors, at least a few farmers and ranchers made a living supplying the presidios of Texas with horses, cattle, and maize. Besides those who received grants from Governor Manuel de Sandoval, or had not been affected by Captain Almazán's redistribution of lands to the Islanders, a group existed with enough wealth to buy out completely some Isleños. It is from this group of men that the first non-Islander officeholders came.

The Canary Islanders stood at the top of the hierarchy but were not a monolithic block. Their bid to exclude anyone else from power was not a unified effort. As the settlers observed, there were deep divisions within the Islander group. Having been brought together in the Mexico City suburbs from at least two different parties, the immigrants were ill prepared to work together. The many civil and criminal proceedings between Islanders, the lawsuits between them and the missionaries, presidio commanders, and governors, all attest to the absence of community in the years following the Canary Islanders' arrival. One frustrated official commented in 1745: "The fourteen families from the Canary Islands complain against the reverend fathers of the five missions, against the Indians that reside therein, against the captain of the presidio, and against the other forty-nine families settled there, so that it seems they desire to be left alone in undisputed possession. Perhaps even then they may not find enough room in the vast area of the entire province." He might well have added that the Isleños complained about each other, too. By the mid-1740s one Islander had renounced membership in the cabildo and departed the province, four had sold their farmland to non-Islanders, and four others had enlisted at the three Texas presidios.

Despite the divisions, social, economic, and political realities broke down the barriers that separated the group and fostered the process of community building. In the year the immigrants arrived, ritual kinship bonds began to be forged. For example, María Rosa Padrón, the first Canary Islander offspring born in San Antonio, had Gertrudes Flores de Valdez, a creole settler, as godmother. More important, the Isleño group's small size determined the inevitability of intermarriage with other settlers. For example, Joseph Leal and Ana de los Santos arranged marriages for their nine children, all of whom were born in San Antonio, to non-Islanders. Among the few Isleño offspring who married each other, their children in turn married into creole families. Within four generations in San Antonio, there remained no pure-blooded Canary Islander descendants.

The Isleño population's biological integration was part of a greater process of racial amalgamation common to the Spanish colonial world in general. In San Antonio, as elsewhere in the Mexican north, being "Spanish" was more a function of socio-economic success than ethnic purity. The continual influx of soldiers and their dependents, the incorporation of Hispanicized Indians, and limited opportunity for marriage within one's declared ethnic group contributed to creating a racially mixed community. Fray Juan Agustín Morfi, during his visit to San Antonio in 1777, described the town's leading men, its cabildo members, as "a ragged band of men of all colors."

Economic integration of the two groups quickly took place as the new arrivals needed the expertise of frontier survival possessed by the presidial population. Apart from learning to tend livestock and to fire guns, skills that Captain Almazán said were lacking in the Isleños, the creole settlers almost certainly introduced the newcomers to the variety of native American crops that made up the frontier diet. Not all were suited to agriculture, however, as evidenced by four young Islanders who left their property for military service in the province's presidios. Other Islanders established business ties with the more powerful members of the greater community, the captain, the governor, or the wealthier creole settlers. . . .

Circumstances, particularly geographic isolation and Indian depredations, also prevented the Islanders from remaining aloof and distinct from the rest of the population. San Antonio was over 250 miles distant from the most important avenue of contact with central New Spain, the presidio-mission complex of San Juan Bautista, over 100 miles from the nearest Spanish settlement, La Bahía, and more than 400 miles from the East Texas area of settlement. Remoteness and isolation were even more tangible during periods when the town was cut off from the outside world. Flooding of streams separating Béxar from San Juan Bautista on the Río Grande, as much as hostile Indians, could delay the mail for months. Distance often precluded the arrival of timely assistance in periods of Indian assault. In the summer of 1768, for example, Captain Luis Antonio Menchaca fended off a twenty-two day siege of the settlement without any help from the outside.

Indian hostilities also had much impact on Béxar's development. A principal reason for establishing Presidio Béxar had been to protect Mission San Antonio de Valero from potential Apache attack. And, only two years after San Antonio's founding, the Apaches were committing depredations against convoys, missions, and the settlement. In the 1760s, Comanches joined the Apaches in making life hazardous in Béxar. Attracting new settlers and recruits under such conditions was extremely difficult. As early as 1724, the presidial commander complained that "it is necessary to seek [recruits] outside the province because here there is no population whatever; and some time is needed to court [recruits] and give them some aid in costs besides their salaries, because of the resignation with which they all come to this country." During periods of extensive violence some of the more faint hearted left Béxar with their families, and there were general threats of abandoning the province. Occupation of the countryside, which did not begin until the 1750s because of hostilities, was often interrupted by renewed depredations.

Despite these problems, population increases did occur. Much of San Antonio's growth during the eighteenth century was inspired by direct government action in response to strategic defensive needs. The Islanders' immigration was the first stage in an abortive scheme to create a large, populous buffer province against both European and Indian intruders. The forced abandonment of East Texas with the relocation of the population to San Antonio in 1773 was also triggered by the government's desire to promote Béxar's development as a strategic outpost. In between these two large additions, and as late as 1780, military reorganizations brought soldiers and their dependents to San Antonio as well. Béxar's population grew from approximately 200 in 1726, to 500 in 1750, to 1,350 in the mid-1770s, before stabilizing at about 1,600 in the 1790s. . . .

Economic opportunities had to be taken where found in remote Béxar. Isolation played a crucial role in sensitizing the population to any perceived threats to the presidio, the town's chief source of livelihood, for even without the Indian problem San Antonio would have been only marginally integrated into the colonial economic system. Although regular export of ranching products began in the 1750s, the traffic was of minor importance, and reliance on the presidial market remained overwhelming. In 1756, for instance, the town council accused the missionaries of wishing to destroy the settlement by moving the presidio, even though the friars knew the town was already isolated by distance and numerous rivers and hostile Indians. Complaints about one parish priest's demands to be paid in cash for services focused on the fact that there was little money in circulation and that there was "no place to find it, this being a solitary and commerceless frontier."

With no more than 1,600 inhabitants in the 1790s, San Antonio's people continued to know each other and continued to exercise a number of economic roles, just as they had in the earliest days. Those who had enough land or cattle to provide the local market sometimes became part-time merchants, converting their profits into goods that they sold out of their homes. Almost everyone did some farming, and even the wealthiest residents went into the field on roundups with their sons and hired hands. Presidial service formed an important economic opportunity for local men, although all residents were expected to contribute to the town's defense. Many residents came to San Antonio as soldiers, and their sons followed them into military service. . . .

Shared roles, kinship ties, and the frontier experience tied much of Béxar's population into a dynamic community. The proximity between presidio and town, and the interdependence between the two, slowly fostered a joint identity for many. The term "Canary Islander" passed from denoting a distinct ethnic group to providing an identifying label for much of the town's core population. While two or three of the Islander descendants called attention to their origins in carrying on personal conflicts, it is inaccurate to portray Béxar in the late eighteenth and early nineteenth centuries as beset by racial conflict. Labels used to divide the population into Islanders and original military settlers slowly fell into disuse. These were generally replaced by the interchangeable *primeros* and *principales pobladores,* that is, first and principal settlers. . . .

Eighteenth-century San Antonio was not the static society so often portrayed, neatly divided into an elite of wealthy Canary Islanders and a mass of mestizo peons. In effect, the hierarchy used to describe early divisions of local society must be modified in order to accommodate a new reality which emerged near the end of the eighteenth century. By 1800 one can distinguish in San Antonio two broad social groups. One group was formed by the mass of the population, made up of poor later arrivals, Hispanicized Indians, and poor relations. Above them stood the better-off members of the community, most of whom were descendants of Islanders and original settlers, but also including merchants and a few other later arrivals who climbed to success. From this second group were drawn the ranchers, large-scale farmers, merchants, and politically active townsmen. For most of these individuals, ancestry and relative economic well being combined to provide status within the community.

As a whole, San Antonio in the eighteenth century reflected, in some aspects in magnified form, social trends apparent in greater Spanish colonial society. Distinctions between Indians, mixed races, and whites in Béxar became increasingly difficult to sort out in the course of the century, just as they were in central New Spain. In the colony as a whole, a socio-economic hierarchy was well on its way to displacing increasingly outdated ethnic distinctions as the principal ingredient in social stratification.

This is not to suggest that Béxar's was a caste-blind or egalitarian society. However, distinctions in social position were based not so much on overarching colonial classifications but on considerations deemed important within the local context. In the absence of a large peninsular-Spanish population, the growing antagonisms between American and European Spaniards was absent. There was, however, a growing sense of separate identity, of being a distinct part of the Spanish world, and of having certain rights and prerogatives earned through constant sacrifice on the frontier. Danger, isolation, limited economic development, and strong kinship structures brought the people of San Antonio close together. The forces that demanded unity of action also worked to bring about a unity of society. The very labels used by individuals to identify themselves within local society attest to the forging of a common identity. As the group that could claim Canary Islander descent grew in the course of generations, that identity was subsumed under the broader concept of a Béxar community. In the town council's words, when it argued in 1793 against a governor who did not want to allow relatives to serve concurrently on the body: "Here [we] are all kin, so that if [we] fixed on that, it would not be possible to form a council."

 *F U R T H E R    R E A D I N G*

Felix D. Almaraz, *The San Antonio Missions and their System of Land Tenure* (1988)
Herbert E. Bolton, *Texas in the Middle Eighteenth Century: Studies in Spanish Colonial History and Administration* (1915)
Carlos Castañeda, *Our Catholic Heritage in Texas,* 7 vols., (1936–1958)
Donald E. Chapman, *Spanish Texas, 1519–1821* (1992)
Gilberto Hinojosa, *A Borderlands Town in Transition: Laredo, 1755–1870* (1983)
Jack Jackson, *Los Mesteños: Spanish Ranching in Texas, 1721–1821* (1986)
Gerald E. Poyo, *Tejano Journey, 1770–1860* (1996)
——— and Gilberto Hinjosa, "Spanish Texas and Borderlands Historiography in Transition," *Journal of American History* 75 (September 1988)
Sandra L. Myres, *The Ranch in Spanish Texas* (1969)
Jesús F. de la Teja, *San Antonio de Béxar: A Community on New Spain's Far Northern Frontier* (1995)
Robert S. Weddle, *San Juan Bautista: Gateway to Spanish Texas* (1968)
———, *The San Saba Mission: Spanish Pivot in Texas* (1964)
David J. Weber, *The Spanish Frontier in North America* (1992)

CHAPTER
4

# Populating Texas During the Late Spanish and Mexican Periods, 1810–1835

*As Anglo Americans began to push westward across the continent in large numbers after their revolution against Great Britain, they began to look covetously at the broad expanse of land to the west owned by Spain. Although the term "Manifest Destiny" would not be coined until the mid-1840s, many Americans, particularly in the southern states, developed a firm ideology of territorial expansion by the early nineteenth century. The outbreak of Mexico's War for Independence in 1810 prompted many Americans to seek to exploit the vacuum of political authority in Spain's northern territories. Filibusters—privately financed and organized military expeditions—entered Texas in 1812 and 1819 with the goal of wresting Texas away from Spanish rule.*

*In an effort to fend off the aggressively expansionist United States, Spain initiated an immigration program designed to bring settlers to Texas. It embraced the principle that "to populate is to govern." The colonization policy, which Mexico continued after winning its independence from Spain in 1821, was designed to attract an international community consisting of Mexican, American, and European immigrants. During the 1820s, however, the overwhelming majority of emigrants to Texas were citizens of the United States who possessed the resources necessary to take advantage of Mexico's offer. Mexico, then, was obliged to resort to the dubious expedient of populating Texas with settlers from the very country whose territorial ambitions its land grant policy was designed to thwart.*

*Initially, the settlement program went forward smoothly as migrants established farming communities and became peaceful, law-abiding citizens of Mexico. The first signs of tensions came in 1825, when American empresario Haden Edwards attempted to remove from his East Texas land grant Mexican families who had inhabited the region for several decades. When the Mexican government rescinded his grant, Edwards declared the region in a state of rebellion and proclaimed the Fredonian Republic. The revolt proved short-lived, and Haden Edwards and his brother Benjamin soon fled to New Orleans. An investigation of conditions in Texas undertaken by Mexican official Mier y Teran soon afterward presented the government with a disturbing picture of a rapidly growing Anglo American popula- tion that displayed only nominal loyalty to Mexico. As a result, the Mexican govern- ment took steps to block further Anglo American settlement in Texas.*

*Were these problems the inevitable result of conflicting and utterly disparate cultures, or were they minor disputes that did not preclude the peaceful settlement of Anglos under the flag of Mexico? Clearly, the Mexican government and many Anglo settlers had widely divergent attitudes about the rights and obligations of citizenship. To what extent did race contribute to the problems that arose between the Anglo American community and Mexico? What role did differences of political and economic philosophy between Anglos and Hispanics play?*

## ⭐ D O C U M E N T S

American filibusters, sometimes acting in concert with Mexican citizens, organized several expeditions into Texas during the early decades of the nineteenth century. Their activities did much to excite the Spanish government's suspicions of the United States. Document 1 is a proclamation issued in Nacogdoches by Bernardo Gutierrez, a Mexican revolutionary who, with Augustus Magee, a former U.S. Army officer, invaded Texas with an army of volunteers in 1812. Although written ostensibly to the soldiers under his command, the document was widely published throughout the southern United States. Its promise of land and other valuable property was undoubtedly intended as an inducement to attract new recruits to the revolutionary cause. The expedition sub- sequently seized San Antonio and declared Texas' independence, but was crushed by a Spanish army in the summer of 1813.

By the mid-1820s, the land grant policy implemented by a newly independent Mexico was beginning to show promising results. Document 2 outlines the terms of settlement in Stephen F. Austin's colony and reveals the empresario's concern that only individuals of upstanding moral character be allowed to settle in Texas. The $12.50 per one hundred acres which Austin charged for surveying and title fees was deemed exorbitant by many colonists, however, and was the cause of considerable grumbling. Document 3 is the Coahuila y Texas Land Colonization Law, which offered prospective settlers more than a league of land for a nominal fee, a highly attractive opportunity for American citizens. Life in Mexico's remote northern province was hard for early settlers, as illustrated in Document 4 by the account of Caroline von Hinueber, whose family purchased land in Austin's colony.

Early signs of friction between Anglos and the Mexican government can be de- tected in Document 5, in which the leaders of the Fredonian revolt state their reasons for insurrection. Employing the rhetoric of liberty reminiscent of the American Revolu- tion, the proclamation is a telling example of the way in which Anglo Americans of the early nineteenth century drew from their political heritage to justify their own economic interests. Although citizens of Mexico, the Fredonian rebels defend their actions on the basis of their rights as Americans.

The Mexican government's response to the Fredonian Rebellion is described in the next two documents. Document 6 is an excerpt from the report of Manuel de Mier y Teran, commandant general of Mexico's Eastern Interior Provinces, who undertook a fact-finding tour of Texas in 1828. Mier y Teran's concerns that Mexico was in danger of losing Texas prompted the Mexican Congress to pass the April 6 1830 law, cited in Document 7, which prohibited further immigration from the United States.

The law prompted a firestorm of protest, as might be expected, from Anglo American settlers and speculators, whose hopes for reaping rich profits from Texas lands were contingent upon the continued migration of Americans into the region. But these former citizens of the United States were not the only residents upset with the new law. As Document 8 reveals, tejano landowners were also anxious to find ways to promote economic development. Complaining of Indian depredations and prolonged neglect by the government in Mexico City, the San Antonio ayuntamiento also argued in favor of a liberal immigration policy in order to bring prosperity to the region.

## 1. Mexican Revolutionary Bernardo Gutierrez Promises Spoils of War to Army Volunteers at Nacogdoches, 1812

*Fellow soldiers and volunteers in the Mexican cause.*

I desire you to receive from me the tribute of my private feelings, and also as the agent of my Mexican brethren, my warmest and most sincere thanks for the activity, zeal, promptitude and courage that you have shewn in the obedience of those orders which you have received from your officers, acting under my command; and I flatter myself with the idea that the line of conduct which you have hitherto observed will be continued in, to the *discomfiture of tyrants,* to the *emancipation* of the *Mexicans,* and to the complete success of the enterprise you have undertaken, which will crown your exertions with glory, honor and fortune. The consolation of the justice of the cause which you support—of the fame and immortality which awaits your success—the idea that all the civilized nations of the world look on your actions with admiration and good will—the reflection that the future happiness or misery of a large portion of the habitable globe is now in your hands, will, I am certain prompt you on, and shew your enemies and the enemies of liberty, in every part of the world, that the spark which lighted the flame of independence in the northern part of America is not extinct in the bosoms of the descendants of those who fought, bled, and prevailed over tyrants; and will at the same time establish, beyond a possibility of doubt, your individual right to that liberty, for the attainment of which for others, you have volunteered your lives, your property, and sacrificed all your social connections.

You are now, fellow-soldiers, in peaceable possession of one of the out-posts established by European tyranny, the more effectually to enslave the oppressed Mexicans. This possession has been obtained without bloodshed on your part, from the consciousness in the minds of the cowardly instruments of tyranny, that they never can prevail in arms against the brave, free, and independent citizens of the United States of America.

This pusillanimity of conduct in the engines of despotism has left in your power, in a weak and defenceless state, all the citizens of the post which you have gained. Your conduct to those citizens has met my entire approbation. It has done honor to yourselves, as men and as soldiers; and if continued, will be more powerful than all the arms in the world—as it will conquer their minds and force them (should they ever feel a doubt) to declare that you are to them as friends, as brothers and as protectors against those who have held them enthralled for ages past, in bondage the most ignominious. From the information which I have received from different quarters, I flatter myself that your stay in this place will not be long—that

"Revolution in Mexico," *Niles' Weekly Register,* vol. III, 104, October 17, 1812.

your numbers will increase to a sufficient extent and enable you to seek the tyrants in their strong holds, and force them to acknowledge this long enslaved country as a free, sovereign and independent government. When this event takes place (and the time is not far distant) you are to look for the reward of your toils, dangers, sufferings and difficulties, in the enjoyment of all the rights of honored citizens of the Mexican republic, in the cultivation of those lands, which I pledge myself will be assigned to every individual among you, or in the pursuit of wealth and happiness, in such way as your inclinations may point out to you. To those who desire it, the right of working or disposing of any mines of gold, silver, or what nature soever, which you may find will be given. The right of taming and disposing of the wild horses and mules which roam unclaimed over an immense tract of country, within the limits of the Mexican republic, will be common to all of you.—The surplus of property confiscated, as belonging to those who are inimical to the republican cause after the expences of the expedition are paid, will be divided amongst you—and those powerful and almost inestimable services which you will render, will further be rewarded from the public treasury of that government which you will have so materially aided in erecting.

JOSE BERNARDO GUTIERREZ.

## 2. Stephen F. Austin Seeks Settlers of "Unblemished Character," 1823

The terms on which Settlers are admitted into the Colony forming by Stephen F. Austin in the Province of Texas are as follows—

No one will be received as a Settler, or even be permitted to remain in the country longer than is absolutely necessary to prepare for a removal who does not produce the most unequivocal and satisfactory evidence of unblemished character, good Morals, Sobriety, and industrious habits, and he must also have sufficient property to begin with either as a farmer or mechanic besides paying for his land—No frontiersman who has no other occupation than that of a hunter will be received—no drunkard, nor Gambler, nor profane swearer no idler, nor any man against whom there is even probable grounds of suspicion that he is a bad man, or even has been considered a bad or disorderly man will be received. Those who are rejected on the grounds of bad character will be immediately ordered out of the County and if the order is not obeyed they will be sent off under guard and their property seized and sold to pay the expences, and should forcible resistence be made by them, the guard will be ordered to fire on and kill them—

Those who are received as Settlers will get one league of land if so much is wanted, to be chosen by the emigrant, which land will cost at the rate of twelve Dollars and fifty cents p$^r$ hundred acres payable in cash or Spanish Cattle or negros on receipt of title, which will be in full for surveying, title deeds, recording, and all other charges.

Terms of Settlement, Eugene Barker, ed., *Austin Papers,* Annual Report of the American Historical Association for the Year 1919, Volume 1, Part I, 705.

The above only applies to men of families—Single men will be examined as to character more particularly than men of families and ten of them must unite to form a family and they will be entitled to one League of land to be divided between them. An exception will be made to this rule in favor of single men who bring a considerable capital into the country all such will be ranked as a family and draw on League—

A person who brings in a large capital and who has a large family will draw more than a league should he wish it. The head of each family will be held personally responsible for the good conduct of every member of his family.

The Roman Catholic is the established religion of the Mexican nation and the law will not allow of any other in this Colony—October 30 1823—

## 3. The Coahuila y Texas Immigration Law of 1824

DECREE, No. 16.—The Congress, assembled for the purpose of forming the Constitution of the Sovereign and Independent State of Coahuila and Texas, desirous of augmenting by all possible means the population of its territory; of encouraging the cultivation of its fertile lands, the raising of stock, and the progress of arts and commerce, in exact conformity with the Act on which the Constitution is founded; with the federal Constitution; and the basis established by the Sovereign Decree of the general Congress, No. 72; decree as follows:—

**Law of Colonization**
OF
*The State of Coahuila and Texas.*

ART. 1.—All those foreigners who in virtue of the general law of the 18th August, 1824, by which security for their property and persons is offered in all the territory of the Mexican Nation, may be desirous of establishing themselves in any of the towns of Coahuila and Texas, are hereby permitted; that State invites and proposes to them so to do.

ART. 2.—Those who shall do so, far from being in any way molested, shall be secured by the local authorities of the above mentioned towns; which shall allow them full liberty to engage in whatever honest calling may suit them, as long as they duly obey the general laws of the nation, and the ordinances of the State.

ART. 3.—Whatever foreigner at present resident in Coahuila and Texas, may determine on settling there, shall make a declaration to that effect, addressed to the municipal authorities of the town in which he is desirous of fixing his residence. The municipal authorities then shall bind him by oath, which he shall make, to abide by and obey the general Constitution, and that of the State; to observe the Religion as stipulated by the former; and in a book (the register of foreigners) which shall be kept for that purpose, his name and those of the members of his family, if he has any, shall be set down; noting the country from whence he comes,

H. P. N. Gammel, ed., *Laws of Texas* (Austin: Gammel Book Co., 1898), 1822–1897, 1:99–105.

whether married or single, his employment; and he having taken the requisite oath, shall be considered thenceforward, and not before that time, a fellow-citizen.

ART. 4.—From the very day in which any foreigner becomes a citizen, agreeably to the preceding article, he may denounce any land belonging to the State, and the proper civil authority being under the obligation of passing to the government, for its approbation, the petition thus made on this subject, shall award it to him; as also to every native of the country, acting in conformity with the laws on that subject.

ART. 5.—The foreigners of any nation and the native Mexicans may undertake to form new settlements on lands belonging to the nation, and even if belonging to individuals under the circumstances stated in Art. 35; but the new settlers, who may demand admission into the nation, must prove, by certificate from the authorities of the place from whence they came, that they are Christians, and also the morality and propriety of their conduct.

ART. 6.—Whatever foreigners shall arrive at a period at which the sovereign general Congress shall have prohibited, as it may do after the year 1840, or previously as regards the natives of any one nation, shall not then be admitted; and all those who shall arrive within the time allowed them, agreeably to this article, shall, nevertheless, be subjected to such measures for the security of the federation as the supreme government may adopt, regarding them without prejudice to the object of this law.

ART. 7.—The government shall take care that no settlement be made within 20 leagues of the boundaries of the United States of North America, and 10 leagues along the coast of the Gulf of Mexico, except such as shall obtain the sanction of the Supreme Government of the Union: for which purpose it shall forward to it every petition on that head, made by Mexicans or foreigners, adding to it whatever remarks it may deem expedient.

ART. 8.—All projects for establishing colonies, on which one or more persons may offer to bring, at their own expense, 100 or more families, shall be presented to the government which, if it finds them agreeable to the law, shall approve of them, and immediately mark out to the projectors the lands which they are to occupy, and the number of years allowed them for presenting the number of families for which they have stipulated, under penalty of forfeiting the rights and benefits offered them in proportion to the number of families they shall omit to provide, and the grant shall be wholly annulled should they not present, at the least, 100 families.

ART. 9.—This law guarantees all contracts made between the projectors and the families brought at their expense, inasmuch as they are in conformity with its provisions. . . .

ART. 11.—A square of land, of which each side is one league of 5,000 yards, or, what is precisely the same, 25,000,000 yards of surface, shall be named a lot, and this shall be considered as the unity in counting one, two, or more lots: thus, also, the unity in counting one, two, or more subdivisions shall be 1,000,000 yards of surface, or a square of 1,000 yards each side, which is the measure of one subdivision: the yard used in these measurements shall be three geometrical feet.

ART. 12.—Supposing the quantity of land above stated to be the unity, and a division of the land being made, when distributed into grazing lands and those adapted for tillage by means of irrigation, or not requiring irrigation;—this law grants to such projector or the projectors of plans for colonization, for each 100 families which they convey, and establish in the State, 5 lots of grazing land, and 5 subdivisions, of which at least one-half shall be arable land, not requiring irrigation; but they shall only receive this premium for as many as 800 families, even if they should introduce a greater number; nor shall any fractional number, be it what it may, which does not amount to 100, give them a right to any recompense, even in proportion to its amount.

Art. 13.—If any one or more projectors shall, on account of the families they have conveyed, obtain, agreeably to the preceding article, more than 11 square leagues, the whole of the land shall be granted to them, but they shall be under the obligation of selling the surplus within 12 years; and should they neglect to do so, the proper civil authorities shall do it, selling it at public auction, and delivering to them the net proceeds, after deducting all the expenses attending the sale.

Art. 14.—To each of the families included in a project of colonization, whose sole occupation is the cultivation of the land, one division of land shall be given; should it also breed cattle, it shall receive also of grazing land a sufficient quantity to complete one lot; and if it only breeds cattle, it shall have of grazing land an extent of 24,000,000 superficial yards.

Art. 15.—Bachelors shall on marrying obtain a similar quantity, and those foreigners who marry Mexican women shall have one-fourth more; but all those who are alone, or forming a part of no family, whether they are Mexicans or foreigners, must content themselves with one-fourth part of the above-mentioned portions, nor will any greater quantity be allowed to them, and the allotments will be assigned to them in this proportion.

Art. 16.—The families, and single men, who having performed the journey at their own expense may wish to join any of the new settlements, shall be permitted to do so at any time; and their assignments of lands shall be to each individual the same as those mentioned in the preceding articles; but if they do so within the first 6 years of the establishment of the colony, one more subdivision shall be given to each family, and each bachelor, in lieu of the one-fourth which the 15th Article designates, shall receive one-third part. . . .

Art. 19.—The Indians of all the tribes on the confines of the States, as also those of the wandering tribes in it, shall be received in the markets without demanding of them any duties on account of the traffic which they carry on in the natural productions of the country; and, if thus induced by kindness and confidence any of them should be desirous (previously making a declaration in favor of the religion and institutions) to establish themselves in any of the settlements which may be formed, they shall be admitted, and obtain the same quantity of land as the settlers mentioned in Articles 14 and 15; the natives being always preferred to the Indians coming from a foreign country. . . .

Art. 22—The new colonist shall, as a species of acknowledgement, pay to the State for each lot of pasture land, 30 dollars; 2½ for each subdivision or arable land not irrigated, and 3½ dollars for each one of irrigated land, each in proportion to the kind and quantity of land which has been allotted to him; but the payment of those sums shall not be made in less than 6 years after their settlement, and in 3 equal installments, the first at the expiration of the fourth, the others at the expiration of the fifth and sixth years, under penalty of forfeiting their lands should they neglect the payment of any one of these instalments: but the projectors and military men, mentioned in the 10th Article, are excepted, with regard to those lands which the former have obtained as a recompense, and the latter agreeably to the documents given them by the government. . . .

Art. 24.—The government shall sell to the Mexicans, and only to them, the lands which they may be desirous of purchasing, but shall not allow more than eleven lots to fall into the hands of one individual, and under the express condition, that the purchaser must cultivate the lands which he obtains by these means within 6 years, under the penalty of losing them: the price of each lot, in conformity with the preceding Article, shall be 100 dollars for grazing, 150 for arable not watered, and 250 for irrigated lands.

Art. 25.—Until 6 years after the publication of this law, the Legislature of the State shall have no power to alter it, inasmuch as regards the measurement of lands, the price to be paid for them, the quantity and description of those which are to be granted to new settlers, and sold to Mexicans.

Art. 26.—It shall be considered, that the many settlers who within 6 years from the date of their grant have not cultivated or occupied according to its quality the land which has been granted to them, have renounced their rights, and the proper civil authority shall resume the grant and the title deeds.

Art. 27.—The projectors, and military men, of whom previous mention has been made, and those who have purchased lands, can sell their lands at any time, on condition that the purchaser oblige himself to cultivate them within the period in which the original possessor ought to do so, including also the time which they have been in his hands; the other settlers may sell theirs when they have cultivated them wholly, and not before that time.

Art. 28.—Every new settler from the very day of his settlement can dispose of his lands by will, made agreeably to the present or then existing law, even although he has not cultivated them; and if he should die intestate, the person or persons who inherit his property agreeably to the laws, shall succeed to them under the same obligations and conditions that he held them.

Art. 29.—The lands granted in virtue of this law can on no account be allowed to pass into the hands of religious communities.

Art. 30.—The new settler who shall determine on quitting the State, in order to establish himself in a foreign country, shall be allowed so to do, together with all his property, but in this case shall not retain his land, and if he has not previously sold it, or the sale been effected agreeably to the 27th Article, it shall be again considered as wholly belonging to the State.

Art. 31.—Those foreigners who agreeably to this law have obtained lands, and established themselves in these settlements, are considered from that moment as naturalized in the country, and should they marry Mexican women will be considered to have established a meritorious claim to obtain the rights of citizenship of the State, except, however, in both instances the cases provided for by the enactments of the Constitution of the State.

Art. 32.—During the first 10 years, counting from the day in which settlements are established, they shall be free from every contribution under whatever denomination, excepting such as in the event of the invasion of an enemy. . . .

ART. 33.—From the very day of their establishment the new settlers shall be at liberty to pursue every branch of industry, as well as to work mines of every description. . . .

ART. 34.—The towns shall be founded on the spots deemed by the government, or the person it names for that purpose, most fitting, and for each of them four leagues square shall be designated, which space shall be either of a regular or irregular shape, according to the locality. . . .

ART. 36.—The sites for houses in the new towns shall be given gratis to the projectors of them, as also to artizans of every description those which they may require for their workshops, and they shall be sold to the others at public auction, an estimate of the value being previously made, on condition of the price being paid in three equal instalments, the first in six months, the second in twelve, and the third in eighteen; but every possessor of sites, including projectors and artizans, shall pay yearly one dollar for each one that he holds, and this sum, as also the product of those sales, shall be collected by the municipalities, and applied to the purpose of erecting a church in the town. . . .

ART. 40.—As soon as at least 40 families are united, they shall proceed to the formal establishment of a new town, all binding themselves by oath, taken before the commissioner, to observe the general Constitution, and that of the State, and subsequently the commissioner presiding for this the first time, shall proceed to the election of the municipality.

ART. 41.—The new town whose population amounts to 200 inhabitants shall elect a corporate body, if there be no other established within the distance of 8 leagues, but if there be one it shall be added to its jurisdiction; the number of members of which the corporation is to be composed shall be regulated agreeably to the existing laws.

ART. 42.—A reservation being made in favour of all the enactments of the Constitution of the State, the foreign settlers are permitted to elect and be elected members of the municipal body. . . .

ART. 44.—The government shall send to the head of that department those individuals who in other parts of the State may be sentenced to hard labour as vagrants or for other crimes, in order that they may be employed in making and repairing the roads in Texas. These persons may also be employed in the services of individuals, who shall in that case pay them the requisite daily allowance, and at the expiration of the period for which they were condemned, they shall be allowed as settlers to join any of the new towns, and to obtain the due quantity of land, if by the improvement of their conduct they shall, in the opinion of the aforesaid chief of the civil department, have rendered themselves fit, but they shall not be admitted without his certificate.

ART. 45.—The government, agreeably to an arrangement with the proper ecclesiastical authorities, shall see that the new towns are provided with a proper number of clergy, and agreeably to an arrangement with the aforesaid authorities, shall propose to the Congress the salary which the new settlers are to pay them.

ART. 46.—As regards the introduction of slaves, the new settlers shall obey the laws already established, and which hereafter may be established on the subject.

## 4. Caroline von Hinueber Describes the Hardship of Life in Austin's Colony, 1832

When my father came to Texas, I was a child of eleven or twelve years. My father's name was Friedrich Ernst. He was by profession a bookkeeper, and emigrated from the duchy of Oldenburg. Shortly after landing in New York he fell in with Mr. Fordtran, a tanner and a countryman of his. A book by a Mr. Duhde, setting forth the advantages of the new State of Missouri, had come into their hands, and they determined to settle in that State. While in New Orleans, they heard that every settler who came to Texas with his family would receive a league and labor of land from the Mexican government. This information induced them to abandon their first intention.

We set sail for Texas in the schooner *Saltillo,* [with] Captain Haskins. Just as we were ready to start, a flatboat with a party of Kentuckians and their dogs was hitched on to our vessel, the Kentuckians coming aboard and leaving their dogs behind on the flatboat. The poor animals met a grievous fate. Whenever the wind arose and the waves swept over the boat, they would howl and whine most piteously. One night the line parted, and we never saw them again.

We were almost as uncomfortable as the dogs. The boat was jammed with passengers and their luggage so that you could hardly find a place on the floor to lie down at night. I firmly believe that a strong wind would have drowned us all. In the bayou, the schooner often grounded, and the men had to take the anchor on shore and pull her off. We landed at Harrisburg, which consisted at that time of about five or six log houses, on the 3d of April, 1831. Captain Harris had a sawmill, and there was a store or two, I believe. Here we remained five weeks, while Fordtran went ahead of us and entered a league, where now stands the town of Industry. While on our way to our new home, we stayed in San Felipe for several days at Whiteside Tavern. The courthouse was about a mile out of town, and here R. M. Williamson, who was the alcalde, had his office. I saw him several times while I was here, and remember how I wondered at his crutch and wooden leg. S. F. Austin was in Mexico at the time, and Sam Williams, his private secretary, gave my father a title to land which he had originally picked out for himself. My father had to kiss the Bible and promise, as soon as the priest should arrive, to become a Catholic. People were married by the alcalde, also, on the promise that they would have themselves reunited on the arrival of the priest. But no one ever became Catholic, though the priest, Father Muldoon, arrived promptly. The people of San Felipe made him drunk and sent him back home. . . .

After we had lived on Fordtran's place for six months, we moved into our own house. This was a miserable little hut, covered with straw and having six sides, which were made out of moss. The roof was by no means water-proof, and we often held an umbrella over our bed when it rained at night, while the cows came and ate the moss. Of course, we suffered a great deal in the winter. My father had tried to build a chimney and fireplace out of logs and clay, but we were afraid to

Caroline von Hinueber, "Life of German Pioneers in Early Texas," *Texas State Historical Quarterly,* vol. 2 (October 1898): 227–230.

light a fire because of the extreme combustibility of our dwelling. So we had to shiver. Our shoes gave out, and we had to go barefoot in winter, for we did not know how to make moccasins. Our supply of clothes was also insufficient, and we had no spinning wheel, nor did we know how to spin and weave like the Americans. It was twenty-eight miles to San Felipe, and, besides, we had no money. When we could buy things, my first calico dress cost 50 cents per yard. No one can imagine what a degree of want there was of the merest necessities of life, and it is difficult for me now to understand how we managed to live and get along under the circumstances. Yet we did so in some way. We were really better supplied than our neighbors with household and farm utensils, but they knew better how to help themselves. Sutherland used his razor for cutting kindling, killing pigs, and cutting leather for moccasins. My mother was once called to a neighbor's house, five miles from us, because one of the little children was very sick. My mother slept on a deer skin, without a pillow, on the floor. In the morning, the lady of the house poured water over my mother's hands and told her to dry her face on her bonnet. At first we had very little to eat. We ate nothing but corn bread at first. Later, we began to raise cow peas, and afterwards my father made a fine vegetable garden. My father always was a poor huntsman. At first, we grated our corn until my father hollowed out a log and we ground it, as in a mortar. We had no cooking-stove, of course, and baked our bread in the only skillet we possessed. The ripe corn was boiled until it was soft, then grated and baked. The nearest mill was thirty miles off.

As I have already said, the country was very thinly settled. Our three neighbors, Burnett, Dougherty, and Sutherland, lived in a radius of seven miles. San Felipe was twenty-eight miles off, and there were about two houses on the road thither.

## 5. Anglo Leaders of the Fredonian Revolt State Their Reasons for Insurrection Against Mexico, 1826

Nacogdoches December 25, 1826.

Fellow citizens!

Having assembled at the town of Nacogdoches under the flag of Independence, and consequently in open hostility towards the Mexican United States, we consider it to be due to you, fellow citizens! in common with all the Inhabitants of the Province of Texas, who are alike interested in the destiny of this our adopted country, to explain the motives and causes, which have impelled us to take this bold and determined stand, without first calling upon you to participate in this holy cause.

It was not from any want of respect and consideration for your character and feelings, it proceeded not from an unworthy suspicion of your patriotism and your sympathies for us. No, fellow citizens! We knew you were Americans, the sons of those long departed patriots, who, when their rights were invaded, nobly grasped their arms, and planted the standard of liberty and Independence in our native land.

"B. W. Edwards and H. B. Mayo to the Inhabitants of Pecan Point," December 25, 1826. Eugene Barker, ed., *Austin Papers, Annual Report of the American Historical Association for the Year 1919*, vol. II, Part 2 (Washington, D.C.: Government Printing Office, 1924): 1542–1545.

Having the same confidence in your patriotism and your valor, believing that the sons of America would never tarnish the proud glory of their fathers, even in a foreign land, and that as brothers far from our homes and removed to a land beyond the maternal protection of our native country, we could not doubt your sympathies for us. We could not question your feelings and your judgments in the present aspect of our political affairs. Placed in a situation peculiar to ourselves and impelled by the most serious necessity; our properties daily seized by violence and injustice, our persons violated, our liberties trampled under foot, and ourselves the destined and immediate victims of the Spanish or Mexican bayonets; we have sprung to arms for our safety.

No longer secure in our properties and our lives, and having long since ceased to hope for liberty and justice under this imbecile, this faithless and perfidious Government, we have planted the standard of liberty and Independence for our protection with a firm and solemn resolve to live or perish with it. Self preservation, the great law of nature, is our justification for planting it thus early, and before we could formally invite our fellow citizens to concur with us in this important matter. Not only the threats of those pretty [sic] tyrants here, who have so long trampled upon the rights of your brother Americans, but the official communications of the Government themselves, now in our possession, prove, that we were selected as the victims of destruction, and that a brutal soldiery were soon to be let loose upon us. . . .

Fellow citizens! We need not here recapitulate the lawless and repeated outrages, that too many of our citizens have had to endure. We were enticed from our native country under the promise of important advantages to our families, and by a guarantee of our rights and liberties. We have been basely deceived in all these promises, and we know not now, that we have a valid title to one foot of land in the province of Texas. Lands have been granted and taken away at the mere will and pleasure of a corrupt and prejudiced Governor without any regard to the forms of justice or the rights of the Judicial Department of the Government. Our slaves have been attempted to be taken from us, and even the most favorable issue of that subject, as is now anticipated, would be the ruin of our country and of our every hope and prospect in it.—Military despotism has been substituted for that liberty which was promised as our shield and protection. Our citizens have without notice of a charge against them, been seized by a brutal soldiery, bound hand and foot and dragged into exile or incarcerated in their dungeons at the will of a petty tyrant, and all these things sanctioned by the Government under which we live. Great God! Can you any longer hesitate, fellow citizens! what to do? Did our fathers, who are now no more, hesitate, what to do, when they were oppressed? No, their blood ran in willing torrents upon the altar of liberty, when their rights were invaded. Shall their sons do less? Forbid it Allmighty God!!! What have we to fear in such a contest? What have we to hope from such a corrupt and perfidious Government as this. Shall we sit with our arms folded in fatal security, untill we are bound in chains and slavery? No! fellow citizens! We have nothing to hope for but in our arms. They will guaranty rights, that will not be wrested from us. Let us then join heart and hand in the noble struggle for our liberties. We are the children of the same mother country. We are Americans in a foreign land, groaning under the galling yoke of injustice and oppression. Our fathers in their struggle for liberty contended against the giant of the world. We have to contend against a corrupt and imbecile Government, now tottering upon its own foundation, and ready to crumble into its former ruins.

We for ourselves have no fears of a speedy establishment of our Independence. We have now the means of making *this empire shake to its very centre.* We ask you not to risk your lives and properties with us in this enterprize, unless your own feelings and your own judgments sanction such a cause. The rights and properties of every American and Spaniard will be held sacred, unless he raises arms against us. We will not dictate to you what course you should pursue.—Should you think proper to leave the struggle to us alone, We are nevertheless willing to fight for your rights and security in common with our own. Should we secure the Independence of this country, of which we have not an earthly doubt, you will of course share its blessings with us. We have undertaken this glorious cause with a determination to be freemen or to perish under the flag of liberty. We at least are determined to live or to die like Americans and like the sons of freemen.

## 6. Mier y Teran Fears Mexico May Lose Texas, 1830

. . . As one covers the distance from Béjar to this town [Nacogdoches], he will note that Mexican influence is proportionately diminished until on arriving in this place he will see that it is almost nothing. And indeed, whence could such influence come? Hardly from superior numbers in population, since the ratio of Mexicans to foreigners is one to ten; certainly not from the superior character of the Mexican population, for exactly the opposite is true, the Mexicans of this town comprising what in all countries is called the lowest class—the very poor and very ignorant. The naturalized North Americans in the town maintain an English school, and send their children north for further education; the poor Mexicans not only do not have sufficient means to establish schools, but they are not of the type that take any thought for the improvement of its public institutions or the betterment of its degraded condition. Neither are there civil authorities or magistrates; one insignificant little man—not to say more—who is called an *alcalde,* and an *ayuntamiento* that does not convene once in a lifetime is the most that we have here at this important point on our frontier; yet, wherever I have looked, in the short time that I have been here, I have witnessed grave occurrences, both political and judicial. It would cause you the same chagrin that it has caused me to see the opinion that is held of our nation by these foreign colonists, since, with the exception of some few who have journeyed to our capital, they know no other Mexicans than the inhabitants about here, and excepting the authorities necessary to any form of society, the said inhabitants are the most ignorant of negroes and Indians, among whom I pass for a man of culture. Thus, I tell myself that it could not be otherwise than that from such a state of affairs should arise an antagonism between the Mexicans and foreigners, which is not the least of the smoldering fires which I have discovered. Therefore, I am warning you to take timely measures. Texas could throw the whole nation into revolution.

Allein Howren, "Causes and Origins of the Decree of April 6, 1830," *Southwestern Historical Quarterly,* vol. 16 (April 1913): 395–397.

The colonists murmur against the political disorganization of the frontier, and the Mexicans complain of the superiority and better education of the colonists; the colonists find it unendurable that they must go three hundred leagues to lodge a complaint against the petty pickpocketing that they suffer from a venal and ignorant *alcalde,* and the Mexicans with no knowledge of the laws of their own country, nor those regulating colonization, set themselves against the foreigners, deliberately setting nets to deprive them of the right of franchise and to exclude them from the *ayuntamiento.* Meanwhile, the incoming stream of new settlers is unceasing; the first news of these comes by discovering them on land already under cultivation, where they have been located for many months; the old inhabitants set up a claim to the property, basing their titles of doubtful priority, and for which there are no records, on a law of the Spanish government; and thus arises a lawsuit in which the *alcalde* has a chance to come out with some money. In this state of affairs, the town where there are no magistrates is the one in which lawsuits abound, and it is at once evident that in Nacogdoches and its vicinity, being most distant from the seat of the general government, the primitive order of things should take its course, which is to say that this section is being settled up without the consent of anybody.

The majority of the North Americans established here under the Spanish government—and these are few—are of two classes. First, those who are fugitives from our neighbor republic and bear the unmistakable earmarks of thieves and criminals; these are located between Nacogdoches and the Sabine, ready to cross and recross this river as they see the necessity of separating themselves from the country in which they have just committed some crime; however, some of these have reformed and settled down to an industrious life in the new country. The other class of early settlers are poor laborers who lack the four or five thousand dollars necessary to buy a *sitio* of land in the north, but having the ambition to become landholders—one of the strong virtues of our neighbors—have come to Texas. Of such as this latter class is Austin's colony composed. They are for the most part industrious and honest, and appreciate this country. Most of them own at least one or two slaves. Unfortunately the emigration of such is made under difficulties, because they lack the means of transportation, and to accomplish this emigration it has become necessary to do what was not necessary until lately: there are empresarios of wealth who advance them the means for their transportation and establishment.

The wealthy Americans of Louisiana and other western states are anxious to secure land in Texas for speculation, but they are restrained by the laws prohibiting slavery. If these laws should be repealed—which God forbid—in a few years Texas would be a powerful state which could compete in productions and wealth with Louisiana. The repeal of these laws is a point toward which the colonists are directing their efforts. They have already succeeded in getting from the Congress of Coahuila a law very favorable to their prosperity: the state government has declared that it will recognize contracts made with servants before coming to this country, and the colonists are thus assured of the employment of ample labor, which can be secured at a very low price in the United States. This law, according to the explanation made to me by several, is going to be interpreted as equivalent to permission to introduce slaves.

In spite of the enmity that usually exists between the Mexicans and the foreigners, there is a most evident uniformity of opinion on one point, namely the separation of Texas from Coahuila and its organization into a territory of the federal government. This idea, which was conceived by some of the colonists who are above the average, has become general among the people and does not fail to cause considerable discussion. . . .

. . . The whole population here is a mixture of strange and incoherent parts without parallel in our federation: numerous tribes of Indians, now at peace, but armed and at any moment ready for war, whose steps toward civilization should be taken under the close supervision of a strong and intelligent government; colonists of another people, more progressive and better informed than the Mexican inhabitants, but also more shrewd and unruly; among these foreigners are fugitives from justice, honest laborers, vagabonds and criminals, but honorable and dishonorable alike travel with their political constitution in their pockets, demanding the privileges, authority and officers which such a constitution guarantees.

## 7. Mexico Seeks to Block Anglo-American Immigration: The April 6, 1830 Law

### The Decree of April 6, 1830

Article 1. Cotton goods excluded in the Law of May 22, 1829, may be introduced through the ports of the Republic until January 1, 1831, and through the ports of the South Sea until June 30, 1831.

Article 2. The duties received on the above mentioned goods shall be used to maintain the integrity of Mexican territory, to form a reserve fund against the event of Spanish invasion, and to promote the development of national industries in the branch of cotton manufacturers.

Article 3. The government is authorized to name one or more commissioners who shall visit the colonies of the frontier states and contract with the legislatures of said states for the purchase, in behalf of the federal government, of lands deemed suitable for the establishment of colonies of Mexicans and other nationalities; and the said commissioners shall make with the existing colonies whatever arrangements seem expedient for the security of the Republic. The said commissioners shall supervise the introduction of new colonists and the fulfilling of their contracts for settlement, and shall ascertain to what extent the existing contracts have been completed.

Article 4. The chief executive is authorized to take such lands as are deemed suitable for fortifications or arsenals and for the new colonies, indemnifying the states for same, in proportion to their assessments due the federal government.

Article 5. The government is authorized to transport the convict-soldiers destined for Vera Cruz and other points to the colonies, there to establish them as is deemed fit; the government will furnish free transportation to the families of the soldiers, should they desire to go.

Allein Howren, "Causes and Origins of the Decree of April 6, 1830," *Southwestern Historical Quarterly,* vol. 16 (April 1913): 415–417.

Article 6. The convict-soldiers shall be employed in constructing the fortifications, public works and roads which the commissioners may deem necessary, and when the time of their imprisonment is terminated, if they should desire to remain as colonists, they shall be given lands and agricultural implements, and their provisions shall be continued through the first year of their colonization.

Article 7. Mexican families who voluntarily express a desire to become colonists will be furnished transportation, maintained for one year, and assigned the best of agricultural lands.

Article 8. All the individuals above mentioned shall be subject to both the federal and state colonization laws.

Article 9. The introduction of foreigners across the northern frontier is prohibited under any pretext whatever, unless the said foreigners are provided with a passport issued by the agents of this Republic at the point whence the said foreigners set out.

Article 10. No change shall be made with respect to the slaves now in the states, but the federal government and the government of each state shall most strictly enforce the colonization laws and prevent the further introduction of slaves.

Article 11. In accordance with the right reserved by the general congress in the seventh article of the Law of August 18, 1824, it is prohibited that emigrants from nations bordering on this Republic shall settle in the states or territory adjacent to their own nation. Consequently, all contracts not already completed and not in harmony with this law are suspended.


## 8. The San Antonio Ayuntamiento Petitions the Mexican Government for a Liberal Immigration Policy, 1832

Honorable Congress

When illnesses occur, the treatment adopted should be proportionate to the gravity of the situation, and application should be immediate. Such is the only rule to be followed when the physical body is attacked by some severe illness. To be consistent, the same procedure should be followed when dealing with ailments of the social body. No doubt exists that ills, similar in nature, have afflicted each of the unfortunate towns of Texas from the very moment they were founded. So it is that some towns have been destroyed while the rest have been unable to attain, even for a single day, that peace or those other guarantees which should have insured population and other resources for their development under the paternal protection of their governments. This town of Béxar was established 140 years ago, La Bahía del Espíritu Santo and Nacogdoches 116 years ago, and the fort of San Sabá, the towns of Jaén, San Marcos, and Trinidad, were founded in the intervening years along with other military establishments on the Guadalupe, Colorado and Brazos rivers. These communities have disappeared entirely; in some of them the residents dying to the last man. One can discern the neglect they always experienced, just by

Conchita Hassell Winn, trans. and David Weber, ed. and trans., *Troubles in Texas, 1832* (Dallas: Wind River Press, 1982): 16–22. Copyright © 1983 DeGolyer Library, Southern Methodist University. Reprinted with permission.

examining the census of the current population of the first three communities, the only ones which still survive, and by retelling the unspeakable stories of the many types of suffering they endured even as they labored for their country. Many early settlers and their descendants have been sacrificed to the barbarians, and not a few others have died of hunger and pestilence, which have caused havoc in this part of the republic due to the inaction and apathy of those who govern. How sad that ninety-seven men have been murdered by Indians within the limits of this city [San Antonio], Bahía, and the new *villa* of González alone (not counting the veterans who perished in campaigns in all the years from 1821 to the present). It should be observed that these [Indian] enemies only waged war from 1825 to 1827, and that peace prevailed during the rest of the time. Other frontier communities, located toward the west have, perhaps, suffered much more, and every last one of us is probably threatened with total extermination by the new Comanche uprising. This very large and most warlike tribe renewed hostilities four months ago, just when the national forces were involved in bloody struggle stemming from the aberrations and Constitutional infractions committed on all sides—especially since the year 1828.

These disturbances have caused us to suffer absolute poverty. Since the troops protecting this part of the frontier have not received even one-tenth part of their salary during the entire past year, it has been necessary to put more than half of them at liberty so they would find means for their own subsistence. Today, in all of Texas, only seventy men are at arms. Their pay in arrears, these troops are a burden on the poor townspeople. To assure themselves that even this limited support will remain available, the poor townspeople are obliged to supply these men with grain and other essential articles from the already meager community resources. By advancing these sums to the troops, however, the settlers jeopardize their ability to hold on to this portion of their own small holdings, since past experience shows they have yet to be repaid for advances they made on several other occasions. . . .

Experience suggests that the first colonization law of this state contains many omissions and contradictions. These have paralyzed population growth in Texas and, because of them, elements of its territorial wealth have failed to develop. Article 26 of that law gives settlers six years to populate and cultivate the lands granted to them; article 27 of said law denies them the right to transfer or give away property that is not totally under cultivation. Who fails to observe, therefore, a contradiction in the spirit behind these two articles with respect to the increase of population? If possible, such rights should be applicable from the first year, be it to the grantee or to any other legally entitled person to whom these lands might be sold or transmitted by any other means.

On the other hand, what inducement, what incentives, or what privileges capable of attracting Mexicans have been written into that or any later law designed to encourage an increase in the population of Mexicans (who doubtless would be the most desirable citizens for Texas)? Not even one. On the contrary, the May 2, 1832 law establishes that lands in Texas are priced at from one to three hundred pesos, according to their quality, while those of Coahuila at only fifteen pesos. What an admirable measure! Principally it serves to keep the Mexican population at a greater distance from Texas, because people from the interior of the Republic have always resisted immigrating to these deserts which they greatly fear. Very few Mexican residents of Texas will be able to afford the indicated fees because of their limited capital. In extreme cases, even those who already acquired concessions of some lands are abstaining from asking for their respective properties. This is due as much to the aforesaid exorbitant price as to provisions in article 13 of the law that demands on quarter of the payment immediately.

And what shall we say concerning evils caused by the general law of April 6, 1830, which absolutely prohibits immigration by North Americans? The lack of troops and other officials capable of supervising it has made it impossible to enforce this law. On the other hand, the law prevents immigration of some capitalists and of some industrious and honorable men who have refrained from coming because of it, but has left the door open to wicked adventurers and others who constitute the dregs of society. Since they have nothing to lose, they have arrived furtively in large numbers and may cause incalculable harm.

The same is true of the numerous tribes of semicivilized Indians. Expelled from the United States of North America, they have crossed the Sabine River and, unchallenged, have established themselves in our territory. It will be very difficult to uproot them and even more so if we intend to make them observe our legal system. Yet, risking all kinds of dangers and inconveniences, North Americans reclaimed a considerable part of these lands from the desert prior to the passage of the law of April 6, 1830, and toiled assiduously to further agriculture and to introduce crafts unknown in these parts since the discovery of this land by the old Spanish government. They planted cotton and sugar cane, introduced the cotton gin, and imported machinery for the cultivation of sugar and sawmills to cut wood economically. We owe these advances to the efforts of these hard-working colonists, who have earned a comfortable living within seven or eight years. Theirs is not a precarious existence, the only kind known in Mexican towns, which depend solely upon the troops' payroll that circulates so slowly among us.

Although it grieves us to say so, we should state that the miserable manufacture of blankets, hats, and even shoes was never established in Texas towns. Lack of these articles has obliged us to beg them from foreigners or from the interior of the republic, two or three hundred leagues distant. The only known loom here is one brought to Béxar two year ago. Meanwhile, residents of La Bahía and Nacogdoches who have never left their communities have no idea of this very simple machine, or the way a hat is made. All these resources came to us with the North American colonists, but if their immigration is blocked who knows how long we will be denied such advances.

Immigration is, unquestionably, the most efficient, quick, and economical means we can employ to destroy the Indians and to populate lands they now occupy—directing the immigrants to the northern interior whenever possible. This goal can only be achieved by freely admitting these enthusiastic North Americans so they may live in this desert. They already are experienced in dealing with the barbarians in their native land, where they have done similar work. Not a single European nation that might be interested in colonizing offers their people similar advantages. Because they have been very regimented, the Europeans' transportation, climate, customs, and forms of government are very different from those of the neighboring republic and are not as suitable for Mexico.

The opening of roads going directly from Texas ports to New Mexico, Paso del Norte, or even Chihuahua, would place Texas at the rank it should occupy in the

Mexican federation. This achievement, too, is the result of the immigration of North American capitalists. They built these at least more economically and in less time than could be accomplished by any other nation and even by Mexico itself. The same is true of direct communication from all the far northern part of our republic with the state of Missouri of the neighboring nation, which is maintained today despite great risk and cost of freight. The population of those lands [between Texas and Missouri, and between Texas and New Mexico] would benefit Texas and would be the best barrier against the Indians. It would thrust population 200 leagues farther north than it is today, and protect the entire line of defense for Coahuila, Nuevo León and Tamaulipas, and even that of Chihuahua.

The advantages that would accrue to this part of the republic, if it could be populated without need of sacrifice by the public treasury or the state, are so numerous they are hard to imagine. Perhaps an entire volume would be insufficient to provide full and minute details of such a beautiful scene. And would not the inhabitants of Texas find it painful and even intolerable to continue envisioning how easily prosperity could be attained in this fertile land—with its mildness of climate, the plenty of its rivers, the abundance of its fish and game, which provides the most beautiful kinds of pelts—and for these settlers to realize that only the government's lack of knowledge and the mistaken measures it undertook to encourage population in this country increasingly separate us from the well-being to which nature invites us? This same apathy and the fatal arrow of the barbarians will probably deprive us of our existence as they did our forebears. Unquestionably, the lack of a government with special sensitivity to the needs of Texas, which would take the necessary and simple measures to increase Texas' population and promote its prosperity and growth in all branches, has been, is, and perhaps will continue to be the source of our suffering.

# ✦ E S S A Y S

The extent to which Anglos and Mexicans coexisted amicably during the years of early settlement is an issue of considerable importance for Texas historians, in view of the political developments that would lead to the separation of Texas from Mexico in the mid-1830s. In the first essay, Arnoldo de León, history professor at Angelo State University and author of several books on Mexican Texans, argues that deeply-rooted Anglo cultural prejudices predisposed settlers from the United States to view Tejanos with hostility. A long tradition of anti-Catholicism combined with a southern attitude that viewed all non-whites as racially inferior made Anglo immigrants incapable of living on a basis of equality with their new Tejano neighbors.

Gregg Cantrell, history professor at the University of North Texas, and the author of a prize-winning study of Stephen F. Austin, offers a very different view of Anglo-Mexican race relations in his analysis of the first empresario of Texas. Although Cantrell concedes that many Anglo Americans subscribed to a racialist ideology that provided a cultural context for political tensions, he cautions against viewing Austin strictly by some of his more inflammatory statements. Cantrell reminds us that, for fifteen years, Austin was an unflagging mediator between Anglo residents, Tejanos, and Mexican authorities; only Mexico's failure to establish effective republican institutions prompted him to reluctantly embrace the cause of independence.

# Early Anglo Settlers View Mexicans with Hostility

### ARNOLDO DE LEÓN

Most whites who first met Tejanos in the 1820s had never had prior experiences with Mexicans nor encountered them anywhere else. Yet their reaction to them upon contact was contemptuous, many thinking Mexicans abhorrent. What caused pioneers to feel this way? Why were their attitudes bigoted instead of neutral? What did they find in Mexicans that aroused xenophobic behavior, or what was it within themselves that generated that response?

According to one Texas historian, Anglo settlers who entered Texas accepted Mexicans on a basis of equality initially and did not react scornfully toward the native Tejanos until the Texas war for independence of 1836. Relationships before then, according to him, were characterized by a marked tolerance, lack of basic antipathy between the two races, and an almost total lack of friction traceable to racial problems. In the opinion of another student of Anglo attitudes during the period 1821–1845, white feelings toward Mexicans were very complex, at times contradictory, and constantly in flux.

The latest scholarship on the subject of racial and cultural attitudes, however, does not sustain these arguments. Americans moving to the west, recent studies indicate, had much more in mind than settling the land and creating prosperous communities. Cultural heirs to Elizabethans and Puritans, those moving into hinterlands sensed an "errand into the wilderness" and felt a compelling need to control all that was beastly—sexuality, vice, nature, and colored peoples. Order and discipline had to be rescued from the wilds in the name of civilization and Christianity. Moving westward with this mission uppermost in their minds, whites psychologically needed to subdue the external world—forests, beasts, and other peoples— for the rational had to be ever in command. Coming into constant encounter with peoples of color in wilderness settings, these sensitive whites struggled against noncivilization. To allow an inverse order and a concomitant surrender of themselves and their liberties to primitive things was to allow chaos to continue when God's will was to impose Christian order.

The desire to bring fields and Indians under submission did not emanate solely from religious passion but was also a product of the individual compulsion to repress instinctual urges. Within humanity were encased base impulses (e.g., sexuality, savagery) that were just as primitive and animalistic as the things of the forest which demanded domination. Killing, destruction, subordination, and appropriation of lands not only brought the external wilderness under control but also served as a form of release for the animal within. In prevailing over primitive things through violence, whites found regeneration, but their efforts also resulted in the uglier manifestations of racism. Therein lay the seed for the perverse responses toward Mexicanos in the first encounter.

Waves of Anglo settlers first entered Texas when the Mexican government in 1821 granted colonization rights in the province to a Missouri entrepreneur named

Moses Austin. Hundreds more followed thereafter, coming to Mexican Texas under the aegis of Moses' son, Stephen, and other empresarios. Most were not radically different from the pre–nineteenth-century pioneers. Like them, they entertained a strong belief in themselves and the superiority of their way of life.

Why, asked the historian Samuel M. Lowrie in his study of culture conflict in Texas, were Americans as narrow and freedom loving as frontiersmen willing to settle in a country as religiously intolerant and undemocratic as Mexico? Perhaps because they felt it their duty to make order of what they perceived as chaos. Certainly they uttered such sentiments many times, though Lowrie did not discern it, given the state of scholarship in the 1930s when he wrote his study. As William H. Wharton, one of the more radical agitators for independence from Mexico, put it in an appeal for American support as the revolution went on in Texas,

> The justice and benevolence of God, will forbid that the delightful region of Texas should again become a howling wilderness, trod only by savages, or that it should be permanently benighted by the ignorance and superstition, the anarchy and rapine of Mexican misrule. The Anglo-American race are destined to be for ever the proprietors of this land of *promise* and *fulfilment. Their* laws will govern it, *their* learning will enlighten it, their enterprise will improve it. *Their* flocks will range its boundless pastures, for *them* its fertile lands will yield their luxuriant harvests: its beauteous rivers will waft the products of *their* industry and enterprise, and *their* latest posterity will here enjoy legacies of "price unspeakable," in the possession of homes fortified by the genius of liberty, and sanctified by the spirit of a beneficent and tolerant religion. This is inevitable, for the wilderness of Texas has been redeemed by Anglo-American blood and enterprise. The colonists have carried with them the language, the habits, and the lofty love of liberty, that has always characterized and distinguished their ancestors. They have identified them indissolubly with the country.

But none was more articulate than Stephen F. Austin, who several times before the war for independence confessed, almost stereotypically, that his intent was "to redeem Texas from the wilderness." In one of his most eloquent expressions, he averred: "My object, the sole and only desire of my ambitions since I first saw Texas, was to redeem it from the wilderness—to settle it with an intelligent honorable and interprising [*sic*] people."

To Austin, redemption could come by "whitening" Texas—or, phrased differently, by making it a cultural and racial copy of the United States. In August 1835, he wrote that the best interests of the nation required "that Texas should be effectually, and fully, Americanized—that is—settled by a population that will harmonize with their neighbors on the *East,* in language, political principles, common origin, sympathy, and even interest." It was well known, he continued, that his object had always been to fill up Texas with a North American population. "I wish a great immigration from Kentucky, Tennessee, *every where,* passports, or no passports, *any how.* For fourteen years I have had a hard time of it, but nothing shall daunt my courage or abate my exertions to complete the main object of my labors—to *Americanize Texas.* This fall, and winter, will fix our fate—a great immigration will settle the question."

At the national level, Americans had never been oblivious to the prospects of rescuing Texas from its alleged primitive status. At all times, there had been those in Washington who had similar thoughts and expressed them publicly. Among them was Henry Clay, who asked in 1821: "By what race should Texas be peopled?" Lest it be settled by others who would make it a "place of despotism and slaves, of the Inquisition and superstition," it should be taken over by settlers from the United States who would transplant to it the free institutions of Anglo-Americans. Should Texas then break off from the United States for some reason, Clay affirmed, at least it would have been rescued from a race alien to everything that Americans held dear.

Clay did not stop at rhetoric. While he was Secretary of State, he and President John Quincy Adams instructed Joel R. Poinsett, the United States Minister to Mexico, to attempt to purchase Texas. Mexico, which had never put Texas up for sale, squarely rejected the proposal, only to see it repeated. When Andrew Jackson assumed office in 1829, he urged Poinsett to renew his efforts, authorizing the minister to offer $5 million for whatever amount of Texas Mexico would surrender. Similar futile attempts at negotiating the purchase of Texas continued until the time of the revolution.

What whites refused to accept was a state of affairs in which chaos presided over them. But what exactly was it that they considered as disorder? Texas was already settled and under the rule of a government, heir to centuries of Spanish civilization. Something else disturbed them, for to them, a connection existed in the new land between the state of civilization and chaos. Thus all the discussion about rescuing Texas from primitivism. The newcomers saw the Tejanos as mongrels, uncivilized, and un-Christian—a part of the wilderness that must be subdued. Living in Mexico and Texas were a sort of people who threatened the march of white civilization.

Incontrovertibly, as far as whites were concerned, order and discipline were missing. For Anglo settlers who arrived in Texas imported certain ideas from the United States, which regarded the native Mexican population as less than civilized. These attitudes ranged from xenophobia against Catholics and Spaniards to racial prejudice against Indians and blacks. Thus Mexicanos were doubly suspect, as heirs to Catholicism and as descendants of Spaniards, Indians, and Africans.

In England, hostile feelings toward the Roman Church originated in the sixteenth century with Henry VIII's religious and political break with the Pope and were hardened by conflict with Catholic Spain. The English mind readily thought in terms of a Catholic-Spanish alliance, conjured by Satan himself, from which nothing less than demonic designs could be expected. Additionally, the English associated the Spanish with cruelty and brutality. Alleged Spanish tyranny in the Netherlands during the latter half of the sixteenth century as well as atrocities toward the Indians in Latin America produced an image of the Spaniard as heartless and genocidal. And, finally, the English saw the Spanish as an embodiment of racial impurity. For hundreds of years, racial mixing or *mestizaje* had occurred in the Iberian peninsula between Spaniards and Moors. At a time when Elizabethans were becoming more and more sensitive to the significance of color—equating whiteness with purity and Christianity and blackness with baseness and the devil—Spaniards came to be thought of as not much better than light-skinned Moors and Africans.

English immigrants to the North American colonies probably brought those ideas with them and were certainly exposed to them through anti-Catholic and anti-Spanish literature constantly arriving in the new society. Men of letters, ministers, and propagandists helped in disseminating such notions. Military clashes along the Georgia-Florida border in the eighteenth century only intensified the hatred.

As for the Mexican aborigines, the English conceived of them as degenerate creatures—un-Christian, uncivilized, and racially impure. From letters, histories, and travel narratives, English writers put together a portrait that turned the people of Mexico into a degraded humanity. The natives subscribed to heathenism, and witches and other devilish agents permeated their culture. They partook of unholy things like polygamy, sodomy, and incest and rejected Christianity outright. Furthermore, they practiced savage rituals like human sacrifice and cannibalism. Of all the Latin American inhabitants, the Mexican Indians seemed the most beastly, for though they were in many ways the most advanced of all the New World peoples, they exercised the grossest violation of civility by these practices. Stories of Aztec gods like Quetzalcoatl who were half man and half beast and accounts of exotic Aztec rites only convinced the English of the Indians' place on the fringes of humankind, with dubious claims to existence, civilization, and Christian salvation.

While such images of the Mexican natives may not have been as widespread as those held of Spaniards, they were nonetheless familiar to many colonists. In newspapers, recent histories, and re-editions of old propaganda materials, furthermore, colonists were able to read things about the origins of the Mexicans which perpetuated enriched images acquired from the mother country.

In addition to ideas that had been fashioned vicariously, there were those that arose from intimate contact with other peoples whom whites esteemed no more than the Mexican aborigines or the Spaniards. The long history of hostilities against North American Indians on the frontier and the institution of Afro-American slavery molded negative attitudes toward dark skin, "savagery," "vice," and interracial sex. The majority of those who responded to empresario calls most assuredly thought along those lines, for they came from the states west of the Appalachians and south of the Ohio River—Louisiana, Alabama, Arkansas, Tennessee, Missouri, Mississippi, Georgia, and Kentucky. A significant number were Eastern born, but had been part of the frontier movement before their transplantation into Texas. From the Southern and frontier-oriented culture they had acquired a certain repulsion for dark-skinned people and a distaste for miscegenation. Believing that the mores of their own provincial institutions should apply in the new frontier, they assumed a posture of superiority and condescension toward the natives. By conditioning, they were predisposed to react intolerantly to people they found different from themselves but similar to those they considered as enemies and as inferiors. Along with dislike for Spaniards and the Indians of Latin America, these perceptions produced a mode of thinking that set the contours of the primordial response.

And what particularly provoked this reaction? Most Tejanos were descendants of Tlascalan Indians and *mestizo* soldiers from Coahuila. Additionally, a few Nacogdoches were the offspring of people from Louisiana and reflected that area's racial amalgam, including Indians and blacks. Throughout the province, Tejanos had intermarried among themselves and with Christianized Indian women from local missions so that the colonists continued as a mixed-blood population. Their contrast to "white" and salient kindred to "black" and "red" made Mexicans subject to treatment commensurate with the odious connotations whites attached to colors, races, and cultures dissimilar to their own.

Manifestly, Americans who immigrated to Texas confronted the native Mexicans with certain preconceptions about their character. Whites believed that the inhabitants of the province had descended from a tradition of paganism, depravity, and primitivism. Mexicans were a type of folk that Americans should avoid becoming.

The fact of the matter was that whites had little contact with Tejanos up to 1836, for most of the Mexican population was concentrated in the San Antonio and La Bahía areas, quite a distance from the Anglo colonies. But whites knew what they would find in Texas before contact confirmed their convictions. They encountered biologically decadent and inferior people because their thoughts had been shaped by the aforementioned circumstances. Thus, Mexicans lived in ways that Anglos equated with an opprobrious condition. They inhabited primitive shelters. William F. Gray, a land agent from Virginia, comparing Mexicans with the black American culture he knew, pronounced some of the Mexican homes "miserable shabby *jacales*" scarcely equal in appearance to the Afro-American houses in the suburbs of his state. Mexicans adhered to a different religion: they were completely the "slaves of Popish superstitions and despotism" and religion was understood not as an affection of the heart and soul but as one requiring personal mortification in such superficialities as penances and other rituals. If Anglos and Mexicans were not inherently different peoples, editorialized the *Texian and Emigrant's Guide* in 1835, habit, education, and religion had made them essentially so.

Additionally, Texians thought that Mexicans' cultural habits clashed with American values, such as the work ethic. Mexicanos appeared a traditional, backward aggregate, an irresponsibly passive people dedicated to the present and resigned not to probe the universe about them. An American arriving in Nacogdoches in 1833 found the citizens there the most "lazy indolent poor Starved set of people as ever the Sun Shined upon." He could not comprehend their lethargy by day nor their inclination to play the violin and dance the entire night. J. C. Clopper of Ohio reasoned in 1828 that Mexicanos were "too ignorant and indolent for enterprises and too poor and *dependent* were they otherwise capacitated." Mexicanos habitually succumbed to indolence and ease and indulged themselves in smoking, music, dancing, horse-racing, and other sports, noted David Woodman, a promoter for a New York and Boston land company, while activity, industry, and frugality marched on in the new American settlements. "The vigor of the descendents of the sturdy north will never mix with the phlegm of the indolent Mexicans," Sam Houston (the future hero of the war for independence) argued in January 1835 in an address to the citizens of Texas, "no matter how long we may live among them." In contrast to the newcomers, Tejanos were chained by custom to complacency, and instead of committing themselves to progress, they preferred fun and frolic. Some three years after Mexico opened Texas to Anglo-American settlement, Anthony R. Clark complained that Spaniards in the District of Nacogdoches, "generally of the lower sort and illitterate [*sic*]," would rather "spend days in gambling to gain a few bits than to make a living by honest industry." William B. Dewees, who lived in San Antonio in the late 1820s, found Bexareños totally hedonistic. "Their whole study seems to be for enjoyment. Mirth and amusement occupy their whole time. If one is fond of balls and theatres, he can here have an opportunity of attending one every evening. Almost every species of dissipation is indulged in, except drinking." In Goliad, the Mexicans had such a strong predisposition for gaming that almost all the inhabitants in 1833 were gamblers and smugglers, said empresario Dr. John Charles Beales. And Alexander McCrae, touring Texas in 1835 under the auspices of the Wilmington

Emigrating Society, remarked in astonishment: "I for the first time saw females betting at a public gambling table; I do not suppose they were of respectable standing in society, from the company they kept; but I am told that it is not all uncommon for Mexican *ladies* to be seen gambling in public."

Acting further to stimulate negative attitudes was the racial composition of Tejanos, who, in the white mind, were closely identified with other colored peoples. For two hundred years, ideas that black men lusted for white women and notions that slaves were of a heathen or "savage" condition had played upon Americans' fantasies; the result had been the institutional debasement of blacks because of their race. Images of the Indian as fierce, hostile, and barbaric similarly affixed themselves in the thoughts of white settlers, and the constant confrontation over land led more to the reaffirmation of these images than to their dissolution. Consequently, when whites arrived in Texas, they unconsciously transferred onto the new "colored" folk they encountered a pseudo-scientific lore acquired from generations of interaction with blacks and Indians.

Travelers, who frequently came in contact with Tejanos, plainly discerned the Mexicans' relation to the black and red peoples. At no time did Americans hold up Frenchmen, or Germans, or themselves for that matter, as a people who physically resembled Mexicans—comparison invariably was with Indians and blacks. Several factors steered discussion in that direction: Anglos were not about to elevate Mexicans to the level of European whiteness; their own sense of superiority turned Tejanos into a people lesser than themselves; and obviously, in any comparison, Mexicans were going to resemble their progenitors. Thus, whites often likened Mexicans to Africans and Native Americans. When Clopper mentioned the complexion of the Tejanos, he thought it "a shade brighter than that of the aborigines of the country." On the other hand, the land agent Gray stamped Tejanos as a "swarthy looking people much resembling our mulattos, some of them nearly black." Sam Houston asked his compatriots (in the aforementioned address) if they "would bow under the yoke of these half-Indians," while abolitionist Benjamin Lundy, in Laredo in 1834, remarked that the Mexicans in the town looked like mulattoes. Even when commentators omitted drawing comparisons about color, they nonetheless made reference to the Mexicans' dark complexion. One traveler asserted that because of it they were "readily designated at first sight."

The same association with Indians and Africans was also apparent in caustic comments about the Mexicans' ancestors. A Texan identifying himself as "H. H." in a letter to the *New Orleans Bee* in 1834 pronounced the people of Mexico the most "degraded and vile; the unfortunate race of Spaniard, Indian and African, is so blended that the worst qualities of each predominate." Two years later, when the Texans were locked in a fateful struggle with the Mexican nation, leaders of the rebellion appealed to their comrades by reminding them that Mexicans were "the adulterate and degenerate brood of the once high-spirited Castilian."

In addition to all their other discoveries about Mexicans, whites in the period between 1821 and 1836 thought Tejanos lax in virtue. A number of aspects of Mexican morality bothered them, including the native *fandango,* a dance of a sinuous sort with sexually suggestive moves. George W. Smyth from Tennessee witnessed it in Nacogdoches upon his arrival in 1830, and was surprised "that the priest and all participated, so contrary to all my pre-conceived notions of propriety." Asahel

Langworthy, a New York lawyer and land speculator, found the dance somewhat uncivilized, identifying it with lack of culture and refinement. "I witnessed one afternoon," he wrote, "a Spanish *fandango* danced in the open air by a party of these people, evidently of a low class."

Because of the apparent revelry of such recreational forms, whites began early on to assume Mexicans had a defective morality, and Mexican attitudes toward sexuality strengthened the white image of Mexicans as sensuous and voluptuous. Despite the close supervision given unmarried girls to prevent intercourse with their male counterparts, Clopper alleged, "soon as married they are scarcely the same creatures—giving the freest indulgence to their naturally gay and enthusiastic dispositions, as if liberated from all moral restraints." To the Ohioan, Mexicans were not cut from the same moral fabric as Americans. . . .

What whites found in the Texas experience during these first fifteen years was that Mexicans were primitive beings who during a century of residence in Texas had failed to improve their status and environment. Mexicans were religious pagans, purposelessly indolent and carefree, sexually remiss, degenerate, depraved, and questionably human. The haunting prospect of being ruled by such people indefinitely explains in part the Texian movement for independence in 1836.

# Stephen F. Austin: Political and Cultural Mediator

### GREGG CANTRELL

The Anglo-American colonists who came to Mexican Texas brought with them some heavy cultural baggage. Most came from slaveholding states and subscribed to southern notions of white supremacy—notions that might easily be applied to dark-skinned Mexicans as well as to African Americans. Many undoubtedly embodied the other forms of ethnocentrism peculiar to the Jacksonian era, such as a strident prejudice against Catholics and an intense hatred of Indians. Moreover, few settlers would have questioned the basic tenets of the ideology that would someday be called "Manifest Destiny:" the belief that the United States would inevitably spread American-style democracy and cultural institutions westward across the continent. Given these realities, many recent scholars have viewed the Anglo settlement of Texas as little more than an American invasion, a racist land grab of Mexico's northern frontier in which Mexicans and Indians were the chief victims.

At first glance, the foremost leader of this "invasion" seems to sustain these interpretations. Stephen Fuller Austin was a Virginia native who had grown up mostly on the Missouri frontier, where he utilized slave labor on a large scale in his family's lead-mining operation. In Texas, he worked repeatedly to ensure that slavery would be protected by the government. He had also served in the Missouri militia during the War of 1812, participating in a military campaign that burned Indian villages in Illinois. His credentials as a white supremacist seemed secure.

The same might be said for his standing as a proponent of Manifest Destiny. In an Independence Day speech in 1818, he delivered an address extolling the virtues

---

Essay by Gregg Cantrell, written for this volume. Reprinted with permission of the author.

of American civilization and the Founding Fathers. Near the end of the oration, he alluded to Mexico's ongoing independence struggle:

> . . . the same spirit that unsheathed the sword of Washington and sacrificed servitude and slavery in the flames of the Revolution, will also flash across the Gulph of Mexico and over the western wilderness that separates independent America from the enslaved colonies of Spain, and darting the beams of intelligence into the benighted souls of their inhabitants awake them from the stupor of slaves to the energy of freemen, from the degradation of vassals to the dignity of sovereigns.

After emigrating to Texas, he frequently defined his mission as that of "[spreading] over it North American population, enterprise, and intelligence."

In addition to his racial beliefs and his pro-American chauvinism, Austin also seemed typically American in his attitudes toward Mexican Catholicism. On his first trip through the interior of Mexico, he wrote that "the people are bigoted and superstitious to an extreem, and indolence appears to be the general order of the day." And in another, oft-quoted passage, he added, "to be candid the majority of the people of the whole nation as far as I have seen them want nothing but tails to be more brutes than the apes. . . . Fanaticism reigns with a power that equally astonishes and grieves a man of common sense."

Austin's words and deeds seemed to confirm his ethnocentrism when Texas began to wage war against Mexico. Not only did he publicly advocate independence several months before the actual declaration, but he justified the revolution on the grounds that "A war of extermination is raging in Texas, a war of barbarism and of despotic principles, waged by the mongrel Spanish-Indian and Negro race, against civilization and the Anglo-American race." He recounted the fifteen years in which he had labored "like a slave to *Americanize Texas*" so that the southwestern frontier of the United States would be safe. "But the Anglo-American foundation, this nucleus of republicanism, is to broken up," he declared, "and its place supplied by a population of Indians, Mexicans, and renegadoes, all mixed together, and all the natural enemies of white men and civilization." In other statements he raised the cry of anti-Catholicism, claiming that the revolution was being fought for "religious liberty" and against the "banner of the inquisition." With such actions and statements coming from the man who initiated the Anglo-American colonization of Texas, who could doubt that racism, imperialism, cultural chauvinism, and greed were the main impulses behind the American occupation of Texas all along?

Despite all of this, the case of Stephen F. Austin—when considered in its entirety—actually tells a very different story. For the better part of fifteen years, the young Missourian served as a political and cultural mediator between Anglo Texans and Mexicans. When examined objectively, Austin's career demonstrates the very real potential for political, economic, and social cooperation across racial and cultural lines. The history leading up to the Texas Revolution emerges as a far more complex story than it appears.

When Austin received permission in 1821 to introduce 300 American families into the region between the Brazos and Colorado, his timing was perfect. The newly independent government of Mexico, as well as the local Tejano leadership of Texas, recognized the need to populate the sparsely settled province with hardworking, taxpaying citizens who would contribute to the economic development of northern Mexico, help fight hostile Indians, and hopefully prevent the loss of Texas to the rapidly expanding United States. Austin's title was *empresario,* which meant that he was responsible for recruiting settlers, surveying and issuing land titles, enforcing the laws, and acting as liaison between his colonists and the Mexican government. From the start, Austin labored tirelessly and took his responsibilities as empresario seriously.

One of the first indications of that seriousness was his approach to the language barrier. Austin spoke little or no Spanish when he first arrived in Texas, but he dedicated himself to learning the language not just passably but fluently. Most of this effort took place in 1822 when he was forced to travel to Mexico City to secure confirmation of his grant from the new government of Mexico. Within a few weeks of his arrival there, Austin was conducting business in Spanish and even acting as spokesman for other Americans in their business with the government.

We get a glimpse of Austin's attitudes toward the language issue in his letters to his younger brother, Brown Austin. Stephen had left Brown, who was only nineteen, behind in Texas when he went to Mexico City. But rather than leave Brown with Anglo friends in the new colony, he placed Brown in the household of the prominent Tejano citizen Erasmo Seguín of San Antonio with instructions to spend every waking moment studying Spanish and learning Mexican ways. "Remember," Stephen lectured Brown, "that all your hopes of rising in this country depend on lear[n]ing to speak and write the language correctly. Without that, you will do nothing," Ten years later he would take a similar course with his teenage nephew, Moses Austin Bryan.

By the time Austin returned to Texas in 1823, he could speak Spanish and was personally acquainted with a host of major Mexican leaders. Arriving home, he issued a proclamation reminding the settlers of their obligation to the government. He instructed them "to remember that the Roman Catholic is the religion of this nation" and urged them to "respect the Catholic religion with all that attention due to its sacredness and to the laws of the land." Two years later, when the new national constitution was published, he summoned the colonists to San Felipe for a grand celebration of the new system of government. There, in the village he had laid out in a traditional Spanish pattern with streets named for Mexican statesmen, Austin raised the Mexican flag, read the constitution, and administered the oath of allegiance. Good order prevailed the entire day, and the people expressed "general enthusiasm in favor of the Government of our adopted Country." Austin made the phrase "fidelity to Mexico" his motto and for years preached it like gospel to the colonists, frequently reminding them that they lived under "the most liberal and munificent government on earth to emigrants."

Austin soon formed harmonious working relationships with important Tejanos as well as Mexicans from the interior. When the national congress combined Texas with Coahuila to form one state, he succeeded in forging an effective three-pronged political coalition between Anglo colonists, Tejanos, and a group of powerful Coahuilan politicians/businessmen headed by the Viesca brothers of Parras. Together, they dominated the politics of the vast frontier state for more than a decade, finding common ground on a wide range of issues.

Prominent Tejano José Antonio Navarro of San Antonio was one of Austin's key allies in this coalition. Navarro represented Texas in the 1828 state legislature, at a time when Austin, along with other Anglo colonists, feared that the state was on the verge of enforcing its prohibitions on slavery. Navarro came to the rescue, quietly securing the passage of a bill that allowed Americans to continue to bring their slaves into Texas. Modern sensibilities will condemn the purpose of Navarro's labors, but the point here is to show the close cooperation and identification of mutual interests between these two men who came from such different cultural backgrounds.

Equally telling is the *personal* relationship that apparently developed between Austin and Navarro. Stephen F. Austin was not the sort who formed intimate friendships easily, and he tended to be a very private and reserved man, rarely mentioning personal matters to business or political associates. But in 1829, he faced one of the greatest personal crises of his life when his beloved younger brother, Brown, suddenly died of yellow fever. The stress of this event triggered a severe attack of fever in Austin, who lingered near death for weeks. When he finally was able to sit up in bed and write a few letters, Navarro was one of the first people he contacted—and one of the few in whom he confided. Austin poured out his grief to his Tejano friend, poignantly writing of the "terrible blow" he had received. That Austin would share his anguish with Navarro (who would later sign the Texas Declaration of Independence) says much about the degree of trust and friendship that existed between the two men.

Similarly strong and enduring was Austin's relationship with the Seguín family. Erasmo Seguín was among a group of Tejanos who traveled to Louisiana in 1821 to escort Stephen F. Austin to the site of his grant. The men became friends, and Brown Austin apparently lived with the Seguíns for the entire year that Austin was gone. Several years later, Austin made efforts to purchase cotton ginning equipment for Erasmo in New Orleans because Erasmo had refused to accept any reimbursement for the time that Brown had boarded with him.

Like the Austin-Navarro relationship, the Austin-Seguín relationship extended into the period of the Revolution itself. In the fall of 1835, when Austin was commanding Texan troops in the field, into the camp galloped Juan Seguín—Erasmo's son—along with a company of Tejano cavalrymen, volunteering their services in the Texas cause. Austin welcomed them into the ranks, commissioning Seguín as a lieutenant colonel. Austin would later praise the Tejano troops, saying that "They uniformly acquitted themselves to their credit as patriots and soldiers."

But Austin did not simply cooperate with Mexicans when they were willing to take the side of Anglos in some conflict. There were also times when he stood by the Mexican government in conflicts with other Anglos. Perhaps the most famous case involved the Fredonian Rebellion of 1826–27. In 1825, an Anglo-American, Haden Edwards, received an empresario contract from the state government to introduce 800 settlers into the Nacogdoches area. Edwards, a reckless and undiplomatic man, soon angered both Anglo and Tejano settlers who had long predated him in the region, and finally the Mexican government canceled his contract and ordered him expelled from Texas. He responded by declaring the independence of the "Fredonian" republic, and he made an alliance with a portion of the local Cherokee Indian tribes who had failed in their attempts to gain land titles from the Mexican government. Political chief José Antonio Saucedo assembled Mexican troops from Goliad and San Antonio, marched to San Felipe where they were joined by Stephen F. Austin and his colony's militia, and together the mixed force marched to Nacogdoches and put down the rebellion with minimal difficulty.

In hindsight, the Fredonian rebellion resembles comic opera, but for those willing to read the lessons carefully, it indicates more about the real nature of the Texas frontier from 1821 to 1835 and of racial and ethnic relations than almost any other incident. The temptation is to look only at surface facts and to see the rebellion as a precursor of the 1836 revolution—a land grab by aggressive, ungrateful Anglos. But the realities are much more complex. Consider several points. Before the granting of the Edwards empresario contract, the Nacogdoches region was occupied by an incredibly diverse population of Tejanos and Anglos, with a sprinkling of other ethnic Europeans. The region was also home to a number of indigenous Texas Indian tribes, plus the semi-Europeanized Cherokees, who were themselves recent emigrants from the American southeast. Edwards's contract was granted by a state legislature in far-off Saltillo, by Mexican elites whose own financial interests depended on the economic development of Texas. Edwards antagonized both Anglos and Tejanos in Nacogdoches, and the actual fighting that took place there was by no means an Anglo vs. Mexican affair. When Austin learned of the revolt, he called the Fredonians "a party of infatuated madmen," and Austin's Anglo colonists turned out unhesitatingly to aid the Mexicans in putting down the rebellion. Furthermore, facts show that the Cherokees themselves were actually sharply divided over the affair, and a sizable portion of them repudiated their comrades who had sided with Edwards and instead aided the Tejanos and Anglos in opposing the rebels. When the revolt disintegrated, the Cherokee leaders who had joined with the Fredonians were condemned by a tribal council, hunted down, and executed by their own people. In the aftermath of the rebellion, Anastacio Bustamante, commandant general of Mexico's northern frontier states, wrote Stephen Austin a letter expressing his gratitude for Austin's colonists' support, saying he wanted personally to give Austin *"un Extrechisimo abrazo"*—a very strong embrace—for "the happy result of the Expedition to Nacogdoches."

Like so much Texas history during this period, the simple dichotomies break down. In the Fredonian episode, Austin and his Anglo colonists marched side by side with Mexican troops against other Anglo-Americans. Even the Indians were bitterly divided. At Austin's suggestion, the Mexicans later granted amnesty to all but the ringleaders of the revolt, and he remained in East Texas several weeks, traveling the region with the Mexican leaders to calm the fears of the inhabitants and restore peace and order. Brown Austin undoubtedly spoke for his brother when he wrote that the insurgents were "treated with a degree of lenity by the Mexicans they had no right to expect from the nature of their crimes—and which I vouchsafe would not have been shewn them in their native country for similar offences." The actions of Austin and his colonists, as well as the response of the Mexican authorities, suggest a degree of cooperation and identification of common interests that transcended cultural differences.

After the notorious Law of April 6, 1830 disrupted the empresario system and initiated a Mexican crackdown on Anglo Texas, Austin once again sought to act as mediator. Although he potentially had more to lose under the law than almost anyone else, he counseled calmness and continued loyalty toward Mexico, even pointing out to his colonists the beneficial aspects of the much-hated decree. Over the next four years, every time that Texans grew dissatisfied with the actions of the government in Mexico City, he tried to forge solidarity between the Tejanos and Anglos of Texas and to encourage the Tejanos to take the lead in petitioning the government for redress. Even after Austin's arrest and imprisonment in 1833, he continued to call for calm in Texas. Indeed, after four months in a dungeon, he was still asking friends in Texas to "Remember me to Ramón Músquíz [the Tejano political chief in San Antonio] particularly—I shall feel grateful to him as long as I live. . . ."

Austin's friendship and respect for a long list of Mexican and Tejano leaders never faltered. His efforts to build a society in Mexican Texas where enterprising men of Anglo and Hispanic backgrounds might live in harmony and prosperity remained constant for fifteen years prior to the outbreak of revolution. He tried to avoid warfare against Indians, and he even accepted a few free blacks as settlers in his colony.

Given these efforts, how are the seemingly bigoted statements that he occasionally uttered to be explained? Take, for example, his famous 1823 complaint about Mexicans being as being as uncivilized apes. It is easy to take such a statement out of context, but if one continues reading that same letter, Austin predicts optimistically that the Mexican nation would soon "assume her rights in full, and bursting the chains of superstition declare that *man has a right to think for himself.*" In other words, Austin directed his criticism at the Church itself and what he perceived as its oppression of the Mexican people, not at Mexicans for any inherent defect of character. In 1833, he was even more explicit on this theme, actually defending Roman Catholicism as "a religion whose foundation is perfect harmony, a union of principles, & of action." But he condemned the *type* of Catholicism then being practiced in Mexico, saying it was "in theory divine, in practice infernal." These were not the words of a knee-jerk nativist.

But what about the harsh racial invective that he employed in 1835–1836? What are we to make of his support for independence, his 1836 outburst about the "war of barbarism" being "waged by the mongrel Spanish-Indian race, against civilization and the Anglo-American race," and his declaration that the non-Anglos of Texas were "the natural enemies of white men and civilization?" Was this the chauvinistic American finally showing his true colors? How do we reconcile such statements with his actions during the previous fifteen years?

Again, context is everything, and placing Austin's racist-sounding comments in context reveals the great tragedy of Anglo-Tejano relations in the Texas Revolutionary period. Austin wrote these words at a point in the Revolution when he was desperately trying to arouse sympathy and support from citizens of the United States. His main audience was made up of Jacksonian Democrats—and *southern* Democrats at that. His rhetorical transformation of the Texian struggle into a war against racially inferior Mexicans was carefully calculated to stir the deepest fears and emotions of southerners. One of the tragic consequences of this war—and of almost all others in which the enemy is of a different race, ethnicity, or culture—is that such wars almost inevitably generate this sort of propaganda. Portray your enemies as somehow less than human, and killing them becomes much easier. Recall how Germans were portrayed in American propaganda during World War I, or the Japanese during World War II, and the genesis of Austin's words can be understood. Was he wrong to resort to racist appeals when his actions over a fifteen-year period clearly contradicted such sentiments? Of course he was. In this one instance, Austin sacrificed his principles in a desperate attempt to reverse the tide of a war that by all appearances was about to be lost. We may wish that he had possessed the superhuman strength of character needed to resist such a sellout, but in the end he was only human.

Returning to his beloved Texas in the critical summer of 1836, Austin reverted to his tried-and-true philosophy of seeking reconciliation and national unity. He never had the opportunity to visit his old Tejano friends in San Antonio, but there is no indication that he would have treated them any differently than before. The harsh rhetoric was never repeated at home. Nothing from his short, ill-fated presidential campaign against Sam Houston that September suggests that he would have changed his longstanding policy of working to build a Texas in which Anglos and Tejanos could honorably cooperate and coexist. And his willingness to accept a cabinet appointment from his rival, Sam Houston, and to support Houston in all broad policy matters, further suggests that he, like Houston, would have resisted the movement toward persecution and recrimination against Tejanos that grew in intensity over the coming years.

However, Stephen F. Austin was a man of his times in one important respect. He believed that American-style democracy—flawed though it may have been by the stain of slavery—was the best system of government yet devised. He only gave up on Mexico when he became convinced that his adopted country had utterly failed to secure the blessings of democracy for its people, Anglo and Hispanic. Having reached that determination, he was willing to employ whatever necessary means to win the Revolution and bring Texas under a better government. That decision—and those means—could give the appearance that he was motivated by an unthinking bigotry against all things not American. But to arrive at such a conclusion, based on a selective reading of the evidence, is to overlook the fifteen-year reality of Austin as a genuine political and cultural mediator.

 ## FURTHER READING

Eugene C. Barker, *The Life of Stephen F. Austin: Founder of Texas, 1793–1836* (1925)

Gregg Cantrell, *Stephen F. Austin, Empresario of Texas* (1999)

Julia Kathryn Garrett, *Green Flag Over Texas; A Story of the Last Years of Spain in Texas* (1939)

Margaret Swett Henson, *Juan Davis Bradburn: A Reappraisal of the Mexican Commander of Anahuac* (1982)

Malcolm D. Maclean, ed., *Papers Concerning Robertson's Colony in Texas,* 17 vols. (1974–1991)

Timothy Matovina, *Tejano Religion and Ethnicity: San Antonio, 1821–1860* (1994)

Manuel de Mier y Terán, *Texas by Teran: The Diary Kept by Manuel Mier y Terán on 1828 Inspection of Texas* (2000)

W. H. Oberste, *Texas Irish Empresarios and their Colonies* (1953)

Rebecca Lee Smith, *Mary Austin Holley: A Biography* (1962)

Noah Smithwick, *Evolution of a State, or Recollections of Old Texas Days* (1900, reprinted, 1995)

Andres Tijerina, *Tejanos and Texas Under the Mexican Flag, 1821–1836* (1994)

Harris Gaylord Warren, *The Sword Was their Passport: a History of American Filibustering in the Mexican Revolution* (1943)

David J. Weber, *The Mexican Frontier, 1821–1846: The American Southwest Under Mexico* (1982)

# CHAPTER
# 5

# *Revolutionary Texas,*

# *1835–1836*

*The early 1830s proved to be years of relative political calm for Texas. Most Anglo Texans demonstrated a willingness to discuss their grievances through the procedures familiar to them as former citizens of the United States. However, a "war party" led by William Barret Travis lobbied for a more militant response to disagreements with local officials. For its part, the federalist government demonstrated a cautious willingness to discuss these issues. In 1834, it repealed the Law of April 6, 1830, which had proved largely unenforceable in any case, and promised to address many of the Texans' long-standing grievances.*

*Relations between Mexico and the communities of Texas deteriorated sharply in 1834, however, when Mexican president Antonio López de Santa Anna abolished the Constitution of 1824 and took steps to establish a centralist, authoritarian system of government. The so-called Plan of Cuernevaca threw the entire country into chaos, sparking federalist uprisings in the provinces of Zacatecas, Coahuila, the Yucatan, and Santa Fe. By October 1835, Santa Anna had moved to further consolidate his power, abolishing the state legislatures and replacing them with military districts. The long-simmering Texas problem now flared into open rebellion. Unlike the other uprisings against the new centralist government, the revolt in Texas drew its support largely from Anglo Americans, many of whom had only recently arrived in Texas.*

*The causes of the Revolution have provoked much debate among historians in both Mexico and the United States. Was the revolution the product of deep-seated cultural cleavages between Anglos and Mexicans, or was it a political crisis occasioned by the collapse of federalism and representative government in Mexico? Although some historians have emphasized the inconsistent and ultimately heavy-handed policies of the Mexican government, others have pointed to the fact that many Anglo Texans willfully disregarded the customs of the country which granted them citizenship. The Texas Revolution, they maintain, was a blatant land grab by Anglo Americans who were determined to wrest the territory from Mexican control by whatever means necessary. Still another question historians have asked is whether the conflict was an inevitable one. Could Anglo Americans have ever lived as dutiful citizens under Mexican rule, or was the conflict the result of short-term crises that could have been avoided had cooler heads prevailed on both sides?*

## ✦ D O C U M E N T S

In 1835, there existed widespread disagreement among Anglo Americans about what course to pursue toward the government in Mexico City. As Gregg Cantrell states in Chapter 4, Stephen F. Austin had long been an effective advocate for conciliation. In 1833, however, Austin was arrested and imprisoned in Mexico City, and did not return to Texas until the fall of 1835. Austin's call for "a general consultation" in Document 1, at a dinner in his honor in Brazoria County, signalled a marked departure from the empresario's previous statements and moved Texas rapidly closer toward the armed resistance that would ultimately lead to independence. Less than a month after Austin delivered this address, Texans would clash with Mexican troops at Gonzales, sparking the Revolution. Document 2 is a map of Texas drafted by Stephen F. Austin when the conflict began. Although the map clearly shows the Nueces River as the southern boundary of Texas, by the end of the war Texans regarded the Rio Grande as the legitimate boundary with Mexico. The boundary dispute would remain unresolved in the years ahead, ultimately providing the pretext for the United States' declaration of war against Mexico in 1846.

The Texas declaration of independence is presented in Document 3. Clearly modeled after the document by which the United States asserted its own independence in 1776, the declaration was designed to inflame public opinion, justifying the Texas action by presenting the policies of the Mexican government in the worst possible light. A rebuttal to the declaration's charges is offered by Jose Maria Tornel, Mexico's Secretary of War in 1836, in Document 4.

The Alamo siege is the most famous episode in Texas history. In Document 5, commander of the Alamo garrison, William B. Travis, appeals for aid in the last of several letters written during the siege. Document 6 is an excerpt from the memoir of José Enrique de la Peña, an officer in the Mexican Army. De la Peña's memoir, which did not come to light until 1955, has been labeled a forgery by some historians and an invaluable eyewitness account of the siege by others. At the center of the debate are the circumstances of the death of former Tennessee congressman David Crockett.

News of the fall of the Alamo, as well as the subsequent capture and execution of another Texas army under Colonel James Fannin at Goliad in March threw Texans into panic and disarray. Document 7 is an account of the "Runaway Scrape," the exodus of Anglo Texans into Louisiana as Santa Anna's army advanced in the spring of 1836. The Texan forces also remained in a fractious frame of mind, and even a stunning victory over the Mexican army at San Jacinto on April 21 did not bring an end to the chaos and disorder of revolutionary upheaval. In Document 8, Mirabeau B. Lamar, who had been appointed commander of the Texas army after San Jacinto, complains in a letter to interim president David G. Burnet of the insubordination that reigned in the ranks in the summer of 1836. A want of discipline among Texas troops, coupled with the ambitions of a number of prominent military leaders, would continue to imperil the stability of the new nation in the years ahead.

Although the Revolution could not have been won without the aid of American volunteers, public opinion in the United States was deeply divided over the struggle for

Texas independence. In Document 9, the prominent American abolitionist Benjamin Lundy attributes the struggle in Texas to a Southern conspiracy bent on expanding the slave empire. This thesis was widely accepted by the Northern antislavery movement, which would furiously oppose any and all efforts to bring Texas into the Union in the years ahead.

## 1. Stephen F. Austin Declares His Support for Independence, 1835

I left Texas in April, 1833, as the public agent of the people, for the purpose of applying for the admission of this country into the Mexican confederation as a state separate from Coahuila. This application was based upon the constitutional and vested rights of Texas, and was sustained by me in the city of Mexico to the utmost of my abilities. No honorable means were spared to effect the objects of my mission and to oppose the forming of Texas into a territory, which was attempted. I rigidly adhered to the instructions and wishes of my constituents, so far as they were communicated to me. My efforts to serve Texas involved me in the labyrinth of Mexican politics. I was arrested, and have suffered a long persecution and imprisonment. I consider it my duty to give an account of these events to my constituents, and will therefore at this time merely observe that I have never, in any manner, agreed to any thing, or admitted any thing, that would compromise the constitutional or vested rights of Texas. These rights belong to the people, and can only be surrendered by them.

I fully hoped to have found Texas at peace and in tranquility, but regret to find it in commotion; all disorganized, all in anarchy, and threatened with immediate hostilities. This state of things is deeply to be lamented; it is a great misfortune, but it is one which has not been produced by any acts of the people of this country: on the contrary, it is the natural and inevitable consequence of the revolution that has spread all over Mexico, and of the imprudent and impolitic measures of both the general and state governments, with respect to Texas. The people here are not to blame, and cannot be justly censured. They are farmers, cultivators of the soil, and are pacific from interest, from occupation, and from inclination. They have uniformly endeavored to sustain the constitution and the public peace by pacific means, and have never deviated from their duty as Mexican citizens. If any acts of imprudence have been committed by individuals, they evidently resulted from the revolutionary state of the whole nation, the imprudent and censurable conduct of the state authorities, and the total want of a local government in Texas. It is, indeed, a source of surprise and creditable congratulation, that so few acts of this description have occurred under the peculiar circumstances of the times. It is, however, to be remembered that acts of this nature were not the acts of the people, nor is Texas responsible for them. They were, as I before observed, the natural consequences of the revolutionary state of the Mexican nation; and Texas certainly did

"Austin to the People of Texas," *The Austin Papers, October 1834–January 1837,* Eugene C. Barker, ed., vol. III (Austin: University of Texas Press), 116–119.

not originate the revolution, neither have the people, as a people, participated in it. The consciences and hands of the Texians are free from censure, and clean.

The revolution in Mexico is drawing to a close. The object is to change the form of government, destroy the federal constitution of 1824, and establish a central or consolidated government. The states are to be converted into provinces.

Whether the people of Texas ought or ought not to agree to this change, and relinquish all or part of their constitutional and vested rights under the constitution of 1824, is a question of the most vital importance; one that calls for the deliberate consideration of the people, and can only be decided by them, fairly convened for the purpose. As a citizen of Texas I have no other right, and pretend to no other. In the report which I consider it my duty to make my constituents, I intend to give my views on the present situation of the country, and especially as to the constitutional and national rights of Texas, and will, therefore, at this time, merely touch this subject.

Under the Spanish government, Texas was a separate and distinct local organization. It was one of the unities that composed the general mass of the nation, and as such participated in the war of the revolution, and was represented in the constituent congress of Mexico, that formed the constitution of 1824. This constituent congress, so far from destroying this unity, expressly recognized and confirmed it by the law of May 7th, 1824, which united Texas with Coahuila *provisionally,* under the especial guarantee of being made a state of the Mexican confederation, as soon as it possessed the necessary elements. That law and the federal constitution gave to Texas a specific political existence, and vested in its inhabitants special and defined rights, which can only be relinquished by the people of Texas, acting for themselves as a unity, and not as a part of Coahuila, for the reason that the union with Coahuila, was *limited,* and only gave power to the state of Coahuila and Texas to govern Texas for the time being, but *always subject to the vested rights of Texas.* The state, therefore, cannot relinquish those vested rights, by agreeing to the change of government, or by any other act, unless expressly authorized by the people of Texas to do so; neither can the general government of Mexico legally deprive Texas of them without the consent of this people. These are my opinions.

An important question now presents itself to the people of this country.

The federal constitution of 1824 is about to be destroyed, the system of government changed, and a central or consolidated one established. Will this act annihilate all the rights of Texas, and subject this country to the uncontrolled and unlimited dictation of the new government?

This is a subject of the most vital importance. I have no doubts the federal constitution will be destroyed, and a central government established, and that the people will soon be called upon to say whether they agree to this change or not. This matter requires the most calm discussion, the most mature deliberation, and the most perfect union. How is this to be had? I see but one way, and that is by a general consultation of the people by means of delegates elected for that purpose, with full powers to give such an answer, in the name of Texas, to this question, as they may deem best, and to adopt such measures as the tranquility and salvation of the country may require. . . .

It is also proper for me to state that, in all my conversation with the president and ministers and men of influence, I advised that no troops should be sent to Texas, and no cruisers along the coast. I gave it as my decided opinion, that the inevitable consequence of sending an armed force to this country would be war. I stated that there was a sound and correct moral principle in the people of Texas, that was abundantly sufficient to restrain or put down all turbulent or seditious movements, but that this moral principle could not, and would not unite with any armed force sent against this country; on the contrary, it would resist and repel it, and ought to do so. This point presents another strong reason why the people of Texas should meet in general consultation. This country is now in anarchy, threatened with hostilities; armed vessels are capturing every thing they can catch on the coast, and acts of piracy are said to be committed under cover of the Mexican flag. Can this state of things exist without precipitating the country into a war? I think it cannot, and therefore believe that it is our bounden and solemn duty as Mexicans, and as Texians, to represent the evils that are likely to result from this mistaken and most impolitic policy in the military movement.

My friends, I can truly say that no one has been, or is now, more anxious than myself to keep trouble away from this country. No one has been, or now is more faithful to his duty as a Mexican citizen, and no one has personally sacrificed or suffered more in the discharge of this duty. I have uniformly been opposed to have any thing to do with the family political quarrels of the Mexicans. Texas needs peace, and a local government: its inhabitants are farmers, and they need a calm and quiet life. But how can I, or any one, remain indifferent, when our rights, our all, appear to be in jeopardy, and when it is our duty, as well as our obligation as good Mexican citizens, to express our opinions on the present state of things, and to represent our situation to the government? It is impossible. The crisis is such as to bring it home to the judgment of every man that something must be done, and that without delay. The question will perhaps be asked, what are we to do? I have already indicated my opinion. Let all personalities, or divisions, or excitements, or passion, or violence, be banished from among us. Let a general consultation of the people of Texas be convened as speedily as possible, to be composed of the best, and most calm, and intelligent, and firm men in the country, and let them decide what representations ought to be made to the general government, and what ought to be done in future.

## 2.  Map of Texas on the Eve of Revolution, 1835

Map of Texas, with Part of Adjoining States (Philadelphia: Henry S. Tanner, 1836), University of Texas at Arlington Cartographic Collection.

# 3. Texas Declaration of Independence, March 2, 1836

When a government has ceased to protect the lives, liberty and property of the people, from whom its legitimate powers are derived, and for the advancement of whose happiness it was instituted; and so far from being a guarantee for their inestimable and inalienable rights, becomes an instrument in the hands of evil rulers for their oppression. When the federal republican constitution of their country, which they have sworn to support, no longer has a substantial existence, and the whole nature of their government has been forcibly changed, without their consent, from a restricted federative republic, composed of sovereign states, to a consolidated central military despotism, in which every interest is disregarded but that of the army and the priesthood, both the eternal enemies of civil liberty, the ever ready minions of power, and the usual instruments of tyrants. When, long after the spirit of the constitution has departed, moderation is at length so far lost by those in power, that even the semblance of freedom is removed, and the forms themselves of the constitution discontinued, and so far from their petitions and remonstrances being regarded, the agents who bear them are thrown into dungeons, and mercenary armies sent forth to enforce a new government upon them at the point of the bayonet.

When, in consequence of such acts of malfeasance and abduction on the part of the government, anarchy prevails, and civil society is dissolved into its original elements, in such a crisis, the first law of nature, the right of self-preservation, the inherent and inalienable right of the people to appeal to first principles, and take their political affairs into their own hands in extreme cases, enjoins it as a right towards themselves, and a sacred obligation to their posterity, to abolish such government, and create another in its stead, calculated to rescue them from impending dangers, and to secure their welfare and happiness.

Nations, as well as individuals, are amenable for their acts to the public opinion of mankind. A statement of a part of our grievances is therefore submitted to an impartial world, in justification of the hazardous but unavoidable step now taken, of severing our political connection with the Mexican people, and assuming an independent attitude among the nations of the earth.

The Mexican government, by its colonization laws, invited and induced the Anglo American population of Texas to colonize its wilderness under the pledged faith of a written constitution, that they should continue to enjoy that constitutional liberty and republican government to which they had been habituated in the land of their birth, the United States of America.

In this expectation they have been cruelly disappointed, inasmuch as the Mexican nation has acquiesced to the late changes made in the government by General Antonio Lopez de Santa Anna, who, having overturned the constitution of his country, now offers, as the cruel alternative, either to abandon our homes, acquired by so many privations, or submit to the most intolerable of all tyranny, the combined despotism of the sword and the priesthood.

---

"The Declaration of Independence Made by the Delegates of the People of Texas," H. P. N. Gammel, comp., *The Laws of Texas, 1822–1897* (Austin: Gammel Book Co., 1898), 1:1063–1066.

It hath sacrificed our welfare to the state of Coahuila, by which our interests have been continually depressed through a jealous and partial course of legislation, carried on at a far distant seat of government, by a hostile majority, in an unknown tongue, and this too, notwithstanding we have petitioned in the humblest terms for the establishment of a separate state government, and have, in accordance with the provisions of the national constitution, presented to the general congress a republican constitution, which was, without a just cause, contemptuously rejected.

It incarcerated in a dungeon, for a long time, one of our citizens, for no other cause but a zealous endeavor to procure the acceptance of our constitution, and the establishment of a state government.

It has failed and refused to secure, on a firm basis, the right of trial by jury, that palladium of civil liberty, and only safe guarantee for the life, liberty, and property of the citizen.

It has failed to establish any public system of education, although possessed of almost boundless resources, (the public domain,) and although it is an axiom in political science, that unless a people are educated and enlightened, it is idle to expect the continuance of civil liberty, or the capacity for self government.

It has suffered the military commandants, stationed among us, to exercise arbitrary acts of oppression and tyranny, thus trampling upon the most sacred rights of the citizen, and rendering the military superior to the civil power.

It has dissolved, by force of arms, the state congress of Coahuila and Texas, and obliged our representatives to fly for their lives from the seat of government, thus depriving us of the fundamental political right of representation.

It has demanded the surrender of a number of our citizens, and ordered military detachments to seize and carry them into the interior for trial, in contempt of the civil authorities, and in defiance of the laws and the constitution.

It has made piratical attacks upon our commerce, by commissioning foreign desperadoes, and authorizing them to seize our vessels, and convey the property of our citizens to far distant parts for confiscation.

It denies us the right of worshiping the Almighty according to the dictates of our own conscience, by the support of a national religion, calculated to promote the temporal interest of its human functionaries, rather than the glory of the true and living God.

It has demanded us to deliver up our arms, which are essential to our defence—the rightful property of freemen—and formidable only to tyrannical governments.

It has invaded our country both by sea and by land, with the intent to lay waste our territory, and drive us from our homes; and has now a large mercenary army advancing, to carry on against us a war of extermination.

It has, through its emissaries, incited the merciless savage, with the tomahawk and scalping knife, to massacre the inhabitants of our defenceless frontiers.

It has been, during the whole time of our connection with it, the contemptible sport and victim of successive military revolutions, and hath continually exhibited every characteristic of a weak, corrupt, and tryannical government.

These, and other grievances, were patiently borne by the people of Texas, until they reached that point at which forbearance ceases to be a virtue. We then took up arms in defence of the national constitution. We appealed to our Mexican brethren for assistance: our appeal has been made in vain; though months have elapsed, no sympathetic response has yet been heard from the interior. We are, therefore, forced to the melancholy conclusion, that the Mexican people have acquiesced in the destruction of their liberty, and the substitution therefor of a military government; that they are unfit to be free, and incapable of self government.

The necessity of self-preservation, therefore, now decrees our eternal political separation.

## 4.  Mexico's Secretary of War José Maria Tornel Rebuts the Texan Reasons for Independence, 1836

Finally a day arrived when, seduced by the happy coincidence of a thousand unforeseen circumstances, the Texas colonists sundered all ties and openly declared themselves independent from the Mexican nation. Their delegates assembled in Washington, in the District of Brazoria, drew up a declaration of independence, March 2, 1836. This is but the admission of a fact and the carrying out of a plan long since recognized. An attempt is made, however, to support this action by an astonishing jumble of impostures. It is stated that the Texans were invited and admitted subject to the observance of a contract by which assurances were given to maintain the written constitution; that this having been annulled, all their obligations ceased. Our country, with ill-advised generosity, acceded to their requests and took them into our midst because they asked and desired to be taken in. We have observed that at the time when the first grants were made the government of the nation was a monarchy and that subsequently several changes have been effected in the government none of which justify them in refusing their obedience because no specific form of government was stipulated in the contracts. An insolent minority cannot arrogate to itself the right of determining the form of government of the republic in violation of the wishes of the great majority. If such a minority was not in accord with the changes effected it was free to leave the country whenever the obligations imposed upon it became too great a burden or a menace to its liberties.

The rebels allege as the principal complaint that they were not permitted to organize themselves as an independent state of the union, governed by a constitution framed and designed by themselves. Granting the stability of the federal system, it was still very questionable whether Texas already possessed the necessary elements and resources to be organized as an independent entity. Furthermore, we cannot ignore the natural distrust which such a forward step inevitably inspired, when we consider the well-known aim of all the petitions of the colonists. A change in the administration of the country having taken place, the Texans should have waited the results of the principal innovations planned, in view of the fact that congress had raised Texas to the rank of a department, separating it from Coahuila to that extent.

They accuse us of having neglected primary education in Texas. This charge clearly shows their bad faith. As is well known, education is left by our laws to the

"Jose Maria Tornel y Mendivil," Carlos Castaneda, trans. and ed., *The Mexican Side of the Texas Revolution* (Austin: Graphic Ideas, 1977), 355–357. Reprint made possible by Ayer Co. Publishers, 2001.

respective *ayuntamientos*. The city councils of Texas not only exercised all the prerogatives allowed them but assumed many that are foreign to such bodies. Why then did they not look after education if it interested them so deeply? Furthermore, the Texas *ayuntamientos* imposed taxes and used their revenues without the least interference on the part of Mexican officials. If they failed to use them for the education of their children, it was clearly their fault. The people of Texas were represented in the legislature of the state. It was there that they should have presented their demands regarding this subject as they did with regard to lands, the prime object of their desires, the obvious aim of their insatiable greed.

The colonists bitterly complain of their having been sacrificed to the interest of Coahuila. This is but a typical untruth. The officers of the state inclined rather to the opposite extreme, indiscreetly favoring the Texans by assenting to their endless petitions. In the course of the preceding pages, the grants of lands made to them have been noted. It is particularly noteworthy, however, that among the grantees there were only two or three citizens of Coahuila, whose grants were in general usurped by other empresarios. The colonists sometimes curse Coahuila for her supposed injustices to them, and at others they curse the nation for its arbitrary acts against Coahuila.

The charges of oppression and tyranny brought against our military officers are false and unfounded. Far from this, our soldiers have, on the contrary, been exposed to the same libelous charges as all our public officers. They have been disarmed and driven from their posts while holding them in the discharge of their duties. Every attempt made to enforce law has been pointed out by the colonists as an attack, while the repression of crime has been called an insult and classed as an attempt upon individual liberties in their newly invented dictionary. Even now they maintain that trade has been hampered by unheard-of restrictions and vexations. During the first seven years they were exempt from paying duties on all goods imported into Texas. After the expiration of this privilege, there has been nothing but contraband trade along the entire coast and the whole frontier.

The prohibition against the erection of places of worship and the practice of other cults than the Roman Catholic was the law of the land at the time when the colonists came and they agreed to conform to it. Why didn't they stay in their own country to raise temples in the vast solitudes of the west? Nations adopt or reject restrictions with regard to religious practices as they see fit. To pretend to force us to promulgate religious toleration is to assume the exercise of a right over us even superior to that of conquest, for the religion and the customs of a conquered country have always been respected.

Lastly, the rebels have tried to justify their criminal uprising before God and before man as the result of the adoption of necessary repressive measures by the easygoing Mexican government. The use of force to restrain the restless, to punish the rebellious, and to maintain obedience is an inherent right of the sovereignty of nations. What other right can the United States invoke in support of the troops sent to Florida to chastise the Seminoles and the Creeks? What is right for one nation should be right for all: The attributes of sovereignty are identical in all nations. The civilized world has already passed judgment upon the usurpations of the Texans, refusing to admit the reasons advanced in support of their declaration of independence.

## 5. Alamo Commander William B. Travis Appeals for Aid, March 3, 1836

Bejar, March 3, 1836.

Sir,—In the present confusion of the political authorities of the country, and in the absence of the commander-in-chief, I beg leave to communicate to you the situation of this garrison. You have doubtless already seen my official report of the action of the 25th ult., made on that day to Gen. Sam. Houston, together with the various communications heretofore sent by express. I shall therefore confine myself to what has transpired since that date.

From the 25th to the present date, the enemy have kept up a bombardment from two howitzers, (one a five and a half inch, and the other an eight inch,) and a heavy cannonade from two long nine pounders, mounted on a battery on the opposite side of the river, at the distance of four hundred yards from our walls. During this period the enemy have been busily employed in encircling us with entrenched encampments on all sides, at the following distances, to wit:—in Bejar, four hundred yards west; in Lavilleta, three hundred yards south; at the powder house, one thousand yards east by south; on the ditch, eight hundred yards northeast, and at the old mill, eight hundred yards north. Notwithstanding all this, a company of thirty-two men, from Gonzales, made their way into us on the morning of the 1st inst., at 3 o'clock, and Col. J. B. Bonham (a courier from Gonzales) got in this morning at 11 o'clock, without molestation. I have so fortified this place, that the walls are generally proof against cannon balls; and I still continue to intrench on the inside, and strengthen the walls by throwing up the dirt. At least two hundred shells have fallen inside of our works without having injured a single man: indeed, we have been so fortunate as not to lose a man from any cause; and we have killed many of the enemy. The spirits of my men are still high, although they have had much to depress them. We have contended for ten days against an enemy whose numbers are variously estimated at from fifteen hundred to six thousand men, with Gen. Ramirer Siesma and Col. Batres, the aids-de-camps of Santa Anna, at their head. A report was circulated that Santa Anna himself was with the enemy, but I think it was false. A reinforcement of about one thousand men is now entering Bejar from the west, and I think it more than probable that Santa Anna is now in town, from the rejoicing we hear. Col. Fannin is said to be on the march to this place with reinforcements; but I fear it is not true, as I have repeatedly sent to him for aid without receiving any. Colonel Bonham, my special messenger, arrived at La Bahia fourteen days ago, with a request for aid; and on the arrival of the enemy in Bejar ten days ago, I sent an express to Col. Fannin, which arrived at Goliad on the next day, urging him to send us reinforcements—*none have yet arrived.* I look to the *colonies alone* for aid: unless it arrives soon, I shall have to fight the enemy on his own terms. I will, however, do the best I can under the circumstances; and I feel confident that the determined valor, and desperate courage, heretofore evinced by my men, will not fail them in the last struggle: and although they may be sacrificed to the vengeance of a gothic enemy, the victory will cost the enemy so dear, that

Mary Austin Holley, *Texas* (Lexington, KY: J. Clarke & Co., 1836), 351–353.

it will be worse for him than a defeat. I hope your honourable body will hasten on reinforcements, ammunition, and provisions to our aid, as soon as possible. We have provisions for twenty days for the men we have—our supply of ammunition is limited. At least five hundred pounds of cannon powder, and two hundred rounds of six, nine, twelve, and eighteen pound balls—ten kegs of rifle powder, and a supply of lead, should be sent to this place without delay, under a sufficient guard.

If these things are promptly sent and large reinforcements are hastened to this frontier, this neighborhood will be the great and decisive battle ground. The power of Santa Anna is to be met here, or in the colonies; we had better meet them here, than to suffer a war of desolation to rage in our settlements. A blood red banner waves from the church of Bejar, and in the camp above us, in token that the war is one of vengeance against rebels: they have declared us as such, and demanded that we should surrender at discretion, or that this garrison should be put to the sword. Their threats have had no influence on me, or my men, but to make all fight with desperation, and that high souled courage which characterizes the patriot, who is willing to die in defence of his country's liberty and his own honor.

The citizens of this municipality are all our enemies except those who have joined us heretofore; we have but three Mexicans now in the fort; those who have not joined us in this extremity, should be declared public enemies, and their property should aid in paying the expenses of the war.

The bearer of this will give your honorable body, a statement more in detail, should he escape through the enemies lines—*God and Texas—Victory or Death!!*

Your obedient servant,

W. BARRETT TRAVIS

## 6. Mexican Lieutenant Colonel José Enrique de la Peña Describes the Fall of the Alamo, 1836

The columns advanced with as much speed as possible; shortly after beginning the march they were ordered to open fire while they were still out of range, but there were some officers who wisely disregarded the signal. Alerted to our attack by the given signal, which all columns answered, the enemy vigorously returned our fire, which had not even touched him but had retarded our advance. Travis, to compensate for the reduced number of the defenders, had placed three or four rifles by the side of each man, so that the initial fire was very rapid and deadly. Our columns left along their path a wide trail of blood, of wounded, and of dead. The bands from all the corps, gathered around our commander, sounded the charge; with a most vivid ardor and enthusiasm, we answered that call which electrifies the heart, elevates the soul, and makes others tremble. The second column, seized by this spirit, burst out in acclamations for the Republic and for the president-general. The officers were unable to repress this act of folly, which was paid for dearly. His attention drawn by this act, the enemy seized the opportunity, at the moment that light was beginning to

José Enrique de la Peña, *With Santa Anna in Texas: A Personal Narrative of the Revolution,* trans. and ed. Carmen Perry (College Station: Texas A&M University Press, 1975), 47–53. Reprinted by permission of Texas A&M University Press.

make objects discernible around us, to redouble the fire on this column, making it suffer the greatest blows. It could be observed that a single cannon volley did away with half the company of chasseurs from Toluca, which was advancing a few paces from the column; Captain José María Herrera, who commanded it, died a few moments later and Vences, its lieutenant, was also wounded. Another volley left many gaps among the ranks at the head, one of them being Colonel Duque, who was wounded in the thigh; there remained standing, not without surprise, one of the two aides to this commander, who marched immediately to his side, but the other one now cannot testify to this. Fate was kind on this occasion to the writer, who survived, though Don José María Macotela, captain from Toluca, was seriously wounded and died shortly after.

It has been observed what the plan of attack was, but various arrangements made to carry it out were for the most part omitted; the columns had been ordered to provide themselves with crow-bars, hatchets, and ladders, but not until the last moment did it become obvious that all this was insufficient and that the ladders were poorly put together.

The columns, bravely storming the fort in the midst of a terrible shower of bullets and cannon-fire, had reached the base of the walls, with the exception of the third, which had been sorely punished on its left flank by a battery of three cannon on a barbette that cut a serious breach in its ranks; since it was being attacked frontally at the same time from the height of a position, it was forced to seek a less bloody entrance, and thus changed its course toward the right angle of the north front. The few poor ladders that we were bringing had not arrived, because their bearers had either perished on the way or had escaped. Only one was seen of all those that were planned. General Cos, looking for a starting point from which to climb, had advanced frontally with his column to where the second and third were. All united at one point, mixing and forming a confused mass. Fortunately the wall reinforcement on this front was of lumber, its excavation was hardly begun, and the height of the parapet was eight or nine feet; there was therefore a starting point, and it could be climbed, though with some difficulty. But disorder had already begun; officers of all ranks shouted but were hardly heard. The most daring of our veterans tried to be the first to climb, which they accomplished, yelling wildly so that room could be made for them, at times climbing over their own comrades. Others, jammed together, made useless efforts, obstructing each other, getting in the way of the more agile ones and pushing down those who were about to carry out their courageous effort. A lively rifle fire coming from the roof of the barracks and other points caused painful havoc, increasing the confusion of our disorderly mass. The first to climb were thrown down by bayonets already waiting for them behind the parapet, or by pistol fire, but the courage of our soldiers was not diminished as they saw their comrades falling dead or wounded, and they hurried to occupy their places and to avenge them, climbing over their bleeding bodies. The sharp reports of the rifles, the whistling of bullets, the groans of the wounded, the cursing of the men, the sighs and anguished cries of the dying, the arrogant harangues of the officers, the noise of the instruments of war, and the inordinate shouts of the attackers, who climbed vigorously, bewildered all and made of this moment a tremendous and critical one. The shouting of those being attacked was no less loud and from the beginning had pierced our ears with desperate, terrible cries of alarm in a language we did not understand.

From his point of observation, General Santa Anna viewed with concern this horrible scene and, misled by the difficulties encountered in the climbing of the walls and by the maneuver executed by the third column, believed we were being repulsed; he therefore ordered Colonel Amat to move in with the rest of the reserves; the Sapper Battalion, already ordered to move their column of attack, arrived and began to climb at the same time. He then also ordered into battle his general staff and everyone at his side. This gallant reserve merely added to the noise and the victims, the more regrettable since there was no necessity for them to engage in the combat. Before the Sapper Battalion, advancing through a shower of bullets and volley of shrapnel, had a chance to reach the foot of the walls, half their officers had been wounded. Another one of these officers, young Torres, died within the fort at the very moment of taking a flag. He died at one blow without uttering a word, covered with glory and lamented by his comrades. Something unusual happened to this corps; it had as casualties four officers and twenty-one soldiers, but among these none of the sergeant class, well known to be more numerous than the former.

A quarter of an hour had elapsed, during which our soldiers remained in a terrible situation, wearing themselves out as they climbed in quest of a less obscure death than that visited on them, crowded in a single mass; later and after much effort, they were able in sufficient numbers to reach the parapet, without distinction of ranks. The terrified defenders withdrew at once into quarters placed to the right and the left of the small area that constituted their second line of defense. They had bolted and reinforced the doors, but in order to form trenches they had excavated some places inside that were now a hindrance to them. Not all of them took refuge, for some remained in the open, looking at us before firing, as if dumbfounded at our daring. Travis was seen to hesitate, but not about the death that he would choose. He would take a few steps and stop, turning his proud face toward us to discharge his shots; he fought like a true soldier. Finally he died, but he died after having traded his life very dearly. None of his men died with greater heroism, and they all died. Travis behaved as a hero; one must do him justice, for with a handful of men without discipline, he resolved to face men used to war and much superior in numbers, without supplies, with scarce munitions, and against the will of his subordinates. He was a handsome blond, with a physique as robust as his spirit was strong.

In the meantime Colonel Morelos with his chasseurs, having carried out instructions received, was just in front of us at a distance of a few paces, and, rightly fearing that our fire would hurt him, he had taken refuge in the trenches he had overrun trying to inflict damage on the enemy without harming us. It was a good thing that other columns could come together in a single front, for because of the small area the destruction among ourselves could be partially avoided; nevertheless, some of our men suffered the pain of falling from shots fired by their comrades, a grievous wound indeed, and a death even more lamentable. The soldiers had been overloaded with munition, for the reserves and all the select companies carried seven rounds apiece. It seems that the purpose of this was to convey the message to the soldier not to rely on his bayonet, which is the weapon generally employed in assault while some of the chasseurs support the attackers with their fire; however, there are always errors committed on these occasions, impossible to remedy. There remains no consolation other than regret for those responsible on this occasion, and there were many.

Our soldiers, some stimulated by courage and others by fury, burst into the quarters where the enemy had entrenched themselves, from which issued an infernal fire. Behind these came others, who, nearing the doors and blind with fury and smoke, fired their shots against friends and enemies alike, and in this way our losses were most grievous. On the other hand, they turned the enemy's own cannon to bring down the doors to the rooms or the rooms themselves; a horrible carnage took place, and some were trampled to death. The tumult was great, the disorder frightful; it seemed as if the furies had descended upon us; different groups of soldiers were firing in all directions, on their comrades and on their officers, so that one was as likely to die by a friendly hand as by an enemy's. In the midst of this thundering din, there was such confusion that orders could not be understood, although those in command would raise their voices when the opportunity occurred. Some may believe that this narrative is exaggerated, but those who were witnesses will confess that this is exact, and in truth, any moderation in relating it would fall short.

It was thus time to end the confusion that was increasing the number of our victims, and on my advice and at my insistence General Cos ordered the fire silenced; but the bugler Tamayo of the sappers blew his instrument in vain, for the fire did not cease until there was no one left to kill and around fifty thousand cartridges had been used up. Whoever doubts this, let him estimate for himself, as I have done, with data that I have given.

Among the defenders there were thirty or more colonists; the rest were pirates, used to defying danger and to disdaining death, and who for that reason fought courageously; their courage, to my way of thinking, merited them the mercy for which, toward the last, some of them pleaded; others, not knowing the language, were unable to do so. In fact, when these men noted the loss of their leader and saw that they were being attacked by superior forces, they faltered. Some, with an accent hardly intelligible, desperately cried, *Mercy, valiant Mexicans;* others poked the points of their bayonets through a hole or a door with a white cloth, the symbol of cease-fire, and some even used their socks. Our trusting soldiers, seeing these demonstrations, would confidently enter their quarters, but those among the enemy who had not pleaded for mercy, who had no thought of surrendering, and who relied on no other recourse than selling their lives dearly, would meet them with pistol shots and bayonets. Thus betrayed, our men rekindled their anger and at every moment fresh skirmishes broke out with renewed fury. The order had been given to spare no one but the women and this was carried out, but such carnage was useless and had we prevented it, we would have saved much blood on our part. Those of the enemy who tried to escape fell victims to the sabers of the cavalry, which had been drawn up for this purpose, but even as they fled they defended themselves. An unfortunate father with a young son in his arms was seen to hurl himself from a considerable height, both perishing at the same blow.

This scene of extermination went on for an hour before the curtain of death covered and ended it: shortly after six in the morning it was all finished; the corps were beginning to reassemble and to identify themselves, their sorrowful countenances revealing the losses in the thinned ranks of their officers and comrades, when the commander in chief appeared. He could see for himself the desolation among his battalions and that devastated area littered with corpses, with scattered limbs and bullets, with weapons and torn uniforms. Some of these were burning together with the corpses, which produced an unbearable and nauseating odor. The bodies, with their blackened and bloody faces disfigured by a desperate death, their hair and uniforms burning at once, presented a dreadful and truly hellish sight. . . .

The general then addressed his crippled battalions, lauding their courage and thanking them in the name of their country. But one hardly noticed in his words the magic that Napoleon expresses in his, which, Count Ségur assures us, was impossible to resist. The *vivas* were seconded icily, and silence would hardly have been broken if I, seized by one of those impulses triggered by enthusiasm or one formed to avoid reflection, which conceals the feelings, had not addressed myself to the valiant chasseurs of Aldama, hailing the Republic and them, an act which, carried out in the presence of the commander on whom so much unmerited honor had been bestowed, proved that I never flatter those in power.

Shortly before Santa Anna's speech, an unpleasant episode had taken place, which, since it occurred after the end of the skirmish, was looked upon as base murder and which contributed greatly to the coolness that was noted. Some seven men had survived the general carnage and, under the protection of General Castrillón, they were brought before Santa Anna. Among them was one of great stature, well proportioned, with regular features, in whose face there was the imprint of adversity, but in whom one also noticed a degree of resignation and nobility that did him honor. He was the naturalist David Crockett, well known in North America for his unusual adventures, who had undertaken to explore the country and who, finding himself in Béjar at the very moment of surprise, had taken refuge in the Alamo, fearing that his status as a foreigner might not be respected. Santa Anna answered Castrillón's intervention in Crockett's behalf with a gesture of indignation and, addressing himself to the sappers, the troops closest to him, ordered his execution. The commanders and officers were outraged at this action and did not support the order, hoping that once the fury of the moment had blown over these men would be spared; but several officers who were around the president and who, perhaps, had not been present during the moment of danger, became noteworthy by an infamous deed, surpassing the soldiers in cruelty. They thrust themselves forward, in order to flatter their commander, and with swords in hand, fell upon these unfortunate, defenseless men just as a tiger leaps upon his prey. Though tortured before they were killed, these unfortunates died without complaining and without humiliating themselves before their torturers.

# 7. Mrs. Dilue Harris Recounts the "Runaway Scrape," March 1836

On the 12th of March came the news of the fall of the Alamo. A courier brought a dispatch from General Houston for the people to leave. Colonel Travis and the men under his command had been slaughtered, the Texas army was retreating, and President Burnet's cabinet had gone to Harrisburg.

Then began the horrors of the "Runaway Scrape." We left home at sunset, hauling clothes, bedding, and provisions on the sleigh with one yoke of oxen. Mother and I were walking, she with an infant in her arms. Brother drove the oxen, and my two little sisters rode in the sleigh. We were going ten miles to where we could be transferred to Mr. Bundick's cart. Father was helping with cattle, but he joined us after dark and brought a horse and saddle for brother. He sent him to help Mr. Stafford with the cattle. He was to go a different road with them and ford the San Jacinto. Mother and I then rode father's horse. . . .

We camped the first night near Harrisburg, about where the railroad depot now stands. Next day we crossed Vince's Bridge and arrived at the San Jacinto in the night. There were fully five thousand people at the ferry. The planters from Brazoria and Columbia with their slaves were crossing. We waited three days before we crossed. Our party consisted of five white families: father's, Mr. Dyer's, Mr. Bell's, Mr. Neal's, and Mr. Bundick's. Father and Mr. Bundick were the only white men in the party, the others being in the army. There were twenty or thirty negroes from Stafford's plantation. They had a large wagon with five yoke of oxen, and horses, and mules, and they were in charge of an old negro man called Uncle Ned. Altogether, black and white, there were about fifty of us. Every one was trying to cross first, and it was almost a riot.

We got over the third day, and after travelling a few miles came to a big prairie. It was about twelve miles further to the next timber and water, and some of our party wanted to camp; but others said that the Trinity river was rising, and if we delayed we might not get across. So we hurried on.

When we got about half across the prairie Uncle Ned's wagon bogged. The negro men driving the carts tried to go around the big wagon one at a time until the four carts were fast in the mud. Mother was the only white woman that rode in a cart; the others travelled on horseback. Mrs. Bell's four children, Mrs. Dyer's three, and mother's four rode in the carts. All that were on horseback had gone on to the timber to let their horses feed and get water. They supposed their families would get there by dark. The negro men put all the oxen to the wagon, but could not move it; so they had to stay there until morning without wood or water. Mother gathered the white children in our cart. They behaved very well and went to sleep, except one little boy, Eli Dyer, who kicked and cried for Uncle Ned and Aunt Dilue till Uncle Ned came and carried him to the wagon. He slept that night in Uncle Ned's arms.

Mother with all the negro women and children walked six miles to the timber and found our friends in trouble. Father and Mr. Bundick had gone to the river and helped with the ferry boat, but late in the evening the boat grounded on the east bank of the Trinity and didn't get back until morning. While they were gone the horses had strayed off and they had to find them before they could go to the wagons. Those that travelled on horseback were supplied with provisions by other campers. We that stayed in the prairie had to eat cold corn bread and cold boiled beef. The wagons and carts didn't get to the timber till night. They had to be unloaded and pulled out.

At the Trinity river men from the army began to join their families. I know they have been blamed for this, but what else could they have done? The Texas army was retreating and the Mexicans were crossing the Colorado, Col. Fannin and his men were prisoners, there were more negroes than whites among us and many of them were wild Africans, there was a large tribe of Indians on the Trinity as well as the Cherokee Indians in Eastern Texas at Nacogdoches, and there were tories, both Mexicans and Americans, in the country. It was the intention of our men to see their families across the Sabine river, and then to return and fight the Mexicans. I must say for the negroes that there was no insubordination among them; they were loyal to their owners.

## 8. Mirabeau B. Lamar Complains of Insubordination in the Ranks of the Texas Army, 1836

Head Quarters
17th July 1836

To His Excellency
President Burnet

Dear Sir—I have just recd several letters from you on various subjects, to none of which have I time to reply at present; I have but five minutes to dictate this note to let you know the dreadful state of affairs in the army. Every thing is in the utmost confusion and rebellion. On my arrival, I was informed that I could not be recognized as Commander in Chief. I proposed to speak to the Soldiers, and did so, but was answered by Rusk, Greene and Felix Houston who carried the popular currant against me. I had an open rupture with Genl. Rusk believing it to be the secret arrangmts of his to supplant me. Some hostile correspondence ensued; which, instead of leading to further difficulties has resulted in this arrangement, viz, that he is to recognise my orders in future; that the regulars and about 6 or 8 volunteer companies are to march to another encampment under my Command; where I shall issue my Orders as Commander in Chief to the balance of the army of Texas, and if Greene and Felix Houston still maintain their present attitude of rebellion to my authority, I shall punish them by Court Martial, if possible, & if not shall report them to Congress. You will perceive from this dreadful state of affairs the high & absolute necessity of Convening a Congress. Nothing else can save the Country from dreadful disorganization and anarchy. The general Officers all seem determined to defy the civil authority of the land; I stand alone in its defense, and in consequence am fast loosing my influence. I hope I shall be able to recall the old citizens of Texas to a sense of their rights and their duty; the volunteers are bent on supremacy. A Vote was taken a few days since on the question of Bringing Santa Anna to the army, which was deter[mi]ned in favor of the measure by a vast majority. They have sent after him. My present purpose is, when I shall take my position with the Regulars and a few companies of the volunteers, to stop him before he reaches the main army, and refer his fate to the Citizens of Texas instead of turning him over to the decision of Greene's soldiers. I believe he has forfeited his life & should die—that is my voice—but I want the Congress to pronounce it and not a rebellious mob of strangers who have been made such by an ambitious and weak General. If I am wrong in any matter, write me your views cordially as I wish to be ruled by the best

Mirabeau Lamar to David G.Burnet, July 17, 1836, *Papers of Mirabeau Lamar,* ed. Charles Adams Gulick (Austin: A. C. Baldwin, 1921–27), 1:417–418.

councils that can be had. I aim only at the interest and glory of my country and whenever it is deemed by the intelligence of that county that I stand in the way of its prosperity, I am ready to retire. I have a dreadful task and duties to perform here, & shall require the aid & support of every friend of Order and Civil government. . . .

Yours

M. B Lamar—

## 9.  American Abolitionist Benjamin Lundy Sees a Southern Slave Conspiracy, 1836

The advocates of slavery, in our southern states and elsewhere, want more land on this continent suitable for the culture of sugar and cotton; and if Texas, with the adjoining portions of Tamaulipas, Coahuila, Chihuahua, and Santa Fe, east of the Rio Bravo del Norte, can be wrested from the Mexican government, room will be afforded for the redundant slave population in the United States, even to a remote period of time. . . .

The breeders of slaves, in those parts of the United States where slave labour has become unprofitable,—and also the traffickers in human flesh, whether American or foreign, desire an extended market, which Texas would afford if revolutionized, and governed as well as inhabited by those who are in favour of re-establishing the system of slavery in that section of country. The northern land speculators most cheerfully co-operate with the southern slave-holders, in the grand scheme of aggression, with the hope of immense gain; and the slave-merchants play into the hands of both, with the same heartless, avaricious feelings and views. The principal seat of operations, for the first, is New York,—though some active and regular agencies are established at New Orleans and Nashville, and minor agencies in other places. The second exercise their influence individually, without any particular organization: while the third cooperate with all, as opportunities present themselves. They have subsidized presses at command, ready to give extensive circulation to whatever they may wish to publish in furtherance of their views. And orators, legislators, and persons holding official stations under our Federal government, are deeply interested in their operations, and frequently willing instruments to promote their cause.

Such are the motives for action—such the combination of interests—such the organization, sources of influence, and foundation of authority, upon which the present *Texas Insurrection* rests. The resident colonists compose but a small fraction of the party concerned in it. The standard of revolt was raised as soon as it was clearly ascertained that slavery could not be perpetuated, nor the illegal speculations in land continued under the *government* of the Mexican Republic. The Mexican authorities were charged with acts of oppression, while the true causes of the revolt—the motives and designs of the insurgents—were studiously concealed from the public view. Influential slave-holders are contributing money, equipping troops, and marching to the scene of conflict. The land speculators are fitting out

Benjamin Lundy, *The Origin and True Causes of the Texas Insurrection* (Philadelphia, 1836), 30–31.

expeditions from New York and New Orleans, with men, munitions of war, provisions, &c., to promote the object. The Independence of Texas is declared, and the system of slavery, as well as the slave trade, (with the United States,) is fully recognised by constitutional regulation. Commissioners are sent from Texas to the United States, to make formal representations, enlist the sympathies of our citizens, and solicit aid in every way that it can be furnished. The subsidized presses are actively employed in magnifying the successes of the insurgents; misrepresenting the character and strength of the Mexican forces; and by inflammatory appeals urging forward the ignorant, the unsuspecting, the adventurous and the daring, to a participation in the struggle.

# ❧ E S S A Y S

In the first essay, Eugene Barker, an early twentieth-century scholar who had an enormous influence on the study of Texas history, presents the traditional interpretation of the Texas Revolution, arguing that the conflict had its roots in a clash between two opposing cultures. Barker gives special emphasis to the wholly disparate political systems of the United States and Mexico, one democratic, the other inclined toward greater centralized authority. Although Santa Anna's decision to abrogate the Constitution of 1824 provided the final rupture between the two sides, chronic political instability in Mexico City had already undermined Anglo American confidence in the national government. Jealously protective of their liberties, the American migrants to Texas, Barker suggests, were bound to resist any central authority that sought to undermine their political sovereignty.

In the second essay, David J. Weber, a professor at Southern Methodist University who has written widely on the American Southwest, offers a critique of Barker's cultural conflict thesis. Although Weber does not ignore deep-seated cultural tensions, he cautions against viewing the Revolution strictly as an upheaval pitting Anglos against Hispanics. Such an interpretation, he argues, serves not only to minimize the significant role that Tejanos played in the events of 1835–36, but has helped to perpetuate the myth that a morally superior Anglo Texan community triumphed over a degenerate Mexico.

Another challenge to the Barker thesis, though an indirect one, is suggested in the third essay by Paul Lack, an historian at McMurry University. Like Weber, Lack argues that the momentum for revolution did not crystallize until 1835, drawing attention to Anglo Texans' fears that the new central government in Mexico would now attempt to undermine slavery. Although the Mexican government did little to actually foment a rebellion in Texas, the widespread perception that it *might* do so, he argues, provided a powerful stimulus for insurrection. Lack's essay offers a valuable reminder that the traditional interpretation of the Revolution as a struggle for liberty against oppressive rule did not apply to Anglo Texans alone. Ironically, as Lack points out, African Americans were inclined to "identify with Mexico as a force of freedom." Lack's essay should also be examined in conjunction with Benjamin Lundy's assessment of slavery's role in the Revolution (see Document 9). Whereas Lundy maintained that slaveowners were engaged in a deliberate, long-term effort to expand the slave empire, Lack views the actions of Anglo-Texas slaveholders during the insurrection as defensive in nature, as an attempt to protect rather than to expand the "peculiar institution."

# Mexico and Texas: A Collision of Two Cultures

EUGENE BARKER

On the one side was the Anglo-American immigrant, blunt, independent, efficient, a rebel against authority, a supreme individualist. On the other side was the Latin American master of the soil, sensitive, secretive, subtle and indirect in his ways, by training and temperament a worshiper of tradition and a creature of authority. With the political ascendancy of the two elements reversed the situation would have held no threatening aspects, but with the Mexicans in the political saddle conflict was certain.

In 1821, after three hundred years of subjection to Spain, Mexico gained its national independence. It was poorly prepared for self-government. In practice, even more than in theory and in law, the Spanish colonial system was rigidly centralized. The highest positions in army, church, and civil service were reserved for Spaniards. [Hubert H.] Bancroft declares, on the authority of Alaman, that from 1535 until 1813 only three creoles became viceroys of Mexico, and he says that out of seven hundred and fifty-four individuals who in the same period held the highest civil and military positions in all Spanish America only eighteen were born in the colonies.

Exclusion from the highest offices need have had little effect upon the political training of the Spanish-blood Mexicans had the subordinate administration been allowed a measure of independent development. But the duties of every officer, down to the *sindico* of the local *ayuntamiento,* were meticulously prescribed and regulated by the omnipotent Laws of the Indies.

In spite of their political incapacity—or perhaps because of it—the Mexicans, after several false starts, declared in 1823 for the most complex form of government ever devised by man, and the next year promulgated the federal republican constitution of 1824.

Greater contrast in the political experience of two peoples could scarcely be imagined than that presented by the Mexicans and their immigrants from the north. The English colonists came to America with a training in local self government already centuries old. Roots of the precinct, the county, and trial by jury go back beyond the dawn of English constitutional history. Parliament and the representative system were developed in all their essential characteristics before the great emigration to America in the seventeenth century. Once on this side, the English colonists settled down to more rather than less local independence and responsibility than they had had in England. Legally no civil office in America was closed to them, from the office of governor down to constable, and only in the royal colonies were they in common practice excluded from the governor's office.

The congregational organization of the churches in the North added its contribution to the political training of the colonists; and even in the South, where the English Episcopal Church was established, sparse population, widely extended parish boundaries, and difficulties of travel and communication combined to foster a high degree of local independence and responsibility in matters of the church.

Eugene Barker, *Mexico and Texas* (Dallas: P. L. Turner, 1928), 1–5, 143–146. Reprinted with the permission of Scribner, A Division of Simon & Schuster.

Generation after generation of thrusting their way through the American wilderness renewed and strengthened the self-reliance and efficiency of the English colonists. On every successive frontier adventurous pioneers re-enacted, with the necessary adaptations of time and circumstance, the experiences and the expedients of the original immigrants. Daniel Boone's colonists at Boonesborough were not less dependent upon their own resources than were Captain Smith's Englishmen at Jamestown. . . .

To men such as these democracy was the breath of political life. As they trudged westward and ever westward to new homes in the wilderness, they shed the property and religious restrictions of the tidewater states on the voting franchise and established manhood suffrage. With political equality went social equality, universally assumed in theory, and commonly conceded in practice. Withal was a rampant nationalism. America and Americans were the best. All foreigners were inferiors.

The causes of popular movements are rarely concrete and simple; on the contrary, they are diffuse and complex. It was so in the Texas revolution. In the end, it was the development of national politics, I think, which precipitated the Texas revolution. Not to mention local and state insurrections and isolated "plans" and pronunciamentoes touching national affairs, there were four major revolutions during the six years from 1829 to 1835. First, . . . the grim old warrior, Vicente Guerrero, overthrew the mild and liberal Pedraza and ruled for nine months, most of the time invested by Congress with the military power of a dictator. Second, General Bustamante succeeded Guerrero by the sword and gave his power a fictitious legality by the sanction of Congress. Third, the republican Santa Anna overthrew Bustamante and restored the accommodating Pedraza to the presidency—all with the approval of Congress—in order to gain time for his own formal election as the champion of liberalism and democracy. Finally, Santa Anna, the Liberal, yielded to Santa Anna, the reactionary Centralist, and a centralized dictatorship took the place of the so-called federal republic—again with the fictitious congressional sanction. The successive eruptions gave no indication of a tendency toward national political stability; quite the contrary—a fact which might be expected to have caused, and which did cause, uneasy reflections in Texas.

The really ominous fact, however, was that each successive change seemed to bring Texas more completely within the blighting sphere of the federal government's attention. Guerrero issued the emancipation decree of 1829; Bustamante approved the fateful Law of April 6, 1830, which, had it been enforced with its original design, would have paralyzed the development of Texas for many years; Santa Anna's Liberal revolt, by a fortuitous chain of circumstances, caused the abandonment of Austin's policy of aloofness and brought the Texans squarely into the national party convulsions that Austin had always tried to avoid; finally, the victory of Centralism threatened, as the Texans would have expressed it, to bring the country under the heel of military despotism.

There are many indications, only three of which can be mentioned now, that Santa Anna's about-face from Liberalism to Centralism was the last unbearable straw upon the proverbial camel's back.

In the first place, I think Santa Anna's overthrow of republican government determined Austin's attitude, and Austin's attitude was decisive. He could have disorganized the resistance of the colonists in the fall of 1835; instead, he organized and united their resistance.

In the second place, a Fourth of July address by R. M. Williamson explaining the circumstances that led to Travis's attack on Anahuac was directed entirely toward the end of convincing the Texans that they were in dire danger from Santa Anna's destruction of the federal system. Williamson was not a radical malcontent chronically bent upon stirring up agitation, but was a man of independent mind and generally of sound judgment. . . .

The third bit of evidence to be mentioned here indicating the importance which the Texans attached to the centralization of the government by Santa Anna is furnished by a set of resolutions drawn by David G. Burnet on August 8, 1835, and adopted by a public meeting on the San Jacinto River. Burnet was a man of judicious temperament, and wrote as a conservative and a pacifist. Assuming it to be true that the federal system was destroyed, he saw no reason, he said, why Texas should not be happy under another form of government. Names were the mere signification of things, he declared, and the people were not "so obstinately prejudiced in favor of the term, 'federal republic' as . . . to reject another government purely because it has assumed a different external sign or denomination."

But, although the overthrow of the nominal republic and the substitution of centralized oligarchy precipitated the revolution, its fundamental causes lie deeper. Always in the background was the fatal fact that the Mexicans distrusted and feared the Anglo-American settlers, while the settlers half despised the Mexicans. A permanent atmosphere of suspicion magnified and distorted mutual annoyances which might otherwise have been ignored or adjusted. The apparent determination of the United States to obtain Texas heightened Mexican apprehensions; and the chronic caprice and instability of state and federal politics and policies exhausted the patience of the Texans. At bottom the Texas revolution was the product of the racial and political inheritances of the two peoples.

## Refighting the Alamo: Mythmaking and the Texas Revolution

### DAVID J. WEBER

The lore surrounding the battle of the Alamo provides the clearest examples of how the Texas rebellion, like so many major events, has been romanticized to take on meanings that transcend the event itself and its principal characters reduced to caricature—to heroes and villains. In certain kinds of history, and in American popular culture, the Texas fight for independence has come to represent a triumph of Protestantism over Catholicism, of democracy over despotism, of a superior white race over a degenerate people of mixed blood, of the future over the past, of good over evil. Heroes of the Texas revolt are portrayed as committed republicans fighting for the noblest of motives (the blood of Davy Crockett, one historian has written, was shed upon "a holy altar"). The conflict over Texas has been reduced to nothing more than a conflict of two incompatible cultures. And the rebellion itself, which was a uniquely successful version of the separatist movements and rebellions that broke

"Refighting the Alamo, Mythmaking and the Texas Revolution," in *Myth and the History of the Hispanic Southwest: Essays,* David J. Weber (Albuquerque: University of New Mexico, 1988), 138–151. Reprinted with permission.

out all over Mexico at this time, has been elevated to the status of a "revolution"—a designation that few, if any, modern social scientists would apply to a revolt that did not seek a profound restructuring of society.

What are the sources of these exaggerated notions about the Texas rebellion? Certainly one source was wartime propaganda—myths invented to stir people to action during conflict. Writing just after the fighting ended, for example, Stephen Austin explained the conflict as "a war of barbarism and of despotic principles, waged by the mongrel Spanish-Indian and Negro race, against civilization and the Anglo-American race." That refrain echoed in nineteenth-century Romantic historiography, and its reverberations can be heard yet today in American popular history and popular culture. . . .

The simple fact that Texas became an independent nation as a result of the rebellion has given Texans enormous pride—perhaps too much pride. Historian T. R. Fehrenbach carried this idea to Texas-size proportions when he wrote, apparently without tongue in cheek: "The great difference between Texas and every other American state in the 20th century was that Texas had a history. Other American regions merely had records of development."

But it is more than a traditional big brag that has led Texans to exaggerate the events of 1836 and to make mortal men into heroes of mythological proportions. This certainly reflects a more universal tendency—the tendency to write pietistic history and to use the past as a kind of Rorschach test, seeing wistfully in the past what we wish to see about ourselves in the present. In the interest of creating a usable past, all peoples seem to engage in the making of myths and passing them off as historical fact. In this country, we begin at an early age to be exposed to such historical figures as Santa Claus, and to learn to tell the truth from the homily about George Washington and the cherry tree. No matter that this fabled episode of the cherry tree did not occur—that the story is a lie. No matter that our teachers lied to us in order to teach us to tell the truth. History was being employed toward good ends. So, in many respects, have the tales of the Alamo been exaggerated to serve particular ends.

Rather than trying to read our present-day concerns into the past, let us try to reconstruct the past and look briefly at the coming of the Texas rebellion as contemporaries might have seen it. What did it mean to them? Certainly there was less heroism, less altruism, less patriotism, less clarity of purpose, and less unity than most of us might imagine. Instead, much as today, events moved along more quickly than contemporaries could grasp them and most Anglo Americans and Mexicans in Texas pursued their private lives, wishing that the entire affair would go away.

Let us look first at the proposition that the Texas rebellion represented a clash of cultures, rendering it nearly inevitable. This line of argument was advanced by some Anglo Texans at the time of the revolt and has continued to receive the support of some scholars.

Certainly it is easy to view the revolt as an "ethnic" conflict, for in some respects it was. Between 1821, when Mexico became independent, and 1836 when the armed struggle between Mexico and Texas began, perhaps 35,000 Anglo Americans had flocked across the border and into Mexican Texas, outnumbering the

Mexican Texans, or tejanos, by a ratio of ten to one. The Anglo Americans, so the argument goes, could not adapt to Mexican culture. Historians have identified a number of sources of cultural friction.

First, Anglo Americans were required to become Catholics, and were not permitted to hold Protestant services.

Second, Anglo Americans, some 75 percent of whom were southerners, were shocked when Mexico prohibited slavery in 1829. Mexicans seemed to have little respect for private property.

Third, Anglo Americans could not tolerate the lack of a jury system and deplored the Mexican system of justice in which alcaldes made decisions on the merits of a case.

Fourth, Anglo Americans could not abide the lack of local autonomy in Texas—of home rule. Since 1824 Texas had been subservient to a larger and more populous state, Coahuila. Both Coahuila and Texas had been joined together as the single state of Coahuila y Texas. Control of state government rested squarely in the hands of officials in the distant state capital at Saltillo, and Coahuila's larger population assured that the state legislature would be controlled by representatives from Coahuila.

Fifth, many Anglo Americans could not abide Mexicans themselves. Stephen Austin, on visiting Mexico City in 1822–23, wrote in private correspondence that "the people are bigoted and superstitious to an extreem [*sic*], and indolence appears to be the order of the day." "To be candid the majority of the people of that whole nation as far as I have seen they want nothing but tails to be more brutes than apes." Many years after the bloody days at the Alamo and San Jacinto, one pioneer who had settled in Texas in 1827, Noah Smithwick, echoed Austin's sentiments. "I looked upon the Mexicans as scarce more than apes," Smithwick recalled.

Anglo Americans made no attempt to conceal their sense of superiority from Mexicans. In 1819, two years before Mexico won her independence from Spain, the Spanish minister who was negotiating with John Q. Adams what became the transcontinental treaty, characterized Americans as an "arrogant and audacious" people who believed themselves "superior to all the nations of Europe," and who were convinced "that their dominion is destined to extend. . . . to the isthmus of Panama, and hereafter, over all the regions of the New World." At the dawn of Mexican independence, in 1821, a Mexican Committee on Foreign Relations warned the government that unless Mexico could populate its northern borders, hordes of North Americans would descend on the fertile province of Texas "Just as the Goths, Ostrogoths, Alans, and other tribes [of barbarians] devastated the Roman empire." As this last statement suggests, many Mexicans believed themselves superior to the uncultured, brash, and barbaric Anglo Americans.

On the surface, then, the two cultures seemed incompatible and, even more important, the fact that some Anglo Texans *believed* the two cultures to be incompatible, contributed to Texas independence. Indeed, there seems little reason to doubt that profound cultural differences, including American racism, contributed to the Texas rebellion and gave it a special virulence.

Nonetheless, it would be easy to exaggerate the importance of cultural differences, incorrectly identifying them as the principal cause of the rebellion. *Within* Texas itself, relations between Mexicans from Texas and the Anglo-American newcomers were generally amicable. A few Anglo Americans had settled in the

Mexican communities of San Antonio and Goliad, where they became assimilated. In the main, however, the two groups lived essentially apart, separated by considerable distance. Most Anglo Americans lived in East Texas and most Mexicans in the area of San Antonio and Goliad. As a result, Anglo Americans enjoyed a good deal of autonomy. Differences in religion, philosophy, or what we have come to call "lifestyles," did not become major irritants.

The alleged "religious conflict" offers a case in point. Some writers have argued that Anglo Americans chaffed at the lack of religious freedom in Texas. In practice, the law requiring immigrants to become Catholics was never enforced. The Mexican government failed to send priests to minister to the Anglo-American colonists, as the Colonization Law of 1824 required, so the colonists were not obliged to practice Catholicism. Nor was the government ever so efficient that it investigated the private or quasi-public worship that went on in East Texas homes, where most Anglo Americans lived far from the watchful eye of Mexican officials.

Indeed, there is some evidence to suggest that Mexico's refusal to allow non-Catholics to worship openly (at least in theory) served as a screening device that kept the most devout or dogmatic Protestants out of Texas. Those who did filter through were less inclined to be irritated by strictures on their religious lives. Indeed, many of those early pioneers who entered Texas may have come precisely because of the lack of religious restraints and the absence of Protestant preachers.

Put simply, the Mexican government never forced Catholicism on the Anglo-American colonists in Texas. To the contrary, in 1834, two years before the revolt broke out, the state of Coahuila y Texas went so far as to guarantee that "no person shall be molested for political and religious opinions provided the public order is not disturbed." Freedom of worship never became an important issue among the foreigners in Mexican Texas and, notwithstanding Anglo-Texan wartime propaganda, the issue of freedom of worship did not directly cause the Texas revolt in 1836.

The idea that cultural conflict caused the Texas rebellion has contributed to the notion that the struggle itself was fought along ethnic lines, pitting *all* Mexicans against *all* Americans in Texas. This was decidedly not the case. Tejanos, for example, contributed substantially to the resistance against centralist forces in the fall of 1835, in the wave of hostilities that preceded Santa Anna's march into Texas. The Texas forces that laid siege to General Martín Perfecto de Cos in San Antonio in the fall of 1835 included as many as 160 *tejanos,* among them companies led by Colonel Juan Nepomuceno Seguín of San Antonio, Plácido Benavides of Victoria, and a group of rancheros from Goliad. The next spring, seven tejanos died inside the Alamo, fighting alongside Anglo Americans *against* Santa Anna. Colonel Seguín and the Second Company of Texas Volunteers, which he raised, performed valuable scouting services prior to the fall of the Alamo and contributed to the defeat of Santa Anna at San Jacinto. (Indeed, Seguín and one Antonio Cruz would have died defending the Alamo had they not been sent on a dangerous ride through enemy lines to seek help from Colonel James Fannin at Goliad.) Tejanos also participated in the famous "Consultation" at San Felipe on November 7 of 1835, which endorsed a conditional declaration of Texas independence. Four months later José Antonio Navarro and Francisco Ruiz, both Texas-born, signed the declaration of Texas independence at Washington-on-the-Brazos.

Thus, the sides did not divide up uniformly along ethnic lines. The issues that caused men to take to arms in 1835–36 may have had to do more with the culture of politics than with the politics of culture. And both tejanos and Anglos *within* Texas found much about politics with which they could agree. Let us look at some areas of agreement.

Elites in the predominantly *tejano* communities of San Antonio and Goliad had apparently *shared* Anglo-American concerns about the need to improve the system of justice and to achieve greater autonomy by separating Texas from Coahuila. Many *tejano* leaders even saw slavery as a necessary evil for Texas if the underpopulated and beleaguered province was going to prosper. Nor, it would appear, did the large influx of Anglo Americans into Texas trouble the tejanos as much as it did the Mexican government. For the tejano *elite*, Anglo-American immigrants meant economic growth. From the *local* perspective Anglo Americans were a necessary evil, and Mexican officials in Texas opposed national laws that would restrict the number of Anglo-American immigrants.

From a *national* perspective, however, officials in Mexico City saw Anglo Americans as aggressive and expansionistic, and as a clear and present danger to Texas. There was no doubt that the United States government wanted Texas. The United States had advanced the absurd claim that Texas was part of the Louisiana Purchase. When that claim could not be sustained, the United States had sought to purchase Texas. Mexico, of course, declined to sell the national patrimony, and Mexican statesman Lucas Alamán feared that the Americans' next strategy would be to take Texas from Mexico by peopling it with Americans. As Alamán wrote in 1830: "Where others send invading armies . . . [the North Americans] send their colonists."

As events would demonstrate, Alamán's fears were quite rational. If Mexican leaders *in Texas* shared those concerns, they subordinated them to their economic interests and called for more immigration to make Texas grow. Francisco Ruiz of San Antonio put it squarely when he wrote in 1830: "I cannot help seeing advantages which, to my way of thinking, would result if we admitted honest, hardworking people, regardless of what country they come from . . . even hell itself."

The evidence is scanty, but it appears that the Anglo Texans and the Mexican-Texan elite shared a number of common concerns. No matter how much mutual interests might tie them together, however, once the fighting began it must have been agonizing for tejanos to decide whether to remain loyal to Mexico or to join forces with Americans and take up arms against fellow Mexicans. Although they might agree with Anglo Texans on certain issues, the idea of separation from Coahuila, much less independence from Mexico came to hold less attraction for tejanos in the mid-1830s than it had in the 1820s. Anglo Americans, who vastly outnumbered tejanos by the early 1830s, would surely dominate the state and tejanos would become, to paraphrase Juan Seguín, "foreigners in their native land." When, however, Coahuila fell into anarchy in the mid-1830s and Santa Anna's centralist dictatorship replaced Mexico's federalist Republic, tejano leaders must have wrung their hands over their unhappy alternatives—domination by Anglo Americans or domination by the centralist dictatorship.

The hard choice must have divided some families. We know, for example, that Gregorio Esparza, who died fighting alongside Americans inside the walls of the

Alamo, had a brother, Francisco, who fought on the Mexican side. Most tejanos, however, probably responded like any residents of a war-torn land. They looked first to their families' welfare, fought on neither side, cooperated overtly with the group in charge at the moment, and hoped for an end to the nightmare.

The same may also be said for most Anglo Texans, who had no desire to fight over political issues until Mexican forces threatened their lives and property. Until autumn of 1835, Anglo Americans in Texas were divided between groups that had come to be called the "war party" and the "peace party." Both parties sought greater political autonomy for Texas in order to enable Texans to adopt measures that would make Texas more attractive to immigrants from the U.S.—measures such as more favorable tariffs, an improved judicial system, and the maintenance of slavery. While they agreed on the goals, the peace and war parties disagreed about the means to achieve them. The "peace party," of which the *empresario* Stephen Austin was the most influential representative, wanted Mexico to grant Texas a divorce from its unhappy and unequal marriage with Coahuila. The radical war party, led by ambitious and sometimes angry young men such as William Barret Travis (who a few years earlier had abandoned a wife and law practice in Alabama after killing a man), sought independence from Mexico itself.

Until the autumn of 1835, the "war party" remained a decided minority, its actions repudiated by most responsible Texans of both Anglo and Mexican background. Then, Mexico committed the blunder of sending troops into Texas under the direction of Santa Anna's brother-in-law, Martín Perfecto de Cos. In part, Mexico had been provoked into that action by the attack on a small Mexican garrison at Anahuac in June of 1835, led by Travis and thirty-some radicals. At first, Anglo-American communities throughout Texas repudiated that attack and professed loyalty to the government, but when Anglo Americans learned that Mexican troops would be sent to Texas, public opinion swung away from the "Tories," as Travis called the peace party, and over to the "war party." Even the foremost Texas "Tory," Stephen Austin, became convinced of the necessity of armed resistance. His private correspondence reveals that by the autumn of 1835 he had come to believe that Texas "must, and ought to become a part of the United States."

Although Anglo Americans in Texas achieved unity of purpose by the fall of 1835, that unity disappeared again after General Cos's forces were defeated in San Antonio. In the spring of 1836, Anglo Americans were in disarray once again, both before, during, and after the tragic events at Goliad and the Alamo.

Clearly, then, the Texas struggle for independence was not a simple conflict of Mexicans versus Anglos, of Mexican culture versus American culture, of democracy versus despotism, or of good versus evil. It was not a conflict in which issues were so clearly drawn that men of good will united readily to fight for principles greater than themselves. That such men existed, I have no reason to doubt, but it should be remembered that many Anglo Americans who came to Texas had more interest in fleeing the law than in changing the law; that they came to Texas for personal gain. Pragmatism rather than principle, self interest rather than political democracy, had driven a disproportionate share of Anglo Americans to Texas in search of opportunity. And the unbridled pursuit of self-interest on the part of some Anglo Americans, rather than the quest for liberty, may have helped to bring on the Texas rebellion. The story is a complicated one, but Professor Malcolm McLean has developed a strong case, in his monumental series, *Papers Concerning Robertson's Colony in Texas,* that land speculation by certain Anglo Americans, and their manipulation of the state government in Saltillo, helped win the wrath of the federal government, bring Mexican troops into Texas, and provoke the Texas revolt. . . .

. . . [I]n a historical event as complicated as the Texas struggle for independence, there are few heroes or villains, but rather men and women much like us, looking after their day-to-day interests and responding to a variety of impulses. By writing romanticized history that magnifies men and events, that simplifies a complicated story of a struggle for political and economic power into an ethnic conflict, and that makes Anglo Americans in the past more altruistic, courageous, patriotic, and united than they were, we not only distort the past, but we diminish ourselves. We come to believe that our own generation, when compared to the giants of yesteryear, is unprincipled and decadent.

Many of the giants of yesteryear—both heroes and villains—are, of course, creatures of our own making, invented to serve salutory ends. First, they provide us with a way to avoid abstractions and complicated issues and to focus instead on the personal, the concrete, the easily understood. As historian Michael Meyer, writing about the villain, has explained: "it is much easier to prepare a diatribe against an antihero than to fathom the actual dynamics of an age." Second, by conjuring heroes of mythic proportions and keeping their memories alive, we hope to offer lessons in morality to the young, or to inspire the young with patriotism and pride. And such lessons have been well learned. As one Texas-educated young man, Lyndon B. Johnson, wrote in his college newspaper, "Down with the debunking biographer. . . . Hero worship is a tremendous force in uplifting and strengthening . . . let us have our heroes. Let us continue to believe that some have been truly great."

Myths are, of course, important to a people. As historian William McNeill has reminded us in a recent essay, myths play an essential role in binding a people together and in serving as a basis for common action. The question, however, is whether a myth is useful or pernicious; whether it drives people to constructive common action or to collective foolishness or disgrace. Perhaps these two extremes are not mutually exclusive, but the mythology surrounding the Alamo has served as rationalization for aggressive behavior toward Mexico and Mexicans that runs counter to our finest national ideals. In the immediate aftermath of the Texas revolt, the enshrinement of the Alamo as a holy place and the popular sanctification of its defenders as martyrs helped reinforce and intensify two complementary articles of faith among Anglo Americans: belief in the moral superiority of Anglos and the degeneracy of Mexicans. From those antipodal myths, which ran strongest among Anglo residents of Texas, it followed that Mexico's conquest by its morally superior neighbor might redeem her benighted citizenry. Their faith affirmed by the windy rhetoric of their elders, young American men of the mid-1840s swallowed the myth of a holy war against Mexico. Entering a fantasy world of promised glory and heroism against a foe they believed to be inferior, many young Americans marched to the Halls of Montezuma. One out of eight never returned.

It may be that by *manufacturing* heroes from the past we do not necessarily "uplift and strengthen" the present generation, as young LBJ supposed, or add to patriotism and pride. Instead, we may only succeed in adding to our self-loathing and cynicism, for as mere human beings we cannot live up to the impossible standards that we set for ourselves when we invent heroes who are larger than life.

# Slavery and the Texas Revolution

PAUL LACK

This study of slavery and the Texas Revolution concentrates on the impact of the 1835–36 struggle on both slaves and slaveholders. The conflict with Mexico raised before Anglos the spectre of slave revolt, created for blacks other avenues to freedom besides rebellion, generated forces that weakened the hold of masters over bondsmen, and placed the very survival of the institution in Texas on the success of Texas arms. In order to understand the events of these two years, some attention will also be given to the status of slavery in the earlier period of Mexican rule and to the difficult question of slavery as a factor leading to the Texas movement for independence.

This latter issue attracted attention as soon as war erupted between Mexico and Texas; antislavery zealots quickly attributed the Texas Revolution to a proslavery conspiracy. The most thoroughgoing of these denunciations, *The War in Texas* by Benjamin Lundy, appeared in 1836. Lundy's suspicions regarding the conflict grew out of a decade-old career as an antislavery writer and his visits in Brazoria, Bexar, and other Mexican provinces in 1833. Lundy viewed the origins of the Revolution as exactly opposite to those identified in public pronouncements in Texas, which stressed liberty and human rights. His historical narrative developed the theme that southern-born immigrants had evaded Mexican emancipation measures and had finally sought separate statehood in order to establish the institution on a firm constitutional basis. When foiled in this and other proslavery efforts, a "vast combination" of slaveholders in Texas, supported by land-jobbers, slave-breeders and dealers, and their political lackeys in the United States, implemented a "treasonable" "scheme" to divide Texas from Mexico and reestablish slavery. Like most abolitionists, Lundy placed blame on individual sin: the Texas war derived from "motives of personal aggrandizement, avaricious adventure, and unlimited, enduring oppression."

When historians like Eugene C. Barker challenged this conspiracy theory, they marshalled not so much new evidence as a new perspective. In fact, Barker acknowledged the southern, proslavery origins of many Anglo-Texans and their resistance in the name of progress to Mexican efforts to limit, exclude, or abolish slavery. He not only recognized other facts—the proslavery features of the constitution of the Republic of Texas, the military support that came from the southern United States, and the Texans' desire for annexation—but published evidence that, if known to Lundy, would have made the conspiracy theory seem irrefutable. On his way from Mexico to Texas in the summer of 1835, Stephen F. Austin had written to his cousin, "The best interests of the United States require that Texas shall be effectually, and fully, *Americanized. . . . Texas must be a slave country. It is no longer a matter of doubt.*" But like other "scientific" historians, Barker doubted the existence of a "slaveocracy" or the prevalence of proslavery crusading zeal among Texas revolutionaries. He asserted that the number of slaves and the frequency of

Paul Lack, "Slavery and the Texas Revolution, *Southwestern Historical Quarterly,* vol. 89 (October 1985): 182–202. Copyright Texas State Historical Association. Reprinted with permission.

Texan-Mexican disagreements over the status of slavery had both declined after 1830. Subsequent scholars have followed this lead so faithfully that they allude to the issue mostly to deride Lundy's theory. Barker's conclusion "that anxiety concerning the status of slavery [does not appear to have] played any appreciable part in producing the Texas revolution" has gone virtually unchallenged.

Whatever doubts they express about the significance of slavery as a causative factor in 1835–1836, historians have acknowledged that disputes over the institution served as a long-standing irritant in relations between Anglo settlers and Mexico. A sense of uncertainty had characterized the status of slavery from almost the beginning of North American colonization of Texas. Throughout the 1820s local authorities blunted repeated but indecisive antislavery measures enacted by the Mexican Congress. In 1822 and again in 1824 the Congress passed legislation to abolish the slave trade and gradually erode the institution. Anglo Texas leaders gained little legal relief by their arguments that these measures undermined economic progress, but they either muted the impact of these laws or simply ignored them. Even the state constitution, which recognized the legality of slavery, outlawed further importations and freed children born of slave parents. Texas memorials then persuaded the Coahuila legislature to sanction a bogus "contract" system allowing imports of bound labor. This apparently successful subterfuge evaporated suddenly on September 15, 1829, with the promulgation of a general emancipation decree by Mexican president Vicente Guerrero. An exemption for Texas was once again granted; however, the pattern of evasion by Texans created alarm regarding the governability of the province. On April 6 of the next year another decree ended all North American emigration to Texas, though it reconized the existence of slavery there.

The 1830s brought something of a respite from the barrage of antislavery measures of the previous decade, partly because of political instability in Mexico. Yet the status of the institution remained in doubt. In April, 1832, the legislature of Coahuila y Texas set a ten-year limitation on the length of labor contracts, thus jeopardizing the evasions of Texas slaveholders and indicating that abolitionist sentiment still prevailed among Mexican authorities. Realization of this fact helped spur a movement in Texas for separate statehood that originated in that year. Texans had blunted some of the effects of governmental hostility to slavery, but defense of the institution ultimately rested on sympathetic and weak local governments that failed to enforce antislavery measures. When a more powerful (authoritarian from the Texas perspective) government arose in Mexico, rebellion broke out. The immediate target of the resistance was John Davis Bradburn, commander at Anahuac. The insurgents included in their Declaration of Grievances a charge that he had encouraged and protected runaway slaves.

Clearly, critics like John Quincy Adams exaggerated in asserting that the Texas Revolution reestablished slavery "where it was abolished." Emigrants from the United States used the indenture system to bring forced labor into Texas, while masters bought, hired, and sold workers without regard for antislavery enactments. In no instance did bondsmen or women become free due to legal procedures. Mexican hostility toward slavery, however, did have some effect. Slaves in Texas had a measure of judicial privilege. Such as the right of petition. A knowledgeable observer like Mary Austin Holley believed that blacks were "invested with more liberty and [were] less liable to abuse" in Texas than in the United States. Flurries of antislavery legislation had other effects as well. The laws slowed the pace of American immigration and possibly the importation of blacks. An estimate from 1834 suggests that the number of slaves had grown at a slower rate than had the white population. Also, continual labor shortages lengthened the period of frontier conditions and retarded the growth of plantations, except for a few instances along the coast.

All things considered, however, Anglo immigrants seem not to have significantly modified their hopes or expectations of slavery, inhospitable laws and government disapprobation notwithstanding. Planters commonly considered their slaves "indispensable," as one traveler noted, and leaders of the province believed that cotton held the key to progress. When Anglo lawmakers came into power in places like Nacogdoches in the mid-1830s, the legal privilege conferred on bondsmen by Mexican law was quickly eroded. And Mexican inattention to slavery after 1830 allowed the institution to grow in at least one area: statistics for the Nacogdoches region reveal a spurt in the slave population between 1831 and 1835. . . .

As political tensions between Texas and the central government grew in the spring of 1835, Texans also began receiving warnings that traditional Mexican restraint with regard to slavery had come to an end. Francis W. Johnson sent a report from Monclova on May 6 concerning impending abolitionist legislation intended for application throughout the republic. "It does appear," he concluded, "that they will stop at nothing short of the ruin of Texas. . . ." William Barrett Travis considered this law as one of a series of "alarming circumstances" produced by "a plundering, robbing, autocratical, aristocratical, jumbled up govt which is in fact no govt at all. . . . There is no security for life, liberty, or property." News of Mexican military preparations created further fear that the expedition intended, in the words of Robert McAlpin Williamson, "to compel you to liberate your slaves" and accept other forms of dictatorial government. . . .

The approach of war was attended by more complaints about Mexican abolitionism and by heightened racial invective. A correspondent of the *Telegraph and Texas Register* pleaded for separation "from a people one half of whom are the most depraved of the different races of Indians, different in color" and inferior in character. From this it took but a short leap of imagination to transform the struggle into one between "Texian freemen" and slaves. "Will you now," John W. Hall asked the people of Texas, "suffer the *colored* hirelings of a cruel and faithless despot, to feast and revel, in your dearly purchased and cherished homes?" Lest any doubt remain about the racial and sexual nature of this reveling, Fannin called Texans to arms to prevent the prostitution of "the *Fair daughters* of chaste *white women*." Given this view of the conflict as one between white and colored races, Anglo-Texans naturally feared slave insurrection. With "war now pending," William H. Wharton compiled a list of evidence of Mexican hostility toward Texas:

> With a sickly philanthropy worthy of the abolitionists of these United States, they have, contrary to justice, and to law, intermedled with our slave population, and have even impotently threatened . . . to emancipate them, and induce them to turn their arms against their masters.

The military events that soon transpired led many to fear that Mexican abolitionism was far from "impotent."

As early as 1828 the Mexican government had considered the relation between slave revolt and Texas independence. General Manuel de Mier y Terán, who believed that bondsmen experienced severe maltreatment and that they knew of the pro-emancipation intent of Mexican law, viewed the slaves as ripe for an uprising. But he argued against abolition, suggesting that the potential for a slave insurrection would restrain both the secession of Texas and the threat of invasion by the United States. Some subsequent officials believed that Mier y Terán had miscalculated. The government of Mexico dispatched Juan N. Almonte to Texas in 1833–34 with secret instructions to inform the slaves of their liberty under Mexican law and to promise them land as freedmen.

By the summer of 1835 many Anglo-Texans concluded that Mexico had acquired the will and power to implement an antislavery strategy. Reports circulated that Thomas M. Thompson, commander of the Mexican schooner of war *Correo,* had intended to impress and subsequently liberate "all the negro slaves in the country that he could get in his possession" when he sailed into Galveston Bay in late July. Even James H. C. Miller, a defender of the Mexican centralists who had believed the government's goals to be pacific, wrote to the people to warn of the Mexican invasion of Texas, which contemplated, among other evils, slave emancipation. More graphically, another Texan recently back from the interior of Mexico reported to the public that a large army had been dispatched. Its numerous oppressive policies included an intent to liberate the slaves and also to "let them loose upon their [the Anglo Texans'] families."

Benjamin R. Milam summarized the emerging consensus of opinion. He too warned that the troops headed for Texas to enforce the centralist constitution planned an unconventional warfare of recruiting Indians and attempting "if possible to get the slaves to revolt." Altogether these forces would "make a wilderness of Texas, and beggars of its inhabitants"; thus the constitutional quarrel had far-reaching implications. "If the Federal system is lost in Texas, what will be our situation? Worse than that of the most degraded slaves." As Milam noted, the political and military crisis posed by the triumph of Santa Anna and centralism in 1835 challenged more than the governmental theories of the Anglo Texans. Over the previous decade unpopular policies emanating from Mexico—whether on immigration, taxation, troop strength, or slavery—had been blunted by sympathetic local officials who ruled with considerable autonomy under the federalist system. This arrangement tacitly protected slavery, an institution that the central government had repeatedly, and officially, condemned. Despite the shroud of uncertainty that hung over it, slavery began to expand aggressively in the two or three years prior to 1835, as evidenced by the invigorated though illegal slave trade. From the Anglo Texan perspective the constitutional changes of that year once again threatened liberty and interrupted economic progress, their version of which included a system of slave labor. Texans took up arms in 1835 against a regime that apparently intended to undermine their political ideals, their emerging prosperity, and their understanding of social and racial peace. Clearly the challenge to slavery contributed to the Texas decision to resist the new order in Mexico. . . .

. . . [V]irtually all the preconditions for rebellion existed in Texas in 1835–1836. As frontiersmen, the slaves of this region had of necessity acquired skills with weapons that in this crisis could be turned against their masters. The slave ranks had recently grown in numbers with the importation of Africans, an element that frequently led uprisings throughout the Americas. The intellectual climate had filled with revolutionary rhetoric emphasizing freedom, rights, and liberty in the struggle against tyranny, despotism, and even slavery. Blacks had apparently acquired some familiarity with the emancipationist leanings of Mexico, which would have prepared them to embrace the invading force as an army of liberation. The internal divisions of the ruling authorities presented a real opportunity; only the whites' continued numerical superiority and success on the battlefield obstructed the chance for a more powerful black revolt.

Threats to slavery posed by political change in Mexico, military efforts to impose this new order, and the upheavals generated by war—these challenges dominated the thoughts of defenders of the institution during 1835 and 1836. Slaveowners also recognized the dangers represented by a growing international antislavery movement. Texas authorities acted quickly to discourage a northern "Abolition society" scheme to establish a free black colony in Texas in 1835, just as they had made their sentiments clear to Lundy on this matter two years earlier. Buoyed by this proslavery consensus, Texas law and constitution makers in 1835 and 1836 moved to the task of protecting property, including the ownership of human beings, while also emphasizing doctrines of freedom. Texas thus entered nationhood with a constitution that defined human rights in racial terms and also provided a long list of positive guarantees of slavery. In deference to world opinion and diplomatic necessity the document prohibited importation of blacks from places other than the United States. The African slave traffic had accelerated in 1835 and 1836, when at least eight vessels, carrying about 600 slaves from the West Indies, disembarked their cargoes at Gulf ports or river plantations. Those who debated the foreign slave trade considered it only as a problem of state; not a delegate expressed a trace of genuine humanitarian feeling for the slaves. The other racial question that drew the attention of the convention, the fate of free blacks, also grew out of concern for the protection of slavery. Texas masters believed that the presence of this class disrupted slave discipline and discouraged slaveholder migration. The constitution, by providing that "no free person of African descent. . . . shall be permitted to reside permanently in the republic, without the consent of Congress," gave the government a free hand to discourage any of this group from tampering with bondsmen.

The events of 1835 and 1836 had shaken slavery considerably, but in the end the Texas victory confirmed the institution. Furthermore, the pattern of race relations that emerged in this period persisted in subsequent years. Blacks continued to identify with Mexico as a force of freedom. Mexican military ventures in Texas and around the Rio Grande attracted the participation of former slaves. Runaways, especially those who fled in groups, still sought their liberty in Mexico in the years just after the Revolution. Troublesome as this outlet for freedom proved to be, white Texans also feared a far worse prospect—that abolitionists would provide financial support to Mexico for a renewal of the war along antislavery lines. . . .

The Texas movement for independence had a dual character in respect to slavery. Ideologically, the Texans displayed mostly reactionary impulses, despite their frequent and fervent identifications with the Spirit of '76. The practical-minded Anglo-Americans applied their version of liberty, equality, and democracy cautiously and only to themselves. This aspect of the Texas Revolution clearly owed a debt to the Great Reaction that swept the southern United States in the early 1830s. By then, radical worldwide abolitionism had also emerged, a development that fostered more reaction and thus reinforced the conservative emphasis on property, order, and white supremacy. However uncongenial in spirit toward black freedom, the Texas Revolution generated other forces—including armed conflict and internal dislocation—that temporarily challenged the slave-labor system and Anglo racial hegemony. Yet the brevity of the war and the sudden collapse of the Mexican invasion effort prevented the disintegration of slavery and allowed Texans three more decades to apply the doctrines of their southern heritage.

# ✦ *F U R T H E R     R E A D I N G*

Alwyn Barr, *Texans in Revolt: The Battle for San Antonio* (1990)
Holly Beacher Brear, *Inherit the Alamo: Myth and Ritual at an American Shrine* (1996)
William C. Davis, *Three Roads to the Alamo: The Lives of David Crockett, James Bowie, and William Barret Travis* (1998)
Ann Fears Crawford, ed., *Eagle: The Autobiography of Santa Anna* (1988)
Stephen Hardin, *Texian Iliad: A Military History of the Texas Revolution, 1835–1836* (1994)
Margaret Swett Henson, *Lorenzo de Zavala, the Pragmatic Idealist* (1996)
Paul D. Lack, *The Texas Revolutionary Experience: A Political and Social History, 1835–1836* (1992)
Jeff Long, *Duel of Eagles: The Mexican and U.S. Fight for the Alamo* (1990)
Timothy Matovina, *The Alamo Remembered: Tejano Accounts and Perspectives* (1995)
Mark E. Nackman, "The Making of the Texan Citizen-Soldier, 1835–1860," *Southwestern Historical Quarterly* 78 (January 1975)
Randy Roberts and James Olson, *A Line in the Sand: The Alamo in Blood and Memory* (2001)
Susan Schoelwer, *Alamo Images: Changing Perceptions of a Texas Experience* (1985)

CHAPTER
6

# The Fragile Republic:
# Building New Communities,
# 1836–1845

After the Battle of San Jacinto, most Anglo Texans assumed that Texas would be speedily annexed by the United States. By an overwhelming margin, Texas voters favored joining the Union in 1837, but the measure was defeated in the U.S. Congress by an antislavery faction that included former president John Quincy Adams. Texas was now obliged to make good on its claim as an independent, sovereign nation. Diplomatic recognition from the United States and the major powers of Europe soon followed. Mexico, on the other hand, continued to insist that Texas was a province in revolt, which it vowed to reconquer. Any attempt by the United States to annex Texas in the future, it warned, would be tantamount to a declaration of war.

During its brief, nine year existence, the fledgling nation was beset with problems. A worldwide depression that lasted into the 1840s severely limited the demand for cotton (the Republic's chief export), while the dire economic situation was aggravated by the government's inability to obtain foreign loans. Border hostilities with Mexico and the depredations of Indian tribes kept Texas's western frontier in a constant state of turmoil, discouraging immigration from the United States and Europe. Internal divisions within the Anglo Texan community also plagued the young republic, as the dissension which had characterized the revolutionary effort continued to undermine political stability and social order.

The challenges Texas faced as an independent nation—a prostrate economy, ethnic conflict, and political strife—all contributed to its reputation as a region where a frontier ethos of self-reliance prevailed. In the absence of well-established political and juridical institutions, according to this interpretation, Anglo Texans were obliged to fend for themselves, establishing a society characterized by a spirit of reckless, anti-authoritarian egalitarianism. Recently, however, some historians have been less inclined to view the Republic as a nation of unfettered individualism. For all their roughhewn qualities, Anglo Texans did not abandon Jacksonian cultural norms when they crossed the Sabine River, but continued to value social conformity and community obligation, much as they had done in the United

*States. What effect, then, did frontier conditions have on the Jacksonian society that emerged in the nascent republic? How successfully did Anglo Texans recreate the world they had known in the United States? More broadly, does Texas deserve to be regarded as a legitimate experiment in nationhood—as Mark Nackman contends in his essay in Chapter One—or merely the westernmost fringe of an ever-expanding American empire?*

## ✪ D O C U M E N T S

In the years immediately following the Revolution, the infant Republic seemed ripe with opportunity. In Document 1, an anonymous visitor to Texas in 1837 describes Houston City, a makeshift boom town that emerged almost overnight after the war along Buffalo Bayou. White settlers, lured by the prospect of cheap land, found an egalitarian culture characteristic of early nineteenth-century American frontier communities, one in which land scrip passed as legal tender and class formation had not yet occurred.

After the U. S. Congress rejected the Republic's overture of annexation in 1837, a number of Texas leaders argued that the new nation should now seek to carve a permanent niche for itself in the American southwest. The most prominent spokesman for Texas nationalism was Mirabeau Lamar, whose presidential inaugural address is excerpted in Document 2. Although the address does not refer specifically to the institution of slavery, Lamar, a slaveholder who had emigrated to Texas from Georgia, had become increasingly alarmed by the tenor of antislavery opinion in the Northern states, and the document should be read with this concern in mind. Lamar's call for an independent republic is consistent with the nationalist fervor in evidence in both the Americas and Europe during the mid-nineteenth century; many Anglo Texans, however, seem never to have abandoned their hope for annexation.

The Panic of 1837 dashed the hopes of an easy fortune for many, prompting the Texas Congress to pass the Homestead Exemption Act in 1839, presented in Document 2. One of the most progressive debtors' protection laws ever passed in North America, and widely copied by other states after Texas joined the Union, the Homestead Exemption Act reflected the egalitarian notion that debtors should be allowed the means to regain their financial independence despite economic hard times.

Anglo Texans sought to establish political hegemony over one of the most racially diverse populations in North America. Document 4 is an excerpt from the memoir of Noah Smithwick, who negotiated a treaty with the Comanche Indians in 1838 that was never ratified by the Texas Senate. In Document 5, Mary Maverick describes the pitched battle known as the Council House Fight that raged on the streets of San Antonio between Comanches and residents of the town in 1840, during which thirty-three Indians and seven townspeople were killed. Tejanos, unlike Native Americans, enjoyed basic rights of citizenship during the Republic period, but were frequently regarded with intense hostility by their Anglo neighbors. Continued clashes with Mexico did not improve the climate of racial suspicion. In the spring and fall of 1842, Mexican forces briefly captured San Antonio. Document 6, an excerpt from the memoir of San Antonio mayor Juan Seguin, reveals the problems many Tejanos faced in the aftermath of the Revolution. They now found themselves "foreigners in their native land."

The border war with Mexico prompted President Sam Houston to issue the bellicose proclamation presented in Document 7. Despite Houston's fiery rhetoric, many Texans believed that the president was lukewarm in his enthusiasm for an aggressive military campaign against Mexico, as illustrated by the poem penned by a Houston critic in Document 8. Opposition to Houston also intensified after his decision to

remove the nation's capital from Austin to Houston City, as well as his public denunciations of Edwin Ward Moore, commander of the Texas fleet, who continued to prey
on Mexican ships in 1843 even after he had been ordered to return to port.

## 1. An Anonymous Visitor Describes Land Speculation in Houston City, 1837

Houston, more properly called the city of Houston, as no place of less denomination exists in all Texas, is situated upon the south side of Buffalo Bayou, at least
sixty feet above the water and about one hundred miles from the coast. The place
stands upon the edge of a prairie which spreads out in a southerly direction to the
timbers of the Brazos and on the east and west, after steering clear of the pines
which flank the city in the shape of a crescent, to a great extent. The bayou immediately below the town assumes the most novel appearance. It does not exceed
thirty yards in width but is very deep, with high steep banks covered with heavy
dense timber, whose limbs interlock from the opposite sides, excluding the sun
from its dark waters. It seems to wind its way under the earth until, encountering a
high bluff immediately below the city, it divides off into two branches, fixing at the
point of separation the head of all navigation. . . .

. . . The place was laid off during the winter and spring of 1837, as the future
seat of government for at least four years to come, and when I arrived, in the latter
part of March, the improvements consisted of a one story frame, two hundred feet
or more in length, which had just been raised, intended by the enterprising proprietors for stores and public offices, several rough log cabins, two of which were occupied as taverns, a few linen tents which were used for groceries, together with three
or four shanties made of poles set in the ground and covered and weatherboarded
with rough split shingles. All, however, was bustle and animation. Hammers and
axes were sounding in all directions, and I heard the trees falling around and saw
some men engaged in laying the foundations of houses, others raising, and a number busily at work marking out the ground and preparing timber for a government
house. I might say that here was concentrated all the energy and enterprise of Texas,
for there were but few improvements making in any other portion of the Republic.
Lots were selling at enormous prices, in some instances as high as four and five
thousand dollars apiece. The spirit of speculation was afloat, which, as a false
medium, distorted and displaced everything. . . .

. . . When the members of Congress saw the immense fortunes which were
likely to be realized out of the sale of lots, they agitated the removal of the seat of
government to some other part of the Republic. All concurred in the propriety of a
change, but all disagreed from conflicting interests as to the place. Should Houston
continue for any length of time to be the seat of government, it will be owing much
to the fact that all the members of Congress cannot be accommodated in the
change. The prospect of a removal will always operate to the disadvantage of the
city, whether it ever took place or not, and that it is agitated at all is much owing to

---

Andrew Forest Muir, ed., *Texas in 1837, an Anonymous, Contemporary Narrative* (Austin: University
of Texas Press, 1958), 26–36.

the course of the proprietors themselves. But notwithstanding all this, when I arrived, Houston was not only the center of most of the spirit and enterprise of Texas, but it seemed to be the focus of immigration from all directions, as it continued to be during the summer. Persons came pouring in until, in a short time, a floating population had collected of some four or five hundred people. Houses could not be built near as fast as required, so that quite a large number of linen tents were pitched in every direction over the prairie, which gave to the city the appearance of a Methodist camp-ground. Some of these tents, such as were used for groceries, were calculated to surprise one from their great size. A number of them measured more than a hundred feet each in circumference, with conical tops, thirty or forty feet in height supported by means of a pole in the center. . . .

During the summer, the money most in circulation was notes of the Louisiana and Mississippi banks and gold and silver. Notes upon most of the southern and middle states passed without difficulty. Bank paper was by no means scarce, as every person coming from the States, especially those who were called speculators, brought it with them in large quantities. But paper of all kinds vanished so soon as the great money embarrassments began to be seen and felt at home. Gold and silver too soon disappeared, being mostly gathered up by speculators to make their purchases of the Mexicans, who would receive no other money, or carried off by the gamblers. From such causes, money of all kinds became exceedingly scarce, which made the issue of shinplasters a matter of necessity. Congress has granted several bank charters, but as yet none has gone into operation, and from present appearances, none is likely soon to do so. A charter was created by the First Congress, with the most enormous powers, and which has been the subject of great excitement in Texas. I think there is little cause for alarm, however, as the act of incorporation requires that the bonus, *twenty thousand dollars,* should be paid within a limited time, which expired, if I have not forgotten, sometime in November last. From appearances in October, there was no probability that the money would be paid, notwithstanding the incorporators were composed of the most wealthy and influential men in the country, who made frequent attempts in person to negotiate for the amount in the United States. . . .

. . . I ought not to omit to mention the *modus operandi* of the speculator, who finds a fine field here for the exercise of his shrewdness and energies. Some were engaged in purchasing the discharges of the soldiers, each of whom is entitled, beyond his pay of eight dollars a month in government paper, to six hundred and forty acres of land for each six months' service and in proportion for a less period. For this he gets a certificate from the government. The discharged soldier comes to Houston, hungry and next to naked, with nothing but his claims upon the government, which his situation compels him to sell. If he gets ten per cent for his money scrip and fifty dollars for a six months' discharge, he receives quite as much as these claims were selling for during the summer. When the storm beaten soldier thus sees the reward of all his sufferings reduced to a few dollars, he has too much reason to lament over the time which he has worse than thrown away and often in despair gives himself up to total abandonment. Upon this subject I might say much, but as Texas may have need for more soldiers, it is well that I should be silent.

Another class of citizens were busy in buying what in the language of the country are called headrights. In order that the reader may understand what these are, I will add that the Constitution of Texas provides that all white males of a specified age who were in the country on the second of March, 1836, the date of the Declaration of Independence, provided such persons are married, shall be entitled to a league and labor of land and if single to one third of a league. As the land office has been closed since the commencement of the Revolution, these rights are nothing more than claims upon the government but are more valuable than soldiers' discharges or government land scrip, as the Constitution provides further that all such rights have a priority of location, for six months, when the office is opened. Such rights have been known to sell for twenty-five cents an acre and in some instances for much more. Those, however, who contracted to take such claims through all the legal steps necessary to procure a title from the government when the land office is opened, for the one half and pay all attendant expenses, made the safest and most profitable speculation.

## 2. Mirabeau Lamar Appeals to Texas Nationalism, November 10, 1838

There is . . . one question of the highest national concernment, on which I feel it a privilege and a duty to address myself to the great body of the people themselves. I mean the annexation of our country to the American union. Notwithstanding the almost undivided voice of my fellow-citizens at one time in favor of the measure, an[d] notwithstanding the decision of the national congress at its last session, inhibiting the chief magistrate from withdrawing the proposition at the cabinet of Washington, yet still I have never been able myself to perceive the policy of the desired connexion, or discover in it any advantage either c[i]vil, political or commercial, which could possibly result to Texas. But on the contrary a long train of consequences of the most appalling character and magnitude, have never failed to present themselves whenever I have entertained the subject, and forced upon my mind the unwelcome conviction, that the step once taken would produce a lasting regret, and ultimately prove as disastrous to our liberty and hopes, as the triumphant sword of the enemy. And I say this from no irreverence to the character and institutions of my native country, whose welfare I have ever desired, and do still desire above my individual happiness, but a deep and abiding gratitude to the people of Texas, as well as a fervent devotion to those sacred principles of government, whose defence invited me to this country, compel me to say that however strong be my attachment to the parent land, the land of my adoption must claim my highest allegiance and affection; her glory and happiness must be my paramount consideration, and I cannot allow myself to speak in any other than the language of freedom and frankness on all matters involving her safety, dignity and honor.

When I reflect upon the invaluable rights which Texas will have to yield up with the surrender of her Independence—the right of making either war or peace; the right of controlling the Indian tribes within her borders; the right of appropriating

Inaugural Address, November 10, 1838, Charles Gulick, ed., *The Papers of Mirabeau Lamar* (Austin: A. C. Baldwin; 1921–27), 2:319–321.

her public domain to purposes of education and internal improvements; of levying her own taxes; regulating her own commerce and forming her own alliances and treaties—when I view her divested of the most essential attributes of free government; reduced to the level of an unfelt fraction of a giant power; or peradventure divided into Territorial districts, with Governors and judges and excise men appointed from abroad to administer laws which she had no adequate voice in enacting, and to gather imposts for the benefit of those who levy them—when I look upon her, as she soon will be, the cornucopia of the world, pouring her abundant treasures into the lap of another people than her own; a tributary vassal to remote and uncongenial communities; communities as widely separated from her in pursuits as in distance, who are known to be opposed to her peculiar and essential interests, and who are daily sending forth their denunciations against her from the fire-side, the pulpit and the council chamber; and when I bear in mind that all this sacrifice of rights and dignity and character is to be made, for what! for the privilege of going into a union in which she carries wealth without proportional influence—for the glory of identifying her fortunes with a government in which a large portion of the inhabitants are alarmed for the safety of the very institution upon which her own hopes of happiness are based; a government embracing conflicting interests and irreconcilable prejudices with lasting causes of domestic quarrel, where Texas can hope for nothing but a participation in the strifes that distract the public councils, and [after] passing through many throes and convulsions be the means perhaps of producing or accelerating an awful catastrophe which none could be more ready to avert or sincerely deplore than herself—when I reflect upon these, the inevitable and fatal consequences of the proposed connection, and then turn from the dark and dreary picture to the contemplation of the high destiny that awaits our country; the great prosperity which lies within her attainment if sh[e] will but appreciate her natural advantages, and not part with the right of developing and controling her incalculable resources: when I view her vast extent of territory, stretching from the Sabine to the Pacific and away to the South West as far as the obstinacy of the enemy may render it necessary for the sword to make the boundary; embracing the most delightful climate and the richest soil in the world, and behold it all in the state of high cultivation and improvement—her mountains of minerals yielding their vast treasures to the touch of industry; her luxuriant pastures alive with flocks and herds, and her wide fields whitening with a staple commodity, in the production of which she can have no rival; with the whole world for her market; and then consider the noble purposes to which this immense and exhaustless wealth may be applied, in adorning and beautifying the country, providing for its safety and defence, endowing institutions for the spread of virtue, knowledge and the arts, and carrying to the door of every citizen of the Republic, peace, plenty, and protection—and when in addition to these glorious and grand results, I look still farther to the important improvements which she will be able to devise in government, and to the entire revolution which her example in free trade will effect in the commerce of other nations, emancipating it from the thralldom of tariff restrictions and placing it upon the high grounds of equitable reciprocity, all of which will as certainly flow from the maintainence of her present independent position as the sun courses the heavens. When I reflect upon these vast and momentous consequences, so fatal to liberty on the one hand and so fraught with happiness and glory on the other, I cannot regard the annexation of Texas to the American Union in any other light than as the grave of all her hopes of happiness and greatness; and if, contrary to the present aspect of affairs, the amalgamation shall ever hereafter take place, I shall feel that the blood of our ma[r]tyred heroes had been shed in vain—that we had riven the chains of Mexican despotism only to fetter our country with more indissoluble bonds, and that a young Republic just rising into high distinction among the nations of the earth, had been swallowed up and lost like a proud bark in a devouring vortex.

## 3. The Homestead Exemption Act Protects Debtors, January 26, 1839

### AN ACT

Sec. 1. Be it enacted by the Senate and House of Representatives of the Republic of Texas in Congress assembled, That from and after the passage of this act, there shall be reserved to every citizen or head of a family in this Republic, free and independent of the power of a writ of fire facias, or other execution issuing from any court of competent jurisdiction whatever, fifty acres of land or one town lot, including his or her homestead, and improvements not exceeding five hundred dollars in value, all house hold and kitchen furniture, (provided it does not exceed in value two hundred dollars,) all implements of husbandry, (provided they shall not exceed fifty dollars in value,) all tools, apparatus and books belonging to the trade or profession of any citizen, five milch cows, one yoke of work oxen or one horse, twenty hogs, and one year's provisions.

## 4. Noah Smithwick Negotiates a Treaty with the Comanche Indians, 1838

The country [the Comanches] considered theirs by the right of inheritance; the game had been placed there for their food. In the true poetry of the simple child of the forest old Muguara said:

"We have set up our lodges in these groves and swung our children from these boughs from time immemorial. When game beats away from us we pull down our lodges and move away, leaving no trace to frighten it, and in a little while it comes back. But the white man comes and cuts down the trees, building houses and fences, and the buffalos get frightened and leave and never come back, and the Indians are left to starve, or, if we follow the game, we trespass on the hunting ground of other tribes and war ensues."

I suggested allotting them land and furnishing them with means to cultivate it like white men.

H. P. N. Gammel, comp., *The Laws of Texas, 1822–1897* (Austin: Gammel Book Co., 1898), 2:125–126.

Noah Smithwick, *Evolution of a State, or Recollections of Old Texas Days* (Austin: University of Texas Press, 1990), 134, 139, 151–154.

"No," said he emphatically, "the Indians were not made to work. If they build houses and try to live like white men they will all die. If the white men would draw a line defining their claims and keep on their side of it the red men would not molest them." . . .

We finally fixed up a treaty, the provisions of which I do not remember, nor is it essential since they were never complied with by either party. One article of the treaty stipulated that a trading post should be established on Brushy [Creek] at the site of the old Tumlinson block house, where the Indians could come and get supplies. They were fast becoming civilized in that respect, bartering buffalo robes and buckskins for blankets and clothing. . . .

Open hostilities ceased for a time, however, and gave the settlers a chance to quarrel among themselves. Dissensions arose, and, lulled by the fancied security, the more venturesome spirits pushed further out, exciting anew the distrust of the Indians. Then, when the time in which the trading post was to have been established passed, and they came in with their skins to trade and found no trading house, they came to call on me to know why the treaty had not been complied with. As there was no plausible excuse for the failure, they held me responsible, saying I had lied to them, which, of course, destroyed any influence I might have previously exercised over them, and the irrepressible conflict recommenced with redoubled vigor. . . .

In 1838 the land office was opened and speculators began flocking into the country, accompanied by surveyors, who at once began an aggressive movement upon the hunting grounds of the wild tribes, thereby provoking them to a more determined resistance to the encroachments of the settlers. Then, too, the Mexican government egged them on, furnishing them with arms and ammunition. It was the same old story of the troubles of the frontiersmen everywhere and destined to the same finale—the survival of the fittest.

True, the Indian mode of indiscriminate warfare was barbarous, but there were not wanting white men to follow their example. Extermination was the motto on both sides. That was President Lamar's avowed policy and Colonel Moore carried it out when he attacked their camp over on the Red fork of the Colorado in 1843. There was a man in Bastrop county whose family had been slaughtered by the Cherokees in the United States, for which he swore eternal vengeance on Indians in toto. He came to Texas and never let an opportunity pass to get a scalp, regardless of the consequences it might entail on others. He was several times apprehended for killing friendly Indians, but could never be convicted.

## 5. Mary Maverick Describes the Council House Fight Between Comanches and San Antonio Residents, 1840

On Tuesday, 19th of March, 1840, "dia de San Jose" sixty-five Comanches came into town to make a treaty of peace. They brought with them, and reluctantly gave up, Matilda Lockhart, whom they had captured with her younger sister in December 1838, after killing two other children of her family. The Indian chiefs and men met

Rena Maverick Green, ed., *Memoirs of Mary Maverick*, (Lincoln: University of Nebraska Press, 1989), 106–113.

in council at the Court House, with our city and military authorities. The calaboose or jail then occupied the corner formed by the east line of Main Plaza and the north line of Calabosa (now Market) Street, and the Court House was north of and adjoining the jail. The Court House yard, back of the Court House, was what is now the city market on Market Street. The Court House and jail were of stone, one story, flat roofed, and floored with dirt. Captain Tom Howard's Company was at first in the Court House yard, where the Indian women and boys came and remained during the pow-wow. The young Indians amused themselves shooting arrows at pieces of money put up by some of the Americans; and Mrs. Higginbotham and myself amused ourselves looking through the picket fence at them.

This was the third time these Indians had come for a talk, pretending to seek peace, and trying to get ransom money for their American and Mexican captives. Their proposition was that they should be paid a great price for Matilda Lockhart, and a Mexican they had just given up, and that traders be sent with paint, powder, flannel, blankets and such other articles as they should name, to ransom the other captives. This course had once before been asked and carried out, but the smallpox breaking out, the Indians killed the traders and kept the goods—believing the traders had made the smallpox to kill them. Now the Americans, mindful of the treachery of the Comanches, answered them as follows: "We will according to a former agreement, keep four or five of your chiefs, whilst the others of your people go to your nation and bring all the captives, and then we will pay all you ask for them. Meanwhile, these chiefs we hold we will treat as brothers and 'not one hair of their heads shall be injured.' This we have determined, and, if you try to fight, our soldiers will shoot you down."

This being interpreted, the Comanches instantly, with one accord raised a terrific war-whoop, drew their arrows, and commenced firing with deadly effect, at the same time making efforts to break out of the council hall. The order "fire" was given by Captain Howard, and the soldiers fired into the midst of the crowd, the first volley killing several Indians and two of our own people. All soon rushed out into the public square, the civilians to procure arms, the Indians to flee, and the soldiers in pursuit. The Indians generally made for the river—they ran up Soledad, east on Commerce Street and for the bend, now known as Bowen's, southeast, below the square. Citizens and soldiers pursued and overtook them at all points, shot some swimming in the river, had desperate fights in the streets—and hand to hand encounters after firearms had been exhausted. Some Indians took refuge in stone houses and fastened the doors. Not one of the sixty-five Indians escaped—thirty-three were killed and thirty-two were taken prisoners. . . .

When the deafening war-whoop sounded in the Court room, it was so loud, so shrill and so inexpressibly horrible and suddenly raised, that we women looking through the fence at the women's and boy's markmanship for a moment could not comprehend its purport. The Indians however knew the first note and instantly shot their arrows into the bodies of Judge Thompson and the other gentleman near by, instantly killing Judge Thompson. We fled into Mrs. Higginbotham's house and I, across the street to my Commerce Street door. Two Indians ran past me on the street and one reached my door as I got in. He turned to raise his hand to push it just as I beat down the heavy bar; then he ran on. I ran in the north room and saw my husband and brother Andrew sitting calmly at a table inspecting some plats of surveys—they had heard nothing. I soon gave them the alarm, and hurried on to look for my boys. Mr. Maverick and Andrew seized their arms, always ready—Mr. Maverick rushed into the street, and Andrew into the back yard where I was shouting at the top of my voice "Here are Indians!" "Here are Indians!" Three Indians had gotten in through the gate on Soledad street and were making direct for the river! One had paused near Jinny Anderson, our cook, who stood bravely in front of the children, mine and hers, with a great rock lifted in both hands above her head, and I heard her cry out to the Indian "If you don't go 'way from here I'll mash your head with this rock!" The Indian seemed regretful that he hadn't time to dispatch Jinny and her brood, but his time was short, and pausing but a moment, he dashed down the bank into the river. and struck out for the opposite shore.

As the Indian hurried down the bank and into the river Andrew shot and killed him, and shot another as he gained and rose on the opposite bank,—then he ran off up Soledad street looking for more Indians.

I housed my little ones, and then looked out of the Soledad Street door. Near by was stretched an Indian, wounded and dying. A large man, journey-apprentice to Mr. Higginbotham, came up just then and aimed a pistol at the Indian's head. I called out: "Oh, don't, he is dying," and the big American laughed and said: "To please you, I won't, but it would put him out of his misery." Then I saw two others lying dead near by.

Captain Lysander Wells, about this time, passed by riding north on Soledad Street. He was elegantly dressed and mounted on a gaily caparisoned Mexican horse with silver mounted saddle and bridle—which outfit he had secured to take back to his native state, on a visit to his mother. As he reached the Verimendi House, an Indian who had escaped detection, sprang up behind him, clasped Wells' arms in his and tried to catch hold of the bridle reins. Well was fearless and active. They struggled for some time, bent back and forward, swayed from side to side, till at last Wells held the Indian's wrists with his left hand, drew his pistol from the holster, partly turned, and fired into the Indian's body—a moment more and the Indian rolled off and dropped dead to the ground. Wells then put spurs to his horse which had stood almost still during the struggle, dashed up the street and did good service in the pursuit. I had become so fascinated by this struggle that I had gone into the street almost breathless, and wholly unconscious of where I was, till recalled by the voice of Lieutenant Chavallier who said: "Are you crazy? Go in or you will be killed." I went in but without feeling any fear, though the street was almost deserted and my husband and brother both gone in the fight. I then looked out on Commerce street and saw four or five dead Indians. I was just twenty-two then, and was endowed with a fair share of curiosity.

Not till dark did all our men get back, and I was grateful to God, indeed, to see my husband and brother back alive and not wounded.

Captain Mat Caldwell, or "Old Paint," as he was familiarly called, our guest from Gonzales, was an old and famous Indian fighter. He had gone from our house to the Council Hall unarmed. But when the fight began, he wrenched a gun from an Indian and killed him with it, and beat another to death with the butt end of the gun. He was shot through the right leg, wounded as he thought by the first volley of the soldiers. After breaking the gun, he then fought with rocks, with his back to the Court House wall. . . .

. . . Captain Caldwell was assisted back to our house and Dr. Weiderman came and cut off his boot and found the bullet had gone entirely through the leg, and lodged in the boot, where it was discovered. The wound, though not dangerous, was very painful, but the doughty Captain recovered rapidly and in a few days walked about with the aid of a stick.

After the captain had been cared for, I ran across to Mrs. Higginbotham's. Mr. Higginbotham, who was as peaceful as a Quaker to all appearances, had been in the fight and had received a slight wound. They could not go into their back yard, because two Indians had taken refuge in their kitchen, and refused to come out or surrender as prisoners when the interpreter had summoned them. A number of young men took counsel together that night, and agred upon a plan. Anton Lock-mar and another got on the roof, and, about two hours after midnight dropped a candlewick ball soaked in turpentine, and blazing, through a hole in the roof upon one Indian's head and so hurt him and frightened them both that they opened the door and rushed out—to their death. An axe split open the head of one of the Indians before he was well out of the door, and the other was killed before he had gone many steps—thus the last of the sixty-five were taken.

## 6. Juan Seguín Flees to Mexico After the Vásquez Invasion, 1842

After the retreat of the Mexican army under Santa Anna, until Vásquez' invasion in 1842, the war between Texas and Mexico ceased to be carried on actively. Although open commercial intercourse did not exist, it was carried on by smuggling, at which the Mexican authorities used to wink provided it was not carried on so openly as to oblige them to notice it, or so extensively as to arouse their avarice.

In the beginning of this year I was elected mayor of San Antonio. Two years previously a gunsmith named James Goodman had taken possession of certain houses, situated on the Military Plaza, which were the property of the city. He used to shoe the horses of the volunteers who passed through San Antonio. Thus the Republic owed him a debt, for the payment of which he applied to the president to give him possession of the buildings referred to, which had always been known as city property.

The board of aldermen passed a resolution to the effect that Goodman should be compelled to leave the premises. Goodman resisted, alleging that the houses had been given to him by the president, in payment for public services. The board could not, of course, acknowledge any power of the president to dispose of the city property and, consequently, directed me to carry the resolution into effect. My compliance with the instructions of the board caused Goodman to become my most bitter and inveterate enemy in the city.

Juan Seguín, *A Revolution Remembered: The Memoirs and Selected Correspondence of Juan Seguín.* Jesús de la Teja, ed. (Austin: State House Press, 1991), 73–74; 92–100. Edited version of the memoirs reprinted by permission of the editor, Jesús F. de la Teja.

The term for the mortgage, that Messrs. Ogden and Howard held on my property, had run out. In order to raise money and comply with my obligations, I determined to go to Mexico for a drove of sheep. But, fearful that this new trip would prove as fatal as the one already alluded to, I wrote to General Rafael Vásquez, who was then in command of the Mexican frontier, requesting him to give me a pass. The tenor of Vásquez' answer caused me to apprehend that an expedition against Texas was in preparation for the following month of March.

I called a session of the board of aldermen (of which the Hon. Samuel A. Maverick was a member) and laid before them the communication of General Vásquez, stating that according to my interpretation of the letter we might soon expect the approach of the Mexicans. A few days afterwards Don José María García, of Laredo, came to San Antonio. His report was so detailed as to preclude all possible doubts as to the imminent approach of Vásquez to San Antonio.

Notice of the impending danger was sent immediately to the government. In the various meetings held to devise means of defense, I expressed my candid opinion as to the impossibility of defending San Antonio. I observed that, for myself, I was going to the town of Seguin and advised everyone to do the same.

On leaving the city, I passed through a street where some men were making breastworks. I told them I was going to my rancho and thence to Seguin, in case the Mexican forces should take possession of San Antonio.

From the Nueces River, Vásquez forwarded a proclamation by Arista to the inhabitants of Texas. At my rancho I received a bundle of those proclamations, which I transmitted at once to the municipality of San Antonio.

As soon as Vásquez entered the city, those who had been determined to defend the place withdrew to Seguin. Among them were James Dunn and Chevallie, both of whom had succeeded in escaping from the Mexican hands into which they had fallen while on a reconnoitering expedition on the Medina River. . . .

On my return to San Antonio, several persons told me that the Mexican officers had declared that I was on their side. This rumor, and some threats uttered against me by Goodman, left me but little doubt that my enemies would try to ruin me.

Some of the citizens of San Antonio had taken up arms on the side of the enemy. Judge John Hemphill advised me to have them arrested and tried but, as I was starting out with the party that was to go in pursuit of the Mexicans, I could not follow his advice.

Having observed that Vásquez gained ground on us, we fell back on the Nueces River. When we came back to San Antonio, reports about my implausible treason were spreading widely. Captain Manuel Flores, Lieutenant Ambrosio Rodríguez, Matías Curbier and five or six other Mexicans joined me to find out the origin of the false rumors. I went out with several friends, leaving Curbier in my house. I had reached the Main Plaza when several persons came running to inform me that some Americans were murdering Curbier. We ran back to the house where we found poor Curbier covered with blood. On being asked who assaulted him he answered that the gunsmith Goodman, in company with several Americans, had struck him with a rifle. A few minutes later Goodman returned to my house with about thirty volunteers but, observing that we were prepared to meet them, they did not attempt to attack us. We went out of the house and then to Mr. Francois Guilbeau's, who offered me his protection. He went out into the street, pistol in hand, and succeeded in dispersing the mob which had formed in front of my house. Mr. John Twohig offered me a shelter for that night. The next morning, I went under disguise to Mr. Van Ness' house. Twohig, who recognized me in the street, warned me to "keep my eyes open." I remained one day at Mr. Van Ness'.

The next day General Edward Burleson arrived at San Antonio, commanding a respectable force of volunteers. I presented myself to him, asking for a court of inquiry. He answered that there were no grounds for such proceedings. In the evening I went to the camp and, jointly with Colonel William H. Patton, received a commission to forage for provisions in the lower ranchos. I complied with this assignment.

I remained, hiding from rancho to rancho for over fifteen days. All the parties of volunteers en route to San Antonio declared "they wanted to kill Seguín." I could no longer go from rancho to rancho, and determined to go to my own rancho and fortify it. Several of my relatives and friends joined me. Hardly a day elapsed without receiving notice that a party was preparing to attack me; we were constantly kept under arms. Several parties came in sight but, probably seeing that we were prepared to receive them, refrained from attacking. . . .

Matters being in this state, I saw that it was necessary to take some step which would place me in security and save my family from constant wretchedness. I had to leave Texas, abandon all for which I had fought and spent my fortune, to become a wanderer. The ingratitude of those who had assumed onto themselves the right of convicting me, their credulity in declaring me a traitor on the basis of mere rumors, the necessity to defend myself for the loyal patriotism with which I had always served Texas, wounded me deeply. . . .

. . . I sent in my resignation as mayor of the city to the municipality of San Antonio, stating to them that, unable any longer to suffer the persecutions of some ungrateful Americans who strove to murder me, I had determined to free my family and friends from their continual misery on my account, and go and live peaceably in Mexico. That for these reasons I resigned my office, with all my privileges and honors as a Texan.

I left Béxar with no obligation to Texas, my services repaid with persecutions. Exiled and deprived of my privileges as a Texan citizen, I was outside the pale of society in Texas. If Texas could not protect the rights of her citizens, they were privileged to seek protection elsewhere. I had been tried by a rabble, condemned without a hearing, and consequently was at liberty to provide for my own safety.

When I arrived at Laredo the military commander of that place put me in prison, stating that he could not do otherwise until he had consulted with General Arista, whom he advised of my arrest. Arista ordered that I be sent to Monterrey. When I arrived in that city, I earnestly prayed the general to allow me to retire to Saltillo, where I had several relatives who could aid me. General Arista answered that, as he had informed Santa Anna of my imprisonment, he could not comply with my request. Santa Anna directed that I be sent to the City of Mexico but Arista, sympathetic to my unfortunate position, interceded with him in my behalf to have the order revoked. The latter complied, but on condition that I should return to Texas with a company of explorers to attack its citizens and, by spilling my blood, vindicate myself.

Under the orders of General Arista, I proceeded to the Rio Grande to join General Woll, who told me that Santa Anna, at his request, had allowed me to go to Texas with Woll's expedition, but that I should receive no command until my services proved that I was worthy.

I set out with the expedition of General Woll. In the vicinity of San Antonio, on the 10th of September, I received an order to take a company of cavalry and block the exits from the city. By this order the city was blockaded and, consequently, it was difficult for any person to escape. When I returned from complying with this order, at dawn of day, the general determined to enter the city with the infantry and artillery. I was sent to the vanguard with orders to take possession of the Military Square despite all obstacles. I entered the square without opposition and, shortly afterwards, the firing commenced on the Main Square. John Hernández came out of Goodman's shop with a message from him to the effect that if I would pardon him for what he had done against me he would leave his place of concealment and deliver himself up. I sent him word that I had no rancor against him. He delivered himself up, and I placed him under the special charge of Captain Manuel Leal. Those who had made some show of resistance in the Main Square surrendered, and the whole city was in General Woll's possession.

The next day I was ordered, with two hundred men, to take the Gonzales road and approach that town. On the Cibolo I divided my forces, sending one detachment up the creek, another down the creek, and with the main body proceeded on the Gonzales road. The following day, these parties joined the main body. Lieutenant Manuel Carvajal, who commanded one of the parties, reported that he had killed three Texans who would not surrender in the Azufrosa [Sulphur Springs].

I returned to San Antonio. A party of Texans appeared by the Garita road and the troops were taken under arms. The general took one hundred infantry, the cavalry under Cayetano Montero, and one piece of artillery and proceeded towards the Salado. The general ordered one hundred *presidiales* [former garrison soldiers from Texas] to attack. The commander of those forces sent word that the enemy was in an advantageous position and that he required reinforcements. The answer of the general was to send me with orders "to attack at all costs." I obeyed. On the first charge I lost three killed and eight wounded, on the second seven killed and fifteen wounded. I was preparing for a third charge when Colonel José María Carrasco came to relieve me from my command. I returned to the side of the general and made my report, whereupon he ordered the firing to cease.

A new attack was in preparation when the attention of the general was called to some troops on our rear guard. The aides reported them to be enemies and near at hand. Colonel Montero was ordered to attack them with his cavalry. He called on them to surrender to the Mexican Government; they answered with scoffing and bantering. Montero formed his dragoons; the Texans commenced firing, killing two soldiers. Montero dismounted his troops, also began firing, and sent for more ammunition. The general angrily sent him a message asking whether his dragoons had no sabres or lances. Before Montero received this answer he had charged, sabre in hand, ending the engagement in a few minutes. Only some ten or fifteen Texans survived. During this time, I remained by the side of General Woll and was there when Montero made his report and brought in the prisoners. At dusk the troops received orders to return to San Antonio.

In accordance with his orders not to remain over a month on this side of the Rio Grande, General Woll began his retreat by the road he came. . . .

After General Woll's expedition I did not return to Texas until the treaty of Guadalupe Hidalgo.

## 7. Sam Houston Threatens Reprisals Against Mexico, March 21, 1842

To His Excellency Antonio Lopez de Santa Anna, President of Mexico:

. . . You touchingly invite Texas to "cover herself anew with the Mexican flag." You certainly intend this as a mockery. You denied us the enjoyment of the laws under which we came to the country. Her flag was never raised in our behalf nor has it been seen in Texas except when displayed in an attempt at our subjugation. We know your lenity—we know your mercy—we are ready again to test your power. You have threatened to plant your banner on the banks of the Sabine. Is this done to intimidate us? Is it done to alarm us? Or do you deem it the most successful mode of conquest? If the latter, it may do to amuse the people surrounding you. If to alarm us, it will amuse those conversant with the history of your last campaign. If to intimidate us, the threat is idle. We have desired peace. You have annoyed our frontier; you have harassed our citizens; you have incarcered our traders, after your commissioners had been kindly received, and your citizens allowed the privilege of commerce in Texas without molestation. You continue aggression; you will not accord us peace. *We will have it.* You threaten to conquer Texas; we will war with Mexico. Your pretentions with ours you have referred to the social world, and to the God of battles. We refer to the same tribunals—the issue involves the fate of nations. Destiny must determine—its event is only known to the tribunal of heaven. If experience of the past will authorize speculations of the future, the attitude of Mexico is more problematical than that of Texas.

In the war which will be conducted by Texas against Mexico, our incentive will not be a love of conquest; it will be to disarm tyranny of its power. We will make no war upon Mexicans or their religion. Our efforts shall be made in behalf of the liberties of the people; and directed against the authorities of the country, and against your principles. We will exalt the condition of the people to representative freedom. They shall choose their own rulers—they shall possess their property in peace; and it shall not be taken from them to support an armed soldiery for the purpose of oppression. With these principles we will march across the Rio Grande, and, believe me, Sir, ere the banner of Mexico shall triumphantly float upon the banks of the Sabine, the Texian standard of the single star, borne by the Anglo-Saxon race, shall display its bright folds in Liberty's triumph, on the isthmus of Darien. . . .

Sam Houston.

Houston to Santa Anna, March 21, 1842, Eugene Barker and Amelia Williams, eds., *Houston Writings*, 2:513–527.

## 8. A Texan Mocks the Houston Administration's Military Record, 1843

Twelve months have passed, since the war blast,
Blown by Sam's threatening letter;
Whose valor found no resting ground,
This side of the Equator.

Then did he swear, that he would bear,
To Darien our Banner—
*Yet* his Religion, *now* takes in dudgeon
All war with Santa Anna.

Some say his courage cooled off like porridge
By oosing through his quill;
And some again, say that he can
Write like a hero still.

He's doubtless read, "Who wields the sword
Shall by the sword be slain."
But who by writing, does his fighting,
Shall live to fight again.

He counts the cost—the millions lost
Orphans and widows made—
And he found paper, and ink much cheaper
Than powder, steel and lead.

To doubt his force, in war, of course
Is wanton defamation,
Since he blockades, likewise invades
With many a *Proclamation.*

"Who arms dare wield, by flood or field
Are pirates and highwaymen."—
Such must prepare, to feel his ire
And hang as high as Haman.

Then let him spill by mouth and quill
The blood of all our foes,
And batter down each walled town
With overwhelming prose.

No fleet does he, require at sea—
No army on the shore,
But just to kill, our *Capital,*
And hang our gallant *Moore.*

---

Untitled Poem, *Morning Star* (Houston), June 6, 1843.

## ✦ E S S A Y S

In the first essay, the late historian William Ransom Hogan, writing in the 1940s, describes Anglo-Texan society during the Lone Star Republic as a bastion of frontier individualism. Borrowing from the triumphalist tradition of Walter Prescott Webb, Eugene Barker, and others, Hogan views the frontier as a space that liberated its white inhabitants from the constraints of established society, an inhospitable environment that forced them to rely on individual initiative and their own resources.

Sam Houston has often been viewed as one of the great exemplars of this frontier ethos. Yet in the second essay by Sam W. Haynes, associate professor at the University of Texas at Arlington, the famed hero of San Jacinto and twice-elected president of the Republic is viewed as a man at odds with the deeply felt community values of his era. The deep-seated, almost rabid hostility which his political enemies felt toward Houston, Haynes argues, is rooted in the Texan leader's penchant for self-aggrandizement. Later generations may have admired Houston's flamboyance, as well as his willingness to make unpopular decisions as both a military and a political leader, but his contemporaries often regarded these same qualities as character flaws. Thus, while Hogan emphasizes a spirit of individualism, Haynes suggests that historians have often failed to appreciate the social dynamics of the Jacksonian community, instead viewing the early years of Anglo Texan settlement by their own modern values.

## Frontier Individualism and the Texas Republic

### WILLIAM RANSOM HOGAN

In February, 1846, when Dr. Anson Jones performed his last official act as president of the Republic of Texas, an old settler could look back upon a decade of partial frustration and disillusion in his economic affairs. To be sure, many changes had occurred. The population of the country had more than quadrupled since 1836. Cotton production was perhaps ten times as great. The line of settlement had been pushed west of the modern cities of Dallas, Waco, Austin, and San Antonio in the face of possible Indian raids and Mexican invasions. Schools, newspapers, and incipient industries had been established. Striking contrasts between the crude and the luxurious had appeared in some of the towns. But these changes did not mean that the ordinary Texan had profited greatly. On the contrary, sound economic growth of his country had been seriously retarded first by a convulsion of speculation and then by the ravages of a devastating financial depression. Immediately following the end of the false boom in lands and townsites, both the government and its citizenry in 1840 had found themselves "land poor" and cruelly afflicted with a disorganized monetary system. The collapse of unsound real-estate values had coincided roughly with governmental issuance of large quantities of paper money, which promptly had undergone violent depreciation. Even in the towns there had been a widespread reversion to barter, which never had been wholly abandoned, as the method of exchange. In the summer of 1842 a leading newspaper had dolefully

William Ransom Hogan, *A Social and Economic History of the Republic of Texas* (Austin: University of Texas Press, 1969), 292–298. Copyright © University of Oklahoma Press. Reprinted with permission.

confessed: "A general gloom seems to rest over every section of the Republic, and doubt and sorrow are depicted on almost every brow."

Aside from dependence on selling land, the Republic's hopes for immediate economic salvation rested upon the exportation of cotton, some cattle, and a few hides. Texas was inescapably an agricultural country; the river valleys and the prairies contained very fertile cotton lands, and cattle were easily raised. But the expectations of most farmers were thwarted in several directions. Though the opinion was widely held that Negro slaves were needed for success in cotton culture, a large majority of Texas farmers were not able to buy even one. In addition to suffering the handicap of an inadequate labor force, they relearned the age-old lesson that farming was an uncertain undertaking which provided no assurance of reasonable returns; some Texas cotton drew the lowest prices in a low-price era because it was found difficult to prepare it properly for the market under frontier conditions, and in the early eighteen forties cotton and corn crops partially failed in two successive seasons. Finally, transporting the staple to shipping points was a time-consuming and onerous task.

Oxen still pulled a large part of Texas cotton to export centers through the mire of unimproved roads. A few steamboats and keelboats negotiated the often obstreperous, snag-blocked rivers, but the inland waterways were largely a failure as a medium of transportation. Although there was much talk of constructing highways, railroads, and canals, few internal improvements resulted. This failure to develop more advanced transportation facilities not only tended to accentuate sectional differences between the eastern and western counties but made stress upon cotton production almost inevitable. More perishable farm products could not have been as safely hauled and stored, and markets for them had not been developed.

Thus the Republic of Texas in the early eighteen forties was virtually impoverished. Its internal transportation system still was largely primitive. Many of its plans for achieving rapid economic maturity came to nothing. What, then, held it together?

Texans felt that their country had struck bottom during the depression years, that any buffeting that the future might bring could not be worse than what had gone before. Like frontiersmen everywhere, most of them were people of unhesitant faith, and their materialism was always tinged with visions of things hoped for in a world that was not only competitive but adventurous and quickly changing. Even new inventions, such as the Colt revolver, were reaching the frontier more rapidly than in an earlier day.

Meanwhile, settlers of both sexes were practicing the art of roughhewing civilization in a semiwooded wilderness, an art that had been almost perfected by past pioneer generations. Many of the women were vigorous products of one or more generations of frontier life, they had been trained from childhood to do their jobs, and they were able to bear hardships. The evidence is strong that most women were both busy and happy, and that they rarely voiced the complaints which some modern historians chivalrously assume that they often made. Even in an economic depression, participation in the process of creating a new country tended to produce resilient spirits and strong muscles.

The poverty of the frontier family undoubtedly differed from the abject poverty of the poorly paid urban artisan of the eastern seaboard. The possessions in a cabin might be few, but they had been fashioned on the adamantine anvil of experience, and they were cherished and owned in a very real sense. Shelter, food, and clothing could always be obtained. Life could be sustained regardless of the price of cotton, and hopes that the future would bring increased security and added value to land-holdings were never abandoned.

The broad distribution of land ownership—an inheritance from the liberal policy of the Mexican regime, reinforced by the typically Western demand for free land—did much to alleviate the pain of the depression years, because ownership of land in this period of American history was viewed as "the key to happiness." The chief source of agrarian discontent arose from uncertainty concerning land titles, and in this matter the government took vigorous steps to rectify an alarming situation.

Although professional speculators partially succeeded in withholding some of the best lands from immediate settlement, their activities in the Republic were hampered by several circumstances. Since the national government, which controlled the public domain, was close to the people, the antispeculation sentiment of the "real cultivators"—who constituted the mass of the electorate—was sufficiently strong not only to secure constitutional guarantees but also to force any politician to think twice before openly associating himself with a land-grabbing scheme. The antispeculation sections of the Republic's constitution, including one which specifically prohibited aliens from acquiring land titles except directly from the government, dealt a blow to rapacious moneyed interests in the United States who hoped to achieve extraordinary returns from unearned increment in Texas land ventures. Thereafter, any attempted land grab involving any group of politicians within the Republic also was subject to condemnation by an opposition group, although neither might be wholly blameless. Moreover, the monetary tightness of the early eighteen forties forced many of the resident "land sharks" to sell their lands. The depression also combined with antagonistic public opinion to cause the Texas Rail-Road, Navigation and Banking Company—considered "the biggest steal ever attempted in Texas" by one historian—to fold up before it began operations.

Large-scale land speculation, commonly condemned by historians of the American West, was not an unmixed evil in the Republic of Texas. Although McKinney, Williams and Company of Galveston and the Allen brothers of Houston acquired thousands of acres of land, they also contributed largely to the development of two important towns, started industries, operated steamboats, set up credit facilities, and established channels for the inflow of productive capital. Matthew Cartwright of San Augustine eventually realized a fortune from land purchases, but he was also a prominent and highly respected merchant who supported many worthwhile local causes. Merchandise firms in nearly every town acquired land at the same time that they combined the functions of banker, shipper, middleman, and retailer. The Mills brothers of Brazoria carried on all of these activities and also became large-scale cotton producers, while members of two leading San Augustine firms, I. D. Thomas and Blount and Price, operated plantations. Regardless of the extensive land acquisitions of some of these firms, they constituted the backbone of the financial and commercial structure of the country.

The public-land system furnished one of the original mainsprings of the intense Texas nationalism that has never subsided. Whereas frontier titles elsewhere emanated from a distant federal government in Washington, free land was obtained in the Republic of Texas from a national government that was close at hand. Most citizens, moreover, were proud that their Republic had shown ability to maintain itself in the face of staggering obstacles, that their laboratory experiment in self-government was proving workable. A sense of participation in the task of "helping to rear up our infant republic" permeated the thinking of all classes. Whether the first professional theater was being opened or the first rail was being laid in a prospective railroad, the orator of the occasion or the local newspaper editor invariably dramatized the event in terms of historical beginnings. This was a popular note, for Texans believed that there was a certain admirable singularity about their frontier commonwealth and that they themselves were a part of history in the making.

While citizens of the Republic demanded that their government see that "all start fair," they were perfectly willing to maintain freedom on a competitive basis, and the pressures of potential insecurity were never so great that they drove the people to any form of collectivism or utopian experiment. On the other hand, cooperative action freely taken by individuals was common. Newly arrived immigrants were aided by houseraisings and similar neighborly frolics. When the Indians or Mexicans threatened, the exodus of volunteers who hurried to join the ranks left whole towns without able-bodied males. Local meetings occasionally expressed community sentiment in regard to political or economic questions, and important political decisions were made by conventions which were proving to be an effective cross between pure democracy and representative government. In the field of religion, camp meetings met both spiritual and social needs. Participation in all of these enterprises was entirely voluntary.

While distance from centers of traditional culture was a handicap, many persons found compensation in the simplicity and freedom of the social mechanism and in the prevailing equalitarian standards that tended to provide broad bases for future development. Cabins were reflections of the personalities of the builders—strong, angular, and open. Both food and clothing usually were rough; refinements in the latter were occasionally seen, but class distinctions in dress were tending to disappear. The chief amusements were square dancing, horse racing and gambling, carousing, practical joking, and yarn swapping—all reflections of a hardy civilization. Imaginative, exaggerative humor aided in withstanding the rigors of frontier life at the same time that malaria, an unbalanced diet, and economic misfortune made life burdensome. The leaders among the lawyers, the doctors, and the teachers were men of ability, but charlatans flourished in all of the professions and standards of apprentice training were low. In the field of education, two achievements that were not petty in a frontier society were recorded: Instruction rose above the secondary level in a few church "colleges," and the substructure of a future educational system for "the whole people" was firmly fixed both in law and in public opinion.

Methodist and "Old School" Presbyterian preachers took the lead in providing facilities for education, and the Methodists, Baptists, and Cumberland Presbyterians dominated the religious scene. In spite of the pertinacity of the indomitable circuit riders, not more than one-eighth of the population were enrolled as church members. Strong forces opposed to the spread of formal religion included postwar social ferment, the riotousness of boom towns, frontier resentment of dogmatic authority, and intradenominational struggles. The religious atmosphere of the Republic was congenial to the skeptics occasionally found among the doctors and lawyers, to those who sought their religion in the open spaces, and to the persons who were repelled by the emotionalism of camp meetings. But the churches were largely responsible for the maintenance of mass moral standards that were conservative in aim, if not always in practice.

Most heads of families were men who sought a productive farm and future comfort for themselves and their families. Every community also had young men who hoped to achieve a more rapid rise in the legal and medical professions and in politics than would be possible in older communities. The most successful among the lawyers and doctors tended to blend into the small planter class, while many others were versatile enough to shift from their professions to other occupations as the occasion demanded. In the larger towns the diversity of occupations was surprising for towns so recently established. On the streets of Houston and Galveston, farmers, small planters, slaves, doctors, and lawyers touched elbows with merchants, clerks, boat crews, actors, barbers, auctioneers, tanners, carpenters, blacksmiths, tailors, teamsters, an occasional friendly Indian, a long-haired scout or two, possibly a group of Germans, rowdies, and loafers.

A small segment of the population gave Texas a reputation for sharp dealing and lawlessness. In the last half of the eighteen thirties the frontier Republic attracted a number of adventure-craving Southern hotheads as well as canny, land-seeking gentlemen who were not overly particular concerning the methods they used to attain an estate. Land frauds by a handful of swindlers were the key factor in igniting the Regulator-Moderator War, which for a time transformed a region centering in Shelby County into an area of law defiance and bloodshed. Some immigrants were shiftless, others had come to Texas to avoid the consequences of discreditable actions, and a few had criminal records. Professional gamblers gravitated to the towns that offered opportunities for the exercise of their special talents. Communities which fortunately failed to attract large numbers of these elements were comparatively peaceful, but individuals everywhere were forced to maintain a hair-trigger regard for their "rights."

The period of the Texas Revolution and the republic which emerged from it bred a temper peculiarly Texan—or "Texian" as it was often spelled in those days. The defense of the Alamo, recently called "the high mark of all times for fearless behavior," the massacre at Goliad, and the subsequent defeat of the Mexicans at San Jacinto gave Texan men at arms rallying cries and a tradition that have persisted for a century. Their fighting spirit arose not alone from national compulsion but also from individual necessity. In the years immediately following the Texas Revolution, law enforcement agencies were still in the process of organization precisely at the time that the country was in a state of postwar unrest and in the grip of a paroxysm of speculation. Disputes between persons with upper-class backgrounds were settled by resort to the Code Duello, and men of all classes engaged in other forms of personal conflict. Indians, Mexicans, desperadoes, drunken ruffians, gamblers, trigger-quick duelists who sought to have their honor offended—any of these might assail normally peaceable citizens. Hence they learned to defend themselves and, if necessary, take the offensive. Their confidence in their ability to look any man in the eye gave them a feeling of strength in their own opinions.

In a society which required strength and self-reliance both in acquiring the necessities of life and in social relationships, everyone was inclined to be self-assertive and restive under restraint. Theoretically one man was as good as another on the frontier, and a feeling of equality prevailed. Although the energy and leadership of business and professional men generally enabled them to exercise dominance, they rarely assumed attitudes of social superiority. The plain people elected few demagogues to high office, but politics was a rough-and-tumble spectacle. In 1838 two candidates for president committed suicide, and the campaign of 1841 was featured by vituperative charges of cowardice, dishonesty, and habitual drunkenness against the candidates.

The Republic was fortunate in its choice of leaders. Houston, Austin, Travis, Lamar, Rusk, Hemphill, Burleson, Burnet, Jones, Ashbel Smith, the Whartons, Henderson—these names only top a long list. The repercussions of the revolution they led and the republic they helped establish have not yet spent themselves, for their actions have impressed themselves indelibly on the consciousness of every Texan to this day. Houston responded to his elevation to the presidency by rising in stature from his former position of speculation-minded adventurer to one of real statesmanship, while Lamar's interest in intellectual matters is still felt in Texas.

So there arose a Texan way of life that still exists, even in the face of all the mass promotion and standardization of machine civilization. Stamina, individualism, "go-ahead" initiative, pride in everything Texan—these were and still are, in varying degrees, among the ingredients of the Texas spirit. Bitter courage, wry or raucous laughter, and kindliness stood out amidst the drabness and coarseness of frontier life. An astonishing number of urbane and intelligent men found a satisfying freedom from compulsion. Indeed, the Republic of Texas worked a curious alchemy with its citizenry, educated and untutored alike. It took the sons and daughters of Tennessee, the Carolinas, Georgia, Mississippi, New York, France, and Germany and set its own ineffaceable stamp on their souls. The same process is still working in Texas today.

## Sam Houston and His Antagonists

### SAM W. HAYNES

By any standard, Sam Houston's career in Texas was a turbulent one. Public figures are rarely strangers to controversy, but few have provoked such deep-seated animosity or been the target of such bitter invective. Houston's appeal today, no doubt, owes much to the fact that for almost a quarter of a century he braved the scorn and vituperative attacks of his political enemies, who routinely denounced the hero of San Jacinto as a charlatan and a fraud. Though his popularity with the electorate remained high, at least until the twilight of his career, to his antagonists he was, in Mosely Baker's phrase, "an incubus upon the land."

Mudslinging and character assassination, of course, were staple features of nineteenth century American politics, and a thick skin was required of all political leaders in order to withstand the calumnies and abuse of campaign opponents. What

Sam W. Haynes, "Sam Houston and his Antagonists" (paper presented at meeting of Texas State Historical Association, Austin, March 1994). Reprinted with permission.

is notable about the attacks on Houston, however, is the dogged persistence of his detractors, some of whom harassed him with a zeal bordering on monomania. For David G. Burnet, Mirabeau Lamar, Thomas Jefferson Green and others, their campaign to discredit Houston became a lifelong preoccupation. Moreover, in contrast to political contests elsewhere, the rancor that characterized Texas politics was intensely personal in nature, creating a climate of contentiousness that was aggravated by, but ultimately extended well beyond, issues of policy or partisanship.

Given Houston's venerable reputation, it is tempting to dismiss such hostility as little more than mean-spirited envy. The hero of San Jacinto cast a long shadow over the landscape of early Anglo Texas, and it is not unreasonable to suppose that there were those who begrudged him his success. But this explanation seems woefully inadequate when one considers how many key military and political figures quarreled bitterly with Houston at one time or another during the course of his career. Nor is it enough to simply assert that nineteenth century Anglo Texans were an independent lot who were inherently averse to all forms of authority, and that some would have chafed under the leadership of any strong-willed individual. Houston's principal antagonists defy ready classification, but they all shared a strongly held belief that the most celebrated figure in Texas did not deserve the laurels bestowed upon him.

The antipathy which many prominent Texans felt toward Houston was due at least in part to the fact that the Republic acted as a magnet for ambitious men eager to make their mark in a frontier society that seemed ripe with opportunity. Although Houston's enemies attacked him on a whole range of issues, they were particularly alienated by his economic and military policies, policies that often had a direct bearing on their own careers. Houston's refusal to sanction an invasion of Matamoros in the fall of 1836 aroused a firestorm of protest from men like Felix Huston, who viewed continued hostilities with Mexico as a means to establish military reputations, a prerequisite for any politically ambitious Texan. Similarly, Houston's opposition to legislation creating a general land office and his stand against the Texas Railroad, Navigation and Banking Company antagonized many speculators and entrepreneurs, among them Branch T. Archer and Thomas Jefferson Green, who hoped to emerge as the country's economic elite. As the consistent advocate of caution and retrenchment, Houston invariably clashed with men who had gravitated to Texas to realize their loftiest ambitions.

Their failure to do so contributed in yet another way to the acrimony that surrounded Houston's leadership. Many had been drawn to Texas as a result of financial problems in the United States, and now experienced further setbacks in the new Republic. Plagued by doubts of self-worth, they often displayed an almost obsessive desire to defend their reputations as men of honor and good standing. In Texas, a young nation beset by economic difficulties, the esteem in which one was held by others in the community took on particular significance in the absence of more tangible determinants of status. To besmirch a man's reputation, to impugn his honor, was to rob him of everything he had.

As a consequence, Houston's enemies exhibited a prickly sensitivity to insult, which allowed arguments with the famous Texan to fester and become lifelong feuds. Duelling, which had once provided immediate satisfaction for injured parties, had fallen into disfavor by the late 1830s, the practice giving way to more democratic, nonviolent means of redress. Men who believed their reputations had been sullied now sought to vindicate themselves before the bar of public opinion, publishing pamphlets or writing open letters to sympathetic newspapers, in which they systematically and thoroughly rebutted each of the charges against them. Sidney Sherman, whose conduct on the eve of San Jacinto was censured by Houston; Thomas Jefferson Green, who Houston accused of leading Texas troops in the sack and pillage of Laredo in 1842; and Commodore Edwin Ward Moore, who was court-martialed by the Houston administration on charges of piracy in 1843, never forgave Houston for the damage they believed had been done to their reputations, and were still defending themselves in blistering attacks against him many years later. For his part, Houston also felt obliged to speak out to protect his "good name," which invariably led to a new round of charges and countercharges. Some of his longest and most impassioned speeches in the United States Senate had nothing to do with national policy or Texas affairs, but were devoted instead to answering allegations that his enemies had been making against him for more than twenty years. His last major address to that body in 1859 was one of several speeches he delivered in response to charges that he was guilty of cowardice and vacillation during the Texas Revolution.

Houston's antagonists may have had personal or self-serving motives for repudiating his leadership, but their implacable opposition was also rooted in a firm antipathy to the man himself. A complete list of the failings ascribed to him by his critics would be too numerous to mention here. Some were little more than scurrilous fabrications—that he deliberately planned the deaths of Travis and Fannin because he saw them as rivals to his command of the Texas army, for example— and do not merit our serious attention. Houston's critics were on much firmer ground, however, when they confined their attacks to questions of character. The hero of San Jacinto, they alleged, was inordinately vain, fond of praise, and eager to take credit for the accomplishments of others. They decried Houston's legendary dissipation, which on occasion rendered him incapable of performing the duties of his office. Above all, they abhorred the utter want of candor, the predilection for artifice and intrigue, that were the hallmarks of Houston's statecraft and which, they maintained, revealed a blatant disregard for the sovereign will of the people.

All of these allegations have been duly noted by students of Houston's career, but they have done little to tarnish his reputation; indeed, such character traits have added luster and color to a persona that has often been described—to use a tired and shopworn cliché—as "larger than life." Still, the fact remains that to many who knew him, Houston was not larger than life, nor was he heroic in stature, and to arrive at a full understanding of the man some effort to account for this discrepancy must be made. The answer lies, I think, not in the kind of man he was, but in the significance we attach to his failings. Whereas later generations have taken, on the whole, a rather charitable view of Houston's foibles, to his contemporary critics such defects of personality were nothing less than unpardonable sins that utterly disqualified him from high office.

If this verdict seems unreasonably harsh to us, it may well be because Houston's enemies judged him by standards with which our own generation is largely unfamiliar. Cultural values are never static, and any attempt to impose the attitudes of one era upon another inevitably leads to fundamental misunderstanding. The need for caution is particularly advisable when dealing with the Jacksonian era, a transitional period in our history which sought to distance itself, with varying degrees of success, from the epoch that preceded it. Any examination of Houston's controversial career must not lose sight of this volatile and uncertain cultural context.

By the early decades of the nineteenth century, Americans had largely rejected the hierarchical, deferential social order of the Revolutionary era in favor of a stridently democratic, egalitarian one. Inevitably, this break with the past was not as easily accomplished as Americans were wont to believe, for it required each citizen to redefine his or her own place within a broad matrix of social relationships. Unfettered by rank, privilege or social pedigree, Americans could now rise or fall according to their innate abilities—or so they believed. But such freedom, as Alexis de Tocqueville noted, was an intimidating prospect for many Americans. Even as they wholeheartedly embraced a brave new competitive world, they also sought refuge from it in a myriad number of voluntary associations, from mass-based political parties to evangelical Christianity to volunteer militia regiments to fraternal brotherhoods. While the opportunities for such institutional networks were necessarily circumscribed by frontier conditions, Texans sought, much as they had done in the United States, to reconcile their new-found freedom as self-directed individuals with their traditional role as members of a larger community.

Houston, it is clear, adapted much more readily to the new ethos of individualism than did many of his counterparts. In both his public and private life, Houston stood alone, shunning the voluntary associations that his generation considered to be the very sinews of a civilized society. His sojourns among the Cherokee Indians are only the most striking examples of Houston's desire to distance himself from the fellowship of his own community. During the course of a long career of public service he formed remarkably few friendships. He does not appear to have been a particularly active Freemason, and only late in life did he seek church membership.

Even his political allegiances were tenuous in nature. Despite his claim to be a "Democrat of the Old School," Houston did not worship at the "shrine of party" as did most stalwart Jacksonians. Although Houston made much of his connections with Andrew Jackson, he proved to be a somewhat fractious protege, and their relationship was not one which he felt required his total candor or cooperation. Houston's decision to run for a second term as Tennessee governor in 1829 against the popular Jackson intimate William Carroll was hardly conducive to party harmony, and indeed caused a rupture in the Tennessee Democracy, at least until the scandal following his estrangement from Eliza Allen cut short his reelection bid. When Texas gained admittance to the Union in 1846, President Polk was unsure if Houston would take his place in the Senate as a Democrat or a Whig. He chose the former, but once seated, Houston showed little inclination to tow the party line if it did not suit him. As the two-party system began to crumble under the weight of the sectional crisis in the 1850s, he was quick to cast about for political support elsewhere, embracing briefly the agendas of two short-lived third parties, and ultimately entertaining the fanciful, if not bizarre notion that he could offer himself in the 1860 presidential campaign as a "People's Candidate," an idea which showed, if nothing else, a fundamental ignorance of the deep-seated attachments which many Americans still felt for the party of their choice.

It was the absence of these ties that enabled Houston to develop the attributes for which he has become celebrated: his pragmatism, his independence, his stubborn determination to follow the dictates of his own conscience. But such qualities were not held in the highest regard in a political culture that placed a premium on institutional and parochial loyalties. Like their revolutionary forebears, Jacksonian Americans tended to view the common good as immutable and absolute. It followed, then, that those who aspired to represent the public interest be men of fixed and unyielding principles. As president of the Republic, however, Houston frequently pursued a wayward course, sending out mixed signals that confounded his friends and enemies alike. During his second term, he pushed for annexation to the United States, even as he sought British aid to ensure that Texas would remain an independent, sovereign state, prompting historians to wonder whether Houston was indecisive, pursuing a master strategy known only to himself, or just keeping his options open. Houston's contemporary critics, on the other hand, viewed his inconsistency in an altogether different light. They condemned his erratic behavior, but not, as one might expect, because it was evidence of a lack of resolve. Rather, in their minds Houston was governed by expediency, which suggested a sinister willingness to subordinate the common good to his own selfish purposes.

Of all the indictments against him, perhaps the most serious was Houston's overweening egotism, a far more damning character flaw in the mid-nineteenth century than it is today. But if Houston's enemies were men of driving ambition, engaged in a relentless pursuit of their own self-interest, why then were they so quick to condemn him for exhibiting similar characteristics? Once again, the answer lies in the fact that Jacksonian Americans were engaged in a process of cultural reorientation, one which pitted conventional values emphasizing public duty against a more permissive, modern set of attitudes that condoned self-aggrandizement. The era has often been described—correctly—as one in which the "anxious pursuit of gain" was universal and all-consuming. To be sure, Americans were engaged in a frenzied pursuit of wealth and distinction, but they nonetheless remained attached to a Jeffersonian political tradition that had imbued the values of republican virtue and social obligation with a sanctity that could not be ignored.

Many remained uncomfortable with the new professionalism which had become a part of American political life. For this reason, aspirants to high office often assumed a pose of passive indifference, allowing their friends and supporters to advance their candidacies on their behalf. No doubt most politicians hungered for the status, power, and honor that were the rewards of high office, but any display of naked ambition was certain to offend republican sensibilities. Similarly, some officeholders felt obliged to step aside and retire—at least temporarily—from public life, thereby offering irrefutable evidence of their lack of ambition. At various points in their careers, Thomas Jefferson Rusk, David G. Burnet, Mirabeau Lamar, Anson Jones, and James Pinckney Henderson either declined to run for office or refused the opportunity to serve second terms.

Houston, on the other hand, was not one to set aside his love of the spotlight for the sake of appearances. The perennial candidate, he pursued high office with an enthusiasm and energy that his detractors found indecorous, to say the least. Try as he might, Houston could not convincingly portray himself as an American

Cincinnatus, who humbly served when called upon, all the while longing to return to simple, agrarian pursuits. One suspects that even his wife Margaret must have come to realize at some point that his repeated promises to retire from public life were less than sincere.

Houston's enemies castigated him not only for the way he sought power but for the way he wielded it. To his critics he seemed more demagogue than democrat; seeking always to manipulate public opinion, but rarely guided by it. Insisting instead on complete control of the decision-making process, Houston made little effort to establish a public consensus for his policy objectives, and as a result some of the most notable achievements of his career failed to receive the widespread approbation one might have expected. Much of the abuse heaped upon him in the wake of the battle at San Jacinto might well have been avoided had he established a dialogue with his subordinate officers. Instead, he held but one council of war, shortly before the battle began. It is, of course, highly unlikely that Houston could have silenced all his critics, given the querulous nature of the citizen-soldier armies of Texas during this period and the resentment many officers felt when he garnered the lion's share of credit for the victory. Nonetheless, the bitter debate over Houston's role in the campaign was fueled by his refusal to divulge his plans to either the provisional government or the officers under his command. "I held no councils of war," Houston wrote in his famous letter to Thomas Jefferson Rusk, "if I err, the blame is mine alone." This statement has often been cited as an example of Houston's stern resolve, but it is also indicative of a brand of leadership that was high-handed and imperious. Said Jess Billingley: "Houston is the basest of all men, as he has, by willfully lying, attempted to rob that little band of men of their well-earned honors on the battlefield of San Jacinto. He has assumed to himself credit that was due others."

Houston's personal conduct also belied his Jacksonian credentials. At a time when even the most aristocratic Whigs found it politically advantageous to promote themselves as models of republican simplicity, Houston cultivated the image of the eccentric showman, flouting conventional forms of behavior. Houston's compulsive desire for attention manifested itself most notably in his manner of dress. While Houston's fondness for flowing capes, garish waistcoats, and enormous rings has often been seen by later generations as evidence of his irrepressible personality, during his own lifetime it was the subject of a great deal of unfavorable comment. His lavish Indian costumes not only earned him a rebuke from John C. Calhoun when he appeared in Washington in 1818, but were ridiculed at the council meetings of the Cherokees themselves. Eccentric behavior could be tolerated in public figures, of course, but only if it reinforced and exemplified acceptable normative values. Houston's antics, however, drew attention to the man, not to the virtues of a larger constituency. His appearance at Mirabeau Lamar's inauguration in a powdered wig and, equally incongruously, as a buckskin-clad frontiersman at the swearing-in ceremony of his second presidential term, were viewed as evidence of Houston's monumental vanity, and thus his desire to set himself apart from, and above, other men.

Nor can the severe criticism heaped upon Houston for his dissipation be lightly dismissed as the feigned outrage of political rivals. To be sure, heavy drinking was endemic in Jacksonian America, and politicians were expected to imbibe freely with the voters as a sign of their "common touch," and to treat their constituents at campaign rallies. Nonetheless, elected officials, then as now, were frequently held to a higher code of behavior than the general public. Leadership carried with it certain responsibilities; and public figures were expected to adhere to standards of probity and decorum as guardians of the people's trust. While Houston was not the only Texas public servant who found such standards too demanding, there is no reason to think that the indignation his opponents expressed at such conduct was mere hypocritical cant. Among the most outspoken critics of Houston's habitual drunkenness were David G. Burnet and *Telegraph and Texas Register* publisher Francis Moore, both of whom were well-known advocates of the fast-growing temperance movement in Texas. That Houston had the temerity to address temperance groups on the evils of alcoholism long before he had made a serious effort to curb his own drinking habits only added to his opponents' ire.

In short, Houston was viewed as an illegitimate leader by some because he lacked the requisite qualities of leadership in a democratic age. Houston's enemies could not deny that he possessed enormous personal charisma, which accounted in large measure for his extraordinary political success. But popular appeal alone did not qualify him to serve as an agent of the people. Like Ralph Waldo Emerson, his critics subscribed to the ideal of the "representative man:" the mantle of leadership could only be worn by one who personified the values of society at large.

The hero of San Jacinto lacked this spirit, his antagonists maintained. Frustrated by his popularity, they never gave up hope that the people would ultimately come to share their opinion of him. In 1854 Mirabeau Lamar wrote wistfully: "His name is now in the transition state; and will, as the light of truth dawns with increasing force upon it, pass from the . . . famous to the notoriously infamous, where it will rest, covered by the dust of oblivion."

Lamar proved to be a poor prophet, for history has been more than kind to the hero of San Jacinto. With few exceptions, students of Houston's career have been inclined to applaud his unwavering faith in his own judgment, his steadfast determination to swim against the tide of public opinion. But this verdict ignores the fact that Houston's independence of thought and action, though undeniably virtues by our own standards, seemed to many of his contemporaries inimical to the precepts of good republican government. Houston's antagonists cannot, therefore, be simply dismissed as reckless firebrands or crankish malcontents. Their furious opposition reminds us that our own admiration for Houston is framed by a modern cultural perspective, one that allows us to be more tolerant of Houston's self-indulgent excesses, his disdain for convention, his talent for self-promotion and relentless pursuit of his own celebrity, than were many members of his own generation.

# ❖ *F U R T H E R     R E A D I N G*

Randolph B. Campbell, *Sam Houston and the American Southwest* (1993)
Jesús F. De la Teja, "Discovering the Tejano Community in 'Early' Texas," *Journal of the Early Republic* 18 (1998)
Llerena Friend, *Sam Houston, The Great Designer* (1954)
Herbert P. Gambrell, *Mirabeau Buonparte Lamar, Troubador and Crusader* (1934)

————, *Anson Jones* (1948)

Sam W. Haynes, *Soldiers of Misfortune: The Somervell and Mier Expeditions* (1990)

Margaret Swett Henson, *Samuel May Williams; Early Texas Entrepreneur* (1976)

Jim Dan Hill, *The Texas Navy* (1937)

John S. Jenkins and Kenneth Keselus, *Edward Burleson: Texas Frontier Leader* (1990)

Andreas Reichstein, *Rise of the Lone Star: The Making of Texas* (1989)

Andreas Resendez, "National Identity in a Shifting Border: Texas and New Mexico in the Age of Transition, 1821–1848," *Journal of American History* 86 (1999)

Stanley Siegel, *The Political History of the Texas Republic, 1836–1845* (1956)

Walter Struve, *Germans and Texans: Commerce, Migration, and Culture in the Days of the Lone Star Republic* (1996)

Elgin Williams, *The Animating Pursuits of Speculation; Land Traffic in the Annexation of Texas* (1949)

John Hoyt Williams, *Sam Houston: A Biography of the Father of Texas* (1993)

# Texas Joins the Union: Changing Roles for Tejanos and Women in the New State, 1845–1860

By 1845, the inability of the Lone Star republic to stand alone as an independent nation-state had become apparent even to the most prominent spokesmen for Texas nationalism. Rumors that Texans might turn for aid to Great Britain had become the subject of great concern in the United States. These reports were particularly alarming to Southern slaveholders, who had always coveted Texas and feared the interference of British abolitionists in the area. Although Northern antislavery forces remained staunchly opposed to annexation, in the spring of 1845 Congress passed by a slim margin a joint resolution offering to admit Texas into the Union as the twenty-eighth state. In July, Texans voted overwhelmingly to accept the annexation offer. Mexico, however, still unreconciled to the loss of Texas, warned the United States that annexation would lead to war. Relations between the two countries continued to deteriorate over the Texas question until the spring of 1846, when a clash between U.S. and Mexican troops along the Rio Grande prompted Washington to declare war against Mexico.

 Texans who had voted for annexation in the hope that statehood would improve the region's economic climate were not disappointed. Access to American capital, as well as a steady flow of immigrants from the United States and Central Europe following the U.S.-Mexican War ushered in an era of burgeoning prosperity unknown during the Republic period. But the state's integration into the economy of the United States was not immediate, nor did it benefit all citizens. For many men and women, life in Texas remained one of considerable hardship and privation. How did these challenges vary, according to one's socioeconomic status and ethnicity? What impact did frontier conditions have on gender roles?

 In the south, Tejanos found themselves in an even more precarious position after the war with Mexico. Denied access to U.S. capital investment and unfamiliar *with the American legal system, Tejano ranchers were often unable to compete with the large-scale business practices implemented by their Anglo counterparts. How did the Tejano community adapt to the rapidly changing power structure in South Texas? What methods did Tejano elites employ to retain their ebbing social and economic status?*

 D O C U M E N T S

By the mid-1840s, the annexation of Texas had become nothing less than a holy grail for Americans who envisioned their nation as a continental empire. Although some writers of the period waxed poetic about the United States' "mission" to expand westward, the phenomenon known as Manifest Destiny had little to do with lofty idealism. In Document 1, Texas politician and adventurer Thomas Jefferson Green calls upon the United States not only to annex Texas, but to push its boundaries to the Pacific Ocean and as far south as the Sierra Madres. Green's utter disregard for Mexican sovereignty, deep-seated feelings of Anglo-Saxon racial superiority, and unabashed sense of entitlement toward the region's economic resources were shared by many Americans, and helped set the stage for conflict between the United States and Mexico. Document 2 is the Brown resolution, passed by the U.S. Congress by a narrow margin in 1845, offering to admit Texas as the twenty-eighth state. Despite the provision to adjust "all questions of boundary that may arise with other Governments," the resolution promptly sparked a boundary dispute with Mexico, providing a pretext for the U.S. declaration of war in 1846.

In the next three documents, the rise of an agricultural capitalist economy and its attendant problems for Tejanos are examined. Document 3 chronicles the rise of the mercantile and cattle empire in South Texas founded by entrepreneurs Richard King and Mifflin Kenedy. In Document 4, Frederick Law Olmsted describes the racial strife that characterized Anglo-Mexican relations in Texas after annexation. The social and economic tensions that Texans experienced during this new era in its history sometimes flared into violence. In 1859, a dispute between a ranchero, Juan Nepomuceno Cortina, and the marshal of Brownsville erupted into a series of skirmishes between the Mexican community on both sides of the Rio Grande and the Texas Rangers. In Document 5, two proclamations issued by Cortina state his reason for leading a revolt against Anglo Texas authority.

In the last two documents, two women give accounts of the sickness, hardships, and absence of creature comforts that were part of daily life for women who immigrated to Texas. In Document 6, Lucadia Pease, a Connecticut native who moved to Brazoria in 1850, writes to her sister after a severe bout of influenza. Her husband, Elisha Marshall Pease, would serve as governor from 1853 to 1857. In Document 7, Ottilie Fuchs Goeth recalls her childhood as a German immigrant in Central Texas.

## 1. Thomas Jefferson Green Dreams of Empire, 1845

All history teaches that the general course of conquest has been from north to south. It was so in the days of Tamerlane, of the Goths and Vandals, and, from the best evidence upon the subject, it has been so already with Mexico herself. Physiology also instructs us, as a general law, that animals are more daring and ferocious in high

Thomas Jefferson Green, *Journal of the Texian Expedition Against Mier,* Sam W. Haynes, ed. (repr., Austin: W. Thomas Taylor, 1993), 185–186, 194–195, 198–200.

than in low latitudes; that as the cold climate makes it the more difficult of subsistence, it nerves the system to an energy commensurate to the want; that while the perpetual produce of the warm climate renders such energy unnecessary, it enervates the system and debases the mind. Nothing can be more true, and a knowledge of the people of the United States and Mexico is strikingly illustrative of the fact. . . .

Two nations so contiguous, so opposite in their policy, and every way so unlike each other, can never live in friendship with a border which invites both to its advantages. The Rio Grande, from its head to its source, from the forty-second to the twenty-fifth degree of north latitude, is capable of maintaining many millions of population, with a variety of product which no river upon the north continent can boast. This river, once settled with the enterprise and intelligence of the English race, will yearly send forth an agricultural export which it will require hundreds of steamers to transport to its delta, while its hides, wool, and metals may be increased to an estimate which would now appear chimerical.

If annexation of Texas to the United States of the North succeeds, this boundary can exist but for a short period; and though there seems to me to be a destiny in the womb of time which marks her southern boundary at the extremity of the north continent, where the two great oceans of the world will unite under a genial sun and a smooth navigation, yet her more *immediate* southern boundary must extend to the *Sierra Madre,* that great Chinese wall which separates the people of the Rio Grande from those of the more southern tablelands. Can this be considered a greedy desire upon the part of the mighty northern nation, when her facilities of communication with those people from her capital in twelve days are superior to their present means of communication with the capital of Mexico in thirty? We say not. This age has merged distance in time, and the people of the Rio Grande at present are as near neighbours to the capital of the United States as Boston was to Philadelphia at the promulgation of President Washington's inaugural message to the first Congress. . . .

The most desirable portion of this continent lies between the 28th and 42d degrees of north latitude upon the Pacific. It presents more than a thousand miles of seacoast, with the important ports of Guaymas, San Diego, San Gabriel, Monterey, San Francisco, and many others, with a soil and climate of unsurpassed capability for grazing and agriculture, and a mineral wealth supposed to be equal, if not superior, to any in the world. This vast country of more than one million of square miles, lying due west of the settled portion of the United States, between the frozen regions of the north and the vertical sun of the south, between the gentle influences of the Pacific Ocean and the great backbone of the continent, capable of giving wealth and happiness to a hundred millions of souls, is now in possession of roaming tribes of unhoused Indians, and a few settlements of less than two hundred thousand Mexican subjects.

If Oregon is important to the United States, this country is a thousand times more so. The extreme northern lines of the states of Pennsylvania, Connecticut, and Rhode Island only reach to the 42d degree of north latitude: that latitude cuts in two the states of Massachusetts and New-York, and Lake Erie and Michigan, while the 28th degree is north of the United States settlements in Florida, and nearly three degrees north of Texas, at the mouth of the Rio Grande. While it is due to the United States that she should not permit this important country to fall into

European hands, it is equally due to her that she should possess it by any and every means necessary thereto.

Let the United States apply, if necessary, the usufruct doctrine of her possession of this country, which Old England and Old Spain practised towards the aborigines upon the discovery of this continent—a doctrine of common sense and sound reason—of human necessity and justice. If the Author of the universe intended the earth for the support of the few, to the exclusion of the greater number, the reverse of this doctrine is true, and then it is right and proper that a very few should hold this country, of which they can make no adequate use, to the exclusion of many millions in other portions of the earth, who may be dying for the want of space to live in. When Spain claimed title and possession to this vast tract of country under this doctrine, that the aborigines had no title in the soil, but only a temporary right to the use and occupancy thereof, such only as the buffalo enjoys, she was justified in such possession only by applying it to a better use. Three hundred years have passed, and neither herself nor those claiming under her have applied it to that better use, and she holds it without such ability so to apply it, to the exclusion of others who have, and whose necessities require it. England, France, or any other nation, whose population is greater than her means of subsistence, has a right, derived directly from the Maker of the earth, to occupy it with her redundant people; and it alone is a question of policy or power whether its present claimants or nearest neighbour will permit it. This era, so marked in the improvements of agriculture, machinery, and navigation—in the knowledge of geography, and the increased necessity of the case, will not allow a perversion of the use of this country. For many wise reasons, the United States should extend her settlements over it; but should she, by a different policy, fail to do so, the all-seeing eye of Great Britain will not let slip such a golden opportunity in possessing herself of this desirable middle ground between home and her vast Eastern possessions. Besides, if the Oregon settlement is important to the United States, without a harbour sufficient for the entrance of her smallest vessels of war, the port of San Francisco, or some other port in the south, is absolutely necessary for her.

It may, however, well be questioned whether either Spain or the present government of Mexico has ever had any other than a nominal possession of this vast region; for only here and there, in a very few isolated spots, has she had a few people in real possession, and those few shut in by fortifications as protection against the aboriginal occupants. If, therefore, she has no power of absolutely possessing herself of this country, her declaration of ownership to it was arbitrary, and the act not justified by her means; and with the same propriety she might have claimed, to illimitable extent, that which she neither had the use of nor power of using, depriving millions of the earth's population of support and the proper uses thereof.

While I hold that it is both just and proper that any nation with an overgrown population may settle these vast wastes with her redundant people, I repeat again that it would be short-sighted policy in the United States to permit it. That nation, with her twenty millions of people, in the ordinary course of events, in fifty years, will have eighty to provide for, and a large country will be necessary for so many within the lifetime of numbers now busy in the politics of that country. With such an acquisition, the United States would not be larger than Brazil with her six millions of people, and about one third of the size of the present British dominions. With such an acquisition, the United States would contain but a fraction over three millions of square miles, and without Texas that would be cut nearly in twain by a narrow slip extending to the 42d degree of north latitude, which is the parallel of Boston. If it be wise policy, and the United States extends her dominions to the 28th degree upon the Pacific, then Texas becomes absolutely necessary to her. Then the *Texas wedge,* making into the centre of her square and compact surface, will appear obviously wrong. It would be a severance of her entirety, which few would be willing to reconcile; and without a union of the two countries, a conflict of interest would inevitably grow up between the separate nations, detrimental certainly to one, and probably to both. This conflict would beget countervailing laws, such as are at present in the bud, and would produce estrangement to the advantage of European powers, which would profit by the quarrel.

## 2. The United States Annexes Texas, March 1845

"Resolved by the Senate and House of Representatives of the United States of America in Congress assembled, That Congress doth consent that the territory properly included within and rightly belonging to the Republic of Texas may be erected into a new State, to be called the State of Texas, with a Republican form of Government, to be adopted by the people of said Republic, by deputies in Convention assembled, with the consent of the existing Government, in order that the same may be admitted as one of the States of this Union.

"2. And be it further Resolved, That the foregoing consent of Congress is given upon the following conditions, and with the following guarantees, to wit:

"First. Said State to be formed subject to the adjustment by this Government of all questions of boundary that may arise with other Governments, and the Constitution thereof, with the proper evidence of its adoption, by the people of said Republic of Texas, shall be transmitted to the President of the United States, to be laid before Congress for its final action, on or before the first day of January, one thousand eight hundred and forty six.

"Second. Said State when admitted into the Union, after ceding to the United States all public edifices, fortifications, barracks, ports and harbors, navy and navy-yards, docks, magazines, arms, armaments and all other property and means pertaining to the public defence belonging to the said Republic of Texas; shall retain all the public funds, debts, taxes, and dues of every kind which may belong to or be due and owing said Republic; and shall also retain all the vacant and unappropriated lands lying within its limits, to be applied to the payment of debts and liabilities of said Republic of Texas, and the residue of said debts and liabilities, to be disposed of as said State may direct; but in no event are said debts and liabilities to become a charge upon the Government of the United States.

"Third, New States of convenient size, not exceeding four in number, in addition to said State of Texas, and having a sufficient population, may hereafter, by the consent of said State, be formed, out of the territory thereof, which shall be entitled to admission under the provisions of the Federal Constitution. And such States as

H. P. N. Gammel, ed., *Laws of Texas* (Austin: Gammel Book Co., 1898), 2:1303–1304.

may be formed out of that portion of said territory lying south of thirty six degrees thirty minutes north latitude, commonly known as the Missouri compromise line, shall be admitted into the Union, with or without slavery, as the people of each State asking admission may desire. And in such State or States as shall be formed out of said territory north of said Missouri compromise line, slavery or involuntary servitude (except for crime) shall be prohibited."

### 3. Entrepreneurs Richard King and Mifflin Kenedy Build a Mercantile and Cattle Empire, 1850

Mifflin Kenedy came to the lower Río Grande in 1846. He was then the commander of the *Corvette,* a steamboat belonging to the United States Quartermaster Department. She was plying between the mouth of the Río Grande and Camargo and Mier. Captain Kenedy had brought her from Pittsburgh, where she had been built. It is needless to say that he did his duty well and that he acquired the confidence and the esteem of all with whom he had transactions.

In the year 1847 Captain Richard King arrived on the Río Grande. He was employed as pilot on the *Corvette.* In this manner the names of these two gentlemen became associated. They remained associated until the close of the war between Mexico and the United States. They had won honor and the confidence of men who controlled affairs. They had won the confidence of the public.

In the year 1850 a company was formed. It was known as M. Kenedy & Co. and consisted of M. Kenedy, Richard King, Charles Stillman, and James O'Donnell. In 1852 Captain Kenedy purchased O'Donnell's interest. This firm continued in existence for about fifteen years. It was the main reliance for navigation from the port of Brazos Santiago to Roma, the center of navigation on the Río Grande in those days.

In 1850 the company had two boats on the Rio Grande—the *Comanche* and the *Grampus.* Captain King and Captain Kenedy each commanded a boat. Whatever could be effected by prudence, foresight, and good management was done. Annually, millions of dollars worth of merchandise entered the customhouse of Brazos Santiago on Point Isabel. The merchandise was transported to Brownsville, Matamoros, Río Grande City, and other points along the river. A large proportion of it was carried into the northeastern States of Mexico. The carrying trade of the Río Grande was extremely lucrative, and those engaged in it soon amassed fortunes. Men possessing capacity, energy, and wealth were not likely to remain silent spectators of events they might control. M. Kenedy & Co. soon became an important factor in the affairs of the lower Río Grande. The firm possessed the requirements calculated to produce good results. It encouraged every enterprise calculated to promote the development of the natural resources of the country.

It must be remembered that in 1850 there was only a single family living on the road made by General Taylor from Corpus Christi to Brownsville—a distance of about one hundred and sixty-five miles. The country was infested with companies of Mexicans who frequently united the business of corralling wild mustangs and murdering and robbing travellers. The Comanches made descents into this district

---

John Salmon Ford, Stephen B. Oates, eds., *Rip Ford's Texas* (Austin: University of Texas, 1963), 457–463. By permission of the University of Texas Press.

ostensibly to capture horses to ride and to eat, but really to kill the men and to make mistresses and slaves of women and children. In 1850 troops were stationed at various points to give protection to the settlers in the valleys of the Río Grande and the Nueces and to those engaged in mercantile pursuits. The writer has spoken of this matter elsewhere.

Life on the border of Texas was wild, rough, and dangerous. There were few points on the border where a family could locate without incurring dangers from which the boldest would recoil. The operations of the troops had inspired a degree of confidence, yet it remained to be seen who would be the first to make the venture to cast his fortunes in a district where life was menaced almost continuously and where property had no security beyond the range of the rifle and the six-shooter. It was Captain Richard King who made the first move in the matter of settling between the Río Grande and the Nueces. He came to the lands of the Santa Gertrudis and became one of the pioneers of that country. . . .

In 1852 Captain Richard King, in company with Captain G.K. Lewis, better known as "Legs" Lewis, established a cattle ranch on the Santa Gertrudis Creek. They made their headquarters near where Captain Ford's old camp stood in 1849. This cattle camp became a stopping-place for wayfarers, a sort of city of refuge for all classes, the timorous and the hungry. The men who held it were of no ordinary mould. They had come to stay. It was no easy matter to scare them. The Indians still made descents upon the country. The regular troops were operating against them. In many of the fights the red men appeared to have been victorious. They fought in a manner at variance with that in which the drilled troops of the United States had been taught to fight. The savages had the advantage in numbers and in movement. But all this had no effect on the brave men who held the ranch of Santa Gertrudis. They had determined to make a ranch on the Santa Gertrudis or leave their bones to tell of their failure.

The company at Brownsville pursued the even tenor of its way. M. Kenedy & Co. aided enterprising men, encouraged the industrious, and was open-handed to the unfortunate and the afflicted. Kenedy and partners had extensive relations with Mexico and were always on the side of those who were struggling against the intolerable oppressions set on foot by the agents of a centralized military despotism, whose instincts and practices were prompted by unmitigated tyranny. On many occasions they took an active part in elections. In State and Federal campaigns they made it a rule to support the Democratic party. It was a difficult matter to be successful against them. They were zealously in favor of advancing the interests of the Río Grande region. . . .

In 1852 Captain Kenedy established a cattle ranch at Valenio on the Nueces River. In 1854 he became the owner of another ranch at San Salvador del Tule, which was one of the first ranches in that country. It was destroyed by General Juan N. Cortina in 1859, when he made war upon the people of the United States and wreaked a bloody vengeance upon Americans whom he could not subjugate.

In 1856 Captain King moved his family from Brownsville to the ranch of Santa Gertrudis. It was an undertaking of great danger. The country between his residence and the Río Grande was thinly settled. The intervening country was raided by Indians. The Mexicans had not acknowledged the supremacy of the Americans. They expected to reconquer the country. For an American to carry his family into the wild country and settle fifty miles from Corpus Christi and one hundred and ten or twenty miles from the Río Grande was looked upon in those days as an act of extreme audacity. . . .

The raids of Cortina caused considerable loss to Captain Kenedy. His ranch of Tula was almost ruined. George and Mr. Cornelius Stillman suffered by the robbers. So did numerous others. Captain King promptly furnished all the supplies and all the intelligence needed by the United States and Texas troops. At that time there were some settlements on the road from King's ranch to Brownsville. It was strongly suspected that many Mexicans employed at the ranches were in collusion with Cortina.

After the Cortina War the vessels of M. Kenedy & Co. attained very respectable proportions. They transported vast quantities of merchandise from Brazos de Santiago to Brownsville and Matamoros and to all the places from the mouth of the Río Grande to Camargo on the San Juan River as well as to Roma on the Río Grande. For a long while Captain Kenedy and Captain King commanded steamboats themselves. Each boat had a full complement of officers and men. All the business of each boat was transacted on board. In process of time the number of boats in their service precluded this manner of transacting business; then it was done to a great extent in Brownsville.

In 1860 Captain Kenedy purchased an equal interest with Captain King in the ranch of Santa Gertrudis. Captain Walworth had an interest of 160 acres which the other partners bought and thus became full owners of the ranch. The firm name was Richard King & Co. The hospitalities extended to travellers and sightseers were undiminished. As genuine a welcome was extended to them as in the days gone by. The ranch on the broad bosom of the prairie maintained its celebrity as the resting place of the weary and as an asylum for the needy and distressed. It had won fairly the confidence and the esteem of the public, and has retained the respect of all classes up to date.

## 4. Frederick Law Olmsted Describes Tejano and Anglo Conflicts in the New State, 1859

The Mexicans were treated for a while after annexation like a conquered people. Ignorant of their rights, and of the new language, they allowed themselves to be imposed upon by the new comers, who seized their lands and property without shadow of claim, and drove hundreds of them homeless across the Rio Grande. They now, as they get gradually better informed, come straggling back, and often their claims give rise to litigation, usually settled by a compromise.

A friend told us, that, wishing, when he built, to square a corner of his lot, after making diligent inquiry he was unable to hear of any owner for the adjoining piece. He took the responsibility, and moved his fence over it. Not long after, he was waited upon by a Mexican woman, in a towering passion. He carried her to a Spanish acquaintance, and explained the transaction. She was immediately appeased, told him he was welcome to the land, and has since been on the most neighborly terms, calling him always her "amigo."

Frederick Law Olmsted, *Journey Through Texas, Or a Saddle-Trip on the Southwestern Frontier* (New York: Dix, Edwards, 1857), 163–165.

Most adult Mexicans are voters by the organic law; but few take measures to make use of the right. Should they do so, they might probably, in San Antonio, have elected a government of their own. Such a step would be followed, however, by a summary revolution. They are regarded by slaveholders with great contempt and suspicion, for their intimacy with slaves, and their competition with plantation labor.

Americans, in speaking of them, constantly distinguish themselves as "white folks." I once heard a new comer informing another American, that he had seen a Mexican with a revolver. "I shouldn't think they ought to be allowed to carry fire-arms. It might be dangerous." "It would be difficult to prevent it," the other replied; "Oh, they think themselves just as good as white men."

From several counties they have been driven out altogether. At Austin, in the spring of 1853, a meeting was held, at which the citizens resolved, on the plea that Mexicans were *horse-thieves,* that they must quit the county. About twenty families were thus driven from their homes, and dispersed over the western counties. Deprived of their means of livelihood, and rendered furious by such wholesale injustice, it is no wonder if they should take to the very crimes with which they are charged.

A similar occurrence took place at Seguin, in 1854; and in 1855, a few families, who had returned to Austin, were again driven out.

Even at San Antonio, there had been talk of such a razzia. A Mexican, caught in an attempt to steal a horse, had been hung by a Lynching party, on the spot, for an example. His friends happened to be numerous, and were much excited, threatening violence in return. Under pretext of subduing an intended riot, the sheriff issued a call for an armed posse of 500 men, with the idea of dispersing and driving from the neighborhood a large part of the Mexican population. But the Germans, who include among them the great majority of young men suitable for such duty, did not volunteer as had been expected, and the scheme was abandoned. They were of the opinion, one of them said to me, that this was not the right and republican way. If the laws were justly and energetically administered, no other remedy would be needed. One of them, who lived on the Medina, in the vicinity of the place of the occurrence, told us he had no complaint to make of the Mexicans; they never stole his property, or troubled him in any way.

## 5. Ranchero Juan Nepomuceno Cortina States His Reasons for Revolt Against Texas, 1859

30 September 1859

An event of grave importance, in which it has fallen to my lot to figure as the principal actor since the morning of the 28th instant, doubtless keeps you in suspense with regard to the progress of its consequences. There is no need of fear. Orderly people and honest citizens are inviolable to us in their persons and interests. Our object as you have seen, has been to chastise the villainy of our enemies, which heretofore has gone unpunished. These have connived with each other, and form, so to speak, a perfidious inquisitorial lodge to persecute and rob us, without any cause, and for no

Jerry D. Thompson, ed., *Juan Cortina and the Texas-Mexico Frontier, 1859–1877* (El Paso: Texas Western Press, 1994), 14–18, 27–28.

other crime on our part than that of being of Mexican origin; considering us, doubtless, destitute of those gifts which they themselves do not possess.

To defend ourselves, and making use of the sacred right of self-preservation, we have assembled in a popular meeting with a view of discussing a means by which to put an end to our misfortunes.

Our identity of origin, our relationship, and the community of our sufferings, has been, as it appears, the cause of our embracing, directly, the proposed object which led us to enter your beautiful city, clothed with the imposing aspect of our exasperation.

The assembly organized, and headed by your humble servant, (thanks to the confidence which he inspired as one of the most aggrieved), we have careered over the streets of the city in search of our adversaries, inasmuch as justice, being administered by their own hands, the supremacy of the law has failed to accomplish its object.

Some of them, rashly remiss in complying with our demand, have perished for having sought to carry their animosity beyond the time limits allowed by their precarious position. Three of them have died—all criminal, wicked men, notorious among the people for their misdeeds. The others, still more unworthy and wretched, dragged themselves through the mire to escape our anger, and now, perhaps, with their usual bravado, pretend to be the cause of an infinity of evils, which might have been avoided but for their cowardice. They concealed themselves, and we were loth to attack them within the dwellings of others, fearing that their cause might be confounded with that of respectable persons, as at last, to our sorrow, did happen. On the other hand, it behooves us to maintain that it was unjust to give the affair such a terrible aspect, and to represent it as of a character foreboding evil; some having carried their blindness so far as to implore the aid of Mexico, alleging as a reason that their persons and property were exposed to vandalism. Were any outrages committed by us during the time we had possession of the city, when we had it in our power to become the arbiters of its fate? Will our enemies be so blind, base, or unthinking, as to deny the evidence of facts? Will there be one to say that he was molested, or that his house was robbed or burned down? . . .

These, as we have said, form, with a multitude of lawyers, a secret conclave, with all its ramifications, for the sole purpose of despoiling the Mexicans of their lands and usurp[ing] them afterwards. This is clearly proven by the conduct of one Adolph Glavecke, who, invested with the character of deputy sheriff, and in collusion with the said lawyers, has spread terror among the unwary, making them believe that he will hang the Mexicans and burn their ranchos, etc., that by this means he might compel them to abandon the country, and thus accomplish their object. . . .

All truce between them and us is at an end, from the fact alone of our holding upon this soil our interests and property. And how can it be otherwise, when the ills that weigh upon the unfortunate republic of Mexico have obliged us for many heart-touching causes to abandon it and our possessions in it, or else become the victims of our principles or of the indigence to which its intestine disturbances had reduced us since the treaty of Guadalupe? When, ever diligent and industrious, and desirous of enjoying the longed for boon of liberty within the classic country of its origin, we were induced to naturalize ourselves in it and form a part of the Confederacy, flattered by the bright and peaceful prospect of living therein and inculcate in the bosoms of our children a feeling of gratitude towards a country beneath whose aegis we would have wrought their felicity and contributed with our conduct to give evidence to the whole world that all the aspirations of the Mexicans are confined to one only—*that of being freemen;* and that, having secured this ourselves, those of the old country, notwithstanding their misfortunes, might have nothing to regret save the loss of a section of territory, but with the sweet satisfaction that their old fellow citizens lived therein, enjoying tranquility, as if Providence had so ordained to set them an example of the advantages to be derived from public peace and quietude; when, in fine, all has been but the baseless fabric of a dream, and our hopes having been defrauded in the most cruel manner in which disappointment can strike, there can be found no other solution to our problem than to make one effort, and at one blow destroy the obstacles to our prosperity.

It is necessary: the hour has arrived. Our oppressors number but six or eight. Hospitality and other noble sentiments shield them at present from our wrath, and such, as you have seen, are inviolable to us.

Innocent persons shall not suffer, no; but, if necessary, we will lead a wandering life, awaiting our opportunity to purge society of men so base that they degrade it with their opprobrium. Our families have returned as strangers to their old country to beg for an asylum. Our lands, if they are to be sacrificed to the avaricious covetousness of our enemies, will be rather so on account of our own vicissitudes. As to land, nature will always grant us sufficient to support our frames, and we accept the consequences that may arise. Further, *our personal enemies shall not possess our lands until they have fattened it (sic) with their own gore.*

We cherish the hope, however, that the government, for the sake of its own dignity, and in obsequiousness to justice, will accede to our demand, by prosecuting those men and bringing them to trial or leave them to become subject to the consequences of our immutable resolve.

It remains for me to say that, separated as we are, by accident alone, from the other citizens of the city, and not having renounced our rights as North American citizens, we disapprove, and energetically protest, against the act of having caused a force of the National Guards from Mexico to cross unto this side to ingraft themselves in a question so foreign to their country that there is no excusing such weakness on the part of those who implored their aid. . . .


[November 23, 1859]

*Mexicans!* My part is taken; the voice of revelation whispers to me that to me is entrusted the work of breaking the chains of your slavery, and that the Lord will enable me with powerful arm to fight against our enemies, in compliance with the requirements of that Sovereign Majesty, who from this day forward, will hold us under His protection. On my part, I am ready to offer myself as a sacrifice for your happiness; and counting upon the means necessary for the discharge of my ministry, you may count upon my cooperation, should no cowardly attempt put an end to my days.

This undertaking will be sustained of the following bases:

FIRST. A society is organized in the State of Texas, which devotes itself sleeplessly, until the work is crowned with success, to the improvement of the unhappy condition of those Mexicans residents therein; exterminating their tyrants, to which end those which compose it are ready to shed their blood and suffer the death of martyrs.

SECOND. As this society contains within itself the elements necessary to accomplish the great end of its labors, the veil of impenetrable secrecy covers "The Great Book" in which the articles of its constitution are written; while so delicate are the difficulties which must be overcome that no honorable man can have cause for alarm if imperious exigencies require them to act without reserve.

THIRD. The Mexicans of Texas repose their lot under the good sentiments of the governor elect of the State, General Houston, and trust that upon his elevation to power he will begin with care to give us legal protection within the limits of his powers.

*Mexicans!* Peace be with you! Good inhabitants of State of Texas, look on them as brothers, and keep in mind that which the Holy Spirit saith: "Thou shalt not be the friend of the passionate man; nor join thyself to the madman, lest thou learn his mode of work and scandalize thy soul."

## 6. Lucadia Pease Recovers from Influenza, 1852

My Dear Sister Augusta,

I have had a long and severe sickness and am now only able to sit up part of the day—I think it is five or six weeks ago, tho' time seems so long to me that it appears like as many months, since I was taken with Influenza, which has been very prevalent here, which settled in my breast, which became very much inflamed and swollen, and at times most excruciatingly painful—The Dr thought it advisable to scatter the tumors and made many applications which caused me great pain in his desire to avoid the necessity of lancing—I had a very high fever for some days, but at length got better except my breast, and as there chanced to arrive, in this remote town, that much desired by us personage a traveling Daguereau Artist, it seemed to me almost like a special providence, for little Carrie's benefit, and we determined to have him try to take her pic—We thought it might be necessary for her to be taken in my arms, and I made the effort, and went to the Court House with her (the Artists room) On my return I went on the bed, which I have scarcely left since, now nearly three weeks—I had so much fever we were compelled to wean little Carrie, who was so much grieved, that she learned to speak at once, most distinctly and piteously ma ma ma ma. Among my other ailments I had the nettle rash, something like the Erysipelas tho not as dangerous, but most exceedingly painful—Marshall is a most excellent nurse, and I know not what I should have done had he not been, as it is not possible here to hire any one to take care of the sick—The baby was kept on the gallery, and away from my room as much as possible. As the weather was very mild they kept her in the open air most of the time, and one night she was taken with all the symptoms of the croup. Her papa gave her all the remedies which we have before tried, but she grew worse so fast, he went in the night for the Doctor, who administered emetics and by morning she was much better—She is not yet

Katherine Hart and Elizabeth Kemp, eds., *Lucadia Pease and the Governor, Letter, 1850–1857* (Austin: Encino Press, 1974), 68–70.

well, has a severe cold, and is very fretful, quite unlike what she has ever been before—Last week Marshall was compelled to go to Galveston to attend Court, having postponed it as long as possible. He will stay only about a week instead of the month which we remained last year—We had made our plans early in winter to go with him, which are now so sadly frustrated. Baby slept with her Aunt Carrie last night, who is now nurse for us both—My breast was finally lanced in three places, and is now I trust getting well, only those who have had a similar one can know how much one suffers—Marshall has writted once since I have been sick, directed to Poquonock where I suppose Maria now is—I was very sorry to hear that Mr Moore's health has failed him, wish he could be induced to stay at Poquonock this year, and leave preaching altogether—We had a short visit from a gent—n from Janesville, who is an invalid, and passing the winter at Galveston for the benefit of his health—he likes the mild weather here much, tho' I think he has the consumption and will not probably be much better—

## 7.  German Pioneer Ottilie Fuchs Goeth Recalls the Hardships of Life in Central Texas, 1859

How tedious and time consuming life was in those earlier days as compared with present. How wonderfully easy things are today when it is possible to buy practically all clothing ready-made, both for grownups and children. How many jackets I had to make for my brothers, as well as for my husband and children. Even a dressmaker could not have had more sewing to do. And as for the kitchen: When one wanted to bake bread, one had first to hand grind corn on a steel mill fitted with two handles. Even then it was more like groats rather than flour. Cooking and baking in an open fireplace was extremely difficult, and one had to watch carefully that baked goods did not burn. Practical as they are now, the first cooking stoves were not completely satisfactory, although they did make things a little easier than before. Food was simple, but wholesome.

We did not have many dishes in our home, and thus there were not many dishes to wash. Our parents had brought along a complete set of pewter dishes from Bremen. It was a terrible job to keep these at least fairly well polished. An American who had dinner at our home related everywhere that at the Pastor Fox house they eat on silver plates. We were very happy when after some years we were able to replace the "silver" plates for porcelain ones. The old pewter plates and dishes were as heavy as lead, and if one did not constantly clean them with soap and lye they turned quite black. We also had an iron stove from Germany which could be used for cooking, but was not usable for baking. This had to be done in the coals in the fireplace. Later the old stove still served as a means of heating.

We had all kinds of meat, such as venison, turkey, lamb, and beef, as well as quantities of fish. There was no lack of milk and butter, so our table was always rather well supplied with food. Guests were always welcome. Flour was more of a problem. It had to be brought from Houston by wagon. This took fourteen days.

Ottilie Fuchs Goeth, *Memoirs of a Texas Pioneer Grandmother* (Austin: Eakin Press, 1982), 61–63.

If we did not wish to sit in the dark at night, we had to make our own candles, having no kerosene or lamps. We prepared a mixture of wax and tallow which was poured into candle moulds. Unfortunately the light was so weak that any reading or fine needlework ruined one's eyes. Probably as a result of the poor light of those days, Father was unable to read anything handwritten when he was old. We did not have any lamps until after the Civil War. After that we even obtained a sewing machine, a very important event!

Not enjoying the luxury of ready-made soap, we had to fabricate our own. Lye balls, which merely have to be dropped into water in order to obtain a solution of lye, were fully unknown. Lye had to be produced in the most cumbersome manner. First one had to build a wooden hopper in which ashes were collected. Then just sufficient boiling water was added to make the lye drip out at the bottom. When it was possible to float an egg on top, fat was added and the mixture was boiled as long as necessary, sometimes taking days until one hit upon the right mixture. Our homemade product turned out very well, for our log cabin was always spick and span.

Fence-building was the most tedious job for the men. Fences were made of split logs, usually set up in zigzag fashion. Wire became available much later. Rock walls were also in use, but building these was even more time-consuming. On the other hand, broken window panes were no problem. This was for obvious reasons, for the log houses had only a few, and these were as carefully guarded as our own eyes.

Wagons were scarce. Everyone rode horseback. Large ox-drawn wagons were used to transport freight as well as passengers, stage coaches in a way, but the postillion unfortunately was less romantic, driving the oxen with his whip, and completely forgetting to sound the post horn. Also women and children were usually seen traveling on horseback. The scene often resembled the movement of a Germanic tribe of ancient times. One woman I saw had made two large pockets, resembling sacks, which she laid across the back of her horse, carrying a child in each one and a third child in her lap as she rode along.

Once to attend a celebration in Cat Spring, Mother, having difficulty in walking, rode on a sled decorated with green branches. The sled was drawn by a large white horse, and it glided smoothly through the tall grass, much as it might have done on the ice in the old country, only there were no accompanying sleigh bells. Instead there was much joking and laughing. In spite of all the hardships, most of the time morale was high, because everyone firmly believed that a better future was in store. This thought made the many hardships easier to endure.

# ❧ E S S A Y S

The first two essays in this chapter examine some of the problems Mexican Americans faced in the years after statehood, as Texas was rapidly transformed from an isolated frontier region into an integral part of the U.S. market economy. The first selection is excerpted from a prize-winning study of Anglo Tejano relations by David Montejano of the University of Texas at Austin. Montejano describes the process by which an Anglo minority managed to establish economic and political control over the tejano majority in the southern part of the state. Although violent clashes between the two ethnic groups periodically occurred, Anglo and Tejano elites often worked together to preserve social order. The emergence of an Anglo-male dominated society in South Texas had a particularly profound impact on the lives of many Mexican women. In the second essay, Jane Dysart, an historian at the University of West Florida, examines the process by which many Tejanas became assimilated into a new American culture through intermarriage. Facing severe economic pressures (which Montejano describes below), some prominent Tejano families viewed the marriage of daughters to Anglo males as a means of maintaining their upper-class status. Such unions, however, did little to prevent the rise of a distinctly Anglo American cultural and economic elite.

In the final essay, Ann Patton Malone, formerly a professor at Illinois State University, studies the Texas frontier from the perspective of Anglo American women. The hardships and primitive conditions of frontier life, she suggests, may have been particularly difficult for women of high social standing, who had been conditioned in the United States to aspire to a Victorian ideal of feminity. Unlike immigrants of central Europe, these well-to-do Anglo American women experienced a "psychic crisis" when confronted with a frontier existence so starkly at odds with the world they had known.

# Anglos Establish Authority over Mexicans in South Texas

## DAVID MONTEJANO

Although the Rio Grande settlements south and west of San Antonio were not directly affected by the Texian struggles for independence, these wars depopulated the coastal areas close to the Nueces River, the boundary between the Mexican states of Texas and Tamaulipas. The livestock industry in this area was completely disrupted as Mexican settlers fled from their *ranchos* to the protected towns of the Rio Grande. As a measure of retribution, the Texas Republic had declared Mexican livestock to be public property, prompting many Texan veterans to conduct stock raids below the Nueces. These "reckless young fellows," according to one old-timer, were the first to be given the name of "cowboys." In short, between 1836 and 1846 the strip between the Nueces and the Rio Grande constituted a veritable "no-man's land," claimed by the Republics of Texas and Mexico but actually controlled by Indian tribes.

Military occupation in 1846 and subsequent annexation replicated, in some respects, the experience above the Nueces after Texas independence. On the one hand, the fate of Mexican property rights was uncertain. Squatters and adventurers were everywhere; tales of fraud and chicanery were common; and deliberations in the Texas Legislature and in Texas courts all suggested an eventual confiscation of Mexican-owned property. The considerable expense of legal proceedings to defend old Spanish and Mexican titles, together with the uncertainty of the outcome, prompted many owners to sell to interested American parties at low prices.

On the other hand, as had happened with the Texas Revolution, there was considerable repatriation after the Mexican War. Mexican refugees moved across the Rio Grande and settled among the old established towns of Paso del Norte, Guerrero, Mier, Camargo, Reynosa, and Matamoros. Other refugees established new towns,

David Montejano, *Anglos and Mexicans in the Making of Texas, 1836–1986* (Austin: University of Texas Press, 1987), 30–40. Copyright © 1987. By permission of the University of Texas Press.

such as Nuevo Monterrey (now Nuevo Laredo) opposite Laredo and Mesilla and Guadalupe, both near El Paso del Norte. Despite these refugee movements, Texas south and west of the Nueces River remained predominantly Mexican in population.

Unlike Texas above the Nueces, where the Mexican population had soon found itself outnumbered, the length of the Rio Grande region remained isolated until the turn of the century. Following the initial Anglo settlement after the Mexican War, there was no continued influx. The only exception was the Civil War period when another layer of ex-soldiers and merchant–camp followers was added to the communities of the Upper and Lower Rio Grande valleys. El Paso served as an important stop for travelers and merchants, but permanent Anglo settlement remained small until the arrival of the railroad in 1881. In South Texas, Laredo and Brownsville were completely away from the westward land movements and no free land existed. As in the case of El Paso, the few Anglo settlers who came were merchants, lawyers, or professionals whose occupation was tied with the northern Mexican trade or the new land business of the border region. . . .

According to the best estimates . . . in 1850 there were 25,000 Mexicans in the state. Approximately 7,000 were concentrated in the region above the Nueces (around San Antonio and Goliad), 5,500 were below the Nueces (Laredo and the lower Rio Grande), 8,500 were in West Texas (El Paso and Presidio), and 4,000 were "floating about" the state. Comparable estimates for the Anglo population were 120,000 above the Nueces and 2,500 south and west of the Nueces. In other words, in 1850 the population beyond the Nueces consisted approximately of 2,500 Anglos and probably 18,000 Mexicans.

In the immediate postwar period, this demographic mix made for an unstable situation. As had occurred earlier (in the 1830s) with the San Antonio and Victoria settlements, the Rio Grande settlements attracted the worst elements among the Anglo pioneers. In Laredo, as José María Rodríguez recalled in his memoirs, some Americans "began a movement to clean out the Mexicans. They would rant at public meetings and declare that this was an American country and the Mexicans ought to be run out." In the Lower Valley, Abbé Emanuel Domenech, who ministered to the religious needs of the Brownsville area from 1849 to 1855, was blunt in his appraisal of the Americans: "The Americans of the Texian frontiers are, for the most part, the very scum of society—bankrupts, escaped criminals, old volunteers, who after the Treaty of Guadalupe Hidalgo, came into a country protected by nothing that could be called a judicial authority, to seek adventure and illicit gains." The *abbé* had especially harsh words about the Texas Rangers and ex-army volunteers in the area, describing them as "the very dregs of society, and the most degraded of human creatures." The Abbé Domenech was equally frank in his judgment of Mexicans: "I could never comprehend the Mexican's submission, supporting, as he did, at once the cruelty and the contempt of a nation which he sovereignly detested, had I not been so often the witness of his incredible *nonchalance* and imperturbable meekness. In these badly-organized regions, the Mexican might have an easy vengeance on his persecutors, who are quite the minority on the Texan frontiers; but vengeance is not in his heart; he would rather forget an injury than take the trouble of avenging it." Notwithstanding the *abbé*'s assessment, the situation along the Rio Grande proved to be extremely volatile. All that was lacking for the emergence of a movement of resistance and retribution was a precipitating gesture or act of defiance. The first Cortina War, which exploded a few years after Domenech had returned to France, had such origins.

According to the well-embossed story, Juan Nepomuceno Cortina, scion of a wealthy landowning family in the Lower Valley, came to the defense of a drunk *ranchero* and former servant from the beating of Brownsville Marshal Bob Shears. Cortina shot the marshal in the arm in self-defense and carried the *ranchero* off to his ranch. Charges of attempted murder were filed, the Brownsville authorities refusing to compromise with Cortina. In response, Cortina and his supporters raided and captured Brownsville, the initial blow of a six-month-long war. . . . Within a month, Cortina had organized an irregular force of five to six hundred men. Many of those involved in the Cortina War, according to a federal report on the matter, were *rancheros* who had been "driven away from the Nueces." Cortina defeated the Brownsville Rifles and Tobin's Rangers from San Antonio, maintaining control of the region until the U.S. Army sent troops in December 1859.

The results of the Cortina War, according to the army commandant, were the depopulation and laying to waste of the whole country from Brownsville to Rio Grande City, 120 miles. Business as far up as Laredo, 240 miles, had been interrupted and suspended for five months. There remained no property belonging to Americans that had not been destroyed. And those *ranchos* spared by Cortina's men had been burned by the Texans.

At the other end of Texas, attempts to assert ownership over several large salt deposits in the mid-1870s ignited a confrontation known as the "Salt War." Anglo merchants and politicians had shown interest in the salt lakes at the foot of the Guadalupe Mountains since annexation, and conflict over various schemes to tax the salt had constituted a volatile element in El Paso politics. For a hundred years or more the residents of Yselta, San Elizario, and other towns along the Upper Rio Grande had hauled salt from the lakes freely. The lakes had created in these towns a group of merchants who plied salt throughout northern Mexico. In 1877 Judge Charles Howard attempted to make the lakes into "a money-making proposition," but his actions, including the public murder of Louis Cardis, the leader of the Mexican opposition, aroused a "mob" to seek revenge. Howard and two of his associates were killed, and the relief troop of Texas Rangers was defeated before order was restored.

Thus, along the border, overt land dispossession, expulsions, and other repressive measures were not safe options. The Anglo pioneers were quite conscious of their small numbers in the region. After the Cortina rebellion, the threat of an uprising formed an important undercurrent in their psychology, a fear that perhaps motivated the practice of benevolent *patronismo* on their part. The "Cortina Wars" of 1859–60 and later of 1873–75 and the El Paso "Salt War" of 1877 were examples of what could happen. In all three episodes, competing claims to land or livestock precipitated a state of virtual warfare, with a mobilized Mexican element matching arms with the local constabulary and the Texas Rangers. The losers in these conflicts were usually the uninvolved civilian population, who bore the brunt of escalating and indiscriminate retaliation and counterretaliation. Indeed, the Nueces Strip of South Texas and the Trans-Pecos region of West Texas remained "untamed" for nearly fifty years after annexation. A frontier battalion of Texas Rangers, stationed in the border zone until 1920, represented the armed force of the Anglo-Texas order. A military unit during the Mexican War, the Texas Rangers functioned as the military police of occupation, waging sporadic warfare whenever the need arose.

Profits and stability, however, could not be maintained under such volatile circumstances. Peace and everyday governance required a more secure arrangement.

### Structure of Peace

The changes brought about by Texas independence and later American annexation were clear: a new political authority, new markets, and new land laws, to mention the most sweeping. A highly conspicuous elite of Anglo merchants, lawyers, army officers, and office-holders now controlled the trade and politics of the annexed Mexican settlements. Whether they lived together above San Pedro Springs in San Antonio, on the bluff overlooking the bay of Corpus Christi, or around Franklin's store opposite El Paso del Norte, the clique of Anglo merchants, military officers, and lawyer politicians constituted a self-conscious foreign enclave. How did they govern?

In the case of the Texas-Mexican border region and generally in the annexed Southwest, the ability to govern in the immediate postwar period was secured through an accommodation between the victorious Anglos and the defeated Mexican elite, with the latter in command of the Mexican communities. In sociological terms, this accommodation was essentially a "peace structure."

By "peace structure" I refer to a general postwar arrangement that allows the victors to maintain law and order without the constant use of force. The concept focuses on the manner in which victors are able to exercise and establish authority over the defeated. In the Texas-Mexican region, such a peace structure was characterized by two major aspects: one, the subordination of Mexicans to Anglos in matters of politics and authority; and two, the accommodation between new and old elites.

**The Fabric of Peace.**    Although the American presence generally represented a new class in an old Mexican society, it did not completely transform the traditional authority structure. On the contrary, the American merchants and lawyers merely affixed themselves atop the Mexican hierarchy. In some cases, they intermarried and became an extension of the old elite. For individual families of the Mexican elite, intermarriage was a convenient way of containing the effects of Anglo military victory on their status, authority, and class position. For the ambitious Anglo merchant and soldier with little capital, it was an easy way of acquiring land. The social basis for postwar governance, in other words, rested on the class character of the Mexican settlements. . . .

The Rio Grande settlements south and west of San Antonio differed little in their social structure. At the time of American occupation in the mid–nineteenth century, there were four major strata: the landed elite; the *arrimados,* or landless relatives of the elite; the *rancheros* and *vaqueros;* and the *pastores.* The society of the time has been described as a "patriarchal" one where the landlord acted as the head and the *vaqueros* and *pastores* acted as "faithful" subjects.

Of the Rio Grande settlements, Laredo represented the peace structure at its best. Although Laredo had suffered from the depredations of "East Texas outlaws" and many families had resettled across the river (thus founding Nuevo Laredo), much of the strife prevailing in the Texas interior had been avoided. To a large extent, the confirmation of twenty land grant titles by the Texas Legislature in the 1850s was responsible for the peace. The wealth and power of landed elite were generally left undisturbed, and considerable intermarriage bound the old and new elites. Thus, in the postannexation politics of the area, ethnic divisions were secondary to those of class. Ordinances were published in both English and Spanish, American and Mexican holidays celebrated, and political offices divided equally; Mexicans ran the city while Anglos ran the county. Likewise, there was a tacit division of labor; Mexicans ranched and farmed while Anglos commerced.

In the Lower Valley, the conservative upper class, fearful of outright confiscation of their property, was divided in their response to the Anglo presence. According to a well-informed source, some landed families "learned to get along with Americans by overlooking whatever misfortunes fell on the lower class of Mexicans." Retaining their property and benefiting from the American presence, the established families had little cause for complaint. Their loyalties were subjected to a difficult test with Cortina's rebellion in 1859. Some lent the "war" quiet approval while others organized the repression of the "uprising." Unwavering support for the Anglo military forces—the Brownsville Rifles, the Texas Rangers, U.S. Army troops, and, later, Confederate troops—came from the Laredo elite in the form of a company of Mexican *rancheros* led by Santos Benavides, grandson of Don Tomás Sánchez, founder of Laredo.

As in San Antonio and Laredo, the accommodation between the old and incoming elites in the Lower Valley manifested itself in tactical marriages. It was customary among the Mexican elite, as Jovita González has noted, that daughters were "married at an early age, and not for love, but for family connections and considerations." On the other hand, for the Anglo settler, marrying a Mexican with property interests made it possible to amass a good-sized stock ranch without considerable expense. The Americans and the European immigrants, most of whom were single men, married the daughters of the leading Spanish-Mexican families and made Rio Grande City "a cosmopolitan little town." Among those who claimed the Spanish language as their own were families with such surnames as Lacaze, Laborde, Lafargue, Decker, Marx, Block, Monroe, Nix, Stuart, and Ellert. As one Texas Mexican from this upper class recalled: "There were neither racial nor social distinctions between Americans and Mexicans, we were just one family. This was due to the fact that so many of us of that generation had a Mexican mother and an American or European father." . . .

For the Anglo settlers, some degree of "Mexicanization" was necessary for the most basic communication in this region, given the overwhelming number of Mexicans. But such acculturation meant far more than the learning of a language and a proper etiquette; it represented a way of acquiring influence and even a tenuous legitimacy in the annexed Mexican settlements. From participation in religious rituals and other communal activities to "becoming family" through godparenthood or marriage—such a range of ties served to create an effective everyday authority, a type that Ranger or army guns alone could not secure.

**Occupation Politics.**    The military occupation established the pattern and climate for civilian rule. This meant that the interim military government of the Mexican settlements of the Upper and Lower Rio Grande valleys did not allow the defeated Mexicans to rule over the victorious American soldiers, however lowly in rank. This applied, by extension, to the American quartermaster employees and merchants accompanying the army of occupation. Mexican civilian leadership may have continued administrative functions but military personnel were under distinct military jurisdiction. Thus in 1850 a sizable fraction of the Anglo population in the Mexican settlements was essentially immune from the acts of civilian authorities. In San Antonio nearly half of the American population was part of the military presence, either as enlisted personnel or as wagon surveyors working for the military. Another 9 percent were merchants or clerks. In the occupied Lower Rio Grande Valley, nearly 40 percent of the American population were army personnel or employees and 15 percent were merchants or clerks.

Once martial law was lifted and troops withdrawn or discharged Americans and Mexicans, former enemies, maintained their distinct statuses in the courts, in the political parties, and in the town administrations of the old settlements. Two questions had to be settled. One concerned the status of Mexican property in the state. Since Texas had, under the terms of statehood in 1845, retained jurisdiction over all the land within its borders, it claimed to be exempted from the Treaty of Guadalupe Hidalgo. Thus the former republic carried out its own deliberations concerning the status of the annexed Mexicans and their land grants.

To adjudicate the matter of land grants, Governor Peter H. Bell appointed William Bourland and James Miller to investigate the validity of Spanish and Mexican titles. In Webb County, site of the first hearings, the Bourland-Miller Commission encountered opposition from Mexican landowners, who believed that the investigation was out to destroy rather than protect their rights. The impartiality of the proceedings and the prompt confirmation by the legislature of the commission's recommendations removed "this unfounded prejudice" and secured the loyalty of the landed elite of the Laredo area to the new order. Other landowners beyond the Nueces were not as fortunate and thus not as loyal as the Laredo grantees. In the Chihuahua Secession, only seven of the fourteen land grants were recognized. Of approximately 350 cases in the Tamaulipas and Coahuila secessions, "some two hundred" were confirmed by the legislature in 1852, and another 50 were subsequently confirmed by 1901. Of course, many of the grants confirmed were already owned, in part or whole, by Anglos.

The second question requiring immediate attention was the political status of the Mexican in Texas. One of the liveliest debates in the Texas Constitutional Convention (1845) concerned whether or not the Mexican should be allowed the right to vote. The debate centered on whether the qualifying adjective "white" should be retained in the constitutional provisions that described the voters of the state. The Harris County representative argued that the qualifier "white" should be kept, not because he feared the Spaniard; he welcomed them as he welcomed any portion of the Caucasian race that desired to settle in Texas. Rather he feared the mass immigration of "hordes of Mexican Indians": "Silently they will come moving in; they will come back in thousands to Bexar, in thousands to Goliad, perhaps to Nacogdoches, and what will be the consequence? Ten, twenty, thirty, forty, fifty thousand may come in here, and vanquish you at the ballot box though you are invincible in arms. This is no idle dream; no bugbear; it is the truth." The proposal failed, however, because of opposition by several Anglo-Texan allies and protectors of the Texas Mexican elite (like Col. Henry Kinney of Corpus Christi). José Antonio Navarro of San Antonio, the only Texas Mexican (and the only native-born Texan) at the Constitutional Convention, argued eloquently against the proposal.

In spite of the formal defeat of disfranchisement at the convention, Mexicans in certain districts were denied the vote or allowed only limited participation. Corpus Christi merchant Henry Kinney observed that in several counties the practice immediately after independence had been to withhold the franchise from Mexicans, even though they may have fought against a people "of their own race." Traveler Frederick Olmsted observed that, if the Mexicans in San Antonio voted, they could elect a government of their own; "such a step would be followed, however, by a summary revolution." Where Mexicans did have the right to vote, protests and threats from Anglo-Americans were constant reminders of a fragile franchise.

A typical protest was exemplified by a hotly contested election for state representative from Nueces and Webb counties in 1863, where S. Kinney of Corpus Christi lost to Charles Callaghan of Laredo by a margin of thirty-five votes. The *Corpus Christi Ranchero* noted that Kinney was the choice of fifteen or sixteen voters where the English language was spoken and that "American men in an American country should have a fair showing in shaping the destinies of the country." The *Fort Brown Flag* of Brownsville joined in the protest, editorializing that "we are opposed to allowing an ignorant crowd of Mexicans to determine the political questions in this country, where a man is supposed to vote knowingly and thoughtfully." Disfranchisement was the usual sentiment of disgruntled losers in electoral politics.

Where Texas Mexicans constituted a significant portion of the male vote, the politicians among the American settlers proceeded to instruct and organize the new voters. A common pattern was the controlled franchise, where Mexicans voted according to the dictates of the local *patrón,* or boss. Since these political machines delivered sizable blocs of votes in state and national elections, the Anglo *patrones* acquired influence far beyond that usually accorded "backwater" county politicians.

Generally, the lesser bosses were members of the wealthy Mexican families who had entered the political arena to maintain and defend their traditional status, as in the "subrings" of Brownsville, San Antonio, and El Paso. But in all these instances, including places where Mexicans controlled most offices, as in Starr and Zapata counties, the figure of an Anglo boss legitimized Mexican political involvement. In the 1850s, the specific arrangements varied. Cameron County in the Lower Valley showed a nearly equal division of county commissioner positions. In Webb County, Anglos ran the county while Mexicans ran the city of Laredo. In El Paso County, the pattern was reversed, and Anglos ran the city while Mexicans ran the county.

The role of the Mexican elite as influential politicians was contingent, of course, on the presence of a large Mexican electorate. In San Antonio, where the Mexican population increasingly declined through the nineteenth century, Mexican representation on the city aldermanic council fell at an exponential rate after 1836. In 1837, for example, all but one of the forty-one candidates running for city elections were of Spanish-Mexican descent; a decade later there were only five.

Table 1.   San Antonio Aldermen by Ethnicity, 1837–1904

| PERIOD | NON-SPANISH-SURNAMED | SPANISH-SURNAMED |
|---|---|---|
| 1837–1847 | 31 | 57 |
| 1848–1857 | 82 | 17 |
| 1858–1866 | 82 | 11 |
| 1867–1874 | 55 | 4 |
| 1875–1884 | 67 | 2 |
| 1885–1894 | 72 | 1 |
| 1895–1904 | 60 | 0 |

Source: Based on listing in August Santleban, *A Texas Pioneer,* pp. 314–321.

Between 1848 and 1866 each aldermanic council included one or two Mexican representatives; after 1866, however, even token representation was rare. Mexican political clubs remained active but constituted minor actors in the city's affairs. Through the early 1900s, the Mexican voice in city politics was symbolically represented by Anglo officials with familial ties to the Mexican upper class—the Lockwoods, Tobins, and Callaghans, for example. The tabulation in Table 1, with city administrations organized roughly in periods of seven to ten years, gives a clear indication of the decline in power of the Mexican elite in San Antonio during the late nineteenth century.

The principle that in all matters of authority the Anglo stood over the Mexican was most evident in the area of law enforcement. Afer the 1840s, for example, there were no Mexican county sheriffs or city marshals in San Antonio but quite a few— again, generally members of the older wealthy families—were deputy sheriffs and assistant marshals. With some exceptions along the border counties, this division of authority was the pattern in the Mexican region of Texas.

# Mexican Women and the Process of Cultural Assimilation

### JANE DYSART

During the course of European expansion, social contact between different ethnic, racial, and national groups initiated a process of assimilation. In those instances where widespread intermarriage occurred, cultural, ethnic, and even racial distinctions were blurred as the two groups incorporated in a common culture. Where prevailing attitudes assuming cultural or racial superiority prevented extensive intermarriage, the assimilation process was only partially complete. Such attitudes on the part of Anglo-Americans inhibited large-scale marriage with Mexicans, and the celebrated frontier melting pot failed to absorb the majority of Mexicans in the southwestern United States.

Jane Dysart, "Mexican Women in San Antonio, 1830–1860: The Assimilation Process," *Western Historical Quarterly* (October, 1976): 365–375. Copyright © 1976 by The Western Historical Quarterly. Reprinted with permission.

The continuing existence of a culturally and visibly distinct Mexican minority in the Southwest can be partially explained by a historical analysis of the relationship between Mexican women and Anglo men. Following the pattern of settlement and conquest in other frontier regions, Anglo immigration into the southwestern frontier was preponderantly male; consequently, intermarriage as well as informal sexual unions almost exclusively involved Mexican women and Anglo men. Focusing this study upon the Mexican women rather than describing male attitudes toward them provides insights into the nature of the assimilation process and delineates more clearly the active role of the women. . . .

Frontier conditions forced limited modifications in traditional sex roles for both Anglo-American and Hispanic societies. When men were absent for extended periods of time—hunting, fighting, or conducting business in distant cities—women had to assume responsibility for managing family and business affairs. . . .

Despite certain liberating tendencies of the frontier, which might have enhanced or modified women's economic and social status, both Anglo and Hispanic cultures remained basically masculine in orientation. They shared a common belief in the subordination of women, and both societies restricted women's political, legal, social, and economic activities. While men dominated business and politics, women's sphere was home and family. In customs and manners the two cultures were markedly different, but an exaggeratedly masculine style of behavior was just as evident among Anglo males as *machismo* among Mexicans. Hero of the Alamo, William Barret Travis, for example, carefully noted in his diary his frequent sexual affairs with young women, both Anglo and Mexican. A double standard of sexual morality enjoined chastity and legal marriage on women but applauded sexual prowess and experience in men. Frontiersmen resolved this dualistic attitude by shielding certain women behind an elaborate code of chivalry while regarding others, especially those with darker skins, as suitable partners in casual sexual relations. Thus, both societies defined appropriate female roles as either wife and mother or mistress. Passive acceptance of such roles was expected, and research to date has not presented evidence that Mexican women in San Antonio deviated from role expectations to any significant degree.

During the 1840s and 1850s American frontiersmen apparently delighted in recounting tales of the passionate and pleasure-loving senoritas of San Antonio. Wishful thinking probably prompted many Anglo males to exaggerate the promiscuity of Mexican women. Different ideas about proper behavior and appropriate dress also accounted for reports of moral laxity. American travelers found the Mexicans' practice of nude public bathing offensive, though judging from their detailed descriptions, few left the scene quickly. Nor did they refrain from attending fandangos, public dances which were held almost nightly in San Antonio, but most expressed shock at the sensuous movements of the Mexican women. (The fandangos, in fact, were taxed by the municipal government and provided the largest single source of public revenue in 1847.) Anglos also regarded the native women's low-cut dresses as provocative and their uncorseted figures immodest. In most instances they did acknowledge that female immorality was largely confined to the lower classes. Fair skin and wealth apparently protected a woman from criticism as well as from unwelcome sexual advances. . . .

Before the outbreak of hostilities in the mid-1830s, upper class Tejanos often identified their own political liberalism with Anglo American ideals and welcomed newcomers from the United States into their homes. In this manner James Bowie met and later wed Ursula Veramendi, daughter of the liberal Mexican governor of Texas. After 1836 it was politically advantageous for Texas Mexicans, often indiscriminately regarded as enemies, to establish family connections with the dominant Anglo group. Several marriages, in fact, united Anglo political influence with Mexican landed wealth. For example, one daughter of José Antonio Navarro married the adjutant general of the state, while one of the De la Garzas married the county clerk, and her sister wed the sheriff. The political benefits of such familial alliances, however, were not entirely one-sided; for although the number of Spanish-surnamed office holders declined after 1840, the Mexican vote remained a significant factor in San Antonio elections. Anglo men with family ties in the Mexican community consistently won election to city office during the 1840s and 1850s.

Mexican *ricos* more than likely regarded retention of political influence an economic necessity. Unfamiliar with American legal practices and suspected of disloyalty to the American cause, many of the wealthy Tejanos undoubtedly viewed an Anglo son-in-law as a protection from the loss of their extensive landholdings. Several of the wealthiest families did indeed marry one or more of their daughters to Anglo men, thereby reinforcing their political as well as economic position. Included among them were the Seguíns, whose family holdings according to the 1840 tax rolls totaled almost twenty thousand acres; the Navarros, who held title to more than twenty thousand acres in addition to fifteen town lots; and the Cassianos with almost twenty-three thousand acres of land and twelve town lots.

The prospect of marrying a Mexican woman from one of the wealthy families was all the more attractive to an enterprising Anglo male, since daughters customarily inherited property, often on an equal basis with sons. Through his marriage to Margarita de la Garza, James Trueheart, a San Antonio politician, acquired a large tract of valuable land, formerly part of the Mission Espada. There he lived in the style of a *patrón* with a number of peon families who maintained his farming operations. Several other Anglo men like Trueheart advanced their own economic position considerably by marrying the daughters of land-rich Tejanos.

Frequent social contacts coupled with a surplus male population promoted intermarriage between Mexican women and Anglo men. During the 1840s and 1850s dances and parties in San Antonio included leading families from both Anglo and Hispanic groups. José María Rodríguez, whose family was counted among the aristocracy, recalled that he was "kept busy acting as an escort" for his sisters, three of whom did marry Anglos. A young soldier stationed in San Antonio during the 1850s reported attending a dance where "two or three of the bloods of Castile were present." Their land-rich parents, he added, were determined that the girls must wed "genuine Americans."

For the upper-class Mexican woman, marriage to an Anglo after 1830 initiated a process of assimilation and acculturation which in the vast majority of cases led to the americanization of their children. This pattern represented a divergence from past experiences and differed markedly from the process which occurred in rural areas of Texas even during the midnineteenth century. The paternal ancestors of the Navarros had emigrated from Corsica and those of the Cassianos from Italy, but both of these prominent San Antonio families were thoroughly hispanicized by 1830. Among the isolated ranchos of the lower Rio Grande Valley, descendants of

Americans who married Mexican wives in the 1850s attended schools in Mexico and were, in fact, thoroughly mexicanized. After 1840, however, San Antonio became a commercial and military center dominated economically, politically, and socially by Anglos.

The trend toward americanization of Anglo-Mexican families in San Antonio developed in spite of certain factors which seemed to lend greater support to a hispanicization process. The familial ties of the men who married upper-class Mexican women were generally weak and their cultural backgrounds diverse. Few of the men who chose high status Mexican brides between 1830 and 1860 had relatives living in San Antonio. Only seven were born in nearby states of the lower South, and judging by their surnames three of those men were of French extraction. Approximately one-third, however, came from the upper South or the North. Europeans were also well represented in these mixed marriages, including five German husbands, two Irish, two French, and one each from England and Scotland. In contrast to the women who maintained close familial ties and whose cultural background was homogeneous, the men seemingly lacked strong reinforcements for americanization of their families. . . .

Nevertheless, the vast majority of these upper-class children of mixed marriages established identity with their father's ethnic group rather than that of their mother. Since the well-to-do Tejano and Anglo-Mexican families did not live in separate residential districts, they had frequent contacts with their American neighbors. School attendance also aided the assimilation process, for according to the 1850 census all of these children between the ages of six and fifteen were attending school. A few children from affluent families were sent to boarding schools and colleges in other states—some as far away as New Jersey, Kentucky, and Virginia. By the time they became adults, the majority had anglicized their given names. At least three families even joined Protestant churches, while five others affiliated with the English-speaking Roman Catholic parish. With rare exceptions both sons and daughters married non-Mexicans. In short, the second generation became assimilated into Anglo-American society.

The pressures urging Anglo conformity on upper-class Mexican women and their children were indeed intense. In addition to the nativist movement of the 1850s, which exacerbated hostilities against non-Anglo-Saxon and Catholic groups, Anglo Texans forced upon the Mexicans an onus of guilt for the Alamo and Goliad. At the root of discrimination and violence, however, was the Anglo's sense of racial and cultural superiority. They considered Mexicans as innately inferior and as obstacles to economic and political progress. Even the high-status Tejanos felt the sting of cultural, if not racial, prejudice. Thus, the majority of Mexicans in San Antonio, even if they desired to become americanized, found that Anglos had erected almost insurmountable obstacles to assimilation. Only the women and children with Anglo surnames, light skins, and wealth had a reasonable chance to escape the stigma attached to their Mexican ancestry. Judging from their actions, many of them considered it important, perhaps even necessary to do so.

Mexican women were not in a position to direct the course of social change that occurred in San Antonio during the midnineteenth century. The male-oriented frontier society limited female role alternatives to either wife and mother or mistress and at the same time determined the racial and class criteria which shaped the nature of relationships between Anglo men and Mexican women. Given the patriarchal family structure of both ethnic groups, the wife's function was child care and home management, while the husband assumed primary responsibility for making decisions affecting the family's relationship to the society. Because the assimilation process in San Antonio demanded conformity to Anglo social and cultural patterns, those few Mexican women whom Anglo men found acceptable as wives lost their own distinctive ethnic identity, and in many cases their children rejected the rich cultural legacy of their Mexican ancestry.

## Victorian Womanhood on the Texas Frontier

### ANN PATTON MALONE

Ironically, the women on the Texas frontier with the greatest social and economic advantages suffered a dislocation and incongruity with their social system which other women were generally spared. The Anglo American woman of the mid-nineteenth century matured within a Victorian society with prescribed feminine roles and expectations. Whenever feasible, they were expected to fulfill the ideals of the "womanly woman." Upper and middle-class women's lives were dictated by these expectations; lower and working-class women also aspired to them and accepted the "womanly woman" as a role model. The strong Southern heritage of most Texas settlers and the scarcity of women on the frontier reinforced the Victorian ideals of womanhood. However, frontier conditions made it nearly impossible for women to achieve them.

According to the Victorian social system, the proper model for men was the "manly man;" for women, the "womanly woman." These two ideals mutually reinforced each other. The "manly man" was aggressive, expansive, and worldly; the entire scope of human endeavors was his sphere. He was actor, leader, defender, and discoverer. Since his primary function was economic, he was forced into the marketplace where he must be strong-willed, rational, inquiring, and occasionally ruthless. The competitiveness, violence, and persistent conflicts of the world made men hard and insensitive. The Victorian code decreed that women should be protected from these hardening influences, and that they should help mitigate such influences for their men. The home served a vital function for the Victorian male. It was a place where he could express himself freely, be soothed, softened, strengthened, cheered, and comforted by domestic tranquility. One of the primary objectives for the "womanly woman" was to assure this peace for her husband; her other primary role was to bear his children.

The ideal Victorian woman was passive, childlike, unreflective, self-sacrificing, and dependent. Whereas men were to be self-possessed, women were to submit to the control of others, principally to their husbands, fathers, and brothers. Above all, women were to be adaptable, able to mold themselves to their husband's expectations and desires. In a Victorian marriage, potential conflict was removed through

Ann Patton Malone, *Women on the Texas Frontier: A Cross-Cultural Perspective* (El Paso: Texas Western Press, 1983), 14–19. Reprinted with permission of the author.

constant wifely adjustment, and this submission sometimes included accompanying husbands to remote frontier regions such as Texas regardless of the wives' personal inclinations.

Since motherhood and wifehood were equally glorified, the Victorian woman was expected to bear children not only dutifully but joyfully. Yet she was to be passionless and submissive in sexual matters. Home and family were her only worlds. She was neither trained nor thought suited for anything else. Even in the sacred spheres of home and family, however, she did not reign as "Queen of the Household" as did women of other cultures on the Texas frontier. Even in household matters the Anglo American woman was expected to defer to her husband or father. Her training from childhood was designed to fulfill the roles prescribed by society. According to the code, female education ceased or was neglected after the age of fifteen because intellectual or opinionated women were considered unwomanly. Her training was almost exclusively in the domestic arts after that point. She learned how to run a household frugally and to direct servants efficiently while performing little of the actual labor herself. She was expected to be charming and pleasing to family and guests, and to this end she was taught a smattering of music, literature, drawing, dancing, and the "art of light conversation." Such skills were generally of little use to the elite women who removed to the Texas frontier.

The mid-nineteenth century Victorian code for female behavior both glorified and oppressed, protected and controlled. Most women, especially in the South, submitted to the code, and some enjoyed the view from the pedestal, but an undercurrent of discontent did exist. An anonymous widely sung Southern rural folk tune of the period, "The Wagoner's Lad," expressed a common attitude among women:

> Hard is the fortune of all womankind,
> They are always controlled,
> They are always confined,
> Controlled by their family until they are wives,
> Then slaves to their husbands
> The rest of their lives.

Women found ways to circumvent some of the male authority. Particularly in the South, women often made a weapon of their womanhood, using coquetry to gain their way. In some cases they could mitigate their husband's authority by appealing to conscience or religion since even husbands could not dictate on such matters. They could gain support by appealing to a formidable array of female kin, the Victorian woman's most constant companions. But on the frontier, the domination of the Anglo woman was almost complete. Coquetry was out of place, organized religion was weak, and supportive kinship networks were removed or dispersed in many cases. If the woman had inherited wealth, she might exercise some independent judgment, but she did so rarely. In Texas a woman's wealth was often absorbed into her husband's estate even if it remained technically in her name.

The Victorian social system was powerful and reached even into the frontier regions. But frontier experiences created challenges to the code, and incongruities developed. The women who had been inculcated from infancy with the feminine ideals of the Victorian code and then found many of the precepts obsolete or inappropriate on the Texas frontier were often torn and bewildered—even traumatized—

by the experience. They were separated from kin, community, and what they considered civilization. Many felt totally inadequate to perform the tasks required of them in their new circumstances, as did Rebecca Pilsbury, a New Englander who accompanied her husband to Brazoria, Texas, in 1848. On November 17, she wrote, "I felt totally incapacitated. I was to perform the duties of chargé d'affaires to slaves." And several days later she confessed that "I am inclined to think that I was not designed for a worker, surely no one ever put their hand to plow more willingly than I. Attempted to preserve some pumpkin today, and surely no one ever met a more total failure."

Even a cursory examination of the voluminous published and unpublished literature of these first-generation frontier women reveals their conflict. A pathetic stream of letters to family and kin plead for more correspondence, any word from "home." They desperately attempted to preserve what they associated with civilized society despite its inappropriateness in the wilderness. It was no accident that frontier wife Harriet Ames wore a black silk dress on the Runaway Scape. And the elite women who were wives of leading colonists dressed in silks, brocades, and diamonds for parties in Columbia and Matagorda Bay. Travelers frequently commented upon the stark contrasts they encountered in Texas, such as fine furniture in crude log cabins, libraries in the wilderness, and elegantly attired and graciously mannered women in remote settlements.

Woman of all social and economic classes accompanied their husbands and families to the frontier during the expansionistic thirties, forties, and fifties, but more is known about the elite women since they left more records. These daughters and wives of planters, merchants, professionals, and army officers had previously performed little physical labor. On the frontier, they had to perform unaccustomed and often untraditional tasks. Although they did not customarily work in the clearing, building, or planting processes, they had to undertake much of the cooking, spinning, gardening, and nursing duties which had been relegated to servants in their distant homes. In addition to their own familial responsibilities, frontier women were frequently expected to care for slaves and neighbors in times of sickness, death, or other crises.

Understandably, the elite women found it difficult or impossible to run a smooth-functioning household on the frontier and to provide what they considered a proper Christian upbringing for their children. Concern for the physical well-being of their families is the most persistent theme in the letters women wrote to relatives. Health, a precarious matter anywhere in the nineteenth century, was especially hazardous on the Texas frontier. Frequent outbreaks of cholera and fevers, frontier lawlessness, wars with Indians and Mexicans, accidents, and childbirth all took a frightful toll on frontier women and their families.

Anglo American women who migrated to the Texas frontier underwent a psychic crisis which their Texas-born daughters could scarcely appreciate. The second generation matured in a new environment, with different expectations and models and with their support groups intact. Lucadia Pease, later the wife of a Texas governor, shortly after leaving her family home to accompany her husband to Texas wrote her sister, "I cannot tell you how sad I felt after parting from you, the last member of our own family, with the prospect of so long a journey before me, and its termination placing me so far from home . . . ." Another homesick transplanted wife wrote that she spent a few hours sewing the garment "wetted by my tears." These first-generation pioneering women, ill equipped for the tasks expected of them, suffered a profound sense of alienation in their new homeland because of the nature of Anglo settlement which tended to be nuclear and scattered rather than organized by family groups, communities, or presidios. Women who had matured while surrounded by relatives and servants found the isolation difficult. Anna Maria Campbell Reynolds recalled that "the first night's camp on the prairies was horrible to me. . . . There was no sound to greet my ears but the howling of wolves. . . . I was frightfully blue." Many women left reminiscences which express feelings of utter loneliness, even terror, in their little cabin homes, miles from the closest neighbors. Considering the frequency of male absences, the unstable and sometimes hostile relations with the Indians, and the general lawlessness of the Texas frontier, the concerns and fears expressed by these women were well founded.

When a social system develops stresses and finally gives way to another, a great burden is placed upon the traditional generation. On the Texas frontier, numerous adjustments were required of these elite women. Some adjusted in a single generation and emerged stronger, more self-reliant than they would have become under less trying circumstances. Mary Austin Holley, a perceptive observer, wrote concerning her 1836 visit to Texas: "Delicate ladies find that they can be useful and need not be vain. . . . Many latent faculties are developed." Other women, however, were unable to satisfactorialy adjust but bore children who faced less conflict with their environment. A few never adjusted and quietly mourned themselves into early graves or returned to their distant familial homes. The latter groups rarely left reminiscences of their bitter experiences, hence we have a rather one-sided and glorified record written by the women who persevered. These accounts unconsciously present a stereotype of pioneer women of unbelievable character—stoic, brave, adventuresome, and ladylike. Their chronicles include confrontations with Indians, runaway slaves, invading Mexican armies, wild animals, and the elements, but they generally avoid comment on confrontations they had with loved ones and themselves. These women who persevered and left records may not have been, in fact, extraordinarily courageous, but they had successfully developed powerful survival mechanisms. Paradoxically, the Victorian social system in some ways prepared these women for the adaptations required of them. The system had conditioned them to develop the traits of patience, acceptance, submission, stoicism, and above all, adaptability. The keen-honing of such traits might explain why supposedly helpless women could defend their cabins with guns and axes against marauding Indians, or could very ably manage businesses, farms, or plantations in their husbands' absences. Since their survival mechanisms had developed within a Victorian framework, the increasingly self-reliant and independent frontier women were also willing, even anxious, to abdicate their authority upon their husbands' return or when the crisis had passed. The submissiveness of the elite women often puzzled foreign visitors. Eugene Maissin, a Frenchman who visited many Texas plantations, observed that the men "talk rarely to the women, and only if they have nothing else to do. The women appear quite accustomed to this neglect and seem astonished if one attempts to converse with them."

In summary, Victorian daughters, wives, and mothers of the first generation became embroiled in social ambiguity on the frontier. Separated from their family and traditional society, they went through multiple migrations and uprootings. They became preoccupied with their health and that of their children and were insecure about their ability to provide a genteel home. Their inculcated instincts told them that the physical and spiritual well-being of their families was foremost, literally their raison d'être. The risks to both were great on the frontier, and the sources of assistance—whether institutional, communal, or familial—were fewer. Because of the absence of community, extended families, and churches, the first generation women came to view themselves as civilizers and felt obligated to bring gentility, culture, and beauty to the raw life of the frontier. In some ways the primitive nature of frontier life inspired a creativity in all women which was expressed in their quilts, pottery, basketry, beadwork, weaving, flower gardens, garments, and in a myriad of other ways.

The elite women of the Texas frontier rose to its many challenges, but at considerable costs. Frequently they submitted to the new demands, attempted to combine old roles with new, and found surprising strength and resolve within themselves. But when reading the diaries, reminiscences, and journals of the pioneer women of Texas, elite or otherwise, one is urged to look for what Lillian Schlissel calls the obscure or hidden patterns. One finds, between the lines, signs of tortured ambiguity. The daughters were less in conflict. They, and the yeoman class women were the self-sufficient Anglo women often commented upon. However, it was not these hardy young women of the soil who were the most remarkable. It may have been instead the first generation elite women—the most reluctant pioneers of all—who made their peace with a hostile world in spite of their fears, conflicts, and insecurities.

The elite woman, or "refined lady" as many nineteenth-century observers called her, eventually achieved a somewhat more liberalized relationship with men on the frontier. The frontier simply precluded the existence of a class of purely ornamental or decorative women. Even planters' wives ultimately became involved in plantation affairs. Immigrant women and Anglo American middle class women developed even stronger economic roles, much like women in Indian society. These hard-working females were much admired by their contemporaries.

Women of varied ethnic groups migrated with their families to the Texas frontier in the thirties, forties, and fifties, and in even larger numbers after the Civil War. Migrants from the German states, from Moravia and Bohemia (areas which later became Czechoslovakia), England, France, Ireland, and Scotland were among the most numerous. They encountered the same basic problems of other newcomers, but their responses to the Texas environment were often as varied as the cultures and circumstances from which they originated. Some generalizations can be extracted from their experiences, however. Separations from homeland, family, kin, and other support groups and institutions were generally acknowledged by immigrating groups to be permanent, thus making the initial adjustment to the frontier doubly trying. Scholars of the immigration process have suggested that immigrants are severely and permanently affected by the loss of community, regardless of any resultant economic or social improvement. Immigrants did attempt to recreate that which was good and familiar from the world they had left, but the motivations behind their migration to a new world were generally much more compelling and concrete than the vague urges of manifest destiny and frontier impulses which propelled Americans to the area. Although they had nostalgia and affection for much of the world they left behind, most migrants had very urgent political, ideological, economic, or religious reasons for leaving. They were not reluctant pioneers, for the most part, as were so many elite Anglo women. Observers frequently commented upon the optimistic demeanor of the immigrants, most of whom were determined to make a new life and to adjust quickly. Mrs. Jesse Houstoun described in 1843 the disembarkment of 115 French settlers in Galveston. She said that they were a "motley group" but "one and all" looked "cheerful and happy." She seemed to think that they were well suited for the frontier experience, commenting upon their "extreme fitness . . . to cope with the inconveniences of a new country, such as Texas. They are more light of heart, and less easily depressed than the British settler . . . (and) their wants are fewer and more easily supplied."

In some ways the immigrant woman did have a psychological advantage over her English and Anglo American counterpart for she was better accustomed to a strong economic role. The peasant or agricultural societies from which many European immigrant women came prepared them well for the hard labor and role adjustments they would encounter in Texas. For example, German women worked in the fields of south-central Texas along with their husbands and servants with no sense of shame or loss of status, since they had worked similarly in their homeland. Furthermore, although the men ruled the family rather autocratically among most European immigrant groups represented on the Texas frontier, the women ruled their households in a like fashion, exercising considerable authority and control in their own realm.

While cultural differences such as language barriers and a lack of frontier know-how presented unique difficulties for the immigrant pioneers, the absence of certain Anglo American cultural biases sometimes resulted in better relations with the Indians, Mexicans, and Blacks on the frontier.

Many immigrants suffered greatly during their first year or so on the Texas frontier. Among them, childbearing women, the elderly, and small children suffered most. Immigration propaganda circulated in Europe had misled many, especially those who came early without an established ethnic community to welcome and advise them. Consequently, most lacked any real understanding of the area, geographically or culturally. Mortality schedules in the leading immigrant areas often contain the notation that most of the dead were infants or new immigrants who had settled in the fever-ridden river bottoms. Once the dangerous period of initial adjustment had passed, the immigrant woman generally thrived on the frontier. Practical, industrious women with few pretensions or grandiose expectations, they contributed much to the development of the region.

Akin to the immigrant woman and between the elite and the poor white woman was a large group of females who were socially and economically of the middle rank. These were the wives, daughters, and other kin of yeomen farmers, small slaveholders, craftsmen, and tradesmen. They were probably more comfortable on the frontier than any other groups of Anglo women. Like the elite women, they, too, were strongly influenced by the feminine role expectations of the Victorian code. It provided them with a sense of duty, loyalty, determination, adaptiveness, and submissiveness, all helpful in adjusting to frontier conditions. But these women also had the advantage of a broader work experience. Because their prior lives had not been ones of either luxury or abject poverty but of hard work and activity, these yeoman-class women were better prepared to fulfill their expected roles on the frontier. Unlike the poor white women, they viewed reversals as temporary and were able to accept hardship with relative equanimity. While the Victorian code made them feel uncomfortable in strictly defined male-related work, they knew how to garden, sew, spin, weave, cook, and raise children without a retinue of servants or kin to assist. And they were accustomed to a division of labor which included demanding economic and familial duties. They were confronted with the same problems as the elite and other women on the frontier. Since these yeomen-class women were generally in a more exposed position on the frontier rather than in a plantation setting, they probably experienced even greater difficulties. They were, however, better prepared by training and experience to meet the challenges, and they developed into strong independent, resourceful, and self-reliant women. Some parallels can be drawn between the yeomen-class frontier Anglo women and Indian women. Both had strong economic roles in addition to their familial roles, acting with their husbands as partners in production. Also, like Indian women, they tended to internalize certain elements of the dominant male culture. These women could not be protected and segregated from worldly events by a secure impenetrable circle of home and family. On the frontier, they witnessed aggression, danger, greed, violence, and death. They experienced fear, undertook varied responsibilities, accomplished new tasks; in short, they were exposed to the whole range of human activities and emotions. But the milieu to which they were exposed was aggressively male-oriented. Males set the goals, provided the criterion for success, and received the rewards. Like the Indian women the yeoman woman adopted some of the characteristics of the dominant male culture. She was, in some respects, masculinized by the frontier experience. . . . Stoic, fatalistic, taciturn, the women who participated most fully in the frontier experience were hardened as well as strengthened by it. Such women could wield a hoe or a rifle nearly as well as their husbands. Such were the women who defended their homes and children against Indian attack with hatchets and guns rather than with feminine appeals for mercy. Such also was the woman who demanded the right to unflinchingly view her scalped son's corpse, or who wept at the birth of a daughter, who urged her sons and husband into battle against the Indians, Mexicans and Yankees, regretting that she couldn't go herself. Frontier men admired her greatly, even though she departed from the prevalent feminine ideal, because she displayed so many of the attributes which they admired in themselves. Yet she rarely failed to defer to her menfolk. The yeoman-class woman was the prototype of the Texas pioneer woman to her contemporaries. . . .

In addition to the genteel and middle-rank yeoman women, a third group which has received little scholarly attention also resided on the Texas frontier. These were the poor white women whose existence was at best marginal. Not much is known about them and their families, but they were occasionally observed and described by travelers and in reminiscences. Most settlers had to endure temporary hard times, but not a debilitating and seemingly hopeless poverty which passed down through the generations. Such poverty was present on every Texas frontier despite abundant natural resources and opportunities. . . .

The experiences of Anglo women on the Texas frontier varied widely according to their backgrounds and circumstances. Some, such as the elite women, were better equipped economically to benefit from the opportunities offered by a developing region. Others, such as the immigrant and second-generation women, were better prepared psychologically for the pioneering experience.

 *F U R T H E R    R E A D I N G*

Armando Alonzo, *Tejano Legacy: Rancheros and Settlers in in South Texas, 1734–1900* (1998)

Ty Cashion, *A Texas Frontier: The Clear Fork Country and Fort Griffin, 1849–1887* (1996)

Arnoldo De León, *Tejano Community, 1836–1890* (1982)

Fane Downs, "Tryels and Trubbles: Women in Early Nineteenth Century Texas," *Southwestern Historical Quarterly,* 90, 564–570.

John Salmon Ford, Stephen B. Oates, eds. *Rip Ford's Texas* (1963)

Joe S. Graham, *El Rancho in South Texas: Continuity and Change from 1750* (1994)

Terry Jordan, *North American Cattle-Ranching Frontiers: Origins, Diffusion, and Differentiation* (1993)

Paula Mitchell Marks, *Hands to the Spindle; Texas Women and Home Textile Production, 1822–1880* (1998)

Timothy Matovina, *Tejano Religion and Ethnicity: San Antonio, 1821–1860* (1995)

Frederick Merk, *Slavery and the Annexation of Texas* (1972)

David E. Narrett, "A Choice of Destiny: Immigration Policy, Slavery, and the Annexation of Texas," *Southwestern Historical Quarterly,* 100, 271–302

David Pletcher, *The Diplomacy of Annexation: Texas, Oregon, and the Mexican War* (1973)

Justin H. Smith, *The Annexation of Texas* (1911)

Thomas T. Smith, *The U.S. Army and the Texas Frontier Economy, 1845–1900* (1999)

Paul N. Spellman, *Hugh McLeod, Forgotten Texas Leader: Hugh McLeod and the Texas Santa Fe Expedition* (1999)

Mark J. Stegner, *Texas, New Mexico and the Compromise of 1850; Boundary Dispute and Sectional Crisis* (1996)

# Secession and Civil War,
# 1861–1865

When Texans joined the Union by virtual acclamation in 1845, it seemed inconceivable that they would vote to leave it a mere sixteen years later. In addition to the manifold economic advantages of annexation, Anglo Texans in the western regions of the state relied upon the U.S. Army to protect them from the tribal bands of Plains Indians. In terms of ethnic composition, too, the population of Texas, with its sizable enclaves of Hispanics and German immigrants, bore little similarity to the other southern states that joined the Confederacy in 1861. Some of its leading public figures, most notably Sam Houston, remained steadfast adherents of Union even as public support grew in the late 1850s for the secessionist cause. Yet for all its unique characteristics, Texas displayed many of the same cultural chromosomes that defined the Lower South. The rich, alluvial soil of east Texas, the most densely populated area of the state, nourished a plantation economy based on cotton and slaves, binding it firmly to the interests of its southern neighbors. In the end, the dominance of the cotton culture led Texans to follow the path of disunion and Civil War.

The extent to which Texas shared in the broader regional identity that made secession possible is an issue that has long intrigued historians, for it calls into question the state's vaunted claim to uniqueness. Some historians have argued that the bitter experience of Civil War prompted Texans in later years to downplay their southern roots. In a subconscious effort to disassociate Texas from the trauma of the "Lost Cause," they tailored their historical memory to give greater emphasis to the state's frontier heritage. In so doing, they laid claim to an artificial brand of exceptionalism, constructing an elaborate and ennobling mythology around the exploits of Anglo Texans in their struggles against Mexico and Native Americans. While this interpretation may not be shared by all historians, Texas' decision to join the Confederacy must be viewed as a significant marker in the formation of the state's identity. In 1861, to be sure, Texas was a state of many competing and disparate identities. What factors contributed to the ascendancy of a distinctly southern perspective? Was the system of slave labor the key ingredient in making Texas a southern state? To what extent did political conditions play a role in convincing Texans that they should take the momentous step of severing their ties to the Union?

In the first two documents, two former Texas slaves recall their lives before emancipation. Both were among the hundreds of former slaves interviewed in the late 1930s as part of an ambitious oral history project conducted by the federal government. Andy J. Anderson was ninety-four years old when interviewed. Lulu Wilson moved to Texas from Kentucky during the Civil War. She was interviewed when she was ninety-seven.

The secession crisis is the focus of the next two documents. In Document 3, the delegates of the state's secession convention present their case for disunion. This document reveals the importance of slavery to the secessionist cause as well as its fear that Lincoln's election would now put the institution in jeopardy. Sam Houston, more fearful that secession would lead to a bloody and destructive war, refused to swear allegiance to the Confederacy and was promptly ousted as governor by a secession convention called by the legislature. Document 4 is an excerpt from Houston's speech at Brenham shortly after his removal, one of the last he gave during a remarkable public career in Texas spanning more than a quarter of a century.

Document 5 is an eyewitness account of the "Great Hanging," which occurred in Gainesville, Cooke County. Although rumors of a unionist conspiracy appear to have been greatly exaggerated, a large non-slaveholding population had voted against secession in Cooke and surrounding counties, creating a climate of intense suspicion in North Texas that culminated in the lynching of 42 individuals in October 1862.

Although most of the fighting between North and South took place in other parts of the United States, the conflict had a wrenching and sometimes violent impact on the civilian population of Texas. In Document 6, Rebecca Ann Adams writes to her husband, a physician serving in the Confederate army. For many Anglo Texas women, the absence of husbands during the war required them to assume new and unfamiliar roles. Accustomed to caring for nine children—a tenth, Robert, was serving with her husband—Rebecca Ann was obliged to take on the added responsibility of running a large East Texas plantation of fifty slaves.

## 1. Andy J. Anderson, Former Slave, Recalls Life During the Civil War, n.d.

The war broke out, and that made the big change on the master's place. He joined the army and hired a man named Delbridge for overseer. After that, the hell started to pop, because the first thing Delbridge did was cut the rations. He weighed out the meat, three pounds for the week, and he measured a peck of meal. And that wasn't enough. He half starved us niggers, and he wanted more work, and he started the whipping. I guess he started to educate them. I guess that Delbridge went to hell when he died, but I don't see how the devil could stand him.

We were not used to such, and some ran off. When they were caught, there was a whipping at the stake. But that Delbridge, he sold me to Massa House in Blanco County. I was sure glad when I was sold, but it was short of gladness, because here was another man that hell was too good for. He gave me the whipping, and the scars are still on my arms and my back, too. I'll carry them to my grave. He sent

Ronnie Tyler and Lawrence Murphy, eds., *Slave Narratives of Texas* (Austin: State House Press, 1974), 98, 126. Copyright © State House Press. Reprinted with permission.

me for firewood, and when I got it loaded, the wheel hit a stump, and the team jerked, and that broke the whippletree. So he tied me to the stake, and every half hour for four hours, they laid ten lashes on my back. For the first couple of hours the pain was awful. I've never forgot it. Then I'd stood so much pain that I did not feel so much, and when they took me loose, I was just about half dead. I laid in the bunk for two days, getting over that whipping, getting over it in the body but not the heart. No, sir, I have that in the heart till this day.

After that whipping I didn't have the heart to work for the massa. If I saw the cattle in the cornfield, I turned them back, instead of chasing them out. I guess that's the reason the massa sold me to his brother, Massa John. And he was good like my first massa; he never whipped me. . . .

Then surrender was announced and master told us we were free. When that took place, it was about one o'clock by sun. I said to myself, I won't be here long. But I had not realized what I was in for till after I'd started, but I couldn't turn back, for that meant whipping or danger from the patrollers. There I was and kept on going. No nigger was supposed to be off the master's place without a pass, so I traveled at night and hid out during the day. I stayed in the brush and got water from the creeks, but didn't get much to eat. Twice I was sure those patrollers were passing while I was hiding.

I was 21 years old then, but it was the first time I'd gone any place except to the neighbors, so I was worried about the right way to Master Haley's place. But the morning of the third day I came to the place, and I was so hungry and tired and scared for fear Master Haley was not home from the army yet. So I found my pappy, and he hid me in his cabin till a week passed, and then luck came to me when Master Haley came home. He came at night and the next morning that Delbridge [the overseer] was sent off the place, because Master Haley saw the niggers were all gaunt and lots had run off, and the fields were not plowed right, and only half the sheep and everything was left. So master said to that Delbridge, "There are no words that can explain what you've done. Get off my place before I smash you."

Then I could come out from my pappy's cabin, and the old master was glad to see me, and he let me stay till freedom was ordered. That was the happiest time in my life, when I got back to Master Haley.

## 2. Lulu Wilson, Former Slave, Describes the Hardships of Slavery, 1938

'Course I was born in slavery, ageable as I am. I am a old time slavery woman and the way I been through the hackles I got plenty to say about slavery. . . .

My paw wan't no slave. He was free man 'cause his mammy was a full blood Creek Indian. Now I ain't saying what his paw was 'cause I ain't knowing. All I know is what my mammy told me and I ain't never seed my paw but one time.

My maw says she was born in slavery to Wash Hodges' paw. He gave her to Wash Hodges when he married. That was the only woman slave he had. He had one man slave, a young buck. My maw says she took with my paw and I was born but

"Lulu Wilson," *The American Slave: A Composite Autobiography,* Supplement, Series 2, vol. 10, Part 9, Texas Narratives (Westport: Greenwood Press, 1979), 191–198.

some time passed and didn't no more younguns come and so they said my paw was too old and wore out for breedin' and they wanted her to take with this here other buck. So the Hodges set the nigger hounds on my paw and run him away from the place and maw said he went to the free state. So she took with my step paw and they must of pleased the white folks that wanted niggers to breed like livestock 'cause she birthed nineteen children. Two died, one when it was a young baby and one when it was a yearling baby. [About one year old.] . . .

Now when I was little chap they was the hardest times. They nearly beat us to death. They took me from my mammy out'n the little house built on to their house and I had to sleep in a bed by Missus Hodges. I cried for my maw but I had to work and wash and iron and clean the house and milk cows when I was so little.

The Hodges had three chilluns. The olderest one they was mean to 'cause she was a gal and so thick headed. She couldn't learn nothing out'n a book but she was kinder and more friendly like than the rest of the lot.

Wash Hodges was mean pore trash and he was a bad actor and a bad manager. He never could make any money and he starved it out'n the niggers. For years all I could get was one little slice of sowbelly, a puny little piece of bread and a tater. I never had enough to stave the hongriness out'n my belly.

My maw would have to cook in the house sometimes and she was a clink. [Cline, best of its kind.] She could cuss and she wan't afeared. Wash Hodges would try to whip her with a cow hide and she would knock him down and bloody him up. Then he would go down to some of his neighbor kin and try to get them to come help him whup her. But they would say, "I don't want to go up there and let Chloe Ann beat me up." Leastways, I heared him tell his wife that they said that.

My step paw used to sit on the rail fence by the yard and hear my maw in a tantrum in the kitchen and wouldn't partialize with her but jest set there laughin' and say, "Chloe Ann is a clink."

My maw did tell me that she was a 'ligious woman and she b'lieved that the time would come when the niggers wouldn't have to be slave to the white folks. She told me to pray for it. She told me she seed a old man what the nigger dogs chased and et the legs nearly off him. She said she was chased by them bloody hounds and she just picked up a club and layed they skull open. She said they had hired her out and they had sold her twice but they brung her back to Wash Hodges.

Now Mrs. Hodges studied 'bout meanness more than Wash done. She was mean to anybody she could lay her hands to, but special mean to me. She beat me and she used to tie my hands and make me lie flat on the floor and she put snuff in my eyes. I b'lieve I ain't lyin' before God when I say that I knows why I went blind. I did see white folks sometimes that spoke right friendly and kindly to me.

I gits to thinkin' now how Wash Hodges would sell off my maws chilluns. He would sell them and have the folks come for them when my maw was in the fields. When she would come back she would raise a rukus. Then many the times I seen her plop right down to a settin' and cry 'bout it. But she 'lowed there wan't nothing could be done 'cause it was the slavery law. She said, "Oh lord let me see the end of it 'fore I die and I'll quit my cussin' and fightin' and rarin'." My maw claimed to me she was part Indian and 'twas 'countable for her ways.

One day they truckled us all down in a covered wagon and started out with the family and my maw and step paw and five of us chilluns. I know I was past twelve year old. We come a long way and we passed through a free state. (Probably Missouri) Some places we drove for miles in the woods instead of the big road and when we come near to folks they hid us down in the bed of the wagon.

We passed through a little place and my maw told me to look and I saw a man going up some steps toting a bucket of water. She said, "Lulu, that man is your paw. He aint such a youngish man but he was good to me and good for me." I ain't never think she was as considible of my step paw as she was of my paw and she gave me to think as much. My step paw never did like me but he was a fool for his own younguns. 'Cause at the end of the wars when they set the niggers free he tramped over half the world gathering up them younguns that they had sold away.

He went to a place called Wadefield (Texas) and settled for some short passing of time and they was a Missionary Baptist church next to the house. When we was there Mrs. Hodges let me go twice and I was fancified with the singing and the preaching. They sang something 'bout the Glory Road. I set it in my mind that some day I'd jine with them and I spoke it over with my maw.

We went on to Chatfield Point. (Navarro County, Texas) Wash Hodges built a log house and covered it with weather boarding and built my maw and paw quarters to live in. They turned to raising corn, taters and hogs. I had to work like a dog. I hoed and I milked ten cows twice a day.

Missus told me I had ought to marry. She told me if I would marry she would togger me up in a white dress and give me a weddin' supper. She made the dress and Wash Hodges married me out'n the Bible to a nigger b'longing to a nephew of his'n. I was bout thirteen or fourteen. I know that it wan't long after that when Missus Hodges got a doctor to me. The doctor told me that less'n I had a baby, old as I was and married, I'd start in on spasms. So it twan't long 'til I had a baby.

In b'twixt that time Wash Hodges started laying out in the woods and swamps all the time. I heared that he was hidin' out from the war and that he was sposin' to go 'cause he had been a volunteer in the first war they didn't have back in Kentucky.

One night when we was all asleep some folks whooped and woke us all up. Two sojers came in and they left more outside. They found Wash Hodges and they said it was midnight. They said to get them something to eat. They 'et and then some more came in an 'et. They tied Wash's hands and made me hold the lamp in the door for them to see by. They had some more men in the wagon with their hands tied. They driv' away and in a minute I heared the reports of the guns three or four times. The next day I heared that they was civil sojers and that they done shot some conscripts in the bottoms back of our place.

Wash Hodges was gone away four years and Missus Hodges was meaner than the devil all the time. Seems like she just hates us worser than ever. She said blobber mouf niggers done cause a war.

Well now things just kind of drift along for a spell and then Wash Hodges come back and he said, "Well now we done whupped the hell out'n them blue bellies and that will teach them a lesson to leave us alone.

Then my step paw done told him that he seen some Federal sojers. I seen them too. They drifted by in droves of fifty and a hundred. My step paw 'lowed as how the Federals told him they ain't no more slavery and he tried to pint it out to Wash Hodges. Now Wash says thats a new ruling but the ruling is that the growed up niggers is free but the chilluns have to stay with the masters 'til they is of age. I have to stay with them but my maw and step paw 'low they ain't. My step paw went out to hunt for his younguns. . . .

I don't never recall just like the real passing of time. I know that I had my little old boy youngun' and he growed up but after he was born I left the Hodges and felt like it was a fine good riddance.

## 3. Texans State Their Reasons for Secession, 1861

A declaration of the causes which impel the State of Texas to secede from the Federal Union.

The government of the United States, by certain joint resolutions, bearing date the 1st day of March, in the year A.D. 1845, proposed to the Republic of Texas, then *a free, sovereign and independent nation,* the annexation of the latter to the former, as one of the co-equal States thereof. . . .

But what has been the course of the government of the United States, and of the people and authorities of the non-slave-holding States, since our connection with them?

The controlling majority of the Federal Government, under various pretences and disguises, has so administered the same as to exclude the citizens of the Southern States, unless under odious and unconstitutional restrictions, from all the immense territory owned in common by all the States on the Pacific Ocean, for the avowed purpose of acquiring sufficient power in the common government to use it as a means of destroying the institutions of Texas and her sister slaveholding States.

By the disloyalty of the Northern States and their citizens and the imbecility of the Federal Government, infamous combinations of incendiaries and outlaws have been permitted in those States and the common territory of Kansas to trample upon the federal laws, to war upon the lives and property of Southern citizens in that territory, and finally, by violence and mob law, to usurp the possession of the same as exclusively the property of the Northern States.

The Federal Government, while but partially under the control of these our unnatural and sectional enemies, has for years almost entirely failed to protect the lives and property of the people of Texas against the Indian savages on our border, and more recently against the murderous forays of banditti from the neighboring territory of Mexico; and when our State government has expended large amounts for such purpose, the Federal Government has refused reimbursement therefor, thus rendering our condition more insecure and harrassing than it was during the existence of the Republic of Texas.

These and other wrongs we have patiently borne in the vain hope that a returning sense of justice and humanity would induce a different course of administration. . . .

In all the non-slave-holding States, in violation of that good faith and comity which should exist between entirely distinct nations, the people have formed themselves into a great sectional party, now strong enough in numbers to control the affairs of each of those States, based upon the unnatural feeling of hostility to these

"Declaration of Causes which Impel the State of Texas to Secede from the Federal Union," Ernest Winkler, ed., *Journal of the Secession Convention of Texas* (Austin: Austin Printing Company, 1912), 61–65.

Southern States and their beneficent and patriarchal system of African slavery, proclaiming the debasing doctrine of the equality of all men, irrespective of race or color—a doctrine at war with nature, in opposition to the experience of mankind, and in violation of the plainest revelations of the Divine Law. They demand the abolition of negro slavery throughout the confederacy, the recognition of political equality between the white and the negro races, and avow their determination to press on their crusade against us, so long as a negro slave remains in these States.

For years past this abolition organization has been actively sowing the seeds of discord through the Union, and has rendered the federal congress the arena for spreading firebrands and hatred between the slave-holding and non-slave-holding States.

By consolidating their strength, they have placed the slave-holding States in a hopeless minority in the federal congress, and rendered representation of no avail in protecting Southern rights against their exactions and encroachments.

They have proclaimed, and at the ballot box sustained, the revolutionary doctrine that there is a "higher law" than the constitution and laws of our Federal Union, and virtually that they will disregard their oaths and trample upon our rights.

They have for years past encouraged and sustained lawless organizations to steal our slaves and prevent their recapture, and have repeatedly murdered Southern citizens while lawfully seeking their rendition.

They have invaded Southern soil and murdered unoffending citizens, and through the press their leading men and a fanatical pulpit have bestowed praise upon the actors and assassins in these crimes, while the governors of several of their States have refused to deliver parties implicated and indicted for participation in such offences, upon the legal demands of the States aggrieved.

They have, through the mails and hired emissaries, sent seditious pamphlets and papers among us to stir up servile insurrection and bring blood and carnage to our firesides

They have sent hired emissaries among us to burn our towns and distribute arms and poison to our slaves for the same purpose.

They have impoverished the slave-holding States by unequal and partial legislation, thereby enriching themselves by draining our substance.

They have refused to vote appropriations for protecting Texas against ruthless savages, for the sole reason that she is a slave-holding State.

And, finally, by the combined sectional vote of the seventeen non-slave-holding States, they have elected as president and vice-president of the whole confederacy two men whose chief claims to such high positions are their approval of these long continued wrongs, and their pledges to continue them to the final consummation of these schemes for the ruin of the slave-holding States.

In view of these and many other facts, it is meet that our own views should be distinctly proclaimed.

We hold as undeniable truths that the governments of the various States, and of the confederacy itself, were established exclusively by the white race, for themselves and their posterity; that the African race had no agency in their establishment; that they were rightfully held and regarded as an inferior and dependent race, and in that condition only could their existence in this country be rendered beneficial or tolerable.

That in this free government *all white men are equal and of right ought to be entitled to equal civil and political rights;* that the servitude of the African race, as existing in these States, is mutually beneficial to both bond and free, and is abundantly authorized and justified by the experience of mankind, and the revealed will of the Almighty Creator, as recognized by all Christian nations; while the destruction of the existing relations between the two races, as advocated by our sectional enemies, would bring inevitable calamities upon both and desolation upon the fifteen slave-holding States.

By the secession of six of the slave-holding States, and the certainty that others will speedily do likewise, Texas has no alternative but to remain in an isolated connection with the North, or unite her destinies with the South.

## 4. Sam Houston Opposes Secession, 1861

Fellow-Citizens: It was not my purpose or desire to address you today upon the great issues now confronting our common country, but old soldier comrades who fought with me at San Jacinto, and other dear friends, insist that I shall explain the reason why I refuse to take the oath of allegiance to the Confederate Government, and why I have been deposed from the Governorship of our beloved State. The earnest solicitations of my old soldier comrades outweigh my desire to remain silent until the whirlwind of passion and popular clamor have subsided and the voice of reason can be fairly heard.

I shall, therefore, speak my honest sentiments and convictions and I now submit to you the reasons why I could not take the oath of allegiance to the so-called Confederate Government, and thereby violate the oath of allegiance I took to the Federal Government when I entered upon the duties of the Chief Magistracy of Texas. It has always been the invariable rule of my life never to form an opinion or verdict upon any great public question until I have first carefully and impartially heard and considered all the evidence and facts upon both sides, and when I have thus formed my verdict, no fear of popular condemnation can induce me to modify or change such verdict. I have never permitted popular clamor, passion, prejudice nor selfish ambition to induce me to change an opinion or verdict which my conscience and judgment has once formed and tells me is right. My only desire is to be right, and for this reason I can not nor will not sacrifice what my conscience and judgment tells me is right. I love the plaudits of my fellow citizens, but will never sacrifice the principle of right and justice for public favor or commendation.

The Vox Populi is not always the voice of God, for when demagogues and selfish political leaders succeed in arousing public prejudice and stilling the voice of reason, then on every hand can be heard the popular cry of "Crucify him, crucify him." The Vox Populi then becomes the voice of the devil, and the hiss of mobs warns all patriots that peace and good government are in peril. I have heard the hiss of mobs upon the streets of Austin, and also heard the hiss of mobs upon the streets of Brenham, and friends have warned me that my life was in great peril if I expressed my honest sentiments and convictions.

"Speech at Brenham," March 31, 1861, Eugene Barker and Amelia Williams, eds., *The Writings of Sam Houston* (Austin: Jenkins, 1970), 8: 295–299.

But the hiss of the mob and the howls of their jackal leaders can not deter me nor compel me to take the oath of allegiance to a so-called Confederate Government. I protest against surrendering the Federal Constitution, its Government and its glorious flag to the Northern abolition leaders and to accept in its stead a so-called Confederate Government whose constitution contains the germs and seeds of decay which must and will lead to its speedy ruin and dismemberment if it can ever secure any real existence. Its seeds of ruin and decay are the principle of secession which permits any one or more of the Confederate States to secede from the parent Confederate Government and to establish separate governments. Can any well-informed man doubt that the time will soon come when several of the Confederate States will secede and establish separate governments? Why will such results follow in the event the Confederate Government is established? Because in all the Confederate States there are ambitious secession leaders who will be aspirants for the Presidency of the Confederacy and to exercise controlling influence in its government and in all cases where their ambitions are frustrated these leaders will cause their respective States to secede and form separate governments wherein they may be able to realize their selfish political hopes. Within ten years we would have ten or more separate Confederate Governments, which would in time fall an easy prey to foreign Governments. The increase of secession leaders will be rapid and large in all the Confederate States and their contests against each other for political leadership will lead to discord, promoting continual conspiracies and revolutions, which will produce many Count Julians, or traitors, who will call to their aid foreign Governments to despoil the people who refuse to help them gratify their selfish ambitions.

Never will I consent to give up our Federal Constitution and our union of States for a Confederate constitution and government whose foundation principles of secession must and will prevent its successful establishment; or if it should triumph, its triumph would be only temporary and its short-lived existence end in revolution and utter ruin.

The Federal Constitution, the Federal Government and its starry flag are glorious heritages bequeathed to the South and all sections of our common country by the valor and patriotism of Washington, and all the brave revolutionary soldiers, who fought for and won American independence. Our galaxy of Southern Presidents—Washington, Jefferson, Monroe, Jackson, Taylor, Tyler, and Polk cemented the bonds of union between all the States which can never be broken. Washington declared for an indivisible union and Jackson made the secession of South Carolina and of other States impossible. Jefferson by the Louisiana purchase added a vast empire of country to our union, and Polk followed his example by further extending our Union to embrace Texas, New Mexico, Arizona, Colorado, and California. Monroe established the Monroe Doctrine which for all time preserves and safeguards the Governments of the Western Hemisphere against foreign conquest. All our Northern Presidents have been equally patriotic and just to the South. Not a single Southern right has been violated by any President or by any Federal Administration. President Lincoln has been elected, because the secession Democratic leaders divided the Democratic party and caused the nomination of two separate Presidential Democratic tickets and nominees.

Both branches of Congress are Democratic; therefore it will be impossible for President Lincoln's administration to enact or enforce any laws or measures that can injure Southern rights. But grant for the sake of the argument that the time may come when both branches of Congress are Republican and laws are enacted and enforced which will injure or destroy Southern rights what shall we then do? I answer that sufficient unto the day is the evil thereof, nor would there be the least danger of the Republican party ever controlling both branches of Congress and all branches of the Federal Government if the secession leaders would permit the Democratic party to remain a solid indivisible party.

But if the day should ever come when Southern rights are ruthlessly violated or injured by the Republican party, we of the South will then fight for our rights under the Stars and Stripes and with the Federal Constitution in one hand and the sword in the other we shall march on to victory.

I believe a large majority of our Southern people are opposed to secession, and if the secession leaders would permit our people to take ample time to consider secession and then hold fair elections the secession movement would be defeated by an overwhelming majority. But the secession leaders declare that secession has already been peaceably accomplished and the Confederate Government independence and sovereignty will soon be acknowledged by all foreign governments. They tell us that the Confederate Government will thus be permanently established without bloodshed. They might with equal truth declare that the fountains of the great deep blue seas can be broken up without disturbing their surface waters, as to tell us that the best Government that ever existed for men can be broken up without bloodshed.

The secession leaders also tell us if war should come that European Nations will speedily come to our relief, and aid us to win our independence because cotton is King and European commerce and civilization can not long exist without cotton, therefore they must help us maintain and perpetuate our Confederate Government. Gentlemen who use such false and misleading statements forget or else are ignorant of the facts that commerce and civilization existed a long period of time before cotton was generally known and used.

They also forget or else are ignorant of the fact that the best sentiment of Europe is opposed to our systems of negro slavery. They also tell us if war comes that the superior courage of our people with their experience of the use of firearms, will enable us to triumph in battle over ten times our number of Northern forces. Never was a more false or absurd statement ever made by designing demagogues. I declare that Civil War is inevitable and is near at hand. When it comes the descendants of the heroes of Lexington and Bunker Hill will be found equal in patriotism, courage and heroic endurance with descendants of the heroes of Cowpens and Yorktown. For this reason I predict that the civil war which is now near at hand will be stubborn and of long duration. We are sadly divided among ourselves, while the North and West are united. Not only will we have to contend against a united and harmonious North, but we will also have to battle against tens of thousands of our own people, who will never desert the Stars and Stripes nor surrender the union of states for a Southern Confederacy of states, whose principles of secession must inevitably lead to discord, conspiracy and revolution, and at last anarchy and utter ruin. When the tug of war comes, it will indeed be the Greek meeting Greek. Then, oh my fellow countrymen, the fearful conflict will fill our fair land with untold suffering, misfortune and disaster. The soil of our beloved South will drink deep the precious blood of our sons and brethren. In earnest prayer to our Heavenly Father, I have daily petitioned him to cast out from my mind the dark foreboding of the coming conflict. My prayers have caused the light of reason to cast the baleful shadows of the coming events before me. I cannot, nor will I close my eyes against the light and voice of reason. The die has been cast by your secession leaders, whom you have permitted to sow and broadcast the seeds of secession, and you must ere long reap the fearful harvest of conspiracy and revolution.

## 5. Dr. Thomas Barrett Describes the Gainesville Lynching, 1862

The arresting continued for about thirteen days and nights. How many were arrested, I have no means of knowing, having kept no account at the time, but I suppose there was not less than one hundred and fifty, and perhaps more.

There was a good many arrested who had connection with the organization.

There were squads of men in every part of the country, and they arrested every man that they suspicioned, and in this way a good many innocent men were arrested.

When I arrived near town, there were crowds in sight in every direction, armed, pressing forward prisoners under guard. The deepest and most intense excitement that I ever saw prevailed. Reason had left its throne. The mind of almost every man I saw seemd to be unhinged, and wild excitement reigned supreme. When I arrived on the square, there were perhaps three or four hundred armed men in town and in sight.

These with the unarmed, constituted a crowd whose words and actions seemed to indicate an upheaving of the most dangerous character, because it was known that the members of that clan were sworn to go to the assistance of any member who was arrested. . . .

Soon after I arrived on the square I heard hanging spoken of. I found the tree had been selected, that same old historic elm, with its long and bending limbs, which was afterwards used for that purpose.

The crowd seemed to be settling down on beginning to hang.

I opposed it with all the power within me. Others also opposed it, and about the time we were in the heat of contention, the church bell rang for a meeting of the crowd for consultation. The ringing of this bell put an end to all plans, in order to see what would be the result of that meeting. This was a military move, sanctioned by soldiers and citizens.

The meeting was called to order and a chairman appointed. A motion was made and carried for the chair to appoint five men to select a jury to decide upon the course to be pursued with these men. This committee selected twelve men, and my name was reported as one of them. My first thought was, not to serve as one of them, when I took the situation under consideration; I at once saw that unless there was considerable influence in that jury against extreme violence, there was great danger of awful work, so I consented to serve, intending to oppose all extreme violence, which I did. And here I will state the excitement was so great that every man found it necessary to exercise much caution in reference to what he said or did. This condition of things had its influence with me in deciding this question.

Thomas Barrett, *The Great Hanging at Gainesville* (Austin: Texas State Historical Association, 1961), 7–9, 13–14, 16–18, 20–21.

The jury was instructed to go into a fair examination and bring accused and witnesses face to face and decide, and they would abide by their decision.

The meeting adjourned, and the jury met and organized, and night came on. The militia and others had been coming in all day, and after dark they continued to come.

Squads of men were sent to different parts of the county to ascertain what was going on, for an attack was expected, which would cause desperate fighting. A double line of sentinels were put around the town. . . .

About fifteen or twenty men had gone about half a mile from the square to stay all night; I was one of the men. We were ordered to the square. When we got there I walked around and to see how the thing was going on. The soldiers were in line of battle and some in the houses making cartridges, others moving to and fro as is always the case in times of great excitement, everyone expecting a desperate fight before morning, for the clan was supposed to be stronger than they were. . . .

After seeing how everything was going on, and not having a gun and not having any desire to be in the fight, I went into a friend's house and asked the lady for a pillow and turning a chair down on the carpet slept til morning. There was no attack, consequently no fighting. . . .

While the multitude did not at this time know the full intention of the clan, enough was known to give the idea that if the clan carried out its designs, the country would be thrown into a bloody war, with neighbor against neighbor, and in some cases the brother against brother, and in some cases the father against the son and the son against the father, and a man's foes would be of his own household.

The second day dawned and no attack being made, the jury met. . . .

The jury met and passed an order that a majority should rule. I opposed this, and wanted it unanimous, or at any rate, two-thirds, but the majority rule was adopted. As far as could be done the leaders were tried first. . . .

The excitement had increased. It was terrible with the crowd outside, and no less so in the jury-room. One man, known to be a leader, was brought in and proven to be guilty. . . . This man was condemned and hung; another was brought and was disposed of the same way, and this was continued till seven were doomed to die likewise. A number of others and I were opposing it with all our powers; I did all the speaking (nearly) but had as well tried to build a dam across Red River in a time of high water with straw, as to resist and control the excitement in the jury-room, and the crowd of soldiers on duty pushed on by influential men. There were eight hundred or a thousand armed men in town by the time the jury condemned seven men.

The crowd were threatening to take the prisoners out and kill all of them. There was a trial made to have me taken off of the jury, because I took the lead in opposing these violent measures. We who opposed hanging insisted to turn the men over to the civil or military authorities instead of hanging, and those not very deep in the thing, to set them at liberty.

The eighth man was tried; he was only slightly in it, but the excitement was so great that he was condemned as readily as the others.

When this was done I concluded that I would stand it no longer; I was determined that I would have a change or leave the jury-room. I rose to my feet and addressed the jury as near as I can recollect as follows: Gentlemen: You are as reckless of human life as though it was a matter of little importance. I am not acquainted with this man, I never saw him till I saw him in the jury-room, consequently my course is not influenced by any particular feelings of partiality. But if you intend to hang all who are no further in this thing than this man is, it is not necessary to do more than bring a man before you and prove him to be slightly connected with this organization and hang him, so you had better pass sentence of death on every man in the prison, for if you continue to carry out the course you have pursued since you came into this jury-room, you will hang all, so you had better dispatch them at once and adjourn. . . .

As soon as I was seated, one of the jurors who had stood shoulder to shoulder with me in opposing the hanging of these men, rose to his feet, took up his hat, and said, he was no longer a member of the jury, and said good bye, and started to the head of the stairs, (we were in an upper room). At this instant two men came rushing to me, one of them caught me by both arms and gave me one of those honest and friendly shakes, which is an indication of deep interest. When this took place the man who had bid the jury good bye, halted. The man who had me by the arms said, for God sake don't break this jury. I asked him why. He said if you break this jury, every man in that prison will be killed before the setting of the sun. The other man who came with him sanctioned what he said. He went on to state that the only chance to save these men, was for the jury to save them, and said he, you can save some. . . .

I perhaps did as much thinking and planning in a few seconds as I ever did. I knew that if a general slaughter was gone into, unless I made good use of my legs I would go up with the rest, as my course in opposing this wholesale hanging had given great offence. The excitement in the jury-room was of that still and deep character which some times takes place every one waiting in silence to see what would be done.

I said to the two men that approached me: Gentlemen, I yield to your judgment, I will try and arrange this thing.

I then went to the man who had told the jury good bye, and told him what these men had told me, and after a short consultation, we agreed to go back and if the jury would adopt the two-thirds rule, we would act with them, but unless the two-thirds was adopted we would leave. The jury readily adopted the two-thirds rule.

We then gave the man who had been condemned to hang, the benefit of the two-third rule and reversed the sentence of death, by deciding to turn him over to the military authority. . . .

Seven had been hung. When we commenced under the two-thirds rule, we had considerable contention till it was found that this rule would prevent hanging. After that was ascertained we got along quietly and speedily till we got through with all the prisoners on hand, and turned some of them over to the military authorities, the rest being set at liberty.

This brought Saturday evening, and the soldiers were beginning to leave. As the excitement had greatly moderated in the jury-room, we thought it was moderating the same outside, and in order to give it time to moderate still more, we agreed to adjourn for a week and come together the next Saturday and let our decision be known, and I was to make a speech to the people to influence them to abide by our decision, for we were fearful of a mob. Our decision was to be kept secret till the next Saturday. Secrecy was enjoined on all, and we were ready to adjourn.

Some person betrayed us, and told the crowd outside of our decision, and a mob rose and sent two men into the jury-room with word that if we did not give up twenty more to be hung, they would kill every man in the prison.

When this demand came, one of the jurors who acted with me, asked what will you do now? I said the Lord only knows what I ought to do; I have risked my life for six or eight days, and gone as far as I dared to go to prevent hanging. I could contend in the jury-room as I pleased, but cannot war against a regiment of men. I oppose it, but if they take them, they will have to do so, I am not going to say a word.

When I failed to oppose the taking of the men, there was no objection.

I thought when the military failed to protect us and suffered a mob to rise and take these men and hang them, contrary to the decision of the jury, I say, when I thought all this over, I concluded that it was in vain for me to raise my voice against it, so I remained silent. I knew my doom if wholesale killing commenced.

One of these men called for a list of the names of the prisoners. Our clerk handed it to him, and he went over it; took such men as he chose and wrote their names down, then handed the list back to the clerk, and called over the names he had and our clerk marked them out. He then counted his names and he had fourteen. He said as he rose from his seat: I reckon this will satisfy them.

These two men went into the prison, called these fourteen men out, put them in a separate room, and notified them that they must hang next day, which was Sunday.

As soon as these men were gone, I said to the jury: Delay, breeds danger if we undertake to send these men to the headquarters of the military they will not get there, they will be killed. I propose that we meet next Saturday to set all the remaining prisoners at liberty. I told them I did not believe that they would be molested, as we had set a good many at liberty, and none of them had been molested.

To this they readily agreed, and passed an order to that effect. I was to make a speech to influence the people to abide by our decision. The jury then adjourned, to meet the next Saturday morning.

I went home that evening, having been absent twelve days and nights. When I arrived at home my wife met me at the gate and asked the news. I attempted to tell her, but my feelings overcame me so, that I choked up and commenced crying. I said I would tell her after I became quiet. And here I will say that no tongue can tell or pen detail what I suffered during those twelve days and nights just closed; not that I had any sympathy for the plans and designs of the organization, for I abhorred and detested their designs. But I considered that it was war times, and as the organization was broken up, all that was necessary was to send them to the military, as the jury at Sherman did, and the county would be relieved. . . .

During this week of adjournment, I went to town every day, and the excitement was moderating, and everything bidding fair for a favorable condition on the next Saturday, the day the jury was to meet.

About the middle of the week, when I got into town I was met with the startling news that a man by the name of Dickson, who was a citizen of Gainesville, had been killed in the brakes of Red River by a squad of men belonging to that organization. This revived the excitement to a flame. I walked in amongst the soldiers; I could hear threats of clearing up the prison that night.

Several, including myself, commenced pursuading them not to do that, for there were men in the prison that were only slightly in this thing, and we continued to pursuade all day, but seemingly to little effect. Late in the evening the talk was that they would clear the prison that night.

I went home that evening with a gloomy feeling, and during the night when I awoke, I listened for the report of guns, but heard none. I was up next morning very early, and went to town, and learned that the prisoners had not been interrupted, but heard the horrible news that Col. Young had been killed by that clan.

The excitement was fearful. Men were swearing they would kill every man in the prison that night. I availed myself of every opportunity that presented itself to pursuade them not to murder the prisoners, but I was compelled to be very humble, in order to effect anything, and finally came down to hard begging.

Late that evening I went home, feeling the prisoners would be murdered that night, and I expected any minute to hear the horrifying report of the death warning guns, but that awful sound failed to reach my ears. When I arrived in town next morning, learned to my great satisfaction, that the prisoners had not been molested.

Saturday morning came, the day for the jury to meet, and when the roll was called, two of the jurors who had opposed the hanging were absent, and their places filled with men who failed to act on the moderate side.

The first thing the jury did, was to reconsider the decision of the jury to set these men at liberty when they met this morning.

This decision was rejected, which placed the prisoners on trial the same as though they had not been tried.

The excitement had reached the jury-room. I and a few others saw the situation at once. The testimony against the men on which they had been tried was all written down, consequently there was nothing to be done but read it, and take the vote. One was put on trial the vote taken and he condemned to hang; a second was disposed of in the same manner. I made a trial to stop the course of things, but I saw that it was useless to make any attempt to save the men by a vote. I then proposed a compromise: I proposed to allow them to select six of the worst ones and hang them, and set the rest at liberty. I saw they were going to hang a good many more than that, and I was striving to save as many as possible, but the jury rejected my proposition. When they rejected it, hope fled, and I took my seat to watch the course of events. I sat sad and silent till six were condemned and not one set at liberty, for it was hang or set at liberty.

The seventh one was put on trial, his was quite a moderate case, and some defended him. While they were talking on his case, they would look at me as though they wanted to say: help us. I thought now is the time to effect something.

I rose to my feet and addressed the jury about in these words: Gentlemen, I have remained silent, and suffered you to take your own course without interruption, but in this moderate case, I would with due respect, ask the question, if it would not be better to set these moderate cases at liberty, and if you must have blood, take the worst cases? We took the vote and set the man at liberty.

I saw that a reaction, to some extent, was taking place in the minds of some of the jury, and right here the day's fight commenced.

I did all I could to save the men, and those with whom I voted came up nobly to the work, and our side gained regularly. After we commenced setting some at liberty, we succeeded in saving about two-thirds.

This was the hardest day's work I ever did, or ever saw done. A portion of the men with whom I acted, contended manfully against all hanging, while others sometimes voted against the men.

This condition of things caused the fight to be fierce, each party striving to get those who sometimes voted for the men, who held the balance of power, and the party that got them, carried their point.

The present condition of things was well calculated to cause the contention to be of the fiercest character. Everything was done and said by each party that it was thought would cause them to succeed. As for myself, I know that I never exerted myself to the same extent as I did that day.

In speaking against the hanging, I said everything I could think of, that I thought would prevent hanging.

I can give substantially any speeches that day. I told the jury what I had often said to them before, that they were laboring under an excitement which had un-hinged their minds. You think you are doing right, but said I, when the war closes and the excitement passes away, and you calmly look back on the course you are now pursuing, for you are bound to come to these sober hours of reflection, you will be astonished that you were so excited as to think that you were doing right. When you come to this, you will then say Barrett was right. All of those jurors that I talked with afterwards came to this sober conclusion. . . .

There were nineteen men condemned to be hung; the balance, about fifty or sixty, were set at liberty.

These nineteen men were hung in consequence of the killing of Dickson and Young. If they had not been killed, all of these men would have been set at liberty that Saturday morning.

The prisoners condemned, were notified that they were to hang next day. . . .

The hanging did not commence very early, and when the last one was hung, the sun was low.

When I started home, my nearest way was to go so as to pass within twenty feet of the tree on which the men were hung, but I took the next street north, to keep from seeing any man hanging.

This day closed this thing, which had caused such an upheaving and excitement for the last twenty or twenty-five days.

There were forty hung, and two who broke from the guard were shot and killed, making forty-two deaths.

## 6. Rebecca Ann Adams Writes to Her Husband About Life on the Home Front, 1863

December 7th, 1863

My Dear Husband,

I received a long letter from you Saturday morning written from Waldeck. I know your visit there this time would have been pleasant if you had only been well enough to enjoy it. I was in hopes from what you wrote in your last letter about your good health that you would not be troubled with chills again. You can cure others, why not cure yourself. I hope you may succeed in breaking them up before you leave that part of the country. How fortunate that you are camped so near Pa's. I wish very much that you could remain there at least during the winter months. How pleasant it would be if I and the children were there to enjoy your many visits

Jo Ella Powell Exley, ed., *Texas Tears and Texas Sunshine, Voices of Frontier Women* (College Station: Texas A&M University Press, 1990), 132–136.

to that place but I know it is best for us to remain at home and try to feel submissive to all privations caused by this cruel war. I think living at this place away from re-lations and friends has been a kind school for me. It has taught me to submit more willingly to inconveniences and privations of all kinds. A lesson which you know I very much needed. I feel that I am entirely a changed being in that respect. My daily prayer now is that you may be protected during this war and spared to return to your family. It is true I would like above all things to have you here at home with us, but I know it is a duty you owe your country. I submit.

You complain of not receiving letters from home. I acknowledge that I have not written as often as I should, but at the time you mentioned I was in bed suffer-ing with severe pain in my face and head. Julia wrote to you that week. This is my fifth letter, but I know your great anxiety to hear from home often. I will try and do better in the future. . . .

I frequently caution the negroes about saving the corn and not wasting it. They have used about half a crib of corn. I sold thirteen bushels of corn, two dollars and a half per bushel. I have sold nothing else since you left home. George hauled ninety-nine loads of corn, putting nine in the government pen. They had twenty sacks of fodder; used all of one sack. Jack is using a good deal of corn to fatten the hogs in the pen, he put them up last week. You said nothing about fattening the hogs on the corn. Not knowing what you intended, I have waited this long expecting you would write. I walked down to see them a few days after he put them up, they are looking very well. I will have some killed the next change in weather. Jack has fifty-three in the pen, says he had three more to put in, leaving just seventy-five year and half old hogs for another year. I write you just as he tells me. Col. Moreland has bought a great many hogs expects to bacon them up for sale. He bought six pair of cards, will pay for them in bacon. I am needing some wool cards, but there is none in the coun-try. The cotton cards that I have been using for wool are nearly ruined. The teeth are pulled nearly straight. The negro women are needing yarn sacks this winter. I have the wood but I don't want to ruin another pair of cotton cards. Mr. Caldwell has returned I hear, he has cards for sale with a good many other goods. Mrs. Garrett went in to see them, she says he has the highest price for everything. It is generally believed that he and Miss Sarah Moreland will marry soon. He brought a great many goods for that family. Amelia was here yesterday morning. It has been some time since Mary had done any weaving, she has a severe bone felon on her finger, but I think it now is getting well. Grayson cut it open twice. I have had Souvenia spinning for some time. Jane cooks in her place four days in the week, she spins faster than any of the others. George thinks he will get through sowing the grain tomorrow or the next day. Fed was badly hurt by one of the oxen. I thought one time it would kill him, but we nursed him well and he finally got over it. Old Black died last week. She was very poor, I think she died with old age. You say you will leave the employment of Mrs. Garrett entirely to me. I must say that I don't feel that I am a competent judge of such a matter, the proper education of our children is very im-portant. It is true I have been with her and ought to know what she is competent to teach. I think she is a good teacher for children beginning. The other children have learned but little, Julia almost nothing. But one thing I do know they have learned no wicked sayings. I think it has been of great service to David to be entirely with his sisters. Julia's great anxiety to go to college has kept her from learning what she might have learned. I don't think Mrs. Garrett can teach her anything but Smith's Grammer. Mrs.Garrett is a *very plain* not neat but I think a well meaning woman. She would like to remain here if she could go to town every Saturday. If I don't hear from *you* before she closes her school I shall employ her another term but I had rather you would decide what is best to be done. I have been very busy lately knitting you some gloves, the thread was spun of mule eared rabbit furs with a little wool. I think the gloves will be warm, pleasant feeling to the skin. David and Old Allen caught the rabbits. Are you wearing your old gloves, or have you bought new ones? Are you or Robert needing anything in the way of clothing? You must let me know in time so I can have them ready. Jennie had another chill yesterday, her skin is yellow, I think her body is swollen. She has been calling for you at night in her sleep. Little Fannie has not looked well since Pa was here.

The children all send love to PaPa and Buddie. Mrs. G. sends respect. Write as often as you can and I hope you will not be sent from that section of the country. Your wife with much love,

R.A.

## ★ E S S A Y S

In the first essay, Randolph Campbell, an authority on Texas slavery at the University of North Texas, provides an overview of the state's "peculiar institution." The slave labor system that emerged in Texas, Campbell argues, differed little from the institution that existed throughout the Lower South. Slaveholders were a privileged minority, enjoying a disproportionate share of economic and political power in the state.

In the second essay, Texas A&M University professor Walter Buenger examines the reasons that prompted Texans to secede from the union. Buenger emphasizes the complex and paradoxical nature of the secessionist movement, in which Texans were torn by conflicting allegiances to their region and the nation. Buenger reminds us that for many Texans, as for many southerners, the decision to secede was not easy nor simple. In the final analysis, however, the state's connections with the Lower South were of paramount importance in the formation of the state's identity, an identity which, most Texans had decided by 1861, was incompatible with Unionism. Thus, both authors view the state's southern heritage as a uniquely formative one.

## An Empire for Slavery

### RANDOLPH B. CAMPBELL

Negro slavery became important in Texas with the arrival of Anglo-American colonists during the 1820s. Most of these settlers came from the Old South and believed that Texas' fertile lands could best be populated and brought into cultivation with the aid of an institution that they knew well. Mexican governments, both federal and state, resisted the development of slavery in Texas and probably retarded its growth during the colonial period. Official opposition was limited and vacillating, however, in the face of insistence by Anglo settlers, led by Stephen F. Austin, that slavery was an economic necessity in Texas. Mexican leaders made concessions that allowed the institution to gain a significant, albeit not completely secure, foothold in the province by 1835.

Slavery constituted one underlying factor in the general clash of Anglo-American and Hispanic cultural traditions that culminated in the Texas Revolution during 1835–36. Had Mexico won the war, slavery almost certainly would have been abolished. As it was, the conflict seriously disturbed slavery in Texas and allowed some bondsmen to escape. Sam Houston's army won the Battle of San Jacinto, however, and Texans succeeded in establishing their new republic with a constitution that guaranteed slavery. The revolution did not begin primarily as a movement to protect the Peculiar Institution, but certainly one major result was, in the words of Justice Abner S. Lipscomb of the Texas Supreme Court, the removal of "all doubt and uneasiness among the citizens of Texas in regard to the tenure by which they held dominion over their slaves."

Slavery expanded rapidly, both numerically and geographically, through the republic and statehood periods from 1836 to 1861. As bondsmen poured into Texas, arriving primarily with immigrant owners, their total population increased from approximately five thousand in 1836 to more than thirty thousand in 1846, when the republic became a state. By 1861, when Texas seceded and joined the Confederacy, the slave population, which had grown more rapidly than the free, was approaching two hundred thousand. Bondsmen lived in largest numbers along Texas' major rivers—the Red in the northeast, the Sabine and Trinity in the east, and the Brazos and Colorado in the south-central region down to the Gulf Coast. By 1860, however, blacks constituted at least 25 percent of the population in all settled portions of the state, except the north-central area centering on Dallas and the southwestern plains extending from the San Antonio River to the Rio Grande.

Perhaps slavery faced, as Charles Ramsdell argued, a barrier to expansion once it reached the semiarid plains of western Texas and the areas within easy reach of the Mexican border, but those limits were not reached by 1861. Slavery was still growing everywhere in the state, and the blackland prairie/Grand Prairie region of north-central Texas offered a vast expanse of suitable acreage relatively untouched by slaveholders and their bondsmen. To open that area, only transportation was needed, and the railroad would have provided that. Texas constituted a virtual empire for slavery, and on the eve of secession Texans talked with buoyant optimism of the millions of bondsmen who would build the state's future.

Slavery existed in antebellum Texas primarily as an economic institution. Those who purchased bondsmen to supply labor on farms and plantations generally found their investments profitable. Slaves produced larger and larger cotton crops, reproduced themselves, and appreciated in value through the late antebellum years. They also produced enough corn and other food crops to provide self-sufficiency in the state's agricultural economy. Finally, slavery was very flexible and highly functional, as witnessed, for example, by the hire system, so that it was economically advantageous in ways that did not appear on a profit-and-loss balance sheet. The institution may have contributed to Texas' relative backwardness in commercialization and industrialization, but there were no important demands that it be ended in order to promote diversification. Slavery flourished in Texas throughout the late antebellum period and was never in danger of failing from its own economic weakness.

Between 1836 and 1861, Texas legislators and judges developed a slave code for the Lone Star state based largely on practices elsewhere in the Old South. The law assured slaveowners of their right to own, buy, and sell bondsmen while protecting their property against criminal interference by others. It regulated the conduct of slaves and prescribed rules for the capture and return of runaways. The legal status accorded free blacks made it clear that, no matter how few, they were an unwelcome minority who would frequently be equated with slaves. Lawmakers and judges recognized that slaves were human and therefore a very special form of property. The weight of the law, however, usually rested with protection of the masters' property rights rather than concern for the slaves' humanity.

Most Texas slaves lived on farms and plantations and worked long hours clearing land, cultivating crops, and taking care of innumerable chores. Many had Saturday afternoons free from labor, but only Sundays, July 4, and Christmas week were regarded virtually without exception as days off. A minority of bondsmen, perhaps 10 to 20 percent of the total, worked as skilled craftsmen or house servants or lived in Texas' towns and few fledgling cities. Compared to agricultural workers, these slaves were less exposed to the elements and performed labor that was less burdensome physically. Some, especially the house servants, may have had longer hours, but few, it seems, wanted to change places with field workers. Slaves frequently were given positions of considerable responsibility as, for example, "drivers" and teamsters. Some had the opportunity, although the practice was illegal for most of the antebellum period, to hire their own time and seek profitable employment for themselves. Many earned at least a little money of their own, especially by working small patches of cotton and food crops.

The state of Texas had constitutional and statutory provisions concerning the material conditions of slaves' lives and the physical treatment accorded them by their masters. In all but the most extreme cases, however, these matters were left, in the words of Justice James H. Bell of the Texas Supreme Court, "to the master's judgment, discretion, and humanity." Texas bondsmen generally had food adequate to provide the energy for work and the nutrition, by the standards of that era, for health. Their housing was usually uncomfortable at best and inadequate for winter weather. Clothing and shoes were made of cheap, rough materials, and slaves found them a source of considerable discomfort. When bondsmen suffered, as they often did, from diseases and accidents, masters generally provided doctors' care. Slaves were, after all, a valuable form of property. Unfortunately, medical science in mid-nineteenth-century Texas could not deal effectively with many of the diseases and injuries that afflicted slaves. Masters, in exercising their right to obedience and submission from their bondsmen, inflicted a variety of punishments, particularly whippings. Any whipping was a fearsome prospect, and all slaves lived with the knowledge that it could happen to them, largely at the whim of their master. At times, punishments became cruel treatment and even murder, but Texas courts were extremely reluctant to interfere with the master-slave relationship. Regardless of the law, slaves' material conditions and physical treatment depended largely upon their individual masters.

Texas slaves endured the psychological pressures of bondage with the aid of strength that came from their families, their religion, and their music. The great majority of bondsmen experienced family ties, and in spite of constant threats and numerous disruptions, depended on those relationships for identity, support, and a sense of worth. Families appear to have been the focal point for survival. Thousands of Texas slaves drew strength too from religion. They listened to white ministers emphasize the virtues of loyal and honest servants, but they heard the underlying message, often brought to them by black preachers, of salvation for all and perhaps even deliverance. Music provided psychological strength also because it served as a means of expression, communication, and protest.

Behavior patterns among Texas slaves varied widely. At one extreme was the loyal servant who apparently loved and identified with his master; at the other was the rebel who resisted bondage at every opportunity, especially by running away. Most common, however, were the bondsmen who, in the words of one woman, did "the best we could." Neither loyal servants nor rebels, they recognized the limitations of their situation and sought to endure on the best terms possible. Such slaves expected certain types of treatment and became rebellious if they did not receive it. Regardless of their behavioral adjustments, the vast majority of blacks wanted freedom, and everyone knew it. In short, the enslaved blacks were simply human. They employed their intelligence and their moral and spiritual resources to survive in an attempt to influence the world in which they found themselves. Some were capable and strong; others were incapable and weak. In any case, the enslaved blacks were not an inherently inferior part of the human race, and slavery was no school for civilization.

A minority of Texans owned slaves, and only a handful achieved elite status as planters. Slaveholders generally found the institution to be a source of tension in their lives. Slaves proved so difficult to manage that owners, while they enjoyed picturing themselves as benevolent paternalists, spent a good deal more time discussing means of punishing effectively. Masters did not labor, it seems, under a great burden of guilt, but constant criticism from outside the South also created tension. Texas slaveholders thus found the institution troublesome and unsettling, but, at the same time, it benefited them to the extent that they would attempt a revolution to keep it.

Slaveholders dominated economic, political, and social life in antebellum Texas. They produced 90 percent of the state's cotton, dominated officeholding at all levels of government, and by virtue of their wealth occupied the top rungs of the social ladder. Not surprisingly under these circumstances, most articulate Texans such as newspaper editors and ministers defended slavery with every imaginable argument, and the vast majority of the state's people either supported or quietly acquiesced in the institution. A few German immigrants found it unworthy of a democratic, liberal nation, but most had no serious objections.

In spite of the proslavery consensus that had no significant opposition anywhere in the state, antebellum Texans often demonstrated the fear and intolerance typical of a society under siege. They struck hard at anyone suspected of preaching abolitionism or fomenting insurrection and were only slightly less tolerant of individuals or groups who did not support the system enthusiastically. As the Galveston *Weekly News* expressed it, "Those who are not for us, must be against us." The potential for terror inherent in this attitude was realized most fully during the summer of 1860, when a series of disastrous fires in north-central counties led to a widespread panic called the "Texas Troubles." Vigilante action to deal with the supposed abolitionist-inspired insurrection plot signaled by the fires claimed an undetermined number of victims, white as well as black. Within a year, "the voice of reason," as Governor Sam Houston termed it, was stilled entirely as Texas seceded and joined the Confederate States of America. The decision for secession involved a variety of considerations for Texans depending on their backgrounds and their circumstances in the Lone Star state, but the fundamental reason for having to decide at all was absolutely clear—it was Negro slavery.

During the Civil War, slavery remained less disturbed in Texas than in other areas of the Confederacy because Federal troops did not invade the state's interior. The most significant disruptions resulted from the impressment of bondsmen to serve Confederate authorities in building fortifications and, to a lesser extent, from the arrival of thousands of "refugeed" slaves fleeing Federal invaders in other states. Most slaves were aware of the war and its implications for their future freedom. They hoped for a Union victory but were in no position to contribute to it or to hinder the Confederate military effort. When the day of jubilee, June 19, 1865, finally came with the arrival of General Gordon Granger at Galveston and the reading of the Emancipation Proclamation, most Texas slaves celebrated their freedom as the answer to a lifelong prayer.

Slavery in Texas did not differ in any fundamental way from the institution as it existed elsewhere in the United States. Claims that somehow Negro bondage was "milder" or "worse" in the Lone Star state are morally pointless and historically inaccurate. Material conditions and physical treatment had nothing to do with making slavery right or wrong. Even if it could be demonstrated convincingly, for example, that Texas slaves had a better diet, worked fewer hours in a milder climate, and were whipped less often than bondsmen elsewhere, the moral nature of a system that held humans as property would remain the same. It was still wrong.

On a day-to-day basis, of course, material conditions and physical treatment were of great importance to Texas slaves themselves. Studies of the institution in other states, however, provide no basis for claiming that it was generally "milder" or "worse" in the Lone Star state. Bondsmen in older southern states were subject to essentially the same laws and, except in very special areas, lived under relatively similar circumstances in terms of work, material conditions, discipline and punishment, formation and preservation of families, religion, and so on. This should be expected. After all, the immigrants who brought slavery to Texas learned its ways in the Old South. They were not likely to change significantly once they reached a new home unless the area was dramatically different from any previously experienced. Granted that Texas constituted a frontier region during the antebellum period, those portions of the state having large numbers of slaves by the 1840s and 1850s were not so different in terms of climate and topography or so wild and unsettled as to change common patterns of labor and management. Slavery in Texas was simply American Negro slavery; nothing about the Lone Star state led or forced slaveholders there to accord their bondsmen appreciably different treatment than the variations common from master to master across the South.

Far from being unimportant, slavery played a vital role in shaping antebellum Texas and determining its future. The state could not have grown as it did without the labor of its slave population. Secession and participation in the tragedy of civil war resulted primarily from the desire to preserve an institution that was flourishing and had seemingly unlimited potential in 1861.

# The Roots of Texas Secession

### WALTER L. BUENGER

Secession remains a mystifying puzzle, a puzzle whose solution in 1861 was a bloody civil war and a puzzle whose solution in our time still defies rational explanation. From the end of the American Revolution until the start of the Civil War, the United States survived a series of intensely bitter internal disputes. Yet within the span of a few months in the winter of 1860–1861 the nation split apart, and a civil war soon began that resulted in over one million casualties. In Texas, secession seemed all the more improbable. Texans had continually asked to become part of the Union from 1836 to 1845. Their precarious position on the southwestern frontier reminded them daily of the value of belonging to a large and powerful nation. Prosperity seemed to preclude a political upheaval in 1860. The burgeoning trade in cotton, hides, and sugar flowing out of the commercial centers of Texas gave promise of making it one of the richest states in the Union. Slavery, while a major part of the social and economic life in some regions of Texas, was almost absent in other regions, and, except for Tennessee and Arkansas, Texas slaves made up the smallest percentage of the total population of any state in the Confederacy. Reflecting its position on the border of the South, politics in Texas on the eve of secession was dominated not by militant secessionists or unionists but by more moderate folk, who wanted to preserve the Union and the status quo if the costs of such action were not too high. At no time before 1860 did these moderates, who comprised a clear majority of the electorate, more persistently and urgently away from their comfortable middle ground. Nonetheless, before the firing on Fort Sumter changed the political question to either defending one's home or defecting to the enemy in defense of principle, Texans voted to secede by a three-to-one margin. . . .

Secession in Texas was part of the central conflict of the nineteenth century, a conflict between forces that encouraged the splintering of the United States into smaller social, political, and economic units and forces that bound the nation more tightly together. Secession, however, was not simply the triumph of localism over nationalism. Nor did it reflect some Hegelian dialectic in which the thesis of localism and the antitheses of nationalism were resolved in the synthesis of secession. Localism and nationalism were the reflex of each other. Factors that nourished localism could also stimulate nationalism. Moreover, a factor that encouraged localism or nationalism could often strengthen both a commitment to the Union and a belief in the necessity of secession. Slavery, for example, was the most prominent feature separating the South from the rest of the nation. Yet its

Walter L. Buenger, "Texas and the Riddle of Secession," *Southwestern Historical Quarterly,* 87 (October 1983), 151–182. Copyright Texas State Historical Association. Reprinted with permission.

slave/cotton economy tied the South to northern merchants and northern mills. The need to defend slavery was one argument for secession. As late as 1861, however, some Texans insisted that in the long run slavery was safer inside the Union than in a smaller more vulnerable southern Confederacy. Thus slavery was both localistic and nationalistic in its implications and could create an impetus toward either secession or preservation of the Union. In a conceptual sense, the secession crisis in Texas involved a struggle among all those elements within Texas society that, like slavery, strengthened unionism or strengthened secession sentiment. What was curious about this struggle was that the two opposing concepts were surprisingly alike. In fact, it was the similarities between the forces behind unionism and secession as much as their differences that accounts for the success of the secession movement in Texas.

If indeed the secession crisis in Texas had two interdependent dimensions, then understanding the cause of secession and the Civil War requires more than understanding the role of individuals, ideology, parochial interests, or instinctual fears. Understanding secession requires envisioning the nature of unionist and secessionist sentiment, and how in the end the imbalance between these two made secession possible.

Though opposite in intent, sentiments for secession and unionism never existed without each other. This dualism grew out of the interlaced nature of localism and nationalism in antebellum Texas. Localism and nationalism coexisted in individual Texans as well as in the collective value system of the state. Texans accomplished this sleight of hand by either compartmentalizing nationalism and localism within nonconflicting spheres of thought and action, or by temporarily subordinating one set of values to the other. Local values related to slavery offer the clearest example of compartmentalization. Texans voted for a unionist ticket in 1859 and at the same time adamantly defended slavery. As long as local notions about slavery or any other divergent point of view were confined within a framework that did not impinge directly upon nationalism, both nationalism and localism existed together. This explains how the La Grange *True Issue* in the midst of the secession crisis ran on its masthead: "Our Country, Our State, the South and the Union."

Texans, however, seldom achieved an exact equilibrium between localism and nationalism. From 1846 to 1848, spurred on by the euphoria of annexation and the Mexican War, Texans were more nationalistic. From 1849 through mid-1850, because of antipathy for President Zachary Taylor and the dispute over the Texas claim to eastern New Mexico, Texans were more localistic. From the closing months of 1850 up until 1854, encouraged by economic growth and stable borders, Texans elevated the Union above their sectional concerns. Then from 1854 through 1857, aroused by the controversy over slavery in Kansas and influenced by a steady influx of people from the plantation South, Texans became more localistic. Worried by the excesses of southern militants, from 1858 until mid-1860 the bulk of the Texas population moved once again toward the Union. About mid-1860 the move toward sectionalism began once more and continued until Texas seceded. In every case, except for the secession crisis, the development of either nationalism or localism was balanced by the resurgence of its countervailing force. This did not happen in the winter of 1860–1861 because of the conflicting and also surprisingly complementary appeal of the Union and secession. . . .

Self-interest, the influence of powerful personalities, ideological conceptions and beliefs, party politics, and certain cultural and regional biases within Texas all combined in 1858 and 1859 to produce a stunning revival of unionism. The force that tended to break the Union into smaller component parts, however, did not disappear from the body politic. Localism was instead only temporarily submerged. It, too, fed upon cultural biases, party politics, ideology, articulate spokesmen, and self-interest. Connecting and intertwining all of these facets of localism was slavery.

Just as Texans from the Upper South seemed to have a cultural bias in favor of the Union, Texans from the Lower South more easily accepted secession. Until 1850, the largest percentage of Anglo immigrants came from the Upper South—primarily from Tennessee, Kentucky, and Missouri. Beginning in 1836, however, people from the Lower South—primarily from Georgia, Alabama, and Mississippi—came to Texas in increasing numbers. By 1860 Texans from the Lower South comprised the largest cultural group in the state. Moreover, these Texans were not equally dispersed among all regions of Texas but were concentrated in specific areas. Not only was the total number of people from the Lower South growing in Texas, but, because their numbers were relatively undiluted by peoples from other groups, their cultural voice remained clear. It would be a voice that would speak ardently for secession in 1860 and 1861.

Slavery and the plantation system were the most distinct features of the Lower South. Texans from the Upper South certainly owned slaves, as did a few Germans. Still, taken as a whole, farm size, crop selection, and lack of capital limited the impact of slavery on both these non-Lower South groups. Germans, while they might raise cotton, farmed less land more intensively, and they usually lacked the capital to buy slaves, or else preferred to invest their limited capital in other things considered more necessary for the efficient operation of their farms. Texans from the Upper South owned cotton plantations. This was especially true if they lived in East Texas, which was ideal for cotton and contained many former residents of the Lower South. If they lived in regions not dominated by lower southerners, however, they typically concentrated on corn, wheat, or livestock. They therefore needed fewer slaves and by habit, and perhaps by preference, were less inclined to acquire more slaves and expand heavily into the production of cotton. A Texas farmer from Alabama, on the other hand, grew cotton by habit and often aspired to the ownership of large numbers of slaves. It was not surprising that Texans from the Lower South who had the most to lose both at the time and in the future by any challenge from the North to slavery increasingly viewed the world from a local and not a national perspective.

Significantly, this local perspective surfaced most clearly in lower southerners, the most dynamic of the four primary cultural groups in Texas. Texas in 1860 was not yet like Alabama, but the future seemed to hold promise that one day it would be so. Counties between Lower South-dominated East Texas, Upper South- or German-dominated North and West Texas, and Mexican-dominated South Texas—counties with a population drawn not only from the Lower South but the other primary source areas as well—seemed to be undergoing a process by which the fecund Lower South culture dominated the entire county. Over a period of years the agricultural and slaveholding habits that distinguished cultures in Texas began to merge into a culture much like that of the Lower South. Perceiving this ascendancy, visionaries talked of a better life tied to slavery, the plantation system, and Lower South culture. Not only the present reality of this culture but also its dynamic characteristic gave secession a strong cultural base.

By 1857 the cultural transformation occurring in Texas society was reflected in the state Democratic party's increasing alliance with the Democratic parties of the Lower South. By 1858 ardent southerners who would be quick to resort to secession at any provocation controlled the apex of the state structure. By 1859 almost all moderate Democrats who had served as party functionaries and who had helped defeat and destroy the Know-Nothings from 1855 to 1858 had left the party and joined the newly formed Opposition party. As an institution the Democratic party was much stronger than the Opposition. Texans supported it out of loyalty and habit. Germans and Mexicans supported the party because it had defended them against the nativist Know-Nothings. Democrats like John H. Reagan still supported the party in 1859 because they hoped to reform its sectional character and revitalize its national heritage. Nor were the Democrats decimated by their losses in August of 1859. The party rapidly bounced back with the election of party war horse Louis T. Wigfall to the U.S. Senate by the Democratic-controlled legislature. Democratic editors continued to dominate the newspapers of the state and to place sectional writings into the hands of the public. All in all, the Democratic party was a powerful force—a force that was harnessed in 1860 and 1861 by its state and local leaders to the cause of secession.

One reason that the Democratic party became an important force in the secession movement was that to a slight but noticeable degree its ideology always stressed the functional nature of the Union and emphasized that local customs and personal liberty must be defended. That is, the Union was a means to an end and not wholly a valuable thing in itself. For Democrats the Union was a means of fulfilling the American destiny. Thus it was that Democrats tended to be moderate secessionists and Whigs moderate unionists. Whigs certainly viewed the Union as necessary for social stability, law and order, and economic prosperity. Yet Whigs, in whatever group they later belonged, stressed more heavily the sacred nature of the Union and spoke in reverential terms of their devotion to the nation. Such sentiments were not absent among Democrats, but they were not as dominant. Thus when Democrats became convinced that the Union threatened the very functions it was meant to achieve, they were more willing to leave behind the old church and seek a new vehicle to achieve salvation.

Here, then, was a perfect example of goals that had once made men unionists converting them to secessionists. Secessionists wanted to change the form of their nation in 1860, but they did not want to change what they interpreted to be the meaning and purpose of a nation of Americans. Indeed, secessionist ideology gained power after November of 1860 because it stressed the dangers that remaining in the United States posed to the traditional purposes of that Union. For secessionists the Republican party symbolized the corruption and decay of their nation. As the presidential elections of 1856 and 1860 proved, it was purely sectional and not a national party. For Texans this sectionalism meant the poisoning of the governmental system whenever Republicans gained control of any branch of government. Texas secessionists had only to point to the chaos generated by the race for Speaker of the U.S. House of Representatives in 1859 or to the failure of the House to allocate money for the defense of the Texas frontier as proof of their arguments. Republicans were also depicted as threats to the nation's role as preserver of law and order and guarantor of social stability. Time and time again secessionists shouted that Republican state governments broke statute law and the dictates of the Constitution when they passed personal-liberty laws that prevented the return of fugitive slaves. They argued persistently that the Republicans' reliance upon some higher moral or divine code was a threat to the very nature of law because it could be interpreted capriciously with no regard for minority rights. Secessionists insisted as well that Republican control of the federal government would eventually destroy slavery in the states where it already existed or would seriously impair the ability of white southerners to control their black slaves. The result of this would be anarchy and chaos. As John Reagan saw it, Texans faced a difficult choice: "The sad alternative is now submitted to us of the unconditional submission to Black Republican principles, and ultimately to free negro equality, and a government of mongrels or war of races on the one hand, or secession and the formation of a Southern Confederacy and a bloody war on the other." . . .

. . . This accelerating movement toward dissolution was not braked by a re-awakened awareness of the pragmatic value of the Union, by the influence of Unionist leaders, by the resurgence of nationalist ideology, by the expression of this ideology in a political party, and by the inherent unionist tendencies of some Texas subcultures. Lincoln's election and the ascendancy of the Republican party made Texans question as nothing had before the ability of the United States to function as an American nation should function. After November of 1860 the Union seemed both unbeneficial and an unfit carrier of nationalist dreams. This perception was reinforced and the balance between attachment to the Union and to region was further endangered when a consensus in favor of secession virtually ended all debate on the matter in many parts of Texas. Still, even so powerful a force as consensus in a democracy could not submerge nationalism. Instead this nationalism caused Texans to focus on the Confederacy as the new hope for the fulfillment of old dreams and needs.

By late 1860 many Texans had come to perceive Republican power in the national government and in the North as eroding both the ideological and pragmatic functions of the Union. Secessionists portrayed the Union as now incapable of providing stabilizing law, social harmony, military protection, and a guarantee of individual rights to its southern citizens. The question of secession became not simply a choice between defending slavery or defending the sanctity of the nation. The point of the secession debate in Texas was what Lincoln's election that November told and foretold about the nature of the Union. The argument that the Union had decayed, backed up by the specific examples of northern attitudes toward slavery, Republican neglect of the frontier, Republican disregard for the law, and Republican fomenting of social discord, weakened attachments to the nation based upon its role as a preserver of order, a promoter of future prosperity, and a keeper of such traditional values as a respect for the law. Thus the impact of parties and people moved by unionist ideology or a rational assessment of the Union's benefits was undercut.

Unionism, however, did not cease to exist either within individuals or within groups, and habit, together with the emotional side of unionist ideology, would have created stronger opposition to secession in 1861 if it had not been for the force of consensus. Human societies, when threatened by an external enemy, have a tendency to require conformity of their members. In the winter of 1860–1861, in regions of Texas with substantial slave populations, a closing off of debate occurred. In that part of Texas most like the Lower South, which was roughly everything east of the Brazos River below a line running from Waco to Texarkana, secessionists, using the apparatus of the Democratic party and the Democratic press, spread their arguments into every hamlet. Meanwhile unionists were disorganized and silent. They lacked the strength of an institutional framework like the Democratic party. The unionists' silence sprang as well from a tactical decision to boycott all discussions of secession and hope that nearsighted visions of the Union would soon be replaced with a healthy nationalism. To an immeasurable degree, however, the silence of unionists arose from various forms of intimidation. Many times this intimidation was direct and overt. Newspaper editors who stridently opposed secession, like Ferdinand Flake of the German- and English-language *Union,* had their presses smashed. In other areas paramilitary groups, such as the minutemen of Harrison County or the Knights of the Golden Circle to which Newcomb took such exception, might have taken part in organized repression of unionist spokesmen and influenced voting. It is a fact, in any case, that secessionists used force to seize the federal government's property in Texas before the statewide referendum on secession, and that they occasionally tried to overtly intimidate or disrupt unionist spokesmen. Unionists also contended that fair election procedures in both the selection of Secession Convention delegates in January, 1861, and in the secession referendum of February 23, 1861, were not used. In such an atmosphere, physical intimidation might have forced some voters to favor secession despite reservations or to simply stay home.

It seems probable, however, that more subtle forms of intimidation and persuasion were primarily responsible for the growing consensus in favor of secession in January and February of 1861. Since even most unionists agreed that secession was legal, the question before the public was whether it was justified. The answer came back a sure and emotion-packed "YES" from the secessionists and a rather timid "perhaps not" from the unionists. The secessionists were aided by their assured and direct approach, and the offering of a simple solution to a universally perceived problem. . . . In the end, either overtly or covertly, unionists were induced to stay home during public discussions and on election day, or they were convinced to quietly support secession.

In some sense the triumph of the secessionists and the existence of a bellicose Confederate States of America for five years was a victory for localism. Texans first began to accept the idea of secession because their local institution of slavery was challenged by the North and by the Republican party. When they came to believe that the Union's proper character would be subverted by the hegemony of the Republican party, Texans moved toward secession. Secessionist propagandizing by the regular Democratic party, the emergence of pragmatic local reasons for supporting secession, the identification of traditional local leaders with secession, the forced consensus in some cultural regions of the state, and the particular ideology of Texas secessionists all had a parochial nature. Even the decision made by many unionists to support the Confederacy was in large measure the result of their realization that their community, their county, their state, or their region was more their physical emotional, and psychological home than the nation as a whole.

To describe the force of localism in creating secession and sustaining the Confederacy in its early days, however, does not negate the existence of nationalism at any time after 1860. Secessionists displayed a widely held assumption that it was only as part of a large and stable nation that Americans could achieve their individual and corporate goals. Almost from the beginning Texas secessionists were nation builders as well as destroyers of the Union. Texans toyed with the notion of restoring the Republic of Texas, but when they made their decision to secede it was clear that Texas would be part of the Confederacy. Six states had left the Union by February, 1861. While some of these states hesitated to leave the Union without a guarantee of cooperation from other southern states, Texans knew they would not be alone. As early as January, 1861, propagandists of secession in Texas began to argue that separate state secession, since it would be the fastest means of removing their state from the Union and uniting it with the other states of the cotton-growing South, was in effect the most efficient form of cooperating in the building of a new nation. In essence, the secession movement did not kill nationalism in Texas, but redirected it toward the Confederate States of America.

Texans did not move toward secession in a straight and simple line. Perhaps only through imagery, then, can secession be reduced to the understandable. If so, the image of Texas and Texans that emerged in 1860–1861 was like the Roman god Janus. Two almost identical faces looking in opposite directions on the same head, secession and the Union, drew sustenance from the same body. Within their common brain secessionists and unionists were localists and nationalists at the same time. Janus, though, evokes an image of balance and inertia—an image that was untrue of Texas in 1861. Commitment to the United States began to evaporate when Abraham Lincoln and the Republican party achieved hegemony within the North and the national government. This event signalled to Texans, as none had done before, the irreparable decay of the Union. All the things that the nation had once done or Texans hoped the nation would do—preventing anarchy, protecting the frontier, insuring the protection of constitutional and legal rights—a Republican-dominated nation promised not to do. In fact, Republicans were perceived as anarchists, as attackers of the frontier as well as all other portions of Texas, and as law breakers. Even so, the pull of the Union was strong, and most Texans might have been willing to give the Republicans a chance to prove themselves worthy of their trust if the momentum of the secession movement had not been constantly accelerated by a growing consensus in favor of secession which ended all debate over its wisdom in many parts of Texas. A greater attachment to one's state and region rather than the nation prompted even secession's critics to accept the dismembering of the Union. In a way that is difficult to measure, however, what made secession acceptable was the realization by most Texans that secessionists were nation builders as well as destroyers. Here again secession was intertwined with notions about the Union. Secession was a continuation of the past, not a radical departure from the past. Its purpose was not simply to tear apart the Union, but to dismantle it in order to construct a purer type of union which would achieve all the goals and purposes of a nation of Americans. Texans did not lose their nationalism in 1861, nor did they cease to define that nationalism in an American fashion. They refocused that nationalism on the Confederacy instead of the United States.

 *F U R T H E R   R E A D I N G*

Alwyn Barr, *Black Texans: A History of African-Americans in Texas, 1528–1995* (1996)

Dale Baum, *The Shattering of Texas Unionism: Politics in the Lone Star State During the Civil War Era* (1998)

Walter L. Buenger, *Secession and the Union in Texas* (1984)

Randolph B. Campbell and Richard Lowe, *Wealth and Power in Antebellum Texas* (1977)

Donald Frazier, *Blood and Treasure: Confederate Empire in the Southwest* (1995)

B. P. Galloway, ed., *Texas, the Dark Corner of the Confederacy: Contemporary Accounts of the Lone Star State in the Civil War* (1994)

Paul A. Levengood, "In the Absence of Scarcity," *Southwestern Historical Quarterly* 101 (April 1998)

James Marten, *Texas Divided: Loyalty and Dissent in the Lone Star State* (1990)

Richard McCaslin, *Tainted Breeze* (1994)

David Pickering and Judy Falls, *Brush Men with Vigilantes: Civil War Dissent in Texas* (2000)

Ralph Wooster, *Texas and Texans in the Civil War* (1996)

# CHAPTER 9

# Race, Politics, and Reconstruction, 1865–1875

*The single most important struggle of the Reconstruction era in Texas focused on defining the role of the state's newly freed African Americans. Freedom, the efforts of blacks to assert their legitimate political and civil rights, and the white backlash against social change provided the foundation for race relations in Texas for the next century. The actors in this drama are well known. Ex-Confederates, now generally identified as conservative Democrats, attempted to regain the political power they had wielded before the war and to restore the social order that the war and emancipation had disrupted. White Texas Unionists, who made up the core of the Republican Party, felt that political power was their due in compensation for their sufferings during the war, even if it required denying the ex-confederates their political rights and extending these rights to the freedmen. Northerners, some genuinely concerned about the need to preserve the Union and prevent a resumption of war, others seeking retribution against southern rebels for the violence and destruction they unleashed, were determined to impose a loyal (and Republican-dominated) government on the defeated South. And African Americans, mostly freed slaves, were in the middle of this conflict, as victims and pawns of political interests, to be sure, but also as active players, pursuing their individual and group interests as they sought to define their role in post-Civil War Texas.*

*Violence existed in Reconstruction Texas, and African Americans were more often the victims of this violence than were whites. And many who avoided becoming victims of racial violence became victims of economic oppression and poverty. However, opportunity also existed and for a time, successful African Americans achieved prominence in politics, and to a lesser extent business and agriculture. In truth, the Reconstruction experience differed, person to person and community to community. Questions remain, however. How pervasive was the violence and to what degree did it undermine efforts of the freedmen to reconstruct their lives after slavery? How real was the opportunity for freedmen to assume positions of leadership, or even to secure a life free from want and fear?*

# ✪ D O C U M E N T S

Document 1 is a section of the Juneteenth Proclamation which dealt with slavery. These orders were issued by General Gordon Granger when he landed in Galveston with federal troops on June 19, 1865 to begin the occupation of Texas following the Civil War. General Granger emancipated all Texas slaves under the terms of President Lincoln's Emancipation Proclamation. The fact that federal troops did not reach Texas until June 19 delayed both emancipation and the organization of civil government. It also underscored the fact that Texas was unoccupied when the war ended. Document 2 consists of three accounts of emancipation as remembered by African Americans more than seventy years later. They are from the collection of interviews with former slaves conducted by the Federal Writers' Project in 1937 and 1938. General Granger's terse announcement on June 19, 1865 set in motion a process that radically altered the lives of Texas' African American population. However, as these slave narratives reveal, a common emancipation experience did not exist, either for whites or blacks.

Emancipation led to a debate over the civil and social status of the former slaves in Texas. This debate affected politics and frequently provoked violence. White Texans were deeply divided over the issue of political and civil rights for African Americans, while blacks, and for the most part the North, were determined to guarantee the rights of the freedmen. In Document 3, John L. Reagan, in an open letter to the people of Texas, advised his neighbors about the need to accept civil and political rights for blacks. Reagan's perspective is unique. He had been an opponent of secession, but had supported the Confederacy loyally, ultimately serving in President Davis's cabinet. After the war, he was briefly imprisoned, along with other members of the Confederate government. Consequently, he was aware of northern expectations on these issues. Documents 4 and 5 chronicle the break down of order and the rise of racial violence. Document 4 is an editorial written by John L. Haynes, a pro-Republican San Antonio newspaper editor who attacks Governor Throckmorton and his administration for their failure to protect the freedmen from the rampant violence. Governor Throckmorton was removed from office by federal miliary authorities four months later, as military authorities under the authority of the Reconstruction Act of 1867, moved to establish governments in the former Confederate states that would enforce the laws and protect the rights of the freedmen. Document 5 consists of two monthly reports filed by Freedmen's Bureau agents, one in Mount Pleasant and the other in Houston, for November 1867. These reports assess the status of freedmen in their respective communities and reveal differences both from one community to another, and from one agent to another.

Documents 6 and 7 reflect the range of feeling among whites. Document 6 is a poem, written by an "unreconstructed" southerner. Its author is unknown, as is its exact date of publication. It appeared in newspapers around the state in the early years of Reconstruction. Document 7 is an excerpt from a handwritten history of Austin county during Reconstruction by Martin M. Kenney. It underscores that conditions varied from community to community, and that some areas experienced the war and postwar period with relatively little disruption. Most residents, black and white, concentrated on efforts to carry on with life after the war.

Under the Reconstruction Act of 1867 and the Texas Constitution of 1869 that followed, the political and civil rights of African Americans were guaranteed, and law and order were restored. However, the political reign of the Republicans in Texas (including their black political allies) was short-lived. By 1873, conservative Democrats were on the verge of regaining political power. The final Document in this collection illustrates the political agenda of African Americans during the last years of Reconstruction. Document 8 was part of a presentation made in Brenham in July 1874 during a "Colored Men's Convention" of leading African American politicians. It expressed the political concerns of African Americans at a time when Republican rule in Texas was beginning to unravel.

# 1. General Gordon Granger Frees All Texas Slaves, June 19, 1865

GALVESTON; June 20th, 1865.

ED. NEWS:—The following are the first five orders issued under the new Administration:

[Official.]

HEADQUARTERS DISTRICT OF TEXAS,
GALVESTON TEXAS, June 19 1865.

*General Orders, No. 3.*

The people are informed that, in accordance with a proclamation from the Executive of the United States, all slaves are free. This involves an absolute equality of personal rights and rights of property, between former masters and slaves, and the connection heretofore existing between them, becomes that between employer and hired labor.—The Freedmen are advised to remain at their present homes, and work for wages. They are informed that they will not be allowed to collect at military posts; and that they will not be supported in idleness either there or elsewhere.

By order of
Major General GRANGER.

(Signed,)

F. W. EMERY, Maj. & A. A. G.

# 2. Three Slaves Remember Emancipation (1865), 1937–1938

**Annie Hawkins:** *Age 90 Years*

We was the happiest folks in the world when we knowed we was free. We couldn't realize it at first but how we did shout and cry for joy when we did realize it. We was afraid to leave the place at first for fear old Mistress would bring us back or the pateroller would git us. Old Mistress died soon after the War and we didn't care either. She didn't never do nothing to make us love her. We was jest as glad as

---

Major-General [Gordon] Granger, "General Orders, No. 3," *Galveston Daily News*, 21 June 1865.

T. Lindsay Baker and Julie P. Baker, eds., *Till Freedom Cried Out: Memories of Texas Slave Life* (College Station: Texas A&M University Press, 1997), 32–33, 41–42; 76–77. Reprinted by permission of the Texas A&M University Press.

when old Master died. I don't know what become of the three gals. They was about grown.

We moved away jest as far away as we could and I married soon after. My husband died and I married again. I been married four times and all my husbands died. The last time I married it was to a man that belonged to a Indian man, Sam Love. He was a good owner and was one of the best men that ever lived. My husband never did move far away from him and he loved him like a father. He always looked after him till he died. My husband has been dead five years.

### Phyllis Petite: *Age 83 Years*

I was born in Rusk County, Texas, on a plantation about eight miles east of Belleview [Bellview]. There wasn't no town where I was born, but they had a church. . . .

Mammy say we was down in Texas to get away from the War, but I didn't see any war and any soldiers. But one day old Master stay after he eat breakfast and when us negroes come in to eat he say: "After today I ain't your master any more. You all as free as I am." We just stand and look and don't know what to say about it.

After while pappy got a wagon and some oxen to drive for a white man who was coming to the Cherokee Nation because he had folks here. His name was Dave Mounts and he had a boy named John.

We come with them and stopped at Fort Gibson where my own grand mammy was cooking for the soldiers at the garrison. Her name was Phyllis Brewer and I was named after her. She had a good Cherokee master. My mammy was born on his place.

We stayed with her about a week and then we moved out on Four Mile Creek to live. She died on Fourteen-Mile Creek about a year later.

When we first went to Four Mile Creek I seen negro women chopping wood and asked them who they work for and I found out they didn't know they was free yet.

### Lewis Jenkins: *Age 93 Years*

That war that freed the niggers started in 1861. I had two young Masters to go. It lasted 4 years. They was figuring on taking me that very next year, and it was so fixed that the war ended. We had a big drought during the war, which made it bad on the soldiers. I never seen the Yankees only when they was passing 'long the road. One day whilst we was eating our dinner, our Master said, "All you, young and old, when you git through come out on the gallery, I got something to tell you." When we got through we all trooped out and he said, "This is military law, but I am forced to tell you." He says, "This law says free the nigger, so now you is jest as free as me by this law. I can't make you all stay wid me 'less you want to, therefore you can go any place you want to." That was about laying-by crop time in June. It was on June 19th an' we still celebrates 'at day in Texas, 'at is "Nigger Day" down there. He say, "I'd lak for you to stay till the crops is laid by iffen you will.["] Iffen it hadn't been for his wife maybe we would've stayed on, but she jest kept bossing the nigger women and we jest didn't lak it and that's what brung on the scatter. I left my old Master and went wid one of my young Masters, which was my uncle.

## 3. Confederate Unionist John H. Reagan Advocates Civil and Political Rights for Blacks, 1865

IN PRISON, FORT WARREN,
BOSTON HARBOR, August 11 1865.

TO THE PEOPLE OF TEXAS:

The condition of the country is such as to awaken the anxious solicitude of every citizen. Portions of you have honored me with your confidence on many occasions. I have tried to repay that confidence by sincere efforts for your good, and by faithful service. Though now a prisoner, in solitary confinement, and far from you, without knowing when, if ever, I shall be permitted to mingle with you again, and my children and relatives and friends among you, my anxiety for their and your welfare induces me to ask the permission of the Government to send you this communication. . . . I need not assure you of my sympathy with you, and I trust I need not doubt your confidence that I would advise you to no course which I did not think best for you. . . .

The State occupies the condition of a conquered nation. State government and State sovereignty are in abeyance, and will be so held until you adopt a government and policy acceptable to the conquerors. A refusal to accede to these conditions would only result in a prolongation of the time during which you will be deprived of a civil government of your own choice. . . .

. . . In order to secure to yourselves again the blessings of local self-government, and to avoid military rule, and the danger of running into military despotism, you must agree:

First, to recognize the supreme authority of the Government of the United States, within the sphere of its power, and its right to protect itself against disintegration by the secession of the States.

And, second, you must recognize the abolition of slavery, and the rights of those who have been slaves to the privileges and protection of the laws of the land.

From what I can see this much will be required as the least that would likely satisfy the Government, and secure to you the benefits of civil government, and the admission of your members into the Congress of the United States.

But even this may fail of the attainment of those ends, unless provision shall be made, by the new State government, for conferring the elective franchise on the former slaves. And present appearances indicate that this will be required by Northern public opinion and by Congress. . . . If you can do this, and secure to yourselves liberty, the protection of the Constitution and laws of the United States,

"To The People of Texas," [John H. Reagan's letter from prison, August 11, 1865] reprinted in *John H. Reagan, Memoirs: with Special Reference to Secession and the Civil War* (New York: The Neale Publishing Company, 1906), 286–295.

and the right of local self-government, you will be more fortunate than many conquered peoples have been. . . .

The adoption of these measures . . . would secure your protection against other
great and pending evils, and is, I am persuaded, of the greatest consequence to your
future peace, prosperity and happiness. And for these reasons:

First, it would remove all just grounds of antagonism between the white and
black races. Unless this is done, endless strife and bitterness of feeling must char-
acterize their relations, and, as all history and human experience teach us, must
sooner or later result in a war of races. . . .

Second, this course would disarm and put an end to interstate, sectional, political agitation on this subject at least, which has been the special curse of our
country for so many years, and which was the cause of the unnumbered woes we
have recently experienced and still suffer, by depriving the agitators of a subject
on which to keep up such agitation, and of the means of producing jealousy, animosity, and hatred between the different parts of the country, and between the
different races. . . .

With these two lines of policy adopted, I think, notwithstanding all your recent
misfortunes, you might look with hope and confidence to the future. The negroes
will, it is hoped, gradually diffuse themselves among the greatly preponderating
numbers of the whites, in the different States and Territories; many of them will
probably go to Mexico, and other countries, in search of social equality, and few
or none of their race will be added to their numbers by accessions from other
countries. While the steady rapid influx of great numbers of the white races, from
other countries, will gradually increase the disproportion in numbers between
them and the whites, and so render this new element in society and government
innocuous, or at least powerless for evil, if they should be so inclined. But from
the general docility of their dispositions we may expect the most of them to be
orderly, and many of them industrious and useful citizens. But to secure these desirable ends, it must not be forgotten that it is an essential prerequisite to confer
on them their reasonable and necessary rights, and to adopt a policy which will
prevent them from becoming an element of political agitation, and strife and danger. And we must bury past animosities with those of our fellow-citizens with
whom we have been at war, and cultivate with them feelings of mutual charity and
fraternal good will. And it will be greatly to your advantage, in many ways which
I cannot trespass upon you to mention now, to hold out inducements to them and
to emigrants from other countries, to come and settle among you, with their labor,
and skill, and capital, to assist in the diffusion of employments, the increase of
your population, and the development of your vast resources into new creations
of wealth and power.

Time, and patience, and wisdom, and justice, mingled with the holy precepts
in the New Testament, are necessary to enable you to secure these great and beneficent ends. That you may by the means I have indicated or others secure these
results, shall have my constant hopes and prayers.

Very truly and respectfully,
JOHN H. REAGAN.

## 4. Republican Newspaper Editor John L. Haynes Berates the Democrats for Failure to Protect Freedman, 1867

*San Antonio Express*, **Saturday, March 30, 1867**

Governor Throckmorton

No one of the Governors of the Rebel States elected under the auspices of the President's reconstruction policy had so fair a chance as Governor Throckmorton of winning the golden opinions of all men and establishing for himself a national reputation. He had worked and spoken against the Ordinance of Secession. In opposing that measure as a Constitutional remedy he was in accord with a large majority of the people of the State who accepted it finally as simply a revolutionary act. When this occurred Governor Throckmorton gave way to local influences, deserted the principles of his whole life, and joined in the rebellion. As a candidate for Governor his former conscience made him acceptable to many Union men, whilst his service as an officer in the Rebel army gave him claim to the confidence of the disloyal. Thus his record was such as to enable him to appeal to both parties, and by moderate and wise action, after his election, he might have had a controlling voice in directing public opinion for the good of the whole people.

But, unfortunately, the Governor had not the capacity and grasp of mind to realize the situation and grapple with a question of such magnitude as that of reconstruction. . . . He is a man of narrow mind, of limited information, and with no fixed political principles. He gravitates to the local majority with the unerring certainty of instinct. He has not the moral courage to face popular clamor. . . .

To throw dust in the eyes of the country and withdraw attention from the lawlessness and anarchy prevalent in the State, Governor Throckmorton has ordered all the judges in the frontier counties to make reports of Indian depredations, which reports are being published weekly in his Austin organ. This is well. But we have no such reports of the hundreds of cases of crime in the interior counties of the State which call as loudly for protection and punishment. For every ten killed on the Frontier, a hundred in other parts of the State are murdered in cold blood by ruffians as ruthless as the Comanche with his tomahawk and scalping-knife. Of these crimes the governor is as silent as the murdered dead.

We have no report from the Judge of Grayson County of the murders and outrages in that county which have proved so many and so atrocious, . . . without any effort on the part of said judge and other civil servants to suppress them, that General Griffin has placed the county practically under martial law. We have no paper from his judge in Red river, or in Lamar county of a Rebel organization in those

---

Editorial, "Governor Throckmorton," *San Antonio Express,* Saturday, 30 March [1867] in Colonel John L. Haynes, Scrapbook, 2J144, The Center for American History, University of Texas at Austin.

and adjoining counties generally known as the "Black Brigade" (from their blackened faces and blacker deeds), whose object is to shoot, flog, or otherwise maltreat Negroes in order to control their labor by terror. . . .

We have no report from Collin County of the outrages upon the freedmen, the stoning and shooting of a quiet gathering of colored Christians by the Governor's immediate neighbors. . . .

The judge of Travis County, the Capital county, and the present residence of the Governor, tells us nothing through the columns of the organ of the several murders in his county, nor whether the "notoriously disloyal" John Ireland has yet found a Union man who might be hung as an example.

Judge Cowan of Caldwell County is so busily engaged in the business of holding public meetings "upon the suggestion of the Governor," that he has no time to report the murder of the freedmen at Prairie Lea, and other outrages upon that class of people, which have caused a garrison to be placed there to protect them. . . .

Victoria county sends no report of the several murders in that county, nor of the fact that three men were killed in one day, it is supposed, by the same man, one of them a Mexican, having been shot, it is said, "just to see how he would kick." . . .

It is not too much to say that the newspapers of the state have reported, since the inauguration of Governor Throckmorton, at least five hundred cases of murder and felony. And many crimes are committed which are unheralded to the world.

These facts cannot be unknown to the Governor, yet he has the audacity to write about them as "occasional" acts of lawlessness. . . .

Nowhere in the state do the civil authorities seem to make any attempt to execute the criminal laws except against the freedmen. For them alone there is speedy trial and swift condemnation. True we had one conviction of a white man in Fayette County for the brutal murder of a freedman, but the governor interposed his Executive pardon, and the criminal goes unwhipt of justice.

The Governor of the state and the editors of the rebel press are justly chargeable, at least, with dereliction of duty in not making some attempt to stem this tide of crime, even if they are not responsible at the bar of public opinion as encouragers and promoters of disorders. They continually cry aloud that peace and law exist when there is no peace and the courts are farces. They denounce those who wish to put an end to this lawlessness as manufacturing northern opinion for our punishment. In his letter to Judge Cowen, the governor says "you are aware that our enemies charge upon us that we do not attempt to protect the lives of freedmen or those who were Union men. *I know these things are false and I have sought every occasion to announce it.*" . . .

Now that the northern elections have passed and the reconstruction policies of Congress have been settled, when there is no necessity for misrepresenting facts and denouncing Union men because they wish to see the laws enforced, let Governor Throckmorton go to work in his appropriate duty of seeing that the laws are fully and impartially executed. If he cannot do this, then we hope to see him set aside, and an Executive appointed who will perform his duty.

# 5. Freedmen's Bureau Agents Report on the Status of Freedmen, 1867

## Report from Freedmen's Bureau Agent, Houston, Texas, December 2, 1867 for the month of November 1867

### Criminal Offenses

| Date | Name and Race of Criminal | Name and Race of Person Injured | Nature of Offense, Statement of Circumstances, Action taken by Courts and Bureau, etc., etc. |
|---|---|---|---|
| Nov 11th | James Potter, fm | Col'd Congregation of the New Zion Church | Swindling—Obtaining money to be applied to the use of said church and using the same for his own personal use, and giving no satisfactory account of the same. |
| Nov. 29th | Albert George, fm | Caroline Doud, fm | Stealing $9 corn. Found guilty of theft by his own acknowledgment. |
| | | | Verdict in both cases: Guilty. Sentenced each to be confined in Camp Guard House for the period of one month. |

*"Report the disposition and feeling of the white people towards the freed people as expressed by words and actions."*

The disposition of the white people is of mixed character, the owners of property and citizens who are educated except violent politicians and partisans entertain a friendly disposition, but I find among the ex-confederate soldiers and the younger part of the community a deep and violent hatred both in actions and words, and only the presence of a military force prevents them from many acts of violence.

### Education

*"Report the feeling upon the subject of education; what steps have been taken to promote the same; what efforts the freed people are making in that direction and in what manner they may be assisted, etc., etc."*

The freed people are deeply solicitous upon the education of themselves and children, but are too poor, owing to the failure of the cotton crop, being made to obtain work they are barely able to earn sufficient to procure the actual necessities of life. The county officials and citizens entertain no desire to assist in the education of

"Report from the Freedmen's Bureau Agent, Houston, Texas, December 2, 1867 for the month of November 1867" and "Report from the Freedmen's Bureau Agent, Mount Pleasant, Texas, December 3, 1867 for the month of November 1867" in Record Group 105, The Records of the Bureau of Refugees, Freedmen, and Abandoned Lands, The National Archives.

either colored or white children, until Teachers are maintained by the government and suitable buildings furnished, I fear that little progress will be made in advancing the cause of education. A few night schools will probably be commenced during the month of December.

## Report from Freedmen's Bureau Agent, Mount Pleasant, Texas, December 3, 1867 for the month of November 1867

### Criminal Offenses

| Date | Name and Race of Criminal | Name and Race of Person Injured | Nature of offense, Statement of Circumstances, Action taken by Courts and Bureau, etc., etc. |
|---|---|---|---|
| Nov 5th | Stephen Shiray, w | Wilson Peppers, fm | Horse stealing. Absconded |
| 6th | Gor. Carter, fm | Church members | Disturbing Public worship, fined five dollars |
| 16th | Tmas. Johnson, w Nancy Johnson, w | John Whitley, fm | Threats of violence, case dismissed |
| 16th | Henderson Hall, w | Marios S, w | Assault & battery. Arrested. Complaint trifling, dismissed |
| 20th | G.S. Irons, w | J. Baldwin, fm | Threats of violence. Not arrested |
| 20th | G.S. Irons, w | Roda Baldwin, fw | Threat to kill. Not arrested |
| 21st | H. Gay, w | C. Hancock, fm | Threat to kill. Dismissed |
| 23rd | Wm. Dodd, w | Green Clay & wife, ff | Threats of violence and false imprisonment. Both parties to blame. Mutual apologies |
| 26th | Luke Carter, fm | Maria Scott | Assault & battery. Committed to jail |
| 28th | Chas. Sheeler, w | R.A. Pleasants, fw | Adultery and obtaining money under false pretenses. Not arrested |
| 29th | M. Hervey, w | G. Saunders, fm | Assault & battery. Trifling, dismissed |

*"Report the disposition and feeling of the white people towards the freed people as expressed by words and actions."*

The feeling is growing worse. The freed people are continually saying, after making complaints that they are afraid to go back to old neighborhood.

### Education

*"Report the feeling upon the subject of education; what steps have been taken to promote the same; what efforts the freed people are making in that direction and in what manner they may be assisted, etc., etc."*

The feeling is unfavorably. I have recommended the establishment of a school at this place and Mount German. At the last place surveyed the freed people have subscribed a small sum for a school which they propose paying toward its support.

*"Give a statement of the official business transacted during the month; its nature and your method of disposing of the same. State your office hours; the number of days absent from office, if any, and occasion for the same."*

Office hours all hours of the day.

*"State the number of Troops at your Post and the necessity for the same; whether or not the freed people would be secure if they were removed; in other words will the civil authorities protect them and give them justice, etc., etc."*

No change since last report. To remove the troops is death to the freed people. Hundreds of crimes are committed against them that they dare not report. They should be emigrated by the government. That is the only way to save them from slaughter.

## 6. An "Unreconstructed" Rebel Laments His Cause (poem), c. 1865

### The Unreconstructed Texan

I am a good old rebel:
    Now that's just what I am,
For this great land of freedom
    I do not care a d—n.
I'm glad I fit agin it,
    I only wish I won,
And I don't ax no parding
    For anything I dun.

I hates the Constitution
    This glorious Union too;
I hates the Freedmen's Bureau
    And everything in blue;
I hates the American Eagle
    With all his bran and fuss
And the lyin', cheatin Yankees,
    I hate them wuss and wuss.

I followed Massa Robert
    For four years nigh about,
Got wounded in three places
    And starved at Point Lookout;
I cotched the rheuma-tis-em
    A campin' in the snow

---

"Poem—Author Unknown—Veteran of the Confed. Army, 1865" in Colonel John L. Haynes, Scrapbook, 2J144, "The Unreconstructed Texan," Colonel John L. Haynes, Scrapbook, 2J144, The Center for American History, University of Texas at Austin.

But I killed a sight of Yankees—
    I'd like to kill some mo'.

Three hundred thousand Yankees
    Is buried in our dust;
We got three hundred thousand
    Before they conquered us.
They died of southern fever,
    And southern shell and shot;
I wish it was three millions
    Instead of what we got.

I can't take up my musket
    And fight 'em now no more;
But I ain't a-goin' to love 'em,
    And that is sartin sure
And I don't ax no parding,
    For what I was I am
And I won't be reconstructed,
    If I do—may I be d—d.

## 7. White Southerner Martin M. Kenney Describes Reconstruction in Austin County, n.d.

The result of the war removed all value from the law and all rural fields of the river valley to the uplands. The river plantations were not abandoned, but greatly depreciated, the small farms in the prairie took a higher value than before the war. The sudden turning loose of so many Negroes did not produce any disturbance. They wandered around for a while in an aimless manner but were soon obliged by want of food to go to work which they performed more inefficiently than before but better than was expected. The fanatical part of the conquering party were much disappointed that the Negroes did not perpetrate brutal outrages on the whites and emissaries came and made speeches at Hempstead and other points designed to incite outrages but the Negroes had the sense or apathy to let good enough alone, or their masters had raised them to better principles. No ill feeling has sprung up between the whites and blacks. The enormity termed reconstruction affected this county less than almost any other which had a considerable Negro population. The military commandant Capt. Whitney proved to be rather an American than a partisan. No exactions were made beyond what was levied in the State at large to secure the election of radical officers. A sufficient number of the opposite party were prohibited from voting. But no false count was effected. Beyond the heavy and unnecessary taxes none graver evils have been complained of attributable to the conquering party than neglect to keep the public roads in repair.

---

Martin M. Kenney, Literary Production, Austin County History—Untitled ZE290, The Center for American History, University of Texas at Austin.

## 8. African American Platform Expresses Concerns About the End of Republican Rule, 1873

### *Colored Men's Convention, 1873*

BRENHAM, July 3 and 4

*Officers:* President, N. W. Cuney. Vice-Presidents, Mathew Gaines, Richard Allen, and John Reed. Secretaries, John N. Coss, and J. H. Washington.

*Committee on Address:* W. C. Richer, W. A. Price, Jacob Freeman, G. T. Ruby, J. J. Hamilton, John DeBruhl, B. F. Williams, P. J. Moore, Cooke Jenkins, L. A. Clope, J. J. Webb. Walter Riptoe, N. W. Cuney, W. H. Holland, J. H. Washington, and Richard Allen, chairman.

ADDRESS

We, the undersigned members of the committee on address, do most respectfully, by leave, report as follows:

That we consider one of the prime objects of our assemblage to be the promotion of good feelings between ourselves and our white fellow-citizens of the State, without whose earnest and sincere efforts in cooperation with our own, to effect our elevation, our progress must be slow and constrained. . . .

. . . It must be borne in mind that the mass of the colored people are in a lamentable state of ignorance, the result of that wicked system of bondage, which shut them out from the acquisition of all knowledge of letters and made it a penal offense to teach them to read the Word of God. They must also remember that they have from the day of the acquisition of our liberty set their faces in steadfast opposition to our political, educational, and social progress, with a blind spirit of malignant opposition not calculated to inspire us with either confidence or affection. . . .

. . . It becomes our duty here to define clearly what is understood by us as civil rights in contradistinction to social privileges. . . . We know perfectly well that a man's social relations cannot be made by legislative enactments. We have no disposition to intrude ourselves upon them, and would *resent as an indignity any intrusion upon ourselves.* But we do demand our Civil Rights Bill of the Hon. Charles Sumner, and shall agitate the question of their concession with unabated ardor until we can celebrate their acquisition. . . .

It is a misfortune for both races that the Southern white men seem determined to leave their colored fellow-citizens nothing to be grateful for, as every right we enjoy has been forced from their grasp, in face of stern opposition and openly expressed hatred. . . . With stolid obstinacy they have clung to their prejudices. Yet we do not despair and feel our duty to ourselves and them render it imperative for us to hold out the olive branch, and express a willingness to cooperate with them in any measure for the advancement of the interests of our State and the welfare of its citizens. We appeal to them to meet us with the free concession of our civil rights in

"Colored Men's Convention, 1873," in *Platforms of Political Parties in Texas,* ed. Ernest William Winkler (Austin: Bulletin of the University of Texas, 1916), 148–151.

their hands, and will thus become a truly homogeneous people, animated by one common purpose, and that purpose the prosperity of the State. . . .

"With charity for all, and malice toward none" of our fellow-citizens, we appeal to the law-abiding and honest people of Texas, of whatever political party, to join with us in deprecating the outrages and wrongs perpetrated upon the colored people in various sections of our State, because of our new relations as freemen and citizens, and we ask that all acts of violence towards us, from whatever source, shall be condemned by the public sentiment of the community in such unequivocal terms as that law and order shall be enforced.

We also recommend to our people the acquisition of land and homesteads, and that they do not support for office any man or set of men who are likely to place obstacles in the way of their success in this direction.

We also urgently recommend to them that they refuse to support for any office whatever any man who is not pledged against repudiation in all its forms. We are not to consider how the State has been brought into debt, or the means by which its obligations were incurred; we only are to consider how we can earliest pay them, and we pledge ourselves to use our humble efforts to the payment of the State obligations, to the last dollar in the treasury, and we will cheerfully submit to any amount of taxation to accomplish that object.

We also express ourselves as being decidedly in favor of internal improvements.

This we also consider an appropriate occasion to disabuse the minds of our fellow-citizens of foreign birth, of the desire that has been attributed to us to lay obstacles in the way of the immigration of their brethren in Europe to this State. We indignantly deny that we cherish any so unworthy or selfish feeling. We look on the Americans as the trustees of this soil for the oppressed of all nations, and we welcome the downtrodden immigrant from wherever he may come with open arms.

We cannot close this address without the strongest expression of our confidence in, and regard for President Grant and reiterate our thanks to him for his efforts to ameliorate our condition and obtain our civil rights.

We also express our confidence in the Federal government and reaffirm our allegiance to the National Republican party.

In conclusion, we tender our grateful thanks to Chas. Sumner for his constant and unwearied efforts for our acquisition of civil rights, and earnestly trust that his existence be so prolonged to win the completed result of his lifelong labors. And we confidently hope and believe that our future will justify his past.

# ESSAYS

These two essays examine African Americans, both as victims of Reconstruction era violence and as effective politicians. Texas experienced more than its share of violence in the months and years that followed the Civil War. Some of this violence was simply the crime and lawlessness that followed the collapse of the Confederacy and the collapse of the frontier. Texas, a relatively sparsely settled region on the southwestern frontier of the Confederacy, was particularly vulnerable due to the lack of an effective police force when civil government vanished in the late spring of 1865. This violence continued because insufficient numbers of federal troops were available to police the Lone Star state.

Although all Texans suffered from the epidemic of postwar violence, African Americans were disproportionately victims. In the first essay by Barry Crouch, of Gallaudet College, two Reconstruction-era reports on crime and violence are used to document, both statistically and narratively, the extent and the nature of the racial violence in Texas. In the second essay, Carl H. Moneyhon of the University of Arkansas in Little Rock explores African American political power through the career of George T. Ruby. Ruby was a "carpetbagger," a northern-born African American who moved South, first to Louisiana, then to Texas, where he initially worked with the Freedman's Bureau. Moneyhon critically examines Ruby's efforts to build a political power base during the turbulent period following the Civil War, as well as his political successes and failures.

# White Violence in Reconstruction Texas

### BARRY A. CROUCH

Southern history, though rich and compelling, is stained by the theme of violence. Both before the Civil War and long after violence was an accepted facet of southern society. Reconstruction, however, may have been that region's most violent era. Blacks and whites struggled to redefine their roles within an atmosphere of bitterness, frustration, and resentment. Racial tensions, always an important characteristic of southern life, reached new extremes that appalled even contemporaries. From Paris, Texas, a year after emancipation, Mrs. L. E. Potts, a native Tennesseean, implored President Andrew Johnson to do something about the plight of the "*poor negro*" and "their persecution." Just a few months out of slavery, she wrote, "their masters are so angry to loose [sic] them that they are trying to persecute them back into slavery." Killing black people was not considered a crime, she continued, and "they are often run down by blood hounds, and shot because they do not do precisely as the white man says." Black Texans needed federal protection, for the area "savors of rebellion." When blacks did work, Potts concluded, they "scarcely get any pay, and what are they to do [?]."

Violence was a major component of postwar race relations. . . . Leon Litwack has been especially forceful in accentuating the role of Reconstruction violence and dramatically portraying some of its effects and results. The number of blacks, "beaten, flogged, mutilated, and murdered in the first years of emancipation," he maintains, "will never be known." . . .

Litwack's graphic description of white violence against blacks is useful in calling attention to this issue, but it has not led to an examination of individual acts of violence. . . . No one has attempted to assess the different aspects of white violence in the immediate postwar era, to analyze the whites who perpetrated it, to ascertain its rationale, or to determine in what social and geographical context the violence occurred. Nor have statistical compilations been undertaken comparing white and black violence, the numbers killed, and the percentage of a specific black population murdered.

Barry A. Crouch, "A Spirit of Lawlessness: White Violence; Texas Blacks, 1865–1868," *Journal of Social History,* 18 (Winter 1984): 217–232. Copyright © 1984 Carnegie-Mellon University Press. Reprinted with permission.

Fortunately, some of these issues can be explored in the case of Texas. Two extant sets of evidence related to the Lone Star state permit a detailed look at white violence against blacks for the years from mid-1865 until mid-1868. The first is the conclusions reached by a special committee on lawlessness and violence established by the 1868 Texas Constitutional Convention. The second is the violence register compiled by the Texas Freedmen's Bureau.

These records reflect certain limitations and biases and must be used with caution. Republican sentiment inspired both documents, and recorders probably stressed rather than minimized white violence against blacks. In addition, the state committee only recorded homicide totals, thus hindering the detection of any statistical errors. Often the Bureau sources provide only minimal background material. Frequently, age and sex statistics of the black victims are missing and have to be inferred. The information about the whites and their backgrounds is sketchy at best. Although the type of assault they committed is included, recurrently the motivation for the crime is ignored. Furthermore, local Bureau agents depended upon various sources for their data, as they did not witness all the violence themselves. Officials throughout the districts submitted reports collected in varying fashion. Surely, some were hearsay and distorted thus skewing the figures.

Another critical difficulty with violence records is that many events were never recorded, so both documents must be weighed against possible omissions. . . . In spite of these problems, these documents represent a rich source of information for the Presidential Reconstruction years. . . .

The special committee's report is less comprehensive than the Bureau's record. Dealing only with homicides, the committee gathered data from state department records (comprising about forty counties) where indictments had been found, Freedman's Bureau materials for approximately sixty counties, and sworn statements of witnesses throughout the state. The committee recognized this was a "very imperfect view of the actual violence and disorder in the State."

According to the committee, the homicide figures reveal a "frightful story of blood." During the three year period from June 1865 to June 1868 Texans killed 939 people. Of this total, 373 were blacks murdered by whites, but only 10 were whites killed by blacks. Additionally, the committee reported 8 blacks killed by unknown assailants. The committee also indicated another 40 homicides where the victim's race was not specified. It concluded that the "great disparity between the numbers of the two races killed, the one by the other, shows conclusively that 'the war of races' is all on the part of the whites against the blacks."

The Texas Freedmen's Bureau compiled the second, and more important, violence record. . . .

The statistical breakdown of the 2,225 offenses catalogued by the Texas Bureau not only corroborates the special committee reports on lawlessness and violence, but reveals much more. The Bureau attempted to describe all physical acts of violence, not simply homicides. Even though there are some minor discrepancies between the state committee's death statistics and those of the Bureau, what should command attention is the high death rate caused by white males killing primarily black males.

More to the point is the meaning of the number of deaths in relation to the Texas black population from June 1865 to June 1868. According to the 1870 census,

253,475 blacks lived in the Lone Star state. Thus, the annual death rate for blacks from white inflicted outrages for these years averaged 65.4 per 100,000. If this same ration is projected to only the 126,278 black males, the violence-specific death rate rises to 131.5 per 100,000. If this ratio is further extended to males in the 15–49 year age range, the rate would be 290.4 per 100,000. This means that a number equal to approximately *one percent* of the black male population between 15 and 49 years old was killed in the early years of Reconstruction. . . .

Of all the southern states at the close of the war, Texas had three distinctive factors that may have affected its violence record: the state's relative immunity from the devastation of the war, location on the frontier, and low population density. Texas is so large that the eastern half of the state is the combined size of Mississippi and Alabama, yet in 1870 only 818,579 citizens resided in the state. Thus, the Army had a difficult responsibility trying to enforce order and protect the ex-slaves, and the Bureau never had more than 100 agents. Moreover, most of the Army's troops were stationed on the vast frontier, not in the heavily populated areas where they could have protected the freedpeople. That Texas was never invaded successfully, and therefore did not accept defeat easily, also helped produce conditions for individual and group attacks by whites against blacks.

The Lone Star state's vast size permitted individuals or groups to elude the law and justice, even when local officials did not connive to aid them in escaping punishment. By 1868 there were 5,000 pending homicide indictments in Texas. Yet from the end of the war until the fall of 1868 only one legal execution occurred in the state, ironically a Houston freedman. . . . Geography, the frontier, a lax system of law enforcement, and inadequate support from the Army or the Bureau all conspired to make rural blacks general targets for white violence.

Did whites commit the violence individually or in groups (a group being defined as two or more people)? Litwack argues that "much of the violence inflicted on the freedmen had been well organized, with bands of white men meting out extralegal 'justice' and anticipating the Klan-type groups that would operate so effectively during Radical Reconstruction." Texas does not bear out Litwack's argument. Of the 1,524 total attacks or threats on blacks during 1865 to 1868, 1,037 (or 68 percent) were perpetrated by individuals. Blacks were terrorized by groups in 301 cases, mostly by desperadoes, some bandits, or in a few instances by the Ku Klux Klan, making its first appearance in early 1868. In 186 actions, the party or parties were unknown. In many of these unsolved outrages the black person was found dead, and no identification of the attacker could be made. Black families were enumerated in only 35 altercations.

White violence against Texas blacks took many forms and resulted from a variety of causes that are difficult to pinpoint precisely. It was, for example, sometimes related to political or labor activities, to social relations and mores. Sometimes it was directed at women and children or institutions such as schools and churches, and, at times by gangs that preyed upon the freepeople. . . .

Two questions might be raised about violence against blacks in the years covered by the sources. First, were certain types of violence more frequently committed by groups of whites or by individuals? Second, were some classes of whites more prone to use group or mob violence than others? Some kinds of violent attacks, or course, were committed by both individuals and groups, but patterns might be established for specific motivations. The question of which classes were likely to commit violence is much more difficult, and a complete answer will need further supporting studies.

In past writings about Reconstruction, historians have too often narrowly focused on politically motivated violence against blacks. This was certainly a central part of the violence equation. There were, to be sure, many other reasons for outrages, ending in injury or death for blacks. At work or play, while drinking, in an institutional setting, or in circumstances when refusing to sanction old social mores, blacks were the subject of numerous outrages. Although black Texans are seen largely as victims in this essay (a concept not without evident pitfalls), the major conclusion to be drawn is that whites used violence in different guises to control blacks politically, economically, and socially. Texas whites resented black political equality, a free labor ideology, or more equitable social relations. Blacks most assuredly responded to white violence and committed individual acts against whites. But the [data] substantiate the judgment that black violence was minimal compared to what whites were doing to them. Obviously not all whites were participants in the outrages, even abhorring the incidents, but the high number of incidents suggest there was little concerted action to stop them. . . .

Once blacks organized, met politically, and were enfranchised, they became sources of potential and real conflict in the political arena. The rise in the death rate of Texas blacks, besides being more carefully tallied, coincides precisely with the Congressional Republicans' struggle to control the Reconstruction process and with the emergence of local blacks as voters, community leaders, registrars, and Union Leaguers. From 1866 to 1867, when freedmen won the right to vote, the total number of blacks slain by whites rose twofold. But worse lay ahead. According to the state committee, sixty-nine percent of the blacks murdered by whites died during 1867 and 1868. Republicans, both black and white, states Otto Olsen, "provoked a hatred from their opponents so intense that it soon turned Reconstruction into an age of violence and terror." White Texans, as one historian has noted, perceived political rights for blacks as a temporary aberration, which "could be taken back by the state after it was readmitted to the Union." Thus, violence, terror, and intimidation became acceptable standards for the destruction of black political equality.

The case of George E. Brooks, a politically active minister from Millican, Texas, is instructive. His decomposing body was found following a racial clash between Millican's blacks and whites in mid-1868. The incident originated after a black man was murdered near the sheriff's residence, the culprit not arrested for two days, and then released on his own recognizance. When blacks protested this lenient treatment, the Ku Klux Klan entered the affray, inciting a racial imbroglio, which resulted in the killing of prominent members of Millican's black community. In the Millican affair, it seems likely that whites, with substantial economic and political interests in the community, were concerned about blacks banding together, asserting their rights, and demanding justice. The killing of Brooks, who was a prominent local politician, registrar, and Union League member, one observer wrote, was a "deliberate murder" and one of a "most outrageous character."

Even if Texas blacks simply wished to learn more about their rights they risked danger. While on his way to hear the Bureau Assistant Commissioner speak, James

Cole of Walker County was beseiged by a mob of "white rowdies," assaulted and pistol whipped. The same thing happened in Harrison County, only the whites involved in that incident were described as "civil officers" and the "disloyal." Where politics motivated violence, whites used both individual and group tactics, depending upon whether blacks had organized and protested denial of rights, served a political function, or attended meetings. The evidence suggests that all classes of whites participated in the attacks, especially where blacks emerged as a vocal segment of the body politic.

Violence associated with labor-related behavior was prevalent in the postwar years. Activities such as contracting, working, moving for better jobs, securing rations, arranging credit bills, seeking wages and dividing shares, or being driven off the land without compensation led to violence. Because of the refusal of blacks to work in gangs, and the dominating presence of sharecropping, much of the violence was committed on individuals. Whites perpetrating the attacks were property-holders, the Bureau records suggest, probably former planters with varying size acreages, who were concerned about maintaining a reliable, dependent, and available labor pool. . . .

Disciplining blacks to the "new" labor relations was another component of white violence. When Texas blacks decided to control their own labor and make the best arrangements with whom and where they worked, their actions provoked physical assaults, injuries, and even death. Again, this type of violence was largely individual. There were rare instances, such as in Davis County, where a gang of white men (perhaps hired by the planters) generally whipped blacks who refused to sign new contracts. Those who controlled the land after the war liberally used the lash to suppress any notions of independence that blacks may have perceived. But not all blacks were only whipped for seeking a new work environment: some were killed, as were a mother and her baby in 1868 in Rusk County when she left her employer. Others were murdered when they refused to return to their "masters."

Allowing Texas blacks total freedom of movement brought indignation from those concerned about a stable labor force. Blacks were not permitted to look for better jobs, or more advantageous share arrangements, and leaving the farm without permission was certainly a transgression of the old pass system. A few owners went to great lengths to find and punish blacks who departed without consent. In Fort Bend and Walker Counties whites used dogs to chase two blackmen (one was shot at twice) because they failed to check with the farm owner before leaving. A Fort Bend County freedman, named Shade, was confined two days in the "calaboose" for attempting to move. Families had to be careful about allowing their offspring freedom of movement. Stephen Bryant and his wife, Liberty County freedpeople, were handcuffed, whipped, and beaten because two of their sons left the farm without asking the owner's permission.

White violence against black Texans, however, involved more than just the contracting process or movement away from the confines of the plantation. It lurked over the freedpeople's everyday working life. Texas blacks were beaten and wounded for being too sick to work, for taking too long to eat breakfast, for being too late coming to work, for hoeing too slowly (100 lashes), for incompetence, laziness, carelessness, or for paying too much attention to an ailing relative. One freedman appeared at the Freedmen's Bureau office in Seguin covered with large scabs and scars. He informed the agent that because he was too sick to pick cotton he had been whipped with a strap that has a two-inch iron buckle. Miles, a Fort Bend Country freedman, told a similar story. His employer beat him over the head and back with a heavy walking stick. Much of this ill-treatment was parcelled out by owners themselves or their hired foremen and managers.

Labor related violence often surfaced at the end of the contracting year or following the harvesting of crops when it was time to collect wages or, more commonly, divide shares. The complaint books of the Texas Freedmen's Bureau contain a large number of cases indicating the role of planters in violence against blacks. Laborers deluged the Bureau with grievances asserting they received too little or no compensation whatsoever from their employers. According to Texas freedpeople, they were shot, struck with pistols, cut with hatchets or knives, whipped, beaten with clubs and chains, assaulted with monkey wrenches, stabbed, or threatened with shotguns and pistols. If a freedperson actually was able to get his/her employer before a Bureau court for non-payment, retaliation was too often the result. Oliver, a Montgomery County freedman, was killed for bringing his employer before the Bureau, while an Anderson County black man, Henry Jones, was waylaid and murdered by his boss because Jones sued him for seven dollars. . . .

Still, anti-black violence was not prompted solely be economics and labor relations. In social relations, whether implementing or maintaining acceptable social mores or monitoring the social activities of blacks, white Texans followed antebellum patterns. Black Texans could not make insulting noises, speak disrespectfully or out of turn, talk back, dispute the word of whites, or disobey a command. Further, they had to stand at attention when whites passed, step aside when white women were on the sidewalk, properly address whites, and remove their hats in their presence. "Improper actions" by blacks resulted in swift retaliation. Although outrages of this sort were not common, the ones that did occur demonstrated to black Texans that social intercourse was still imbued with prescribed rules. . . .

Texas whites who attempted to guard and maintain the old social mores generally did so individually, though there were a few exceptions. Whites who attacked blacks at dances, parties, or social functions did so in groups, apparently angered that blacks found ways to enjoy themselves. These "gangs," as the Bureau referred to them entered a Palestine saloon where local blacks were dancing and threw several of them through the upper story windows. A similar occurrence in Panola County in 1868 ended with three black men dead and four wounded. The white ringleader was the county sheriff. Freedmen were also murdered at celebrations.

Texas whites did not respect sex when committing outrages. Whites victimized black women in 183 incidents, according to a tabulation of the Bureau records. Too often in discussions of anti-black violence following the Civil War, males are the major focus. The rather significant number of offenses perpetrated on black women strongly indicates that there was a deep rage underlying many of the attacks and that much of the violence was purposeless, almost elemental and irrational. In addition to this violence, black women at times received gruesome treatment. A Limestone County freedwoman, Jo Brooks, had her ears cut off and her arms burned to a crisp, for no stated provocation. Others, if not so horribly violated, were nonetheless brutalized beyond rationality. These attacks, when women were not engaged in a specific activity such as labor, were perpetrated by individuals, who, the sources

suggest, had little economic standing in communities and were of a desperate, socially irresponsible class.

Nor were children immune from white violence. They suffered as did adults
from whipping, flogging, beating, assaults, castration, and murder. Much violence
against children seems to have a random quality, with whites motivated by nothing
more than a deep rage. This may lead to the surmise that whites who brutalized
black children were from the lower economic echelon and thus presumably more
frustrated than wealthier persons, but this conclusion is not entirely valid. For example, three prominent citizens of McLennan and Bosque Counties, two of whom
were doctors, committed what a Bureau agent called one of the "most atrocious
deeds in the annals of barbarity," castrating a freedboy. Perhaps in the same social
strata was the planter who shot a freedchild because the mother left his employ.
However, child assault instigated by influential whites remained rare. Most of the
other recorded outrages were as brutal, but there is nothing to indicate that those
who performed them were of the same class as those who castrated the boy or the
planter who shot a child because of a labor incident. Children were whipped and
kicked, stabbed to death, shot at, and had turpentine placed on their "fundaments"
in a random pattern of violence. In the fall of 1866, a Bosque County black boy
was whipped to death, while a seven year old girl, Dolla Jackson, suffered an
attempted rape and was robbed of twenty-five cents. The Bureau viewed the whites
who precipitated these cases as characters of a desperate and mean sort, with no
established economic or community standing.

Two treasured institutions of the black community, schools and churches, also
were the objects of white violence. In Anderson County, with an almost equal
black and white population, a white mob stoned the black church, twice broke the
windows, and threatened the minister. In Washington County congregation members were beaten. A white mob attacked a Harris County Baptist Church in September 1868. The whites assaulted the former minister, an "old man," his son, and
daughter-in-law, brutally kicking, mauling, and mangling them, nearly killing the
elderly preacher and his daughter-in-law. Teachers and schools suffered the same
fate. The former were driven from counties or killed. The latter were trashed and
burned. Northern white soldiers, apparently not immune to the deep racial hatred
of Texas whites, fired on a school on their way to the outer frontier, leading to a
"regular skirmish" between the two races with four wounded, two on each side.
Whites also entered schools with drawn pistols, disrupting classes.

Although individual acts of violence accounted for over two-thirds of the total,
white desperadoes committed the most destructive forms of group violence against
blacks. In the immediate postwar years these bandits robbed, plundered, harassed,
and murdered blacks who lived in Northeastern Texas and along the Arkansas
border. Marauding bands, composed of ex-Confederate soldiers and other economically dispossessed social elements, hated both blacks and Yankees. Blaming the
war and Northern invaders for their depressed plight and bleak circumstances, their
attacks bordered on the fanatical. . . . Many of these desperadoes, as one contemporary observed, would kill a freedman for seventy-five cents and boast of the deed as
a "laudable one to high minded chivalry." . . .

Texas whites often killed blacks for no obvious reason other than racial hatred
or the satisfaction of sadistic fantasies. Some reportedly shot freedmen to "see a

d——d nigger kick" or because they just wanted to shoot a "damned nigger." Others shot them, apparently, to test their skills as marksmen. The very presence of free blacks led to murders. In Grayson County, for instance, where blacks comprised only eighteen percent of the population and therefore were not a political threat, three whites murdered three freedmen because, they said, they felt a need to "thin the niggers out and drive them to their holes."

Texas anti-black violence, in the years 1865 to 1868, was significant because of its high yearly death toll and the percentage of the population affected. . . .

Probably due to the size of the state and the isolation of many sections, more than any other factors, white attacks on blacks were largely individual and only partially by groups. Certain patterns emerge, however, in relation to the motivations behind the various categories of white violence.

Politically motivated white violence had a varied background, with three distinct patterns. The one major group confrontation occurred at Millican involving a cross-section of both the white and black communities. Much of the political violence was perpetrated by individuals or by quite small groups that harassed, intimidated, and sometimes murdered black Texans who participated in some fashion in politics or simply desired to live a free life. Those blacks directly involved in politics, such as registrars, were subjected to the violence of small groups, described as bullies and rowdies. The nature of the particular circumstances dictated which whites engaged in this type of violence. Prominent members of the community were apparently part of the Millican affray, and perhaps where blacks were attacked when they held some official position.

Labor violence, or its related categories, was largely individual, perpetrated by planters. The constant references in the source to former "owners" and "masters" suggest this clearly. In this struggle of economic independence versus continued dependence, with racial and class overtones, whites could not hope to emerge victorious without the complete subordination of blacks. Although this cannot be definitely ascertained from the records, there are indications that those who perpetrated much of the labor-related violence were landowners of some type. Indeed, almost all may have been previous slaveholders. Occasionally there were attacks on working blacks that can be classified as random, but most were purposeful. Whipping was still widely practiced as a means of discipline and punishment, but other ingenious ways of using violence to keep blacks working and tied to the land were found.

Anti-black violence directed against persons who violated prewar social relations or mores is much more difficult to classify. Those whites who committed outrages against blacks for violating the "old" ways seem to have been from a different economic strata than those who attacked blacks who were enjoying themselves socially. Another difference is that the former were performed largely by individuals, while "gangs" accounted for the latter, according to the sources. When attacks focused on schools and churches, lower class white crowds or mobs were the villains. Desperadoes were the final element in the violence equation, and they wreaked havoc upon individual blacks and communities. . . .

During the early years of Texas Reconstruction conditions were " 'anomalous, singular, and unsatisfactory,' " according to General Philip H. Sheridan. He also reputedly remarked that if he had owned both Texas and hell he would have rented out Texas and moved to hell because of Lone Star state terror. Texas was all this and more, particularly for blacks who tried to take advantage of their supposed freedom. Clearly more studies of violence in other Southern states are necessary before we can conclude, as does James M. Smallwood, that an "examination of sources" suggests "there was little difference in the degree of harassment suffered by Texas blacks and those of other states." If the remainder of the old Confederacy had a scale of violence similar to Texas, then the Southern black populace faced an even more desperate situation than earlier assumed. All this serves as a reminder that Reconstruction elicited remarkable and wrenching experiences. Texas blacks needed extraordinary resilience because their potential social, economic, and political losses surpassed even the fetters of slavery.

# George T. Ruby and African American Politics During Reconstruction

## CARL H. MONEYHON

In the post–Civil War era no black man in Texas exercised more political power than did George Thompson Ruby. An astute politician, Ruby built a base of power in the black community of Galveston, then used that support to make himself a major force in the state at large. He was a forceful advocate of civil and political rights for his race, but he knew when to compromise to gain his larger goals, and he moved carefully among hostile white politicians in his efforts to expand opportunities for black people. In the context of his time and place, his goals were radical, but he was hardly a political fanatic. His entire career demonstrated responsibility and moderation. In the end his work failed and he left Texas for a more favorable environment, but rather than any personal character flaws or lack of depth in his vision, forces outside his control undercut his efforts. The refusal of whites to compromise on racial matters, the white majority of the state, and Ruby's steadfast willingness to adhere to democratic politics prevented his attaining the goals he sought. His career is instructive, not only in that it shows how at least one black politician gained power during Reconstruction, but also because it indicates the problems that beset both Ruby and the southern Republican movement in their efforts to establish a viable political alternative to the white-dominated Democratic party.

Ruby was not a native Texan, but arrived in the state after the Civil War. . . .

In September 1866, . . . Ruby joined the Freedmen's Bureau schools in Texas. . . . He received an appointment as school organizer and operated in Galveston and the surrounding counties. This job placed him in the heart of the black belt of Texas and helped him establish contacts with the local black community. During this time he gained a reputation, even among whites, as a man of integrity. A Unionist newspaper cited him as "a colored man of education, character, and ability, and . . . an honest man." One local Democratic newspaper begrudgingly viewed him as a

Carl H. Moneyhon, "George T. Ruby and the Politics of Expediency in Texas," in *Southern Black Leaders of the Reconstruction Era*, ed. Howard N. Rabinowitz (Urbana: University of Illinois Press, 1982), 363–392. Reprinted with permission of the author.

good fellow among a bad lot. General Charles Griffin, assistant commissioner of the Freedmen's Bureau in Texas, wrote of his agent, "He is an energetic man and has great influence among his people." At this time Ruby began to build the base for his later political activities.

In spring 1867 Ruby turned from education to politics. . . . The introduction of black people into the political process [through the Reconstruction Act of 1867] meant that successful politicians would have to attract their votes. Ruby, who had emerged as an individual with contacts throughout the black belt, proved an excellent intermediary between the freedmen and ambitious white politicians.

Ruby's first office was president of the Galveston chapter of the Union League, and the league would thereafter remain the center of his power. . . . The league was a secret organization with elaborate rituals—mechanisms that allowed freedmen to be instructed in patriotism toward the Union and the Republican party, marched to the polls, and protected from outside white interference.

At the beginning Ruby appears to have been little more than an instrument used by the Unionists and other white politicians. . . . His relationship with political leaders in Galveston during the period affirms this. . . . These men, although they publicly supported the doctrine of political and civil equality of blacks, hardly carried out these ideas in practice. With few exceptions they did not approve of black officeholding and did not see blacks as filling leadership roles even within the party. . . .

While Ruby probably realized the incongruity of his friends' public and practical positions, he defended them nonetheless, leading to accusations that he was nothing more than "a yellow negro, a tool." He may have been just that, but at that time his political power lay with the white Republicans, no matter how insincere they may have been, and he remained loyal. He faithfully turned out the league for party rallies and conventions.

Eventually he began to receive rewards, although modest. At the first state Republican convention, in July, he received an honorary vice-presidency. Later he solicited and obtained an appointment as a notary public for Galveston. . . . Although the beginnings were small, Ruby had shown that he could organize black voters, and he had been rewarded. The offices, as minor as they were, in turn showed blacks that he had access to white political leaders, and this bolstered his support among them.

The composition of the electorate following the initiation of Congressional Reconstruction added to Ruby's importance to white politicians. The required registration of voters proceeded through the spring and summer of 1867 and certified over a thousand blacks in Galveston. Potential white registrants outnumbered blacks, but restrictions imposed by the Reconstruction Act passed March 23 and the refusal of many, who were otherwise qualified, to swear to the oath provided by that law, limited the number of those actually registered to about two-thirds of the blacks. To be elected required the support of black voters; therefore, the man who could deliver that support possessed political power.

As Ruby used his bureau position to organize local Union leagues around the Galveston area in preparation for the convention election, he became less satisfied with his role as a spokesman for white interests. In autumn 1867 he finally announced that he intended to run for one of Galveston's seats in the convention. His associates argued against a black man representing such an important county, suggesting that if he ran, the men in business and industry whom they hoped to attract to their party would be dissuaded from joining. Ruby countered that he was the only true representative of the great majority of loyal men in Galveston, and it was his right to run and their right to have him run. He refused to back out of the race and, thus, precipitated a vitriolic fight between himself and his friends in the Galveston Republican Association.

To minimize Ruby's threat and undercut his power, association leaders immediately attempted to broaden white participation in the organization's activities by bringing in individuals not yet eligible to vote. When Colonel A. P. Wiley, a "father of secession," applied for membership [they] . . . heartily endorsed his admission and called for the acceptance of all converts to the Republican cause. If enough such men came in, black power would be severely reduced. Ruby, along with B. Rush Plumly, who . . . considered himself a protector of blacks, fought the move. . . . When the association admitted Wiley anyway, Ruby resigned and charged that the association's leaders had sold out to the rebels.

Cut out of the Republican association, Ruby determined to run for the convention without its backing. He believed that the Union League actually controlled black voters, and he knew that he controlled the league; therefore, he believed that he could win the election despite the opposition of white Republicans. He obtained some white support. Plumly continued to work with him, and a convert to his cause was Dr. Robert K. "Revenue" Smith of the customhouse. On December 21, 1867, the Galveston Union League met to decide whom it would support for the convention election. Ruby demanded that it endorse him, whereas association leaders desperately tried to prevent such a move. However, Ruby showed that he controlled this group when the members announced that their choices for the convention were he and Smith.

But the nominee was not satisfied simply with the league's endorsement; he quickly moved to take over the rest of the machinery of the local Republican party. He and Smith called a meeting of the Galveston Republican Association to ratify the league nominations. . . . Over opposition of the white leadership, the association joined with the league and approved Ruby and Smith as the convention nominees.

The campaign that followed was relatively quiet, with the election of Ruby a foregone conclusion. . . .

Ruby had run for constitutional convention as a candidate of the black community. When he arrived at Austin, most people believed he was a radical politician who was primarily interested in securing equal rights and suffrage for blacks. His actions proved him a strong advocate of both of these goals, but he did not turn out to be the firebrand that whites had expected. He was an active participant in debate, a forceful behind-the-scenes manipulator, yet an acute observer of the political situation and a spokesman for moderation. His work in the convention made him an important figure in the state Republican political scene for the next five years and marked his transformation to the state level of leadership. . . .

The Constitutional Convention of 1868 provides the first opportunity to examine Ruby's ideas concerning the problems of blacks and the ways to rectify them. He envisioned a comprehensive program of education, economic development, and legal protection. Perhaps because of his background in education, he placed the development of a system of public schools at the center of his program. In this he was typical of others, of both the North and the South, who believed that education was the panacea that would help blacks climb out of the darkness of slavery. After the convention's committees had already been named, he solicited an appointment as an additional member of the Committee on Education, and he helped draft the constitutional mandate for a public-school system for the children of all races.

Yet Ruby was not content to rely solely upon education. He supported provisions to make available public lands for homesteading, which would give blacks an opportunity to become landowners. Understanding from personal experience how artificial and legal barriers could be built to exclude blacks from full participation in the community, he also worked to prevent legal or other kinds of discrimination. Just prior to the convention he had been denied first-class passage on a steamship to New Orleans. Now he obtained a place on the Committee on General Provisions and helped draft a section that would have made the exclusion of blacks from public conveyances, places of public business, and businesses licensed by the state illegal. That committee also produced a section that called for equal rights for all free men, with no man or set of men entitled to exclusive separate offices or privileges.

On the convention floor, Ruby also repeatedly supported investigations of violence and favored all measures to suppress these less subtle actions against blacks. While he believed in democratic political processes, he thought the restoration of former Confederates to their civil rights would lead inevitably to the imposition of limits on his own race; consequently, he argued that their continued exclusion from the franchise and officeholding was necessary and proper as punishment for their treason. With some modification, Ruby worked for these goals in 1868 and continued to pursue them through the rest of his career.

Given the fact that in the convention eighty of the ninety delegates were white, Ruby had little chance to secure the provisions he sought. Unable to carry out his plan in full, Ruby's major accomplishment in the convention was working for a coalition with whites that would aid him in carrying out as much of it as possible. He demonstrated in this effort mature political abilities, successfully exploiting for his own ends the factionalism among the white members of his own party. . . .

The factionalism of the white Republicans . . . provided an avenue along which Ruby could move to greater power. Two events aided him in this rise—his unexpected takeover of the state Union League on June 15, 1868, only two weeks after the beginning of the constitutional convention, and the formal split of the white Republicans into two parties in the state convention in August.

Under the leadership of white Unionist politicians, the state Union League had never been particularly responsive to the aspirations of its black members. Following the removal of Governor Throckmorton in 1867 and his replacement with E. M. Pease, these unionists had been even less interested in the blacks and went about their business distributing offices among white loyalists. Pease's administration and, consequently, the state league under the direction of Pease's associate Bell lost popularity among blacks because of its reluctance to give public offices to blacks, its weak stand on civil rights, and its hesitation in prosecuting white terrorists. This discontent provided the background for the annual league convention at Austin in 1868, where Ruby became the spokesman for those wanting change.

When Ruby discovered the extent of the unrest, he announced his candidacy for Bell's office. The action caught administration supporters by surprise and, unaware of Ruby's potential challenge, they were unprepared to beat him back. White leaders tried to restrain the black delegates and managed to hold many in line; but by a vote of 91 to 90, Ruby took over the state league organization. . . .

The regular party leadership realized too late the extent of Ruby's power and the importance of his league presidency. In an effort to rectify the situation, they attempted, after the party convention adjourned, to undermine his base of power at Galveston. Smith, Ruby's running mate the previous spring, led the attack, returning to Galveston, where he accused his colleague of corruption and selling out his black constituents. Ruby denied the accusations and appealed to league members for support. Smith quickly found himself in the midst of outraged blacks who refused to believe the charges and, when called upon to affirm the course of their leader at Austin, overwhelmingly voted their approval. . . . He had easily survived the first attack upon his base of power.

The constitutional convention continued despite the Republican party's collapse. . . . The regulars controlled the convention; therefore, the document they produced reflected their interests. . . . Rather than Ruby's proposals for a clear statement on the extent of an individual's civil rights, the draft incorporated a general resolution recognizing the equality of all persons before the law. A proposal by blacks to include a resolution that would not require mandatory segregation . . . was not included. Most portentous for blacks, the proposed constitution included a provision allowing all adult males to vote, except those explicitly disqualified by the United States Constitution. Given the white majority in Texas, this section paved the way for the ultimate failure of Ruby and his program.

Ruby, who considered the draft constitution a disaster for blacks, joined with twenty-two other convention delegates who opposed it on other grounds. . . . He urged league leaders to instruct members to vote against the constitution but to select candidates in legislative races who favored the Radical cause in the event a majority of voters ratified the document. As president, Ruby issued new league charters and harangued members throughout the state to reorganize, meet regularly, and prepare for an active campaign.

A major task was to break away any residual black support from Pease and Hamilton. Hamilton became the focus of Ruby's attacks upon the administration's forces after he announced his intention of running for governor. Ruby characterized Jack Hamilton as the archetypal white man who could be anything he wanted to be, rebel or loyalist, a man without principles and totally untrustworthy. In a speech at Galveston, Ruby warned blacks that they could never vote for a politician who had tried to convince Congress that no Negroes were being killed in Texas. . . .

By spring of 1869 the ground upon which Ruby was fighting was quicksand. Ruby discovered, as he warmed to the fight, that political conditions were rapidly changing. Through the Galveston Republican Association, Ruby had helped to plan a convention of bolting Republicans for May 11, 1869. He supported Morgan Hamilton, brother of Jack, who urged that the Radicals organize to oppose the constitution but make no nominations for public office until the president called for an election. . . .

Within the Radical group, however, a strong movement had emerged . . . to accept the constitution and bring about a compromise between the two factions. The middle-road movement had strong support, including General Joseph J. Reynolds, commander of the Fifth Military District, and, implicitly, Reynolds's close friend, President Grant. Grant appears to have tired of the internal squabbles within the southern-state party organizations and, unable to decide which group to back, began to pressure them to cooperate. . . .

Ruby realized that a shift was taking place. If General Reynolds and the president wanted compromise, to stick with Morgan Hamilton opened up the possibility of being left isolated. As a result, Ruby attended the middle-party convention and backed its nomination of E. J. Davis for governor, and its decision no longer to oppose the constitution. Ruby indicated that he believed united action was now necessary to settle the local political situation, and he was willing to compromise. "Whenever unnecessary," he wrote to Morgan Hamilton, "I do not believe in open force among those claiming to be with us, *at this time.*" . . .

Having joined the middle-party movement, Ruby was at the center of activity after President Grant, in midsummer, ordered the Texas election for the following November. Ruby quickly found that mobilizing the Union League was a task of considerable difficulty and encountered a problem that plagued the Republican organization throughout its early history. At the heart of the problem was inadequate financing. . . . Ruby sought alternative funding in the North, but found Republicans there reluctant to help. He called upon the national council of the league, claiming that the perpetuation of freedom in Texas depended upon their willingness to give money; but the support did not come. . . . Without financing, organization was practically impossible, and Ruby would discover that the league was always more efficient in its reputation among its antagonists than it was in actuality.

In addition to handling league work, Ruby decided to run for a seat in the Senate from the Twelfth District. The Twelfth consisted of Galveston, Brazoria, and Matagorda counties; and while Galveston did not contain a large black population upon which to draw support, the other two were old black-belt counties with large black majorities. Ruby faced the same arguments he had encountered in his run for the convention, in particular that the time had not come for black men to put themselves forward for public office. Even friends who had urged him to take over the state league and to run for the constitutional convention now opposed him. . . .

Although facing strong opposition, Ruby responded vigorously and refused to abandon the race. Accusing his opponents of being motivated by their own thwarted ambition, he effectively manipulated league chapters in his district to keep voters in line behind him. His candidacy created an excited response throughout the black community. . . . Ruby's campaign raised fears among whites, who complained that throughout the district blacks had become more defiant.

The chances of success for Ruby appeared good, but the campaign of the middle-party languished through the summer of 1869. Ruby possessed good possibilities for election to the state Senate, but unless the Davis ticket did well throughout the state he would be in the minority. The middle-party movement received a major boost in September, when President Grant . . . finally gave his open support to it.

Grant's decision to back Davis worked immediately to Ruby's advantage. At Galveston the Treasury replaced the pro-Hamilton collector of customs with a Davis man, Nathan Patten, who had worked with Ruby in the constitutional convention; and Patten appointed the senatorial candidate a special deputy collector. For the next four years Ruby would be the chief arbiter of appointments to positions as clerks, inspectors, weighers, watchmen, and messengers in the customhouse. The president's recognition of the middle-party group placed in Ruby's hands the ability to provide tangible rewards to his supporters and thus gave him another powerful tool to promote party loyalty. . . .

Ruby still faced a difficult election campaign and the candidate had to adjust to changing political realities if he hoped to maintain power. Whites who had been reluctant to register and vote in 1867 were returning to the polls. While black voters still outnumbered white voters in adjacent counties, last minute registration in Galveston placed more whites than blacks on the lists. . . . When the returns came in, Ruby's opponent carried Galveston County, 1,597 to 1,554; but Ruby's majority in Brazoria and Matagorda insured him the seat he sought. Despite the victory, the election of 1869 indicated that politics based solely on black power was no longer possible in the Twelfth District and that Ruby would have to adjust his politics to meet the new situation. . . .

When the state Senate met at Austin in a special session, George Ruby faced a difficult problem. He had to work for measures that would insure his continued control over his black constituency but at the same time act to make inroads among white voters. As senator from the Twelfth District, Ruby would work to develop a new image, one of a conservative politician who looked after not only the interests of blacks, but also whites in his community. During his four- year term he worked to tie himself and his constituents closer to the white business interests of Galveston in particular, seeking an alliance that would benefit all three.

Ruby tried several new approaches and techniques in rearranging his base of power. A major goal was to decrease his reliance upon the Union League. Whites did not like the organization because they saw it as a somewhat corrupt institution in which they could have little say. . . . He began efforts to weld blacks in his district into an organization that whites could not ignore and would have to deal with politically and economically—a labor union. He believed that if he could create a situation of mutual economic interdependence between blacks and white businessmen blacks would have a greater chance to maintain political power. In his effort the urban nature of his district was important; black workers in an urban economy could make demands that unskilled and unorganized workers in rural areas could not. Dependence on organized black labor would, theoretically, force white businessmen and industrialists to help maintain black political rights.

Ruby turned to the docks in his efforts to organize blacks. Whites had dominated the work on the Galveston wharf prior to the war, but in the postwar period large numbers of blacks moved into these jobs. If he could control this labor force, he would obtain power that even the most grudging white politician would have to recognize. . . .

Ruby's organizational activities unified black workers on the docks, but the philosophy of the local union movement limited its effectiveness. Ruby did not see the union as a device for confrontation, but rather as an institution to make possible an alliance with Galveston's white businessmen. The Galveston union denied the need for strikes but argued, rather, that the union provided capital with an organized work force. Politically, the union suffered from many of the charges of corruption and political manipulation that plagued the league, charges that worked against the alliance Ruby envisioned. Information about black activities on the wharf during this period is practically nonexistent, but at least one former dock worker remembered how he was used politically. On election days, leaders appeared and took the workers to picnics, gave them whisky, cigars, and marked ballots, then took them to cast their votes. . . . Despite his hopes, Ruby never used the union effectively to support his own political power. The work he accomplished, however, would provide a base for his young protégé, N. Wright Cuney, who would dominate the wharf in the 1880s and 1890s.

In addition to seeking economic interdependence that would link blacks and whites, Ruby tried to build his ties to whites by establishing himself as a power broker between them and the newly installed Davis administration. While Davis was in power, Ruby was the intermediary between the state government and the local community, providing direct access to Governor Davis when appealed to. Ruby also oversaw the appointment of local officials and worked tirelessly to insure that they acted in the party's interest. Unfortunately, rather than strengthening his position, this role worked against him, for it irritated many whites who complained of having to rely upon a black man. . . . Another weakness of his particular approach to the local businessmen was that it required continuation of the Davis administration to remain effective. . . .

Ruby also attempted to improve his connections with white business interests by working for them in the legislature. He held major assignments on committees concerned with the judiciary, militia, and public lands. He was assiduous in his efforts in behalf of railroads, banks, and insurance companies connected with Galveston. . . .

While trying to establish some sort of working relationship with the economic leaders of Galveston, Ruby had few illusions about the benevolence of these or any other white Texans. He made concessions on such issues as railroads, but he remained a strong advocate of measures designed to protect blacks in their civil rights and to provide equal opportunities. With Matthew Gaines, the other black member of the Senate, and backing from the Davis administration, Ruby helped pass bills that created a state militia, the state police, and a public-school system. He never believed these were enough to protect blacks, but he found whites unwilling to go further. When he attempted to pass a bill that would have enforced the compliance of public carriers with constitutional provisions that demanded equal access by all peoples, he found that his most ardent white supporters were not interested in helping. Ruby worked this bill through the Judiciary Committee and saw it reported to the floor, but the bill never even came up for a vote. Thus, while he was willing to compromise with whites, he did not forget his black constituents and pushed as far as he could in trying to protect them.

But in spite of his work for blacks, as Ruby tried to appease the white community his position among blacks became less secure. The interests of a landless agrarian, and urban work force, which comprised the bulk of Ruby's backing, were inimicable to the interests of the planter and merchant groups Ruby had to approach for support. The education and self-help programs Ruby sought for his black constituents were hardly in the interest of the whites, since they would serve to make the former slaves more independent. The state aid for railroads and public improvements demanded by white business men, on the other hand, took away money needed to support the programs intended to aid blacks. Funding to support the interests of both groups was not possible, since the tax base in the state was too narrow. Ruby was forced to make concessions; and as he provided support for white interests, he sacrificed some of the goals of his black constituents, who were denied educational opportunities, office, and greater economic freedom. As a result, his position drew fire from blacks. Compromise gained him little from whites also; for no matter what he did, businessmen continued to view him as an upstart and a threat. . . .

Ruby also appropriated a new mechanism for political purposes, the newly created public-school system. This activity greatly offended whites, who feared Ruby's increased power. The school system was a potentially important political tool because of the valuable patronage associated with it. The supervisor of schools in each district appointed local school boards that had tremendous power—they chose teachers, leased buildings, and made contracts for books and construction. At Ruby's request, Davis appointed Captain William H. Griffin supervisor of education at Galveston because he was a party loyalist, in addition to being a good school officer. When Griffin arrived at Galveston, he joined Cuney's chapter of the Union League, legitimizing its official status, and appointed a proadministration school board: Ruby; George Lawrence, a Union League organizer; Nathan Patten of the custom-house; N. Wright Cuney; and F. C. Mosebach, a German Republican businessman. From this position Ruby used school patronage to party advantage. Already hostile to the costs of public education, white businessmen were further alienated by Ruby's blatant use of the schools for political ends. Ruby managed to hang onto power, but he also undid work that was aimed at pacifying local whites. . . .

Despite his efforts . . . the changing electorate threatened Ruby. . . . The growing white majority turned the election [of 1871] into a Republican debacle. . . . When all the returns were in, the Democrat[s] had won by a narrow margin. . . . In Galveston County, intimidation and black distrust of Clark had cut into the number of Republican votes, decreasing the party poll from nearly one thousand in 1869 to only 304. Other counties made the election close, but the Galveston returns indicated approaching disaster for Ruby. Despite what he had done for Galveston's business leaders, they were not coming into the Republican party and he could not count on them for votes. It was also apparent that he could no longer muster black voters in full strength. While he would continue to be an important figure in state politics until 1874, the election of 1871 marked the collapse of his independent power. His political base had been eroded, both in real numbers and in the importance of the black vote relative to the total electorate.

After 1871 Ruby's power depended increasingly upon his connections with the national Republican leadership and with the Davis administration. In his continued bid for power, he now turned to Washington and Austin rather than to activity in the local community. . . .

However, neither Grant nor Davis could protect Ruby's office in his predominantly white district. From members of his own party, pressure increased for the senator to step aside in 1873 for a white candidate in the general election. A group of German Republicans, who demanded that the party recognize their claims to office, advocated that Judge Chauncey B. Sabin be put up for the Senate instead of Ruby. Because Ruby himself realized the unlikelihood of his reelection and thought that Sabin might have a chance, he refused to stand for renomination. . . .

In the general election of 1873, Texans voted Davis out of office. Sabin lost despite Republican hopes that the judge was attractive enough to be elected. The Democratic administration of Richard Coke set about dismantling much of the Republican administration's programs, including the final dismemberment of the police force that had been introduced to protect black voters. Under Coke, Texas was not a promising place for a former black senator. . . .

[In 1874], Ruby moved to New Orleans, where he found conditions more congenial to his efforts in behalf of blacks. He received an appointment in the customhouse, perhaps a reward from Grant for his prior services; but he spent most of his time working on newspapers in behalf of Republican and black causes. . . .

The Exoduster Movement of the later 1870s occupied must of Ruby's time. He became a prominent figure in the promotion of black migration from Louisiana to Kansas. In his newspaper, at public meetings, and before Congress he argued that the only way for blacks to obtain complete freedom was to leave the South. . . . Clearly, by 1880 Ruby had come to see improvement in the social relations of races in the South as hinging on increased respect of whites for black economic power. . . .

Ruby's work in New Orleans continued the fight that had occupied him from his youth—for economic opportunities and civil rights for black people. His politics were those of expediency; the men he supported and the course he pursued changed with shifting conditions. But his political opportunism always aimed at securing goals to which he remained dedicated. Alliances changed, but the ends changed very little. Unfortunately the people he had to work with were not as willing to compromise. In 1882, at forty-one years of age, Ruby promised to be a prominent leader among blacks for many years to come, a man who could lead, a model of educated and astute political ability. That promise would never be fulfilled, however, for on October 31, 1882, after a short attack of malaria, Ruby died in his home at 125 Euterpe Street.

## ✯ *F U R T H E R*     *R E A D I N G*

Alwyn Barr, *Black Texans: A History of African Americans in Texas, 1528–1995* (1996)
Randolph B. Campbell, "Carpetbagger Rule in Reconstruction Texas, *Southwestern Historical Quarterly,* 97 (1994)
———, *Grass-Roots Reconstruction in Texas, 1865–1880* (1997)
Gregg Cantrell, "Racial Violence and Reconstruction Politics in Texas, 1867–1868" *Southwestern Historical Quarterly,* 89 (1986)
Paul D. Casdorph, *A History of the Republican Party in Texas, 1865–1965* (1965)
Barry Crouch, " 'All the Vile Passions': The Texas Black Code of 1866," *Southwestern Historical Quarterly,* 97 (1993)
———, *The Freedmen's Bureau and Black Texans* (1992)
———, " 'Unmanacling' Texas Reconstruction: A Twenty Year Perspective," *Southwestern Historical Quarterly,* 98 (1995)

Carl Moneyhon, "Public Education and Texas Reconstruction Politics, 1871–1874"
    *Southwestern Historical Quarterly,* 89 (1986)
——, *Republicanism in Reconstruction Texas* (1980)
William C. Nunn, *Texas Under the Carpetbaggers* (1962)
Merline Pitre, *Through Many Dangers, Toils and Snares: Black Leadership in Texas,*
    *1870–1890* (1997)
Charles W. Ramsdell, *Reconstruction in Texas* (1910)
Williams L. Richter, *The Army in Texas During Reconstruction, 1865–1879* (1987)
——, *Overreached on All Sides: The Freedmen's Bureau Administrators in Texas,*
    *1865–1868* (1991)
James M. Smallwood, *Time of Hope, Time of Despair: Black Texans During Reconstruction*
    (1981)
Ernest Wallace, *The Howling of the Coyotes: Reconstruction Efforts to Divide Texas* (1979)

CHAPTER
10

# Conquering and Populating
# the Frontiers,
# 1860–1890

What Texas experienced during Reconstruction was not unlike that of other
southern states; however, its frontier experience in the late nineteenth century
linked it to the west. Like other western states in the late nineteenth century,
Texas was defined more by the pacification and settlement of the frontier than
by efforts to define and create a "New South." In this process the black-white
racial dichotomy of Reconstruction gave way to a far more complex blending
of race and gender on the frontier. Furthermore, the Texas frontier was more
complex than that of many other western states. It consisted of a western frontier
and a southern frontier, and the last decades of the nineteenth century witnessed
the conquest, settlement, and economic exploitation of both. On each frontier,
men and women endured danger and hardship as they settled and developed
new lands. Settlement also involved conflict with other inhabitants of the new
lands—Mexicans and Mexican Americans in South Texas, and Native Americans
in the West.

Traditionally, historians have focused on the settlement of the western frontier.
Two waves of settlers, cattlemen who moved north from South Texas and farmers
who moved west from the East, spread into the western areas of the state in the
1870s, 1880s, and 1890s. More recently, historians have modified this interpretation,
noting that the process of settlement was far more complex, that it involved issues of
gender as well as the complex interaction of diverse peoples and cultures, and that
it must be understood through the stories of individuals and families as well as
through the conflict of classes and races. The traditional outline, though, remains
relatively unchanged. When the Civil War ended, the frontier line extended from
the Red River north of Dallas southwestward past Waco to the hill country west of
Austin and San Antonio, and then southeast to the Nueces River and into South
Texas. Post-Civil War expansion involved the subjugation of Tejano and Mexican
settlers in South Texas and the removal of Native Americans. The cattle industry

*moved into the plains of the west and northwest in the post-Civil War period.
Hundreds of thousands of farm families followed, spreading west of the 100th
meridian as the century came to a close.*

*The process of frontier settlement raises issues of conquest and racial dominance
as well as questions about the nature of the conquest and settlement of the Texas
frontier. Was the Texas frontier experience dominated by the westward extension of
southern culture and mores, or did other forces define it? What role did men and
women play in this process, and how were they changed by it? What was the interaction of African Americans, Mexican Americans, Anglo Americans, and Native
Americans?*

 D O C U M E N T S

In 1870 Hugh Harmon McElvy moved his family from southwest Georgia to Collin
County, Texas. McElvy was one of thousands of southerners who abandoned war-
ravaged areas of the former Confederacy for the promise of wealth and opportunity
on the Texas frontier. Document 1 describes McElvy's impressions of Texas and
indicates that the promise of Texas was not always realized. In Document 2, Emily K.
Andrews, presents her first impression of West Texas as she traveled with her new
husband from Austin to Fort Davis in the late summer of 1874. Andrews was accompanying her husband Colonel George Lippitt Andrews to his post as commander of
Fort Davis. Her diary chronicles her impression of the land, its scattered settlements,
and its people. Especially compelling is the sense of emptiness, stark beauty, and
ever-present danger.

The next three documents consist of the recollections of three "cowboys"
who describe their lives and their work. Document 3 is the story of Will Crittendon,
an African American, who was introduced to the life by his father, who came to
Texas after emancipation to start a horse ranch. Crittenden took up the cowboy life
at the age of five and set out on his own at the age of fifteen. Document 4 tells the
story of Elario Cardova, a descendent of a family that began farming and ranching
in the Nacogdoches area during the Spanish colonial period. At the age of ten,
Cardova left home to find work in South Texas as a ranch hand where he experienced
the turmoil and conflicts that characterized that region in the post-Civil War period.
Lastly, in Document 5, Mrs. Ben Miskimon tells of entering the cattle business
when she was a child. After her marriage she ran the family cattle business and
directed the move west from Jack county in North Central Texas to Tom Green
county near San Angelo. Each of these selections de-romanticizes the cattle business,
focusing on it as work.

Document 6 satirizes the myths about Texas and its cowboys and Indians.
Alexander Sweet was a late-nineteenth-century Texas humorist who describes a "Wild
West Show" that he witnessed in the Polo Grounds, in the heart of New York City
in 1884. The central feature of this show was a mock-battle between cowboys and
Indians. Document 7 vividly describes the last battle between the Apache and the
Texas Rangers. In 1880 Apaches attacked the Overland Stage in Southwest Texas near
Eagle Springs. Captain George Wythe Baylor of the Texas Rangers commanded the
posse sent out to track the Indians and deliver punishment. Here the conflict between
whites and Indians is presented unadorned by myth.

## 1. Hugh Harmon McElvy, a Georgia Farmer, Reports on the Hardships Farmers Faced on the Texas Frontier, 1871

Sunday Evenig August 27th 1871
Collin Co Texas

Well Lawson your letter reached us yesterday being out just as long again as it Should have bin. I have nothing much to write you. We are all well & our country burned up with drouth. We have not had any rain Since the 28th of May. We had on that day a ground Soker & it lasted tell a bout the 4th of July. Since then we have suffered beyond any thing I ever new in the way of drouth. There is maney places the ground is cracked open tell it is daingrous to ride through the grass. Your horses feete can if he happens to Strike one of thoes cracks fall in to his belly. Our forward corn is maid a bout half crop whare it was will tilled. Late corn & half tended corn will yeald from 10 to 15 bushels per acre. Cotton is no go. There was verry little planted & what was has maid a flash. It grew up verry rapid full of sapp & had just commenced to fruite when the drouth set in & it threw of[f] the forms & the boles that stuck has swiveled & opened. The lint is short & nearly all pickd out now. . . .

You ask me a bout Maj Hines. I do not no any thing of the Maj. When he got here last winter the Maj was out of funds & he could not git in business & he was in a tite. So he engaged to drive a 6 mule gin which he did for 20 dollars per month. He drove tell he got money enoug to leave on & he left for the frontier. He never has written back but once & then said he had an offer to drive stock to Kansas. Whether [he] acceped it or not we do not no. I would not be surprised if the Indiens got his scalp. He left heare with two other Georgians, young men from Mitchell County, Eavans & Willingham. We have not heard from none of the party. They were verry much dissatisfied with this part of the State. If they got a birth to drive stock to cansis citty they will not git back to Texas soon.

You ask me to give you the report of the country at Waco. We Set out the 3rd day of this Inst. & travel down to the edge of the plain which is a bout 60 miles wide, one etarnal pariar [prairie]; no water only in wells & it worth or cost 10 cents a bucket full for our stock; the grass all dried up & nothing mid [made] only in the valley of the Brases [Brazos] River. We met Sitizens from that sexion & they told us it was a fine country all up and down the Brases but it was subject to this drouths. It is a wheete country & the winter rains make the wheete. Corn there is 2.00 dollars per bushel at the railroad 40 miles from Waco and as we have all maid corn a plenty to do us an other year & one dollar is all we can git for it we concluded we would turn our cours & look for a more plesent portion of country & rent one more year. . . .

There is one thing I can Say for the Sitizens of Texas. They are a longs ways a head of the Sitizens of Ga in Schools. Evry kneighborhood I Saw they had large fine Schools & churches houses & the School rooms ware all occupied. Thes frontier

---

"'I Am Tired of Writeing,' A Georgia Farmer Reports on Texas in 1871," ed. William Warren Rogers, *Southern Historical Quarterly* 87 (October 1983): 185–188.

counties we traveld in are nearly all Settle up from the old States mostly from Kentucky, Tennessee & Missourea & a good chance of north Georgians. Some fiew from South Carolina & a fiew from North C.

I am tired writeing & will Close.

I remain as Ever
H. H. McElvy

Send this letter to your farther.
It will Save me a long letter to him.

## 2. Army Wife Emily K. Andrews Gives a Woman's View of the Texas Frontier, 1874

Our Trip from Austin to Fort Davis Texas

'Sunrise'
"Dripping Springs"
'In Camp' Augt. 11 1874

My Dear Father,

Feeling sure that some little account of our trip through Texas would be entertaining to you, I have tried to note down each days doings, and herewith send them to you. . . .

"Half way House" "Adams Creek"
Wednesday evening, Augt 12th

We have now arrived at our second camping ground, and while the tents are being pitched I am waiting in a real Texan house.

It is made of logs, with daylight peeping in at the many crevices. The chairs are covered with skins, while the rest of the furniture is primitive in the extreme. Hens and chickens are running in and out the doors, and the pigs in the yard would I think be quite as friendly were it not for the old darkie who sits at the door and keeps away all such intruders. . . .

Friday Morning, Augt 14th

A good bath, plenty of sound sleep, a breakfast of rabbit and squirrel, and we are ready to start again—I find . . . a good deal of pleasure in this out of door life, and I often wish you could see us in camp especially at night. The men who are marched carefully, are never to weary to dance and sing about their camp fires. Their voices are many of them, so rich and full of melody that I am very glad if I can hear them as I go to sleep—. . .

"A Women's View of the Texas Frontier, 1874: The Diary of Emily K. Andrews," ed. and annotated by Sandra L. Meyers, *Southwestern Historical Quarterly* 86 (July 1982): 49–80.

"Seven Mile Creek" Friday Evening 14th

Fredericksburg is a small German town filled with Lager beer saloons, and beer gardens, with more blue eyed round faced fraüleins about, than anything else—

At the only Hotel in the place we had a real German dinner, highly seasoned with herbs and onions, but our appetites were sharp enough to enjoy anything. . . .

Peg Leg Station, Monday evening Augt 17th

This morning we broke camp at half past six and were soon "en route" again. . . .

After traveling about twelve miles we came to "Rock Springs Station", where an old man 75 years old with his wife and one child, live all by themselves, certainly it was the most broken down, and homeless looking place. However they were so kind as to give us plenty of delicious milk. Just before reaching this place we espied a body of horsemen descending the hill in front of us, I must say I was a little frightened, but we soon discovered by their dress, that they were a band of Rangers under command of Major Jones, with two Tonqua [*sic*] Indians, acting as guides. As the Col. desired it I went forward and looked at the brave red man, but knowing their desire for light haired scalps I kept a good distance from them. . . .

Kickapoo Springs Wednesday evening, 19th, Aug.

After a breakfast of Rabbit as we were off at an early hour this morning. We started just before the Cavalry and with their wagon train and ours made quite an imposing sight—. . .

The troops are all to move early in the morning over the same road as we do, so if possible we start by half past four, to avoid the dust. Last night, 12 Indians made a raid on a train encamped here, and captured 17 mules. As soon as the troops arrived this morning a company was detailed to recapture them, but the Indians having 12 hours the start there is not much chance for the soldiers success. . . .

Thursday Evening, August 20th
"Fort Concho"

This morning we were all up at half past three and at half past four after a hasty cup of coffee, taken by starlight . . . we were ready to move—

Just as we were starting Col. Anderson sent word to our Camp, that he feared the Indians were nearer than he supposed as one of his men had been chased the evening before. So we had to creep along using extra precautions. . . .

We lunched at rather a poor looking place, called Lipan Springs, with not a very inviting looking house, so we preferred making an eating house of our ambulance. The woman here tried to make me believe that if I walked far from the house I should be carried off, but as I have not found many persons in this country who really tell the truth, I paid very little attention to her, and walked as I liked. . . .

Friday evening, Augt 21st
Johnson's Station—

The ride of today has been much pleasanter [sic] than that of yesterday. The country has mountains, with very beautiful interval lands, while the grass and trees were very green. . . . We met an immense Mexican train today going to Concho, there were 15 teams each 8 or ten yoke of oxen. These carts are similar to our tip carts only very much heavier carrying 3500 pounds each. . . .

We have just heard that a Mexican was killed here last night by an Indian, not very pleasant news, and I, for one shall sleep with one eye open, not withstanding we are to have a special guard round our tent. I does seem strange to think that in this beautiful country where every thing is apparently so peaceful, each man sleeping or waking must have his carbine loaded just at hand. . . .

Central Station, Stake [*sic*] Plains
Augt. 23rd. 10.45 P.M. *Full moon*

Ten hours ago we left the head of the Concho, and entered at once the dense Chaparral. In any other country I should have enjoyed this ride very much, for the road was very beautiful and the moon at its full, but these thickets are such dangerous places, so well fitted for an ambush, that I was not sorry when we struck out on the famous Staked Plains. . . . [W]e arrived here at the "Central Station", where we are resting and taking a bit of lunch—This is a queer house, looking more like a small fortress than anything else. Standing here alone in the midst of this great Desert. Nothing to break the view as far as the eye can see. We are rather a strange looking party as we stand or sit, taking our midnight cup of tea, while in the back ground are the keeper and guard of the house who have come out of their beds to see us pass—But I am sure it is impossible to give you any correct idea of the scene—

Leon Hole's, Sunset
September 5th

Now after a week or so of garrison life [at Ft Stockton] we are again in Camp, and sitting at my tent door, just at sunset enjoying the luxury of out of door freedom.

I must tell you a little of Stockton. To me it is not as pleasantly situated as Concho. The lack of shade and the want of grass, on the Parade make a glare as you look upon it almost intolerable, and we found many of the officers suffering from the effect of it on the eye. They, and also their wives I found the most agreeable, cultivated people, hospitable in the extreme. They reminded me very much of home people, and sitting chatting in their pleasant parlors, I could easily fancy myself in Boston again. . . .

Fort Davis
Tuesday Evening Sept. 8. 1874

Every body was stirring bright and early this morning, and in the best of spirits while trying to make the travel worn harnesses and carriages presentable to drive into the Post. . . .

About two miles from the Post, near the Station House we were met by three of the officers, who had come out to receive their Colonel, and very heartily they did it. From here we had a good view of the cleanly cut mountain known as "Mitre Peak," and which on a clear day can be easily seen from Stockton.

In less than an hour, we dashed into the garrison where officers and men were eagerly waiting to welcome us. So here I am safe and sound and so ends my pleasant camp life, to which I shall ever look back as one of the happiest epochs in my life, and as I sit here in my homelike quarters, I cannot but be thankful to that Kind Providence, that has brought us in safety to our Journey's end.

Affec yr daughter
Emily K Andrews—

### 3. Will Crittenden, an African American Cowboy, Describes Life on the Range, 1870s–1880s

Do I know anything about the range? Why, man, I made a trail drive right through Fort Worth when it wasn't even a whistle-stop and I was only nine years old! I learned to ride a hoss on my pap's stock farm at Cedar Grove, Texas. I was born on December 12, 1868, right after Pap came to Texas from Alabama, where he was a slave of Governor Crittendon.

It was while he was a slave that he got his love of good hoss flesh from the governor. He always had a good surrey team and used Pap to drive it. When freedom came, one of the governor's sons had already taught Pap to read and write, so he came to Texas to start a hoss ranch and to get himself a school to teach. We did all right about the school by getting one at Cedar Grove. He was the first teacher in the county at that time. He didn't do so well about the hoss ranch. He only got around twenty to thirty head and forty to a hundred cattle critters at a time. . . .

When I got to be fifteen, I'd got fifty mules together and set out to make my fortune. I traded those mules around and busted hosses on the side. Among the places I busted hosses was the Tom King ranch at Greenville, Texas. Tom King had thousands of critters. Jim Harris, a banker at Terrell, Texas, had a ranch in West Texas but bought his hosses at Terrell and always had me bust them for him. . . . The Manning hoss ranch had me bust all his hosses. His place was close to Terrell, and I'd contract to bust forty at a time. Many a time I'd have the money gambled off before I'd busted half of what I'd contracted for. . . .

The last man I worked for busting hosses was Lindsey, at Elmo, Texas. He was a big hoss man and ran a regular hoss ranch. He'd gotten a big order for so many head of hosses, and I was hired to round them up for him. Well, I rounded his hosses up for him, but I cut back a few for myself, and after the sale was made, I went back and got the stuff and took it to Abilene, Texas, and sold it.

### 4. Elario Cardova, a Mexican American Cowboy, Remembers Working as a Ranch Hand in South Texas, 1870s–1880s

I was born on November 3, 1861, at my father's farm seven miles east of Nacogdoches County. . . .

The Spanish government made a grant of land to my grandmother, Rachel de los Santos Coez, and her three brothers. The grant consisted of eleven leagues of land in the Nacogdoches section. . . .

Jim Lanning and Judy Lanning, eds., *Texas Cowboys: Memories of the Early Days* (College Station: Texas A&M University Press, 1994): 169–75.

Jim Lanning and Judy Lanning, eds., *Texas Cowboys: Memories of the Early Days* (College Station: Texas A&M University Press, 1994): 177–182.

Our farm consisted of about fifty acres under cultivation and about fifty acres in pasture for our milk cows and work stock. In addition to our farming, we owned longhorn cattle which ranged on the unsettled land. Farms were all fenced and were situated far apart, leaving great tracts of land for the cattle to graze on. . . . We didn't give the cattle any attention. The cattle bred and multiplied at their will and found their own living on the range where it suited their taste. All we did to hold the herd was to provide salt licks in the section we desired the animals to make their bedding ground. When we needed a little beef or made a sale, we held a little roundup and cut out the critters desired. . . .

As part of our farm work we raised hogs, using the same method we employed raising the cattle. The hogs bred, ranged, and obtained their living in the woods. . . .

. . . My mother married the second time when I was ten years old, and then I left home to make my own living. That I have done ever since.

The cattle range was about the only place a young farm boy could secure employment. Consequently, I went to the open-range country where large ranches were established, and I chose Goliad County as the place to find work. I was successful and was given work on a ranch owned by the Hughes brothers. That was in 1871. . . .

My career on the range was during the period when there was a great deal of conflict among the ranchers of the Goliad range territory. I happened to secure a job with an outfit which was not only called rustlers, but were classed as one of the leaders of the rustlers. However, they maintained that they were defending the rights of the small ranchers against the impositions of the large ranchers [Pures]. . . .

During the Civil War and for a period after the war ceased, branding was neglected by many cattlemen. Also, very few cattle were sent to market, because the market was cut off from Texas. The lack of sales resulted in a large increase of cattle. Therefore, the two conditions produced thousands of cattle which were unbranded.

A few years after the war ceased, railroads extended west into Kansas, and markets were established within driving distance of Texas. Then the prices went up which resulted in a scramble to brand those cattle without a brand. Naturally, ranchers maintained they had a superior claim to the unbranded cattle within the section which they called their home range, and any unbranded cattle grazing with the cattle carrying their brand. This claim was generally accepted as proper, but there were some folks who did not confine their branding strictly within their territory. Branding cattle in territory claimed by some other rancher led to trouble and many killings. The conflict developed two contending parties.

The small fellows claimed that the Pures were claiming too much territory, for the purpose of excluding the small ranchers and to take undue advantage with the unbranded cattle. The small ranches, and some people who never had a herd, ignored the Pures' claims to territory and branded cattle where found. . . . These conditions started arguments, which progressed into quarrels and ended in many shootings and killings.

The Pures organized vigilante committees which operated secretly and set out to clean out the rustlers. In the section were some thieves, but when the vigilantes began to operate, they classed many cattle branders as rustlers, and many men were run out of the country who were not real thieves.

## 5. Mrs. Ben Miskimon, a Woman on the Range, Recounts Her Experiences Running the Family Cattle Business in Texas, 1874

When I was nineteen years old I married W. A. Miskimon. I had property and cattle, too. We lived in Jack County seventeen miles below Jacksboro. We had a mighty hard time, loss of cattle, and dry weather. My husband wasn't no cowman; I tried to teach him about cows, but he never could learn, not even to feed one. At last God gave me a boy. We would have to stay by ourselves on many instances. Once my husband went to Missouri on business. The severe drouth had caused all the water holes to sink and all wells to dry up. I strapped the baby on my back, papoose style, and would walk a mile or two for water. The wild hogs rooted in the low places, and water would come up in small holes. With my baby on my back and a teacup in my hand I would dip water here and there until I filled my buckets and carried the weary load home. . . . I didn't stay out of the saddle long. I began riding the range again when my baby (papoose, I called him) was quite small.

We started to Tom Green County on September 1, 1889. We had about one thousand head of cattle and three hundred head of horses. I had five cowboys to help; as I've said, my husband was no cowman, couldn't ride nor cut out cattle, so he wasn't much help. . . . When we neared the Brazos River, . . . I sent my husband on with the horses, and he crossed and put them in the corral. Me and the boys were to hold the cattle. We drove them down to the river and camped with intentions of pushing them across the next morning. The cowboys were from the malarial country, and when they got cold and wet they took chills. I got on my horse and logged the wood up, built a fire for the sick boys and made blankets down, the poor boys with high fever and me with the cattle. That was one awful night, trying to hold the cattle all alone, with wolves howling and panthers screaming and boys sick. I stayed on my horse, rounding the cattle, keeping them down. The boys were better next morning, and we pushed the bellowing herd across the swollen stream. . . . We continued our journey on to Tom Green County, which was comprised of several counties then. We came to Red Creek, which looked very desirable for camping. There was plenty of water and fresh fall grass. . . .

We herded the cattle on that area until the fence was built and ranching started. In the later part of 1889 we built the old ranch house that now stands on the corner of Randolph and First Street. I traded a little old red bull for that lot.

Jim Lanning and Judy Lanning, eds., *Texas Cowboys: Memories of the Early Days* (College Station: Texas A&M University Press, 1994): 200–201.

## 6. Texas Humorist Alexander Sweet Scoffs at the Images in an Eastern "Wild West Show," 1884

November 15, 1884

New York City
To Big Foot Wallace,
Chacon Creek, Texas

Those who dwell in the busy haunts of men are tormented with a morbid curiosity to know all about the habits of their fellowman in his savage state. It is this that stimulated the manufacture of dime novels. . . . Buffalo Bill reproduces the wild nomadic life of the border, using real Texas cowboys and *bona fide* Indians, both of whom look as true to nature as if they had never seen the inside of a barber shop, much less that of a wash basin, and who furnish their own hair.

The most refined and cultured people attend these performances. I, myself, attended several of them. It is pleasant to sit in perfect safety and observe the pale-face cowboys murder the poor Indian in cold blood with blank cartridges. . . .

One of the most surprising features of the performances is the utterly unexpected attack by wild Indians, on the log cabin of a sturdy pioneer, who had established himself right in the midst of the Polo Grounds, far beyond the confines of civilization. . . .

. . . In this wild, lonesome spot, near Harlem, lived the heroic backwoodsman, with his solitary wife and fearless boy, exposed to the ravages of confidence men, in constant danger of policemen and other wild animals that prowl at nights around the jungles of New York. . . . The opening scene is supposed to occur at the peep of day. A large audience, who have just dined, are seated on the benches. The door of the cabin opens, just as the peanut boy walks around among the audience and offers three cents worth of peanuts for a dime. The wife of the frontiersman, who does not wear any bustle, now emerges from the cabin, and shading her eyes with her hand, looks at the roofs of the distant tenement houses for Indian signs. . . .

A distant rifle shot is heard in the corner of the Polo Grounds near Gimpel's beer saloon. . . .

The solitary hunter comes galloping up on a pony. Tied behind his saddle is a big fat buck, which, if it is not stuffed, must have fallen before his unerring rifle at the provision store opposite Gimpel's saloon. The wife and boy assist the hunter in hanging up the fat buck. The huntsman then performs his ablutions, several of them, in a tin wash basin. The boy stakes out the pony to graze. . . . The pony, however, is not staked out to graze. He is staked out to tempt the redskins to steal him. Even now two dusky forms can be seen emerging from their hiding places near Gimpel's saloon. . . .

The stealthy redmen of the forest have got near the pony. A man in the audience, perceiving that the horse is about to be stolen calls out "Police! Police!" The audience laughs vociferously, but, owing to Gimpel's beer, the Indians do not hear the racket.

---

"Alexander Edwin Sweet and the Wild West Show," ed. Virginia Eisenhour, *Southwestern Historical Quarterly* 93 (October 1989) 199–207.

At last the Indian seizes the rope. He knows the ropes. He looks at the roof of the tenement house to see if the frontiersman is watching. Not seeing him there, the Indian is about to go off with the horse, when the boy seizes a pistol and fires at the Indian. The husband takes a pop, and even the old woman blazes away as if it was a regular Fourth of July celebration. The Indian drops dead, and kicks about on the ground, like a decapitated chicken. The other Indian climbs up on the roof of the cabin, probably to see if there is another horse staked out to graze.

Thirty red devils, mounted on ponies, emerge from the vicinity of Gimpel's saloon. . . . The white family and the redskins exchange several tons of imaginary lead. The fight looks as if it were a real one. . . .

Now is the time for Buffalo Bill and his cowboys to take part in the canvass. Here they come, brandishing their revolvers, as fierce as so many United States deputy marshals. The first thing they do is to exchange a few thousand shots with the illegal voters—that is, the Indians who are not allowed to vote. Buffalo Bill kills a number of Indians single handed. Several Indians send in their resignations. The rest seek safety in flight, closely pursued by the cowboys. The hunter and his family are saved from a fate worse than death. The Indians did not even get away with the venison.

"Darned funny sort of a log cabin," said a rough looking customer behind me: "No chickens and no dogs about the place, and only one boy. All the log cabins I ever seen had about forty chickens, the same number of dogs and more'n a dozen children of different sizes. Maybe the Injuns stole 'em," he added philosophically.

Yours,
Alex E. Sweet

## 7. Captain George Wythe Baylor, Texas Ranger, Gives a Stark Account of the Last Battle Between the Apache and the Rangers, 1880

The writer having been promoted captain of Company A, Frontier Battalion [of the Texas Rangers], in October 1880, the strength of the company was increased to twenty men, stationed at Ysleta. The Overland Stage, then carrying United States mail and passengers between San Antonio and El Paso, was attacked in Quitman Canyon, between Eagle Springs and the Rio Grande. . . .

[John] Ford at the time, with a few of the ranchmen and Overland employees, went out to look for the stage when it failed to show up at the proper time, feeling pretty sure the Apaches had either captured or killed the driver and passengers. The searchers found the stage . . . the mailbags cut open and mail scattered over the ground, a leather boot cut up and carried off, but did not find the bodies of the men. Examining the signs, Ford believed there were only four Indians, and they had left the road and gone off southwest toward the river. The party took it for granted the

George Wythe Baylor, *Into the Far, Wild Country: True Tales of the Old Southwest*, ed., Jerry D. Thompson (El Paso: Texas Western Press, 1996): 304–322 driver and passenger had been taken prisoners and carried off to be tortured, and followed five or six miles, expecting to find their bodies.

Ford wrote to me, and Rangers were soon on the road. I had twelve of my men and three Pueblo Indians, making our force sixteen, quite small enough. . . .

By sunrise we were off and took a trail that left the river and wound through some rough hills. Coming in below again, we struck the trail where the Indians had come from the southeast, and picked up a small, handsome fur-tipped [red] glove, and our conjecture was it had been dropped by the passenger for the benefit of pursuers, and gave us hopes that both the men were alive. The trail showed one fresh shod mule, which had been taken by the Apaches from a colored soldier who was repairing the telegraph wire in Quitman Canyon. I once overheard him relating the affair to an admiring crowd on a San Antonio street. He was up the telegraph pole and did not see the Indians until they had him treed and were getting ready to shoot him like a 'coon, when the Rangers charged and saved his life, but he lost his mule. . . .

On reaching the river pretty well supplied with water, we followed a ledge of rocks crossing diagonally and making a splendid ford, and followed the trail down the river, they taking the old trail used by the Mexican customhouse guards. Where this leaves and strikes the rough hills we found the first camp of the Apaches after the murder in the canyon. . . .

Following the trail, we came to a wide gravely stream that came from the mountains to our right, and the trail led to the west, but when we struck the creek bed we found a fresh trail going east of some fourteen unshod ponies and knew in reason they were the game we were after, and we followed the fresh sign. We had with us old Bernardo Olguín, Domingo Olguín, his son, and Aniceto Durán, a nephew of the old Pueblo chief.

Bernardo, [who] had for a long while been acting as scout and trailer for the United States troops, was familiar with the whole county, brave, sober and reliable, and could read wood signs like a book. . . .

The three Pueblos had a score to settle with these same Apaches, as Simón Olguín, a brother of Bernardo and noted guide for the United States Army, was killed at Ojo Viejo when a company of Pueblos under a Lieutenant Bell was ambushed, or rather surprised, in a camp that Simón begged the Lieutenant not to stop at. But to go back to our trail. . . .

The chase was now becoming very exciting. The signs showed the Mescaleros had left that morning and were traveling slowly and carelessly, having come to the conclusion their last murders would be unavenged. We passed plenty of deer and antelope, but orders not to shoot anything but an Indian were positive. The Pueblos rode ahead a quarter of a mile, and often were strung up to highest pitch. Every coyote, antelope or moving thing seen was eagerly scanned.

In the evening we came to their camp, and an examination of the ashes showed that live coals of fire were still burning. In hunting large game, as the pleasure of the chase is in proportion to the danger, so we felt all the eagerness of tiger or lion hunter, but I doubt much if either comes up to the Apache warrior with his Winchester and fierceness and cunning.

Rushing ahead, by sunset we had covered a good deal of ground. . . .

Taking Old Bernardo and a couple of men with me we went up to where the trail crossed the crest of the mountains and with our glass scanned the hills in front of us, but no head of ponies, smoke, nor Indian could be seen. Whil'st we were standing there a flock of doves came sweeping by our heads and I said: "Boys, where those are going to water we will find the Indians in the morning." No fire could be seen from our front, so we cooked and were soon asleep, the sentinel instructed to waken us before day-break.

We were good tired and it seemed I had hardly been asleep an hour until we were awakened and had a hasty breakfast and were off on the trail. It was bitterly cold, so we walked and led our horses. . . . Old Bernardo was ahead and I and Lieutenant Nevill just behind, and just as day began to dawn, the Old Pueblo squatted down and said: *"Hay, están los Indios,* captain," and looking in the direction he pointed we distinguished two camp fires burning up brightly.

Luckily we were just on the crest of a hill and turning back, were soon out of sight. . . .

. . . My squad by following in Indian file and stooping as low as possible got within a hundred yards of the eastern camp. Here we came to a swag or low place between us and the Indians, who were huddled up around their fires cooking breakfast and not conscious of a Ranger being within a hundred miles. One was just coming to the fire with some wood and looked as big as a skinned horse, having an army cape on taken from some Negro soldiers killed at Hot Springs on the Rio Grande. It proved to be a little girl not over five years old, and goes to show how easily one can let his imagination run away with him. I was afraid if we passed down this swag some of the Apaches would see us and being just on the crest of the hill with a deep canyon beyond a few jumps would take them out of sight. So I kneeled down and motioned to the men to fall into line on my right and passed the word down the line when I fired to turn loose.

Old Bernardo's eyes were glistening like a panther's at the chance of getting even with the murderers of his brothers, his son and nephew by his side. . . . It was a complete surprise to the Indians, and there was plenty of blood all around their camp fire, showing some of us had good aim. Sergeant Carruthers got three at the other fire. Nearly all the men had Winchester carbines and rifles, but I used a Springfield rifle with hair trigger such as the United States officers used and I doubt if a better army gun was ever made for reliability.

We only had a few shots when the Apaches broke over the hill like a herd of deer and we charged the camp, as did the other squad, and when we got where we could see, the Indians were making two-forty time down the steep canyon. . . . The Apaches ran, some to the west and some east down the deep canyon and one warrior went up the opposite side of the canyon.

He bore along the hill in full view and drew the fire of every one and occasionally would turn around and shoot back at us. All we could do was to hold our breath until he shot, not knowing which one was his target. I took five pops at him myself. Frank De Jarnette and another Ranger followed his trail for over a mile and said he was bleeding like a beef, but still making big jumps toward the Tularosa Agency. . . .

Finding we could make no further progress in that direction, and the firing in the canyon ceasing, we turned back to the arroyo, and soon saw Sergeant Carruthers and a squad of Rangers coming up the bed of the arroyo with two squaws and a child, prisoners. . . .

. . . [Sam] Graham came up, and he was perfectly wild with rage at the sight of them, for this same band had . . . shot his brother, making him a cripple and killing his sister-in-law, . . . and killed an old man named [James] Grant. . . .

Of course, young Graham, a hot headed boy, wanted to kill the women. The prisoners soon took in the situation and cowered behind me as they saw his angry face and hostile attitude, but I told him I could never agree to killing women, crying and begging for their lives, but would go with him after the warriors willingly. . . . We started up the arroyo, and soon heard such a roar of Winchesters we thought the Apaches must have rallied and returned to their camp. We were pretty badly scattered, for the Indians went in every direction and the Rangers after them, but as we were afoot we were not in it in a race with fleet-footed Apaches, especially as they were running for dear life, assisted by a lively fusillade of Winchester bullets. . . .

We found in their camp women and children's clothing, showing we had struck the band that murdered Mrs. [Margaret] Graham and robbed their wagons. We found five United States cavalry saddles, showing that they had killed the six colored soldiers at the Hot Springs below Fort Quitman. We found the tops of old Morgan's boots which, no doubt, would have been used to make moccasins, and the pants of the passenger who was on the stage. They had cut them off at the body and above the knees and made them into sacks filled with tobacco and such little trinkets as delight the Indians. We had got the identical Indians that had killed ten people we knew of within a few months. . . .

We put the squaw on her horse and the little girl produced her saddle, quirt and army cape and selected her pony, and appeared as contented as if with her own people. We strung out and by 11 o'clock that night were back at Victorio's tank, pretty well tired out, thankful that none of the men were hurt, and satisfied we had given the Apaches a lesson that they would remember; in fact, they never committed another murder in Texas.

# ❖ E S S A Y S

In the first essay, geographer Terry Jordan of the University of Texas at Austin uses migration patterns and other social data to challenge the traditional argument that the Texas and U.S. cattle industry was born in South Texas and was based on Spanish/Mexican cattle raising practices. Instead Jordan argues that the cattle industry originated in South Carolina, was influenced by British, African, and Spanish herding techniques, and spread westward into east and southeast Texas in the early nineteenth century. Spanish influences were absorbed primarily in the southeast and in Louisiana, not in Texas. In the second essay, historian Arnoldo De Léon and sociologist Kenneth Stewart, both of Angelo State University, analyze employment data and economic data to assess the clash between Hispanics and Anglos in South Texas. They argue that Anglo settlers relied on their domination of the political process and the presence of American military force to wrest control of South Texas from Mexicans and Mexican Americans. Both groups migrated to South Texas for economic opportunity. Historical racial and cultural antagonisms resulted in one group succeeding at the expense of the other. In the third essay, Jacqueline Reinier, Professor Emeritus at California State University at Sacramento, examines in detail the experience of forty women who migrated to the plains of the Panhandle and northwest Texas. She concludes that these women did not challenge existing social or political mores, but served primarily to transplant institutions and domestic practices to the Texas frontier.

# Southern Origins of the Texas Cattle Industry

TERRY G. JORDAN

The continued westward expansion by herders following Texas statehood in 1845 created, as early as 1860, the first two clusters of Anglo cattle ranching within the Great Plains. One of these clusters lay in the Coastal Bend area, along and between the lower courses of the Guadalupe, San Antonio, and Nueces rivers, a region that formed the northeastern part of the South Texas "diamond." In the process the Anglos overran, not for the first time in their spread westward from Carolina, a formerly important Hispanic ranching region. The Coastal Bend had been the scene of a thriving Spanish cattle industry, particularly in the 1700s, and some vestiges remained in the middle nineteenth century. The Anglos, like the Hispanos before them, found the prairies and brush country *chaparral* of the northeastern diamond well suited to cattle raising. . . . By 1870, Anglos had expanded up the Nueces and San Antonio valleys, enlarging this South Texas ranching region to include, roughly, the northern half of the diamond area. In that year, the northern diamond housed fully one-third of the cattle population of Texas, a total of well over one million head.

By contrast, the southern half of the diamond, which remained an Hispano stronghold, did not witness an increase in cattle ranching during these decades. Instead, the purest Mexican-American counties, those lining the Rio Grande, formed a sheep-ranching district. . . .

The second major new cattle-ranching cluster by 1860 lay on the central-western frontier of Texas, in a block of rolling to hilly counties drained by the middle courses of the Brazos and Colorado rivers, a region including a northern part known in the vernacular as the Cross Timbers and a southern section called the Heart of Texas. . . . Cultural geographer D. W. Meinig and historian R. N. Richardson designated the Cross Timbers-Heart of Texas as a "main source region" of the western cattle industry, noting that it produced "more notable cattlemen than any other region of equal size in America." At the same time, the region formed one of the purest southern Anglo-American districts in Texas, lacking as it did any significant numbers of blacks, Hispanos, or European immigrants. . . .

The two major cattle-ranching regions implanted within the southeastern margin of the Great Plains between 1850 and 1870 were created by cattlemen migrating from eastern Texas, from the three areas where Anglo herding had developed during the first half of the nineteenth century. The Coastal Prairie corridor played a key role in this westward thrust.

## Diffusion from the Coastal Prairie of Southeast Texas

The creolized herding culture rooted in the Texas Coastal Prairie east of the Guadalupe or Lavaca rivers before 1845 subsequently made a significant contribution to the rise of ranching in the Great Plains. In the last decade and a half of the antebellum era, these lower southerners were largely responsible for developing the Coastal Bend ranching area in the South Texas diamond. . . .

When Anglo herders began entering the trans-Guadalupe country in the 1840s, they found a war-ravaged land from which most of the former Mexican ranchers had fled. Remaining behind were numerous longhorn cattle, as well as a relatively small population of *vaqueros,* some Irish-born ranchers, and a few Hispanic *rancheros,* such as the Navarro and de León families. The cattle industry of the Coastal Bend was all but dead. . . . Between 1850, and 1860, Anglos from the Coastal Prairie corridor rebuilt the cattle industry of the trans-Guadalupe country, elevating it to a magnitude previously unknown. By the time of the Civil War, Coastal Prairie settlers had created the cattle-ranching focus in the Coastal Bend. . . .

Even beyond the Guadalupe River, Anglo cattlemen in the South Texas diamond did not forget their traditional lower-southern markets. New Orleans remained their chief goal as late as the Civil War, and drives to Louisiana continued even in postbellum times. The Crescent City's hold on the receding coastal cattle frontier strengthened with the advent of steamship cattle transport, and the port town of Indianola thrived as the major handler of Texas cattle shipped by sea to New Orleans. Other cattle drives from the Guadalupe and San Antonio river valleys in the 1860s and early 1870s reached Mobile, Natchez, Shreveport, and Woodville in Mississippi. . . .

## Continuing Diffusion after 1870

Many Anglos paused only briefly in South Texas and the Cross Timbers-Heart of Texas areas before continuing their migration. From these two clearly defined bases in the margins of the Great Plains, they spread rapidly westward and northward after 1870. In the wake of the decimation of the Plains Indians and the bison herds, Anglo herders, continuing the thrust that had long before brought their genealogical and cultural ancestors out of Carolina, surged through much of the Great Plains.

In this expansion, cattlemen from the two regions followed different paths westward. The primary goal of ranchers emigrating from South Texas was the trans-Pecos country, including the Davis Mountains and Big Bend. These inheritors of the coastal cattle tradition rarely ventured north of the thirty-second parallel, clinging instead to counties on or near the Mexican border. In South Texas and the Coastal Prairie, many of them had become accustomed to using Mexican *vaqueros,* a dependence which may help explain their migration pattern. In semiarid Southwest Texas, near the border, they could continue to ranch in the manner they had known in the valleys of the Guadalupe, San Antonio and Nueces rivers. Theirs remained a far southern, creolized herding culture, and they were not major participants in the spread of ranching through the Great Plains.

Instead, the Cross Timbers-Heart of Texas cattlemen provided the main westward and northward movement after 1870. The spread of ranching into the Texas South Plains and Panhandle was largely their work, as was a major thrust up the Concho Valley, across a low divide to the Pecos River, and northward along that stream into eastern New Mexico. Many soon expanded their ranching operations into states north of Texas, carrying the Anglo herding system through the Great Plains. . . . West Texas, in very considerable measure, was colonized from East and Central Texas, a pattern initially established by cattlemen from the Cross Timbers-Heart of

Texas. More than that, these sons of the Piney Woods and Upper South were chiefly responsible for bringing Carolina to the Great Plains.

## Anglo Herding Traits in the West

As Anglo cattle herders spread westward after mid-century, they did not forsake the Carolina heritage. Rather, they introduced elements of their cattle tradition, passing on to descendants in the west many ancestral herding traits from the southeastern seaboard. They remained, in goodly measure, Carolina's children.

One typically Anglo custom imported to the west was the use of herder dogs. Tilden, the county seat of McMullen in the South Texas diamond, was called Dog Town in the 1870s, due to the local ranchers' habit of using packs of dogs to round up cattle in the surrounding brush country. Even the Mexican *vaqueros* on the famous King Ranch in South Texas had herder dogs by the 1940s, using them to find cattle that strayed into brush thickets. To the north, also, in the Cross Timbers-Heart of Texas ranching region, leopard dogs were common. Their use declined to the west, on the open grasslands, and relatively few major ranches in West Texas kept such canines. One late nineteenth-century rancher in the Texas Panhandle did own a pack of seventy-five "greyhounds," but their job was to protect his cattle from wolves and coyotes rather than to herd stock. These hounds lived in a low, elongated "mush house," and the man in charge of them was called a "mush-pot wrangler."

Black cowboys made a more effective transition to the west. Famous Cross Timbers cattlemen such as Dan Waggoner and Oliver Loving used black cowhands before and after the Civil War. On his Wichita County ranch in 1880, Waggoner employed thirty-one Anglos, one black, and one Mexican as cowboys. Even in the South Texas diamond, where *vaquero* labor was common, black cowboys were occasionally found. For example, C. C. Cox, a rancher in Live Oak County in the Coastal Bend area, used Negro help in the late 1850s. Blacks accompanied the Anglo rancher migration to West Texas, where sixty-eight of them worked as cowboys by 1880. While these blacks made up only 4 percent of the cowboy work force, a far lower proportion than claimed by some historians, their presence in West Texas is undeniable. . . . Eventually, a few blacks even became ranch owners in West Texas, and Negro cowhands continued to find employment on ranches there into the present century. . . .

Hispanic-derived longhorns, according to the commonly accepted account, provided the livestock for the early cattle industry of West Texas and the Great Plains. Only later, after the advent of barbed wire, were improved breeds introduced to displace the longhorn, goes the traditional argument. My evidence suggests, on the contrary, that West Texas cattle were not pureblood longhorns in the pre-fence era and that bloodlines derived from the Anglo-American East were always present. Dan Waggoner's experience in the Cross Timbers region is illustrative. . . . Waggoner began as a cattle raiser in the Blackland Prairie corridor of Northeast Texas, then moved his herds to the Cross Timbers of Wise County in the 1850s. About 1865 he became aware of a "slow change in appearance" in his cattle from one year to the next. Seeking the cause of this change, Waggoner finally located a single feral longhorn bull among his stock. This bull fought and defeated Waggoner's smaller bulls, presumably of British origin, and collected a sizable entourage of cows. Supposedly,

Waggoner's uninvited longhorn was the first of his breed to appear as far north as Wise County. Thus, on the very eve of the surge by Anglo ranchers onto the Great Plains, one of the legendary cattle kings noticed the first appearance of longhorn traits in his herd. It seems very likely that other cattle introduced to the Cross Timbers from Northeast Texas, such as the herd brought from Fannin to Palo Pinto County about 1858, were also dominantly British.

Nor were the cattle trailed west from the Piney Woods of unmixed Hispanic ancestry—and the East Texas area remained a major source of western cattle throughout the nineteenth century. In the 1880s cattlemen from West Texas came to the southern Piney Woods looking for herd replacements, and one East Texas resident recalled that "every once in a while somebody would go along the big road" in front of his house, "with a small herd of cattle, drifting them west to grass and prairie country."

Further diluting the longhorn parentage of early West Texas herds were cattle introduced directly from eastern states. One early rancher in the Cross Timbers had come from Alabama with some nonlonghorn stock, and Lum Slaughter, the cattle baron of Palo Pinto County in the Cross Timbers, imported shorthorn bulls from Kentucky as early as 1871 to improve his herd. It may well be true that Texas ranchers sent their purer longhorn animals north to stock the Great Plains ranges between 1870 and 1890, keeping the superior, part-British cattle to restock their own ranges. In this way, Texas cattle could have gotten the reputation in the north of being longhorns, even though the actual makeup of the herds reflected a mixture of Spanish and British stock. At any rate, the claim that pure longhorn cattle prevailed on the West Texas ranges between 1870 and 1890 deserves to be challenged. Not even the crucial Coastal Prairie corridor, the southernmost of the Anglo routes westward, was stocked with pure longhorns. . . .

Carolina, then, was abundantly represented in the Great Plains cattle industry. But so, too, was Latin America. Western ranching vocabulary abounded with Spanish loanwords such as "corral," "ranch" "remuda," "morral," "lariat," "bronc," and "pinto," and various other aspects of nonmaterial and material herding culture on the Great Plains reflected Hispanic influence. Traditionally, the South Texas diamond has been designated as the primary scene of Hispanicization.

It is not my intent to deny the Hispanos a role in the evolution of Great Plains ranching. Rather, the argument presented here . . . is (1) that the role of the South Texas diamond as an arena of Hispanicization has been greatly overemphasized and (2) that the case for Hispanic influence in the Great Plains has been consistently overstated.

Absorption of Spanish herding traits by lower southern Anglos began in the late eighteenth century, far to the east along the creole coast. . . . Hispanicization began in earnest in southern Louisiana and the Natchez area of Mississippi, and the process continued in the Coastal Prairie corridor of Southeast Texas, where Anglos employed Mexican herders and used lariats by 1830. Census marshals working the Coastal Prairie counties of Southeast Texas in 1850 found additional evidence that Hispanicization was well advanced there. They listed the profession of a Fort Bend County Anglo as "owner of ranch," while in nearby Jackson County one of the nine Mexican-American inhabitants declared himself to be a 'becero' (*vaquero*). The creolized herding culture carried west of the Guadalupe River by Anglos after

1845 or 1850 probably differed only in minor respects from the remnant Hispanic system already rooted there.

Moreover, the Mexican rancheros of the South Texas diamond had very nearly disappeared before 1850. In the Guadalupe, San Antonio, and Nueces river valleys—the crucial Coastal Bend area in the northeastern part of the diamond—only 10 persons of Spanish surname owned 100 or more cattle at mid-century, and the total number of resident Hispanic "herdsmen' was but 181, of whom 92 lived south of the Nueces River. In the most purely Mexican portion of South Texas—the Rio Grande Valley between Laredo and the Gulf—only 12 Spanish-surnamed persons owned as many as 100 cattle in 1850, and this southern part of the diamond remained inconsequential as a cattle-ranching region. Moreover, banditry, lasting from the 1850s through the middle 1870s, made cattle ranching in the district between the Nueces River and the Rio Grande next to impossible for Hispanos and Anglos alike.

A culture in rapid decline, such as that of the South Texas Hispanic rancheros between 1840 and 1880, is unlikely to exert much shaping influence on a vital, expanding neighbor culture. It is therefore more appropriate to regard the cattle industry that thrived in the northern part of the diamond area by 1860 and 1870 as mainly an Anglo-American achievement, as a successor of the creolized lower-southern herder culture. The diamond was the westernmost in a succession of arenas where coastal Anglos met Hispanos, and not demonstrably the most important.

The overemphasis on South Texas as a scene of Hispanicization has, in turn, led to an incorrect view of that region as the "cradle" of the Texas and Great Plains cattle industry. In fact, a better argument can be made for the South Texas diamond as a cradle of Texas sheep ranching. The combination of sheep and cattle on the same range, a combination in which sheep not infrequently exceeded cattle in importance, was typical of Hispanic-American ranching. In the southern half of the South Texas diamond, exactly such a situation existed in the middle nineteenth-century, as was suggested earlier. One result, perhaps, was that some Anglo ranchers in the northern half of the diamond, by 1870, combined cattle and sheep raising. Sheep outnumbered swine almost two to one in the northern diamond, a major departure from coastal southern Anglo tradition. Perhaps the sheep-ranching industry which developed in the Edwards Plateau region by 1880 can be traced to this experience gained in the South Texas diamond.

The principal Hispanic-American contribution to western cattle ranching lay in horsemanship and related paraphernalia and vocabulary. Anglos thereby acquired equestrian techniques well suited to open grassland country. Most likely, this acquisition began far to the east, perhaps even in Florida and South Georgia, and was largely completed in the Coastal Prairie of southern Louisiana and Southeast Texas. When Anglo and Hispano ranchers met again in the trans-Guadalupe country, both were mounted herdsmen.

Not only has South Texas been falsely designated as the cradle of the western cattle kingdom and overrated as a scene of Hispanicization, but also (and perhaps consequently) the extent of Spanish influence in the Great Plains ranching industry has been overestimated. The incorrect assumption that Anglos were neophytes who adopted intact the Hispanic herding system has led scholars of that school of thought to look for a Mexican behind every sagebrush. A good example of such overstatement is Sandra Myres's claim that the *mesta,* an Hispanic stockraisers' guild traceable to medieval Spain, was the forerunner of such Anglo cattlemen's organizations as the Panhandle Stockmen's Association, established in 1880, and the Texas and Southwestern Cattle Raisers Association, founded in the Cross Timbers area in 1877. This extravagant claim has no documented factual basis. The Cross Timbers-Heart of Texas was the less Hispanicized of the two major cattle-ranching districts of Texas by 1870, and yet it produced the first Anglo stockmen's organization. It is more logical to seek the origin of such associations in the traditional communalism of the Anglo frontier, the same communalism that produced claim clubs, house raisings, wagon trains, and home-guard militia. . . .

Still, as suggested earlier, Hispanic influence existed in the Great Plains, most notably in horsemanship. Agents and routes of diffusion must be found to account for the presence of these Spanish traits. Since Anglos ranching in the South Texas diamond were more thoroughly Hispanicized than any others, as a result of their long experience on the creole coast, they would seem to provide the key. Closer inspection, however, reveals several apparent problems with this diffusion model. First, a number of Hispanic traits failed to spread northward from the diamond area. Among these was the "Mexican plan" of herding, adopted by some Anglos in the Nueces Valley of South Texas in the 1850s. It involved a roundup or *rodeo* "once a week or oftener," instead of only once or twice each year, as was the Anglo custom.

Nor did large-scale sheep raising or the use of Mexican *vaqueros* spread notably north of the thirty-second parallel. Only 2 percent of the cowhands employed north of that parallel in 1880 were Hispanos. In fact, when Anglo ranchers in the Texas Panhandle were confronted by Hispano sheepmen from another source— New Mexico—in the late 1870s and early 1880s, Anglo-Texas ranchers stuck by their cattle and rejected the opportunity to give sheep a major place in their range operation. The Panhandle's Hispano *pastores,* who numbered 358 in 1880, had recently arrived from New Mexico. Though they accounted in that year for 22 percent of the Panhandle's total population—70 percent in the four western border counties—the Hispanos were quickly shunted out and their sheep replaced by Anglo cattle. They left behind only some place names.

Another problem with accepting South Texas Anglos as a major source of Hispanic traits lies in their migration routes. As we have seen, their principal path in the latter part of the nineteenth century led westward to the trans-Pecos country, not north into the Great Plains proper. Relocation diffusion in the form of migration from South Texas cannot explain the spread of Hispanic traits, since migration routes ran at right angles to the presumed direction of trait diffusion.

This apparent problem is resolved by a consideration of marketing routes. After the Civil War, South Texas Anglo cattlemen broke their longstanding allegiance to New Orleans as a market and began trailing herds northward to Missouri and Kansas, following the earlier example of ranchers in northern and central Texas. The principal cattle trails serving South Texas led directly north, through the Cross Timbers-Heart of Texas region (fig. 10A). Hispanic horsemanship skills, with the related items of material culture and vocabulary as well as the word "ranch," appear to have diffused northward along the cattle trails and to have been implanted in the Cross Timbers-Heart of Texas. Another potent force in the northward diffusion of Hispanic herding traits was the Mexican War of 1846–48, in which numerous Texans from the northern and central portions of the state saw action in the south. These

**Coastal prairie corridor**

**Northeast Texas prairies**

**Southern Piney Woods**

**Cross Timbers-Heart of Texas**

**Northern part of "Diamond"**

**Major cattle trail, 1865–1880**

**Major migration thrust**

**Minor migration thrust**

**Fig. 10A**   The major postbellum cattle trails ran at right angles to the direction of migration, encouraging south-to-north cultural diffusion.

contacts with South Texas were renewed during the Civil War, when the blockade of Texan ports forced a variety of goods to be shipped out through Mexican ports. So, while migration routes ran east to west, important north-south avenues of communication were opened by two wars and a new marketing pattern. These avenues brought selected Hispanic traits and huge numbers of longhorn cattle north without noticeably influencing migration. Principally in this manner, the techniques of the Creole coast cowmen reached the Great Plains.

## Conclusion

Great Plains cattle ranching in the open-range era during the latter part of the nineteenth century contained an important Anglo-American component, a component that derived ultimately from seventeenth-century South Carolina. A spatial and temporal continuity between the colonial South Atlantic seaboard and western Texas has been demonstrated. Great Plains open-range cattle ranchers belonged in part among South Carolina children, both genealogically and culturally.

Geographer Donald Meinig enumerated "about twenty" nuclei of colonization on the Atlantic coast of North America in which distinct local cultures developed, later to spread westward and contribute to the shaping of the United States. Boston and its environs, for example, gave us the Puritan work ethic; the Delaware Valley provided the log cabin and family-operated farm; the Chesapeake Tidewater was the source of the plantation. Among the twenty, too, was Charleston and its hinterland, though its importance has generally been underestimated. Henceforth, colonial South Carolina, whose legacy reached the grassy expanses of the Great Plains, should be regarded as a cultural hearth of great significance to the evolution and understanding of both the South and the West. It should take its rightful place alongside the other major colonial nuclei as one of the major shapers of American culture and institutions. . . .

In ethnic terms, western ranching reflects a unique mixture of groups, a blending of British, African, Hispanic, and probably also French, German, and Amerindian influences. The crucial early mixing occurred in one confined locality, lowland South Carolina, the southern fringe of the English colonial empire in North America, where a favorable juxtaposition of Britons and West Africans occurred. Westward along the creole coast of the Lower South, as far as the Nueces Valley of Texas, vigorous ethnic blending continued for two centuries.

Environmentally, a subtropical belt of pine barrens better suited to grazing than cultivation provided a hospitable, though certainly not determinant, physical setting for the incubation of Carolina cattle herding. The same pine barrens, together with canebrakes, small prairies, and grassland corridors, offered suitable pathways to the west. Ultimately, ranching reached the greatest stretch of grassland on the North American continent, an environment that encouraged expansion of herding on a scale previously unknown.

Frontier conditions, most notably a shortage of labor, contributed to the rise of ranching in South Carolina, but large-scale cattle herding was not typical of other English colonial frontiers in America. Often, but not always, in the areas where it was implanted, ranching was confined to a pioneer stage and disappeared with the passing of the Anglo frontier. While helpful in certain instances, the concept of cattle herding as an occupance stage is not universally applicable in the westward diffusion to the Great Plains.

A desire to participate in the market of the Thünenian World City, coupled with the difficulty of access typical of frontier areas, helps explain the viability of an extensive form of land-use such as livestock ranching. The market, emanating initially from western Europe through the West Indian plantations, was essential to the rise and spread of open-range herding. But in the final analysis, the market model cannot explain the precise character of a frontier economy.

In sum, western ranching was the product of ethnic creolization occuring in a frontier setting and a suitable physical environment, under favorable market conditions. Had any one of these elements—culture, contact, remoteness, environment, or market—been fundamentally different, western ranching would also have been different, or quite possibly would not have come to exist at all. Indeed, when one element—remoteness—was broken down by railroads and the industrial age around the turn of the present century, traditional open-range cattle ranching quickly disappeared. Carolina's reign on the western grasslands was short, limited to the brief, pleasant interlude between the arrival of the first cattlemen and the coming of the machine age.

# Power Struggle in the Valley:
## Mexicans and Anglos in South Texas, 1850–1900

ARNOLDO DE LÉON AND KENNETH L. STEWART

The history of Spanish Texas is now well documented. First outlined by the pioneer Borderlands historian Herbert E. Bolton and advanced by Carlos E. Castañeda, the story takes up much space in Texana collections. . . .

Less well known is the story of Spanish-Americans in Texas following the arrival of Anglo settlers from the United States in 1821. The dissertations of James E. Crisp, Arnoldo De León, Fane Downs, Andrew A. Tijerina, Gilberto M. Hinojosa, and Mario T. García, however, have broadened historical understanding of social attitudes toward Tejanos and of Mexican-American demographic patterns in the Lone Star State during its formative decades in the nineteenth century. Many more works are in progress among them a comprehensive quantitative analysis of social life among Mexican Americans in Texas between 1850 and 1900.

This analysis of immigration into south Texas during the last half of the nineteenth century comes from that larger study. It attempts to trace the destiny of two immigrant groups—one from Mexico, the other from the United States and Europe—as they arrived in south Texas following the Mexican War. It seeks to describe how the two peoples fared, considering the fact that they came to south Texas bent upon making something of themselves in a frontier region that promised them an equal start. In explaining the eventual inequalities that developed, the study probes into the historical forces that determined the destiny of the two groups.

Understanding the fate of immigrant groups descending upon south Texas in the last half of the nineteenth century requires much more than grasping the dynamics of local historical forces. The fact is that the experience of newcomers to the region was determined by a host of patterns and events far beyond the section's immediate surroundings and reaching far back into time. Thus, the context inherited by the population ingressing into the region during the latter nineteenth century is outlined in the first part of the article.

Spain first took an interest in the northern part of Tamaulipas (or modern-day south Texas) in the 1740s, some thirty or forty years after establishing permanent settlements at Nacogdoches in east Texas and San Antonio and Goliad in central Texas. . . .

Arnoldo De Léon and Kenneth L. Stewart, "Lost Dreams and Found Fortunes: Mexican and Anglo Immigrants in South Texas, 1850–1900," *Western Historical Quarterly* 14 (July 1983): 291–309. Copyright © 1983 by The Western Historical Quarterly. Reprinted by permission.

Though hot and dry and unfriendly to farmers, the region proved beneficial to settlers with a penchant for raising livestock. Its topography offered an abundance of grazing land for cattle and mustangs, and ranching activities soon provided the bounty that made the Escandón settlements permanent. As the region became an active livestock center, it took on the features of other Hispanic enclaves. . . . By the dawn of the nineteenth century, . . . the settlements in the Rio Grande Valley were "on the threshold of an upward thrust from the Rio Grande to the Nueces River."

What signaled an incipient change for all of Texas was the arrival of Stephen F. Austin in 1821. Implementation of colonization plans for Anglo-Americans produced a wave of immigration from the United States that dramatically altered the social and cultural fabric of the entire state. By 1835, the demography of the region east of the Hispanic settlements in San Antonio and Goliad was radically different from before. The Anglo-American population centered in this eastern region numbered some 35,000, far more than the estimated 4,000 Hispanos located primarily in the central Texas area.

Though the influx of Anglo-Americans created a different kind of world for the Nacogdoches, Béxar, and Goliad areas, northern Tamaulipas, or what is present-day south Texas, was touched only peripherally. The Tamaulipecos took little interest in the changes occurring to the northeast. In fact, the region experienced a brisk expansion between 1821 and 1835. The settlements originally concentrated in a wedge of land along the Rio Grande extended outward. . . . The region now consisted mainly of ranching communities, including approximately 350 rancherías where settlers carried on a customary way of life and identified with the familiar institutions of the Spanish-Mexican tradition. . . .

Until the 1840s, residents of the section lived remotely from American influences as Mexico's claim to the region discouraged Anglo-Americans from entering. Within a few years, however, it became an area where immigrants from both Mexico and the United States came to mold their destinies. . . .

Americans came to the region with a decided edge, however. To begin with, troops came along with them to secure the area for the United States. Anglo appreciation for this military presence remained constant even after the end of the Mexican War when it was seen as crucial to their prosperity. . . .

Encouraged by the military fortifications and the support they could count on from Austin, Anglos scoured the territory in efforts to acquire lands held by the former Tamaulipecos. In Nueces County, where some land was acquired by Anglos while the war raged, original grants to Mexicans were displaced through a combination of methods including litigation, chicanery, robbery, fraud, and threat. . . .

Along the lower border, similar mechanisms were used. . . . In part, such indiscreet misuses of power incited the Juan Cortina "revolt" of 1859. One of Cortina's major grievances during the rebellion was that no justice existed for Tejanos in south Texas.

. . . By various means, then, Anglos transformed the formerly isolated south Texas region, and by 1860 it had become a part of Texas where the Mexican-American majority was militarily and politically subordinated to the Anglo-American minorities. Once the pattern was established, it held for the rest of the century.

The military and political advantages enjoyed by Anglo-Americans as they arrived in south Texas ultimately led to a new regional economic arrangement.

Within just twelve years after the Treaty of Guadalupe Hidalgo, large tracts of the most valued real estate in the region had been acquired by a few Anglo immigrants. Estimates based on the Census of 1860 show that immigrants, including those from Mexico, Europe, and the United States, comprised about 64 percent of the nonslave population in that year. Newcomers also held about 95 percent of the assessed real estate value of south Texas. . . .

What these figures show is that Anglo-American immigrants to south Texas rapidly appropriated not just lands but the foundation of the region's economy. Through the transfer of land ownership from Mexicans, they gained economic control of an area where persons rooted in the older Spanish-Mexican heritage comprised at least 73 percent of the total population through the last half of the nineteenth century. Moreover, it was military and political power, not entrepreneurial opportunities created by the transformation in agriculture during the 1870s and 1880s, that was responsible for the takeover of the means of production. The region remained almost exclusively a ranching area without adequate access to commercial markets during the 1850s and 1860s, and not until the decades following 1870 did it make the transition to commercialized farming and ranching. By the time the agricultural transformation reached the southern portion of Texas, both the economic and political processes were solidly held by the Anglo-American minority, which could reach out and reap its benefits.

Another aspect of post-Mexican War economic change in south Texas was the appearance of a complex process of occupational differentiation. Two contrasting patterns of diversification occurred simultaneously during the time the region came under the domination of Anglo-Americans and commenced the transition to a commercial agricultural base. First, economic and political conditions wrought changes in the demand for labor, and all gainful workers felt this impact regardless of their ethnic heritage. Second, ethnic cleavages became deeply drawn, with ominous consequences for both immigrants from Mexico and Mexican Americans born in Texas.

. . . The spread of the railroads and the growth of commercial farming operations meant improved technologies and greater mechanization, and the labor force as a whole paid the price for these developments in the form of job displacement. The proportion of workers specializing in agricultural pursuits, for example, decreased from nearly 30 percent in 1850 to only 17 percent in 1900. Declines also occurred in specialized trade, transportation, manufacturing, and mechanical employment. Only one category of workers—unspecialized laborers—increased rapidly between 1850 and 1900. An insignificant segment of the labor force in 1850, this group multiplied to over 40 percent of all workers in south Texas by 1900. The total effect of the agricultural transition was to reduce the degree of specialization required of the largest number of workers. Levels of skill among south Texas workers declined in accordance. . . .

As these dramatic changes took place in the overall labor force, a second pattern of more direct consequence for Mexicans was manifest. Divergent roles in the economic process developed in close correspondence to varying national origins of the region's immigrants, and an ethnic division of labor emerged. Subsequently, the stream of *inmigrantes* (immigrants from Mexico) crossing into the area faced distressing employment prospects, and their hopes for a better life in Texas were thwarted. . . .

In 1850 Mexican immigrants, together with native Tejanos, literally served as the backbone of the labor force. Over half (54.2 percent) of the immigrants were engaged in specialized agricultural pursuits, and the same was true of the native population, nine out of ten of whom were of Mexican descent. Together, the indigenous Tejanos and the *inmigrantes* comprised about 90 percent of the entire agricultural labor force of 1850. Only 4.6 percent of the Anglo-American immigrants were similarly employed, and they constituted less than 5 percent of the total workers specialized in agriculture.

A similar labor arrangement also held true in the area of manufacturing and craftsmanship. Over 40 percent of both the *inmigrantes* and Tejanos were involved in manufacturing and mechanical occupations in 1850, and the two groups together made up about two-thirds of this labor sector. The incoming Anglo-Americans, in contrast, were employed in manufacturing and mechanical endeavors at a rate of 17.4 percent, and they comprised only about 16 percent of all workers in the category. . . .

. . . The most notable change in the ethnic composition of labor between 1850 and 1900 was an extensive decline in the percentage of *inmigrantes* and indigenous Tejanos committed to agricultural labor. As noted, the agricultural segment of the total labor force dwindled from 29.8 percent in 1850 to just 17 percent in 1900. As the overall decline set in, however, the percent of Anglo-Americans entering south Texas to take up agricultural pursuits increased from less than 5 percent to 17.6 percent. Consequently, the reduction in the proportion of *inmigrantes* involved in agriculture was extreme. Where 54.2 percent of them were engaged in this labor segment in 1850, only 18.4 percent performed specialized agricultural tasks in 1900. Of course, a similar trend occurred among the indigenous workers, about 85 percent of whom were Mexican Americans in 1900.

Manufacturing and mechanical occupations also formed a waning sector of the total labor force of south Texas. This group dwindled from 33 percent to 11.6 percent of the working population in the years between 1850 and 1900, and once again, those coming from Mexico experienced a more radical decline than those from the United States. The proportion of *inmigrantes* pursuing manufacturing and mechanical employments decreased by 30 percent. The decline among Anglo-American immigrants, in contrast, was only 2 percent. The fact that Tejanos, who comprised a large majority of the indigenous Texans, underwent a reduction paralleling that of the incoming Mexicans makes the overall pattern of shifting labor in south Texas tellingly clear.

The labor displacement, associated intrinsically with the transition to commercial agriculture, focused primarily on the commodity production sectors of the economy. Agriculture and manufacturing and mechanical occupations, all with heavy concentrations of Mexican immigrant and native Tejano workers in 1850, were especially reduced. The result was a movement of *inmigrantes* and Tejanos into the general mass of unspecialized laborers. Over 40 percent of all Mexican and Tejano workers were confined to the general labor pool by 1900, and together they made up about 99 percent of its members. Meanwhile, immigrants from the United States continued to stream into service, trade, and transportation endeavors and even increased their participation in the declining commodity production segments of the labor force. The Mexicans and Tejanos, then, suffered a severe downturn in occupational standing during the agricultural transition, while opportunities for immigrants from the United States were apparently enhanced.

Such an ethnically stratified occupational structure obviously affected the personal and collective lives of Mexicanos in the lower strata. The jobs they came to have surely touched on their personal well-being, for certainly a nexus exists between vocation and standard of living. Given the correlation between ethnicity and labor that emerged in south Texas between 1850 and 1900, it should be expected that Mexican immigrants suffered not only in terms of occupational status but in terms of wage and wealth benefits as well. Indications are that this was the case exactly. . . .

Estimates of personal wealth in the south Texas area show that in the years between 1850 and 1870 the standard of living among the workers who arrived from Mexico fluctuated violently in comparison to that of Anglo-American immigrants. The proportion of Mexicans who reported possession of personal wealth totaled 2.6 percent in 1850. The number increased to 16.4 percent in 1860, but declined by more than 10 percent by 1870. A similar pattern of wealth ownership took place among the American immigrants, but the number reporting assets was not less than 16 percent in any one year. Thus, the relative percentage of the American immigrant population that was able to accrue some degree of wealth consistently surpassed that of the *inmigrantes.*

In addition, the relative amount of personal wealth concentrated in the hands of the Anglo-Americans remained constant over the years. Anglos controlled about 31 percent of all personal wealth in the region, though they composed only about 9 percent of the population. Wealth owned by *inmigrantes,* on the other hand, amounted to only 10.4 percent of the regional total in 1850, increasing to 37.1 percent in 1860, and then dropping sharply to 18.2 percent in 1870. At the same time, the Mexicans composed 31 percent of the region's population in 1850, and by 1870 they made up 50 percent. Hence, while immigrants from Mexico composed the fastest growing single ethnic group in the region, they were the ones most habitually consigned to a marginal level of existence or less. It cannot be argued, moreover, that the *inmigrantes* were unwilling to work hard toward personal betterment. Their participation in the labor force increased consistently, even as their standard of living, as reflected in wealth statistics, remained unstable. In 1850 the percentage of Mexican immigrants over the age of twenty pursuing gainful employment was 23.1 percent. This increased to 52.7 percent by 1870 and to 56.5 percent by 1900. As in the case of other immigrant groups streaming into the developing territory of nineteenth-century south Texas, they undertook work as a way of realizing their aspirations. An improved standard of living, however, was not a dependable outcome for them. Dreams for a better life in Texas escaped them.

During the twentieth century, numerous academicians and government policy makers concerned with the effects of migration from Mexico to the United States have tried to profile the essential characteristics and qualities of the *inmigrantes.* . . .

Since the earliest efforts to construct profiles of the character of the Mexicans coming to the United States, American scholars and public officials have been guided by the fundamental assumption that "Mexican" culture somehow does not mix well with "American" culture. . . .

. . . [T]he presumption of antipathy between Mexican and American cultures has been forged into a more sophisticated technical rhetoric by more recent scholars and bureaucrats, but the notion nonetheless remains. . . . Only in the last two decades, since the resurgence of interest in Mexican-American historical studies, have viewpoints impugning this belief in cultural antipathy been cultivated.

Rodolfo Acuña's book, *Occupied America,* serves as an excellent illustration of the kind of challenge being advanced in the more recent works of Chicano historians. As Acuña sees it, Mexico since the 1870s has been a sort of colony of the United States, and Mexican workers have been transformed into "migrants" by the push and pull of fluctuating labor demands in the powerful American economy. Inconvenient as it may be from the American perspective, the challenging connotations of Acuña's views are self-evident. Less apparent, however, is the lesson in methodology or historiography to be drawn from Acuña's observations. Where earlier approaches explained conditions among immigrants from Mexico in terms of the *internal nature of their culture and personalities,* Acuña explains them in terms of their *relations to American social and economic patterns.* Instead of looking only inside the lifeways of Mexican Americans, Acuña explores the relationships between Mexican-American and Anglo-American behaviors.

This study falls within the fold of the . . . revisionist understanding of the Mexican-American heritage introduced by Acuña and others. Committed to a comparative analysis of the destinies of both Mexican and American immigrants to south Texas, it points to several things that Texas historians have long suspected but neglected to document. Perhaps most important among these is the speculation that "Mexican" workers provided the massive amounts of general and unskilled labor required by the switch to commercial agriculture that eventually sent south Texas into the twentieth-century industrial age. *Inmigrantes* and indigenous Tejanos made up the largest part of the swelling, unspecialized labor pool in south Texas between 1850 and 1900. They supplied work demanding only general skills in large quantities to the agricultural sector and the burgeoning manufacturing and personal service sectors of the regional labor force, while the incoming Anglo-Americans streamed more frequently into the more skill-intensive areas of trade, transportation, and civil service. Corresponding to these differences in the occupational endeavors of the *inmigrantes* and Tejanos on the one hand and the Anglo-American immigrants on the other were inequalities of wealth and living standards.

Though support for long-standing speculation about labor patterns and standards of living in south Texas is important per se, such documentation does not constitute the most significant aspect of this study. Of greater importance is the understanding it makes possible of the sequence of historical events that determined the destinies of Mexicans and Anglos in the former region of Tamaulipas. South Texas, as indicated, was a relatively isolated territory steeped in at least one hundred years of Spanish-Mexican heritage before mid-nineteenth century when immigrants from the United States and Europe first arrived. Its institutional patterns were forged in that heritage, and its people identified with that legacy. In this tradition, the foundations of politics and economy in south Texas rested.

With the coming of Anglo-Americans, however, a veritable revolution in the social structure of the region occurred. The transformation was not so much the product of the Anglo-American influx; whites were, after all, relatively few in number and never comprised a majority of the region's population in the nineteenth century. Rather, it was the military, political, and economic ambitions and traditions pursued by Anglo-American newcomers that created the alteration of society in south Texas. Anglos showed too little regard for the rights and property of Mexicans and Tejanos, and they usurped control of both the political process and the means of production within a decade after their arrival. It was, in effect, a continuing conquest extending the legacy of the Mexican War over the remaining decades of the century.

This confrontation, . . . fostered the rise of an ethnic division of labor and subsequent impoverishment of the *inmigrantes*. For by the 1870s and 1880s Anglos were in a position to reap the benefits of the change to commercial agriculture and to insulate themselves from the transformation's less advantageous effects. The Mexican population, having lost control of the political and economic base in the 1850s and 1860s, became vulnerable to the negative effects of the transition. In comparison to Anglos, Mexicanos found themselves crippled in their ability to secure benefits from the new order. This vulnerability was more the result of displacement of control over crucial economic and political resources at an earlier period than it was from the tyranny of a ruling Anglo-American economic class of the time of the economic transition.

## Women on the Texas Frontier

### JACQUELINE S. REINIER

Definitions of "domesticity" and "the woman's sphere" in nineteenth-century America have been the subject of recent scholarly scrutiny. Nancy Cott has discovered that prescriptive literature published early in the century described woman's proper "sphere" as the domestic setting where her superior moral influence could restrain the vices of her husband and mold the character of future citizens, her children. Although most areas of public life were closed to nineteenth-century women, their "sphere" did include the church, the schoolroom and the religious or benevolent voluntary association. Katherine Kish Sklar's biography of Catherine Beecher has explained how Beecher elaborated these role definitions and extended them to single women by exalting the American mothers and schoolteachers who would play a special role in transmitting cultural values to the rapidly expanding Western frontier. Anne Firor Scott has demonstrated how the institution of slavery made acceptance of "woman's sphere" particularly urgent for Southern women. During and after the Civil War, Southern women were forced by necessity to extend their "sphere" beyond the domestic setting; some worked for wages, some enjoyed widened opportunities for education, and others participated actively in women's clubs and organizations. Nevertheless, even those who advocated female suffrage did not significantly challenge nineteenth-century definitions of femininity, arguing that women could use the vote to enhance their role as wives, mothers, and the nation's moral guardians.

Recent studies in women's history have investigated whether emigrating nineteenth-century women followed, altered, or abandoned these definitions of "woman's sphere" under the pressures of migrating and building new homes on the

Jacqueline S. Reinier, "Concepts of Domesticity on the Southern Plains Agricultural Frontier, 1870–1920," in *At Home on the Range: Essays on the History of Western Social and Domestic Life.* (Westport, CT: Greenwood Press, 1985), 57–68. Copyright © 1985 by John R. Wunder. Abridged and reprinted with permission.

frontier. In his study of midwestern farm families who crossed the plains on the Overland Trail to the Pacific Northwest, John Mack Faragher described "woman's sphere" in the rural setting, suggesting that feminine ideology that filtered into the Midwest essentially reinforced traditional agricultural sex roles and division of labor. Even on the trail, he found that sex roles did not change but were transferred to the new agricultural environment. . . .

Other historians, however, have suggested that the experience of women who settled the Great Plains might present a special case. Some time ago, Walter Prescott Webb argued that settlers who ventured into the "level, timberless, and semiarid" region west of the ninety-eighth meridian "were thrown by Mother Necessity into the clutch of new circumstances." Women, he conjectured, who left the humid regions they had known and were forced to cope with the isolation of the vast, empty prairie, the lack of wood and water, and problems caused by excessive dust and wind, found the Plains "peculiarly appalling." Mary Hargreaves has emphasized the loneliness and the domestic hardship experienced by women who settled the northern plains. And, disagreeing with the conclusions of Faragher and Jeffery, Christine Stansill has argued that plains women, who lived in sod huts and dugouts and lacked cultural supports, "failed to reinstate their own sphere" because of "the duration as well as the severity of cultural disruption" that they experienced. . . .

This case study is based on materials left by forty women who participated in the agriculturalization of one of the United States' later frontiers, the high Southern plains. It seeks to examine whether this plains environment did so disrupt the lives of women that they found establishment of conventional female culture especially difficult. These forty women lived in twenty-five Texas and three New Mexico counties which constitute a level, treeless, semi-arid plains region that the Spanish labeled the Llano Estacado. They were born or arrived during the years when this last frontier was being settled, largely between 1880 and 1910. Only two of the forty women migrated in the late 1870s; ten arrived in the 1880s, eight in the 1890s, eleven in the first decade of the twentieth century, and only one after 1910. Although their birthdates ranged from 1840 to 1903, most of the women were born between 1860 and 1890, with the largest number of their birthdates clustered between 1869 and 1878. Three of the women were born in Europe, three in the northeastern United States, and three in neighboring plains states; but most of them, the remaining thirty-one, came from east or central Texas, the border states, or the South.

Twenty-one of the women were wives and daughters in what could be called "ranching" families; their husbands or fathers were owners of large or small ranches or workers in the cattle industry. Ten of these "ranching" women married cowboys. Eleven of the forty were wives and daughters of "homesteaders"; two briefly had been homesteaders themselves before they married. These families generally engaged in a combination of stock farming and production of a small cotton crop. The remaining eight women best could described as "townswomen"; their husbands or fathers were merchants, lawyers, judges, or town founders.

Eight of the forty women were born in or set up housekeeping in a dugout, and only one, from Kansas, in a sod house. After an initial period of living in either a tent or a covered wagon, the rest of them lived in wooden houses of one or two rooms. Several of them were educated; five had been schoolteachers and one had been a governess. Of the forty, only one never married and only three gave up pioneering on the southern plains and returned "home." Unfortunately, the sources do not provide enough information to determine numbers of children and their birth intervals.

The experience of these forty pioneer women certainly was influenced by the plains environment they sought to settle. Once they climbed the escarpment of the Llano Estacado, they encountered a vast, empty grassland, with few rivers, sparse rainfall, and almost no trees, that was swept by hot dry winds in summer, blizzards in winter, and dust storms in the spring. However, this late frontier was opened when Eastern technology already was well advanced. By the late 1880s, railroads reached Amarillo in the north, and Colorado City in the south; many of these pioneering families began their trek west by rail. Technology could provide not only barbed wire and windmills, but also canned goods and sewing machines. Families could order manufactured items from mail-order catalogues. By 1910, the automobile brought relief from rural isolation. Mary Perritt Blankenship arrived in Hockley County in 1902; ten years later her life changed dramatically when her family purchased their first Ford. By 1910, the "frontier" period was essentially over in West Texas, although it lingered into the 1920's in eastern New Mexico. These forty women, then, were pioneers under unique circumstances. Largely of Southern background, they attempted to build homes under the difficult conditions created by a plains environment, at a late date when industrialization was of some help.

Southern plains women worked long and hard to recreate in their new homes the values of the particular cultural setting in which they had been socialized. Technology aided them, when they could make use of it, and temporary modifications were made to cope with the plains environment. The better educated pioneer women tended to focus on their role as educators rather than as experts in domestic production. One of the three women from the northeastern United States made a deliberate and conscious attempt to transplant northeastern feminine ideology. Margaret Adams McCollum Mooar was born in New York state and, according to her daughter, Lydia Louise, was "a highly educated lady both academically and musically" before she married John W. Mooar, a buffalo hunter who settled down to become a prominent rancher in Scurry County.

Margaret Mooar chose to spend much of her time at her town home in Colorado City, Mitchell County, where she became an active club woman. In 1892, she helped organize the "Up-to-Date History Club", which attempted to keep abreast of national issues concerning women. Members of the Up-to-Date Club were proud of being the first federated women's club in West Texas. They felt their spirits ennobled by their plains environment, those "vast prairies . . . in whose lap this child club of the West has been rocked and nourished—broadminded, full souled, big and generous hearted." Euphemistically, they considered themselves "as active in body, mind, and soul as the gentle zephyrs" that blew through their West Texas town. Catherine Beecher would have lauded Mooar's civic emphasis on molding citizens through motherhood rather than seeking the vote: "In this day when we hear so much of woman's sphere," wrote Mooar, "let us not forget that it is eminently her [concern] to teach her sons and daughters to be patriots." Members of the Up-to-Date Club gave reports on English and American history, on activities of the Texas Federation of Women's Clubs, and on eminent nineteenth-century women such as Margaret Fuller. On George Washington's birthday, they dressed up in colonial costumes and made speeches praising Washington's mother whose good influence clearly had molded his noble character.

Although less up-to-date on northeastern feminine ideology, West Texas pioneer women born in Europe worked as diligently to transmit learned cultural values to their new homes. Constance Aldous arrived from England in 1901 with a side saddle, a Singer sewing machine, and a tin bathtub, to keep house for her brother who had been herding sheep in Collingsworth County since 1887. A year later, she married a second English sheep herder, Albert Manby, fourteen years her junior. Constance Aldous Manby was a well-educated English "lady" who learned her limited domestic skills from her new husband. Throughout her years on their Elm Creek cattle ranch, she endeavored to instruct her only daughter, Mary, in English culture and values. In 1911, a governess came from England to occupy Mary with mornings of rigorous lessons and afternoons of reading and needlework. When this first teacher went to Canada to marry a cowboy in 1913, a replacement was quickly sent for from England.

Juliana McGregor, born in Munich, came to live on her American husband's Haskell County ranch in 1904. Dismayed by the hot, dry West Texas environment, she sought to beautify it according to European standards. Her daughter commented: "Julie so loved things to be pretty that she took a wheelbarrow down into the canyons where she gathered up the lace-like white caliche rocks and built 'rockeries' in which she planted flowers so that they looked like fountains. She also lined the walk-ways around the house with the rocks and made flower beds. . . . She drew the well dry, bucketfull by bucketfull [sic] carrying water to her garden."

Educated women of Southern and border state background, although less conscious than Margaret Mooar of feminine ideology, also worked diligently to transmit learned cultural values, especially to their children. Mollie Wylie Abernathy came to Lubbock County in 1902 with her husband, James Jarrott, who sought to settle twenty-five families on a strip of land missed in the early surveys. After Jarrott's murder by a paid assassin, Mollie stayed, living on her four sections of land, eventually increasing them to eighteen, and building a thriving cattle ranch. Mollie's strength was not in domestic skills: "I never did any hard house work," she said, "I never did wash and iron, scrub and scour, but I cooked a little bit." Nevertheless, she prided herself on providing an education for her three children. Although not a Catholic, she sent them to a convent school in Stanton, Texas. "It was the nearest place I could find that would take my children and take care of them," she said; "they stayed there four years and they got wonderful training and a fine start in school." Mollie had attended Add-Ran College near Fort Worth; "I come from an educated place," she declared, and "I educated my children."

After her marriage to Monroe Abernathy in 1905, Mollie lived part-time in the town of Lubbock where she became an active businesswoman in real estate and development, and a charter member of Lubbock's Business and Professional Women's Club. Like most of the forty women, she favored prohibition, but was unusual not only in her business career, but also in her advocacy of female suffrage. Her support of her beliefs neatly summarized the entire nineteenth- and early twentieth-century suffrage argument: "I was born a suffrager and almost a prohibitionist," she said. "When we were born, we were born equal. Women got as much sense as men. May not be the same kind, but its usually a better kind." And she acted on her views by organizing Lubbock chapters of the Women's Christian Temperance Union, and later, the League of Women Voters.

Other educated women born in Southern and border states also saw themselves essentially as educators. Texas-born Margaret Collins had been trained in a New York City conservatory of music. Shortly after she came to Cochran County as a governess at the Byrd Bar N Bar Ranch in 1905, she met and married Hiley T. Boyd, foreman on the nearby Slaughter Ranch. Her son later commented that single schoolteachers in West Texas generally married cowboys: "I . . . can't remember but one . . . or two at least that ever escaped some cowpuncher for the next twenty years." Margaret Collins Boyd was deeply concerned about the health, diet, and education of her three children in the isolated conditions of their ranch life. She put up hundreds of gallons of canned peaches, cherries, and plums in order that her children would have a proper diet even in drought years. Realizing that she was too busy with domestic chores to educate her children properly herself, she arranged for a "slight tax" in her area, hired and boarded a teacher, and set up a school in her front yard.

Julia Sutton taught school for thirteen years in Oklahoma before she homesteaded as a single woman in Curry County, New Mexico, in 1907. Within a year, she married U. S. Land Commissioner, Thomas Carter. While raising five children and helping with the family's "trading post" after their move to DeBaca County, she organized an interracial, interdenominational Sunday school. Her daughter explained: "Julia always had been a teacher at heart. Here in this even further west location, she extended herself into bringing some form of culture to her community." In her later years, Julia was postmistress of her town and Democratic chairperson of her county while her husband served as Republican county chair.

Yet, what of the southern Plains pioneer women less educated than these fortunate few? What cultural values did they endeavor to transmit? These women were not unlike the midwestern farm women described by John Mack Faragher; although they exhibited scant consciousness of feminine ideology, they were well trained in methods of domestic production and profoundly versed in traditional feminine lore. An excellent example would be Winnie Harris Rush, who carefully described the medical treatments, food processing, soap making, laundry procedures, and cloth production that she had learned during her Arkansas girlhood in the 1890s. Although her mother had a sewing machine, this introduction of technology followed a pattern frequently found in this group of forty women. It was the only such machine in the neighborhood and women came from miles around to use it: "People from all over the country would bring their sewing and sew all day, which was a little irritating. Some would bring their children to run the treadle."

After her father's death in 1909, Winnie, her mother, and her brothers homesteaded in Curry County, New Mexico. The two women valiantly transmitted their rich domestic knowledge to the new environment. On the plains, they made some interesting temporary domestic adaptations. Winnie's mother worked hard to make their dugout more comfortable. She put wagon sheets over joists to create a ceiling, "covered the dirt walls with gunny sacks," and then "papered over that with remnants of wall paper that she had brought along. She brought some cement and plastered the whole floor completely." Winnie later marveled, "it is still a mystery to me where she got all the stuff to work with."

Mrs. Arthur Duncan, one of the first women to come to Floyd County in 1884, lived with her husband and children in an abandoned sheep herder's dugout for seven years. She, too, attempted to make her new home "attractive and livable" by nailing towsacks covered with newspapers to the walls and building a partition that would divide her home into a kitchen and a "bedroom-parlor." She even managed to smile when a steer's leg penetrated the dug-out roof and spoiled the first meal for company she had prepared in three years. When the family moved to a two-room wooden house in Floydada in 1891, Mrs. Duncan was ecstatic: "A queen in all the splendor of her palaces," she said, "could not have glorified in her riches as much as I did in that home."

Other Plains women in the Llano Estacado environment followed a similar pattern, working diligently to transplant domestic values and procedures, yet being forced by circumstances to make temporary adaptations. For example, on the West Texas homestead, the windmill became an important focus for women. Mary Perritt Blankenship, who came to Hockley County in 1902, climbed the windmill tower when her husband was away, hoping for a glimpse of company. She hung a lantern on the windmill to direct her husband home, hung a towel to signal dinner for field hands, used the windmill tank for a cooler for milk, and the tower as a place to hang and dry beef. Before a church was built in her area, baptism took place in the windmill tank. Emma B. Russell was born in a dugout in Dickens County in 1890. Her mother attempted to use the power generated by the windmill to churn butter, attaching the dash of the churn to the windmill rod. She had trouble, however, controlling the wind.

Child care in the plains environment could be difficult for these busy pioneer women, and they evolved ingenious methods to make their task easier. Jane Lowe Quillan came to Hale County in 1888 when she was two. After her mother's death, she was raised by an aunt who insisted that Jane wear a bright red sunbonnet with two holes cut out for her braids so that she could not take it off. Then, whether Jane was in her playhouse by the cow lot or sailing homemade wooden boats in the pond in the pasture, her aunt could climb the windmill tower and spot her. Nanny Jowell came to West Texas with her cattleman husband in 1886 and moved with him from place to place, frequently living in a tent, while he sought pasture land unsettled by homesteaders. Her great worry in caring for her young children was the constant presence of snakes; finally she hit on the solution of using a mule for a babysitter. With her two toddlers high on the mule's back, she could concentrate on her domestic chores. Later, she said, "Old Jen was a dandy. She raised all the kids. That's a fact."

Another woman who practiced traditional domestic skills in an unusual way was Mrs. J. P. McDonald, wife of the foreman of the XIT Ranch, which covered ten counties in northwestern Texas. In 1904, she lived at the ranch headquarters, Las Escarbadas, where she cooked for the cowboys and measured out supplies for the line camps. McDonald was delighted with her domestic arrangements at XIT headquarters; later she commented: "I loved living in that house. It was cool in the summer and warm in the winter. . . . That was the nicest little ranch place that I've ever been in . . . everything was convenient." She lovingly described her 500 chickens, her splendid big black cookstove, her neat bins to keep supplies with the biscuit-rolling board that covered them, and her butter churn on a frame in which she made ten to fifteen pounds of butter a day. The cowboys helped her by clearing the table, and she, too, worked out arrangements for child care. While she cooked, either her husband cared for the children or three-year-old Raymond pulled baby Mary around the ranch yard in a little red wagon. Mrs. McDonald had learned home medical remedies, domestic skills, and methods of maintaining family harmony from her Southern mother-in-law. "We have always had harmony," she said, "I know people can live together without fussing."

These frontier women worked diligently to transmit learned cultural values and methods of domestic production to their new arid environment. Although they discovered ingenious ways of coping with the isolation of the empty prairie, the lack of wood and water, and the weather, their goal was always reestablishment of the conventions of female culture they had known. Although advanced technology was available to them, only a few with sufficient means were able to use it prior to 1910. A sewing machine mentioned in a memoir always was the only one in the county; women came from miles around to share in its use. Canned goods were considered a luxury and were not included in lists of supplies brought by wagon every six months. Some women thought that only cowboys and bachelors used store-bought canned goods; others were convinced that such provisions were unhealthy.

With the exceptions of Mollie Abernathy, businesswoman; Julia Carter, homesteader and postmistress; and Martha Killough Conaway of Mitchell County, who managed the family ranch after her husband's death, these women did not venture from nineteenth-century definitions of "woman's sphere." Although only Margaret Mooar consciously transplanted feminine ideology, most of the women implicitly followed it. Educated women of southern background concentrated on transmitting values and knowledge to children, as mothers and as schoolteachers. Less educated Southern women diligently transplanted their complicated methods of domestic production and their rich medical lore. Only three of the forty women even mentioned female suffrage. Instead of creating new gender definitions, they concentrated on recreating the world they had known. With the men who accompanied them, in a short span of thirty years, defying heat, wind, snakes, and dust storms, they transformed the vast and empty Llano Estacado into an extension of mainstream Anglo-American rural culture.

## ❖ *F U R T H E R   R E A D I N G*

Armando C. Alonzo, *Tejano Legacy: Rancheros and Settlers in South Texas, 1734–1900* (1998)

T. Lindsay Baker and Billy R. Harrison, *Adobe Walls: The History and Archeology of the 1874 Trading Post* (1986)

Arnoldo De León and Kenneth L. Stewart, *Not Room Enough: Mexicans, Anglos, and Socioeconomic Change in Texas, 1850–1900* (1993)

———, *Tejanos and the Numbers Game: A Socio-Historical Interpretation from the Federal Censuses, 1850–1900* (1989)

Jo Ella Powell Exley, ed., *Texas Tears and Texas Sunshine: Voices of Frontier Women* (1985)

Neil Foley, *The White Scourge: Mexicans, Blacks, and Poor Whites in Texas Cotton Culture* (1997)

Joe S. Graham, *El Rancho in South Texas: Continuity and Change from 1750* (1994)
William T. Hagan, *United States-Comanche Relations: The Reservation Years* (1976)
Theodore D. Harris, ed., *Black Frontiersman: The Memoirs of Henry O. Flipper* (1997)
Jack Jackson, *Los Mesteñeros: Spanish Ranching in Texas, 1721–1821* (1986)
Terry G. Jordan, *North American Cattle Ranching Frontiers* (1993)
Sara R. Massey, ed., *Black Cowboys of Texas* (2000)
Sandra Meyers, *Westering Women and the Frontier Experience* (1982)
Sandra L. Myres, ed., *Cavalry Wife: The Diary of Eveline M. Alexander, 1866–1867* (1977)
Charles M. Robinson, III, *Satanta: The Life and Death of a War Chief* (1998)
Robert Wooster, "The Army and the Politics of Expansion: Texas and the Southwestern
    Borderlands, 1870–1886, *"Southwestern Historical Quarterly* 93 (1989): 151–167
———, *Soldiers, Sulters, and Settlers: Garrison Life on the Texas Frontier* (1987)

C H A P T E R
11

# Suffrage and Beyond: Texas Women and Reform, 1885–1925

*During the last decade of the nineteenth century and the first two decades of the twentieth century, social, political, and economic reform movements addressed the problems that Texans confronted as the state moved from a frontier, agricultural society to an urban, industrial one. The immediate political result of these reform movements brought an end to the series of conservative Democratic administrations that had controlled Texas government since the end of Reconstruction. Discontent and protest among the rural population led to organizations such as the Grange and the Greenback party in the 1870s. By the late 1880s the Farmers' Alliance had become the primary vehicle for agrarian protest. The election of James Stephen Hogg in 1890 and the emergence of the People's party (or the Populist party) reflected the strength of reform sentiment. In the mid-1890s the Farmers Alliance and populism gave way to the progressive movement. While progressives in Texas were still deeply rooted in the issues of rural communities, they also addressed the issues of the rapidly growing urban communities. Issues such as good government, increased social services, regulation of child labor and women's labor, and prison reform, were added to the earlier agenda of regulation of big business and the railroads, extension of democracy, and banking and currency reform. Reformers from both movements addressed the issues of women's suffrage and prohibition.*

*One aspect of the reform movements of the late-nineteenth and early twentieth centuries was the increasing role of women both in reform movements and in politics. The role of women in the Texas reform process is complex. Women undoubtedly supported reform—especially when it addressed moral issues such as prohibition or issues related to traditional women's concerns, such as education and the welfare of children. The extent to which Texas women pushed into mainstream reform issues, even the extent of the suffrage movement in Texas, are more complex issues. In the past three decades historians have developed a deeper understanding of the role women played in these movements. At the national level women unquestionably were active in, and occasionally in the forefront of, the agrarian unrest that preceded the Populist uprising. Women's organizations also played a major role in defining the social agenda of the progressive movement, and without question women took the leadership in the crusades for prohibition and women's suffrage. What is less clear is the role that women played in reform at the local level. Specific questions remain about the relationship of women to reform movements. How effectively did they function within male-dominated organizations? What was the impact of women's clubs and other women's organizations? What were the origins and the impact of the suffrage movement in Texas?*

## ★ D O C U M E N T S

The Farmers' Alliance and its journal, the *Southern Mercury*, introduced many Texas women to the political arena. Document 1 is an example of the correspondence that filled this journal during the late 1880s. This letter to the *Mercury* from Ann Other of Ennis, Texas, illustrates the growing concern of these women with the suffrage issue. The next three documents reveal the importance of the women's clubs. Document 2 is a poem about the virtues and utility of "The Club" that appeared *The Club Monthly* of Tyler, Texas in 1897. In Document 3, Pauline Periwinkle (Isadore Miner Callaway) uses her column in the *Dallas Morning News* to encourage the trans-formation of women's clubs from social clubs to organizations for civic improve-ment and reform. Calloway transformed her newspaper column from one devoted to fashion to one that advocated political and social activism. She also was active in the suffrage movement and in other women's political causes. Document 4 describes the involvement of the Texas division of the General Federation of Women's Clubs in environmental work. By 1914 women had transformed their clubs into effective forces for reform.

Eventually the struggle for suffrage overshadowed all other women's reform issues. The next four documents trace the final stage of the struggle for the right to vote, and also illustrate the political sophistication of the suffrage movement and the connection of suffrage to other political issues. In Document 5, Texas suffrage organizer Jane McCallum describes a detour in the suffrage campaign—the rally for the impeachment of Governor James Ferguson, an absolute opponent of women's suffrage. Following Ferguson's impeachment, women achieved a partial victory in their campaign when Texas allowed women to vote in primary elections. By the early twentieth century, Mrs. Percy V. Pennybacker, founder of the Tyler Women's Club in 1894, had become active in the women's club and suffrage movement at both the state and national levels. In Document 6 she lobbies fellow Texan, Colonel Edward M. House, a key advisor in the Wilson White House, on the political impli-cations of loosing the vote in Congress for the suffrage amendment. In Document 7 she explains to national suffrage leader Carrie Chapman Catt the danger to the suf-frage movement of ex-Governor Ferguson's efforts to resurrect his political career. In this letter to Catt and again in Document 8 from fellow Texas suffragist Minnie Fisher Cunningham, Pennybacker begins planning for political activity in the post-suffrage era.

## 1. Texas Pioneer Ann Other Describes Women's Political Interests in the Farmer's Revolt, 1888

May 31, 1888. Ennis, Texas. Ann Other.

EDITOR MERCURY: As we are searching for facts on this subject, and I sincerely believe that none of us are writing for argument's sake, let us look candidly on the matter and sift each point, and try to give fair and unprejudiced opinion on the arguments. . . . Now, Sister Rebeca . . .

You class the decline of patriotism with the rise of the popularity of universal suffrage and "woman neglecting her duty in her proper sphere." Now will someone kindly tell me what is her proper sphere? I have always heard the expression, but have failed to locate it by any series of studies I have taken up. I am obliged to conclude it is whatever the state of society dictates to her.

Men have intruded and wrestled from her what were formerly her legitimate occupations. And her present effort is only to recover a useful sphere in life by those who have become weary for others to do that which God intended she should do for herself.

Women used to be our bakers, brewers, dry-salters, butter-makers, cooks, dressmakers, cheese-makers, confectioners, jam and jelly makers, pickle makers, soap makers, spinners, weavers, sock makers, lace makers, embroiders, and midwives. Thus crowded out of her old fields of labor by men's intrusion and invention, she must either accept a life of idleness, and be satisfied with such as her brothers see proper to give her, or she must demand a more useful and energetic life. The woman in idleness naturally loses the bright vigor of her mind, and a "scheming mama" must look for an "eligible partie" for her daughters, for society in its present state has so limited her sphere of usefulness in life that there is nothing left for her to do but marry, and the mother knowing there is no comfort or happiness in the married life without an eligible partie, naturally aspires to that.

But when society becomes enough advanced in marking the bounds of woman's sphere to give her the untrammeled right to write her name as high on the book of fame in any sphere her tastes dictate, as her brothers, then we will see mothers having higher aspirations for their daughters than marriage only as it may come by the dictates of their own lofty sentiments.

Yes, I am aware that the W.C.T.U. has the suffrage plank a movable plank, but when our leaders are boldly advocating it, what effect will those who cling to their shirts and cry against it have but to slightly impede its progress in that one direction?

Have you not seen Frances E. Willard's address before the senate committee? For fear you have not, I will quote a little from it: "I suppose these honorable gentlemen think that we women want the earth, when we only want one half of it. Our brethren have encroached upon the sphere of women. They have very definitely marked out that sphere and then they have proceeded with their incursions by the power of invention, so that we women, full of vigor and full of desire to be active

Ann Other, Ennis, Texas, letter to the *Southern Mercury*, May 31, 1888, in *Women in the Texas Populist Movement: Letters to the Southern Mercury* (College Station: Texas A&M University Press, 1997); 108–111.

and useful and to react upon the world around us, finding our industries largely gone, have been obliged to seek out new territory and to preempt from the sphere of our brothers, as it was popularly supposed to be, some of the territory that they have hitherto considered their own. So we think it will be very desirable indeed that you should let us lend a hand in their affairs of government." It is said that if women are given the right to vote, it will prevent their being womanly; how it is a sentiment of chivalry in some good men that hinders them from giving us the ballot. They think we should not be lacking in womanliness of character, which we most certainly wish to preserve but we believe that history proves they have retained that womanliness, and if we can only make men believe that, the ballot will just come along sailing like a ship with the wind beating every sail.

Again see her [Willard's] letter in *Union Signal* to the Kansas women urging them to let no false modesty keep them from registering and voting, as now the eyes of the world were upon them, to see if women would exercise the right of franchise if they had it.

"It is inconceivable to me why some women, simply because they do not wish to vote, should clamor so loud against giving the right to those who do, as there would be nothing compelling any to vote who did not think they could benefit the laws by doing so."

You "fear that men will lose their respect for women who assemble with them at the ballot box." Now I think those men who could think less of a woman because she took a judicious interest in the laws of her country would not be worth the while to mourn over; whether they respected her or not they would be obliged to respect her laws. When you hear men talking of women losing men's esteem by using the highest and most sacred right of an American citizen, you can rest assured that his esteem is not worth having. . . . If you are obliged to associate with all whom you meet at the polls, do not go there, for your soul is just as liable to be contaminated as mine.

I have written these few thoughts from a sick-bed. I do not think anyone can do justice to their subject when the physical machinery is out of repair but I do hope you will candidly consider the few thoughts I have tried to sketch out for you. Your loving friend,

## 2. Tyler Women's Club Presents the Virtues of the Club in a Poem from *The Club Monthly,* 1897

### The Club

[With apologies to Edgar Allen Poe and everyone else]

> Hear the kick against "the club"
> Literary club:
> For solid information I guess it is the "hub."

"The Club," in *The Club Monthly,* published by a Tyler, Texas women's club for the new Texas Federation of Women's Clubs 1 (November 1897): 15 in Austin American History Club Papers, Austin History Collection, Austin Public Library.

How they study, study, study,
Intricacies of the day!
How the mind so strong and ruddy,
Clears the stream that's deep and muddy,
Fades the mysteries all away:
Like a dream, dream, dream.
Like a sudden spurt
From a teapot on the table just before you eat
    your grub,
Is the club, club, club,
Club, club, club,
When you're yearning for learning, see the club.


Hear the literary club,
Woman's club:
The men are quite forgot—and "there's the rub"
'Till the balmy air of night,
They must rock the cradle quiet,
They must pay two promised notes
    Very soon.
And unless a woman votes,
The world will go to thunder—and she dotes
    On the moon,
Oh, that man could take a club
And fight forbidden usage—compel his wife to rub!
And to scrub
For her grub
Then the erstwhile "dearest hub"
Would be called Beelzebub,
For the bringing and the swinging
    Of the club, club, club,
Of the club, club, club, club,
Club, club, club.
For the buying and applying of the "club."


"There are others"—
Real Clubs,
And the women call them wicked, with
    irreverential "dubs"
In the silent of the night
These clubs are "out-er-sight."
But they take the Men away—that is wrong:
His place, you know, is Home—
But a Woman, she can roam.
Doing "clubwork"—off a clubbing all
    day long.

## 3. Newspaper Columnist Pauline Periwinkle Celebrates Transforming Social Clubs into Civic Reform Organizations, 1904

It almost takes one's breath to contemplate the evolution of the Texas federation. Seven years ago the word "culture" comprehended its broadest meaning, and a book was its symbol. One would imagine that society had no ailment, spiritual or moral, that could not be relieved by a good strong dose of culture, administered in book capsule. Dooley's vision of Carnegie handing out a library to a starving man on his back doorstep, would have served as a pen-portrait of the club idea. Do you remember the "yard of roses," "yard of pansies," et al.—those popular gift litho-graphs that once cemented the friendship of women for their favorite journal? Well, the papers read at those old-time club occasions were like that—sentimen-tally rounded periods interspersed with flowery quotations, and set in formal rows, a yard, yes, two or more tiresome yards in length.

Now the federation counts its philanthropies by the scores—libraries and scholarships, kindergartens and civic betterment, music and art for the enjoyment of those unable to supply their own. Aesthetic science, patriotic endeavor, work for home and schools, and for that unfortunate element that has known the influences of neither good homes nor schools. The federation has awakened to the fact that the progress of the world does not depend on the acquirement of a little more culture on the part of a limited number of fairly well-educated women, but on the amount of leavening those women are enabled to impart to the masses.

As for prosy papers and flowery reports, the convention will have none of them. "Cut the papers and give the time to discussion" is the cry. When the presiding officer of the northeastern division presented the work for her division, the federation listened with eager attention to a concise statement of what each club in the district had accomplished, and I could but recall the listless interest once exhibited in the long, rambling reports that evaded the issue in the attempt to achieve literary distinc-tion. And whereas great stress was always laid on the social side of club gatherings, one long instance of where "eatables and wearables" got the best of "thinkables and doables" raised a smile of toleration. Verily, we are coming on.

## 4. Mrs. R. W. Simpson, Chairman of the Texas General Federation of Women's Clubs, Presents the Federation's Environmental Agenda, 1914

The aim of the department representing the conservation of our national resources, has been to include forests, waters, birds, soils, ores, and minerals and the vital resources.

During the past two years the committee has tried to leave no stone unturned that would impress upon the people of Texas the importance of this great ques-tion. Personally, beside sending telegrams and writing letters, I have addressed 1400

Pauline Periwinkle [Isadore Miner Callaway], *Dallas Morning News,* November 28, 1904 in *Pauline Peri-winkle and Progressive Reform in Dallas* (College Station: Texas A&M University Press, 1998), 73–74.

General Federation of Women's Clubs, Reports of State Chairmen of Conservation, 1912–1914: Texas: 54–57. Center for American History, University of Texas (2L505).

circular letters, including a few postcards, each letter containing condensed leaflets and other enclosures. . . .

While the inspiration of our state convention of 1912 at Fort Worth was still warm in the hearts of Texas women, a hasty call to arms came from our beloved National Conservation Chairman, Mrs. Crocker. Preparations were being made by a clique of politicians, representing selfish interests, to introduce into Congress bills under the guise of "States rights," which asked that the Federal government turn over to state control parts of our national forests. At once, the efforts of our committee were directed to prove that if such bills should pass, the whole system of conservation would be weakened and the national forests themselves would soon be frittered away; that the functions and uses of the forest extend far beyond state lines and involve the welfare of many people exterior of the state, for often they cover the headwaters of streams in one state, thus protecting the riverflow in another. . . . Circular letters, with resolution models, protesting against these measures, were mailed to every club in Texas, requesting that copies of these resolutions be sent to our representatives in congress. . . . We felt assured that we merited some credit in the battle that caused the authors of this proposed legislation to back down.

Requests were mailed to all clubs in the state to observe Arbor Day. Arbor Day programs, including birds and waterways as well as forestry and tree-planting, were sent to clubs requesting them. . . . Members of the legislature were interested in the project of introducing a bill to arrange the date of Arbor Day to suit the varied climate of our state. . . .

When the summons came to me from Mrs. Crocker to work for the revision of Schedule N so that it would mean protection to the birds all over the country, letters earnestly beseeching this revision were at once rushed to Washington to our representatives on the Ways and Means Committee. I also wrote to Hon. Oscar W. Underwood of Alabama, chairman of the committee; his courteous reply was reassuring. . . . After Schedule N was revised as conservationists desired, your chairman wrote to every Texas congressman asking that they use their influence to keep the desired revision, because it was loudly whispered that the National Millinery Association was preparing to have it stricken out. After the battle was won, we were happy to think of the memorable hour which soon afterward came, when President Wilson placed his signature to the new tariff bill.

There is a steady interest among children in the building of Jenny Wren bungalows, a pattern of which I sent to all Texas clubs last year, for the winter protection of birds. Pilot Point school children constructed fifty bungalows at one time. . . .

From the first our plea for cooperation has been given hearty response from Texas club women. Some have adopted a study course on national forest reservation and all other phases of conservation. Many clubs have placed conservation programs in yearbooks. Local conservation committees write articles for their city newspapers and report conservation items monthly to their respective clubs. School faculties have been asked that children be taught the importance of conservation. . . .

Resolutions urging that beautiful Palo Duro Canyon in the Texas Panhandle become a national park, endorsing the Lever Agricultural Bill, praising the action of custom officials in enforcing the new Federal law in regard to plumage and pleading for the protection of Hetch Hetchy, offered by this committee, have been adopted by the State Federation. . . .

In the controversy over Hetch Hetchy, Texas women worked valiantly to aid in preserving the natural beauty of this wonderful valley. I telegraphed to Senators Sheppard and Culberson asking them to vote against granting the valley to San Francisco for a reservoir. Pleas were mailed to every Texas club to write letters of protest to Washington and numerous were the letters thus sent from Texas women. Resolutions of protest were sent from the San Antonio City Federation. Similar resolutions and telegrams went from our state convention to the two senators and to President Wilson. This fight, though lost, leaves an influence gratifying to all conservationists.

The three hundred and fifty circular letters which our committee sent to Texas clubs in October, 1913, were accompanied by the same number of forest-fire circulars, showing how the careless tossing of a match or cigarette into a forest begins a flame which not only destroys all young trees and wild flowers, nuts, berries, and fruits, but all the wee birds in their nests and all young animal life.

The people of Texas have resources of enormous value in fruits and nuts, which should be planted along our highways emphasizing the growth of the already famous Texas pecan.

At the November state convention at Corpus Christi, 1913, I requested that the pecan tree be adopted as the Texas Federation Tree, to be planted henceforth at our annual meetings. . . .

We also urge the sowing of flower seeds along our watercourses and by the highways. This would add a glow of beauty, even to Nature's profusion of blossoms in Texas, where the blue bonnets grow.

## 5. Texas Suffrage Organizer Jane Y. McCallum Describes the Impeachment Rally Against James Ferguson, July 28, 1917

Friends of higher education rushed to the capital city in response to the clarion call. Ferguson looked to rural residents for his chief support. In the midst of preliminaries to the legislative session called for "impeachment purposes," a "Farmer's Institute" attended by over two thousand farmers and their families assembled in the capitol.

The times were very exciting. In addition to the residential population, there were the senators and representatives, members of the tribunal before which the offending governor would have to give an account of his stewardship; hot-headed University students milling about, and kept in bounds only by calmer ex-students gathered in Austin by the hundreds . . . —and everywhere . . . were towering figures, shod with cowboy boots, covered with "Texas Stetson," and armed with honest-to-goodness guns. They were Texas rangers; said to have been summoned by the governor from the border and the "badlands" for his "protection."

In the midst of this perfervid, chaotic situation, women, who were friends of the State University and not particularly sympathetic toward the gentleman whose record was up for discussion, decided to take a hand.

Led by their State president, Mrs. Minnie Fisher Cunningham, the members of the Equal Suffrage Association had during preceding years built up a State-wide

Jane Y. McCallum, "A Texas Suffragist" in *Texas Democracy,* 474–476. Reprinted in Janet G. Humphrey, ed., *A Texas Suffragist: Diaries and Writings of Jane Y. McCallum* (Austin: Ellen C. Temple, 1988), 89–91.

organization which was a marvel of efficiency. Ferguson probably had another name for it, in the light of later events and the remark of the expert stage-driver that "a fly is a fly, and a leaf is a leaf, but a hornet's nest is an organization." By whatever name, this machine, which included in its files the background of every lawmaker in the State capital, was brought to Austin and placed at the disposal of the committee, along with the services of a Woman's Committee.

"If only we might have an opportunity of placing the facts before the farmers they would never support Ferguson," was the committee's cry when the Farmers' Institute referred to was assembling.

It was when they were denied this opportunity, after announcement that "Farmer Jim" would address the farmers, that an ingenious method was devised by the women political leaders, joined by women patriotic organization leaders, of placing the facts before the public, especially the farmers whom Ferguson was using all of his wits to prejudice against their State school. . . .

When morning dawned of the day "Farmer (?) Jim" was to address the Institute in the afternoon, early arrivals on Congress Avenue at 13th Street stared in wonderment. They rubbed their eyes and looked again. *"Women of Texas Protest."* It was no optical illusion. There it loomed on the corner of the city's main thoroughfare, right in front of the capital grounds and flanked on the West by a State Park.

The words blazed from two orange colored banners, eight feet long, that were attached to scaffolding on either side of a large dray, further embellished with orange and white bunting, colors of Texas University.

Continued observation disclosed a unique procedure: without intermission except for brief introductions by a feminine presiding officer, one man and woman after another climbed on the dray and made a speech; not perfunctory talks, but addresses that were earnest, able, and in many instances impassioned. . . .

The gathering crowds pushed nearer to within sound of the voices of the speakers in their eagerness to learn what it was all about. They were not kept in doubt. . . . The farmers got the facts, and the crowd[,] because [the surrounding streets were] so dense with traffic[,] was blocked despite the commodious park to the side, and the "continuous protest" had to cease long enough to adjourn to the city's largest park where shortly before midnight it came to a rousing close with a speech by "fighting Bob Shuler," the well-known Methodist evangelist.

## 6. Mrs. Percy V. Pennybacker, Texas Suffrage Organizer, Writes About Political Implications of Losing the Suffrage Amendment in Congress, 1918

January 31st, 1918.

Dear Mr. House:—

For the good of the cause, may I take a few moments of your time?

I returned last night from Washington. While there, in a conference with Mrs. Carrie Chapman Catt, she told me that there was special need of making sure of

Mrs. Percy V. Pennybacker to Edward M. House, January 31, 1918. Center for American History, University of Texas (2M12).

Senator Culberson on the question of the Federal Amendment for Suffrage. Remembering the great influence of Mrs. Culberson over her husband, as I was to lunch with her the next day, I promised Mrs. Catt to ascertain how Mrs. Culberson stood. To my delight, I found that she was unequivocally in favor of Woman Suffrage, but was a bit uneasy as to the effect of the negro women as to suffrage and the Federal Amendment. I tried as best I could to show her how to-day the suffrage question was a war measure and how the vote of the negro woman was no more to be feared than the vote of the negro man. Aside from my earnest desire to see justice done us by means of the Federal Amendment, I am made each day more cognisant of the danger to our Democratic Party if this Amendment fails to pass, owing to the opposition of Democratic Senators. During the last two weeks I have heard from at least twenty sources, of work that is being socially done by Republican leaders to imbue the mind of women all over the country with the fact that if the Amendment is defeated, it will be the Democrats who defeat it. I can but feel that a word from you to Senator Culberson would bring about the result for which thousands and thousands of women are earnestly praying. Mrs. Catt spoke with deep appreciation of the attitude you and Mrs. House held towards the Suffrage Cause.

Apropos of the work of our Republican friends, I happened to learn a few days ago that certain Republican leaders are watching closely as to the reappointment of certain high naval and military officers. A group was discussing the reappointment of Gen. George Barnett, Commandant of the Marine Corps. It was universally conceded that his ability was beyond all question and that he was especially needed in his present position during these times of danger. The point was made that if the Secretary of the Navy should fail to reappoint him, it would throw superb campaign materials for the Republicans. Knowing what happened four years ago, I am venturing to call this matter to your attention in the hope that even in the midst of your busy life, you will find time to see about to it that the man who has so eminently filled the position as Commandant be continued in his post.

With kindest regards to you and Mrs. House, I am,
Ever cordially yours.

## 7. Mrs. Percy V. Pennybacker Explains the Dangers of Fergusonism to the Suffrage Movement, 1918

June 13th, 1918

Dear Mrs. Catt:

It seems a crime to ask your time to read a single letter, but this matter is urgent and so I must ask your indulgence.

Texas has never been in a more critical position. Mr. Ferguson and his cohorts are waging a most vigorous campaign and while you and I cannot realize how sane, sensible people can dream of supporting him, yet he has succeeded, by his half-truths

---

Mrs. Percy V. Pennybacker to Carrie Chapman Catt, June 13, 1918. Center for American History, University of Texas (2M12).

and whole falsehoods in arousing such bitter class, and town versus country prejudice, that there is no telling what the results may be. If he is elected his candidates
for the Legislature and his candidates for the Supreme Court will also be elected.
This will mean the repeal of the Primary Suffrage law. Mrs. Cunningham wisely
feels that the State Suffrage Assn. cannot work under any party name, but the Texas
suffragists are organizing "Good Government Clubs" over the State and getting in
excellent work. Really, however,—and here is the crux of the situation—we are
sadly hampered by lack of means. We came near losing Mrs. Cunningham as President at the State meeting in Austin. One of the main reasons was the fact that the
load of finances has always been laid upon her shoulders; that she has had to give as
security her own personal property. The Association was in debt $2700.00. Some
of us pledged ourselves to raise this indebtedness but this leaves Mrs. Cunningham
with virtually nothing for expenses and you know the work she is capable of doing
cannot be performed without money.

Now since the suffrage cause is in jeopardy, could you, as President of the
Leslie Commission, help out? I believe it is true that few states have ever financed
a suffrage campaign without some outside assistance. Were we to lose Mrs. Cunningham, I would look upon it as a calamity. Unless some definite budget can be
offered her there is no telling what may happen. Please let me hear from you as
soon as possible.

Your telegram was most welcome. Mr. Baster had written that he was hoping
to secure you for Saturday, July 20th. If you are engaged from Saturday, I am hoping that you could come the day before so we could have the privilege of you and
Dr. Shaw sharing the Women's Club hour and giving us the greatest session we
have ever had in all the history of the Club.

Ever yours,

## 8. Suffragist Minnie Fisher Cunningham Begins Planning Political Activity in Texas in the Postsuffrage Era, 1918

July 4, 1918.

My Dear Mrs. Pennybacker:

Yours of the 29th of June, with enclosures, to hand. Since you are so good as
to ask me to make suggestions, I offer a very radical one for the Club program. It is
that they take the book, "The Brewers and Texas Politics" as their text and around
*it* "gather current articles and thus make it very present day and practical." Such a
course of study adopted by the clubwomen if this state could and would revolution-
ize conditions in Texas, now that the women have the vote as a safe and sane
method of making their information effective. And there are a number of available

Minnie Fisher Cunningham to Mrs. Percy V. Pennybacker, July 4, 1918. Center for American History,
University of Texas (2M12).

lecturers who could supplement the book work, Gen. M. M. Crane, for instance. You, of course, realize that to have the vote is not enough if good men continue to refuse to stand for election to office, and corrupt men continue to wield the power and influence of the party machinery. We are going to have to devise some way of changing this situation, and letting the light of publicity in on it is at least a step in that direction. I feel quite certain that it would strike horror to the hearts of our friend, the enemy, if they knew the women were sitting down in cold blood to examine into their past record and study the conditions which permitted them to flourish and grow fat off the state's resources, with a view to "doing something about it." Cannot you put some such idea before the State Federation convention this fall and get a state program adopted?

Mrs Bass's letter is interesting. . . . I was especially interested to learn that in none of the Suffrage states, except Colorado, have the women really been taken into the party organization. You know, I am opposed to the separate organization plan, and hope to see the women of Texas go right into our Democratic party organization and "take over as a war measure" a reasonable number of party offices and a reasonable proportion of party power; only so can we be advised as to the machinations within the party, and only so can we hope to defeat them, as I see it. . . .

Very truly yours,
Minnie Fisher Cunningham
President.

 E S S A Y S

The Farmers' Alliance, initially organized in Texas in 1875, evolved into the most important national voice of agrarian discontent in the late 1880s and was instrumental in the organization of the Populist party in 1892. Women played an important role in the movement, first by encouraging the involvement of their husbands, but more significantly as members in their own right with their own perspective on the reform program. Marion Barthelme, a journalist, historian, and independent scholar from Houston, documents the evolution of the political agenda of these women through the letters they wrote to the *Southern Mercury*, the official organ of the Farmers' Alliance. Through this outlet, a community of women emerged who developed a sophisticated analysis of the economic and political issues confronting the farmer. They also expanded their sense of the role of women in addressing these problems.

Following the collapse of the Farmers' Alliance and the Populist party in the mid-1890s, progressive reformers defined reform politics in Texas. Although many of the issues they addressed reflected the continued dominance of rural interests in the state, progressives were also well organized in the state's urban centers. Progressives tended to be more politically moderate than the Populists, but women in the progressive movement were more aggressive and assertive than their Populist sisters, especially as they pushed for prohibition and suffrage. Another historian and independent scholar, Betty Chapman, examines the evolution of women's clubs as a vehicle for the reform efforts of urban women during the progressive era.

# Texas Women and the Farmers' Alliance

## MARION K. BARTHELME

To most Americans, industrialization was a painful process. In the last quarter of the nineteenth century, many of the nation's groups developed alternatives to the emerging design of American industrial society. The farmers' effort—the brief but powerful Populist movement—was the largest and most significant endeavor of the era. It originated on the Texas farming frontier in 1877, as farmers, trying to improve their lot through cooperation and education, created the Southern Farmers' Alliance. In 1892, they turned to politics and formed the Populist party. The movement had peaked by 1896, but not before it had swept like wildfire through the South and West and out into the Great Plains, igniting the hopes of followers one to three million strong. . . .

## Alliance and Populist Women

In pioneer agricultural states such as Texas, women often worked alongside men as equals in the business of farming, shouldering burdens traditionally deemed unwomanly. The Alliance recognized this and offered membership to white rural women over sixteen years of age. . . . Significant numbers of women, perhaps as many as 25 percent of its membership, joined the Farmers' Alliance and later supported the Populist party. . . .

At the heart of this reform press . . . was the sixteen-page *Southern Mercury,* a Dallas-based weekly under various editors and publishers. . . . The paper was published between 1884 and 1907. It became the official organ of the state Southern Farmers' Alliance in 1886. . . . [F]rom 1890 to 1892—its peak years—the paper had a circulation of twenty-six to thirty thousand. Although most subscribers lived in Texas, the large number of letters from elsewhere indicates that the *Mercury* had a sizable readership in other states. It cost one dollar a year.

From 1886 to 1907, with varying intensity and dedication, the *Mercury* singled out correspondence from women by devoting one page (usually the second page) of each weekly issue to their letters and concerns. . . .

A prodigious amount has been written about the Farmers' Alliance and the Populist party, but until recently historians have neglected the part played by women in the agrarian movement. . . .

In the 1960s, a handful of historians began to take a look at old records, creating a "new history" of Southern women. It was a "brave beginning," said historian Anne Firor Scott, yet on the subject of women and rural reform in the 1880s and 1890s, this sort of brave new work consists for the most part of a few biographical studies, two essays, one doctoral dissertation, and a master's thesis. . . .

The women of Texas, among the Southern states, were the most active and influential Alliance participants. A number of them—such as Fannie Moss of Cleburne;

---

Marion K. Barthelme, "An Introduction" in *Women in the Texas Populist Movement: Letters to the Southern Mercury,* ed. Marion K. Bartheleme (College Station: Texas A&M University Press, 1997), 3–76. Reprinted by permission of Texas A&M University Press.

Fannie Leak, a physician in Austin; and Mary Clardy of Sulphur Springs—held offices in the order. Bettie Gay of Columbus and Ellen Dabbs, a physician also from Sulphur Springs, represented the state at national conventions, while Bessie Dwyer from San Antonio was a staff writer for the *National Economist*. . . . But the Alliance movement was a mass movement, a grassroots effort, made by rank-and-file "plain" people. These people were marginal farmers and their families—tenants, land-owners, teachers, preachers, and doctors operating farms in economically depressed sections of the country. Among them were ordinary women. . . .

Women's letters to the *Southern Mercury* . . . provide a rare look into the thoughts and daily life of rural Texas women. One comes away from a reading of the letters with a greater understanding of rural Populist women and a tremendous appreciation of their resilience, their attention to detail and duty, their light humor, their strong convictions, their compassion, and their growth. . . .

Over the six years in which the women correspond, they undergo political and personal growth, due in part to their participation in the movement and in part to the act of writing and communicating in the *Southern Mercury*. The letters suggest that many of the women emerge from the experience with a stronger sense of self. Their individual and collective self-esteem is augmented by the act of writing and by the mutual reading of each other's written words. The letters also reveal, among "conservative" rural women, far greater enthusiasm for suffrage than generally has been attributed to them. Scholars looking for the roots of the suffrage movement in Texas have overlooked suffrage sentiment in the countryside and have theorized that urbanization was an essential precursor. . . .

The Alliance's stated expectation that women would join as equal members did much to bring these women into public life, even while they remained linked to a domestic setting. They entered the public arena as representatives of private life, bringing private-life concerns such as education, morality, and temperance; but they also entered with broader public-life issues, such as equal representation and the fairer division of the young nation's resources. . . . Women in these associations and reform movements were expected to practice the basic skills of public life—to speak and to listen, to analyze issues in relation to structures of power, and to de-velop agendas and strategies for action.

## Southern Farmers' Alliance

In the 1870s, caravans of beleaguered farmers—almost 100,000 each year—migrated across plank roads and rutted trails into Texas in search of fresh farmland and a better life. From 1870 to 1890, close to 1,500,000 newcomers flocked in, some from Germany and Mexico but most from Alabama, Arkansas, Louisiana, Mississippi, Missouri, and Tennesse. . . .

Women who joined the Alliance formed part of this amalgam. In carving homesteads and farms from the unsettled forests and prairies, they and their families faced the vicissitudes of uncertain rainfall, primitive housing, vicious feuds, cattle rustling, loneliness, and economic dislocation. . . .

Beginning in 1870, the price of cotton—the farmers' economic mainstay—began to drop steadily in price. Many cash-strapped farmers turned to the crop-lien method of financing, by which a furnishing merchant or landlord would advance supplies and goods to the farmer in return for a lien on the future crop. . . . The effect of the crop-lien system was to establish a condition of peonage, for women as well as men. Appreciating money and diminishing returns, drought, depression, or northers often meant loss of ownership, and the number of landless tenant farmers began to rise. Even those who fared well enough to avoid lien financing and debt complained bitterly about the agricultural depression. Some farmers formed organizations of economic self-help, such as the National Grange of the Patrons of Husbandry, a secret society that officially eschewed partisan politics but called for cooperative endeavor and state railroad regulation. Other farmers pioneered new political institutions, such as the Greenback Party or the Union Labor Party.

The Farmers' Alliance originated in Lampasas County, Texas, in 1877, to thwart cattle rustling. In 1880, it was moved to Parker County and chartered as the nonprofit Farmers State Alliance organization. . . . By 1885, it had been forged into a cohesive system of approximately two hundred thousand members in more than two hundred suballiances. . . .

In 1886, the Alliance recruited in Louisiana. The next year, representatives from Texas and Louisiana organized alliances throughout the South. . . . The movement expanded into Kansas and in 1889 merged with strong state agrarian organizations in North Dakota and South Dakota. . . . In December 1889, farmers' organizations met in St. Louis to constitute a truly national alliance called the National Farmers' Alliance and Industrial Union. In the next four years, it attained a strength of between one and three million members.

Throughout its lifetime, the Alliance struggled with the issue of political insurgency versus nonpartisanship. As early as 1886, a series of political demands was formulated, then modified by conservatives who hoped to avoid political divisions and promote harmony. These were the Cleburne Demands, and they became the agrarian gospel that organizers preached throughout the nation. They included calls for: legislation against alien land ownership, laws to prevent trading in agricultural futures, the immediate forfeiture of railroad lands, the removal of illegal fences from public lands, tax reforms on corporate holdings, unlimited coinage of both gold and silver, an expanded money supply based on legal tender notes issued by the federal government, passage of an interstate commerce act, and abolition of convict labor. . . .

In many ways, the Alliance was an ideal movement for women. "No other movement in history—not even the antislavery cause—appealed to the women like [Populism]," wrote novelist Hamlin Garland. The doctrine of "separate spheres" gave women responsibility for morality and a higher purpose in life, a leitmotif clearly sketched in and by the order's teachings concerning sobriety, morality, benevolence, and cooperation. Its constitution announced the need "to develop a better state, mentally, morally, socially and financially," and placed much stress on the moral conduct of its members. Protection of the family was another goal. Women were a valuable component of these aims. Harry Tracy, a national lecturer, told Alliance members: "The ladies eligible must join the order before we can succeed." . . .

It was disconcerting at first for these early letter writers to have their words and names appear in public print. Nineteenth-century middle-class American society was based upon widespread acceptance of a particular image of the "ideal lady"— modest, submissive, educated in the genteel and domestic arts, supportive of her husband's efforts, physically weaker, probably mentally inferior but morally superior to men, uncomplaining, a perfect wife and mother, and, most certainly, private and never public. Good women were not to be seen or heard outside the sacred confines of the family circle. But the traditional view of the submissive, virtuous Southern lady, set apart in her "woman's sphere," had begun to crumble under the impact of the traumatic Civil War and post-Civil War conditions. As well, these were farm women who, for the common good, often were required to undertake tasks outside the circumscribed sphere of woman's place. Despite literature produced in the East, which promoted the woman's sphere, many farm women continued to work in the fields and pastures and to exchange their domestic produce for essential goods. Doing so created contradictions for them, and their letters reveal their struggles to reconcile their actual roles with the feminine ideal. Paradoxically, the separate sphere also gave them a special identification with Alliance goals.

Initially the women were hesitant to appear in public. Some used pen names. Again and again, they apologized for their correspondence, their presumption of a place in the public eye, but they clearly felt that it was a duty required by the Alliance. . . .

As time passed, the women became less timid and less self-effacing. The painful apologies ceased, and confidence in their public stance grew. Their increasing numbers fortified them. . . .

As farm women began to see themselves as part of a class, they expressed concern for urban working people and organizations such as the Knights of Labor. The Knights encouraged the participation of women in its own ranks and supported women's suffrage in ways not unlike the practices of the Alliance. The women were aware of the activities of the labor movement and its demand for an eight-hour day and national events such as the 1884 Haymarket Square Riot in Chicago and the Great Southwest Strike of 1886. Some were radicalized and spoke of the brighter future that could be created by an organized working class. "I hope the day is not far distant when the downtrodden farmer can look back and say, we have gained the victory at last, for if any class of people have been slaves it is the farmers. If ever there was a time when the farming and labor elements should stick together it is now," wrote Ida Jones from Mansfield in May 1888. . . .

At first the Texas Alliance focused on economic strategies of protest. It attempted local trade agreements with merchants, local cotton bulking, and local cooperative stores which could lower the costs of goods to the farmer. In 1887, when Alliance President Charles W. Macune realized that such disjointed efforts would not improve the position of the farmer in the market, he proposed the Exchange, a statewide Alliance-owned cooperative, based in Dallas, in which farmers would unite to buy supplies, store their crops in giant warehouses, and send them to market when the price was right. The exchange was to have the dual effect of increasing the supply of money at harvest time, when it usually was scarce, and granting the farmer credit at a low rate of interest, thereby breaking the grasp of crop-lien. . . .

### Women's Concerns

Alliance leaders believed American democracy to be in moral and political decay, corrupted by the professional politician and slick financier. The farmer was the last repository of the true values—the very humanity—of American culture. Education was needed not only to bolster agrarian self-esteem and to protect the unschooled farmer against merchandising fraud; it also was central to an understanding of urban, financial, and industrial capitalism and to the creation of a sophisticated political movement based upon unity, cooperation, and independence. . . .

Education also was a logical extension of women's traditional roles as child rearers and as moral and cultural guardians. Children constituted the next generation of voters and politicians, and they needed to be trained at the earliest age. Women were expected to shield home and family from the rapidly changing values of an increasingly materialistic society. Alliance and Populist platform demands included a uniform, inexpensive system of textbooks and free public schools. . . .

In the April 19, 1888, issue of the *Mercury,* "A Country Girl" from Belton wrote that there was one thing farmers "could go into debt for if we cannot obtain it otherwise, that is an education. Knowledge is power. . . . Educate your girls that they may be independent. Educate your boys that they may perform the work assigned them through life with intelligence and then our country homes will be a paradise surrounded by the beauties of nature and enlightened sons and daughters of toil and prosperity." . . .

The women discussed the propriety of working in the fields, an activity that conflicted with the notions of woman's sphere. In April 1889, Frankie Bradford of Luna Vista had written:

> . . . I am not ashamed to confess that I work on the farm, for I am sure it is no discredit to do so; and whoever thinks so, have some lack of knowledge. I believe a girl can work in the field and be so full of grace as one that dwells in a palace. . . . Let those who say it is a disgrace to a girl to work in the field take heed. . . .

Times got rougher as the currency contracted. Among other things, the dollar continued to appreciate, its value rising steadily, while prices for agricultural products, especially cotton, declined. The farming community, noted for its hard work and industry, worked harder. The women urged each other to economize, to be more frugal. "We can be the most independent people in the world if we will only try," said Eddie, from the Round Pound Alliance. "First, we must economize. If we want to accomplish anything, raise everything that we can at home, wear old clothes and keep out of debt." . . .

In June 1888, Bettie Gay from Columbus suggested boycotting coffee until the price fell, something she had done during the Civil War. She had a blunt response to a contributor's suggestion that women return to the spinning wheel and loom. "I am in sympathy with every economical move," she said, but

> . . . It will take three days to weave one yard of cloth; at twenty-five cents per day, it would cost seventy-five cents per yard to spin and weave a yard, besides the expense of the machinery, so you see there is no economy. It would be more healthful to raise a cotton patch, work in the open air and buy calico or muslin for five cents per yard. . . .

The Cleburne Demands of 1886 and later Alliance and Populist platforms were disseminated widely among the Alliance membership. Moreover, after 1888 the Alliance's educational campaign efforts intensified, and the many reform journals and suballiances embraced new roles as schools for education. Alliance newspapers carried voluminous eighteen- to twenty-part series on the history of democracy or on the economic theories of Ricardo, Mills, and Smith. Long and capable—if somewhat mythological—letters, such as Ann Other's earnest two-column synopsis of civilization's development, reflect a reading of Macune's similar multi-part educational accounts of history. . . . She went on to trace the arrival and decline of the Greeks and Romans, the development of family and government, as well as the growth of vast corporations. . . .

Some of the letters were sophisticated and explicit, and writers asked important, thoughtful questions. Other opinions were abstract, as indeed the whole Populist theme could be, again with the discussion of economic issues cast in moral or Christian terms and expressed in statements filled with Old Testament imagery and Christian metaphor. To some, the "money power" indicated particular individuals—for example, the legislators who had passed the bill for the demonetization of silver. For others, the phrase loosely denoted not only politicians on the wrong side but also all wealthy men and corporations—Wall Street brokers, bankers (American and British), small and large business owners, railroads, mortgage companies, mine owners, and landlords. . . . Always the letter writers urged the farmers on in the struggle.

The land belonged to the farmer—not the government, the speculator, the banker, the London financier, or the railroad magnate. "It is good to discuss the why's and wherefore's of the exceeding scarcity of money but there is another question of great magnitude," advised Mary of Limestone County. "Why is it that there are so many homeless men and women, men who would till the soil for a living, and yet there are thousands of acres of land lying idle. Why did our state officials give the railroads so much of the people's land, and compel the poor to rent? Why did they give so much land to build a state house? Would it have not been better policy to have given that 3,000,000 acres of land to the poor renting farmer and built a less palatial house by direct taxation?"

The women articulated economic theories and financial legislation well, but in their personal analyses and final conclusions, they emphasized the human aspects of poverty among all classes and its effects upon the family and home. They never doubted that impersonal industrial capitalism caused family poverty and the poverty of single women. . . .

### Bettie Gay

In many ways, Bettie Gay epitomizes the ordinary Alliance woman—the stolid, independent, strong-willed, resourceful Texas farmer who heard the challenges of the Alliance and embraced its promises. In other ways, she is different, representing a smaller group of women who were radicalized first by the movement and then by its failure to deliver on its promises. . . .

Her first appearance in the pages of the *Mercury* may have been June 14, 1888, and signed "B. G." She was urging people to boycott coffee. In June 1889, she and Mrs. Shaw proposed that the Alliance women sell poultry and dairy items for money to save the Exchange. In 1891, she angrily complained about the decline of women's letters in the *Mercury*. When Nelson Dunning published his history of the Farmers' Alliance that same year, he included a chapter by Gay on "The Influence of Women in the Alliance," which summed up the status of women. It has been interpreted by McMath, among other historians, as accepting women's conventional roles, because in it Gay speaks of woman as man's companion and helpmeet. However, she did not marry again after her husband died, choosing not to become someone's "helpmeet." Read from a different perspective, her essay seems strongly feminist, almost revolutionary. "Nature has endowed women with brains," she wrote. "Why should she not think . . . why not act? If allowed to act, what privilege should men enjoy of which she should be deprived?" She looked to the Alliance to redeem woman from her "enslaved condition," insisting that "what we need is a better womanhood . . . acknowledging no master and accepting no compromise." Bettie Gay strongly espoused suffrage and eventually became a Socialist.

Historians of Alliance and Populist women have found that, despite the movement's official support of expanded roles for women, the meaning of equality was constricted by and to the organization's major goal of reviving Southern agriculture. It has been understood that political rights within the Alliance were not seen by women as the first step toward political rights outside the Alliance. . . . Despite the equality of membership in the Alliance and its promise of democracy, Alliance and Populist women were not able to convert the party—or even each other—to unequivocal support for suffrage. . . .

Success, however, is not the only criterion of importance. If an accelerated transformation of consciousness among a group of oppressed people was vital to the formation of the Alliance movement, it was to the suffrage movement as well. . . .

It is precisely this movement of awakening consciousness that these rural Texas letters illustrate. . . . Very possibly these letters about suffrage represent the first articulation of feminist consciousness for many rural women. Ann Other, one of the most frequent letter writers, confessed that "when I began to study suffrage . . . I thought women's only ambition should be to read the latest novels, work green dogs with pink eyes on cardboard and other ornamental work, keep her house and children clean and healthy and 'always meet your husband with a smile' but now I am satisfied that with suffrage, she can benefit her country, keep her own womanly traits and have more just laws for herself and better protection for her children."

Between April 19, 1888, and April 18, 1889, women were stirred to write to the *Mercury* about suffrage and women's rights, more than about any other topic. Fifteen percent of the women's letters focused on female suffrage or women's rights. Of the Texas letters, 56 percent were in favor of suffrage, while 44 percent were against it. . . .

Widespread support for prohibition existed among Populist women and was linked with suffrage sentiment, pro and con. "I have been reading sister Ann Other's letters and I think they're splendid," said Mary M. of Greer County in another letter published on June 28. "I can't understand why some are so opposed to us ladies voting. One good sister thinks it would be a downfall to the female sex to go there among so many grades of people. Well, have we not got all kinds of people in our country and do we have to stop and shake hands with them and tell them we are on their side? No Sir. . . . . Where would whiskey have gone if women had been allowed to vote? There would not have been a drop of whisky now in existence."

Eva J. Sims of Sault Creek Alliance, Indian Territory, also blamed the failure to pass prohibition on women's inability to vote. . . .

The June *Mercury* was full of interesting letters, including a heated antisuffrage message from Rebecca of Jefferson, Texas. "Please withhold your vials of wrath while I reassert that there are corrupt women as well as men," she wrote, in defiance of the traditional view of female perfection. . . . "Lady Macbeth whose unholy ambition (I think she wanted female suffrage) caused her to suggest and help execute the murder of her king, and which finally resulted in the ruin of herself and the overthrow of her family. Thus it is often the case when a woman obtrudes herself beyond her legitimate sphere." . . .

For Dianecia Jones of Dallas County, the discussion had gone on long enough. "Women's rights!" she exploded. "Now sisters, let that question rest. As for my part I don't think it would improve things for the ladies to vote. Let us allow the men to make laws. We can certainly live by their laws if they can. As to woman's suffrage, that is something we will never get in this world. I say look up and trust for our rights in a better world."

Despite Jones's weary surfeit, the Alliance and the Populist party awakened in other women the powerful drive to participate in the more formal realm of politics through suffrage, and aroused a discontent with purely private identities and definitions of femininity. . . . Women took their voting privileges seriously and looked to the Alliance to increase their political understanding. Through the order, women were able to practice the arts of participation and experience themselves as visible and effective. . . .

## The Alliance Begins to Decline

The number of women's letters peaked during the fall of 1888 and declined swiftly thereafter. Several issues during the following few months of that year contained no letters at all from women, although a woman's page still existed. . . .

Some students of the agrarian movement have suggested that, as the Alliance became politicized, its social function declined in importance. . . . As things got tougher, the resilience and dedication of Alliance women became even more necessary to the order, if not to the *Mercury*. This suggests that the women's contribution had assumed an importance far beyond the social arena: the women had become a vital nexus of the organization, an essential segment of its spiritual backbone, a component, possibly, of its very survival. . . .

The *Mercury,* as well as the Alliance, was in crisis over the Exchange. A cryptic paragraph from the editors in an October issue said, "A great many of our readers are holding back the money they have saved to renew their subscription to the *Mercury* until everything was clear to them, or until the executive committee secured control of the paper. As the latter has been accomplished, all should renew at once." The reference is to the charge that Macune and other Exchange directors were incompetent, an accusation that had replaced the original explanation—merchant-banker opposition—for the failure of the Exchange. Alliance members had been warned not to put their hard-earned money into the doomed venture. The *Southern Mercury,* . . . took up this idea and, by the late summer of 1888, was taking a definite anti-Exchange stance, lambasting Macune and other Alliance leaders. . . .

An investigatory committee fully vindicated Macune and the Exchange of any wrongdoing, and Macune in turned accused the *Mercury* of betraying the Alliance to avoid losing advertising patronage. The reaction of the rank-and-file Alliance members to the controversy was bitter, however, and the consequences devastating. Local alliances began reporting immediate declines in membership. Although control of the *Mercury* passed into the hands of the state Alliance, the new editors never reversed the editorial position of the ousted editors. . . .

. . . Women's issues no longer appeared on the front pages of the *Nonconformist*, for example, and the remaining women's columns devoted themselves to fashions and cooking, rather than women's rights and politics. . . .

The failure of the Exchange led Macune to develop the most significant proposal in Alliance history: the subtreasury plan. The plan called for the establishment of locally situated federal subtreasuries, along with warehouses and elevators in which farmers could store certain nonperishable commodities. The government would provide short-term credit at low interest, giving the farmer more independence in marketing his crop. As projected, the system would end the deflationary glut of commodities on the market at harvest time and create an expanded, flexible currency that would reverse the decline of farm prices.

The proposal was a watershed for the Alliance. It brought the order directly into party politics, a move that, as many had predicted and feared, generated friction and divided the Texas Alliance. It precipitated the final protest strategy of the Alliance movement—the Populist party. The party siphoned off Alliance energy and led to the movement's demise. Then the party itself fused with the Democrats in the 1896 presidential election, lost the support of Texas Populists who refused to fuse, and eventually died out. . . .

Before the Populist conventions [in 1892], women had been excited about the potential of a new party—a party which included them, which might give them suffrage, which recognized the importance of home and family and woman's central role, which might support prohibition, and which would solve the economic problems of the farmers. . . .

However, in an opening speech in St. Louis, Ben Terrell of Texas urged delegates to consider only questions of "economic" reforms. "Moral reforms" should be put off until a later date, while other differences between Northern and Southern elements in the movement were bridged. . . . Many Democrats whom the Populists were wooing opposed women's suffrage; it was considered a fatally divisive issue that should be sacrificed for the Populist cause. The other major moral reform, prohibition, also was lost. . . .

The official platform was drawn up later that summer, on the Fourth of July, at the national nominating convention in Omaha, Nebraska. . . . It did not include women's suffrage or temperance. . . .

The Populists did not fare well in the 1892 presidential election against Republican Benjamin Harrison and Democrat Grover Cleveland. In only five Southern states did the total Populist vote amount to more than one half of the Alliance's potential voting strength at its peak. In Texas, the order was split, as many moderate Alliancemen remained loyal to the Democratic party and looked to the popular young governor, James S. Hogg, for leadership. . . .

. . . In 1896, the Democrats co-opted the free-silver issue and nominated Nebraska's William Jennings Bryan for president. The national party fused with the Democrats; the Texas Populists preferred to stay in "the middle of the road" between the major parties. Neither strategy worked. Bryan lost the election to William McKinley, although he received more popular votes than Grover Cleveland had garnered in 1892. It was essentially the end of the party. The Alliance already had died.

Strong urban agitation for suffrage had begun in Texas in 1893, when the Texas Equal Rights Association (TERA), an auxiliary of the National American Woman Suffrage Association, was formed. It is not surprising that Bettie Gay was among the rural women who moved from the Alliance into TERA. Joining her were Alliance sisters Grace Danforth, Ellen Dabbs, and Margaret Watson. Nor is it surprising that the rhetoric of TERA tended to be more radical on the redefinition of sex roles than that put forth two decades later by the suffrage organizations that resuscitated the movement after TERA had died. . . .

Lawrence Goodwyn has suggested that the most important contribution of the agrarian revolt was to create "the visible evidence of community that gave meaning and substance to all lesser individuals." Politically, women were among those lesser individuals. But the Populist movement challenged the status quo; with the help of the *Southern Mercury,* it provided many women with community, meaning, and a stronger sense of self. . . . Rural women's participation in the Alliance and the Populist party undoubtedly helped break the ground for later social legislation, including that for women's suffrage.

## Women's Clubs as Vehicles for Reform in Houston, 1885–1918

### BETTY T. CHAPMAN

During the latter decades of the nineteenth century and the early years of the twentieth, the lives of middle-class Southern women changed significantly. Before then they had existed in a separate sphere, described by historian Barbara Welter as the "cult of true womanhood," which had kept them confined mostly to the home. Piety, purity, submissiveness, and domesticity were considered the most desirable feminine attributes. Events outside the home were, however, sowing seeds for change.

Exigencies of the Civil War had moved women beyond the domestic realm and had exposed them to new experiences, which in turn had made them eager for more knowledge and a broader education. Increased industrialization eased the burden of homemaking and resulted in more leisure time for middle-class women. A rapidly urbanizing society raised new concerns and caused unrest among citizens of growing cities and towns. Women were confronted with the new challenge of escaping from their separate sphere into a broad new world. These trends were evident not only nationally, but also in Houston.

How did these women move from their Victorian parlors into the public arena where they would become full-fledged instruments of change and civic reform? One channel through which this extraordinary journey occurred was provided by female organizations that offered women opportunities to shape their ideas within

Betty T. Chapman, "From the Parlor to the Public: New Roles for Women in Houston, 1885–1918," *Houston Review* 15 (1993), 31–44. Copyright © 1993 University of Houston. Reprinted with permission.

the safe confines of a sisterhood and to expand them into the broader framework of the community.

In February 1885, nine women concerned about their need for greater knowledge and for female companionship met in Houston and announced that "the name of this Association shall be The Ladies' History Class and its object shall be intellectual and social culture." Two months later, their membership having grown to 24, they drafted a constitution, changed their name to the Ladies' Reading Club, and adopted a plan for study.

Before that time, Houston had offered few forums for women to collectively voice their opinions and to act on their convictions. Organized female activity was almost entirely within the churches. Most noticeably, two groups—the Ladies' Parish Association of Christ Episcopal Church and the Ladies' Association of First Presbyterian Church—had recognized the needs of their congregations and had acted to meet those needs. Records of Christ Episcopal Church show that in 1875 the Ladies' Parish Association succeeded in raising enough money to purchase an organ and to initiate a fund to erect a larger church building. Similarly, the Presbyterian ladies decided in 1880 that a dwelling was needed for their minister and his family. After securing a charter enabling them to hold property, they bought three lots and erected a manse at a cost of approximately $8,000. This is not to imply that women had any official voice in the transactions of the church body. Indeed, Presbyterians had been cautioned by their General Assembly that "It is not proper for girls and young women to preside over a meeting of a society or to make an address or to lead in prayer." However, it is apparent that these women, acting within their own organizations, had achieved a marked degree of independence and were making significant contributions to the entire congregation.

Interestingly, over half of the charter members of the Ladies' Reading Club were from these two congregations. Soon after their organization, however, it was apparent that their bond was more than just religious. Several had brought daughters and sisters into the group, most had husbands prominent within the business community, and many were descendants of Houston's first families. Though most were matrons, they welcomed unmarried women, declaring that "the new thoughts, strong sympathies, wider views, and the expression of mind and character . . . would be a gain for all women." While little is known of their schooling, it appears that most had had the advantage of a more extensive and formal education than many of their contemporaries. Several were employed as teachers.

The Ladies' Reading Club uniformly and firmly believed—as stated by their first president, Adele Briscoe Looscan—that a woman should be "one whose mind shall be trained to form her own opinions, to organize her own household and, if need be, to make her own living." At one of the meetings the topic for debate was "Resolved: That the education of our daughters for an independent career will unfit them for the duties of wife and mother." Club minutes show that this view was soundly defeated.

Chroniclers of the nineteenth-century women's club movement have stated that one of its more far-reaching results was that it stimulated women to think and gave them the opportunity to articulate their views. The substance of this statement can be seen in the Ladies' Reading Club, which pursued in-depth studies of subjects such as "The Progress of Art During the Reign of the Four Georges" and "The Cause of Spain's Low Rank in the Fields of Science and Philosophy." All members were required to participate; they presented carefully researched papers, engaged in lively debates, and prepared informative statements on assigned topics with which to answer roll call. It was an opportunity to teach and to be taught. This mutual exchange gave every woman in the club equal consideration and respect. While the meetings may not have produced avid scholars, careerists, or social critics, they did provide a means for the members to view themselves as something more than moral guardians of their homes. This club attracted intelligent women for whom turning from the realm of abstract thought to the arena of practical action was a natural progression.

In March 1887, four members of this club—Adele Briscoe Looscan, Harriet Fitzgerald, Eva McIlhenny, and Julia Huston—helped establish the Woman's Exchange, which advertised that it was the only organization in Houston assisting females. The Exchange secured employment for women who were forced to earn their own livings and served as a commission house selling goods produced by women. Though it frequently suffered financial problems, it managed to stay open with funds derived from the 25-cent monthly dues paid by its members, the commissions on sales of goods, periodic entertainments, and donations from local businessmen. It stated in its first annual report that it had 161 members 14 honorary members—males who had made donations—and 37 persons with goods for sale. Records for the next year indicated that the number of consignors had doubled, 23 women had been placed in jobs, and a sewing class for young girls was being successfully conducted. In spite of criticism, which they felt was unjustified, the Women's Exchange continued to offer a dignified means of support to women in need.

The Woman's Exchange and other female-related groups were supported by *The Ladies' Messenger,* a local publication begun in 1887. It proclaimed itself to be "the exponent of woman's thought and woman's work." While the publication did contain the usual amount of domestic advice, it also advocated equal educational opportunities for females and touted the advantages of calisthenics for young women in defiance of those who insisted that the female brain was smaller than the male and the female physique was frail. It encouraged the formation of women's literary clubs and offered to publicize and promote their causes. The Ladies' Reading Club accepted the offer and published its President's Annual Report in *The Ladies' Messenger.*

This support became less visible in 1890 when the name of *The Ladies's Messenger* was changed to *The Gulf Messenger.* The female editor explained the change by saying that the publication would be "no less devoted to women but the name change will give us a wider field and more readers, for many men still have a silly prejudice that a journal devoted to women has nothing in it pertaining to 'the grand thoughts that shape mankind.'" Despite the editor's stated intent, the paper became an organ divided between sentimental literary offerings and promotional information for males in the business community. Though the women of Houston had lost a strong voice in the public arena, they did not become invisible.

In an address to the Ladies' Reading Club on its tenth anniversary in 1895, Adele Looscan admonished its members, "Do we exercise . . . influence as largely as we might? Are we not inclined to be too conservative? . . . Ladies, failing to recognize a responsibility does not lessen the reality of a duty, which, from the very nature of our organization, becomes ours."

One of the greatest concerns of Mrs. Looscan and her fellow club members was that Houston had no public library. In 1894, they had requested that the books of the Houston Lyceum, a private, predominantly male literary organization, be made available to nonmembers and that its library be moved from the Market House to a location more accessible to the women of the community. Though the first request was granted, and a woman was hired as librarian, the Lyceum library remained where it had been. The ladies continued their campaign for new quarters, and finally in September 1897—almost three years after the initial request—the Lyceum allowed its library to be relocated. The Ladies' Reading Club paid for the move. To build a treasury for the new facility, each member of the club became a monthly subscriber, the club donated its magazine files and its own collection of 150 books, and they voted to give the library five dollars worth of new books each month. This provided the nucleus of the library, but it soon became apparent—at least to the women of the city—that a more substantial base was essential. When the city council reneged on its promise to include in its 1899 budget a provision for stocking and maintaining the library, the women used the strategy of both appeasing and chiding the male officials of the city. They invited them to an entertainment where they served refreshments, politely reminded them of their pledge, and then pointed to the empty bookshelves. The following week Mamie Ewing, one of the two club members who had personally invited the officials, recorded in the club minutes that she "believed the embarrassment of meeting an army of women re-solved itself into a pleasure to all of them . . . because the Mayor admitted he would deem it an honor to be the first mayor to recommend an appropriation for the library." Whether he felt it an honor or an obligation may never be known; one alderman was heard to comment that women would not have time to read books if they took care of their homes and families. Nevertheless, a monthly appropriation of $200 was made, and a free public reading room became a reality.

Encouraged by this victory but still dissatisfied with what they considered an inadequate facility, the ladies deluged the mayor with letters. Perseverance, though, seemed to accomplish little until two members of the Woman's Club, Belle Kendall and Mamie Gearing, wrote to Andrew Carnegie. In response to their solic-itation, he agreed to furnish money for a building if the city would provide a site. To support the city in this undertaking and "to give aid to the material welfare of the community," representatives of five women's clubs—the Ladies' Reading Club, the Woman's Club, the Current Literature Club, the Ladies' Shakespeare Club, and the Mansfield Dramatic Club—met in January 1900 to form the City Federation of Women's Clubs. The new federation joined with the Lyceum to coordinate their efforts to raise funds for the library site. Lectures, ice cream socials, musicales, bazaars, and a "home circus" produced funds that were applied to the $7,880 cost of the proposed site on Travis and McKinney streets. On May 1, 1902, the women of Houston could feel a real sense of accomplishment when the first brick was laid; the Houston Lyceum and Carnegie Library would soon be available to residents of the city.

The organization of the City Federation led to the formation of other groups. In March 1900, Emma Richardson Cherry was instrumental in founding the Public School Art League. Drawing its membership primarily from clubwomen and public school teachers, the group endeavored to encourage art education in the schools.

Still working within the accepted realm of home and family, they took as their inspiration these lines from the poem "Mother to a Child":

> For the sake of my child I must hasten to save
> All children on earth from the jail and the grave.

Convinced that one way to accomplish this was by introducing the children to great works of art, they began to acquire reproductions of art masterpieces, which they presented to the public schools. They were instrumental in having art courses added to the curriculum, and they brought noted artists to the city to lecture. While the children were receptive—five thousand students attended one lecture at the City Auditorium—the adult citizens, from whom the League had hoped to receive funding, showed little interest. To combat this indifference, the women of the Public School Art League resorted to creative means of raising money. They first solicited the help of a prominent businessman who provided a building where they could hold art exhibits to which they would charge admission. Then each school was allotted certain days on which it would sponsor attendance and sell artwork created by its own students. Thus, by creating a friendly rivalry within a coalition of students, parents, and teachers, they were soon able to raise the needed funds.

Not every attempt to promote art was so favorably received. When the Public School Art League ordered a replica of the Venus de Milo to place in one of the schools, it was rejected by the school administration for fear that it might adversely affect the morals of the children. Not to be deterred, the League gave the statue to the public library where its presence 89 years later attests to the determination of these women. Houston's Museum of Fine Arts, which evolved from the Public School Art League, further attests to their vision.

Affirming the values of art and literature led to more aggressive female-inspired programs. By 1900, Houston's population was approaching 45,000 and the city was experiencing rapid growth. This growth brought problems that would only intensify during the next two decades. Public health, education, and city services continued to be addressed only sporadically by the city government. In 1901, Margaret Hadley Foster published a call for action imploring clubwomen throughout the city to put aside their petty rivalries and to join forces in an effort aimed toward "improving and advancing the city." Realizing that men would still be essential to their efforts, she invited their participation. "Men," she declared, "are very useful—at times—and if they could only be stirred up to do something for the beauty and cleanliness of the city, what a world of good they could do!" Though they still realized that males made policy and controlled purse strings, women were becoming bolder about prodding men into action. Mrs. Foster then appealed to a broader segment of the female population. The strategy for implementing improvements was to organize a civic club in each of Houston's six wards. Each ward club would, in turn, determine the needs of its own neighborhood.

One of the first concerns of the Houston Civic Club was the scarcity of parks and playgrounds in Houston. The city's first park had been established in 1899 after a group of women, led by Elizabeth Ring, had flouted convention and appeared in a body at City Hall to request that land be purchased for a park. Using this as a precedent, the women in the ward clubs succeeded in placing parks in several neighborhoods. Then they purchased playground equipment, sponsored free concerts, and beautified the grounds of public buildings throughout the city. Operating in essence as a city recreation department, the women assumed the responsibility for establishing and maintaining parks but continually reproached city officials for their failure to do so.

Sanitation was another grave concern of the Houston Civic Club. In a 1906 report, they credit their group with the successful passage of two city ordinances: the anti-expectoration ordinance and the uniform garbage can law. Clearing trash and debris from the streets became an ongoing project of these energetic women. Though they insisted that "they had carefully abstained from meddling in politics," it is obvious that they were constantly reminding city officials that public services were less than adequate and that action was needed.

The increased population, which now included a growing number of immigrants, changed the demographics of many neighborhoods. This was especially true of the Second Ward where former residents had moved into the newly developed South End neighborhoods and had been replaced by immigrant families. Houses were divided into cramped apartments; poverty was readily apparent. Believing strongly that the expansion of educational opportunities was one of the keys to improving the lives of Second Ward citizens, the 26 members of the Woman's Club, under the leadership of Mamie Gearing, opened a free kindergarten in the neighborhood in 1902. The first quarters, a lean-to shed, were quickly outgrown. The club members rented land, solicited building materials from local businesses, and secured volunteer labor to erect a larger facility. With limited income at their disposal, the Woman's Club instituted an innovative system of securing the needed personnel to assist the one paid teacher. They opened a training school for volunteer teachers, thereby laying the foundation for future community volunteerism. Five years later, the program was expanded when the local school board gave the club permission to open a kindergarten in a newly constructed public school. These women steadfastly believed that a significant step in educating the city's young had been taken.

In 1907, as the Second Ward became increasingly crowded and impoverished, 12 women, recognizing a critical need for health and education in that area, organized the Houston Settlement Association. Alice Baker was selected to head the Association and, as one account states, she brought to this endeavor "intelligence, vision, and a tenacity of purpose." The women's first task was the inevitable one of raising funds. Their bylaws stated that "Monthly dues shall not be stipulated, each member subscribing as her pleasure dictates." This encouraged liberal giving from the more economically privileged members. It is also evident that these women tapped resources that were familiar to them. Their first outside donation was from the Ladies' Association of First Presbyterian Church, of which Mrs. Baker was a member.

Feeling strongly that the neighborhood should work for its own improvement instead of merely accepting charity from others, the Houston Settlement Association established the Second Ward Women's Club. This created a unique opportunity for cross-class cooperation, as members of the ward club, sustained by the experienced and affluent clubwomen, now provided volunteers and at least some financial support for its projects. These included assuming responsibility for the Woman's Club kindergarten and establishing a visiting nurses program. The Settlement Association focused its attention on the needs of children with a new intensity, but also broadened its horizons to include adult education classes, programs for the deaf and dumb, Houston's first branch library, community-sponsored manual training and domestic science programs, and a school for delinquent boys.

By first establishing programs through its own initiatives and then keeping them before the public, the Settlement Association was able to realize the creation of permanent institutions by 1918. Its visiting nurses program had been integrated into the city's newly organized Public Health Department. The Association's work with delinquent boys had led to the Seabrook School for Boys in Clear Lake. The Association had lobbied successfully to establish a City Recreation Department to oversee parks and playgrounds across the entire city. The Settlement Association believed that a neighborhood approach that depended on "the philanthropic whim of the individual giver" was not the most efficient one and they continued to work for the development of permanent agencies.

Clubwomen, who by now had become crusaders for their causes, realized that it was critical to their success to keep the public informed of what they viewed as the city's needs. Since the demise of *The Ladies' Messenger* in 1890, women's activities, other then those of a purely social nature, had received little attention from the press. This lack of publicity had not at first displeased the organized women's groups. The Ladies' Reading Club had even declared in their minutes of October 13, 1896, that "the *Post* may contain the exercises of the Ladies' Reading Club but the names may not be given." Club members had been acutely sensitive to the ridicule which had resulted from the less-than-serious articles printed about them in their formative years. By 1906, however, they realized that they needed a public voice; and Stella Christian brought together 11 women with a dual interest in literary writing and community improvements. Thus was born the Houston Pen Women, who took it as their objective "to proclaim the glory and sublimity of righteousness." If righteousness can be defined as combating poverty, ignorance, disease, indifference, and exploitation, these female writers achieved their goal; they regularly submitted articles to Houston publications and sponsored a weekly column by Mrs. Christian in the *Houston Post*. They were no longer reluctant to be mentioned in print.

Clubwomen realized that legislation was ultimately the key to ensuring permanent reforms in the community. Through the networking of the City Federation of Women's Clubs and its allied group, the Texas Federation of Women's Clubs, they kept issues before the appropriate legislative bodies. As a result, local storekeepers were required to shorten working hours and to provide seats for their clerks during breaks, a women's restroom was maintained in the Market House, and matrons were placed in both the jail and the railroad station for the protection of women. More kindergartens were opened and traveling libraries were sent into rural areas. Additionally, the need for pure food and milk laws was publicized and a municipal livestock fencing ordinance was enacted. Between 1909 and 1917, women's groups across the state came together to form powerful coalitions. These determined women lobbied successfully for legislation including a state child welfare commission, child labor laws, a juvenile court system, public kindergartens, compulsory school attendance laws, pure food inspection, and a state library commission. Always concerned about the quality of life, women broadened their role as guardians of the home to include being caretakers of the community.

What were the necessary components for the journey these women made in moving out of the narrow sphere of home and family into the real and troubled world around them? In order to succeed it was essential that they gain public acceptance, acquire financial support, and establish strong leadership. At the same time they had to operate within the bounds of propriety, never forgetting their roles as homemakers.

While they faced some opposition, not only from men but also from women who felt that too much public exposure would lead to a deterioration of home and family, it is apparent that many of the women were strongly supported by male family members, who contributed not only financially, but also through their influence within the business and political communities. Although most women's clubs avoided controversial issues that might overshadow their own more immediate goals, certainly some of their members individually supported the woman suffrage movement and strongly agreed with their fellow clubwoman, Elizabeth Ring, that "we could all do this work much better and quicker with less loss of time and dignity and self-respect by casting our vote as full-fledged citizens. It is not pleasant to have to wheedle and cajole or flatter men to give us these sensible and practical things. It takes too much of our time and energy and it makes us think less of ourselves and them." Though they might deplore it, they understood the necessity of having the support and approval of the male population, and they became experts at the art of persuasion. In a broader sense they appealed to middle-class society by emphasizing their goals and their spirit of service to the community in an attractive and, perhaps more importantly, nonthreatening way.

While the Ladies' Reading Club had firmly declared in their minutes of November 8, 1895, that they did not wish to become ticket sellers, clubwomen soon realized that the need for funds would be a perpetual reality and they became persistent and innovative money raisers. They entertained, decorously of course. They begged, always appealing to the goodness and generosity of the hoped-for benefactor. And they taught, feeling that funds would more readily come from an educated citizenry. Eventually they realized that by reproaching those in authority, they could persuade government to assume financial responsibility for improving the quality of life within the city.

Leadership, of course, was the ultimate key to success. Women like Adele Looscan, Elizabeth Ring, Emma Cherry, Margaret Foster, Alice Baker, and Mamie Gearing, who began with the desire for self-improvement, came to the realization that community improvement could enhance the general welfare. Though they lacked power in the conventional sense, they combined perseverance, intelligence, and an astute sense of timing to effect coalitions that would actively work for the good of the entire population.

From our late-twentieth-century perspective, these clubwomen may have acted conservatively, addressed a narrow segment of the population, and failed to achieve true equality. Within the ideological and political framework of the time, however, they helped to lay the foundation for the feminist expression of the future. The club movement provided a socially acceptable way for many women to begin moving out of the domestic realm and gain a public voice, without taking on the public notoriety that was attached to the crusading feminists of the time. Through their clubs, women learned the importance of joining together to effect change. In them, women found the strength to become autonomous persons.

# ✦ F U R T H E R   R E A D I N G

Evan Anders, *Boss Rule in South Texas: The Progressive Era* (1982)

Donna K. Barnes, *Farmers in Rebellion: The Rise and Fall of the Southern Farmers' Alliance and the People's Party in Texas* (1984)

Alwyn Barr, *Reconstruction to Reform: Texas Politics, 1876–1906* (1971)

Marion K. Barthelme, ed., *Women in the Texas Populist Movement: Letters to the* Southern Mercury (1997)

Debbie Mauldin Cottrell, *Pioneer Woman Educator: Annie Webb Blanton* (1993)

Elizabeth York Enstam, *Women and the Creation of Urban Life, Dallas, Texas, 1843–1920* (1998)

James R. Green, "Tenant Farmer Discontent and Socialist Protest in Texas, 1901–1917," *Southwestern Historical Quarterly* 81 (1977): 133–154

Patricia E. Hill, "Women's Groups and the Extension of City Services in Early Twentieth Century Dallas," *East Texas Historical Review* 30 (1992): 3–10.

Janet G. Humphrey, ed, *A Texas Suffragist: Diaries and Writings of Jane Y. McCallum* (1988)

James D. Ivy, "The Lone Star State Surrenders to a Lone Woman: Frances Willard's Forgotten 1882 Texas Temperance Tour," *Southwestern Historical Quarterly* 102 (1998): 44–61

Judith N. MacArthur, *Creating the New Woman: The Rise of Southern Women's Progressive Culture in Texas, 1893–1919* (1998)

Jacquelyn Masur McElhaney, *Pauline Periwinkle and Progressive Reform in Dallas* (1998)

Elizabeth Hayes Turner, *Women, Culture and Community: Religion and Reform in Galveston, 1880–1920* (1997)

CHAPTER
12

# Oil, Industrialization, and Urbanization, 1900–1940

*In the twentieth century, the traditional Texas of farms and ranches, cotton and cattle, gave way to an increasingly urban and industrialized Texas. Although urban growth in Texas has been spectacular, the change from rural to urban did not occur as soon or as quickly as it sometimes appears. In 1900 Texas was still 83 percent rural. In 1940 the state was approaching an even split between its rural and urban population, but it remained 54 percent rural. The balance of power between urban and rural shifted permanently in the decade of the 1940s. Not only did a majority (63 percent) of Texans in 1950 reside in urban areas for the first time, but rural population actually declined during the 1940s and has continued to decline ever since. Urban population growth can also be measured in the growth of individual cities, especially the growth of the state's two major metropolises, Houston and Dallas. At the turn of the century, San Antonio (population 53,321) was the state's largest city, followed by Houston (44,633), Dallas (42,638), and Galveston (37,788). By 1930 Houston (292,352) and Dallas (262,475) had emerged as the state's two largest cities.*

*Urban growth in Texas was directly related to the state's industrialization. Simply put, Spindletop and the resulting oil boom triggered unprecedented economic and urban growth. Before the end of the 1920s, industrial output had replaced agricultural output as the main source of the state's wealth. World War II created a second economic boom as aircraft manufacturing, shipbuilding, steel, chemicals, and electronics broadened the industrial base and accelerated the state's transition from rural to urban.*

*While many Texans embraced the boom times brought by oil, industry, and urban growth, others were concerned by the challenges that these developments introduced. Urbanization and industrialization shifted political power from rural areas and rural concerns to the cities and towns and their concerns. Urbanization increased the need for services and infrastructure to accommodate rapid population growth. In addition, it raised questions about the adequacy of traditional political structures and policies. Racial and ethnic conflict often followed rapid population shifts to the cities, and overall social change led to efforts to preserve traditional social and racial mores, law and order, and standards of moral behavior.*

*What Texas experienced with urbanization and industrialization has raised questions. First, what triggered urban growth? Was it solely the result of economic factors and economic advantage or did it arise from wise leadership and careful planning? Was rapid urbanization a blessing or a curse? Could the traditional image of Texas individualism survive the pressures of an urban society? How would the state deal with the problems that surfaced with economic growth and urbanization?*

 D O C U M E N T S

Industrialization and the Texas oil industry began to slowly develop in the last quarter of the nineteenth century, but it was the Spindletop discovery in 1901 that transformed Texas unlike any other economic event. The first two documents attest to the almost mythic aspects of Spindletop. Document 1 illustrates how this event was reported in Dallas, which along with Houston, most successfully reaped the economic benefits of the oil boom. Document 2 presents the worker's perspective on this event. It consists of the oral history testimony of two of the three men who were on the oil platform the day that the Spindletop gusher came in.

Interest in urban planning blossomed during the first quarter of the twentieth century as a logical outgrowth of the Progressive era reform philosophy. Both Houston and Dallas initially flirted with planning during the years immediately preceding the First World War. In Document 3 the *Dallas Morning News* reports favorably on the plan that a Kansas City urban designer, George Kessler, developed for the City of Dallas. The Kessler Plan would serve as the basis for Dallas planning efforts for the next twenty years. Three years later, Arthur Comey, a Boston city planner, provided Houston with its first city plan as Document 4 presents. Both of these plans were developed by national planning firms and reflect the approach to urban planning typical of the Progressive Era. Neither plan was fully implemented.

The next three documents address the racial and social conflicts that accompanied early twentieth-century urbanization. Document 5 presents the initial reports of the worst race riot in Houston history, the 1917 mutiny of African American troops stationed in the city. The revived Ku Klux Klan enjoyed considerable power and influence in Texas cities in the early 1920s. Document 6 attempts to explain the nature of the Klan and its popularity. Document 7 presents an African American perspective on urban promise and problems. In 1928 Houston proponents of urban planning established a magazine to promote a new city plan. Clifford F. Richardson, an African American newspaper publisher, businessman, and civil rights activist, was asked to contribute an article on the state of "Negro Houston." Richardson's contribution mixed a combination of black Houston "boosterism" with a fairly accurate assessment of the needs of black neighborhoods.

The final document, 8, details the growth of the Texas oil industry and its connection to the growth and prosperity of Houston. It was written by John R. Suman, a vice president of Humble Oil and Refining Company, and published in the magazine of the Houston Chamber of Commerce.

## 1. The *Dallas Morning News* Reports a Big Oil Discovery at Spindletop, January 11, 1901

### A BIG OIL GEYSER
#### STREAM SIX INCHES IN DIAMETER SHOOTING 100 FEET INTO THE AIR NEAR BEAUMONT.

### ALL RECORDS BROKEN
#### IT IS ESTIMATED THAT ITS DAILY OUTPUT IS ABOUT FIVE THOUSAND BARRELS.

### BEAUMONT IN TRANSPORTS
**Road to the Well Is Lined with Vehicles Carrying Delighted Citizens.**

Beaumont, Tex., Jan. 10.—A stream of oil six inches in diameter is shooting over 100 feet into the air from a well located about three miles south of the city and the people of Beaumont, of every sort and condition, are in a feverish state of excitement. Nothing in point of general interest ever before so wrought up the population of this city. The throng on the streets appears to be childishly happy and grown men are going about smiling and bowing to each other like school girls and oil geyser is the sole topic of conversation among men, women and children. . . .

The well was sunk by Capt. A. F. Lucas of Washington, D.C., who has been operating for oil in this territory for more than a year. It was dug by Hammil Bros. of Corsicana, professional oilwell men, and one of these gentlemen told the correspondent of The News this afternoon that he has not in all his experience seen a well that equaled this one. He said Corsicana's wells were insignificant compared with this well, if the size and force of the flow are indications of its value.

Capt. Lucas is fairly delighted. To the correspondent, who called upon him, he said he hardly knew what to say. "We've struck oil, is about all I know to tell you," said he. "You can see the well yourself and except for my experience; you can tell almost as much about it as I can tell you. I have had experience in nearly every oil field in the United States, and I never saw a well to equal this. It is a larger geyser than I ever saw in West Virginia or Pennsylvania, and I believe it is the strongest stream ever found in the United States. Our first step now will be to anchor the well by process familiar in all fields. I have two large well rigs on the road here now and will at once sink other wells."

## 2. Oil Workers Al Hamill and Curt Hamill Give Eyewitness Accounts of the Spindletop Gusher, 1901

**Al Hamill:**    We put it on and was running this string of drill pipe back in, at about seven hundred feet or a little over in, when the drilling mud commenced to boil up through the rotary. And it got higher and higher and higher up through the top of

---

"A Big Oil Geyser," *Dallas Morning News*, 11 January 1901.

Mody C. Boatright and William A. Owens, *Tales from the Derrick Floor: A People's History of the Oil Industry* (Garden City: Doubleday, 1970): 40–42.

the derrick and with such pressure, why, the drill pipe commenced to move up. It moved up and started to going out through the top of the derrick. . . . The pipe went up through the derrick, then would break off in sections of three and four lengths at a time and fall over. Course, after that got out of the way, why, the rocks began to come out and gas to beat the cars.

It didn't last so awful long, but it died down very gradually. Well, we three boys then sneaked back down to the well after it quieted down and surveyed the situation, and I don't think I'm exaggerating to say that the mud was six inches deep on the derrick floor. And I had turned around to get a shovel to start to clean up, get some of that off the floor. And all of a sudden, a chunk of mud came out of the six-inch hole, full-size, with an explosion just like a cannon popping off. And that blew up with a little blue gas following it for a little bit, and then it quieted down, ceased altogether again.

. . . I walked over and looked down in the hole there. I heard—sort of hear something kind of bubbling just a little bit and looked down there, and here this frothy oil was starting up. It was just breathing like, you know, coming up and sinking back with the gas pressure. And it kept coming up and over the rotary table and each flow a little higher and a little higher and a little higher. Finally it came up with such momentum that it just shot up clear through the top of the derrick.

**Curt Hamill:**　I was in the derrick at this time, and I couldn't tell you how I got down, but when I got down the driller had left the clutch in the draw works, and I got down in time to kick the clutch out. And by this time the pipe was going out the top of the derrick. And the other men had run and got out of the way, and, of course, I did the same thing. I ran as hard as I could and got away from the falling pipe, and no one was hurt from any of the blowout or the falling pipe.

**Al:**　At first when we went down there to see all that mud and our drill pipe ruined— it was Mr. Galey's drill pipe, Guffey and Galey's, but it was our responsibility—we didn't know how much of the hole was ruined or what was in it. I rather expect that I was pretty disgusted. Of course, after the oil came in then and kept flowing and flowing we sent Peck on the run down to Mr. Lucas again. . . . And he immediately jumped in his old buckboard with his old horse and beat it for Spindletop. . . . Well, when he got so close, why, he just—well, . . . the old horse stopped, and Cap fell out and ran up. Of course, he was very heavy, you see, and by time he got up to me he was just about out of breath.

And he says, "Al! Al! What is it?"

And when I says, "Why, it's oil, Captain," well, he just grabbed me and says, "Thank God, thank God."

I daresay it wasn't over an hour, maybe, till people began to come. Some heard it, you see. You could hear this roar. And that afternoon they came in all kinds of conveyances. Lot of them walked. Young fellows walked out there from town and come on horseback and wagons and buggies. Practically everybody came from town because from where we were for miles and miles there wasn't another dwelling. That afternoon, there was a big crowd there.

## 3. The *Dallas Morning News* Praises Urban Planning for the City of Dallas, 1910

### FEASIBILITY OF CITY REVISION
#### MR. KESSLER'S TENTATIVE PLANS
#### PRESENT HUGE, BUT
#### POSSIBLE TASK.

### BENEFITS EXCEED OUTLAY
**Thought Is to Help All Sections,**
**Citizens and Interests—What Seattle**
**Has Done.**

When we were merely looking forward to the presentation of a city plan by Mr. Kessler, the landscape artist, there were many people in Dallas who expected it to be something in the nature of an Utopian dream, something impractical, a scheme merely of beautification, adornment and ornamentation. Now that Mr. Kessler has made his preliminary announcement and has given the Dallas public a glimpse of the studies thus far worked out, changes of opinion have come. For one thing, it is seen that Mr. Kessler has begun with two intensely practical ideas—facilitation of the traffic of the city, ordinary vehicular, traction, steam rail and boat, and the protection of the city's lower levels from overflow—and with them he has carried along the idea of converting unsightly places into scenes of beauty. . . .

**Mr. Kessler's Suggestions.**

1. The removal of the steam railroad lines which now cross the city in many directions.
2. The creation of a belt railroad, encircling the city beyond its boundaries, but affording access to the railroads along the river front only. The provision of passenger terminals along the river front: of a union passenger station in the vicinity of the Dallas County court house, creating in that district one of the civic centers of the city, the same to include besides the passenger station, the county court house main postoffice building, public library, City Hall and a large plaza. It is contemplated that local freight yards shall be placed in the territory contiguous to the river front and south of Commerce street, and transfer yards on the belt line outside the city. . . .
3. To protect the city from overflow and at the same time to provide room for the railroads and for rail and steamboat terminals along the river front, Mr. Kessler has tentatively planned the creation of a new, straight and broad channel for the Trinity River further west than the present channel and in the neighborhood of the foot of the bluffs on the west side and the keeping open of the bottoms on the west side.

---

Tom Finty, Jr., "Feasibility of City Revision," *Dallas Morning News,* 16 October 1910.

**Parks and Boulevards.**

4. A boulevard and park system, the main features of which are as follows:
    (1) A parkway along Turtle Creek, with a driveway on either bank, starting from a park which is to be created from the grounds of the present City Hospital, the grounds surrounding the present waterworks station and possibly some other land which may be acquired, and extending through Oak Lawn and Highland Park, taking in Oak Lawn Park.
    (2) A boulevard running south from the lower end of Turtle Creek parkway, through a territory between Maple avenue and the river bottoms to Masten street, thence along that street, St. Paul street, Evergreen street and Harwood street to some point in Colonial Hill, say South Boulevard or Pennsylvania avenue; thence east to Fair Park; thence, north, say along Carroll avenue, to a connection with the Turtle Creek parkway. It is contemplated that this boulevard shall be 100 feet wide and eleven miles long.
    (3) A cross boulevard of the same width, starting at the west from the Masten street boulevard and extending along Ross avenue to the city limits and thence to the White Rock reservoir, where it is planned to create the city's chief park, completely surrounding the reservoir with a driveway and beautiful grounds.
5. The widening of certain streets, the cutting of other streets through one or more blocks which now bar them, and the extension of others so as to produce needed diagonal ways, freer and shorter cuts than are now available. . . .

Mr. Kessler's tentative plans contemplate two things, basically: Revision to overcome existing defects; planning ahead to avoid defects in the future. . . .

. . . There are very few places such as Washington, which were planned as cities from the jump. Most of our cities started as villages and grew more or less illogically.

Dallas is of that class. It was not planned as a city; instead it began as a "settlement," and evolved through hamlet, village and town stages into the city class, bearing the marks of each. The bonds fastened upon it in its youth chafe and hamper it now. They ought to be removed; everybody admits that. The feasibility of removing them can scarcely be doubted by any one who contemplated the Titanic tasks performed by the people in scores of American cities.

# 4. Boston City Planner Arthur Comey Presents a Plan for the Development of Houston, 1913

The twentieth century is an age of cities. In thirty years from 1880 to 1910 the proportion of urban population in the United States has risen from 29.5 to 46.3 per cent. . . .

People live in the city primarily because it offers better facilities for trade and industry, . . . and, secondarily, because it provides better opportunities for enjoying the amenities of life. Trade and industry are dependent mainly upon a market and

Arthur Coleman Comey, *Houston: Tentative Plans for Its Development: Report to the Houston Park Commission* (Boston: Press of Geo. H. Ellis, Co., 1913): 5–8 facilities for communication with that market. Therefore, the cities which have grown most rapidly are those with the largest tributary areas and the most efficient means of transportation, where possible utilizing both water and rail. These fundamental causes for growth have frequently been supplemented by others, such as . . . the adoption of progressive measures in civic development.

In Houston we find all these and many other agencies combining to create a great city. The territory for the marketing of its commodities is vast in area and increasing in population at a rapid rate. Its radiating railroad lines give ready access to all this territory; and upon completion of its ship channel it will have a combination of rail and water facilities second to none in the State of Texas. Strategically considered, Houston's location assures it of becoming the metropolis of the great South-west. Its steady, rapid increase in population in the past indicates a keen appreciation of this fact.

With the growth of cities there has come a great increase in the mutual interdependence of their inhabitants. Whether we believe in socialistic doctrines or not, we all recognize the value of commercial activity in a great variety of directions, such as preserving law and order, safety from fire, provision for pavements, sewerage, and the other usual municipal departments. But it is only recently that any thought has been given toward correlating these activities and planning on broad lines in advance to secure the greatest public good, as would be done by a private corporation.

This, then, is city planning,—to study and determine in advance the physical needs of the growing city, and lay out a scheme of development in such a way that each improvement will dovetail into the next, thus gradually forming an organically related whole. The complex activities of a city demand an equally complex plan for development, so that each of its functions may be fulfilled without undue interference with any other. . . .

In the co-ordinated development of a city plan the underlying framework must be its means of communication. First the waterways must be determined, as they are rather rigidly fixed by the topography. Then the railroads, which are also located in large measure by existing grades, must be so planned as to best serve the needs of passengers and freight. . . . Finally, the thoroughfares must be laid out,—the net of traffic streets that will give access by foot, vehicle, or electric car to every portion of the city. . . .

Given such a plan, the next concern will be for the provision of homes and places to work. . . . A certain type of street plan is best adapted to factories, another to office buildings, and a third to workingmen's homes. If the class of building is determined in advance, great economies will result from this differentiation, and each section will benefit by having its special plan. The improvement of the working places and homes themselves should next be considered, for they constitute the normal environment of most of the city dwellers. Industrial welfare and housing are each in themselves subjects demanding exhaustive study.

The intense activity of city life and the increasingly artificial conditions under which its citizens live make more and more essential the introduction into daily life of recreation. . . . Such recreation facilities are for the most part to be provided by the city's park system, though school centres, public baths, and other agencies may contribute no small share of the opportunities for play.

Finally there will be needed in the modern city a large number of administrative and other public and quasi-public buildings, such as the city hall, post-office, railway station, institutional buildings, and the like, over whose design and location more or less direct control can be exercised.

The architectural treatment of individual buildings has recently been raised to a high standard in the United States. But the opportunity for an immeasurably enhanced effect due to the grouping of several buildings is as yet seldom availed of, despite the numerous reports lately issued in various cities urging this principle. In a rapidly growing city such as Houston . . . if these occasions are utilized to erect buildings on locations conforming to prearranged plans, in a few years monumental civic centres will be produced . . . in place of the usual haphazard "spotting" of public building about the city.

. . . In the case of Houston great increase in size is so assured that plans can be drawn along very broad lines. . . . Houston's problems can now be dealt with before the serious mistakes are made which have hampered so many American cities.

## 5. The *Houston Post* Reports the Mutiny of African American Troops, 1917

### MARTIAL LAW DECLARED
**Result of riot started by negro regulars who mutinied, fired upon their officers and left camp, slaying 13, wounding 19. One officer of Illinois regiment slain and seven policemen are dead or wounded.**

As a result of a riot which began early in the evening at the camp of the negro regulars of the Twenty-fourth infantry, Houston and its environs are today under martial law with Brigadier General John A. Hulen in command. This action was taken by Governor Ferguson, upon request by acting Mayor D. M. Moody, at about 12:30 this morning; and this was later followed with an order by General James Parker naming General Hulen as the officer in command.

General Hulen at once gave orders for the dispersing of the crowds who still thronged the streets at that hour, for the prompt arrest of such of the negro soldiers as were not in the camp under guard, for the closing of all saloons and drinking places until such time as he may direct.

Crowds are not to be permitted and incendiary oratory will be promptly suppressed.

Men bearing arms will be arrested.

Sheriff Frank Hammond hurried to the city from his home at Seabrook and has summoned a posse of citizens. This posse is to see to the suppression of excitement among the citizens. There are rumors that a great number of people from other counties are hurrying to Houston—and they are not wanted. If they come to Houston bearing arms they will be promptly arrested and put in jail. . . .

---

"Martial Law Declared," *Houston Post,* 24 August 1917.

## THE DEAD.

### At C. J. Wright's Morgue.

IRA D. RAINEY, mounted police officer.

RUFE DANIELS, mounted police officer.

MIDDLE AGED MAN NAMED SMITH.

S. SATTON, barber, 1207 Rusk.

### At Wall & Stabe's Morgue.

CAPTAIN J. W. MATTES, battery A, Second Illinois Field artillery.

E. J. MEINEKE, police officer.

### At Westheimer's Morgue.

EARL FINLEY.

A. R. CARSTEN, painter.

MANUEL GARREDO, 4903 Washington.

FRED E. WINKLER, 3910 Lillian street.

BRYANT WATTSON, negro soldier, company K, Twenty-fourth infantry.

### Dead at Hospitals.

M. D. EVERTON, battery E, a local company.

C. W. WRIGHT, 3701 Wood street.

## THE WOUNDED.

William J. Drucks, 4910 Lillian street, shot in right arm, amputation necessary; very low from loss of blood and surgical shock.

W. H. Burkett, Runnells streets, shot in left side, sprinkled on side and back with shotgun shot; condition serious.

E. A. Thompson of Hempstead. Gunshot in right leg; condition serious.

J. E. Richardson, 1203 Waverly street, shot in the head with rifle by negro soldier; condition not serious.

Asa Bland of Park Place, shot over left eye; injury slight.

Wylie Strong, negro private, company I, Twenty-fourth negro infantry, shot in right side accidentally by another soldier of his company; condition not serious.

Horace Moody, mounted police officer, wounded in left leg.

D. R. Patton, mounted police officer, received five or six wounds in hip, thigh, leg and shoulder.

Sammie Foreman of Livingston, company F, Fifth Texas infantry, shot in leg; not serious.

James Edwin Lyon, 4427 Walker street, employe of Cotton Belt office, shot in leg and arm.

Unidentified negro trooper, shot through abdomen

Unidentified negro trooper, shot in leg with buckshot.

G. W. Butcher, Cottage Grove, shot in left chest and right loin; seriously wounded.

W. A. Thompson, shot through right hip; condition serious.

Wiley Strong, negro soldier, Twenty-fourth infantry, wounded.

City Detective T. A. Binford, shot in the knee.

Sam Salensky, 105 Hamilton, badly hurt in auto accident going to camp.

Alma Reichert, white girl, 8001 Washington avenue, shot in stomach.

George Beavens, negro soldier, wounded in leg.

---

Thirteen known dead and 19 wounded make the toll of race troubles that reached a climax Thursday night when negro soldiers of the Twenty-fourth infantry raided through West End.

The riot got its starting spark from trouble Thursday afternoon between negro soldiers and city police. That it had been brewing for several days is the general belief.

That the list of dead and wounded will grow with the coming of daylight is highly possible. . . .

All citizens will remain in their homes or usual places of business at once.

No citizen not an officer will appear on the streets with arms.

Parties will not assemble on the streets.

Saloons will not be permitted to open.

Places of business where arms and ammunition are sold, kept or stored will remain closed.

[General] Hulen.

---

I call upon every citizen of Houston, white and colored, to preserve the peace, to go quietly about their business and to rest assured that there is going to be full inquiry and proper punishment for the crimes which have been committed.

It is time for coolness and for careful avoidance of further trouble.

It is no time for further excitement.

The city is under martial law, a condition which is most regrettable; but it is necessary.

There will be no further trouble if every citizen will carefully see to his own conduct. Incendiary speech is of no avail.

The situation is well in hand—unless there be studied effort to cause more trouble.

Dan M. Moody, Acting Mayor

## 6. Texans Tell Reporter Edward T. Devine That Some of "the Best People" Belong to the Klan, 1922

The New York World is quoted by the Searchlight of Atlanta as "chortling" to the effect that "now that the mask has been torn from the Ku Klux Klan, it has ceased to be a menace." In this county seat in the interior of Texas where I have been spending a week the Klan seems to be considered a very serious menace indeed—to evildoers.

Edward T. Devine, "The Klan in Texas," *The Survey* 48 (April 1, 1922): 10–11; "More About the Klan," *The Survey* 48 (April 8, 1922): 42–43.

I am still rubbing my eyes and questioning my ears. This is surely not the same fantastic embodiment of anti-Catholic, anti-Jewish, anti-Negro, anti-labor prejudice which I have read about, the masked hundred percenters who are so free with whips and tar and feathers, or worse, whose lawless methods have become proverbial. . . .

. . . My next jolt came when a student in this Texas town . . . came to my room for a long evening talk, in the course of which he launched into a warm eulogy of the Ku Klux Klan. He is not a member, but that is only because a certain girl whose opinions are important to him had vetoed it. . . .

The Klan, this ardent college youth insists, is not against Negroes but in their interest, not against Catholics but only for Protestantism—as the Knights of Columbus are for their religion. It is for one hundred per cent Americanism, for law and order, and for white supremacy. He admitted that it sometimes upholds law and order by extra-legal means. He knew of the cases in Houston; for example, the tarring of a doctor who was known to be guilty of criminal practices. What the boy insisted upon was that the doctor was guilty, that he was a menace, and that the Klan rid the city of his presence and his practices when the authorities by their milder measures had failed to do so. . . .

It began to seem to me important to understand the point of view of this southern community. I therefore sounded next the Methodist minister. "I understand," I remarked casually, "that some very good people get into the Ku Klux Klan in these parts." "The very best people get into it," he replied emphatically. The good doctor who said this is not a bigot. . . . He is active in the inter-racial commission. He neither condemned nor advocated the Klan, but with discrimination expressed both his doubts and his appreciation of some of their acts. He is deeply distressed by the lawlessness of the time. He thinks that the intention of the Klan is to combat lawlessness and that . . . its ordinary method is to try to secure the election of capable and honest officials and to cooperate with them in furnishing evidence of criminal acts. . . .

I had a whole afternoon of serious talk with half a dozen men of the faculty of a school for the training of teachers. We talked about the race question and the Ku Klux Klan. All these men are southern in ancestry, birth, education and life-long residence. They are in sympathy with efforts to improve racial cooperation. They are taking part in them persistently. They would no doubt subscribe to the shibboleth of white supremacy, but they would narrow its meaning in practice in such a way as to make it comparatively unobjectionable to self-respecting Negroes. They are for equal justice in the courts and in economic relations; for better schools, for the colored, for better accommodations on railways. . . .

What these gentlemen, . . . had to say about the mysterious organization is no doubt as fair an estimate as one will find. They are confident that stories of lawless acts by the Klan published in northern newspapers are exaggerated; that hereabouts, at least, it does not represent anti-Jewish prejudice nor anti-Catholic bigotry nor antagonism to Negroes; that it is not hostile to labor; . . . that its main purpose, however, is to inculcate a wholesome respect for law and order. . . .

I had, finally, an interview with one representative business man, who was so well informed and so outspoken in his advocacy as to leave little doubt of his active membership. In his eyes it is a righteous crusade. It makes no mistakes. It will use whatever means are necessary. . . .

It is easy to laugh at the absurdities of the Klan, its childish follies, its illiterate nomenclature, its fallacious conception of law and order. But it is not easily laughed out of existence. Close at hand it is serious. It has a certain dignity of purpose. It is not sheer bigotry or stupidity or charlatanry or fraud. Perhaps it may be short-lived. I hope so; for the evils which it professes to attack are certainly for the most part to be overcome only by very different means.

**More About the Klan**

I have been hearing more about the Ku Klux Klan in Texas towns. . . .

I notice that there is rather more anti-Catholic sentiment in the complex than appeared to be the case in the first community studied. . . .

On the other hand, further evidence confirms my first impressions that the Ku Klux movement hereabouts is not conspicuously anti-Negro. . . .

Everywhere I hear, as I heard in my first Texas town, that "the best people" are among the Klansmen. . . .

Notwithstanding the repeated assurance that "the best people" join, it may not be entirely without significance that in fact only one of all the "best people" whom I have happened to meet appears actually to have done so. . . . With the one exception all have taken pains to make it clear that they are not members, though several of them have expressed strong sympathy with the purposes of the Klan and some had given serious consideration to an invitation to join. What has deterred them in the last analysis is the mask, and the resort to what are politely called "extra-legal methods of upholding law and order" when the ordinary processes do not avail, or are not sufficiently prompt and drastic.

## 7. African American Activist Clifford Richardson Assesses the Needs of Black Neighborhoods in Houston, 1928

With the largest colored population of any city in Texas—variously estimated from 55,000 to 60,000—"Heavenly Houston" can rightfully boast of as intelligent, thrifty, substantial, upstanding, law-abiding and patriotic a group of colored citizens as can be found in any other city in America, without regard to geographical lines or location. This is as it should be, for the progress, peace, growth and well-being in this community are indissolubly linked and intertwined with the black race. . . .

A recent survey of colored business enterprises in twenty Southern cities . . . reveals that Houston tops the list with business concerns owned and operated by members of the colored race. . . .

According to available statistics, more colored citizens own or are acquiring homes in Houston than in any other purely Southern city. It is further estimated that Houston's colored population has approximately $7,000,000 deposited with local banks and financial houses. . . .

Clifford F. Richardson, "Houston's Colored Citizens: Activities and Conditions Among the Negro Population," *Civics for Houston* 1 (August 1928): 5, 14, 29–30.

The residential sections inhabited by colored citizens, which, during the last two or three years, have received considerable civic consideration and physical improvement are still lacking (many of them) in the permanent type of improvements so essential to the moral, physical, civic and aesthetic welfare of the community. Rent houses are built in such close proximity to each other that one can stand in one house and hear the inmate in the adjacent house change his mind. . . .

If the City of Houston has an ordinance on its statute books regulating and prohibiting this method of building houses for tenants, the law is neither invoked nor enforced when it comes to rent houses for colored citizens. Surface privies are still ubiquitous in many sections occupied by colored residents, while drainage is extremely bad in most of these colored sections, with cess-pools and ponds of stagnant water which seldom dry up between rains.

Street lights are few and far between, and the resultant darkness obtaining in these colored neighborhoods becomes a[n] . . . incubator of crime and criminals. . . . These districts have very little fire and police protection, and it is becoming increasingly difficult for colored Houstonians to get much fire insurance upon their homes and household effects. . . .

In the face of such unhealthy and unsavory living conditions the death rate among colored Houstonians is alarmingly high. . . .

Emancipation Park, located at Dowling, Tuam and Elgin, Third Ward, which the colored citizens of the community bought years ago and turned over to the city . . . is the only colored park in the city; and, though under municipal management and control, the city has done very little towards beautifying and improving this park. . . .

Civic improvement associations are being fostered in some of the populous colored residential sections and, though rather sporadic in their activities, they are doing much to inspire the race along the lines of civic beautification, health, hygiene and sanitation.

Houston has three colored senior high schools (something that no other city in America possesses) . . . and the only municipally owned and operated colored junior college in the entire world. . . .

Houston offers the colored group the greatest opportunity of any Southern city for industrial employment and commercial and professional activity. . . .

Additional parks should be provided in the Fourth and Fifth wards for colored citizens, and the colored residents of the Heights should have a park. There is no swimming pool provided for our colored population, although playground activities are being conducted at two or three of the ward public schools.

Housing and living conditions among the colored residents of Houston should be surveyed and studied in the immediate future, and the findings made a basis for a well-defined program for the amelioration of these shameful, shocking and startling conditions under which thousands of colored Houstonians are forced to live and eke out a bare existence.

Additional colored patrolmen should be added to the local police force to patrol colored districts on all beats, and thus minimize the danger of clashes between minions of the law and colored citizens.

With its extremely large colored population and their various and varied activities and achievements, it is next to impossible to give a free and full account in such an article as this, but the writer has endeavored to give the readers of this magazine a graphic cross-section of Houston's colored citizenry, who constitute an important and integral part of our heterogeneous and polyglot population.

## 8. Humble Oil Vice President John Suman Relates Prosperity in Houston to the Growth of the Texas Oil Industry, 1940

Since Houston has become recognized as the oil capital of the world, in spite of the dying claims of cities in neighboring states, a brief discussion of the importance of world-wide, national, and state activities in petroleum will also be indicative of the importance of petroleum to Houston.

It has been estimated that the United States has produced over 21,000,000,000 barrels of the 33,200,000,000 barrels of oil produced for the entire world. To produce this volume of oil, investments amounting to $14,500,000,000 have been made, which consist principally . . . in crude-oil-producing properties, . . . in pipe lines, . . . in refineries, and . . . in marketing and transportation facilities. Although the industry is 80 years old, the principal activities in petroleum and consumption of products have extended over the past two decades. . . . Although the population of the United States is only 6.5 percent of the world population, it accounted for 55 percent of the total consumption. Also, it produced 61 percent of the world production and supplied 13 percent of the requirements of the remainder of the world. . . .

The world reserves of petroleum at present are placed at approximately 34,000,000,000 barrels and the American Petroleum Institute placed the reserves of the United States at 17,348,146,000 barrels as of January 1, 1939, or approximately 51 percent of the total reserve. . . . At the present rate of consumption, our reserves will not supply demand beyond a 15-year period. . . . Keeping reserves ahead of demand has largely been accomplished through intensive application of science and technology to oil production. When it is understood that such a large percentage of our population is directly or indirectly dependent on the oil industry for a livelihood and that a good percentage of governmental activities is supported through taxation of the oil industry, it will readily be agreed that the high standards of living in this country were considerably aided by developments in petroleum.

Although the petroleum industry is among the top-ranking industries in the United States, it occupies a position of greater significance in the state of Texas. Since the discovery of oil in Texas at Nacogdoches in 1866, shortly after the first discovery of oil in the United States, Texas has produced five and one-half billion barrels of the 21 billion barrels of crude produced in the United States. . . .

Petroleum is now considered to be the most valuable mineral resource of the state and petroleum refining holds the distinction of being the largest manufacturing industry, with its products accounting for over 40 per cent of all manufactured

From John R. Suman, Vice President, Humble Oil and Refining Company, "Importance of Oil and Gas Industry to Houston," *Houston* 11 (April 1940): 52–54. Copyright © 1940. Reprinted with permission of the Greater Houston Partnership.

products. This is somewhat in contrast to the former conception of Texas being principally an agricultural state. . . . Texas produced . . . during 1938, 40 percent of the total crude produced by the United States. . . . The petroleum income provides a livelihood directly or indirectly for approximately 1,000,000 people in Texas, 175,000 of which are employed directly in the production, transportation and refining branches of the industry. . . . In spite of large production in the past, Texas offers one of the most fertile fields of oil exploration and possesses, according to the American Petroleum Institute, 9,447,764,000 barrels of the 17,348,146,000 barrels of reserve in the United States as of January 1, 1939, or more than 54 percent of the national reserve. With this picture of reserve and prospective fields for development in the state, it can be seen that the industry will continue to occupy a position of great importance in the business of the state for many years to come.

You have probably wondered why Houston has been designated the oil capital of the world. This came about due principally to three main reasons as follows: (1) the location of Houston in regard to shipping facilities; (2) the location of Houston in regard to petroleum activities; and (3) the location of Houston in relation to future prospective petroleum activities. Due to the strategic location of Houston, a large number of companies interested in every phase of the petroleum industry have located here. Included among these are oil and gas producing, refining, transportation, marketing companies, and manufacturing plants supplying oil-field equipment. Houston is the largest concentration point in the world for oil field supply companies. The oil industry furnishes a means of livelihood to more than one-half the population of the city with something like 50,000 people being employed directly. The petroleum industry is by far the biggest customer of incoming and outgoing freight to railroads, and. . . . approximately 81½ per cent of all the tonnage handled through the port, and this amounts to 30½ per cent of all the oil produced in Texas. Oil is delivered by pipe lines to Houston from the states of New Mexico, Oklahoma, Kansas, Arkansas, and Louisiana, and there is also considerable tank car traffic. Tank steamers from California, Mexico, and other foreign countries bring special grades of crude for refining and blending and crude to be processed for consumption in the markets of the world. Besides serving the coastal area and Texas, Houston is rapidly becoming the center of oil equipment distribution for a considerable portion of the Mid-Continent area.

The reserves of oil have been maintained during the past 30 years principally by exploring structures of progressively greater depths, and geologists now agree that the Gulf Coast area in which Houston is located is one of the most promising areas in the United States for future development of crude reserves.

The desirable location of Houston for the oil industry has, in turn, been greatly enhanced for other industries by the petroleum industry through development of gas reserves within the near-by area. The gas available . . . within 50 miles of Houston . . . is adequate to supply the area with low-cost industrial fuel . . . for over 130 years. Additional large reserves of gas are located beyond the 50-mile radius from Houston and within distance for supplying cheap industrial fuel gas.

There is no other large city in the world that possesses the combined desirable transportation and fuel facilities so favorable to industrial growth. This should go a long way to insure the continued progress and growth of our city.

# ⬧ E S S A Y S

The two essays focus on different aspects of urbanization in Texas and reflect different approaches to this issue that historians have taken. The historian Bruce Beauboeuf examines the factors that transformed Houston into a rapidly growing industrial city. Like many urban historians he stresses the city's natural economic advantages and its transportation system. However, he also argues that World War I and the needs and policies of the federal government were the catalysts that transformed Houston into a major industrial center and placed the city with it's two major industries, cotton and oil, into the international economic arena. In the second essay, Robert Fairbanks of the University of Texas at Arlington addresses a different aspect of urbanization. He examines the efforts of Dallas business, political, and civic leaders to use planning to mold their city into a major urban center. He argues that economic advantage must be matched with enlightened civic leadership to create a great city.

## World War I and Houston's Emergence as an Industrial City

### BRUCE ANDRE BEAUBOEUF

The economic mobilization of the First World War . . . propelled the economy of the city of Houston into its modern position within the international community. . . . The war effort provided a . . . window of opportunity through which local business greatly accelerated the process of industrialization. Cotton and oil, both vital to the war effort, spurred Houston's economic growth during and after the war. The demand for these items during the war meant immediate profits, but that demand also brought about fundamental structural changes in the local cotton and oil industries, including expansion of operations and an unprecedented degree of cooperation between business and government at both state and federal levels. The renewed commitment to improve the Houston Ship Channel was a key aspect of this federal-local alliance, as was the federal government's encouragement of the merchant marine, whose vessels were instrumental in bringing international cotton trade to the Port of Houston. In both instances, and in many others, these economic transformations resulted from the process of mobilization during the First World War. This then set the stage for Houston's economic growth in the 1920s, enabling the city to become the model of the New South sought by Southern modernization proponents since Reconstruction. . . .

Initially, the war created an economic crisis in the United States, especially in the South. With the disruption of international trade caused by the war, national export trade decreased by over 58 million dollars. The country lost vital markets in Europe, and surplus amounts of cotton, oil, and other products grew, with prices falling sharply. . . . Bales of cotton piled up in the streets of Houston and many other Southern cities, and the price of cotton fell from 12 cents to under 7 cents per pound. . . .

Bruce Andre Beauboeuf, "War and Change: Houston's Economic Ascendancy During World War I," *Houston Review* 14 (1992): 89–112. Copyright © 1992 University of Houston. Reprinted with permission.

While domestic attempts to alleviate the "cotton crisis" availed little, the foreign policy of the federal government, regarding the nations at war, proved to be very beneficial. The decision of the Wilson administration to forgo strict neutrality and assume a de facto . . . alliance with Great Britain and France, would revive international trade and bring a return of prosperity from the economic recession of late 1914 and early 1915.

Cotton was crucial to a modern war effort for its value in making smokeless powder, as well as military clothing, medical supplies, tenting for encampments, and a myriad of other uses. As the United States became economically tied to the Allied war effort, the cotton economy of Houston and the South rebounded dramatically. . . . Cotton prices grew from their low of under 7 cents per pound to over 35 cents per pound by 1919, increasing more than five times in price.

. . . This dramatic price increase, then, unchecked by ceilings, resurrected the Southern cotton economy. In turn, these new profits enabled Houston cotton merchants to expand their operations in significant and lasting ways.

With regard to cotton, the war placed renewed emphasis on improving the Port of Houston in two important ways. First, the economic recession of late 1914 to early 1915 made Houston cotton merchants realize the need to improve storage and compress facilities on the Ship Channel for surplus cotton. Second, the congestion of the railroad system because of the war effort made clear the need to use the nation's waterways as an alternative route for the transportation of goods. . . .

To fund this expansion, cotton merchants were able to take advantage of new investment assets as Allied purchases of U.S. goods and supplies transformed the United States from a debtor to a creditor nation. The Wilson administration's decision to allow U.S. industries to trade with the Allies brought a historic reversal to the U.S.-European financial relationship. Through Allied war purchases, bank deposits in the United States and in Houston increased dramatically. . . . Bank deposits in Houston grew from $32 million in 1915 to $50 million in 1916. With U.S. entrance into the war, Houston bank deposits reached $61 million in 1917, and were over $94 million by 1919.

This new financial backing also allowed Houston cotton merchants to increase the vertical integration of their operations and thus gain greater efficiency and stability. During and after the First World War, Houston cotton merchants such as Anderson, Clayton & Company, George McFadden & Company, and Alexander Sprunt & Sons developed closer ties to the growing, ginning, and milling of cotton. Of even greater importance was that this influx of capital to Houston banks enabled Houston cotton merchants to expand their cotton compresses, storage, and wharf facilities along the Ship Channel, making Houston more attractive as a seaport. A growing alliance between Houston banks and local cotton merchants provided the latter with the capital they needed to expand their operations along the Ship Channel continually during the period 1916 to 1930.

In 1916, Ship Channel warehouses could store roughly 400,000 bales of cotton, and at least 13 cotton merchants had facilities in the Port of Houston. . . . By 1920, there were 80 cotton merchant firms in the city, there were 9 cotton compresses along the Ship Channel, and storage capacity had increased to 600,000 bales. Houston emerged from the war as the largest spot cotton market in the world, and the largest inland seaport in the nation.

Seizing the opportunity, Anderson, Clayton & Company moved its headquarters from Oklahoma City to Houston in 1916, and designated the Houston Ship Channel as its primary clearinghouse for all the cotton it dealt with. William Clayton later explained the move, stating that "Houston was the little end of the funnel that drained all of the Texas and Oklahoma territory . . . we were at the back door, and we wanted to be at the front door."

The Anderson, Clayton company's commitment to the burgeoning Port of Houston at this time was a sign that Houston's cotton economy and port activity were not only reviving; they were undergoing fundamental structural change. This economic expansion fostered a growth in Houston's cotton trade that played a large role in driving Houston's economy during the 1920s. Exports of cotton bales increased dramatically in that decade, growing from 45,000 bales in 1920 to just over 1,000,000 in 1924. By 1929, exports of bales of cotton were approximately 2.3 million; they stayed high into the 1930s.

Port facilities expanded to handle the increased traffic. Use of the city's public terminals and facilities increased 97.6 percent from 1921 to 1924. A number of firms built private facilities for cotton shipping during the 1920s. In 1922 and 1923, Alexander Sprunt & Son established the Ship Channel Compress Company; the following year, the Houston Compress Company, owned by Anderson, Clayton & Company, built the "Long Reach" facility that remained the largest cotton terminal and warehouse system on the channel for decades. In 1928, Joseph W. Evans completed the Manchester Terminal, with a storage capacity of 250,000 bales; by that year, Ship Channel facilities could hold 1,250,000 bales of cotton. By 1930, warehousing facilities along the Ship Channel could hold 2,000,000 bales of cotton, equal to 40 percent of all cotton produced annually in Texas.

With this tremendous growth in cotton facilities along the Ship Channel during the 1920s, net receipts of cotton—meaning cotton actually handled, compressed, and stored by Houston merchants, as opposed to being merely en route to Galveston and therefore not profiting Houston firms—increased significantly. As a percentage of gross receipts, net receipts of cotton increased from 27 percent at the beginning of the war to . . . 54 percent by 1919–20. . . . By the 1926–27 season, net receipts of cotton were over 3.5 million bales, equal to 99 percent of all the cotton that entered Houston to be exported. Now nearly all the cotton that entered Houston was exported from the Ship Channel; now Houston was a port in its own right, no longer merely a transition point to Galveston.

In addition, the void created by World War I allowed Houston cotton merchants to fill the role that European import firms had once held. During the war, the Anderson, Clayton company established its own selling organizations in such traditional European markets as Liverpool and Le Havre, as well as in other Allied countries: Russia, China, and Japan. The federal government worked with the nation's shipping interests to promote trade and expansion of U.S. shipping into foreign markets during and after the war. To this end, the government increased the size of the merchant marine, which had declined since the Civil War. With the passage of the Shipping Act of 1916, Congress created the United States Shipping Board, an agency designed to promote the development, construction, and regulation of the merchant marine. . . .

At the end of the war, Daniel Ripley saw a need to make the Port of Houston more widely known to shipping interests. Through contacts made by his business, the Ripley Steamship Company, he lobbied the Shipping Board to direct trade to the port. Ripley's efforts paid off when he was able to charter the Shipping Board vessel *Merry Mount,* which came into the port in November 1919 and sailed away with 23,319 bales of cotton destined for Liverpool. With the navigability of the waterway thus proven, the *West Chetac,* the *Bethlehem Ridge,* and the *Montgomery* soon followed, all under the authorization of the United States Shipping Board, carrying over 46,000 bales of cotton to Liverpool. Under the aegis of the Shipping Board, Ripley also expanded his own shipping concerns into such foreign markets as Liverpool, Le Havre, Bremen, and Barcelona in 1920. In this way, federal aid helped accelerate the growth of the cotton trade in the Port of Houston and enabled the city to significantly increase its ties to international ports. . . .

The Lykes Brothers Steamship company, which began operations as a charter shipping concern in Galveston in 1906 and in the Port of Houston in 1920, also became involved in the war-shipping effort. Lykes, abandoning its former practice of chartering foreign vessels, was the first Gulf Coast shipping company to charter the newly built Shipping Board vessels in the war effort. In 1922, Lykes purchased its first five vessels—ships that had been built as part of the federal government's wartime economic expansion. In 1923, Lykes transferred the bulk of its Texas Gulf Coast operations from Galveston to Houston, tangibly symbolizing the emerging Port of Houston overtaking the Port of Galveston.

After the war, Anderson, Clayton & Company renewed its connections with Bremen, Germany, and established ties to the newly formed nation of Czechoslovakia. The firm also bought a 40 percent share of a Liverpool importing firm, D. F. Pennefather & Co., which would later become a controlling 60 percent interest. As the owners of this firm, Anderson, Clayton dealt directly with the cotton spinners in Great Britain and the European mainland, effectively avoiding the overseas middlemen. Addressing the interrelated growth of shipping and the cotton trade in the postwar Port of Houston, Fleming commented that the transfer of wealth from Europe to the United States had "called for the assumption by American cotton interests of a much broader role than before in merchandising, storing, carrying, financing, and retail distribution to the ultimate consumer."

Assessing the overall expansion and transformation of Houston's cotton economy, Fleming stated that the Houston cotton merchants found that "at the close of the war . . . the previous handicaps of American cotton firms, with respect to banking, storing and handling surpluses, had been replaced by advantages." With federal support of the cotton trade in these ways, due to the war effort, merchant firms in Houston and throughout the region found themselves with opportunities for expansion of operations that would transform their industry.

The war effort also transformed the Texas oil industry. A modern, mechanized military depended heavily upon petroleum products. . . . [D]emand for petroleum products increased dramatically. . . .

As with the cotton industry, the initial disruption of trade and economic recession brought on by the war affected the oil industry. . . . Although exports of petroleum from the Port of Houston did not suffer significantly, this was largely because the Ship Channel was not yet the major petroleum port it would become. . . . Yet the Gulf Coast oil industry did suffer, as the price of crude oil fell from 95 cents per barrel in 1913 to 64 cents in 1914, before finally bottoming out at 48 cents in 1915. . . .

Yet after the U.S. economy became tied to the Allied war effort, exports and oil prices improved swiftly. In 1917, the United Stated exported 65.4 million barrels, with Great Britain and France the principal buyers. Shipments of petroleum products from the Port of Houston, both foreign and coastwise, grew dramatically from 31,584 short tons in 1915 to 293,400 in 1916. During the war, Houston oil concerns used their own ships to reach northeastern U.S. ports to supply the navy; in 1917, 288,503 short tons of crude oil were shipped coastwise from the Port of Houston.

With the war-related increase in demand, Gulf Coast oil prices rose from 48 cents per barrel in 1915 to 75 cents in 1916, and in some areas along the Texas Gulf Coast prices were even higher. . . . Will C. Hogg, writing to Cullinan and Thomas P. Lee (all three were involved with Cullinan's Farmer's Petroleum Company), announced: "Dollar oil has arrived." . . . By March 1917, the price of crude oil at Goose Creek, an increasingly productive field located along the banks of the Ship Channel, had reached $1.25 per barrel. By 1919, Gulf Coast oil prices had risen to $1.70 per barrel of crude oil.

The oil industry, like the cotton industry, also benefited from an absence of federally mandated price ceilings throughout the war. Again, the federal government allowed this inflation to spur production, and increasing prices did stimulate oil production in the Houston area. At the Goose Creek field, where the newly formed Humble Oil and Refining Company was predominant, production increased from 397,000 barrels of crude oil in 1916 to over 7,000,000 in 1917; then to nearly 9,000,000 by 1918; and continued at around the 6,000,000 barrel mark annually into the middle of the 1920s. Production at the Humble field, just north of Houston, spurred on by Farmers Petroleum Company, increased from roughly 3,000,000 barrels in 1914 to over 11,000,000 by 1916; annual production there varied from 6,000,000 to 10,000,000 barrels for the rest of the war. . . .

The oil industry acquired power as well as profits during the wartime era, particularly in its governmental relationships. The war effort, highly dependent upon the production of oil, meant that the oil industry dealt from a position of strength in its cooperative wartime relationship with the federal government. Furthermore, unlike coal, price hikes or shortages of oil brought relatively little public protest. Coal was the primary domestic consumption fuel; oil was more important to the army and navy. This helped to strengthen the oil industry's bargaining leverage with the federal government and allowed Houston-area oil companies to deal with their concerns of efficiency, stability, and integrated operations without the threats of either adverse public opinion or government sanctions.

Labor-management relations were to be a key example of the oil industry's new political muscle, as was manifest in the Gulf Coast oil strike of 1917. As oil field production, oil prices, corporate profits, and inflation all began to soar in 1916–17, oil field workers in Texas and Louisiana seized the opportunity to demand improvements in working conditions. The Houston-Goose Creek area oil concerns, however, such as the Producer's Oil Company, the Gulf Production Company, and the newly incorporated Humble Oil and Refining Company, all refused to recognize the oil workers' union or their demands. When 10,000 oil field workers in Texas and Louisiana went on strike on November 1, 1917, the local oil companies remained intransigent. . . .

A number of factors would work in favor of local oil management. One critical fact was that management could readily keep the refining process going by using the vast reserves of crude oil already pumped and stored, in large part a result of the high levels of production that had recently been attained. . . . Oil management also found it easy to replace the strikers, as many low-wage farm workers from Texas and Oklahoma were only too willing to accept the comparatively high-wage oil field work.

Local business and civic leaders stressed the danger of a reduction in oil production to the federal government. . . . With the rumor of local activities by the Industrial Workers of the World (IWW), with its incendiary ideology, state and local government leaders requested the War Department to send federal troops to Gulf Coast oil fields on November 2, after the strike was only one day old. The War Department quickly responded, deploying more than 2,000 federal troops at Goose Creek and other Houston-area oil fields.

Due to the perceived threat of "radical" and "disloyal" labor unions, local oil concerns were able to exploit both the federal government's need for oil and the general public opprobrium toward strikers during a war effort. The deployment of federal troops into the Gulf Coast oil fields to protect corporate assets, and strike-breakers, from rumored threats of sabotage by "alien enemies" was one of the more dramatic examples of wartime cooperation between business and government. The full impact of federal military influence was evident when, after a violent clash between union and nonunion men, martial law was declared in Houston on November 21.

The strike, however, had faded before that episode. . . . As oil field workers began to return to their jobs, the Department of Labor announced that it had no intention of intervening in the dispute, since the operators had convinced them production would be unaffected.

The presence of federal troops in this Gulf Coast labor-management dispute helped resolve the crisis into an unmitigated victory for local oil concerns. It resolved the immediate crisis in favor of the local oil industry; it symbolized the power relationship between the oil interests and the federal government; and, by suppressing the nascent oil field workers' union, it set the tone for the management-controlled labor relations of the 1920s.

During and because of the war effort, Gulf Coast oil companies were able to take full advantage of those aspects of the federal intervention that they valued, such as federal demand for oil products and federal troops to protect their operations, while they effectively ignored other aspects that tended to work against them, as with federal attempts to arbitrate the oil field workers' demands. Oil companies on the Gulf Coast and throughout the nation were also able to take advantage of the wartime emphasis upon production to free themselves from previous government restraints on establishing vertically integrated operations.

Antitrust policy was perhaps one of the first casualties of the war. The antitrust policies that had existed at the federal and state levels and in public sentiment before the war were of secondary importance to maintaining consistent and sufficient production levels. Vertically integrated operations, for petroleum concerns, meant consolidating production in the fields, the refining process, transportation, and the marketing of the ultimate product, such as gasoline. Corporate desires for consolidation were heightened by the economic recession of late 1914 and early 1915, since such integrated operations were seen as necessary to achieve stability and efficiency in times of economic disruption. As the economy began to improve in 1915–18, a desire to benefit from the wartime federal contracts was also an important motivation for consolidated operations.

At the federal level, the Fuel Administration allowed for and even encouraged ostensibly collusive activities. For example, the Oil Division of the Fuel Administration, in order to ensure adequate supply at a "fair price," encouraged the pooling of oil reserves. In early 1918, the Oil Division also suppressed an attempt by the Federal Trade Commission to begin litigation against Standard Oil-Indiana for violation of the Clayton Antitrust Act.

In February 1917, the Texas legislature passed a law allowing for the operations of production, refining, and marketing within one firm. The Texas Company, in an effort to legitimize its close relationship with smaller production companies, was the primary proponent of the bill. . . . Just a few months later, the Producers Oil Company was openly dissolved and absorbed into the Texas Company. Also in 1917, the Texas Company incorporated the Texas Pipeline Company as a wholly owned subsidiary. The company that Cullinan had founded (but had left in 1913) was becoming a fully vertically integrated petroleum concern. Standard Oil of New Jersey, no longer afraid of Texas antitrust statutes that they had suffered from in the past, in 1919 bought a 50 percent share of interest in the Humble Oil and Refining Company. . . .

Increased tax relief at the federal level was also made available as a spur to production. The Revenue Acts of 1916 and 1918 increased the "oil depletion allowance," a tax deduction which allowed the oil industry to recover production and discovery costs. Thus the war effort had reversed earlier antitrust policy, and had fostered a new era of conciliation and cooperation between business and government, a cooperation that facilitated the economic expansion of the 1920s.

With this expansion of the oil industry, oil-related industries grew and flourished in Houston during and after the war. The highly profitable tool company owned by Howard Hughes had existed at least a decade before the war, but the wartime expansion of the Gulf Coast petroleum industry greatly accelerated the growth of the oil-tool industry in Houston. For example, in 1916, Texas Iron Works established operations in the Goose Creek field. Also in 1916, the Reed Roller Bit Company and the Howard Smith Company were founded in Houston. In 1919, WKM Manufacturers began operations in Houston; in 1920, the Oil Well Supply Company, then the largest manufacturer of oil tool supplies in the world, established operations in Houston. Cameron Iron Works, which would become one of the world's largest producers of oil tool supplies, began operations in Houston that same year. The Lucey Manufacturing Company and the Mack Manufacturing Company had operations in Houston by 1920. In January 1921, the Wilson Supply Company was founded in Houston. In 1927, the Penick brothers, Arthur and Kirby, founded the Oil Tool Company in Houston; in 1928, the Houston Oil Field Material Company was established, adding to the growing list of oil-tool supply concerns in the city. In addition, in 1925 and 1926, the Houston Gulf Gas Company, owned by the Moody-Seagraves interests of Galveston, and the Houston Pipeline Company, a subsidiary of the Houston Oil Company, began to build extensive pipelines and supply natural gas to the Houston area.

Oil interests also expanded their operations along the Ship Channel in a period of fervent activity during and shortly after the war. The Texas Company, the Farmer's Petroleum Company, and the Merchants and Planters Oil Company had existed along the channel before the war, but during and immediately after the war oil companies greatly expanded their operations or established new ones. In 1916, the Gulf Oil Company transferred its offices to Houston and built a refinery along the Ship Channel. . . . By 1927, there were 8 oil refineries with a daily capacity of 125,000 barrels of crude oil located along the Ship Channel. Throughout the 1920s, the Shell Petroleum Corporation, Humble Oil, the Texas Company, the Gulf Refining Company, and virtually all the oil interests in southeast Texas expanded their facilities in the Port of Houston.

The growth of petroleum exports from Houston after the war was meteoric. While estimates vary, official Port of Houston figures showed 1,789 short tons of oil and oil products exported during 1919. Exports of petroleum products from the Port of Houston in 1925 were 1,044,824 short tons. By 1930, 27 tanker lines had operations in the port, and petroleum exports had risen dramatically to 3,918,927 short tons. The growth of the oil industry during the war brought the process of industrialization to Houston in the 1920s.

Indeed, the Port . . . would play an even larger role in the future economic growth of the area. The federal-local alliance to dredge and improve the Ship Channel was renewed during the war, and the rationale of aiding the war effort gave the business and civic leaders of Houston—the "boosters"—an added credibility, enabling them to overcome congressional opposition to funding "pork barrel" projects.

Starting in 1915, J. S. Cullinan led the efforts of Houston "boosters" to obtain federal funding for renewed Ship Channel improvement projects. Cullinan, other members of Chamber of Commerce, congressmen from Texas, and local oil men such as Ross Sterling of Humble Oil, were frequently in Washington lobbying Congress and writing letters to the United States Corps of Engineers for federal aid to channel improvement projects. . . .Cullinan emphasized that improving the Houston Ship Channel would aid the shipment of petroleum to France; that the channel's 25 foot depth, unable to accommodate the growing number of ships that drew 27 to 30 feet of water, hindered the war effort. . . .

The efforts of Cullinan and other boosters of Houston finally paid off with the Rivers and Harbors Act, passed by Congress in March 1919. The federal government had increased its role with the promotion of the merchant marine; now it also expanded its cooperative role in the development of the nation's waterways. With the Rivers and Harbors Act of 1919, Congress designated . . . the Houston Ship Channel to be dredged to 30 feet, among other improvements. [Federal funding] was to be matched by local funds. . . . By 1925, the Houston Ship Channel boasted a depth of 30 feet.

Port of Houston freight activity, just over 1,000,000 short tons in 1920, increased to over 9,000,000 short tons by 1926, after the Ship Channel had achieved its new depth. By 1930, activity in the Port of Houston increased to nearly 15,000,000 short tons; by 1940, freight tonnage in the port was over 27,000,000. This cooperative relationship between the federal government and the local leaders of Houston, increased by the war effort, continued afterwards and enabled the Houston Ship Channel to become a first-class port, facilitating the growth of the economy of Houston into the 1920s and beyond.

The . . . alliance of the United States with Great Britain and France created an almost limitless demand for U.S. products, including Houston cotton and oil. As part of the war effort's need for economic expansion, the government promoted centralization and integration of business operations while relaxing antitrust statutes, emphasized production over labor demands, and cooperated with the private sector to expand shipping and trade. These decisions left several important postwar legacies: a federal-municipal relationship committed to economic growth, which continued in infrastructure projects such as waterways; the transformation of structural relationships within and between businesses; and the facilities and expertise needed for business to serve a wider international market.

These legacies set the stage for Houston's astonishing economic growth in the 1920s, and indeed became the foundation of its economy for many decades. Cotton continued to be a mainstay of the city's trade through the 1930s, while oil became the catalyst of Houston's economy throughout most of the twentieth century. The growing oil economy, now geared to industrial production as well as simple shipping, generated an increasing number of related industries in Houston. The process would be further stimulated by another war effort, but the groundwork was laid during the First World War by the federal government's alliance with the business and civic leaders of Houston. This national and civic commitment to economic mobilization and expansion enabled the city to increase its importance as a commercial trading center for the mid-continent interior of the United States, hasten the process of industrialization, and follow the model of the New South that Southern modernization proponents had sought since Reconstruction.

## Boosterism, Reform, and Planning in Dallas in the 1920s and 1930s

### ROBERT B. FAIRBANKS

Despite its location in a largely rural and agricultural state, Dallas experienced rapid growth in the early twentieth century and approached problems associated with that growth in ways compatible with approaches embraced by cities in the more urbanized north. Undeniably committed to growing their city as much as Texas farmers were to raising cotton, Dallas boosters probably shared more in common with civic leaders in St. Louis or Chicago than they did with their county cousins. Dallas leaders also looked outside of Dallas for help in responding to perceived urban needs. Moreover, their changing definition and response to urban problems from the 1900s to the 1920s appears to reflect a national trend. By the 1920s, notions about the city emphasized the inextricable linkage of its parts and the need for comprehensive and coordinated solutions to urban problems.

Dallas's rapid development in the first three decades of the twentieth century mirrored the growth typical of Texas cities of this time. In 1900 the North Texas city had a population of 42,638, but by 1920 census takers there found 158,976 residents. That growth wetted the city's appetite for more and Dallas experienced another

Robert B. Fairbanks, "Dallas Confronts the Twenties: Boosterism, Reform, and the Urban Network," original essay drawn from Robert B. Fairbanks, *For the City as a Whole: Politics and the Public Interest in Dallas, Texas, 1900–1965* (Columbus: Ohio State University Press, 1998), especially pp. 37–72. Copyright © 1998 by Ohio State University Press. Reprinted with permission.

surge of population to 260,475 during the 1920s. Such an increase in population can be explained in part by the city's new dominant retail and wholesale position in North Texas. Connected to national markets through its rail system which also brought migrants to North Texas and helped establish it as a regional financial center, Dallas experienced spectacular growth. Oil and the textile industry also fed the city's growth at this time.

The city's expansion was neither accidental nor inevitable. City boosters, mainly businessmen working through their organizations, promoted Dallas to the region and the nation. For instance, one of the most active bodies in the first decade of the new century was the 150,000 club, committed to securing the city a population of 150,000 by 1910, a figure railroad magnet Jay Gould in 1887 predicted that Dallas would reach in his lifetime. Other businessmen-led organizations, such as the Chamber of Commerce established in 1909, also promoted the city with great zeal and commitment.

Not content with merely publicizing the city, turn-of-the-century civic leaders also embraced the Progressive era reform movements of city planning and governmental reform to further encourage the city's development. And they regularly participated in a variety of associations committed to improving the cities throughout the nation. However, Dallas leaders were selective in regard to the kinds of movements they embraced and participated most enthusiastically in efforts that promised to further encourage the city's rapid growth and development.

Growth, of course, accelerated a variety of urban problems and tensions that demanded attention. When the earlier solutions of the Progressive era did not satisfactorily meet the city's needs, civic leaders rethought the problems and searched for better solutions. The 1920s were a particularly critical time in the city's history. Not only did Dallas's population continue to mushroom, but its physical size more than doubled from 23 square miles to 45 square miles. Such expansion heightened local government's inability to provide adequate paved streets, sanitary and drainage sewers, as well as needed water, fire, and police protection. For example, the National Fire Protection Association found that among its survey of twenty-five of the nation's cities, Dallas experienced the highest per capita loss of all cities examined between 1922 and 1926. An undermanned police force made to patrol the much larger city of the 1920s also helps explain why Dallas suffered a particularly nasty wave of crime in 1927.

Growth also encouraged a variety of social problems as the large number of newcomers and the city's changing social geography seemed to threaten the old timers' sense of community. In addition, increasing numbers of blacks attracted to the city's economic opportunities found little adequate housing, and the expanding pockets of black dwellings created real serious racial tension in the city by the 1920s. The textile industries and their low wages also expanded the rolls of people near or below the poverty level in the city. Fearful that the city's increasing diversity, as well as the widening gulf between the haves and have-nots threatened to undermine the civic order, civic leaders turned to a growing volume of expert advice from outside of Dallas on how to operate that city. Indeed, how Dallasites responded to these challenges in the 1920s ultimately reminds us that Dallas and other Texas cities, despite their unique Texas qualities, were part of a larger urban network that defined and responded to problems in similar ways.

Unfortunately, many Dallas citizens chose not to embrace a reform strategy and followed the guidance of another national movement in the early 1920s, the Ku Klux Klan. Organized in late 1920 by Hiram Wesley Evans, a local dentist, and Z. E. Marvin, an owner of a chain of drug stores, the Dallas Klan enrolled approximately 13,000 members and dominated city and county government in the early 1920s. The Klan preached "one hundred percent Americanism" and focused its animus on Catholics, Jews, African Americans, and immigrants as well as transgressors of traditional morality. The organization had special appeal to working class Dallasites overwhelmed by the rapid changes in the city and unhinged by the growing new morality associated with city life in the 1920s. The Klan also offered sanctuary to Dallasites uprooted by neighborhood transformations and insecurity in the workplace, who confronted a growing, more heterogeneous population than ever before and the accompanying perceived loss of community. It responded to that loss by campaigning for a more homogeneous Dallas and promoting intolerance of those who were different. Although some leading businessmen and established politicians initially supported the Klan, this group's vigilante efforts throughout the city alienated many Dallas civic leaders who organized the Dallas County Citizens League in opposition. Their efforts, as well as some statewide political defeats, ultimately seriously weakened the Klan in 1924 and led to the waning of its influence.

If the Klan proved one type of response to rapid growth and change, not only in Dallas, but in the rest of urban America during the 1920s, civic leaders took a different tact. Dallas leaders in the 1920s consulted urban professionals and national associations to maintain the city on its course of proper growth and development. Two areas that illustrate this new commitment in the 1920s were city planning and governmental reform. Frustrated by the city's haphazard physical growth, as well as its inadequate streets, parks, and constant threat of flooding, Dallas leaders renewed their commitment to physical planning, yet went about it differently than they had earlier. Unhappy with the way city government seemed unable to respond effectively to a host of urban needs, civic leaders also embraced structural reform of their government promoting a more efficient and coordinated city hall that would better govern the city as a whole. Neither concerns were entirely new to the 1920s but the specific approach taken that decade mirrored an urgency in Dallas and elsewhere for a more comprehensive and better coordinated approach to the larger city. The rhetoric and emphasis of the new movements also reminds us how closely tied Dallas was to the national network of cities and the pronouncements of national planning and government improvement associations created to address modern urban problems.

Dallas had embraced planning since at least the first decade of the twentieth century when unhappiness with a variety of physical problems led to the development of the Kessler Plan published in 1911. George Dealey of the *Dallas News,* later tabbed "the father of planning in the southwest," played the most critical role in securing the plan. At first Dealey was interested in merely improving the city's surface sanitation, but after corresponding with J. Horace McFarland of the American Civic Association, the newspaperman became committed to planning and employed the *Dallas News* and the Chamber of Commerce to promote enthusiasm for planning in the city. The result of his efforts was the Kessler Plan, a document that proposed nine improvements including a Union railroad station, a levee system for the Trinity River, and a comprehensive system of parks and parkways.

The plan, then, focused on providing a variety of public works for the city but offered no systematic strategy to carry out a coordinated program. In a single paragraph, it discussed financing. Kessler warned against relying too much on bonds and called for special assessments and local improvement districts to fund most of his recommendations. Some projects rallied citywide support, such as the Union railroad station completed in 1916, but others languished because of the lack of such support, including the levee/reclamation project. The lack of clarity on how to proceed with planning along with the distraction of World War I stalled local enthusiasm for carrying out the Kessler Plan.

Frustrated by the delay in public improvements that would affect their property holdings, businessmen in the west end of downtown Dallas decided to reinvigorate planning after the war with special emphasis on the needs of their area. As a result, in 1919 they created a new organization, the Dallas Property Owners' Association (DPOA), and brought in Kessler to revise his earlier plan with more attention given to harnessing the nearby Trinity River with levees and reclaiming the foul-smelling bottoms. Uptown businessmen responded by organizing the Central Improvement Association which promoted Kessler Plan improvements for their eastern section of the central business district. The two groups saw little accomplished but did manage to stir up sectional animosity.

Soon these groups came to the conclusion that such piecemeal planning was not adequate for the demands of the new city, so they joined forces and created several new planning bodies including in 1919 the Dallas Metropolitan Development Association (DMDA), a Dallas Chamber of Commerce, and the Kessler Plan Association, a citywide planning body established in 1924 by the efforts of the DPOA. The DMDA helped engineer the establishment of a permanent City Plan Commission as part of city government, and together the two bodies worked diligently to develop the city's comprehensive zoning ordinance modeled on those written for New York City and Saint Louis. In order to produce the best zoning ordinance possible, the DMDA employed not only George Kessler but also prominent zoning consultant Robert Whitten for such a task. These actions, prompted by civic leaders and urban boosters, acknowledged that even in individualistic Texas, land use regulation was needed to order the city better. After Kessler's death in 1924, the city also sought, though never successfully hired (until 1943), a planner of national reputation to develop another plan for the city. Although court decisions delayed zoning, Dallas did finally secure its first comprehensive zoning ordinance in 1929. Unlike earlier efforts which were more limited in scope, the planning movement of the 1920s both in Dallas and elsewhere emphasized the inextricable linkage of all the parts to the whole and underscored the need to coordinate and plan for the entire city, both private and public lands. Earlier planning had focused on the comprehensive planning of public works but now with the addition of zoning, emphasis shifted toward managing all of the city's land.

The Kessler Plan Association (KPA) proved to be the other significant planning body to appear in the 1920s. At first, it seemed to be just another arm of the business community to secure support for planning projects and bond issues. Established in 1924 by the efforts of the DPOA after that group realized it could never get citywide support for its west end improvement projects, the KPA was the most ambitious effort yet to overcome the petty sectional jealousies that seemed to dominate the city at the time. This organization under the able leadership of John Surratt not only tried to secure support for projects such as the levee district and street openings in downtown, but it also attempted to educate the community to identify with the city as a whole rather than with neighborhoods. Its initial goal was to secure the completion of the Kessler Plan, but it quickly concluded this could be achieved only after educating the city of the interconnectedness of the city's parts. Borrowing freely from citizen planning movements in Chicago, Los Angeles, and St. Louis, the KPA focused on educating the public about the benefits of planning. Toward that end, it brought in nationally known speakers, such as J.C. Nichols of Kansas City and E. M. Bassett of New York, and it secured the prestigious National Conference on City Planning for Dallas in 1928.

Even more important, it developed a school textbook. *Our City Dallas—A Community Civics* focused on promoting a heightened sense of civic consciousness within the city and on educating readers how an improvement in one area of the city benefited the entire city. Written by former school superintendent Justin F. Kimball, this book, adopted for the city's seventh graders, examined not only the Kessler Plan but a variety of other civic issues including government, education, and even public utilities. The book also retold Dallas history and emphasized the importance of cooperative and civic-minded citizens in the city's development. Such an effort attempted to instill in the children a sense of civic pride and loyalty so that they could support and serve the city. Indeed, a flyer promoting the book called it "a guide to citizenship."

In order to secure citywide support for planning, the KPA sought to be the most representative civic body in Dallas. Unlike the Klan, which wanted to eradicate the city's diversity, the KPA embraced it and helped both black and white neighborhoods, rich and poor. Indeed, the association's board of directors included representatives from 115 civic groups such as labor unions, manufacturing associations, and mother's clubs. The KPA also provided a forum that allowed various neighborhood groups in the city to bring their planning concerns to civic leaders. In addition, the KPA acted as a resource for those groups and helped them to improve their neighborhood. First KPA president, Dr. E. H. Cary, was probably not off the mark when he claimed his organization was "the most democratic in Dallas."

The efforts of the KPA apparently paid off when citizens approved a $23.9 million bond package as part of the Ulrickson Program in 1927. That comprehensive program of long-range financial planning modeled after one developed by St. Louis attempted to not only complete the Kessler Plan but develop other projects such as a municipal airport, a library, and improved water purification. Not a traditional plan with maps and predictions of future growth patterns, the Ulrickson Program called the city to develop "mature, scientific and orderly plans." The comprehensive nature of the proposals, as well as the document's emphasis linking all these urban needs together, illustrates the prominent focus of comprehensive planning in Dallas in the 1920s, a strategy that civic leaders thought would guarantee the city's continuous growth.

Not only did the Ulrickson report identify and offer solutions to many of the city's physical needs, but it proposed charter amendments to give Dallas adequate "legal and financial power to plan, prosecute and complete the entire program in an orderly and connected way." With the help of massive support from the Kessler Plan

Association, voters on December 15, 1927 approved the program's fifteen bond proposals and the thirty-two amendments to the city's charter needed to implement the bond program and other planning strategies, such as comprehensive zoning.

During the time of the Ulrickson program and the culmination of the city's commitment to comprehensive planning in the 1920s, another movement occurred that also emphasized a comprehensive approach. Many of the same motives behind the efforts for comprehensive planning and zoning also help to explain the city's new interest in council-manager government. In an earlier reform movement to secure more effective government, Dallas citizens in 1907 had approved a city commission government. Under it, five commissioners were elected by the voters, each given a specific responsibility. One would be a commissioner of police and fire, another commissioner of streets and public property, a third would serve as waterworks and sewage commissioner, while a fourth would serve as commissioner of finance and revenue. The mayor would serve as the fifth commissioner. Together these five had both legislative and executive powers over city government.

Despite the implementation of the city commission government, and the nearly complete domination of businessmen's slates associated with the Citizens Association for the next eleven years, supporters of "good government" criticized both its form and its personnel. As early as 1918, a *Dallas Morning News* planning reporter complained to Dealey that an ineffective government hampered the completion of the Kessler Plan. Others criticized the politicization of a government structure based on administrative function. Instead of looking out for the city as a whole, commissioners were usually too busy looking out for their departments. Instead of focusing on long-term projects, commissioners were caught up in the day-to-day grind of administering their departments and taking care of their workers.

City government, then, paralleled pre-1920s planning. As we have seen, the Kessler Plan also had been a type of comprehensive citywide planning approach, but its execution focused on certain planning needs and/or city districts and failed to treat adequately the city as a whole. Only in the 1920s did civic leaders embrace more comprehensive strategies for the physical city through comprehensive zoning and a comprehensive bond package to ensure coordinated planning for the entire city.

The city commission form of government had centralized government over the fragmented and apparently impotent council/mayor form of government Dallas previously experienced. Yet its functionally divided treatment of the whole proved unsatisfactory to a growing number of people by 1920 because it appeared not to be working the way supporters had hoped. As a result, in the very year that the Ulrickson Program was proposed, civic leaders also initiated a movement to better city government.

The decision to alter government, then, did not stem from an attempt to destroy a political machine, or even to rid the city of incompetent public officials. Nor was it an attempt to weaken neighborhood influence through the destruction of wards—that had been achieved in 1907. Rather, the movement, which was widely publicized by the National Municipal League, focused on creating a more efficient and comprehensively administered government through structural change—a government capable of action on immediate problems and long-term planning for a healthy future. Toward this end, local leaders embraced the council-manager government as the best hope for the city. During the 1920s the popularity of this form of government soared as the emphasis turned from accountability and the ability to get things done to efficiency and comprehensive treatment. Indeed, by 1926, Cleveland, Cincinnati, and Kansas City had adopted city manager government. The government structure provided administrative powers to the city manager, and legislative powers to a city council elected at large without partisan labels.

In his textbook *Municipal Government,* Harvard Professor William Bennett Munro emphasized that council-government established "a real pivot of administrative authority," and it placed "this under expert control." Munro also argued that the city manager plan improved upon the commission form of government because it provided "a better basis for cooperation and harmony," another concern of Dallas leaders. Indeed, the rhetoric of the city manager supporters suggested that politics in city government caused fragmentation, and if politics were eliminated (as the city manager government promised to do), then fragmentation would decline.

The momentum for city government reform slowed as civic leaders decided to focus on securing charter amendments for the Ulrickson Program in 1927. After that election, however, it resumed when the city's mayor named a twenty-member Charter Committee to "make a systematic study of the charter of the city . . . and evolve a document consistent with a population of 300,000 instead of 90,000." Because under the state constitution cities could amend their charters once every two years, no charter election could be held until December 16, 1929, giving the committee ample time to do its job. The committee issued a report on March 5, 1929 that recommended Dallas adopt a nine member council-manager government. The charter committee advised that all councilman should be elected at large rather than just by wards "to eliminate the possibility of sectional jealousies and so-called log-rolling."

On October 10, 1930, 13,179 voters turned out for the election and approved the new government by a 2-1 margin (8,962–4,217). Supporters of the city manager movement, calling themselves the Citizens Charter Association (CCA), also offered a list of candidates to run the new government. Dallas voters endorsed the entire CCA slate in the first city manager election in 1931. The council selected John Edy as its inaugural city manager. The former president of the International City Managers Association had held a similar post in Flint, Michigan and Berkeley, California.

Edy and the council-manager government promoted a better coordinated and more professional government than earlier, something civic leaders believed critical for the city's continued health. Unhappy with the ineffectiveness of the city's fire and police departments, Edy consulted outside experts to improve them. He also implemented changes in the budgetary procedures, including the development of a budget office with budgetary control, that led to more efficiency and coordination. And unlike the commission form of government, where each commissioner fought for allocations for his department and often traded votes for budgetary favors, the council had no particular incentive to protect specific departments. Even more important, the city manager "brought all expenditures of the city together in one place and considered them as a whole." The procedure reflected the new emphasis on governing the city as a whole.

Not only did Edy try to coordinate better the city's finances, but he did the same for the staff. The city manager held bi-weekly meetings primarily to keep department heads informed of what others were doing. This simple act, according to one observer, marked "the first time in the history of Dallas that department heads were brought together to attack problems concertedly."

Those CCA sponsored councils operating under a new charter governed differently than the city commissioners. The city commissioners seemed more interested in protecting their little fiefdom, the department that they oversaw, than in governing for the city as a whole. For the most part, the commissioners acted as politicians and attempted to increase their power within the city. The new council, composed of prestigious businessmen and professionals, saw their entry into government as a service rather than a career, and did not, according to one outside observer, seek to reward their friends with the petty favors and special services as the commissioners had. The new system, on paper, set up procedures to treat all areas of the city equally, so no one had to depend on the influence of individual councilmen. Unlike earlier governments, the city now had, according to a 1939 report by Committee on Public Administration of the Social Science Research Council, "an administrative staff that was prepared to present a well-rounded program of municipal policy for its consideration and to produce on short notice information relating to all departments without favoring or neglecting the interests of any of them." As a result, the report concluded that: "For the first time the affairs of the city were determined by a deliberate body that considered municipal policy as a whole rather than in relation to the needs of individual administrative departments or minority pressure groups."

Although this system was clearly not without defects, and the administrative reality of government and planning never treated everyone equally, the rhetoric behind these programs suggests that changing assumptions about the city altered the nature of planning and government reform from that of the turn of the century. Efficiency replaced responsiveness and comprehensiveness overshadowed specificity.

The rhetoric of the 1920s emphasized comprehensive treatment of the city and called for a new civic consciousness emphasizing the city-as-a-whole. Manifestations of this included a new planning emphasis that called on coordinated planning for both public and private land and structural reform in government that attempted to better coordinate and administer government while at the same time de-politicizing it. The last goal proved particularly difficult due to a major dispute between civic leaders over the city's role in the Trinity River reclamation/levee project as approved by the Ulrickson bond program. Despite the implementation of a new form of government, and despite voter approval of a comprehensive bond program to better coordinate the development of Dallas, tensions developed among Dallasites about policy priorities. A conflict over the timing of the city's contribution to the Trinity River levee/reclamation program, authorized by the Ulrickson bond program, badly divided the city's civic leadership.

Ever since the Kessler Plan of 1911, there had been interest in leveeing the unpredictable Trinity River and reclaiming the nearby bottoms land. In 1926 a group of 1,300 property owners of the Trinity River bottoms organized the City and County Dallas Levee Improvement District for such a task. It worked out a coordinated program with the city, county, and utilities company for an ambitious undertaking costing more than $21 million to rechannel and levee the river. The city agreed to help and provide storm sewers, water mains, and other infrastructure for the district. Based on that agreement and similar arrangements with the county and the utilities, the reclamation district broke ground on July 24, 1928 for a project that would move the Trinity River three and one-half miles from its current course and salvage more than 10,000 acres of smelly, overgrown river bottoms.

However, controversy over the city's role in this project erupted during the Great Depression when the levee district insisted that their needs be taken care of first even though other parts of the city needed the infrastructure supported by the bonds. And when flamboyant Mayor J. Waddy Tate, the last mayor under the commission form of government, announced in 1930 that he would have to raise taxes to cover debt service on the bonds sold for drainage sewer development in the reclaimed land, outraged citizens protested. Among those opposed to the immediate funding of the levee were leading members of the Kessler Plan Association including president E. H. Cary, board member Karl Hoblitzelle, and executive secretary John Surratt. They argued that the Kessler Plan Association had supported the reclamation plan as part of a broader comprehensive package of improvements, but now it feared that reclamation was being singled out for special attention while other populated areas in south and east Dallas, in desperate need of sewers, were being ignored. Kessler Plan officials also reminded city officials that the Ulrickson Plan called for a comprehensive sewer system plan before any money was allocated and noted that it simply had not been done.

Proponents of the levee/reclamation, including newspaperman George Dealey, countered that that not only would the project bring needed flood protection to Dallas but launch significant economic expansion that would ultimately help the entire city. Such a response was unsatisfactory to opponents and by 1930, bad feelings about the reclamation project had polarized the city. One side viewed the excessive preoccupation with it as damaging to the development of the rest of the city while the other side saw the project as the key to more rapid development of Dallas. What is significant about this conflict is that the KPA became the leading opponent of the levee district, standing as an advocate for the needs of neighborhoods who would suffer if the city proceeded with using the bond money for the levee district.

Unable to resolve the problem, both sides agreed to wait and let the new council-manager government resolve the dispute. City manager John Edy proceeded cautiously and this alienated him from the levee supporters who wanted the city to immediately commit the funds to finish the levee/reclamation project. What the city council eventually did was to bring in an outside consultant from St. Louis, W. W. Horner, to develop a general plan for the city's drainage sewers. Only after that project was completed, did the city provide money for the reclamation drainage sewers. By that time the depression as well as the erosion of the levees stalled efforts to develop the area as an industrial district, and it remained undeveloped until after World War II.

Representing the neighborhoods of the working classes, the Kessler Plan Association had successfully stood up to some powerful business interests and persuaded them to protect the neighborhoods. But the KPA's involvement in the controversial issue proved costly, as its membership and financial support declined. Although the civic organization continued its work of helping neighborhood organizations and promoting planning in Dallas, it never regained the presence it had in the 1920s.

The levee/reclamation controversy reminds us that despite the rhetoric of both planning advocates and governmental reformers in Dallas during the 1920s, which stressed developing public policy for the entire city as opposed to special privileges for factions and special interests, a new age of urban consensus did not emerge. Even though Dallas leaders turned to the guidance of national bodies such as the National Conference on City Planning and the National Municipal League, and brought in an assortment of experts to help solve knotty problems, such a new commitment to professionalism and outside expert guidance did not eliminate controversy within the city. Different groups in Dallas continued to hold different notions of what constituted the public interest. The supporters of the levee/reclamation district argued that their massive project would not only protect much of the city from floods, but make access to the downtown from neighborhoods in Oak Cliff, on the other side of the Trinity River, much easier. In addition, they believed that the levee would salvage thousands of acres for industrial use at a time that the city desperately wanted more industry for its tax base. On the other hand, the Kessler Plan Association argued that the development of vacant land should not be taken at the expense of neighborhood needs for drainage sewers and adequate water. For that group, the quality of life for those already in Dallas took precedent over the promise of future growth offered by the levee advocates.

For many, the new structural changes in local government that promoted efficiency and coordination proved problematic even though the actions of the council-manager government sided with neighborhood interests in the levee controversy. Quite simply, council members elected at-large came primarily from business and professional backgrounds and adopted city booster notions of the public interest emphasizing pro-growth policies. With the city's strongest advocate of neighborhood interests, the Kessler Plan Association, greatly weakened by the levee fight, no strong voice was heard in Dallas during the 1930s to provide an interpretation of the public interest different from the city's boosters. Although neighborhood unhappiness with the CCA council did contribute to the defeat of that body in 1935, only four years after charter reform took place, that would prove to be the last gasp of neighborhood power in Dallas for a long time. When that CCA returned to power in 1939, it developed an even closer relationship to the city's business interests after the establishment of the Dallas Citizens Council. Meanwhile, many of the voices for neighborhood interests were quieted. As a result, Dallas experienced both the best and worst results from the planning and governmental reform movements of the 1920s. It received a more effectively administered city with a new commitment to professionally overseen comprehensive planning. But it also inherited a governmental structure increasingly occupied by professionals rather than representatives of the people, and a political ethos directed toward growth rather than quality of life issues.

# FURTHER READING

Charles C. Alexander, *Crusade for Conformity: The Ku Klux Klan in Texas, 1920–1930* (1962)

Mody C. Boatright and William A. Owens, *Tales from the Derrick Floor: A People's History of the Oil Industry* (1970)

Norman D. Brown, *Hood Bonnet, and Little Brown Jug: Texas Politics, 1921–1928* (1984)

Garna Christian, *Black Soldiers in Jim Crow Texas, 1899–1917* (1995)

Robert B. Fairbanks, *For the City as a Whole: Planning, Politics and the Public Interest in Dallas, Texas, 1900–1965* (1998)

Robert V. Haynes, *A Night of Violence: The Houston Riot of 1917* (1976)

Michael V Hazel, *Dallas: A History of "Big D"* (1997)

Patricia Evridge Hill, *Dallas: The Making of a Modern City* (1996)

Shawn Lay, ed., *The Invisible Empire in the West: Toward a New Appraisal of The Ku Klux Klan in the 1920s* (1992)

David G. McComb, *Houston: A History* (1981)

Char Millar and Heywood Sanders, eds., *Urban Texas: Politics and Development* (1990)

Harold L. Platt, *City Building in the New South: The Growth of Public Services in Houston, Texas, 1830–1915* (1983)

Marlyn Sibley, *The Port of Houston* (1968)

Johm Stricklin Spratt, *The Road to Spindletop: Economic Change in Texas, 1875–1901* (1955)

# Defining Mexican American
# Identity in Texas, 1910–1950

*Relations between Anglo Americans and Mexicans and Mexican Americans have been one of the defining elements in Texas history. The first half of the nineteenth century witnessed first the demographic, then the military conquest of Texas by immigrants from the United States. In the second half of the century, the borderlands of South Texas remained sparsely populated and culturally dominated by Texans of Mexican descent, many of whom were descendents of families who settled there during the Spanish period. Anglo migration to the region threatened the economic and social dominance of the Mexican residents. The clash of cultures in the borderlands left a legacy of suspicion, hostility, and violence.*

*In the early twentieth century, the demographics of Texas began to change as Mexican immigrants began to move northward in large numbers. The immigrants were an economic resource and valued as a cheap and supposedly docile work force for the fields, railroads, and growing industry of the region. As the Mexican American population grew, racial and ethnic tensions also increased. Mexican Americans suffered as victims of racial and ethnic prejudice, and political and economic oppression.*

*As Mexican Americans attempted to define their identity and assert their rights in Texas during the first half of the twentieth century, they faced a number of political and ideological options as well as pressures from the left and the right. The Mexican Revolution, which precipitated large-scale migration northward, also instilled a sense of nationalism and political radicalism in the Mexican and Mexican American population. Likewise, in the years around the First World War the International Workers of the World attempted to bring their radical labor movement to the largely Mexican and Mexican American agricultural and industrial workers of the southwest. The Red Scare that followed World War I contributed to the wave of anti-radicalism and nativism that lingered throughout the 1920s, deepening the historical antipathy towards Mexican Americans. The economic growth of the region led to increasing urbanization and the emergence of a Mexican American middle class that sought respect and equal rights, but rejected the extreme nationalism and radicalism of the lower classes.*

*The political ferment within the Mexican American community led to a variety of approaches to their social and political problems. On one extreme nationalists dreamed of reconquering the Southwest. Moderates sought assimilation and civil rights. Workers and labor organizers struggled to improve the economic plight of the Mexican American worker, and perhaps build a workers' paradise in the process. In the midst of the social, political, intellectual, and international upheaval that characterized this place and time, how did Mexican Americans define themselves and envision their role in this turbulent land? How did they organize and struggle for their rights?*

## D O C U M E N T S

As the revolutionary struggles in Mexico spread across the Rio Grande during the first two decades of the twentieth century, Mexican Americans in South Texas became caught up in the turbulence of this period. Document 1 is a recruiting poster for the "Plan of San Diego," a plot that surfaced in 1915 among extreme nationalists who proposed to separate Texas and the other border states from the United States and create an independent Republic. While this plan had little chance of success, it was associated with a brief but intense period of extreme violence and reprisal that spread fear through the South Texas borderlands. Document 2 maps the areas in northern Mexico where Americans were murdered and also notes the incursions of Mexican revolutionaries into Texas and New Mexico. Document 3 presents another perspective on this nationalist perspective. This brief excerpt from Lionel G. Garcia's 1987 novel, *A Shroud in the Family,* sets up a radically altered vision of key elements in Texas mythology—the Alamo, San Jacinto, the heroes of the Texas Revolution. This "fantasy" of early-twentieth-century South Texas Mexican Americans redefines the history of the 1836 clash between Mexicans and Anglos in Texas.

The next two documents reflect more traditional expressions of political activity among the growing Mexican American middle class. Document 4 presents two statements of the League of United Latin American Citizens (LULAC) beliefs: "Objetos y Fines de la Liga De Cuidadanos Unidos Latin-Americanos" (Objectives and Goals of LULAC) from 1932 and "The LULAC Code" from 1933. Document 5 lists the political concerns of the Chapultepec Club, a Mexican American women's club in Houston. This particular letter of grievances was likely inspired by the June 1937 acquittal of two Houston policemen charged with the death of a Mexican national. It may also be a reaction against the resurgence of Texas nationalism stimulated by the Texas Centennial celebrations the previous year.

Document 6 presents a more traditionally leftist/labor perspective on the Mexican American struggle for equal rights. Emma Tenayuca and Homer Brooks, respectively the chair and the secretary of the Texas Communist Party, outline their vision of a "movement for Mexican unification," a worker-led movement of equal rights and economic justice in Texas and the southwest. This manifesto appeared a short time after Emma Tenayuca won fame for her leadership in the San Antonio Pecan Shellers' Strike and confirmed her association with the Communist Party. In Document 7, the poet Américo Paredes Manzano presents his vision of the Mexican Texan, reviled and oppressed on both sides of the Rio Grande. The last document in this chapter, Document 8, presents the purpose of the American G.I. Forum, a civil rights organization created by Mexican American World War II veterans. The G.I. Forum took the leadership in the Mexican American struggle for civil rights in the immediate postwar period.

# 1. Mexican American Nationalists Call for a Separate Republic in the Southwest, 1915

To Our Fellow-Citizens
Mexicans in Texas

A cry of genuine indignation and rage has sprung from the very depths of our souls at the sight of the crimes and assaults committed on a daily basis against the defenseless women, old people, and children of our race by the bandits and contemptible Texas Rangers who patrol the banks of the Río Grande.

A righteous and just indignation inflames the blood which circulates in our veins. That rage drives us, no, compels us to punish—with all the energy we can muster—the pack of savages who would put even a starving tiger or a disgusting hyena to shame.

How could one remain calm and indifferent in the face of such criminal attacks? Who could permit such offenses to be inflicted on our race? Perhaps the feeling of humanity and patriotism has died out among us? No! It might be asleep, but it is easy enough to wake up.

Enough of tolerance, enough of suffering insults and derogatory remarks. We are men conscious of our actions; we know how to think as well as the "gringos" do; we could be free and we will be. We are sufficiently educated and strong to be capable of electing our own public authorities and we will do so.

The moment has arrived. It is necessary that all good patriotic Mexicans, all those who still have a sense of shame and self esteem, it is necessary, I repeat, that we resort to our weapons and to the cry of "Long live the Independence of the states of Texas, New Mexico, California, Arizona, and parts of the states of Mississippi and Oklahoma, which from today forward will be called the "Republic of Texas." We join our comrades in arms who are already waging the battle, proving their valor and patriotism.

Long Live Independence!
Land and Liberty
General Barracks at San Antonio, Texas

First Chief of Operations            Second Chief of the General Staff
Luis de la Rosa                      Aniceto Pizaña

Handbill, 1915, from David Montejano, *Anglos and Mexicans in the Making of Texas, 1836–1986* (Austin: University of Texas Press): 154. Translated by Francine Cronshaw. Copyright © 1987. By permission of the University of Texas Press.

## 2. Map Showing Where Americans Were Killed in Ethnic Violence in Northern Mexico, Texas, and New Mexico, 1910–1919

From "Map depicting killings of Americans in northern Mexico and South Texas and New Mexico, 1910–1919" in David Montejano, *Anglos and Mexicans in the Making of Texas, 1836–1986* (Austin: University of Texas Press): 124. [Based on "Murder Map of Mexico," U.S. Congress, Senate, *Investigation of Mexican Affairs*, Document 285, 66th Congress, 2nd Session, 1920, 1: 845]

## 3. Novelist Lionel G. Garcia Presents the Battle of the Alamo and San Jacinto from a Fictional Twentieth-Century Perspective, 1987

Father Procopio, early into the night, arrived with Andres Garcia and with the four other gentlemen that had been helping Andres Garcia at the creek. They were: Faustino, the drunkard, who had noticed Andres Garcia at the creek in the first place; Amandito, the fat one, who had already been there helping Andres Garcia placate the disturbed locusts; Bernabe, the crazy one, who was helping at the creek when the Priest had arrived; and Fecundo, the prolific, the man with many children, who had also joined the other three in helping Andres Garcia. Andres Garcia walked erectly in the center of the group as they neared the house. "This reminds me," he said making a circle with his arms to signify the group, "of the death of James Bowie after the battle of the Alamo. Just as you are surrounding me, so did General Santa Anna's men surround the hated Bowie. Do you know that Bowie had the nerve to spit on my father's boots, while my father was trying to convince Travis that Santa Anna did not want a battle at the Alamo? What ignorance! There you had Captain Agustin Garcia, right hand man to the great General Santa Anna, educated in Spain at the most prestigious academies. . . . And then the ignorant Bowie, whose claim to fame was that he made a knife."

"What happened to the man?" Faustino asked him, as they walked.

"What man?"

"Bowie."

"Bowie was found alive after the Alamo. So was Crockett. Crockett hated Sam Houston for what Houston had done to General Santa Anna at the Alamo. Hated him so much that he joined Santa Anna's troups at San Jacinto." Andres Garcia adjusted his collar with both hands and tried to walk even more erect. "By that time Crockett had changed his name officially to David Cruz."

"This man knows everything," Bernabe said in awe. "Didn't I tell you that he knows everything?" . . .

"What happened to Bowie?" Fecundo asked. . . .

Don Andres Garcia stopped abruptly to gather his thoughts. He had been think-ing of what Father Procopio had said about purgatory. Everyone stopped with him. At the same time he thought that he could still smell the honeysuckle blossoms from the front of his house. "My father killed James Bowie with his trusty derringer," he said. "Shot him in the head after he tied him to a horse ring on the wall of the Alamo. General Santa Anna asked him to. My father had been very pleased that Bowie had begged for his life . . . that Bowie had lied and said that his mother was a Mexican and he should be allowed to live. Bowie's death was the highlight of my father's life up to that point. . . .

". . . I had other men in mind, the priest's cousin who came to visit from Spain. How educated he was. I could sit and talk to him for hours without being bored. He understood the history of Texas as I explained it to him. The treachery of Sam

Lionel G. Garcia, *A Shroud in the Family* (Houston: Arte Publico Press, 1987): 23–28, 47–48. Reprinted with permission from the publisher of *A Shroud in the Family*.

Houston. The integrity and honor that dominated General Santa Anna's life. I could explain to him the battles of the Alamo and Goliad and San Jacinto. Logically, as my father had lived them. He knew that the Texas Rangers were men that were not to be trusted. He knew how the Mexican people had been exploited by Anglo justice. I could make him understand the destruction of culture that took place when the ignorant Anglo came to Texas. How they made everyone into an animal of greed and avarice. This is mine, the Anglo would say to the Mexican. Give it to me or I'll kill you. How much is that? Sell it to me or I'll kill you or I'll steal it. Through hook or crook, I'll get it. With or without the law. And if the law is against me, why I'll change the law. That's what a gentleman of breeding understands. That no one of culture ever came to save Texas from Mexico. They were castoffs of other states, dumb enough to come here just to die." . . .

## 4. The League of Latin American Citizens (LULAC) States Its Objectives, Goals, and Code, 1932, 1933

### Objectives and Goals of the League of United Latin American Citizens

The goals and objectives of this Organization will be:

1. –To develop among the members of our race the best, purest and most perfect type of true and loyal citizen of the United States of America.
2. –To yank from the roots of our political body any tendency to make distinctions among our fellow citizens based on race, religion or social position, as contrary to the true spirit of Democracy, our Constitution and our Laws.
3. –To use all the legal means at our disposal to ensure that all citizens of our nation enjoy equal rights, equal protection under this nation's laws, and equal opportunities and privileges.
4. –The acquisition of the English language, which is the official language of our nation and necessary for the full enjoyment of our rights and privileges, is declared for that reason to be the official language of this Organization. We affirm our intention to learn it, to speak it, and to teach it to our children.
5. –To define clearly and with absolute precision our indisputable loyalty toward the ideals, principles, and citizenship of the United States of America.
6. –To assume complete responsibility for the education of our children in the knowledge of their rights and responsibilities as well as knowledge of the language and customs of this nation in terms of their good features.
7. –We solemnly declare once and for all to pay respectful and sincere homage to our racial origins, of which we are proud.
8. –Secretly or openly, by all legal means at our disposal, we will help with the cultural level and guidance of Latin Americans. We will protect and defend their lives and interests whenever necessary.

From "Objectos y Fines de la Liga de Cuidadanos Unidos Latino-Americanos," *LULAC News* (September 1932) and "L.U.L.A.C. Code," *LULAC News* (January 1933). [E. E. Mireles and Jovita Gonzalez de Mireles Papers, Special Collections and Archives, Texas A&M University—Corpus Christi Library]. "Objectives and Goals" translated by Francine Cronshaw. Reprinted with permission from the League of Latin American Citizens (LULAC).

9. –We will block any momentum leading to the creation of racial prejudices against our people. We will fight any degrading stigma imposed on them. We claim on their behalf the respect and the prerogatives granted to all under the Constitution of our nation.

10. –Each one of us is considered to have equal responsibility in our Organization, to which we voluntarily pledge our subordination and obedience.

11. –We will create funds for our mutual protection, for the defense of any among us who might be unfairly indicted, and for the education and cultural development of our people.

12. –This Society is not a political club, but as citizens we will participate in the electoral contests at local, state and federal levels. However, in the process we will always keep in mind the general welfare of our people. We disavow and renounce once and for all any commitment of a personal nature not in harmony with the above principles.

13. –We will lend our votes and influence to building the political stature of individuals whose actions show respect and consideration for our people.

14. –We will elect as our leaders those among us who show by their integrity and cultural attainments that they are capable of guiding and leading us in an upright manner.

15. –We will maintain publicity efforts to communicate these principles, increase the number of branches of our Organization, and work for its consolidation.

16. –We will pay our share of the poll tax for ourselves and our families in order to fully enjoy our political rights.

17. –We will spread the word about our ideals through the press, conferences, and pamphlets.

18. –We are opposed to any kind of racial and violent demonstration that might tend to create conflicts and consequently infringe on the peace and tranquility of this nation.

19. –We will respect the religious ideas of each individual and moreover we refer to religious ideas in our institutions.

20. –We will stimulate the creation of educational institutions for Latin Americans and we will lend our support to those already in existence.

21. –We will work toward obtaining equal representation for our people on juries and in public administration in general.

22. –We will denounce all instances of peonage and mistreatment as well as child labor among our people.

23. –We will resist and forcefully combat all machinations tending to prevent our social and political unity.

24. –We will unite against any effort leading to the segregation of our children in the schools of our nation.*

25. –We will set up statistics to orient our people in regards to working and living conditions and agricultural and business activity in different parts of the country.

---

*The original Spanish uses the verb "combinaremos" (we will unite). The resulting translation says that LULAC will unite to support any effort to segregate their children. Obviously, either the negative was omitted (we will unite against), or the writers meant to use the verb "combatiremos" (we will fight).

## L. U. L. A. C. CODE

Respect your citizenship and preserve it: honor your country, maintain its traditions in the spirit of its citizens, and embody yourself into its culture and civilization;

Love the men of your race, be proud of your origin and maintain it immaculate, respect your glorious past and help to defend the rights of your own people.

Learn how to fulfill your duties before you learn how to claim your rights; educate and make yourself worthy, and stand high in the light of your own deeds; you must always be loyal and courageous;

Filled with optimism make yourself sociable, upright, judicious, and above all things be sober and collected in your habits, cautious in your actions and sparing in your speech;

Study the past of your own, and of the country to which you owe your allegiance, learn how to master with purity the two most essential languages—English and Spanish.

Always be honorable and high-minded, learn how to be self-reliant upon your own qualifications and resources;

Believe in God, love Humanity and rely upon the framework of human progress, slow and sound, unequivocal and firm;

In war serve your country, in peace your convictions; discern, investigate, meditate and think, study, at all times be honest and generous.

Let your firmest purpose be that of helping to see that each new generation of your own shall be of a youth more efficient and capable, and in this, let your own children be included.

## 5. The Chapultepec Club, a Mexican American Women's Club in Houston, Lists Complaints Concerning Treatment of Minorities, 1937

June 11, 1937

Miss Leona B. Hendrix
2219 Tracy Street
Kansas City, Missouri

My dear Miss Hendrix:

The Chapultepec Club of the Houston Y.W.C.A. has the following to offer as findings from their study of minorities. Here in Texas they [the club members] happen to constitute a minority group themselves and are called Mexicans. Some of the group were born in Mexico and have not taken out citizenship papers. [The] reason [is as] follows: Many were born in Texas and are therefore American citizens but are

Thomas Krenick, "The Chapultepec Club: A Mexican American Women's Club in Houston" from *Houston Review* 3 (Summer 1981): 269–71. Copyright © 1981 University of Houston. Reprinted with permission.

still called Mexicans. The group is made up of an excellent cross section of the Mexican colony in Houston. There are several high school graduates in the group and of course every year more Mexicans are staying in school until graduation.

These are the problems which these young Mexican girls and women face in Texas and they wonder what the future will be for them and their children. From this study, they hope sincerely for recommendations from the National B. & P. Council on action they can take to better understanding, respect and opportunity. They recognize that minority groups elsewhere in the United States face some, though not all, of the same problems.

1. Texas is next door to Mexico and there are border town problems to be considered, historically as well as at present.

    Texas history is founded on troubles, oft created by Texans, to get land and cattle from the Mexican people. [N]ow the problem of stolen automobiles is causing the same problem and also the water power of the Rio Grande River is causing hard feelings.

2. Texas cannot, due to Chamber of Commerce and patriotic society activities, forget that Texas lost a tragic battle at the [A]lamo in San Antonio and won a battle at San Jacinto. This causes teachers to preach a patriotism not kind to Mexican children. Mexicans have been known to stay out of school [in Houston] when that part of history was being taught because of abuses inflicted by pupils and even teachers.

3. Mexicans in [a] desire to get ahead have at times denied their nationality calling themselves French, Italian, and Spanish. This induces the Mexican colony's disfavor. Nationalistic spirit [is] being cultured at present [and] this of course can be as dangerous an attitude as the denial [of] one.

    If they should move back to Mexico they are considered traitors for having lived in Texas.

4. They do not take out citizenship papers because those who have are still called Mexicans and treated as such.

5. The Mexican people find it impossible to rent or buy in any decent section of town and are forced to live in dirty crowded conditions in houses out of which Americans have moved.

6. Playgrounds and parks show distinct distaste to their presence on them and in some cases they are ordered off or forbidden on. This problem is caused by the youth and not the recreation leaders.

7. Falsely accused of many crimes in the city and because of some difficulty with the English language they are taken advantage of frequently.

8. Mexican people are paid less in wages on all jobs and a great many jobs and industries are closed to them.

9. Mexican lawyers receive no respect from other lawyers nor even from our judges. It is a well known fact that a case is practically lost if a Mexican lawyer handles it. Justice is very one-sided, and they have had some rather serious cases recently.

10. They are called "brown people," "greasers," et cetera and of course want to be called white.

This letter is also going to Beatrice Langley and at the same time the group is also sending a letter to the American Youth Congress protesting certain movies which have been shown in Texas portraying the Mexicans in a very bad light.

Very truly yours,
Stella Quintenella
Carmen Cortez
Olive Lewis

P.S. These statements were verified by outstanding men in the Mexican colony, such as the consul, doctors, and teachers.

## 6. Emma Tenayuca and Homer Brooks, Officers of the Texas Communist Party, Outline Their Vision for Mexican Unification, 1939

Upon what is this movement for Mexican unification based? What are its main objectives?

It is a people's movement, uniting the interests of large and important sections of the population, over two million strong, who, in alliance with the country's democratic forces, in the Southwest and nationally, can free themselves from the special oppression and discrimination in all its phases that have existed for almost a century.

The struggle is directed:

1. Against economic discrimination—extra low wages; expropriation of small land holders; discrimination in the right to work in all trades and crafts, particularly skilled trades; discrimination against professional and white collar workers; discrimination in relief and right to employment in W.P.A.
2. For educational and cultural equality—equal educational facilities for the Mexican population; no discrimination against children of Mexican parentage; a special system of schooling to meet the needs of the migratory families; the study of the Spanish language and *the use of Spanish as well as English in the public schools and universities* in communities where Mexicans are a majority; the granting of equal status to the Spanish language, as has been done in New Mexico and in those counties and states where the Mexican people form a large part of the total population.
3. Against social oppression—for laws making illegal the various forms of Jim-Crowism, segregation in living quarters, schools, parks, hotels, restaurants, etc. This struggle must be linked with that of the Negro people.
4. Against political repression. The struggle for the right to vote is divided into two phases:
    (a) The majority of the Mexicans are American-born. The problem is, therefore, one of enforcing their citizenship right. This means demanding that all

Emma Tenayuca and Homer Brooks, "What Path to Follow" in "The Mexican Questions in the Southwest," *The Communist* 18 (March 1939): 264–265.

legal and extra-legal restrictions to the free exercise of the ballot be removed. These include residence qualifications, difficult for semi-migratory workers to meet; and in Texas, the elimination of the poll tax.

(b) Those who are foreign born must join with all of the immigrant groups in the United States to secure the democratization of the federal regulations pertaining to *length of time, cost,* and *language conditions* required for citizenship; the aim being to simplify the process whereby all who intend to remain permanent residents of the United States—and this includes nearly all of the Mexicans—and who express a desire for naturalization, can become citizens.

In some states, as in Texas, it may become feasible to restore, at least until federal requirements for becoming citizens become less onerous, the provisions in the Texas state constitution which, until 1921, granted voting rights to all Mexicans and other foreign born, citizens and non-citizens, providing they met residence requirements and declared their desire for American citizenship.

In this general movement the leading role will undoubtedly be played by the proletarian base of the Mexican population, its overwhelming majority. This is already evident from the impetus given the movement for Mexican rights by the large strike struggles in Texas, California and Colorado. The surest guarantee for the full and successful development of the people's movement will be in further trade union organization among the Mexican workers.

## 7. Poet Américo Paredes Manzano Laments the Oppression of the Mexico-Texan, 1939

"The Mexico-Texan, he's one fonny man
Who lives in the region that's north of the Gran';
Of Mexican father, he born in thees part.
For the Mexico-Texan, he no gotta lan';
And sometimes he rues it, deep down in hees heart.
He stomped on da neck on both sides of the Gran';
The dam gringo lingo he no cannot spick,
It twista da tong and it maka heem sik;
A cit'zen of Texas they say that he ees!
But then,—why they call heem da Mexican Grease?
Soft talk and hard action, he can't understan',
The Mexico-Texan, he no gotta' lan'."

—Américo Paredes Manzano
"The Mexico-Texan," 1939

Américo Paredes Manzano, "The Mexico-Texan," 1939 in David Montejano, *Anglos and Mexicans in the Making of Texas, 1836–1986* (Austin: Arte Publico Press, University of Texas Press, 1991): 158. Reprinted with permission from the publisher.

## 8. The Constitution of the American G.I. Forum of Texas Seeks Equal Rights for Mexican Americans in the Post-World War II Era

### Section 1: NAME

The official name of this organization shall be "The American GI Forum of Texas, Inc." and can be shortened for practical use to "GI Forum".

### Section 2: PURPOSE

As veterans, this organization will strive for the procurement, of all veterans and their families, regardless of race, color or creed, the equal privileges to which they are entitled under the laws of our country. Also, this organization will strive for the preservation of the Democratic ideals for which this country has fought in all wars, and we propose to ever maintain as well as advance these ideals wherever possible; to foster the training and education of our citizens in order that a true and real democracy may exist in the lowest as well as the highest unit so that our loyalty to these principles may never be questioned.

As loyal citizens of the United States of America, we sincerely believe that one of the principles of Democracy is religious and political freedom for the individual and that all citizens are entitled to the right of equality in social and economic opportunities and that to produce a stronger American society we must advance understanding between the different nationalities.

## ✦ E S S A Y S

By the 1920s, the growing Mexican American population began organizing to achieve economic, social, and political rights. In the first essay, Mario T. Garcia of the University of California at Santa Barbara, discusses the efforts of the rising middle class to create an organization that would enable them to win the respect of the Anglo majority and smooth their assimilation into American life. In spite of the underlying conservatism of LULAC, it did give voice to the Mexican American demand for civil rights and an end to discrimination. Mexican American workers also addressed the injustices they confronted in Texas. In the second essay, the late Irene Ledesma, who was a professor at the University of Texas Pan American, examines the efforts of Mexican American women to organize in defense of their rights in the workplace and to achieve economic and social justice. Ledesma argues that as they became labor activists, Mexican American women confronted a mixed response from the media. She analyzes the complex and often contradictory response to the workplace struggles for these women, not only in the mainstream press, but also among the labor press and the Mexican American newspapers.

---

From "Constitution of the American G.I. Forum of Texas," Article I, Section 2, "Purpose" 1949. [Dr. Hector P. Garcia Papers Special Collections and Archives, Texas A&M University—Corpus Christi Library].

# LULAC, Mexican American Identity, and Civil Rights

## MARIO T. GARCÍA

The search for America and their place in it shaped the consciousness and politics of the Mexican-American Generation. Mexican Americans, however, did not define "Americanization" in the patronizing and ethnocentric terms characteristic of many Anglo-American educators and welfare workers. They interpreted Americanization in light of the perceived need to forge a movement that would help break the economic, political, and cultural isolation of Mexican Americans in the United States during the early twentieth century. The Mexican-American Generation aspired to move into the mainstream of American life. They recognized that Mexican Americans could no longer adequately function in the marginal ethnic enclaves of the Southwest that had survived the nineteenth century or in the immigrant culture superimposed after 1900 as thousands of Mexicans crossed the border seeking work and political asylum. Instead, the Mexican-American Generation sought to advance from their past and to see themselves as permanent citizens of the United States with all the rights and privileges of American citizenship. . . . No Mexican-American organization better exemplified this search for America than the League of United Latin American Citizens, founded in 1929 and the oldest Mexican-American civil rights association in the United States.

## Origins of a Political Generation

The Mexican-American Generation, as a political entity, began to come of age in the 1930s, but its embryo can be detected in the Roaring Twenties. In this decade, Mexican Americans already stressed the need for a new political direction for themselves based on two basic needs: the importance of instilling a new consciousness among Mexican Americans—to develop a "new Mexican" in the United States—and the need to organize new forms of political and civic organizations—a "new politics"—that would best serve their interests separate from those of Mexican immigrants. The confluence of these two needs can be seen in south Texas, the cradle of the Mexican-American Generation.

The importance of a new political movement for Mexican Americans in south Texas was emphasized by the economic and social transformations affecting the region. Increased agricultural production during World War I integrated south Texas into the market economy of the United States. Possessing a year-long warm climate, south Texas became the "winter garden" of the nation, producing a variety of commercial fruits and vegetables. Economic development along capitalist agricultural lines in turn changed the class structure of south Texas. Texas-born Mexican-American farmers and ranchers as well as sharecroppers found themselves unable to compete with agribusiness and some lost what small family lands they possessed. In their place, or alongside them, came thousands of Mexican immigrant

Mario T. García, "In Search of America: The League of United Latin American Citizens (LULAC)," in *Mexican Americans: Leadership, Ideology & Identity, 1930–1960.* (New Haven: Yale University Press, 1989): 25–61. Copyright © 1989 by Yale University Press. Reprinted with permission.

wageworkers to pick the crops produced by the new mode of production. The introduction of this large immigrant work force plus the need to segregate Mexican immigrants and dislocated Mexican-Americans as a cheap agricultural labor force responsible for producing surplus value intensified earlier patterns of discrimination and racial hostility toward people of Mexican descent.

Indeed, the "Mexican problem" emerged in the 1920s. Anglos adversely affected by the rise of agribusiness vented their resentments and frustrations toward Mexican immigrants, whom they characterized as an economic and social threat to Texas and the rest of the country. They charged mexicanos with introducing crime, illiteracy, and diseases and with mongrelizing the social-ethnic base of American society. . . .

Such antagonisms in conjunction with labor exploitation directed at people of Mexican descent during the 1920s, plus a previous history of racism in Texas and elsewhere, created objective conditions for efforts toward Mexican-American political unity. M. C. González . . . categorized five types of discrimination faced by all Mexicans in Texas during the 1920s. These included (1) public school segregation of Mexican-American children; (2) segregation and discrimination in public facilities such as restaurants, movie theaters, swimming pools, and barbershops; (3) the establishment of "white man's" primaries to prevent blacks and Mexican Americans from exercising their right of suffrage; (4) discrimination in housing by not allowing Mexicans to purchase real estate in certain sections of towns and cities such as San Antonio; and (5) discrimination in the administration of justice by preventing Mexican Americans from serving on juries. . . . Of course most Mexicans also faced job discrimination. Both rural and urban employers profited from Mexicans as cheap unskilled labor and refused to jeopardize such a lucrative labor pool by supporting educational and job opportunities.

Yet, despite heightened discrimination against Mexicans in south Texas, economic development plus the needs of an expanding Mexican population produced some advances and even relative prosperity for a few Mexican Americans in the growing towns and cities of the region. Those whose families had previously been merchants or who had recently migrated from the rural areas with sufficient capital to open small stores shared, although unequally, in the south Texas boom. Most catered to the Mexican communities—the "Mexiquitos"—and hence experienced mobility within a Mexican-American context. A few *comerciantes,* especially along the border, expanded enough to also serve Anglo customers. An even smaller number with better opportunities for education became lawyers, teachers, journalists, and politicians. In effect, a small Mexican-American middle class emerged or survived from an earlier period.

The Mexican-American middle class, however, confronted a contradiction. It participated in the new prosperity of south Texas but still faced racial, cultural, and social discrimination. The notice No Mexicans Allowed affected them just as it did immigrant workers. Hence, the Mexican-American middle class sowed the seeds of discontent over the magnitude and persistence of racial discrimination and called for its eradication. Yet the middle class recognized that the struggle against racism would have to take a different form and have a different emphasis than before. Mexicans through older forms of organization such as mutual aid societies and through Mexican consulates had historically protested against discrimination.

But antidiscrimination was never effectively linked with the issue of integration. This was mainly because previous generations of both native-born citizens, still living in a predominantly Mexican world, and recent immigrants from Mexico did not share an interest in Americanizing their experiences. . . .

Besides a change of consciousness, a "new politics" was in order. Unlike the older generation of Mexican-American politicos who subordinated themselves to Anglo political machines, purchased the Mexican-American vote, and literally herded Mexican Americans to the polls, those involved in the "new politics" hoped to cleanse Mexican-American politics by stressing nonpartisan civic action and avoidance of machine politics. . . . This new consciousness and new politics would give birth to a new citizen: the Mexican American.

## The Formation of LULAC

The initial effort at a new political movement among Mexican Americans commenced in 1921 with the organization of the Sons of America in San Antonio. Comprised of mostly lower middle-class professionals, the Sons stressed socializing Mexican Americans to their rights as U.S. citizens and obtaining equal rights for them. Unfortunately, personal rivalries within the Sons soon splintered the organization. . . . To remedy the situation and redirect efforts toward political unity, Ben Garza of Council No. 4 of the Sons of America and González of the Knights took the lead in advocating a merger of the different organizations. . . . With Perales's* support as well as that of González,** . . . Garza . . . called for a unity convention to be held in Corpus Christi on February 17, 1929, for the purpose of founding a new Mexican-American association.

Twenty-five designated delegates attended the convention held in Obreros Hall. An additional 150 Mexican Americans participated as nonvoting members. They came from throughout south Texas. . . .

The convention unanimously agreed to fuse all three represented organizations and to form . . . the League of United Latin-American Citizens (LULAC). The convention also agreed to restrict its membership to U.S. citizens of Latin extraction. English would be the official language of LULAC. . . .

Mexican Americans were to be socialized to U.S. citizenship. The goal was "to develop within the members of our race the best, purest and most perfect type of a true and loyal citizen of the United States of America." However, Mexican Americans could not assume their rightful place alongside other Americans as long as they faced discrimination. LULAC committed itself to a campaign, if not crusade, against such un-American practices. Reforms would be achieved not by radical measures but within the confines of the law. Americanization for LULAC meant struggling within the system not outside it and certainly not against it. Of course, Americanizing the Mexican-American experience also involved a cultural question. LULAC emphasized a dual cultural approach. For one, LULAC emphatically reiterated its support of English as the organization's official language and noted that

---

*Alonso S. Perales
**M. C. González

only by learning English could Mexican Americans be integrated as full citizens. Yet, organizers of LULAC believed that they were of such an ethnic, class, and cultural background that they did not have to apologize for their Mexican roots and cultural traditions. Lulacers were not begging for integration. They were proud middle-class Mexican Americans who at the same time understood the need to adapt to American conditions. Consequently, Americanization was not perceived as a one-way street. Anglo Americans would also have to accommodate to the best of middle-class Mexican-American life. "We solemnly declare once and for all to maintain a sincere and respectful reverence for our racial origin of which we are proud." The LULAC constitution reaffirmed the need to maintain bilingualism and ethnic pride.

Despite the affirmation of their ethnicity, or what Conzen regards as the invention of ethnicity, Lulacers still recognized the controversial nature of their exclusion of Mexican nationals and their adoption of English as LULAC's official language. Indeed, the exclusion of Mexican nationals had not been a unanimous decision. M. C. González, for example, had argued that ethnic unity required inclusion of Mexican nationals and that LULAC could utilize the support of the Mexican consulates along with mexicano self-help organizations. . . . Alonso Perales stressed that exclusion of Mexican nationals was based solely on pragmatism. . . . State and local authorities, especially in Texas, did not respect or fear groupings of noncitizens. Perales argued that only an association of U.S. citizens, such as LULAC, could effectively pressure and lobby for concrete reforms. Practicality also involved a recognition that Mexican Americans and Mexican nationals possessed certain distinct political interests that separated them. Whereas Mexican nationals looked toward their eventual repatriation to Mexico, Mexican Americans hoped for integration within the United States. . . .

On the question of the use of English, Lulacers reemphasized that this did not imply an abandonment of Spanish. Instead, *La Verdad* of Corpus Christi, a LULAC supporter, advocated bilingualism and called on Mexican Americans as well as Mexican nationals to retain their knowledge of Spanish. English, however, could not be avoided. It was indispensable for adjusting to life north of the border and it behooved Mexicans—of whatever nationality—to learn it. Moreover, Mexican Americans would be aided in their efforts to secure their rights and privileges as U.S. citizens by learning English and the customs of the country. . . .

Finally, the Corpus Christi constitutional convention underscored the need for Mexican-American unity. Without it, LULAC efforts to remove the barriers excluding Mexican Americans from full participation in American life would come to naught. "We should resist and attack energetically," the constitution proclaimed, "all machinations tending to prevent our social and political unification." . . .

From a few initial chapters in south Texas, LULAC expanded throughout the 1930s. By the commencement of World War II, it included more than 80 councils in Texas, New Mexico, Arizona, California, and Kansas. "Tejanos" with their more numerous councils, however, continued to dominate the organization. Indeed, most of LULAC's principal issues and activities took place in Texas until the postwar period. . . .

As pioneers searching for a Mexican-American place in the American sun, LULAC leaders attempted to define what Americanization meant to them. This involved both the evolution of a set of principles, what one historian has termed the "Mexican-American mind," as well as a praxis through particular struggles. Mexican Americans in LULAC desired integration and acceptance as U.S. citizens but at the same time wanted to negotiate maintaining their Mexican heritage, or portions of it. Could such a pluralistic assimilation be accomplished? This was one of the questions faced by the initial LULAC generation. This and other issues were magnified by the pressures and transforming conditions of the Great Depression, World War II, and the cold war. LULAC's responses to these historical periods set the tone for much of the politics of the Mexican-American Generation. Although more radical Mexican Americans would challenge LULAC for political hegemony, they supplemented rather than replaced LULAC's basic reformism. Reform not revolution characterized Mexican-American politics. . . . Devoid of a radical political culture such as existed in California, which was characterized by the greater activism of white radicals as well as a more militant labor movement, Texas proved to be less than fertile ground for a more radical form of Mexican-American politics. . . . Fundamental to LULAC's reform initiatives was the stress on Americanization as LULAC's interpretation of Americanization, for the purpose of preparing Mexican Americans for their roles in American society and proving to other citizens the assimilable character of people of Mexican descent. Americanization for LULAC revolved around the following issues: (1) adjustment to American values and culture, (2) political socialization, (3) cultural pluralism, (4) desegregation, and (5) education. . . .

Fundamental to LULAC's effort to assimilate American democratic ideals was the need to reinforce the idea among Mexican Americans that they were as American as anyone else in the United States. . . . Mexican Americans had to see themselves as Americans not Mexicans. LULAC rejected any suggestion that "real Americans" belonged to a particular ethnic group. "When Columbus came here he brought with him our forefathers," one LULAC official wrote, "but he did not bring a blood. Later, when Americo Vespucius named the country America, he had no particular racial blood in mind. So therefore we are all Americans because we live in America, and don't let anyone kid you." No basic human differences existed between the average Mexican American and the average Anglo American.

LULAC accentuated the inherent Americanism of Mexican Americans but still had to confront ethnic labeling. This involved the term "Latin American." The *LULAC News* acknowledged that the term had been a compromise to accommodate the particular position of Mexican Americans in the Southwest. LULAC needed a term that would not offend Anglos but at the same time convince them that Mexican Americans were American citizens and not just "Mexican." . . .

Acculturation also meant rejecting competing ideologies. During the 1930s, LULAC condemned both fascism and communism. In an editorial entitled "Beware of Communism," M. C. González pledged that LULAC would not only be an agent of Americanization, but that it enlisted in the combat against "communistic propaganda that is so destructive of the basic principles of Democracy and of American ideals." At its 1938 convention in El Paso, LULAC furthered its antitotalitarian posture by adopting resolutions opposing "all seditious propaganda courting our subscription to the un-American doctrines of Communism, Nazism, fascism, and all other 'isms' detrimental to the present and future well-being of all Americans." . . .

As part of its effort to Americanize the Mexican-American image, LULAC upheld middle-class role models. "Most of us in LULAC enjoy a fairly good standard of living," the *LULAC News* reported in 1954, "bringing about our desire to 'keep up with the Jones.'" Both middle-class and working-class Mexican Americans joined LULAC, but the middle class dominated leadership positions at the local and national levels. Attorneys, for example, formed the overwhelming majority of national LULAC presidents. In addition, the *LULAC News* extolled the life histories and achievements of its middle-class leaders. A composite picture of such role models included the following characteristics: American born, rising from poor backgrounds to achieve education, veterans of World War I or World War II, high school or college graduates, and professionally either a lawyer, teacher, physician, or government employee. In all, LULAC equated Americanism with middle-class success and believed that true leadership could emanate only from the middle class.

Although an organization of Mexican Americans, LULAC also aimed to Americanize Mexican nationals. Mexicanos could not be official members of LULAC, but they could become honorary members and some apparently joined under this status. LULAC in Victoria, Texas, in 1944 sponsored a meeting chaired by the Mexican consul of Corpus Christi that discussed discrimination against Mexican nationals and organized a committee composed of Mexican nationals to investigate the situation. Moreover, LULAC through the Spanish-language sections of the *LULAC News* during the 1930s counseled Mexican nationals about adjustment to life in the United States. It organized English and citizenship classes for Mexican nationals. LULAC councils in south Texas in the post-World War II period, for example, expressed shock at the number of Mexican nationals who failed citizenship examinations due to lack of both English and a knowledge of American civics. Consequently, Laredo Council No. 12 commenced its own adult night school for Mexican nationals. In 1953 the school taught English and citizenship to more than two thousand persons. LULAC teachers provided citizenship classes in both English and Spanish. "I teach them in English hoping they will pick up the language," one teacher in El Paso told a reporter about his students, "and I teach Spanish to be sure they learn the essentials of the American form of government in which they will be tested when they apply for naturalization." . . .

Although LULAC's constitution prohibited councils from engaging in electoral politics, still, men and women members were encouraged to participate in politics. However, they had to do so in a nonpartisan fashion. LULAC believed that it would lose effectiveness if perceived as a partisan front for a political party. According to M. C. González, given the hostile climate against Mexican Americans in Texas, LULAC could organize politically only by stressing citizenship and Americanism and avoiding being labeled as "political agitators." Hence LULAC reacted strongly to implications that it was a political organization. When the *Harlingen Morning Star,* in noting the formation of a LULAC council in this south Texas city, referred to it as a "Vote League," the neighboring Brownsville LULAC council quickly refuted the statement. "This is absolutely wrong," officer Federico Recio wrote the Chamber of Commerce. "The League of United Latin American Citizens is not a political organization, it stands for something better and higher than that; it is a Civic and Patriotic Organization." Shunning the label of "political club,"

LULAC insisted that members as individuals actively work in local, state, and national politics. In doing so, they should be guided by LULAC principles. T. G. Giron of El Paso stressed that nonpartisan political activity conformed to the need for a new political direction and abandonment of machine politics that had characterized much of Mexican-American politics, especially in Texas. Under the "old politics," politicians saw Mexican Americans only as commodities to be bought or sold during election time. This was also the politics of "old Mexico" and it had to change and become Americanized by Mexican Americans acting independently in politics.

LULAC considered voting to be the most important political act. Voting was a right and a duty for citizens. For Mexican Americans, it was also an Americanizing exercise. Good citizenship was more than fighting to protect one's country in war or being patriotic in time of peace. Good citizenship also involved participating in the making of the country's laws. Citizens did this through voting and electing their representatives. . . .

In Texas, however, voting was no simple matter. Like other southern states. Texas required a poll tax until the 1960s. The tax in the South prevented blacks from voting, but in Texas it likewise discriminated against thousands of poor Mexican Americans. Some counties excluded Mexican Americans from voting in "white primaries" of the Democratic party until the 1930s. LULAC detested the poll tax but faced a dilemma. It could boycott the tax and attempt to eliminate it or it could encourage Mexican Americans to pay the tax and build up Mexican-American political strength. Recognizing that not to pay would be the greater evil, LULAC organized Poll Tax Committees and conducted voter registration drives. . . .

Voting also assumed importance in encouraging Mexican Americans to run for office. LULAC acknowledged that one of the main political problems faced by Mexican Americans was their lack of representation. However, Mexican-American candidates had to run free of entangling alliances with machine politics. M. C. González, who unsuccessfully campaigned in San Antonio for the Texas legislature in 1930, sought votes under the banner of the Citizens League, a reform political movement. "It is obvious from my name that I am of Mexican descent," González told a reporter during the campaign. "I was born and raised in Texas, however; I served my country during the war. I am an American and am proud of it." Other Mexican American candidates ran for office and failed, but in time some succeeded. LULAC celebrated the election in 1932 of Mexican-American Griff Jones as county commissioner of Maverick County in south Texas. "As he is Vice President of the Eagle Pass Council of LULAC," the *LULAC News* observed of Jones, "rumor has it that LULAC is responsible for his election, as all the Eagle Pass Lulacers supported him individualby [*sic*]." . . .

LULAC's efforts at political socialization finally consisted of getting Mexican Americans to become interested and involved in state and national politics. The economic crisis of the 1930s, of course, and the activist response by President Roosevelt's New Deal attracted Mexican-American adherents, as they did Afro-American and other previously unrecognized minorities, to FDR and the standard of the national Democratic party. LULAC furthered the nationalization of Mexican-American politics by passing resolutions at its national conventions endorsing federal legislation that would benefit Mexican Americans. In all, LULAC through its political socialization sanctioned the Mexican-American Generation's need to engage in a new type of politics in the Southwest aimed at its integration into American life. . . .

## Desegregation Struggles

Desiring to be integrated as first-class citizens, Mexican Americans in LULAC, like their middle-class Afro-American counterparts in the NAACP, struggled against various forms of racial discrimination. . . . They did not want to be singled out for discrimination or for patronization. All they aspired to was equal access to the rights enjoyed by other Americans. Lulacers believed that Mexican Americans were entitled to first-class citizenship not only under the Constitution but also under guarantees of the Treaty of Guadalupe Hidalgo (1848), which ended the Mexican War. . . .

LULAC in particular protested against discrimination in public facilities, considered a major affront to Mexican Americans. Not shy about resorting to the courts, LULAC preferred diplomacy and pressure group politics to achieve desegregation. . . . Lockhart Council No. 38 in Texas, for example, after hearing in 1938 that a new movie theater was going to segregate Mexicans and blacks in the balcony, vehemently objected to the management and succeeded in desegregating the theater, at least for Mexican Americans. . . .

On certain occasions diplomacy and pressure group politics had to include the threat of an economic boycott to achieve desegregation of public facilities. In 1940 LULAC again protested in San Angelo over the efforts of a new movie theater to segregate Mexicans along with blacks in the balcony. President General A. M. Fernández at first counseled firm diplomacy. He advised LULAC's newly created Public Relations Board headed by E. D. Salinas to investigate the issue and "courteously" request that the theater drop its segregated policy toward Mexicans. Fernández also proposed publicizing this local affront to Mexican Americans by linking it with the harm such a case of prejudice did to President Roosevelt's efforts to advance the Good Neighbor Policy. If the management still demurred, Fernández proposed appealing to Washington, where Senator Dennis Chávez, the lone Mexican American in the Congress, and other supporters of the Good Neighbor Policy might be able to intervene. These political channels would first be exhausted before possibly pursuing adjudication. Yet diplomacy had to be reinforced by more direct action. Fernández called on Mexican Americans to boycott the theater until its segregated policies ended. LULAC's strategy succeeded. The management agreed to seat Mexicans throughout the theater and publicly apologized for the controversy. Besides theaters, LULAC protested, in many cases successfully, the segregation of Mexican Americans in swimming pools, restaurants, hospitals, and other forms of public accommodations.

In these antisegregation efforts, LULAC rejected any attempt to segregate Mexican Americans as a nonwhite population. Mexican Americans expressed ambivalences about race identity and possessed their own prejudices against blacks. However, they also recognized that irrespective of how they saw themselves, reclassification as colored, especially in Texas, would subject Mexicans not only to de facto segregation but to de jure as well. This was intolerable. Lulacers consistently argued that Mexicans were legally recognized members of the white race and that no legal or physical basis existed for racial discrimination. Lulacers specifically objected to Anglos excluding Mexican Americans from the political process because Mexicans were colored. In 1937 Council No. 69 in Wharton, Texas, successfully stopped the county tax collector from designating Mexican Americans holding receipts as "colored." . . .

Public discrimination against Mexican Americans likewise involved the exclusion of Mexican Americans from juries in Texas. Although this practice had a long history, Mexican Americans in LULAC vowed to eliminate this blatant type of discrimination. Despite earlier efforts to achieve proportional representation on grand juries in Texas counties with significant Mexican-American populations, by 1951 LULAC concluded that only through court action could jury discrimination be abolished. In September of that year, LULAC lawyer Gus García agreed to represent Pete Hernández, a laborer charged with murdering another Mexican American in Jackson County, Texas. García defended Hernández not only because he believed that authorities were determined to condemn the 26-year old to the electric chair, but because García concluded that he could use the case to combat the systematic exclusion of Mexican Americans from jury commissions, grand juries, and petit juries in Texas. Exclusion could be attacked as a violation of the Fourteenth Amendment, which insisted on equal protection of the law. With the assistance of Houston lawyer John J. Herrera, who also served as first national vice president of LULAC, García defended Hernández in his preliminary hearing and in the initial trial. . . . Despite García's and Herrera's labors, a Jackson County jury, containing no Mexican Americans, found Hernández guilty and sentenced him to life imprisonment.

Not discouraged, García and Herrera filed a motion for a new trial with the Texas Court of Criminal Appeals. In the appeal process, Carlos Cadena, a law professor at St. Mary's University in San Antonio, assisted García and Herrera. The court heard the Mexican-American arguments but still rejected Hernández's request for a new trial. It argued that the Fourteenth Amendment did not apply to the case. The amendment, so the court asserted, recognized only two classes under its equal protection of the law clause: whites and blacks. Mexican Americans were considered whites, hence they could not claim that they had been discriminated against in jury selection. As long as other whites served on these juries, Mexican Americans were represented. . . .

Despite some misgivings over the case, García and Cadena filed an application for a writ of certiorari (review) with the U.S. Supreme Court on January 19, 1953. . . . The U.S. Supreme Court on May 3, 1954, in a decision written by Chief Justice Earl Warren, overturned the Texas Court of Appeals and ruled that Hernández had not received a fair trial due to jury discrimination against Mexican Americans depriving him of the equal protection of the laws under the Fourteenth Amendment. Warren and the Court rejected the "two classes" theory and stated that the Fourteenth Amendment did not restrict itself to whites and blacks.

The Hernández decision represented a major legal victory for Mexican Americans. . . . The Supreme Court's rejection of the "two classes" theory under the Fourteenth Amendment meant that other ethnic groups besides blacks could appeal for protection under the amendment. . . .

Besides acting against discrimination in public facilities and on juries, LULAC struggled against varied forms of job discrimination. It investigated charges of discrimination in WPA jobs during the 1930s depression. LULAC also protested efforts to exclude Mexican Americans from skilled jobs. In 1941 El Paso Council No. 132 expressed anger over the Southern Pacific Railroad's refusal to provide skilled apprenticeships to Mexican Americans. . . .

Yet eliminating discrimination would not mean much unless accompanied by education. Consequently, education became basic to LULAC's ideology and the foundation of its Americanization program. As political liberals, Lulacers perceived education as the key solution to the social problems facing Mexican Americans. LULAC linked its commitment to education to the belief that Americans possessed a universal right to education with no limit to individual educational achievement. Mexican Americans would no longer accept, as they had experienced for many years, limited education in inferior Mexican schools throughout the Southwest. Such an education reproduced a low-skilled work force and kept Mexican Americans in a state of economic underdevelopment. . . .

LULAC also visualized education as a means of developing permanent leadership for the Mexican-American community. This leadership would, of course, be based on a professional middle class. The linkage of education with leadership, however, would require access to university education. Carlos Castañeda of the University of Texas expressed delight with the increased number of young Mexican Americans studying at Austin in the 1930s. He especially noted the importance of many of them studying law. "This is essential to the best interests of our Latin American citizens," he wrote to lawyer M. C. González. "What we need most of all in this state is a group of well trained and representative Latin-American lawyers to whom our people can go for legal advice and who can defend their rights when these are trampled upon."

Embracing education as perhaps the chief vehicle for the integration of Mexican Americans, LULAC at the same time understood that Mexican Americans would have to wage desegregation struggles to achieve quality education. . . .

LULAC pursued dual strategies in its attempt to achieve educational integration and quality education for Mexican-American children. It first sought through a combination of protests, negotiations, and community pressure to convince school authorities to institute changes voluntarily. LULAC councils, for example, investigated charges by Mexican parents concerning discriminatory acts by teachers against their children and when warranted brought such incidents to the attention of the proper authorities. Councils also publicized the unequal distribution of educational resources between schools predominantly attended by Mexican Americans and those attended by Anglos. Moreover, councils protested against de facto segregated schools for Mexican-American children. In particular cases, local community pressure by itself succeeded in desegregating the schools. In 1934, Goliad Council No. 21 assisted by Lulacers from San Antonio obtained the integration of Mexican-American students into the primarily Anglo Goliad High School. Five years later, Council No. 2 of San Antonio achieved the desegregation of the high school in Beeville, Texas. Still other actions involved meetings with state educational authorities concerning desegregation and increased resources for Mexican-American students as well as the hiring of attorneys to investigate segregated conditions. Some of these efforts resulted in reforms, while others encountered more obstacles.

Because of the difficulties in eradicating de facto school segregation in Texas and throughout the Southwest, LULAC also pursued a policy of instigating or assisting in legal actions. In 1930, one year after its formation, LULAC organized its first school desegregation case in Del Rio, Texas. Jesús Salvatierra and several parents, assisted by LULAC lawyers . . . requested and obtained a local injunction from a state court prohibiting the Del Rio School District from using recently approved bond monies to construct new facilities that Mexican Americans claimed would only further the existing segregation of Mexican-American children. . . .

After hearing the arguments, a local trial court ruled in favor of Salvatierra and the other Mexican-American appellants and issued an injunction restraining the school district from expanding the de facto segregated Mexican school. However, on appeal the court of appeals in San Antonio overturned the injunction. The court in the Salvatierra case dismissed the contention by the appellates that the Del Rio school district deliberately segregated Mexican-American children on the basis of race. . . . The Salvatierra case had displayed LULAC's ability to lead in this matter and to organize support. Numerous individuals as well as local LULAC councils throughout Texas contributed to the legal defense fund. The Salvatierra case became the first step in a legal campaign for school integration.

Sixteen years later, in 1946, LULAC helped achieve a major legal breakthrough in the Westminster case in California. . . . LULAC endorsed and supported a class suit by Gonzalo Méndez and other Mexican Americans against the school districts of Westminster, Garden Grove, El Modeno, and Santa Ana of Orange county. Mexican Americans alleged that these districts' policies of segregating Mexican-American students throughout most if not all the elementary grades was discriminatory and a violation of the Fourteenth Amendment. . . .

The Federal District Court agreed and ruled that such segregation not only violated California educational laws that prohibited segregation of Mexican-American children, but also violated the Fourteenth Amendment of the U.S. Constitution. . . .

On appeal the Ninth Circuit Court of Appeals one year later affirmed the decision in the Westminster case. Closely resembling the more famous Brown case in 1954, in which the U.S. Supreme Court declared separate schools for blacks unconstitutional, the Westminster case signaled a major victory for Mexican Americans and for LULAC, which had helped provide the funding support for the adjudication of the case. . . .

The Westminster case had a ripple effect and in 1948 LULAC sponsored and funded a similar legal challenge to school segregation in Texas. In *Delgado v. Bastrop Independent School District,* a federal district court again ruled, as in the Westminster case, that the segregation of Mexican-American pupils violated the Fourteenth Amendment. The Delgado case went one step further and specifically declared unconstitutional the segregation of Mexican Americans in separate classrooms within "integrated" schools. . . .

. . . LULAC's legal battles did not end educational underdevelopment for many Mexican Americans. They continued to face inequalities in comparison to Anglo students. Still, LULAC's path-breaking litigation forced the southwestern education system on the defensive and obtained the force of law behind Mexican-American efforts to achieve educational equality. It also furthered the "nationalization" of Mexican-American politics through LULAC's reliance on the powers of the federal courts to institute changes for Mexican Americans.

## Conclusion

For over thirty years LULAC served as the principal and most visible Mexican-American organization in the United States. Although founded in Texas and initially concentrating on Mexican-American issues in that state, LULAC by 1960 had become a national organization with councils throughout the Southwest and Midwest, the regions containing the majority of Mexican Americans. In later decades it would spread even more and include other Latino peoples such as Puerto Ricans and to a lesser extent Cuban Americans. As one of the few organizations working on basic civil rights for Mexican Americans, LULAC, despite its idealistic faith in the ability of the American system to reform itself, provided a degree of ethnic protection for Mexican Americans and through its struggles achieved breakthroughs in advancing civil rights.

# Race, Gender, Class, and Image in the Chicana Labor Struggle, 1918–1938

IRENE LEDESMA

During the 1935 organizing of Dorothy Frocks workers in San Antonio, Mexican women, members of the International Ladies Garment Workers Union (ILGWU) advertised for a fund-raising dance in the local labor-union paper. In the advertisement, union leaders described the women workers as "some of the most comely of the female sex to be found anywhere. They are good seamstresses besides." Although the editors of the paper recognized the women's struggle, they portrayed the dance merely as a social event. This incident was not unique. The press image of Mexican women workers frequently diverged from the women's pronouncements and actions. In this article, I would like to show that Texas-press images of Mexican-American strikers depended on Anglo, "American," and male criteria, and therefore touched only peripherally on the women's experiences. . . .

Texas newspapers reported numerous union disputes and constructed images of Chicana strikers. . . . In El Paso, in 1919, Mexican laundry women protested the firing of two workers for union activity. During the 1930s, Mexican women in San Antonio—cigarmakers, pecan shellers, and dressmakers—went on strike for higher wages and for improved working-conditions. . . .

The Mexican women strikers in El Paso contended with a particularly antagonistic, Anglo-dominated economy. World War I anti-foreign propaganda and Pancho Villa raids into New Mexico generated hostile anti-Mexican sentiments. Accordingly, in 1919, the Anglo-American population of El Paso generally viewed Mexican

Irene Ledesma, "Texas Newspapers and Chicana Workers' Activism, 1918–1974," *Western Historical Quarterly* 26 (Autumn 1995): 309–332. Copyright © 1995 by The Western Historical Quarterly. Reprinted with permission.

immigrants as an alien force. This hostility was compounded by the anti-labor sentiments of local officials, who expressed themselves by creating an ordinance against picketing.

Organized labor also resented Mexican immigrants. Union officials blamed them for low wages, claimed they took jobs from Americans, and declared that they served as strikebreakers. El Paso's light industrial economy and the discriminatory practices of American employers placed unskilled Mexican workers in low-paying, segmented, and stratified jobs. Married Mexican immigrant women usually did not work; young, single Mexican women were employed in domestic service and in laundries.

When the Mexican women's laundry strike broke out, however, xenophobic labor leaders momentarily stopped their racially-based campaigns against the employment of Mexicans. The story of the laundry workers is a good example of how labor leaders seemingly change their attitudes toward Mexican workers. On 24 October 1919, Mexican women workers organized a local of the International Laundry Workers Union. Soon after, the Acme Laundry of El Paso fired two veteran workers—one sorter and one marker—because they were recruiting new members to the union. According to sorter Francisca Saenz, the remaining Mexican women at Acme then refused to cooperate with Acme's attempt to send their work to other local laundries. Within a few days, almost five hundred laundry women walked out of the six laundries in the city.

On the evening of the walkout at Acme, several hundred Mexican laundry women voted to stay out until the company reinstated the two fired workers. Subsequently, William Moran, editor of the labor paper and head of the Central Labor Union (CLU), the labor leadership in El Paso, assumed control of the strike. He took responsibility for all public statements on the strike and created a fund-raising committee from the CLU membership. A few Mexican women were assigned the task of persuading strikebreakers to refrain from taking the places of union members; all other Mexican women union members were relegated to the union hall. The CLU leadership takeover reflected a belief generally held among unionists that working women could be dominated by male leaders. The takeover further suggested that Anglo CLU leaders perceived Mexicans as docile people.

From previous experience, labor leaders understood the difficulty of presenting a favorable image of Mexican immigrants to the Anglos in El Paso. Like many Progressive reformers of the era, the editors of the *El Paso City and County Labor Advocate* called on employers to prevent vice among the unmarried Mexican women workers. Labor leaders focused on the low wages of the laundry strikers, asking, "What chance has a girl or woman to live a decent respectable life at the wages of this kind?" In another article concerning wages, the union leadership claimed that many of the laundry stockholders were two-faced in calling for "clean-up campaigns" while "breeding prostitution and every thing that can possibly be vicious" and by paying a four dollar a week wage. As the strike intensified, the paper attempted to counter El Pasoans' notions that Mexicans were morally lax. To do this, they imposed on the public images of the women's vulnerability.

In this attempt to help, the labor leadership itself ignored other roles of the Mexican women unionists. In November, a Texas Welfare Commission study of wages—in a variety of industries—revealed that many of the laundry women supported their families. One laundry worker told the committee, "I find it difficult to live on my wages, which I turn in to the family budget." Despite the report and personal testimony, union leaders continued to portray these workers as women in need of moral protection and guidance. . . .

In their attempt to create new images of the women, the labor press fought employer practices that were acceptable to business-dominated civic leaders. The labor paper raised the issue of the women's citizenship, hoping to turn the public against the practice of hiring Mexican aliens to replace strikers. Labor leaders intended to reach any reform-minded unionist through the use of Progressive rhetoric. These leaders emphasized that the striking women were asking for fundamental rights expressed in the Constitution. They admitted, too, that many Americans regarded all Mexican Americans as Mexicans. . . . Acknowledging members' prejudices, the labor paper sought its members' support by defining Mexicans in a manner consistent with Progressive ideals.

Labor leaders used the citizenship angle to reverse other working El Pasoans' chronic antagonism toward Mexican immigrants. Pressing the issue, the *Labor Advocate* insisted that "nothing will be left undone to see that they receive just treatment and a square deal . . . which the Constitution of the American government guarantees to its every citizen." Fortunately for El Paso labor leaders, Theodore Roosevelt's Progressive language and Americans' ideal vision of the Constitution proved perfect for turning Mexicans from aliens into American citizens.

The laborites did not limit to editorials their representation of the strikers. Having banished the Mexican women strikers to the union hall or to the picket line, the CLU leadership sent out agents to garner support from other locals, Mexican-American civic groups, and Anglo-American organizations. The American Federation of Labor (AFL) sent in C.N. Idar to help. Idar, in a speech before the El Paso Ministerial Alliance, took the opportunity to impress upon his listeners the image of the strikers as both morally vulnerable women and as citizens. He told the group that prevailing wages did not permit the Mexican laundry women to "live decent and respectable lives as American citizens." Both appeals succeeded: locals sent funds totaling more than $3,000. Local ministers promised to look into the situation.

But union leaders' appeals on the issue of morality posed a problem. When Mexican women strikers positioned themselves at the El Paso-Ciudad Juarez border bridge to prevent Mexican citizens from taking their places, they contradicted union images of vulnerability. Those that remained picketing at plant sites issued verbal threats. They told one worker they would "pull her hair out if she crossed the line." They also knitted and sold items for strike coffers, even as a male unionist took a leave of absence from his job to raise strike funds. Such actions clearly contradicted the prevailing image of these workers as defenseless women.

On the issue of anti-Mexican biases, the union faced overwhelming obstacles. In 1919, Anglo El Pasoans regarded Mexicans as foreigners, regardless of their citizenship status. Anglos saw non-English speaking Mexicans as unlikely Americans. They perceived a link between corrupt local government officials and Mexican votes. Protestant Anglos considered Catholics non-Christians, and Mexicans were mostly Catholics. These Protestants also held Mexicans responsible for bootlegging and for the excessive drinking in the area. And Anglos believed that Mexicans, as dark-skinned people, expressed a threatening sexual licentiousness through prostitution.

Clashes between Mexican revolutionaries and American citizens in Columbus, New Mexico, added to Anglo El Pasoans' convictions that Mexicans spelled trouble. Despite Anglo preconceptions, the Mexican strikers in El Paso saw themselves to be Americans, and they viewed those crossing over from Juarez to be the "aliens."

Laundry owners rallied, turning the tables on their opponents by seizing these negative preconceptions and applying them to union members. The daily press was quick to echo the owners' cause. Reiterating that the strike had no effect on his business, the owner of the Excelsior Laundry boasted in the *El Paso Herald,* "[S]ome of my Mexicans quit and I put Americans in their place. The American used just half as much materials as the Mexican. The work was cleaner and whiter and better in every way." In a news advertisement in the same paper, the owner of the Elite Laundry reinforced notions of Mexican workers as less capable of good work. He argued that the walkout had started when a girl was fired for not doing her work. The *El Paso Herald* added to the negative image by describing strikers as "Mexican girls" who "are enjoying their vacation." The paper declared, "At the central Labor Union hall the girls are singing and dancing." In these depictions, the Mexicans seemed childlike. As one school principal said of them, "The Mexicans are particulary gifted in art work and music."

Without evidence, the commercial press disparaged the Mexican strikers by linking them to radical groups. The *Herald* published the mayor's instructions to the police chief "to permit no disorders of rioting in this city no matter what the cause." The *El Paso Morning Times,* at least, noted that the women had acted peacefully during the strike. The press gave inordinate attention to materials written in Spanish that had been seized from the Industrial Workers of the World (IWW). The daily papers played up the actions of scab laundry drivers as a first blow against Bolshevism. Although the Mexican women strikers had not gone beyond verbal jousting against strikebreakers, the daily press insisted on associating them with so-called un-American activities.

The daily press fueled ethnic slurs by quoting employers. One such quote included the Acme Laundry owner's pernicious statements on wages to the Welfare Commission. In his testimony, he argued that Mexican women worked too slowly, lacked interest in their work, and completed less items than American employees. He referred to twenty striking women from his plant as, "the cheaper sort of work." He said he found it difficult to find workers for the better jobs because Mexican women could only do routine back labor. Although the two Mexican women he fired had worked (one as a sorter and one as a marker) for at least six years, he testified that American women served better at those positions. Such public observations fueled existing prejudices, intensifying the image of the Mexican women strikers as "un-American," subversive, or inept.

The sentiments of Anglo-American society complicated the strike situation for the women. These El Pasoans seemed to share with other Americans a fear that organized labor might lead the way to Bolshevism. The local American Legion members searched the city for "Reds" but found none. The press, meanwhile, exploited strike stories involving the IWW, and the hysteria reached such heights that the press interpreted unintelligible graffiti found in a men's room as the advance guard of the IWW. Stories such as these gained credibility in light of the other negative images of Mexicans.

The Spanish-language press, with its largely Mexican audience, was enthusiastic, but patronizing, in its portrayal of laundry strikers. The paper covered the visit of Mexican women strikers to local Mexican civic groups, proudly and frequently referring to the women's Mexican antecedents and emphasizing their goals as a struggle for respect for their rights. Stressing the women's peacefulness, the press claimed, "pero no han pasado de eso[1] [shouting at scabs]," the papers expressed outright admiration for them, saying "nuestras mujeres están dando un ejemplo de carácter, energía y solidaridad racial."[2] Interestingly, the Mexican umbrella union that supported the women declared itself the voice of the Mexican community, announcing that the latter was "muy dignamente representada en las sociedades."[3]

For all its posturing in support of the laundry strikers, *La Patria* was often condescending. An article calling the women "compatriots" expressed appreciation to all who had helped the women in their struggle and exhorted the latter to remain united in the view of the union's efforts on their behalf. Earlier in the article, *La Patria*, recounting how the mayor had ordered the police to enforce peace on both sides, considered the situation grave. The journalist stressed that the women "se han portado con toda corrección."[4] This writer added that the violence would be eschewed by the organizers and indicated that any violence would undercut the women's final goal. The ones who wrote these words offered solidarity only because the strikers behaved correctly, and such writers took upon themselves the task of showing to whom the women ought to be grateful as well as what the women's goals should be.

Editors of *La Patria,* and others, appeared intent on educating the women on the conduct of labor disputes. In a discussion of the problems facing the strikers, they predicted the negative outcome of the strike. With a hint of censure, they concluded that too many unemployed women resided in El Paso and Ciudad Juarez. Both strikers and the union realized the extent of the unemployment problem. The CLU sought a solution, asking city officials to demand that laundry owners not hire alien labor. The effort was rebuffed. Another Mexican-American organization added a *machismo* element. In calling for a conference on the strike, the umbrella civic group noted the high percentage of *women* [my emphasis] strikers and asked that "no por esa misma razón [deben] abandonarlas en este momento."[5] Thus, they implied the women needed their help. Mention of the strike by the press had diminished by early December, an indication that the prediction of the Spanish press that the strike would fail had been realized.

Those civic groups to whom *La Patria* appealed clearly reflected the class interests of the Spanish press and of their own membership. In particular, the Mexican Alliance's denial of rumors that it was contemplating supporting a general strike by Mexican workers showed the members' eagerness to appease the owners. When questioned on the issue, members responded that "they were in full sympathy with the striking girls [but] no proposition of a sympathetic strike by local Mexican workers was favored or had even been considered." Seeing themselves as

---

[1]But they have not gone beyond this.
[2]Our women are giving an example of character, enthusiasm, and racial solidarity.
[3]Very well represented in the groups.
[4]They have behaved quite correctly.
[5]For the same reason, we should not abandon them at this time.

representatives of El Paso's Mexican community, the Mexican Alliance quickly discounted any connection to extremist actions.

By 1920, many CLU members withdrew into an alliance with a Ku Klux Klan-dominated good-government movement. With this retreat, organized labor and Mexican immigrants lost the opportunity for an alliance. Nativism in the 1920s and bad economic conditions in the 1930s widened the rift. It would not be until the 1950s that organized labor in El Paso allied itself once again with those workers of Mexican heritage.

Labor union activity in the United States increased enormously in the 1930s because of economic conditions and encouragement from the national government in the form of the Wagner Act. The creation of the Congress of Industrial Organization (CIO) made trade unionism possible to the "unorganizable." In San Antonio, between 12,000 and 15,000 mainly unorganized pecan shellers worked in the pecan industry. Pecan shelling was normally a young, single woman's job, but Depression conditions had forced men into the industry, and home-shelling by entire families became common. When the CIO began unionizing efforts among the shellers, business and community leaders, who touted the city as a haven of cheap labor and who relied on bought Mexican votes, worried that the Chicano masses might become politically conscious.

Conditions and pay in pecan plants in San Antonio early in this century can best be described as poor, but the economic situation of the 1930s made it worse. Workers sat in filthy rooms on backless benches with boxes of pecans in front of them. They were surrounded by the dust from broken shells, and they cracked the nuts by hand. The average weekly wage was $2.25. In 1934, and again in 1935, the pecan shellers forced companies to rescind pay cuts. The owner of Southern Pecan Shelling Company solved this problem by funding the president of the largest local, making it, for all intents and purposes, a company union. In 1936, the president of Southern Pecan proclaimed that five cents a day was plenty for the shellers, who, he said, daily consumed nuts as they worked. That year the company made a profit of $500,000.

On 1 February 1938, thousands of pecan shellers walked out in protest of yet another wage reduction. The pecan shellers chose a non-sheller, twenty-three-year-old Emma Tenayuca, as strike committee chair. The shellers told the Spanish paper that, "la repetida líder no ha tomado participación en este movimiento de manera espontánea, sino obedeciendo la persistente solicitud de los obreros."[6] Tenayuca had earned the Mexican-American workers' respect through her activities as secretary of the local chapter of the Workers' Alliance. During the 1937 winter layoff of relief recipients on public works projects, Tenayuca and the Alliance staged a workers' protest in front of city hall. Additionally, in Tenayuca's words, "the Workers' Alliance continued, carrying grievances, meeting on Sunday." According to Tenayuca, the Alliance "had more than 10,000 members," and its attempts to inform Mexican-American workers of their rights and to alleviate their work-related problems angered city government officials. For years, they had counted on an acquiescent Mexican-American work force to prop their political machine.

---

[6]The above-mentioned leader did not take part in this movement spontaneously but to obey the persistent requests of the workers.

In support of city government's contention that no strike existed, police committed violence on the picket line almost daily. San Antonio did not have Mexican policemen in the 1930s, but strikers, and most of their leaders, came from the Mexican community. Both male and female strikers were arrested during the strike, although on occasion police released from jail women with children. The governor of Texas initiated an investigation on blatant police harassment after the Mexican consul and a U.S. congressman protested the worker's treatment.

Police used lawful and unlawful means to suppress the strike. Capturing national attention with their actions, they tear-gassed pickets indiscriminately, jailed pecan shellers for days without charging them, and took workers outside city limits, forcing them to walk miles back to town. At one point, the police chief doused male strikers with hoses for protesting jail conditions. A local study by a woman's group revealed that Mexican women strikers were crowded into cells with prostitutes. The treatment of the women reflected city officials' bias in categorizing women into what historians call the whore/Madonna complex. The police chief justified his handling of the strike situation by claiming, "It is my duty to interfere with revolution, and communism is revolution." The archbishop of San Antonio, Arthur Drossaerts, praised the chief's efforts.

Fearing the political consequences of a successful strike, the Democratic machine at city hall denounced the strikers and their leaders as outsiders and Communists. The local papers published the police chief's comment that no strike existed because Communist leaders—and he named Tenayuca and Minnie Rendon, the local's secretary—duped the Mexican-American workers. In addition, the mayor and the head of the city vigilance committee questioned the credentials of Cassie Jane Winifree, state chairperson of the Women's National League for Peace and Freedom, after she requested approval to seek funds for strikers' meals. The daily paper wrote approvingly of the mayor's visit to pecan sheds, where he told workers,

> I am convinced that you will not be able to receive calm and dispassionate hearing if you permit Communistic leaders to excite and agitate your people . . . I have reference to such well-known Communistic leaders as Mrs. Emma Tenayuca Brooks, Jim Sager and their co-workers and advisors in the Communist or Red movement.

The police chief told a state inquiry commission, "if the [Mexican] westside workers were organized by UCAPAWA [United Cannery, Agricultural, Pacing and Allied Workers of America], 25,000 persons would be lost to the 'Red Banner.'" The daily press accepted the mayor's and the chief's characterizations and disseminated them without further inquiry. Refusing to consider the frustrations of a destitute people, the mayor and chief gave voice to Anglo San Antonians' views of Mexican immigrants as ignorant, tractable people open to subversive influences.

Daily press accounts of the strike focused on similar allegations about Tenayuca. They centered on Tenayuca's connection to Communism. Even after UCAPAWA's national president, Donald Henderson, took over the strike, the papers continued to allude to Tenayuca's Communist affiliations. The journalists concentrated on her marriage to Homer Brooks, onetime candidate for governor on the Communist ticket. Tenayuca's marriage to an Anglo failed to endear her to other Anglos, not only because she was breaking a social taboo with the marriage but because the marriage reflected her ties to outsiders and Communists. The Mexican community preferred to see her in terms of her activism on their behalf. It typically referred to her as "la pasionaría" rather than by her married name.

In addition to frequent references of her marriage to a Communist, the press detailed Tenayuca's protest activities as chair of the state chapter of the Workers' Alliance. The *San Antonio Express,* reporting the findings of the state industrial commission on police harassment, noted that she had previously been "acquitted of a charge of unlawful assemblage and disturbing the peace." In this article on police wrong-doing, the journalist discredited Tenayuca by associating her with anarchy, lawlessness, and even subversion.

In contrast to the obviously hostile attitude of the Anglo press and aggressive actions of the police, the middle-class Spanish-language paper *La Prensa* expressed some support for the Mexican strikers. The paper approvingly described them as "los miembros de la Texas Pecan Shelling Workers Union han guardado completo orden durante su huelga, sin recurrir a actos de violencia."[7] The journalist at *La Prensa* attempted to dilute the negative images of the strikers by noting that "unos cuantos radicales, sin conección alguna con la industria de nuez, intentaron de tomar parte en la huelga y algunos fueron aprehendidos."[8] The paper, however, also noted that two Mexican-American civic groups—the League of Loyal Americans and the Mexican Chamber of Commerce—demanded that strike leaders sign a loyalty pledge. These groups proclaimed, "We are interested in Mexican workers getting a living wage because we want them to be loyal and progressive citizens of the United States." Two weeks later a worker's rally featured the archbishop, a University of Mexico student, and two representatives from Mexican civic groups. Speakers denounced Communist support and reinforced middle-class Mexican-Americans' stance.

At the same time, the paper offered stories on other aspects of the strike that showed the Mexican unionists' viewpoint. The paper published the workers' defense of Tenayuca and a statement of their intent to protest her arrest. *La Prensa* also published references to the strike that the daily press ignored, such as a charge by Henderson that city opposition was racially motivated. In addition, *La Prensa* proudly noted that the Mexican vice-consul defended the rights of arrested Mexican strikers by attending their court appearances. As had *La Patria* in El Paso in 1919, *La Prensa* offered support only when the women behaved according to middle-class standards. Additionally, by the 1930s, the owner of the paper, favoring American citizenship, lost interest in returning to Mexico. His editors reflected this shift in mindset by emphasizing that the Mexican strikers were peaceful, citizenship-worthy people.

The Anglo-labor leadership in San Antonio shared city government fears that the Mexican masses might revolt. This concern explained the labor paper's lack of coverage of the shellers' strike. In the four years prior to the 1938 strike, the labor press occasionally expressed its dismay over work conditions in the pecan industry,

---

[7]The members of the Texas Pecan Shelling Workers Union have maintained complete order during their strike, without resorting to violence.

[8]A few radicals without connection to the pecan industry have tried to take part in the strike and a few were apprehended.

and referred to the Mexican strikers as "that class of citizenship that are located on our West side." This was a weak gesture made to represent the strikers as Americans. Laborites knew that during a depression American workers' resentment of aliens increased. In the case of Mexicans, this animosity was so intense that repatriation efforts in some cities had succeeded.

When the unionist newspaper did take up the topic, labor leaders' resentment was clear. The paper had indicated its biases in the 1934 strike by declaring that a "more intelligent class of workers" would not have brooked the interference that the sheriff had inflicted on the Mexican strikers' rights. The attorney for the ILGWU may have expressed local labor leaders' attitude most cogently by saying that the pecan strike concerned "un grupo de radicales que se declararon en huelga bajo la guía de Emma Tenayuca de Brooks y Homer Brooks."[9] During the dispute some presidents of locals joined pecan-sheller representatives at behind-the-scenes meetings with town officials. But, in fact, by 1938, the AF of L leadership had done nothing to organize the largely female shellers, and it expressed surprise and perturbation in the *Weekly Dispatch* over CIO efforts to do so that year.

The Mexican pecan shellers won the dispute. Three Mexican women—Amelia De La Rosa, Natalia Camareno, and Velia Quinones—served on the committee arranging for an arbitration board settlement that restored wages to pre-strike levels. Other women did not fare as well. Tenayuca left San Antonio in 1939 when in August a mob stormed the city auditorium in a successful effort to prevent an Alliance rally. Tired of her protest activities, city leaders advised her to leave or face the consequences. Pecan-shelling companies reverted to machine labor in 1939 to avoid paying the wage rates of 25 cents an hour that had been set by Fair Labor Standards Act. This measure reduced the work force in the sheds by thousands. . . .

Guided by accepted ideas of gender, class, and ethnicity in American society, Texas newspapers expressed unwarranted assumptions in their representations of the Chicana strikers. The daily, local papers maintained a consistent profile of the strikers as outside mainstream America—as Bolsheviks, Communists, and as evil and filthy foreigners. When the local press was not focusing on the alleged anti-social and anti-American behavior of the women, it tended to ignore them and concentrate on the males instead. San Antonio and El Paso papers emphasized the Mexican heritage of the strikers in negative ways, usually through the comments of company owners or city officials. These papers pictured the Chicanas as lazy, impressionable, and stupid—or simply as "Mexicans." The daily paper's representations illustrated their bonds with Anglo government at the local level.

The daily press did not seem bothered by their contradictory depictions of the strikers. Their efforts *meant* to alienate the women from the rest of the community. At times, the papers portrayed the women as the antithesis of American good. In the next breath, the papers called them gullible and too indolent even to realize the American work ethic. Anglo readers could be comfortable with these representations because they fit into the accepted notion of Chicanas as an alien and unassimilable

---

[9]A group of radicals who went on strike under the guidance of Emma Tenayuca Brooks and Henry Brooks.

element. It was this shared understanding with other establishment institutions that the commercial press pushed incomplete images of the striker.

To gain support, the labor press would periodically change its image of the Chicana strikers. It would select what was socially palatable in an effort to make acceptable a group of strikers who stood on the margins of society. . . . [T]he labor papers overlooked the Mexican heritage of the strikers to stress their American citizenship and their roles as vulnerable women and mothers. . . .

Labor editors operated with many of the same prejudices as the rest of the community. In 1919, the labor paper pulled back from earlier anti-Mexican diatribes and supported the Mexican women strikers only to retreat into a KKK alliance by 1920. In the pecan strike of 1938, the labor paper, run by AFL leaders, gave coverage only in reaction to CIO interest or involvement in it. . . .

Spanish-language papers . . . caught between their Mexican origins and ties to Chicana strikers and their hopes of becoming Americans, tried to play it both ways be stressing the Mexican heritage of the women in a positive way and at the same time stressing their good behavior. By emphasizing proper behavior, the Spanish press, with its own middle-and-upper class management, clearly exhibited patronizing attitudes towards the strikers as women and as working-class people.

In reality, the seeming ambivalence of the Spanish press lay purely on the surface. Its concerns over its own status in the U.S. inhibited its sense of solidarity, as evidenced by the civic club's attitude in 1919 that the women's good behavior had earned them the former's support as representatives of the Mexican community. The striking women's often violent responses served to place them beyond the pale of traditional middle-class ideology, and the male hierarchy in the Spanish language press preferred instructing the women on strategy and conduct. Particularly after the 1920s, the middle- and upper-class Mexican immigrant embraced American ideals, and they pushed their ideals on their less well-placed ethnic sisters. . . .

The newspapers in El Paso and San Antonio proved unable to move beyond established notions of gender, class, and ethnicity in their coverage of the Chicana strikers . . . but in the process, the press provided information on the overwhelming forces the women faced during protest situations. The Chicanas fought not only great opposition from the companies, but a powerful daily press ready to condemn their actions in support of the established order. Even their supporters, the unions and Spanish-language papers, expected certain behavior from them based on each paper's particular agenda in a given period. Despite these complex odds arrayed against them, Chicanas in Texas demonstrated the power of persistence in the battle for labor justice.

---

# ✪ F U R T H E R   R E A D I N G

Carl Allsup, *The American G.I. Forum: Origins and Evolution* (1982)

Francisco E. Balderrama and Raymond Rodríguez, *Decade of Betrayal: Mexican Repatriation in the 1930s* (1995)

Julia Blackwelder, *Women of the Depression: Caste and Culture in San Antonio, 1929–1939* (1984)

Armando C. Alonzo, *Tejano Legacy: Rancheros and Settlers in South Texas, 1734–1900*
  (1998)
Arnoldo De León, *Ethnicity in the Sunbelt: A History of Mexican Americans in Houston*
  (1989)
———*The Tejano Community, 1836–1900* (1982)
———*They Call Them Greasers: Anglo Attitudes toward Mexicans in Texas, 1821–1900*
  (1983)
Arnold De León and Kenneth L. Stewart, *Not Room Enough: Mexicans, Anglos, and
  Socioeconomic Change in Texas, 1850–1900* (1993)
———*Tejanos and the Numbers Game: A Socio-Historical Interpretation from the Federal
  Censuses, 1850–1900* (1989)
Neil Foley, *The White Scourge: Mexicans, Blacks, and Poor Whites in Texas Cotton Culture*
  (1997)
Mario T. García, *Desert Immigrants: The Mexicans of El Paso, 1880–1920* (1981)
———*Mexican Americans: Leadership, Ideology & Identity, 1930–1960* (1989)
Richard Griswald del Castillo and Arnoldo De León, *North to Aztlán: A History of Mexican
  Americans in the United States* (1996)
Thomas H. Kreneck, *Mexican American Odyssey: Felix Tijerina, Entrepreneur and Civic
  Leader, 1905–1965* (2001)
Benjamin Marques, *LULAC: The Evolution of a Mexican American Political Organization*
  (1993)
David Montejano, *Anglos and Mexicans in the Making of Texas, 1836–1986* (1987)
Guadalupe San Miguel, Jr., *"Let All of them Take Heed": Mexican Americans and the
  Campaign for Educational Equality in Texas, 1910–1981* (1987)
Emilio Zamora, Cynthia Orozco, and Rodolfo Rocha, eds., *Mexican Americans in Texas
  History: Selected Essays* (2000)

CHAPTER
14

# The African American
# Struggle for Civil
# Rights in Texas,
# 1940–1960

*The African American civil rights movement is generally viewed as a post-World
War II phenomenon that followed the Supreme Court decision against school
segregation in* Brown v. Topeka Board of Education *and was dominated by the
leadership of Martin Luther King. In Texas the struggle for racial equality was
well underway in the 1930s, and achieved major victories in the 1940s and early
1950s under the leadership of local NAACP (National Association for the Advancement of Colored People) organizers like Lulu B. White of Houston and Juanita
Craft of Dallas. Black Texans never accommodated themselves to discrimination
and disfranchisement. Primarily through the NAACP, which established its first
local chapter in the state in 1912 and had grown to 31 chapters and 7,000 members
by 1919, blacks organized themselves on the local level to resist the attack on their
civil and political rights.*

*In the 1920s and 1930s the struggle for civil rights in Texas took several
forms. First, beginning in 1924 in El Paso local blacks, with support from the
national NAACP, launched a legal challenge to the white primary, the principal
tool used to disfranchise African Americans. Blacks would win this battle in
1944. Meanwhile in a number of communities, blacks challenged segregation
in public transportation; others campaigned to improve segregated facilities like
schools and hospitals. In the 1940s conflict developed about the appropriate
strategy to combat discrimination. Should African Americans accept equal funding
or even high quality segregated facilities, or should they insist on desegregation,
even if it meant that existing black institutions would suffer? This conflict
divided the black community when the state legislature voted in 1947 to create*

*the Texas State University for Negroes in an effort to block the lawsuit to desegre-*
*gate the University of Texas Law School. Blacks also faced serious opposition*
*from whites anytime they demanded equal rights. Although highly publicized*
*confrontations between civil rights activists and political leaders were rare in*
*Texas, resistance to racial equality was widespread, both among white supremacist*
*fringe groups and public officials. Still, black Texans won their major civil rights*
*battles and, for the most part, won them sooner with less violence than did blacks*
*in the deep South.*

*How did the civil rights struggle in Texas differ from that of other former*
*Confederate states? How significant were local leadership and local movements*
*compared with the struggle at the national level? How was the struggle for civil*
*rights in Texas affected by national political and civil rights movements?*

## ✪ D O C U M E N T S

The first three documents illustrate the campaign of African Americans to regain
the right to vote. This struggle to regain the right to vote in Texas began in 1924
when an El Paso dentist, Lawrence A. Nixon, filed suit challenging the white
primary. Document 1 is a memo from NAACP attorney Thurgood Marshall to the
NAACP describing efforts to organize a new legal challenge to the white primary
in 1940. Document 2 presents the 1944 Supreme Court decision in the case of
*Smith v. Allwright* that declared the white primary unconstitutional. Document 3
illustrates the resurgence of African American political activity in the late 1940s
following the decision.

The next three documents relate to the struggle for equal access to higher education in Texas. As in the struggle against the white primary, local NAACP chapters
worked with the national office of the NAACP to organize a legal challenge to segregate colleges and universities. In 1947 Heman Sweatt filed suit when he was denied
admission to the University of Texas Law School. As Document 4 demonstrates, in a
ploy to maintain "separate but equal" facilities, the Texas legislature voted to create
the Texas State University for Negroes (with a law school) in 1947. Three years later,
in a decision that anticipated *Brown v. The Topeka Board of Education,* the Supreme
Court ruled against the state of Texas (Document 5). As desegregation spread in the
1950s, reactionary groups organized to resist the assault on white supremacy. In
Document 6, an unidentified El Paso investigator gathered intelligence on civil rights
activities in that community, including the efforts to desegregate Texas Western
College (now the University of Texas at El Paso).

Texas civil rights groups and their political allies attempted to resist efforts
of segregationists and white supremacists to derail the civil rights movement. In
Document 7, the Texas Citizen's Council of Greater Houston attempted to link
civil rights to communism and arouse fears of miscegenation. When the Texas
legislature introduced a series of anti-desegregation bills in 1957, liberal state
senator Henry B. Gonzalez employed the favorite legislative weapon of southern
segregationists, the filibuster, in an effort to defeat the proposals. In Document 8,
*The Texas Observer* describes Gonzalez's filibuster. Document 9 describes the
Dallas NAACP's fundraising efforts aimed at combating the state's segregationist
legislation.

## 1. NAACP Attorney Thurgood Marshall Describes Efforts to Challenge the White Primary, 1941

November 17, 1941.

Memorandum: to office
From: Thurgood Marshall
Re: *"Saving the Race"*

### *Background*

Left New York October 31 for two days in Washington with enough clothes for one day and a tooth brush—still on the road.

### *Old Texas Primary Case*

Only way to get to Dallas in time for the meeting on Wednsday, [sic] November 5th was to fly by way of New Orleans to Houston and then to Dallas. On Tuesday night before I arrived in Dallas Charlie Brackins and some other members of the local committee made some rather bad statements about "messing up" the case etc. Had to take most of the time Wednesday pointing out to Brackins and others the true difficulties in the case and the benefits of filing another case. All agreed that if we did not get another case started all of us would have to leave the U.S. and go live with Hitler or some other peace loving individual who would be less difficult then the Negroes in Texas who had put up the money for the case.

### *New Case????*

The gang in Dallas swore that they had a good plaintiff for a new case. We immediately started drafting a new complaint to fit this situation. By the time the man returned to town we discovered that he was not sure when he tried to vote. On checking the dailies we found that he had attempted to vote in the "run-off" primary in 1940 and we were right where we started—out in the street. Checked again and could find no cases in Dallas. Next stop Houston—still not anxious to go live with Hitler. This was on November 8th.

In Houston talked with Dr. L. E. Smith who is alleged to have attempted to vote at the right time. Checked his story as best I could. Started drafting complaint. Davis' stenographer can't type worth a dime. Tried for a day to get a stenographer who specialized in typing—no such animal available. Called Carter Wesley and drafted his secretary who really can type.

Had to go to Court House to find names of officials involved in case. Got the name of the County Clerk. Tried to get the names of the elections judges. Could only get the name of the election judge. Called this man and told him I was a reporter

---

"Saving the Race," Memo, Thurgood Marshall to [NAACP] Office, November 17, 1941, in NAACP Collection, Manuscript Division (8–16) Library of Congress. Available from lcweb.loc.gov/exhibits/odyssey/archive/08/0816001r.jpg.

for a local daily and wanted the name of his associated judge. Got the name and called this man who admitted he was the associate judge in the particular precinct. Drafted complaint Thursday.

## 2. *Smith v. Allwright* Declares the White Primary Unconstitutional, April 3, 1944

Mr. Justice Reed delivered the opinion of the Court.

This writ of certiorari brings here for review a claim for damages in the sum of $5,000 on the part of petitioner, a Negro citizen of the 48th precinct of Harris County, Texas, for the refusal . . . to give petitioner a ballot or to permit him to cast a ballot in the primary election of July 27, 1940. . . . The refusal is alleged to have been solely because of the race and color of the proposed voter. . . .

The State of Texas by its Constitution and statutes provides that every person, if certain other requirements are met which are not here in issue, qualified by residence in the district or county "shall be deemed a qualified elector." . . . Primary elections for United States Senators, Congressmen and state officers are provided for by Chapters Twelve and Thirteen of the statutes. Under these chapters, the Democratic Party was required to hold the primary which was the occasion of the alleged wrong to petitioner. . . .

The Democratic party, on May 24, 1932, in a state convention adopted the following resolution: . . .

> Be it resolved that all white citizens of the State of Texas who are qualified to vote under the Constitution and laws of the State shall be eligible to membership in the Democratic party and, as such, entitled to participate in its deliberations.

It was by virtue of this resolution that the respondents refused to permit the petitioner to vote.

Texas is free to conduct her elections and limit her electorate as she may deem wise, save only as her action may be affected by the prohibitions of the United States Constitution or in conflict with powers delegated to and exercised by the National Government. The Fourteenth Amendment forbids a state from making or enforcing any law which abridges the privileges or immunities of citizens of the United States and the Fifteenth Amendment specifically interdicts any denial or abridgement by a state of the right of citizens to vote on account of color. . . .

The statutes of Texas relating to primaries and the resolution of the Democratic party of Texas extending the privileges of membership to white citizens only are the same in substance and effect today as they were when *Grovey v. Townsend* was decided by a unanimous Court. The question as to whether the exclusionary action of the party was the action of the State persists as the determinative factor. . . .

We are thus brought to an examination of the qualifications for Democratic primary electors in Texas, to determine whether state action or private action has

---

*Smith v. Allwright,* 321 U.S. 649 (April 3, 1944).

excluded Negroes from participation. . . . Texas requires electors in a primary to pay a poll tax. Every person who does so pay and who has the qualifications of age and residence is an acceptable voter for the primary. . . . Texas requires by the law the election of the county officers of a party. . . . The county chairmen so selected are members of the district executive committee and choose the chairman for the district. Precinct primary election officers are named by the county executive committee. . . . Texas thus directs the selection of all party officers.

Primary elections are conducted by the party under state statutory authority. . . .

We think that this statutory system for the selection of party nominees for inclusion on the general election ballot makes the party which is required to follow these legislative directions an agency of the state in so far as it determines the participants in a primary election. . . .

The United States is a constitutional democracy. Its organic law grants to all citizens a right to participate in the choice of elected officials without restriction by any state because of race. This grant to the people of the opportunity for choice is not to be nullified by a state through casting its electoral process in a form which permits a private organization to practice racial discrimination in the election. Constitutional rights would be of little value if they could be thus indirectly denied. . . .

The privilege of membership in a party may be, as this Court said in *Grovey v. Townsend*, . . . no concern of a state. But when, as here, that privilege is also the essential qualification for voting in a primary to select nominees for a general election, that state makes the action of the party the action of the state. . . . Here, we are applying, contrary to the recent decision in *Grovey v. Townsend*, the well established principle of the Fifteenth Amendment, forbidding the abridgement by a state of a citizen's right to vote. *Grovey v. Townsend* is overruled.

*Judgment reversed.*

### 3. Broadside Documents Political Action of African Americans After Defeat of the White Primary, 1948

# CITY-WIDE
# Political Rallies

Hear ATTORNEY C. B. BUNKLEY, Jr., candidate for Precinct Committee-man, Precinct 6, and MR. GEORGE ALLEN, candidate for Precinct Committeeman, Precinct 45, along with other Candidates on the following dates and places:

## Tuesday, July 20th, 1948     8 P. M.
## ST. PAUL A. M. E. CHURCH
Rev. F. W. Grant, Pastor

## Friday, July 23rd, 1948     8 P. M.
## ST. JOHN BAPTIST CHURCH

Allen Street                    Rev. E C. Estelle, Pastor

Every citizen and voter is invited to hear the candidates discuss the issues in this campaign. After hearing the issues discussed then go to the polls and vote your honest conviction for the best qualified candidate.

Attend these meetings and hear the facts concerning certain political leaders in this campaign.

## TEXAS CLUB OF DEMOCRATIC VOTERS
### BY: CAMPAIGN COMMITTEE

D. B. Garner, President; Raymond Rogers, Lynn Townsend, Mrs. Mary Clark, Mrs. R. V. Smith, Mrs. Edith Richardson, Rev. J. R. McGee, Rev. B. E. Joshua, Rev. C. D. Knight, C. A. Ventress, Jimmie Walker, Mrs. J. E. Craft, W. J. Durham.

"City-Wide Political Rallies," Dallas, TX, July 20, 1948 and July 23, 1948, Juanita Jewel Shanks Craft Collection, The Center for American History, The University of Texas at Austin. (3N325). Reprinted with permission.

## 4. The Founding of Texas Southern University Affirms "Separate But Equal" Education, 1947

### Art. 2643b. Texas Southern University; The Prairie View Agricultural and Mechanical College of Texas

#### Purpose of act

Sec. 1.   The Legislature of Texas deems it impracticable to establish and maintain a college or branch of the University of Texas for the instruction of the colored youths of this state without the levy of taxes and the use of the general revenue for the establishment, maintenance and erection of buildings as would be required by Section 14 of Article VII of the Constitution of Texas, if such institution were established as a college or branch of the University of Texas. Further, the Legislature of Texas deems that establishment of a negro university with such limitations as to funds and operation would be unfair and wholly inadequate for the purpose of providing an equivalent university of the first class for negroes of this state. Therefore, it is the purpose of this Act to establish an entirely separate and equivalent university of the first class for negroes with full rights to the use of tax money and the general revenue fund for establishment, maintenance, erection of buildings and operation of such institution as provided in Section 48, Article III of the Constitution of the State of Texas.

#### Establishment; courses; governing body of agricultural and mechanical college

Sec. 2.   To provide instruction, training, and higher education for colored people, there is hereby established a university of the first class in two divisions: the first, styled "The Texas State University for Negroes" to be located at Houston, Harris County, Texas, to be governed by a Board of Directors as provided in Section 3 hereof; the second, to be styled "The Prairie View Agricultural and Mechanical College of Texas" at Prairie View, Waller County, Texas, formerly known as Prairie View University, originally established in 1876, which shall remain under the control and supervision of the Board of Directors of The Agricultural and Mechanical College of Texas. At the Prairie View Agricultural and Mechanical College shall be offered courses in agriculture, the mechanic arts, engineering, and the natural sciences connected therewith, together with any other courses authorized at Prairie View at the time of the passage of this Act, all of which shall be equivalent to those offered at The Agricultural and Mechanical College of Texas. The Texas State University for Negroes shall offer all other courses of higher learning, including, but without limitation, (other than as to those professional courses designated for the Prairie View Agricultural and Mechanical College), arts and sciences, literature, law, medicine, pharmacy, dentistry, journalism, education, and other professional courses, all of which shall be equivalent to those offered at The University of Texas.

---

"Legislation Establishing Texas State University for Negroes," in *Coordinating Board, Texas College and University System. Compilation of Constitutional and Statutory Laws Affecting Public Colleges and Universities* (Austin: November 1967): 305.

Upon demand being made by any qualified applicant for any present or future course of instruction offered at The University of Texas, or its branches, such course shall be established or added to the curriculum of the appropriate division of the schools hereby established in order that the separate universities for Negroes shall at all times offer equal educational opportunities and training as that available to other persons of this state.

## 5. The Supreme Court Rules Separate Education Is Unequal in *Sweatt v. Painter,* April 4, 1950

Mr. Chief Justice Vinson delivered the opinion of the Court.

This case and *McLaurin v. Oklahoma State Regents, post,* p. *637,* present different aspects of this general question: to what extent does the Equal Protection Clause of the Fourteenth Amendment limit the power of a state to distinguish between students of different races in professional and graduate education in a state university? Broader issues have been urged for our consideration, but we adhere to the principle of deciding constitutional questions only in the context of the particular case before the Court. . . .

In the instant case, petitioner filed an application for admission to the University of Texas Law School for the February, 1946, term. His application was rejected solely because he is a Negro. . . . At that time, there was no law school in Texas which admitted Negroes.

The state trial court recognized that the action of the State in denying petitioner the opportunity to gain a legal education while granting it to others deprived him of the equal protection of the laws guaranteed by the Fourteenth Amendment. The court did not grant the relief requested, however, but continued the case for six months to allow the State to supply substantially equal facilities. At the expiration of the six months, in December, 1946, the court denied the writ on the showing that the authorized university officials had adopted an order calling for the opening of a law school for Negroes the following February. . . .

. . . We granted certiorari, because of the manifest importance of the constitutional issues involved.

The University of Texas Law School, from which petitioner was excluded, was staffed by a faculty of sixteen full-time and three part-time professors, some of whom are nationally recognized authorities in their field. Its student body numbered 850. The library contained over 65,000 volumes. Among the other facilities available to the students were a law review, moot court facilities, scholarship funds, and Order of the Coif affiliation. The school's alumni occupy the most distinguished positions in the private practice of the law and in the public life of the State. It may properly be considered one of the nation's ranking law schools.

The law school for Negroes which was to have opened in February, 1947, would have had no independent faculty or library. The teaching was to be carried on by four members of the University of Texas Law School faculty, who were to maintain their offices at the University of Texas while teaching at both institutions.

*Sweatt v. Painter,* 339 U.S. 629, (April 4, 1950).

Few of the 10,000 volumes ordered for the library had arrived, nor was there any full-time librarian. The school lacked accreditation.

Since the trial of this case, respondents report the opening of a law school at the Texas State University for Negroes. It is apparently on the road to full accreditation. It has a faculty of five full-time professors; a student body of 23; a library of some 16,500 volumes serviced by a full-time staff; a practice court and legal aid association, and one alumnus who has become a member of the Texas Bar.

Whether the University of Texas Law School is compared with the original or the new law school for Negroes, we cannot find substantial equality in the educational opportunities offered white and Negro law students by the State. In terms of number of the faculty, variety of courses and opportunity for specialization, size of the student body, scope of the library, availability of law review and similar activities, the University of Texas Law School is superior. What is more important, the University of Texas Law School possesses to a far greater degree those qualities which are incapable of objective measurement but which make for greatness in a law school. Such qualities, to name but a few, include reputation of the faculty, experience of the administration, position and influence of the alumni, standing in the community, traditions and prestige. It is difficult to believe that one who had a free choice between these law schools would consider the question close. . . .

In accordance with these cases, petitioner may claim his full constitutional right: legal education equivalent to that offered by the State to students of other races. Such education is not available to him in a separate law school as offered by the State. We cannot, therefore, agree with respondents that the doctrine of *Plessy v. Ferguson*, (1896), requires affirmance of the judgment below. Nor need we reach petitioner's contention that *Plessy v. Ferguson* should be reexamined in the light of contemporary knowledge respecting the purposes of the Fourteenth Amendment and the effects of racial segregation.

We hold that the Equal Protection Clause of the Fourteenth Amendment requires that petitioner be admitted to the University of Texas Law School. The judgment is reversed, and the cause is remanded for proceedings not inconsistent with this opinion.

*Reversed.*

## 6. An Unidentified Investigator Gathers Intelligence on Desegregation Activities in El Paso, 1955

April 9, 1955

Subject:   Segregation.   *(Suit Thelma White)*

Pursuant to instructions the undersigned contacted a number of information sources regarding the back ground of the *Ray White Family.* I secured through several reliable sources the following information regarding activities of Ray White and his family back ground.

---

"Segregation Suit: Thelma White," April 9, 1955, Juanita Jewel Shanks Craft Collection, The Center for American History, The University of Texas at Austin. (3N164). Reprinted with permission.

*Ray White* (Negro male) was born in Marlin, Texas about 1908, and was one of a family of five children. His parents were common working people and worked for wages on various farms and worked a small farm on shares with the [l]and for the land-lord. White obtained a 5th grade education in the colored school of Marlin, Texas, and worked on the farm with his parents, and worked some odd jobs receiving a laborers wage. White, moved away from his parents at the age of 19 years old and worked on farms, and at other jobs and in the early part of 1931 married a Marlin colored girl. Two children were born to this family—namely *Ray White Junior,* who is serving in the United States Navy at this time, and *Thelma White*—party involved in the suit against Texas Western College. White's wife died when the two children were very young. . . .

From a reliable source the under signed learned that Ray White had financial difficulties and secured a number of loans as indicated below . . .

Investigation revealed that *Thelma White* was an honor student of the Douglas High School and was give two Scholorships of $100.00 each from the Las Amigas Club for application to any school she chose and a $75.00 scholarship to Prairie View A & M College. At registeration time in the fall of 1954 she (Thelma White) accompanied by Mrs E. M. Williams (Widow of the late Dr. E. M. Williams), Council for National Association for Advancement for colored people for the El Paso area, went to the Registar, Texas Wester[n] College, El Paso, Texas and attempted to enroll where she was refused admittance due to her *color.* . . .

Investigation reveals that Thelma White, began to associate with Mrs. E. M. Williams by meeting her at the Church, and Mrs E. M. Williams taking a liking to Thelma White and began to push her for advancement and encouraged her to seek admittance to a *White State College or University.*

Thelma White, was also promised the support and backing of the Local Chapter of National Association for Advancement of Colored People, and on a state level also. This writer learned from a reliable source that Doctor Vernon Collins, Acting President, of the National Association of advancement of Colored People (NAACP) through Mrs. E. M. Williams got interested in Thelma White and began to seek support of the local groups, regional, State and National level of the National Association for Advancement of Colored People to get her enrolled in one of the *State Colleges, or Universities.* . . . The undersigned recieved information from a reliable informant that after Thelma White attempted to secure admission to Texas Western College and finally entered New Mexico A & M that Dr. Vernon Collins, U. Simpson Tate and other leaders of the NAACP, State level organization met and discussed the case of Thelma White, this leading up to the suit being filed in the U.S. District Court, El Paso, Texas. . . .

At the time that the petition was filed in the United States District Court (Texas Western District), El Paso, Texas, wide publicity was given by the El Paso Times, El Paso Herald Post, and some Radio Station on their news cast. This writer received information from a relieable source that Airforce Personnel (NEGRO) station at Biggs Field, contacted Social Workers at agencies located on the base and complained of discrimination against the negro personnel in El Paso, naming places of businesses as *Bar-rooms, eating establishments, theaters and hotels and other places,* and some places of *recreation.* Negro airmen accompanied by one or two white airmen entered some of the first class eating establishments and demanded service and due to existing laws the management refused service due to subjects being incompany with negro personnel. After a lengthy argument between the management and the negro subjects the white personnel would take up the argument and ask the management if they did not respect the United States Air Force Uniform and not the color or race of the man that was wearing it. And upon leaving the establishment would threaten the management with having them put off limits for not serving the colored personnel. This same type disturbance occurred at a local first class theater.

This writer received information that during the second week of March 1954, the speech class at TWC were assigned the topic of "BROTHERHOOD." With the assistance of the instructor, Mrs. Ball, many of the students chose to discuss the problem of *segregation*. The idea of the talks, according to Mrs. Ball, was to encourage *kindness* and *understanding* for the fellow-man. Since the issue of admitting colored students to TWC has been much publicized, several students used this as the subject for their talks. None of the students who spoke on this issue were against it. . . .

This writer contacted a informant (Reliable). . . . This informant is a colored man and is a business man in El Paso and owns a large amount of property. He stated to this writer that as far as he was concerned that he was happy as he was and had no desire to be come involved in a segregation questions and also had no desire to mix and mingle with the white race and they have always been good to him and that he knew he was a negro and was going to stay in his place. . . . This informant stated that as far as Doctor Vernon Collin's was concerned that the only reason that he wanted to be on the equal with the white man was that he wanted to move upon the hill along with the white doctors and have the opportunity to examine and *play*, and when he stated play, he stated you know what I mean, as he thinks that he is a lady's man either white or black. . . . This informant stated that a large number of the local members of the NAACP are the young buck negros that have the same desire as Dr. Collins, and are former Army, Navy, or Marine personnel and want to get an education and live off of the Government taxes that you and I are paying.

## 7. White Backlash: The Texas Citizens' Council of Houston Describes Links Between Civil Rights Activities and Communists, 1956

Our guest speaker for last Thursday night, Feb. 23, 1956, was Mr Curt Copeland. Mr Copeland is editor and publisher of "Arkansas Faith", 111 Caddo St., Crossett, Ark. Subscription to this publication—$3.00 per year. We urge our members and their friends to subscribe to this and other publications that will furnish you with the only source of truth and imformation about what is taking place on our side of this fight to preserve the racial integrity of the White people of this country. Send Mr Copeland a postcard thanking him for his speech—it will cost you only two

"Newsletter," Texas Citizens' Council of Greater Houston, February 27, 1956, Juanita Jewel Shanks Craft Collection, The Center for American History, The University of Texas at Austin. (3N164). Reprinted with permission.

cents, but will be worth many many times that amount to him. We must encourage all of our people who have the courage and intestinal fortitude to lead this fight. . . .

JOIN US NOW * BECOME ACTIVE!
IF YOU ARE TOO TIMID TO GET INTO THIS FIGHT THEN
LEND US YOUR FINANCIAL, MORAL AND SPIRITUAL HELP.

If the communists are allowed to lead the negro into such unwise participation as their transportation boycott in Alabama, to force their unwelcome association upon the majority of American White people, to corrupt our Churches and our schools, and to eventually lead our children into the BLACK HELL of miscegenation—without our willingness to resist this communist inspired and directed plot—THEN WE SHALL DESERVE THE HOUSE FULL OF MULATTO GRANDCHILDREN WE SHALL HAVE. . . .

. . .—*YOU BE THE JUDGE.* Senator James O. Eastland of Mississippi, said in a speech on the floor of the U.S. Senate, Thursday May 26, 1955, quote;

"Mr President, somewhat more than 1 year ago I pointed out in an adress on this floor that the Supreme Court had been indoctrinated and brainwashed by left-wing pressure groups; that individual members of the Court *were influenced by and were guilty of* grossly improper conduct in accepting *awards and emoluments* from groups and organizations interested in political litigation before the Court and bent on changing and destroying our American way of life; that such reprehensible conduct placed a question mark by the validity and integrity of their decisions in cases which these groups were interested, of which the school segregation case is one.

Today, I am calling upon the members of the Senate to consider an even more serious problem. *The Court has not only arrogated to itself powers which were not delegated to it under the Constitution of the United States* and has entered fields of the legislative and executive branches of the Government, but they are attempting to graft into the organic law of the land the teachings, preachments, and social doctrines arising from a political philosophy which is the antithesis of the principles upon which this Government was founded. The origin of the doctrines can be traced to Karl Marx, and their propagation is part and parcel of the conspiracy to divide and destroy this Government through internal controversy. The Court adopts this propaganda as "modern scientific authority". Emphasis added.

Texas Citizens' Council of Greater Houston
P.O. Box 2316
Houston 1, Texas

## 8. Liberal State Senator Henry B. Gonzalez Uses the Filibuster to Oppose Anti-Desegregation Bills, 1957

No one in the capitol this week will deny that Henry Gonzalez registered it—that through him and Sen. Abraham (Chick) Kazen of Laredo and four other senators who spelled the two talkers-in-chief during their 36-hour marathon on the Senate floor, the minorities were heard with eloquence and impact as never before in Texas.

Ronnie Dugger, "The Segregation Filibuster of 1957," reprinted in *The Texas Observer* 66 (December 27, 1974): 46–47. Copyright © 1974 by The Texas Observer. Reprinted with permission.

In the larger way the filibuster was the splitting up of the Texas culture into some of its varied ways of life. On one side of the Senate chamber stood South and far West Texans with more than a million Latin-Americans behind them—Latin-Americans they think are threatened by general segregation bills which do not say they aim at Negroes. On the other side of the chamber were white East Texans with a million Negroes behind them, some of them restive for what the Supreme Court says are their rights. In the middle stood senators of moderate persuasion, some of whom voted with the minorities, some of whom voted with the East Texans—then switched at the last minute to vote their personal convictions. . . .

The talkers won their point for the week: Sen. Wardlow Lane, Center, who originally wanted to pass out all five bills before the Senate, except the one barring NAACP members from public employment, gave in when Gonzalez refused all blandishments and importations and talked on into early Friday morning. Only HB 231 was passed. . . . It was due Wednesday.

Monday, Senate State Affairs passed out two more bills but (by a 9-7 vote) referred to Atty. Gen. Will Wilson one requiring some advocates of integration and segregation to register with the secretary of state.

"I intend to fight every one of 'em to the last ditch—every one of 'em. It's the least I can do," said Gonzalez after 22 hours and 2 minutes of continuous argument. . . .

Sen. Wardlow Lane of Center, the Senate leader of the East Texans, explained very briefly that H.B. 231 permits school boards to use 17 factors (not including race) in assigning students to schools. It ought to be passed. . . .

As passed by the House, HB 231 also permits parents who object to integration to withdraw their children from the public schools, all other laws to the contrary notwithstanding, and says they will then get education grants as provided by law. . . .

The argument was advanced, Gonzalez said, that the bills had to be passed of necessity. "Necessity is the creed of slaves and the argument of tyrants. They have sown to the wind and reaped a whirlwind!" he shouted. . . .

Gonzalez told of times he had been discriminated against because of his ancestry. "The Irish have a saying, 'It's easy to sleep on another man's wounds,'" he said. "Well, what's the difference? Mexican, Negro, what have you. The assault on the inward dignity of man, which our society protects, has been made . . . We all know in our hearts and our minds that it is wrong." . . .

About 3:30 negotiations started for a compromise. At 5:07 Lane asked him if he had yielded the floor because he was sitting against his desk. At 5:13 his friends came to him and asked him to quit. . . .

"Henry," said Reagan to Gonzalez, "I think we ought to go." Willis told him they were going to move the previous question. Reagan said something to him about getting "urban renewal up." Hudson said, "We've done all we can, Henry." Owen said to him, "It's how far we're gonna push the chair."

Gonzalez replied to them: "I think compromise on one, you're sunk on all. They're fanatical!" . . .

About 1:45 Lane came in unhappily. They would pass only HB 231. The call for a quorum went out, and the senators started dragging in sleepily. The voting was finished, the Senate adjourned. . . .

He held the floor 22 hours and two minutes. He and Mrs. Gonzalez, and Senator and Mrs. Kazen, went on home to bed.

*Later in the year, Gonzalez was filibustering again—this time alone—in opposi-
tion to a bill allowing local boards to close schools if they thought violence or the
threat thereof could not be controlled without military troops. Gonzales talked all
night long, and when he sat down at 7 a.m., the Senate passed the bill. A total of
nine segregation bills were passed in 1957.*

## 9. The Dallas NAACP Organizes
## Against the Segregationists, 1957

1. The recent session of the Texas Legislature passed certain laws which the Legislators, in debate, admitted were directed at the NAACP and Negro citizens for
   the purpose of preventing Negroes from lawfully pursuing a course for the
   protection of their constitutional rights.
2. The State of Texas has already appropriated an initial sum of $50,000.00 to be
   used and spent by the Attorney General to prevent Negroes from enjoying rights
   and privileges which the United States Constitution guarantees and the Supreme
   Court of the United States has already declared that Negroes are entitled to.
3. The Registration Law was passed for the sole purpose of destroying the NAACP
   and its work; the most powerful organization in the world today fighting to protect the rights of Negro citizens.
4. The Registration Law does not only affect the NAACP and its members, but the
   same can and will be used by unscrupulous politicians and hate masters against
   any other organization that works for and advocates equal rights for Negroes.
5. The Registration Law can be used against a church when the minister and the
   members advocate justice for Negroes if the manipulators of this law so choose.
6. The Registration Law can be used to intimidate members of social clubs, fra-
   ternities, sororities, labor unions, charitable, educational, literary and any other
   type of organization that the officials of the State consider to be against their
   interest, or is advocating justice for Negroes.
7. The most vicious effect of the Registration Law is that unscrupulous politicians confederating with the members of the White Citizens Council will have
   their power to examine the lists of members of any organization since the list
   of membership of any organization, under the Registration statute, is to be
   made public, thus, when any Negro is compelled to take an examination by
   any board set up by the State or City, to wit, Plumbers, Barbers, Beauticians,
   Morticians, Electricians, Doctors, Lawyers, Teachers, Pharmacists, et cetera,
   will be subject to the whims of the members of the examining boards. No
   Negro applicant would be able to pass any examination given by unscrupulous
   members of the board where it was shown that he was affiliated with or a
   member of a church or other organization fighting for the protection of the
   rights of Negroes.

"Information: For Use by the Members of the Finance Department and Workers in Raising the Special
Defense Fund," [Dallas NAACP Chapter] c. 1957, Juanita Jewel Shanks Craft Collection, The Center
for American History, The University of Texas at Austin. (3N321). Reprinted with permssion.

8. Negroes in the State of Mississippi, for many years, it has been disclosed, are allowed to pass the examinations given provided they will settle only in areas where white applicants do not desire to locate.

9. To further emphasize that such laws can and will be used against other organizations, is the incident which occurred at Jackson, Mississippi, when the charter of an all-Negro American Legion post was cancelled because of alleged "radical agitators" in the membership and because the post's commander was "very much active in the NAACP." This is a patriotic organization.

10. It is reliably reported that the leaders of the White Citizens Council have reached the conclusion that the bulk of the money furnished for the fight for Negroes' rights comes from Negro citizens who are required to pass examinations such as Plumbers, Barbers, Beauticians, Morticians, Electricians, Doctors, Lawyers, Teachers, Pharmacists, and the like, and that the effective way to destroy the NAACP and other organizations is to make it impossible for Negroes to pass these examinations and enter into and engage in the above professions and callings.

11. It is the plan of the reactionaries to whip the Negro into submission economically, and a part of their strategy is above indicated. These laws must be attacked in the courts on the grounds that they are unconstitutional. *It will require money to do this!*

## ⭐ E S S A Y S

The two essays in this chapter examine the leadership of the civil rights movement in Texas' two largest cities, Houston and Dallas. Merline Pitre, of Texas Southern University, emphasizes the local nature of the civil rights struggle. She describes how Lulu White of Houston confronted opposition both from within the leadership of the African American community and from white segregationists. Pitre also describes how national events and issues affected local movements. Yvonne Davis Freer, a doctoral candidate at Texas A & M University, argues that while there was a successful grassroots civil rights movement in North Texas under the direction of Juanita Craft, this movement was essentially a local manifestation of the national civil rights struggle and drew its strength from national events, especially the Supreme Court decision in *Brown v. The Topeka Board of Education.*

## Lulu B. White, the NAACP, and Launching the Fight Against Segregation in Houston

### MERLINE PITRE

Lulu White, female and civil rights activist, was a significant force in the struggle against Jim Crow in Texas during the 1940s and 1950s. A mobilizer, organizer, and foot soldier, White dedicated her entire life to fighting to dismantle the apartheid system in this country and used almost every means necessary to accomplish this

Merline Pitre, original essay drawn from Merline Pitre, *In Struggle Against Jim Crow: Lulu B. White and the NAACP, 1900–1957* (College Station: Texas A&M University Press, 1999). Reprinted by permission of the Texas A&M University Press.

goal. She led mass movements, delighted in controversies, and encouraged coalitions. Her name was far more likely to appear in a headline than a byline. Yet her role as a radical, black leader, as one of those giants on whose shoulders Barbara Jordan and other civil rights leaders have stood, has been obscured and ignored by historians. White's activities and positions with the NAACP, as well as her philosophy of integrating African Americans into the mainstream of American life is no less substantial for its lack of publicity. It is the purpose of this essay to provide a glimpse of the activities and ideologies that made White vulnerable to charges that she was a participant in the Communist conspiracy.

Born in 1900 in Elmo, Texas to Henry Madison, a farmer, and Easter Madison, a domestic worker, Lulu Belle Madison White, received her early education in the public schools of Elmo and Terrell, Texas. Following her high school graduation, she attended Butler College for one year before transferring to Prairie View College where she received a bachelor's degree in English in 1928. After her marriage to Julius White and teaching school for nine years, White resigned her post to devote full time service to the NAACP. In 1937 she became Director of Youth Council and field worker and in 1939, acting president of the Houston branch of the NAACP. In 1943, she was elevated to full-time executive secretary of the Houston branch, making her the first women in the South to hold such a post. Finally, in 1946, she was named director of state branches for the state of Texas.

In size and appearance, Lulu White presented a formidable image to confront the state of Texas. Standing five feet, six inches tall and weighing more than two hundred and fifty pounds, she was bold, brave, and loud, but also amiable, dignified, and respected by friends and foes alike. An acid tongued individual who was not afraid to speak her mind to powerful whites and to differing black factions, White combined political radicalism with the administrative skills needed to effect change. When milder techniques did not work, she became openly defiant. To many, she seemed exactly what the doctor ordered for the civil rights movement in Houston and in Texas during the 1940s and 1950s.

Lulu White's political sensibility was informed by a belief in racial equality and in federally protected citizenship rights. Guided by this philosophy, she was not hesitant about raising her voice on any issue pertaining to the civil rights of blacks. She publicly advocated the right of blacks to vote and to participate at all levels of government. She pushed for equal access to jobs and education. She defended the political and civil rights of blacks and complained loudly whenever anyone trampled upon them. In her various capacities with the NAACP, White increasingly adopted an outspoken, almost deliberately provocative style. Both her natural speaking talent and her defense of free expression reinforced her candor. The NAACP's legal success in breaking down racial barriers in the 1940s, the growth of its branches, an increase in the number of black organizations and liberal labor unions—all of these broadened the parameters of Lulu White's activism. Needless to say, White thrived on the activities of her office, as the city of Houston and the state of Texas offered new opportunities and challenges to those working to move the South beyond the politics of racial differences.

Upon assuming her post as head of the NAACP, Lulu White acquired firsthand knowledge of how deeply race prejudice was embedded in the American economic and political system. Moreover, she was cognizant of the fact that the NAACP had waged a two-decade struggle to garner support for an anti-lynching bill, all to no avail. She knew that although the white Democratic primary had been overturned via *Smith v. Allwright* (1944), there were still impediments to the black franchise, such as poll taxes. With these facts in mind, Lulu White reasoned that if blacks were to overcome such obstacles, assistance from other sources was imperative. They would need to unite or join forces with other groups with shared political and economic interests.

As Lulu White traversed Texas' racialized terrain and experimented with different groups, strategies, and tactics, she embraced organized labor, the leftist proclivities of the Congress of Industrial Opportunities (CIO) notwithstanding. For as she put it: "You take your friends where you find them." White's idea to coalesce with labor was neither novel nor original. Blacks and labor faced many common problems in the South during the first half of the twentieth century. The South was a stronghold of antiunion, antiblack and antifemale sentiments. Its powerful elected officials, from the local to the national level, defied the political winds of change that threatened to undermine the established order and way of life. Facing this reality, the national office of the NAACP and labor entered an alliance in 1941. This alliance was a marriage of convenience because blacks and labor were facing some of the same enemies—city halls, state legislatures, Congress, southern Democrats, conservative Northerners, western Republicans, and other individuals who saw the two as a threat to their jobs and the status quo.

With few exceptions, efforts to organize workers, white or black, remained extremely weak in Texas, including in Houston until 1930, at which time both the American Federation of Labor (AFL), a craft-oriented union, and the Congress of Industrial Opportunities (CIO) a semiskilled union, initiated a general campaign in Dixie. Prior to 1935, the International Longshoreman's Association, a separate affiliate of the AFL, conducted most union activities in the city involving blacks. After 1935, the CIO would be most visible in union activities among blacks. Between 1935 and 1945, the CIO was responsible for organizing blacks in several industries including workers in oil and sugar refineries, and in fruits and tobacco industries. CIO field workers proved especially effective in organizing black steelworkers at Hughes Tool Company, Sheffield Steel Company, and the Dedman Foundry. Through these industries, almost two thousand blacks had joined the United Steel Workers of America Local Union by 1945.

While these efforts of the CIO's campaign to attract formerly unorganized black workers would prove beneficial in the early 1940s, labor unions still posed a problem for blacks, whites, and the NAACP. Sometimes, black workers joined enthusiastically; but in other cases, they were skeptical and distrustful, as wisdom born from the bitter experience of discrimination had taught them. The CIO's interest in and activities with black workers impressed the NAACP, but the Association was hesitant to commit to a total alliance with the union because of the latter's alleged communist ties. Likewise, many whites opposed unions in general and the CIO in particular for its interracial character and Communist affiliation. To many white southern conservatives, the push for civil rights by the CIO and the NAACP was nothing more than a communist conspiracy. In their mind, both the NAACP and the CIO were communist—led, inspired, and dominated.

Because of this recurring Communist label, by 1945 the NAACP leadership began to wean itself from the CIO. This was not so, however, for Lulu White, who retained her relationship with labor and used the Communist threat to her advantage.

While White was willing and eager to say that she did not embrace Communism, she used the threat posed by Communism to press the NAACP agenda against racism and discrimination in the workplace. In a word, she became more visible and more vocal in her support of labor.

Through an association with a number of friends who were members, supporters, and organizers of union activities, Lulu White had acquired some knowledge of the labor movement in Houston and in Texas. Yet it was not until she became executive secretary that she acquired firsthand knowledge of the activities of the major unions, especially those of the CIO. White was impressed with the educational program of the CIO, a program that increased blacks' militancy by making them more desirous of waging the struggle for racial equality and less willing to tolerate gradualism. Administering this program was a CIO Political Action Committee (PAC), formed in the summer of 1943. The purpose of the PAC was to build a political machine rooted in the national network of local unions, and city and state industrial councils that embraced liberal, progressive, and civil rights activities. This PAC divided the nation into fourteen regional centers and organized branches in states, cities, and wards. Operating under the premise that organized, informed, and active voters were essential for meeting antiunion conservatives at the polls, the PAC had voter education and registration as the core of its activities.

These PAC activities went hand in hand with the civil rights movement in Texas and were very encouraging to Lulu White. The CIO union's campaign for voting rights was creative and wide-ranging, combining such activities as education, organizing, and publicity strategies. Partially due to PAC's campaign efforts in 1943, three powerful southern congressmen lost their house seats. Two lost their bid for reelection and Texas Congressman Martin Dies, Chairman of the House Un-American Activities Committee, withdrew from the race once he learned that the CIO PAC was campaigning against him. Recognizing their effectiveness, White utilized PAC members as teachers for the many citizenship classes that the local chapter NAACP sponsored before and after *Smith v. Allwright* (1944). Also, PAC aided union members in paying poll taxes and in sponsoring rallies to get out the vote in elections held after 1944.

Because Lulu White established a special bond with labor early in her career, it did not take much prodding for her to support the CIO-led United Steel Workers Strike of 1946 and the 1946 Houston Municipal strike engineered by the AFL. For Lulu White, to the extent that these and other labor unions protected all workers from discrimination by employers and raised the wages of lower paid workers, they advanced the interests of their black workers and furthered the cause of the NAACP in eradicating economic injustice.

By 1946, White had come to view the labor movement as a liberalizing force in the civil rights struggle, a force that could help bring the country nearer to the reality of democracy. Because she viewed the movement as a voice of domestic liberalism, White helped to organize a Houston Area Labor Conference on September 28, 1946. She was the only female on the program when the conference adopted resolutions that called for unity of labor; an end to Jim Crow schools, poll taxes, lynching; and the abolition of the House Un-American Activities Committee. The conference also adopted a controversial resolution calling for "World Peace and the Freedom of Oppressed People." This resolution literally raised the eyebrows of Gloster Current, national director of branches of the NAACP, who sent a memorandum to Walter White noting that the "Houston NAACP Labor Committee saw fit to take a position on foreign policy which paralleled that of Moscow. This is friendship and collaboration of USSR." Current commented further that the political orientation of several of these unions was obvious.

While the above resolutions expressed the philosophy of Lulu White, they do not shed much light on her active role in the labor movement. When viewed from the perspective that the labor movement among blacks in Houston was a combination of public spokesperson and network activators, rather than simply people following an articulate leader, one gets a better sense of Lulu White's activities in the movement. To be sure, White's effectiveness was closely connected to the work of advance men in the labor movement such as Richard Grovey, Sid Hilliard, Sidney Hasgett, Heman Sweatt, and Moses Leroy. These men worked publicly in organizing black workers and privately in negotiating with white employers for better wages and working conditions. They risked their reputations and livelihoods by accepting leadership roles in the fledgling labor movement, by informing Lulu White of the discrimination heaped on black workers, and by developing strategies with her that were designed to reach economic parity. Lulu White's sharp tongue and bold speeches made her widely popular with the labor movement. Yet she was essentially a network activator and gadfly for the movement. For example, in the elections of 1946, she posed the following question to many candidates: "Are you in favor of equal opportunity? Do you support organized labor? Will you support or oppose legislation planned to curb organized labor in our state?" Depending on the response given, White elicited support for or against the candidate.

Lulu White's pro-labor stance was probably magnified most during the summer of 1946 when the death of a black man gave rise to the largest mass protest demonstration that the city of Houston had ever witnessed. White and the NAACP converted the funeral for Berry Branch, killed by a white bus driver, into a rally, but used this occasion to denounce discrimination and to call for the need to build a coalition with labor. Blacks of all classes, as well as socialists, labor leaders and white radicals were there. Not only were all labor unions in the city present at the funeral, but representatives from the CIO and AFL participated on the program and served as pallbearers. What was interesting about this funeral was not that both of Houston's white newspapers carried stories about it, but that both branded Lulu White as an agent of the "red" movement.

At this point, the communist label seemed not to have bothered Lulu White, for she continued to stand up for labor. In response to strikes throughout the city and state, in 1947 the Texas legislature passed a Right to Work Act designed to curtail and restrict labor unions' activities. More specifically, this law denied public employees the right to bargain collectively. To add insult to injury, the state of Texas embraced the Taft-Hartley Bill that outlawed the closed shop but allowed a measure of union security. This bill called for a contract that required workers to join the union after signing a contract, as opposed to joining before employment. It also legalized the right to work by which states could forbid the requirement of union membership as a condition of employment. Additionally, the bill provided for a "cooling off" period for both sides before they resorted to strike. Labor leaders throughout the country denounced the law. Lulu White joined the chorus and made several speeches across the state, trying to garner support for its repeal. When she appeared in Galveston, to speak on this subject, Carter Wesley, who White had chided for supporting Taft-Hartley, reported in the *Informer* that "the Galveston Branch had been taken over by Communists like the Houston Branch." White shrugged off this allegation by saying these newspaper writers (including Wesley) and the FBI were present at the meeting at the urging of a "stool pigeon black woman who wanted to discredit [her]." In part because of such black critics as Carter Wesley, most whites interpreted Lulu White's support for labor as the work of outside agitators who were using White to surreptitiously change the economic order of this country. Hence, the Communist label would come to haunt White like a fire bell in the night.

To make matters worse, in June 1947, Arthur J. Mandell and Herman Wright, labor lawyers, added the civil rights struggle to their list of reforms in America and joined the local chapter of the [NAACP]. Needless to say, the membership of these radical, socialist labor lawyers was not greeted by instant jubilation in the black community. In fact, their membership attracted the attention of many members of the NAACP, especially those caught up in the anticommunist hysteria. But White responded to this criticism by noting again that in the struggle against Jim Crow, "you take your friends where you find them." Furthermore, at the time that Mandell and Wright joined the NAACP, Lulu White and Carter Wesley were in a bitter dispute over the integration of the University of Texas versus the establishment of a separate black University in Houston. White was opposed to creating another black university because in her opinion, "there could be no equality in separation." Wesley held just the opposite view—blacks could force the state to make separate equal and thus African Americans could have an institution of their own and still attend the University of Texas. Because White did not agree with Wesley on this issue, he began an unrelenting attack against her for what he called "Communist influence in the NAACP." In July 1947, he wrote in his *Informer* that "our NAACP [is] taken over by the infiltration of the Communists through the stupidity and nearsightedness of our leaders." In Wesley's opinion, these Communists were not merely allies of Lulu White, but they were dominating her thinking and aiding the formulation of policies. "They [helped] mimeograph sharp attacks against race prejudice and organized committees to go before City Council and protest discrimination. Our leaders think they are God," wrote Wesley.

Wesley would later admit that he did not know if White was a Communist, but that he knew the company she kept: "When a Communist is willing to go to Negro houses and drink liquor with them and call them by their first name, they know that as far as these white people are concerned, the race question is solved," wrote Wesley. Everyone in town knew that Lulu White and Herman Wright had established a close friendship, and that Wright was one among many whites who frequented her house and attended her twentieth wedding anniversary. Lulu White's history and demeanor indicate she that could hardly be accused of allowing anyone to do her thinking. Whatever White did, she did because it was what she wanted or because of her belief in integration, criticism notwithstanding.

While Wesley was making his allegations, the Federal Bureau of Investigation (FBI) was launching a concerted effort to monitor all black organizations and individuals whom it deemed as subversive. The surveillance of black Americans was established as part of the FBI's responsibilities during Franklin D. Roosevelt's administration, but it would intensify during the cold war era. Thus, in 1938, in the area of domestic intelligence, Roosevelt both expanded and encouraged the FBI to gather information on the activities of individuals labeled as subversive. In that same year, the FBI included a special Negro Question Category as part of its regular Communist infiltration investigations. One year later, President Roosevelt expanded the FBI's civil and criminal jurisdiction to include at least a cursory examination, if not a complete investigation of almost every type of civil rights case from voter registration to police brutality and lynching. For more than twenty years, the FBI and its director, J. Edgar Hoover, pursued these dual mandates at their own discretion, investigating the political affairs of black activists and organizations thoroughly, while treating civil rights investigations nonchalantly (if at all). Such was the fate of Lulu White and the NAACP.

In September 1947, the FBI sent out a circular letter to all its directors and field workers "to submit to the Bureau any information obtained from reliable and established sources indicating Communist infiltration, influence or connection of the local NAACP chapters." While admitting that the national office of the NAACP was not associated with Communist activities, the FBI was adamant that some local chapters were "under the direct influence of the Communist elements." Because of this belief, whether real or imagined, the FBI began a "dead file" designed for local chapters but entitled "Communist Infiltration of the National Office." Information contained in this file was sent to the attorney general's Loyal Review Board, which had been established to analyze the information and to make a determination if any of it was subversive to the government. Once such analysis was completed, the attorney general published a list of individuals and organizations that were deemed antigovernment. The list, published in December of 1947, named the Civil Rights Congress and all of its affiliates as antigovernment forces. One of the affiliates mentioned was located in Houston and had the same office and address as the Houston chapter of the NAACP.

The Civil Rights Congress was formed in April 1946 as a merger between two organizations, the International Labor Defense and the National Federation of Constitutional Liberties. According to FBI records, this organization was not "dedicated to the broader issue of civil liberties, but to the defense of individual Communists and the Communist Party, and controlled by individuals who were either members of the Communist Party or openly loyal to it." In December of 1947, the Civil Rights Congress put out a call for a legislative conference scheduled in Washington, D.C. on January 17–18, 1948. Members of the Civil Rights Congress asked Lulu White to sign the call for this conference, but she failed to respond. Nevertheless, when the flyer was sent out announcing the conference, White's name was listed as one of its sponsors. No doubt, this was one of the reasons why the local branch was viewed as an affiliate of the Civil Rights Congress.

Upon hearing and reading that the Civil Rights Congress was being linked to the Houston branch, Thurgood Marshall moved quickly to squash any speculations of the FBI. First, he contacted Lulu White, then relayed her reply to J. Edgar Hoover in order "to keep the record straight." "I have received the following report form our Houston Branch," wrote Marshall. "Neither at this time nor any other time has this office been affiliated with the Office of the Civil Rights Congress. It is true that they did hold about three meetings here about a year ago [but they are not part of the organization]." When Hoover replied and denied that the list had been sent from his office to the Dallas newspaper or that his office had anything to do with the compilation of the list, Marshall then responded in kind, either facetiously or naively saying, "I am happy to know that the listing does not appear in your file."

Evidence reveals that when Marshall requested that Hoover clear up this matter, he probably was unaware that Hoover had instructed a field agent to make a "very discreet check on the Pilgrim Building #228" the day after the Dallas newspaper published the subversive list, and instructed the agent "to furnish the results [to Hoover] telephonically." The agent reported his finding the same day he received the communiqué. There was nothing in the office to the effect that the Civil Rights Congress maintained an office in Houston. But "a check at the post office reflect[ed] that P.O. Box 1988 was rented on July 1, 1946. The application was signed by [an unidentified woman] who gave as her business address: Civil Rights Congress, 228 Pilgrim Building, Houston Texas . . . On the letterhead she is listed as the Temporary Executive Secretary." A further check showed that White had received two copies of the pamphlet, *The Southern People's Congress Program.* Throughout this investigation, Lulu White maintained that neither she nor the Civil Rights Congress was Communist, and that her association with any labor organization reflected her concern for civil liberties. So strong were the communist attacks from both whites and blacks that Lulu White could no longer ignore them. Responding to Carter Wesley's charge of her affiliation with Communists (Mandell and Wright), Lulu White wrote Gloster Current: "I have talked to Maceo about this Communist business. He told me that the NAACP did not ask persons to declare their party affiliation before they join the organization." In this civil rights movement, White was of the opinion that "Negroes are supposed to take friends where they find them."

To many, Lulu White moved even further to the "left" when she openly supported Henry A. Wallace's candidacy for president of the United States in 1948. Wallace, the Progressive Party presidential nominee, was a former Secretary of Agriculture in the 1930s and a former Vice President during Franklin Roosevelt's third term. The four individuals who ran for the presidency in 1948 were Republican governor Thomas E. Dewey, Democratic incumbent Harry S Truman, Progressive Party candidate Henry A. Wallace, and the anti–civil rights Dixiecrat candidate, Strom Thurmond. Neither Dewey's personality nor his campaign aroused enthusiasm among his supporters. As far as Truman was concerned, there were signs as early as 1946 that he and lost control of the economic and political situation in this country. Labor resented his reaction to the railroad strikes. Farmers attempted to roll back Truman's meat prices. Conservatives denounced his civil rights proposals, and his "Doctrine of Containment" outraged communist sympathizers in the North. Because of these views, the Progressives thought that their candidate, Henry Wallace, had a good chance of winning.

Between 1941 and 1945, there were few politicians more highly praised by the NAACP than Wallace. He was lauded for his stance on racism, poll taxes, and Jim Crow. Even when President Harry S Truman dropped him from the ticket, the NAACP still supported him. This situation changed, however, when it became apparent to the NAACP in 1948 that Wallace's candidacy would take black voters away from the Democratic party. Yet, a number of blacks continued to support Henry Wallace. Included were such notables as Lulu White, W.E.B. Du Bois, Lena

Horne, Roscoe Dunjee, Margaret Bush Wilson, Paul Robeson, and Gordon Hancock. For these individuals, Wallace's campaign represented a radical, forward-looking approach to solving the race problems and to bringing about economic parity in this country. Moreover, Wallace's platform included demands for a one-dollar per hour minimum wage, abolition of the poll tax, desegregation, repeal of the Taft-Hartley labor law, day care centers for working mothers, and opposition to the military draft.

The day after Wallace announced his candidacy, the pro-Wallace forces began working to establish a Texas Wallace campaign headquarters. This project came to fruition on March 21, 1948, when the Wallace for President Committee held its first state meeting in Austin. The organizers included Elvierto Bela of Laredo, Harriet Leary of San Antonio, H. K. Deuchare of Galveston, Pat Lunford of Baytown, and Herman Wright of Houston. There were reports that Lulu White was a party to this group, rumors which she denied. When the news media heard of Lulu White's alleged involvement with this group, all pandemonium broke loose. Many newspapers carried headlines such as "An NAACP Official Endorses Wallace." *The Austin American Statesman* reported that the "Director of the NAACP was elected Vice Chair of a Statewide Movement for Wallace." The hierarchy of the NAACP became very disturbed over this matter and called Lulu White's actions into question. White denied such involvements and asked these newspapers for a retraction. Never cast as a moderate, in writing to the editors of these newspapers, Lulu White made it clear that she did not endorse Wallace in her official capacity, but that she "reserve[d] the right to support the candidate of her choice in any election."

With her position made clear to the public and to the NAACP, Lulu White was active and visible in Wallace's two-day whistle stop tour of Houston on September 28 and 29, 1948. The first of these hectic days included a Wallace press conference, speeches by the candidate at radio station KPRC, at the Black Businessmen Club's luncheon, and at a tea in the home of Lulu White. Present at White's reception was Paul Robeson, black actor, singer, and a professed socialist, whose passport had been revoked. Already a thorn in the side of many white conservatives, White now became a menace to be reckoned with as a result of publicly supporting Wallace, embracing Paul Robeson, and holding a mixed audience reception at her home. White's position was undergirded by Wallace on the next day of his tour when he spoke to approximately four hundred persons—blacks and whites—at the Music Hall.

While in Houston, Wallace encountered many hecklers who threw omelets and eggs at him and almost forced him out of town. The newspaper account of his two-day visit could give one the impression that Wallace was a viable candidate, although he was only a Third Party candidate who stood no chance of winning. Although Lulu White supported Wallace, along with a small number of blacks throughout the country, there is no evidence that she persuaded other blacks to do likewise. She took a fearless stand on Wallace's candidacy because she believed that Wallace shared some of her views on bettering the conditions of "the common man and woman." In part, because of Wallace's campaign, Wesley's labeling of White as a communist, and her affiliation with several socialists, Lulu White's name appeared on the list of the House Un-American Activities Committee in 1948.

The indomitable Lulu White was not one to walk away from a struggle, and silently endured the pains of discrimination. She resolved to fight back, the Communist label notwithstanding. But her fortitude and courage were equally matched by the doggedness and cynicism of many of her critics, not the least of whom was

Carter Wesley. Wesley's constant bashing in his newspaper was enough to convince many blacks that in the struggle for civil rights, Lulu White's behavior had moved from disorderly conduct to radicalism. In his June 11, 1949 editorial citing yet another case of her flirtation with socialists, Wesley pointed out that Lulu White had joined forces with the CIO, the Civil Rights Congress, and the Texas Progressive Party in signing a petition to protest Judge Harold Medina's jailing of *The Daily Worker's* editor along with three socialists for contempt of court in a New York conspiracy trial. In Wesley's opinion, the actions of the petitioners did not result from spontaneous protest of aggrieved citizens, but were carefully orchestrated. Wesley was partially right in his assessment. Lulu White was an adept practitioner of coalition-building politics and would ally herself with almost any group if it would bring about political and economic parity for blacks. Her action in the above case, however, only fueled further speculation that she was doing the bidding of the Communists. Because of this incident, Carter Wesley again called for White's resignation as executive secretary of the Houston Branch. This time she acquiesced. She stepped down almost immediately after the publication of his editorial.

Even after Lulu White left the helm of the local branch of the NAACP in 1949, the FBI still followed her. In 1951 an informant reported that although she was no longer working in the office of the local chapter, Communist literature was still being sent to her at that address. In 1953 the same informant reported that Lulu White was not as active in the Communist Party as she had been in the past; and that she did not influence her successor, Christia Adair, who was described as anticommunist. In 1956, when students at Texas Southern University (TSU) staged a protest against Governor Alan Shivers, who was the guest speaker for the inauguration of Samuel M. Nabrit, the University's second president, Lulu White was listed by the FBI as the instigator of that activity. The field agent confirmed and enhanced this speculation by sending a newspaper clipping to the FBI director that carried the following headline: "New President Inaugurated: Shivers Ignores Pickets to Give T.S.U. Speech."

The TSU demonstration was a reaction to a speech made by Shivers against the Supreme Court's decision in *Brown v. Board of Education* (1954) and against his stance on the integration of schools in particular. A poll taken by the informant revealed that most of the student body at Texas Southern University favored the protest because of the governor's pro-segregationist stand. When Shivers arrived on campus on March 14, 1956, he met the protestors carrying placards that read "We want integration, not Shivers"; "Not anti-T.S.U., just anti-Shivers"; "Alan Shivers, you sent your boy to an integrated school, but why object to others." The local chapter of the NAACP, along with TSU students, supposedly staged this demonstration. But as Carter Wesley would later write: "Those on the inside knew that Lulu was the reason why the picketing came off. The people of the local chapter gave every indication of not wanting the picket to go forward . . . but Lulu consulted her lawyers and when told it would not be illegal to picket, she gathered her forces and went out to Texas Southern University." The demonstration went on without incident, but the FBI hounded Lulu White until her death.

There is no hard data to support the claim that White was a Communist. But as was true for many whites, the combined forces of the Great Depression, the New Deal, and World War II pushed black political activists and thought in a leftward direction. Like their white counterparts, a number of African American reformers were affected by Marxist and non-Marxist class theories. Neither the NAACP nor the Urban League was immune to the economic and political impulses of the thirties and forties. Within the ranks of both organizations were individuals who advocated a more militant course of economic action. Young intellectuals such as E. Franklin Frazier and Ralph Bunch held that an expanded federal authority in the economy required new strategies and a more radical response by blacks for a more comprehensive economic program. Made somewhat impatient by what she felt was the unwillingness of the federal government to provide blacks with equal economic opportunities, Lulu White turned to building coalitions with other groups of similar fate. What complicated her willingness to embrace an alternative economic perspective was her inclination to entertain an organized political struggle outside the traditional, legal, educational and personal lobbying tactics associated with the NAACP. But if the means she employed were different, her objective was the same as that of the NAACP: to force the government into extending and expanding the scope of its efforts to become more inclusive of African Americans. Lulu White's flirtation with alleged Communists in relation to her role in the NAACP was one of loyal opposition. There is no record to indicate that she tried to convince anyone to join the leftist cause. In fact, her husband's business venture would have militated against that course. Her association with individuals with socialist proclivities was sometimes used for coalition building. At other times, it amounted to little more than White's own personal protest when government policies appeared antithetical to black needs.

# Juanita Craft and the Struggle to End Segregation in Dallas, 1945–1955

### YVONNE DAVIS FREER

Until the middle of the twentieth century, Jim Crow laws defined race relations in the South and many of the border states. These laws and de facto practices of segregation in housing, public accommodations, transportation, politics, and education, denied most blacks the right to vote and restricted blacks to segregated, low-paying, unskilled jobs. In 1954, the United States Supreme Court handed down the landmark decision, *Brown v. Board of Education of Topeka*, 347 U.S.483 (1954), which brought an end to Jim Crow, at least in *de jure* form. *Brown v. Board of Education of Topeka* reversed the racist "separate but equal doctrine" handed down fifty-eight years prior in the *Plessy v. Ferguson* case. In 1896, the jurists in *Plessy v. Ferguson*, 163 U.S.537 (1896), held that racial segregation of public train passengers in separate but equal facilities complied with the equal protection clause under the Fourteenth Amendment. This decision served as legal justification of segregation in public facilities and accommodations until the Supreme Court ruled in the *Brown* case that mandatory racial separation contradicted the guarantee of equal protection

Yvonne Davis Freer, original essay based on "'The Fight Is On!': One Woman's Battle to End Segregation in Dallas, Texas, 1945–1965," a paper presented at the annual meeting of the Texas State Historical Association, Dallas, March 4, 1999. Reprinted with permission.

laws outlined in the Fourteenth Amendment. In short, the ruling held that the discriminatory laws that enforced the segregation of the races were unconstitutional, thus providing the legal basis of dismantling the system of Jim Crow laws.

The Supreme Court's decision in *Brown* energized the existing struggle against racial segregation in the United States. Blacks had struggled both in the political and legal arenas against segregation ever since the *Plessy* decision, but had not established a successful strategy to challenge racial segregation. African American leadership in the United States saw the *Brown* decision as the catalyst to end segregation in the public schools, one of the areas where segregation was most visible and most resented. Unfortunately, the end of segregated schools occurred all too slowly after the ruling.

Despite the 1954 court ruling in *Brown v. Board of Education,* segregation survived in Texas for a number of years. While the state's civil rights movement certainly was stimulated by the *Brown* decision, its origins predated that decision by several decades. For many years prior to *Brown,* the state's African American leaders concentrated their physical, emotional, and financial resources on efforts to gain racial equality through a statewide movement. Black leaders in most cities and counties in Texas challenged the degrading practices of segregation that undermined their basic constitutional and human rights. In 1954, the struggle escalated as the national civil rights movement gained momentum in the post-*Brown* years. African Americans seized the opportunity not merely to scale the walls of segregation, but to tear the walls down. With a national mandate and statewide momentum, significant political and social transformation in Texas was inevitable.

Texas African American leaders recognized the significance of the Supreme Court's decision and the opportunity it provided in their struggle for the total integration of the state's educational system. In the same year as the *Brown* decision, these civil rights leaders attending the General Convention of the National Association for the Advancement of Colored People (NAACP) outlined their long range plans for the fight for first-class citizenship at all levels. This struggle brought to the forefront already established civil rights leaders such as Lulu White of Houston, and Antonio Maceo Smith and Juanita Craft of Dallas. White, Smith, and Craft understood that segregation implied the inferiority of African Americans and that it restricted the educational, mental, and social development of the race. In the aftermath of *Brown,* the elimination of de jure segregation in Texas schools was no longer an unattainable dream, but a constitutional reality.

One woman who was particularly influential in the battle to end segregation in Texas was Juanita Jewel Shanks Craft. Craft had lived in Dallas for more than twenty-five years prior to the *Brown* decision, so she experienced firsthand segregation in all of its forms. She had attended a segregated high school in Austin, a segregated college in Prairie View, and experienced discrimination at her job at the Adolphus Hotel in Dallas. These experiences, as well as the Court's ruling and the burgeoning civil rights movement fueled the fervor that Craft brought to the struggle to end segregation in Dallas and to establish a more egalitarian social order. Her dream was a social order that would extinguish the racial caste system that had penetrated a significant portion of Craft's life and prevented African Americans from interacting with whites. Her struggle to achieve this dream began years before the *Brown* decision and continued throughout her life.

During the postwar years, Dallas rose to prominence as one of the nation's leading textile, technological, and financial centers, and the state's second largest city. Spread over 893 square miles with an estimated metropolitan area population of greater than 600,000, Dallas offered its population real opportunities in the economic, political, and educational arenas, but only if they were white. However for thirteen percent of the city—the African American population—opportunities in these areas were quite limited, not because of competition, but because of entrenched racial segregation and discrimination. Segregation was as fundamental to Texas's identity as the bluebonnet, the state flower. African Americans in Dallas suffered from segregation in the workplace, public accommodations, housing, and education. Although individuals of both races protested segregationist policies in Texas, the majority supported the system, arguing that it was easier and safer to establish and implement "separate" policies and facilities for the races than to integrate them. Despite this belief, key leaders in Dallas's African American community made significant strides to remove these antiquated barriers and move toward racial equality.

African Americans in Dallas concluded that the process of desegregation could only begin if they presented an organized and unified front and demanded that supporters of segregation recognize the legal and constitutional rights of African Americans. Juanita Craft, as the NAACP field organizer in Dallas, organized and led the struggle against segregation in Dallas. Craft joined the Dallas chapter of the NAACP in 1935, and by 1942 she had become instrumental in increasing the city's recorded membership to 1,200. Under her guidance, it grew to an amazing 7,000 members by 1946. This increase in NAACP membership reflected the unity among African Americans in Dallas as well as their commitment to confront inequality and racial injustice in Dallas through systematic organization. Craft's strident oratorical style at membership rallies infused the public with a desire for justice. Donald Jones, a local leader in Dallas, recalled that Craft's membership campaigns were "like a blood transfusion," that she invigorated individuals to join the NAACP in its campaign against segregation and for civil rights.

Craft's success in increasing the NAACP membership in Dallas provided her with a formidable army for the battle against segregation. Craft had lived under varying forms of segregation for most of her life and personally abhorred the institutional barriers that limited her access to the political, social, and economic benefits that Texas and Dallas had to offer. Reacting against her early years as a marginalized citizen, Craft emphasized action through activism. However, she recognized that the implementation of any action would take more than the efforts of one woman. Craft, along with Lulu White, executive secretary of the Houston branch of the NAACP, merged their energies and traveled thousands of miles throughout Texas on massive NAACP membership campaigns. Craft and White organized membership meetings, collected membership fees, and established local chapters. They employed the oratorical style of the pulpit and infused the masses they met, primarily at church meetings and voter registration drives, with the passion and courage to rebel against the stagnated structure of segregation and join in the fight for full civil rights. Their successful grassroots approach increased NAACP membership across the state and informed the new members about NAACP programs for equality in politics and educational opportunity. By garnering interest in the NAACP and increasing the membership rolls, Craft and White gathered the resources they needed to launch a well-organized and coordinated attack on the "old" segregationist leadership of the state and their bastions of racial injustice and discrimination.

To launch her civil rights campaign in Dallas, Juanita Craft joined forces with Antonio Maceo Smith, executive secretary of the Texas State Conference of Branches, NAACP. Craft and Smith understood that revitalization of the Dallas Chapter of the NAACP was essential to the successful promotion of its statewide efforts. Smith was instrumental in reviving the foundering state branches and worked tirelessly to encourage participation among African Americans in the state's political, economic, and civil rights affairs. Craft and Smith focused their initial efforts on securing public sector jobs for African Americans in Dallas. They reasoned that if members and potential members saw the NAACP achieve success in integrating public sector jobs, then they would commit their energy and resources to the civil rights struggle.

During the mid-1940s to early 1950s, Craft joined the NAACP in challenging racial discrimination in employment and education. The Texas State Conference of Branches of the NAACP targeted the inequity in teachers' salaries as their first point of attack. This was a moderate approach, which did not directly confront segregation, but which demanded equality in pay for black and white teachers and principals. In 1942, Craft allied with the Texas State Conference of Branches and the Dallas Council of Negro Organizations (DCNO), which consisted of about twenty other African American organizations in Dallas, to support a lawsuit against the Dallas school board for its racially biased salary structure. Prominent black civil rights activist and attorney William J. Durham, with the cooperation of the Texas State Conference of Branches and the DCNO, filed the civil action on the behalf of plaintiff, Thelma Page and the Negro Teachers Alliance of Dallas.

In the late 1930s, the African American teachers and principals in Dallas had organized to challenge salary discrimination in the Dallas public school system by forming the Dallas Teachers Alliance. By the early 1940s, the Alliance had raised a legal defense fund and after several special meetings agreed that it was time to enter into legal proceedings against the Board of Education, City of Dallas. William Durham and Thurgood Marshall, representing the NAACP legal team, argued for a summary judgment against the Board of Education for its system of salary discrimination. In a judgment rendered by the court in February 1943, African American teachers were granted salary increases designed to equalize pay over a two-year period.

The early judgment by the United States District Court for the Northern District of Dallas in 1943 forced an out of court settlement with a three-step plan. The key element of the plan that signaled victory for the NAACP and the DCNO was that one third of the amount needed for salary equalization would immediately be added to African American teacher salary contracts. The settlement forced the Dallas school board to pay African American teachers on the same scale as its white teachers. This victory set the precedence for other school districts in Texas to adjust their pay scales and pay African American teachers an equitable salary.

The success in getting the Dallas school board to equalize pay for black and white teachers encouraged Craft to seek additional changes, especially in education. Craft was appointed the advisor of the Dallas NAACP Youth Council in 1946. Although the primary purpose of NAACP youth councils was to act as social organizations, Craft organized the Dallas chapter to be active in the civil rights movement. She instructed the members about the importance of education and its connection to ending discrimination. In that same year, Craft organized the youth to raise money and picket in support of ending segregation in higher education. Heman Marion Sweatt, a Houston letter carrier, had applied for admission to the all-white University of Texas law school in 1946 and was denied admission based on his race. The University of Texas offered the best legal education in the southern region of the United States, but routinely denied admission to African American applicants. Initially, the state legislature tried to appease Heman Sweatt and provide legal education for blacks by establishing a law school at the colored Prairie View University. Then they created a makeshift school in a basement office building that was located blocks from University of Texas in Austin, and finally, in 1947 created the Texas State University for Negroes in Houston with a law school. Sweatt and the NAACP refused to accept a segregated law school and continued their suit against Jim Crow education. Again, William Durham and Thurgood Marshall directed the lawsuit.

Craft's grassroots involvement in the Sweatt case was effective. Youth Council members demonstrated and helped raise money for the NAACP's legal fees, and Craft used the struggle to educate them about the importance of confronting racial segregation in public higher education. Craft supported the tempestuous four-year battle to gain Sweatt's admission into the Texas law school because she believed that a truly first-class education was impossible in segregated facilities. Sweatt and the NAACP won their case June 6, 1950. The Supreme Court ruled that a black law student must be admitted to the all-white University of Texas because separate facilities for Negroes were inherently not equal. The Court's ruling paved the way for a series of education desegregation cases that would lead to the landmark *Brown* ruling and defiance of segregation.

The *Sweatt* decision may have ignited the embers in the battle against segregation, but it was the *Brown* decision that fueled the fire of interest and support for the civil rights movement. Craft's participation in the battle to end segregation increased as the problems of African Americans in Dallas escalated. The national push toward civil rights for African Americans confirmed to Craft that "there was a lot to be done." Craft disliked being discriminated against because of her color or her condition. She fervently believed that she and others of the African American race deserved an opportunity to participate fully and equally in all the rights and privileges outlined in the United States Constitution and that drawing arbitrary lines based on prejudicial traditions or opinions served only to strengthen injustice and discrimination. Unfortunately, proponents of segregation in Dallas did not share Craft's beliefs and they worked vigorously to maintain a segregated city.

The legal assaults for racial equality orchestrated by the NAACP were virtually ineffective as racial discrimination in Dallas continued unabated. The Dallas Board of Education refused to comply with the 1954 Supreme Court school desegregation order. The local chapter of the NAACP responded with a petition demanding that the school board immediately comply with the Supreme Court ruling. However, Dallas School Superintendent W. T. White refused to provide equal education for African American children and white children because, he argued, the Dallas schools operated solely under state legislation, not federal law. The obstinacy exhibited by the Dallas school system in refusing to end segregation filtered into other public arenas in the city. Retail stores in downtown Dallas refused to allow African American customers to try on clothing. The NAACP responded by peaceful protests and sit-ins, but was relatively unsuccessful in attaining speedy desegregation of the stores. Not until the early 1960s did most downtown department stores desegregate in Dallas, and then only to "promote a good national image of the city." Housing codes and localized acts of violence deterred African Americans from moving into in nonsegregated residential neighborhoods in Dallas. Housing for African Americans in Dallas was never a great priority of the city's leaders, but a restrictive process. Segregated housing patterns forced at least ninety percent of the African American population in Dallas to reside in South Dallas. Despite the legal maneuvers of the NAACP and federal legislation, most African Americans who could afford housing remained in the southern sector of the city for fear of being bombed, like several other African Americans who attempted to move into North or East Dallas. The only visible gesture to provide better housing for blacks was the development of Hamilton Park in 1954, a model, segregated residential housing community for those middle-class African Americans who could afford to purchase a home. Even though the outlook on ending segregation in Dallas looked bleak based on these setbacks experienced by the NAACP and other key African American organizations, Craft continued to commit herself to the struggle for equality.

As the struggle for civil rights continued, Craft continued to use her position as advisor of the Youth Council to involve African American students in the process of school desegregation. She continuously lectured the youth about their rights as Americans and the importance of ending segregation in Dallas and opening the doors of equal opportunity in politics, employment, and education. In 1955 she directed her attention to the desegregation of North Texas State College (now the University of North Texas). Joe L. Atkins, a member of the Youth Council and high school honor student, applied for admission to North Texas State College in Denton, Texas, approximately forty miles north of Dallas. Atkins, his mother, Mable Atkins, and Craft traveled to Denton to meet the school's president, James Carl Matthews and Vice President Arthur Sampley about Atkins' admission. According to Craft, a week later Atkins received a letter from the president of North Texas State University refusing to admit him because of his race. This correspondence from President Matthews blatantly violated the Supreme Court mandate in the *Brown* decision. However, President Matthews intended to avoid desegregation of his campus as long as possible, despite the Court's ruling. Joe Atkins responded to the letter by filing a lawsuit against North Texas State College for failing to admit him based on his race.

The Dallas NAACP legal team headed by U. Simpson Tate, a Howard University graduate and confidant of Thurgood Marshall, represented Atkins in his case. Tate filed an immediate motion to force North Texas to allow Atkins to be admitted for the fall semester. He also argued that the school violated the Fourteenth Amendment by admitting African American students only to the college's doctoral program, not its undergraduate and masters level programs. Counsel for the university replied to the injunction by stating that the campus was not prepared administratively or financially to address the needs of approximately two hundred or more African American students, especially since Texas Southern University and Prairie

View A&M University were available to this group. The order overruling Tate's request for an injunction forced Atkins to enroll at the integrated Texas Western College in El Paso so he would not lose a semester of study during the trial.

By late fall semester 1955, federal magistrate Judge Joe Sheehy in the Eastern District court ruled that North Texas had to admit Atkins without delay. Judge Sheehy ruled that North Texas had admitted many other white students to its campus without any administrative or financial difficulties since Atkins made application to the campus and that any further delay of admissions to African Americans directly violated the Fourteenth Amendment, the Supreme Court ruling in *Brown,* and subsequent desegregation cases. The permanent injunction rendered by Judge Sheehy ended the exclusion of admission to the university based solely on race. For Atkins, the judge's ruling was bittersweet, as he already was attending the integrated Texas Western College and did not wish to transfer. However, for Craft, the victory was sweet justice, because she had played an instrumental role in ending segregation in education and opening North Texas State College's doors to African American students.

Juanita Craft focused the public's attention on the inequitable treatment of African Americans because of segregationist policies and practices. Because of her own experiences with segregation and racial discrimination, Craft worked unselfishly to end segregation and to increase equal opportunities regardless of race. Her contributions stimulated by her participation in the NAACP, the *Brown* decision, and the burgeoning civil rights movement catapulted her into the mainstream battle for racial equality. In a ten-year span, her battles against segregation in Dallas pecked away at the bastions of exclusion and segregation. Despite deeply-rooted resistance to desegregation, Craft, along with others, continued to press for full integration in education, politics, housing, and public accommodations. *"The Fight is On!"* served no longer as a catchy membership slogan, but as an electrically charged statement of action. This statement of action would dominate the civil rights movement in Dallas well beyond the 1950s.

## EPILOGUE

Juanita Craft's vision and dedication to ending segregation in Dallas did not go unnoticed. On the national level she received personal invitations from Presidents Kennedy, Johnson, Nixon, and Carter to attend conferences focusing on the escalating problems among the nation's youth. The national office of the NAACP presented her with two major awards for her guidance in the Dallas Youth Council's fight against segregation. And locally in Dallas, Mayor Erik Jonsson invited Craft to attend several of the conferences, "Goals for Dallas."

Craft's continued interest in and love for her city pushed her into the political arena at the age of seventy-three. She ran for city council in 1975, winning over six opponents. Although critics chided her for her age, she resisted their verbal attacks and became the second African American female elected to the Dallas City Council. During her two council terms, she carried out her election platform of cleaning up the deteriorating inner-city areas of Dallas and revitalizing downtown Dallas.

Juanita Craft held what scholars identify as a utopian vision. She pushed for African American civil rights because she knew something was wrong and she "had to help change the system." The events that occurred during the civil rights movement were inevitable actions that Craft was able to use in her arsenal for the assault on segregation. Her involvement in the battles became infectious actions that encouraged youth and adults to envision a life that went beyond merely hoping for a desegregated society, to actively seize the opportunity promised by the Constitution. Craft believed in and insisted race relations improve in her city, so that racial tolerance and harmony was not an elusive goal, but a potential reality.

 *F U R T H E R    R E A D I N G*

Alwyn Barr, *Black Texans: A History of African Americans in Texas, 1528–1995,* 2d ed. (1996)

Howard Beeth and Cary D. Wintz, eds., *Black Dixie: Afro-Texan History and Culture in Houston* (1992)

Thomas R. Cole, *No Color Is My Kind: The Life of Eldrewey Stearns and the Integration of Houston* (1997)

Vicki Crawford, Jacqueline Anne Rouse, and Barbara Woods, eds., *Women in the Civil Rights Movement: Trailblazers and Torchbearers, 1941–1965* (1990)

W. Marvin Dulaney, "Whatever Happened to the Civil Rights Movement in Dallas, Texas?" in *Essays on the American Civil Rights Movement,* eds. John Dittmer, W. Marvin Dulaney, Kathleen Underwood, and George C. Wright (1993)

Michael L Gillette, "The Rise of the NAACP in Texas," *Southwestern Historical Quarterly* 81 (1978): 393–416

William Henry Kellar, *Make Haste Slowly: Moderates, Conservatives, and School Desegregation in Houston* (1999)

Robyn Duff Ladino, *Desegregating Texas Schools: Eisenhower, Shivers, and the Crisis at Mansfield High* (1996)

Ronald E. Marcello, "Reluctance versus Reality: The Desegregation of North Texas State College, 1954–1956," *Southwestern Historical Quarterly* 99 (1996): 153–185

Ernest Obadele-Starks, *Black Unionism in the Industrial South* (2000)

Merline Pitre, "Black Houstonians and the 'Separate But Equal' Doctrine: Carter W. Wesley versus Lulu White" *The Houston Review* 12 (1990): 23–36

———, *In Struggle against Jim Crow: Lulu B. White and the NAACP, 1900–1957* (1999)

William H. Wilson, *Hamilton Park: A Planned Black Community in Dallas* (1998)

Ruthe Winegarten, *Black Texas Women: 150 Years of Trial and Triumph* (1995)

# The Rise of the Republican Party and the Transformation of Texas Politics, 1960–2000

*The most surprising development in the late-twentieth-century Texas politics was the emergence of the Republican Party. Texas, once the home of "yellow-dog Democrats," did the unthinkable in 1978 when it elected the first Republican governor since Reconstruction; twenty years later, Republicans held all of the major statewide elected offices. The rapid political rise of George W. Bush to the governor's mansion in 1995 and then to the White House in 2001 symbolized the degree to which Texas politics had changed since the days of Sam Rayburn, Lyndon Baines Johnson, and Democratic Party political dominance.*

*The rise of the Republicans began when John Tower won the U.S. Senate seat vacated by Vice President Lyndon Baines Johnson in a 1961 special election. This was the first victory of a Republican in a statewide election since Reconstruction. However, there were precedents to Tower's surprising win. Texans had voted for Republican presidential candidates—Herbert Hoover in 1928 and Dwight Eisenhower in 1952 and 1956. But to many, these were aberrations. Some attribute this transformation to conservatives abandoning the Democratic Party as it turned liberal on the national level. In this scenario, the rise of the Republican Party in Texas was a reaction against civil rights, social welfare, women's rights, and gay rights. It signaled the capture of the party by the religious right and political and social conservatives, and was part of a political trend that swept the Sun Belt in the late twentieth century. Others believed that Republican ascendancy related to the failure of the Democratic Party in Texas. A succession of political missteps and economic disasters undermined confidence with Democratic leadership in the postwar period. The Sharpstown stock scandal, the savings and loan scandal, and the collapse of the oil economy undermined the political status quo. A deepening split within the party between conservatives and liberals, and demographic changes including the re-emergence of African American and Mexican American political strength destabilized the essentially conservative coalition that had dominated the party since the end of Reconstruction.*

*As dramatic as these changes have been, they have yet to attract much attention or analysis from historians or political scientists. Was this turnaround due to the failure of Democratic Party leadership, or were Republicans more attuned to the social and demographic changes affecting Texas in the last half of the twentieth century?*

## ❧ D O C U M E N T S

The first document examines the Sharpstown Stock Scandal, a complex blend of financial shenanigans and political bribery that rocked the Democratic Party in the early 1970s. *The Texas Observer*, a left/liberal political bi-weekly helped expose the scandal, which ultimately ended the careers of the governor, lieutenant governor, speaker of the house, a former Texas attorney general and U.S. Senate candidate, and dozens of members of the legislature—a generation of the leadership of the Democratic Party. Document 2 reports on the election of Texas' first Republican governor since Reconstruction.

The 1980s in Texas were characterized by a series of economic blows that had political implications. First the collapse of oil prices pulled the rug out from under Texas's oil-based economy. Then the peso devaluation created a severe depression in the Texas borderlands and hurt retail sales throughout the state. Finally, the savings and loan scandal ruined the Texas real estate market. Document 3 examines the crash in oil prices, while Document 4 discusses the impact of high profile bankruptcies on the culture of the state.

In the 1990s, the political impact of the events of the proceeding decades became clear. Documents 5 and 6 provide two assessments and explanations for political novice George W. Bush's shocking upset of popular Democratic governor Ann Richards in 1994. The first, an election analysis in *The Texas Observer* notes the disappearance of "yellow-dogs Democrats" (those Democrats who would vote for an old yellow dog rather than a Republican), and blames Richard's for running a poor campaign and voter realignment for the Republican's victory. The second, from the *Houston Chronicle*, attempts to explain the changes taking place in Texas politics. Document 7, a January 1998 editorial from the popular *Texas Monthly*, assesses the total collapse of the Democratic Party in Texas, accurately predicting the November election. In Document 8, the *Houston Chronicle's* political analysts attempt to explain the Republican sweep in the November 1998 elections.

## 1. The Sharpstown Stock Scandal Shakes the Texas Democratic Party, 1971

### The Plot

It all started, according to the SEC, back in June, 1968, when Frank Sharp acquired a publicly-held life insurance company, to wit, Olympic. This acquisition was financed by Sharp through a loan made in the name of his son-in-law. W. D. Haden II at SSB. Sharp's involvement in the arena of publicly-held companies was further expanded in July of 1968 when he acquired more than 50% of NBL. This company, which had a rather shaky history (it was once part of Billie Sol Estes' empire) was

---

Molly Ivins, "The Stock Fraud Scandal: The Plot—As Written by the SEC," "A Chronology," "The Cast of Characters," and "Bankers Life Blues," *The Texas Observer* 63 (February 12, 1971): 2–4, 7, 11. Copyright © 1971 by The Texas Observer. Reprinted with permission.

at the time Sharp bought it from Allan Shivers, a reasonably successful life insurance company. . . . After acquiring NBL, Sharp made Novotny a director of the company and a member of its executive and finance committees, along with Osorio and Stock. All three became trustees of the NBL Plan.

The stock of NBL Sharp acquired, some 519,000 shares outstanding, was issued in the name of SRC. When Shivers sold the company to Sharp, part of the contract stated that the stock was investment letter stock—not for resale. Soon after acquiring NBL, Sharp, acting through Novotny, Osorio and Stock, caused NBL to loan SRC $2 million. The collateral for this loan was 150,000 shares of SSB stock. Subsequently the Texas State Insurance Dept. indicated to the management of NBL that this was not a legal loan. . . .

Osorio, Carr and Novotny did agree to purchase control of SAC from Southeastern Funding Co., a Florida corporation. To accomplish this, Osorio, on behalf of Carr and himself, borrowed $500,000 from CB&T, secured by 220,000 shares of SAC stock.

Next the defendants had DB&T finance their ownership of CB&T. Bank regulatory authorities objected and the loan was moved to SSB.

This act and others by the FDIC caused Sharp to become dissatisfied with FDIC regulation. He therefore suggested to Osorio that a bill be introduced in the Texas Legislature creating a state-chartered insurance corporation to insure state banks. Osorio's and Carr's firm drafted the bill and it was introduced in the House in September, 1969, during the special session. Prior to the introduction of the bill, SSB loaned large sums of money to Tommy Shannon, who sponsored the bill, Preston Smith, Gus Mutsher Jr. and Sr., Elmer Baum, Rush McGinty and F. T. Schulte. The proceeds of these loans were used to purchase NBL stock from Ling & Co. through Adams. The bill was passed by the legislature on Sept. 9, 1969. On Sept. 11, 1969, Shannon, Mutscher, Jr. and Sr., McGinty and Schulte sold 39,800 shares of their NBL stock to the Jesuit Fathers at a profit of from $6 to $8 a share. On Sept.12, 1969, Smith and Baum sold a portion of their stock to the Fathers at a similar profit. The market price of NBL stock at this time was approximately $5 under the price paid by the Fathers. On Sept. 29, 1969, Governor Smith vetoed the bill.

## The Cast

### THE PLAINTFF:

SEC—The Securities and Exchange Commission, a federal regulatory agency established in 1934 to police stock transactions.

### THE DEFENDANTS:

NBL—National Bankers Life Insurance Co., chartered in Texas on June 13, 1945, and does business in several other states.

SAC—South Atlantic Corp., a Delaware corporation controlled by Waggoner Carr, John Osorio, Joseph Novotny and Frank Sharp. SAC was used as a holding company for stock of the Dallas Bank & Trust Co. (DB&T) and for stock of Ric International Industries, Inc, a publicly owned company formerly listed on the American Stock Exchange and currently the subject of a voluntary petition under the Bankruptcy Act.

SRC—(Sharpstown Realty Co.), . . . —all privately owned Texas corporations owned or controlled by Frank Sharp.

SSB—Sharpstown State Bank, chartered by the State of Texas. Approximately 80% of the stock of SSB was issued in the name of SRC, a holding company 100% owned by Sharp and his family.

Frank W. Sharp—chairman of the board of NBL and owner of 53% of the outstanding stock of NBL and of MCI. Controls Olympic . . . and; . . . Sharp controls Nashwood; . . . Sharp controls SAC through his control of SSB. . . .

Since November, 1967, Sharp has exercised control over and conducted securities transactions through the Jesuit Fathers.

John Osorio—until July 1, 1970, president of NBL, part owner of Nashwood and of SAC. Former insurance commissioner of Texas and former aide to ex-Gov. Allan Shivers.

Waggoner Carr—part owner of SAC and vice-president, director and controlling person of RIC. Former Texas Atty. Gen.

CB&T and DB&T—Dallas Bank & Trust Co. and City Bank & Trust Co. in Dallas are both bank-chartered by the state of Texas. They are controlled by Frank Sharp and owned by Nashwood due to a series of maneuvers that will make your head swim.

## SUPPORTING PLAYERS:

Preston Smith—Governor of Texas

Dr. Elmer Baum—friend and business partner of Smith, member of the State Banking Commission, chairman of the State Democratic Party.

Gus Mutscher, Jr.—speaker of the Texas House of Representatives.

Gus Mutsher, Sr.—father of Junior.

S. Rush McGinty—aide to Mutscher.

F. T. Schulte—same.

Tommy Shannon—chairman of the House Administration Committee.

Bill Heatly—chairman of the House Appropriations Committee.

Ben Barnes—Lieutenant Governor of Texas.

The Fathers—Jesuit Fathers of Houston, Inc., a non-profit corporation organized to construct and operate Strake Jesuit College Prepatory in Houston.

And a Cast of Thousands

## The Chronology

Gus Mutscher, Jr.,

> July 22, 1969—bought 10,000 shares of NBL at $13 a share.
>
> Sept. 11, 1969—sold 7,500 shares of NBL at $20 a share.
>
> Oct. 8, 1969—bought 17,000 shares of NBL at $20.50 a share.
>
> Nov. 10, 1969—sold 2,000 of MCI for $22,000 profit.

He said last week that his loss on the NBL shares he still holds is about $200,000.

Tommy Shannon:

> July 22, 1969—bought 4,115 shares of NBL at 11-1/8 a share.
>
> Sept. 11, 1969—sold 3,500 shares of NBL at $20 a share for a profit of $31,125.

J. S. Heatley:

    Aug. 4, 1969—bought 8,813 shares of NBL at 14¼ a share.

    Sept. 30, 1969—Sold 7,813 of NBL at 19¾ for a profit of $42,971.50.

Elmer Baum and Preston Smith jointly:

    July 25,1969—bought 20,000 shares of NBL at 13¾.

    Sept. 12, 1969—sold 14,000 shares of NBL at $20 a share for a profit of $87,500.

    Oct. 6, 1969—sold 6,000 shares of NBL at $20 a share for a profit of $37,500.

    Total profit: $125,000.

Elmer Baum individually:

    Oct. 6, 1969—bought 2,000 shares of NBL at 20½ a share.

    Oct. 31, 1969—sold 1,000 shares of NBL at 26½ for profit of $6,000.

S. Rush McGinty:

    July 22, 1969—bought 4,115 shares of NBL at 11-1/8.

    Sept. 11, 1969—sold 3,000 shares of NBL at 20 for profit of $26,625.

    Oct. 30, 1969—sold 1,646 shares of MCI at 5¼ a share for a profit of $8,641.50.

F. C. Schulte:

    July 22, 1969—bought 2,000 shares of NBL at 11-1/8 a share.

    Sept. 11, 1969—sold 2,000 shares of NBL at $20 a share for profit of $17,750.

All the politicians who sold their stock on Sept. 11, 1969 sold it to the Jesuit Fathers at approximately $5 above the quoted market price that day.

### The Score: Bankers Life Blues

There was a real sharp businessman
Who lived in Houston town
Who thought he'd help some legislators
Pass a bill around
He lended them some money free
To buy a stock or two
They, being public servants, rushed
To help their country through.
    Sellin stocks
    Is like stackin' blocks
    And if the blocks fall down
        Well I'll be darned . . .
        Who'da thought it . . .

And they did pass a law to help
Our friendly local banks
Although the law itself was writ
With certain empty blanks.
Just send your cash to Texas, folks
It's guaranteed just fine
By hindsight, P. T. Barnum,

And the lost San Saba mine.
  Golly gee
  Nothing is free
  But we're gettin' close . . .
      real close . . .

Now this sharp businessman did talk
Unto a Jes-u-ite
About the ways mysterious
That God moves towards the right.
He put a million dollars in,
The stock went on the skids:
The market was adjusted for
A thousand orphaned kids.
  Gosh, oh gee
  A new Theodicy
  About the ways of Preston
      Smith to man . . .

And they did get some astronauts
To front for that stock soon
Before you could shout "Countdown!"
It took off for the moon
And there it would be soaring still
Except but for the fact
That wholly innocent factors
Got into the act.
  Five Four Three Two One
  Liftoff is done:
  One giant step for
      Olympic Life . . .

The statesmen bought and sold their stocks
In a peculiar way
And they replied when asked "Well gosh,
It takes your breath away
To think this was accomplished
By sheer providence and chance
And gently guiding pressures
And the laws of happenstance."
  Casting dice
  Is very, very nice
  Statistics are
  A fellow's only friend . . .

The bets went off, the stocks went down
At one stride came the Feds
And now our Glorious Leaders hide
Beneath their glorious beds

Now and then they rise to say
They do not want out lip
But National Bankers Life Insurance
Is in conservatorship.
The whole world enjoys
   Good honest country boys
   Why, they was only funnin'
     . . . honest

Well now the story's ended
The moral's plain to see
If you don't like the stench, friend
Then sing along with me
Newsprint's soon forgotten
So's yesterday's t.v.
But what men sing they think about
Right on. In middle C.
   La la dee dum
   Ben, won't you at least hum!
   All together now . . .

Aristarchus of Samos

## 2. Charles Deaton Analyzes the Election of Republican Governor William Clements, 1978

In one of the *biggest political upsets* in Texas history, Republican Bill Clements has narrowly defeated Democrat John Hill in the governor's race. The 61-year-old multimillionaire oilwell drilling contractor from Dallas will be sworn in to a four-year term as the state's chief executive next January, the first Republican to occupy the Texas Governor's Mansion *in 105 years.* . . .

It is, of course, much too early to say what this all means for Texas politics in the future. It could, quite easily, become the single most important event in Texas politics in decades. The key to this is whether Bill Clements can use his gubernatorial powers to forge a strong and lasting Republican Party in Texas. If he doesn't, chances are pretty good that Clements will be remembered someday as nothing more than a footnote in the history books. If he does, though, it's likely that people will look back at this election as the real beginning of two-party politics in Texas. John Tower, after his victory in 1961, flew off to Washington to get involved in national politics, returning to Texas every six years to run as an incumbent, not as a Republican. He was, as something of a political curiosity, always more interested in self-preservation than in building a strong Republican Party. Indeed, some Republicans argued that he didn't really want any other Republican stars, since they would only draw Republican support and campaign dollars away from him. At any rate, he was never involved much in Texas political wars, preferring to remain above it all in Washington.

From Charles Deaton, "The Republican Upset!" *Texas Government Newsletter*, vol. 6, no. 38 (November 13, 1978), 1–2.

Clements, on the other hand, will be in a position to do some real foundation-building for the party. Over the next four years, he'll have the opportunity to put some 4,000–6,000 Republicans into various state appointive offices, thereby creating a strong core of publicity-generating Republican leaders, all with a vested interest in keeping the party victorious. This, in turn, will likely attract more and more people into the party, since their will at last be tangible rewards for those who become known as movers and shakers in Republican circles. If Clements and his cadre of officeholders perform creditably and do things like reducing spending and cutting state taxes, then the voters will probably not hesitate to return them to office.

Clements will also be in a position to make his party's influence felt in the Legislature, something that hasn't happened much in years. The Republicans, for example, would like to have another presidential preference primary in 1980, something that proved disastrous for conservative Democrats in 1976 when thousands of Texans ignored the Democratic primary to go vote for Ronald Reagan in the GOP primary. . . . And just consider, if you will, what will happen in 1981, when a Republican governor has veto power over the Democratic legislature's attempts to redistrict the various legislative districts after the 1980 census. Just the threat of his veto should be enough to prevent any blatant anti-Republican gerrymandering, a rather normal fact of past legislative wars.

## 3. *Time* Reports the Collapse of the Oil Industry in Texas, 1982

It was not a moment of pride for Texas, or for Republican Governor William Clements, who is in the midst of a tough re-election fight. Growing layoffs have brought the state unemployment compensation fund to the edge of bankruptcy. Clements last week was forced to summon a special session of the legislature to bail out the fund. . . .

Democrats, who control both houses, went along with the deal, but not before having some rhetorical fun at Clements' expense. . . . Clements' opponent in November, State Attorney General Mark White, noted that the incumbent "has the dubious distinction of being the first Governor in the Southwest to preside over the bankruptcy of a state unemployment compensation fund, and this is a disgrace." . . .

At long last the recession has caught up with a state that had seemed immune to the general economic malaise. A year ago the major industrial cities of Texas were meccas for workers from the Midwest who migrated south in search of jobs. In August, the state's unemployment rate was 7%—significantly; below the national average of 9.8%, but up from last December's 4.6%. Today labor leaders are warning would-be immigrants not to consider Texas as a new home unless they have jobs solidly lined up.

A major factor in Texas' new economic blues has been depression in the energy industry. A worldwide glut of crude has brought a sharp drop in oil prices, killing incentives to drill new wells. The number of active drilling rigs in the state has dropped 40% since December, and refineries and petrochemical plants in the state's eastern counties have been operating at about 70% capacity for at least a year. In the Houston bankruptcy court, 98 energy-related companies have filed for Chapter 11 protection so far this year.

In the East Texas town of Lone Star (pop. 2036); the Lone Star Steel Co. shut down last month, laying off 3,500 workers. Nearly 75% of the town's residents work at the plant, and most of the others are employed by firms that depend on the factory, which made tubular steel for oil pipes. But when no one is drilling, no one is buying tubular pipes. . . .

Says Dale Crumbaugh, a labor-market analyst for the Houston branch of the Texas Employment Commission: "Blue-collar workers tied to the oilfield industry are the ones suffering the most from layoffs here." . . .

Other events beyond the control of Texans added to the economic gloom. Spring rains and hail caused an estimated $686 million damage to cotton and wheat crops in the state. The threat of bankruptcy in Mexico and last month's devaluation of the peso sent shoppers south of the border in search of bargains, thereby bringing stores in El Paso and other cities along the Rio Grande to the edge of insolvency. Joe Castro, manager of an El Paso camera store, says the devaluation cut his business 50%. . . .

The persistent economic troubles should help Democrats at the polls in November, but the experts are not sure how much. State Democratic Party Chairman Robert Slagle advises that the anger of the unemployed may not automatically translate into an anti-Republican tide. "It's hard to gauge what people will do who lose their jobs. You wonder if they'll vote at all."

## 4. *Newsweek* "Laments" the Demise of the Texas Millionaire, 1986

There was a certain sameness when news of another Texas bankruptcy came over the radio in Leon Adams's black Chevy pickup one morning last month. "Here we go again," thought Adams, owner of the Acme Rubber Stamp Co. in downtown Dallas and victim of 12 customer collapses so far this year. But this one turned out to be no mere replay, for it illustrated to Adams that "nobody's too big to crash and burn." Placid Oil Co., the corporate cornerstone of the Hunt brothers' fabled empire, had gone to federal court to seek protection from its creditors. Acme Rubber Stamp was among them. Strip away the labyrinthine finance and the legal technicalities, and what's left is an irony both humble and immense: Bunker Hunt, regarded as the world's wealthiest businessman in the 1970s, now owes Leon Adams $67.71. And Adams, whose storefront firm employs four people, is writing it off as a loss. . . .

*There was a time Texans believed you could turn dirt into diamonds and one of the reasons was the old man, H. L. Hunt, the most successful of all the maverick wildcatters, now dead a dozen years. . . . He went broke more than once, but H. L. finally managed to turn a $5,000 inheritance into a fortune that grew to $4 billion. He led a life of bigamy, gambling and such unbridled success in the oil patch that Texans, notes historian T. R. Fehrenbach, were left with a grudging sense of admiration for this man no one ever called nice. . . . His 12 living children by three different wives*

Daniel Pederson, "The Fall of the Texas High Roller," *Newsweek*, September 29, 1986, 28–29. Copyright © 1986 Newsweek, Inc. All rights reserved. Reprinted with permission.

*divided the estate, but sons Bunker, Herbert and Lamar inherited the mantle and mission: invest in tangible goods—oil, land, silver—rather than less controllable stocks or currency. After H. L.'s death, that messianic faith in commodities caused the brothers' holdings to soar to $12 billion by 1980. But that year their abortive attempt to corner the world's silver market began a so far uninterrupted decline.*

The neighborhood of Highland Park is Dallas's old-money enclave. . . . The fellow who owes Leon Adams $67 wasn't talking about his troubles last week. But his next-door neighbor for the past two decades, H. R. (Bum) Bright, confesses that the cratering of large Texas fortunes. . . . isn't helping the neighborhood or his state of mind. "It's just made me more wary, more apprehensive, more attentive to my own business"—which includes lead ownership in the Dallas Cowboys bought two years ago from Clint Murchison Jr., heir to another epic Texas fortune that has gone down the drain.

*Chapter 11 is a slow kind of dying. Clint W. Murchison Jr., the man who first brought "America's Team" to town, awaits from a wheelchair the final impact of the bankruptcy he declared 19 months ago. In 1983 Forbes magazine had estimated his net worth at $350 million. Under terms of a reorganization plan approved in court last June, Murchison will emerge with roughly $3 million left—the value of his 43,000-square-foot home which sits on the market in a moribund Dallas economy. Murchison's overextension in highly leveraged real-estate deals had only been the natural extension of his wildcatting father's most famous words: "Money is like manure. If you spread it around, it does a lot of good. If you pile it up in one place, it stinks like hell."*

That dictum was Texas's as much as it was Murchison's. "What's happening to the Hunts and the Connallys is a macrocosm of what's happening all across the oil patch," notes Bernard Weinstein of the Center for Enterprising at Southern Methodist University. The highly inflationary decade of the '70s encouraged heavy debt and a commodity-based investment strategy. In Texas, benefiting at the time from a commodity economy, the strategy fit perfectly with the never-blink, high-rolling mentality ingrained in the culture. . . .

As the old mystique evaporates, some Texans argue that a massive jolt in the world economy may yet restore the state's commodity-driven power. More contend that a new kind of entrepreneurial energy will have to replace it—"Look at Ross Perot" Texas's self-made, computer-age man, being the most common rallying cry among the latter. If that view is correct, Texas won't be manufacturing any more H. L. Hunts. . . . Another way to put it is Texas has finally lost its innocence and what lies ahead is a more mature—and far blander—future.

## 5. *The Texas Observer* Proclaims the Death of the Yellow-Dog Democrat, 1994

Reports of the death of the Democratic Party in Texas may have been somewhat exaggerated but the Yellow Dog, if not dead, at least is a sick puppy. Republican businessman George W. Bush in the recent general election routed Democratic

James Cullen, "Sick Yellow Dogs," *The Texas Observer,* 25 November 1994, 7–10, 21. Copyright © 1994 by The Texas Observer. Reprinted with permission.

Governor Ann Richards, despite her personal popularity and the generally positive trends in the state, Lieut. Gov. Bob Bullock, Attorney General Dan Morales, Comptroller John Sharp, Land Commissioner Garry Mauro and Treasurer Martha Whitehead, all Democrats, managed to win re-election and Democrats maintained majorities in the state House and Senate, albeit with the traditional tilt toward business interests in both chambers. Still, Republican victories in races for agriculture commissioner, two railroad commissioners' seats and five benches on the Texas Supreme Court and Court of Criminal Appeals are proof that no Democrats can take re-election for granted.

Bullock claimed the title of the state's most popular official, gaining 2,629,497 votes, or 61.5 percent of the total, just ahead of Senator Kay Bailey Hutchison, a Republican who got 2,601,733 votes, or 60.8 percent of the total, and Agriculture Commissioner Rick Perry, a Republican who won a second term with 2.5 million votes, or 61.9 percent.

Critics generally agreed that Richards botched her re-election campaign by allowing Bush to define the issues and failing to present a clear vision of her plans for a second term. The impact of Bill Clinton upon Texas Democrats was harder to gauge. While a poll the week before the election found the President's approval rating in Texas at a tepid 38 percent, Tex Lezar was unable to hang Clinton around Bullock's neck and Greytok was unable to unseat Mauro despite the fact that the Land Commissioner reportedly had stretched state ethics rules when he ran Bill Clinton's Texas primary campaign out of his state office.

Texas counted about 450,000 more voters than in 1990 and they were almost all from Republican areas. Richards carried Central Texas and South Texas while Bush swept other areas of the state. . . .

The poll by Blum & Welpin Associates Inc. of New York found that 44 percent called themselves Republicans or Republican-leaning independents; 34 percent called themselves Democrats or Democrat-leaning independents; and 18 percent were independents. Richards got substantial support from black and Hispanic voters, as exit polls showed 76 percent of the Latino vote and 88 percent of the African-American vote went to the Democrat. The four Lower Rio Grande Valley counties voted 63.1 percent for Richards but other exit polls indicated that almost a quarter of the Texas voters who supported Richards in 1990 shifted their vote to Bush this year. . . .

"She ran such a poor campaign you just wonder what in the world was going on while [Bush] ran a textbook perfect campaign." Polinard said. Bush put Richards, the incumbent, on the defensive and he governed the pace of the campaign as well as the issues. " They almost had no passion in her campaign until the last week or so and the emphasis on attacking his business record, although I understand her focus groups showed movement with that, didn't motivate people to get out and vote," Polinard said.

"It's just unprecedented in my experience to have a candidate with an almost 60 percent positive rating, with a moving economy and crime down three years in a row, with no personal scandal around and immigration wasn't playing here like it was on the two coasts; it was inexplicable why those things could not be reduced to 30-second sound bites." . . .

"I think you can still see Democratic strength in South Texas while Republicans do awfully well in the ring counties around the big cities," Murray said, "but we still see the confirmation of the pattern that's been developing over a quarter-century, where the Republicans have strength with white suburban voters and the Democrats have strength with the minorities, and the rural and small-town whites tend to be up for grabs. They went Republican in '94." . . .

**What Next?**

The Democratic party has to make some changes to appeal to the Texas electorate, but talk about realigning the party on the left is "suicidal thinking," Polinard of UT-Pan American said. The Texas Poll has consistently found less than 20 percent of Texas identify themselves as liberal. . . . "One rule that still does hold is who captures the center holds the winning hand, I don't think the Democrats should ignore the traditional Democratic constituency but you don't want to be isolated and six out of every 10 [white] men are voting against you."

## 6. The *Houston Chronicle* Explains the Political Realignment in Texas, 1994

Austin—Gov. Ann Richards' two biggest political legacies likely will be that she pioneered women's elections to statewide offices and that she was the final outpost in almost 120 years of Democratic dominance over Texas government.

As the smoke cleared from Richards' defeat Tuesday by Republican George W. Bush, it was clear the political landscape of Texas had changed dramatically from when Richards first won election as state treasurer in 1982.

Richards was the only woman on the ballot in her 1982 statewide race and the first to win state office in 50 years.

But on Tuesday, Democratic and Republican women up and down the ballot won and lost races for statewide offices, including U.S. Senate and the Texas Court of Criminal Appeals. Two Democratic women and four Republican women will now hold statewide office.

And for the Republican Party, the election marked a dramatic change from the year Richards first came into office, when U.S. Sen. John Tower was the only Republican holding statewide office. After the oaths of office are taken in January, Republicans will hold almost half of all statewide offices and control of the Texas Supreme Court, Railroad Commission and State Board of Education.

Republicans also are bragging that Bush got 37 percent of the traditionally Democratic Hispanic vote.

Bush also broke the lock on Democratic East Texas by more than 158,000 votes. He won five East Texas counties that had never voted Republican in a governor's race: Bowie, Hardin, Harrison, Shelby and Titus.

Down the ballot, Republicans won county judgeships in rural conservative counties like Wilbarger and Van Zandt counties in North Texas and took control of the Bexar County Commissioner's Court.

---

Republicans now also hold all three of the state Senate districts along the Louisiana border.

"I don't even think at the height of Reconstruction did Republicans hold every Senate seat from Texarkana to Beaumont," said Republican consultant Karl Rove.

Republican Party Executive Director Gary Bruner predicted Texas will by Republican by the year 2000.

"In the past, the Democratic Party had a conservative wing and a liberal wing. The conservative wing is gone," Bruner said.

"If you are a conservative in Texas and share conservative values, the only home you have is in the Republican Party."

But Democratic Party Chairman Bob Slagle said the election just proves Texas has become a two-party state that either party can win.

"Most Texans move back and forth on that ballot and look for people they know of," Slagle said. "The days of electing people who don't have able-person characteristics are gone for both parties."

One of the biggest questions for both parties is what will happen with the state's fast-growing Hispanic population.

While Hispanics traditionally have been one of the core Democratic constituency groups, there has been a growing tendency among younger, more affluent Hispanics to vote Republican.

Rove said tracking polls conducted by the Bush campaign found 37 percent of Texans with a Hispanic heritage were planning to vote for Bush.

Rove said the tracking polls found that Democrats were still strong among Hispanics living in the Lower Rio Grande Valley. But he said Republicans are making gains among "middle-class Hispanics" who live in "heavily integrated neighborhoods" in Houston and the Dallas-Fort Worth area. . . . .

[Southwest Voter Research] Institute Director Robert Brischetto said higher income Hispanics do tend to vote more Republican. But he said they make up a small group of the total Hispanic population.

Brischetto said continued growth of the state's Hispanic population should help Democrats. . . .

While the future of the Hispanic vote remains in question, Republicans definitely are benefiting from rapidly growing activism among the state's religious right.

Burner described the Christian Coalition as a "key ingredient" in the Republican victories.

"They were very instrumental in providing key grass-roots support," Bruner said. "They printed voter guides and encouraged voters to vote early."

Slagle also described the religious right as effective.

"A lot of their work showed up in the early vote totals, and a lot of their work showed up in the state board of education," Slagle said.

At least three Republican State Board of Education candidates won their elections with the backing of Christian conservatives. . . .

Dick Weinhold, president of the Texas Christian Coalition, said his organization does not support candidates of either party but tries to inform voters about how candidates stand on moral issues.

He said the Christian Coalition put out 2.3 million voter guides.

"Our whole purpose is to encourage Christians to be involved in the process of government," Weinhold said.

Weinhold said a speech that Richards delivered to the State Democratic Convention in June against what she called the "radical right" probably had as much to do with stirring up Christian voters as the coalition's voter guides.

"One thing that came through loud and clear is anti-Christian bigotry does not work," Weinhold said. "Ann Richards' attack . . . did more to energize Christian voters and Roman Catholics than anything I could have done."

Exit polls showed almost a quarter of the state's voters said family values and morality were among the top issues that motivated them to vote in this election. Voters who said that overwhelmingly supported Bush.

Texas arguably has been leaning toward the Republican Party for more than two decades.

President Richard Nixon's re-election landslide almost carried Republican Henry Grover into the governor's office in 1972. Democrats responded by moving the governor's race to nonpresidential years.

Many Republicans believe Texas would have gone Republican in 1990 if it had not been for the gaffe-prone campaign that Clayton Williams ran against Richards.

Republican political consultant Mark Sanders said now that angry voters have swept many of the Democrats out of office, it is time for the often-critical Republicans to put up or shut up.

"If the Republicans who got elected this time don't deliver, they'll be kicked out of office just like the Democrats were," Sanders said. "George Bush carries the weight of the future of the Republican Party in Texas on his shoulders."

## 7. The *Texas Monthly* Assesses the Collapse of the Democratic Party in Texas, 1998

At least Dan Morales knew that the mere proclamation he was going to have a press conference was not likely to stop the world in its tracks. The night before and all that morning, some supporters, as well as the attorney general himself, were busy calling around to say that at the press conference Morales would announce the startling news that he would not run for reelection. The calls worked well enough. The room at the Capitol was overflowing well before Morales' scheduled appearance at noon. The daily press was there, as well as others, such as myself, who had come just to be present at what could be a small, improbable but still significant historic event. Morales entered the room suddenly, announced he would retire to private life at the end of his term, and made December 2, 1997, the day the Democratic party of Texas finally collapsed, not with a bang but a whimper.

Morales said he had decided not to run so he could spend more time with his new wife and her two children, who were standing beside him. The four presented such an appealing picture, it was reasonable to take him at his word. After all, he

Gregory Curtis, "The Last Whimper," *Texas Monthly,* January 1998. Reprinted with permission from Texas Monthly.

had never seemed to burn with political ambition. Even though he had won three terms as a state legislator and two as attorney general, he always seemed remote, even uncomfortable as a politician. He is not a party man is the classic mode, nor is he a bold, charismatic politician. Even so, he has never lost an election, he enjoys a 69 percent approval rating as attorney general, he is honest and free of scandal, he is a Hispanic with a Harvard law degree, and he is only 41 years old. The Democrats, who had never completely embraced him, suddenly realized with his leaving that they had lost the strongest candidate they had.

This fall the Democrats will have no incumbent seeking to retain his statewide office. . . . But the carnage does not stop there. The state Senate already has a Republican majority. The House now has 82 Democrats and 68 Republicans. A shift of just eight seats leaves Republicans in control. . . . Both U.S. senators are Republican, and thirteen out of thirty members of Congress are Republican, almost a majority. In 1996, more people voted in the Republican primary than the Democratic.

It has been a truism for several years that contemporary Texas is more a Republican state than a Democratic one. That seemed a natural enough evolution. Conservative Democrats, who had ruled the Southern states since Reconstruction, were giving way to Republicans throughout the South, including Texas. But now the rout is so complete it's not enough to say that the times have changed. The Democratic party is so weak that Morales' exit, which just a few years ago would not have left a scratch, now appears to be a mortal wound. What happened?

It's clear that the pinnacle of the party in Texas was the three 2-year terms of John Connally from 1963 to 1969. During most of that time, Lyndon Johnson was in the White House. On the whole, Connally was an effective and farsighted governor, sophisticated rather than provincial. Then came four years of Preston Smith and six years of Dolph Briscoe. They were neither effective, farsighted, or sophisticated, although they were provincial. They were nice enough fellows, and a quarter century later it's easily to be amused by their idiosyncrasies. Smith liked to shoot pool in local halls and often answered his own phone. At least the call got answered. Briscoe's office was a black hole that never got organized enough to answer mail routinely. Both governors were incapable of understanding the intricacies of power, and during Smith's terms, corruption flourished. Nor could they recognize and attract people of ability and situate them to assume major roles when the time came. And what most needed to be done—to create and communicate new goals, ideas, programs, philosophies for the state party so that it stood for something— they were most incapable of doing.

Then came Billy Clayton and Gib Lewis. Clayton was Speaker of the House from 1975 to 1983 and Lewis was Speaker from 1983 until 1993, a total between the two of eighteen years in power. Those years included the most difficult economic period for Texas since the Depression. They saw the election and subsequent reelection of the first Republican governor since Reconstruction. Instead of finding this a spur to action, they took their own long years in office as a sign that the basic politics of the state would never change. Nor would it ever need to change. For almost two decades they embraced and rewarded a system of wait your turn, go along to get along in the Legislature that stopped the ambitious and talented dead in their tracks. New blood could not get ahead by hard work and ability—that is, on merit—but only by being in line behind whoever had gotten there first. That created an ossified party rather than a dynamic one. One Democrat who was unable to find an outlet for his talent and was unwilling to wait is Rick Perry, the Republican agricultural commissioner who is running now for lieutenant governor. He came to the Legislature during those years as a Democrat. But he could make no headway as a Democrat, so he switched parties and quickly became a statewide political figure. Speaking privately about the switch, he said that the Democrats didn't seem to want him, though the Republicans did.

Since John Connally there have been exactly four Texas Democrats of the first rank. Two, Bill Hobby and Lloyd Bentsen, were the sons of established families with histories of prominence in business and politics. The other two, Barbara Jordan and Ann Richards, were women without family wealth or connections who rose by their own abilities and personalities. As a group, they represent the party at its best—a solid traditional legacy of welcoming and encouraging the common citizen of any race or gender.

The first three spent most of their political life while the party was still strong. Ann Richards, elected governor in 1990 in what seemed a certain Republican year, was in a perfect position to reformulate the party by returning it to its roots. She talked the talk by proclaiming a New Texas. But it didn't happen. As governor she had the opportunity to appoint a U.S. senator and a railroad commissioner. These appointees would then have the advantage of running for reelection as incumbents. These appointments were the perfect opportunity to catapult a rising star into prominence and strengthen the party in future elections. She chose Bob Krueger for senator and Lena Guerrero for railroad commissioner; both miserably failed to hold the office. Nor did state government in Austin see the arrival of fresh, new talent with fresh, new energy and ideas. Richards was a symbol, not a woman of ideas. As a symbol, she could attract people to herself but she could neither attract nor choose people with staying power in the Democratic party.

Referring to the Republican dominance of the state at his press conference, Dan Morales said, "I don't think it's good for the vast majority of elected officials in Texas to come from one party." This is just what Republicans used to say not so long ago, when the Democrats controlled Texas completely. But any single party that controls Texas sleeps uneasily. Texas Democrats were one party in name only. The fights between the conservative and liberal wings were spectacular and bitter. Again and again the conservatives had to rally their troops to win in the primary only to have to placate the liberals and minorities enough to defeat the Republicans in the general election.

A similar division exists among the Republicans between the social and religious conservatives on the right and the moderates in the center. The Republicans will have to follow the same pattern of defeat and conciliation to win since, just as a liberal cannot win a statewide race in Texas, neither can a candidate of the far right. The Democrats might win a race or two next fall simply because the Republicans, who are new at this specialized political game, could lose their way in these often intricate maneuvers.

But the Democrats will never return to power by hoping for the Republicans to beat themselves. Now it's the Republicans who seem to have the depth to produce promising candidates and a platform that appeals to Texas voters. During her time in office, Ann Richards said, speaking of democratic institutions, that Democrats need to "bring them into a new decade that requires new thinking and new resolutions. . . . There is a way to make it work, but we have not found it yet." Unless they do, the Democrats could lose every statewide election, and it will be the end of the hundred years of Democratic domination in Texas. Republicans could control Texas as long as the Democrats did, and the Democrats will have nothing to do but learn, as the Republicans had to, just how long a century really is.

## 8. The *Houston Chronicle* Explains the Republican Sweep, 1998

Austin—Optimism, believe it or not, infected a few Texas Democrats on Wednesday, the morning after their party's most disastrous showing at the polls in more than 120 years.

"The resurgence of the Texas Democratic Party begins today," said Texas Democratic Chairwoman Molly Beth Malcolm, putting the best face—or spin—on the future of a party that has almost no place to go but up.

Not surprisingly, Jim Mattox was a bit less optimistic. . . .

"The Democratic Party is going to have a hard time in statewide offices resurrecting itself for a period of time," he said.

Mattox blamed Gov. George W. Bush's popularity, Republican attorney general nominee John Cornyn's negative television ads and newspaper endorsements and the Republicans' wealth of campaign money for denying his comeback bid for the attorney general's post that he once held. . . .

Bush's overwhelming defeat of Democratic challenger Garry Mauro helped propel every Republican statewide candidate into office. . . .

For the first time since Reconstruction ended in the 1870s, Republicans were elected lieutenant governor, attorney general, state comptroller and land commissioner.

The GOP also captured all the statewide court seats on the ballot. The last remaining Democrat holding a statewide elective office, Texas Supreme Court Justice Raul A. Gonzalez, announced before the election that he will resign Dec. 31. . . .

Democrats could take some consolation from the legislative races.

The Democrats retook one state Senate seat, but Republicans will still hold a 16–15 majority when lawmakers convene Jan. 12.

Democrats will still have a majority in the Texas House and apparently be able to save Democrat Pete Laney's speakership. But the GOP gained three House seats to trim the Democratic majority to eight—79–71.

And Democrats held on to their 17–13 margin among congressional seats from Texas. . . .

Austin political consultant George Christian said Texas was "still a very competitive state between the two parties." And he predicted the Republican gains could be

Clay Robinson, R. G. Ratcliffe, and John W. Gonzalez, "Election Aftermath: Democrats Try to Smile," *Houston Chronicle*, November 5, 1998, A1. Copyright © 1998 by the Houston Chronicle. Reprinted with permission.

short-lived as the state's minority population, which votes heavily for Democrats, continues to grow.

"The battleground from now on is going to be for the Hispanic vote, and Democrats have a headstart there," he said.

Nevertheless, Bush captured almost half the Hispanic vote in Texas, which he could use to prove Republicans can attract Hispanic support. Former Texas Secretary of State Tony Garza, who was elected to the Texas Railroad Commission on Tuesday, became the first Hispanic elected to statewide office in Texas as a Republican. . . .

Christian and others believe the two Texas Democrats with . . . potential to recapture statewide offices for their party are Comptroller John Sharp and Houston businessman Paul Hobby.

Each lost close races on Tuesday—Sharp to Republican Rick Perry in the lieutenant governor's race and Hobby to Republican Carole Keeton Rylander in the comptroller's contest. . . .

Other observers also believe that retiring Democratic Attorney General Dan Morales, who did not seek re-election but has not ruled out a return to political life, also could help revive his party. . . .

Mattox said the Texas Democratic Party, without incumbents in statewide offices, will have difficulty raising money for future elections.

He said the dominant role that money now plays in political campaigns made him more concerned about the future of democracy than the future of the Democratic Party.

"It's going to be difficult for our democracy in the long run to survive not being bought if we don't have some campaign finance reform," he said.

Austin businessman Greg Hartman, a former Democratic political operative and aide to Sharp, said some of the state's mayors could be potential statewide Democratic candidates.

But before the Democrats start rebuilding, Hartman predicted that the party will go through "some crazy bloodletting."

## ✦ E S S A Y S

Historians have not yet developed a comprehensive analysis of the late-twentieth century political alignment in Texas. In the first essay presented here, Chandler Davidson, a political scientist from Rice University, attempts to assess Texas politics through the lens of V. O. Key who argued in 1940 that Texas (and southern politics) would evolve into a viable two-party system with issues and programs defined largely in terms of class rather than race. Davidson argues that the rise of the right-wing Republicans in the second half of the century not only reflected a political realignment of the Democrats, as the liberal party, but also reflected the emergence of a religious, anti-civil rights, anticommunist faction that became the dominant force in the Republican Party. Next, George N. Green of the University of Texas at Arlington and John Kushma, an historian and independent scholar, discuss the rise of Senator John Tower within the context of the changes in Texas politics. They essentially argue that Tower's political success owed more to divisions and miscalculations within the Democratic Party than to the political appeal of either Tower or the Republican Party.

# An Anatomy of Right Wing Republicans

### CHANDLER DAVIDSON

When [Lloyd Bentsen, Sr., father of the U.S. senator] first moved to the Valley, he went to see R. B. Creager of Brownsville, state chairman of the Republican party during its dormant years.

"I told Mr. Creager that I wanted to join the Republican party since my daddy had always been a rock-ribbed Republican in South Dakota. He said, 'Young man, do you want to do what's best for Texas?' I said I did. And he told me, 'You go back to Mission and join the Democratic party, because what's best for Texas is for every state in the union to have a two-party system and for Texas to be a one-party state. When you have a one-party state, your men stay in Congress longer and build up seniority.' I took his advice."

The Modern Texas Republican party was born in 1961 with the election of John Tower to the U.S. Senate, although there were adumbrations of it in the 1950's. Tower in 1960 had opposed Lyndon Johnson, the incumbent, who ran simultaneously for the Senate and the vice presidency thanks to a law the legislature had passed the year before at Johnson's behest. Tower was thoroughly beaten, but he entered the race for LBJ's vacated seat, took advantage of a large field that included two well-known liberal candidates, and won a runoff against a reactionary Democrat whom many liberals would not support. Tower was thus the first Republican since Reconstruction, not only in Texas but in the South, to win a Senate seat.

Until then, the Texas Republicans were more a paper party than anything else, although ticket-splitting in rich urban precincts was already common in presidential elections and spread further down the class structure after Eisenhower had twice carried the state. But the establishment saw no need for a two-party state. Indeed, like Creager and his able pupil, the elder Bentsen, it saw much to be gained by one-partyism. Not only did the one-party arrangement obscure class issues, but under the old seniority system Democratic congressmen, lacking serious opposition, worked their way up to powerful committee chairmanships where they did a world of good for the tightly knit upper class, whatever party the rich paid public homage to.

Tower's victory, followed by the Goldwater movement over the next three years, augured a new day in Texas. Just as the events of 1944 within the Democratic party had given rise to a liberal movement culminating in Ralph Yarborough's Senate career and LBJ's Great Society, the very triumph of liberalism nationally, as well as the many excesses of the political and cultural "revolutionaries" of the 1960's, gave rise to a powerful countermovement.

The scope of this movement can be seen in three trends. The first is the growing electoral successes of Republicans in a traditionally Democratic state, which underscore the extent of party realignment. The second is the influence on Texas Republicanism of its extreme Right—those elements that in the McCarthy period were known as the "Radical Right." The third is the staying power of racial politics. . . .

---

Texas Republicanism has had a remarkable history. After 1928, none of its presidential candidates carried Texas again until 1952; yet in the nine elections between 1952 and 1984, the GOP ticket took the state's popular vote five times. At the senatorial level, Tower proved his 1961 victory was not happenstance by winning every succeeding election he contested until he bowed out in 1984. He was succeeded by Republican Phil Gramm, a congressman recently converted to the party whose conservatism proved to be even more hard-line than that of Tower. The governor's mansion was captured by the Republicans in 1978 with Bill Clements's upset victory over Democrat John Hill. Clements lost to Democratic moderate-conservative Mark White in 1982 and then defeated him in 1986. The Republican groundswell continued to grow.

True, by the mid-1980's the GOP had failed to win any important statewide offices below the level of governor. . . . But it had made deep inroads into the state legislature and congressional delegation. . . . At the time of Tower's 1961 election, only a tiny fraction of Republicans were in either body. The change was gradual, although Nixon's 1968 and 1972 victories, along with Reagan's smashing landslides in 1980 and 1984, were accompanied by sharp Republican gains among Texas lawmakers.

What is the significance of this important and long-prophesied evolution toward a two-party state? What is the nature of Texas Republicanism? How does it compare with the Democratic party from which it sprang? . . .

### Sources of Texas Republicanism

When the liberals set out in the 1940s to reform the state's Democratic party, they appeared to believe that if they were successful, conservatives would migrate to the Republicans. The resulting two-party system would resemble that of the nation. In those days the national Republican party was dominated by eastern moderates on the order of Thomas Dewey and, later, Nelson Rockefeller—a dominance that continued into the early 1960s. The idea that realignment might give rise to a different kind of Republican party locally seemed not to have occurred to Texas liberals then. . . .

In retrospect, liberals' failure to anticipate this possibility is curious, because the very logic of their argument pointed to it. The coming realignment in Texas, they had explained, would result from the liberalization of the Democratic party, which would drive economic conservatives and unreconstructed racists into the arms of the GOP. But the Texas Republicans, unlike many northern state parties, did not have a liberal wing to moderate the excesses of the converts. . . .

The realignment that actually came about owed much to the rapid growth of a Texas Republicanism that was deeply reactionary, when seen in the light of optimistic liberal expectations. In a number of elections in the 1960s, many liberals had either refused to vote rather than support conservative Democrats against Republicans such as Tower, or they had tried to rally fellow liberals to Republican candidates, for the tactical purpose of driving conservatives out of the Democratic primaries and conventions. This, they had hoped, would enable liberal candidates to win the party's nomination more easily.

"I want you to realize [that] there are no liberals in this party," outgoing Texas Republican chair Chet Upham told his state committee in April 1983, and "there are no moderates. We're all conservatives." It was a statement the committee obviously wanted to hear. And it was at least true of the party's activist core. . . .

There were of course factions, some of which coalesced around personalities. John Tower, George Bush, James Baker, and Anne Armstrong were among those whom less well-connected Republicans accused of being part of the country club set, and this seemed to imply a conservatism more attuned to considerations of wealth and status than, for example, their positions on race, homosexuality, "secular humanism," or abortion.

To be sure, there were stylistic differences that sometimes distinguished the social elite. Bush and Baker, important members of Reagan's team in the 1980s, were more pragmatic in temperament and more adept in the give-and-take of American politics than were ideologues like Henry Grover, Clymer Wright, or Nancy Palm in Houston or Jim Collins in Dallas.

But it is doubtful that the country club set as a whole was more moderate in its basic values than were its "populist" critics. When Bush, who as a congressman represented an extremely wealthy district that included Houston's River Oaks, announced his intention in 1968 to vote for a federal open housing provision—one of the few liberal stands he took during his tenure—office was deluged with hate letters and anonymous death threats, many from his district. After the vote, he had to face down his own crowd—a group of angry businessmen at the exclusive Ramada Club. . . .

The differences that split Republicans involved disputes over means as often as ends. For example, Bush, humane in his personal views, nonetheless was an ardent Goldwaterite in 1964 and attacked that year's Civil Rights Act in its entirety, arguing that the strong George Wallace vote in the Wisconsin presidential primary was not so much a sign of extremism as of general concern over government civil rights measures. In the same campaign he criticized Medicare as "socialized medicine." As vice president he eagerly sought the endorsement of the religious firebrand Jerry Falwell—praising his "moral vision for America"—and other right-wing leaders and fringe groups in his quest for the 1988 presidential nomination, reminding them of his earlier Goldwater support. . . .

Tower, despite his talk between 1964 and 1976 of Republicans' capturing the center, had a Senate voting record during those days that placed him at the right edge of his own national party. As Texas's favorite son at the Republican convention in 1968, he supported Reagan's candidacy before finally backing Nixon. . . .

If there was a spectrum of Texas Republican beliefs, its "Left" was firmly anchored in what might be called the establishment conservatism of John Connally, who had migrated from the Tory Democratic wing in the 1970s. The Republicans' right flank consisted of militant religious fundamentalists, racial bigots, current or former members of the John Birch Society, homophobes, financial backers of mercenary anti-Sandinista troops, and advocates of conspiracy theories linking the Illuminati with the Trilateral Commission.

Somewhere between these two poles, numerous Texas took up political residence in the decades following Tower's election to the Senate. Many of the new Republicans were decent Americans worried or frightened by the economic and social problems of the times, who hoped for a return to "traditional" values. Others were apostles of discord: paranoid, anti-intellectual, intemperate, full of hatred for outgroups, and contemptuous of fair play. While probably a minority, the latter were influential in setting the tone of Texas Republican politics in the early 1960s, the formative years of the modern party. Although as a group their influence declined after Goldwater was buried in the LBJ landslide of 1964, they returned to prominence as part of the New Right—sometimes under the same leaders—in the late 1970s. In consequence, the Texas GOP developed into an unabashedly right-wing party.

Where did the recruits who swelled the GOP rolls come from? Two separate groups of "immigrants" accounted for much of the increase. The first consisted of erstwhile Democrats who found their party too liberal for their liking. They included the rich and the upper-middle class whose families had been "presidential Republicans" for decades and who made up the establishment. They also included those less-affluent Texans who had left the party in 1968 and 1972, many voting for George Wallace under the American party label before moving into Republican ranks.

Wallace, an erstwhile economic liberal in Alabama who later tried to turn the racial backlash to his advantage, drew substantial support in his 1968 presidential bid in the South from Birchers, former Goldwaterites, and Democrats who had sat out the 1964 presidential race. In Texas, half of Wallace's state executive committee consisted of John Birch Society members, according to the organization's state chairman. It was to the Wallace supporters, among others on the Far Right, that Reagan's forces in Texas made strong overtures in 1976, and they attributed Reagan's stunning defeat of Ford in the state's primary to Reagan's appeal to these groups.

The nature of the second "immigrant group" is suggested by the fact that the number of Texas whites born outside the South rose from 9 percent in 1950 to 20 percent in 1980. Among the latter were a disproportionate number of Republicans from other states. Many had moved to Texas from the Midwest during the boom years of the late 1970s and early 1980s. The immigrants seemed to be somewhat less conservative than natives but were unwilling to challenge the rightward drift of the Texas Republican party.

The growth of Republicanism was also a result of broad social currents sweeping across Texas and the nation, and it laid claim to the allegiance of a disproportionate number of new voters as well. Key's theory of southern realignment seemed premised on the assumption of continuing, perhaps expanding, support for New Deal or similar principles. Yet many developments created crosscutting loyalties among New Deal constituencies. The Cold War and McCarthyism gave rise to an emotional anticommunism in America beyond anything warranted by Russian threats to American interests at the time. Anticommunist jingoism was at the heart of the Radical Right revival in the 1950s.

At the same time, the civil rights movement was gathering force. Its epochal achievements were first expressed in Supreme Court decisions: *Smith v. Allwright*, which struck down the exclusively white Democratic primary in Texas; and *Brown v. Board of Education*, which declared state-enforced school segregation unconstitutional. After much travail and violence, Congress passed the Civil Rights Act of 1964 and the Voting Rights Act of 1965, the first abolishing Jim Crow and the second enfranchising hundreds of thousands of new black voters. Many white southerners were deeply alienated from the national Democratic party that, through passage of these two measure, reluctantly, then with increasing purpose, imposed a second Reconstruction on the South.

Another contemporary political current was the conservative reaction to the 1960s—including political excesses of the Left and the "counterculture"—and to subsequent social and economic trends that the Right blamed on the Democrats, particularly liberals. High on their bill of particulars were the women's equal rights movement, including the right to abortion; the perceived decline in religion; the rising divorce rate; the alleged permissiveness of the courts toward criminals; the homosexual rights movement; and America's failure to win the Vietnam War. These perceived results of liberal culture fueled both traditional conservatism and the Radical Right. The Republicans capitalized on the fear, anger, and uncertainty these factors engendered across the socioeconomic spectrum.

## The Radical Right

The distinction between the radical and the traditional Right is sometimes fuzzy. In Texas, historically both groups have opposed racial desegregation, inveighed against "big government" as the defender of the disadvantaged and against labor unions, and vehemently attacked the USSR as a military threat to the United States. According to David W. Reinhard, a student of the Republican Right, "it is the Radical Right's all-encompassing conspiratorial view of American politics that places it apart from Right Wing Republicans, who may themselves entertain limited conspiratorial notions." Earlier students of the Radical Right such as historian Richard Hofstadter referred to a "paranoid style"—a tendency to imagine Communists around every corner, to harbor theories of vast conspiracy, and to use ethnic minorities and other outgroups as scapegoats for their problems. Their simplistic views of the world and even more simplistic solutions to its problems set them apart from sophisticated conservatives. Even so, both types of rightists have often worked together in common cause.

It is the thesis of this chapter that the Radical Right in Texas, always a minority but sometimes including rich and influential members of the elite, has had a marked influence on the state's modern Republican party. It has not taken over the party, but its influence is significant and gives the Texas Republicans their particular stridency and, at times, their appearance of a Know-Nothing movement. This influence is wielded by virtue of the radicals' importance in winning elections. Given the Republican decision, for all practical purposes, to write off minority voters, their party relies more heavily than it otherwise would on the radicals.

Until the end of World War II, the Radical Right in Texas operated primarily within the Democratic party. Since then, it has often tied its hopes to third parties—such as Strom Thurmond's Dixiecrats and Wallace's American party—or joined with the Republicans. The John Birch Society, to take one example, was firmly ensconced in the Texas GOP by the early 1960s. Its founder was Massachusetts candy manufacturer Robert Welch, who was keenly interested in the Republican party. In his book, *The Politician*, he concluded that Dwight Eisenhower was " a dedicated conscious agent of the Communist conspiracy."

Birch Society organizational operations in the 1950s and 1960s were quite similar to those of the American Communist party a generation earlier. Membership was largely secret; front groups were used to infiltrate respectable organizations; local chapters were "designed to operate as isolated islands, impervious to penetration by outsiders"; members were expelled if they did not follow the official line; "dirty tricks" were employed against opponents; and a grand conspiratorial theory of evil forces explained events. But instead of Wall Street bankers, as the Communists had believed, communism itself had taken control of American government, in the Birchers' version. At its height, the Birch Society had numerous chapters in Texas. Several thousand members were reported in Houston, Dallas, and the Panhandle. Uniquely Texan were teenage chapters in high schools. By the mid-1960s, the Birch magazine, *American Opinion,* had a press run per issue of about 50,000. Among the magazine's owners was Nelson Bunker Hunt of Dallas.

Historian George Norris Green asserts that it was easier for the Birchers to gain entry to the state's Republicans than it was for the Democrats because there was no connection between the liberal wing of the national Republican party and the local GOP activists. In addition, the state party's fast expansion made it vulnerable to Birch infiltration. By the time Tower was elected to the Senate, the state Republican party, especially in West Texas, was heavily influenced by the society. And while there were liabilities for public officials in becoming openly identified with it, the leading elected Republicans of the time—Dallas congressmen Bruce Alger and Tower—"maintained voting records indistinguishable from the Birch line," according to Green. . . .

## God, Politics, and the Reverend Criswell

The Reverend Dr. W. A. Criswell, longtime pastor of the First Baptist Church of Dallas . . . has been called "the best-known, most heeded, most influential preacher of the Southern Baptist persuasion." The Southern Baptists are the largest Protestant denomination by far in Texas and, in the aggregate, the most conservative of the major religious groups. In the mid-1980s, an estimated 2.3 million Texans were Southern Baptists. Their state newspaper, the *Baptist Standard,* was mailed in 1984 to 350,000 subscribers. . . .

The First Baptist Church of Dallas is a wonder in its own right. It houses the world's largest Southern Baptist congregation, with a membership of twenty-five thousand, and sits on real estate valued at $200 million. It counts evangelist Billy Graham among its more distinguished members. In 1986 the church had a budget of $12 million. Criswell's salary was $90,000. He was also given money for his wardrobe and a new car each year.

The flamboyant minister gained renown in the days following *Brown v. Board of Education* by using his pulpit to attack school integration as evil and contrary to biblical command, thus aligning himself against that group of Baptists that "steadfastly refuses to believe that God is behind the identifiable streams of brutality, bigotry, and vicious chauvinism that course their way through the Bible," as a Texas professor of religion—also a Baptist—put it. In 1956 Criswell declared that "the idea of the universal brotherhood of man and the fatherhood of God is a denial of everything in the Bible." The same year he thundered against desegregation before the South Carolina legislature, where he had been introduced by Senator Strom Thurmond. The speech gained national press coverage. During the days of the civil rights struggle, he was one of its most outspoken and vituperative opponents. Billy Graham, a racial moderate, took care to distance himself from Criswell over the matter.

John F. Kennedy's presidential race created a stir among Protestant Evangelicals in 1960. Southern Baptists, in particular, had a long history of anti-Catholic hostility, and until JKF met with Baptist ministers in Houston that summer and somewhat defused the issue, his candidacy was a fertile ground for religious bigotry. . . .

Later in the summer, Criswell told reporters that Kennedy was "lying" when he said he would not take orders from the Catholic hierarchy. The preacher advocated barring all Catholics from public office and endorsed Nixon. Nonetheless, when the November votes were tallied, the Kennedy-Johnson ticket swept most Texas counties with the largest Baptist concentrations.

By 1968 a spirit of moderation was evident among Southern Baptists who controlled the annual convention in Houston. The group issued "the strongest statement" ever on racial discrimination by the denomination, which had split from its northern counterpart in 1845 over the slavery issue. It committed its members to "open" church membership and urged them to work for equality in "employment, housing and education." Almost three-quarters of the voting delegates supported the statement in a secret ballot, after defeating an amendment that blamed racial tension on "Communist infiltration."

At this meeting, Criswell was elected president of the convention, which coincided with the hundredth anniversary of his church. Given his reputation on race, this development struck many observers as incongruous. Within weeks of his election, his church opened its doors to blacks, although Criswell denied that this had anything to do with his attempt to win the presidency. He also pledged to support the convention's statement on race. . . .

. . . Criswell at one time called himself a Democrat, but it is not clear if he has ever backed a Democratic presidential candidate. When asked in 1960 if he had voted for FDR, he said "yes and no," and he refused to clarify the answer when probed. Beyond that, he would not name a Democrat he had voted for. He admitted not liking Truman and voting for Eisenhower. . . .

. . . By the 1970s, it was clear that Criswell was firmly in the Republican camp. At a time when Jimmy Carter's Evangelical background was getting widespread attention, Criswell endorsed Ford, an Episcopalian, in the 1976 presidential race, criticizing Carter's proposed social programs and the "social policies of the Democratic party." When Clements was fist elected governor, Criswell presided at an inaugural prayer service, and on that cold January day in 1979 delivered what a reporter described as a "thunderous diatribe against the welfare state and government intrusion."

It was an auspicious year for Criswell. A deep schism was developing in the Southern Baptist convention between conservatives on one side and moderates and liberals on the other. The battle was fought ostensibly on theological grounds over inerrancy, but it clearly had political overtones that spilled into the secular realm. Indeed, the rise of a militant right-wing faction within the convention coincided with the rise nationally of the New Religious Right, whose most prominent spokesman was Falwell, an independent Baptist who founded the Moral Majority with help from Richard Viguerie, a Republican direct-mail expert and erstwhile Goldwater supporter from Houston. . . .

The 1980s were good to Criswell. Not only did his faction within the convention come to prevail, but in the world of temporal powers so did his party—and a presidential candidate he obviously admired. As the crowning political honor to the aging preacher's career, he was asked to give the benediction at the Republican convention in Dallas in the summer of 1984, following President Reagan's acceptance speech. . . .

## The Radical Right and the Respectable Right

The modern Texas Republican party was not wholly or primarily made up of reactionary fringe groups, even though it was overwhelmingly a right-wing party . . . "in arch opposition to the domestic, foreign, and political changes wrought by Franklin Roosevelt and later the Great Society of Lyndon Johnson." Nonetheless, the radicals' fervor, organizing talents, showmanship and energy—not to mention the money of right-wingers like the Hunts and the institutional prominence of Criswell and some of his fellow zealots—gave them an important voice in the party's affairs. Their numbers, while difficult to estimate precisely, were large enough to make them an essential part of any serious effort by Republicans to win statewide, so long as the party wrote off potential converts among minority groups and moderates.

Moreover, the respectable Right and the Radical Right often intermingled. The shriller evangelists had become an integral part of the Republican party in Texas, as in the nation. Both Clements and former state chairman George Strake were publicly associated with Falwell—as was Bush—and attempted to use him for their political purposes, just as he tried to use them for his. . . .

[In 1980], John Connally was a featured speaker at the Religious Roundtable political action seminar in Dallas, which also drew presidential candidate Reagan, Helms, Phyllis Schlafly, Falwell, Robison, and evangelist Pat Robertson. In 1979 Connally had met with Falwell and other right-wingers at his ranch and agreed to participate in Robison's TV special, "Wake Up America." . . .

Especially noteworthy about the intimacy between the Radical Right and the respectable Right was the virtual absence among the Texas party's mainstream of any outspoken opposition to this confluence—opposition like that voiced in 1986 by Republican news columnist Doug Harlan of San Antonio who wrote that "religious fundamentalists are to Republicans what LaRouchites are to Democrats, but the threat to Republicans from the religious right is far greater than the threat to Democrats from [right-wing demagogue Lyndon] LaRouche." Harlan—who earlier had criticized Gramm for homosexual baiting in his 1984 senatorial contest—was a lonely voice in the Republican wilderness. Perhaps the extent of radical right-wing influence in the state's party was no better illustrated than by the fact that it was almost unthinkable, by the mid-1980s, that a Republican candidate would make a statement such as that of Harlan.

The perpetual tendency of the Texas Radical Right to move as far on the fringes of the political spectrum as they could go pulled the entire party in their direction. The result was that one day's traditional rightists were always in danger of becoming the next day's "liberals," at least as the radicals saw it.

# John Tower and the Rise of the
# Texas Republican Party

## GEORGE N. GREEN AND JOHN J. KUSHMA

John Tower often joked about his stature, introducing himself to campaign audiences early in his political career with the stock greeting, "My name's Tower, but I don't." In a state that has traditionally prided itself on bigness, especially among its political leaders, the diminutive John Tower presented an improbable physical image, one that was only enhanced by his slicked-back hair and Savile Row suits and English cigarettes that gave him the look of a London dandy. His political career was as remarkable as his appearance. John Tower was the first Republican U.S. senator since Reconstruction to be elected from a former Confederate state. He was among the architects of the Republican "Southern Strategy" in the 1960s that, although it led to that party's electoral success, turned the nation's attention away from the problems and challenges of racial injustice. As chairman of the Senate Armed Services Committee, John Tower provided the ideological rationale for and then presided over the huge defense spending increases if the first Reagan administration that shaped both foreign and domestic policies during the 1980s. Following his retirement from the Senate, he was subsequently tapped by President Ronald Reagan to serve as a negotiator to the Strategic Arms Reduction Talks and chairman of the President's Special Review Board that investigated the Iran-contra scandal. John Tower's political conservatism was not remarkable. Many of the Texans who preceded him in Washington were conservatives, albeit Democrats. Tower's amorous affairs with women, the bottle, and defense contractors were also unremarkable. When they were widely publicized during the Senate hearings on his nomination as Secretary of Defense, one of his supporters summed them up by simply concluding: "He's a Texan, make no mistake, and he's no angel." Personal indiscretions had never stood in the way of Texans' political success, nor had they been sufficient grounds to disqualify previous cabinet nominees. What was remarkable was that questions about his character resulted in John Tower becoming the first cabinet nominee of an incoming president to be rejected by the Senate.

John Goodwin Tower was born in Houston on September 25, 1925, the son and grandson of Methodist ministers. Growing up during the Great Depression of the 1930s, he spent his childhood in various towns in East Texas in which his father preached. . . . Following his wartime service, he enrolled in Southwestern University in Georgetown and was graduated in 1948 with a bachelor of arts degree in political science. He worked . . . on political science faculty at Midwestern University in Wichita Falls in 1951. Tower continued his studies in political science. . . . The focus of Tower's attention was the British Conservative party, whose study he viewed "as an opportunity to pursue my own academic and practical interest in the mechanics of building a broad-based political movement." . . .

. . . Although he began his political life as a Democrat, . . . John Tower abandoned the Democratic party between 1948 and 1951 and joined the Republicans. . . .

The Texas Republican party that John Tower joined was a moribund organization that had offered no competition for the dominant state Democratic party throughout the twentieth century. For example, in the six gubernatorial elections between 1940 and 1950, the Republican party's candidate for governor averaged less than 10 percent of the popular vote. Lacking the ability to contest statewide offices and with only a few isolated pockets of voting strength, the party had degenerated into little more than a patronage machine. But winds of change that fanned the fires of racism would soon shake the structure of the dominant Democratic coalition. The strong civil rights platform adopted by the Democrats in 1948 led some Texas conservative Democrats to bolt to "Dixiecrat" presidential candidate Strom Thurmond. Others voted for Thomas E. Dewey, resulting in the state's highest Republican vote in a presidential election since 1928. Although the Democratic party's hegemonic control of the state was not immediately threatened, race would ultimately become the issue that would lead to the resurgence of the Republican party of Texas.

John Tower's conversion to Republican activist thus coincided with the emergence of race as an important political question in Texas. Although he claimed to have thrown off "deep seated prejudices," Tower did admit to being profoundly influenced by his paternal grandfather, an "unreconstructed rebel." He was never known as a race baiter, but by the 1950s all but the most crude segregationists had learned to substitute code words like states' rights, local control, and constitutional government. . . .

The Eisenhower movement also energized Texas Republicans. Eisenhower carried the state in both 1952 and 1956, the first Republican victories in presidential elections since 1928, when an anti-wet and anti-Catholic backlash placed the state in Herbert Hoover's column. The "presidential Republicanism" that had its origins in unhappiness with the liberal New Deal and Fair Deal policies of the Roosevelt and Truman administrations did little initially for the state Republican organization. Conservative Democrats like Governor Allan Shivers, who endorsed Eisenhower's candidacy, operated independent organizations. The national Republican party, cognizant of the need to secure Democratic votes, did little to help the state party. A majority of Eisenhower voters simply returned to their Democratic moorings in state and local contests. In the three gubernatorial elections from 1954 to 1958, the Republican candidate averaged only slightly more than 12 percent.

It was not surprising, then, that Thad Hutcheson and other party leaders declined to make a hopeless race against Lyndon Johnson in his reelection bid to the Senate in 1960. John Tower offered himself as the party's sacrificial lamb. The party's leadership agreed to endorse him, provided he "lost" his panama hat, giant cigar, and Vandyke goatee. . . . Despite his inauspicious beginning, Tower campaigned tirelessly and effectively. He was able to tap the public resentment at how Johnson had contrived to change the state election laws to provide himself a safe return to the Senate in case the voters spurned the Kennedy-Johnson national ticket. Johnson was elected vice-president and senator, but Tower captured over 41 percent of the ballots in the Senate race, losing to Johnson 1,307,000 to 927,000. It was a startling performance by a poorly funded, unknown college professor. The success of his initial race carried him through to the special election held in the next year. . . .

. . . [A]ll Tower needed to do was to avoid making any stupid mistakes. He campaigned around the clock, frequently accompanied by fellow conservative, Arizona Senator Barry Goldwater. . . . Tower also covered his left flank and appealed to moderates by enlisting Connecticut Senator Prescott Bush to campaign on his behalf. Bush's appearances and a warm endorsement from former President Eisenhower undermined the allegation that Tower was a right-wing kook who would be ineffective in the Senate. Tower desperately needed this backing, for only fourteen out of the approximately five hundred newspapers in the state supported him.

In May 1961 runoff resulted in a remarkable ten-thousand-vote victory by Tower. He carried only seventy-one counties, but ran well among white-collar Anglo voters in the state's burgeoning metropolitan areas and especially among newcomers to the state. . . .

Liberal and moderate Democrats had no incentive to vote for Blakley, [the Democratic candidate] who was every bit as conservative as Tower. Many were consequently willing to help defeat Blakley in order to drive conservative Democrats into the Republican party and thus bring about a more responsible two-party system in Texas. They assumed Tower would be merely a one-term oddity who would be easily defeated in 1966. Therefore an initial Tower victory would demonstrate to autocratic and high-handed conservative Democrats that the days of cooptation were over. A significant proportion of moderate and liberal Democrats either voted for Tower in the runoff or, in the vernacular of the day, "went fishing" on election day. Blakley might have staved off these defections and drop-outs had he moved slightly to the left, but instead he pulled such stunts as using a dinner in Waco, in the central Texas farm belt, as a platform to attack the relatively popular Democratic farm program.

Arriving in Washington as the new junior senator from Texas, Tower basked in his newfound celebrity status as the first Republican to be elected from the South in nearly ninety years. Although conventional wisdom recognized Tower's victory as a fluke (Richard Nixon labeled it a "pure accident"), conservative Republicans proclaimed his triumph as the initial breakthrough that would allow them to challenge the Democrats' dominance not only in the South but throughout the nation. Tower was feted as many party functions, and he spent more time being toasted and appearing on behalf of other Republican candidates than he did attending to his Senate duties. He soon acquired a reputation of being lazy and indifferent in the chamber and a playboy outside of it. It was not until March 1, 1962, that he introduced a series of bills and resolutions that identified his policy objectives. They represented little more than a statement of conservative Republican verities. . . .

From the time he entered the Senate, Tower was more interested in foreign policy than domestic issues. He was an unabashed and unapologetic cold warrior who viewed victory over communism as the principal goal of U.S. foreign policy. . . .

. . . Tower quickly joined Senators Goldwater and Thurmond as a champion of the far right, whose banner he was initially happy to carry. Tower's affiliation with the extremist groups and neglect of his Senate duties suggested to many observers that he too had come to regard his victory as a fluke and saw no realistic chance for his reelection. Ken Towery, who joined Tower's staff in 1963, convinced him that he had a chance for a second term, and he helped to steer the senator away from parties and toward committee meetings.

Tower had indeed had good reason to question his chances for reelection. The incredible series of events that led to his victory in 1961—a low-turnout special election with a nonpartisan ballot, a highly factionalized Democratic opposition, and help from liberal and moderate Democrats—would not be repeated, so he would be running for reelection as a Republican in a state that was still overwhelmingly Democratic. Moreover, his victory had jolted Texas Democrats into action, particularly Lyndon Johnson, whose control of the state had been threatened not only by the surging Republicans but also by the restive liberal Democrats. Conservative Democrats recognized that they needed a strong gubernatorial candidate in 1962, and they tapped heretofore unknown John Connally, a Johnson protege. The handsome and charismatic Connally triumphed easily in the gubernatorial election but not nearly as easily as previous Democratic candidates.

Although the state was still safely Democratic, Texas Republicans had reason for optimism. Tower's Senate victory had broken a psychological barrier that had discouraged conservatives from joining the Republicans if they wished to win political office in Texas. A spate of conservative activists now found a congenial home in the GOP, and they carried their enthusiasm to the grass roots. More important, the racial issue had once again emerged as a lever for Republicans to use in order to pry conservative Democrats away from their traditional partisan roots. In 1962 white backlash over the Kennedy administration's civil rights initiatives helped the Republicans win two congressional seats in Texas and significantly increase their strength throughout the state. . . . Three special elections for seats in the Texas House went to Republicans in 1963, bringing the GOP total to 10 in that 150-member body. Tower's 1961 victory and the subsequent increase in the Republican voting strength in Texas provided the raw materials out of which the "Southern Strategy" began to develop. The right wing of the Republican party under the leadership of Tower's mentor, Goldwater, would employ this strategy in 1964. The political amorality of manipulating racial antagonisms for partisan advantage that underlay the divisive "Southern Strategy" would provoke a bitter debate within the national GOP ranks, but there was no denying that the strategy had worked. The only recent Republican gains had come in the South, and it appeared that the Democrats' commitment to civil rights would make them vulnerable there in 1964. Texas became the heart of the Goldwater-for-president movement, and John Tower became the first Republican senator to endorse Goldwater's candidacy.

President Kennedy's assassination on Texas soil and Lyndon Johnson's elevation to the presidency temporarily deflated Texas Republicans. All of the incumbent Republicans save one were defeated in 1964, the same year that Lyndon Johnson called for the passage of a basic civil rights law as a monument to the slain President Kennedy. Johnson was returned to the presidential office in an overwhelming victory over Goldwater. But the "Southern Strategy" did partially succeed. Five southern states deserted the "solid South" and awarded their electoral votes to Goldwater. The issue of race would continue to be the Republican party's trump card in building up electoral strength in the southern states.

John Tower's only mention of civil rights in his memoirs is a brief concession that he joined the filibuster and voted against the 1964 civil rights bill because he believed the provision guaranteeing equal access to public accommodations to be unconstitutional. He apologized for this vote in hindsight. However, he was much too modest about . . . the importance of racial issues in the growth of the Republican party in Texas. Tower had long opposed integration. . . . As a Nixon delegate to the 1960 national Republican convention, Tower led a group of Texans and Southerners who threatened to bolt to Goldwater after Nixon acceded to Nelson Rockefeller's progressive civil rights planks. . . . Tower was the only Republican to join the southern Democrats' filibuster against the 1964 civil rights bill. . . . The unabashed hostility of Goldwater's supporters toward civil rights shocked many moderate Republicans who showed their displeasure by supporting the victorious Lyndon Johnson that year. Tower and Strom Thurmond of South Carolina were the only Republicans who tried to block the Voting Rights Act of 1965, and Tower subsequently opposed the civil rights act of 1968 as well.

A few days after the Republican election debacle of 1964, Tower stunned a private gathering of state party leaders by offering not to seek reelection in 1966 if, they felt that another GOP candidate (presumably George Bush, who had just lost a Senate race to incumbent Ralph Yarborough) would have a better chance of holding the seat. The group declined Tower's offer and resolved to enhance his reelection chances by focussing the party's attention and resources on his senatorial campaign. . . . Republican prospects did not look particularly bright, however, when the John Kraft organization, hired by Tower to conduct a poll of Texas voters in the summer of 1965, reported that only a third of Texans were conservative and that Tower's political ideology was viewed as controversial.

Chastened by the poll's findings and recognizing the need to moderate his reactionary stands, Tower did attempt to position himself somewhat closer to mainstream Republican conservatism. He broke with the extremist John Birch Society, labeling it a liability to the conservative cause, and his supporters discouraged ultraconservatives from volunteering their services at party headquarters. Before the 1964 election, Tower would fly anywhere in the country in order to assail Lyndon Johnson, but afterwards he never mentioned the president except to praise his staunch leadership against the Communists in Vietnam. In 1965 he voted for the Johnson administration's omnibus farm bill, his first affirmative vote on farm legislation. He suddenly saw fit to support federal aid to higher education and even voted for the administration's omnibus housing bill that contained a controversial rent supplement section. Tower joined Ralph Yarborough in introducing a GI Bill for Vietnam veterans that would entitle them to educational and loan benefits similar to those that had been made available to veterans of previous wars. His gestures toward political moderation increased during the election year of 1966. . . . By 1966 Tower had positioned himself well within the mainstream conservatism, and if he could disassociate himself from the reactionary label that had brought down the 1964 Republican presidential ticket, he had a fair shot at reelection. Asked early in 1966 if he would invite Barry Goldwater to campaign with him, Tower replied with a smile, "Barry Who?"

Most political pundits agreed that a strong moderate-to-conservative Democrat would be clearly favored against Tower in the 1966 Senate race. The state remained predominantly Democratic, and the expected higher voter turnout than in the 1961 special election would bring that Democratic majority to the polls. . . . [T]he Democratic senatorial nomination fell to state Attorney General Waggoner Carr. Connally and Johnson quickly lined up almost all of the state Democratic leaders behind Carr, an impressive demonstration of party unity that did not bode well for Tower's chances.

Carr, however, had no experience in the federal government, and he quickly proved himself an ineffective campaigner. He was no match for the eloquent Tower as a public speaker, and he was unable to state his positions clearly and concisely. Nevertheless, Tower recognized the need to expand his base of support beyond the normal Republican ranks in order to stand a chance of winning. He departed from traditional Republican campaign practices by organizing an outreach program to court the vote of Mexican Americans, especially in those areas in which they were employed on military installations. Tower campaigned actively in Hispanic areas traditionally ignored by Republicans and introduced a resolution to enlarge the Equal Employment Opportunity Commission by adding a Hispanic member. . . .

Tower trounced Carr 843,000 to 642,000, while half the electorate stayed at home. White-collar, urban voters were again the bulk of Tower's support: he captured all the urban counties with ten thousand or more votes except McLennan (Waco). Nearly half of Tower's votes came from Democrats and Independents. The liberal-labor backlash was particularly evident in Jefferson and Travis counties, and Tower did very well with the Mexican-American vote in El Paso and Bexar counties. . . .

The next phase of the GOP's "Southern Strategy" was hammered out . . . on May 31, 1968. Richard Nixon reached an understanding with Tower, Thurmond, and thirteen southern and border state Republican party chairmen. In return for their support on the first ballot at the upcoming Republican national convention, Nixon promised to slow down the desegregation of the public schools, select a conservative as his running mate, continue hefty defense expenditures, and provide considerable patronage and appointments for southern Republicans and other conservatives. . . .

Tower had worked on behalf of Nixon's candidacy for years and had played a major role in devising the strategy that had led to his nomination, but Tower was all but ignored once Nixon was in the White House. During Richard Nixon's first few months as president, Tower, Thurmond, and a very few others bluntly told the president that he was going too far in the enforcement of the U.S. Supreme Court decision that ordered American schools to desegregate immediately. . . .

By the 1970s Tower had gravitated away from the Goldwaters and Thurmonds, the purist outsiders, and toward the Texas corporate and country club elite. The Texas country club wing of the Republican party, primarily Dallas-based and decidedly pro-Nixon, wanted to avoid diverting money and effort away from Nixon's and Tower's reelection efforts. Their prospective gubernatorial candidate, Albert Fay, had agreed to wage a low-keyed campaign in 1972. This was the same top-of-the ticket strategy that had worked for Tower six years earlier. But grass-roots Republicans were no longer willing to write off their chances elsewhere on the ballot. Fay was upended in the Republican primary by Houston Reaganite Hank Grover who came from the obstreperous, right wing "Lions Club" of the party that was beginning to flex its muscles. Tower, resenting the challenge to his control of the party, did nothing to help Grover in his race and all but ignored him during the election campaign.

In 1972 Tower was once again confronted with the results of a secret poll that showed him to be vulnerable. He was also faced with an able Democratic opponent in Dallas attorney Barefoot Sanders, a former state legislator who had served as an assistant attorney general and White House aide during the Johnson administration. Sanders was gravely handicapped by the absence of name identification and lack of money. He had never run for statewide office in Texas, and Sander's campaign war chest was less than half the size of Tower's. But Sanders was hurt most of all by the Democrat's presidential nominee, anti–Vietnam War liberal, George McGovern. Although Sanders endeavored to distance himself from McGovern, Tower's campaign continually linked the two. . . . One historian has argued that "George McGovern cost the Texas Democrats a United States Senate seat" in 1972. Money was a crucial factor in Tower's success; he reported spending over $2.5 million, making his campaign the most expensive nonpresidential one in the nation that year. Tower defeated Sanders rather easily by a popular vote of 1,823,000 to 1,512,000, but he ran a half million votes behind Richard Nixon in Texas. . . . Although Texas Republicans had carried Nixon and Tower to victory, their candidate-centered campaigns probably cost Grover the governor's race. . . . The growth of the state party was temporarily halted by this lack of unity. The subsequent revelations of the Watergate scandal also stymied the Republican party's development.

During the Nixon and Ford presidencies Tower moved into leadership roles in the national Republican party and in the Senate. In 1970 he chaired the Senate GOP Campaign Committee, which distributed funds to senators facing reelection fights. (The maverick Republican Senator Charles Goodell of New York was not provided any financial assistance by the Committee.) Tower assumed the chairmanship of the Senate Republican Policy Committee in 1973, an office that required him to downplay his personal ideology in favor of party loyalty. . . .

Tower loyally backed incumbent Gerald Ford over Ronald Reagan for the Republican presidential nomination in 1976. . . . Tower's country club wing feared that Reagan might drag the party into an election debacle just as Barry Goldwater had done in 1964. . . . But country club Republican fears about Reagan were unfounded. Texas was Reagan country, and the California governor smashed Ford (and Tower) in the state's primary. It was a resounding vote of no-confidence in Tower's party leadership. . . .

Nevertheless, Tower was well positioned for his reelection campaign. Although the Reagan-Grover faction was still rankled, Tower faced no serious Republican opposition. . . .

Tower's opponent was a two-term Democratic congressman, Robert Krueger, who had garnered considerable publicity in Texas through his ardent but unsuccessful attempts to deregulate the price of natural gas. A tireless and effective campaigner, Krueger's television spots portrayed him as an energetic, small-town Texas boy—in contrast to the divorced, high-living, and effete Tower. . . .

Tower outspent Krueger by more than two-to-one ($5.1 million to $2.3 million) during the campaign, but managed only a razor-thin victory, 1,151,000 to 1,139,000. His margin of 12,000 votes was less than one-half of one percent. . . . Indeed, it was oilman Bill Clements's stunning but narrow upset of Democrat John Hill in the governor's race that probably pulled Tower through, especially in the rural areas. Minority and traditional Democratic turnout was low, and the Republicans did a much better job in turning out their voters. Tower once again courted Hispanic voters, claiming to be "un amigo sincero," but he fell far short of the 35 percent he sought, securing only about 20 percent of the Mexican-American vote in the election.

Following the election, East Texas Congressman Charles Wilson pointed out the improbable character of Tower's election victories: "Tower would never have made it without Clements. . . . He got elected on a fluke to start with. Then the next time he had a Democrat more conservative than he was, and all the liberals voted for him. Then the next time he got to run when his opponent was strapped with McGovern. He's just lucky." Lucky or not, John Tower returned to the Senate where his seniority ensured him a starring role in the legislative wars. . . .

Tower stunned Texans in August 1983, when he announced his intention to retire from the Senate at the end of his fourth term. He cited burnout as his reason for declining to seek reelection. Republican leaders privately predicted that Tower would have faced another difficult reelection campaign, but Tower had never shied away from tough challenges. His successor, Republican Phil Gramm was elected easily with 59 percent of the vote. Tower professed to find the Senate a less congenial place to work, lacking the courtesy and collegiality that had characterized the chamber when he first entered it.

 *F U R T H E R    R E A D I N G*

Walter Buenger and Joe Pratt, *But Also Good Business: Texas Commerce Banks and the Financing of Houston and Texas* (1986)

Paul Burka, "The Year Everything Changed," *Texas Monthly* 11 (1983):100–109

Chandler Davidson, *Biracial Politics: Conflict and Coalition in the Metropolitan South* (1972)

———, *Race and Class in Texas Politics* (1990)

Kenneth E. Hendrickson, Jr. and Michael L. Collins, eds., *Profiles in Power: Twentieth Century Texans in Washington* (1993)

John R. Knaggs, *Two Party Texas: The John Tower Era 1961–1984* (1984)

Char Millar and Heywood Sanders, eds., *Urban Texas: Politics and Development* (1990)

Mary Ann Norman, *The Texas Economy Since World War II* (1983)

M. Ray Perryman, *Survive and Conquor, Texas in the 80s—Money—Power—Tragedy . . . Hope!* (1990)

Kirkpatrick Sale, *Power Shift: The Rise of the Southern Rim and Its Challenge to the Eastern Establishment* (1976)